MAC OS X PANTHER

IN A NUTSHELL

Other Macintosh resources from O'Reilly

Related titles

AppleScript: The Definitive Guide
Inside .Mac
Learning Unix for Mac OS X Panther
Mac OS X Panther for Unix Geeks
Mac OS X Unwired
Mac OS X Panther Hacks
Running Mac OS X Panther
GarageBand: The Missing Manual
iPod and iTunes: The Missing Manual
Mac OS X: The Missing Manual

Macintosh Books Resource Center

mac.oreilly.com is a complete catalog of O'Reilly's books on the Apple Macintosh and related technologies, including sample chapters and code examples.

A popular watering hole for Macintosh developers and power users, the Mac DevCenter focuses on pure Mac OS X and its related technologies, including Cocoa, Java, AppleScript, and Apache, to name just a few. It's also keenly interested in all the spokes of the digital hub, with special attention paid to digital photography, digital video, MP3 music, and QuickTime.

Conferences

O'Reilly brings diverse innovators together to nurture the ideas that spark revolutionary industries. We specialize in documenting the latest tools and systems, translating the innovator's knowledge into useful skills for those in the trenches. Visit *conferences.oreilly.com* for our upcoming events.

Safari Bookshelf (*safari.oreilly.com*) is the premier online reference library for programmers and IT professionals. Conduct searches across more than 1,000 books. Subscribers can zero in on answers to time-critical questions in a matter of seconds. Read the books on your Bookshelf from cover to cover or simply flip to the page you need. Try it today with a free trial.

MAC OS X PANTHER

IN A NUTSHELL

Chuck Toporek, Chris Stone,
and Jason McIntosh

with contributions from Leon Towns-von Stauber,
Andy Lester, Wei-Meng Lee, Brian Jepson,
and Ernest E. Rothman

Beijing • Cambridge • Farnham • Köln • Paris • Sebastopol • Taipei • Tokyo

Mac OS X Panther in a Nutshell
by Chuck Toporek, Chris Stone, and Jason McIntosh

Published by O'Reilly Media, Inc., 1005 Gravenstein Highway North, Sebastopol, CA 95472.

O'Reilly books may be purchased for educational, business, or sales promotional use. Online editions are also available for most titles (*safari.oreilly.com*). For more information, contact our corporate/institutional sales department: (800) 998-9938 or *corporate@oreilly.com*.

Editor:	Chuck Toporek
Production Editor:	Mary Anne Weeks Mayo
Cover Designer:	Emma Colby
Interior Designer:	Melanie Wang

Printing History:

January 2003:	First Edition, originally published as *Mac OS X in a Nutshell.*
June 2004:	Second Edition.

ISBN: 0-596-00606-3
[M]

Table of Contents

Preface .... **xiii**

Part I. Lay of the Land

1. **Using Mac OS X** **3**
   Starting Up and Logging In 3
   Startup and Shutdown Keys 4
   The Mac Desktop 5
   The Menu Bar 5
   The Application Switcher 23
   Exposé 23
   The Dock 24
   Windows 34
   Opening and Saving Documents 43
   Services 46
   Logging Out and Shutting Down 47

2. **Using the Finder** **49**
   Finder Overview 49
   Finder Views 56
   Relaunching the Finder 67
   Menus and Keyboard Shortcuts 68
   Searching for and Locating Files 74
   File Types 82

Folders 85
Bundles 86
Aliases 87
Moving and Copying Files and Folders 88
The Get Info Window 92

3. **Mac OS 9, Mac OS X, and Classic** 96
Changes to Mac OS X from Mac OS 9 96
What Is Classic? 100
Starting Classic 101
Controlling Classic 103
Managing Classic Applications 106
Using Classic Applications 108
Printing from Classic 112
Dual-Booting with Mac OS 9 113

4. **System Preferences** 115
Using System Preferences 115
The System Preference Panels 118
Speech Recognition and Speakable Commands 177
Adding Panes to System Preferences 181

5. **Applications and Utilities** 182
Applications 183
Installing Applications 191

6. **Task and Setting Index** 200

Part II. System and Network Administration

7. **Filesystem Overview** 245
Mac OS X Filesystems 245
Filesystem Organization 248
Hidden Files 255
The File Permissions System 261

8. **Networking** 265
Networking Basics 265
Accessing Network Disks 280
Web Browsing 285
Using FTP 288

Remote Logins 290
Virtual Private Networking 291
Rendezvous 293

9. Printer Configuration and Printing **295**
How Printing Works 295
The Print Dialog 296
Printer Setup Utility 303
Page Setup 309
Print & Fax Preferences 310
ColorSync 312
PostScript Converter 317
Alternative Printer Interfaces 318
Printer Sharing 320
Configuring CUPS 321
Printer Drivers 322

10. System Administration Overview **324**
Acting as Root 324
Managing Users and Groups 326
Network Administration 334
NFS 337
Single-User Mode 347
cron Tasks 349

11. Directory Services **351**
Understanding Directory Services 351
Programming with Directory Services 352
Configuring Directory Services 355
NetInfo Manager 358
Directory Services Utilities 358
Managing Groups 360
Managing Users and Passwords 362
Managing Hostnames and IP Addresses 365
Exporting Directories with NFS 365
Flat Files and Their Directory Services Counterparts 366
Restoring the Directory Services Database 367

12. Running Network Services **369**
Network Services Overview 369
Running Services in Mac OS X 369
Mail Services 371

Web Services 375
File Transfer Protocol (FTP) 376
Remote Login Services 377
File Sharing Services 378
Daemon Management 380

13. Security Basics 385
General Security 385
Authentication 387
Filesystem Security 392
Physical Security 394

Part III. Scripting and Development

14. AppleScript 397
The Script Menu Extra 397
Programming AppleScript 398
Script Editor 403
Folder Actions 406
AppleScript Studio 408
Scripting the Terminal 409
AppleScript Resources 410

15. Xcode Tools 411
Getting the Xcode Tools 411
The Developer Folder 412
Developer Applications 413
Xcode 416
Programming Languages 425
Interface Builder 428
Libraries and Frameworks 429
The Info.plist File 430

16. Java on Mac OS X 431
Java Tools and Applications 431
Running Mac-Friendly Java Programs 433
Running Generic Java Applications 438
Java on the Command Line 440
Customizing Java Applications 442

17. **CVS** **444**
Basic Concepts 444
CVS Command Format 446
Common Global Options 447
Gotchas 447
CVS Administrator Reference 447
CVS User Reference 465

Part IV. Under Mac OS X's Hood

18. **Using the Terminal** **493**
Using the Terminal 493
Process Management 502

19. **Shell Overview** **507**
Introduction to the Shell 507
Shell Flavors 508
Common Features 509
Differing Features 510

20. **bash: The Bourne-Again Shell** **511**
Invoking the Shell 512
Syntax 514
Variables 521
Arithmetic Expressions 525
Command History 526
Job Control 529
Built-in Commands 530

21. **tcsh: An Extended C Shell** **559**
Overview of Features 559
Invoking the Shell 560
Syntax 561
Variables 564
Expressions 574
Command History 577
Command-Line Manipulation 581
Job Control 584
Built-in Commands 585

22. Pattern Matching **607**
Filenames Versus Patterns 607
Metacharacters, Listed by Unix Program 608
Metacharacters 609
Examples of Searching 610

23. The vi Editor **613**
Review of vi Operations 614
vi Command-Line Options 616
ex Command-Line Options 618
Movement Commands 619
Edit Commands 622
Saving and Exiting 624
Accessing Multiple Files 625
Window Commands 625
Interacting with the Shell 626
Macros 626
Miscellaneous Commands 627
Alphabetical List of Keys in Command Mode 627
Syntax of ex Commands 629
Alphabetical Summary of ex Commands 631
vi Configuration 647

24. The Emacs Editor **651**
Emacs Concepts 651
Typical Problems 652
Notes on the Tables 653
Summary of Commands by Group 653
Summary of Commands by Key 659
Summary of Commands by Name 663

25. The Defaults System **670**
Property Lists 670
Viewing and Editing Property Lists 673

26. The X Window System **680**
About Apple's X11 681
Installing X11 681
Running X11 681
Customizing X11 683

X11-Based Applications and Libraries 688
Connecting to Other X Window Systems 689
Virtual Network Computer 691

27. Installing Unix Software 698
Package Managers 698
Installing from Source 701

28. Unix Command Reference 703
Alphabetical Summary of Commands 704

Part V. Appendixes

A. Special Characters 969

B. Resources 972

Index 979

Preface

Although Apple Computer ushered in the PC revolution in 1980 with the Apple II computer, the inventions that are most synonymous with the company are the Macintosh computer and its ground-breaking graphical operating system, both released in 1984. Let's think of this operating system as Mac OS 1, though Apple wouldn't coin the term "Mac OS" to describe its operating system until the 1990s. The early Mac made its mark in a world where all other popular computer interfaces were obscure.

In the years following the Mac's release, much has changed. Both bad and good things have happened, and some company in Washington called Microsoft started to take over the world. By 1996, Apple knew it needed to modernize the Mac OS (and make it more worthy competition to Windows) from the bottom up, but previous attempts and partnerships to bring this about had ended in failure. So, it made an unusual move and purchased NeXT. This company had made a nice Unix-based operating system called NeXTSTEP, in which Apple saw the seeds of its own salvation. As it happened, NeXT's leader was the ambitious Steve Jobs, one of Apple's founders, who left the company after a political rift in the 1980s. To make a long and interesting story short, Jobs quickly seized control of Apple Computer, stripped it down to its essentials, and put all its resources into reinventing the Mac. Five years later, the result was Mac OS X: a computing platform based around an entirely new operating system that merged the best parts of the old Mac OS, NeXTSTEP, and nearly two decades of user feedback on the Mac OS.

Mac OS X initially may seem a little alien to long-time Mac users; it is, quite literally, an entirely different operating system from Mac OS 9 and earlier versions (even though Mac OS X retains most of its predecessor's important interface idioms, such as the way the desktop and the user interface works, as covered in the first two chapters of this book). However, the Mac is now winning more converts than ever, not just from Windows, but from other Unix systems such as Linux, Solaris, and FreeBSD (from which Mac OS X's Unix core is derived).

Mac OS X brings all of the great things from earlier versions of the Mac OS and melds them with a BSD core, bringing Unix to the masses of the world. Apple has created a rock-solid operating system to compete both on the user and enterprise level. In days gone by, the Mac was mostly looked at as a system for "fluffy-bunny designers." It's now becoming the must-have hardware and operating system of geeks and designers everywhere.

With Mac OS X, you can bring home the bacon and fry it up in a pan. Your Mac can be used not only for graphic design and creating web pages, but also as a web server. Not into flat graphics? Fine, Mac OS X sports Quartz Extreme and OpenGL. Want to learn how to program? Mac OS X is a developer's dream, packing in Perl, Python, Ruby, C, C++, Objective-C, compilers, and debuggers; if you're an X jockey, you can also run X Windows on top of Mac OS X using Apple's X11 distribution or with other installations of XFree86. In addition to the standard programming languages, Mac OS X comes with a powerful set of frameworks for programming with Cocoa, Mac OS X's native language (adopted from NeXT).

The Layers of Mac OS X

As mentioned earlier, Mac OS X is a multilayered system, as shown in Figure P-1. At its core is the Kernel Environment, or Darwin (*http://opensource.apple.com/darwin*), Apple's own open source operating system, which is based on the Mach 3.0 microkernel and BSD 4.4 Unix. Darwin gives Mac OS X its Unix core, along with features such as a protected memory environment, support for multithreaded applications, and stability that just wasn't attainable in earlier versions of the Mac OS.

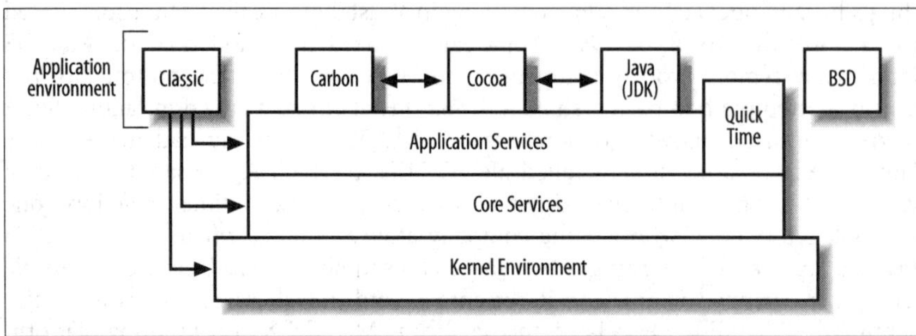

Figure P-1. The layers of Mac OS X

Next up is the Core Services layer. The Core Services provide a set of application program interfaces (or APIs) that allow applications to speak with and take instructions from the kernel. Unless you're a developer, the Core is something that you'll never have to touch or deal with. For programmers, though, the Core provides access to such things as Core Foundation, Core Graphics, Core Audio, CFNetwork, Carbon Core, and Apple Events, to name a few.

The Application Services layer gives Mac OS X its slick Aqua interface. The components in this layer include Quartz Extreme (which replaces QuickDraw from earlier versions of the Mac OS), QuickTime, and OpenGL. Quartz Extreme draws and renders graphics, performs anti-aliasing, and provides services for rendering and printing PDF. Quartz actually has two components: the Quartz Compositor and Quartz 2D. The Quartz Compositor is the window server, while Quartz 2D provides a set of APIs for rendering and drawing two-dimensional shapes.

OpenGL—the workhorse of the graphics community—provides services for three-dimensional (3D) graphics. If you've played any games created in the last 10 years or so, chances are they were based on OpenGL. QuickTime is used in the OS to handle multimedia, such as streaming graphics and movies. Quartz, OpenGL, and QuickTime work together to render all you see in the graphical world of Mac OS X.

On top of it all is the Application Environment. This final layer is where you do all your work and where the applications are run. Apple provides two native APIs for applications to run on Mac OS X: Carbon and Cocoa. Carbon applications are older C and C++ applications that have been Carbonized to run natively on Mac OS X. Cocoa is Mac OS X's "pure" environment: Cocoa applications rely only on the frameworks provided by the system and not on an older code base.

The Application Environment contains a pure Java system—not a virtual machine, as in older Mac systems—that allows you to run 100 percent–pure Java applications on Mac OS X. The current implementation in Mac OS X Panther is J2SE Version 1.4.1.

If you have an older Mac application that hasn't been Carbonized and isn't Cocoa- or Java-based, you're not out of luck. If your system also has Mac OS 9 installed (9.2.2 to be exact), you can run older Mac applications in the Classic Environment (or just Classic). When you're running Classic, you're basically running a watered-down implementation of Mac OS 9 on top of Mac OS X. Classic is covered in Chapter 3.

Also running at the application layer is the Terminal application (*/Applications/Utilities*), which is your command-line interface to the Unix shell. For users, the new default shell in Panther is *bash*, the very same shell that Linux and FreeBSD users worldwide rely on every day.

This multilayered architecture gives Mac OS X its power and elegance. Each layer—and in some cases, the components within each layer—is independent from the other, resulting in a system that hardly ever crashes.

Audience for This Book

No book can be everything to everyone, but *Mac OS X Panther in a Nutshell* does have an audience: one that first needs some clarification.

A question that came up a while back is "Why do I need a Nutshell book if I already have the Missing Manual?" We explain some of the reasoning and the audiences for both books here.

The Missing Manuals (copublished by Pogue Press and O'Reilly) are a series of books aimed at the beginner- to intermediate-level user. The books are written in friendly prose and cover everything users want to know and more.

O'Reilly's Nutshell series is the opposite of that. These books take a more terse approach to the topic. They give you what you need to know in as few words as possible, while at the same time covering things that are useful not only to beginners, but also advanced users.

The resulting package—the combination of the Missing Manual and the Nutshell book—provides you with the depth and coverage not attainable in a single book (unless, of course, you don't mind lifting weights).

So, to get back to the original question, the answer is: to truly master Mac OS X, you probably do need both the Missing Manual and the Nutshell book. Each book takes a different approach to covering Mac OS X, and each offers something the other can't.

Who This Book Is for

Due to the unusual pedigree of Mac OS X, readers might meet it in a number of ways. This book is aimed at folks with a more technical bent than the average user—the *power user*. This book will come in handy as a quick reference guide for those who are curious about what happens under Mac OS X's hood (and how you might tinker with it) and will be useful to those who are using Mac OS X as a server or development platform.

It's important to note that this book doesn't cover Mac OS X Server; it covers only the client version, Mac OS X Panther. For more information on Mac OS X Server, see Apple's online documentation at *http://www.apple.com/macosxserver*.

Who This Book Isn't for

This book focuses mainly on topics that aren't likely to interest those who use Mac OS X primarily to run applications, such as word processing, graphic design, browsing the Web, and so on. These users might be better served by more user-friendly volumes, such as *Mac OS X: The Missing Manual, Panther Edition* (Pogue Press/O'Reilly) or the *Mac OS X Panther Pocket Guide* (O'Reilly), both of which were recently revised for Panther.

How This Book Is Organized

This book is broken down into 5 parts, 28 chapters, and 2 appendixes.

Part I, *Lay of the Land*
: This first part of the book introduces users to Mac OS X Panther, showing you what's there and how to get your system configured to your liking.

: Chapter 1, *Using Mac OS X*
: : We begin our exploration of Mac OS X at its surface, by describing and documenting Aqua, the system's liquid-themed graphical user interface. This chapter covers the visual metaphors and window features that every

native Mac OS X application uses, as well as onscreen objects that are available from every program, such as the Dock and the menu bar.

Chapter 2, *Using the Finder*
: The Finder is Mac OS X's graphical file navigation application, which presents your computer's filesystem through the familiar visual metaphor of folders and files. This chapter explores this application, including a wealth of subtle tips and tricks.

Chapter 3, *Mac OS 9, Mac OS X, and Classic*
: Meant especially for longtime Mac veterans, this chapter covers the major differences between Mac OS X and its predecessors, of which Mac OS 9 was the final version.

Chapter 4, *System Preferences*
: This chapter covers the System Preferences application as it appears in Mac OS X Version 10.2 and details how it works as a frontend to the file-based preferences system.

Chapter 5, *Applications and Utilities*
: Mac OS X comes with a wealth of core applications, more than any Mac OS before it. This chapter lists the contents of a fresh Mac OS X installation's Applications folder and discusses the system's unique approach to application integration, as well as ways to install new programs onto your Mac.

Chapter 6, *Task and Setting Index*
: This chapter provides a quick index of common operating system activities in a question-and-answer format.

Part II, *System and Network Administration*
: Now that you've set up your Mac, it's time to dive deeper into the operating system. This part of the book introduces you to the basic concepts of networking and system administration, including coverage of Directory Services.

Chapter 7, *Filesystem Overview*
: Like any Unix system, much of Mac OS X's functionality is based on its filesystem layout. This chapter tours the various folders found on a typical Mac OS X volume, including the Unix-centric directories that the Finder usually keeps out of sight.

Chapter 8, *Networking*
: This chapter covers the user's part in establishing and using a network connection with Mac OS X. It centers on the system's Network preferences pane and touches on the programs you can use to take advantage of an active connection.

Chapter 9, *Printer Configuration and Printing*
: This chapter details the Mac OS X printing system. It covers printing documents through the standard Print dialogs (as well as through a handful of command-line programs) and discusses configuring the printing system.

Chapter 10, *System Administration Overview*

Now that Macs are actually Unix machines at the core, it pays to know the fundamentals of administrating a multiuser system (even if you're the only human user on it). This chapter also covers the basics of monitoring and maintaining your Mac's network connections, whether they are to a LAN or the Internet.

Chapter 11, *Directory Services*

This chapter details the ways Mac OS X stores and accesses its administrative information, ranging from the NetInfo system of network-linked databases to the "old-school" file-based system familiar to Unix administrators.

Chapter 12, *Running Network Services*

Mac OS X's suite of open source Unix software includes a full complement of network services programs (what the Unix wizards call daemons). This chapter details the major categories of services Unix supplies, including web servers, file sharing, and mail servers. This chapter also covers the control that Mac OS X gives you through either the Sharing preferences pane or the command line.

Chapter 13, *Security Basics*

Mac OS X Panther includes many new security-related features, from Kerberos authentication to the new FileVault and Secure Empty Trash. This chapter provides a basic run-down of how you can keep your Mac and the data on it more secure.

Part III, *Scripting and Development*

Mac OS X is a developer's dream come true. This part covers the basics of AppleScript, the Xcode Tools, Java, and the concurrent versioning system (CVS) for managing your source code.

Chapter 14, *AppleScript*

The Mac's native scripting language, AppleScript, gives you control over the environment and the applications on your system. This chapter introduces you to AppleScript, describing Apple Events and showing you how to use the Script Editor to write AppleScripts.

Chapter 15, *Xcode Tools*

Mac OS X is a developer's delight, and each new Mac and OS box comes with Apple's own Xcode Tools. This chapter provides a basic overview of the applications and tools that ship as part of the Xcode Tools, including Xcode and Interface Builder, the integrated development environment (IDE) for programming Cocoa-based applications for Mac OS X.

Chapter 16, *Java on Mac OS X*

This chapter covers the various ways you can run Java programs in Mac OS X, either as full-fledged Aqua applications, JAR files that provide their own interfaces, or even command-line programs.

Chapter 17, *CVS*

CVS, the concurrent versions system, gives users and developers an easy way to manage changes made to project files. Under CVS, each person working on a project gets their own "sandbox" copy of every file involved, which they can modify and experiment with however they please; a central, untouchable file repository keeps the canonical files safe. This chapter introduces you to CVS and includes both the administrator and user commands.

Part IV, *Under Mac OS X's Hood*

Now it's time to roll up your sleeves. This part of the book goes deeper into the BSD Unix side of Mac OS X.

Chapter 18, *Using the Terminal*

With Mac OS X, you'll normally use one way to gain access to the Unix core: the Terminal application. This chapter introduces you to the Terminal application and shows you how to issue commands and tweak its settings.

Chapter 19, *Shell Overview*

This chapter provides a quick overview of the differences between *bash*, Mac OS X Panther's default shell, and *tcsh*, the default shell for earlier versions of Mac OS X.

Chapter 20, *bash: The Bourne-Again Shell*

This chapter provides a quick overview of the *bash* shell, along with a listing of its built-in commands for shell scripting.

Chapter 21, *tcsh: An Extended C Shell*

This chapter provides a quick overview of the *tcsh* shell, along with a listing of its built-in commands for shell scripting.

Chapter 22, *Pattern Matching*

A number of Unix text-processing utilities let you search for, and in some cases change, text patterns rather than fixed strings. These utilities include editing programs such as *vi* and *Emacs*, programming languages such as Perl and Python, and the commands *grep* and *egrep*. Text patterns (formally called *regular expressions*) contain normal characters mixed with special characters (called *metacharacters*).

Chapter 23, *The vi Editor*

vi is the classic screen-editing program for Unix. In Mac OS X Panther, *vim* is the default version of *vi* and runs when you invoke *vi* from the command line. This chapter covers some of *vi*'s most commonly used options and features.

Chapter 24, *The Emacs Editor*

The *Emacs* editor is found on many Unix systems, including Mac OS X, because it is a popular alternative to *vi*. For many Unix users, *Emacs* is more than "just an editor." While *Emacs* provides a fully integrated user environment, this chapter focuses on its editing capabilities.

Chapter 25, *The Defaults System*

Like the old saying goes, there's more than one way to skin a cat. In this case, the cat we're skinning is Panther. When you configure your system or an application to your liking, those preferences are stored in what's known as the *defaults database*. This chapter describes how to gain access to and hack these settings via the Terminal application and the *defaults* command.

Chapter 26, *The X Window System*
: This chapter highlights some of the key features of Apple's X11 distribution and explains how to install Apple's X11 and the X11 SDK. It also explains how to use X11 in both rootless and full-screen modes (using the GNOME and KDE desktops). You'll also learn how to connect to other X Window systems using Virtual Network Computer (VNC), as well as how to remotely control the Mac OS X desktop from other X11 systems.

Chapter 27, *Installing Unix Software*
: While Mac OS X is Unix-based, most Unix applications need a little help to get them installed and running. This chapter describes some of the issues you'll run into when installing a Unix application on Mac OS X and guides you through what's needed to make them run.

Chapter 28, *Unix Command Reference*
: This final chapter lists descriptions and usage terms for nearly 300 Unix commands found in Mac OS X. The commands have been painstakingly run and verified against the manpages for accuracy; this is the most complete and accurate Mac-based Unix command reference in print.

Part V, *Appendixes*
: The book also has the following appendixes.

Appendix A, *Special Characters*
: This appendix lists the special characters you can create using the various special keys (Shift, Control, Option, Command, and combinations thereof) to create special characters without having to use the Character Palette.

Appendix B, *Resources*
: This appendix is a listing of resources for Mac users, including books, web sites, and mailing lists applicable to Mac OS X users, developers, and administrators.

Conventions Used in This Book

The following typographical conventions are used in this book:

Italic
: Used to indicate new terms, URLs, filenames, file extensions, directories, commands and options, program names, and to highlight comments in examples. For example, a path in the filesystem appears as */Applications/Utilities*.

`Constant Width`
: Used to show the contents of files or the output from commands.

`Constant Width Bold`
: Used in examples and tables to show commands or other text that should be typed literally by the user.

`Constant Width Italic`
: Used in examples and tables to show text that should be replaced with user-supplied values.

Menus/navigation

Menus and their options are referred to in the text as File→Open, Edit→Copy, etc. Arrows are also used to signify a navigation path when using window options. For example, "System Preferences→Desktop & Screen Saver→Screen Saver" means that you would launch System Preferences, click the icon for the "Desktop & Screen Saver" preference panel, and then select the "Screen Saver" pane within that panel.

Pathnames

Pathnames are used to show the location of a file or application in the filesystem. Directories (or folders for Mac and Windows users) are separated by a forward slash. For example, if you see something like, ". . . launch the Terminal application (*/Applications/Utilities*)" in the text, this means the Terminal application can be found in the Utilities subfolder of the Applications folder.

The tilde character (~) refers to the current user's Home folder, so *~/Library* refers to the Library folder within your own Home folder.

↵ A carriage return (↵) at the end of a line of code denotes an unnatural line break; that is, you should not enter these as two lines of code, but as one continuous line. Multiple lines are used in these cases due to printing constraints.

$, # The dollar sign ($) is used in some examples to show the user prompt for the *bash* shell; the hash mark (#) is the prompt for the *root* user.

Menu symbols

When looking at the menus for any application, you will see some symbols associated with keyboard shortcuts for a particular command. For example, to open a document in Microsoft Word, you can go to the File menu and select Open (File→Open), or you can issue the keyboard shortcut, ⌘-O.

Figure P-2 shows the symbols used in the various menus to denote a keyboard shortcut.

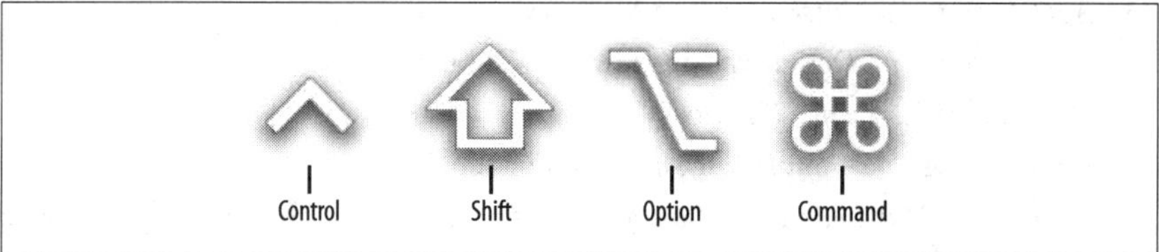

Figure P-2. Keyboard modifiers for issuing commands

Rarely will you see the Control symbol used as a menu command option; it's more often used in association with mouse clicks or for working with the *bash* shell.

Indicates a tip, suggestion, or general note.

Indicates a warning or caution.

Comments and Questions

Please address comments and questions concerning this book to the publisher:

O'Reilly Media, Inc.
1005 Gravenstein Highway North
Sebastopol, CA 95472
800-998-9938 (in the U.S. or Canada)
707-829-0515 (international/local)
707-829-0104 (fax)

There is a web page for this book that lists errata, examples, or any additional information. You can access this page at:

http://www.oreilly.com/catalog/macpantherian

To comment or ask technical questions about this book, send email to:

bookquestions@oreilly.com

For more information about books, conferences, Resource Centers, and the O'Reilly Network, see the O'Reilly web site at:

http://www.oreilly.com

Acknowledgments

The authors would like to acknowledge the masses who helped make the book possible, and also would like to thank the authors of other O'Reilly books, from which some portions of this book were derived; including:

- *AppleScript in a Nutshell* (Bruce M. Perry)
- *AppleScript: The Definitive Guide* (Matt Neuburg)
- *CVS Pocket Reference* (Gregor N. Purdy)
- *Essential System Administration* (Æleen Frisch)
- *Linux in a Nutshell* (Ellen Siever, Stephen Spainhour, Stephen Figgins, and Jessica P. Hekman)
- *Mac OS X Panther Pocket Guide* (Chuck Toporek)
- *Mac OS X Panther for Unix Geeks* (Brian Jepson and Ernest E. Rothman)
- *DNS & BIND* (Paul Albitz and Cricket Liu)
- *Running Mac OS X Panther* (James Duncan Davidson)
- *SSH, The Secure Shell: The Definitive Guide* (Daniel J. Barrett and Richard E. Silverman)
- *Unix in a Nutshell* (Arnold Robbins)

Acknowledgments for Chuck Toporek

There are many people to thank for their contributions to making this book happen:

- Jason McIntosh, who initially took on this book and welcomed me as a coauthor, in addition to my recurring role as editor, on the first edition
- Chris Stone, who along with Scott Gever and Dave Carrano, helped put together a solid *Unix Command Reference* for the first edition
- Chris Stone (again) for coming back to work on the second edition as a coauthor with me on revising the book for Mac OS X Panther
- Leon Towns-von Stauber, who gave some vital contributions to the *Unix Command Reference* chapter for both editions of the book
- Andy Lester and Wei-Meng Lee for taking on the task of updating the *Unix Command Reference* chapter for Panther
- Daniel Steinberg, who penned the *Java on Mac OS X* chapter for this edition
- Wacom, for the loan of a Graphire 3 tablet for testing with Ink

Next, I have to thank my wife Kellie Robinson for putting up with her "geek" of a husband while I took on yet another project. My DIY attitude often gets me in trouble, and you'd think that after having spent four years in the U.S. Navy, I would have learned that "NAVY" stands for "Never Again Volunteer Yourself"—but I didn't. Thanks, Kellie, for putting up with my long nights and weekends of working at home, and for supporting me when I needed it. Thanks also to my family and friends for their support with everything I do.

Thanks to the many people at O'Reilly for their involvement in this project, in particular: David Chu, Claire Cloutier, Mary Anne Weeks Mayo, Julie Hawks, Melanie Wang, Emma Colby, C.J. Rayhill, Bob Amen, Sue Willing, and Lorrie LeJeune for drawing Vinny (the dog on the cover).

Thanks to our great friends at Apple Computer, not only for giving us a killer operating system to work with, but also for their assistance, guidance, and input on some of the technical details we couldn't find answers to.

And last, but not least, I'd like to thank Tim O'Reilly for getting "The Mac Religion," backing all the work I'm doing, and for making O'Reilly a truly awesome place to work (even if I'm now working remotely from a 120-square-foot "office" in Portland, Oregon).

Acknowledgments for Chris Stone

I wouldn't have gotten very far with this book without the support of my incredible wife and kids, Miho, Andy, and Jonathan; to them I dedicate this book, my work, and my life.

For even getting me started on the book, I have to thank editor and coauthor Chuck Toporek, who did an amazing job of putting this whole tome together, and whose support and faith in me were all it took to keep my nose to the grindstone. I must also thank the three other people who were responsible for getting me into print: Troy Mott, Derrick Story, and David Pogue. Without the encouragement and guidance of all four gentlemen, I'd still be only a reader of O'Reilly books.

My thanks also go to the other contributors to this book, namely Jason McIntosh, Leon Towns-von Stauber, Daniel Steinberg, Wei Meng Lee, and Andy Lester, as well as Scott Gever, Dave Carrano, and David Brickner, who helped so much with the first edition. I also have to thank all the kind and talented people at O'Reilly with whom I work as a systems administrator. It's a privilege to be able to do the work I love, and do it with such great colleagues. I'd put the entire company roster here if space (and Chuck) permitted, but special thanks go to Bob Amen, C. J. Rayhill, and Laurie Petrycki for allowing and encouraging me to take on this project.

Finally, I know it would have been impossible to work through all the hours put into this book without having my (almost) weekly disc golf game to look forward to. For that I have to thank my good friends, golf partners and just nice guys, Carlos Chavez and Jon Robbins.

Acknowledgments for Jason McIntosh (from the First Edition)

Chuck Toporek provided great guidance and insight as an editor, and knew when to step in and help write once my life changed in unexpected ways (i.e., I suddenly stopped being unemployed); this book is much better for his active efforts. Chris Stone took on the *Unix Command Reference* chapter before any of us realized the magnitude of that task, and yet he and his cohorts did a smashing job. I mean, just look at that thing.

John Keimel and Andrew "Zarf" Plotkin tech-reviewed this book. Jim Troutman and Andy Turner at Arcus Digital in Waterville, Maine, hosted my email, web, and CVS server, which was crucial to this project (and my life). They also tossed me some freelance programming jobs to gnaw on, and pitched in with tech reviewing. Karl von Laudermann and Derek Lichter assisted with last-minute fact checking. The filler text in several examples is excerpted from Erik T. Ray's The Lambda Expressway and used with permission.

Derrick Story at the O'Reilly Network let me write some Mac OS X articles for macdevcenter.com, helping me stave off financial ruin until Erik Brauner and the Institute for Chemistry and Cell Biology at Harvard Medical School hired me into a wonderful job midway through this book's production. They showed great patience with me as I pulled odd and antisocial office hours in order to complete the book on time.

Reprising their roles from my work on *Perl & XML* (with Erik T. Ray, published by O'Reilly), Julia "Cthulhia" Tenney acted as my personal principal gadfly, and the 1369 Coffee House in Cambridge and the Diesel Cafe in Somerville again served as my alternate offices.

Mary Agner, Denis Moskowitz, and the whole regular crowd at the House of Roses game nights made sure I got my biweekly ration of sanity-maintaining game playing.

My housemates Melissa Kibbe and Noah Meyerhans (and, before them, Charles Peterman and Carla Schack) continually encouraged me to hurry up and finish the book, if only so I'd stop moping about it.

If you've made a web page (or even posted to a mailing list) about Mac OS X, I've probably read it and used its information somehow. Thanks.

Mike Scott at the University of Maine first introduced me to Macintosh computers back when System 7 was brand new. Andy England of Mac Advantage in Bangor and Jeff Wheeler of the Town of Hermon gave me my first Mac-centric, post-college jobs. Jason Lavoie and Andy Turner of the late Maine InternetWorks got me into Unix (by way of Linux and Perl) with my first programming job. O'Reilly then hired me, after which they unhired me, but not before getting me irrevocably entangled with technical writing. This is more or less how I got here.

I did all my work for this book on my iBook running Mac OS X. The text is courtesy the *Emacs* text editor, working in raw DocBook XML, and the screen shots come from Apple's Grab application. The Omni Group's OmniOutliner application helped me organize my thoughts and notes for every chapter I wrote.

All remaining thanks go to my parents Dorothy and Richard, my brothers Peter and Ricky, my aunt Jan, and all of my friends both local and remote, whose network of love and support I relied heavily upon throughout this project, and upon which I shall no doubt continue to draw for whatever silly thing I do next. Yay!

I

Lay of the Land

As any newcomer can attest, Mac OS X's user interface can be overwhelming at first. This part sets the stage for the rest of the book, in that you'll learn the lay of the land for the Mac that sits before you. It introduces the Mac OS X landscape, providing details about the user interface elements, such as the windows, buttons, and various controls, along with information on using the Dock and Finder. For Mac OS 9 users who are coming to Mac OS X, Chapter 3 will be of particular interest to you. This part wraps up with a task and setting index, which includes nearly 300 hints, tips, and tricks for using and configuring your Mac OS X System.

The chapters in this part include:

- Chapter 1, *Using Mac OS X*
- Chapter 2, *Using the Finder*
- Chapter 3, *Mac OS 9, Mac OS X, and Classic*
- Chapter 4, *System Preferences*
- Chapter 5, *Applications and Utilities*
- Chapter 6, *Task and Setting Index*

1
Using Mac OS X

There are actually two interface layers to Mac OS X. One is *Aqua*, the system's native graphical user interface (GUI); the other is a command-line interface (CLI), which is most commonly accessed via the Terminal application (*/Applications/Utilities*). This chapter provides a quick overview of Mac OS X's Aqua environment; later chapters in the book will introduce you to the Terminal and the BSD Unix side, with a full examination of these deeper OS layers in Part IV.

Mac OS X offers a feature-rich graphical user environment that makes it easy for people to interact with the operating system. This chapter starts out with a discussion of Mac OS X's Desktop, and introduces things like the menu bar, the Dock, and basic window controls. Chapter 2 covers the Finder, Mac OS X's file manager.

Starting Up and Logging In

When you turn on your Mac (or restart it), it takes a minute or so for the system to start up. During this time, various processes and services are started before the user is presented with a login window. Unix veterans are used to seeing the startup phase displayed as a cascade of text messages spilling down the screen, but Mac OS X hides all this information behind a plain white screen with a gray Apple logo on it.

You *can* see all that startup text if you really want to, by booting into single-user mode (hold down ⌘-S as your Mac starts up). This can be a useful diagnostic tool for hardcore Unix-heads who know what they're doing, or a way for the merely curious to watch the strange sight of their Mac rolling out of bed and stumbling around in pure-Unix mode before it puts on its Mac OS face. Use the *exit* command at the single-user shell to resume the normal Mac OS X boot process. You can also view some of the machine's startup messages after the fact by looking at the file */var/log/system.log*; only users with admin privileges can read this file.

Eventually the system either settles on the login screen or logs in a specific user, depending upon the machine's configuration (System Preferences→Accounts→Login Options). If presented with a login screen, you need to provide your username (either by choosing it from a list or typing your username into a text field) and password.

Once you've successfully logged in, Mac OS X loads your user account and presents you with your Desktop using the settings you've provided in System Preferences. You are now in your Home folder.

Generally speaking, everything in your Home folder (which you can always go to through the Finder's Go→Home (Shift-⌘-H) option) belongs to you, and you are unrestricted in how you read, modify, create and delete the files and folders within it (and the files and folders within those folders, and so on). Everything *outside* your Home folder is another matter. For example, all users can run the applications stored in the */Applications* folder, but only admin users can modify that folder's contents; no regular user, admin or otherwise, has full access to any other user's Home folder. See Chapter 8 for more information on the structure of Mac OS X's filesystem and permissions.

Startup and Shutdown Keys

For most users, starting and shutting down your Mac is fairly routine: press the Power-On button to start, and go to →Shut Down to turn off the machine at night. But there are times when you need to do more, for whatever reason. Table 1-1 lists some of the additional keys you can use when starting, restarting, logging out, and shutting down your system.

Some of the keyboard shortcuts listed in Table 1-1 work only on newer hardware. If you are using an older Mac, these keyboard shortcuts might not work.

Table 1-1. Keyboard shortcuts to start, restart, log out, and shut down

Key command	Description
C	Holding down the C key at startup boots from a CD (useful when installing or upgrading the system software).
N	Attempts to start up from a NetBoot server.
R	Resets the display for a PowerBook.

Table 1-1. Keyboard shortcuts to start, restart, log out, and shut down (continued)

Key command	Description
T	Holding down the T key at startup places your Mac into Target Mode as a mountable FireWire drive. After starting up, your screen will have a blue background with a floating yellow FireWire symbol. Target mode makes the hard drive(s) of your Mac appear as mounted FireWire drives when connected to another system. To exit Target mode, press the Power-On button to turn off your Mac. After your Mac has shut down completely, press the Power-on button again to restart normally.
X	Holding down the X key at startup forces the machine to boot into Mac OS X, even if Mac OS 9 is specified as the default startup disk.
⌘-S	Boots into single-user mode.
⌘-V	Boots into verbose mode, displaying all the startup messages onscreen. (Linux users will be familiar with this.)
Shift	Holding down the Shift key at startup invokes Safe Boot mode, turning off any unnecessary kernel extensions (*kexts*) and ignoring anything you've set in the Accounts→Login Options preferences pane.
Option	Holding down the Option key at startup opens the Startup Manager, which allows you to select which OS to boot into.
Mouse button	Holding down the mouse button at startup ejects any disk (CD, DVD, or other removable media) that might still be in the drive.
Shift-Option-⌘-Q Option + →Log Out	Logs you off without prompting you first.
Option-Power-On Option + →Shut Down	Shuts down your system without prompting you first.
Option + →Restart	Restarts your machine without prompting you first.
Control-⌘-Power-On button	Forces an automatic shutdown of your system; this should be used only as a last resort, because it could mess up your filesystem.[a]
Control-Eject (F12)	Opens a dialog box that contains options for Restart, Sleep, and Shutdown.

[a] Mostly, you'll just wait forever at the gray Apple startup screen while an *fsck* happens in the background, unless you have journaling turned on (see Chapter 7).

Once you've successfully logged in to your user account, you are presented with the famed Macintosh Desktop. It's here where your Mac experience begins.

The Mac Desktop

When you first log on to your Mac, you are presented with the *Desktop*, as shown in Figure 1-1. By "Desktop," we're referring to the entire screen and all its interface elements, including the menu bar, the Dock, the Desktop, disk and file icons, and the various windows used by the Finder and other applications.

The Menu Bar

Regardless of which application you use, Mac OS X's menu bar is always located across the top of the screen. This is different from Microsoft Windows or Linux GNOME or KDE desktop environments, where the menu bar is attached to each individual window. There are some standard items you'll always find in the menu

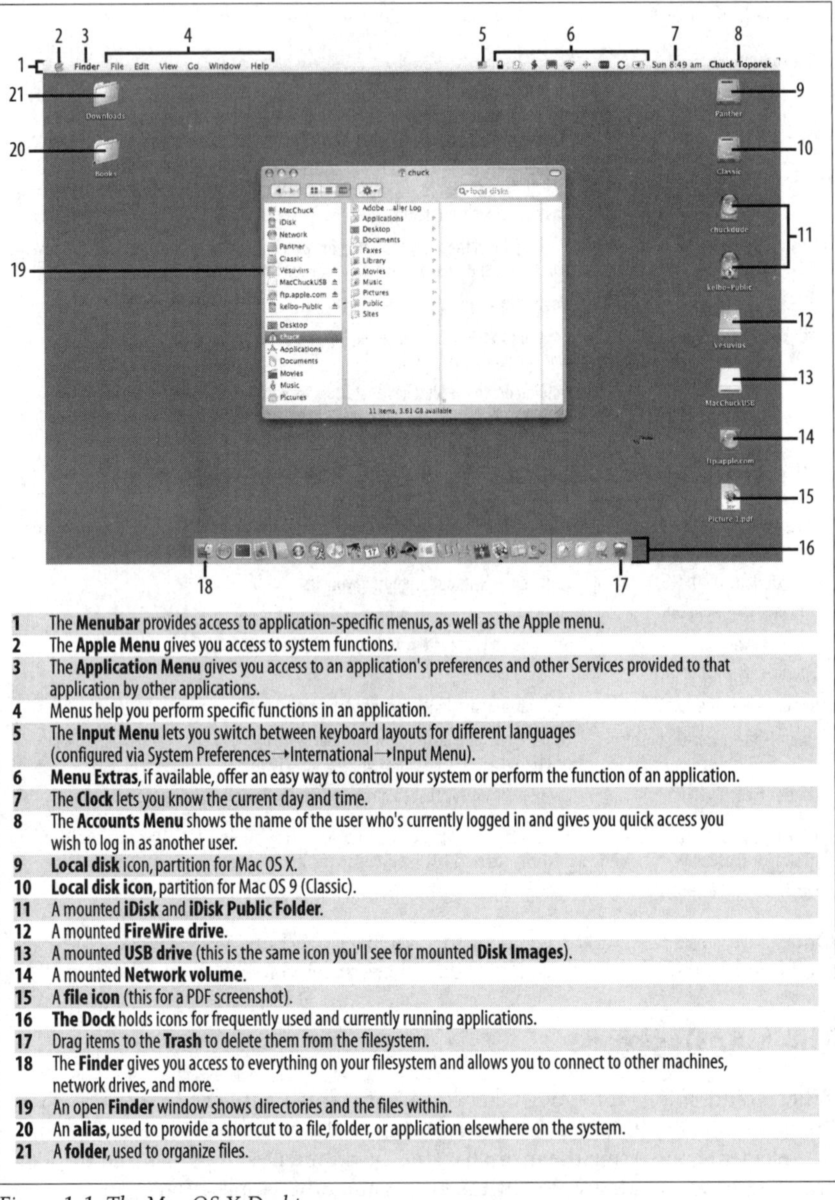

1 The Menubar provides access to application-specific menus, as well as the Apple menu.
2 The Apple Menu gives you access to system functions.
3 The Application Menu gives you access to an application's preferences and other Services provided to that application by other applications.
4 Menus help you perform specific functions in an application.
5 The Input Menu lets you switch between keyboard layouts for different languages (configured via System Preferences→International→Input Menu).
6 Menu Extras, if available, offer an easy way to control your system or perform the function of an application.
7 The Clock lets you know the current day and time.
8 The Accounts Menu shows the name of the user who's currently logged in and gives you quick access you wish to log in as another user.
9 Local disk icon, partition for Mac OS X.
10 Local disk icon, partition for Mac OS 9 (Classic).
11 A mounted iDisk and iDisk Public Folder.
12 A mounted FireWire drive.
13 A mounted USB drive (this is the same icon you'll see for mounted Disk Images).
14 A mounted Network volume.
15 A file icon (this for a PDF screenshot).
16 The Dock holds icons for frequently used and currently running applications.
17 Drag items to the Trash to delete them from the filesystem.
18 The Finder gives you access to everything on your filesystem and allows you to connect to other machines, network drives, and more.
19 An open Finder window shows directories and the files within.
20 An alias, used to provide a shortcut to a file, folder, or application elsewhere on the system.
21 A folder, used to organize files.

Figure 1-1. The Mac OS X Desktop

bar, but as you switch from application to application, you'll notice that the menu names and some of their options change according to which application is active. Figure 1-2 shows the menu bar as it appears when the Finder is active.

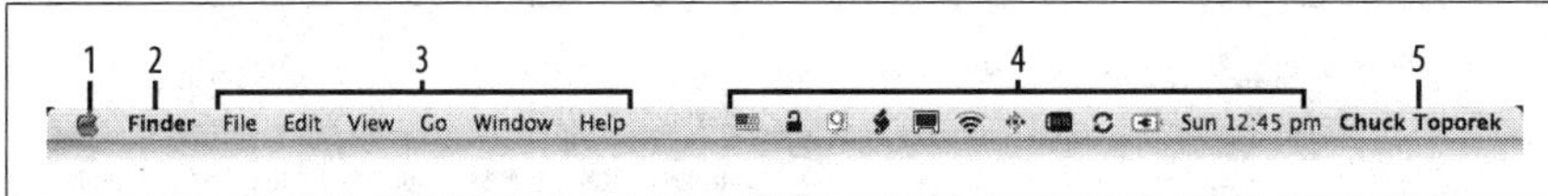

Figure 1-2. The Mac OS X menu bar (with the Finder active)

Using Mac OS X

As Figure 1-2 shows, these menus and items can be found in the menu bar:

1. The Apple menu (see the section "The Apple Menu")
2. The Application menu (see the section "The Application Menu")
3. A default set of application menus (see the section "Standard Application Menus")
4. Menu extras (see the section "Menu Extras")
5. The Accounts menu (see the section "The Accounts Menu")

Active and Inactive Applications

A running application can have one of two possible states: *active* or *inactive*.

An *active application* is the application you're currently using—in other words, the application that receives any input you generate through the keyboard or mouse (with the exception of clicks or keystrokes that switch between applications). An *inactive application* has been launched but is running in the background.

You'll typically run many applications at once, using the Dock to track and manage them as described later in "The Dock." For example, let's say you're browsing the Web with Safari (the active application) and have Mail running in the background (inactive). When new mail arrives, Mail alerts you by playing a sound and by placing a small red dot on its icon in the Dock with a number inside to let you know how many new messages you have. To see what those new messages are, you click on Mail's icon in the Dock to bring Mail forward, thus making it the active application and relegating Safari to the background.

Menu Basics

All menus in Mac OS X work the same way: click once on a word or symbol in the menu bar, and the appropriate menu pops down beneath it. The menu closes when you select something by scrolling down and letting go of the mouse button, select a different menu in the menu bar, or click somewhere outside the menu.

Each menu contains a set of *commands* for the application, as shown in Figure 1-3's example of the Finder's File menu. Menus can also contain *submenus* that lead to other commands, and special commands that have an ellipsis (...) after them, which typically require more information from the user before they can do anything.

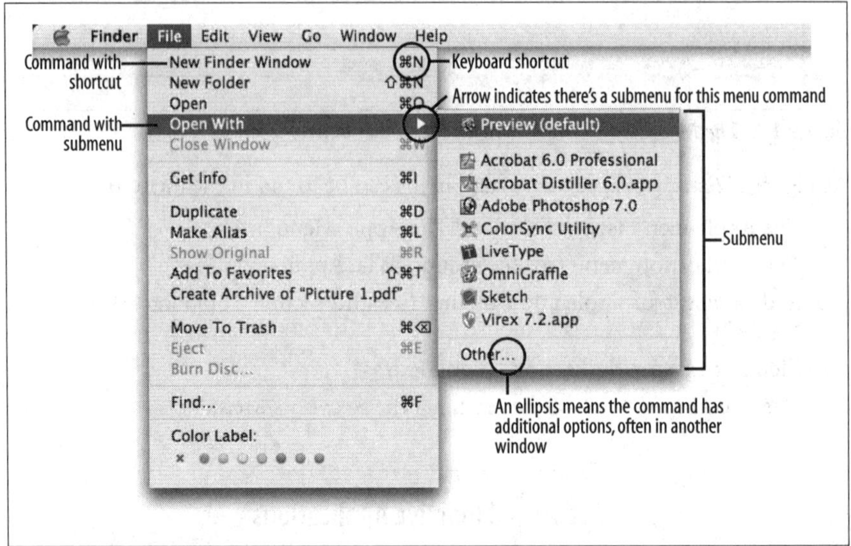

Figure 1-3. The Finder's File menu has regular commands, commands with submenus, and special commands, such as Find..., followed by an ellipsis.

Commands

Every row that's not a submenu heading is a *command*. When you move the mouse over a command, the command is highlighted with a colored bar (the color of which is set in System Preferences→Appearance→Appearance). The command is selected and invoked when you let go of the mouse button.

If you have invoked a command in error, most applications offer the Edit→Undo option (⌘-Z) as a way of undoing the last command or action performed.

Commands that end in an ellipsis (...) require more information from the user before they can do anything. Typically, these menu items summon a dialog box requiring the user to do something else. For example, if you select File→Find..., the Find window appears, giving you options to search for a particular file. If you decide that you don't want to search for a file (or if you've selected the wrong menu item), you can click on the Cancel button to close the window.

Most menu commands have keyboard shortcuts (also known as *key bindings*). The keyboard shortcuts, if available, are on the right edge of the menu and act as an alternate way to invoke a menu command without using the mouse. The most commonly used keyboard shortcut is ⌘-Q, used to quit an application.

Bindings for common commands, such as ⌘-Q, are the same across all applications (with the exception of the Finder, which you cannot quit). This is in accordance with Apple's *Aqua Human Interface Guidelines*, more commonly known as "the HIG." The HIG specifies the default key bindings for standard menu options and should be the interface design Bible of every Macintosh developer.

If you've installed the Xcode Tools on your system, a copy of the HIG can be found in */Developer/Documentation/UserExperience/Conceptual/AquaHIGuidelines* in both HTML and PDF form. The HIG can also be accessed online at *http://developer.apple.com*.

Submenus

Submenus appear as menu choices with little gray triangles at the right edge of the menu. When you move the mouse over a submenu heading, another menu appears to the right, as seen earlier in Figure 1-3. Submenus can contain additional menu items or even more submenus.

Contextual Menus

Many objects in Mac OS X offer *contextual menus*, which are special lists of commands and submenus that appear only when you Control-click (or right-click) on the item. When you're in the Finder (or on the Desktop) and you hold the Control key down over an object, the mouse pointer's shape changes to include an image of a menu, as shown in Figure 1-4. If you Control-click on an object, a context menu appears, giving you various options to select from, as shown in Figure 1-5.

Figure 1-4. When the mouse is hovering over an object, the pointer changes to include a menu image if you hold down the Control key

Context menus are also available within applications as well. For example, if you Control-click on a hypertext link in Safari, a context menu appears giving you various options to select from, such as copying the URL to the clipboard or the ability to quickly bookmark a link without viewing the page (see Figure 1-6).

The Apple Menu

The Apple menu, shown in Figure 1-7, is displayed as a blue Apple symbol (), and is always the left-most item in the menu bar.

If you've used an earlier version of the Mac OS, you'll notice that the Apple menu is now completely different. You can no longer store aliases for files, folders, or applications there. Its new purpose is to provide you with information about your system, and to give you quick access to system preferences, network locations, and recently used files and applications, as well as a means to log out, put your system to sleep, or shut down.

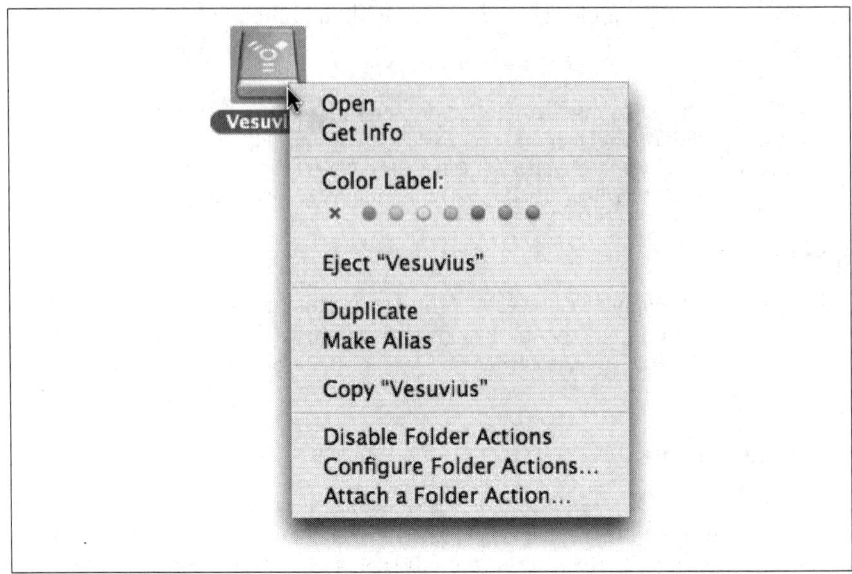

Figure 1-5. The context menu for a FireWire drive is revealed by Control-clicking on the drive's Desktop icon

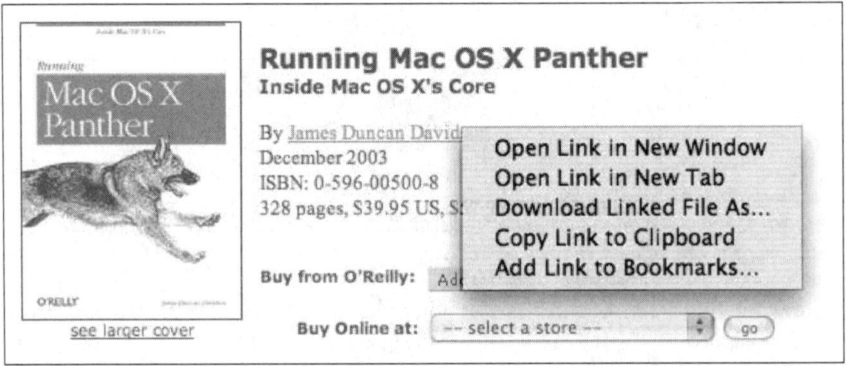

Figure 1-6. A contextual menu in Safari

The following items can be found in the Apple menu.

About This Mac
: This window, shown in Figure 1-8, provides you with useful information about your Mac. Here you'll find details about the version of Mac OS X you're running, how much memory your machine has, and the speed and type of processor in your computer. Clicking on the More Info button launches the System Profiler application (*/Applications/Utilities*), which reveals specific details about your hardware, as well as its devices, applications, and extensions. The System Profiler is covered in Chapter 5.

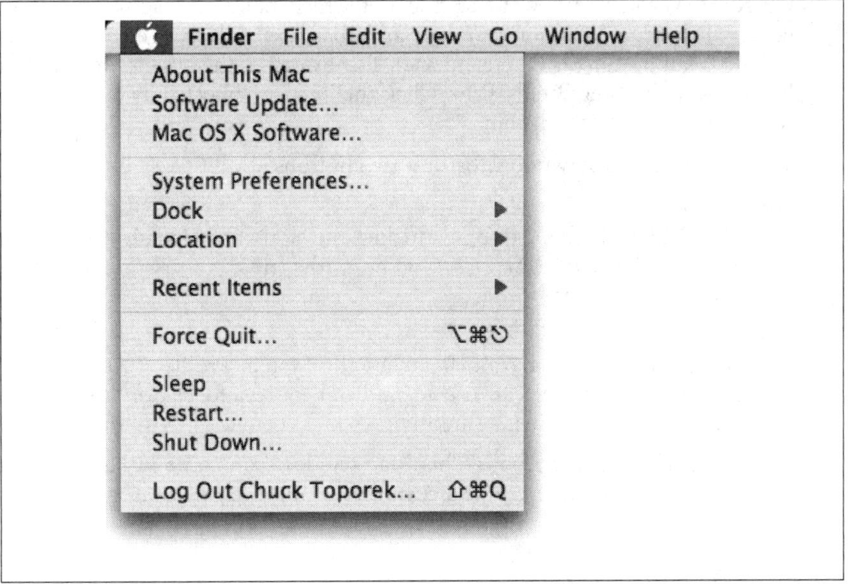

Figure 1-7. The Apple menu

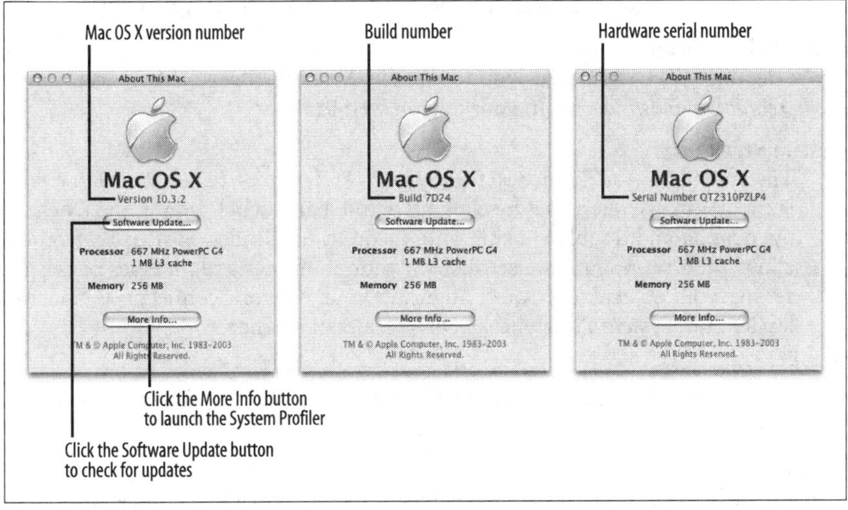

Figure 1-8. The About This Mac window

In earlier versions of the Mac OS, the About box would change depending on which application was active. For information about the application, you now have to use the application menu (located to the right of the Apple menu) and select the About option.

When you first select →About This Mac, the window shown on the left side of Figure 1-8 shows you the currently installed version number of Mac

OS X. However, if you want to find out which build of Mac OS X you're using, click on the version number, and that text will change to show the versions' build number (center image). For example, the system depicted in Figure 1-8 is running Build 7D24. Click the build number, and you'll see the serial number for your machine.

The About This Mac window features two buttons:

Software Update
: When clicked, this button launches the Software Update application (*/System/Library/CoreServices*) without the need to use its panel in System Preferences.

More Info
: When clicked, this button launches the System Profiler (*/Applications/Utilities*), which you can use to find out more information about your Mac and the software it's running.

The information in the About This Mac window can come in handy when you're on the phone with Apple's customer support, trying to troubleshoot a problem.

Software Update
: This launches the Software Update application and checks for updates for Mac OS X and other Apple software installed on your system. For more information about using Software Update, see Chapter 5, *System Preferences*.

Mac OS X Software
: Selecting this option takes you to Apple's Mac OS X page (*http://www.apple.com/downloads/macosx*) in your default web browser.

System Preferences
: This menu option launches the System Preferences panel. (You can also launch System Preferences by clicking on the light switch icon in the Dock, or by locating and double-clicking on its icon in the Finder. System Preferences allow you to configure the settings on your computer and includes panels for setting your screen saver or configuring your network connection. You will learn about System Preferences in greater detail in Chapter 4.

Dock
: This menu offers a quick way to change settings for the Dock (see the later section "The Dock").

Location
: This allows you to quickly change locations for connecting to a network and/or the Internet. This is similar to the Location Manager Control Panel from earlier versions of the Mac OS.

Recent Items
: This menu option combines the Recent Applications and Recent Documents options from Mac OS 9's Apple menu into one convenient menu. The Clear Menu option allows you to reset the recent items from the menu, giving you a clean slate to work from.

Force Quit

This window lets you force-quit any running Aqua application. See the section "Force-quitting applications," later in this chapter.

Sleep

Just as its name implies, this menu item will instantly put your Mac into sleep mode. Selecting this option will result in your screen going dark; the hard drive on your system will spin down and go into energy saver mode. This is different from the settings you dictate in the Energy Saver preference pane (see Chapter 4 for more on auto-sleep functionality).

To "wake" your computer from sleep mode, simply press any key, or click the mouse if you have a desktop system. However, clicking the mouse on an iBook or PowerBook as an attempt to wake your system from sleep mode is useless; it won't do anything. Instead, you need to press one of the keys on the keyboard (or the Power-On button) to revive your laptop. Opening a sleeping and closed Mac laptop will also wake it up.

Sleep, Restart, Shutdown, and Log Out have moved from Mac OS 9's Special menu into Mac OS X's Apple menu. If you're looking for a menu option for the Empty Trash option, you need to be in the Finder (Finder→Empty Trash or Shift-⌘-Delete).

Restart

Selecting this option opens a window (shown in Figure 1-9) to restart your Mac. If any applications are running, they will be automatically shut down, and you will be prompted to save changes for any files that were open.

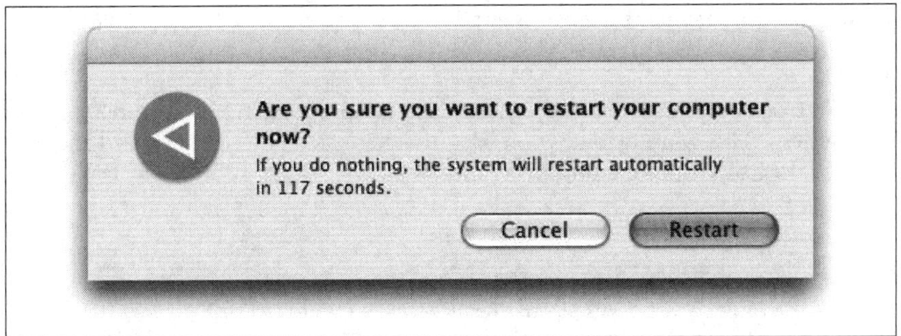
Are you sure you want to restart your computer now?
If you do nothing, the system will restart automatically in 117 seconds.
Cancel
Restart

Figure 1-9. The Restart window

System administrators can remove the Restart and Shut Down items from the Apple menu, as described in Chapter 4.

Shutdown

Selecting this option pops up a window (shown in Figure 1-10) for shutting down your Mac. You can also shut down by pressing the Power-On button, which opens the dialog box shown in Figure 1-11 with the options for restarting, shutting down, or putting your Mac to sleep.

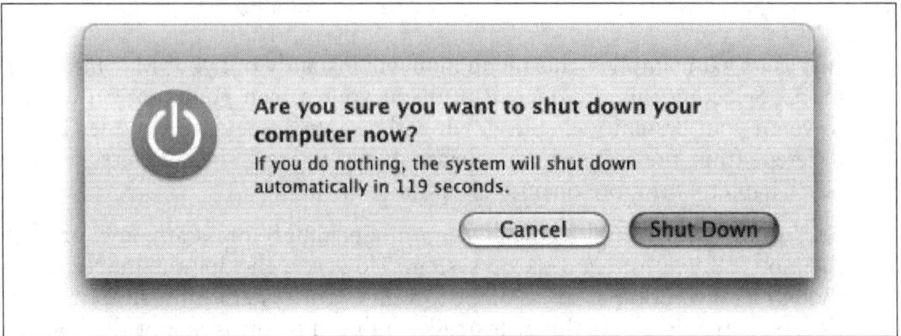

Figure 1-10. The Shutdown window

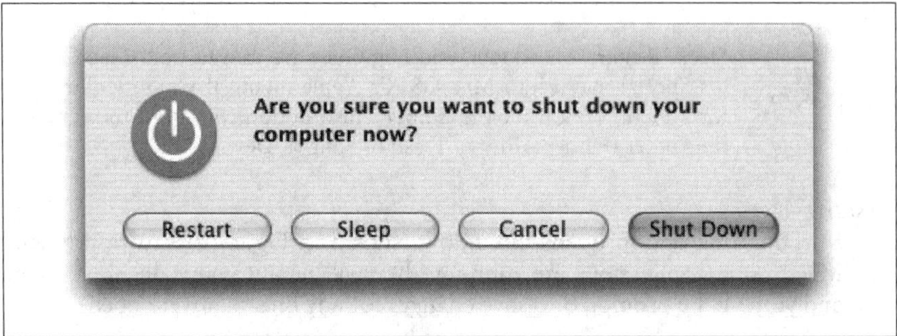

Figure 1-11. This Shutdown window is displayed after pressing the Power-On button

Log Out
: This option pops open the window shown in Figure 1-12 to log out of your system. This window takes you back to a login screen. The keyboard shortcut for the Log Out menu option is Shift-⌘-Q.

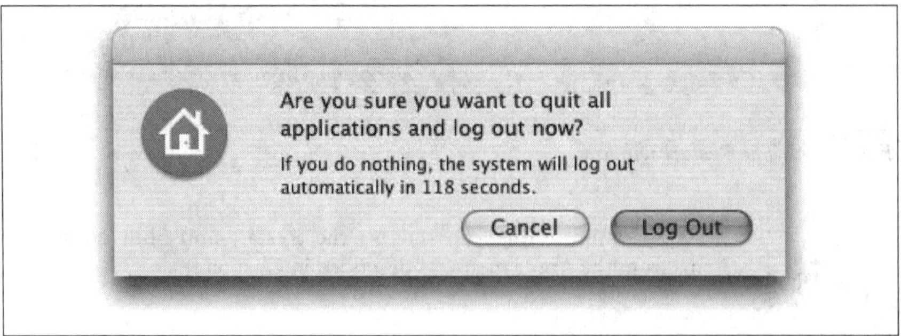

Figure 1-12. The logout window

If you hold down the Option key while selecting the Apple menu, you will see that the ellipsis have disappeared from the Restart, Shut Down, and Log Out items.

Selecting one of these menu items while holding down the Option key causes that action to take effect immediately, without prompting you first. For example, if you hold down the Option key and select →Shut Down, your Mac will shut down as it normally would, except you won't see one of the Shut Down windows shown earlier in Figure 1-10 or Figure 1-11; your Mac will shutdown immediately.

Force-quitting applications

Thanks to Mac OS X's protected memory, you don't have to restart the entire system if an application crashes or freezes. If an application freezes for some reason, you can force it to quit without affecting the other applications you're running.

In Mac OS 9 and earlier, force-quitting an application tended to throw the whole system off-kilter, prompting users to save all their work and restart the machine before continuing. Mac OS X's protected memory scheme makes force-quitting a lot safer, affecting nothing but the application itself. Veteran Mac users trained to be hesitant about force-quitting can now do so with impunity with Mac OS X.

However, force-quitting a Classic application can spell trouble to any other Classic applications running at the same time, due to the Classic environment's emulation of Mac OS 9's unprotected memory handling. See Chapter 3.

To force-quit a stuck application, you can either select →Force Quit, or use the keyboard shortcut Option-⌘-Escape to open the Force Quit window, shown in Figure 1-13

Figure 1-13. The Force Quit window

You then follow these steps:

1. Select the application name in the Force Quit Applications window.
2. Click on the Force Quit button.
3. A warning sheet, shown in Figure 1-14, appears, which alerts you that force-quitting the application will cause you to lose any unsaved changes.
4. If you're sure you want to quit the application, click on the Force Quit button; otherwise, click on the Cancel button (or hit ⌘-.).

Figure 1-14. A warning sheet appears before you can force an application to quit

Once you've forced the application to quit, use the keyboard shortcut ⌘-W to close the Force Quit Applications window. (This keyboard shortcut didn't work in earlier versions of Mac OS X.)

In addition to using the Force Quit window, there are two other ways you can force an application to quit:

- If you Option-click on the Dock icon for a running application, you can select Force Quit from the contextual menu.
- Use Shift-Option-⌘-Escape to immediately force the application you're using to quit. This is particularly handy because it's often the application you're working in that gets a brain freeze.

Be careful with these options, because neither questions you before the application is forced to quit. Any unsaved changes will be lost.

Force-quitting the Finder

Unlike applications, you cannot force-quit the Finder by Control-clicking on its icon in the Dock. You can only restart the Finder. When you select the Finder in the Force Quit Applications window, the Force Quit button changes to Relaunch as shown in Figure 1-15; click that button to restart the Finder.

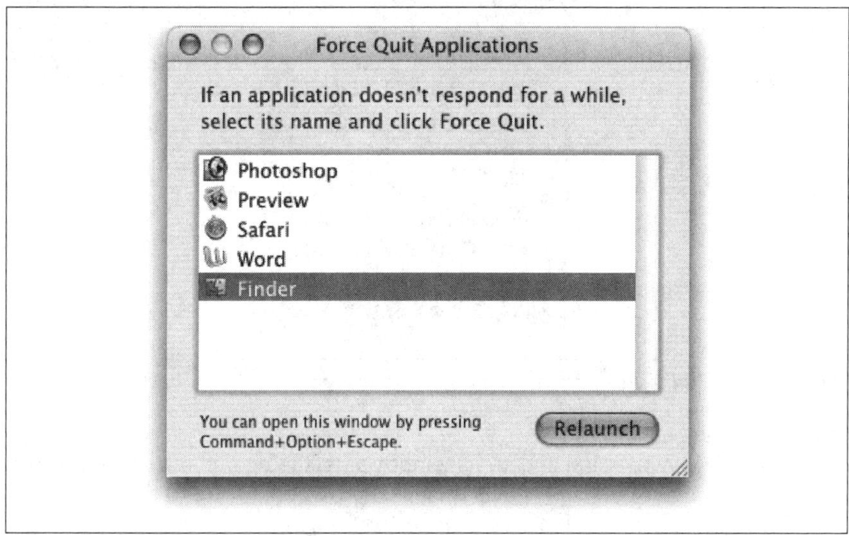

Figure 1-15. Select the Finder item in the list, and then click on the Relaunch button to restart the Finder

Once you've forced the Finder to restart, use the keyboard shortcut ⌘-W to close the Force Quit Applications window.

The Application Menu

Immediately to the right of the Apple menu in the menu bar is the Application menu, shown in Figure 1-16. As the Apple menu holds commands relevant to the whole system, the Application menu, which is rendered in boldface and named after the active application, holds commands relevant to the active application itself and not any of its windows or documents.

The following are some typical Application menu commands:

About "Application Name"
: Displays a small window that typically features the application's name, icon, version number, authors, copyright information, web links, and whatever else the developers felt appropriate.

Preferences...
: Calls up the application's preferences window. The standard keyboard shortcut to open an application's preference window is ⌘-, (Command-comma).

Services
: Brings up the Services submenu, covered later in "Services."

Figure 1-16. The Finder's Application menu

Hide "Application Name"
: Makes the application and all its windows (including minimized windows on the Dock) invisible, and brings the next active application to the foreground. Clicking this application's Dock icon (or bringing forth any of its individual windows through its Dock menu) reveals it once again. The standard keyboard shortcut for hiding an application is ⌘-H.

Hide Others
: Hides all running Aqua applications besides the current one. The standard keyboard shortcut to hide other applications is Option-⌘-H.

Show All
: Reveals all hidden applications.

Quit "Application Name"
: Quits the application. The standard keyboard shortcut to quit an application is ⌘-Q.

  When selected, every open window belonging to that application receives the signal to close. Windows with unsaved changes will alert the user with a dialog sheet (as seen in Figure 1-35). Hitting Cancel (or ⌘-.) on any of these sheets dismisses that sheet and keeps the window open, canceling the application's Quit request.

  The one exception to this rule is the Finder. The Finder lacks a Quit option in its application menu because the Finder is constantly running. However, if the Finder is frozen or otherwise acting up, you can force it to relaunch as described earlier.

Standard Application Menus

In addition to the Application menu, each application (including the Finder) has at least four additional menus in the menu bar:

- File
- Edit
- Window
- Help

The following list touches on the common menu commands found in many Mac OS X applications:

File

This menu contains commands for working with documents on disk:

New (⌘-N)
: Opens a new, empty document window.

Open... (⌘-O)
: Summons a dialog box for selecting a document from the filesystem. Once selected, its content appears in a new window.

Open Recent
: Contains the names of the last few documents this application worked with. Selecting one quickly opens it into a new window.

Close (⌘-W)
: Asks to close the foremost window; this is equivalent to hitting the window's red titlebar button. Some menus also offer Close All (Shift-⌘-W), which is equivalent to Option-clicking the window's Close button.

Save (⌘-S)
: If the foremost window represents an existing file (i.e., its titlebar has a real title and a proxy icon), it resynchs its contents with the file, writing all changes made since the last save. Otherwise, it presents the user with a sheet for creating a new file.

Save As... (Shift-⌘-S)
: Presents the user with a file-creation sheet, regardless of whether the window already has a file associated with it. After saving, the system reassociates the window with this new file, though the previous one continues to exist in the state in which it was last saved.

Page Setup... (Shift-⌘-P)
: This command sets up how the window presents its contents to a printing device.

Print... (⌘-P)
: Prepares a document for printing. Chapter 9 covers document printing in more detail.

Edit

The Edit menu almost always holds the all-important clipboard controls and text-editing commands:

Undo action (⌘-Z)
: This handy command undoes the last action you performed in this application, be it typing, moving stuff around, drawing a circle, and just about anything else. (This is within limits; it can't, for example, unsend an

emotional email you find yourself suddenly regretting.) If you invoke this command repeatedly, you can undo a whole sequence of actions.

Redo action (Shift-⌘-Z)
: This command is simply the antidote of Undo, restoring the last thing you undid, should you change your mind (or go one step too far while performing a multiple Undo). Note that this command is available only immediately after you perform an Undo.

Cut (⌘-X)
: Copies the selected text or images onto the system's clipboard and then deletes it from the window.

Copy (⌘-C)
: Copies the selected text or images onto the system's clipboard, leaving it in place in the window.

Paste (⌘-V)
: Tries to copy the current clipboard contents to the cursor's current position in the window.

Select All (⌘-A)
: Selects all text or objects in the window.

Find, Spelling
: These submenus usually hold some standard interfaces for finding text and using the system's built-in spellchecker.

Special Characters
: This option opens the Character Palette, used for finding and inserting special characters into documents, email messages, etc.

Window
: Like the application's Dock menu, the Window menu usually holds a list of all the windows currently open; selecting one brings it into focus. The menu also often holds the Minimize Window option (⌘-M), which, when selected, minimizes the window to the Dock. You can also minimize a window by clicking on the yellow button in the window's titlebar or by double-clicking on the titlebar. To bring the window back into focus, simply click on its icon in the Dock.

  Some applications also assign keyboard shortcuts to open windows. For example, the Terminal application assigns a Command-`number` keyboard shortcut for each open Terminal window (see Figure 1-17). This allows you to quickly switch back and forth between windows when you need to.

Help
: This menu varies greatly among applications. Some offer just a single command, Application Help (⌘-?), which usually displays the application's documentation in Help Center or your web browser. Other applications fill this menu with commands that let you browse various pieces of documentation and tutorials.

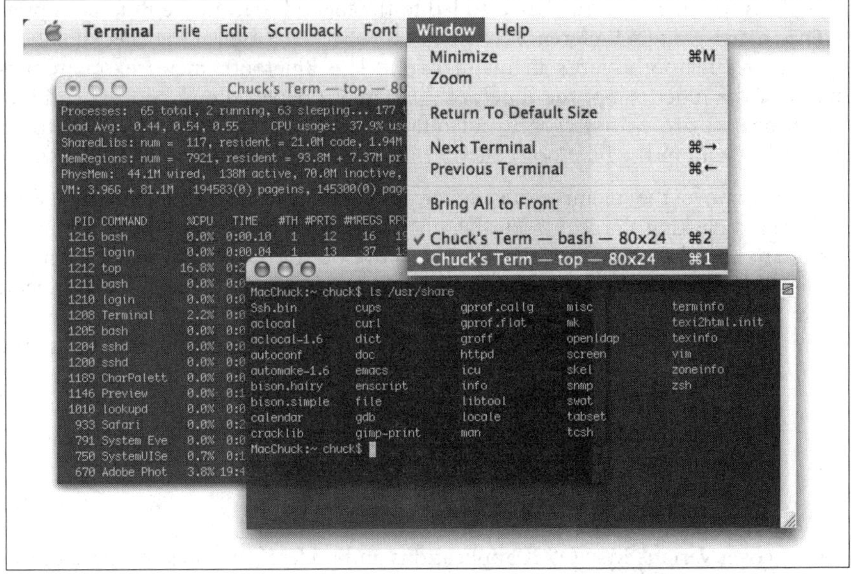

Figure 1-17. The Terminal's Window menu offers keyboard shortcuts to open windows

Menu Extras

Mac OS X programs and services can place menu extras on the right side of the menu bar. Like the Apple menu, these little symbols remain constant on the menu bar, regardless of which application you're using.

Menu extras' appearance typically reflects their function, and they often carry menus loaded with commands, just like the other menus. Figure 1-18 shows the Bluetooth menu extra.

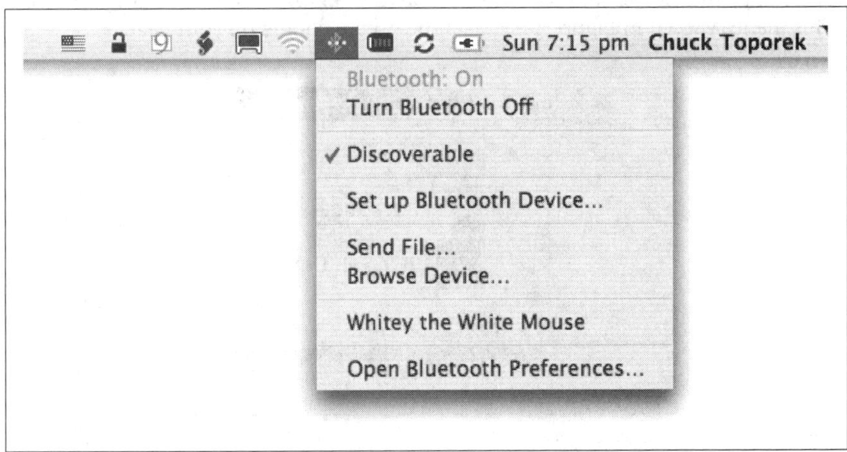

Figure 1-18. The Bluetooth menu extra

The Bluetooth menu extra can be added to the menu bar from the Bluetooth preference panel (System Preferences→Bluetooth→Settings→select the checkbox next to "Show Bluetooth status in menu bar"). The Bluetooth menu extra mimics many of the functions of the Bluetooth preference panel, shows you which Bluetooth devices are within range, and offers quick ways to launch the Bluetooth Setup Assistant or the Bluetooth File Exchange utilities (*/Applications/Utilities*).

You can move the menu extras to a different location in the menu bar by Command-clicking the icon and dragging it left or right. As you move the menu extra around, the other menu extras will move out of the way to make room for the menu extra you're moving. When you let go of the mouse button, the menu extra will take its new place in the menu bar. To remove a menu extra from the menu bar, Command-click on the icon, drag it off the menu bar, and release the mouse button.

For reference, executables for most of the standard menu extras can be found in */System/Library/CoreServices/Menu Extras* as folders with *.menu* extensions.

As we cover various Mac OS X applications and preference panes throughout this book, we'll note those that offer menu extras.

The Accounts Menu

One of the many new features added to Mac OS X Panther is something called Fast User Switching. This lets you have multiple users logged into the same system without having to log out.

If your Mac has more than one user account (set up via System Preferences→Accounts), you can turn on Fast User Switching, as well as specify which user is automatically logged in when the system starts up. When you enable Fast User Switching, the Accounts menu appears at the far right corner of the menu bar. This menu, shown in Figure 1-19, lists the user accounts on your Mac.

Figure 1-19. The Accounts menu

To switch to another user account, simply click on the bolded name of the currently logged in user, and select another user account name from the Accounts menu. A login window will appear, prompting you for that user's password. If your Mac supports Quartz Extreme (and has enough RAM), your display will rotate with a 3D cube effect to the other user's Desktop. You will be required to enter a password each time you switch user accounts from the Accounts menu. See Chapter 10 for more on Fast User Switching.

The Application Switcher

You can also cycle forward through active applications by pressing ⌘-Tab from within any application. This opens the Application Switcher, shown in Figure 1-20, which lists the applications currently running on your Mac.

Figure 1-20. The Application Switcher

In earlier versions of Mac OS X, ⌘-Tab (and Shift-⌘-Tab) cycled through active application icons in the Dock, highlighting them as you hit the Tab key.

To select an application in the Application Switcher, hold down the Command key and press the Tab key until the application you want to use is highlighted; then release the Command key to bring that application forward. If you hold down Shift-⌘ and press Tab, you will cycle backward through the active applications.

You can also use the mouse in combination with the Application Switcher. For instance, you can use ⌘-Tab to bring the Application Switcher into view, and then use the mouse to click on one of the application icons in the screen. When you click on an icon in the Application Switcher, that application comes to the foreground, and the Switcher fades away.

To toggle back and forth between the same two applications, press Command and Tab briefly and let go. When you don't hold the keys down, you'll be switched to the previously used application. Pressing them again brings you back to the other one.

Exposé

Another new feature added to Mac OS X Panther started out as a little system hack and eventually got pulled into Mac OS X as something called Exposé. If you've ever wished for a quick way to get at your Desktop or just the windows for a single application, Exposé (shown in Figure 1-21) is your answer.

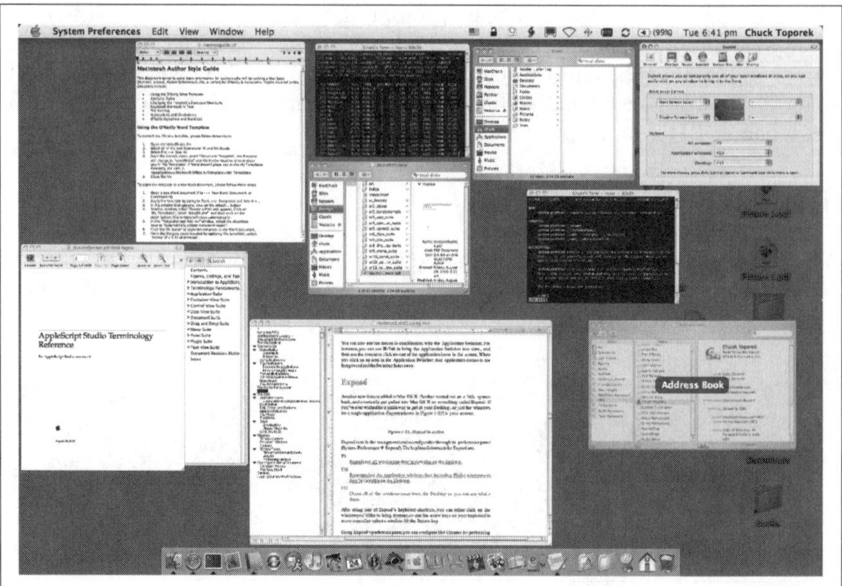

Figure 1-21. Exposé in action

Exposé runs in the background and is configurable through its preferences panel (System Preferences→Exposé). The default keyboard shortcuts for Exposé are:

F9 Spreads out all windows so they're viewable on the Desktop.

F10
: Separates just the active application's windows so they're viewable on the Desktop.

F11
: Clears all windows from the Desktop so you can see what's there.

After using one of Exposé's keyboard shortcuts, you can either click on the window you'd like to bring forward or use the arrow keys on your keyboard to move around; to select a window, hit the Return key.

Using Exposé's preference panel, you can configure Hot Corners to perform the actions of the function keys, or you can change the default key settings to something more convenient.

The Dock

One of Mac OS X's most visually distinctive features is its Dock, a highly customizable strip of icons found (by default) along the bottom of the screen. Even if you choose to temporarily hide or change its location, the Dock remains active and always available.

As Figure 1-22 shows, the Dock can contain many different kinds of icons, several of which are described in the list that follows.

Figure 1-22. The Dock

1. The Finder icon
2. Application icons
3. An active application
4. An inactive application
5. The Divider
6. Folders that have been placed in the Dock
7. A Quick Link
8. Minimized windows
9. The Trash icon

The icons found in the Dock allow you to quickly launch and maneuver among applications, as well as provide shortcuts to frequently used folders and documents. These icons also sometimes act as applications in their own right. The Dock is the new home of the Trash, which used to reside at the lower-right corner of the Desktop in earlier versions of the Mac OS.

Application Icons

Application icons live to the left of the Dock's divider bar. Each represents an application, either one that is currently running or one that's idle but "docked" (meaning that you've chosen to let its icon have a permanent home on the Dock).

To launch an application whose icon is in the Dock, just click on the icon. If an application's icon doesn't reside in the Dock, you can launch an application (or open a file) by locating it in the Finder and performing one of the actions in the following list.

- Double-clicking its icon
- Selecting the icon and selecting File→Open from the menu bar
- Selecting the icon and hitting ⌘-O

When you launch an application, its icon bounces in the Dock to let you know the program is loading. After the application has launched and is ready to use, a black triangle appears beneath its icon to let you know that the application is active. (The Finder will always have a black triangle under its icon because it's always available.) When you quit the application, the black triangle disappears, as will the application's Dock icon if it hasn't been selected to stay in the Dock.

When you have more than one application running, you can bring another application forward by clicking once on that application's Dock icon. That application and all of its open windows will come to the foreground.

Not Every Program Gets an Icon

Like any other Unix system, Mac OS X is usually running dozens of programs—more correctly known as *processes*—at any given time. Many of them, however, receive no representation in the Dock. These programs have no Aqua-based user interface, and some have no UIs at all.

Processes in this class include all the little daemons and low-level Unix programs that support network services and core OS-level functionality. Additionally, command-line programs that have only console-based UIs—nearly every shell or Perl script and AppleScript you encounter, for example—won't appear in the Dock when running, even though you may be interacting with them through the Terminal or some other interface.

You can get a glimpse of the true layout of active processes through the Process Viewer (*/Applications/Utilities*). Each line in its window represents an active process. Some you may recognize as belonging to running Aqua applications, while others have more esoteric names.

When a background application needs your attention, its Dock icon will bounce frantically. To see the application, bring it to the foreground by clicking on its Dock icon.

Interactive Dock Icons

While most applications identify themselves with a single icon, some can change their icons to different images, or even redraw themselves on the fly, as needed.

For example, the Activity Monitor's Dock icon can be changed into many different icons to reveal information about the processor load, memory and disk usage, and network activity. When Mail is running in the background, it posts the number of unread messages in your Inbox in its icon, as seen in Figure 1-22.

Adding and removing applications from the Dock

The Dock gives you two ways to permanently add application icons:

- You can drag any application's icon onto the Dock from the Finder. The original icon will stay where it is, and the Dock creates a pointer to it, much like an alias.
- If you are running an application that doesn't normally have an icon in the Dock, Control-click on the application icon to reveal its Dock menu. Select "Keep In Dock" from the menu to make the icon stay there after the application quits, as described in the next section.

To remove an item from the Dock, simply drag an inactive application's icon off the Dock and release the mouse button. The icon will disappear in a puff of smoke. This has no effect on the actual application; it simply removes the application's icon from the Dock.

You can also remove an active application from the Dock by dragging it off, although the effect is less obvious because it will snap back into place (since all active applications' icons must appear on the Dock). However, the system will remember your action, and quietly remove the icon from the Dock once the application quits (unless, of course, you change your mind by choosing "Keep In Dock" from its Dock menu).

The Dock Is an Application

While it doesn't work like other applications on Mac OS X, the Dock is in fact an application that lives in */System/Library/CoreServices*.

You can find a record of all the applications kept on the Dock, as well as other interesting information, by looking at the Dock's property list file (*~/Library/Preferences/com.apple.dock.plist*). If you know what you're doing, you can tweak this file to control the Dock's behavior by editing the file or using the *defaults* command from the Terminal.

Dock Menus

Every active application icon has a *Dock menu*, which you can call up by either Control-clicking the icon or clicking on the icon and holding the mouse button down. An application's Dock menu is attached to the icon, as shown in Figure 1-23.

Dock menus contain, as commands, the titles of all the windows an application has open, each marked with a little "window" symbol. Select one to bring it forth, along with its parent application. The top window will have a checkmark next to it; there is no distinction for minimized windows.

Classic applications have only a basic Dock menu without the window list. Instead, a Classic application's Dock menu gives you only the options of Show in Finder and Quit (or Force Quit).

Every application's Dock menu typically contains at least a couple other commands, including:

Quit
: Quits the application, even if it's not in the foreground. The application reacts as if you had selected Quit from its application menu or used the keyboard shortcut ⌘-Q to quit the application.

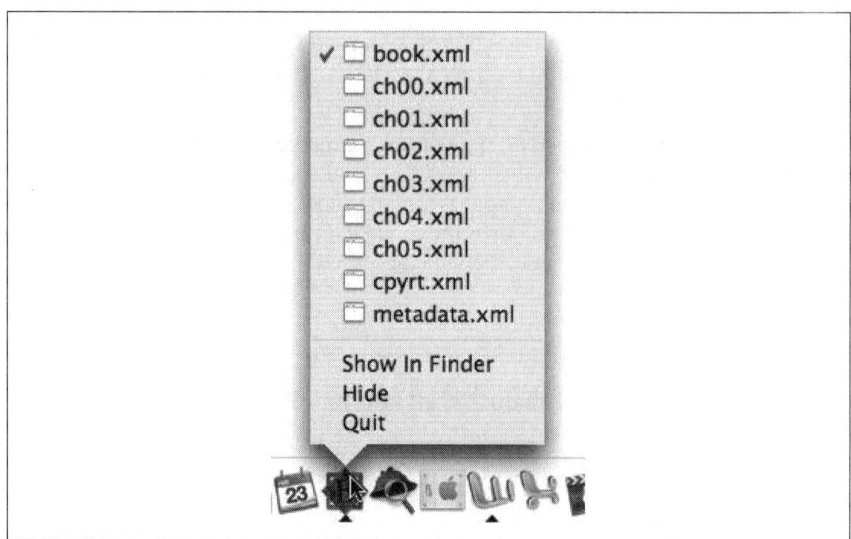

Figure 1-23. A typical Dock menu; this one for BBEdit includes a list of open document windows

If you hold down the Option key while looking at an application's Dock menu, Quit changes to Force Quit; selecting this option instantly kills that application.

The Finder's icon lacks a Quit or Force Quit option. (In fact, all it has is a list of open Finder windows and a Hide option to hide all open Finder windows.) If you need to restart the Finder for some odd reason, do so by selecting →Force Quit (Option-⌘-Escape). Then select the Finder and click on the Relaunch button, as described earlier.

Show In Finder
: Opens a Finder window, showing the location of the application on your system.

Keep In Dock
: This option appears only for icons whose applications aren't permanently docked. Normally, the icon of an undocked application vanishes once that application exits. Select this option to give the application a permanent home in the Dock, where it will remain as an inactive application icon once its corresponding program has quit.

Beyond these basic selections, an application can put whatever it likes in its Dock menu. Among the standard Apple suite, for example, iTunes is notable for cramming a basic audio control panel in its Dock menu, including information about the song that's currently playing, as shown in Figure 1-24.

Disk, Folder, and File Icons

Beyond applications, documents, folders, and disks can also be placed in the Dock to the right of the divider, as shown in Figure 1-25. Clicking on a document

Figure 1-24. The Dock menu for iTunes

in the Dock opens the file using the appropriate application; disks and folders will open a new Finder window bearing their contents. If you click on a folder in the Dock and hold down the mouse button, its contents are revealed in a Dock menu, allowing you to select from its contents.

One folder you might consider placing in the Dock is your Home folder, which gives you rapid access to everything stored within. To add your Home folder to the Dock, follow these steps:

1. Open a Finder window by clicking on its Dock icon.
2. Click on the Home icon in the Finder's Sidebar.
3. Drag your Home folder's proxy icon (the little house in the window's titlebar) into the Dock and drop it on the right side of the divider. (Proxy icons are covered later in this chapter in "Document Windows.") Your home folder's icon now appears in the Dock.
4. As Figure 1-26 shows, you can now Control-click (or click and hold) on this icon at any time to see your entire Home folder represented as a hierarchical Dock menu. Selecting any file or application opens it, just as if it had been double-clicked from within the Finder.

You can follow these basic steps to add other folders to your Dock, depending on which ones you need access to more often.

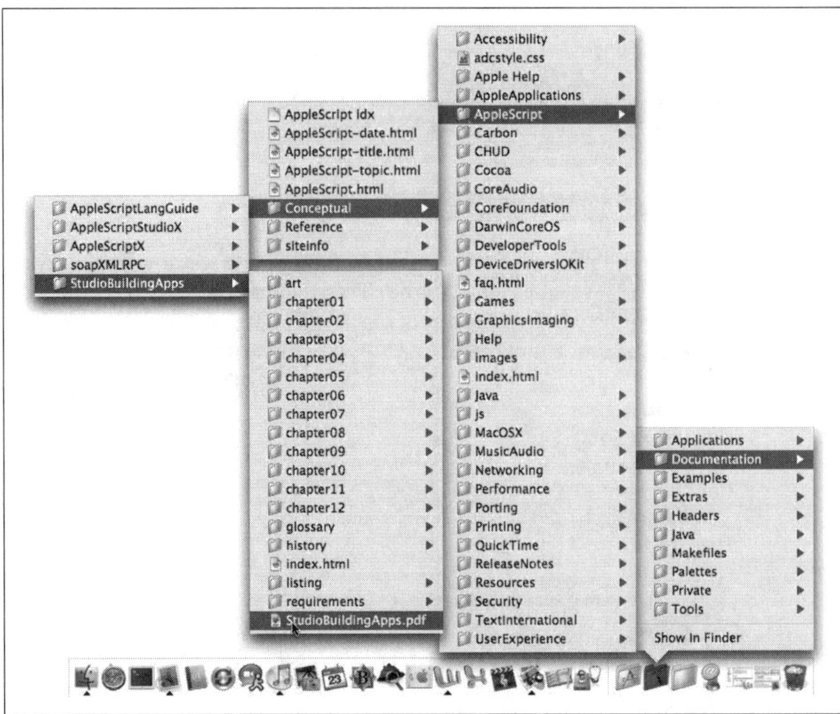

Figure 1-25. Disks, folders, and files can be located to the right of the divider in the Dock

Figure 1-26. Accessing your Home folder from the Dock

Minimized Windows

There are a number of ways to minimize a window, including:

- Clicking the yellow Minimize button in a window's titlebar
- Selecting Window→Minimize
- With the ⌘-M keyboard shortcut, which most native Mac OS X applications offer

When a window is minimized, a miniaturized version of the window is placed in the Dock immediately to the left of the Trash icon, as shown earlier in Figure 1-22. (The most recently minimized window appears in the Dock next to the Trash icon.) There's not much you can do with minimized windows except click on them, which opens the window and places it at the top of the window stack. If you Hide an application that has minimized windows, those windows will fade away but will return when the application is made active again.

Minimized windows feature a tiny icon of the application to which they belong. This makes it easy to tell at a glance which windows belong to which application.

The Finder

As mentioned earlier, the Finder is located on the far-left edge of the Dock. Unlike other applications, the Finder's icon cannot be removed from the Dock. (The same applies to the Trash icon.) The Finder also has a limited Dock menu, which displays only the Finder's current window list. Chapter 2 covers the Finder in detail.

The Divider

In its basic form, the Dock's divider bar is used to segregate application icons to the left, (quick links, folders, minimized windows, etc.) and the Trash to the right. However, if you place the mouse pointer over the divider bar, you'll see that the pointer changes shape, providing you with the ability to:

Resize the Dock
: If you click-drag the divider up or down, you can make the Dock larger or smaller.

Access the Dock's context menu
: If you Control-click on the divider, as shown in Figure 1-27, you'll see a boiled-down, textual version of the Dock's preference panel (see Chapter 4) pop up as a contextual menu.

Relocate the Dock
: If you Shift-click on the divider bar and hold down on the mouse button, you can drag the mouse to the left or right edge of the screen to quickly relocate the Dock there.

These are just shortcuts to things you do in the Dock's preferences panel, detailed in Chapter 4.

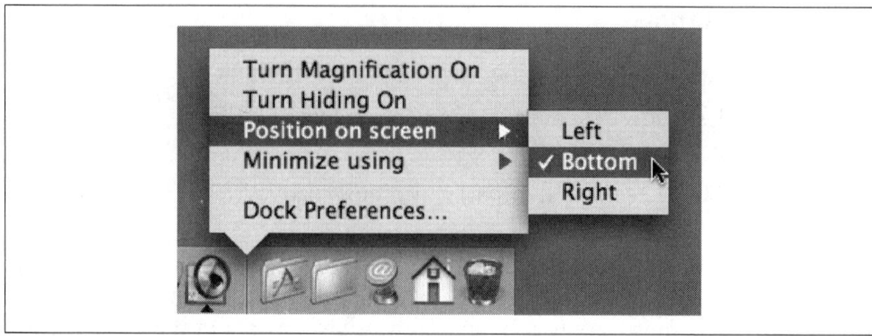

Figure 1-27. The Dock divider's Dock menu

Trash

The Trash icon is one of the few remnants of the original Mac desktop metaphor that still looks like what it does. Like the Finder icon on the Dock's opposite end, the Trash icon is a permanent fixture in the Dock, ignoring any of your attempts to drag it elsewhere.

Deleting files

The Trash serves many functions, all having to do with removing stuff from your filesystem. You can mark files for deletion in one of the following ways:

- Drag an item from a Finder window onto the Trash icon in the Dock.
- Select an item and use the ⌘-Delete keyboard shortcut.
- Select an item in the Finder and selecting File→Move to Trash.
- Control-click an item and select Move to Trash from its context menu.

To see the contents of the Trash, click on the Trash icon to open a Trash window with the Finder. To rescue an item from the Trash, simply drag its icon from the Trash to the Desktop or to another location in a Finder window. If you move a file to the Trash and decide that you don't want to delete it, you can select the file and hit ⌘-Z (Undo) to move the file back to its original location in the filesystem. However, this works only with the most recently trashed item. If you trash a second item and decide that you want to move the first trashed item back, the Undo command won't help you out.

The Trash icon acts as a graphical frontend to the *.Trash* folder in your Home directory. As with all "dotfiles" (a file or folder whose name begins with a period, or *dot*), you can't normally see the *.Trash* file in the Finder, but you can access it with the Terminal.

You can't open files that have been trashed. If you can't remember what the item contains and want to look at it before you empty the Trash, drag the item out of the Trash and onto the Desktop (or anywhere else in the filesystem). Once you're sure this is the file you want to dump, select the file and press ⌘-Delete to move it back into the Trash.

To permanently erase files, you must *empty the trash*. The Trash's Dock menu provides an Empty Trash option, seen in Figure 1-28, which deletes all the files and folders contains. In the Finder, you can also hit Shift-⌘-Delete to accomplish the same thing.

Figure 1-28. The Trash's Dock menu Empty Trash option

One of the many new features added to Mac OS X Panther is the Secure Empty Trash option, which can be accessed only from the Finder's application menu (Finder→Secure Empty Trash). If you select Secure Empty Trash, the system deletes the file, and then overwrites the location where the file was located on the filesystem a number of times, making it next to impossible to ever recover that file.

In the background, the Secure Empty Trash option invokes the *srm* command to delete the files in the *~/.Trash* directory.

You should use the Secure Empty Trash option judiciously, because the chances of recovering a file deleted from the filesystem using this option is practically nil. It takes a little longer to delete files using Secure Empty Trash, but the added security is well worth the wait if you're working with sensitive data.

Unmounting disks

If you drag a disk image (CD, DVD, USB or FireWire drive, or a mounted disk image file) to the Trash, the Trash icon changes to an Eject icon. However, rather than retaining the disk image in the Trash, the disk is ejected, or unmounted, from the system. You can also unmount or eject disks while in the Finder by selecting their icons and hitting ⌘-E.

If you have an iBook or PowerBook, the F12 key also functions as an eject button; however, this works only for ejecting CDs and DVDs, not unmounting drives, partitions, or network shares.

Dock Shortcuts

Table 1-2 contains a listing of keyboard shortcuts for use with the Dock and when clicking on an application's Dock icon.

Table 1-2. Dock shortcuts

Keyboard shortcut	Description
Option-⌘-D	Quickly toggle the Dock's state between visible and hidden.
⌘-drag	Force docked icons to stay put when dragging other icons onto them.
⌘-click	Opens a Finder window to the application's location in the filesystem. This is similar to Control-clicking a Dock icon to and selecting Show In Finder from its context menu.
Control-click	Opens an application's Dock menu.
Control-Option-click	If you press the Option key while Control-clicking an icon in the Dock, the Quit option is toggled to Force Quit, and the Hide option toggles to Hide Others; this wn't work with Classic applications (i.e., it works only with native Mac OS X applications).
Option-click	Hide the foreground application before bringing this application forward; Option-clicking the same application icon again brings the previous application forward.
Option-⌘-click	Hides the windows of all other open applications and switches (if necessary) to the clicked application; similar to selecting Hide Others from an application menu.

Windows

Windows in Mac OS X have an entirely different set of controls than those from earlier versions of the Mac OS. Controls for closing, minimizing, and zooming a window to a larger size are all grouped together at the left edge of a window's title bar, and the dialog windows, alerts, and sheets have changed as well.

This section introduces you to the basic features and types of windows you'll encounter while using Mac OS X.

Window Controls

Each window has a set of common controls, as shown in Figure 1-29.

The controls are listed as follows:

1. Close button (red)
2. Minimize button (yellow)
3. Zoom button (green)
4. Proxy icon
5. Filename
6. Toolbar button (not available on all windows)
7. Scrollbars and scroll arrows
8. Resize window control

The top part of the window is known as the *titlebar*. The titlebar is home to the three colored window control buttons used for closing (red), minimizing (yellow), and zooming (green) the window. Mousing over the buttons changes their state to be either an X, a minus sign (–), or a plus sign (+), respectively. These are visual cues of the function the button performs.

With some applications, you'll notice that the red Close window button has a dark-colored dot in its center. This means that the document you're working on

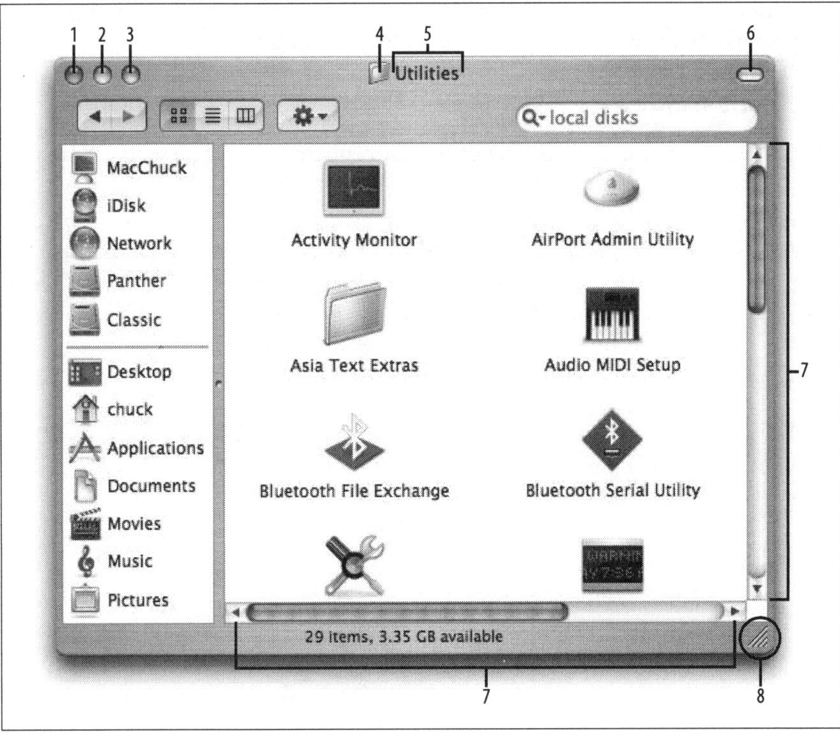

Figure 1-29. Common window controls

has unsaved changes; if you save the document (File→Save, or ⌘-S), the dot goes away.

A window's titlebar runs across the top edge and, as its name implies, features the title or name of that window. Window names are usually unique within a single application. For example, word processor windows are named for the documents they represent, while web browser windows take their titles from the `<title></title>` tag in the HTML web pages they display.

In earlier versions of the Mac OS, double-clicking the titlebar invoked the *windowshade* feature. Everything below the titlebar would hide, leaving just a floating titlebar, which you could leave in place or drag around as needed. If you double-click on the titlebar of a window in Mac OS X, the window minimized to the Dock.

The only Mac OS X application that still retains the windowshade feature is Stickies (found in */Applications*). However, if you miss this feature, you can download a third-party application called WindowShade X (*http://www.unsanity.com*).

Titlebars are a window's simplest control. You can move a window around just by dragging its titlebar, and double-clicking the titlebar minimizes the window to the Dock. Beyond this built-in functionality, however, the titlebar is home to several other controls, such as the close, minimize, and maximize window buttons, the proxy icon, and in certain circumstances, a toolbar button.

Document Windows

A window's titlebar gains a couple of special properties if it represents something in the filesystem:

Path view and selection
: Command-click the window's title (the actual text in the middle of the titlebar) to produce a pop-up menu showing the object's path (as seen in Figure 1-30), with one menu row for each enclosing folder or disk. Selecting any of these folders or disks opens that object's window in the Finder.

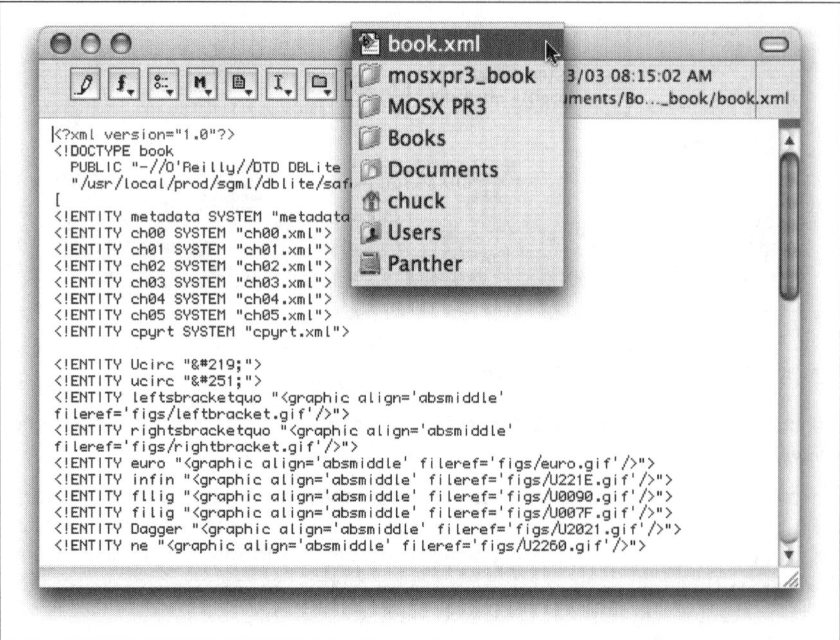

Figure 1-30. The titlebar path menu exposed by Command-clicking on the proxy icon or title

The final item in this pop-up menu is always a disk icon (most often that of a hard disk, or a disk partition); selecting it opens a Finder view of that disk's *root*. See the earlier section "Disk, Folder, and File Icons" for more about disk icons in the Finder.

This also works with Finder windows, as a rapid way to navigate to any point in an open folder's path.

Proxy icon

Any window that represents a file, folder, or disk gets a miniature version of its Finder icon to the left of its title in the titlebar, as seen in Figure 1-29; this is its *proxy icon*. (New document windows don't get a proxy icon until the first time they are saved.) While this can be useful for visually determining a document's file type, it's more than a mere label.

You can click and drag this icon and get the same effect as if you were dragging its "real" Finder icon around. Hence, you can drop its icon into another document window, onto another application's icon, place it in the Dock, and so on. In all cases, you'll receive the same effect as if you performed the same action from the Finder.

The one exception to this rule is that you can't drag an open document window's proxy icon to the Trash.

Modifier keys for moving, copying, and making aliases all apply when dragging a proxy icon, as detailed in the section "Moving and Copying Files and Folders" in Chapter 2.

Some nondocument windows put proxy icons to other clever uses. Internet Explorer, for example, uses an @-shaped proxy icon in the titlebar of web pages. Dragging it is equivalent to dragging the page's URL string, letting you quickly paste it into an email message or drop it on the Desktop as a "Web Internet Location" document.

If the window is not in sync with its document (i.e., it contains unsaved changes), the proxy icon is grayed out and untouchable. Saving the document returns it to its opaque and interactive state.

Toolbars

Some applications assign a *toolbar* to its windows, giving you quick access to various commands. As seen in Figure 1-31, the System Preferences window has a toolbar, which you can use to hold the preference panels you use frequently.

Windows with toolbars have a transparent button on the right side of their titlebars, as shown in Figure 1-31. If you click on the toolbar button, the toolbar disappears; click on it again, and the toolbar reappears.

Most applications that use toolbars make them customizable by way of a "Customize Toolbar..." option in their View menu. Selecting this summons a *sheet* that contains a palette of all the buttons you can place in that particular window's toolbar (including a predefined default set, at the bottom) as well as options to control their appearance and organize them into groups. You can now make the toolbar look just how you want. Figure 1-32 shows the Finder's Customize Toolbar window.

You can also customize a toolbar to some extent without using this dialog. If you hold down the Command key (⌘), you can drag toolbar icons left or right to rearrange them, or drag and drop them from the toolbar to make them go away in a

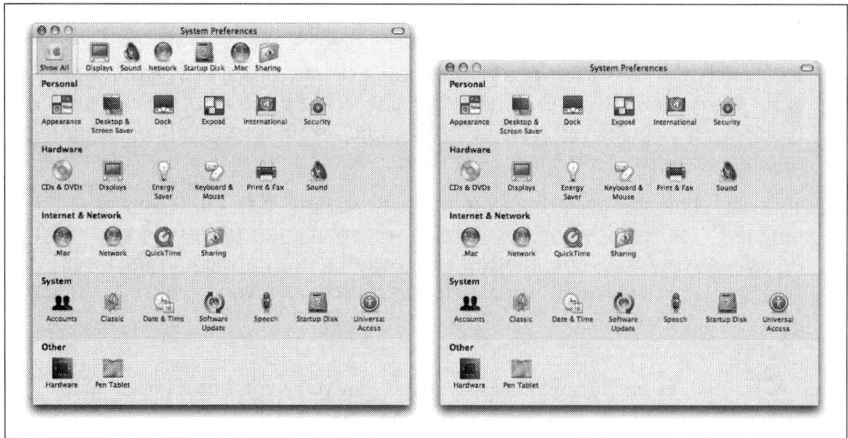

Figure 1-31. The System Preferences toolbar

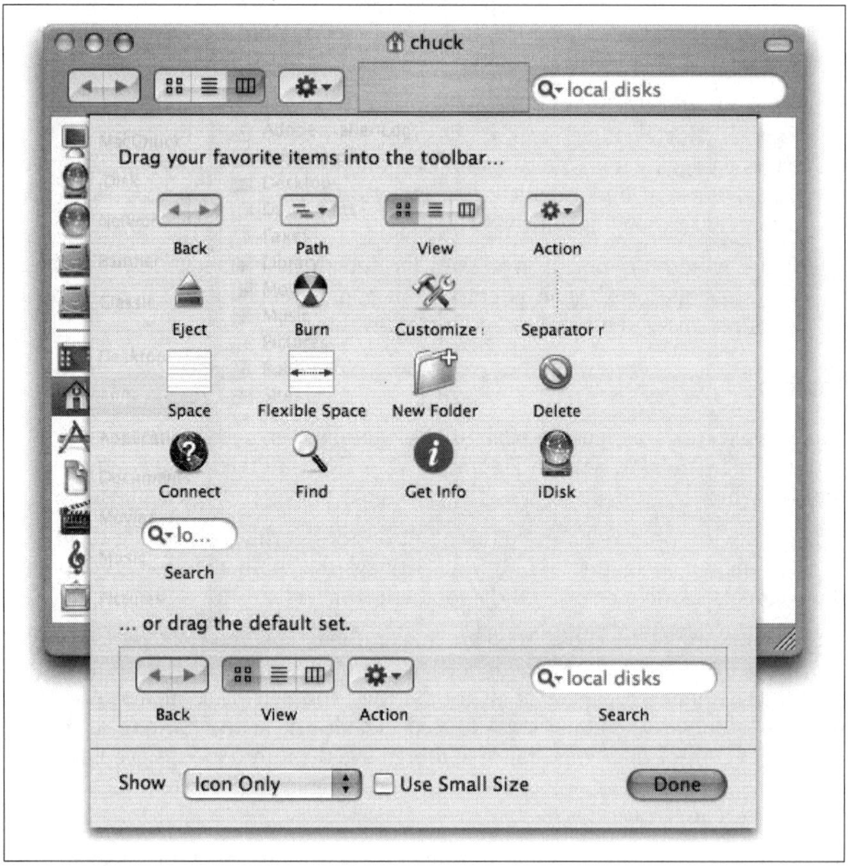

Figure 1-32. The Finder's Customize Toolbar window

puff of smoke. (You can add them back again later by visiting the Customize Toolbar... sheet.) Some applications, such as System Preferences and the Finder, let you drag icons on and off the toolbar.

Window Types

When using Mac OS X, there are a variety of windows you'll encounter. Everything ranging from your standard Finder window (discussed in Chapter 2) to document windows, palettes, dialogs, alerts, sheets, and drawers. These include all the buttons and controls that help give the Mac interface its ease-of-use reputation.

Dialogs: windows and sheets

Dialogs are a common sight in any GUI. When an application requires you to make a decision or otherwise needs your attention, it interrupts its activities to display a special window. Thereafter, it won't let you perform any other activities within that application until you give it due attention, whether that involves making a choice, or merely acknowledging or dismissing the dialog.

A common example of a dialog window (or *dialog box*), is what you see when you select File→Open (⌘-O) in any document-editing application, as shown in Figure 1-33.

Open dialogs in Mac OS X Panther now offer many of the features of the Finder window, including:

- The Finder's Sidebar to the left for navigating through drives and folders; all of the items in the Finder's Sidebar are available in the Sidebars of Open and Save dialogs in Mac OS X Panther.
- Back and Forward buttons to go up or down through folders.
- View buttons, to change the view from Column View (the default) to List View.

When you locate the file you wish to open, either select the file and hit the Open button, or dismiss the dialog by clicking on the Cancel button (or using the ⌘-. keyboard shortcut).

A *sheet* is a special kind of dialog that flops out from beneath the window's titlebar, partially covering its view (see Figure 1-34). As with the Open window, the Save (and Save As) sheets incorporates Finder features to help you navigate through the filesystem and select a location to save files.

A window loses most of its interactivity when displaying a sheet; the sheet requires your input on some decision (even if it's just to dismiss the sheet through its Cancel button), although you can still use window controls to move, resize, and minimize the window. However, you can continue using other windows, even those belonging to that application.

The sheet you'll see most often is the Save sheet; look for it when you first save a new document to disk or whenever you choose Save As... from an application's File menu. When you try to close a document window that contains unsaved changes, the sheet shown in Figure 1-35 appears.

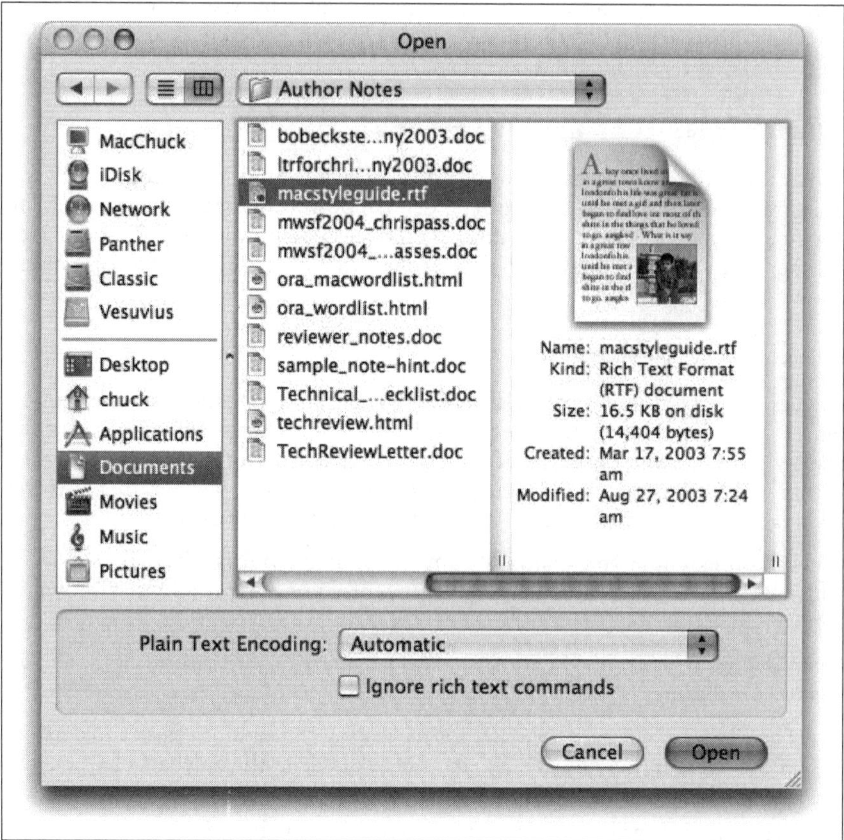

Figure 1-33. The Open window

This sheet offers three possible options:

- Save, which is the default as noted by its blue color. If you click on the Save button (or hit the Return key), this sheet is replaced with a Save sheet so you can save the file.
- Cancel, which dismisses the sheet and returns you to the document window.
- Don't Save, which closes the document window without saving the file or any changes you've made.

Whenever you see a sheet similar to the one shown in Figure 1-35, you can hit the Return key to invoke the button that has the *focus* (meaning, the colored button), or use ⌘-. to invoke the Cancel button and ⌘-D to invoke the Don't Save button.

Drawers

Windows can choose to hide parts of themselves in *drawers*, which slide out from the left or right side of a window. Drawers contain information and controls secondary to the window's main function. One such application that uses drawers is Preview. For example, if you select a bunch of JPEG images in the Finder and

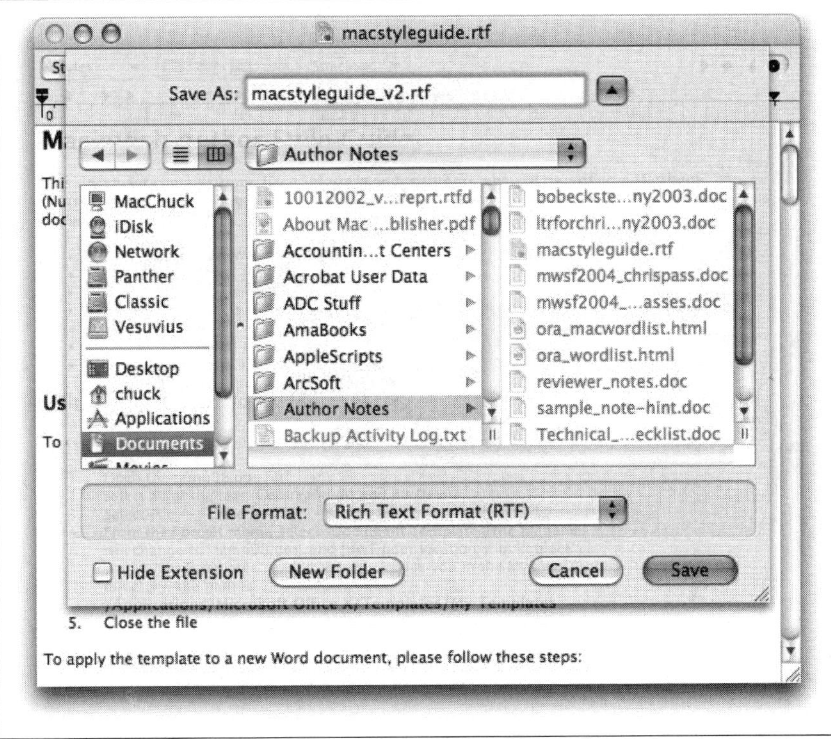

Figure 1-34. A typical dialog sheet

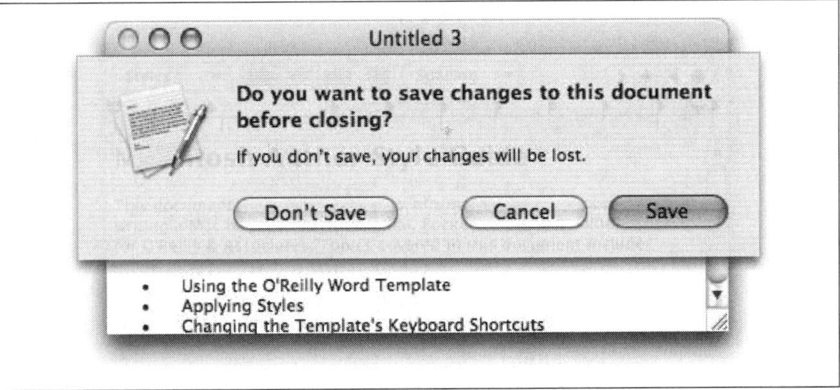

Figure 1-35. This sheet appears when you attempt to close a window with unsaved changes

hit ⌘-O (short for File→Open), all the images will open in a single Preview window, and the individual images are displayed in the drawer, as shown in Figure 1-36. If you open a multipage PDF document in Preview, each page of the document is represented in Preview's drawer.

Figure 1-36. Preview's drawer

Other applications that make great use of drawers include Mail, iCal, and Backup's QuickPicks drawer. (Backup is only available to .Mac members; use it to back up data to an iDisk, CD/DVD, or an external drive.)

As with sheets, a drawer remains attached to its window, even if you move or resize the parent window. You can change the width of a drawer by clicking and dragging on one of its edges. (You can also close it entirely by dragging it to the window's edge, but usually it or its window provides faster ways to close it.)

Interleaving windows

Unlike previous versions of the Mac OS, Aqua windows can *interleave* freely. This means that windows belonging to a given application don't insist on sticking together as they did in earlier versions of the Mac OS. Bringing one window of an application into focus won't automatically pop all other windows of that application to the top of the stack. This can prove useful when working with two applications side by side. You can arrange the windows so you can see the contents of both without having to wrestle with any other open windows belonging to either application.

> If you do want to bring all of an application's windows to the top of the window stack, just click once on that application's icon in the Dock.

Mac OS X windows follow the usual behavior of forming into a single stack, with one window at a time possessing focus and ready for user interaction. Subtle visual cues are used, however, to make the top window visually distinct, giving it an opaque titlebar with red, yellow, and green control buttons (see "Window Controls" earlier in this chapter), as well as a drop shadow.

Most of the time, you bring a window into focus by clicking on it, which makes it snap to the top of the stack. You can also call it forth by selecting a window from an application's Dock menu (accessed by Control-clicking on the Dock icon) or choosing it from its application's Window menu, if the application offers one.

You can use ⌘-` to cycle through all of the application's open windows. (That's the "backtick" key, located in the upper-left of your keyboard, just below the Escape key.)

You can interact with a window in the background by holding down the Command key (⌘); when you move the mouse over any of the window's controls, that control temporarily receives the focus. You can always move, resize, or scroll it by ⌘- dragging its various controls; if it uses standard Cocoa interface widgets, you can even press buttons and select text without losing focus from the top window! Similarly, you can also access the close, minimize, and zoom window control buttons by just mousing over them; no keypress required.

Opening and Saving Documents

As mentioned earlier, all Open and Save dialogs in Mac OS X Panther use features of the Finder's user interface, making it easy to navigate through the filesystem until you find the folder or file you're seeking. This section discusses the Open and Save dialogs in more detail, showing you how to find what you're looking for on your Mac.

The Open Window

The Open dialog, shown in Figure 1-33, is very similar to the Finder. The dialog features the very same Sidebar that the Finder has and opens in a Column View for navigating through disks and folders for the item you want to open. Above the Column View is a pop-up menu that shows the path the folder or disk that's selected in the View's path, as shown in Figure 1-37.

As you can see from Figure 1-37, the pop-up menu is split in two. The top portion shows the path to the current folder, while the bottom half lists Recent Places that you recently opened a file from. In addition to using this pop-up menu, you can also use various keyboard shortcuts to switch the view or go to a different folder, as noted in Table 1-3.

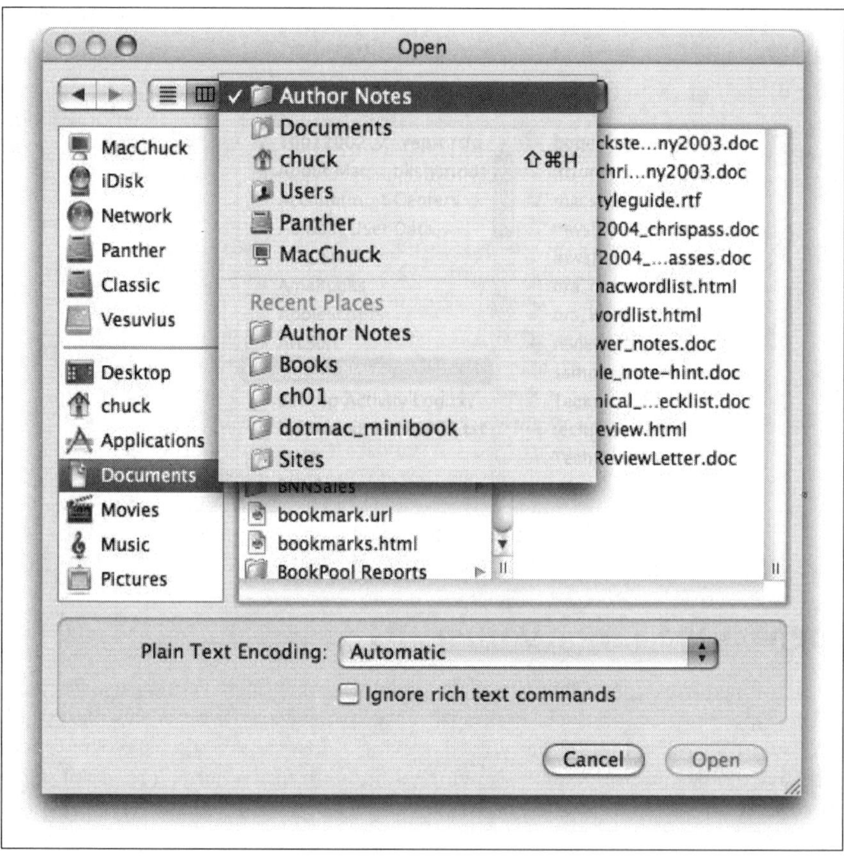

Figure 1-37. The pop-up menu above the Open dialog's Column View lets you select a folder from which to open a file

Table 1-3. Keyboard shortcuts to use with the Open window and Save sheets

Keyboard shortcut	Action
⌘-2	Switches the dialog to List View.
⌘-3	Switches the dialog to Column View.
⌘-D	Switches the location to your Desktop folder.
Shift-⌘-H	Switches the selected location to your Home directory.
Shift-⌘-I	Switches the selected location to your iDisk, if you have a .Mac account. If your iDisk isn't mounted, the iDisk is mounted for you, based on the settings you've entered in the .Mac preference panel (System Preferences→.Mac).
Shift-⌘-G	This keyboard shortcut opens a "Go to Folder" sheet, from which you can enter the path to a particular folder (for example, *~/Documents*, or */etc*). If you include a filename as part of the path, the application tries to open that file. If you type a filename the application can't open, the open dialog will close as if you had clicked the Cancel button. If you type in a path to a file that doesn't exist, the alert sound is played.

The Save Sheet

The Save sheet appears when you first try to save a new document using File→Save (⌘-S), or if you select File→Save As... (Shift-⌘-S, in some applications) with a previously saved document. The Save sheet in its basic form, shown in Figure 1-38, provides a text field for entering a filename and a pop-up menu for selecting a location in the filesystem to save the file.

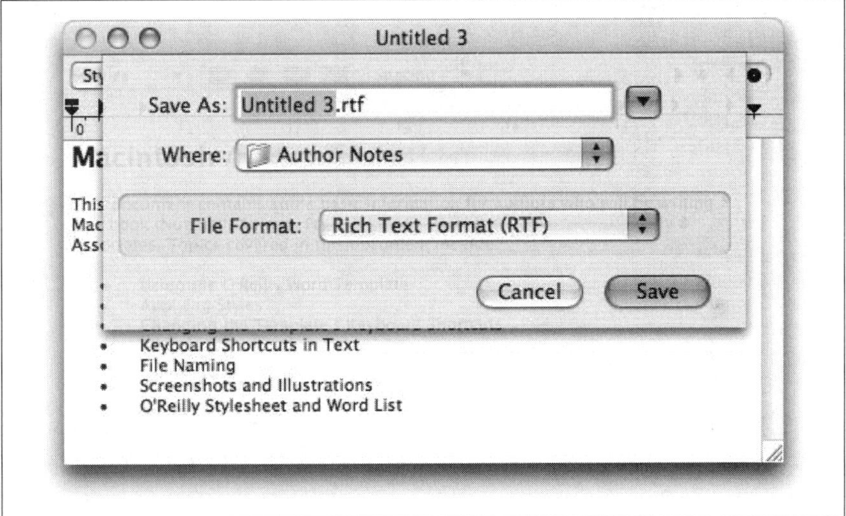

Figure 1-38. The Save sheet with the "Finder" view hidden

If you look closely at Figure 1-38, you'll see a button to the right of the "Save As:" text field. If you click on this button, the Save sheet expands to give you a Finder-like view that provides better access to the filesystem (see Figure 1-39).

The dialog's interface looks and works a lot like that of an Open window, with one major difference: its purpose is not to let you open a file, but to let you name and save the file to a location in the filesystem.

The keyboard shortcuts listed earlier in Table 1-3 also apply to Save sheets, with one addition; ⌘-N can be used to create a new folder (saving you from having to click on the New Folder button).

The Save sheet also features a Hide Extension checkbox at the bottom, leaving it unchecked lets the application choose and assign the file extension (e.g., *.txt*, *.doc*, *.html*, etc.). If you opt to use your own file extension, the application may refuse to accept your replacement or simply ignore you, tacking its own extension on the end of the filename. The default state of the Hide Extension checkbox depends on what you've specified in the Finder's preferences (via the "Show all file extensions checkbox, found in Finder→Preferences→Advanced).

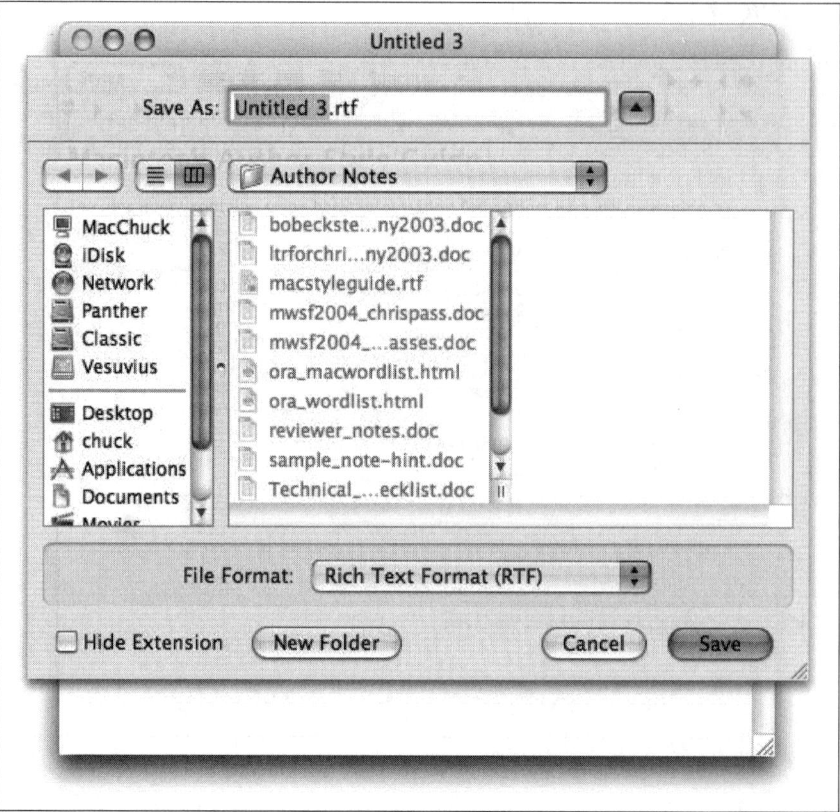

Figure 1-39. The expanded Save sheet includes a Finder-like view

Services

The Services menu is available as a submenu in a program's Application menu. It allows the foreground application to invoke functions of other applications, usually while passing along user-selected text or objects to them.

The Service menu's contents depend on the applications installed on your Mac and the services they offer to other applications. When installed, some applications such as Mail, Safari, and BBEdit, place entries in the Services menu. If an application provides more than one service, those items are placed in a submenu named after that application. For example, Mail offers two services from its Application menu, Send Selection and Sent To, as shown in Figure 1-40.

With some text selected in a TextEdit document, if you select TextEdit (the application menu)→Services→Mail→Send Selection, Mac OS X copies that text and places it in the body of a new message in Mail. Then all you need to do is enter the email address of the person you want to send the text to and click on the Send button. (The Services→Mail→Send To option places the selected item in an email message's To field.)

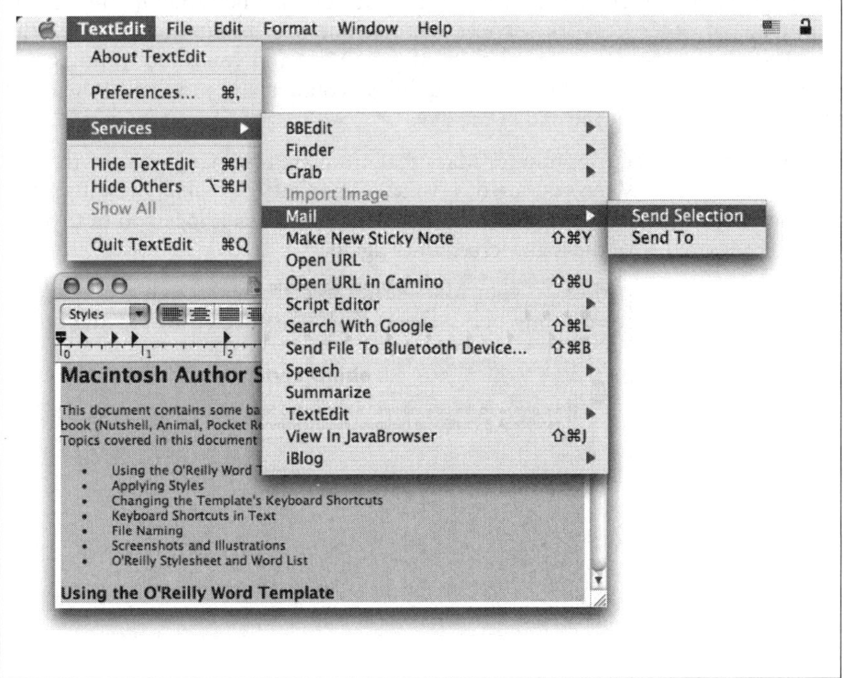

Figure 1-40. The Services menu

Some Services also offer key bindings, which makes it easy to send some selected text to a Bluetooth device (Shift-⌘-B), or to create a new sticky note (Shift-⌘-Y).

An application's own key bindings always trump those in the Services menu. Services know when the current application has a binding that conflicts with theirs and might try to offer alternative keystrokes, changing its binding indicator in the Services menu to reflect this. If all of its bindings raise conflicts, it stops trying altogether and can then be used only through the Services menu for that particular application.

Logging Out and Shutting Down

When you're done using your Macintosh, there are two ways to bring your session to a close: shutting down and logging out.

Because Mac OS X is a multiple-user system and a server platform, you should choose to shut down the computer *only* if nobody else on the network is using it or the services it provides. This includes both the other human users on the system, who might be logged into it remotely using network-shared volumes, as well as people or programs using any running network services.

For example, if you have enabled USB Printer Sharing so that others in your home or office can use the printer connected to your Mac, shutting down the Mac will also make that printer unavailable to the other users. The same applies to any web, mail, or other network services the machine may be running. On the flip side, if you are the sole account holder of your Mac, and you're not running any public network services, then you shouldn't encounter any problems when you shut your Mac down at the end of the day.

Logging out is the better option for Macs that are shared by many users or that act as network servers. When you log out (via →Log Out *Username*, or Shift-⌘-Q), all programs you haven't quit will be quit by the system as it logs you out; you'll then be presented with the login screen once again.

If other users are logged on to your Mac, either directly or through the network, they (and the programs running under them) won't be affected by logging out of your account locally.

2
Using the Finder

In earlier versions of the Mac OS, the Finder was located in the application menu at the far-right edge of the menu bar. The Finder was the application responsible for displaying the contents of a drive or folder; when it was double-clicked, a window opened, displaying either an Icon or List View of the contents. Mac OS X's Finder really isn't that different from Mac OS 9's Finder. It still displays the contents of drives and folders; however, now it is much more powerful.

With each new version of Mac OS X, Mac users have been presented with a new iteration of the Finder. Just as the Finder's icon is anchored in the Dock, the Finder is truly the cornerstone that marks the progress of Mac OS X's evolution through time. The same holds true in Panther, in which the Finder got a fresh new metal interface, a Sidebar, expanded search capabilities, and better functionality to make it easier for you to connect your Mac with other devices and other computers, including Windows machines.

This chapter covers the use of the Finder, and includes tips and tricks to make you a more efficient Mac user.

Finder Overview

The Finder serves as a graphical file manager, which offers three ways (or Views) to look at files, folders, applications, and other filesystems (or volumes) mounted on your system. If you've used an earlier version of Mac OS X, you'll notice that Panther's Finder, shown in Figure 2-1, has changed dramatically.

Panther's Finder has three main sections:

Toolbar
: Located across the top of the Finder window, the toolbar offers buttons that let you go back or forward to previous views, buttons for changing the three views (Icon, List, or Column), the new Action menu, and a search field for

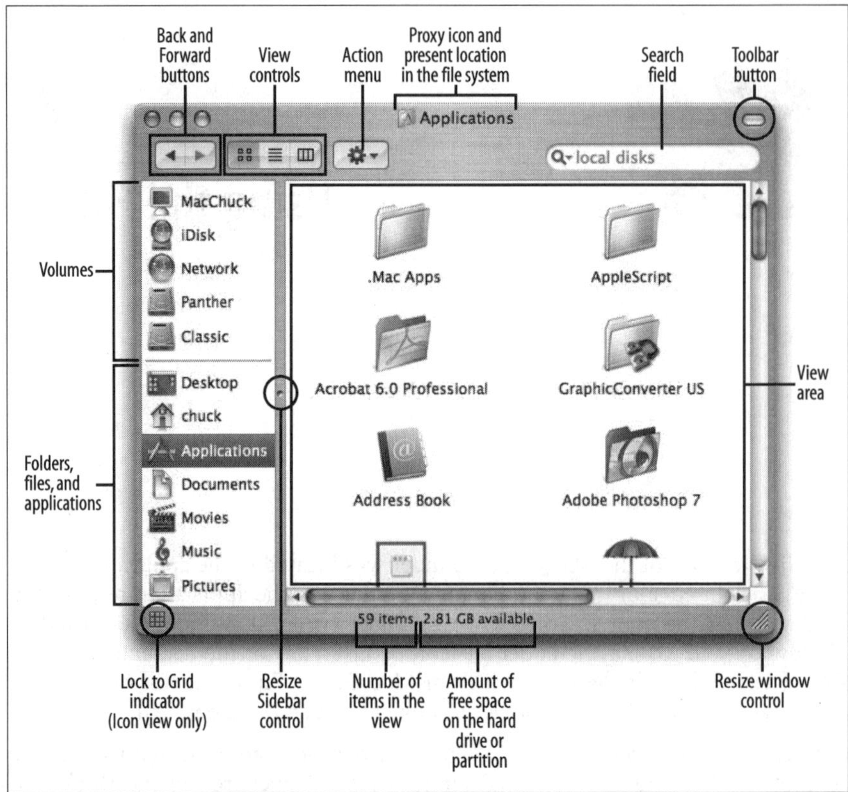

Figure 2-1. Panther's new Finder and its controls

quickly finding files and folders on your Mac. See the section, "The Finder Toolbar" for more information on using the toolbar.

Sidebar

Located at the left edge of the Finder window, the Sidebar offers a split view for accessing drives and other items on your Mac.

The top portion of the Sidebar has icons for any volumes connected to your Mac. This includes hard drives and partitions, FireWire and USB drives, CDs and DVDs, iDisks, disk images, and networked drives, such as FTP sites or Samba shares.

The bottom portion of the Sidebar includes clickable icons to quickly take you to your Desktop, Home folder, the Applications folder, or to the Documents, Movies, Music, or Pictures folder. This lower half of the sidebar is also user-customizable, which means you can add items (including files, folders, and applications) by simply dragging an item from the View area to this part of the Sidebar. See the section, "The Finder's Sidebar" for more information on how to use the Sidebar effectively.

The View

This area of the Finder is the big section to the right of the Sidebar. The View displays the contents of the drives and folders of your system. The default View is Icon View, which displays the files and folders as named icons. You can change the view to either List or Column View by clicking on the appropriate button in the toolbar. See the section, "Finder Views" for more information about how to use the different Views of the Finder.

You can quickly change the Finder's viewpoint by using ⌘-1 for Icon View, ⌘-2 for List View, or ⌘-3 for Column View.

To open a new Finder window, click on the Finder icon in the Dock or click on the Desktop and then select File→New Finder Window (⌘-N) from the menu bar.

The Finder

The Finder Toolbar

Along the top of the Finder window is a toolbar, shown in Figure 2-2, which offers a quick way to switch between the View modes mentioned earlier, perform an action on a selected object, or search for files on your Mac. You can add a file, folder, or application to the Finder's toolbar by dragging and dropping its icon on the toolbar. Application icons that get added to the toolbar will launch with a single click, just as they do in the Dock.

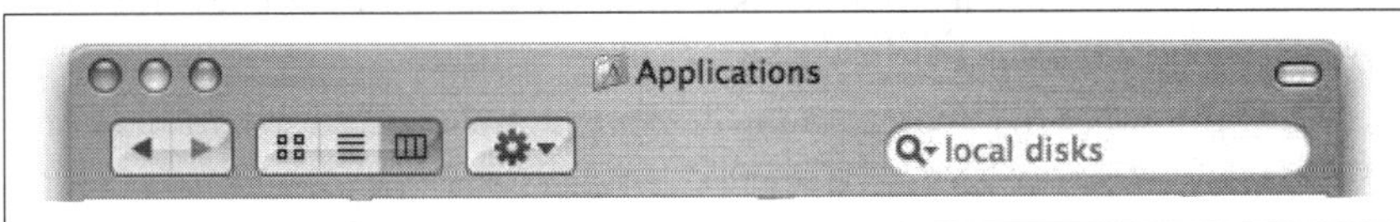

Figure 2-2. The Finder toolbar

The Finder toolbar has the following controls and icons by default (you can refer back to Figure 2-1 to determine what's where in this list):

Back
: Takes you to the previous view in the same Finder window.

Forward
: If you've gone backward in a Finder window, clicking the Forward button will take you forward in the view.

View
: The three Finder View buttons let you switch from Icon View, List View, or Column View, respectively, from left to right.

Action menu
: This new menu, which looks like a cog, is one of the marvels of the new Finder. If you select an object in the Finder and then click on the Action menu, a pop-up menu appears, which lets you do any of the following:

    - Create a new folder within the selected folder or within the same folder if the item selected is a file.

- Open the Get Info window to see details about the selected item.
- Apply a color label (yes, labels are back in Panther) to the item.
- Move the selected item to the Trash.
- Duplicate (or make a copy) of the item.
- Create an alias of the item.
- Create a Zip archive of the selected item. This is particularly handy when you want to quickly create a Zip archive of only a few files within a folder.

Command-click on the files you want to archive, and then select Create Archive from the Action menu. To unzip an archive, just double-click its icon, and the Finder will extract its contents to the same folder.

- Copy the selected item to the pasteboard. If an item has been copied to the pasteboard, a Paste option then becomes available in the Action menu; you can then paste a copy of the item in another location on your Mac.
- Show the available options for the View.

Search
: The Search field offers users a way to perform context-based searches on the filesystem. See the later section "Searching for and Locating Files" for more information on using this field.

Located at the upper-right corner of the Finder window is a clear, elliptical button that can be used to hide the Finder's toolbar, as shown in Figure 2-3.

If you are in Icon or List View with the toolbar hidden, double-clicking a folder icon opens a new Finder window for that folder, displaying its contents. Column View will function normally.

Customizing the Toolbar

In addition to hiding the toolbar, users can customize the Finder's toolbar in a variety of ways. As mentioned earlier, the easiest way to customize your Finder's toolbar is to drag and drop icons in the toolbar. To remove an icon, drag it away from the toolbar, and it disappears in a puff of smoke.

Another way to customize the Finder's toolbar is to switch to the Customize Toolbar window, shown in Figure 2-4, by selecting View→Customize Toolbar or Option-⌘-clicking on the toolbar button.

Here you can choose from a plethora of icons to place in the Finder's toolbar, along with an option to revert back to the default set. At the lower left of the Customize Toolbar window is a pop-up menu with Show next to it. This menu is used to set how the icons appear in the toolbar. By default, Show is set to "Icon & Text". Other options available are "Icon Only" and "Text Only". When finished customizing the Finder toolbar, click the Done button to go back to the previous Finder view (but with the newly customized toolbar, if you've made any changes).

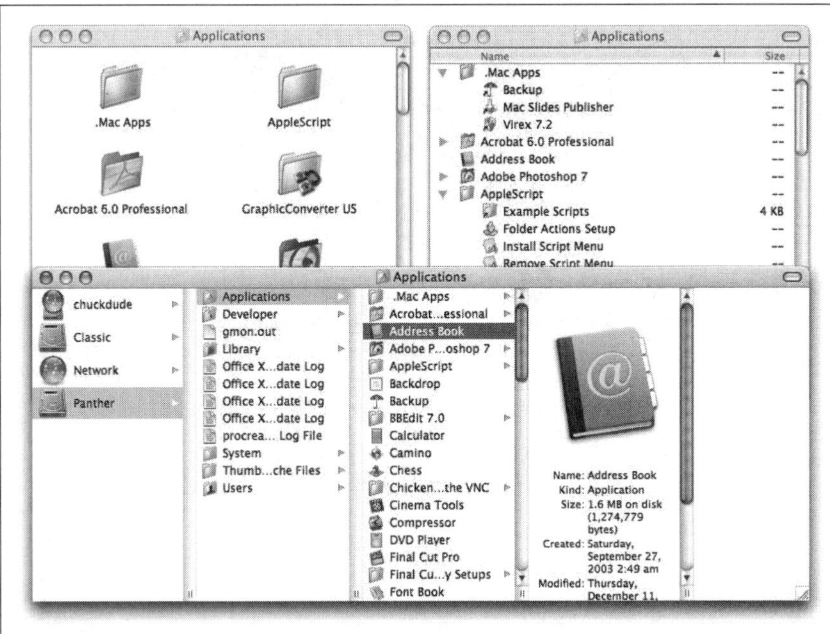

Figure 2-3. Finder windows with hidden toolbars (in the background, Icon View and List View; in the foreground, Column View)

If you see a double-arrow (>>) icon at the right edge of the Finder's toolbar, click on it to reveal its contents. This menu shows up when you have too many items in the Finder's toolbar for them to appear in the Finder window. To remove an icon from the side menu, you need to resize the Finder window to make your icons appear. Then ⌘-click on the undesired icon and drag it off the toolbar.

The Finder's Sidebar

The Finder's Sidebar, shown earlier in Figure 2-1, makes it easier for you to access volumes mounted on your Mac (internal, external, and networked) and provides quick access to the items you use most often. The top half of the Sidebar manages volumes, while the lower can contain icons for files, folders, and applications.

When you mount a networked or external drive, or a CD or DVD, that volume appears in the upper portion of the Sidebar, as shown in Figure 2-5.

External drives, CDs/DVDs, iPods, and FTP sites show up in the Sidebar as separate items with little Eject icons to their right. When you want to eject one of these items, just click on the eject button or select the item in the Sidebar and select File→Eject (⌘-E). You can also select the item and use the Finder's Action menu to eject items as well.

By default, the lower half of the Sidebar contains the following folder icons:

- Desktop
- Your Home folder

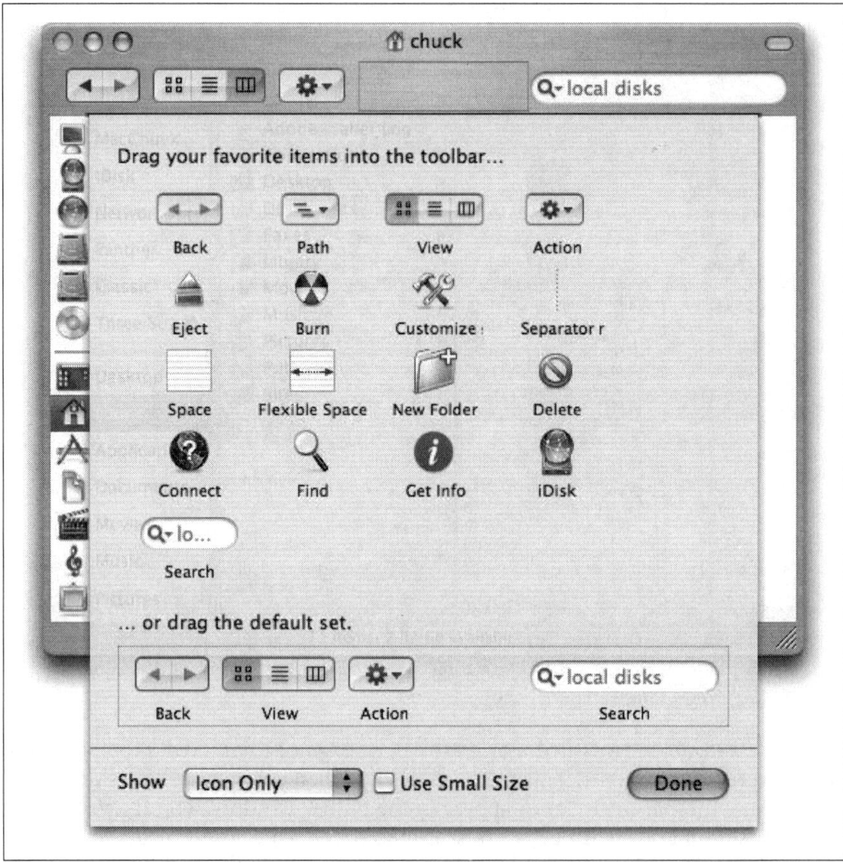

Figure 2-4. The Finder's toolbar customization sheet

- Applications
- Documents
- Movies
- Music
- Pictures

To view the contents of a folder, simply click on its icon in the Sidebar, and the Finder's View changes to display the items within. As mentioned earlier, the lower portion of the Sidebar can be customized by the user. All she needs to do is drag a file, folder, or application to the Sidebar. Depending on what the item is, one of the following three actions will take place when an icon in the Sidebar is clicked:

- Files will open in their native application; if the application isn't already running, the application will be launched as well.
- Folders reveal their contents in the Finder view.
- Applications will launch with a single click, just as if they were in the Dock.

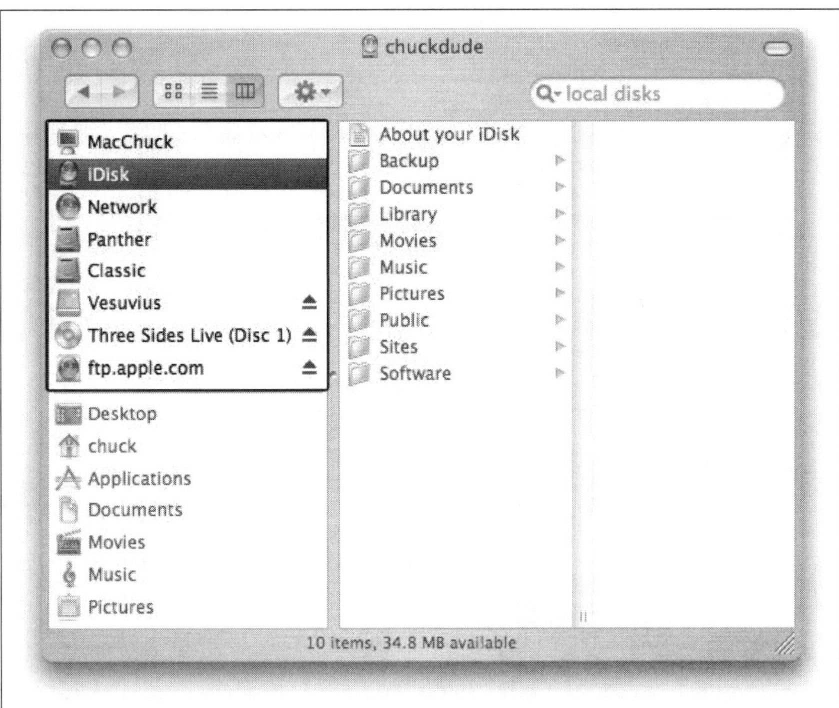

Figure 2-5. Disk volumes and network shares show up in the top portion of the Finder's sidebar

When you drag an item to the lower portion of the Sidebar, an insertion marker is placed between existing items, as shown in Figure 2-6.

If you drag an item over an existing folder, that folder is highlighted in the Sidebar. You can either drop the item on the folder or wait for the folder to flash a few times. When the folder stops flashing, the Finder goes to that folder's location in the view. You can either drop the item in place, or you can hover it over another folder and repeat the process until you find the location where you'd like to move the item.

To remove an item from the Sidebar, simply drag the icon away from the Finder window and release the mouse button; the icon disappears in a puff of smoke.

Resizing the Sidebar

As you can see from Figure 2-6, some item names in the Sidebar have been cut short, and have an ellipsis (...) at the end. To make the Sidebar wider so you can see an items' full name, click on the resize control (the little dot at the middle of the bar to the right of the Sidebar), and drag the bar to the right, as shown in Figure 2-7.

When you place the mouse over the resize control, the pointer changes to a vertical bar with arrows pointing left and right. As you drag the bar to the right,

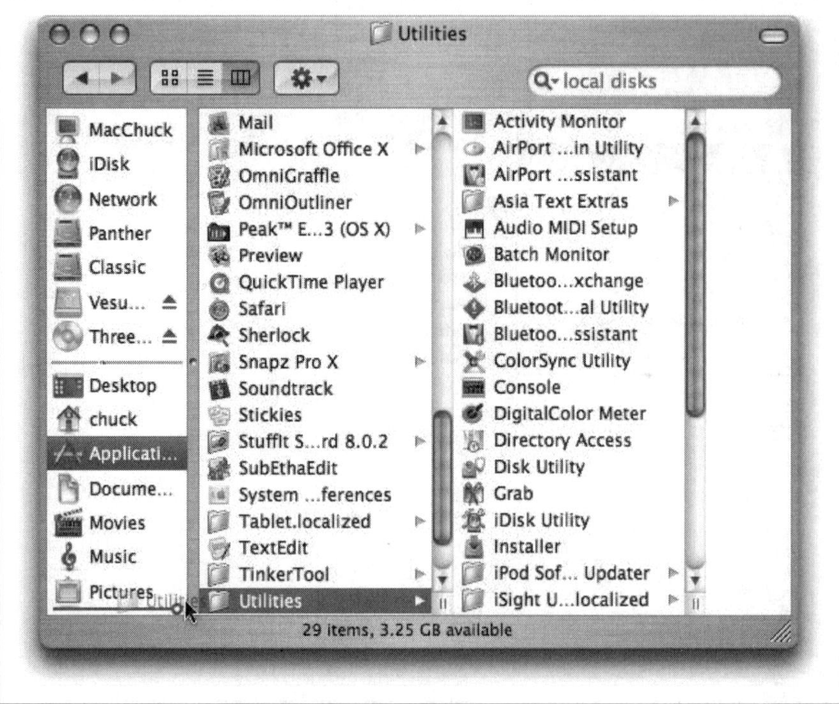

Figure 2-6. Drag files, folders, or application icons to the lower portion of the Sidebar

you'll notice that it seems to catch on some invisible force when it reaches the edge of the item with the longest name.

Likewise, you can also hide the names of the items in the Sidebar by dragging the resize control to the left, so you just have a row of icons in the Sidebar. When you move the mouse over an item in the Sidebar, a little balloon window pops up, displaying the full name of the item, as shown in Figure 2-8.

Double-clicking on the resize control collapses the Sidebar entirely; double-clicking on it again opens the Sidebar to its previous state.

Finder Views

The Finder serves as a graphical file manager, which offers three ways (or Views) to look at the files, folders, applications, and other filesystems mounted on your system. The Finder's Sidebar gives you quick access to frequently used files and directories.

The three Views available in the Finder window are Icon, List, and Column View. To select any of these views for a Finder window, click on the View menu, and select "as Icons" (⌘-1), "as List" (⌘-2), or "as Columns" (⌘-3), respectively.

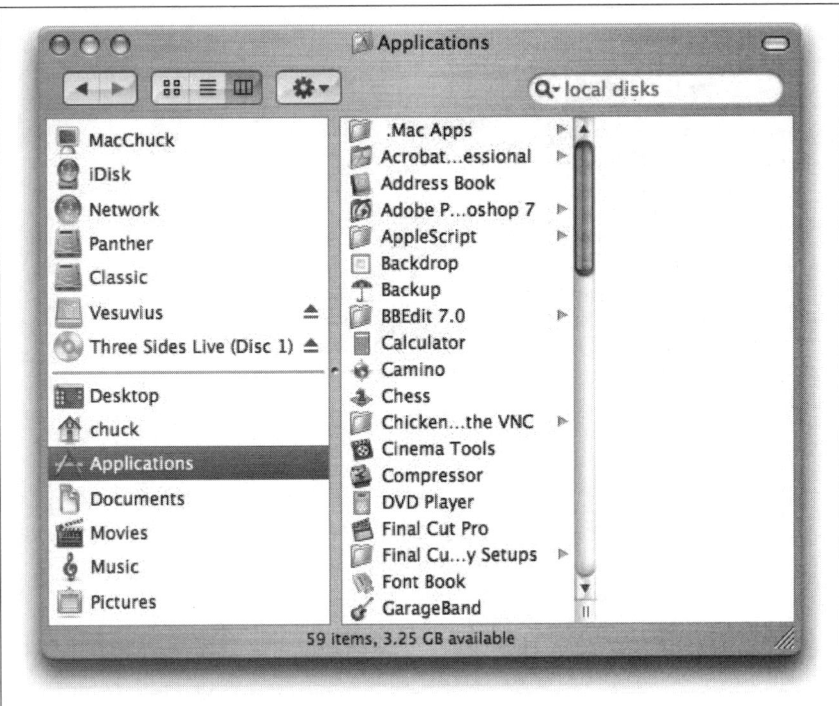

Figure 2-7. Resize the Sidebar to reveal the full name of the items within

Depending on the View you select for your Finder window, you can also tweak the settings for that view by selecting View→Show View Options (⌘-J). The View Options for each View will be discussed in the sections that follow.

Icon View

This view shows the contents of a directory as file, folder, or an application icons, as shown in Figure 2-1. In this view, every Finder object appears as an icon of a variable size. Icons can be arbitrarily arranged within a window by dragging and dropping them to different locations. If you find that icons are overlapping or out of order, you can clean up the view by selecting View→Clean Up or View→Arrange (by Name, Date Modified, Date Created, Size, Kind, or Label).

Double-clicking on an icon will do one of three things, depending on its type: launch an application, open a file, or display the contents of a double-clicked folder in the Finder window. If the Finder window's toolbar is hidden when you double-click on a folder, the contents of that folder are displayed in a new Finder window, rather than the same Finder window.

Table 2-1 lists some keyboard shortcuts for navigating within the Finder's Icon View.

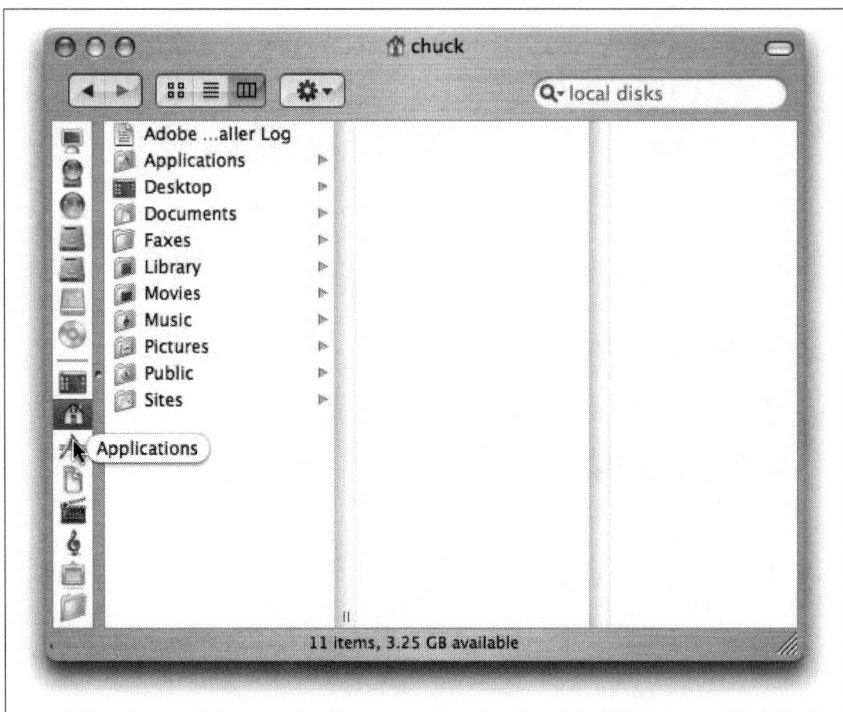

Figure 2-8. Mousing over an icon without a name in the Sidebar pops open a balloon to display the items' name

Table 2-1. Icon View's keyboard shortcuts

Keyboard shortcut	Description
Left Arrow	Select item to the left of the currently highlighted icon.
Right Arrow	Select the item to the right of the currently highlighted icon.
Up Arrow	Select the item above the currently highlighted icon.
Down Arrow	Select the item below the currently highlighted icon.
⌘-Up Arrow	Used to go backward in the filesystem (e.g., if an application is highlighted and you hit ⌘-Up Arrow, the view switches to */Applications*).
⌘-Down Arrow	Used to launch a highlighted application icon or to open a folder in the view.
Letter or Number keys	Select the item in the list that begins with that letter or number.

Icon View's options

With a Finder window in Icon View, you can select from the following options by selecting View→Show View Options (⌘-J), as shown in Figure 2-9.

At the top of the Options window are two radio buttons. Depending on which is selected, the changes you make in this window will apply to "This window only" or to "All windows" (the default). If you select "This window only," the options

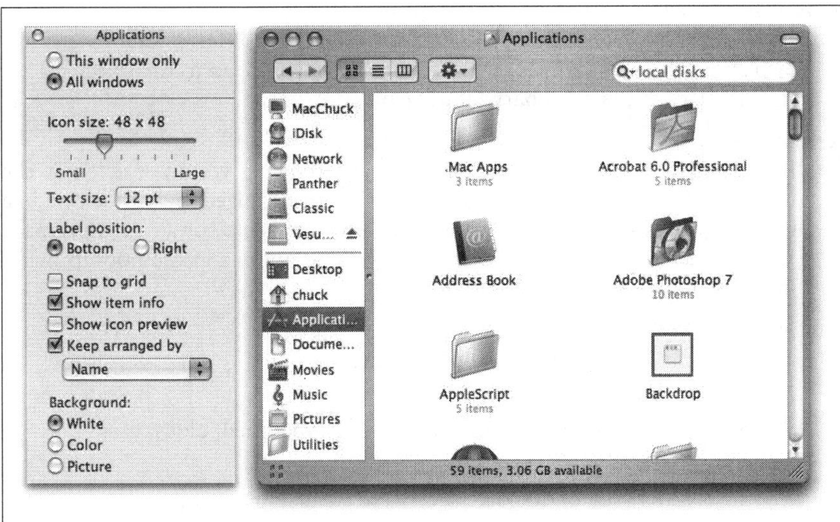

Figure 2-9. Icon View's View Options palette

you set will apply to that particular folder or drive every time you open that window in Icon View in the Finder. This lets you color-code folders by setting the background color (or image) for individual folders.

Other options for Icon View include:

Icon size
: This slider controls the size of all the window's icons. If dragged all the way to the right, the icons resize to 128 × 128 pixels. Dragging the slider all the way to the left reduces them to 16 × 16 pixels (which happens to be the same size as the Column View icons, or the smaller List View icons). The default size is 48 × 48 pixels.

Text size
: A pop-up menu for choosing the size of the icon's text label. The default size is 12-point type.

Label position
: Lets you select where an icon's label is placed: Bottom (the default) or Right.

Snap to grid
: With this option selected, the icons will stick to a strict grid layout. Dropping an icon in the window makes it appear in the nearest empty spot of this grid, unless you've selected one of the options from the "Keep arranged by" pop-up menu. When "Snap to grid" is selected, a small grid icon appears in the lower-left corner of the Finder window, as shown in Figure 2-1.

Show item info
: If selected, the Finder displays a brief piece of information about certain kinds of items beneath their labels. Folders display how many files and folders are contained within, disks show their capacity, and images display their dimensions in pixels.

Show icon preview

If this checkbox is selected, document icons that offer a simple preview display (such as image files) will use this preview (scaled to the selected icon size) in place of their ordinary Finder icon.

Keep arranged by

If selected, a pop-up menu becomes active, allowing you to select how the icons in the view are arranged. When "Keep arranged by" is selected, a grouping of four mini icons appears in the lower-left corner of the Finder window, as shown in Figure 2-9. The available options in the pop-up menu include:

Name

Sorts the icons alphabetically, by name.

Date Modified

Sorts files based on the date they were last modified, oldest first.

Date Created

Sorts files based on the date they were created, oldest first.

Size

Sorts files by their file size, smallest first.

The "Keep arranged by size" option can cause some visual confusion in a window containing lots of folders. Determining the total size of a folder and everything inside it can take a while. As the Finder works on the problem, it arranges all the icons based on the information it's received up to that second. Thus, the Finder usually ends up shuffling everything in the window several times while you watch (which can frustrate your attempts to select something).

Kind

Sorts by the type of object.

Label

Sorts objects by their colored label.

Background

By default, the background for Finder windows is set to White; however, there are two other options available:

Color

If you select Color, a box appears next to this label, which when clicked on, opens a color picker that you can use to select a color.

Picture

If you select Picture, click on the Select button to be taken to your Pictures folder (*~/Pictures*) so you can select a picture to use as the background.

List View

List View, shown in Figure 2-10, displays the contents of a folder or drive in a table list, with one row for each file or folder and one column for each bit of information about the object.

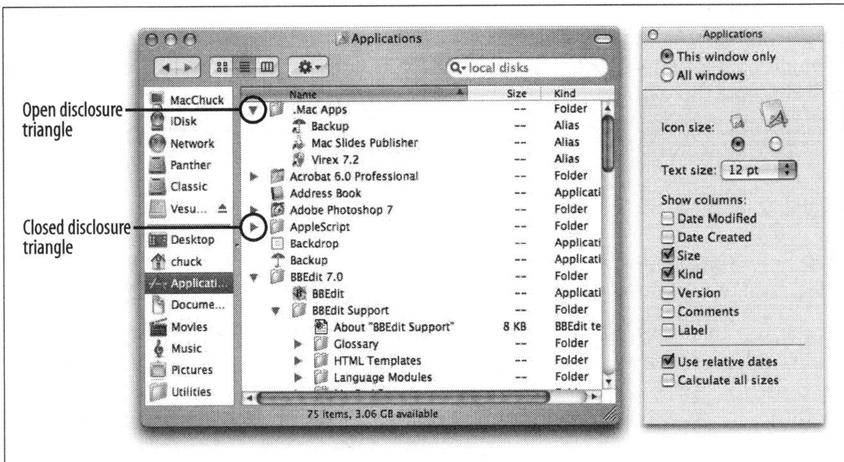

Figure 2-10. The Finder in List View along with its View Options window

Next to each folder in a List View is a black disclosure triangle. To view the items within the folder without opening a new Finder window, click on the disclosure triangle to view the folder's contents. Another way to navigate through the icons and folders in the Finder's List View is by using the keyboard, as noted in Table 2-2.

Table 2-2. List View's keyboard shortcuts

Keyboard shortcut	Description
Down Arrow	Move down through the list of items.
Up Arrow	Move up through the list of items.
Right Arrow	Open a folder's disclosure triangle to reveal its contents.
Left Arrow	Close a folder's disclosure triangle to hide its contents.
Option-Right Arrow	Open a folder and any subfolders to reveal their contents.
Option-Left Arrow	Close a folder and any subfolders to hide its contents.
Letter or Number keys	Select the item in the list that begins with that letter or number.

To open all the folders in the View, select all the View's contents (⌘-A) and use Option-Right Arrow (likewise, Option-Left Arrow to close them again). To open all the folders in the View including subfolders, add the Shift or Command key (e.g., Shift-Option-Right Arrow or Option-⌘-Right Arrow to open, Shift-Option-Left Arrow or Option-⌘-Left Arrow to close).

Sorting a List View

A List View is sorted alphabetically by the name of the file or folder by default. This corresponds to whichever column heading is highlighted. If you click on a different column heading, that one takes on the highlight, and all the view's rows rearrange themselves according to this new sort criteria.

Clicking the highlighted column a second time reverses the sort order. A little triangle on the right side of the highlighted header suggests the sort order. When pointing up, the window sorts the data in alphabetical (A–Z), numerical (0–9), or chronological order (oldest to most recent). Click on the column head again to reverse the sort order.

List View's options

With a Finder window in List View, you can select from the following options by selecting View→Show View Options (⌘-J), as shown in Figure 2-10.

At the top of the Options window are two radio buttons. Depending on which one is selected, the changes you make in this window apply to "This window only" or to "All windows" (the default). If you select "This window only," the options you've set will apply to that particular folder or drive every time you open that window in List View in the Finder. This lets you color-code folders by setting the background color (or image) for individual folders.

Other options for List View include:

Icon size
: Choose between small (16 × 16) or large (32 × 32) size. The default is small.

Text size
: Selects the size of the text in the view. The range is 10–16 point type, with 12 point being the default size.

Show columns
: These six checkboxes, listed here, let you specify which columns the Finder should display in the List View. Note that the Name column always appear in the List view.

  Date Modified
  : The date and time the file was last modified.

  Date Created
  : The date and time the file was created.

  Size
  : Shows the file size.

  Kind
  : Displays the file type (e.g., Alias, Application, Folder, etc.).

  Version
  : If applicable, this displays the version number for the file or application.

Comments

Displays any comments attached to the file (typically entered via the file's Get Info window).

Label

Sorts objects by their colored label.

Use relative dates

In a List View, the dates are typically displayed using the date and time format specified in the System Preferences (International→Formats→Dates, and International→Formats→Times); for example, 12/07/03, 9:11 a.m. However, if you select "Use relative dates," the date for newly created or recently edited files will change to Yesterday or Today, as applicable.

Calculate all sizes

If checked, the Finder digs through each folder in the view, calculating its total size, and then displaying it in the view's Size column. This box is unchecked by default because it takes the system a fair amount of time (and processor power) to calculate the size of the folder's contents. If left unchecked, every folder's size shows up simply as "– –". However, you can always find the size of a folder (or file) by selecting it and going to File→Get Info (⌘-I).

The Finder

Arranging columns in List View

When you select an item in the "Show columns" section of List View's Options, you'll notice that the columns appear in the order in which the buttons are listed in Figure 2-10. But what if you wanted the Version column to appear next to the name column without turning all the other columns off? To do this, click on the column header you'd like to move, and hold down the mouse button. Now drag that column left or right, and drop it where you would like it to appear; the other column(s) will move out of its way.

The only column you can't move is the Name column. By default, the Name column is always the left-most column in the List View display; you can't place another column to the left of the Name column.

Column View

Column View, shown in Figure 2-11, displays a directory's contents in column form. This is similar to List View, except that when you click on an item, a new pane opens to the right and either exposes the contents of a folder or displays some information about a file, including its name, type, and file size.

Column View divides a Finder window into several columns, similar to the frames on a web site, each with its own vertical scrollbar (if needed). As Figure 2-11 shows, drives and folders have a gray arrow at the right edge of their column. Clicking on a drive or folder reveals its contents in the next column to the right, ending with a selected object in the Preview column. The Preview column displays some basic information about the file or application, including its name, size, date created and modified, and version number if it is an application icon.

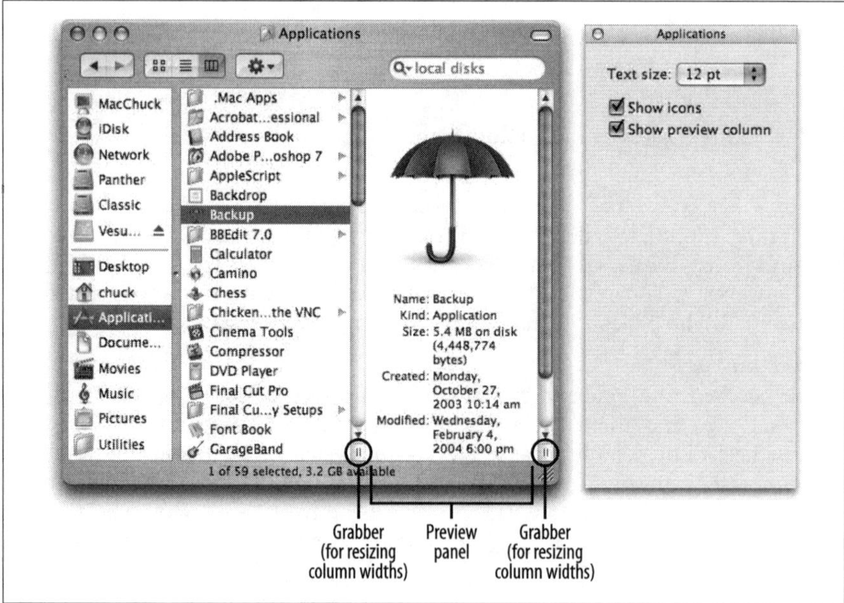

Figure 2-11. The Finder's Column View

The advantage to using Column View is its ability to rapidly scroll back and forth through the filesystem. It allows you to use a combination of the scrollbars and the titlebar's proxy icon (see "Document Windows" in Chapter 1) to quickly switch to a different location. (Remember, if you ⌘-click on the proxy icon, a context menu will pop up, showing where you are in the filesystem.)

Column View's options

Unlike Icon and List View, the Finder's Column View has only three items in its Show View Options window:

Text size
: Selects the size of the text in the view. The range is 10–16 point type, with 12 point being the default size.

Show icons
: This option decides whether icons will be displayed in the Column View along with their appropriate text label. "Show icons" is enabled by default; if you deselect this checkbox, the icons in the Column View will disappear, leaving you with text labels only.

Show preview column
: The far right column shown in Figure 2-11 is known as the Preview column. If you disable this option, file and application icons won't be displayed in the Column View.

Table 2-3 lists the keyboard shortcuts that can be used within the Finder's Column View.

Table 2-3. Column View's keyboard shortcuts

Keyboard shortcut	Description
Right Arrow	Move to the next column.
Left Arrow	Move to the previous column.
Up Arrow	Select the above item in the column.
Down Arrow	Select the next item down in the column.
Letter or Number keys	Select the item in the next column that begins with that letter or number.

Resizing column widths

Between each column is a vertical bar with what looks like a sideways equals sign at the bottom, which is known as a *grabber*. To adjust the width of a column, click and hold on the grabber and drag the mouse left or right to make the column width decrease or increase, respectively. To adjust the width of all of the columns simultaneously, hold down the Option key when you click and drag the grabber. To reset the columns so they're all the same width, simply double-click (or Option–double-click) on any available grabber.

Finder Preferences

As with most other applications, the Finder keeps its preferences command in the application menu under Finder→Preferences (⌘-,). This command brings forth the Finder's preferences window, as shown in Figure 2-12.

In earlier versions of Mac OS X, the Finder's preferences were all in one window. With Panther, however, the Finder's preference window has a toolbar with four categories: General, Labels, Sidebar, and Advanced.

General preferences

The following options can be found in the Finder's General preferences pane:

Show these items on the Desktop

This category gives you three checkboxes for controlling the types of disk icons displayed on your Desktop:

- Hard disks
- Removable media (such as CDs)
- Connected servers

By default, all three are checked, which means icons for those disk types will be displayed on your Desktop. Uncheck an item, and its icon will disappear from your Desktop, but you can still see them in the Finder's Computer window (Go→Computer, or Shift-⌘-C).

New Finder windows open

This pop-up menu lets you select the default location in which new Finder windows will open: either Home (your home directory) or the Documents folder.

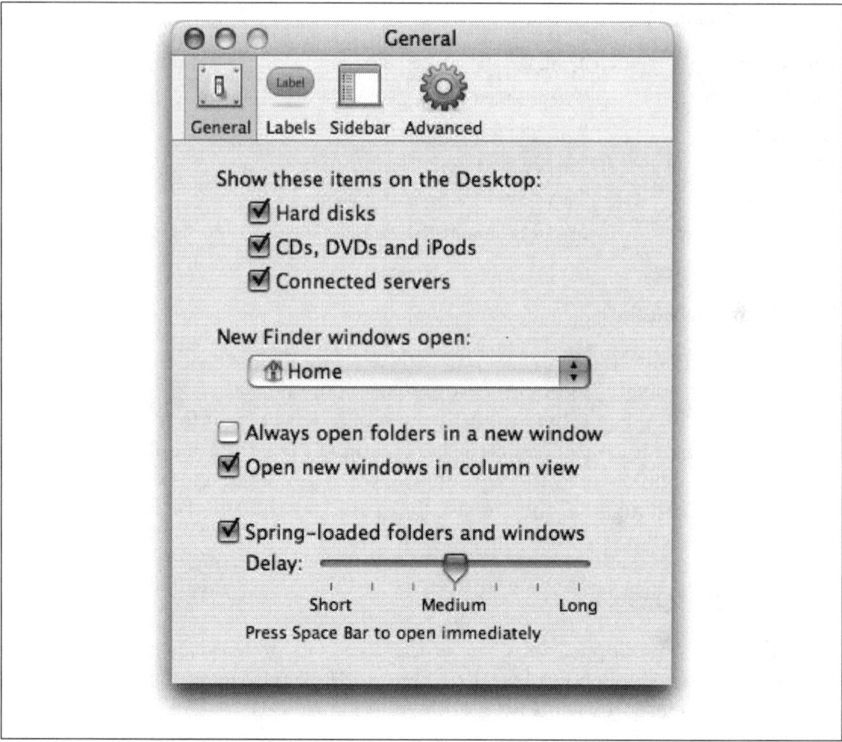

Figure 2-12. The Finder's preferences window

Always open folders in a new window
: If checked, any folder you double-click on in a Finder view will open in a new Finder window (rather than appear in the same Finder window). This is how Mac OS 9's Finder reacted when a folder was double-clicked. If you leave this item unchecked, you can open a folder in a new window by holding down the Command (⌘) key when double-clicking a folder icon.

Open new windows in Column View
: If you select this checkbox, all new Finder windows will open in Column View (described earlier).

Spring-loaded folders and windows
: This determines how folders and windows will react when you drag an item over its location. If unchecked, dragging an item to another folder or window just places that item there. However, if this option is checked, the location to which the item is dragged will open in a new Finder window.

You can use the slider to specify the Delay before the new Finder window appears. By default, the Delay is set to a Medium time frame. If you have the Delay set for Long, but you're sure of where you're moving the file, hold down the spacebar to open the new location immediately.

Labels preferences

Mac OS X Panther brings back the use of colored labels, which were commonplace in earlier versions of the Mac OS. Labels can be applied to any item on the filesystem, including files, folders, and applications. This panel lists the colored labels you can use (Red, Orange, Yellow, Green, Blue, Purple, and Gray). Each color label has a text field next to it, in which you can enter some other text to describe the label. For example, you could rename the Red label as "Critical."

Sidebar preferences

This panel lets you select which items show up in the Finder's Sidebar. To enable or disable an item, simply click on its checkbox.

Advanced preferences

The following options can be found in the Finder's Advanced preferences pane:

Show all file extensions
: This item is not checked by default, although we recommend that you check it. Leaving it unchecked allows the Finder to chop off file extensions (e.g., *.doc*, *.xls*, *.psd*, *.txt*, *.html*, etc.) when displaying filenames; checking this option appends the appropriate file extension.

Apple prefers to hide extensions from nontechnical users so they can't accidentally break the association between documents and their assigned applications. This is much easier to do in Mac OS X than in previous versions of the Mac OS because it is now based on easy-to-edit file extensions and not more arcane creator codes (see "Type and Creator Codes").

Show warning before emptying the Trash
: When checked, the Finder makes emptying the Trash a two-step process, displaying a dialog box asking you to confirm the deletion of files in the Trash. If you don't want to be bothered by that warning note, uncheck this box.

Languages for searching file contents
: The lone item for this option is a Select button, which, when clicked, pops open a window that lists the languages supported by Mac OS X. The fewer languages you select in this window, the faster your content indexing and searching will be.

Relaunching the Finder

The Force Quit window (see "Force-quitting applications" in Chapter 1) is the quickest way to restart the Finder if it seems to be stuck or if you want to apply some change you've made by hacking the Dock's preferences (see Chapter 5).

To restart the Finder, go to →Force Quit (Option-⌘-Esc), select the Finder, and click on the Relaunch button. As with force-quitting other applications, a warning sheet will slide down from the window's titlebar asking you to confirm the operation. If you still want to restart the Finder, click on the Relaunch button; if not, click on the Cancel button or hit ⌘-. (Command-period) to cancel the operation.

Menus and Keyboard Shortcuts

On the Mac (as with Windows and Linux desktops), you have two ways to invoke commands in the GUI: by using the menus or by issuing shortcuts for the commands on the keyboard. Not every menu item has a keyboard accelerator, but for the ones that do—the more common functions—using the keyboard shortcuts can save you a lot of time.

Aside from its application menu, the Finder has these menus in its menu bar:

- The Finder's application menu
- File
- Edit
- View
- Go
- Window
- Help

The commands found in these menus are highlighted in Tables 2-4 through 2-10. While most of these commands function the same across all applications, the functions of some, such as ⌘-B and ⌘-I, can vary between programs, and others may work only when the Finder is active. For example, ⌘-B in Microsoft Word turns on boldface type or makes a selection bold, while in Xcode, ⌘-B builds your application. Likewise, ⌘-I in Word italicizes a word or selection, while hitting ⌘-I after selecting a file, folder, or application in the Finder opens the Get Info window for the selected item. Table 2-11 lists keyboard shortcuts that should work across most applications.

The Finder's Application Menu

As with other applications, options found in the Finder's application menu (Table 2-4) give the user access to its Preferences and the Services menu, and provide information about the Finder, options for hiding and showing windows, and options for emptying the Trash.

Table 2-4. The Finder's application menu

Menu option	Keyboard shortcut	Description
About Finder	None	Displays the Finder's About Box.
Preferences	⌘-,	Opens the Finder's Preferences window.
Empty Trash	Shift-⌘-Delete	Empties the Trash.
Secure Empty TrashNone		Empties the Trash and writes over the location of the file numerous times, reducing its chances of ever being recovered.
Services	None	Gives you access to Services provided by other applications on the system.

Table 2-4. The Finder's application menu (continued)

Menu option	Keyboard shortcut	Description
Hide Finder	⌘-H	Hides all open Finder windows.
Hide Others	Option-⌘-H	Hides the windows for other open applications.
Show All	None	Brings all Finder windows to the forefront.

The File Menu

The Finder's File menu lacks the usual Open, Save, and Print commands found in most other applications. Instead, the commands for the File menu, listed in Table 2-5, contain commands for dealing with files and folders.

If you've been using the Mac OS prior to Mac OS X, you'll notice that the keyboard shortcut for creating a new folder has changed; ⌘-N now opens a new Finder window, while Shift-⌘-N creates a new folder.

Table 2-5. The File menu

Menu option	Keyboard shortcut	Description
New Finder Window	⌘-N	Opens a new Finder window.
New Folder	Shift-⌘-N	Creates a new folder.
Open	⌘-O	Opens a file or folder; can also be used to launch applications.
Open With	None	If the selected item is a file, this submenu displays Mac OS X and Classic Mac applications you can use to open the selected file.
Close Window	⌘-W	Closes the window.
Get Info	⌘-I	Opens the Get Info window for the selected item.
Duplicate	⌘-D	Creates a duplicate copy of a selected item. This command adds the word "copy" to the filename before the file extension.
Make Alias	⌘-L	Creates an alias of the selected file.
Show Original	⌘-R	Opens a Finder window that takes you to the original of an alias.
Add to Sidebar	⌘-T	Adds the selected item to the lower-half of the Finder's Sidebar.
Create Archive of "..."None		When selected, this option creates a zipped archive (*.zip*) of the items selected in the Finder view.
Move to Trash	⌘-Delete	Moves the selected item to the Trash.
Eject	⌘-E	Ejects or unmounts the selected disk.
Burn Disc	⌘-E	Initiates a Finder burn session, for creating CDs and DVDs.
Find	⌘-F	Opens a Find window for searching through the filesystem.
Color LabelNone		Lets you assign a colored label to the selected item in the Finder.

The Edit Menu

Commands found in the Edit menu, listed in Table 2-6, allow you to perform actions on a file in the Finder window.

Table 2-6. The Edit menu

Menu option	Keyboard shortcut	Description
Undo	⌘-Z	Undoes the previously issued command.
Cut	⌘-X	Deletes the selected item or text and copies it to the clipboard.
Copy	⌘-C	Copies the selected item or text to the clipboard.
Paste	⌘-V	Pastes the contents of the clipboard at the currently selected location.
Select All	⌘-A	Selects all items within the Finder view or text document.
Show Clipboard	None	Displays the contents of the clipboard.
Special CharactersNone		Opens the Character Palette, which you can use to place special Unicode characters into a document, or use in a file or folder name.

The View Menu

The items in the View menu, listed in Table 2-7, offer shortcuts for changing the Finder's view.

Table 2-7. The View menu

Menu option	Keyboard shortcut	Description
as Icons	⌘-1	Changes the Finder to Icon View.
as List	⌘-2	Changes the Finder to List View.
as Columns	⌘-3	Changes the Finder to Column View.
Clean Up	None	Aligns the items within the Finder view.
Arrange	None	Only an available option in Icon View. Grayed out if the View Option's "Keep arranged by" option is checked; otherwise, it lets you arrange the icons in the View by Name, Date Modified, Date Created, Size, Kind, or Label.
Hide Toolbar	Option-⌘-T	Hides the Finder's toolbar.
Customize Toolbar	None	Used for customizing the Finder's toolbar.
Hide/Show Status Bar	None	Hides or shows the status bar in the Finder view.
Show View Options	⌘-J	Opens the Finder view's View Options window.

The Go Menu

The Finder's Go menu offers a number of shortcuts (listed in Table 2-8), some hardcoded and some user-definable, to various folders and disks on your system. This menu also contains commands to mount disks via a network connection, and for users willing to speak a little Unix, a quick way to view the contents of any folder in the filesystem in the Finder.

Table 2-8. The Go menu

Menu option	Keyboard shortcut	Description
Back	⌘-[	Goes backward in the Finder view.
Forward	⌘-]	Goes forward in the Finder view.
Enclosing Folder	⌘-Up Arrow	Goes backward in the Finder view to the folder that contains the selected item.
Computer	Shift-⌘-C	Shows which volumes are mounted on the computer.
Home	Shift-⌘-H	Takes the user to his home directory (*/Users/username*).
Network	Shift-⌘-K	Opens a Finder window, showing the local network
iDisk	Shift-⌘-I	The iDisk menu item has a submenu with three options: • My iDisk (Shift-⌘-I); this mounts the user's iDisk based on the settings made in System Preference→.Mac→.Mac. • Other User's iDisk. • Other User's Public Folder.
Applications	Shift-⌘-A	Takes the user to the Applications folder (*/Applications*) in the Finder view.
Utilities	Shift-⌘-U	Takes the user to the Utilities folder (*/Applications/Utilities*) in the Finder view.
Recent Folders	None	This submenu displays a list of the recently accessed folders; the submenu also features a Clear Menu option which resets the list of folders in this menu.
Go to Folder	Shift-⌘-G	Displays a sheet that lets the user quickly change the Finder's view to the location of a specific folder.
Connect to Server	⌘-K	Lets the user connect to another computer on the network via AppleTalk, AFP, Samba, IP, and WebDAV.

The Window Menu

Items found in the Window menu (Table 2-9) give you access to the open Finder windows.

Table 2-9. The Window menu

Menu option	Keyboard shortcut	Description
Minimize Window	⌘-M	Minimizes the window to the Dock.
Bring All to Front	None	Brings all of the Finder windows to the front of the window stack.
[List of Open Windows]	None	All open Finder windows are listed at the bottom of this menu, allowing you to quickly select a Finder window based on its title.

The Help Menu

The Finder's Help menu (as with most, but not all applications) gives you access to the Mac's Help Viewer application. Some applications' Help menus, such as Microsoft Word, include quick links to the product's web site or a means for checking for software updates. The Finder's lone Help menu item is listed in Table 2-10.

Table 2-10. The Help menu

Menu option	Keyboard shortcut	Description
Mac Help	⌘-?	Opens the Help Viewer.

Basic Keyboard Shortcuts

Table 2-11 lists some additional keyboard shortcuts that will work the same across most applications on Mac OS X.

Table 2-11. Additional keyboard shortcuts for Mac OS X

Keyboard shortcut	Description
Option-⌘-Escape	Opens the Force Quit window.
⌘-Tab ⌘-Tab+Right Arrow	Cycles forward through active applications.
Shift-⌘-Tab ⌘-Tab+Left Arrow	Cycles backward through active applications.
⌘-.	Cancels operation.
⌘-?	Opens Mac Help.
⌘-[	Goes back in the Finder view to the previous item.
⌘-]	Goes forward in the Finder view to the previous item.
⌘-Up Arrow	Goes to the folder that contains a selected item.
Shift-⌘-G	Goes to a folder in the Finder.
⌘-A	Selects all.
Option-⌘-T	Hides/reveals the Finder's toolbar.
⌘-C	Copies.
⌘-D	Duplicates; creates a duplicate copy of a selected item. This command adds the word "copy" to the filename before the file extension. For example, if you selected the file *file.txt* and hit ⌘-D, a new file named *file copy.txt* (with a space in the filename) is created in the same directory as *file.txt*.
⌘-L	Creates an alias of a file.
Option-⌘-D	Turns Dock hiding on/off.
⌘-Delete	Moves item to Trash.
Shift-⌘-Delete	Empties Trash.
⌘-E	Ejects the selected disk image, CD, etc.
F12	Ejects a CD or DVD (on iBooks and PowerBooks).
⌘-F	Finds.
⌘-H	Hides application.
⌘-I	Gets Info.
⌘-J	Shows View options in the Finder.
⌘-K	Connects to Server.
Shift-⌘-K	Connects to a specific network.

Table 2-11. Additional keyboard shortcuts for Mac OS X (continued)

Keyboard shortcut	Description
⌘-M	Minimizes window.
Option-⌘-M	Minimizes all open windows for an application.
⌘-N	Opens a new Finder window. (This is a change from earlier versions of the Mac OS, where ⌘-N was used to create new folders.)
Shift-⌘-N	Creates new folder.
⌘-O	Opens file or folder; can also be used to launch applications.
⌘-P	Prints file.
⌘-Q	Quits application.
⌘-R	Shows original.
⌘-V	Pastes.
⌘-W	Closes window.
Option-⌘-W	Closes all open windows for an application.
⌘-X	Cuts.
⌘-Z	Undoes.
Shift-⌘-Z	Redoes (not available in all applications).
Shift-⌘-A	Goes to the Applications folder in the Finder.
Shift-⌘-U	Goes to the Utilities folder in the Finder.
Shift-⌘-C	Goes to Computer View in the Finder.
Shift-⌘-H	Goes to Home View in the Finder.
Shift-⌘-I	Goes to iDisk View in the Finder (requires a *.Mac* account).
Shift-⌘-3	Takes a screenshot of the entire display and save the image data to a file.
Control-Shift-⌘-3	Takes a screenshot of the entire display and save the image data to the clipboard.
Shift-⌘-4	Takes a screenshot of a selection of the display and save the image data to a file.
Control-Shift-⌘-4	Takes a screenshot of a selection of the display and save the image data to the clipboard.

Keyboard Navigation

When working with Finder windows, you can perform almost all the navigation you need via the keyboard, speeding up things considerably.

Selecting icons

You can select a file by starting to type its name. When looking at a Finder window, typing (for example) "S" will select the first file in the view whose name begins with the letter "S." If you quickly follow that with an "H," then the first file whose name begins with "SH" will be highlighted, and so on.

Alternately, you can change the selection via the arrow keys, which switches the selection depending on its icons' window position, or with Tab, which selects the next alphabetical icon. Shift-Tab selects the previous alphabetical icon in the view.

Opening icons and navigating folders

Once you've selected the file, folder, or application you want to open, hit ⌘-O, which has the same effect as double-clicking on the icon or choosing Open from the File menu (File→Open).

Note that you can do this with folders to drill down through your filesystem. If you find yourself too deep, use the keyboard shortcut ⌘-Up Arrow or ⌘-[to go backward in the view.

Searching for and Locating Files

Mac OS X gives you five ways to find files—two easy-to-use methods through the Finder, and three more as Unix commands you can invoke through the Terminal.

Searching from the Finder

As shown earlier in Figure 2-1, the Finder's toolbar sports a Search field, which was added to the Finder in Mac OS X 10.2 (Jaguar), replacing Sherlock's old system search functionality. The Search field in Panther has been enhanced to allow you to search in the following places:

- On any local disks mounted on your system, including external drives
- Within your Home folder
- Within a selected disk or folder
- Everywhere on the system, including all three previously mentioned locations

To change the location of the search, click on the magnifying glass at the left edge of the Search field, and then select the location where you'd like to conduct your search. Your choices of places where you can search include:

Local disks
: Searches through all the disks attached to your Mac, including hard disks, CDs, DVDs, FireWire, and USB drives.

Home
: Searches for files located in your Home folder and any of the folders within, including the Desktop, Documents, Library, Movies, Music, Pictures, Public, and Sites folders.

Selection
: Use this option if you've selected a folder or disk volume in the Finder and just want to search the contents of a folder or volume.

Everywhere
: Selecting this option forces the Finder to search not only through your hard drive, but also through any other volume mounted on your system, including networked drives.

Use the Everywhere option sparingly for conducting your searches because the search will look at every file, in every folder, and on every disk attached to your Mac, which could take a long time to finish and return its results.

To search for a file on your system, select where you'd like the search conducted, and then type a word in the Search field. As soon as you start typing what you'd like to search for, the Finder kicks into high gear and immediately returns its results.

Search results are displayed in a split Finder window, as shown in Figure 2-13. Clicking on one of the items in the search results in the upper pane displays its path in the lower pane. If a folder is part of the search results, simply click once on the folder to see its contents in the Finder window; double-clicking an application icon launches the application, and double-clicking a file opens the file in the appropriate application (and launches that application too, if it isn't already active).

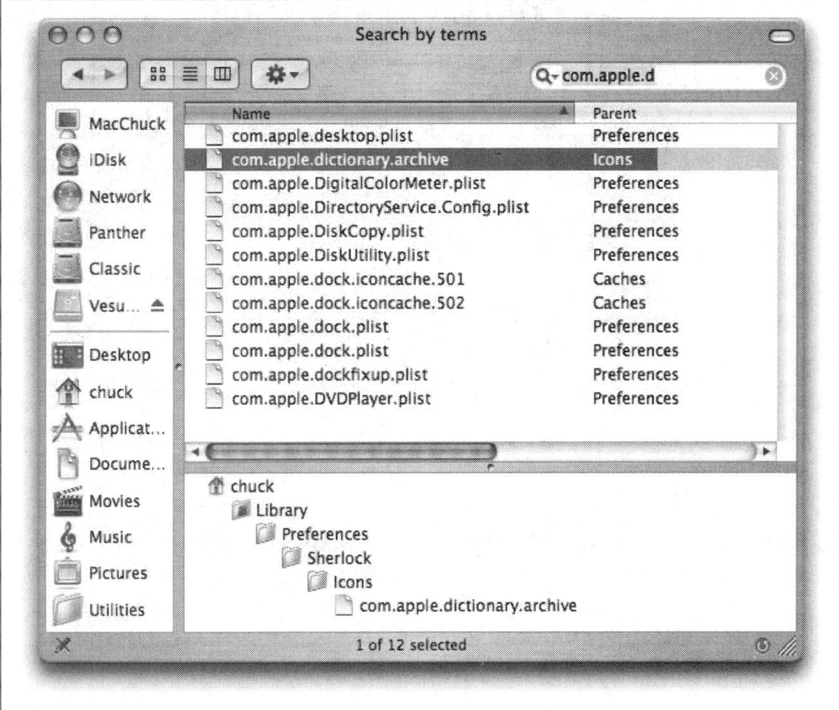

Figure 2-13. The Finder's search results window

You can also do a more advanced search by opening up the Find window (shown in Figure 2-14), by selecting File→Find (⌘-F).

At the top of the window is a "Search in" pop-up menu that lets you select where you want the search to be conducted (options are Everywhere, Local Disks, Home, or Specific places). With up to 15 lines of search criteria to offer, the "Search for items whose" area can help you refine your searches to find exactly what you're looking for. Options for the first pop-up menu in the "Search for items whose" area and their options are listed in Table 2-12.

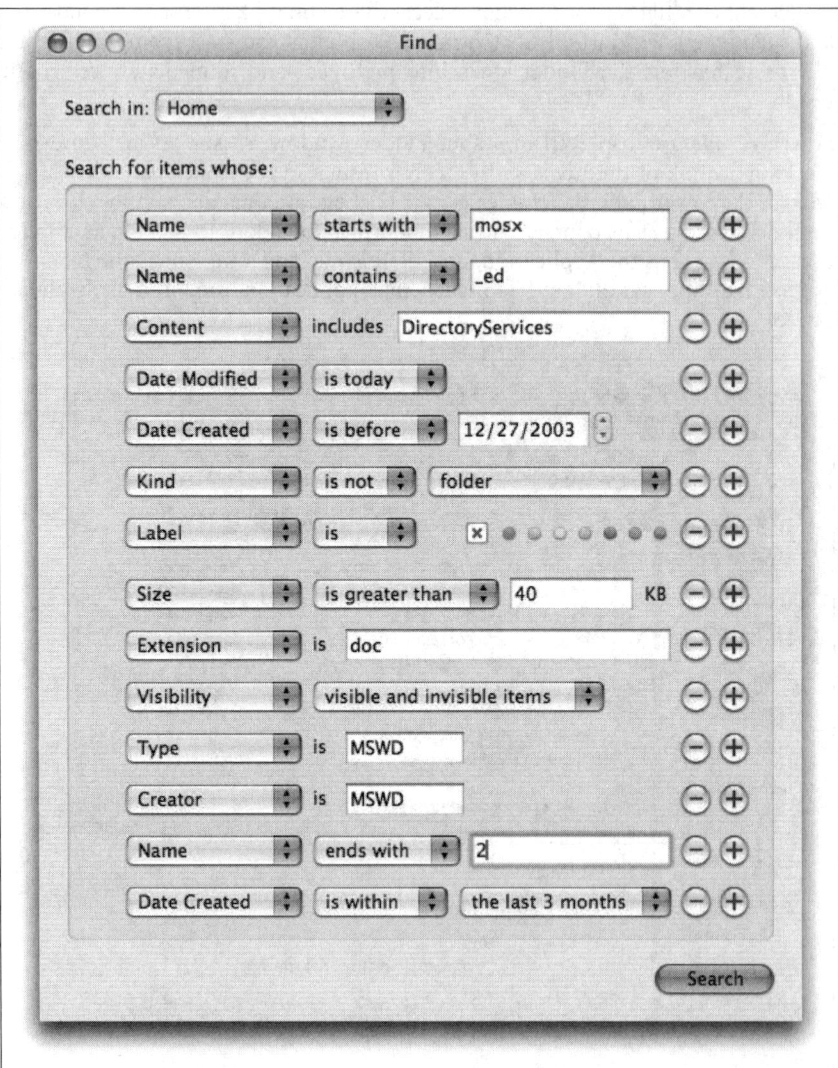

Figure 2-14. The Finder's Find window offers hundreds of options for searching for the right file

Table 2-12. Options to select from in the "Search for items whose" area

Criteria pop-up menu	Second option	Third option
Name	contains	[text field]
	starts with	[text field]
	ends with	[text field]
	is	[text field]
Content	includes	[text field]
Date Modified	is today	None

Table 2-12. Options to select from in the "Search for items whose" area (continued)

Criteria pop-up menu	Second option	Third option
	is within	the last day
		the last 2 days
		the last 3 days
		the last week
		the last 2 weeks
		the last 3 weeks
		the last month
		the last 2 months
		the last 3 months
		the last 6 months
	is before	[date selection field]
	is after	[date selection field]
	is exactly	[date selection field]
Date Created	is today	None
	is within	the last day
		the last 2 days
		the last 3 days
		the last week
		the last 2 weeks
		the last 3 weeks
		the last month
		the last 2 months
		the last 3 months
		the last 6 months
	is before	[date selection field]
	is after	[date selection field]
	is exactly	[date selection field]
Kind	is	alias
		application
		folder
		document
		audio
		image
		movie
	is not	alias
		application
		folder
		document5
		audio
		image
		movie

The Finder

Table 2-12. Options to select from in the "Search for items whose" area (continued)

Criteria pop-up menu	Second option	Third option
Label	is	[label color selector]
	is not	[label color selector]
Size	is less than	[text field] KB
	is greater than	[text field] KB
Extension	is	[text field]
Visibility	visible items	None
	invisible items	None
	visible and invisible items	None
Type	is	[text field]
Creator	is	[text field]

For example, if you want to search your Home directory for invisible files that have "bash" in the filename, the Find window can be configured as shown in Figure 2-15. Clicking on the Search button opens a Search Results window, which in this case yields the *.bash_history* and *.bash_profile* files, as shown in Figure 2-16.

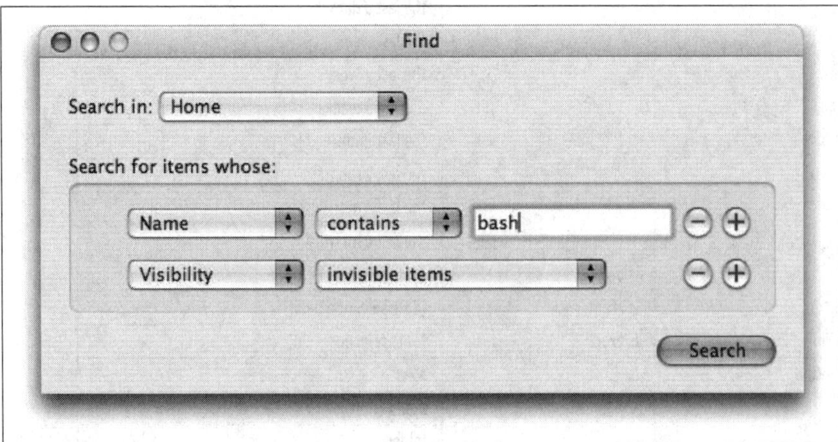

Figure 2-15. The Finder's Find window

Finding Files by Content

When you use the "Content→includes" criteria in your Finder search, the Finder doesn't just look at the names and attributes of files, folders, and disks, it looks inside a file for whatever the criteria is.

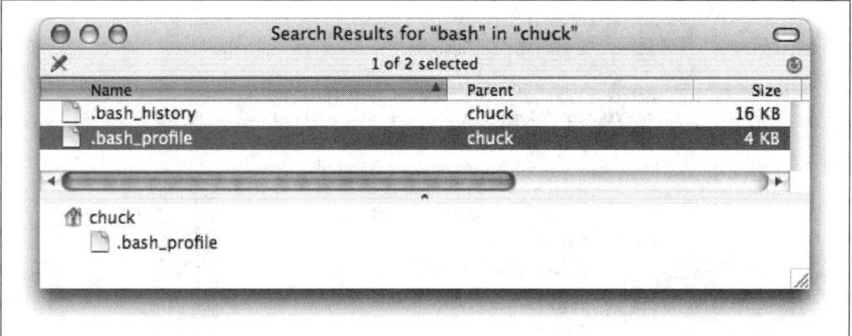

Figure 2-16. The Finder also lets you search for invisible files, such as Unix dot files

When you perform a by-content search, the Finder launches an invisible application called *ContentIndexing*,* which proceeds to crawl through the disks and folders you defined as the search domains. The first time *ContentIndexing* searches through a folder, it creates a Finder-invisible dotfile called *.FBCIndex*, holding (in an opaque binary format) an index of various words and strings. On its next pass through, if the folder hasn't changed, then *ContentIndexing* (very quickly) learns about the folder's contents from that existing index file. Otherwise, it crawls the folder again and updates the index.

If the text in the files you work with tends to be in only one or two languages, you can speed up content indexing by selecting Finder→Preferences (⌘-,)→Advanced, and then clicking on the Select button beneath "Languages for searching file contents" at the bottom of the window. Another window, shown in Figure 2-17 pops up, with a list of languages you can enable or disable by clicking on the appropriate checkbox. When performing content indexing, the system scans for word stems and language constructs appropriate to any of the checked languages. By unchecking some, you decrease the complexity of *ContentIndexing*'s job and increase its speed.

Finding Files with the Terminal

You can quickly find files on your system using the Unix commands, *locate*, *grep*, or *find*. To learn more about these commands, see their respective manpages.

The locate command

The *locate* command finds files not just by filename, but by full path. It's also *very* fast—easily the fastest method for finding files—because it reads from a database that it builds as a result of an earlier filesystem crawl.

You invoke *locate* using a pattern (see Chapter 22), and it instantly returns a list of all paths across the filesystem that match it. In its most simple (and perhaps most

* For certain values of "invisible," anyway. In one example, using a 500-MHz G3 computer, *ContentIndexing* causes a notable, general slowdown while it runs, as it monopolizes the hard disk for the many minutes it takes to crawl through all the necessary directories.

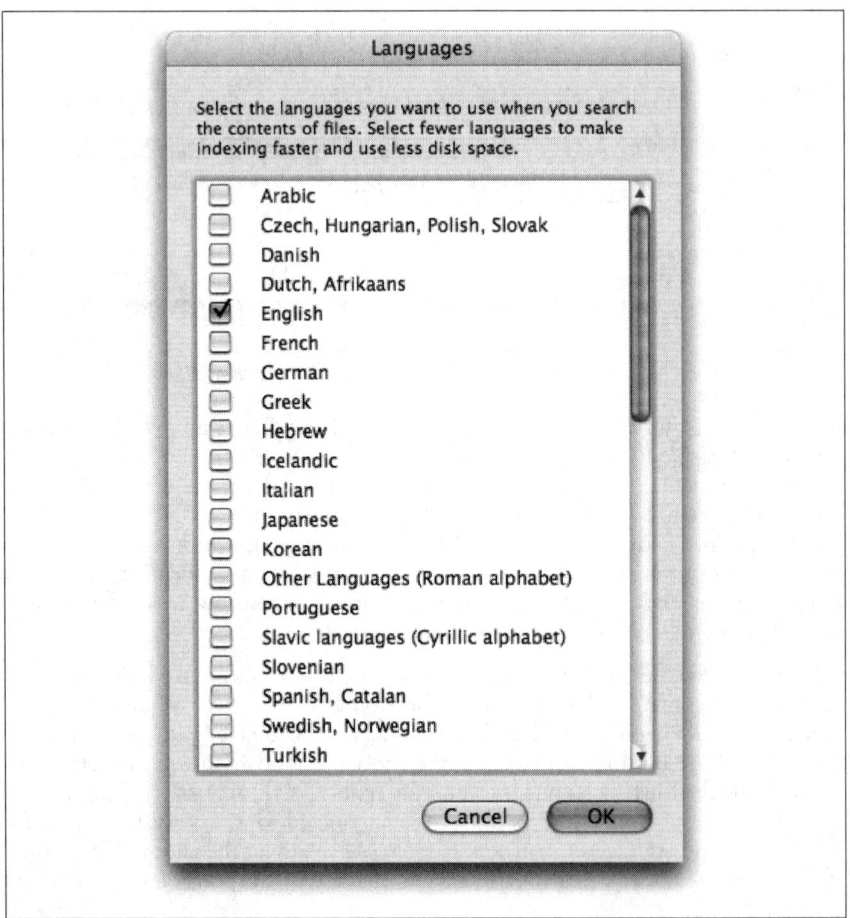

Figure 2-17. The Finder's list of indexable languages

The locate Database

Building the *locate* database—a single file found at */var/db/locate. database*—takes a while. You can manually run the database-updating script (*/usr/libexec/ locate.updatedb*) any time you want (you'll need to use *sudo* to invoke the *locate. updatedb* command; see Chapter 10), but the default Mac OS X *cron* setup will run this script for you every week (every Saturday at 4 a.m. local time, to be precise) as part of *root*'s regularly scheduled system maintenance tasks.

common) use, you can feed it a literal string and see every path that contains it. For example, to quickly scan for a file or directory with "bash" somewhere in its path:

```
MacChuck:~ chuck$ locate bash
/bin/bash
/Library/Documentation/Commands/bash
/private/etc/bashrc
/System/Library/Frameworks/JavaVM.framework/Versions/1.4.2/
Home/lib/zi/Africa/Lubumbashi
/Users/chuck/.bash_history
/Users/chuck/.bash_profile
/usr/bin/bashbug
/usr/share/emacs/21.2/etc/emacs.bash
/usr/share/info/bash.info
/usr/share/man/man1/bash.1
/usr/share/man/man1/bashbug.1
/usr/share/zoneinfo/Africa/Lubumbashi
/usr/share/zsh/4.1.1/functions/bashcompinit
/usr/share/zsh/4.1.1/functions/_bash_completions
MacChuck:~ chuck$
```


Searching file content with grep

As its entry in Chapter 28 shows, *grep* is an enormously flexible command; one application of it involves the Unix command line's own version of by-content file searching. Through the syntax *grep pattern files*, you can search fairly rapidly through text files for a certain string or regular expression (see Chapter 22).

Useful *grep* options for file searching include:

- *–r*, which searches recursively through directories.
- *–i*, used for case-insensitive searches.
- *–l*, which lists only filenames, suppressing *grep*'s default behavior of printing out every line in which it finds a match.

For instance, you can search through your entire Home directory for the string "bash" (or "Bash") with this command:

```
MacChuck:~ chuck$ grep -ril bash ~
```

Note that this search can take a long time, because *grep* doesn't use content indexing. (Nor should it, really; it's meant to be a general-purpose tool for not just file searching but also filtering out interesting lines from large volumes of program output, through the clever application of Unix pipes.)

find

The *find* command is roughly equivalent to the interface described earlier in "Searching from the Finder," but ten times as sophisticated and one-tenth as easy to use. Generally speaking, you run *find* with a list of paths, options, arguments, and operators (of which there is a bewildering variety), and it outputs a list of filenames that match your criteria. While useful for simply finding files, a veteran Terminal user can then pipe this output into other programs to use as input, but this is again a topic for Chapter 21.

Chapter 28 sorts out the complexities of the *find* command.

File Types

A file is a basic unit of filesystem currency in any modern operating system. The following sections discusses some of the file types you'll find in Mac OS X.

> ### Mac OS X's Application-to-Document Map
>
> The system determines a document's *kind* in one of two ways. First it sees if the document has an *attribute fork*, a data attachment possessed by documents created by Classic and Carbon applications that provides information about the document's type (among other things). If the file lacks a attribute fork, it looks to the document's filename extension; Mac OS X maintains a system- wide map between these extensions and recognized document types.
>
> The system's map that binds particular filename extensions to certain Aqua applications is made from two sorts of files. Each application's *Info.plist* file (see Chapter 22) can define the filename extensions its documents use. For example, Terminal application files have the extension *.term*, and it says as much in its Info file (located, for the curious, at */Applications/Terminal.app/ Contents/Info. plist*. If only one application lays claim to a particular file extension (as is the case with *.term*, at least in a fresh Mac OS X installation), the system will recognize a binding between that application and all files with that extension; double-clicking these documents in the Finder will open them through that application.
>
> These claims, however, may be overruled by the contents of another file: *com. apple.LaunchServices.plist*, which is another XML property list file that exists in your Home folder's */Library* folder (see Chapter 9). It lists the preferences that you have stated (through the Finder's Show Info window, and other means) regarding what applications to use with which files, or classes of files.
>
> If the Finder encounters an ambiguity due to two or more applications recognizing the same file extension (as is the case with Acrobat Reader and Apple's Preview application with *.pdf* files), the system again looks to this file, seeing if the user has a stated preference. If not, it will favor a Carbon or Cocoa application over a Classic one and, failing that, an application with a more recent modification time on the filesystem.
>
> Based on this attached information, a document's icon gets its image, its "Kind" label (as it appears in List view; see "List View" later in this chapter), and knowledge of which application it will activate when double-clicked. You can, however, adjust any of these connections through the document's Info window, as detailed in "The Get Info Window."
>
> See Chapter 7 for further detail on how Mac OS X manages its files.

Applications

Most applications live in the filesystem as bundles (discussed later) of executable files and the code libraries, pictures, sounds, and other resources they need to run.

Most application designers take the trouble to give an application a meaningful icon; for example, a postage stamp for Mail, or a life preserver for Apple's Help Viewer. The default application icon, however, looks like two pieces of paper with a ruler, pencil, and paint brush forming an "A," as shown in Figure 2-18.

Figure 2-18. A generic application icon

Double-clicking an application's icon in the Finder or single clicking on an application icon in the Dock will launch it. If the application is already running, it comes to the foreground as the active application.

Documents

Documents are files that you read from, write to, and otherwise manipulate with an application. A document can, but doesn't have to, associate itself with an application residing elsewhere on your Mac. If it does, then the document's icon reflects the application that can work with it. The generic document icon is a blank white piece of paper with a dog-eared upper-right corner, while the icons of documents created by a specific application often reflect the program that opens the file, as shown in Figure 2-19.

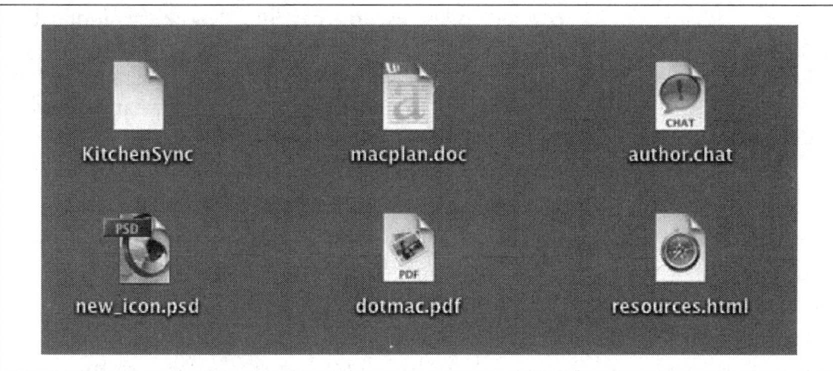

Figure 2-19. A generic document icon, and a few application-specific ones

Double-clicking a document's icon in the Finder opens that file with the appropriate application. The Finder tries to find this application by examining the document's extension, if it has one, its resource fork, and its type and creator codes.

Type and Creator Codes

Every file on your Mac has a specific filetype. The Type code is a four-character code that gets assigned to a file when it is created and is used by the filesystem to denote what type of file it is. Type codes are exactly four characters in length, and are case-sensitive. Table 2-13 lists some common Type codes. In this table, an open square (❐) means that you should insert a space where a character should be (remember, Type codes have to be exactly four characters).

Table 2-13. Common Type codes to be used when searching for files

File extension	Type of file	Type code
.pdf	PDF file	PDF❐
.doc	Word document	W8BN
.xls	Excel document	XLS8
.psd	Photoshop file	8BPS
.dmg	Disk image	devi
.txt, *.html*, *.htm*, *.rtf*, *.rtfd*	Raw text, HTML, and rich text files	TEXT
.tiff	TIFF image file	TIFF
.jpeg, *.jpg*	JPEG image file	JPEG
.gif	GIF image file	GIF
.avi	Video file	VfW❐
.mov	QuickTime movie	MooV
.mp4	MPEG 4 movie	mpg4
.aif	AIFF audio	AIFF
.m4p	Audio files purchased through iTunes Music Store	M4P❐

Creator codes are similar to Type codes, except that they denote the application used to create a particular file. Type codes and Creator codes are different. Their only similarity is that Creator codes are exactly four characters in length and are case sensitive. Table 2-14 lists some common Creator codes you can use when searching for files.

Table 2-14. Common Creator codes

Application or file type	Creator code
Preview	prvw
Adobe Acrobat	CARO
Microsoft Word	MSWD
Microsoft Excel	XCEL
Adobe Photoshop	8BIM
Disk Image	ddsk
Text files (including files saved as RTF)	R*ch
QuickTime movies and *.avi* files	TVOD
.mp4 files	TVOD

Table 2-14. Common Creator codes (continued)

Application or file type	Creator code
.aif audio files	stlu
.m4p audio files purchased through iTunes Music Store	hook

If you're not sure what a file's Type or Creator code is, you can use the *GetFileInfo* command-line utility that gets installed with the Xcode Tools. If you have installed the Xcode Tools, *GetFileInfo* can be found in */Developer/Tools*. For example, to use *GetFileInfo* on a TIFF file in your Pictures folder, follow these steps:

1. Launch the Terminal application (found in */Applications/Utilities*).
2. Change directories to */Developer/Tools* with the following command:

```
$ cd /Developer/Tools
```

3. Issue the command as follows:

```
$ ./GetFileInfo ~/Pictures/poweron.tif
file: "/Users/chuck/Pictures/poweron.tif"
type: "TIFF"
creator: "8BIM"
attributes: avbstClinmed
created: 11/03/2003 15:11:16
modified: 11/03/2003 15:23:43
```

If you haven't installed the Xcode Tools, you can do so by inserting the Xcode Tools CD that came with Panther (or your system) and double-click on the *developer.mpkg* file within.While you might think of the Xcode Tools as being something that only programmers and geeks might need, some of the utilities are actually quite useful for everyday Mac users.

If you look at the command issued, *./GetFileInfo ~/Pictures/poweron.tif*, you'll see that it contains two parts, separated by a space. The first part, *./GetFileInfo*, tells the Terminal that you want to issue the *GetFileInfo* command. The *./* (or dot-slash, in Unix terms) tells the shell to issue the command that follows (in this case, *GetFileInfo*). The second part, *~/Pictures/poweron.tif*, tells *GetFileInfo* to look for the *poweron.tif* file in your Pictures folder. If the file is found, as in this case, the command's results are returned to the Terminal window.

In looking at the results for the command, you can see that the file Type is `TIFF`, which means that the file has been saved in the Tagged Image File Format (better-known as a TIFF). On the next line, you can see that it's Creator code is `8BIM`, which, in looking back at Table 2-14, is the Creator code for Adobe Photoshop.

Folders

Folders, also referred to as *directories* (especially in a Unix context), give disks a hierarchical structure. A disk can hold any number of files and folders, and these folders can contain more files and other folders, ad infinitum.

Folders are colored blue by default, although some applications like to include their icon on the folder as well. This is similar to the default folders in a user's Home directory, which have icons to suggest their intended use. For example, the Documents folder has a generic document icon, the Library folder has four book icons, etc.

If the Finder is in Icon or List View, double-clicking a folder causes its contents to appear in a Finder window. Double-clicking a folder in Column View just displays the contents of the folder in the next pane to the right, as if you had single-clicked on the folder. If you double-click a folder on the Desktop, that folder opens in a new Finder window of its own in the default View (which is Icon View, unless you've selected Column View in the Finder's preferences; see earlier). You can go back to a folder's parent folder or disk by selecting Go→Enclosing folder in the menu bar or with the keyboard shortcut, ⌘-Up Arrow.

If you hold down the Command key (⌘) and double-click on a folder, the folder opens in a new Finder window and brings that window to the front of the window stack.

Bundles

Under the hood, folders are actually Unix directories. However, not all Unix directories on the filesystem are folders; some are bundles, holding application resources or special multiple-file document types that the Finder doesn't think you really need to know about. For example, many of the programs in the Applications folder are bundles, though they may appear to be just a single file in the Finder. Other examples include:

- Rich text documents you create with TextEdit that contain images and graphics (which end with a *.rtfd* extension).
- Keynote presentation files (which end with a *.key* extension)
- Data contained in a backup set, created with .Mac's Backup application (which end with a *.backup* extension)

To view the contents of a bundle, simply Control-click on the file and select "Show Package Contents" from the contextual menu, as shown in Figure 2-20. When you select this option, a new Finder window opens in Icon View, revealing the bundle's contents. You can also select an item in the Finder and then select "Show Package Contents" from the Action menu in the Finder's toolbar.

Another way to view a bundle's contents is from the command line, using the Terminal application (*/Applications/Utilities*). For example, to view the resources associated with Safari, do the following:

```
MacChuck:~ chuck$ cd /Applications/Safari.app/Contents
MacChuck:/Applications/Safari.app/Contents chuck$ ls -la
total 40
drwxrwxr-x    7 root  admin    238  5 Dec 12:00 .
drwxrwxr-x    3 root  admin    102  5 Dec 14:56 ..
-rw-rw-r--    1 root  admin  10493 21 Jan 16:29 Info.plist
drwxrwxr-x    3 root  admin    102 30 Jan 07:58 MacOS
```

Figure 2-20. Control-click on a bundle and select the "Show Package Contents" option to see what's inside

```
-rw-rw-r--    1 root  admin     8 21 Jan 16:29 PkgInfo
drwxrwxr-x  152 root  admin  5168  5 Dec 12:00 Resources
-rw-rw-r--    1 root  admin   459 30 Jan 14:30 version.plist
```

Aliases

An *alias* is a special file that acts as a pointer to its original file, folder, or disk elsewhere on your Mac. Opening an alias has the same effect as opening its original file. For example, the icons in the Dock are nothing more than aliases to their original application, file, or folder icons elsewhere in the filesystem. Step through the following list to create an alias.

1. Select an item in the Finder by clicking on it once, and then hold down on the mouse button.
2. With your other hand, hold down the Option-⌘ keys.
3. Drag the item to another location, such as your Desktop; when you move the item, the mouse pointer changes to a curved arrow.
4. When you release the mouse button, an alias of the original item is created wherever you dropped it.

This action is depicted in Figure 2-21. As you can see, the alias's icon matches that of its original, with the addition of a small arrow in its lower-left corner.

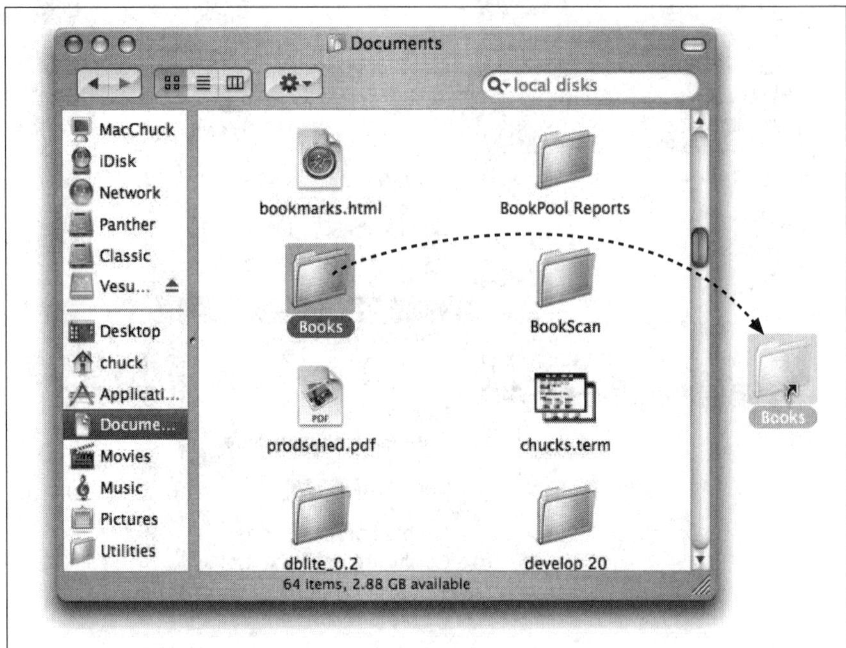

Figure 2-21. Create an alias by holding down Option-⌘ and drag an item to another location, such as to your Desktop

You can also create an alias of any item you select in the Finder using File→Make Alias (⌘-L) in the menu bar, or by selecting Make Alias from the Action menu in the Finder's toolbar. In each case, the aliased file is created in the same directory as the original, which you can then drag to another location.

Moving and Copying Files and Folders

To move an item from one folder to another, just click and drag it to another location in the filesystem. For this, it's sometimes easier to open two Finder windows, one that contains the item you want to move, and the other set to the location where you want to move it.

Aliases and Symlinks

Aliases are similar, but not identical, to the Unix concept of *symbolic links*, better known as *symlinks*. Like aliases, symlinks (created through the Unix *ln* command) are shortcuts between distant parts of a filesystem.

Symlinks, however, are pointers to paths, not to actual filesystem objects. A symlink, when opened, will resolve to whatever happens to reside at its pointed-to path at that moment—which might be nothing at all. Mac OS X aliases, on the other hand, always refer to a specific file, folder, or disk, and are able to keep their links alive even if the original object moves elsewhere in the filesystem. (An alias will break if its original is deleted or unmounted, of course.)

In this way, aliases act more like Unix *hard links*, but that's the limit of their similarity; unlike aliases, hard links are completely indistinguishable from their originals, and can't refer to files on different volumes.

The Finder is aware of Unix symlinks and displays their icons as aliases. This allows you to work with both the Mac and the Unix notions of filesystem shortcuts from the Finder. However, when working with Mac OS X's Unix side through the Terminal, only Unix symlinks will work as shortcuts; aliases show up as meaningless binary files. (In truth, they contain the filesystem ID number of the objects they point to, but your Mac's Unix side can't use this information by itself.)

If you drop an icon in the same window it started in, its position in the filesystem doesn't change at all. However, if you're in Icon View, the position of the icon shifts to wherever you dropped the item.

Dropping an icon into a different folder on the same disk moves the file, while dropping it into a folder located on a different disk *copies* it, keeping the original file in place while creating a duplicate in the destination folder. This is useful for when you want to copy a folder onto an external FireWire drive or an iPod.

To make a copy of a file or folder, select the item in the Finder view and either:

- Hold down the Option key, and drag the item to a new location
- Select File→Duplicate (⌘-D) from the menu bar
- Select Duplicate from the Action menu in the Finder's toolbar

When you use the Option-drag combination, the standard mouse pointer changes to an arrow with a little green bubble with a plus-sign inside, as seen in Figure 2-22.

If you are dragging the file to the same location, the Finder inserts a space after the filename and adds the word "copy" to the filename. For example, in Figure 2-22, the copy of *cone_nebula.jpg* would be named *cone_nebula copy.jpg*. Otherwise, if you are copying the file to another location, the file retains its original name.

Figure 2-22. Option-drag a file in the Finder to create a copy

Renaming Objects

To rename an object in the Finder, select its icon, and then either hit the Return key or click once on the item's text label. If you have write permission to this object, the text label transforms into a highlighted text field (as shown with the second image from the left in Figure 2-23), letting you type what you wish. Once you've modified the filename, press Return or click elsewhere to make it permanent.

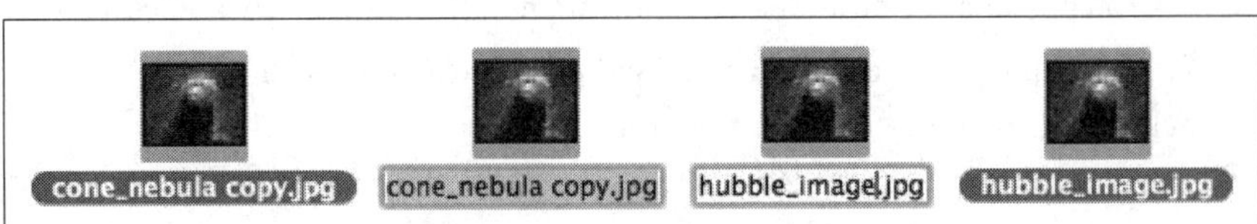

Figure 2-23. Renaming a file in the Finder

While in the item's text label, you can use the Up and Down arrow keys on your keyboard to go to the beginning or end of the filename, respectively. Double-clicking the filename selects the filename, and if the item is a file with an extension, only the filename (not the period or extension) is selected.

Filename Rules

Mac OS X limits the length of a filename to 255 characters. In the interest of saving screen real estate, the Finder abbreviates long filenames when displaying icons in the Finder views by replacing characters from its middle with an ellipsis (...), as shown in Figure 2-24.

Figure 2-24. A long filename in a short window

You can view the entire filename by mousing over the label; after a second or so, the complete filename appears in a floating tooltip.

There are two characters the Finder won't let you use in a filename: a colon (:) anywhere in a filename or a period (or dot) at the beginning of a filename. If you try using a colon as part of a filename, the Finder pops up an alert window, telling you that the filename can't be used and that you should try using a filename with fewer characters or no punctuation marks. If you try to insert a period at the beginning of a filename (for example, *.my_folder*), the Finder pops up an alert message telling you that filenames that begin with a dot are reserved for use by the system. You can, however, create dot files (files or folders that begin with a dot in their name) using the Terminal.

One trick that many Mac OS 9 users are accustomed to is placing a space at the beginning of a file, folder, or application name to give the item better ranking in the Apple menu. If you really want a file or folder name to begin with a period, you can trick the Finder by placing a space before the period, followed by the filename.

You can see an example of this earlier in Figure 2-1, where you see a folder named "Mac Apps" in the Applications folder. (Aliases of Backup, iDisk Utility, Mac Slides Publisher, and Virex were placed in this folder. The folder was then dragged to the right side of the Dock's divider to offer quick access to these apps without having to place their individual icons in the Dock.)

Moving Objects to the Trash

The Finder gives you several ways to toss things into the Trash:

- Drag icons onto the Trash icon in the Dock.
- Select Move to Trash from an icon's contextual menu.
- Select Move to Trash from the Action menu in the Finder's toolbar.
- Select File→Move To Trash.
- Use the keyboard shortcut, ⌘-Delete (which is the same as File→Move To Trash).

Likewise, you can empty the Trash with one of the following methods:

- Select Finder→Empty Trash.
- Select Finder→Secure Empty Trash.
- Use the keyboard shortcut, ⌘-Delete (which is the same as Finder→Empty Trash).

When you select Empty Trash, the files in the Trash are deleted from your system. The Trash can icon used in the Dock is a graphical frontend to the *.Trash* folder, found in your Home directory. Since the file begins with a dot, the *.Trash* folder is hidden from view, but its contents can be viewed by clicking on the Trash icon in the Dock.

When you select Secure Empty Trash (for which there is no known keyboard shortcut), the files in the Trash are deleted from the hard drive, and the space that the file previously occupied is overwritten a few more times. This reduces the chances of someone coming along later and trying to recover that file from your hard drive. While this gives you some added security, it also reduces the chances that *you'll* ever recover that file. As such, you should use this option judiciously, and only when you're certain you'll never need that file again.

The Get Info Window

Get Info gives you access to all sorts of information about the files, directories, and applications on your system. To view the information for an item, click on its icon in the Finder and go to File→Get Info or use its keyboard shortcut, ⌘-I. The

Get Info window, shown in Figure 2-25, has six different panes, which offer different kinds of information about the file.

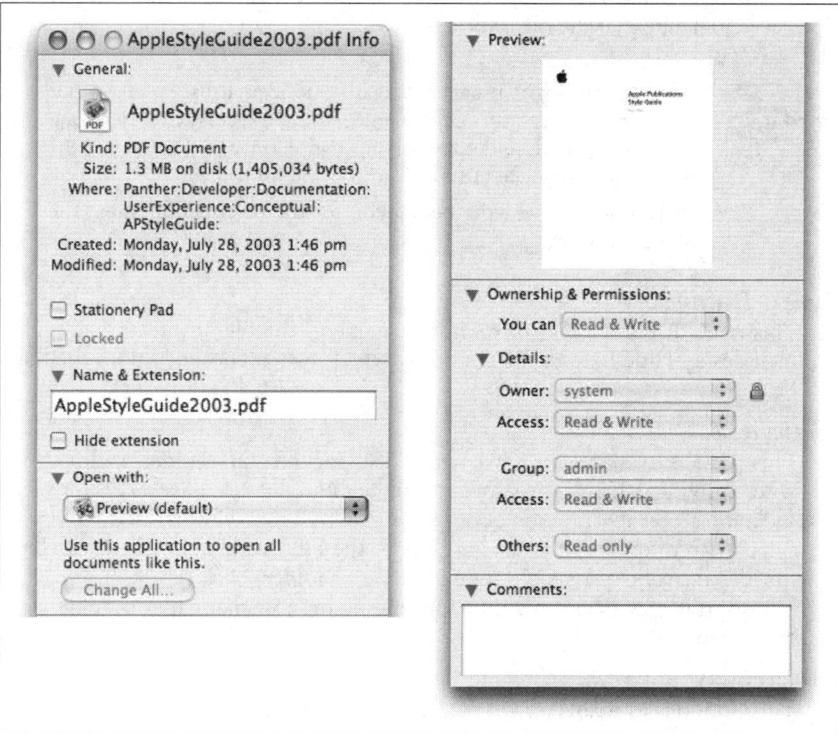

Figure 2-25. The Get Info window for a PDF file

To reveal the content of one of these items, click on its disclosure triangle to expand the pane. The panes of the Get Info window include the following:

General

This pane tells you the basics about the file, including its kind, size, where it's located in the filesystem, and when it was created and last modified. The General section also includes two controls for attaching the following special properties to an object:

Stationary Pad

This checkbox appears only in a file's Info window. One of the most obscurely useful Finder commands that survived the transition to Mac OS X, this checkbox signals applications to treat this file as a template instead of an editable file. If opened with an application capable of working with stationary pad files, it copies the files' contents into an untitled new document window, leaving the original file as is on disk.

Locked

When checked, the object becomes hard to modify or delete. Applications can read from, but not change, a locked document. Locked folders will let you explore them, but you cannot add or remove anything from them. The Trash doesn't allow you to add a locked item to it. A locked object gets a tiny padlock added to the corner of its icon, which is a visual clue that the file is locked.

Locking an object protects it against accidental user damage but offers no real security because unlocking it is as easy as unselecting this checkbox. Use the Ownership and Permissions section of the Get Info Window to make a file truly write-protected.

If you don't have write permission for the object in question, the controls are grayed out.

Name & Extension
: This pane displays a text box with the name of the file or directory and also includes a "Hide Extension" checkbox which, when checked, hides the file's extension.

Content index
: This pane is available only when you use Get Info on a folder or drive (not with individual files); it tells you whether its contents have been indexed. Indexing stores information about the files contained within that directory or drive in an information database used by the Find command when searching for files on your system. To index a drive or folder, click on the Index Now button; this may take some time, depending on how many files or folders are contained within.

Open with
: This option is available only if you select a file (i.e., not a folder or an application). Here you can specify which application will open this file or all similar files.

Preview
: Depending on the file type, you can view the contents of the file here (this also works for playing sounds and QuickTime movies).

Changing the Preview Icon

If you have a single object selected, you can change its icon through the Get Info window. You can invoke clipboard commands on it. Edit→Copy (⌘-C) copies the icon image, at its full size, to the clipboard. Edit→Paste (⌘-V) changes the object's icon to whatever image (if any) is in the clipboard.

You can also set the icon by simply dragging an image file's icon onto the Get Info window's displayed icon.

Ownership & Permissions
: This displays the name of the owner and the name of the group to which the file belongs. It also allows you to set access privileges to that file for the

Owner, Group, and Others on the system (see "The File Permissions System" in Chapter 7).

Comments

This field can contain some basic information about the file, folder, or application. If you have your Finder set to List View, you can opt to have the Comments displayed within the view.

The Get Info window for applications has the General Information, Name & Extension, and Ownership & Permissions options mentioned previously (although the Ownership & Permissions options are disabled by default), as well as one or both of the following options:

Languages

Shows the languages supported by that application.

Plug-ins

If applicable, this lists the available plug-ins for the application. Applications that have a Plug-ins section in their Info windows include iMovie, iPhoto, iDVD, Image Capture, Keynote, and Final Cut Pro, just to name a few.

Noticeably missing from a Mac OS X application's Get Info window is the Memory option. Because memory for applications is assigned dynamically by virtual memory, you no longer have to specify how much memory an application requires. However, if you use Get Info on a Mac OS 9 application, the Memory option will be there.

3

Mac OS 9, Mac OS X, and Classic

Mac OS X is way ahead of its time. When Apple developed this hybrid operating system, they knew it would take a while for application developers to Carbonize their applications to run on Mac OS X. Rather than locking out older software entirely, Apple made it possible to run both Mac OS 9 and Mac OS X on the same system, and took it a step further by building a Mac OS 9 *virtual machine* into Mac OS X, called *The Classic Environment*, or just Classic.

This chapter covers some of the changes between Mac OS 9 and Mac OS X, and introduces you to Classic.

Changes to Mac OS X from Mac OS 9

There are many noticeable changes in the user interface from earlier versions of the Mac OS to Mac OS X, while others may not be so apparent. Two of the biggest changes from Mac OS 9 to Mac OS X can be found in the Apple menu and the Control Panels.

The Apple Menu

The Apple menu, displayed as an apple symbol () in the menu bar, is completely different. For Mac OS 9 users, the thing that will probably impact you most is that you can no longer store aliases for files, folders, or applications at this location. Here's what you'll find in Mac OS X's Apple menu:

About This Mac
: This option pops open a window that supplies you with information about your Mac. Aside from telling you that you're running Mac OS X on your computer, the window shows you which version of Mac OS X is installed, how much memory you have, and the speed and type of processor in your computer. Clicking on the More Info button launches the System Profiler

(*/Applications/Utilities*), which gives you a greater level of detail about your computer.

As mentioned in Chapter 1 and shown in Figure 1-8, clicking on the version number in the About This Mac window will reveal the build number of Mac OS X; clicking it again will show the hardware serial number for your computer. These small details are important to have when contacting Apple Customer Service and when reporting a probable bug.

In earlier versions of the Mac OS, the About box would change depending on which application was active. For information about the application, you now have to use the Application menu (located to the right of the Apple menu) and select the About option.

Software Update
: This launches the Software Update preferences panel (System Preferences→Software Update) and checks for updates for Mac OS X and other Apple software installed on your system. For more information about using Software Update, see Chapter 4.

Get Mac OS X Software
: Selecting this option takes you to Apple's Mac OS X page (*http://www.apple.com/macosx*) in your default web browser.

System Preferences
: This launches the System Preferences application, which replaces most of the Control Panels from earlier versions of the Mac OS. See Chapter 4 for more details.

Dock
: This menu offers a quick way to change settings for the Dock, described in Chapter 1.

Location
: This is similar to the Location Manager Control Panel in earlier versions of the Mac OS; it allows you to change locations quickly for connecting to a network and/or the Internet.

Recent Items
: This menu option combines the Recent Applications and Recent Documents options from Mac OS 9's Apple menu into one convenient menu. A Clear option allows you to reset the recent items from the menu.

Force Quit
: Thanks to Mac OS X's protected memory, you don't have to restart the entire system if an application crashes or freezes. Instead, you can come here (or use Option-⌘-Esc) to open a window that lists the applications running on your system. To force-quit an application, simply click on the application name, then click on Force Quit.

Unlike applications, you cannot force-quit the Finder by Control-clicking on its icon in the Dock. Instead, you need to restart it from here. When you select the Finder, the Force Quit button changes to Relaunch; click that button to restart the Finder.

Sleep
Selecting this option immediately puts your Mac into sleep mode. This is different from the settings you dictate in System Preferences→Energy Saver for auto-sleep functionality. To "wake" your computer from sleep mode, simply press any key.

If you close the lid (or display) on your iBook or PowerBook while it is running, the computer will go into sleep mode. Opening your laptop will wake up your system automatically; if it doesn't, try hitting the spacebar or the Return key a couple times.

Restart
This restarts your Mac. If any applications are running, the system will quit them automatically, and you will be prompted to save changes for any files that were open.

Shutdown
This shuts your Mac down. You can also shut down your Mac by pressing the Power-On button, which opens a dialog box with the options for restarting, shutting down, or putting your Mac to sleep.

Log Out
This option logs you out of your system, taking you back to a login screen. The keyboard shortcut to log out is Shift-⌘-Q.

As you can see, Sleep, Restart, Shutdown, and Log Out have all moved from Mac OS 9's Special menu into Mac OS X's Apple menu. In addition, if you're looking for a menu option for Empty Trash—which also used to be in the Special menu—you need to be in the Finder (Finder→Empty Trash, or Shift-⌘-Delete).

Think System Preferences, Not Control Panels

One of the most notable changes in Mac OS X is the Control Panels (→Control Panels) aren't in the Apple menu. The Control Panels of old are now replaced by System Preferences. Table 3-1 lists the Control Panels from Mac OS 9 and shows their equivalents in Mac OS X.

Table 3-1. Mac OS 9's Control Panels and their disposition in Mac OS X

Mac OS 9 Control Panel	Equivalent in Mac OS X
Appearance	System Preferences→Desktop & Screen Saver System Preferences→Appearance
Apple Menu Options	System Preferences→Appearance
AppleTalk[a]	System Preferences→Network→AppleTalk
ColorSync	System Preferences→ColorSync
Control Strip[a]	Gone; replaced by Dock.
Date & Time	System Preferences→Date & Time
DialAssist[a]	System Preferences→Network→Show→Internal Modem
Energy Saver[a]	System Preferences→Energy Saver

Table 3-1. Mac OS 9's Control Panels and their disposition in Mac OS X (continued)

Mac OS 9 Control Panel	Equivalent in Mac OS X
Extensions Manager	Gone. With Mac OS X, you no longer need to manage your extensions. To view the extensions on your system, launch the Apple System Profiler (*/Applications/ Utilities*), and click on the Extensions tab.
File Exchange[a]	Gone; use Bluetooth File Exchange (*/Applications/ Utilities*).
File Sharing	System Preferences→Sharing
File Synchronization	Gone.
General Controls	System Preferences→Appearance
Infrared[a]	System Preferences→Network→Show→infrared-port.
Internet	Gone.
Keyboard	System Preferences→Keyboard & Mouse System Preferences→International→Input Menu
Keychain Access	Applications→Utilities→Keychain Access
Launcher	Gone; replaced by Dock.
Location Manager[a]	System Preferences→Network→Location (This applies only to network settings, unlike Location Manager.) →Location
Memory[a]	Gone.
Modem[a]	System Preferences→Network→Show→Internal Modem
Monitors	System Preferences→Displays
Mouse[a]	System Preferences→Keyboard & Mouse
Multiple Users[a]	System Preferences→Accounts
Numbers	System Preferences→International→Formats→Numbers
Password Security	System Preferences→Security
QuickTime Settings	System Preferences→QuickTime
Remote Access[a]	Applications→Internet Connect
Software Update[a]	System Preferences→Software Update
Sound[a]	System Preferences→Sound
Speech	System Preferences→Speech
Startup Disk[a]	System Preferences→Startup Disk
TCP/IP[a]	System Preferences→Network
Text	System Preferences→International→Language
Trackpad[a]	System Preferences→Mouse
USB Printer Sharing	System Preferences→Sharing→Services→Printer Sharing
Web Sharing	System Preferences→Sharing→Services→Personal Web Sharing

[a] Not supported under Classic.

See Chapter 4 for additional information about Mac OS X's System Preference panels.

Other Missing Items

Some other things you'll find missing from Mac OS X include:

Apple CD Audio Player
: This has been replaced by iTunes.

The Chooser
: To configure a printer in Mac OS X, you need to use the Printer Setup Utility (*/Applications/Utilities*). To connect to a server or another computer on your network, you need to use Go→Connect to Server (⌘-K). The Chooser still exists for printing and networking from the Classic environment (described later).

Put Away (⌘-Y)
: This command had two functions: to eject a disk (floppy or CD) or to move an item out of the Trash back to its place of origin. Instead, ⌘-E can be used to eject a CD or unmount a networked drive.

On newer iBooks and PowerBooks, pressing the F12 key ejects a CD or DVD.

Note Pad and SimpleText
: These have been replaced by the more versatile TextEdit application. However, if you've installed the Developer Tools, SimpleText can be found in */Developer/Applications/Utilities/Build Examples* but isn't available otherwise.

If you want to see the code used to create SimpleText, you can find it in */Developer/Examples/Carbon/SimpleText/SimpleText.pbxproj*.

Scrapbook
: Gone; at present there's no equivalent replacement from Apple for Mac OS X.

SimpleSound
: This has been replaced by the Sound preferences panel, which can be accessed from System Preferences→Sound; this is where you can select an alert sound and set its volume.

Now that we've shown you what's changed between Mac OS 9 and Mac OS X, it's time to learn more about Classic so you can run your Mac OS 9 applications *on top of* Mac OS X.

What Is Classic?

To help bridge the application gap between Mac OS 9 and Mac OS X, Apple has built a *virtual machine* that enables you to run older Mac software under Mac OS X in the Classic Environment, or just Classic. Classic is an emulator that looks and feels just like Mac OS 9, and, in fact, it is—just slightly watered down.

Classic allows you to run most older Mac applications on Mac OS X without requiring you to boot directly into Mac OS 9. The big difference is that Classic applications won't benefit from the features of Mac OS X, such as protected memory and its advanced printing capability. Meaning, if a Classic application crashes, it can bring down everything else running under Classic; just as a crash under Mac OS 9 could affect your entire system.

Additionally, some Control Panels (→Control Panels), such as Control Strip, Memory, and Remote Access, are disabled. However, if you boot into Mac OS 9 instead of Mac OS X, you will be using a full version of the OS. See the section "Dual-Booting with Mac OS 9" later in this chapter for details on how to choose your Startup Disk.

If you want Mac OS 9 and Mac OS X on separate partitions, you need to partition your hard drive and reinstall both systems. In most cases, the biggest benefit to installing Mac OS 9 and Mac OS X on separate partitions is being able to choose which version of the OS to boot at startup by holding down the Option key. Otherwise, you can choose which OS to boot using the Startup Disk Control Panel (Mac OS 9) or System Preferences→Startup Disk (Mac OS X).

Until all Mac applications are Mac OS X–compliant, you will need to install a version of Mac OS 9 (9.2.2, to be exact) if you want to run older Mac applications. Most new Apple hardware ship with Mac OS 9 and Mac OS X preinstalled on the same disk partition. However, the boxed release of Mac OS X Panther doesn't include a copy of Mac OS 9. If you find yourself in need of Classic, you can probably find a copy of Mac OS 9 on eBay at *http://www.ebay. com*. (Apple no longer sells this version of the Mac OS.)

Starting Classic

When Classic is started, it doesn't actually boot Mac OS 9. Instead, it launches the Classic Startup process, found in */System/Library/CoreServices*. In turn, the Classic Startup process looks for a Mac OS 9 system folder on the system. If one is found, Classic will start; if not, you will receive an error message, letting you know that Classic can't be started because there isn't a valid Mac OS 9 system folder on your computer.

There are four ways to launch Classic:

Launch a Classic application
: When you launch any Classic application (one of the three application flavors the Finder recognizes; see Chapter 2), Mac OS X automatically starts Classic if it isn't running already.

The Classic preferences panel
: Go to System Preferences→Classic→Stop/Start, and click on the Start button to launch Classic.

: The table view under "Select a system folder for Classic:" lists every disk or partition on the filesystem that holds a Mac OS 9 System Folder. (If you've gone the usual route of installing Mac OS 9 and Mac OS X on the same disk or partition, then you'll see just one choice here.)

From the Classic menu

If you select the checkbox next to "Show Classic status in menu bar," a Classic menu extra appears in the menu bar at the top of the screen as shown in Figure 3-1. From this menu, you can start, stop, and restart Classic; open the Classic preference panel; and gain access to Mac OS 9's Apple menu.

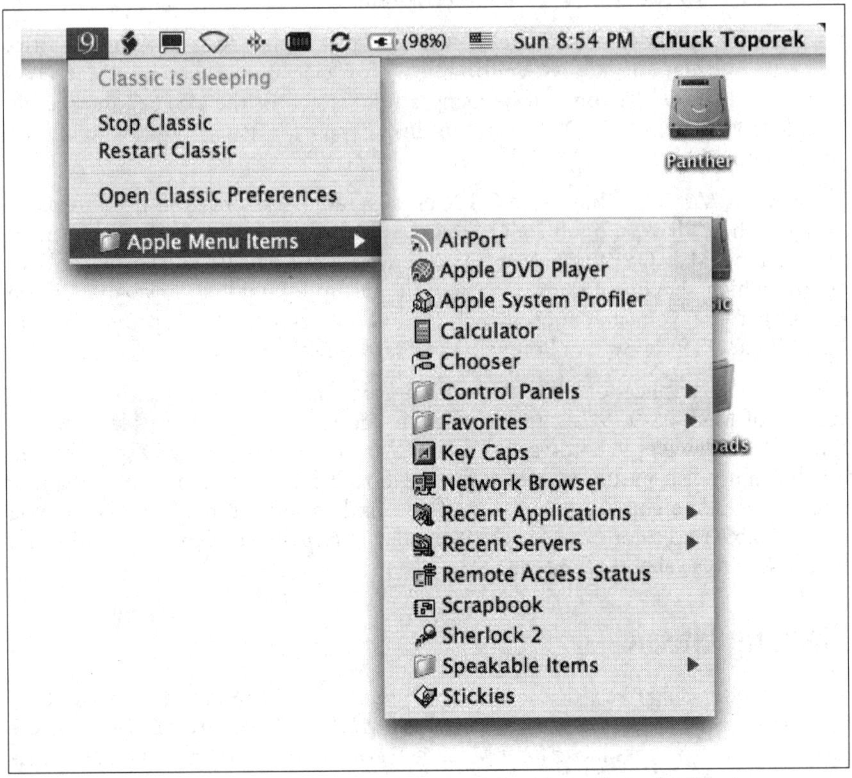

Figure 3-1. In Panther, you can enable a menu extra for Classic from the Classic preferences panel

Starting Classic when you log on

Select the checkbox next to "Start Classic when you login" to have the Classic environment launch automatically when you log in to your account.

Savvy Unix users will see a fifth way to launch Classic: from the command line. If you launch the Terminal (*/Applications/Utilities*), you can launch the Classic Startup process (*Classic Startup.app*) by switching directories to */System/Library/CoreServices* and issuing the following commands:

```
$ cd /System/Library/CoreServices
$ open "Classic Startup.app"
```

As the Classic Startup application launches, you'll see a window containing the virtual Mac's startup sequence, as shown in Figure 3-2.

Figure 3-2. Classic Startup's window

While Classic is starting, you will see Classic's icon bouncing in the Dock; once Classic has finished loading, the icon disappears. To verify that Classic is running, you can go to System Preferences→Classic→Start/Stop and look for a bolded message that says:

```
Classic is running using folder "System Folder" on volume "Classic".
```

This message tells you that Classic is using Mac OS 9's System Folder, which it found on the disk volume named Classic.

Controlling Classic

Classic's preference panel, shown in Figure 3-3, has three tabs, or panes, from which you can control its settings and monitor its activities. To launch the Classic preference panel, go to System Preferences→Classic.

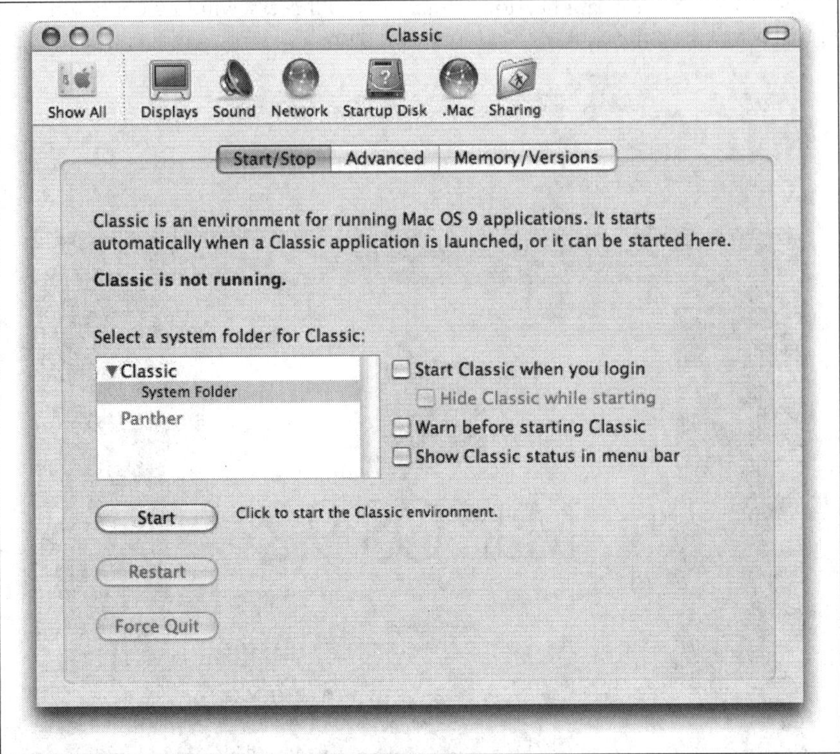

Figure 3-3. The Classic preference panel

The three tabbed panes found in the Classic preference panel include:

Start/Stop
: This pane, shown in Figure 3-3, provides controls for starting, stopping, restarting, and force-quitting Classic. A bolded message near the top of this pane lets you know whether or not Classic is running, and the text box below it displays a valid Mac OS 9 System Folder.

Advanced
: This pane, shown in Figure 3-4, gives you more granularity and control over how Classic will run on your system.

  The controls found in the Advanced pane include:

  Startup Options
  : This pop-up menu can be used to specify whether Mac OS 9's extensions will be turned off by default, or whether to open the Extension Manager as Classic starts up, which allows you to select which extensions to load. A third item in this menu is "Use Key Combination," which lets you specify a keyboard shortcut (up to five characters) for stopping and restarting Classic.

  Restart Classic
  : When clicked, this button restarts Classic.

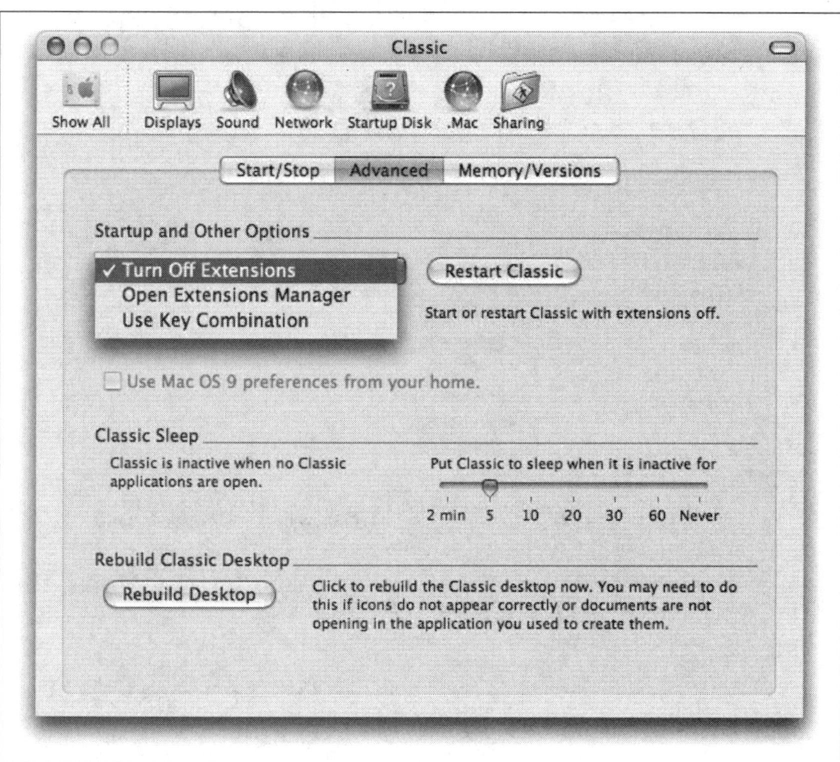

Figure 3-4. Classic's Advanced pane

Use Mac OS 9 preferences from your home folder
: Selecting this checkbox forces Classic to use the preferences stored in *~/Library/Classic* instead of */System Folder*, thereby providing each OS X user his own OS 9 preference set.

Classic Sleep
: This slider allows you to set the amount of time Classic is inactive before its process is put into sleep mode. By default, this is set to five minutes. Move the slider left or right to specify the delay before Classic will be put to sleep (from two minutes to never).

Rebuild Classic Desktop
: For Mac OS 9 users, rebuilding the Desktop is something of a regular occurrence: once or twice a week you hold down Option-Command during the startup process to rebuild the desktop database. However, clicking this button will do the same thing for you, without forcing you to boot into Mac OS 9.

Memory/Versions
: This pane, shown in Figure 3-5, lets you keep track of the processes running in the Classic environment.

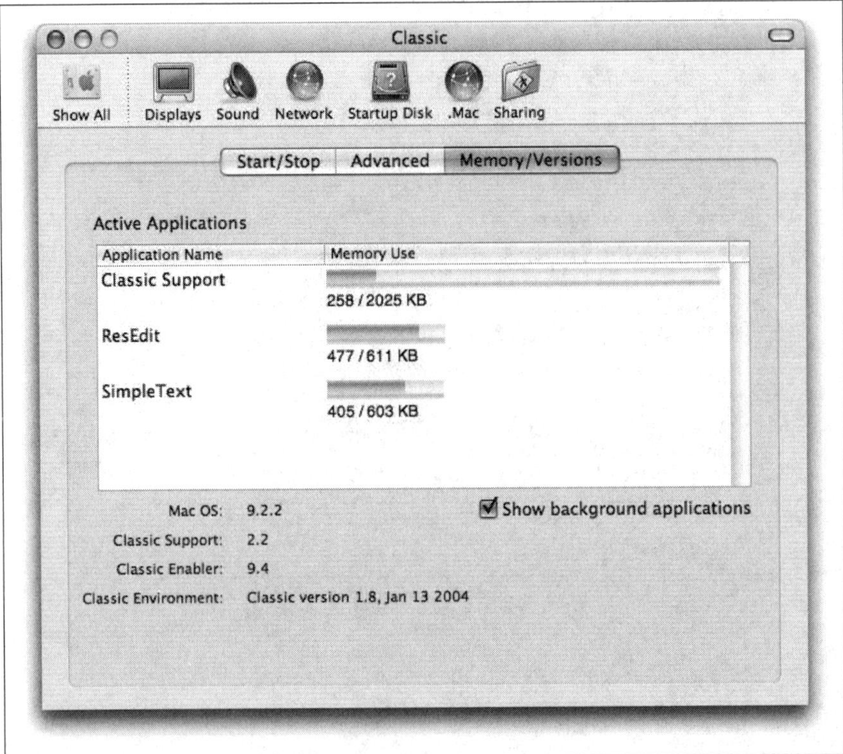

Figure 3-5. Classic's Memory/Versions pane

By default, the checkbox next to "Show background processes" is unchecked. To view the Active Processes running under Classic, check this box. When Classic is running, there will always be one background application: Classic Support.

The bottom of this window shows details about the version and build of Classic, as well as the Mac OS version it's using.

Managing Classic Applications

Mac OS X's Finder manages your Classic applications like any other; the only difference is that they're stored in */Applications (Mac OS 9)*, not in */Applications*. When Classic is running, you won't work with the old Mac OS 9 Finder; however, when a Classic application is running in the foreground, the menu bar changes to that of Mac OS 9. Similarly, the Dock provides space for the icons of Classic applications and even lets you keep them in the Dock.

You can easily identify a Classic application in the Dock, because its icon has a Mac OS 9–style (32 × 32 pixel) icon, which looks "jaggy" if viewed at a higher resolution.

Classic Applications and Memory

As mentioned earlier, Mac OS 9 applications don't benefit from Mac OS X's protected memory space or its dynamic memory allocation. In Classic, a Mac OS 9 application is still a Mac OS 9 application, requiring you to assign memory the old way: via the Get Info window. Figure 3-6 shows the Get Info window for Mac OS 9's Script Editor (*/Applications (Mac OS 9)/Apple Extras/AppleScript*).

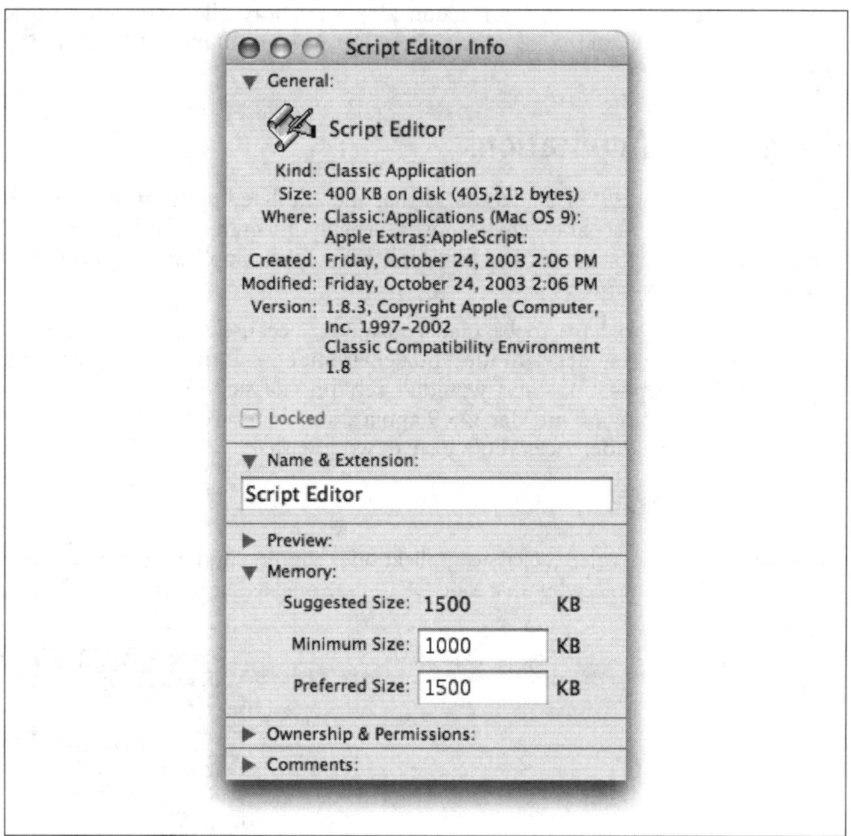

Figure 3-6. Mac OS 9's Script Editor's Info window, showing the Memory section

The Memory section of the Info window (available only for Classic applications) lists the following three items:

Suggested Size
: This number represents the amount of RAM (in kilobytes) that the application's developers suggest to get optimum performance from the application. This number always remains constant and can't be changed.

Minimum Size
: This field holds the minimum amount of memory the application needs before it can launch.

Preferred Size
: This field holds the amount of RAM this application uses when it is running. By default, this number is set to match the applications' Suggested Size. You can make this number larger or smaller, but the Preferred Size shouldn't be smaller than the Minimum Size.

Normally, the only time you should modify these is if the Classic application in question complains about a lack of memory, either during runtime or by failing to launch altogether. For more information about memory allocation for Classic applications, see Chapter 5 of *Mac OS 9: The Missing Manual* (Pogue Press/O'Reilly).

Using Classic Applications

Classic is unlike other OS emulators in that the emulated applications, though running in their own separate environment, visually integrate with the Mac OS X workspace. You use the Finder and the Dock with Classic application icons just as you would with any other.

Some concessions do have to be made, however, because Classic applications don't know how to interact with the Aqua environment. (If they did, they would be true Carbon applications and wouldn't rely on Classic.) While we certainly won't cover everything about Mac OS 9 applications here, we will cover some of the more noticeable differences you'll have to work with.

Classic's Menu Bar

As mentioned earlier, when a Classic application is running in the foreground, Mac OS X's menu bar is replaced with a Mac OS 9–style one, as shown in Figure 3-7.

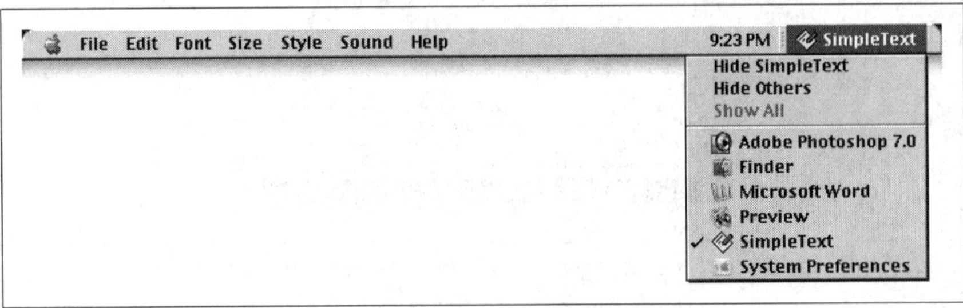

Figure 3-7. A typical Classic application's menu bar

Mac OS 9's menu bar is structurally quite different from Aqua's (which you'll see again as soon as you switch back to an Aqua application or click on the Desktop). Here's a brief rundown of what you'll find in Mac OS 9's menu bar:

- The rainbow-colored Apple menu contains the application's About box, as well as all the objects within */System Folder/Apple Menu Items* on the Classic startup volume, including a path to Mac OS 9's Control Panels.
- Standard application menus, such as File, Edit, and Help. Note the lack of a Mac OS X–style application menu here.

- The only menu extra you'll see when in Classic mode is the Clock.
- The application menu, which is located to the right of the Clock. Mac OS 9's application menu is entirely different from the one in Mac OS X. This menu contains a list of all active applications (including Aqua ones, as shown in Figure 3-7), and options for hiding the current or other applications, as well as a Show All option to unhide any hidden applications. As such, it mixes some of the functionality of Mac OS X's application menu and Dock.

One function that some Mac OS 9 users might miss while in Classic mode is the Applications palette, which you can get in Mac OS 9 by clicking on the Application menu and slowly dragging it away from the menu bar. While this works if you boot into Mac OS 9, it isn't available under Classic; however, you can still use the Dock to switch back and forth between running applications.

Classic Application Windows

Classic application windows use Mac OS 9's "Platinum" theme for their look, as shown in Figure 3-8.

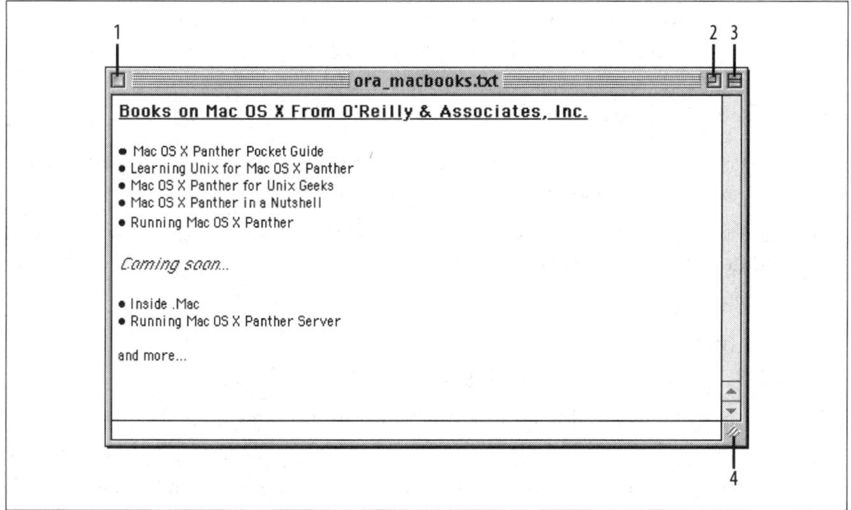

Figure 3-8. A typical Classic window (this is from SimpleText)

Most of their controls are analogous to Aqua windows; however, there are a few differences listed here as they appear, from left to right:

1. Close window button
2. Zoom window button
3. Windowshade button
4. Resize window control

The windowshade button collapses the window into its titlebar, which remains in place. Clicking this button again brings the full window back into view. Try as you might, you cannot minimize a Classic window to the Dock, as you can with the yellow minimize button on Aqua windows.

Here are some other oddities you'll find with Classic application windows:

- Compared to Aqua applications, fewer document-centric Classic applications offer proxy icons in their titlebars, as noticed in Figure 3-8. When they do appear, however, you can use them in all the ways detailed in Chapter 1.
- Although they look different, Classic windows share the window stack with all open Aqua windows; however, they don't interleave. This means that when a Classic application is running in the foreground, all its windows are in the foreground. If you bring an Aqua application to the front, either by its Dock icon or by clicking on one of its windows, that application comes to the foreground as well, and the Classic application windows are placed in the background.
- Classic applications also lack certain windowing features common to Mac OS X applications, such as sheets and drawers. Since Mac OS 9 doesn't use threaded processing, when a Classic application's dialog box appears, you cannot do anything else in Classic until you give the window the attention it deserves. (You can still step out and use other Aqua applications while Classic waits for a dialog box response, of course.)

The Dock and Classic

Active Classic applications' icons appear on your Dock like any other, and nearly all the tricks covered in Chapter 1 apply to them.

The biggest difference is that Classic icons on the Dock receive only a limited Dock menu, containing just the four basic items:

- Keep In Dock
- Show In Finder
- Hide (or Hide Others, if you hold down the Option key)
- Quit (or Force Quit, if you hold down the Option key)

Noticeably missing in a Classic application's Dock menu is a listing of its open windows. Unlike Aqua applications in which you can interleave windows, Classic forces you to bring all its windows forward when you click on an application's Dock icon.

If a Classic application is running in the background (i.e., you're using a Mac OS X application in the foreground), and it needs your attention, its Dock icon won't bounce. Instead, the Classic application interrupts what you're doing to display its dialog boxes.

Force-Quitting Classic Applications

Although they put on airs of equality with Aqua applications, appearing side by side with them in the Finder and on the Dock, Classic applications get much different treatment from Mac OS X.

If you launch the Activity Monitor (*/Applications/Utilities*), you will see a process named "(null)" in the second column; this is the Classic process and all its running applications lumped together. You can also locate Classic's process in the Terminal by issuing the *top* command and looking for a process named *TruBlueEnv* (which is short for *True Blue Environment*). Classic applications aren't given their own, separate Unix process ID, as with Cocoa and Carbon applications. Instead, all Classic applications run within the process for the Classic environment.

As mentioned earlier, if you want to see which Classic applications are running, go to System Preferences→Classic→Advanced, and look in the Active Processes window.

Despite this, all active Classic applications still appear as choices in Mac OS X's Force Quit window (which you can make appear even when a Classic application is in the foreground using the Option-⌘-Esc key combo).

Should you quit a Classic application this way, though, you run the risk of pulling down the entire Classic environment with it, especially if the application you are trying to force-quit has crashed. Mac OS 9's lack of memory protection means that applications can corrupt memory that belongs to other applications, or to the Classic system itself. The Force Quit window pops up a sheet to remind you of this whenever you attempt to force-quit a Classic application. (You can get around this warning by Option-clicking the Classic application's Dock icon and selecting Force Quit there.) Before force-quitting a Classic application, you should save all your work in other active Classic applications, if you can.

Since it's just another Mac OS X application, if the whole Classic environment does crash, it doesn't affect any Cocoa or Carbon applications, or any other part of the Mac OS X system. You can just restart Classic through the Classic preference pane or by opening a Classic application from the Finder or Dock.

Force-Quitting TruBlueEnv

Of course, sometimes the Classic Environment dies all by itself, the result of the virtual Mac OS 9 machine entering an unstable state, often after a specific Classic application crashes or force-quits. When Classic goes down in flames like this, it sometimes leaves its *TruBlueEnv* process running, even though its interface has gone away (along with any Classic applications that were active).

If you find your Mac's CPU seems a little busier than it needs to be after Classic has crashed, check for the presence of *TruBlueEnv* with the Terminal or a process named "(null)" with the Activity Monitor, and force-quit that process to clear the remnants of Classic from memory.

Printing from Classic

While we cover printing in Chapter 9, we note here that the interface for printing from a Classic application works entirely differently than printing from Aqua.

In Classic, as in Mac OS 9, you use an application called the Chooser to connect to file servers, manage printers, and perform other network-related tasks. In Classic, most of this is moot because Mac OS X handles Classic's networking needs. However, if you want to print from a Classic application, you need to use the Chooser to select and configure a printer.

The Chooser, shown in Figure 3-9, can be found in the Apple menu of any Classic application (assuming that you haven't moved the Chooser icon out of */System Folder/Apple Menu Items*).

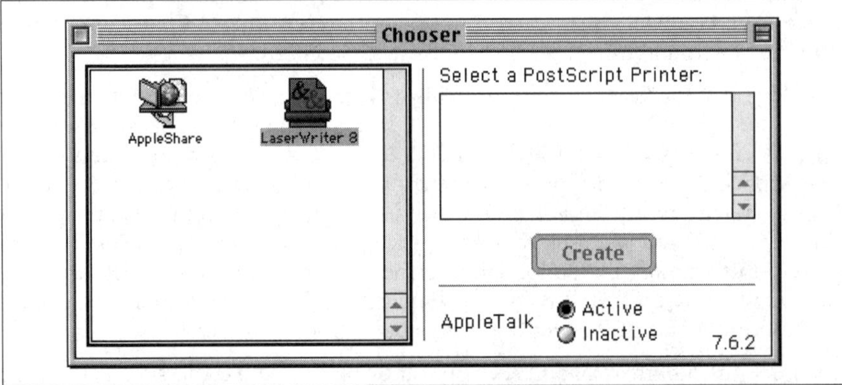

Figure 3-9. The Chooser (with the LaserWriter 8 driver loaded)

If your printer driver isn't available, you need to boot into Mac OS 9 and install the printer's drivers (which you can usually download for free from the printer vendor's web site, if you don't have the printer's bundled software CD). Then restart and boot back into Mac OS X.

Use the following steps to configure your printer using the Chooser; these depend on the type of connection between your Mac and the printer:

USB (non-PostScript) Printers

These steps apply to USB-connected, non-PostScript printers, such as most inkjets or low-end laser printers.

1. With a Classic application active, choose →Chooser.
2. In the upper-left section of the Chooser, select your printer type.
3. In the field to the right, select the printer name or printer port (either may appear, depending on the printer driver).
4. Close the Chooser.

AppleTalk Printers

Follow these steps to connect to a printer available over a legacy AppleTalk network:

1. With a Classic application active, choose →Chooser.
2. In the upper-left section of the Chooser, select your printer type.
3. If AppleTalk Zones appear on your network, select one from the lower-left section of the Choose.
4. In the field to the right, select the printer by name.
5. Close the Chooser.

LPR or PostScript USB

These steps apply when connecting to a printer over TCP/IP or to a USB-connected printer that uses PostScript:

1. Open the Desktop Printer Utility (*/Applications (Mac OS 9)/Utilities*).
2. Select the printer type "LPR" to connect to a printer via IP address or "USB" to connect via direct USB connection.
3. Click OK.
4. Click the upper Change button to select a PPD file, and then click Select.
5. Click the lower Change button to select your printer. USB users choose the printer from a list. LPR users select the printer by entering its DNS name or IP address for the printer in the Printer Address field. Then click OK.
6. Click Create to make the printer connection.

Classic

Dual-Booting with Mac OS 9

There are times when you may need to use Mac OS 9 as an actual operating system, rather than just in Classic mode. In these situations if your hardware is old enough to support it, you can still opt to boot into Mac OS 9 by selecting a startup disk in the Startup Disk preferences panel (System Preferences→Startup Disk), shown in Figure 3-10.

To boot into Mac OS 9, select its system folder and click the Restart button. When your Mac restarts, and every time thereafter, it will boot into Mac OS 9. To reset your computer so it boots into Mac OS X, you need to use Mac OS 9's Startup Disk Control panel (→Control Panels→Startup Disk). As with the Mac OS X's System Preferences panel, select Mac OS X's system folder, and click Restart to boot back into Mac OS X.

If you have Mac OS X and Mac OS 9 installed on separate partitions (or drives), you can subvert the process of going through the System Preferences and Control panels by using the following startup keyboard shortcuts.

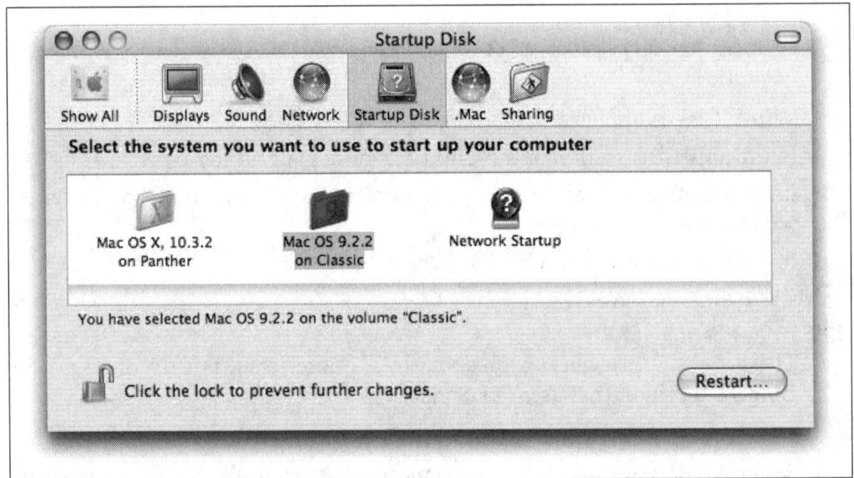

Figure 3-10. The Startup Disk preference panel

Option
: Holding down the Option key at startup opens the Startup Manager, which detects the System Folders on any partitions or drives connected to your Mac, allowing you to select which one to boot into.

X
: Holding down the "X" key at startup forces your Mac to boot into Mac OS X, even if Mac OS 9 is selected as the default startup disk.

4
System Preferences

After finding your way around the Mac's interface, the next thing you'll want to do is configure your system to suit your needs. The primary way to do this is with Mac OS X's System Preferences application. Using the System Preferences and the panels within, you can configure and customize your system and how you interact with it. You can perform actions such as set your Desktop image, configure your network settings (including those for your .Mac account), and manage user accounts if your system has more than one user.

This chapter covers the use of the System Preferences application and describes all the individual panes that Mac OS X ships with. It also explains how the application works, including ways to add panes of your own to its display.

Using System Preferences

The System Preferences application, as seen in Figure 4-1, contains many individual *preference panels*, each represented by its own icon in the application's main display window. Long-time Mac users will recognize that most of the panels in the System Preferences application are similar to the Control Panels found in earlier versions of the Mac OS. For a listing of the differences between Mac OS X and earlier versions of the Mac OS, see Chapter 3.

The System Preferences are divided into four categories: Personal, Hardware, Internet & Network, and System. There is also a toolbar at the top of the window. If you find yourself using a particular System Preference often, drag its icon to the toolbar. Likewise, if there is one you use rarely, or can add a menu item for (such as the Displays panel), drag the icon away, and the icon disappears in a puff of smoke, similar to what happens when you remove an icon from the Dock.

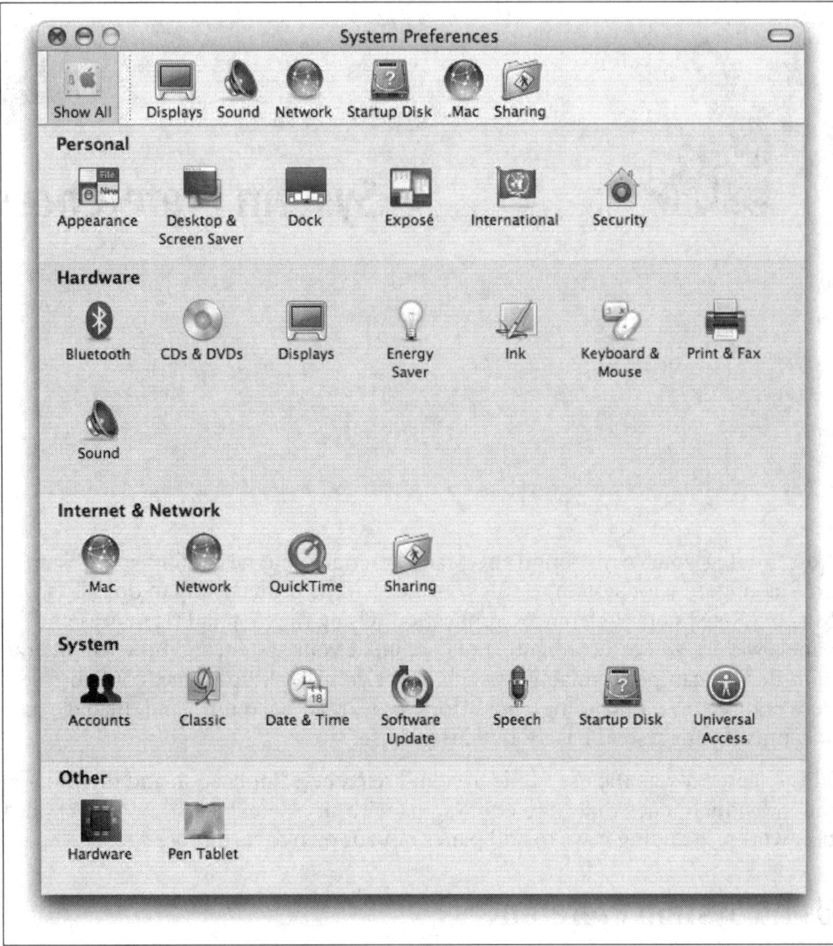

Figure 4-1. The System Preferences application

System Preferences' Default Toolbar

As seen in Figure 4-1, the System Preferences window has a toolbar at the top of its window, which by default contains four panel icons: Displays, Sound, Network, and Startup Disk. These are Apple's best guess at the four items you'll need the most. However, after using Mac OS X for a while, you may find that having Displays in the toolbar is useless because you can make its controls available via a menu extra. For example, system administrators might want to have Accounts, Network, Software Update, and Sharing as a useful set of toolbar icons for System Preferences.

You can launch the System Preferences application by:

- Clicking on its icon in the Dock; the System Preferences icon is the one that looks like a light switch with a gray Apple logo next to it.
- Selecting ->System Preferences in the menu bar.
- Double-clicking on its icon in the Finder (found in */Applications*), as shown in Figure 4-2.

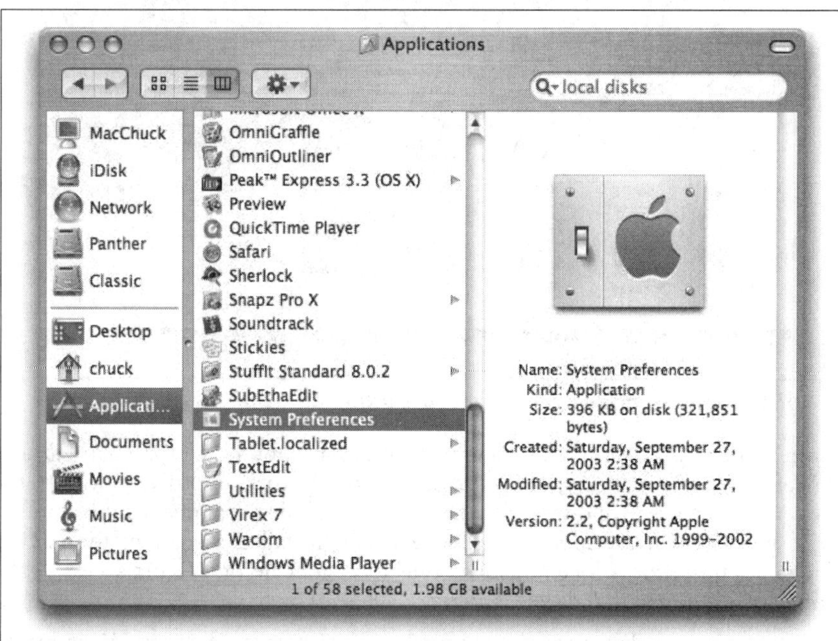

Figure 4-2. The System Preferences application, as found in the Finder

There is one undocumented way to launch the System Preferences application. If you hold down the Option key and hit one of the volume controls on your keyboard, the System Preferences application will launch and quickly go to the Sound preferences panel.

When you click on one of the icons, the window changes to reflect that particular panel's settings, but the toolbar remains in place. To hide the toolbar, click on the transparent button in the upper-right corner of the window. To go back to the main view, click the Show All button (View→Show All Preferences, or ⌘-L). You can also select View→Organize Alphabetically; this menu option changes the view of the System Preferences window to that shown in Figure 4-3.

If you Shift-click on the Toolbar button, System Preferences' toolbar will hide and reveal itself slowly. You won't gain anything by this, but it's kind of fun to do once or twice.

Figure 4-3. The System Preferences, listed alphabetically

Each panel is really a separate application, found in */System/Library/PreferencePanes*; however, they are designed to work exclusively within the System Preferences window rather than as standalone programs. Add-on preference panels, such as Apple's Hardware panel (installed as part of the CHUD tools), or those for Adobe Creative Suite's VersionCue or Wacom's Pen Tablet software, are stored in */Library/PreferencePanes*.

To open a panel, click once on its icon, or select its name from the View menu. This causes the System Preferences window to change into an interface for that particular panel. To return to the main System Preferences window, click the Show All icon in the upper-left corner of the window's toolbar or select View→Show All Preferences (⌘-L).

When you've completed setting your Mac's preferences, you can quit System Preferences by selecting System Preferences→Quit (⌘-Q) or by simply closing the System Preferences window, using Window→Close (⌘-W).

The System Preference Panels

System Preferences breaks the different panels down into four categories, each of which appears as its own row of icons in the program's main display window. The four categories are:

- Personal
- Hardware
- Internet & Network
- System

If you or another application needs to add panels to the System Preferences window (see the later section "Adding Panes to System Preferences"), they appear in a separate category row called Other.

The changes you make to the various panels in the System Preferences are saved as XML data in the form of a *property list*, or *plist*. These plists can be found in your *~/Library/Preferences* directory, and can be further tweaked and manipulated using a text editor or the Property List Editor application if you've installed the Xcode Tools. Look for filenames that begin with *com.apple.something.plist* in this directory.

The panels found in System Preferences are discussed in the sections that follow. Some System Preferences panels require administrator privileges. If you attempt to change a setting and are asked for a password, try using the password you used to log in to the computer. If that doesn't work, contact your system administrator for assistance.

Personal

These panels allow you to configure various aspects of the Aqua "look and feel" of your system, such as the placement and behavior of the Dock, window appearance, language preferences, and the ability to customize some features of user accounts.

The panels included in the Personal section include:

- Appearance
- Desktop & Screen Saver
- Dock
- Exposé
- International
- Security

These Preference panels are explained further in the following sections.

Appearance

The Appearance panel, seen in Figure 4-4, used to be the General panel in Jaguar. This panel lets you select the color to use for text highlighting, configure window scrollbar appearance and behavior, specify the number of entries the Apple Menu should keep under its Recent Items submenu, and control text smoothing (anti-aliasing) throughout the system.

The Appearance pull-down menu lets you select from either Blue (the default) or Graphite as the color Mac OS X uses for its interface elements, such as buttons, scrollbars, and menus. Likewise, the Highlight Color pull-down menu lets you choose the background color the system uses when you select an item or double-click on some text in a document. The default is Blue, but you can choose from

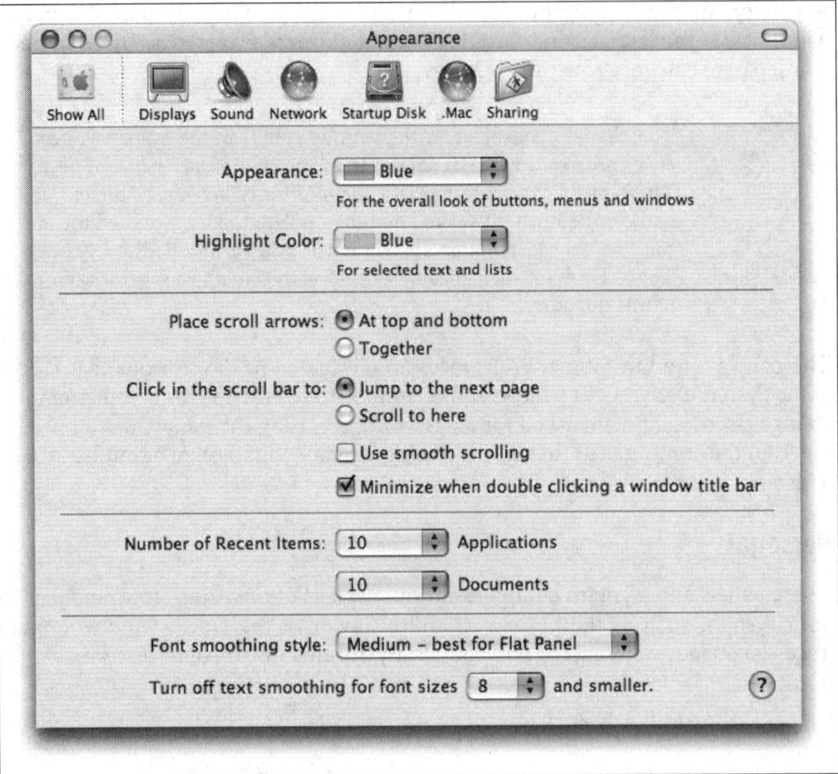

Figure 4-4. The Appearance preference panel

one of eight preset colors, or specify a custom color by selecting Other... from the pull-down menu.

You can also specify the number of recent items to be remembered and listed in the →Recent Items menu for Applications and Documents, as well as determine which font-smoothing style and size is best for your type of display. For example, if you use an iBook or PowerBook, you should set your "Font smoothing style" to "Medium — best for Flat Panel."

Desktop & Screen Saver

This panel combines the Desktop and Screen Effects panels from Jaguar. It has two panes you can use to set the background image for your desktop and to select your screensaver.

The Desktop pane, shown in Figure 4-5, lets you choose the background image that appears on your desktop. You can choose from several preinstalled collections, an image you've saved in your Pictures folder (*~/Pictures*), and with Panther, the Desktop pane includes quick access to iPhoto's libraries.

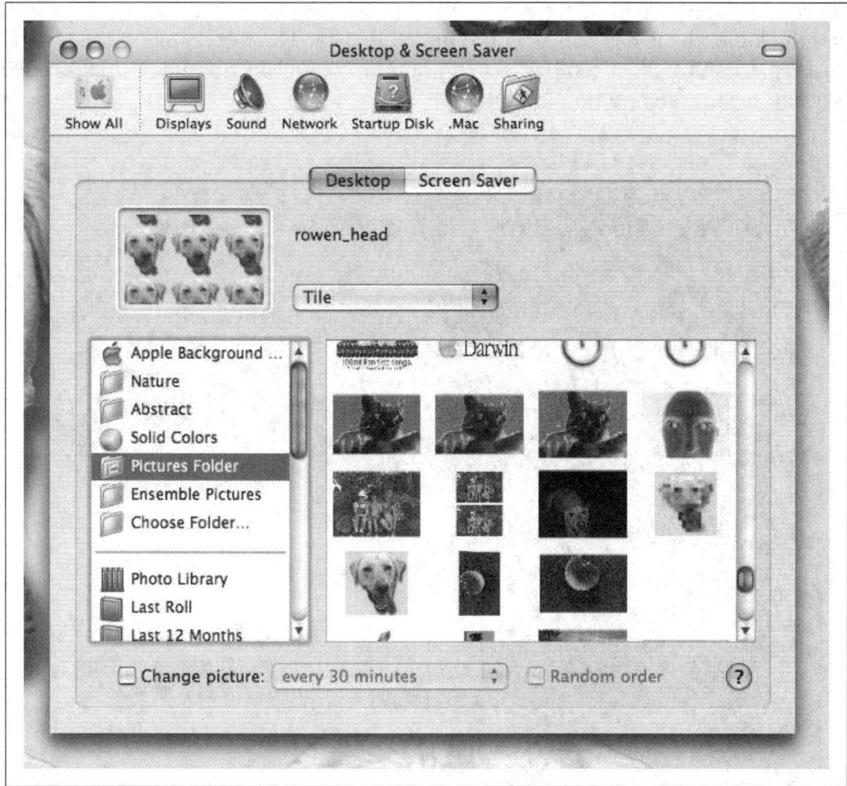

Figure 4-5. The Desktop pane

If you click on the checkbox next to "Change picture" at the bottom of the window, the desktop picture changes automatically based on the timing you select in the pull-down menu.

Additional features of the Desktop pane in Panther include:

- A pull-down menu that allows you to specify whether an image will fill the screen, stretch to fill the screen (thus changing the proportional size of the original image), center the image on screen, or tile the image (if needed).
- The ability to change the Desktop picture automatically. For example, if you have a bunch of JPEG images saved in your Pictures folder or an iPhoto library, you can specify that as the target source for your background image, and then select the checkbox at the bottom of the Desktop window. Clicking on the "Change picture" checkbox enables the pull-down menu, which lets you set the timing rotation of the images.
- If you Control-click (or right-click) on the Desktop itself, a context menu will appear with an option to Change Desktop Background. Selecting this menu item opens the Desktop panel.

If you have more than one display connected to your system, selecting the Desktop panel opens a separate panel in each display, as shown in Figure 4-6.

This panel allows you to set a separate Desktop picture for the other display. If you look closely at Figure 4-6, you'll notice that the Desktop pane on the second display doesn't have a toolbar. For more information on running a dual-headed system, see the later section "Displays."

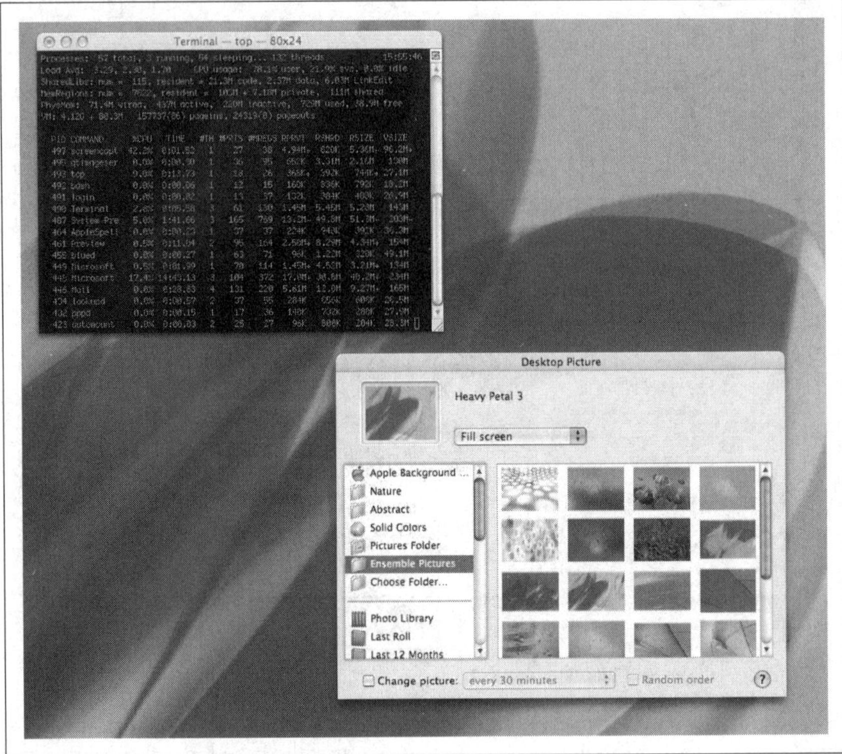

Figure 4-6. The Desktop panel as displayed on a second monitor

The Screen Saver pane, shown in Figure 4-7, lets you select one of Mac OS X's default screensaver modules. Here, you can set the amount of time your system must be inactive before the screensaver kicks in, require a password to turn off the screensaver, and specify Hot Corners for enabling/disabling the screensaver.

If you have a .Mac account, you can also choose from the .Mac Screen Effects or subscribe to another .Mac member's public slide show. To do this, click on the Configure button and enter the members' name (for example, *chuckdude*).

If you click on the Hot Corners button (located at the lower-left corner of the pane), you can specify which corners of your screen to use to quickly enable/disable the screensaver, as shown in Figure 4-8. This is a handy feature because it allows you to immediately activate the screen saver, rather than wait for the time you've specified in the slider.

You can also specify Hot Corners to invoke the effects for Exposé (discussed later) or opt to leave a corner without any function at all.

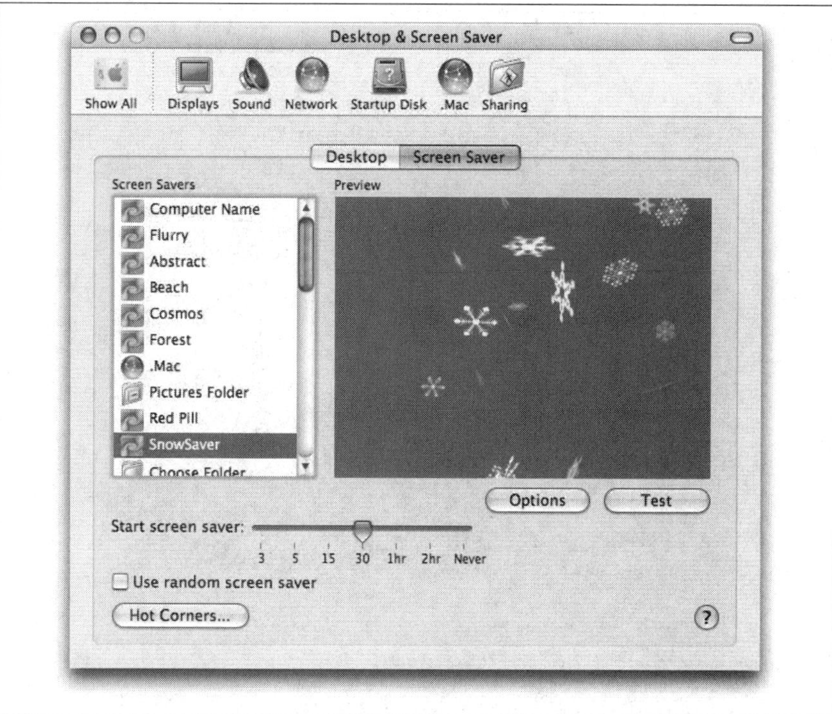

Figure 4-7. The Screen Effects preferences panel

Screensavers are essentially a collection of JPEG image files, bundled together and saved in */System/Library/Screen Savers*. If you have a .Mac account, you can create a screensaver of your own from images in an iPhoto library. To create and publish your screensaver using iPhoto, follow these steps:

1. Make sure you're connected to the Internet.
2. Launch iPhoto by either clicking on its icon in the Dock, or double-click its icon in the Finder (*/Applications*).
3. Select the images you'd like to use in the screensaver.
4. Click on the .Mac Slides button, located at the bottom of iPhoto's window.

iPhoto creates the screensaver slides and publishes them to your iDisk, saving them in the */Pictures/Slide Shows* folder. You can then opt to use the slide show you just created as your own screensaver. Other .Mac users can use it as well, as long as they know your username.

Dock

The Dock panel lets you control the Dock's appearance and behavior, including its size, icon magnification, and screen position. As Figure 4-9 shows, you can also dictate the animation style used for minimizing windows (choose between the Genie Effect or the Scale Effect).

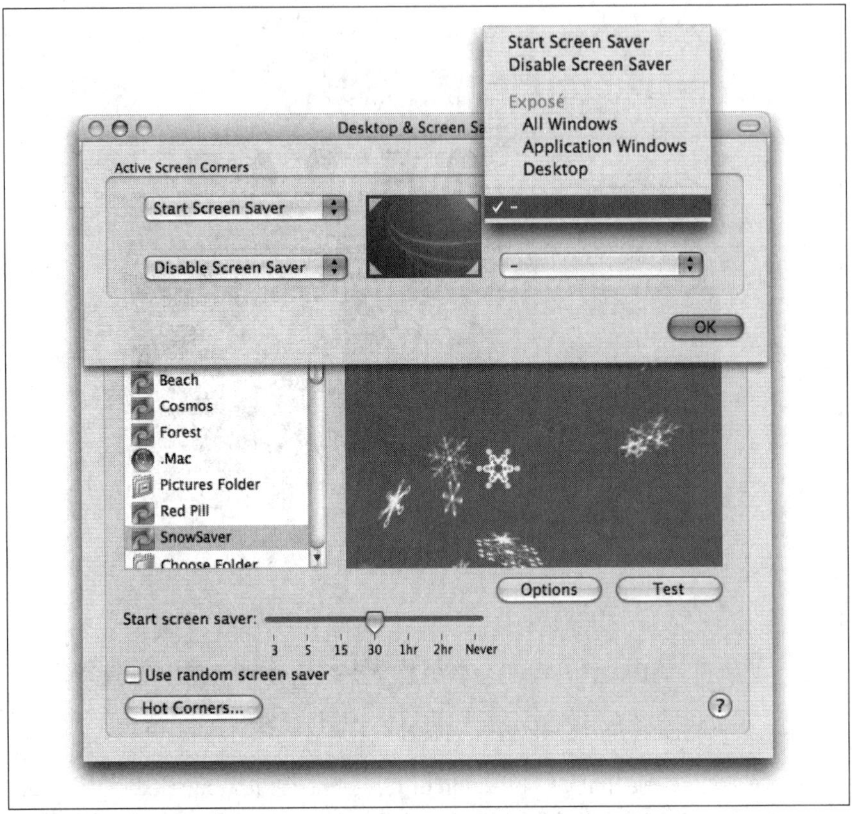

Figure 4-8. The Hot Corners pane of the Screen Saver preferences pane

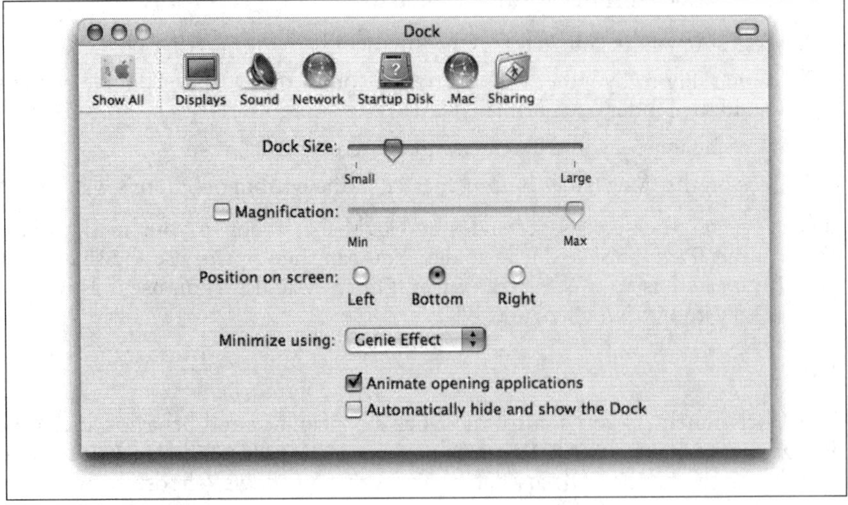

Figure 4-9. The Dock preferences panel

The checkbox next to "Animate opening applications" is checked by default. This option causes an application icon to bounce in the Dock as it starts up. If you uncheck this box, the icon won't bounce, but the black triangle beneath the icon will pulse instead to indicate that the application is launching.

If you find that the Dock takes up too much space on your screen, you can check the box next to "Automatically hide and show the Dock" to make it hide when you don't need it. When you need to launch an application, use the Finder, or unminimize a window, just move your mouse to where the Dock should be and it will reappear.

As Chapter 1 states, abbreviated versions of the Dock panel appear in the Apple Menu submenu, and the Dock divider's Dock menu, shown in Figure 1-27.

Don't forget that you can always quickly toggle the Dock's hidden/shown state by pressing Option-⌘-D.

The plist file for Dock preferences is saved as *~/Library/Preferences/com.apple.dock.plist*.

Hacking the Dock's plist File

Suppose you want your Dock to appear at the top of the screen, beneath the menu bar. While this isn't one of the positions available (as shown in Figure 4-9), you *can* do this by hacking the Dock's *plist* file. To do so, follow these steps:

1. Open the *com.apple.dock.plist* file (*~/Library/Preferences*) by double-clicking on its icon in the Finder. This opens the file using the Property List Editor if you have installed the Xcode Tools; otherwise, the file opens in TextEdit.
2. Click on the Dump button.
3. Click on the disclosure triangle next to Root, and look for a key item named `orientation`.
4. Change the value of `orientation` from `bottom` (or `left` or `right`, depending on where you have it placed) to `top`, hit Return to accept the change, then save the file and quit the Property List Editor.
5. Logout (→Log Out), and then log back in.

When you log back in, the Dock appears at the top of the screen, just below the menu bar. To move it back, you can edit the *plist* file again or use the Dock's preferences panel to select Left, Right, or Bottom as its location; you can also select →Locate at (Bottom, Left, or Right) to change the position of the Dock.

System Preferences

Exposé

What started out as a nifty little hack turned out to be one of the most talked-about features added to Mac OS X Panther. Exposé uses Quartz Extreme rendering to quickly give you access to all of the open windows for running applications or to scoot them out of the way so you can quickly see what's on your Desktop.

Exposé lets users separate open windows on their system so they can quickly select a different window or view the items on their Desktop. All this is accomplished with the aid of keyboard shortcuts and Hot Corners, which you can configure through the Exposé preference panel, shown in Figure 4-10. You can also program the buttons of multibutton mice to invoke Exposé's features through the Keyboard & Mouse preference panel.

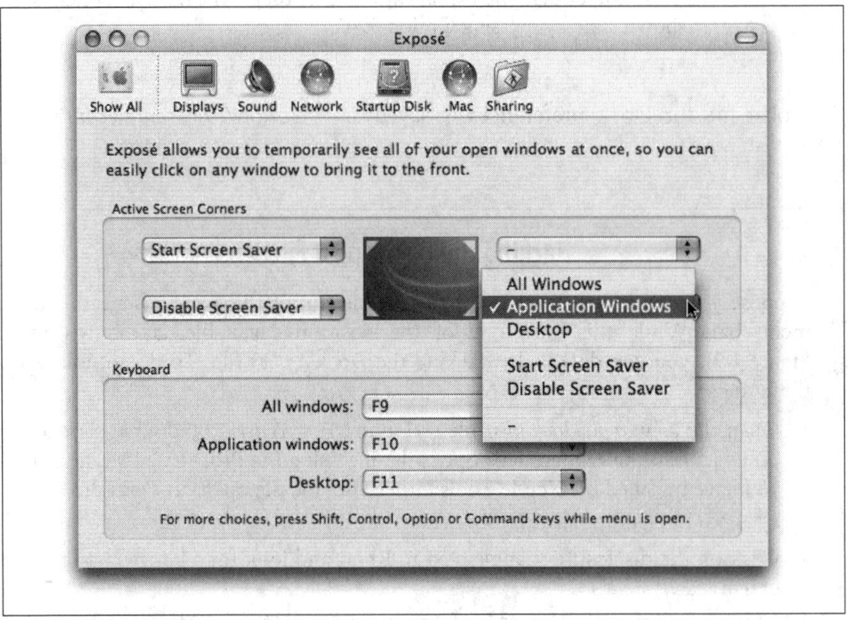

Figure 4-10. Exposé's preference panel

By default, Exposé's keyboard shortcuts are mapped as listed in Table 4-1; Figure 4-11 shows what the desktop will look like if F9 (All windows) is pressed. However, the keyboard shortcuts can be mapped to other keyboard shortcuts using the pop-up menus in the Keyboard area at the bottom of the window.

Table 4-1. Exposé's default keyboard shortcuts

Key	Action
F9	Separates and resizes all open windows; use the arrow keys to highlight individual windows and use the Return key to select that window and bring it to the front of the window stack.

Table 4-1. Exposé's default keyboard shortcuts (continued)

Key	Action
F10	Separates the windows for each application; use the Tab key to bring the next application's windows to the front of the stack.
F11	Scoots all open windows off to the side of the display so you can see the files on your Desktop.

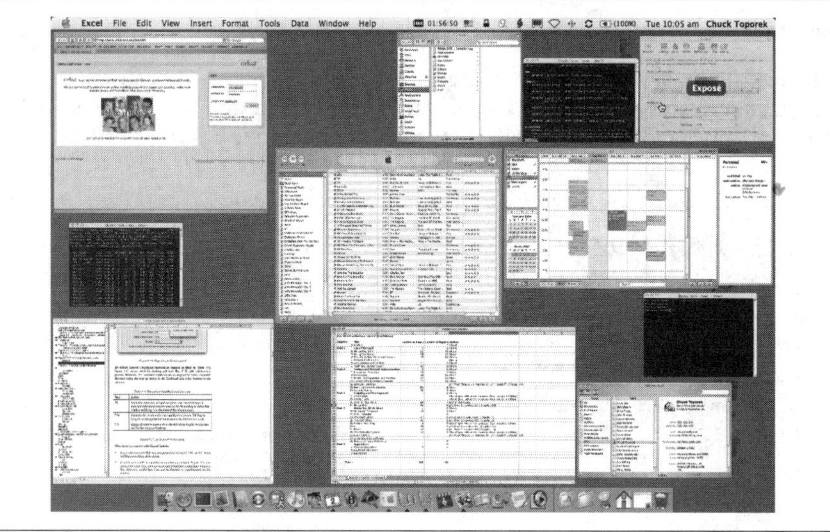

Figure 4-11. An Exposé-tiled desktop

Here are some other tricks you can try with Exposé:

- If you hold down the Shift key and press either of the F9, F10, or F11 keys, Exposé starts working in slow motion.
- If you press F9 to separate the windows as shown in Figure 4-11, you can use the arrow keys on your keyboard to highlight a particular window. The window is shaded light blue, and its filename is superimposed on the window.
- If you press F10 to separate the windows for the current application, you can hit the Tab key to switch to another application and bring its windows—again, separated by Exposé—to the front. Also, Shift-Tab cycles backwards through the window stack, so if you've gone too far with the Tab key, try hitting Shift-Tab to go back to the application you need.
- If you've done the last trick, combine that with the previous and use the arrow keys to highlight a window; pressing Return brings that window to the front of the stack.
- If you've used F11 to push the windows out of the way so you can see the Desktop, the window that previously had the focus is still active, even though it isn't really visible. For example, if you have a Terminal window open and you hit F11, try issuing a simple command like *ls*, then hit F11 to bring the windows back; you should see the output of *ls* in the Terminal window. (F9 and F10 take the focus away.)

If you have an additional display connected to your Mac, Exposé's option for viewing the Desktop works a little differently. For example, if you have your second display configured so that it appears to the right of your main display, the windows on your main display will scoot off to the left edge of that display, while the windows in the second display will shift to the right edge of that display. For additional information on working with two displays, see the Displays section later in this chapter.

International

The international pane, shown in Figure 4-12, is Mac OS X's user interface to its localization features. Through it, you can set your preferred language, as well as the date, time, and number formats most appropriate to the part of the world you live in.

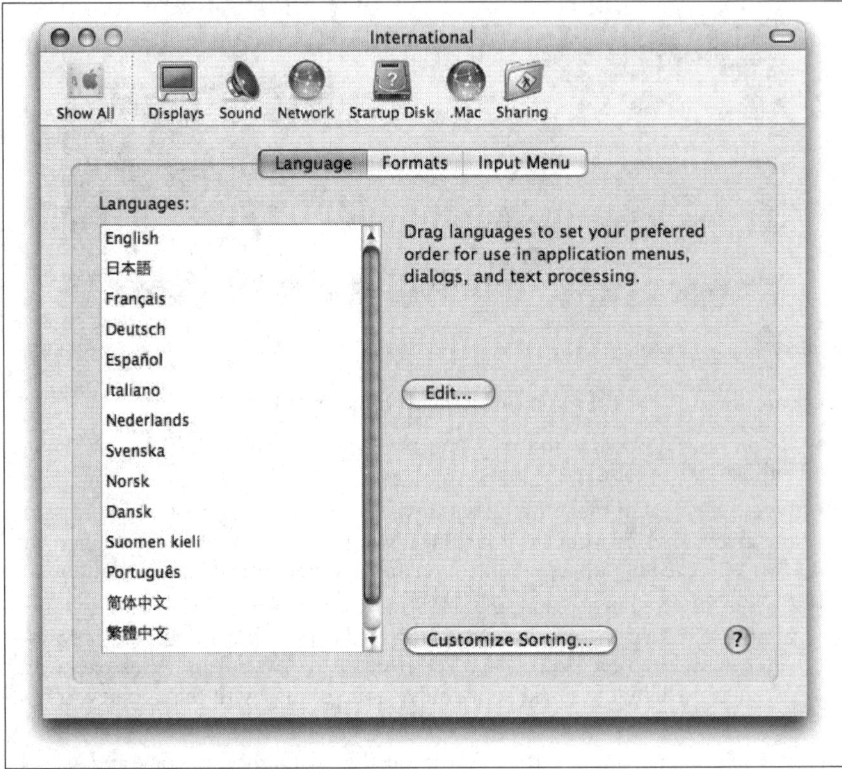

Figure 4-12. The International preferences panel

Mac OS X uses a fairly elegant strategy for implementing systemwide *localization*, letting the system and its various applications modify their text and interfaces depending on the user's native language. For example, a person from the United States would probably prefer to use an English-language system, whose controls and text flow from left to right and top to bottom. Likewise, a person from Saudi

Arabia would benefit from applications with Arabic-language interfaces and a right-to-left flow of text and controls.

There are three panes to the International preferences panel, whose functions are as follows:

Language
: This pane, shown in Figure 4-12, is used to select the languages you prefer to use in your application menus and dialogs. The language at the top of the list is your default language, which is established when you install Mac OS X. To change your preferred language, click on another and drag it to the top of the list (the mouse pointer will change to a hand symbol).

  If you don't see a language in this list, or if you would like to make it shorter, click on the Edit button. A sheet will slide down, containing a checkbox list of the more than 90 languages supported by Mac OS X Panther. You can also use this listing to reduce the number of languages that appear in the Languages window by deselecting their checkboxes.

  If you decide to switch languages (say from English to Polish), you will need to log out and log back in to your account for the change to take effect.

Formats
: This pane lists options for how the following items are displayed, based on the Region you've selected from the pop-up menu at the top of the panel:

  Dates
  : The Dates section lets you specify how the system date appears in the menu bar clock.

  Times
  : This section lets you specify the format for your clock.

  Numbers
  : The Numbers section lets you specify the Separators numbers (Decimal and Thousands), the symbol to be used for Currency, and whether your Measurement Units will be standard or metric. Typically, you won't have to change the items under Separators, Currency, or Measurement System, as their defaults are based on the Region you select from the pull-down menu.

Input Menu
: This pane is used to select the keyboard layout for your system, based on the language you've specified as the default. Initially, you will have only one language selected here. However, if you select other languages by clicking on their checkboxes, the Input Menu will appear in your menu bar.

  One item you'll want to add to your Input Menu is the Character Palette, especially if you frequently need to add international characters or mathematical symbols to your documents. If you select the Character Palette from the Input Menu, the palette will open in a separate window. To add a character to a document, find the symbol you're looking for and drag it to where you would like it inserted.

Clicking on the Options button opens a sheet with Input Menu Shortcuts (keyboard shortcuts for switching the default keyboard layout or input method), and an option to synchronize the font and keyboard scripts.

Mac OS X has the textual base covered by making Unicode its native text-encoding architecture. To make localized user interfaces, application developers can build groups of interface widgets or text strings to use depending on the user's local settings. These resources are built into *.lproj* folders found within the application's */Resources* folder.

Security

The Security panel, shown in Figure 4-13, is used to configure FileVault for setting up system- and user-specific passwords to protect the data on your computer.

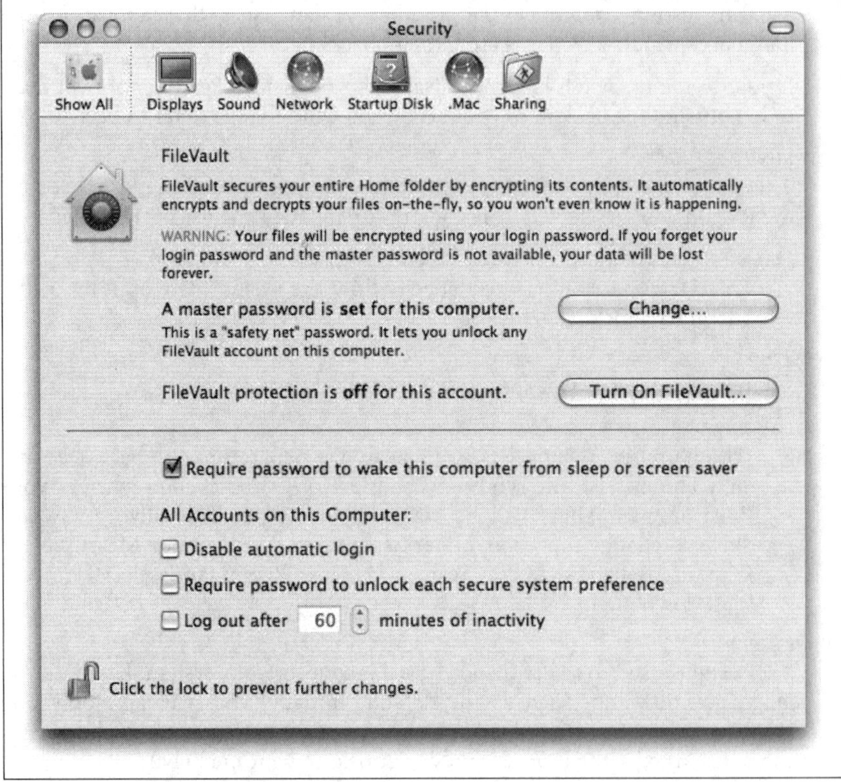

Figure 4-13. The Security preference panel

With FileVault enabled, the data in your Home folder will be encrypted in a single disk image that can be accessed only with the proper password, even if your Mac is mounted in target disk mode. The only exception to this rule is if you have set the Master Password for the computer. If the Master Password has been set, and if you have administrator privileges on the system, you can unlock any user's FileVault account.

The lower portion of the window provides a series of checkboxes for added security, which include:

Require password to wake this computer from sleep or screen saver
: If your Mac is in sleep or screensaver mode, and someone tries to gain access to your computer, they will be challenged for your login password.

  Selecting this option is a quick way to improve your account's security, if your Mac is in an office or other setting where you'd rather not risk prying eyes, and you need to leave the keyboard for a little while.

All Accounts on this Computer:
: This section of the Security panel is available only to users with administrator privileges; it's grayed out for normal users. The following options apply across the board to all user accounts on the system:

  Disable automatic login
  : If checked, this option makes it so users *must* use their account password to log in to the system.

  Require password to unlock each secure system preference
  : If checked, this option disables secure system preference panels from being used without first authenticating with an administrator's username and password, as shown in Figure 4-14.

  Log out after [60] minutes of inactivity
  : If checked, this option automatically logs other users out of their accounts if their account has been inactive for a specified amount of time. The default period of inactivity is 60 minutes.

System Preferences

Hardware

Apple has used the term "digital hub" as a marketing slogan to describe its computers' zero-configuration plug-and-play abilities with various devices. The Hardware preference panels let you control your Mac's behavior when you connect or insert various kinds of media or devices (such as a digital camera or iPods), or insert a CD or DVD.

The standard set of panels in the Hardware section include:

- CDs & DVDs
- ColorSync
- Displays
- Energy Saver
- Keyboard
- Mouse
- Sound

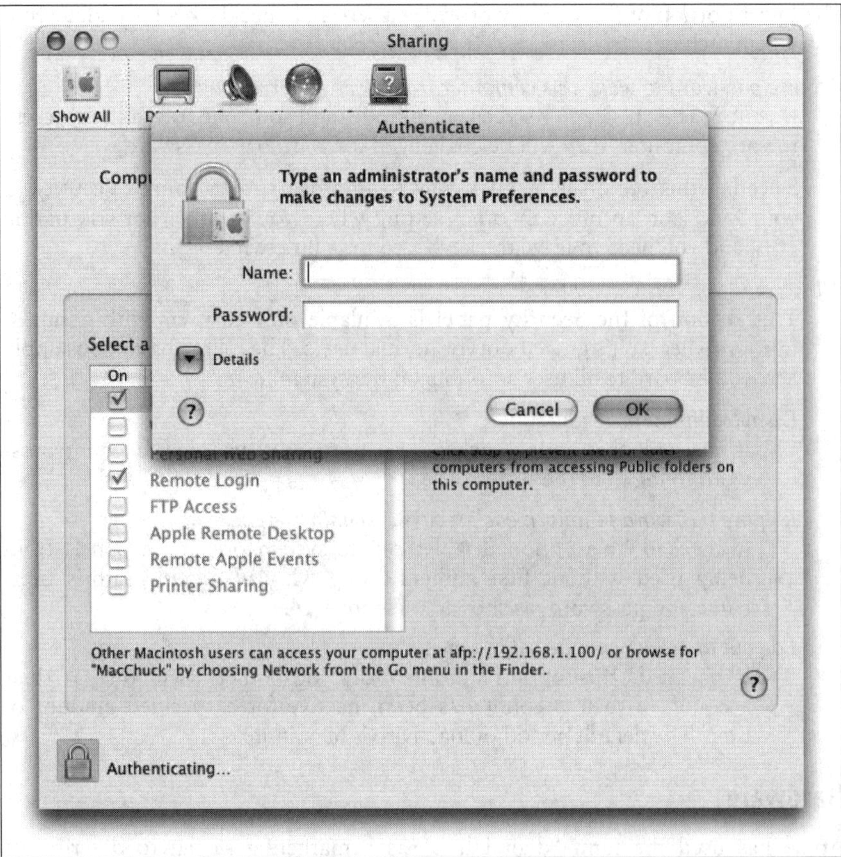

Figure 4-14. Typical password challenge when "Require password to unlock each secure system preference" is enabled

In addition to the standard set of Hardware preference panels, there are two more that you might find, depending on additional hardware or peripherals attached to your system. These are:

- Bluetooth
- Ink

The standard set of Hardware preference panels, along with Bluetooth and Ink are discussed in the following sections.

CDs & DVDs

The CDs & DVDs preferences panel, shown in Figure 4-15, lets you determine what action (if any) will be taken when you insert a CD or DVD.

The items in the CDs & DVDs panel all share the same basic interface: a pull-down menu that lets you choose what the Mac does when it mounts various kinds of disks. You can choose to have it simply open the new media volume as a Finder

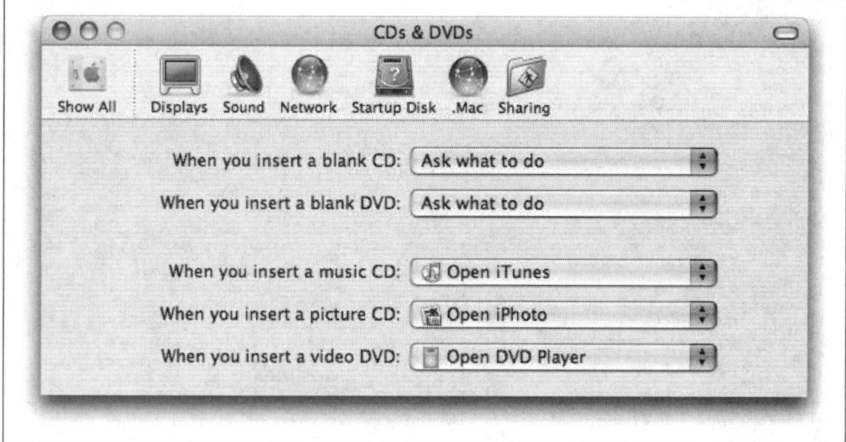

Figure 4-15. The CDs & DVDs preferences panel

window, launch an appropriate application (such as iTunes for music CDs and Disk Copy for blank discs), run a script, or prompt you for some other action to take. The pull-down menus ask you what action to take when you perform one of the following actions:

Insert a blank CD
: Specifies the Mac's behavior when you insert a blank, recordable CD or DVD. By default, this is set to "Ask what to do"; however, you might want to change the action for this to "Open Finder", "Open iTunes", or select another application, such as Disk Utility (*/Applications/Utilities*).

Insert a blank DVD
: Specifies the Mac's behavior when you insert a blank, recordable DVD or DVD. By default, this is set to "Ask what to do"; however, you might want to change the action for this to "Open Finder," "Open iDVD" (if you have iLife '04 installed on your Mac), or another application.

Insert a music CD
: Specifies the Mac's behavior when it mounts an audio CD (including an MP3 CD). The default is to open the CD with iTunes.

Insert a picture CD
: Specifies the Mac's behavior when it mounts a picture CD; the default is to open the CD with iPhoto.

Insert a video DVD
: Specifies the Mac's behavior when it mounts a DVD with a movie on it; the default is to open it with the DVD Player.

Displays

The Displays panel configures the resolution, color depth, and refresh rates available to the currently connected monitor (see Figure 4-16.)

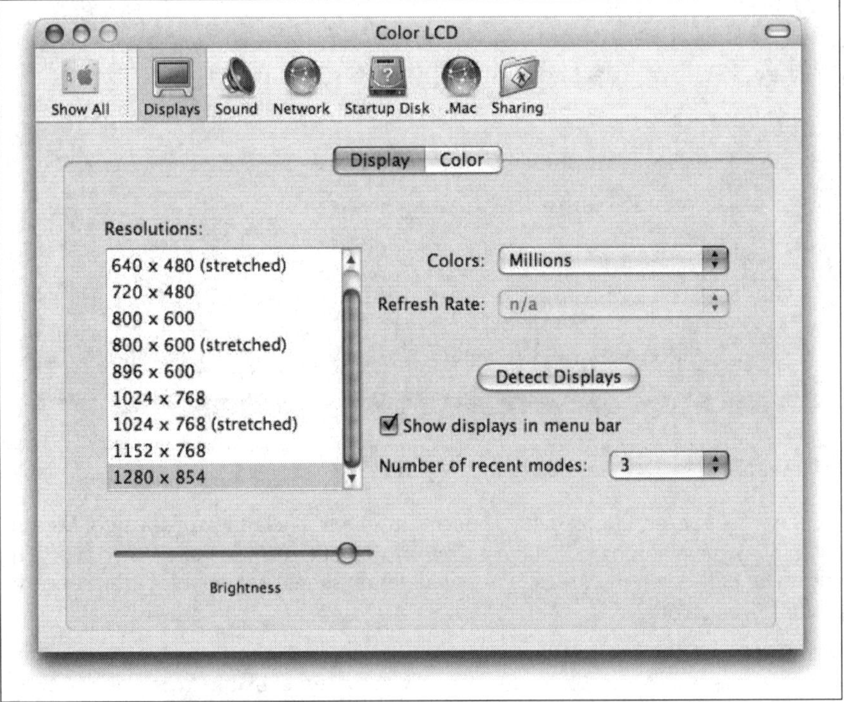

Figure 4-16. The Displays preference panel

The Color tab contains controls for associating and calibrating a ColorSync profile with the current display. Clicking the Calibrate button launches the Display Calibrator application, which allows you to create a custom ColorSync calibration for your particular monitor and needs.

It's wise to check the "Show profiles for this display only" item in the Color tab, because it will keep you from selecting a screen resolution that may not be supported by your monitor.

If you check the "Show displays in menu bar" checkbox, the Displays menu extra shown in Figure 4-17 will appear in the menu bar.

If you connect more than one display to your computer, you'll notice some differences in the some of the System Preference panels, described in the next list.

- An Arrangement tab, shown in Figure 4-18, is added to the Displays preferences panel. This tab allows you to select the placement of the second monitor in relation to the primary display.

  If you select the Mirror Displays checkbox, the second monitor will mirror the main display. This is particularly useful when you connect your computer to an overhead projector to give a presentation.

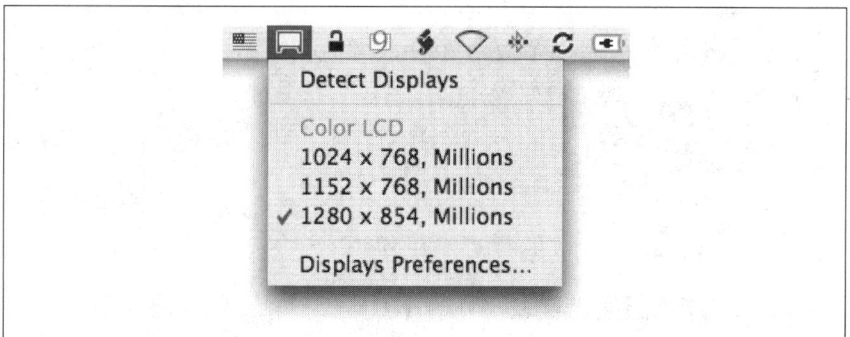

Figure 4-17. The Displays menu extra, located in the menu bar

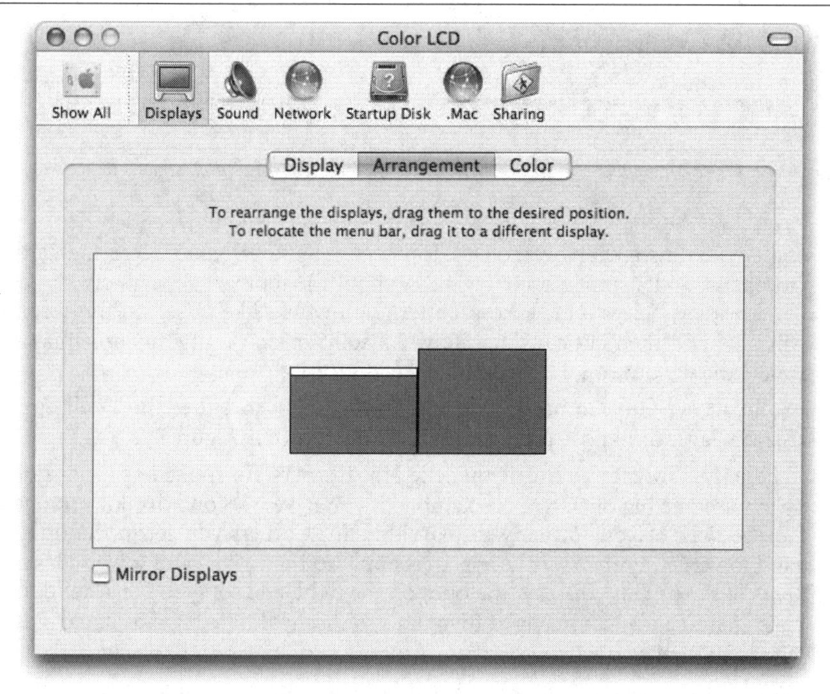

Figure 4-18. The Arrangement tab; available only if more than one monitor is connected to your system

- A watered-down version of the Displays panel appears on the second monitor, as shown in Figure 4-19.

  To interact with this window, move your mouse over to the second monitor by moving the cursor in the direction you placed the second display in the Arrangement tab.

  If you click on the Show All icon in the System Preferences toolbar on the main display, the Displays panel disappears from the second monitor.

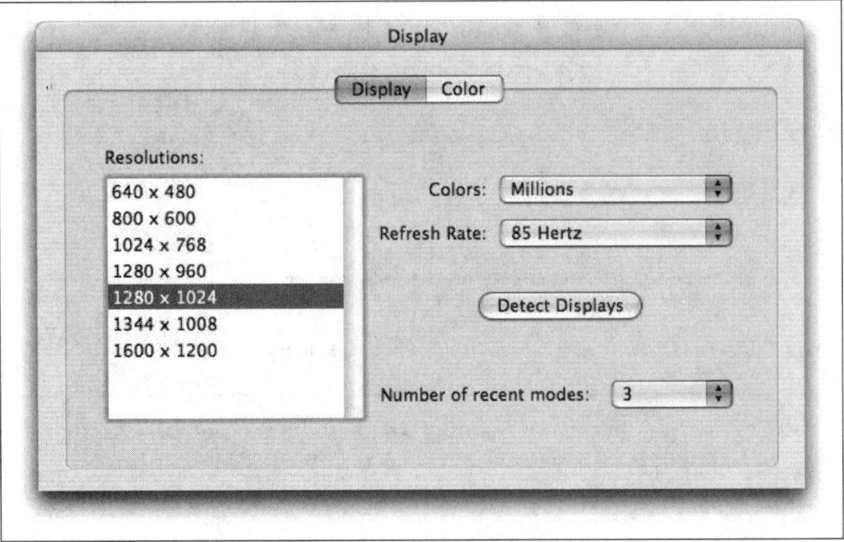

Figure 4-19. The Displays preference panel as shown on a second monitor

- You can set the Desktop pictures for both displays independent of each other. To do so, click on the Desktop & Screen Saver panel, go to the Desktop pane, and a similar pane (again, without the toolbar) appears on the second display. Select the Desktop pattern you would like to see on the second display, and then click on the Show All toolbar icon in the main display to make the window on the second display disappear.
- You can set Hot Corners for the second display in either the Desktop & Screen Saver or Exposé preference panels, as shown in Figure 4-20.

  The only downside to this is that the Hot Corners are applied as if both displays are one big display. For example, if you have a second display arranged to the right of your primary display, the Hot Corners you set in the upper- and lower-left corners of these panels apply to the upper- and lower-left corners of the primary display; the ones on the right side apply to the second display. This can be confusing at first and is radically different from Jaguar (Mac OS X 10.2), which let you set Hot Corners for each display independently.

  While at first glance this might seem like you can enable the screensaver on the second monitor independently from your main display, you can't. If you move the mouse into the Hot Corner to enable the screensaver, both monitors will display the same screensaver simultaneously.
- The Displays menu extra in the menu bar allows you to control both displays from the same menu, as shown in Figure 4-21.
- When you minimize a window in the second display, you can watch as it's whisked away to a place in the Dock on the primary display. Likewise, when you unminimize that window, it will spring back to its former placement on the second display.

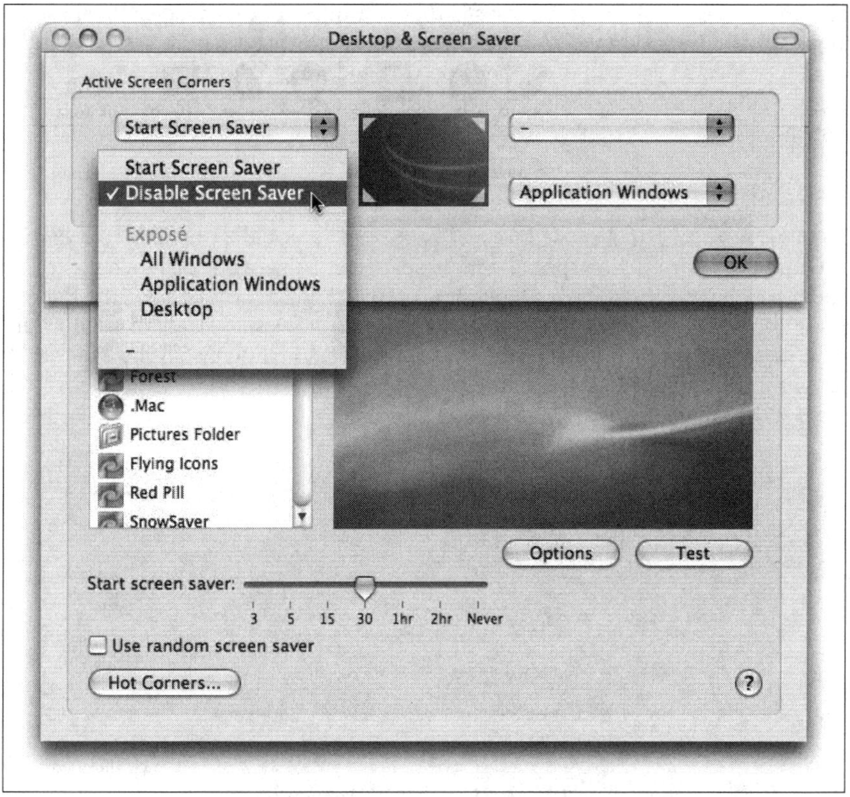

Figure 4-20. *Setting the Hot Corners for the second monitor from the Screen Savers panel*

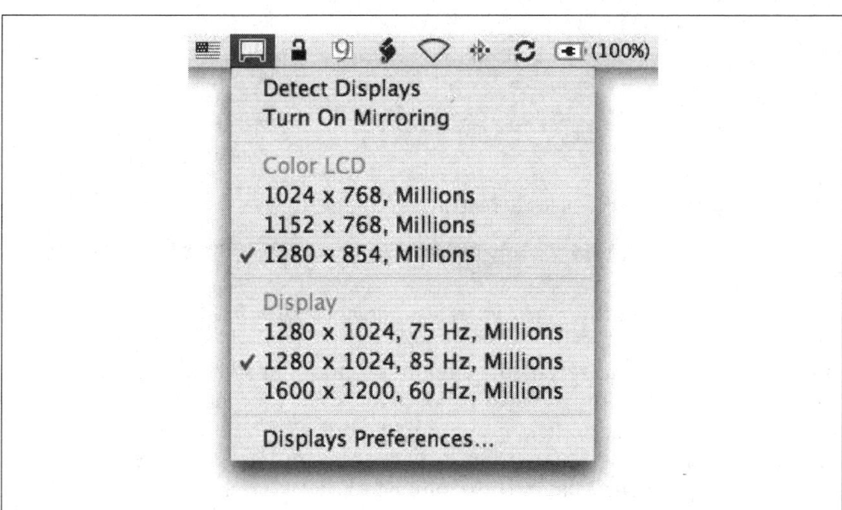

Figure 4-21. *The Displays menu extra, showing controls for two displays*

The advantage of using two displays is that you have additional screen real estate to work with. For example, you can use the second display to have various Finder windows open so you can drag and drop text and image files into a dynamic web page builder (such as Dreamweaver MX) that you're running on your main display.

Energy Saver

The Energy Saver panel is used to specify the machine's idle time before it enters sleep mode and to define special conditions (such as network or modem access) under which it awakens itself. Depending on which machine you have, the Energy Saver panel you see may be different. If you have a Desktop system such as an iMac or a desktop Mac (such as a G4 or G5 tower), the Energy Saver panel you'll see is shown in Figure 4-22; if you have an iBook or PowerBook, the panel you'll see is shown in Figure 4-23.

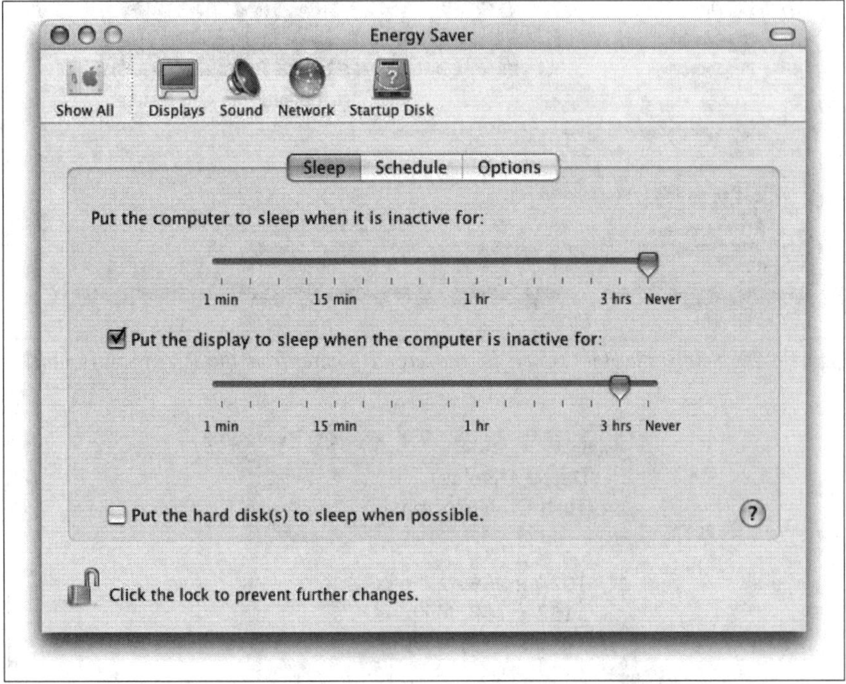

Figure 4-22. The Energy Saver preferences panel as displayed on a G4 tower

This panel allows you to specify the amount of time your system is inactive before your computer or monitor is put to sleep. If you want your monitor to go to sleep sooner than the computer, click on the checkbox next to "Use separate time to put the display to sleep." Another option, "Put the hard disk to sleep when possible," allows you to put your Mac into the ultimate Energy Saver mode, in which the hard disk spins itself down, reducing the power consumption even more.

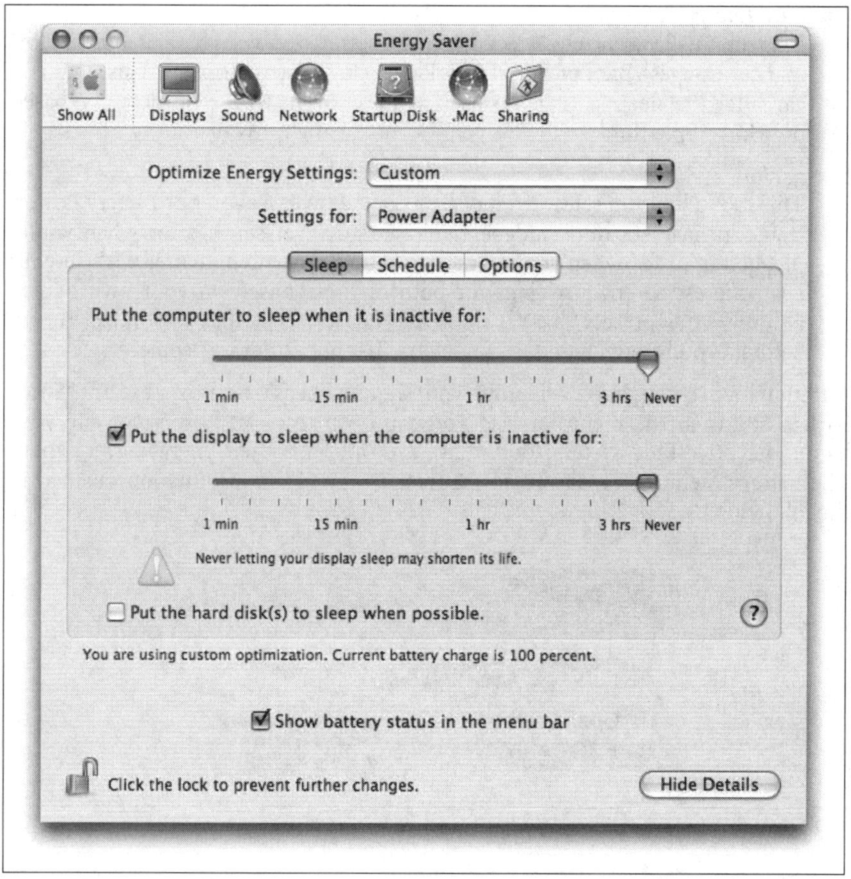

Figure 4-23. The Energy Saver preferences panel as displayed on a PowerBook G4

Because the settings defined by the Energy Saver panel take effect for the entire system (and not just while your login is active, as with the Desktop & Screen Saver preferences panel), you must open the pane's authentication lock before making any changes here.

As noted earlier, iBook and PowerBook users will see the Energy Saver panel shown in Figure 4-23. The reason for this change is to give laptop users the ability to set the sleep time for when they're plugged in or when they're operating on battery power. Note the two pull-down menus at the top of the window:

At some point, Apple removed the ability to configure the hard drive spindown time in Energy Saver: the value is stuck at 10 minutes. This can be changed by editing */var/db/SystemConfiguration/com.apple.PowerManagement.xml* or by using the command *pmset –a spindown n* (where *n* is a number in minutes) to write the `config` value. See *man pmset* for more information.

Optimize Energy Settings

This menu allows you to select one of six settings: Automatic, Highest Performance, Longest Battery Life, DVD Playback, Presentations, or Custom. You can alter the sleep settings for each of these or go with their defaults, based on what Apple thinks will give you the most bang for your battery's buck.

Settings for

This menu lets you select from two options: Power Adapter or Battery Power. You can have separate, independent Energy Saver settings for when you're plugged in or for when you're unplugged and running on battery. It's in your best interest to enter settings for both of these based on your own habits, although the presets, based on what you select in the "Optimize Energy Settings" pull-down menu, should work just fine for most people.

Additionally, if you have a laptop, you should check the box next to "Show battery status in the menu bar" so you can keep track of how much life your battery has. (Desktop systems don't have this option in their Energy Saver panel.) The battery menu extra, shown in Figure 4-24, gives the information detailed in the following list.

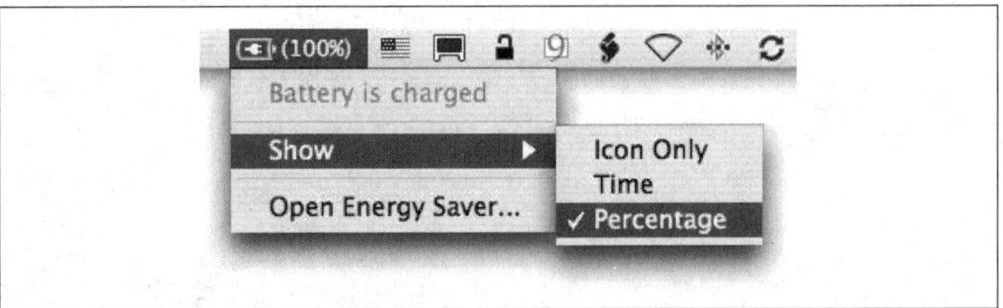

Figure 4-24. The battery menu extra, found in the menu bar

- The icon in the menu bar shows whether the computer is plugged in, running on battery, or if the battery is charging:
  - If you are plugged in, the battery icon has a plug symbol inside.
  - The battery icon displays a progress meter to show the amount of life remaining in your battery. As the energy in the battery depletes, the indicator bar moves to the left.
  - The battery icon has a small lightning bolt inside it when the battery is charging.
- When your battery is below 25 percent, the progress meter inside the battery turns red, prompting you to plug in somewhere (and soon).

  You will receive one final warning when your battery hits 8 percent, telling you that you are running on reserve power. If you get this warning, and you fail to plug in soon, your computer will be put to sleep automatically to preserve the contents of memory.
- The menu extra allows you to select how the time remaining on your battery will be displayed next to the battery icon in the menu bar. You can choose from Show Icon Only, Show Time, or Show Percentage; the menu also has an

option to open the Energy Saver preferences panel. Show Icon Only displays a battery icon. Show Time displays the time remaining on your battery in hours and minutes (e.g., 2:36 is the equivalent of 2 hours and 36 minutes); Show Percentage displays the percent remaining of your battery's life.

Depending on which item you select in the menu extra, Show Time or Show Percent, the opposite will be shown as gray text as the first item in the menu extra. For example, if you select Show Percent, the percentage will be shown in the menu bar, while the time remaining on your battery will be displayed as gray text at the top of the menu extra. If you select Show Neither, the time remaining will be shown as hours and minutes in gray text at the top of the menu extra.

The Schedule pane, shown in Figure 4-25, allows you to configure your Mac so it starts up or shuts down automatically at a specified time. This is particularly useful if you want your Mac to start up and shut down during the night for backups scheduled via *cron*, or just so your Mac starts up before you arrive at work.

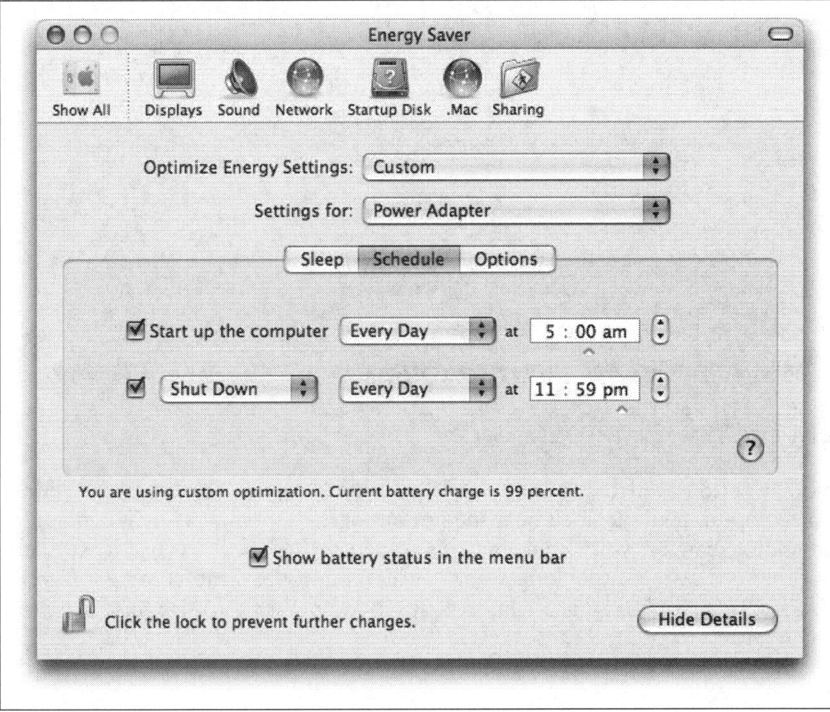

Figure 4-25. Energy Saver's Schedule pane

The Options pane, shown in Figure 4-26, has two Wake Options and an option that automatically restarts your Mac if there is a power failure that forces it to shutdown prematurely. For iBook and PowerBook owners, though, the auto restart option is moot if your Mac is plugged in because your laptop will run on battery until the power connection is reestablished.

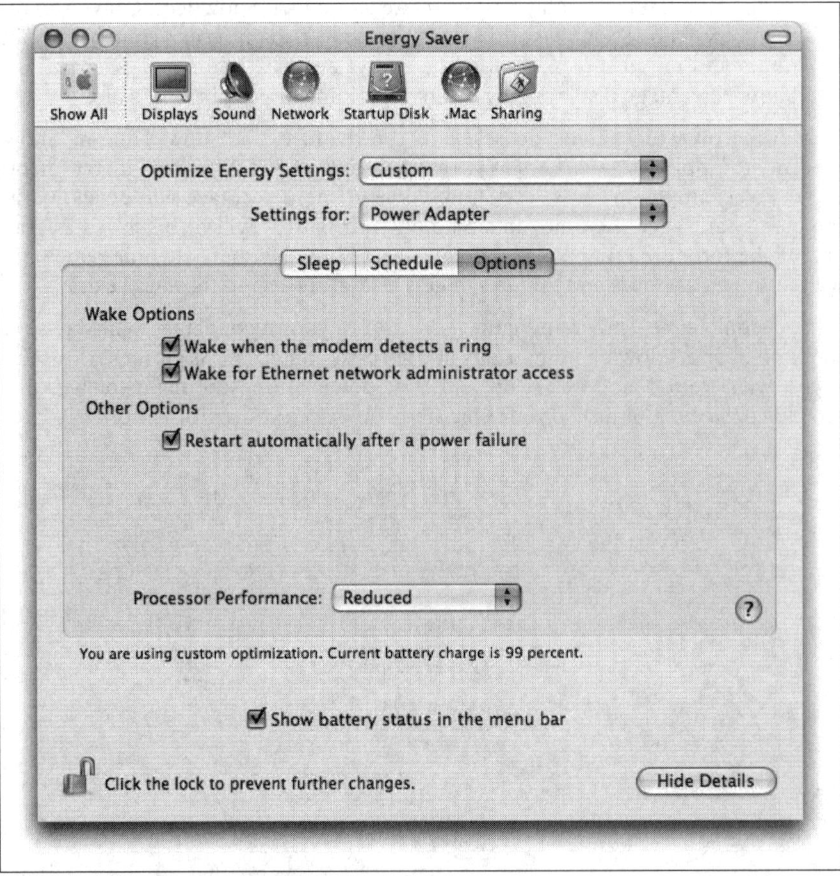

Figure 4-26. Energy Saver's Options pane

Another option available to iBook and PowerBook users is the Processor Performance pop-up menu located near the bottom of the Options pane. When you're running on battery, you should set this option to Reduced because it will help your battery last a little longer (and will reduce the heat coming off your processor). If you're plugged in, set this pop-up menu to Highest for peak performance.

Keyboard & Mouse

The Keyboard & Mouse panel combines the separate Keyboard and Mouse preference panels from Jaguar into one panel, shown in Figure 4-27. The Keyboard pane controls the repeat rate when you depress a key and hold it down. You can specify the speed of the repeat (from slow to fast) and the delay between the time the key is first depressed until the repeat option kicks in (from long to short). If you select the Off option for Delay Until Repeat, the repeat feature will be disabled entirely.

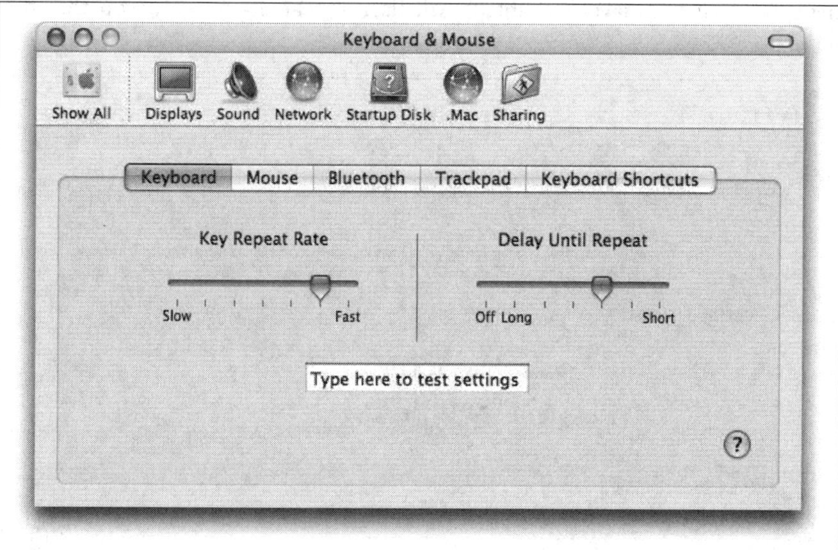

Figure 4-27. The Keyboard preferences panel

The Mouse panel, shown in Figure 4-28, lets you specify the speed of the mouse, as well as the delay between double-clicks.

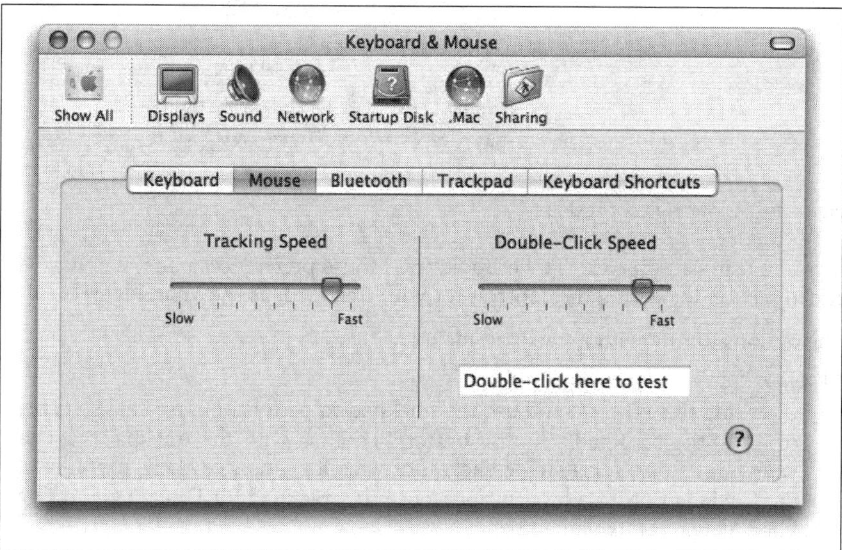

Figure 4-28. The Mouse pane

The Bluetooth pane, shown in Figure 4-29, monitors the battery life of the Apple Bluetooth Mouse and Keyboard, if you have one. You can also use this pane to assign a name to these devices. When the battery starts to run low, the Bluetooth menu extra (if you have it enabled) will flash repeatedly to warn you that the battery is low.

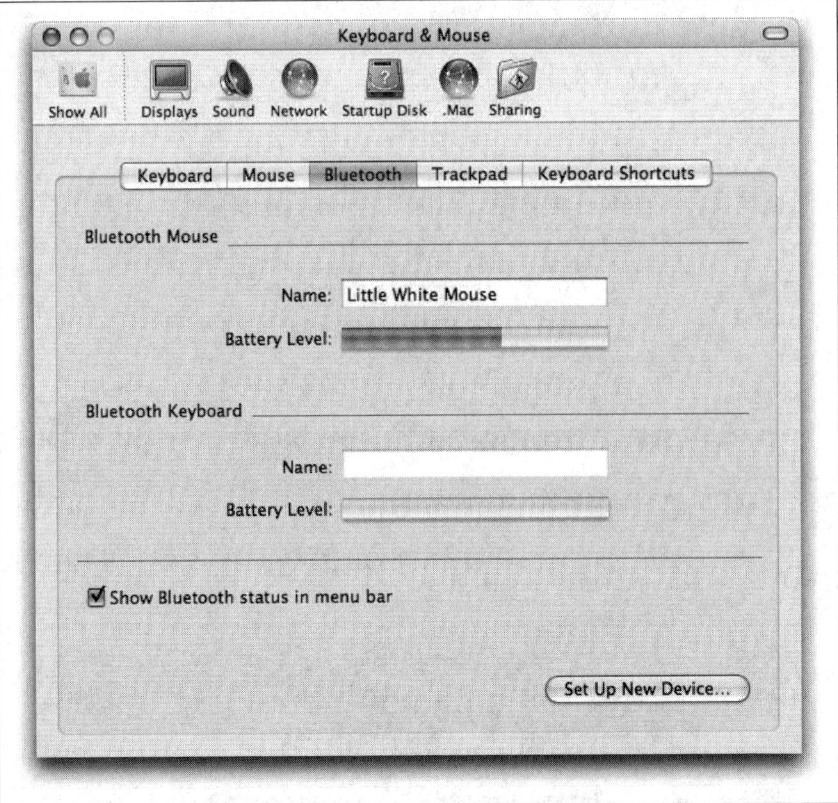

Figure 4-29. The Bluetooth pane

If you're using an iBook or PowerBook, the Mouse preferences panel will have an added section for setting the controls for your trackpad, as shown in Figure 4-30.

The options for use with a trackpad include:

Clicking
: Checking this box lets you use the trackpad to perform mouse clicks, instead of using the trackpad's mouse button. To click with the trackpad, just tap your finger once for a single-click and twice for a double-click. If you select the Clicking option, you can opt to use the trackpad for Dragging and Drag Lock, which are explained here:

  Dragging
  : This option allows you to use the trackpad to drag-select items, either in the Finder or on your Desktop. To drag-select, tap twice with your

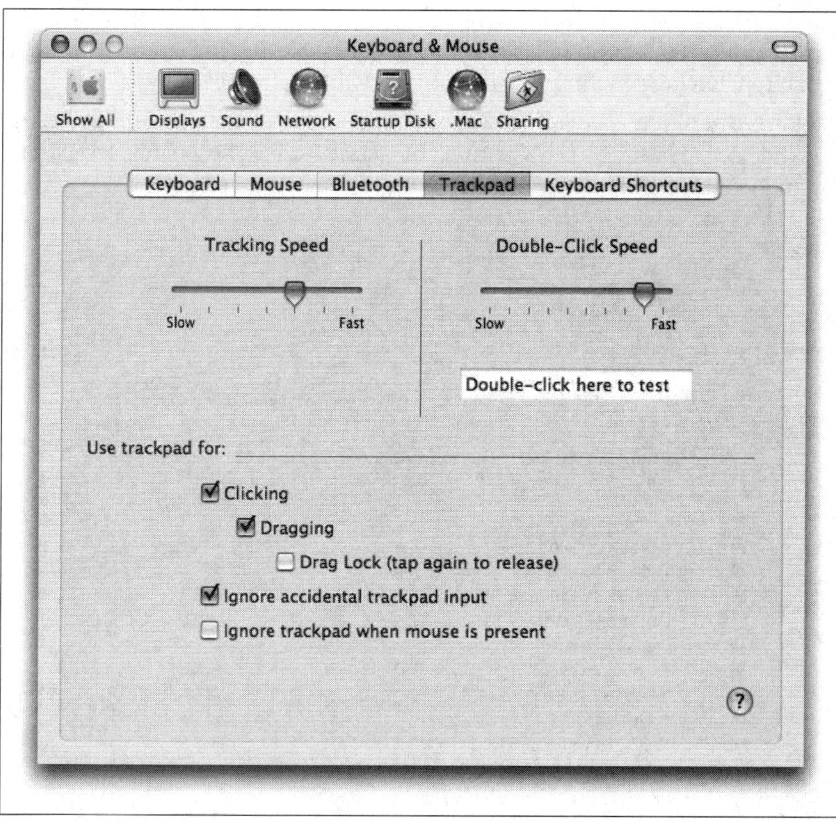

Figure 4-30. The Mouse preferences panel, with options to control the trackpad

finger, hold your finger down on the second tap. Then move your finger on the trackpad to select the items. To deselect the items, tap once to release.

Drag Lock

This option allows you to drag-select (as with the Dragging option) and drag the files to another location (such as over the Trash icon in the Dock). To use Drag Lock, tap twice with your finger and hold down on the second tap and move your finger on the trackpad to select the items, and then tap once to end the selection. With the items selected, tap your finger on the trackpad twice to "grab" them, and then drag the items to where you want to move them. To release the items, tap your finger on the trackpad once; to deselect the items, move the pointer elsewhere, and tap the trackpad once.

Ignore accidental trackpad input

Selecting this item disables input to the trackpad while you're typing. This is particularly useful if you have a tendency to move or rest your hands next to the trackpad while typing.

Ignore trackpad when mouse is present

Checking this box disables the trackpad if a mouse is connected to your laptop, forcing you to use the mouse instead of the trackpad.

The Keyboard Shortcuts pane, shown in Figure 4-31, lists the standard keyboard shortcuts available for Screen Capture, Universal Access, Keyboard Navigation, the Dock, and for other Application Keyboard Shortcuts.

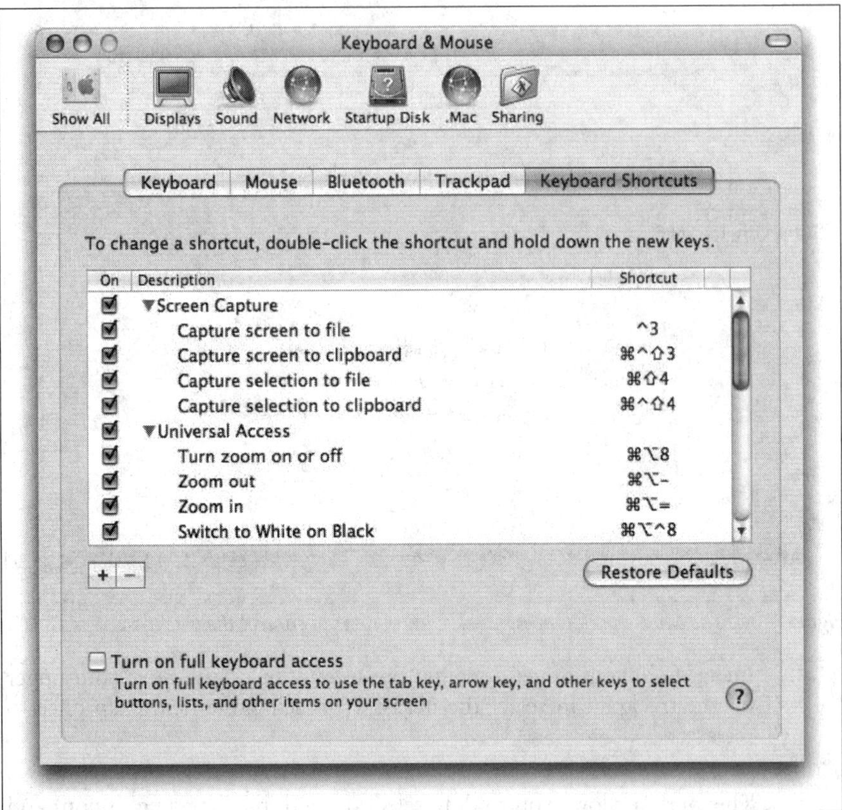

Figure 4-31. The Keyboard Shortcuts pane

You can toggle the keyboard shortcuts off or on by clicking on their respective checkboxes in the On column. This is particularly useful for system administrators who might not want to let users take screenshots (for security purposes or otherwise). If you want to add a keyboard shortcut to a menu item that doesn't have one, you can do so by clicking on the add button (the one with the plus sign, +, on it). This opens a sheet that lets you select the specific application (or All Applications) and the menu item, and assign a keyboard shortcut (as shown in Figure 4-32).

If you click on the checkbox next to "Turn on full keyboard access" (at the bottom of Figure 4-32), you can use the Control key with either Function keys,

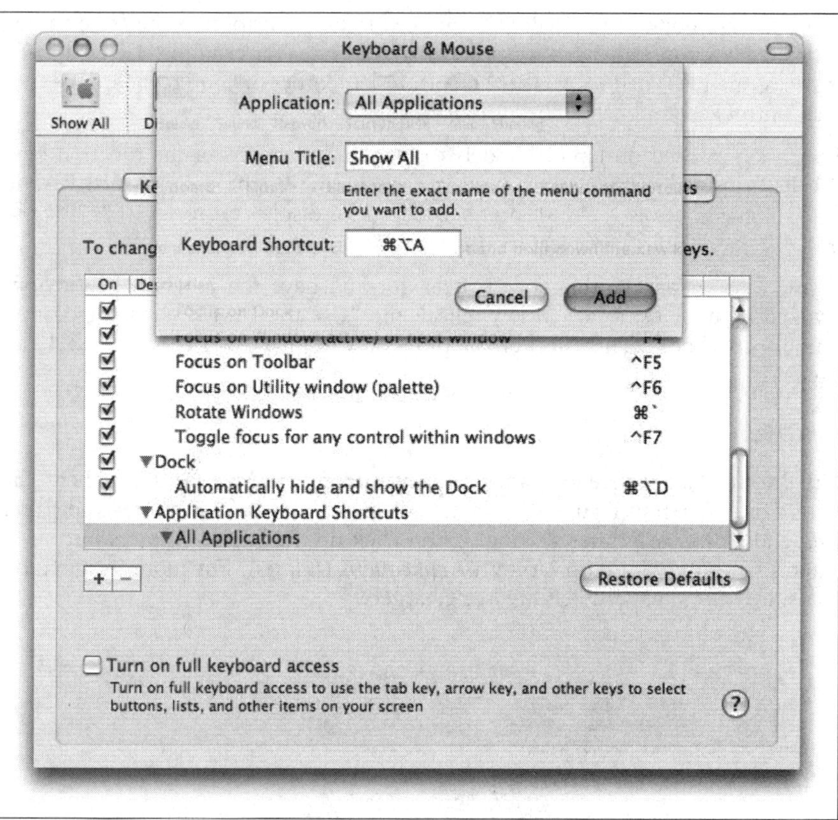

Figure 4-32. Click on the plus sign button (+) to add a keyboard shortcut and apply that to a specific or all applications on your Mac

Letter keys, or Custom keys instead of using the mouse. These key combinations and their functions are listed in Table 4-2.

Table 4-2. Keyboard access key combinations

Function keys	Letter keys	Description
Control-F1	Control-F1	Enable/disable keyboard access
Control-F2	m	Control the menu bar
Control-F3	d	Control the Dock
Control-F4	w	Activate the window or the window behind it
Control-F5	t	Control an application's toolbar
Control-F6	u	Control an application's utility window (or palette)
Control-F7	Control-F7	Used for windows and dialogs to highlight either text input fields and lists, or for any window control
Esc	Esc	Return control to the mouse, disabling the Control-*Fx* key combination
Spacebar	Spacebar	Perform the function of a mouse click

If you use an iBook or PowerBook, you need to use Control plus the *fn* key along with the Function or Letter key for keyboard access—for example, Control-fn-F2 to access menus. The *fn* key is at the bottom-left corner of your keyboard, next to the Control key (and below the Shift key).

The *fn* key is used on laptop models to invoke the actions of the function keys (F1–F12) instead of their other functions, including brightness controls (F1 and F2), volume controls (F3–F5), number lock (F6), display mirroring (F7), Exposé (F9–F11, by default), and eject (F12).

If you wish to reverse this default behavior and have the function key actions invoked without using the *fn* key, check the "Use the F1–F12 keys for custom actions" checkbox. (This checkbox appears only in Mac OS X Version 10.3.3 and later.)

Print & Fax

The Print & Fax preference panel is a new addition in Mac OS X Panther. The Print pane, shown in Figure 4-33, is used to select your default printer and paper size, and to enable printer sharing. If you click on the Set Up Printers button, it launches the Printer Setup Utility (*/Applications/Utilities*). For more information on using the Printer Setup Utility, see Chapter 9.

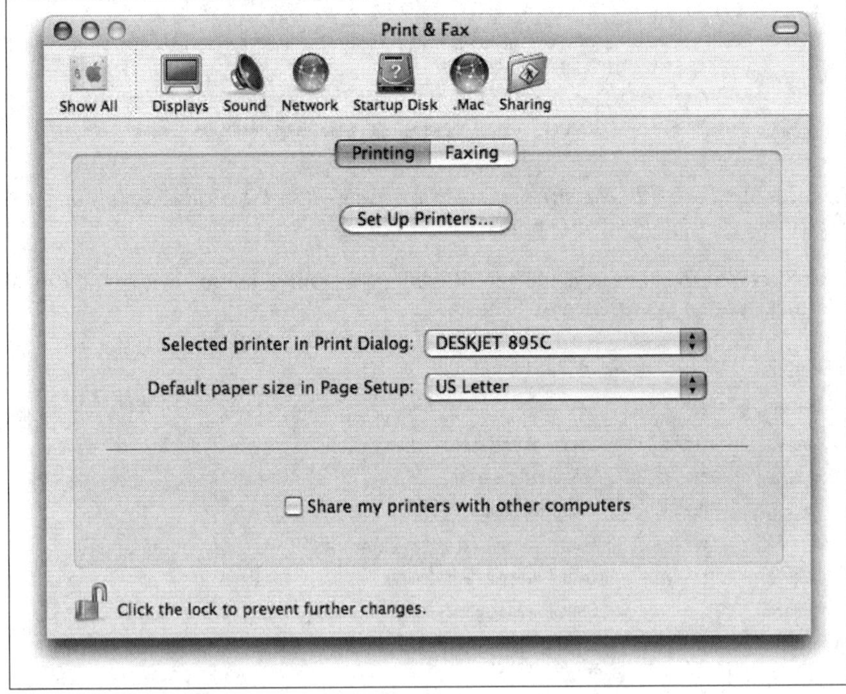

Figure 4-33. The Printing pane

If you have an internal modem, the Faxing pane, shown in Figure 4-34, is used to configure your Mac for sending and receiving faxes.

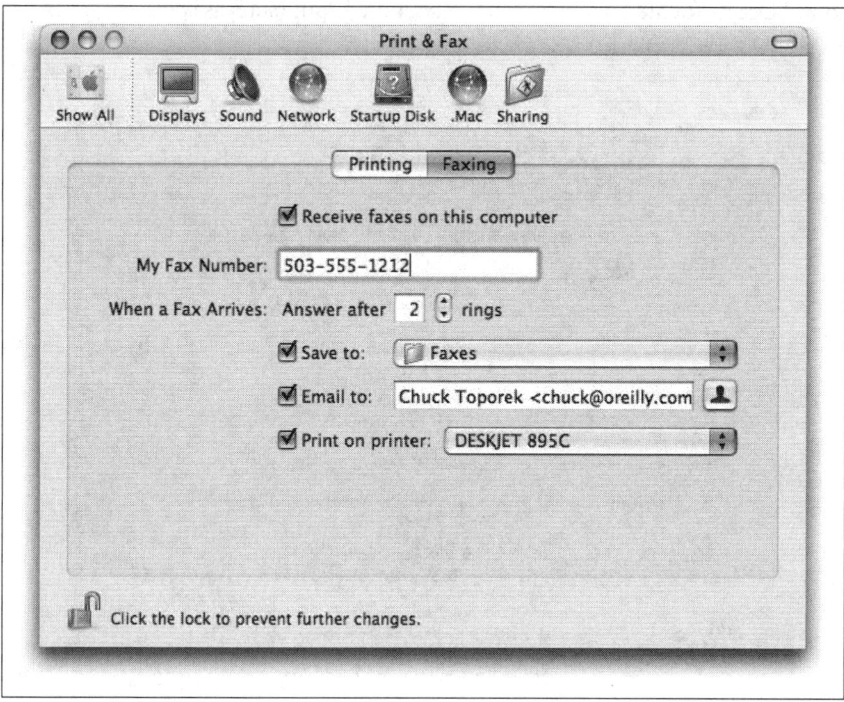

Figure 4-34. The Faxing pane

Here are some options you can configure on this pane:

- Your fax number (i.e., the number for the phone line you've plugged in to your modem port)
- What to do when a fax arrives, including:
  - The number of rings before your Mac answers the line to receive a fax
  - Where incoming faxes will be saved to (the default is the Faxes folder, located within your Home folder)
  - An option to redirect the incoming fax as an attachment via email
  - An option to print the fax automatically after it arrives

Incoming faxes are saved as PDF documents, with a filename that reflects the phone number from which it came (e.g., *Fax from 503 555 1212.pdf*). The only downside is that when a fax arrives, there is no way, by default, that the system alerts you to an incoming fax. To solve this oversight, you can download and install the Fax Alert script, created by Rainer Brockerhoff (*http://www.brockerhoff.net/fai/index.html*). Once installed, this Folder Action script pops open a dialog window to let you know when a fax is received in the folder you specify.

Sound

The Sound panel, shown in Figure 4-35, offers three panes: one for configuring Sound Effects (or alert sounds), one for sound Output (such as speakers), and one for sound Input.

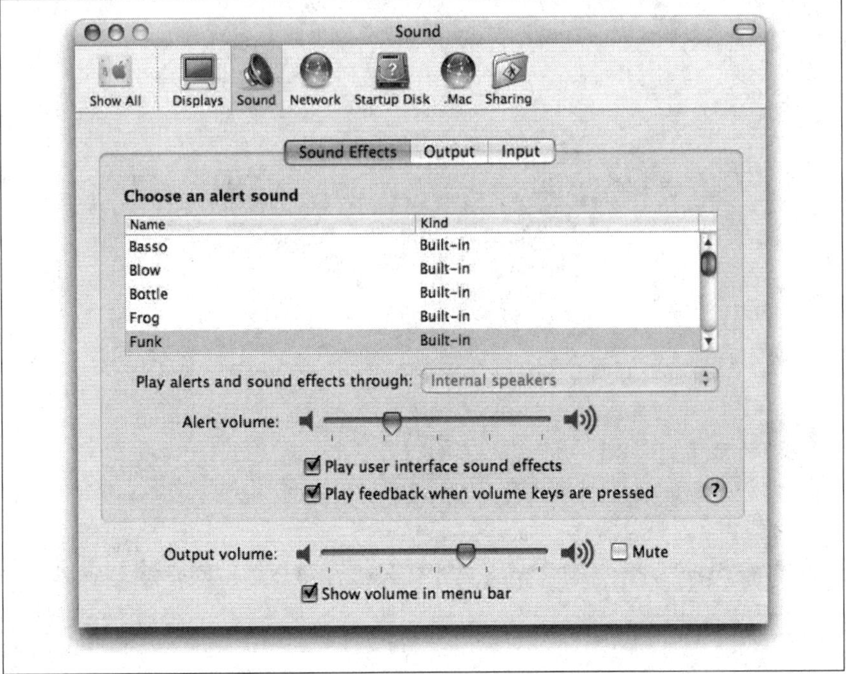

Figure 4-35. The Sound preferences panel

The three Sound preferences panes are described as follows:

Sound Effects
: The Sound Effects pane lets you select the alert sound your Mac emits when an error occurs. It also offers a slider control for setting the volume level for the alert sound.

Output
: The Output pane lets you choose a device for sound output (typically, the built-in audio controller) and includes a slider for controlling the left-right balance.

Input
: The Input pane lets you specify the sound input device, or microphone, for your computer. If you have a laptop, the internal microphone is selected by default. If you use an external microphone, you need to select the Line In option. You can even adjust the sound input level for an iSight camera from this panel as well.

All three panes include the same lower portion, with a slider control for setting your computer's Output volume. The volume you set here applies to all sound output, including system sounds and the audio content you play via iTunes. There is also a checkbox for enabling a sound volume slider as a menu extra in the menu bar. The number of "sound waves" in the menu extra's icon corresponds to the current system's volume setting.

All newer Macs have sound controls on the keyboard that allow you to decrease, increase, or mute the sound level. On laptops, you can use F3 to mute the sound, F4 to decrease it, and F5 to increase the output sound level. If you're using a Desktop system with an extended keyboard, the output sound controls are located across the top of the number pad.

If you hold down the Option key and press any of the sound controls on the keyboard, the System Preferences application will launch and open to the Sound preferences panel.

Bluetooth

Bluetooth is a short-range wireless technology for communicating with devices, such as cellular phones, PDAs, keyboards, mice, and other computers. The Bluetooth panel, has the following tabbed panes:

Settings
: This pane, shown in Figure 4-36, is used to control the settings for how your computer will be recognized via Bluetooth, whether authentication is required, if 128-bit encryption should be used for transmitting data over Bluetooth, and if your computer will support connections to older Bluetooth phones.

  This pane also tells you that the Bluetooth Device Name is the same as the Computer Name set up in the Sharing preferences and offers an option to place a Bluetooth menu extra in the menu bar.

File Exchange
: This pane, shown in Figure 4-37, is used to configure what to do with the files you receive via Bluetooth and where to store them.

Devices
: If there are any Bluetooth devices within range of your computer, and you're able to connect to them, they will appear in the Devices pane, as shown in Figure 4-38.

  To see detailed information about a device, click on the device name in the Bluetooth Devices box; information about the device is displayed in the box below. Click on the "Set Up New Device" button to configure a new Bluetooth device with your Mac. Likewise, click on the "Delete Pairing" button to unpair a device.

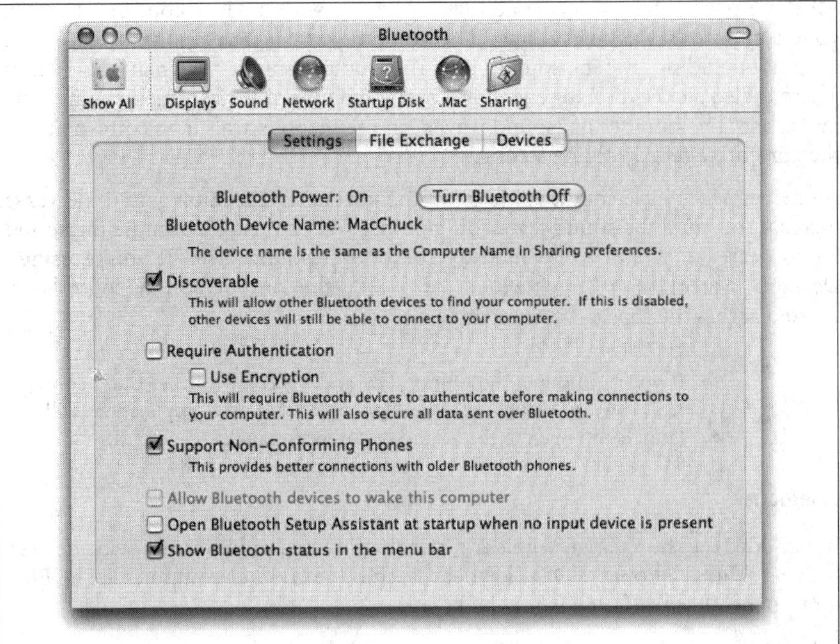

Figure 4-36. The Bluetooth Settings pane

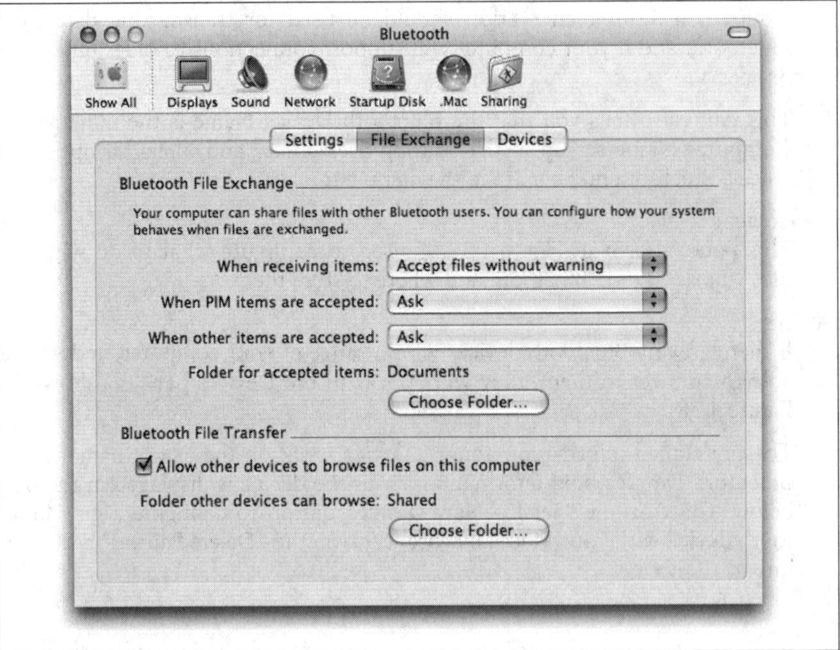

Figure 4-37. The Bluetooth File Exchange pane

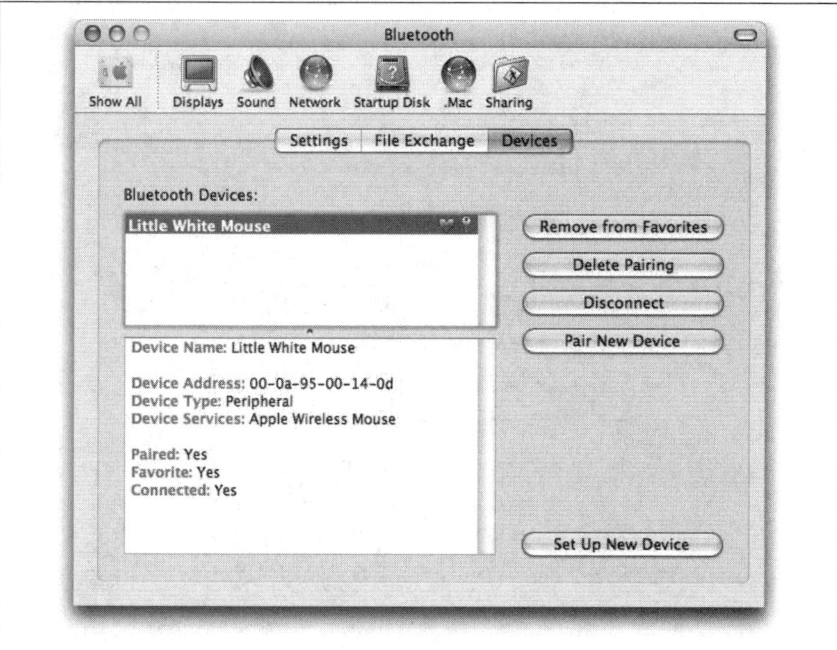

Figure 4-38. The Bluetooth Devices pane

Ink

One of the newer panels and features added to Mac OS X is an application called Inkwell, whose actions and controls are managed by the Ink preferences panel. Ink allows you to take input from a graphics pen and/or tablet (such as the Graphire 3 from Wacom), and either write directly into that application or to the InkPad, which is accessible through a small floating palette on your Desktop.

In order to use Ink (and Inkwell), you must first install the drivers and connect the tablet to your computer (typically via one of its USB ports).

At the top of Ink's panel is a radio button that allows you to turn handwriting recognition on or off. The three panels for Ink offer the following settings:

Settings
: The Settings pane, shown in Figure 4-39, is used to control how Inkwell will handle your handwriting. The panel has the following controls:

  My handwriting style is:
  : Here you have a slider control, which you can move left or right, depending on how closely or widely spaced your writing is, respectively.

  Allow me to write anywhere
  : If this option is checked, you can write anywhere onscreen into what looks like a yellow, lined sheet of paper, as well as to the InkPad, if you have that open. If unchecked, you can only write in the InkPad via its floating palette.

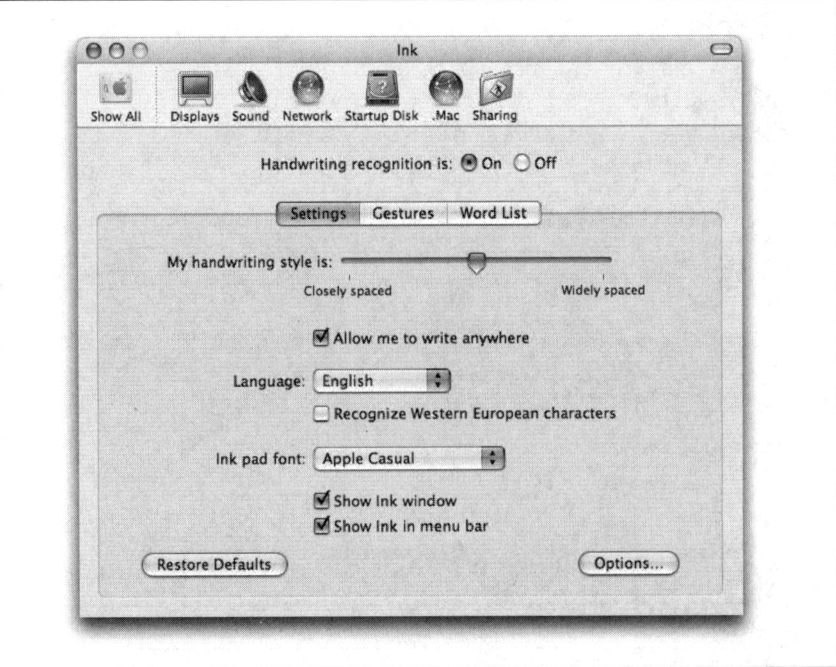

Figure 4-39. Ink's Settings pane

Language
: This pop-up menu lets you select the language that you will write with in InkPad; you can select from English, French, or German.

Recognize Western European characters
: When checked, this option allows you to use characters from languages such as Polish or Russian when using Ink.

Ink pad font:
: This menu lets you select the font to use when writing in the InkPad; the default is Apple Casual. (Next to this control is a checkbox, giving you the option to "Play sound while writing.")

Show Ink window
: When enabled, this option displays Ink's floating palette.

Show Ink in menu bar
: When enabled, this option places a menu extra for Ink in the menu bar, which has options for Write Anywhere, Hide Ink Window, and Ink Preferences (which opens Ink's preference panel).

Options...
: Clicking this button reveals a sheet that gives you finer control over how your handwriting is recognized.

When you first start using Ink, this panel will be your friend. Here you can set the delay for how quickly recognition begins after you've stopped writing, how far the pen must move before the writing begins, and how long the pen must be still to be used as a mouse. We strongly encourage you to play around with these settings to tune Ink to your writing style.

Gestures

The Gestures pane, shown in Figure 4-40, shows the handwriting gestures you can use to perform certain actions while writing, such as add a space, insert a carriage return (or "Vertical Space"), etc.

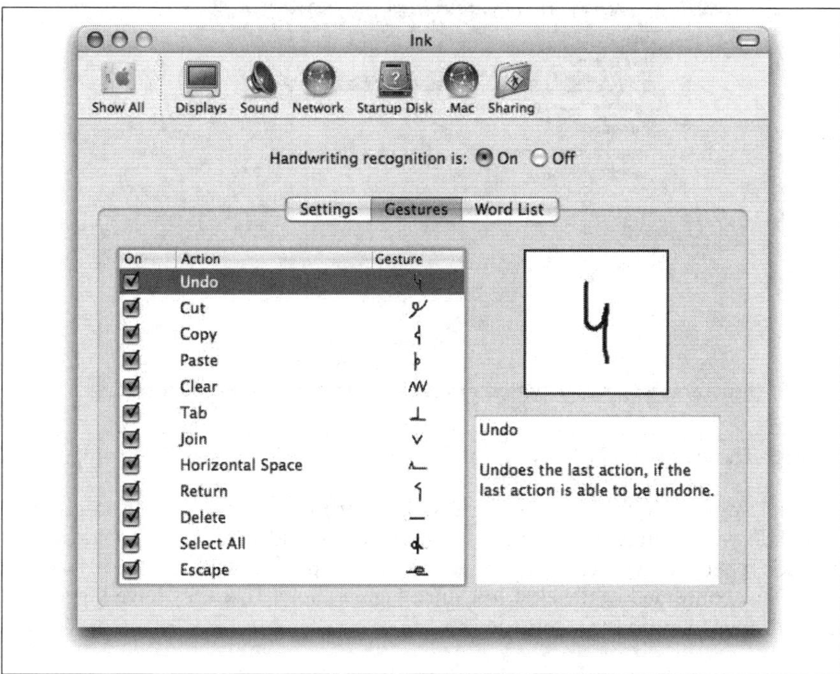

Figure 4-40. Ink's Gestures pane

When you click on an Action to the left, the gesture will be drawn in the little box to the right to show you how you should enter that gesture while writing.

If you plan to use Ink often, you might want to take a screenshot of the Gestures tab and keep that handy until you have memorized the gestures.

Word List

The Word List panel, shown in Figure 4-41, allows you to add common words to Ink's dictionary.

The button controls to the right of the text field are fairly self-explanatory; click Add to add a word, Edit to change the spelling of a word, Delete to remove a word, etc. If you try to add a word that's already in Ink's dictionary, you will be alerted as such.

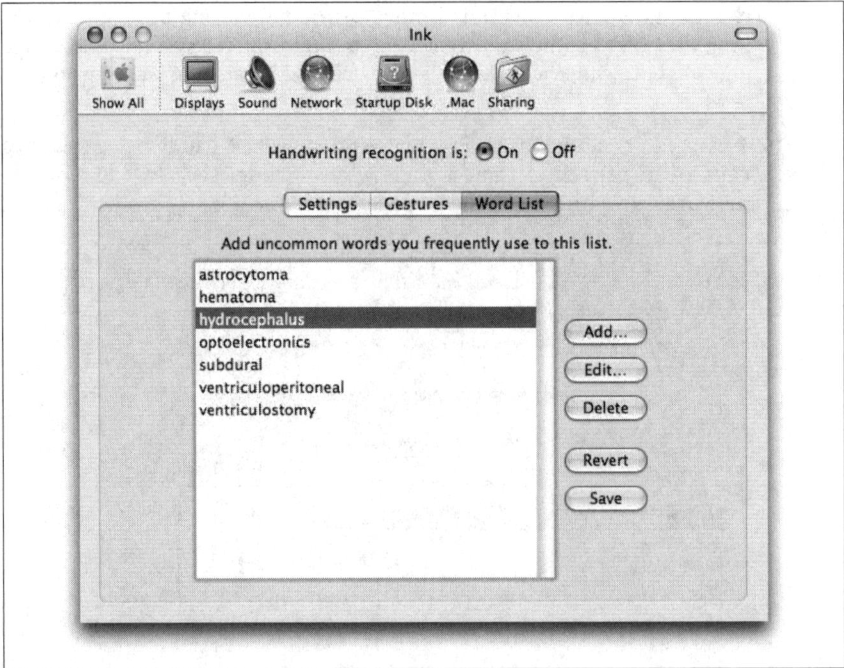

Figure 4-41. Ink's Word List pane

The only downside to Ink is that it's still a work in progress. For example, you can't add your own gestures to the Gestures panel, and while you can add words to Ink's repertoire, you can't add a gesture for them. That said, the mere fact that Apple has continued to develop Ink since Jaguar shows that they have bigger and better things in mind for it someday.

Internet & Network

Through these panes, users can set up and manage their .Mac accounts, set up their email account, select a default web browser, and configure how QuickTime handles incoming streaming media. System administrators can further use the Sharing panel to activate file sharing, web serving, and remote login services.

The standard set of panels in the Internet & Network section include:

- .Mac
- Network
- QuickTime
- Sharing

These panels are explained in the sections that follow.

.Mac

The .Mac panel is where to configure your settings for your .Mac account and the applications you use to access the Internet. There are two tabbed panes to this preference panel.

.Mac
: The .Mac panel, shown in Figure 4-42, is where to set up your .Mac account.

Figure 4-42. The .Mac pane

If you already have a .Mac account, you can just enter your .Mac member name and password; if you don't, you can sign up for a .Mac account by clicking on the Sign Up button.

.Mac is Apple's subscriber service, with an annual cost of $99 (US). To learn how to use the services included with a .Mac membership, see *Inside .Mac* (O'Reilly), or go to *http://www.mac.com*.

iDisk
: This pane, shown in Figure 4-43, gives you information about your iDisk, if you have a .Mac account.

  The top-half of the window shows how much space you've used on your iDisk. If you need more space and wish to purchase some, click on the Buy More button.

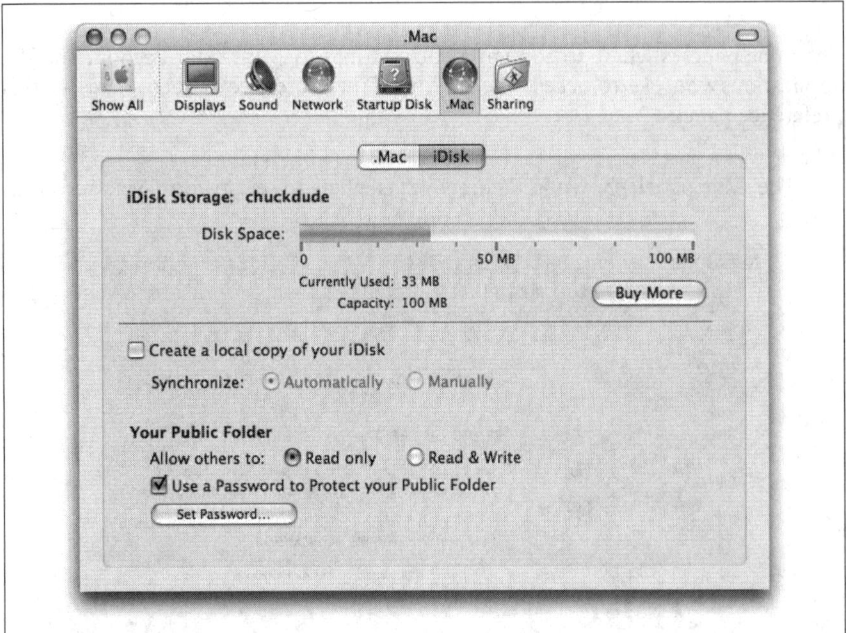

Figure 4-43. The iDisk pane

Clicking on the Buy More button takes you to .Mac's Upgrade storage page, where you can purchase additional space for your iDisk and your .Mac email account, and additional *mac.com* email-only accounts.

If you select the checkbox next to "Create a local copy of your iDisk," your iDisk will be mounted to your Mac, and a local copy will be created on your Desktop. Bare in mind, though, that you will need enough free hard-drive space to match the size of your iDisk (which is a minimum of 100 MB). You can also opt to synchronize your local iDisk either Automatically or Manually by selecting the appropriate radio button. If you select Automatically, the Finder will synchronize your iDisk with your local copy (and vice versa) any time a change is made. If you select Manually, you will need to click on the synchronize icon next to your iDisk in the upper portion of the Finder's Sidebar.

The lower portion of this window allows you to specify the permissions for your iDisk's Public folder. The three options for your Public folder include:

Read only
: Allows others to view and download the contents of your Public directory.

Read & Write
: Allows others to view, download, and save files to your Public directory.

Use a Password to Protect your Public Folder

Allows you to set a password for your Public folder, which means that anyone who tries to access your Public folder has to supply a password before they're given access. Note that the Read-Only and Read-Write options still apply, even if password protection is turned on.

Network

The Network panel, shown in Figure 4-44, is the interface to the Mac's basic network interfaces, including Ethernet, AirPort, and dialup modems. At least one of these interfaces has to be configured properly to get the Mac into a network environment or the Internet.

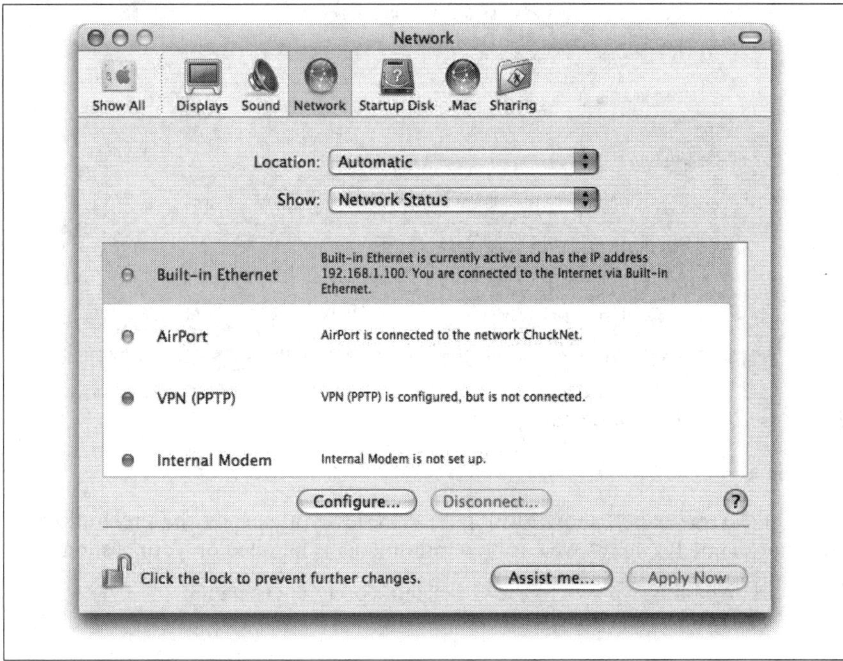

Figure 4-44. The Network preferences panel

A green dot to the left of a network interface means that the service is up and available; a red dot indicates that the service isn't in use or is unavailable. You will sometimes see a yellow dot appear as a network service, such as AirPort; it starts up by connecting from your laptop to a wireless base station. To view the detail about a network interface, double-clicking on an item in the list changes the window to reveal more options for configuring network settings, as shown in Figure 4-45.

The Network preferences panel is described in detail in Chapter 8.

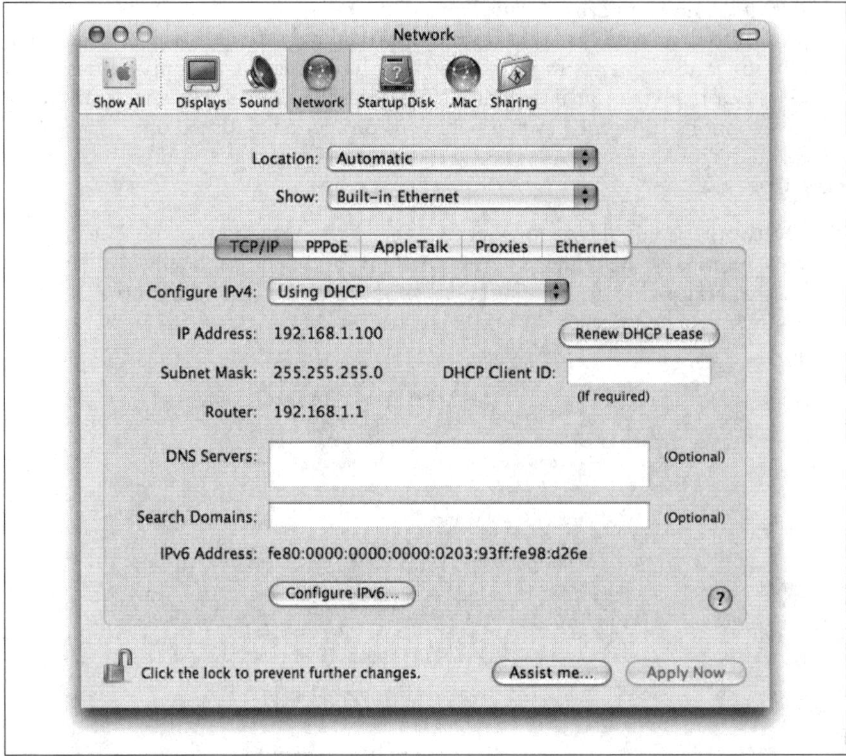

Figure 4-45. The Built-in Ethernet panel

QuickTime

The QuickTime panel, shown in Figure 4-46, lets you specify the preferences for the QuickTime Player, as well as how multimedia is handled on your system.

There are five tabbed panes to the QuickTime preferences panel:

Plug-In
: Configures the settings for the QuickTime plug-in for your web browser. Clicking on the MIME settings button reveals a sheet (shown in Figure 4-47) that changes how your browser will handle various file types, including streaming media, audio, MPEG movies, MP3 files, image files, and miscellaneous multimedia.

  To select all the types for a category, click on the checkbox so a check appears. If a category box has a minus sign in it, it means that one of the options inside is unchecked. To reveal all the file types for a category, click on the disclosure triangle.

Connection
: This is where you specify the speed of your network connection. Clicking on the Instant-On button reveals a sheet that lets you choose whether streaming media is played automatically as it starts to download, and if so, you can

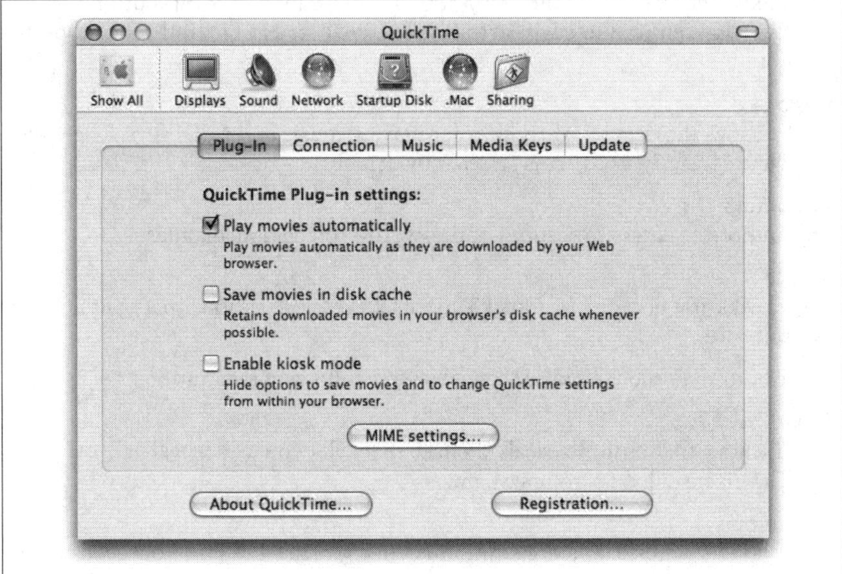

Figure 4-46. The QuickTime preferences panel

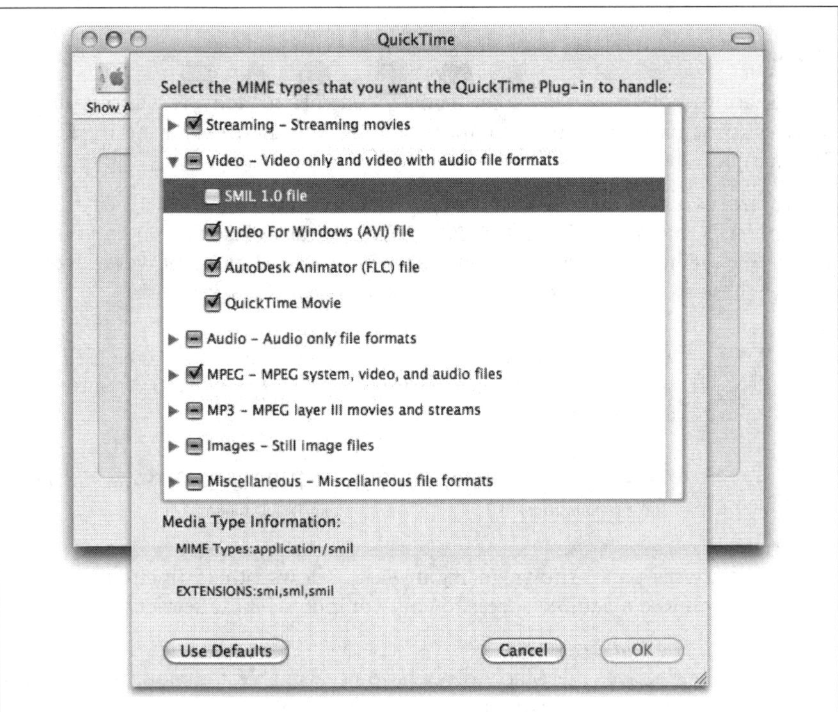

Figure 4-47. The QuickTime panel's MIME settings sheet

System Preferences

choose whether to set the delay period. The Transport Setup button reveals a sheet for setting the transport protocol (UDP or HTTP) and their respective ports.

Music
: Specifies the default synthesizer for playing music and MIDI files. The QuickTime Music Synthesizer is selected by default.

Media Keys
: Authorizes access to secured or password-protected media files.

Update
: Checks for updates to QuickTime itself, as well as third-party QuickTime software.

At the bottom of the QuickTime panel are the following two buttons:

About QuickTime
: Clicking this button reveals a sheet that tells you which version of QuickTime is installed on your system.

Registration
: If you've purchased a registration key for QuickTime Pro, you need to click on this button to enter your registration number. For more information about QuickTime Pro, see Apple's QuickTime web site (*http://www.apple.com/quicktime*).

Sharing

The Sharing panel provides some simple controls to activate various *network services* (programs that other computers can connect to over a network or the Internet).

There are two text fields at the top of the Sharing panel for specifying your Computer Name and Rendezvous Name. By default, these are set to your username (e.g., Chuck Toporek's Computer) after installation; however, you can change these to whatever you'd like (for instance, MacChuck).

> The name you specify in the Computer Name field will be used as your machine's hostname when your IP number does not resolve to a hostname in DNS.

In addition to these basic text fields, the Sharing panel has three tabbed panes, described as follows:

Services
: The Services pane, shown in Figure 4-48, allows others (including yourself from a remote machine) access to your computer. These services include:

  Personal File Sharing
  : When active, the Mac's disks become available for mounting on other machines over the network.

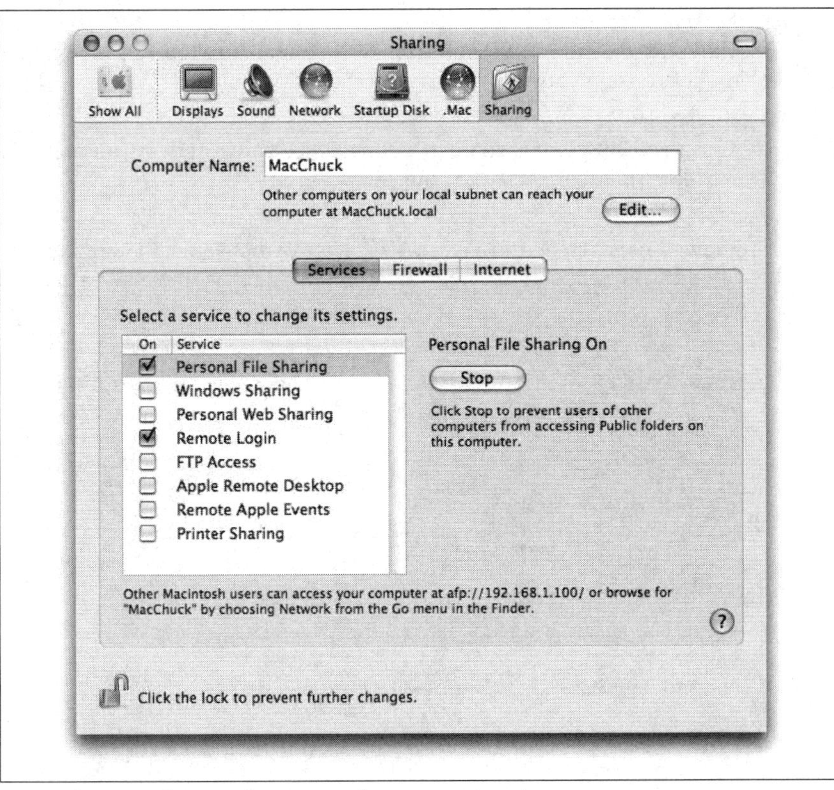

Figure 4-48. Configuring the Tomcat plug-in

Windows Sharing
: Lets you share folders on your computer with Windows users via SMB and CIFS.

Personal Web Sharing
: Turns on the Apache web server so people on the outside world can view web pages stored in your *~/Sites* directory.

Remote Login
: Controls *sshd*, which allows users to connect remotely to your Mac via the secure shell (SSH).

FTP Access
: Controls the machine's FTP server.

Apple Remote Desktop
: Allows others to access your Mac using Apple Remote Desktop (ARD). If you click on the Access Privileges button, you can specify which users can use ARD to access your Mac, as well as what they are allowed to do once connected. For example, if the "Control and observe" option is selected, an administrator can control your Mac remotely or watch what you are doing without your ever knowing.

Remote Apple Events

Allows applications on other Mac OS X systems to send Apple Events to applications on your system via AppleScript.

Printer Sharing

Activates USB printer sharing, letting other computers on the network use the printer connected to your Mac.

Firewall

The Firewall pane, shown in Figure 4-49, lets you activate and configure the firewall on your Mac. For more information on the Firewall pane, see Chapter 13.

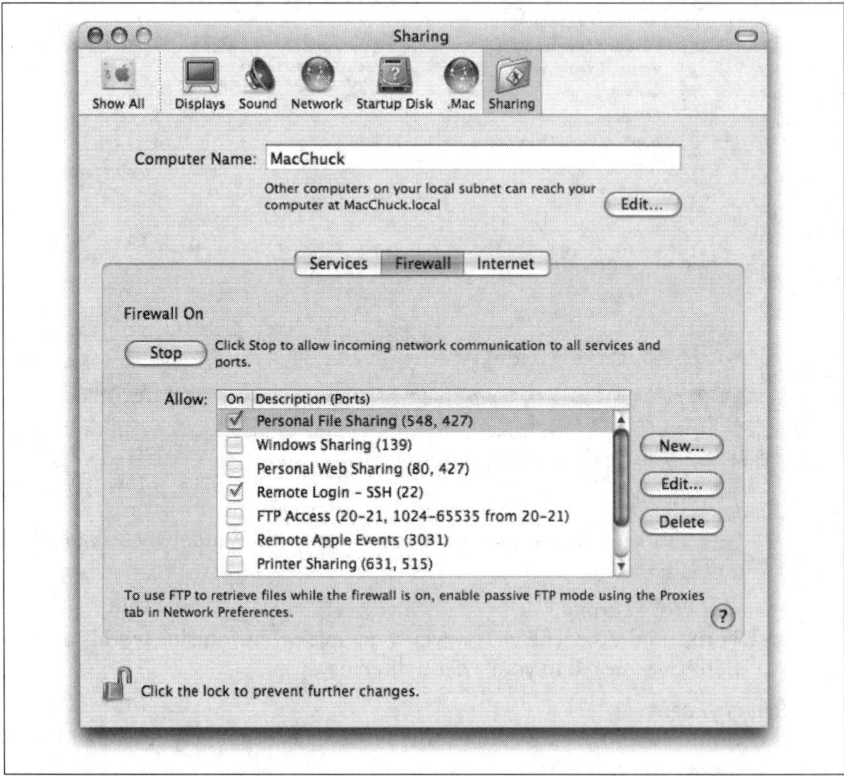

Figure 4-49. Sharing's Firewall pane

Internet

The Internet pane, shown in Figure 4-50, lets you share your Internet connection with other Macs on the same network, even via AirPort. Enabling Internet sharing lets you turn your Mac OS X machine into a router.

System

This final category of preinstalled preference panes lets system administrators manage the machine's user accounts, adjust the system clock, and set the Mac's

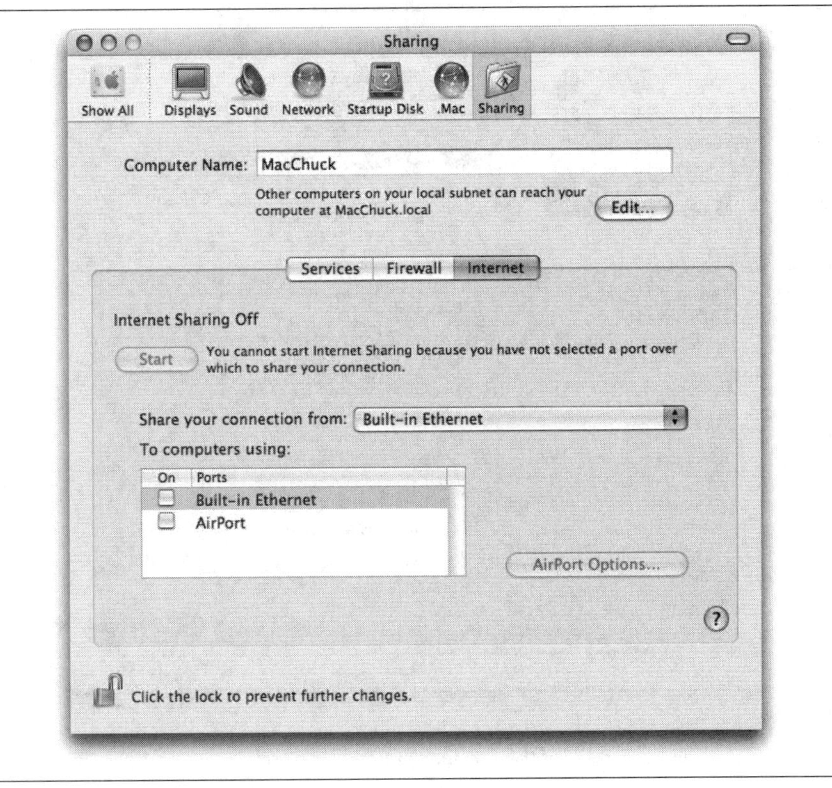

Figure 4-50. Sharing's Internet pane

startup disk. It also serves as the main interface for obtaining system software updates from Apple. Some of these panes involve systemwide settings, and require administrator privileges.

The standard set of panels in the System section include:

- Accounts
- Classic
- Date & Time
- Software Update
- Speech
- Startup Disk
- Universal Access

These panels are explained in the sections that follow.

Accounts

The Accounts panel, shown in Figure 4-51, lets users with administrator privileges create and delete users from the system, as well as manage user accounts.

Figure 4-51. The Users pane of the Accounts preferences panel

The column on the left displays the user accounts on the system, listing their full name and what type of user account they have. If a username has an orange circle with a checkmark inside next to their name, it means that the user is logged in to the system.

There are four types of user accounts on Mac OS X Panther: Admin, Standard, Managed, or Simplified. The user type is determined by how the account is configured in the Security or Limitations panes:

- Admin users are allowed to do pretty much anything they want on the system, as long as they provide the proper administrator's password when prompted. You can grant a user Admin privileges by selecting the checkbox next to "Allow user to administer this computer" near the bottom of the Security pane.
- Standard users are restricted somewhat from installing and updating the system software, as well as from changing vital settings on their system. Standard users have the No Limits button selected in the Limitations pane.
- Managed users have the Some Limits button selected in the Limitations pane, and may be restricted from performing certain tasks, such as burning CDs and DVDs, or using certain applications and utilities.
- Simplified users have the Simple Finder button selected in the Limitations pane, and are at the bottom of the rung among the class of users. They are

restricted from every angle; they can't use all of the System Preferences and can use only the applications found in a My Applications folder in the Dock.

If you are an Admin user, you can't alter the settings for another user account while that user is logged in.

To add a new user account on the system, click on the plus sign button (+) at the bottom of the accounts column on the left. To delete a user account from the system, select the username in the Accounts column, and click on the minus sign button (–). When deleting a user account from the system, you have two options: you can opt to immediately delete the user account and all the information in her Home directory or you can package the contents of her Home directory and place it in */Users/Deleted Users*.

When a user is logged in, there are four tabbed panes he can select from to alter and change settings for his account:

Password
: This panel, shown in Figure 4-51, lists the user's full name, short name, password, and password hint.

Picture
: This pane lets users select a picture that will be associated with the user account in the Login window; this picture is also attached to any emails they send with the Mail application. Users can select a picture from the collection Apple provides (stored in */Library/User Pictures*), or they can select one of their own by clicking on the Edit button.

Security
: This pane lets users change the Master Password for the computer (if they have administrator privileges) and turn FileVault protection on or off for their Home directory.

Startup Items
: This pane lets users select applications to automatically launch at startup. For Mac OS 9 users, the Startup Items pane is similar to dragging an application alias to the */System Folder/Startup Items* folder.

: The interface for the Startup Items pane is fairly self-explanatory. To add an item to launch or mount upon startup, you can drag an item from the Finder or click the plus sign button (+). To remove an item, select it with the mouse and click on the minus sign button (–). You can also specify the order in which the items will launch by dragging them up or down in the listing.

Clicking on the Login Options button at the bottom of the Accounts column on the left lets you manage login options for a multiuser Mac OS X system. The Login Options pane, shown in Figure 4-52, has the following options:

Display Login Window as:
: If you select "List of users," users will see a list of the users for that system. All they need to do to log in is click on their name, enter their password, and

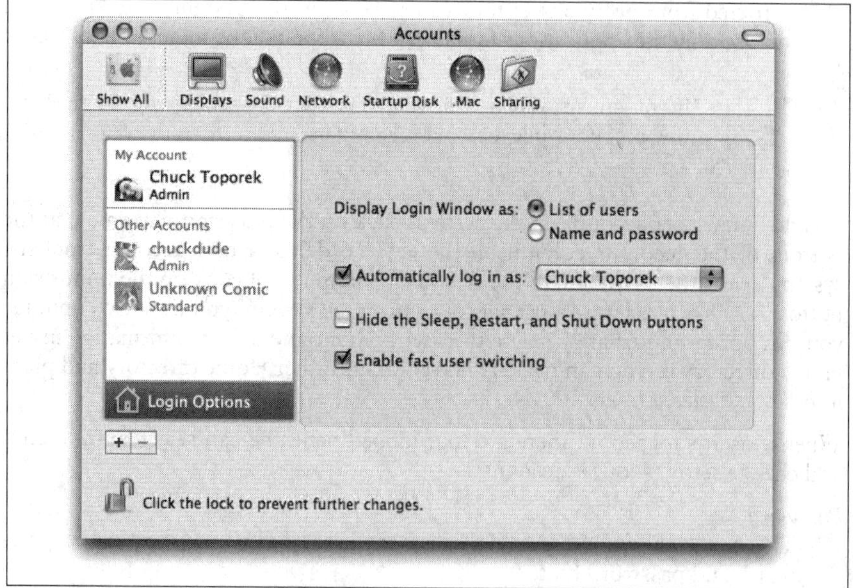

Figure 4-52. The Login Options pane

press Return. If you select "Name and password," users will be required to enter their username and password before they can log in.

Automatically log in as:
: If the checkbox next to this item is selected, the user whose name is selected in the pop-up menu is automatically logged in when the system starts up.

Hide the Sleep, Restart, and Shut Down buttons
: If this item is selected, these buttons will not show up in the login window.

Enable fast user switching
: If enabled, this option places the Accounts menu at the far right edge of the menu bar, which allows multiple users to log in to the same system without requiring another user to log off.

If your Mac supports Quartz Extreme, you will see the cube effect as you switch from one user's Desktop to another; see Figure 10-5.

Classic

The Classic panel lets you manually start, stop, and configure the Classic environment that runs Mac OS 9 applications within Mac OS X. Use of the Classic panel is described in Chapter 3.

Date & Time

If you have administrator privileges, the Date & Time panel, shown in Figure 4-53, lets you set the system clock and time zone, as well as select an NTP (Network Time Protocol) server.

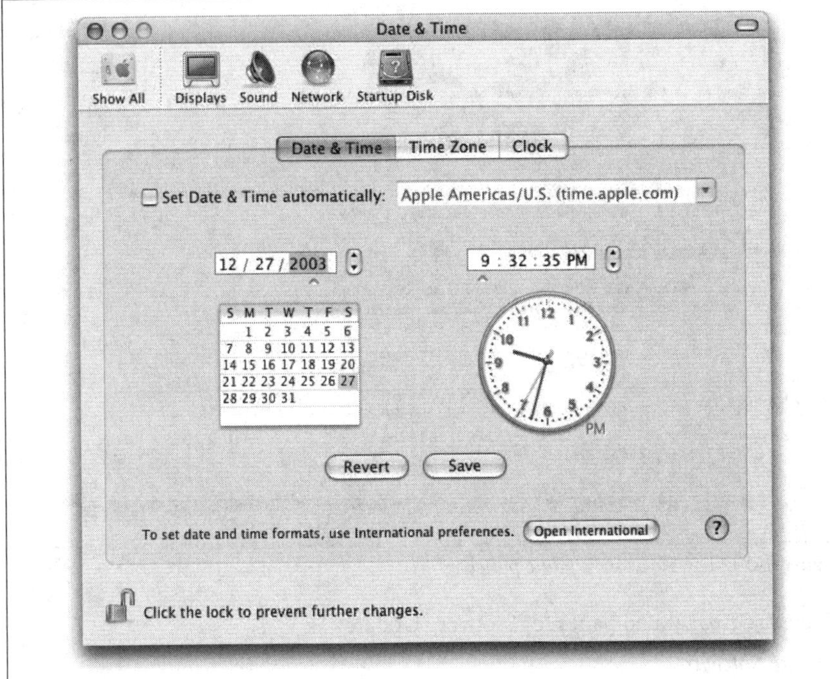

Figure 4-53. The Date & Time preferences panel

The Date & Time panel has four tabbed panes, described as follows:

Date & Time
: The Date & Time pane is where you set the date and time for your system. If you select the checkbox next to "Set Date & Time automatically," you can use an NTP server to automatically set the date and time of your computer if it is connected to the Internet.

Time Zone
: The Time Zone pane provides you with a map of the continent you live in so you can select your time zone, either from the pull-down menu or by dragging the time-zone bar left or right.

Clock
: The Clock pane lets you determine whether the date and time will show up in the menu bar, as well as the manner they appear there. You can also opt to have your computer announce the time for you on the hour, half hour, and quarter hour.

Software Update

The Software Update panel, shown in Figure 4-54, lets you contact servers at Apple to check for updates to Mac OS X system software, updates to security, and updates to the iApps.

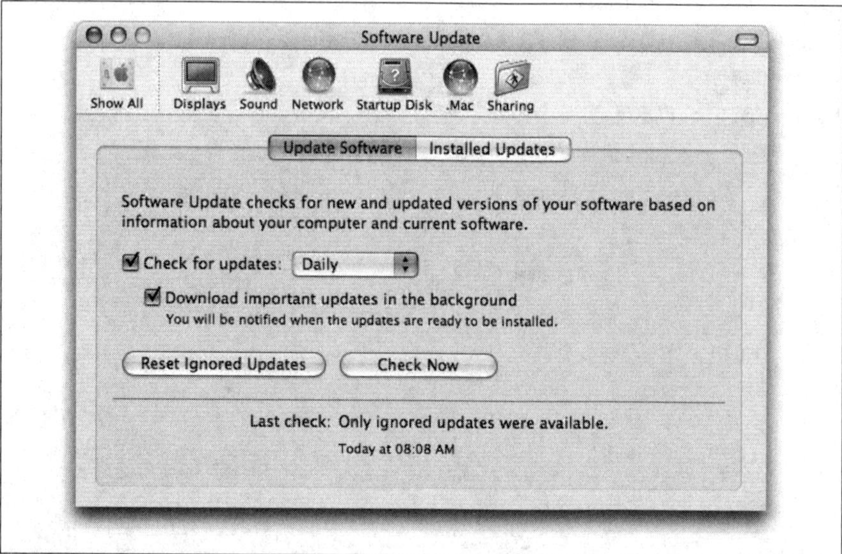

Figure 4-54. The Software Update panel

There are two tabbed panes for Software Update:

Update Software
: The Update Software pane checks for updates and configures your system to automatically check for updates (Daily, Weekly, or Monthly) when your system is connected to the Internet, and also to automatically download important updates (such as security patches) in the background. To check for available updates, click on the Check Now button.

Installed Updates
: The Installed Updates pane lists the updates you've installed on your system. This list is stored in */Library/Logs/Software Update.log*. You can view the *Software Update.log* file by clicking on the Open as Log File button, which opens the log file in the Console application (*/Applications/Utilities*).

If Software Update detects an available update when you click on the Check Now button, a separate window pops up that shows the available updates (see Figure 4-55). To find more information about the update, click on its name; its description will appear in the text field below the listing of updates.

To install an available update, select the checkbox next to the package and click on the Install button (administrator privileges are required for most updates). Some other tips for using Software Update include the following:

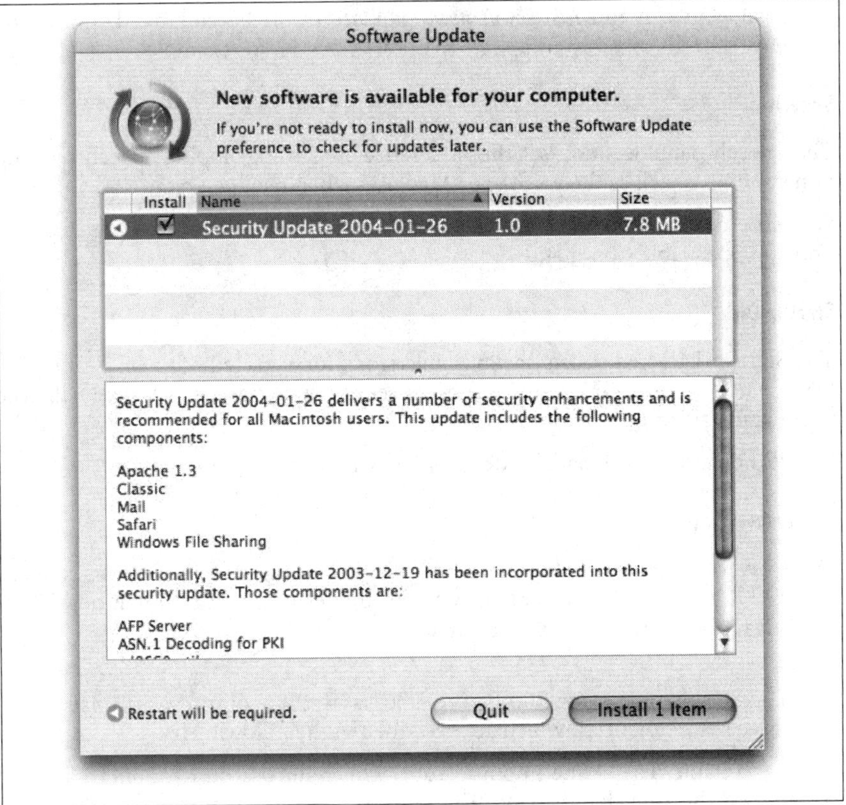

Figure 4-55. Software Update's window lists available updates

- If there is an update you want to install at a later time, unselect its checkbox and install the other updates (or quit Software Update with ⌘-Q). The next time you run Software Update, the update you deferred will show up as an available update.
- If there is an update that you feel you will never install, such as a foreign language update, click on the update's name and choose Update→Make Inactive. The next time Software Update is run, that update won't appear in the list of available updates. However, if you decide later that you do want to install it, you can do so by selecting Update→Make Active.
- To view a list of Inactive updates, go to Update→Show Inactive Updates.
- To save an update rather than install it (say, for archive purposes), place a checkmark in the box next to the update and then select Update→Download checked items to Desktop.
- Apple maintains a listing of available updates for Mac OS X on their web site, *http://www.apple.com/downloads/macosx/apple*.
- You can tell Software Update to immediately check for updates by holding down the Option key as you click its icon in the System Preferences window.

Also, you can run */usr/sbin/softwareupdate* from the command line if you have a need (to apply an update remotely via SSH, for example).

Speech

The Speech panel lets you set the preferences regarding Apple's speech recognition system, as well as the voice your Mac uses when reading text to you.

For more details about the Speech panel, see the later section "Speech Recognition and Speakable Commands."

Startup Disk

The Startup Disk panel lists the available icons for detected Mac OS X and Mac OS 9 system folders. This panel is used to select which operating system will boot when you start or restart your Mac.

Use of the Startup Disk panel is described in Chapter 3.

Universal Access

The Universal Access panel lets you activate and configure many options to make Mac OS X easier to use by persons with disabilities or physical limitations. There are four tabbed panes, described as follows:

Seeing

The Seeing pane, shown in Figure 4-56, is used to control the display. It has three main functions, which are described in the following list.

- Enable/disable the Zoom feature, which allows you to zoom in and out of the viewable display. When Zoom is enabled, clicking on the Zoom Options button gives you more control over the Zoom feature. There are slider controls for specifying the maximum and minimum zoom range, a checkbox for adding a preview rectangle to the display as a target area for zooming in, and an option for smoothing images.

  The size of the preview rectangle is based on the Maximum Zoom setting, and takes the shape of your display. If you enable the preview rectangle, your mouse pointer is placed at the rectangle's center. When you zoom in, the area defined by the preview rectangle is the focus of the display. The keyboard shortcuts for Zoom are shown in Table 4-3.

  Table 4-3. Keyboard shortcuts for using Zoom

Keyboard shortcut	Description
Option-⌘-8	Toggle Zoom on/off
Option-⌘-=	Zoom in
Option-⌘-–	Zoom out
Option-⌘-\	Toggle display smoothing on/off

- Switch the screen mode to White on Black, and vice versa (essentially giving the user a view that looks similar to a black-and-white film negative).

- Set the display to grayscale (clicking the button a second time returns your display to full-color mode).
- Increase or decrease the contrast of the display. Keyboard shortcuts for changing the contrast are Control-Option-⌘-. to increase the contrast, and Control-Option-⌘-, to decrease the contrast.

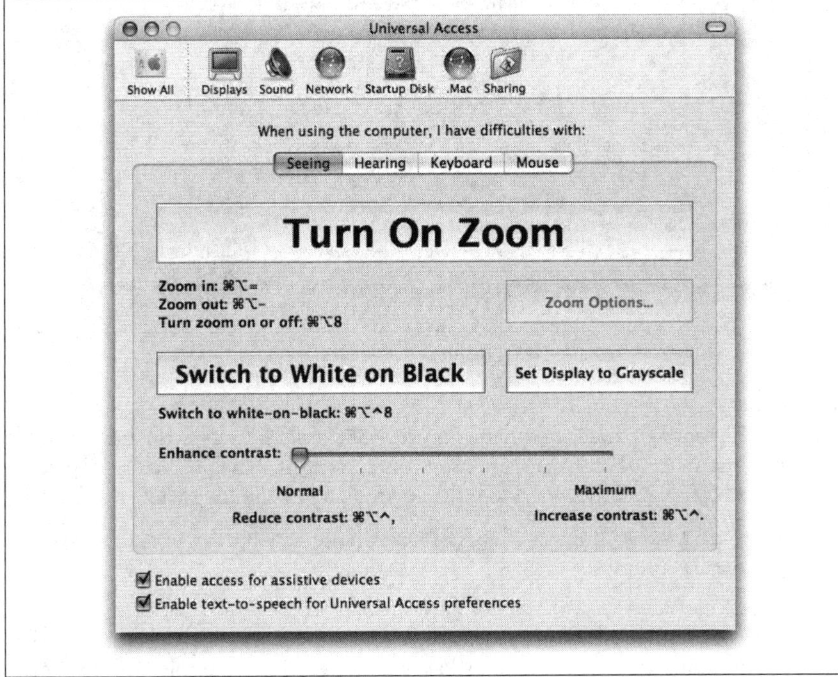

Figure 4-56. Universal Access's Seeing pane

Hearing

The Hearing pane, shown in Figure 4-57, offers a checkbox that, when activated, causes the screen to flash (with a single white pulse) instead of playing an alert sound.

Starting with Mac OS X 10.2.*x*, the display flashes (regardless of this setting) if the system tries to play an alert sound and the sound is muted, or if there is no sound output device connected to the Mac.

Clicking the Adjust Volume button changes the System Preferences window to the Sound panel, described earlier in this chapter in the "Hardware" section.

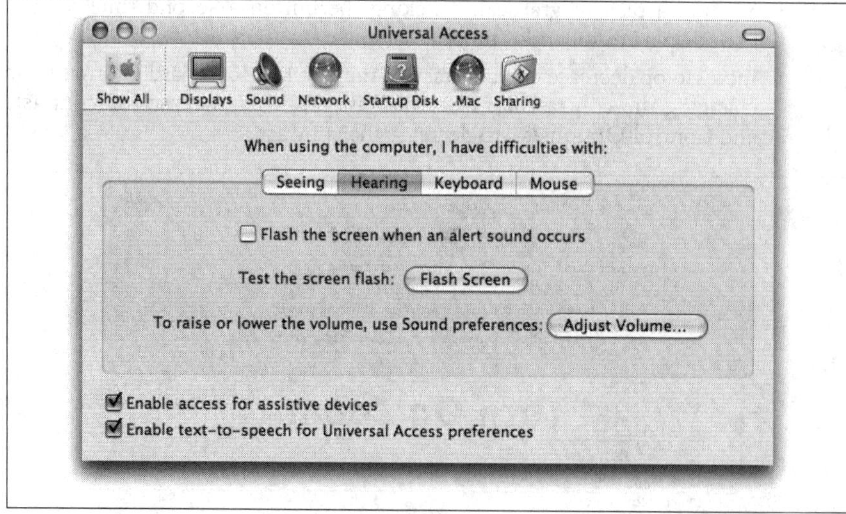

Figure 4-57. Universal Access's Hearing pane

Keyboard

The Keyboard pane, shown in Figure 4-58, assists users who have trouble pressing more than one key at a time, and/or have difficulty repeating keystrokes (e.g., if they tend to hold down on a key too long while pressing it).

There are two sections to the Keyboard pane: Sticky Keys and Slow Keys, described as follows:

Sticky Keys

Switching on the Sticky Keys radio button causes Mac OS X to treat key combinations as individual key sequences. For example, the keyboard shortcut Option-⌘-W closes all open windows for an application. Typically, these keys are pressed together, or you can hold down Option-⌘ and then press W. However, with Sticky Keys enabled, you can press these keys one at a time to invoke the command.

If you press a modifier key (Control, Shift, Option, or Command) twice, the key will be *super-sticky*, so that it remains active after you issue a key combination. This is useful when you want to use the same modifier key but invoke a different command; for example, when using Word, you might want to make some text bold (⌘-B) and italic (⌘-I). Typing a modifier key three times removes it from the current key combination's list of modifier keys. If you remove all the modifier keys from the combination you are constructing, the keyboard returns to its usual typing mode.

Slow Keys

These controls are an addendum to those found in the Keyboard & Mouse preferences panel (see the earlier section "Hardware"). If you enable Slow Keys, the slider lets you set a delay between key presses.

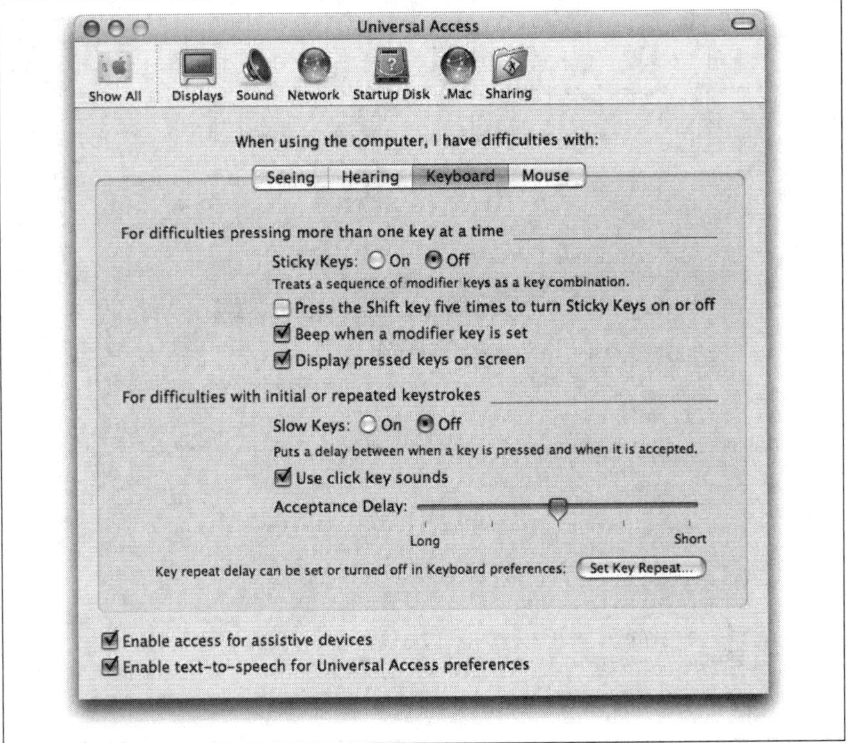

Figure 4-58. Universal Access's Keyboard pane

Using this feature along with the Keyboard preferences panel can reduce accidental letter repetition while typing.

Pressing the Set Key Repeat button opens the Keyboard preferences panel. In earlier versions of Mac OS X, this button was the only control available for Slow Keys.

Mouse

If you have trouble using the mouse, you can enable Mouse Keys via the Mouse pane (shown in Figure 4-59). Mouse Keys allows you to use your keyboard's number pad instead of the mouse.

By holding down the number keys as detailed in Table 4-4, you can move the mouse pointer in eight different directions, and use the 5 and 0 (zero) keys as the mouse button. (Conversely, the keypad ceases to function as a device for typing numbers; you need to turn off Mouse Keys to enter numbers.)

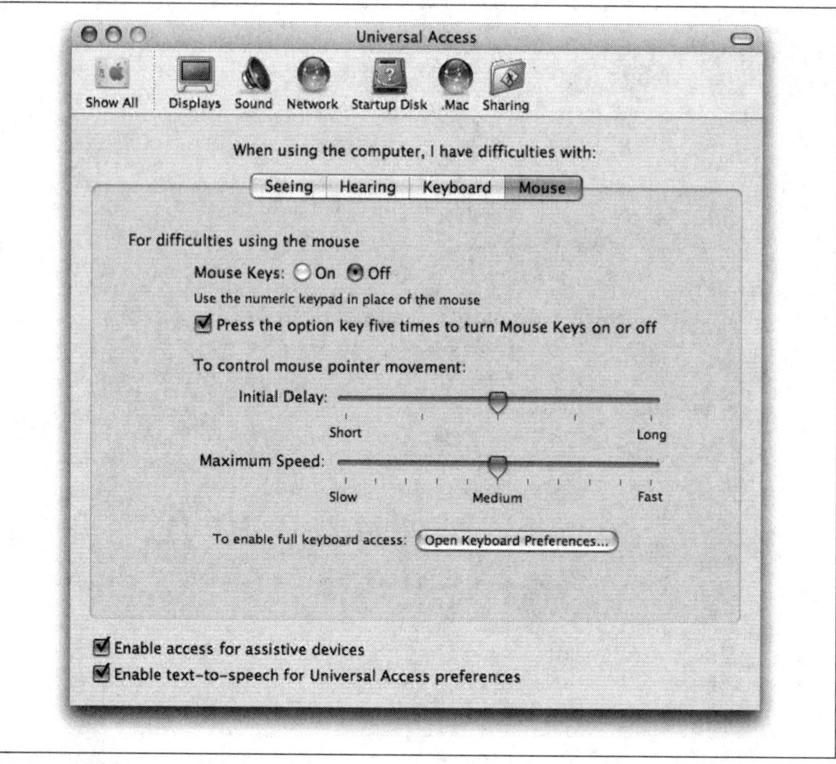

Figure 4-59. Universal Access's Mouse pane

Table 4-4. Mouse Keys numeric mouse controls

Number key	Action
1	Move pointer down and to the left
2	Move pointer down
3	Move pointer down and to the right
4	Move pointer left
5	Mouse click
6	Move pointer right
7	Move pointer up and to the left
8	Move pointer up
9	Move pointer up and to the right
0	Mouse click

Mouse Keys can come in handy if the Mac's mouse breaks or goes missing. You may want to select the checkbox next to "Press the option key five times to turn Mouse Keys on or off", even if you don't normally use the Universal Access options regularly.

Speech Recognition and Speakable Commands

Mac OS X's built-in speech recognition software lets you execute various system and application commands by speaking them (assuming you have a microphone attached to or built into your Macintosh). The system includes many commands. Application developers can also define spoken commands that work within their own programs, and users can expand the machine's speakable repertoire by writing and installing scripts.

The speech recognition system is primarily useful for defining voice-activated macros and shortcuts. It doesn't let you use your microphone as a complete alternative to the keyboard and mouse. The system can't, for example, take dictation into a word processor. For that level of functionality, you need a third-party application, such as IBM's ViaVoice (*http://www.ibm.com/software/speech/mac/osx/*).

Activating Speech Recognition

You can configure and activate the speech recognition through the three tabbed panes of the Speech preferences panel, shown in Figure 4-60.

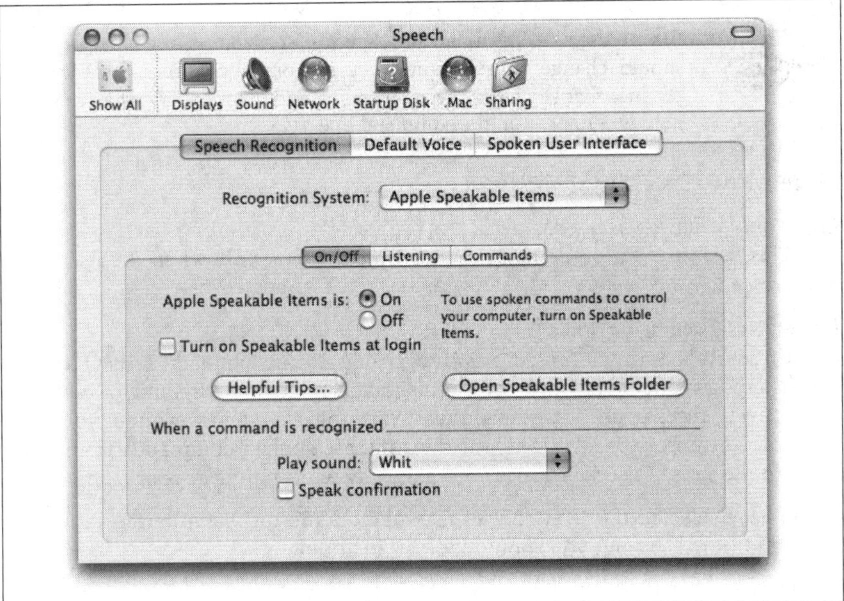

Figure 4-60. The Speech preference panel, showing the Speech Recognition pane

To turn speech recognition on, set the "Apple Speakable Items is" radio button to On. This causes the speech systems' round "listener" window (Figure 4-61) to appear. Note that the listener floats over all your active windows, but you can drag it anywhere you like. It remains visible until you switch the Apple Speakable Items button back to Off.

Figure 4-61. Speech's microphone

The system doesn't try listening for commands until you put it into listening mode via the Speech panels' Speech Recognition→Listening tab. By default, the listening key is set to Esc (the Escape key). Until you press the Esc key, the microphone is grayed out; however, when the Esc key is pressed, the listener looks similar to Figure 4-61, complete with a sound input indicator (the blue-, green-, and red-colored bars) and indicator arrows showing that sound is being received by the microphone. If you don't want to have the Esc key as the default key for listening, click on the Change Key button and enter a new key or key combination (e.g., ⌘-Esc).

If you use the Terminal and Speech Recognition together, you should change your listening key to something other than Esc because that key has a special meaning and functionality when running programs from the command line.

There are two Listening Methods:

Listen only while key is pressed
: This setting is an on-demand mode, which listens only when the Esc key is pressed.

Key toggles listening on and off
: Under this setting, pressing and releasing the listening key (Esc) toggles listening mode on or off. Because this means the computer's microphone will actively receive and analyze sounds over longer stretches of time, you must set two more controls to help it discriminate spoken commands from background noise (or other things you might say while sitting at your computer).

If you have selected the "Key toggles listening on and off" radio button, there are some additional settings you should look at, including:

Name
: By default, this is set to the *Star Trek*-esque Computer, which means you must first say "Computer, ..." before issuing a spoken command. You can change the Name; however, you should choose a name that's easy to say and unlikely to appear in any conversation your Mac might overhear.

Name is
: This pop-up menu defines how the computer differentiates spoken commands from other sounds. Here are the options in this menu:

Optional before commands

When this setting is selected, the machine doesn't listen for its Name and tries to interpret everything it hears as a potential command. For example, in order to check your mail and then switch to iTunes, you only need to say, "Get my mail. Switch to iTunes."

This setting is actually rather dangerous because if you are in listening mode, anything you say that the computer hears can be interpreted as a command.

Required before each command (the default)

This setting has the speech system listen for the name defined in the Name field before interpreting every command. For example, to hear a knock-knock joke, you could say "Computer, tell me a joke." (If you try this, remember that you need to say "Computer, ..." before each step of the joke. For example, "Computer, who's there?" and "Computer, Thea who?")

Required 15 seconds after last command
Required 30 seconds after last command

These settings also require that you speak the Name that you chose in the Name text field. Once you have said it, however, the machine will continue to interpret sounds as possible commands until either 15 or 30 seconds have elapsed without recognizing a command. Thus, you can launch multiple commands like this: "Computer, get my mail. Switch to iTunes."

The last two items at the bottom of the Listening pane allow you to specify which microphone to use (Line In or Internal microphone) and to set the volume for the microphone's input. Pressing the Volume button pops open a window that lets you test and adjust the volume level by having you say some sample commands.

Speakable Items

To see which commands are available to you at any time, click on the triangle at the bottom of the listener window, as shown in Figure 4-62.

Figure 4-62. Clicking on the listener's triangle opens its context menu

The Speech Commands window, shown in Figure 4-63, has two parts:

- The top section shows a log of the speech commands issued.
- A Commands section (at the bottom of the window), which shows a list of available commands, collapsed into categories with disclosure triangles to reveal the speakable commands.

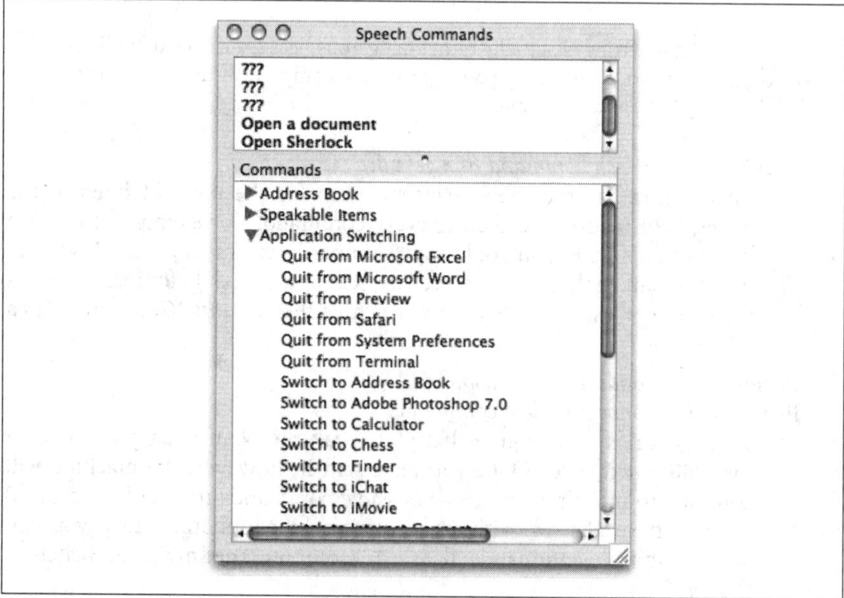

Figure 4-63. The Speech Commands window

By default, there are two categories in the Commands section:

Speakable Items
: This is a catch-all category for commands you can invoke throughout the system.

Application Switching
: This lists the special commands for switching (and launching) between applications, based on the application icons in the Dock.

Applications such as the Finder, Mail, and Safari define their own speakable items when they are the active (i.e., front-most) application. When that application is active, its list of speakable items shows up in the Commands section.

Customizing Speakable Items

If you click on the Open Speakable Items Folder button located on the Speech→Speech Recognition→On/Off pane, a Finder window pops open, listing the speakable items on your system. The speakable items available exist as files in *~/Library/Speech/Speakable Items*. Files residing within that folder directly represent systemwide items. Those inside the Application Speakable Items folder are specific to various applications on your system.

Each speakable item can either be a property list (*.plist*) file, an AppleScript, or some other type of Finder object. Property lists simply execute the commands predefined by the system or speech-friendly application. AppleScripts are executed by the system.

In other words, users can make their own voice-activated commands by writing (or finding on the Internet) an AppleScript that performs a particular task or series of tasks, giving that script a pronounceable name. The AppleScript can then be placed into the *~/Library/Speech/Speakable Items* directory.

Finally, any other Finder object—arbitrary files, folders, disks, or aliases to one of these—acts as if it was double-clicked in the Finder when its name is spoken.

Adding Panes to System Preferences

Preference panes are really just slimmed-down Mac OS X applications, and as such, can be installed from a source disk (or a freshly downloaded disk image) to your local hard drive with a simple drag-and-drop procedure (see Chapter 5). They can even be launched like other applications; double-clicking a *.prefPane* file's icon while in the Finder causes it to open within System Preferences (launching that application first, if it wasn't already running). However, the System Preferences application won't display preference panes' icons as part of its main view (Figure 4-1) unless you add them into one of the filesystem's Library folders.

Placing a *.prefPane* file in the *~/Library/PreferencePanes* folder located within your own Home folder causes it to appear listed among the System Preferences' pane icons for you alone. If you want to let all users of the machine use the pane (and you have admin privileges), you can place it in */Library/PreferencePanes*. (Note that this shares only the interface; unless the pane explicitly sets systemwide preferences, it will read from and write to only the appropriate preference file within the */Library* folder of any user who uses it.)

5 Applications and Utilities

Apple has included a set of native applications and utilities for Mac OS X, including the famous iApps, including iMovie, iPhoto, iTunes, iCal, and iSync.

There are applications for such things as viewing and printing PostScript and PDF files, basic word processing, sending and receiving email, creating movies, and a suite of utilities to help you manage your system.

Use the Finder to locate the applications (*/Applications*) and utilities (*/Applications/Utilities*) on your system. You can quickly go to the *Applications* folder by clicking on the Applications icon in the Finder's Sidebar or by using the Shift-⌘-A keyboard shortcut. To quickly go to the Utilities folder, use its keyboard shortcut Shift-⌘-U, or you might consider dragging the Utilities folder to the lower portion of the Finder's Sidebar.

These aren't the only programs Mac OS X ships with. The underlying Darwin system involves hundreds of commands, tools, and system service programs (also known as *daemons*) that run behind the scenes to make the operating system work. These Unix utilities can be invoked as command-line programs through the Terminal (*/Applications/Utilities*). Chapter 28 covers command-line tools and system daemons.

If you've installed the Xcode Tools, you have access to another suite of applications, located in */Developer/Applications*. These programs can create Mac OS X applications; two of which, Xcode and Interface Builder, are described in Chapter 15.

This chapter provides a basic overview of the Applications and Utilities that ship with Mac OS X Panther (Version 10.3 and its point releases) and also covers installing applications from disk images (*.dmg* files), uninstalling applications, and the use of StuffIt Expander for uncompressing application archives.

Applications

This section very briefly touches on Mac OS X's standard-issue productivity and utility applications, even though some of them (such as iMovie) are sophisticated enough to have entire books written on them already.

Address Book

This application is a simple frontend to the current user's Address Book database, which stores email addresses and associated information. The database is primarily used by Apple's Mail application, but other applications run by the same user can read from and write to it as well. (The actual database exists as binary data files in *~/Library/Application Support/AddressBook*.)

If you have a .Mac account, you can use iSync (discussed later) to synchronize your Address Book contacts to your iDisk (stored in */Library/Application Support/Sync/CONT*). Once synchronized to your iDisk, your contacts are available online for use with the .Mac web-based Mail. For more information about Address Book syncing, see O'Reilly's *Inside .Mac* or Apple's .Mac web page (*http://www.mac.com*).

AppleScript

This folder contains the Script Editor application, which is used for writing AppleScripts, as well as subfolders holding example scripts. If you have installed the Xcode Tools, you can also build applications using AppleScript Studio. To learn more about AppleScript, see O'Reilly's *AppleScript: The Definitive Guide*.

Calculator

The Calculator is a fully functional scientific calculator. It also has a Paper Tape sheet that allows you to view the math functions, which you can copy and paste into another document window.

Other Calculators on Mac OS X

If you have Mac OS 9 installed, you can use the Graphing Calculator, found in */Applications (Mac OS 9)*, which lets you plot equations and watch the results in 2D or 3D space.

Through the Terminal, you can run a command-line program called *bc*, which is the GNU project's calculator that ships with Mac OS X. You can use it either as an interactive calculator or a complete mathematical scripting language involving variable substitution, Boolean logic operations, binary and hexadecimal computation, and many other features. Consult *bc*'s manpage (*man bc*) for complete documentation.

Chess

An implementation of the GNU project's chess program, a staple of many other Unix distributions, and good enough to consistently crush at least one author of this book at its easiest skill level. It features 2D and 3D modes, and can document games' progress using chess notation.

Apple also uses this application to demonstrate its speech recognition technology. If you select the "Allow Player to Speak Moves" checkbox in Chess' preferences (Chess→Preferences, or ⌘-,), the speech recognition microphone window (as described in Chapter 4) lets you play chess by speaking your moves.

DVD Player

If your Mac has a DVD drive, use this application to play DVDs. When active, you can use menu commands and a control panel window to navigate through the active disc and its features. You can also activate the DVD's own menu selections simply by pointing to and clicking on them.

Font Book

New to Panther, the Font Book application offers an intuitive way to preview fonts on your Mac, as well as the ability to create font collections. Personal font collections are stored in *~/Library/FontsCollections*.

iCal

iCal is a calendaring application (similar to Outlook's Calendar, if you're a Windows convert) that allows you to manage and publish your calendar to any WebDAV-enabled server (including your .Mac account). You can also subscribe to other calendars (such as a listing of holidays, the schedule for your favorite sports team, or that of another user).

If you have a .Mac account, you can use iSync (discussed later) to synchronize calendar and To-Do list items to your iDisk (stored in */Library/Application Support/Sync/ICAL*). Once synchronized to your iDisk, your calendars are viewable online through most standard web browsers. The URL for viewing your iCal items is *http://ical.mac.com/dotMac_memberName/calendarName* (for example, *http://ical.mac.com/chuckdude/Softball*). For more information about iCal syncing, see O'Reilly's *Inside .Mac* or Apple's .Mac web page (*http://www.mac.com*).

iChat

iChat allows you to chat with other .Mac members, as well as with AOL Instant Messenger (AIM) users. iChat also supports messaging via Rendezvous for dynamically finding iChat users on your local network.

If you have an iSight camera, you can also use iChat for video conferencing over the Internet. To learn more about iSight, visit Apple's web site at *http://www.apple.com/isight*.

Image Capture

This program can download pictures and video from a digital camera to your Mac. New in Panther, you can share input devices such as digital cameras and scanners attached to your Mac with other users on a network. To enable device sharing, go to Image Capture→Preferences (⌘-,)→Sharing, and then click on the checkbox next to "Share my devices".

iMovie

This application lets you create digital movies by sequencing and combining video and audio sources (either from on-disk files or linked in from iPhoto and iTunes), and gives you basic tools for working with title overlays, scene transitions, and other effects. It can export your creations to the cross-platform QuickTime (*.mov*) file format, as well as upload movies to your .Mac HomePage. To learn more about iMovie, see *iMovie 4 & iDVD 2: The Missing Manual* (Pogue Press/O'Reilly) or go to Apple's page at *http://www.apple.com/imovie*.

Internet Connect

This application is used to connect to the Internet or to another computer via a dial-up modem or an AirPort connection. You can also use Internet Connect to connect your Mac to a Virtual Private Network (VPN) via File→New VPN Connection. In Panther, Internet Connect supports Point-to-Point Tunneling Protocol (PPTP) and Layer 2 Tunneling Protocol (L2TP) over IPSec for connecting to a VPN.

Internet Connect shows your current dial-up status and settings (as configured in the Network preferences panel) and provides a Connect/Disconnect button for opening or closing a connection.

Internet Explorer

Microsoft's Internet Explorer 5.2.1 web browser. In Panther, Safari (discussed later in this section) is the default web browser. If you so desire, you can opt not to install Internet Explorer when installing Panther on your Mac. That, or you can always drag it to the Trash if you don't plan to use Internet Explorer.

iPhoto

iPhoto allows you to download, organize, and edit images taken with a digital camera. iPhoto is much more powerful than Image Capture, described earlier. New with iPhoto 4 (included as part of iLife '04), you can now share your iPhoto Libraries with other Macs on a local network via Rendezvous. To learn more about iPhoto, see *iPhoto 4: The Missing Manual* (Pogue Press/O'Reilly) or Apple's iPhoto page at *http://www. apple.com/iphoto*.

iSync

iSync can be used to synchronize the following items with your .Mac iDisk, iPod, or with Bluetooth devices such as cellular phones and PDAs:

- Contact information stored in Address Book
- iCal calendars and To-Do list items
- Safari's bookmarks

Once synchronized with your .Mac iDisk, this data can be accessed from most standard web browsers after logging in to the .Mac web site (*http://www.mac.com*). You can also synchronize this data between two Macs with the aid of an iDisk by registering both Macs with the .Mac synchronization server (from within iSync), synching one Mac first to .Mac, then the other. For more information on how to use iSync with a .Mac account, see O'Reilly's *Inside .Mac*.

iTunes

iTunes can be used to play CDs, listen to Internet radio stations, import (rip) music from CDs, burn CDs from music you've ripped or purchased through the iTunes Music Store (ITMS), and to store and play MP3 files. If you have an iPod, you can also use iTunes to synchronize your music files to your iPod.

iTunes also serves as the virtual storefront for the iTunes Music Store (ITMS). If you have an Apple account, you can use the ITMS to purchase AAC-encoded music files for $.99 each. For more information about the iTunes Music Store, visit Apple's page at *http://www.apple.com/music/store*.

Mail

Mail is the default email client for Mac OS X. It supports multiple accounts per user, which can be either local Unix mail accounts or remote mail accounts updated through the POP or IMAP mail protocols.

Preview

Preview received a major revision with Panther and is now more than just a simple image viewer or PDF reader. Preview lets you open (and export) files that have been saved in a variety of image formats—including PICT, GIF, JPEG, and TIFF, to name a few—and can also be used to view raw PostScript files. Preview is the default application for opening and viewing PDF files, the standard format now for the screenshots you create with Shift-⌘-3 or Shift-⌘-4.

QuickTime Player

QuickTime Player is the default viewer for QuickTime files (both locally stored and network-streamed) as well as a handful of other video formats (such as MPEG and AVI). QuickTime Player can also play audio formats such as MP3, but it lacks the sophisticated audio-friendly cataloguing features of iTunes.

Safari

Safari is a fast Cocoa-based web browser, built by Apple specifically for Mac OS X. Safari is the default web browser that ships with Panther; if you want to use another browser as the default, you can change this in Safari's preferences (Safari→Preferences→General→Default Web Browser).

If you have a .Mac account, you can use iSync (discussed later) to synchronize Safari's bookmarks to your iDisk (stored in */Library/Application Support/Sync/BKMK*). Once synchronized to your iDisk, your bookmarks are viewable online through most standard web browsers. For additional information about bookmark syncing, see O'Reilly's *Inside .Mac*, or Apple's .Mac web page (*http://www.mac.com*).

Sherlock

Sherlock 3 is Apple's venture into web services. (As mentioned earlier, the search functionality has been built into the Finder, and indexing is done via the Get Info window for drives, partitions, and folders.) To use Sherlock, you *must* have a connection to the Internet. Sherlock 3 can conduct searches on the Internet for:

- Pictures
- Stock quotes
- Movie theaters and show times
- Locating a business in your area (based on the address information you provide in Sherlock's preferences), along with driving directions and a map to the location
- Bidding on eBay auction items
- Checking the arrival and departure times of airline flights
- Finding the definition or spelling for a word in the dictionary
- Searching in AppleCare's Knowledge Base to solve a problem you're having with your computer
- Getting a quick translation from one language to another

Stickies

Stickies is a simple application that lets you create sticky notes on your screen. Like the notes stuck to your desk or computer, Stickies can be used to store important notes and reminders, as well as any pictures or movies you drag into a note.

System Preferences

System Preferences is a frontend to all the system's preference panels, as described in Chapter 4.

TextEdit

TextEdit also received a bit of an upgrade for Panther and is the default application for creating text and rich text documents. TextEdit now sports a ruler bar with text-formatting buttons for changing the alignment, leading, and indentation of text. By default, TextEdit documents are saved rich text format (*.rtf* and *.rtfd*), but you can also save documents as plain text (*.txt*) via the Format→Make Plain Text menu option. TextEdit replaces the SimpleText application from earlier versions of the Mac OS.

Best of all, TextEdit can open Word files (*.doc*), making it possible for you to read, print, and edit Word files even if you don't have Microsoft Office. However, TextEdit's compatibility with Word is limited; for example, TextEdit can't interpret Word files that use change tracking.

Utilities

The tools found in the Utilities folder (*/Applications/Utilities*) can help manage your system:

Activity Monitor

Panther's Activity Monitor combines the CPU Monitor and Process Viewer utilities from earlier versions of Mac OS X. The Activity Monitor lets you view the processes running on your system and lets you see the CPU load, how memory is allocated, disk activity, disk usage, and network activity. If you click on a process name, you can see additional information about that process, or you can cancel (*kill*, in Unix-speak) by highlighting a process and choosing Process→Quit (Option-⌘-Q).

AirPort Admin Utility
: This utility is used to administer AirPort Base Stations.

AirPort Setup Assistant
: This utility is used to configure your system to connect to an AirPort wireless network.

Asia Text Extras
: This folder contains two tools (Chinese Text Converter and IM Plugin Converter) for converting Chinese text.

Audio MIDI Setup
: This utility is used to add, set up, and configure Musical Instrument Digital Interface (MIDI) devices connected to your Mac.

Bluetooth File Exchange
: This utility allows you to exchange files with other Bluetooth-enabled devices, such as cellular phones, PDAs, and other computers. To exchange a file, launch this utility and then drag a file from the Finder to the Bluetooth File Exchange icon in the Dock. A window will appear, asking you to select a recipient (or recipients) for the file.

Bluetooth Serial Utility
: This utility keeps track of the serial ports used on your computer for incoming or outgoing connections with Bluetooth devices.

Bluetooth Setup Assistant
: This utility is used to configure Bluetooth devices (such as mice, keyboards, mobile phones, etc.) with your Mac.

ColorSync Utility
: This utility has four main functions. By pressing the Profile First Aid icon, it can verify and repair your ColorSync settings. The Profiles icon keeps track of the ColorSync profiles for your system, and the Devices icon lets you see which ColorSync devices are connected, as well as the name and location of the current profile. The Filters icon lets you apply filters to selected items within a PDF document.

The ColorSync Utility combines features that were in the ColorSync preference panel and the Display Calibrator utility in Jaguar.

Console
: One of the many system utilities to get an overhaul for Panther, the primary use of the Console application is to log the interactions between applications on your system as well as with the operating system itself. The Console gives you quick and easy access to system and crash logs via the Logs icon in its toolbar. The crash log created by the Console application can be used by developers to help debug their applications and should be supplied to Apple if you come across a bug in Mac OS X.

DigitalColor Meter
This small application lets you view and copy the color settings from any pixel on your screen.

Directory Access
This utility controls access for Mac OS X systems to Directory Services, such as NetInfo, LDAP, Active Directory, and BSD flat files, as well as Discovery Services such as AppleTalk, Rendezvous, SLP, and SMB.

Disk Utility
In Panther, Disk Copy and the Disk Utility have been combined. This utility now lets you create disk images (*.dmg*) for batching and sending files (including folders and applications) from one Mac user to another. It can also be used to repair a damaged hard drive, erase rewriteable media such as CD-RWs, and initialize and partition new drives.

Grab
This utility can be used to take screenshots of your system. Two of its most useful features include the ability to select the pointer (or no pointer at all) to be displayed in the screenshot and the ability to start a 10-second timer (which you can invoke with the shortcut, Shift-⌘-Z) before the screenshot is taken, to give you the necessary time to set up the shot.

Installer
This program launches whenever you install an application on your system.

Java
The following Java utilities can be found in this directory:

Applet Launcher
This utility lets you run Java applets on your Mac.

Java Plugin Settings
This controls Java settings when Java runs in a browser. Panther ships with two versions of this utility, one for Java 1.3.1 and another for Java 1.4.1.

Java Web Start
Java Web Start (JWS) can be used to download and run Java applications.

Keychain Access
This utility can be used to create and manage your passwords for accessing secure web and FTP sites, networked filesystems, and other items, such as password-encoded files. You can also use Keychain Access to create secure, encrypted notes that can be read only using this utility.

NetInfo Manager
The NetInfo Manager is mainly a tool for system and network administrators to view and edit the settings for a system. You need to have administrator privileges to use NetInfo Manager. See Chapter 11 for more information on using NetInfo Manager.

Network Utility

This utility is a graphical frontend to a standard set of Unix tools such as *netstat*, *ping*, *lookup*, *traceroute*, *whois*, and *finger*. It also lets you view specific information about your network connection, view stats about your AppleTalk connections, and scan the available ports for a particular domain or IP address.

ODBC Administrator

This tool allows you to connect to and exchange data with ODBC-compliant data sources. ODBC, which stands for Open Database Connectivity, is a standard database protocol, supported by most database systems such as FileMaker Pro, Oracle, MySQL, and PostgreSQL. You can use ODBC Administrator to add data sources, install new database drivers, trace calls to the ODBC API, and configure connection pooling.

Printer Setup Utility

This is used to configure and control the printers connected to your computer, either locally or on a network via AppleTalk, Open Directory, IP Printing, Rendezvous, USB, or Windows printing. In Panther, you can also configure printers from the Print & Fax preference panel (System Preferences→Print & Fax→Printing→Set Up Printers).

For users who are coming over from Mac OS 9, the Printer Setup Utility replaces the Chooser for managing printers.

StuffIt Expander

This is the popular utility for expanding, or decompressing, files. To launch StuffIt Expander, simply double-click on the compressed file. StuffIt Expander can open files saved as *.bin*, *.hqx*, *.sit*, *.zip*, *.tar*, *.tar.gz*, and *.tgz*, to name a few.

System Profiler

This tool (formerly known as the Apple System Profiler) keeps track of the finer details about your system. Here, you can view information about your particular computer, the devices (e.g., Zip or Jaz drive, CD-ROM drives, etc.) and volumes (i.e., hard drives and partitions) connected to your Mac, as well as listings of the frameworks, extensions, and applications on your Mac.

Terminal

The Terminal application is the command-line interface (CLI) to Mac OS X's Unix core. For more information about the Terminal, see Chapter 18.

X11

This is Apple's Mac OS X–compatible distribution of the X Window System. Since X11 is something used more by veteran Unix users, this utility isn't installed by default with Panther, but it is available as one of the Custom options during the install.

Installing Applications

Because each Mac OS X application keeps itself and all its resources inside a single bundled (see the section *Bundles*, in Chapter 2), installing them onto a local hard disk is often just a manner of dragging an application icon from its original medium (such as a CD-ROM or a mounted disk image) into the Applications folder (*/Applications*).

Theoretically, you can install an application anywhere on the filesystem, but the system's application database won't automatically register it unless you place it in one of the system's predefined Applications folders (either */Applications*, or *~/Applications*). If you have administrative privileges and wish to make an application available to all the Mac's users (or if you are the Mac's sole user), you should install applications in */Applications* (the one that the Finder's Applications Sidebar button leads to). To make an application accessible to you alone, place it in an Applications folder within your Home folder (creating it first, if necessary).

Software Installers

Some software packages, particularly those that update core system software or install several applications at once, require the use of special installer applications to get them onto a machine's local disk. Using these applications is as simple as launching them and then following the prompts.

Many installers, especially if they place files outside your Home folder, require that you have admin privileges before the software can be installed. If you do, these installers will prompt you for your username and password before the software can be installed.

Uninstalling applications

Uninstalling the majority of applications is easy: just drag their Finder icons into the Trash, or use the Unix command, *rm –rf*, to delete the application and its resources from the Terminal. If you used an installer application, however, it may be more complicated because the application may have placed other files in the filesystem.

As in previous versions of Mac OS, applications do tend to leave a legacy behind in the form of *preference files*. If you've run an application at least once, chances are good that it wrote a property list (or *plist*) file in your *~/Library/Preferences* folder (see Chapter 25), as well as performed other actions, such as create a folder for itself in *~/Library/Application Support*.

These files are usually small in size (just a few kilobytes) and won't affect the system if the application it belongs to has been deleted. They're arguably even useful at times: if you ever reinstall the software (or other software that shares or imports the other application's preferences), the property list is accessed as the application starts up, and the program will use your old settings. If you are still concerned about clutter, you can manually sift through your Preferences folder every so often or use a utility like Aladdin Systems' Spring Cleaning (*http://www.aladdinsys.com*) to do it for you.

If you used a package installer, though, things can get trickier because it's not obvious how many files it wrote and where they were written. Fortunately, Mac OS X does feature a rudimentary package management system. Package installers (which have a *.pkg* file extension) write a list of their contents in a "bill of materials," or *.bom* file, which can be found within the .pkg file in */Library/Receipts*. To view the list of files installed by an installer package, use the *lsbom* command in the Terminal:

```
MacChuck:~ chuck$ lsbom /Library/Receipts/Backup.pkg/Contents/ Archive.bom
.       41775   0/80
./Applications  40775   0/80
./Applications/Backup.app       40775   0/80
./Applications/Backup.app/Contents      40775   0/80
./Applications/Backup.app/Contents/Frameworks   40775   0/80
./Applications/Backup.app/Contents/Frameworks/XRModel.framework 40775   0/80
./Applications/Backup.app/Contents/Frameworks/XRModel.framework/Resources
120775   0/80    26      3302263027      Versions/Current/Resources
./Applications/Backup.app/Contents/Frameworks/XRModel.framework/Versions
40775    0/80
./Applications/Backup.app/Contents/Frameworks/XRModel.framework/Versions/A
40775    0/80
...
```

Depending on the size of the application, the output from the *lsbom* command may give you numerous screens of output. To make this easier to sift through, you can redirect *lsbom*'s output to a file that gets saved on your Desktop, as follows:

```
MacChuck:~ chuck$ lsbom /Library/Receipts/Backup.pkg/Contents/
Archive.bom > ~/Desktop/backup_lsbom_output.txt
```

This command uses the > symbol to redirect the output of the *lsbom* command to a file named *backup_lsbom_outut.txt*, which gets saved on the Desktop.

To actually do something with the information contained therein, install the OSXGNU project's *pkgInstall* utility (*http://www.osxgnu.org*). This command-line tool knows how to read receipt files, and (if run as root or under the *sudo* command) act upon it to seek out and remove all of the files that the package installed. The same organization also offers the OSXPackageManager, a graphic utility that lets you select and delete installed packages with a single click.

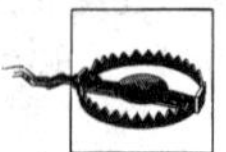

Don't uninstall packages unless you know exactly what they are. (Opening the bundle and browsing its *Info.plist* can give you clues, if you really have forgotten.) Among the bundles in */Library/Receipts* are installers of your Mac's Developer Tools, printer drivers, Darwin software, and other things you probably wouldn't want to see go away.

The authentication lock

Many Mac OS X applications and their functions require an administrator password. For example, only users in the machine's admin group can add new users to the system or install software from a CD-ROM into the machine's */Applications* folder. Before you can perform these actions, you must *authenticate* yourself to prove you are a user with administrative privileges.

Figure 5-1 shows a typical example of the Mac OS X *authentication lock* button in action. When you first visit this panel, this button bears an image of a closed padlock and the message "Click the lock to make changes." (Unfortunately, it displays this rather vague message even if you're installing software or doing other things you don't normally associate with "making changes," often leading to confusion among new users.) If you're a member of the system's admin group, you can authenticate yourself by clicking on the padlock icon, which summons the dialog shown in Figure 5-2.

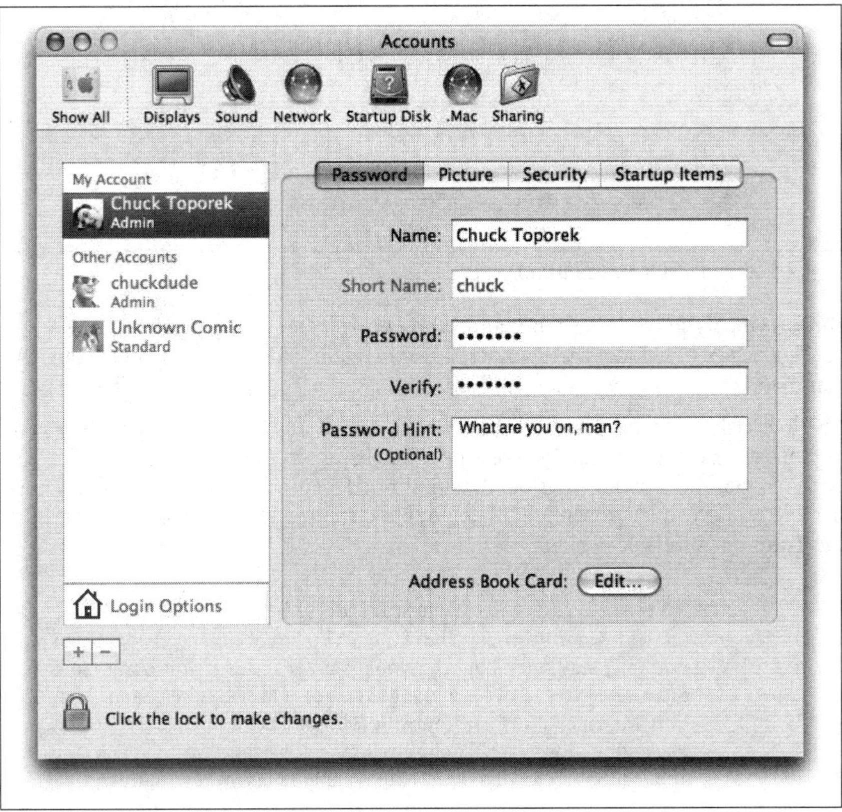

Figure 5-1. The Accounts preference panel, with a closed authentication lock

You can enter your real name or username in the top field (the Mac actually places your real name there for you) and your account password in the bottom field. Clicking OK completes the authentication and results in an open padlock

Applications and Utilities

Figure 5-2. The lock's authentication challenge

and previously grayed-out commands and controls becoming available, as shown in Figure 5-3. Clicking the padlock button again closes it and locks out the commands that require authentication.

The lock asks for your account's password even though you've already used it to log into your current Mac OS X session. This is just to make sure you're who you claim to be and not an interloper who slipped behind your keyboard to cause trouble while you left for lunch. This double-checking strategy works similarly to the Terminal's *sudo* command.

Some applications' authentication locks, however, choose to be a bit less security-strict. The System Preference panels' locks, for example, stay open between your login sessions if you don't close them after you're done making changes. On the other hand, NetInfo Manager's authentication lock takes the opposite approach, presenting you with a closed lock every time you launch the application, regardless of its state when you last quit the utility.

Installing Mac OS 9 Applications

Thanks to the Classic Environment (see Chapter 3), Mac OS X can run most Mac OS 9 applications without a hitch. However, due to philosophical differences between the two operating systems, installing Mac OS 9 software within Mac OS X doesn't always work as smoothly.

Because Mac OS 9 is a single-user system, software installers treat the whole root volume the same way Mac OS X treats the current user's Home folder and often

Figure 5-3. The Accounts preference panel, with an open authentication lock

try writing software directly under the *root* folder. Even if you do have write permission to the *root* directory (as all admin users do, by default), you likely won't want arbitrary applications cluttering that space, so you'll need to move the results into */Applications* (or wherever it should go) once the installer exits.

Furthermore, even if you're an admin user, you might not have write permission to the */System Folder* directory, which many Mac OS 9 software installers add files to.

Worse, since Mac OS 9 has no concept of user permissions, that system's installers assume that the person behind the keyboard has full write access to the Mac OS 9 System Folder sitting under *root*. In Mac OS X, this usually isn't true because System Folder is owned by root. Even admin users will see an error dialog if the installer wants to add files to it.

While Mac OS X also has a */System* folder of its own, it is a sacred space that not even software installers can modify (except for Apple's own system software updaters). Modern Mac applications and their installers instead use the filesystem's various */Library* folders to store auxiliary, system-dependent files. See Chapter 7 for more information.

You can skirt these issues by modifying your filesystem's permissions: make the System Folder writeable by the *admin* group, through a command like this:

```
$ sudo chgrp -R admin "/System Folder"
$ sudo chmod -R g+w "/System Folder"
```

However, if you seldom install new Mac OS 9–only applications (an increasingly likely condition as Mac software developers switch their focus to creating Carbon and Cocoa applications), you may be better off simply booting into Mac OS 9 just to perform these installs, and otherwise leaving your Mac OS X filesystem as it is.

Disk Images

While the concept of disk images exists in both Mac OS 9 and Unix, Mac OS X uses it more than either system as a standard software installation idiom. Quite often, a freshly downloaded file will decompress into a single *disk image* file (with a *.dmg* extension), representing an entire, compressed disk volume.

When opened with Disk Copy (or just double-clicked from the Finder), the system spends a moment verifying the image's data integrity and then mounts it as a disk volume. When mounted, disk images show up in the top portion of the Finder's Sidebar, as well as on the Desktop, as shown in Figure 5-4.

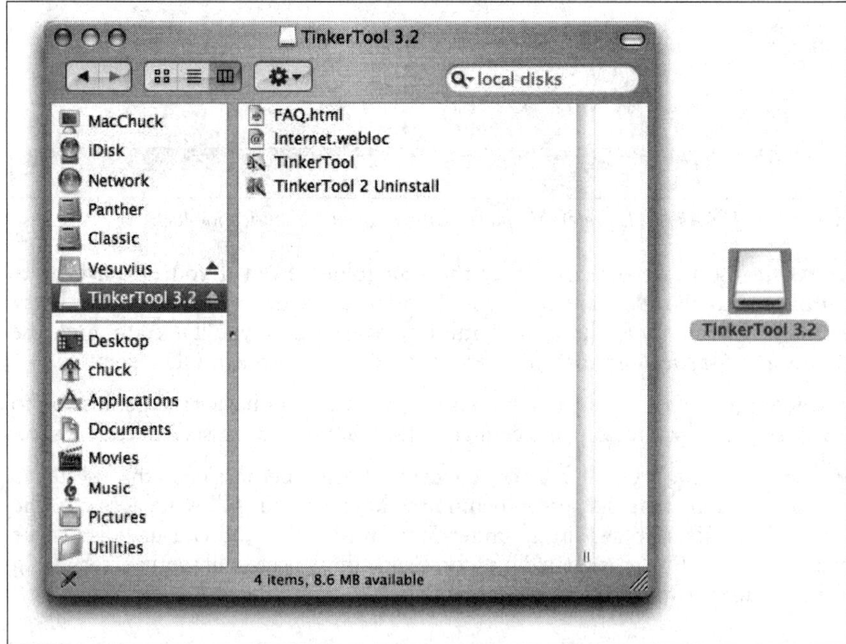

Figure 5-4. Mounted disk images show up in the top part of the Finder's Sidebar

If you haven't enabled the "Removable media (such as CDs)" checkbox in the Finder's preferences (Finder→Preferences→Sidebar), the disk image won't show up in the Finder's Sidebar; however, it will show up on your Desktop. To view the disk image's contents, simply double-click on the disk image icon on your Desktop.

Once a disk image is mounted, it behaves like any other Finder disk. You can open files and applications on the image, and they work as expected. However, you'll need to copy any files and folders you wish to permanently keep onto a more stable location (such as the Applications folder of your machine's hard drive) if you'd like to install them on your system.

You can quickly install an application from a disk image by dragging the application's icon to the Applications icon in the lower-half of the Finder's Sidebar. The Applications icon is highlighted when the dragged item is placed over it, and when you let go of the mouse button, the application is moved from the disk image to the */Applications* folder on your hard drive.

File Compression

Applications downloaded over the Internet are nearly always available only in some sort of compressed file format. Through file compression, several files can be melded into one, which itself is shrunk through reversible compression algorithms to a compact size.

Mac OS X supports both the StuffIt (*.sit*) compression and BinHex (*.hqx*) file encoding formats that were ubiquitous with Mac OS 9 file sharing, and can handle the tar (*.tar*) and *gzip* (*.gz*) formats often seen in the Unix world, as well as the PKZip (*.zip*) format usually seen in Windows.

The downside to using these formats has always been that you needed to run a third-party application or a Unix command line utility to create an archive. In Panther, you can select files, folders, and even applications in a Finder window, and then select File→Create Archive of "items" to create a Zip archive of the items you've selected. You can also access the Create Archive feature from the Action menu in the Finder's toolbar, as shown in Figure 5-5.

If you are just zipping one file, the Finder uses the original filename and extension, zips the file, and then tacks on a *.zip* extension at the end. For example, *supernova.jpg* becomes *supernova.jpg.zip* when archived alone. However, if you are zipping a bunch of files, as shown in Figure 5-5 (the Action menu item says "Create Archive of 9 items"), the Finder zips all the files into a file named *Archive.zip* and places that in the same folder as the original files. Because this is a fairly basic filename that can easily get confused with other archives, you should consider renaming the Zip file, as described in Chapter 2.

To unzip an archive in the Finder, simply double-click on the Zip archive. If the Zip archive contains one file, the file within is saved in the directory or folder that contained the Zip archive. If the Zip archive contains more than one file, the Finder creates a folder based on the Zip archive's name and places the contents of the archive within that folder. The Finder doesn't automatically delete the *.zip* file

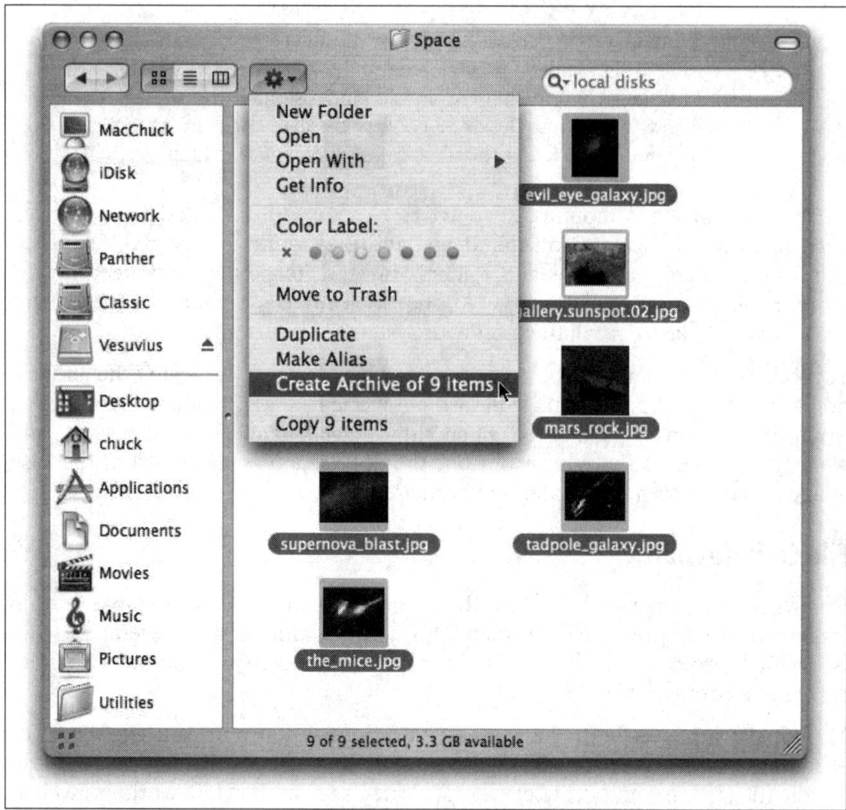

Figure 5-5. Using the Create Archive option in the Finder's Action menu

after it has been unzipped. To get rid of the *.zip* file, simply click on it once, and then hit ⌘-Delete to move the file to the Trash for later disposal.

For other types of compressed files, Mac OS X comes with StuffIt Expander, which can uncompress *.sit*, *.hqx*, *.tar*, *.gz*, and *.tgz* files (to name a few) by simply double-clicking on them. You can also Control-click on one of these archive files and select Open With→StuffIt Expander from the contextual menu, as shown in Figure 5-6.

By default, StuffIt Expander leaves the compressed files alone once it has expanded them, which can lead to a cluttered Desktop or downloads folder in short order, especially when dealing with *.tar* and *.gz* files that are both compressed and encoded, leaving behind an extra, intermediate file. StuffIt Expander can be configured to automatically delete archive files after expanding them by selecting the "Delete after expanding" checkbox in its preferences (StuffIt Expander→Preferences→Expanding).

Figure 5-6. Control-click on an archive file and select Open With to choose StuffIt Expander

Cleaning Up

Once your new software is in the */Applications* folder, you still have a bit of cleanup to do.

You can safely delete the *.gz* and *.tar* files that might be lying around after a successful download-and-install procedure. You can also get rid of installer applications and *.pkg* packages; Mac OS X's package manager doesn't need these original files to track the packages' presence on your system, as the earlier section "Uninstalling applications" details.

Disk images can be a little confusing because some require a two-step process to be deleted. Once you're done using a mounted disk image, you can unmount it through the Finder by:

- Dragging its icon to the Trash
- Clicking on the eject icon next to its name in the Finder's Sidebar
- Selecting the disk image and choosing File→Eject (⌘-E) from the menu bar
- Selecting the disk image in the Finder and choosing Eject from the Action menu in the toolbar

However, this just unmounts the disk image; the actual disk image file remains on your filesystem until you move it to the Trash.

6
Task and Setting Index

After rooting through all the System Preferences and looking at the Applications and Utilities that come with Mac OS X, you'll quickly find that there are literally hundreds of ways to configure the settings for your system. Finding all these items in the interface can sometimes be a challenge.

This chapter provides a comprehensive listing of settings and tasks that can be performed with System Preferences, Applications, and Utilities and from the command line in the Terminal application. In some cases, we've provided instructions for how to perform tasks using the GUI tools and by issuing Unix commands in the Terminal. It's up to you to decide which is faster or easier to use (but you're likely to realize quickly that the power of Unix is unmatchable by most GUI tools).

The tasks in this chapter are sorted alphabetically by their function, rather than by the application or utility name. Headings show major functional groupings (such as "Accessibility" or "Display"). These group miscellaneous entries up until the next functional grouping.

This section provides shorthand instructions to help you configure and use your Mac OS X system as quickly as possible. Each task is presented as the answer to a "How do I..." question (for example, "How do I change the color depth of my display?"), followed by the shorthand way to execute the answer (e.g., System Preferences→Displays).

If you're new to Mac OS X, or if you just want to jog your memory when you can't quite remember where a particular setting is located, this is the place to start.

Accessibility

Change the settings for a person with disabilities?
System Preferences→Universal Access

Enable full keyboard access so I can navigate through and select menu items without using a mouse?
System Preferences→Keyboard & Mouse→Keyboard Shortcuts→select the checkbox next to "Turn on full keyboard access"

Enable Universal Access keyboard shortcuts?
System Preferences→Keyboard & Mouse→Keyboard Shortcuts→select the checkbox next to "Universal Access" in the scroll list

Set the voice for my system?
System Preferences→Speech→Default Voice→select a voice style from the Voice scroll list

Change the rate at which the default voice speaks?
System Preferences→Speech→Default Voice→Rate (move the slide control left or right to make the voice speak slower or faster, respectively; click on the Play button to test the speed)

Turn on speech recognition?
System Preferences→Speech→Speech Recognition→On/Off→Apple Speakable Items is→select the On radio button

View the speakable items?
System Preferences→Speech→Speech Recognition→On/Off→Apple Speakable Items is→select the On radio button→click on the button named, Open Speakable Items Folder

Finder→Home→Library→Speech→Speakable Items

Where does an application store its speakable items?
In *~/Library/Speech/Speakable Items/Application Speakable Items/application*

Enable accessibility devices to be used with the system?
System Preferences→Universal Access→select the checkbox next to "Enable access for assistive devices"

Change the display settings for person with a visual impairment?
System Preferences→Universal Access→Seeing

Provide a visual alert cue for a user with a hearing impairment?
System Preferences→Universal Access→Hearing→select the checkbox next to "Flash the screen when an alert sound occurs"

Place the scrollbar controls together so they're easier to access?
System Preferences→Appearance→Place scroll arrows→Together (this is the default setting)

Change the display from color to grayscale?
System Preferences→Universal Access→Seeing→Set Display to Grayscale

Change the display so everything is white on black?

System Preferences→Universal Access→Seeing→Switch to White on Black

Use the keyboard shortcut, Control-Option-⌘-8.

Zoom in on items on the screen?

System Preferences→Universal Access→Seeing→Turn On Zoom

Use the keyboard shortcut, Option-⌘-8.

With Zoom enabled, use Option-⌘-= to zoom in, and Option-⌘-– (a hyphen) to zoom out.

Change the display's contrast?

System Preferences→Universal Access→Seeing→Enhance Contrast→move the slider left or right

Press Control-Option-⌘-, to decrease the contrast and set it to Normal.

Press Control-Option-⌘-. (period) to increase the contrast to its Maximum setting.

Use the numeric keypad instead of the mouse?

System Preferences→Universal Access→Mouse→Mouse Keys→select the On radio button

Have the system "read" an email message to me?

Select the text in the email message, or select all with Edit→Select All (⌘-A). Then go to Mail→Services→Speech→Start Speaking Text.

Allow menu bar commands to be spoken and recognized?

System Preferences→Speech→Commands→Select a command set→select the checkbox next to Menu Bar in the list

Accounts and User Management

Add another user to the system?

System Preferences→Accounts→click on the plus sign button (+) at the lower-left of the window (requires administrator privileges)

Unix administrators might be tempted to use the *useradd*, *userdel*, and *usermod* commands to add, remove, and modify a user, respectively, from the Terminal. However, those commands don't exist on Mac OS X.

Remove a user from the system?

System Preferences→Accounts→select the user's name in the left column→click on the button with a minus sign (–) to delete the user

While logged in, you can't remove yourself from the system. If you want to remove your user account from the system, you have to log out and log back in as another user.

Configuring my login?
: System Preferences→Accounts→select your username in the left column→Login Options

Change my login password?
: System Preferences→Accounts→select your username in the left column→Password

Use the *passwd* command in the Terminal.

When choosing a password, you should avoid using dictionary words (i.e., common, everyday words found in the dictionary) or something that can be easily guessed. To improve your security, we recommend that you choose an alphanumeric password. Remember, passwords are case-sensitive, so you can mix upper- and lowercase letters with your password as well.

Turn on fast user switching?
: System Preferences→Accounts→Login Options→select the checkbox next to "Enable fast user switching"

Give a user administrator privileges?
: System Preferences→Accounts→select the username in the left column→Security→click on the checkbox next to "Allow user to administer this computer" (requires administrator privileges)

Take administrator privileges away from a user?
: System Preferences→Accounts→select the username in the left column→Security→uncheck the box next to "Allow user to administer this computer" (requires administrator privileges)

Restrict which applications a user can use?
: System Preferences→Accounts→select the username in the left column→Limitations→This user needs→select either Some Limitations, or Simple Finder

Keep this in mind if you have a user you'd like to restrict from issuing Unix commands. You can cut off their access to using the Terminal application by clicking the disclosure triangle next to Utilities, and then unchecking the box next to the Terminal.

Keep a user from changing his password?
: System Preferences→Accounts→select the username in the left column→Limitations→Some Limitations→make sure that the "Change password" option is unchecked

Turn off automatic login?

System Preferences→Accounts→select the username in the left column→Login Options→uncheck the box next to "Automatically log in as"

On a multiuser system, specify which user will be automatically logged on?

System Preferences→Accounts→select the username in the left column→Login Options→make sure that "Automatically log in as" is checked→select a username from the pop-up menu→enter that user's password in the sheet that appears

Require users to type their username and password when logging in?

System Preferences→Accounts→select a username in the left column→Login Options→Display Login Window As→select the radio button next to "Name and password"

If you have your Mac configured for automatic login, the login screen will not appear after the system has finished booting. Instead, your Mac will automatically log in as the user specified in the pop-up menu next to the "Automatically log in as" option; if you want the login screen to appear, uncheck this option.

Allow a user to access files on my Mac from a Windows system?

System Preferences→Sharing→Services→check the box next to Windows Sharing

Set a password hint?

System Preferences→Accounts→select a username in the left column→Password→select the text in the Password Hint field. When you try typing something, you'll be prompted to enter the account's password; enter the password, click OK, and then type in a new hint.

Find out which users have admin privileges?

System Preferences→Accounts; users with administrator privileges will have Admin beneath their name in the list of users in the left column

Launch NetInfo Manager (*/Applications/Utilities*). In the Directory Browser at the top of the window, select `/`→`groups`→`admin`. In the lower-half of the window, look at the Property value next to `users`; you will see something like (`root,` *`username`*) in the Value(s) column.

Add a new group?

Launch NetInfo Manager (*/Applications/Utilities*), and follow these steps:

1. Click on the padlock icon in the lower-left corner of the window, and enter the administrator's password. This allows you to make changes.
2. In the Directory Browser pane, select `/`→`groups`.
3. From the menu bar, go to Directory→New Subdirectory (⌘-N).
4. In the Directory pane below, select the `new_directory` name by double-clicking on it, and type in a new group name (e.g., *`editorial`*) and press Return.

5. Go to Domain→Save Changes. A message window appears, asking if you want to save the changes; click on the "Update this copy" button. The name of the new group appears in the Directory Browser pane.
6. Click on the padlock to prevent further changes from being made, and quit NetInfo Manager (⌘-Q).

As with the user-related Unix commands, Unix users will notice that the various group commands (*groupadd*, *groupdel*, *groupmod*, *gpasswd*, *grpconv*, and *grpunconv*) are missing from Mac OS X. Use NetInfo Manager to manage groups.

Enable the root user account?

Follow these steps to enable the *root* user account from NetInfo Manager:

1. Launch NetInfo Manager.
2. To make changes to the NetInfo settings, click on the padlock in the lower-left corner of the NetInfo window. You will be asked for the administrator's name and password; enter those, and click OK.
3. In the menu bar, select Security→Enable Root User.
4. You will be asked to enter a password for the root user; the root password must be more than five characters in length.
5. Enter the password again to confirm the password for the root user account. Click on the Verify button to confirm the password and enable the root account.
6. If you have no further changes to make in NetInfo Manager, click on the padlock at the lower-left of the window to prevent further changes from being made, and quit the application (⌘-Q).
7. To enable the *root* user account using the Terminal, enter the following command:

```
MacChuck:~ chuck$ sudo passwd root
Password: *******
Changing password for root.
New password: ********
Retype new password: ********
MacChuck:~ chuck$
```

The first time you're asked for a password, enter the password you use to log in to your Mac. Once you're verified by the system to have administrator privileges, you will be asked to enter and confirm a new password for the *root* user account.

The asterisks shown in this example won't appear onscreen when you enter the passwords; actually, nothing will happen onscreen. If you make a mistake while entering the password, you can always hit the Backspace or Delete key to go back over what you typed; then just re-enter the password.

Once the root account has been assigned a password, you can use it to log in with the username *root*.

Restrict a non-admin user to using the Simple Finder?
System Preferences→Accounts→select a username in the left column→Limitations→Simple Finder

AirPort

Find the MAC address for my AirPort card?
System Preferences→Network→AirPort; the AirPort ID should appear at the top of that window

Applications→Utilities→Network Utility→Info→Hardware Address

Configure an AirPort Base Station?
Applications→Utilities→AirPort Admin Utility

Configure my AirPort settings for wireless networking?
Follow the steps for connecting to an Ethernet network first, and then use the AirPort Setup Assistant (*/Applications/Utilities*). The settings you've applied for your regular network will be applied to your AirPort settings.

Quickly switch to an AirPort network after disconnecting the Ethernet cable from my iBook?
System Preferences→Network→Show→Network Port Configurations. Click on the checkboxes next to the network ports you want to enable, and drag the ports in the list to place them in the order in which you're most likely to connect to them. (The Automatic location should do this for you.)

Share my modem or Ethernet connection with other AirPort-equipped Macs?
System Preferences→Sharing→Internet panel; click on the Start button to turn Internet sharing on

Display the AirPort strength meter in the menu bar?
System Preferences→Network→AirPort→select the checkbox next to "Show AirPort status in menu bar"

Enable a computer to set up AirPort networks?
System Preferences→Network→AirPort→select the checkbox next to "Allow this computer to create networks"

AppleScript

Find out which version of AppleScript I'm using?
Launch the Script Editor (*/Applications/AppleScript*)→Script Editor→About Script Editor→the version of AppleScript appears beneath Script Editor's version number

Enable the Script Menu in the menu bar?
Applications→AppleScript→double-click on the item named "Install Script Menu"

Remove the Script Menu from the menu bar?

Applications→AppleScript→double-click on the item named "Remove Script Menu"

Command-click on the Script Menu icon and drag it off the menu bar.

Locate the scripts found in the Script menu?

Finder→Macintosh HD→Library→Scripts

Create a place for my AppleScripts in the Script menu?

Go to the Scripts folder (*/Library/Scripts*) and create a new folder (File→New Folder) to place your scripts in.

Find out which Scripting Additions are on my system?

Look in */Library/ScriptingAdditions*.

Background Images

Change my Desktop image?

System Preferences→Desktop & Screen Saver→Desktop

Control-click (right-click) on the Desktop itself and select Change Desktop Background from the context menu.

Applications→iPhoto→select an image from one of your photo libraries→click on the Desktop icon at the bottom of the window

Have the pictures on my Desktop change automatically?

System Preferences→Desktop & Screen Saver→Desktop→click on the checkbox next to "Change picture" and select an interval from the pull-down menu

Use one of Mac OS 9's background images for my Desktop instead of the ones that come with Mac OS X?

System Preferences→Desktop & Screen Saver→Desktop→Choose Folder. A Finder sheet slides down; use this to navigate to Mac OS 9 System Folder→Appearance→Desktop Pictures. Then select one of the following folders, and click the Choose button: 3D Graphics, Convergency, Ensemble Photos, or Photos. The images in that directory appear as part of the Desktop Collection.

Add a new background pattern, making it available to all users?

Create or save the image to the */Library/Desktop Pictures* folder.

Change the background of a Finder window to a different color or to an image?

Finder→View→as Icons; then use View→Show View Options (⌘-J); select either Color or Picture for the Background option

Classic

Launch Classic?

System Preferences→Classic→Start/Stop→click on the Start button

Finder→Macintosh HD→System→Library→CoreServices→double-click on the Classic Startup item

Quit Classic?

System Preferences→Classic→Start/Stop→click on the Stop button

Restart Classic?

System Preferences→Classic→Start/Stop→click on the Restart button

System Preferences→Classic→Advanced→click on the Restart Classic button

Create a command alias for starting Classic from the command line?

Follow these steps:

1. Launch the Terminal application (*/Applications/Utilities*).
2. Issue the following command:

   ```
   $ vi .bash_profile
   ```

   This creates the *.bash_profile* file in your Home directory if it doesn't already exist; if it does, the file will open up using the *vi* editor.
3. Hit the "i" key to put *vi* into insert mode.
4. Enter the following:

   ```
   alias classic='open -a "Classic Startup.app"'
   ```

   This command creates an alias named *classic*, which uses the *open* command to launch the Classic Startup application, located in */System/Library/CoreServices*.
5. Hit the Escape key (esc); this takes *vi* out of insert mode and places it in command mode.
6. Enter **:wq**, and then hit the Return key. The colon (**:**) tells *vi* that you're going to issue a command, the **w** tells *vi* to write the changes to the *.bash_profile* file, and the **q** tells *vi* to quit, which places you back on the command line. (The **:wq** command appears at the bottom of the Terminal window as it is being typed.)
7. Type in **exit** and hit the Return key to close the Terminal window.
8. Open a new Terminal window with ⌘-N.
9. Type in the command, **classic**, to launch Classic.

Find out what version of Mac OS 9 I'm running?

Open the Finder and go to Mac OS 9's System Folder→System→File→Get Info (⌘-I)→look next to Version near the top of the window

In the Classic environment, use →Apple System Profiler→System Profile panel; look in the System overview section

System Preferences→Classic→Start/Stop→click on the Start button to start Classic→after Classic has started, go to the Memory/Versions tab→look for

Mac OS near the bottom of the Memory/Versions tab for Mac OS 9's version number

See whether Classic is running?

System Preferences→Classic→Start/Stop; look for a bolded message that says "Classic is not running" or "Classic is running using folder "System Folder" on volume (name of the disk volume that contains Mac OS 9's System Folder)"

Set a keyboard shortcut for starting and restarting Classic?

System Preferences→Classic→Advanced→Startup Options and Other Options→select "Use Key Combination" from the pop-up menu, and enter a keyboard shortcut (up to five keys) in the text field

Include an option in the menu bar for starting Classic?

System Preferences→Classic→Start/Stop→click on the checkbox next to "Show Classic status in menu bar"

Keep the Classic icon in the Dock?

Control-click (right-click) on the Classic icon while Classic is starting up and select Keep In Dock from its context menu

Finder→Macintosh HD→System→Library→CoreServices→drag the Classic Startup icon to the Dock

Start Classic automatically when I start up my computer?

System Preferences→Classic→Start/Stop→select the checkbox next to "Start Classic when you login"

Rebuild Classic/Mac OS 9's Desktop without booting into Mac OS 9?

System Preferences→Classic→Advanced→Rebuild Classic Desktop→click on the Rebuild Desktop button

See how much memory a Classic application is using?

System Preferences→Classic→Memory/Versions

Allocate memory to a Classic application?

Finder→select the drive or partition→Applications (Mac OS 9)→select the application icon→File→Get Info→Memory→change the value for Preferred Size to a larger number

Start Classic with the extensions off?

System Preferences→Classic→Advanced→Startup and Other Options→select Turn Off Extensions from the pop-up menu→click on the Start Classic button

View the background processes running under Classic?

System Preferences→Classic→Memory/Versions→select the checkbox next to "Show background applications"

Configure a printer so I can print from a Classic application?

From Mac OS 9's →Chooser→select the printer

Colors

Find the 8-bit hexadecimal value for a color from an image?

Open the image with Preview (*/Applications*)→launch DigitalColor Meter (in */Applications/Utilities*)→select "RGB As Hex Value, 8-bit" from the pull-down menu→move the mouse pointer over an area in the image→ Shift-⌘-H (for Hold Color) holds the RGB value in the application window

Copy an RGB color value from an image and paste it into an HTML document?

Open the image with Preview→launch DigitalColor Meter→select "RGB A Hex Value, 8-bit" from the pull-down menu→move the mouse pointer over an area in the image→Shift-⌘-C (for Copy Color)→switch to the text editor you're using to edit the HTML page→use ⌘-P to paste in the hex value (e.g., "#FFCC00")

Convert a full-color PDF document to grayscale?

Follow these steps:

1. Launch the ColorSync Utility (*/Applications/Utilities*).
2. Click on the Filters button in the toolbar.
3. In the Filters list (left column) select Gray Tone.
4. Click on the "View file with Filter..." button.
5. Select a PDF document to open.
6. A Preview window opens with the PDF document in view; in that window:
    a. Select Gray Tone in the Filters list on the left.
    b. Select the checkbox next to Preview at the top of the window; all of the text and images in the document will be viewable as grayscale instead of color.
    c. Click on the Apply button; this converts the color to grayscale,
    d. Select File→Save As (Shift-⌘-S); give the file a new name and then click on the Save button.
    e. Close the Preview window (⌘-W).
7. Quit the ColorSync Utility (⌘-Q).
8. Open the grayscale PDF file in Preview.

This works only with PDF documents, not image files, such as GIF, JPEG, PNG, TIFF, etc. However, it is worth noting that, by default, Mac OS X saves any screenshots as PDF files, so these can be converted to grayscale using this method.

Date and Time

Change the date/time?

System Preferences→Date & Time→Date & Time

Specify how the date and time will appear in the menu bar?
System Preferences→Date & Time→Clock

Specify the date and time settings for another country while I'm traveling?
System Preferences→International→Formats→select a country from the Region pull-down menu

Have my computer speak the time out for me?
System Preferences→Date & Time→Clock→select the checkbox next to "Announce the time"→select an increment from the pop-up menu (choices are "On the hour," "On the half hour," and "On the quarter hour")

Use a network time server to set my clock's time?
System Preferences→Date & Time→Date & Time→select the checkbox next to "Set Date & Time automatically"→select an NTP Server in the scroll list

You must be connected to the Internet to use a network time server. One helpful hint is to first use the network time server to set an accurate time for your system, then uncheck the "Set Date & Time automatically" box.

Set my time zone?
System Preferences→Date & Time→Time Zone

Display the current date and time from the command line?
Use the *date* command:

```
MacChuck:~ chuck$ date
Thu Dec 25 12:34:56 PST 2003
```

Display the time in military time?
System Preferences→Date & Time→Clock→select the checkbox next to "Use a 24-hour clock"

Display the calendar for a specific month and year from the command line?
Use the *cal* command, followed by the number of the month and the year:

```
MacChuck:~ chuck$ cal 10 1965
    October 1965
 S  M Tu  W Th  F  S
                1  2
 3  4  5  6  7  8  9
10 11 12 13 14 15 16
17 18 19 20 21 22 23
24 25 26 27 28 29 30
31
```

Disks

Find out how much disk space I have left?
Applications→Utilities→Disk Utility→select hard drive or partition (e.g., Macintosh HD)→click on the Info button in the toolbar

Launch the Finder and look in the status bar at the bottom of the window. You will see something that says how many items are in that directory, and how much space is available on your hard drive.

Finder→select the hard drive icon in the Sidebar→select File→Get Info (⌘-I).

Issue the *df –m* command in the Terminal to display disk usage in megabytes.

Find out whether a drive is formatted with HFS?

Applications→Utilities→Disk Utility→select the drive or partition→click on the Info button in the toolbar (look for the "IO Content" item in the Info list)

Create a disk image?

To create a disk image, follow these steps:

1. Launch Disk Utility (*/Application/Utilities*).
2. In the menu bar, select Images→New→Blank Image, or click on the New Image button in Disk Utility's toolbar.
3. In the Save As field, enter a name for the disk image.
4. From the Where pop-up menu, select the location where you'd like to save the disk image.
5. Set the Size, Encryption method, and Format from their respective pop-up menus.
6. Click the Save button to create the disk image; the dial image file (with a *.dmg* file extension) will be saved in the location you selected, and the image itself will be mounted on your desktop.
7. Double-click on the disk image to open its Finder window.
8. Drag and drop the items you would like included in the disk image into the image's Finder window.
9. When complete, close the Finder window and Eject the image (⌘-E) to complete the process.

To create a disk image from an actual disk, such as your hard drive or a CD, follow these steps:

1. Launch Disk Utility (*/Application/Utilities*).
2. In the left side of Disk Utility's window, select the disk you'd like to create an image of.
3. In the menu bar, select Images→New→Image from *`disk name`*.
4. In the Save As field, enter a name for the image you want to create.
5. From the Where pop-up menu, select the location where you'd like to save the disk image.
6. Select the Image Format and Encryption Type from their respective pop-up menus.
7. Click the Save button to create the disk image.

Display the contents of a shared folder on another volume in my network?

Finder→*`volume`*→*`folder`*

From your home directory in the Terminal:

```
MacChuck:~ chuck$ ls -la /Volumes/volume/folder
```

Partition a new hard drive?
Applications→Utilities→Disk Utility→select the new drive→Partition

Partition an existing drive?
Follow these steps:

1. Back everything up, because partitioning the drive requires a reinstall of the system and reformatting of the hard drive (don't skip this step).
2. Insert the Mac OS X installation CD.
3. Restart the computer and hold down the C key to boot from the CD.
4. Select Installer→Disk Utility.
5. Select the hard drive and specify the partition sizes, names, and the format of the partition (HFS+ is recommended).
6. Click on the Partition button.
7. When that's completed, finish installing Mac OS X and then load your data back on from the backup.

Unmount an external drive or partition?
Click on the unmount button next to the volume in the Finder's Sidebar.

Drag the disk icon from the Desktop to the Trash.

Applications→Utilities→Disk Utility→select the drive or partition→File→Unmount Volume (Option-⌘-U); you may need to enter the administrator's password

Erase a CD-RW disc or hard drive?
Applications→Utilities→Disk Utility→select the CD or disk→Erase

Create a redundant array of independent disks (RAID) for my system?
Applications→Utilities→Disk Utility→select the drives→RAID

Hide the hard disk (or partition) icons on my Desktop?
Finder→Preferences→General→Show these items on the Desktop→uncheck the box next to "Hard disks"

Task & Setting Index

Display

Change my Desktop size/resolution, or the color depth of my display?
System Preferences→Displays→Display→Resolutions

Get a menu extra in the menu bar for changing my display's settings?
System Preferences→Displays→select the checkbox next to "Show displays in menu bar"

Configure the settings for a second monitor?
System Preferences→Displays→click on the Detect Displays button

Click on the Displays icon in the menu bar→Detect Displays

Change the display from color to grayscale?
System Preferences→Universal Access→Seeing→click on the "Set Display to Grayscale" button

Change the display from color to white on black?
System Preferences→Universal Access→Seeing→click on the "Switch to White on Black" button

From the Finder, use the keyboard shortcut Control-Option-⌘-8.

Change the contrast of the display?
System Preferences→Universal Access→Seeing→move the Enhance Contrast slider right or left (from Normal to Maximum, respectively)

From the Finder, use the keyboard shortcut Control-Option-⌘-, to decrease the contrast or Control-Option-⌘-. to increase the contrast.

Enlarge the display?
System Preferences→Universal Access→Turn On Zoom

From the Finder, use the keyboard shortcut Option-⌘-8.

Use Option-⌘-+ to zoom in and Option-⌘- – to zoom out.

Change the brightness of the display?
System Preferences→Displays→Display→move the Brightness slider left or right to decrease or increase the brightness, respectively

Press the F1 key to decrease the brightness.

Press the F2 key to increase the brightness.

Calibrate my display to ensure its colors are accurate?
System Preferences→Displays→Color→click on the Calibrate button

Applications→Utilities→ColorSync Utility→click on Profile First Aid in the toolbar→click on the Verify button; if needed, repair any ColorSync profiles and then Verify again

The Dock

Change the Dock's preferences?
→Dock→Dock Preferences

System Preferences→Dock

Control-click on the Dock's divider bar, and select Dock Preferences from the context menu.

Quickly resize the Dock without launching its System Preferences panel?
Place the mouse over the divider bar in the Dock; the pointer will change from an arrow to a horizontal bar with arrows pointing up and down. Click

on the divider bar and move the mouse up or down to make the Dock larger or smaller, respectively.

Add a program to the Dock?

Drag and drop an application's icon in the Dock from a Finder window.

After launching an application that isn't normally in the Dock, Control-click on that application's icon, and select "Keep in Dock" from the pop-up menu.

Remove a program from the Dock?

Drag the application icon from the Dock, and drop it anywhere.

Change the Dock's location from the bottom of the screen to the left or right side?

System Preferences→Dock→Position on screen (Left or Right)

→Dock→Position on (Left or Right)

Control-click on the Dock's divider, and select "Position on screen→Left or Right.

Shift-click on the Dock's divider and move the pointer to the left or right edge of the screen.

Control the magnification of icons in the Dock?

System Preferences→Dock→select the checkbox next to Magnification and move the slider left or right to decrease or increase the amount of magnification

→Dock→Turn Magnification (On/Off)

Control-click the Dock's divider and select Turn Magnification (On/Off).

Make it so the Dock hides when I'm not using it?

Option-⌘-D

System Preferences→Dock→Automatically hide and show the Dock

→Dock→Turn Hiding (On/Off)

Control-click the Dock's divider and select Turn Hiding (On/Off).

Stop application icons from bouncing when a program is launched?

System Preferences→Dock→Animate opening applications

Quickly go to an application's location in the Finder?

⌘-click on the application's icon in the Dock.

View a list of the windows an application has open?

Control-click on the application's icon in the Dock.

Force quit an application?

Option-click on an application icon in the Dock.

Hide the windows of all running applications?

Option-⌘-click on the Desktop.

Hide the windows for other active applications?

Option-⌘-click on the Dock icon for the application you're using, and the open windows for all other active applications instantly go into hiding. To bring another application's windows to the front, click on that application's icon in the Dock. To reveal the other windows, select Show All from the application menu of the application you're currently using (e.g., Finder→Show All).

Faxes

Configure my Mac to receive faxes?
System Preferences→Print & Fax→Faxing→select the checkbox next to "Receive faxes on this computer"

Set my computer's fax number?
System Preferences→Print & Fax→Faxing→enter the phone number of the line that's connected to your Mac in the "My Fax Number" text field

Have incoming faxes print on my printer?
System Preferences→Print & Fax→Faxing→select the checkbox next to "Print on Printer"→select a printer from the pop-up menu

Specify the number of rings before my Mac picks up the line to receive a fax?
System Preferences→Print & Fax→Faxing→When a Fax Arrives→enter a number in the text field

Specify where incoming faxes are saved to?
System Preferences→Print & Fax→Faxing→When a Fax Arrives→Save to→select either Faxes (*~/Faxes*), Shared Faxes (*/Users/Shared/Faxes*), or choose another folder where you'd like them saved to

Unfortunately, Mac OS X doesn't alert you when there is an incoming fax; instead, you need to check the folder to which you want faxes saved if you think one may have arrived.

To solve this oversight, you can download and install the Fax Alert script, created by Rainer Brockerhoff (*http://www.brockerhoff.net/fai/index.html*). Once installed, this Folder Action script pops open a dialog window to let you know when a fax is received in the folder you specify.

Fax a Word document to a friend?
Within the Word document, select File→Print; click on the Fax button at the bottom of the Print dialog→fill in the information→click on the Fax button

Files and Folders

Create a new folder?
File→New Folder (in the Finder)

Control-click→New Folder (in a Finder window or on the Desktop)

Shift-⌘-N.

In earlier versions of the Mac OS, ⌘-N was used to create new folders; now ⌘-N is used to open a new Finder window.

Select New Folder from the Finder's Action menu.

Rename a file or folder?

Click once on the icon and hit Return, type in the new name, and then hit Return to accept the new name.

Click once on the icon, and then click once on the name of the file to highlight it (or press Return). Type in the new name for the file or folder, and hit Return to accept the new name.

Click on the icon, and then use ⌘-I to open the Get Info window. Click on the disclosure triangle next to Name & Extension, enter the new file or directory name, and then close the Get Info window.

In the Terminal, use the following command:

```
MacChuck:~ chuck$ mv myFile.txt yourFile.txt
```

The *mv* command changes the name of *myFile.txt* to *yourFile.txt*.

Change the program associated with a particular extension?

Click on a file, and then use File→Get Info (or ⌘-I). Click on the disclosure triangle next to "Open with" and select one of the applications from the pull-down menu, or choose Other to select a different program. If you want to specify that application as the default for opening files with that particular extension, click the Change All; otherwise, close the Info window to save the changes.

Change the permissions for a file or directory?

Click on a file or directory, and then use File→Get Info (or ⌘-I). Click on the disclosure triangle next to "Ownership & Permissions" to change the access for the Owner, Group, and Others.

Use the *chmod* command. To learn more about *chmod* and its options, see its manpage (*man chmod*).

Copy a file to the Desktop instead of moving it or creating a shortcut?

Select the file, then Option-drag the icon to the Desktop (notice a plus sign will appear next to the pointer in a green bubble), and release the mouse button.

In the Finder, select the file→Edit→Copy `filename`→click on the Desktop icon in the Finder's Sidebar→Edit→Paste item

Find out where an open file exists in the filesystem?

Command-click on the proxy icon in the titlebar. This pops open a context menu, showing you where the file exists. Selecting another item (such as a hard drive or a folder) from the proxy icon's context menu opens a Finder window that takes you to the location.

Quickly create a directory and a set of numbered directories (such as for chapters in a book)?

```
MacChuck:~ chuck$ mkdir -p NewBook/ {ch}{01,02,03,04,05}
MacChuck:~ chuck$ ls -F NewBook
ch01/ ch02/ ch03/ ch04/ ch05/
```

Try doing that in the Finder: you can't! After issuing the first command, *ls –F NewBook* lists the folders within the *NewBook* directory, which shows that five separate subdirectories have been created.

Quickly delete a directory (and its subdirectories) without sending it to Trash?
Issue the following command in the Terminal:

```
MacChuck:~ chuck$ rm -rf directory_name
```

Make the Trash stop asking me if I'm sure I want to delete every file?
Finder→Preferences (or ⌘-,)→Advanced→uncheck the option next to "Show warning before emptying the Trash"

Empty the trash of locked items?
Shift-Option-⌘-Delete. The addition of the Option key forces the deletion of the contents of Trash.

Give a file or folder a custom icon?
Open an image file, and copy it with ⌘-C. Select the icon→File→Get Info (⌘-I). Select the file icon in the General section, and then paste (⌘-V) in the new image.

The proper image size for an icon is 128 × 128 pixels.

Quickly create an alias of an open file, or move it, depending on the application (e.g., Word)?
Click and drag the file's proxy icon to a new location (i.e., the Desktop, Dock, Finder, etc.). The file must first be saved and named before an alias can be created.

Dragging a folder's proxy icon from a Finder window's titlebar moves that folder to the new location instead of creating an alias. If you want to create an alias for a folder, you should select the folder in the Finder, then Option-⌘-drag the folder to where you'd like the alias to be. As a visual cue to let you know you're creating an alias, the mouse pointer changes to a curved arrow.

Create a zip archive of some image files I want to send via email?
Select the image files in the Finder, and then select File→Create Archive of *x* items; a zip archive file will be created in the same directory as the image files.

Finder

Hide the Finder toolbar?

View→Hide Toolbar (Option-⌘-T)

Click on the transparent button in the upper-right corner of the titlebar.

Customize the Finder toolbar?

Finder→View→Customize Toolbar

Control-click within the toolbar, and select Customize Toolbar from the context menu.

Option-⌘-click on the toolbar button.

Option-⌘-clicking on the toolbar button again closes the Customize Toolbar window and returns to the previous Finder View.

Always open the Finder in Column View?

Finder→Preferences (⌘-,)→General→select the checkbox next to "Open new windows in column view"

From Icon View, open a folder in a new Finder window?

⌘-double-click the folder icon.

Force folders to open in a new Finder window when they're double-clicked?

Hide the Finder toolbar (only works in Icon or List View).

Quickly switch to my home directory?

Go→Home (Shift-⌘-H)

Quickly go back or forward in a Finder view?

Use ⌘-[or ⌘-] to go back or forward, respectively.

This also works in most web browsers, including Safari, Internet Explorer, Netscape Communicator, Mozilla, and Firefox.

Show only the icons or text labels of items in the toolbar?

View→Customize Toolbar→Show; select Icon Only or Text Only from the pull-down menu

Control-click on the toolbar, and select Icon Only Mode or Text Only Mode from the context menu.

Speed up Finder searches?

Finder→Preferences (⌘-,)→Advanced→click on the Select button at the bottom of the window; this pops open a window that lets you select the languages to use when searching a file's contents. The fewer languages you select, the faster your search.

Locate a specific folder in the Finder?

Go→Go to Folder (or Shift-⌘-G)

Where is the database file saved for use with context searches from the Finder?

It's saved in *~/Library/Indexes/FindByContent*.

Fonts and Font Management

Share fonts with other users on my system?

If you are the administrator, move the font from */Users/username/Library/Fonts* to */Library/Fonts*.

Where can I store new fonts I've purchased or downloaded from the Internet?

Save them to */Users/username/Library/Fonts* for your personal use or to */Library/Fonts* to allow everyone on the system access to them.

Why aren't my bitmap fonts working?

Mac OS X doesn't support bitmapped fonts; it supports only TrueType, OpenType, and PostScript Level 1 fonts.

What does the .dfont extension mean on some of my Mac OS X fonts?

The extension stands for "Data Fork TrueType Font." Basically, this just tells you that this is a TrueType font.

Turn off font antialiasing?

You can't, but you can adjust the minimum font size to be affected by font smoothing in System Preferences→Appearance→"Turn off text smoothing for font sizes *x* and smaller" (Eight points is the default setting).

Create a Font Collection?

Applications→Font Book→File→New Collection (⌘-N)→type in a name for the new collection (such as BookFonts)→hit Return→click on All Fonts at the top of the Collection column→select the fonts you want to add to your collection→drag the fonts to your collection

Where are my Font Collections stored, in case I want to share them with another user?

They are stored in */Users/username/Library/FontCollections*.

If you want to share a collection, place a copy of the collection in the Shared folder. All font collections have a *.collection* file extension.

Add a new font to the system?

Applications→Font Book→File→Add Fonts (⌘-O)→select the font(s) you want to add→select one of the three options for installing the fonts ("for me only," "for all users of this computer," or "for Classic Mac OS")→click on the Open button

Remove a font from the system?

Applications→Font Book→select the font in the Font column→File→Remove Font

Make Classic's font available for Mac OS X applications?

Applications→Font Book→File→Add Fonts (⌘-O)→navigate to /System Folder/Fonts→select all the fonts (⌘-A)→select one of the three options for installing the fonts ("for me only," "for all users of this computer," or "for Classic Mac OS")→click on the Open button

Make a Mac OS X font usable for Classic applications?

Applications→Font Book→File→Add Fonts (⌘-O)→select the fonts you want to share with Classic applications→select "Install fonts for Classic Mac OS"→click on the Open button

Disable a font from being used?

Applications→Font Book→select the font in the Font column→click on the Disable button beneath the column (or use Edit→Disable Font)

Disable a font collection from being used?

Applications→Font Book→select the font collection in the Collections column→click on the Disable button beneath the column (or use Edit→Disable Collection)

Find out who made a particular font?

Applications→Font Book→select the font in the Font column→Preview→Show Font Info (⌘-I)→details about the font appear beneath the font preview area on the right; the creator of the font is displayed next to the "Foundry" item

Why is there a bullet to the right of a font name in Font Book?

This means that there are duplicate copies of that font on your system. To resolve this, select Edit→Resolve Duplicates.

Groups

Add a group?

See the section "Accounts and User Management."

Internet, Web, and Email

Change the default email client and web browser from Mail and Safari, respectively?

To select a different email client:

1. Launch Mail (*/Applications*).
2. Select Mail→Preferences from the menu bar.
3. Click on the General icon in the toolbar.
4. From the pop-up menu next to "Default Email Reader," select a different email application, if you have another installed on your system.

To select a different web browser:

1. Launch Safari (*/Applications*).
2. Select Safari→Preferences from the menu bar.
3. Click on the General icon in the toolbar.
4. From the pop-up menu next to "Default Web Browser," select a different web browser, if you have another installed on your system.

Specify where Safari saves files downloaded from the Internet?

Safari (*/Applications*)→Safari→Preferences→General→Save downloaded files to→select a location on your system where you'd like to save the files

Change Safari's default home page?
Safari→Preferences→General→Home page→enter a URL in the text box

Turn on web sharing?
System Preferences→Sharing→Services→click on the checkbox next to Personal Web Sharing to start this service. Enabling this service allows others to access your Sites folder (*/Users/username/Sites*) from the Internet.

Register my license number for QuickTime Pro?
System Preferences→QuickTime; click on the Registration button and enter your license number

Listen to an Internet radio station?
iTunes→Radio; click on the Radio option in the Source pane to the left, the right pane changes to show you a list of different music genres from which to choose. Click on the disclosure triangle next to a music type to reveal the available stations.

Use my own stylesheet for viewing web pages in Safari?
Safari (*/Applications*)→Safari→Preferences (⌘-,)→Advanced→Style Sheet→ locate and select the Cascading Style Sheet (CSS) you want to apply

Connect to an FTP site?
Finder→Go→Connect to Server (⌘-K)→enter the address for the FTP site (e.g., *ftp://ftp.oreilly.com*)→click on the Connect button→the FTP site mounts on your Desktop and a Finder window opens for that site

Create shortcuts on my Desktop for web sites I visit often, or for people I email frequently?
Open the TextEdit application, enter a URL (such as *http://www.oreilly.com*) or an email address (such as *chuckdude@mac.com*), then triple-click on the address to select the entire line and drag that to your Desktop. This creates an icon on your Desktop for whatever you drag there. When you double-click on the icon, your default web browser opens that URL, or your email client creates a new message window with the address specified by the shortcut.

.Mac

Set up a .Mac account?
System Preference→.Mac→.Mac→Sign Up (you must be connected to the Internet to set up a .Mac account)

Find out how much space I have available on my iDisk?
System Preferences→.Mac→iDisk

Require a password from others before they can access my iDisk's Public folder?
System Preferences→.Mac→iDisk→Your Public Folder→click on the checkbox next to "Use a Password to Protect your Public Folder," and then click on the Set Password button to set a password

Create a local copy of my iDisk?

System Preferences→.Mac→iDisk→click on the checkbox next to "Create local copy of your iDisk"→select one of the radio buttons to Automatically or Manually synchronize your local iDisk with the online iDisk

Quickly access my .Mac email from Safari?

Enter the URL *http://webmail.mac.com*, and log in using your .Mac member name and password.

Mount my iDisk?

Click on the iDisk icon in the Finder's Sidebar.

Finder→Go→iDisk→My iDisk

Use the keyboard shortcut Shift-⌘-I.

Mount another .Mac member's iDisk?

Finder→Go→iDisk→Other User's iDisk

Mount another .Mac member's iDisk Public folder?

Finder→Go→iDisk→Other User's Public Folder

Unmount my iDisk?

Drag the iDisk icon from the Desktop to the Trash.

Finder→iDisk→Action menu→Eject "*dotMac_MemberName*"

Unmount another user's iDisk Public folder?

Drag the iDisk icon from the Desktop to the Trash.

Click on the eject icon next to the iDisk name in the Finder's Sidebar.

Finder→select the iDisk or Public folder in question from the Sidebar→Action menu→Eject "*dotMac_MemberName*-Public"

Go to a .Mac member's HomePage?

Point your browser to *http://homepage.mac.com/dotMac_MemberName*, for example, *http://homepage.mac.com/chuckdude*.

Create a .Mac Slide Show?

Here's how you can create a .Mac Slide Show, otherwise known as a screensaver:

1. Launch iPhoto (*/Applications*).
2. Select the images you want to use for your screensaver.
3. Click on the .Mac Slides button at the bottom of iPhoto's window.

iPhoto creates a slide show from the pictures you selected and posts them on your iDisk in */Pictures/Slide Shows/Public*.

Configure my Mac to use a .Mac member's Slide Show?

System Preferences→Desktop & Screen Saver→Screen Saver→select .Mac in the left column→click the Options button→enter the member's name in the .Mac Membership Name field→click OK

Back up to my iDisk automatically with a modem connection when I'm not around?

System Preferences→Network→Show→Internal Modem→PPP→PPP Options→select the checkbox next to "Connect automatically when needed"→select the checkbox next to "Prompt every XX minutes to maintain connection"→configure Backup to do a scheduled backup to your iDisk

Publish a movie I've created with iMovie to my .Mac HomePage?
iMovie (*/Applications*)→File→Share→HomePage→click on the Share button

Use iPhoto to create a Photo Album page for my .Mac HomePage?
iPhoto (*/Applications*)→select the images→click on the HomePage button at the bottom of the window→edit the page as necessary

Menu Extras

Remove a menu extra from the menu bar?
Command-click on the icon, and drag it off the menu bar.

Switch the position of a menu extra with another?
Command-click on the icon, and drag it left or right; the other menu extra icons will move out of the way, giving you room to drop the icon where you want it.

Change the settings for the clock's menu extra?
System Preferences→Date & Time→Clock

Click on the clock menu extra→View as (Icon/Text)

Remove the clock from the menu bar?
Command-drag the clock off the menu bar.

System Preferences→Date & Time→Clock→deselect the checkbox next to "Show the date and time"

Add a menu extra to show the status of my iBook's battery?
System Preferences→Energy Saver→select the checkbox next to "Show battery status in the menu bar"

In the Finder, go to */System/Library/CoreServices/Menu Extras*, and double-click on the *Battery.menu* item.

Add a menu extra for controlling the displays connected to my Mac?
System Preferences→Displays→select the checkbox next to "Show displays in menu bar"

In the Finder, go to */System/Library/CoreServices/Menu Extras*, and double-click on the *Displays.menu* item.

Add an AirPort menu extra?
System Preferences→Network→AirPort→select the checkbox next to "Show AirPort status in menu bar"

In the Finder, go to */System/Library/CoreServices/Menu Extras*, and double-click on the *AirPort.menu* item.

Add a menu extra for the different keyboard language types?
System Preferences→International→Input Menu→select the languages you would like to turn on by clicking on their checkboxes→select the checkbox next to "Show input menu in menu bar"

Access the Character Palette from the menu bar?

System Preferences→International→Input Menu→select the checkbox next to "Character Palette"→select the checkbox next to "Show input menu in menu bar"

Add an eject button for my CD/DVD drive to the menu bar?

In the Finder, go to */System/Library/CoreServices/Menu Extras*, and double-click on the *Eject.menu* item.

Add a sound control to the menu bar?

System Preferences→Sound→select the checkbox next to "Show volume in menu bar"

In the Finder, go to */System/Library/CoreServices/Menu Extras,* and double-click on the *Volume.menu* folder.

Get that little lock icon in my menu bar for quickly locking and unlocking my keychain?

Keychain Access (*/Applications/Utilities*)→View→Show Status in Menu Bar

Control-click on Keychain Access (*/Applications/Utilities*)→select "Show Package Contents"→change the Finder view to Column View (⌘-3)→Contents→Resources→double-click on the *Keychain.menu* item

Add the Script Menu to the menu bar?

In the Finder, go to */Applications/AppleScript*, and double-click on the item named *Install Script Menu*.

Remove the Script Menu from the menu bar?

Command-click on the Script Menu, and drag it off the menu bar.

In the Finder, go to */Applications/AppleScript*, and double-click on the item named *Remove Script Menu*.

Add a menu extra for iChat?

iChat (*/Applications*)→Preferences (⌘-,)→General→Settings→click on the checkbox next to "Show status in menu bar"

In the Finder, go to */System/Library/CoreServices/Menu Extras*, and double-click on the *iChat.menu* item.

Add a menu extra for Bluetooth?

System Preferences→Bluetooth→Settings→select the checkbox next to "Show Bluetooth status in the menu bar"

In the Finder, go to */System/Library/CoreServices/Menu Extras*, and double-click on the *Bluetooth.menu* item.

Display the modem status in the menu bar?

System Preferences→Network→Show→Internal Modem→Modem→select the checkbox next to "Show modem status in menu bar"

In the Finder, go to */System/Library/CoreServices/Menu Extras*, and double-click on the *PPP.menu* item.

Add a menu extra for my PPPoE (Point-to-Point Protocol over Ethernet) connection?

System Preferences→Network→PPPoE→select the checkbox next to "Show PPPoE status in menu bar"

In the Finder, go to */System/Library/CoreServices/Menu Extras*, and double-click on the *PPPoE.menu* item.

Add a menu extra for use with an infrared port?

In the Finder, go to */System/Library/CoreServices/Menu Extras*, and double-click on the *IrDA.menu* item.

Add a menu extra for viewing the status of the PCMCIA card in my PowerBook?

In the Finder, go to */System/Library/CoreServices/Menu Extras*, and double-click on the *PCCard.menu* item.

Add a menu extra for Ink?

System Preferences→Ink→Settings→select the checkbox next to "Show Ink in menu bar"

In the Finder, go to */System/Library/CoreServices/Menu Extras*, and double-click on the *Ink.menu* item.

If you don't have a USB graphics tablet plugged in to your Mac, you can still double-click on the *Ink.menu* item and open Ink's preference panel in System Preferences. However, if you click on the Show All button in System Preferences' toolbar, you won't see an icon in the Hardware section for Ink.

Mice, Trackpads, and Scrollwheel Mice

Change the double-click speed of my mouse?

System Preferences→Keyboard & Mouse→Mouse (or Trackpad if you're using a PowerBook or iBook)

Change the scrolling speed for my scrollwheel mouse?

System Preferences→Keyboard & Mouse→Mouse→Scrolling Speed

Change the settings on my iBook's trackpad so it can emulate mouse clicks?

System Preferences→Keyboard & Mouse→Trackpad→Use trackpad for:→select the checkbox next to Clicking, and Dragging and Drag Lock, if you'd like to use the trackpad for those functions as well

Set up my PowerBook so it recognizes my Apple Wireless Mouse?

System Preferences→Keyboard & Mouse→Bluetooth→click on the "Set Up New Device" button

Check the battery status of my Apple Wireless Mouse?

System Preferences→Keyboard & Mouse→Bluetooth

Configure my iBook so I can't use the trackpad if I'm also using a mouse?

System Preferences→Keyboard & Mouse→Trackpad→select the checkbox next to "Ignore trackpad when mouse is present"

Modems and Dial-Up Networking

Configure a modem for dialing into my ISP?

Go to System Preferences→Network, and follow these steps:

1. Select New Location from the Location pull-down menu. Enter a name for the new location (for example, My ISP), and click OK.
2. Select Internal Modem from the Show pull-down menu.
3. Fill in the blanks on the PPP panel.
4. In the TCP/IP panel, select Using PPP from the Configure IPv4 pull-down menu.
5. Select your modem type from the Modem panel.
6. Click the Apply Now button.

Show the modem status in the menu bar?

System Preferences→Network→Show→Internal Modem→Modem→click on the checkbox next to "Show modem status in menu bar"

Make sure my modem is working?

Internet Connect (*/Applications*)→Internal Modem→check the Status area at the bottom of the window

Connect to my ISP automatically when my Mac needs to (e.g., for use with Software Update or .Mac's Backup application for late-night backups to your iDisk)?

System Preferences→Network→Show→Internal Modem→PPP→PPP Options→select the checkbox next to "Connect automatically when needed"→select the checkbox next to "Prompt every [30] minutes to maintain connection" and change the time from 30 minutes to 10 minutes

Set my computer to wake up from sleep mode when the modem rings?

System Preferences→Energy Saver→Options→Wake Options→click on the checkbox next to "Wake when the modem detects a ring"

Find out the speed of my dial-up connection?

Internet Connect (*/Applications*)→Internal Modem→check the Status area at the bottom of the window

Disable call waiting on my phone when using the modem?

System Preferences→Network→PPP; insert `*70` at the beginning of the telephone number you're dialing (e.g., `*70, 1-707-555-1212`).

Where are my modem configuration files stored?

They are stored in */Library/Modem Scripts*.

Specify how many times my modem will redial if it detects a busy signal?

System Preferences→Network→Show→Internal Modem→PPP→PPP Options→Session Options→Redial if busy→enter a number in the "Redial *X* times" field

Networking

Find the media access control (MAC) address for my Ethernet card?

Finder→Applications→Utilities→System Profiler→Network Contents→Configuration Name→Built-in Ethernet→look at the bottom half of the display for the "Ethernet Address"

System Preferences→Network→Ethernet pane, look for a sequence of numbers and letters next to Ethernet Address

Configure my system to connect to an Ethernet network?

Go to System Preferences→Network and follow these steps:

1. Select New Location from the Location pull-down menu. Enter a name for the new location (for example, ORA-Local), and click OK.
2. Select Built-in Ethernet from the Show pull-down menu.
3. From the Configure pull-down menu in the TCP/IP panel, select Using DHCP if your IP address will be assigned dynamically, or Manually if your machine will have a fixed IP address. (In most cases, particularly if you have a broadband Internet connection at home, your IP address is assigned via DHCP.)
4. If you're on an AppleTalk network, select the Make AppleTalk Active option in the AppleTalk panel, and select your Zone (if any).
5. Click the Apply Now button.

Configure my system to connect to a virtual private network (VPN)?

Here's how to set up your Mac OS X system for connecting to a VPN:

1. Launch Internet Connect (*/Applications*). (If you haven't used Internet Connect before, you will be prompted to configure the modem settings, or a VPN connection if a modem can't be found.)
2. Click on the VPN (PPTP) icon in the toolbar.
3. In the VPN Connection window, enter the Server Address, Account name, and Password you will use to connect to the VPN. If your VPN is on an older Windows-based server, you have to enter the domain as well; e.g., *domain\chuck*.
4. Click the Connect button to try connecting to the VPN.
5. Open the Network preference panel (System Preferences→Network) and select Location→New Location; supply a name for your VPN (such as Work VPN) and hit OK.
6. Select Show→VPN (PPTP) in the Network preferences panel.
7. In the TCP/IP tab, select Configure IPv4→select Using PPP from the drop-down menu.
8. Click the Apply Now button on the Network preferences panel.
9. Go back to Internet Connect by clicking on its Dock icon, and select File→New VPN Connection Window (Shift-⌘-P).
10. Click on the Connect button to connect to your VPN server. (The Status indicator in this window will tell you whether you're connected.)

When you want to connect to the VPN in the future, follow these steps:

1. Apple→Location→*VPN Name* (e.g., Work VPN).
2. Launch Internet Connect (*/Applications*); if you use the VPN frequently, you should consider adding Internet Connect to your Dock.
3. File→New VPN Connection Window (Shift-⌘-P).
4. Click on the Connect button.

When you've completed the work you need to do over the VPN, click the Disconnect button in the VPN Connection window, quit Internet Connect, and then change your network location to your regular network setting.

Change my Rendezvous name from my full name to something else?
System Preferences→Sharing; enter the new name in the Rendezvous Name text box. Your Rendezvous name will have a *.local* extension; for example, *MacPanther.local*.

Configure my AirPort settings for wireless networking?
Follow the steps for connecting to an Ethernet network first, then use the AirPort Setup Assistant (*/Applications/Utilities*). The settings you've applied for your regular network will be applied to your AirPort settings.

Find out the speed of my network connection?
Network Utility (*/Applications/Utilities*)→Info panel; look next to Link Speed in the Interface Information section.

Find out what's taking a site so long to respond?
Network Utility (*/Applications/Utilities*)→Ping panel; enter the network address for the location (e.g., *www.macdevcenter.com* or *10.0.2.1*).

Use the *ping* command:

```
MacChuck:~ chuck$ ping hostname
```

Trace the route taken to connect to a web page?
Network Utility (*/Applications/Utilities*)→Traceroute panel; enter the URL for the location.

Use the *traceroute* command:

```
MacChuck:~ chuck$ traceroute hostname
```

Restrict access to my computer so others can get files I make available to them?
System Preferences→Sharing→Services→click on the checkbox next to Personal File Sharing to give others access to your Public folder (*/Users/username/Public*). The Public folder is read-only, which means other people can only view or copy files from that directory; they can't write files to it.

Where can my coworkers place files on my computer without getting access to the rest of my system?
With file sharing turned on, people can place files, folders, or even applications in your Drop Box, located within the Public folder (*/Users/username/Public/Drop Box*).

Quickly switch to an AirPort network after disconnecting the Ethernet cable from my iBook?

System Preferences→Network→Show→Active Network Ports. Click on the checkboxes next to the network ports you want to enable, and drag the ports in the list to place them in the order in which you're most likely to connect to them. (The Automatic location should do this for you, but it doesn't always work.)

Share my modem or Ethernet connection with other AirPort- equipped Macs?

System Preferences→Sharing→Internet panel; click on the Start button to turn Internet sharing on

View what's inside someone else's iDisk Public folder?

Go→Connect to Server. At the bottom of the dialog box, type `http://idisk.mac.com/`*`membername`*`/Public`. Click Connect or press Return; the Public iDisk image will then mount on your desktop.

Not all iDisk Public folders are created equal. An iDisk owner can choose to make her Public folder read-only, or read-write, which allows others to place files in her Public folder. The Public folder can also be password protected, which means you need to enter a password before you can mount the Public folder.

Connect to a networked drive?

Click the /Networks icon and browse for the server name within it or its subdirectories. When you've found it, double-click its icon (or in column view, click the Connect button in its preview column), enter your username and password when prompted and the shared volume will appear on your desktop and in the sidebar.

Connect directly to an SMB share?

Finder→Go→Connect to Server (⌘-K)

If you want to connect to a Windows server directly, you can specify the Address in the text box as follows:

```
smb://hostname/sharename
```

After clicking the Connect button, you will be asked to supply the domain to which you wish to connect as well as your username and password. You can speed up this process by supplying the domain and your username, as follows:

```
smb://domain;username@hostname/sharename
```

Where *`domain`* is the NT domain name; *`username`* is the name you use to connect to that domain; and *`hostname`* and *`sharename`* are the server name and shared directory that you have or want to access. Now when you click on the Connect button, all you need to enter is your password (if one is required), and the networked drive will appear on your Desktop.

Before pressing the Connect button, press the button with a plus sign (+) in it to add the server to your list of Favorites. This will save you time in the future if you frequently need to connect to the same drive, because you won't have to enter that address again.

Printer Configuration and Printing

Configure a printer?

Printer Setup Utility (*/Applications/Utilities*)→click on the Add button in the Printer List window, or select Printers→Add Printer from the menu bar. Select how the printer is connected using the pull-down menu (AppleTalk, Bluetooth, IP Printing, Open Directory, Rendezvous, USB, or Windows Printing).

- If you select AppleTalk, select the zone (if any) using the second pull-down menu, choose the printer in the lower pane, and then click the Add button.
- If you select IP Printing, you need to know and fill in the IP address of the printer; select the printer model, and click the Add button.
- If you select Open Directory, you can choose a printer listed in the NetInfo Network. Select the printer name, and then click the Add button.
- If you select Rendezvous, USB, or Windows, choose the name of the printer and the printer model, and then click the Add button.

View the jobs in the print queue?

Printer Setup Utility→double-click on the name of the printer to see the print queue

Cancel a print job?

Printer Setup Utility→double-click on the printer name→click on the name of the print job→click on the Delete button

Halt a print job?

Printer Setup Utility→double-click on the printer name→click on the name of the print job→click on the Hold button. (Click on the Resume button to start the job where it left off.)

Share the printer that's connected to my Mac with another user?

System Preferences→Sharing→Services→click on the checkbox next to Printer Sharing

System Preferences→Print & Fax→Printing→select the checkbox next to "Share my printers with other computers"

Configure my system so I can print from the command line using the Terminal?

To do this, you must first issue the cryptic *at_cho_prn* command either with the *sudo* command or as *root*:

```
[dhcp-123-45:~] chuck$ sudo at_cho_prn
Password: ********
1  East_Ora_EtherTalk      2  West_Ora_EtherTalk
```

```
ZONE number (0 for current zone)? 1
Zone:East_Ora_EtherTalk
   1: 0002.83.9dtpenguin1:LaserWriter
   2: 0002.86.9d DODO1:LaserWriter
   3: 0002.82.9d Chicken1:LaserWriter
   4: 0002.08.9d Rheas1:LaserWriter
   5: 0002.85.9d weka1:LaserWriter
ITEM number (0 to make no selection)? 5
Default printer is:weka1:LaserWriter@East_Ora_EtherTalk
status: idle
[dhcp-123-45:~] chuck$
```

In the example shown here, I've specified *East_Ora_EtherTalk* as my AppleTalk zone and *weka1* as my default printer for printing from the command line.

Send a text file to a PostScript printer?

For this, use the *enscript* and *atprint* commands:

```
[dhcp-123-45:~/Desktop] chuck$ enscript -p- textFile.txt | atprint
Looking for weka1:LaserWriter@East_Ora_EtherTalk.
Trying to connect to weka1:LaserWriter@East_Ora_EtherTalk.
atprint: printing on weka1:LaserWriter@East_Ora_EtherTalk.
[ 3 pages * 1 copy ] left in -
[dhcp-123-45:~/Desktop] chuck$
```

The *enscript* command is used to translate plaintext into PostScript so the file can be printed. The *atprint* command lets you stream any Unix output to an AppleTalk printer. In this example, the commands are piped together (using the standard Unix pipe, |), which formats the file and sends it to the default AppleTalk printer. Additional information about *enscript* and its options can be found in its manpage (*man enscript*).

There is another Unix facility, *lpd*, for printing from the command line. However, configuring *lpd* is beyond the scope of this book. For information on how to configure *lpd* and use its associated commands (*lpr*, *lpq*, *lprm*), see *Learning Unix for Mac OS X Panther* (O'Reilly).

View a list of available AppleTalk printers on my network?

From the command line, use the *atlookup* command.

If you're on a large AppleTalk network, *atlookup* shows you everything: printers, servers, computers...*everything*. You will have to look through the output to find the item you're looking for.

Screensavers

Adjust the amount of time my system needs to be idle before the screensaver kicks in?

System Preferences→Desktop & Screen Saver→Screen Saver→Start screen saver→move the slider left or right

Quickly activate my screensaver when I know I'll be away from my desk for a while?
System Preferences→Desktop & Screen Saver→Screen Saver→Hot Corners→in Active Screen Corners sheet, mark a corner of the screen to activate or disable the screensaver by selecting one of the pop-up menus

Configure my Mac to use a .Mac member's Slide Show?
System Preferences→Desktop & Screen Saver→Screen Saver→select .Mac in the left column→click the Options button→enter the member's name in the .Mac Membership Name field→click OK

Protect my system from prying eyes while I'm away from my computer?
System Preferences→Security→select the checkbox next to "Require password to wake this computer from sleep or screen saver"

Store a .saver file for a third-party screensaver I've downloaded from the Internet?
Place the *.saver* file in */Library/Screen Savers.*

Locate the default screensavers that come with Mac OS X?
Look in */System/Library/Screen Savers.*

Use the images in one of my iPhoto libraries as a screensaver?
System Preferences→Desktop & Screen Saver→Screen Saver→in the Screen Savers column, scroll down→select the iPhoto library name

Screenshots

Take a screenshot of everything on my display?
Shift-⌘-3

Take a screenshot of a certain portion of my display?
Shift-⌘-4; the mouse pointer will change to a set of crosshairs, which you can use to drag-select the area you desire.

Convert a PDF screenshot into a JPEG image?
Double-click on the screenshot to open it in Preview (*/Applications*)→File→Export (Shift-⌘-E)→enter a new name for the file in the Save As field at the top of the window→select JPEG from the Format pull-down menu→click on the Save button

Take a screenshot of the topmost window, including its shadow?
Shift-⌘-4; position the crosshairs outside the upper-left corner of the window and drag-select the window, including its drop shadow.

Take a screenshot and copy it to the pasteboard without actually creating a screenshot file?
Shift-Control-⌘-3 to take a screenshot of the entire display, or Shift-Control-⌘-4 to select a screenshot area, and then use File→Paste (⌘-V) to paste the screenshot from the clipboard into another document.

Get my regular mouse pointer back after hitting Shift-⌘-4 without taking a screenshot?
Click the mouse once without drag-selecting an area with the crosshairs.

Searching for and Locating Files

Find a file when I don't know its name?

Finder→enter a keyword in the Search field in the toolbar→hit Return to start the search

Finder→File→Find (⌘-F)

Index my hard drive to allow for content-based searching?

Finder→select hard drive→File→Get Info→click on the disclosure triangle next to "Content index"→click on the Index Now button

The Finder doesn't index filenames—only the contents of files. However, you can still search for filenames.

Where is the content index stored?

It's stored in *~/Library/Indexes/FindByContent/00001/.FBCIndex*.

Find a file when I can't remember where I saved it?

Use the *locate* command in the Terminal. However, you must first update the *locate* database as follows:

```
MacChuck:~ chuck$ cd /usr/libexec
MacChuck:/usr/libexec chuck$ sudo ./locate.updatedb
```

If you haven't built the *locate* database yet, this command could take a few minutes to run; afterwards, you will be returned to the command line.

The *locate.updatedb* command is executed weekly by default, as noted in the */etc/weekly* file. However, you might want to issue this command shortly after installing Mac OS X.

Now you can use the *locate* command; for example:

```
MacChuck:/usr/libexec chuck$ locate temp98.doc
/Users/chuck/Books/Templates/temp98.doc
MacChuck:/usr/libexec chuck$
```

In this example, we used *locate* to search for the file *temp98.doc*; in return, the command tells us where the file is located.

Indexing your hard drive via Get Info allows you to do context searches; building the *locate* database helps speed things up when you're searching for a filename. Use both the Finder and the command line to your advantage.

Where is the locate database stored?

It is stored in */var/db/locate.database*.

Clear the Finder's search field?

Click on the X at the right edge of the search field.

Security

Delete a file, making it nearly impossible to be recovered?
Finder→Secure Empty Trash

You should use the Secure Empty Trash option judiciously, keeping in mind that once it is used, the chances of ever recovering that file again is practically nil.

Manage my Keychains?
Keychain Access (*/Applications/Utilities*)

Enable the firewall on my system?
System Preferences→Sharing→Firewall→click on the Start button

Enable my firewall, but make it so I can still use Rendezvous with iChat and iTunes?
System Preferences→Sharing→Firewall→click on the Start button→click on the checkboxes next to "iChat Rendezvous (5297, 5298", and "iTunes Music Sharing (3689)"

Allow people access to my Public folder?
System Preferences→Sharing→Services→click on the checkbox next to Personal File Sharing

Set a master password for my Mac?
System Preferences→Security→FileVault→click on the Set button

Turn on FileVault protection for my user account?
System Preferences→Security→FileVault→FileVault protection is off for this account→click on the "Turn On FileVault" button

Make it so a user has to enter their password to wake their Mac up from sleep or to disable the screensaver?
System Preferences→Security→click on the checkbox next to "Require password to wake this computer from sleep or screen saver"

Have my Mac automatically log me off if I haven't used it within a certain amount of time?
System Preferences→Security→click on the checkbox next to "Log out after [60] minutes of inactivity→change the number of minutes as desired (the default is 60 minutes)

Add a menu bar item for Keychains?
Keychain Access (*/Applications/Utilities*)→View→Show Status in Menu Bar

Create a password-protected note to store some information in?
Keychain Access (*/Applications/Utilities*)→File→New Secure Note Item (or click on the Note icon in the toolbar)→enter a name for the note in the Name field→enter the text of the note in the Note field→click on the Add button

Keep other applications from detecting my keystrokes when I'm using the Terminal?
Terminal (*/Applications/Utilities*)→File→Secure Keyboard Entry

System Information

Find out how much memory I have?

→About This Mac

Find out what version of Mac OS X I'm running?

→About This Mac

→About This Mac→click on the version number (e.g., 10.3.2) to reveal the build number (e.g., 7D24)

System Profiler (*/Applications/Utilities*)→click on the Software item in the Contents column on the left→look in the System Software Overview section on the right to see the exact build of Mac OS X

Find out what processor my Mac has?

→About This Mac

System Profile (*/Applications/Utilities*)→click on the Hardware item in the Contents column on the left→look in the Hardware Overview section on the right

What type of cache do I have and how big is it?

System Profile (*/Applications/Utilities*)→click on the Hardware item in the Contents column on the left→look in the Hardware Overview section on the right

Find out what programs (or processes) are running?

Activity Monitor (*/Applications/Utilities*)→select "My Processes" from the pop-up menu in the toolbar

Terminal (*/Applications/Utilities*)→use the *ps –aux* command

Terminal (*/Applications/Utilities*)→use the *top* command

Display the status of the computer's used and free memory?

Activity Monitor (*/Applications/Utilities*)→System Memory

Terminal (*/Applications/Utilities*)→use the *top* command. The *top* command gives you a real-time view of the processes running on your system, as well as processor and memory usage. To stop the *top* command from running, hit Control-C or ⌘-. (Command-period).

View the hardware connected to my system?

System Profiler (*/Applications/Utilities*)→click on the black disclosure triangle next to the Hardware item in the Contents column on the left→select the appropriate device from the list below (e.g., click on FireWire to see information about an external drive or device connected to your Mac's FireWire port)

Quickly generate a report about my system so I can submit it to Apple along with a bug report?

From the Terminal, issue the following command:

```
MacChuck:~ chuck$ system_profiler > sysprofile.txt
```

The *system_profiler* command runs and redirects the output (with the > symbol) that would normally print in the Terminal window and saves it in the *sysprofile.txt* file in your Home directory. Now you can open, view, and print the file using TextEdit, or copy and paste this into a bug report:

```
MacChuck:~ chuck$ open -e sysprofile.txt
```

System Status

Find out how long my system has been running?

Use the `uptime` command:

```
MacChuck:~ chuck$ uptime
3:34PM  up  10:09, 2 users, load averages: 0.09, 0.12, 0. 09
```

The `uptime` command displays, in the following order: the current time, how long the system has been running (`up 10:09`, or 10 hours 9 minutes), the number of users logged in to the system, and the load averages on the processor.

Display the battery status for my PowerBook in the menu bar?

System Preferences→Energy Saver→select the checkbox next to "Show battery status in menu bar"

Display a volume control in the menu bar?

System Preferences→Sound→select the checkbox next to "Show volume in menu bar"

Change the name of my computer?

System Preferences→Sharing→enter the new name for your computer in the Computer Name text field

Automatically check for updates to the system?

System Preferences→Software Update→Update Software→select the checkbox next to "Check for updates" and then select the frequency (Daily, Weekly, Monthly) from the pop-up menu

Automatically download important updates, such as system and security updates?

System Preferences→Software Update→Update Software→select the checkbox next to "Download important updates in the background"

View a list of the updates I've installed on my Mac?

System Preferences→Software Update→Installed Updates

Have an application start up automatically after I log in?

System Preferences→Accounts→select your username in the left column→Startup Items→the Add button (the one with a plus sign, +)→ use the Finder to select the applications you want to start after you log in

Drag an application icon from the Finder to the window in the Startup Items pane of a user's Accounts preference panel.

Terminal Settings

This section offers advice on how to configure the settings for the Terminal application (also covered in Chapter 20). To configure the Terminal's settings, you need to have an open Terminal window, and then select File→Show Info. You'll then use the pop-up menu at the top of the Terminal Inspector window.

Change the style of the cursor?
Display→Cursor Style→(Block, Underline, Vertical Bar)

Stop the cursor from blinking?
Display→Cursor Style→deselect the checkbox next to Blink

Change the background color and font colors of the Terminal window?
Color→click on the color selection boxes next to Cursor, Normal Text, Selection, and Bold Text to open another window with the color wheel. To change the background color of the Terminal window, select the color selection box next to "Use this background color".

Assign a different title to the Terminal window?
Window→enter a name for the window in the Title text field

Assign a different title to the current Terminal window?
With an open Terminal window, select File→Set Title (Shift-⌘-T). The Terminal Inspector window opens with Window selected in the pull-down menu. Enter a new title for the window in the Title field, and hit Return or Tab to change the title of the current window.

Specify the number of lines a Terminal window can contain in the scrollback buffer?
Buffer→Buffer Size. You can either specify a number of lines in the field provided (10,000 lines is the default) or select either an unlimited scrollback or no scrollback at all.

Set the Terminal's emulation mode to VT100?
Emulation→Strict VT-100 keypad behavior

Automatically close the Terminal window after I've exited?
Shell→When the shell exits→select from either "Close the window" or "Close only if the shell exited cleanly"

Where is the history file for the shell?
It is in *~/.bash_history*.

Where can I create a profile for my shell?
If you use *bash* (which is the default shell for Panther), create a file named *.bash_profile* and save that in your home directory (so *~/.bash_profile*).

Set the transparency of my Terminal window?
Color→Transparency→move the slider left or right for less or more transparency, respectively

Display a keyboard shortcut in the titlebar of my Terminal windows so I can quickly switch between windows?
Window→Title→select the checkbox next to Command Key

Troubleshooting and Maintenance

Force quit an application that's stuck?

Option-⌘-Escape opens a window showing all of the running applications. Select the troublesome application, and click the Force Quit button.

Option-click the application's icon in the Dock, and select Force Quit from the context menu.

Activity Monitor (*/Applications/Utilities*)→select the process that's causing the problem→click on the Quit Process button in the toolbar→select Quit or Force Quit from the alert window

Restart my computer automatically after a power failure?

System Preferences→Energy Saver→Options→select the checkbox next to "Restart automatically after a power failure"

Where are crash logs kept?

~/Library/Logs/CrashReporter

Fix a disk that won't mount?

Disk Utility (*/Applications/Utilities*)→select the disk that won't mount→First Aid→Verify Disk Permissions; after Verify has run, click on the Repair Disk Permissions button if prompted

Restart my system when it has completely frozen?

Hold down the Shift-Option-⌘ keys, and press the Power-On button.

Access command-line mode and bypass Aqua?

There are two ways to access the command-line interface:

1. Hold down ⌘-S when starting up the system; this is known as *single-user mode*.
2. At the login window, type **>console** as the username, don't enter a password, and click on the Login button. This is known as *multiuser mode* and is just like being in the Terminal, except that your entire screen is the Terminal.

When you've finished diagnosing your system, type **reboot** and press Return to reboot your system into Aqua.

Rebuild Classic's Desktop?

System Preferences→Classic→Advanced→Rebuild Classic Desktop→click on the Rebuild Desktop button. There is no need to rebuild Mac OS X's Desktop; holding down Option-⌘ keys at startup is futile.

There is a question mark icon in the Dock. What is this?

A question mark icon in the Dock or in one of the toolbars means that the application, folder, or file that the original icon related to has been deleted from your system. Just drag the question mark icon away from the Dock or toolbar to make it disappear.

View the processor load on my dual-processor G5 machine?

Activity Monitor (*/Applications/Utilities*)→CPU→each processor will have its own meter bar

View a log of software updates?
System Preferences→Software Update→Installed Updates

Connect an external monitor or projector to my PowerBook without restarting?
Select →Sleep to put your laptop to sleep, plug in and turn on the external monitor, and then hit the Escape key to wake your system and the display. You can then use the Displays panel (System Preferences→Displays) to turn display mirroring on or off as needed, or click on the Detect Displays button so your system can probe the external monitor.

Windows

Open a new window?
File→Open (⌘-O)

Close a window?
File→Close (⌘-W)

Close all open windows for an application?
Option-click on the close window button.

If there are changes that need to be saved in any of the windows being closed, you will be prompted to save. Either hit Return to save the changes, or enter ⌘-D to invoke the Don't Save button.

Minimize a window?
Window→Minimize Window (⌘-M)

Double-click on the window's titlebar.

Minimize all open windows for a single application?
Option-⌘-M

With some applications, Option-⌘-M may function differently. For example, issuing Option-⌘-M in Microsoft Word (Office v.X) opens the Paragraph format window (Format→Paragraph). Instead, you can minimize all of Word's windows by holding down the Option key and double-clicking on a document's titlebar.

To be safe, you should save changes to the file before trying to minimize all the application's windows with Option-⌘-M.

Slow down the genie effect while minimizing a window to the Dock?
Shift-click on the minimize button in the window's toolbar. (This works in reverse, too; shift-clicking a minimized window icon in the Dock opens it up slowly.)

Really slow down the genie effect while minimizing a window the Dock?
Shift-⌘-click on the minimize button.

Hide the windows for other active applications?

Option-⌘-click on the Dock icon for the application you're using; the open windows for all other active applications will instantly hide. To bring another application's windows to the front, click on that application's Dock icon. To reveal all the other windows, select Show All from the application menu (e.g., Finder→Show All).

System and Network Administration

Now that you've learned your way around Mac OS X, it's time to put your system to work. This part of the book provides an overview of Mac OS X's filesystem and shows how to configure your system for printing and networking. You'll also get a quick overview on system administration, the Directory Services infrastructure and a lesson on security topics, including use of Mac OS X Panther's FileVault.

The chapters in this part include:

- Chapter 7, *Filesystem Overview*
- Chapter 8, *Networking*
- Chapter 9, *Printer Configuration and Printing*
- Chapter 10, *System Administration Overview*
- Chapter 11, *Directory Services*
- Chapter 12, *Running Network Services*
- Chapter 13, *Security Basics*

7
Filesystem Overview

This chapter examines how Mac OS X works with files, both in the lower level of its filesystems, and more generally in the specific directory layouts it uses to organize its most important files and keep track of installed applications.

Mac OS X Filesystems

Like earlier versions of Mac OS, Mac OS X filesystems favor the Mac OS Extended Format, better known as HFS+ (Hierarchical File System),* but they also work well with the Universal File System (UFS) that most other Unix-based operating systems use as their primary filesystem.

Most Mac OS X volumes use HFS+ as their format for two reasons. First, until Mac OS X 10.3, HFS+ has performed much better than UFS (though UFS performance in Panther has improved greatly, close to matching that of HFS+). The other reason is that HFS+ natively supports multiple file forks (see the later section "File Forks.") Still, through strong UFS support, a Mac OS X machine can work seamlessly with other Unix volumes, such as network-mounted ones that may be accessible over NFS.

Differences Between HFS+ and UFS

Here are the most noticeable differences between the HFS+ and UFS file formats:

- UFS is case-sensitive in its file path interpretation, while standard HFS+ is not. The paths */tmp/foo*, */tmp/Foo*, and */TMP/FOO* all point to the same location on an HFS+ system but to three different ones on a UFS filesystem. However, using Mac OS X Server 10.3, you can format case-sensitive HFS+

* Mac OS 8.1 and later used HFS+, while versions prior to 8.1 used the older Mac OS Standard Format, known as just HFS (without the plus).

volumes, and these volumes will maintain case-sensitivity when mounted on a Mac OS X client system.

Some software from the UFS world might assert case-sensitivity despite HFS+'s permissiveness. The Tab-completion feature of the *bash* or *zsh* shell command lines, for example, is case-sensitive, even if the filesystem they're working with is not.

- UFS uses slashes (/) as its path separator, while HFS+ uses colons (:). However, various Mac OS X applications accept slash-using path notation no matter the underlying filesystem format. The Finder's Go→Go To Folder (Shift-⌘-G) command lets you type a path to travel to that point on the computer's filesystem. On the other hand, the Finder's Get Info window displays the real, colon-based path of the selected Finder object if it's on an HFS+ system.

  The two filesystems have a different concept of "root," or what the path / or : means, respectively. A UFS system's root directory is the top level of some designated disk volume, while the root to an HFS+ filesystem contains no data but has a list of available volumes. This is why absolute filenames expressed in HFS+ terms always lead in with a volume name, such as `Volume:tmp:`*foo*. (It's also philosophically similar to the filesystem *root* as the Finder displays it, through its Go→Computer (Shift-⌘-C) command.)

Mac OS X often expects absolute paths to act as they would look on a UFS system. In the Terminal, *cd /* takes you to the top level of the boot volume, not to the HFS+ *root*. (Other volumes are accessible from */Volumes*.)

- HFS+ stores two time-related pieces of metadata with each file: its creation date and its modification date. UFS stores only modification dates.

File Forks

HFS+ is perhaps most distinctive among filesystems concerning how it allows files to store information in multiple *forks*. A typical non-Carbonized application for Mac OS 9 stores its executable binary code in a *data fork*, and supplemental information—such as icons, dialogs, and sounds—is stored in a *resource fork*. Each fork is a separate subsection of the file. Documents can also have both data and resources forks, which applications can read from and write to as they see fit.

However, Mac OS X is based on Unix, which was built to work with single-forked files, holding nothing except their own data. Modern Mac OS applications eschew all use of resource forks, instead taking one of two paths. They either store all their resources in a separate file with an *.rsrc* extension, kept inside the application package, or they simply store their resources as separate files inside the package. Carbon applications usually take the former, single-file route for their resources, and Cocoa applications favor the latter.

To accommodate traditional Macintosh applications and files, Mac OS X provides native support for multiple forks on HFS+ volumes, and native-like support on

UFS volumes. Copying and moving such files with the Finder works as expected, whether the files reside on an HFS+ or a UFS volume.

Under the hood, however, you'll find that this task required some special engineering on Apple's part. Mac OS X stores any resource fork that happens to reside on a UFS volume as a separate *file*, whose original name is prefixed with `._`. For example, when a copy of the SimpleText application resides on a UFS volume, it's comprised of a data file named *SimpleText*, and a resource file named *._SimpleText*. The Finder shows only the data file but does the work of splitting, moving, and recombining both files as they move between UFS and HFS+ volumes.

Similarly, because the Unix subsystem can't directly recognize multiple file forks residing on HFS+ volumes, the OS handles them differently. When viewed from the Unix command line, resource forks appear as separate files of the same name, but with */rsrc* appended. These special files will not show up in a directory listing, but will when explicitly listed (for example, `ls Simpletext/rsrc"`).

For both of these reasons, then, special care is required when handling dual-fork files from the command line. Traditional Unix file-transfer tools such as *cp*, *mv*, *tar*, *cpio*, and *rscync*, do not recognize resource forks and will leave them behind when moving the data fork, rendering application files useless. Apple provides the *CpMac*, *MvMac*, and *ditto* utilities that do handle resource forks properly, and these are detailed in Chapter 28.

Attribute forks

HFS+ files can store metainformation in a third fork, called an *attribute fork*. Most commonly, this fork, if used, holds the file's application and creator codes.

As with resource forks, Mac OS X supports this fork and its codes but considers them deprecated. Modern Mac applications link files to themselves through filename extensions, not creator codes. As a user, you can also modify these application-document links as you wish, through the "Open with application" page of the Finder's Get Info window (as described in "The Get Info Window" in Chapter 2).

Journaling

The Disk Utility application enables *journaling* on HFS+ volumes. Disk journaling is a feature that both increases filesystem stability and decreases recovery time in the event filesystem directory damage occurs.

With journaling enabled, the OS keeps a record, or *journal*, of all write operations to the disk. If the system ever stops unexpectedly due to a crash or power failure, the OS automatically "replays" the journal upon restart, ensuring that the disk and its directory are again consistent with each other, a processes that takes only a few seconds.

Without journaling enabled, the OS must perform a check of the entire filesystem following a crash to restore consistency. This can take up to several hours, depending on the size of the disk.

Journaling does slightly decrease disk-write performance, but this should only be an issue when working with high-end multimedia, for example, when disks need to perform as fast as possible.

Other Supported Filesystem Formats

Mac OS X can recognize and work with several local filesystem formats beyond UFS and HFS+, as listed in Table 7-1.

Table 7-1. Mac OS X's supported filesystem formats

Filesystem type	Description
HFS+	Mac OS Extended Format. The standard filesystem format for Mac OS Versions 8.1 and later (including Mac OS X).
HFS	Mac OS Standard Format. Used by Mac OS versions prior to 8.1.
UFS	Universal File System, used by most Unix-based systems.
UDF	Universal disk format, used by DVDs.
ISO 9660	Used by CD-ROMs.
FAT	Used primarily by DOS and older versions of Windows, sometimes other media (such as some digital cameras).
FAT32	Used by newer versions of Windows.
NFS	The Network File System (see Chapter 10).

This list doesn't include the remote filesystems that Mac OS X can mount as network-shared volumes. See "Mounting Network Disks Through the Terminal" in Chapter 8.

Filesystem Organization

Mac OS X defines several folders across the filesystem as holding special significance to the system. Individual applications, as well as the system software itself, consult these directories when scanning for certain types of software or resources installed on the machine. For example, a program that wants a list of fonts available to the whole system can look in */Library/Fonts* and */System/Library/Fonts*. Font files can certainly exist elsewhere in the filesystem, but relevant applications aren't likely to find them unless they're in a predictable place.

Domains

You might also have a */Library/Fonts* folder inside your home folder and perhaps yet another inside */Network/Library/Fonts*. Each *Fonts* folder exists inside a separate *domain*–Mac OS X's term for the scope that a folder resides in (in terms of both function and permission from the current user's point of view). The system defines four domains:

The term "domain" is a contender for the most overloaded word used to describe Mac OS X. While reading this section, try not to confuse the concept of filesystem domains with that of Internet domain names (such as *oreilly.com*) or NetInfo domains (as covered in Chapter 11). None of these have anything to do with each other.

User
: Contains folders that are under complete control of the current user. Generally speaking, this includes the user's Home folder and everything inside it.

Local
: Holds folders and files usable by all users of this machine, which may be modified by system administrators (users in the admin group) but are not crucial to the operating system.

  Folders directly under the *root* directory (/) that don't belong to other domains fall into the Local domain. On most systems, these include the */Library* and */Applications* folders.

Network
: Works like the Local domain, except that its folders are hosted on the network, accessible to users of that network and modifiable by network administrators. Usually, this domain extends to cover all folders (but not the servers) found within the */Network* directory.

System
: Contains folders and files that exist to support the computer's operating system and are not intended for direct human use. Nobody except the root account has permission to modify anything in the */System* domain.

  The */System* folder contains a typical Mac OS X machine's System domain.

Not every folder on the system lies in a domain. Other users' Home folders, for example, are always out of reach, even for administrative users, and the system has no special use for them. From the current user's point of view, they have no relevance; hence, they have no domain.

When an application needs to scan a system-defined folder for information, it usually seeks that folder in each of these four domains and scans its content, if it exists. The search order it uses is usually as follows:

1. User
2. Local
3. Network
4. System

An individual application can use a different order if it wishes, but this order suffices for most. It starts at the User domain (the scope where the current user has the most control), continues through the Local and Network domains (where system administrators might have put files for users' shared use), and ends at the

System domain (where files critical to the operating system live and whose presence is usually a decision of Apple's).

For example, a program that wishes to find a particular font knows that it can find that font's file in a */Library/Font* folder. This folder can exist in any of the four domains, so it scans the following directories, in order:

1. */Users/username/Library/Fonts/*
2. */Library/Fonts/*
3. */Network/Library/Fonts/*
4. */System/Library/Fonts/*

If it finds the font, it stops its search. If that same application wishes to build a list of all fonts available to the user, it scans all the previous folders in their entirety. In the case of duplicates—for example, `Courier` is defined in both the User and System domains—the earlier domain in the search order (User, in this case) takes precedence.

Special Folders

There are two interpretations of the *root* directory on Mac OS X: one that's displayed for Finder views, and a Unix one that is mainly accessible from the Terminal. For more information on accessing the Unix *root* directory from the Finder, see "Exploring root" later in this chapter.

When you click on the icon of the boot hard drive in the Sidebar, you will see the folders listed in Table 7-2. These folders contain essential system files, applications, and the directories for all the system's users.

Table 7-2. Special folders in the root directory

Directory	Domain	Description
Applications	Local, System[a]	Holds applications available to all users of this machine.
Library	Local	Contains resources available to all users of this machine, such as fonts, plug-ins, and documentation.
System	System	This is the system folder for Mac OS X.
Users	User	Contains user home directories
System Folder	System	This is the system folder for Mac OS 9. Present only if Mac OS 9 is also installed on this volume.
Documents	-	Miscellaneous files from a Mac OS 9 installation.
Applications (Mac OS 9)	-	Applications from a Mac OS 9 installation.

[a] This folder exists in both the local and system domains. Most of its content belongs to the admin group, but some applications, such as Printer Setup Utility, can't be modified by even admin-group users.

User directories

Once created, each user is provided with a series of subdirectories in the home directory (*/Users/username*). These directories, listed here, can be used for storing anything, although some have specific purposes:

Desktop
: This directory contains the items found on your Desktop, including any files, folders, or application aliases placed there.

Documents
: While it isn't mandatory, the */Documents* directory can be used as a repository for any files or folders you create.

Library
: This directory is similar to the */System/Preferences* directory found in earlier versions of the Mac OS; it contains resources used by applications but not the applications themselves.

Movies
: This is a place to store movies you create with iMovie or hold QuickTime movies you create or download from the Internet.

Music
: This directory can store music and sound files, including *.aiff*, *.mp3*, and so on. This directory also stores the iTunes Library.

Pictures
: This directory can store photos and other images. iPhoto also uses the */Pictures* directory to house its iPhoto Library directory, which contains the photo albums you create.

Public
: If you enable file or web sharing (System Preferences→Sharing→Services), this is where you can place items you wish to share with other users. Users who access your */Public* directory can see and copy items from this directory. Also in the */Public* directory is the Drop Box (*/Public/Drop Box*), a place in which other users can put files for you. If you have file sharing enabled, guest users anywhere on the network can also view and copy from */Public* and add items to the Drop Box.

Sites
: If you enable Personal Web Sharing (System Preferences→Sharing→Services), this is the directory that houses the web site for your user account.

The Shared user directory

Because users are allowed to add or modify files only within their own home directories, the */Users/Shared* directory exists as a place to drop items to be shared with other users on the system. Guest network users can't access this directory.

The Library folder

Every domain contains a Library folder. Applications searching for additional resources and software available to it scan through the Library folders in the order noted in the earlier section "Domains."

Library folders hold system-specific application resources. Unlike the application-specific icons, sounds, and other resource files found within an application's package, Library resources are either shared among many applications (as fonts are) or are specific to both individual applications and the current system (as user preference files are).

A running application has access to the resources in all the Library folders within the domains the current user can see. Thus, if the user *chris* is running an application, the application combs through */Users/chris/Library*, */Library*, */Network/Library*, and */System/Library* for resource files. If searching for a particular resource, such as a font or a configuration file, it looks through the folders in the usual User→Local Network→System domain search order, unless the application specifies a different order.

Anything a user places in her own User domain's Library folder, either directly or through an application, is available to that user alone. For example, all applications on the system are stored in */Applications*; however, a user's preferences for an application are stored in */Users/username/Library/Preferences*, usually as *plist* files. This separation allows multiple users on the system to use the same applications and yet have a different set of preferences to suit their needs. A system administrator can place resources in the Local domain's Library folder to allow all users of that computer access to them, and a network administrator can place files in the Network domain's Library so that all users of all computers across a network can use them. Nobody should ever need to modify the System domain's Library folder; leave that up to Apple's own system software installer and updater applications.

Mac OS X's Library folders are somewhat analogous to the *lib* directories found in key places around a typical Unix system, such as */usr/lib* and */usr/local/lib*. Unix *lib* directories usually hold code libraries and modules, and Mac OS X Library folders hold frameworks (the dynamic code libraries that Cocoa applications can link to in their Frameworks subfolders; see Chapter 15). As this section illustrates, though, Library folders also hold all manner of other application resources.

It's worth noting that a typical Mac OS X system does, in fact, have a number of more traditional Unix *lib* directories in the usual places, which the underlying Darwin OS uses when compiling software.

The following list briefly describes the folders often found in Library folders. Unless otherwise noted, they might be found in any domain.

Application Support
: This folder acts as a "scratch pad" for various applications. By convention, each application creates its own subfolder in this one, within which it can write whatever files it wishes.

Some applications do, however, place their own folders directly underneath the Library folder, rather than in */Library/Application Support*. (For example, Apple's iTunes application does this.)

Assistants
: Programs that assist with the configuration of other applications or services (also known as *wizards*).

Audio
: Audio-related resources, including system alerts and audio plug-ins for various applications' use.

ColorPickers
: Programs for choosing a color according to various models. The available color pickers appear as choices when an application displays a color well panel (Figure 7-1). Mac OS X's default pickers, including the color wheel, slider, and image-based pickers, live in */System/Library/ColorPickers*.

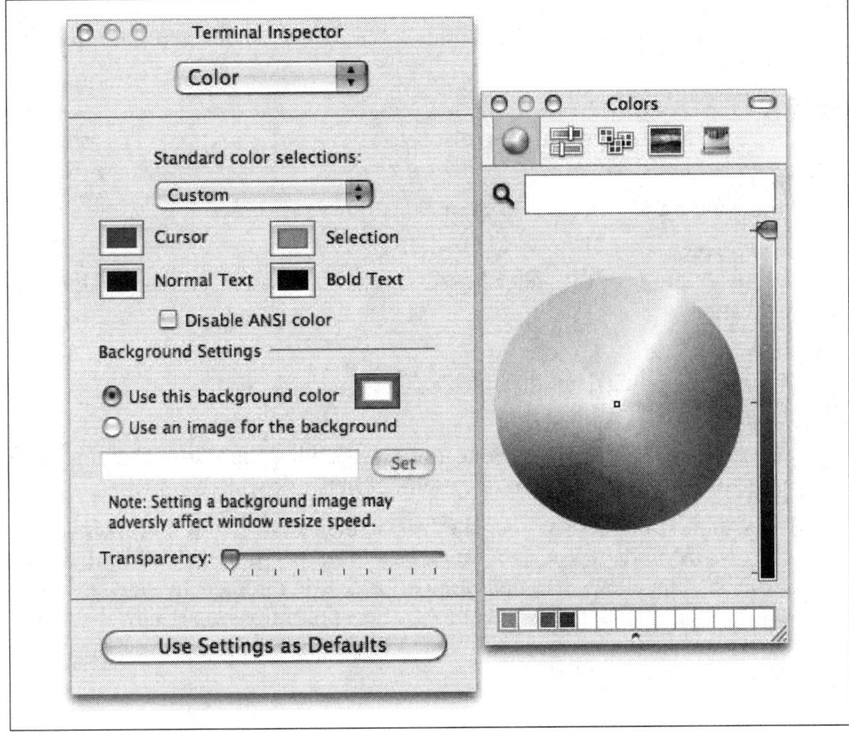

Figure 7-1. A color well panel

ColorSync
: ColorSync profiles and scripts.

Components
: Miscellaneous components and extensions. This folder tends to exist solely in the System domain.

Documentation

Documentation files. Can be in Apple Help format, plaintext files, collections of HTML, or just about anything else.

As with */Library/Application Support*, applications usually place their files within their own, eponymous subfolders.

Extensions

Device drivers and kernel extensions. Appropriate only in the system domain.

Don't confuse the */System/Library/Extension* folder with Mac OS 9's */System Folder/Extensions* folder. The two are somewhat analogous in that both contain device drivers and low-level system extensions, but Mac OS 9's */Extensions* folder often contains all the sorts of things that Mac OS X's Library folders now hold, in one big, unsorted directory.

Favorites

Found only in the User domain, this folder contains aliases to files, folders, and disks.

Fonts

Font files, for both printing and display.

Frameworks

Frameworks and shared code libraries.

Internet Plug-ins

Plug-ins, libraries, and filters used by web browsers and other Internet applications.

Keyboards

Keyboard mapping definitions.

Preferences

Preference files for various applications. Depending upon the domain, these can be for an individual user, or system- or network-wide.

Applications can use whatever file format they wish for storing their preferences. Many modern Mac applications use XML property list files, with a *.plist* extension; this allows its application to access it through the standard user-defaults programming APIs and allows other applications to see how that application is configured. (Unix's permission system prevents users from spying on one another's config files!)

The files in */Library/Preferences* usually apply to system-wide things, such as login window preferences. However, a system administrator can place an individual application's preferences file here to override individual users' preferences for that application.

See Chapter 25 for more information about Mac OS X's preferences system known as the defaults database.

Printers
: Printer drivers and PPD plug-ins, organized by printer vendor.

  Setup for individual printers doesn't go here; see Chapter 9 to learn how that works.

QuickTime
: QuickTime components and extensions.

Scripting Additions
: AppleScript extensions (see Chapter 14).

Scripts
: Scripts to display under the Script menu extra (see Chapter 14). The menu extra's content is an aggregation of all the filesystem domains' */Library/Scripts* folders. Subfolders show up as submenus.

WebServer
: */Library/WebServer* is the default document *root* of the Apache web server that ships with Mac OS X. See Chapter 12 for more on running Apache.

Hidden Files

By default, the Finder hides many files and folders from view, including the entirety of Darwin's directory layout, under the philosophy that most Mac OS X users will never need to access the system's Unix underpinnings. Savvier users, on the other hand, have a number of ways to see and work with all the filesystem's files.

Seeing Hidden Files

There are two ways to see files that don't appear in the Finder. The most direct way involves simply viewing a folder's contents by running the *ls* command on it in the Terminal. The Terminal sees the world simply as a tree of directories and files, and nothing more; files that have special, Mac-specific system roles appear like any other file. (However, you'll have to run *ls* with the *-a* flag.)

The other way involves changing the Finder preference that keeps these files hidden from sight. (Apple gets points for making this a user-adjustable preference, albeit not a very obvious one.) You'll need to add a value to the Finder preferences' file. You can accomplish this by operating the *defaults* command-line program on your *com.apple.finder* user defaults domain (described in Chapter 25), or by directly editing your */Users/username/Library/Preferences/com.apple.finder.plist* file with the Property List Editor application, as shown in Figure 7-2.

To add a value to the *com.apple.finder.plist* file, follow these steps:

1. Launch the Property List Editor (*/Developer/Applications/Utilities*).
2. Open the *com.apple.finder.plist* file located in */Users/username/Library/Preferences*.
3. Click on the disclosure triangle next to Root to reveal the values and keys for the Finder's preferences.

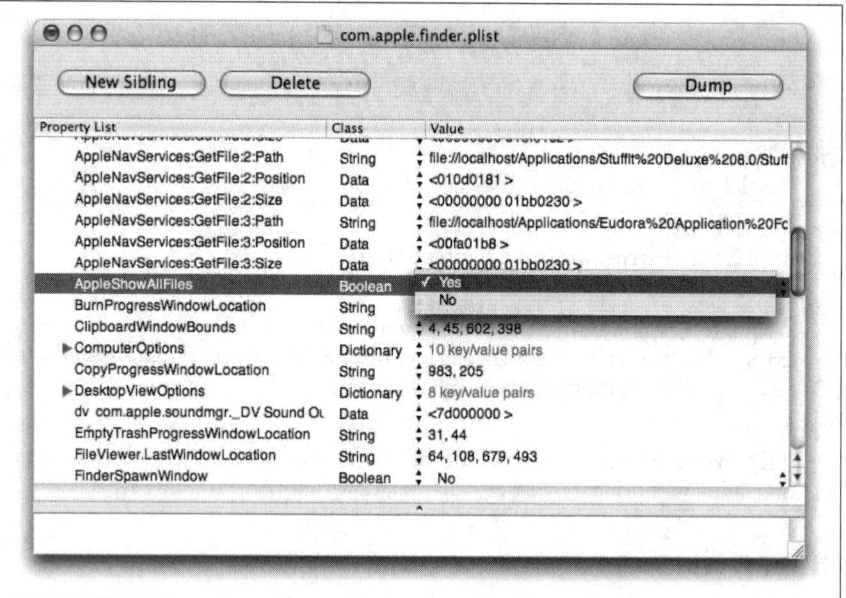

Figure 7-2. The Finder's preferences, as seen in Property List Editor

4. Select Root by clicking on it once.
5. Click on the New Child button.
6. In the first column, enter `AppleShowAllFiles`.
7. Change its class to `Boolean`.
8. Change its value to `Yes`.
9. Save the changes to the *plist* file (File→Save, or ⌘-S).
10. Quit the Property List Editor (⌘-Q).

Your work's almost over. To make the changes take effect, you need to relaunch the Finder, as follows:

1. Go to →Force Quit (or Option-⌘-Esc).
2. Select the Finder.
3. Click the Relaunch button.

There will be a short pause while the process for the Finder quits and restarts, after which the changes you made will take effect.

If you already know about a Finder-hidden folder's existence, you can view its contents in the Finder by choosing Go to Folder (Shift-⌘-G) and then typing the path to that folder. Typing */bin*, for example, reveals the contents of that directory.

Dotfiles

Following the traditional Unix model, the Finder hides all *dotfiles*, which are simply files (or folders) whose names begin with a period (dot) character. Applications can access dotfiles like any other file.

Your Mac's filesystem will likely accrue many dotfiles over time, particularly in users' Home folders, since this is the typical location for legacy Unix applications to store preference and configuration files. (Mac OS X–specific applications prefer to store this sort of information in Library folders, as described in the earlier section "The Library folder.") The following list covers some of particular interest:

.bash_history
: Found in the user's Home directory, this file is used by the *bash* shell to record previously entered commands.

.FBCIndex
.FBCLockFolder
: The Finder creates these dotfiles in each directory that it indexes by content. The binary file, *FBCIndex,* acts as an index to the content of all the folder's files. When performing a by-content search via the Finder's Find command, the Finder quickly reads from these index files, rather than picking through all the individual files again.

.ssh
: When you access another computer via the Secure Shell (SSH), an encrypted RSA key is stored in the *known_hosts* file within this directory.

.Trash
: Found in users' Home folders, this directory contains all the files and folders that a user has sent to the Trash (through either the Dock's Trash icon or the Finder's Move to Trash (⌘-Delete) command) but not yet deleted. When a user clicks once on the Dock's Trash icon, this folder's contents appear in a special Finder window labeled Trash.

  This knowledge is useful for accessing users' Trash folders from the Terminal, or doing it programmatically through Perl or a shell script.

Mac OS 9, if present, also keeps its system-wide Trash as a hidden folder, separate from the Trash folder in each Mac OS X user's Home folder. See the section "Hidden Mac OS 9 files," later in this chapter.

Exploring root

The *root* directory of a Mac OS X boot disk has the most to hide, from the Finder's point of view; it may play *root* to as many as three separate operating systems' filesystems, all at once! Beyond holding the lowest-level directories of the Mac OS X filesystem, such as the */System* and */Library* folders, the *root* directory also contains the basic directories that Darwin—the pure Unix system running at Mac OS X's core—needs. These include the directories that any Unix user would recognize, such as */etc* and */tmp*. Compare Figure 7-3 with Figure 7-4.

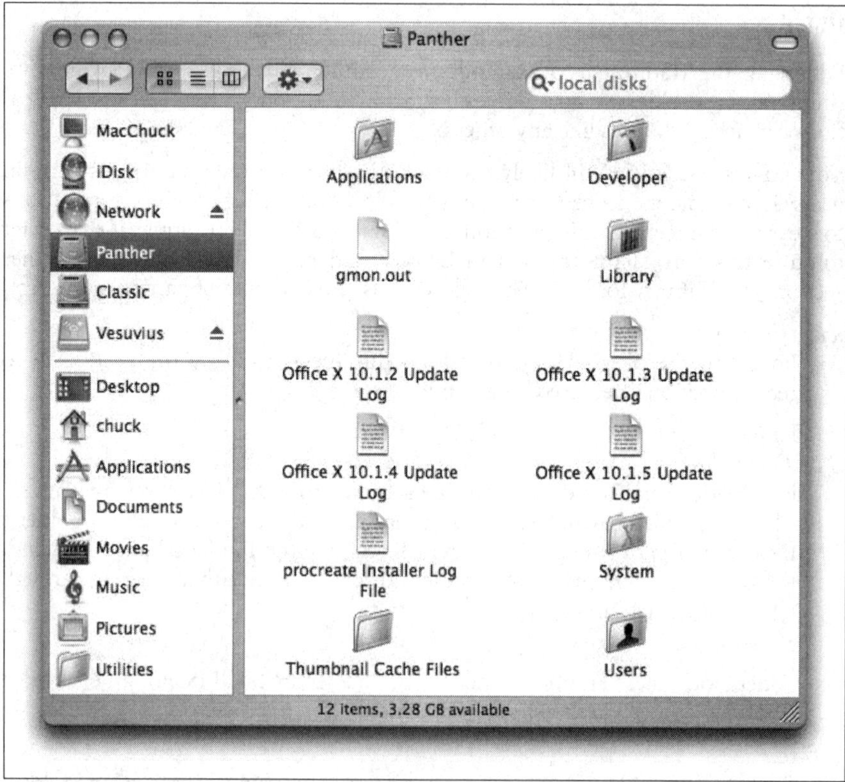

Figure 7-3. A typical Finder view of the boot disk's root

Furthermore, if Mac OS 9 is installed on the boot disk, its System Folder appears under the *root* directory, as do several Mac OS 9 configuration files. Other arbitrary files and folders created by the Mac OS 9 application might also exist at *root* because that operating system lacks Mac OS X's permission system and doesn't view the *root* directory as "sacred ground." For example, many Mac OS 9 software installers create new folders directly under *root*; Mac OS X installers place their software in locations such as */Applications/Library*.

Mac OS X's Finder, when displaying the boot disk's *root* folder, will show most of the low-level Mac OS X and Mac OS 9 filesystems' folders, but keep several special files hidden from sight, and it won't show any of Darwin's directories.

Hidden Mac OS 9 files

This isn't a book about Mac OS 9, so we won't go into detail about these files' functions. However, it's worthwhile to point out their presence on disks on which Mac OS 9 and Mac OS X are both installed because their mysterious existence might otherwise prove confusing.

Figure 7-4. The same view, with hidden files revealed

All of these exist under the boot volume's *root* directory (/). Mac OS 9 is a single-user system, so it finds no fault in writing files directly to /, even though that's considered sacred ground to any Unix system, including Mac OS X.

Here are a few of the more common Mac OS 9 hidden files:

- Cleanup At Startup
- Desktop DB
- Desktop DF
- Temporary Items
- TheFindByContentFolder
- TheVolumeSettingsFolder
- Trash

As a rule of thumb, if you see mysterious, hidden files lurking directly under the *root* directory, they're probably the doing of Mac OS 9.

Hidden Darwin files

This book frequently mentions "traditional Unix systems" when comparing Mac OS X to other Unix-based operating systems. The truth is that Darwin (already noted) *is* a rather traditional Unix system, when considered all by itself. It has its own directory structure that subtly shares disk space with the more visible Mac OS X structure covered in the earlier section "Filesystem Organization."

All these files and directories exist under the *root* directory (*/*). (This may make them sound like the hidden Mac OS 9 files described in the previous section, but they're quite different. They serve as the core of the Darwin system, and hence of Mac OS X itself, in a way.)

mach
mach.sym
mach_kernel
: These files make up the Mach kernel, the heart of Darwin and Mac OS X.

etc
private/etc
: */etc* is actually a symbolic link to */private/etc*, a directory that holds Darwin's system configuration files. While many of these files, such as *hosts* and *passwd*, have roles superceded by Mac OS X's Directory Service technologies, others, such as *hostconfig*, are central to the whole operating system's configuration, especially during the startup process.

tmp
private/tmp
: Again, */tmp* is a symbolic link to */private/tmp*. The usual Unix *tmp* directory is readable and writeable by all users and processes, despite the fact that it's hidden in the invisible */private* directory. Lots of command-line programs and utilities use this directory as a scratch pad to write temporary files to disk. (Modern Mac OS X applications are more likely to use users' *Library* folders.)

var
private/var
: */var* is a symbolic link to the */private/var* directory, which holds logs, spools, PID files, and other file-based resources used by active processes. Most importantly, */private/var/db* holds vital configuration data including the NetInfo databases.

bin
: Core Terminal commands, such as *cp* and *mkdir*. (As with all Unix command-line functions, all these commands, even the seemingly simple ones such as *ls*, are executable program files.)

sbin
: Command-line utilities to perform basic filesystem and other administrative operations, such as mounting, unmounting, configuring, and diagnosing disks. Because these commands affect the whole system, they must usually be run as *root* (see the section "Acting as Root" in Chapter 10).

automount

The system uses this directory as a mount point when statically mounting networked volumes; see Chapter 10.

dev

Device files, each a pointer to some kind of Unix device the system supports, are both real (such as disks and their partitions) and virtual (such as */dev/null*).

Volumes

This is the default mount point Mac OS X uses for the filesystems of disks and partitions other than the boot volume. One subdirectory appears here for every disk (except for the boot disk and Network icon) that the Finder displays in the top-half of the Sidebar.

The File Permissions System

Mac OS X uses the Unix file permission system to control who has access to the filesystem's files, folders, and disks, and what they can do with them.

Ownership and permissions are central to security. It's important to get them right, even when you're the only user, because odd things can happen if you don't. For most users' interaction with Mac OS X, the system will do the right thing, without their having to think much about it. (Things get a little trickier when viewing the system as an administrator, though.)

Permissions refer to the ways in which someone can use a file. There are three such permissions under Unix:

Read

Allows you to look at a file's contents.

Write

Allows you to change or delete a file.

Execute

Allows you to run a file as a program. (This isn't so important when using Mac OS X's GUI, though; see the sidebar "What About the Execute Bit?" later in this section.)

When each file is created, the system assigns some default permissions that work most of the time. For instance, it gives you both read and write permission, but most of the world has only read permission. If you have a reason to be concerned, you can set things up so that other people have no permissions at all.

There are times when defaults don't work, though. For instance, if you create a shell script or Perl program in the Terminal, you have to assign executable permission so that you can run it. We'll show how to do that later in this section, after we get through the basic concepts.

Permissions have different meanings for a directory:

Read
: Allows you to list the contents of that directory.

Write
: Allows you to add or remove files in that directory.

Execute
: Allows you to make that directory your working directory and list information about its contents.

If you allow people to add files to a directory, you are also letting them remove files. The two privileges go together when you assign write permission. However, there is a way you can let users share a directory and keep them from deleting each other's files: you can set that directory's *sticky bit*. (See the entry for *chmod* in Chapter 28.)

The differences between the Read and Execute bits allow you to set up special kinds of directories such as drop boxes and pickup boxes. A *Drop Box* is a directory with only write and execute access allowed. Users are therefore able to place items inside the directory but not see what's inside. A *Pickup Box* has only execute access allowed, forcing users to specify a full pathname to access any items inside and preventing them from adding anything to the directory.

There are more files on Unix systems than the plain files and directories we've talked about so far. These are special files (devices), sockets, symbolic links, and so forth; each type observes its own rules regarding permissions. However you don't need to know the details on each type.

Owners and Groups

Now, who gets these permissions? To allow people to work together, Unix has three levels of permission: *owner*, *group*, and *other*. The *other* covers everybody who has access to the system and who isn't the *owner* or a member of the *group*.

The idea behind having groups is to give a set of users, such as a team of programmers, access to a file or set of applications. For instance, a programmer creating source code may reserve write permission to himself, but allow members of his group to have read access through a *group* permission. As for *other*, it might have no permission at all.

Each file has an *owner* and a *group*. The *owner* is generally the user who created the file. Each user also belongs to a default *group* that has the same name as the user account, if that account was created in Panther (older versions of Mac OS X assigned the group *staff* to new accounts). Therefore, by default, each user is the only member or their group. That *group*, then, is assigned to every file the user creates. You can create other groups, though, and assign each user to multiple groups. By changing the *group* assigned to a file, you can give this level of access to any collection of people you want.

Mac OS 9 had something similar to this system with its Users & Groups Control panel, but this was relevant mainly to configuring who could mount your machine's hard drive over a network. Mac OS X's permission system also applies itself to this use but is far more pervasive, affecting every user's interaction with every part of the filesystem whether they are logged in locally or over a network.

Viewing and Modifying File Permissions

The permissions system is another part of Mac OS X with two distinct interfaces: you can either use the traditional Unix command-line tools through the Terminal to view and change a file's permissions, or you can use the Finder's Get Info window for a graphical interface to the same task.

Figure 7-5 shows the Finder's interface to the permission system, a section of the Finder's Info window (see the section "The Get Info Window" in Chapter 2).

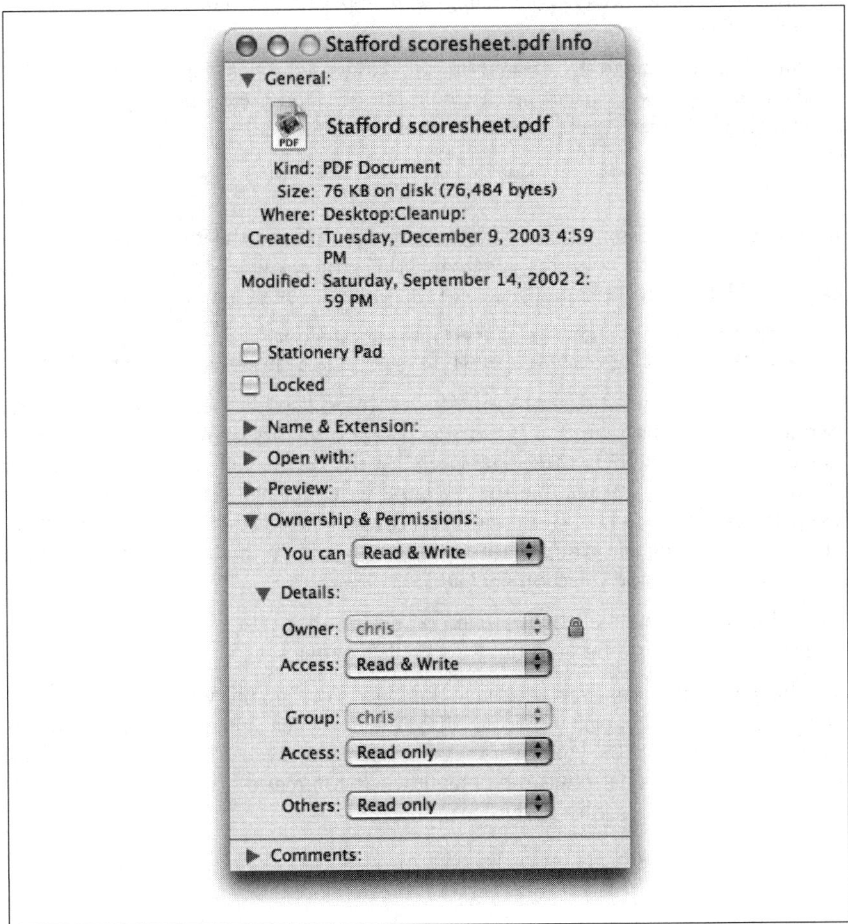

Figure 7-5. The Get Info window's Ownership & Permissions view

The pop-up menus display the object's current owner and group, as well as the owner, group, and other access permissions.

If you are the file's owner, you can modify the three permission menus, setting them to Read & Write, Read Only, or No Access for that type of user. If you have administrative privileges, you can also modify the object's owner and group.

What About the Execute Bit?

Unix veterans will note that the Finder offers no interface to any of a file's "execute" bits, which determine whether someone is allowed to try launching a file as a program. Simply put, this type of distinction doesn't exist in Mac OS X's Aqua layer, in which the Finder recognizes only certain kinds of files or directories as launchable, including *.app* application bundles and *.jar* Java archive files.

Furthermore, directories created in the Finder—through File→New Folder (Shift-⌘-N)—always have their execute bits set, and there's no way to unset them in the Finder. Again, you have to use *chmod* for that.

If you run the *ls* command with the *–l* option, it lists the requested files in a tabular format, with columns specifying the group, owner, and permissions of each file. Here is the Terminal's view of the same file depicted in Figure 7-5:

```
MyPB:~/Documents chris$ ls -l Stafford\ scoresheet.pdf
-rw-r--r--  1 chris  chris  76484 14 Sep  2002 Stafford scoresheet.pdf
```

The code of letters and dashes in the first column lists the permissions. The first hyphen means it's a plain file (as opposed to a directory, which would be designated with a *d*). The next three characters list the read, write, and execute bits for the file's owner; `rw-` means that the read and write permissions are active, but the execute permission is not. (If it were, you'd see `rwx` instead.) Then there are three characters showing the group permissions (read-only, in this case) and three more for "other" permission (read-only, again).

After this, we see the file's owner (`chris`) and group (`chris`), followed by the file's size in bytes, a timestamp, and finally, the file's name.

To change permissions, you must use the *chmod* command, while the *chown* and *chgrp* commands change a file or directory's owner and group, respectively. Consult Chapter 28 or your Mac's manpages for more information on these commands. You may also wish to consult the *ls* command's documentation to see other ways you can list files in the Terminal.

8
Networking

These days, using a computer and using a network are nearly synonymous concepts. Since Unix has always been a network-oriented operating system, Mac OS X supports networking (and Internetworking) at its core, and provides many friendly interfaces to let users take advantage of this.

This chapter covers the basics of getting a Mac OS X machine connected to a network, particularly the Internet, from a user's perspective. Chapter 10 covers network administration in more detail.

Networking Basics

Connecting to a network basically involves telling your Mac where on the network it belongs by giving it a network IP address (which might belong to the Internet or maybe just the local area network) and telling it where it can find its router (which lets it speak to the network outside of the immediate subnetwork). Depending on your network's configuration, you might have to enter this and other information manually, or you can have a network server configure your network setup for you through DHCP, as described in the later section "Configuring TCP/IP."

In any case, Mac OS X's main interface for setting and displaying all this information is the Network preference pane, described in the next section. Though network administrators can also use *ifconfig*, *route*, and other command-line tools to display a machine's network settings, changes made with these tools don't always work as expected because they don't report their changes to the *configd* daemon, which is responsible for storing the systems' network settings and providing them to other processes. (See Chapter 28 for more about *configd*.)

Mac OS X networking primarily involves TCP/IP, the family of protocols upon which the Internet is built. When configuring a Mac's network connection, you'll often work with IP addresses. These are dot-notated numbers, such as

`192.168.0.1` or `66.101.11.57`, which (with an exception or two) are unique for every computer that belongs to a network. Chapter 10 describes this concept in detail. Mac OS X machines can also use AppleTalk, the legacy set of communication protocols more often found on networks of older Macs. You may see AppleTalk used in Mac-centric local area networks. A Mac OS X machine can communicate through TCP/IP and AppleTalk simultaneously over the same interface, though AppleTalk isn't active by default.

The Network Pane

As Figure 8-1 shows, the Network pane has three elements: a Location menu (whose function we describe in the later section "Locations"), a Show pop-up menu, and a large center area, which shows either the Network Status, a separate tabbed view, or the Network Port Configurations, depending on what's chosen in the Show pop-up menu.

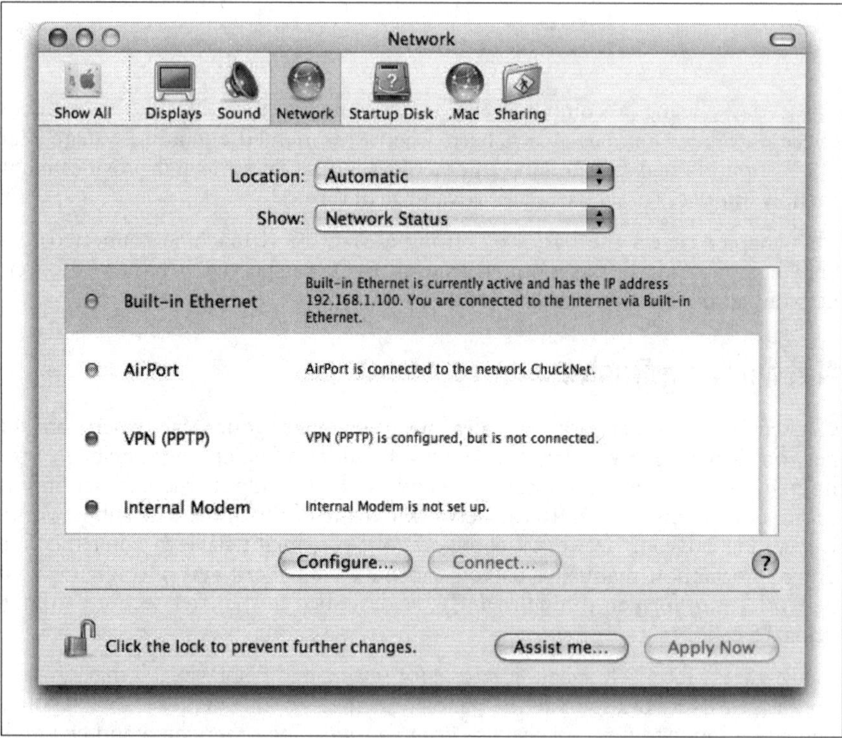

Figure 8-1. The Network preferences pane

When Network Status is selected from the Show pop-up menu, the center area lists the status of each network interface that exists for the chosen location (such as Ethernet, AirPort, modems, or VPN interfaces). Each interface is listed with a colored dot indicating its general status: red if not connected, yellow if connected but not fully active, and green if connected and active. Listed also for each interface is a brief textual description of its status, reporting any associated IP number or wireless network name for example, and if the interface is currently the primary connection to the Internet.

The Network Status list updates itself nearly instantly when changes to the network status occur. For example, unplugging an Ethernet cable from an active interface immediately causes the status dot to change from green to red. Plugging the cable back in changes the dot to yellow (if that interface is configured via DHCP), until an IP address is received, and then it changes back to green.

In addition to the Network Status item, the Show pop-up menu also contains one item for every network interface (such as Ethernet, AirPort, or modems) within your machine, and its current selection dictates the tabbed view's content. In Figure 8-2, the tabbed view displays configuration information relevant to an Ethernet interface.

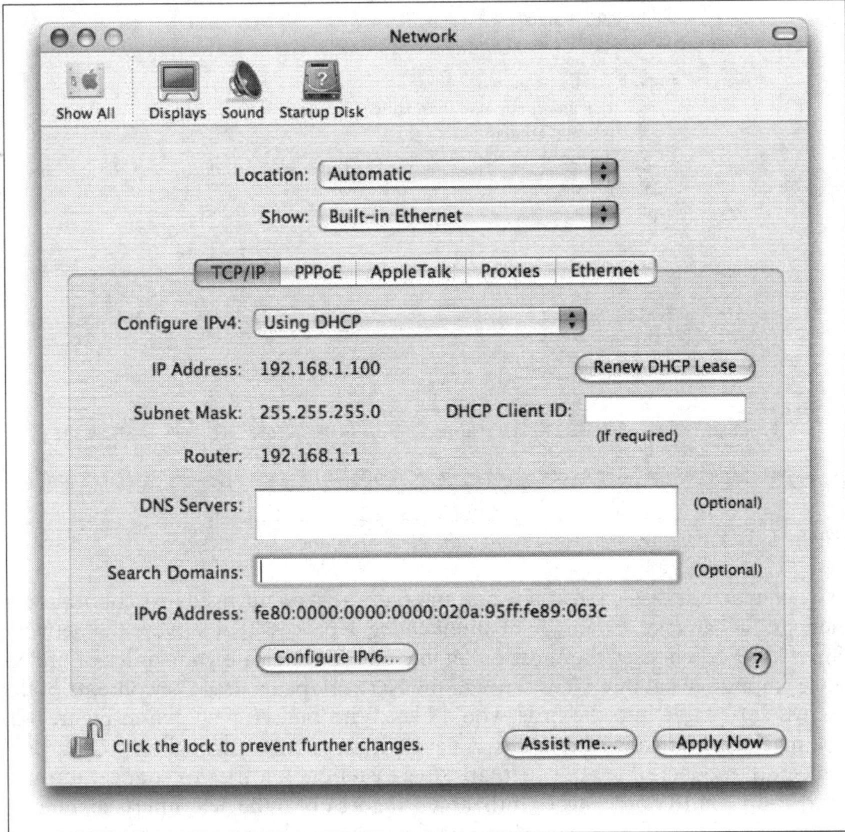

Figure 8-2. The built-in Ethernet interface configuration

Choosing network interfaces

The final (and ever-present) option of the Network pane's Show menu is Network Port Configurations. When selected, the pane's view changes to look like Figure 8-3. The Network Port Configurations table lists all the network interfaces available to this machine. The checkbox to the left of each indicates whether it's active or inactive.

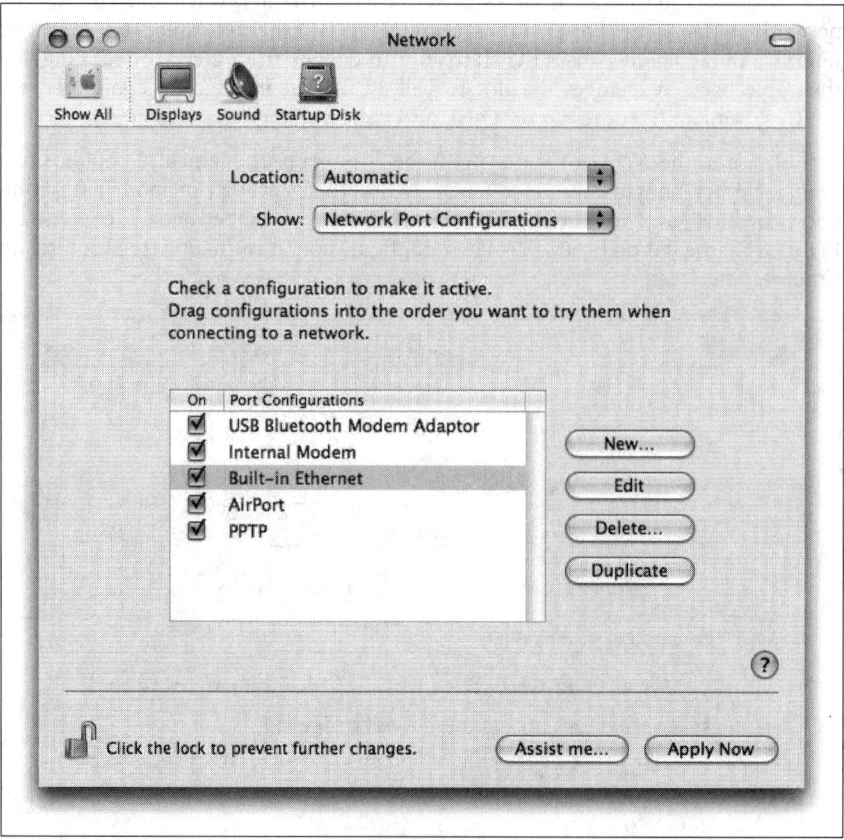

Figure 8-3. Activating interfaces through the Network pane

If your machine has more than one interface active and needs to connect to a network, it can take advantage of *multihoming*, a process that surveys the network interfaces and chooses the most preferable one. To indicate your order of preference among several interfaces through the Network pane, drag the contents of the Active Ports table into the order you'd like. With the setup shown in Figure 8-3, the machine first tries to establish a network connection through any connected Bluetooth modem. If it can't (perhaps, there isn't one), it tries to connect through its dial-up connection instead. If that fails, it goes on to the next interface, Built-in Ethernet and then the next, AirPort, until it either is able to connect through one, or it gives up because no more interfaces are active.

These settings still allow you to have multiple network interfaces active at once, but the system will use the topmost functioning interface in the list as the default route for network traffic.

To see a precise (and more technical) summary of your machine's network interfaces' current status and configurations, consult the Info tab of the Network Utility application, as described in Chapter 11. For still more status information, run *ifconfig* in the Terminal, as described in Chapter 28.

Configuring TCP/IP

Because all Mac OS X network interfaces use the TCP/IP communication protocols, every interface's representation in the Network pane includes a TCP/IP tab view, as seen in Figure 8-2. It contains the following text fields:

IP Address
: The machine's network address, unique across the network.

Subnet Mask
: The IP mask of the machine's subnetwork.

Router
: The IP address of the machine's router, which gives it access to the network outside its subnet.

DNS Servers
: A newline-separated list of all the domain name servers the machine can use to resolve IP addresses into human-readable hostnames, and vice versa. This allows you to, for example, point a web browser at `www.oreilly.com` instead of `209.204.146.22`, the raw IP address of that same web server machine.

Search Domains
: A comma-separated list of domain names that the machine can try appending to hostnames that don't resolve into IP address by themselves. For example, if you access machines in the `morgul.net` domain often, listing `morgul.net` as a search domain lets you refer to `spider.morgul.net` as `spider`, `cricket.morgul.net` as `cricket`, and so on.

  This is basically a domain-wide way to accomplish the machine-by-machine aliasing you can do with the */machines* entry in NetInfo; see Chapter 12.

IPv6 Address
: If you're on an IPv6 network, your IPv6 address appears in this field. The button below it, "Configure IPv6," allows you to configure an address manually.

The Configure pop-up menu at the top of this view determines who fills in the values of these various fields: you the admin-allowed user, or an automatic, network-based configuration system. The menu's contents depend on the selected interface, but here are the more common options:

Manually
: All the IP text fields are editable and contain no values by default, leaving it up to you to set them all.

Using DHCP
: DHCP is the Dynamic Host Configuration Protocol; it allows network servers to tell client machines how they ought to be configured. When you select this option, the machine will, when trying to establish a network connection, search for a DHCP server by broadcasting a request to the whole network.

  Only the DNS Servers and Search Domains text fields are editable (though optionally, as required by your network administrator or ISP); the DHCP server provides the values of the other text fields once a connection is established.

  The "Renew DHCP Lease" button allows you to manually release your current IP address and request a new IP address from the DHCP server.

Manually Using DHCP Router
: This option is the same as Using DHCP, but you specify your machine's IP address manually. This information is used to seek a specific DHCP server, which in turn supplies a router address you can use.

Using BootP
: This option works just like Using DHCP, except that it uses the BootP protocol, intended especially for network-booting computers.

Using PPP
: PPP, the Point-to-Point protocol, lets TCP/IP run over a serial link, usually a dial-up modem connection. Commonly, a PPP server also provides IP configuration information to a client upon connection, just as DHCP can do through Ethernet.

When selected, only the DNS Servers and Search Domains text fields are editable (though optionally, as required by your ISP); the PPP server provides the values of the other text fields for you.

Other configurations

The TCP/IP tab contains the most important information for any network interface's setup. Other tabs contain configuration information specific to different interfaces.

AppleTalk
: Controls whether AppleTalk is active on that interface (along with TCP/IP), and defines the current AppleTalk zone. Unlike TCP/IP, however, AppleTalk can be active only on one interface at a time.

Proxies
: If your location requires proxies for different kinds of Internet traffic, you can define them in this tab. See Figure 8-4.

  This is also where you'll find the checkbox that lets you activate passive FTP mode; see the section "Passive FTP Mode," later in this chapter.

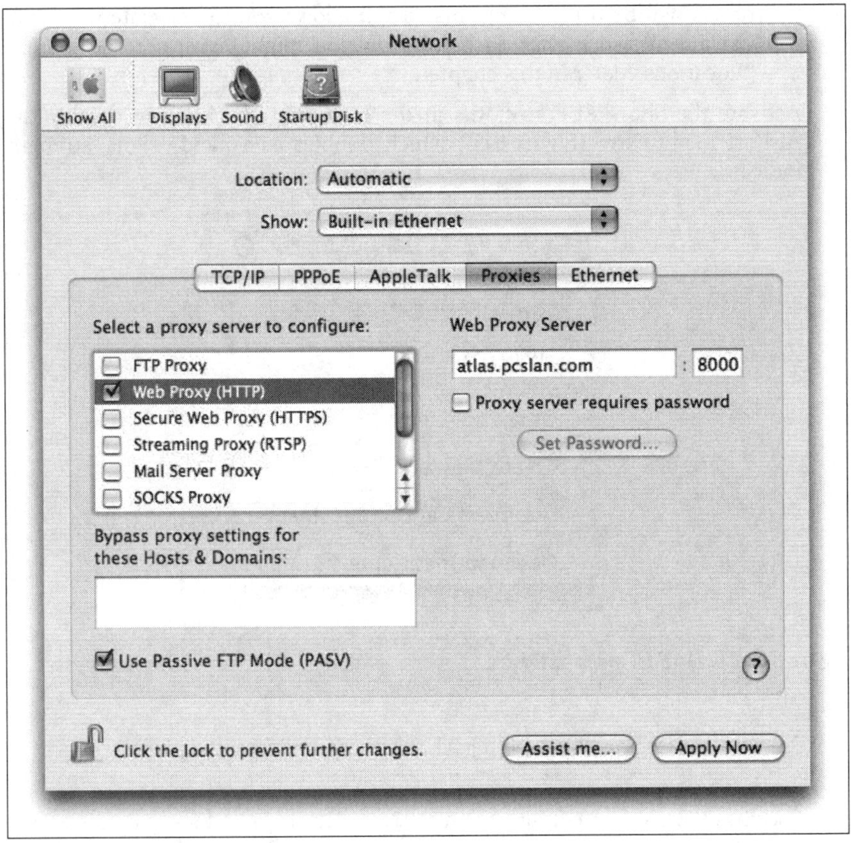

Figure 8-4. The Network Pane's Proxies tab

AirPort

Here, you can view and specify settings particular to AirPort usage.

First listed is the "AirPort ID," your AirPort card's MAC address, which is further described later in the Ethernet tab section.

The "By default, join" pop-up menu lets you define which of the following methods the AirPort software uses to seek and choose an 802.11b or 802.11g wireless network to join automatically after a restart or wake from sleep:

Automatic

The default setting. Of all the wireless networks available, try to join the one most recently used. This would be the best setting to use if, for example, you moved between a wireless network at home and one at work. Once you join both networks, you can move between the two networks seamlessly, without doing a thing.

Join a specific network

Join only the network named in the Network pop-up menu, using the specified password, if any. If the specified network is not available, no

others will be tried. Using this option allows you to associate a specific wireless network with each location you might have; see the section "Locations," later in this chapter.

Activate the Show AirPort status in the menu bar checkbox to display the AirPort menu extra (Figure 8-5), which doubles as a handy signal-strength indicator.

Figure 8-5. The AirPort menu extra

PPP
: See the later section "Connecting Through Dialup" for an explanation.

Modem
: Specifies the modem configuration to use when making dial-up connections. The Modem pop-up menu contains references to all the configuration files in */Library/Modem Scripts*.

  Activate the Show modem status in the menu bar checkbox to reveal the modem menu extra.

PPPoE
: If your network uses PPP over an Ethernet connection (as with some DSL connections), use this tab to configure your account information as provided by your ISP.

  When the Show PPPoE status in menu bar checkbox is active, the PPPoE menu extra appears. Just as with dialup-based PPP, this menu extra lets you quickly make and break your PPPoE connection.

Ethernet
: When an Ethernet interface is chosen from the Show pop-up menu, the Ethernet tab appears (Figure 8-6), allowing you to configure advanced Ethernet settings for that interface.

  Listed first in the Ethernet tab is the interface's *Ethernet ID*, also known as a MAC address (Media Access Control) or hardware address. This is a

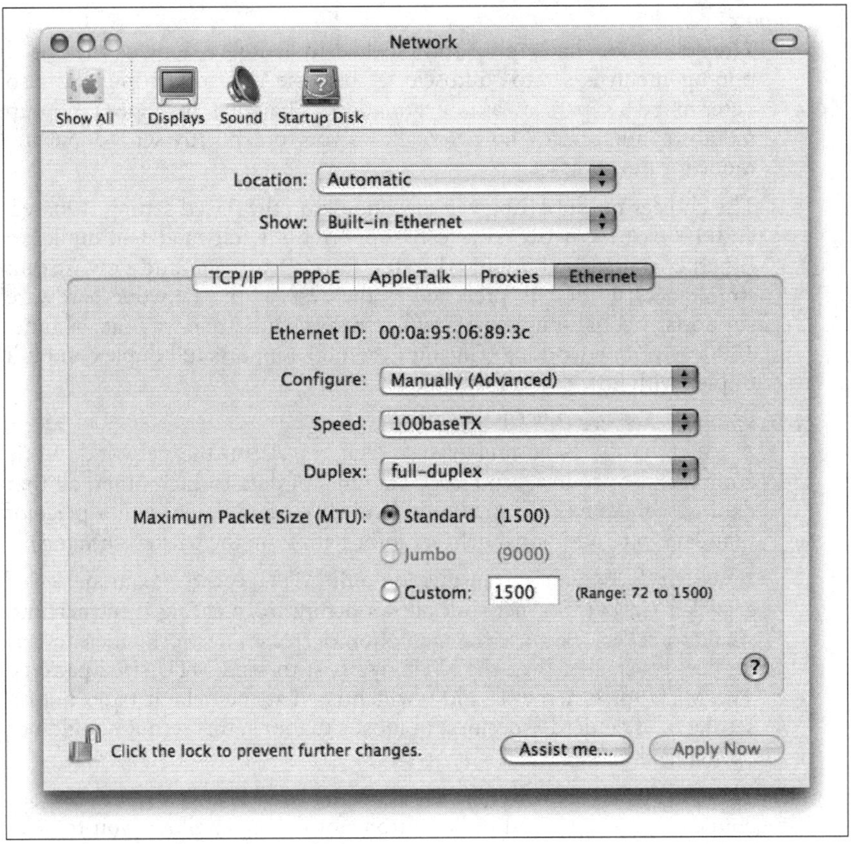

Figure 8-6. The Ethernet configuration tab

colon-notated hexadecimal number assigned to the hardware interface itself. It is globally unique and can't be modified, generally speaking.

The remaining item on the tab is the Configure pop-up menu, which is set to "Automatically" by default. For most cases, this is the proper setting. However, if you need to tweak your Ethernet connection for maximum performance or compatibility, you can choose "Manually (Advanced)" from the Configure pop-up menu and make adjustments. Be aware, though, that setting these incorrectly can interfere with Ethernet traffic on your computer and possibly other computers on your network.

Speed
: The default setting for this pop-up is "Autoselect," which forces your Mac's Ethernet interface and the port on the switch, hub, or other Ethernet device at the opposite end of the link to auto-negotiate the highest speed offered by both devices. In cases where this is not desirable (when the switch isn't behaving, for example), you can explicitly set the speed by selecting from this pop-up. The choices available here vary depending on the type of interface.

Duplex

The setting for this pop-up stays locked to "auto" as long as the Speed pop-up menu is set to "autoselect," because the duplex mode is also determined as part of auto-negotiation. Changing the Speed pop-up menu to "autoselect," however, allows you to explicitly set a duplexing mode for the interface.

The choices for duplexing vary depending on the Speed setting. 10baseT and 100baseTX networking can support both full- and half-duplexed Ethernet traffic. Full-duplexed traffic travels upstream and downstream simultaneously and is preferred if the rest of the network hardware supports it; half-duplexed traffic travels only one-way at a time. 1000baseTX networking (Gigabit Ethernet) supports full duplex and full duplex with flow control.

Maximum Packet Size (MTU)

A packet is the basic unit of data that travels on the network. While computers, of course, send large amounts of data to each other, all that data is segmented into smaller individual packets, each with a piece of that data, plus additional delivery information (in the packet's *headers*).

A network's maximum transmission unit (MTU) is the maximum size of a packet (in bytes) a network allows before fragmenting it further into smaller packets. Because fragmentation decreases network efficiency, as do packets smaller than the MTU, it's best to send MTU-sized packets. The MTU for Ethernet is 1500, which is what the default radio button setting of "Standard" specifies. In most situations, this setting should not be changed.

There are cases, however, when changing the MTU can optimize your connection. The second radio button, for example, allows you to send "Jumbo Frames"; these are 9,000-byte packets that are allowed on some Gigabit Ethernet networks.

The third radio button allows you to reduce your MTU from the standard 1,500 bytes. There are several reasons why you might need to do this, typically to maintain compatibility with a network with a lower MTU. For example, some broadband connections using PPPoE work best with a lower MTU.

Locations

The Network pane (Figure 8-1) is actually a frontend that lets you create and manage several independent profiles of network configuration information, called *locations*. The default location is called Automatic; if your machine isn't the traveling type, you can just leave it be. Otherwise, you might need to create a list of locations.

Mac OS 9 users may recall the Location Manager control panel. Part of its functionality, that involving network configurations, is found in Mac OS X's Network pane, as well as the Location submenu under the Apple menu.

Adding and using locations

To create a new location, select New Location... from the Location menu. A sheet prompting you with a text field will appear. Fill it out with an appropriate name ("Home," "Office," "Carlos' house," and so on), and click OK.

That location will now appear as a selectable choice in the Network pane's Location menu, as well as in the Apple menu's Location submenu. Selecting a location either way will adjust your Mac's network settings.

Selecting a location from the Apple menu applies its network settings immediately. Selecting one from the Network pane won't change the Mac's behavior until you click the pane's Apply Now button. This behavior lets you adjust a location's settings before they take effect.

Changes you make to your network settings via the Network pane also apply to the currently selected location. If you, for example, change the next time you select the original location, the Configure menu will snap back to Manually.

Even if your Mac does travel among different networks, it's likely that it uses DHCP to dynamically fetch its IP address from each one. In this case, you can get away with sticking to the Automatic location.

Editing and removing locations

Selecting Edit Locations from the Location menu displays the sheet shown in Figure 8-7. It offers controls for modifying the list of network locations stored on your Mac. (To change the actual settings under a particular location, just select that location from the Network pane's Location menu, and make the necessary changes.)

Duplicate
: Clicking this button duplicates the selected location. This can be handy if you'd like to base a new location off an existing one that's different by only one or two settings or if you'd like to make a backup copy of a location you're about to modify.

Rename
: This button makes the selected location's name editable.

Delete
: Click this to remove the selected location from the list.

Connecting Through Dialup

Compared to the immediacy of Ethernet or AirPort-based network connections, connecting to a network through a modem requires the additional step of the computer dialing up a server through a phone line. You can choose to have your computer perform this step automatically or only when you request it, but either

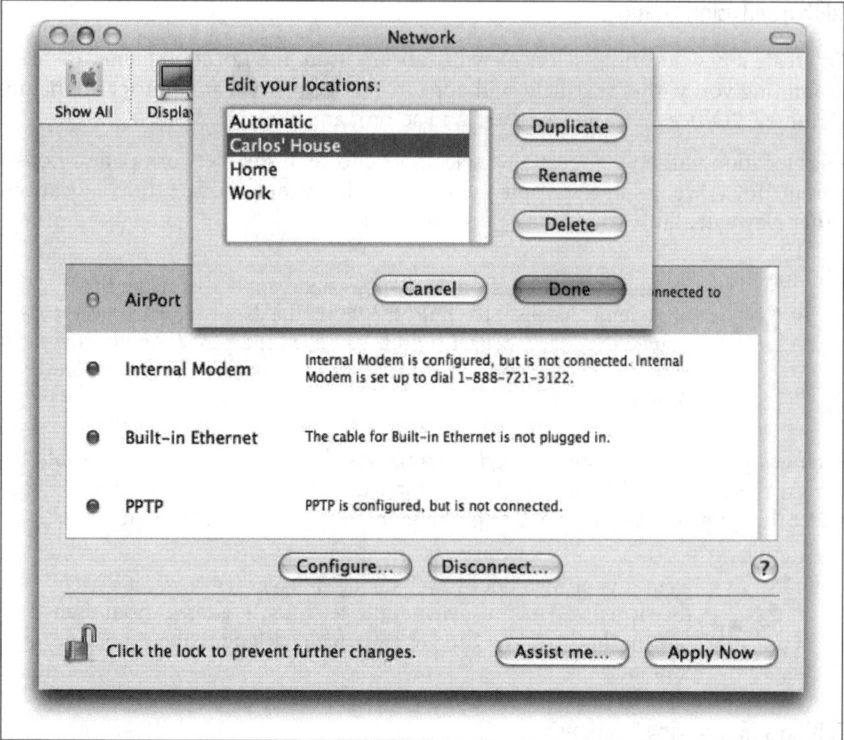

Figure 8-7. Editing network locations

way you need to set up some additional configuration information using either the Internet Connect application (found in the Applications folder) or the PPP tab of the Network pane's modem section, seen in Figure 8-8.

If you set up a dialup connection using the latter method, that configuration will automatically becomes the new "Main Number" list item in the Configuration popup menu of Internet Connect's Modem pane. (The new configuration gets its name from the value entered for "Service Provider.")

The reverse, however, is not true. That is, if you add or modify a configuration in Internet Connect, nothing will change in the Network pane. This behavior maintains a single dialup configuration associated with each Network location. If you need to store multiple dialup configurations and use any of them regardless of the current location setting, you can do so with Internet Connect.

Configuring the PPP tab

If you usually dial up the same server, it's best to configure that connection using the Network pane's PPP tab. In any case, if you want the computer to dial up automatically whenever an application requires Internet access, your only choice is to configure that connection using the Network pane's PPP tab. Here's how to do it:

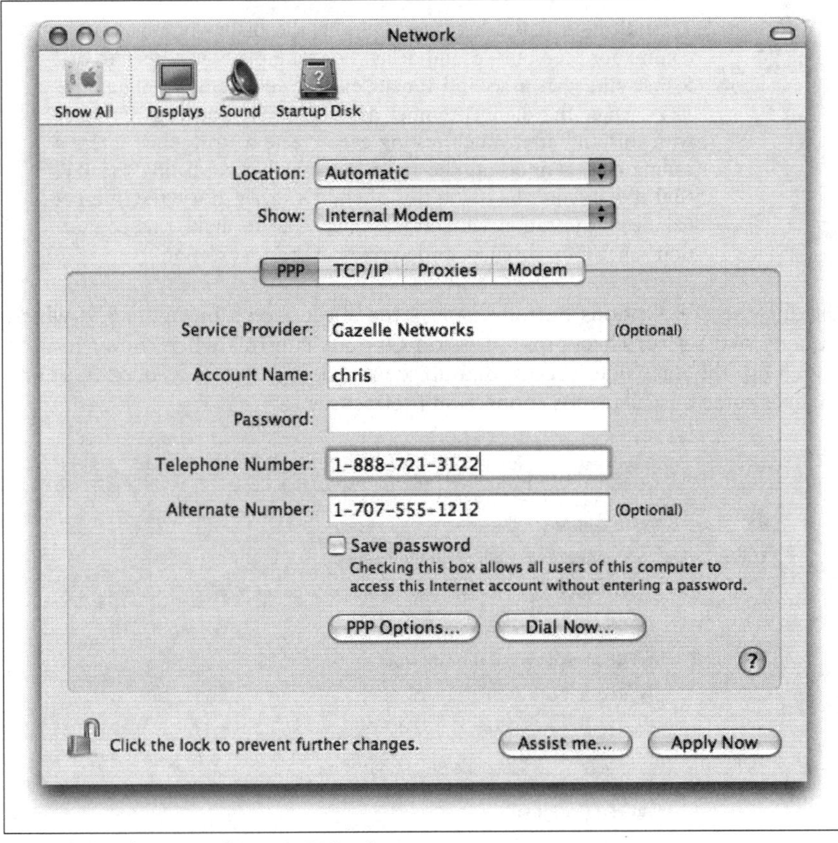

Figure 8-8. The Network pane's PPP tab

1. Select the modem interface from the Show menu.
2. Type the PPP server's telephone number into the Telephone Number field.
3. Provide the service provider's name and an alternate phone number in the appropriate fields, if you wish.
4. Enter a PPP account name and password into the last two text fields (your Mac's PPP client is usually able to supply them to the server at the appropriate time, but if it's not, you can connect through a terminal window, as described in the following section, and supply them manually when prompted).

To indicate a pause between digits in the dialup number, use a comma for each one-second delay. For example, if you need to dial 9 first and wait a second for an outside line before dialing 123-1234, enter the dialup number as 9,1231234. You can get fancy with this and after much testing even create a string that enters a calling card number at the right moment before dialing the ISP. (But if you won't be doing this often, it's easier to use the Internet Connect application with its "Manual Dial to make this connection" checkbox checked, as described in the next section.)

Clicking the PPP Options button displays the sheet shown in Figure 8-9, which contains two sets of checkboxes. Session Options controls when, how, and for how long the machine makes dial-up connections, and Advanced Options manages some miscellaneous connection preferences.

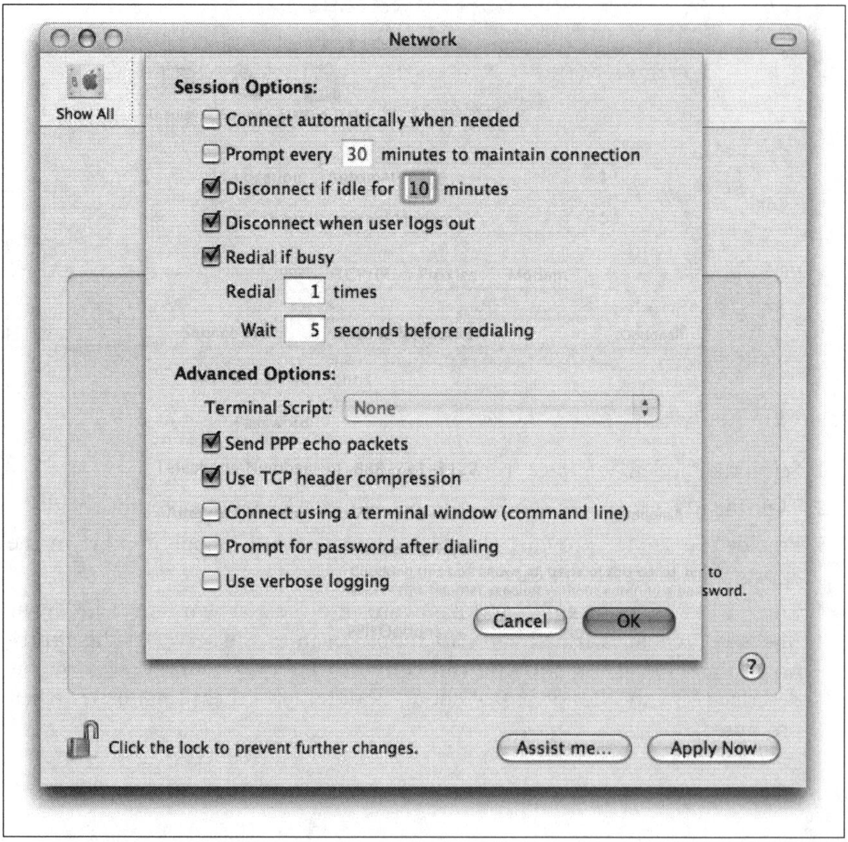

Figure 8-9. The PPP Options sheet

Two checkboxes are of particular interest:

Connect automatically when starting TCP/IP applications
: When checked, the Mac automatically uses the modem to dial in to the PPP server when any program wishes to use the network (for an explanation of what to do if any other active network interface fails to work, see the earlier section "Choosing network interfaces"). If it's not checked, you must use a program like the Internet Connect application and launch the dial-up process yourself.

Connect using a terminal window (command line)
: If checked, the Mac presents a simple terminal window (with no affiliation to the Terminal application) that lets you manually log in and authenticate with the PPP server. If you leave it unchecked, Mac OS X will use the username and password you supplied in the Network pane's PPP tab to try authenticating itself.

  You'll need to resort to this option only if connecting through an office's custom in-house PPP setup or the like; almost all ISPs keep their PPP authentication protocol simple enough to let Mac OS X's PPP software work without user assistance.

If you are experiencing problems when dialing into your ISP, you can try connecting via the PPP terminal to see what its authentication process looks like. If it's something more complicated than a username prompt followed by a password prompt, you might have to connect through the terminal; talk to your ISP about it.

Clicking the Dial Now button at the lower right of the PPP tab is actually just a shortcut to the Internet Connect application, which will allow you to dial the main number or any other you have stored there.

Configuring Internet Connect

The Internet Connect application allows you to keep something similar to an address book of all your dialup connections and quickly connect with any of them, regardless of your current network location setting.

To add a configuration, click the modem tab (probably labeled "Internal Modem"). If you've already configured the Network Preferences pane, you'll see that a "Main Number" configuration already exists. This configuration can't be changed from within Internet Connect. If you make changes to any of its fields, you'll be prompted to save the changes into a new configuration when you close the tab.

From the Configuration popup-menu, select "Edit Configurations." Click the "+" icon at the bottom left of the window to add a new configuration item. (Notice that the Main Number configuration is not editable.) Fill the fields as you did in the Network pane.

Checking the "Manual Dial to make this connection" checkbox allows you to use the number pad on your telephone to dial the number of your ISP. When this box is checked, and you click Connect on the Modem tab, the computer will prompt you to pick up your phone and dial the appropriate numbers. This can be useful when the computer can't dial the number correctly for some reason, or you need to enter additional information like a credit card number to complete the call.

Once you save the configuration by clicking OK, you can then dial it or any of your configurations by selecting one from the Configuration popup-menu on the Modem tab and clicking Connect.

Accessing Network Disks

Mac OS X gives you a number of ways to connect to a remote filesystem (or a segment of one) using the Finder, an Open or Save dialog box, of even from the command line. The remote system need not run under Mac OS; you can, for example, use SMB to connect to Windows machines, and NFS to access filesystems on Unix computers.*

Browsing Network File Servers

Mac OS X allows you to browse local network fileservers that use any of the supported service discovery protocols: Rendezvous, AppleTalk, SLP, and SMB. To configure the service discovery function of these protocols on your Mac, use the Directory Access application, found in */Applications/Utilities*. Note that turning off a protocol in Directory Access doesn't keep you from connecting to and using a server if you already know its name; it only prevents you from discovering the server using that protocol.

In a Finder window or an Open or Save dialog, click the Network icon in the Sidebar to browse your local network for discoverable file servers. What you'll find inside Network depends on the complexity of your network. Even if you're not connected to any network, you'll always find at least one item, named "Servers," which is a mount point for remote home directories and not the location of any file servers.

If you have only AppleShare servers (AFP over IP or AppleTalk) on your network, and your network is without AppleTalk zones, those servers will appear loose within Network alongside the Servers item. If you do have AppleTalk zones, each zone appears as a folder inside Network, with each folder holding server icons representing the servers in that zone.

Similarly, Windows workgroups and domains appear as folders in Network, each holding icons of the file servers found in those groups. If you are on a mixed network, you'll find another folder inside Network called Local, which holds icons for the servers found in your current AppleTalk zone, primary Windows domain, SLP scope, and Rendezvous subnet.

* On the other hand, Mac OS X isn't unique in offering cross-platform file-sharing options, so it's quite possible to find yourself connecting to Unix machines via SMB, for example.

Double-click a server icon, and you'll be prompted for your username and password on that server. (In column view you'll also find a "Connect" button in the preview pane). Once you've successfully authenticated, you'll be prompted to select the shared volumes to mount. Those you select will appear as icons on your desktop and in the sidebar, where you can browse the available subfolders.

Using Connect to Server

When you can't browse a desired server or you want one mounted on the desktop, you can use the Finder's Connect to Server (⌘-K) command, which gives a simple interface for mounting remote disks locally. As Figure 8-10 shows, the Connect to Server window contains three ways to specify the server you'd like to mount:

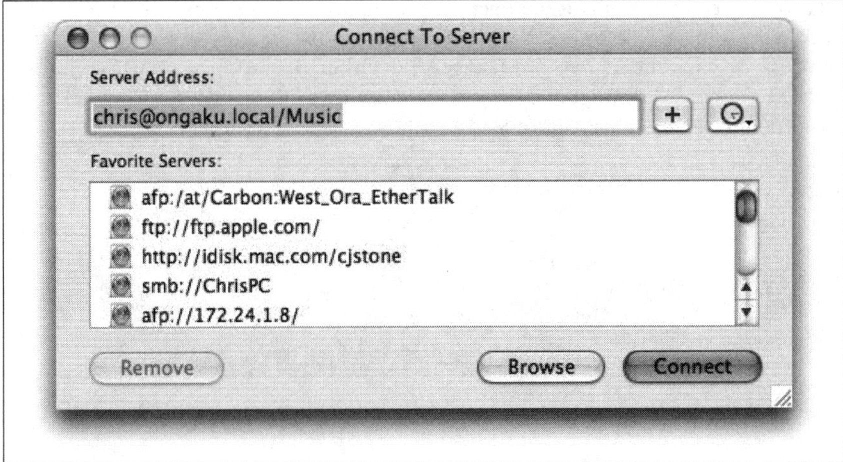

Figure 8-10. Connecting to an AFP server

Address text field
: Here you can type in the URL that points to the disk you wish to mount. The Finder knows what type of disk it is (and which network protocol to use) by the URL's prefix, such as `afp://` or `smb://`; if you don't use a prefix at all, the Finder assumes AFP.

: Clicking Connect when this field contains a URL will connect to the shared disk to which it points.

Recent Servers Pop-up menu
: This menu, indicated by the clock icon, contains a list of the last few servers you've connected to through the Finder. Selecting one and then clicking the window's Connect button will connect to it.

Favorite Servers
: Once you've specified an address in the server address field, clicking the + icon to its right adds that server to the Favorite Servers list below it. Items in that list will stay until you select them and click the Remove button.

Clicking the "browse" button opens a new Finder window with the Network Sidebar icon selected, which allows you to browse servers as described in the previous section.

Like browsed volumes, network volumes accessed this way will appear in the Finder's Sidebar alongside the local volumes, and on your desktop if you've configured that in the Finder. To unmount a volume, select its icon, and drag it to the Eject icon in the dock or use the ⌘-E shortcut.

The next few sections cover the kinds of remote filesystems the Finder recognizes.

Connecting to AFP shares

AFP is the Apple Filing Protocol,* the native file-sharing protocol for Macintosh computers since Mac OS 6. Until System 7.5.3, AFP worked only over AppleTalk, but since then has worked over TCP/IP as well. When you turn on Personal File Sharing using Mac OS X's Sharing preferences pane (see "File Sharing Services" in Chapter 12), you're using AFP. Other operating systems, including Mac OS Versions 7 through 9.2, as well as Windows 2000 and Windows NT, can also run AFP services. See Figure 8-11.

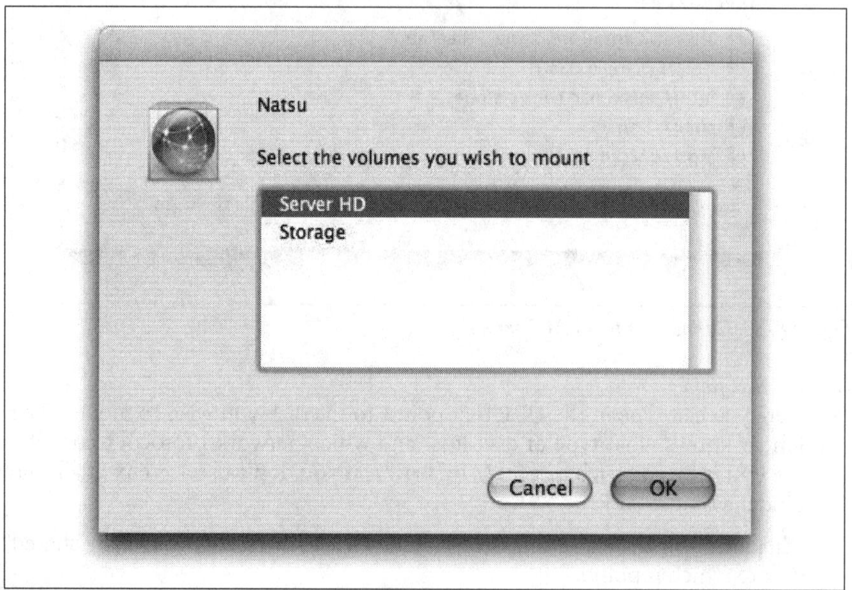

Figure 8-11. Choosing a volume from an AFP server

* Available online at *http://developer.apple.com/documentation/Networking/Conceptual/AFP/AFP3_1.pdf*, or if you have installed the Developer Tools, this document can be found on your system in */Developer/Documentation/Networking/Conceptual/AFP/AFP3_1.pdf*.

Connecting to SMB/CIFS shares

Windows-based file servers communicate through SMB, the Server Message Block protocol. (It's also known as the Common Internet File System (CIFS)). You can connect to these servers through the Finder's Connect To Server command, just as described in the previous section. As Figures 8-12 and 8-13 show, the process differs only slightly.

The URL you type into the Address text field takes the form `smb://`*`host/sharename`*. For the hostname, you can use the server's DNS name, its IP number, or its Windows machine name. You can specify the name of the share you wish to connect to after a slash (/) character; otherwise, like AFP, you'll get a menu of shares to choose from.

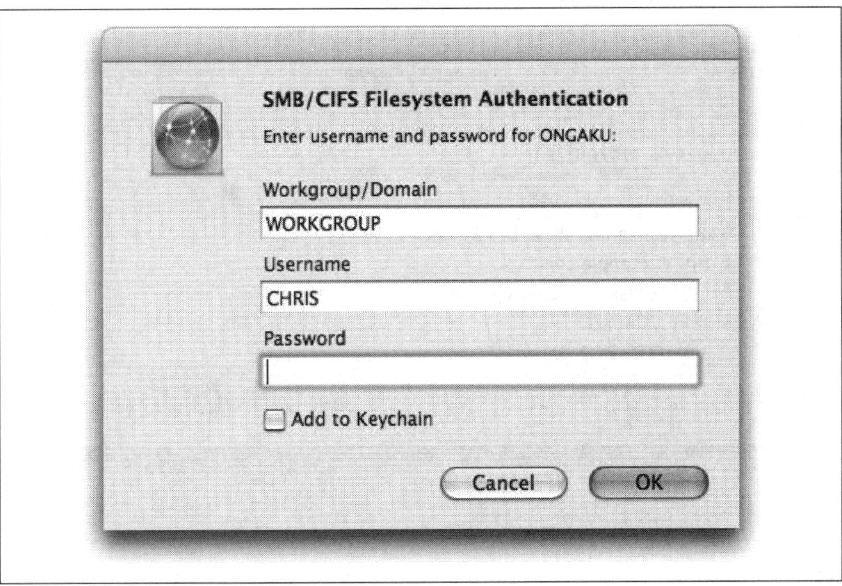

Figure 8-12. Authenticating with an SMB server

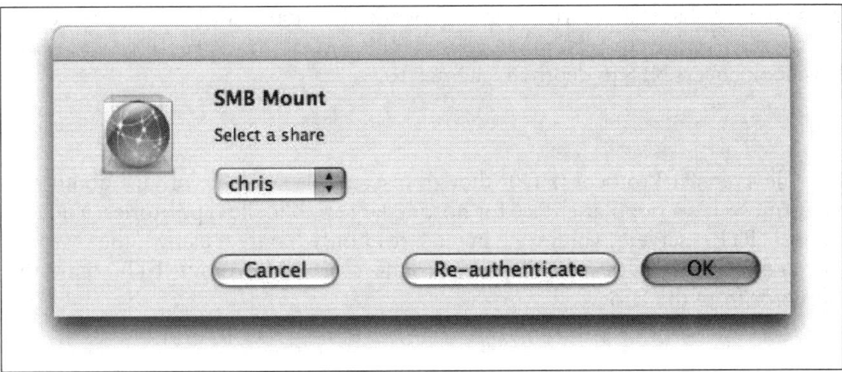

Figure 8-13. Selecting an SMB share

Once you connect and authenticate, the SMB share shows up as a disk in the Finder, and you can use it like any other.

Mounting WebDAV sites

The Web-based Distributed Authoring and Versioning system (WebDAV; *http://www.webdav.com*) extends HTTP (the protocol on which the Web runs) with version-control commands (much like RCS). This allows several web developers to simultaneously and safely work on the same set of files over a network connection, rather than edit them locally and then FTP them to a server (thus eliminating the risk of conflicting changes).

To mount a WebDAV site, call up the Connect to Server (⌘-K) window, and type in its URL, prefixed with `http://`, as shown in Figure 8-14.

Figure 8-14. Connecting to a WebDAV site

NFS

For many years, the Network File System (NFS) protocol has let Unix machines transparently share directories over a network. To mount an NFS volume, use a URL in the Connect to Server dialog box in this format: *nfs://hostname/pathname*. This book covers NFS in depth in Chapter 10.

FTP

The File Transfer Protocol (FTP), though insecure, is available on just about any platform, so it's a popular choice for hosting large public file repositories. You can mount FTP server volumes in a read-only state using the `ftp://`*username@hostname/pathname* URL. To connect via anonymous FTP, omit the *username@* from the URL.

Mounting Disks Through the Terminal

Advanced users who wish finer control over mounting these remote filesystems can instead use the *mount* command or one of the *mount_fstype* Terminal commands to graft them to arbitrary points in the filesystem, or specify special arguments to pass to the mounting programs.* Table 8-1 lists the specific *mount_fstype* commands for each kind of remote filesystem you can mount. Use *mount* (with a *–t* argument appropriate to the target filesystem) if you've defined mount points through NetInfo, as described in the section "NFS through automount" in Chapter 10.

Table 8-1. Remote filesystem types

mount –t argument	Handler program	Filesystem type
smb	mount_smbfs	SMB share
afp	mount_afp	AFP (AppleShare) shared disk
webdav	mount_webdav	WebDAV site
nfs	mount_nfs	NFS export

Refer to Chapter 28 for the proper arguments for each of these commands. For example, to mount the SMB share from Figure 8-13 to the local directory *~/mnt/chris*:

```
$ mount_smbfs
//chris@ongaku.internal.morgul.net/chris ~/mnt/chris
Password: myBigSecretPassword
```

If *~/mnt/chris* is already defined as an SMB mount point through NetInfo, you can just run this command:

```
$ mount ~/mnt/chris
Password: ********
```

Web Browsing

Web browsing on Mac OS X is as easy as launching Apple's own Safari, which ships with Mac OS X. You can find it in */Applications*, and the Dock displays its icon (a compass face) among its default icons for new users.

Alternative Browsers

Safari is a fine browser, but curious users may want to investigate some of the alternative browsers available for Mac OS X. They all serve the same basic function of letting you view HTML files on the World Wide Web, but each has its own style and set of unique, fine-tuned features.

* If you simply want a mounted disk to appear at some arbitrary place in the local filesystem, you can mount it, as described in the earlier section "Accessing Network Disks," and then make an alias of it (see the "Aliases" section in Chapter 2), placing it wherever you wish.

Network Disks and Security

All these remote disk-mounting methods are great for safely sharing information with other computers located elsewhere on a closed intranet, when you and they are all tucked safely behind a firewall or grouped together through a virtual private network (VPN). When sending information (including the passwords you use to connect to these network services) over the worldwide Internet, however, the packets that make up this information must potentially pass through many points unknown. A malicious eavesdropper sitting somewhere in between and running a network packet-sniffing program could intercept your passwords and other sensitive information, which would be Bad. When possible, consider using a secure Internet protocol, such as *ssh* for remote logins or *sftp* for file transfers. Unfortunately, this precludes the connections that the Finder makes super-easy. Express due paranoia when appropriate.

This warning counts double for AirPort-enabled Macs, by the way; the Airport protocol, 802.11b and 802.11g (the same used by nearly all popular IP-over-radio devices, Apple or otherwise, at the time of this writing), has been shown to be easily crackable at any level of its built-in WEP encryption,[a] giving network snoops another potential door into your network. SSH, SSL, and other secure connection layers work just as well as they do over a wired network, though; so use them (through the *ssh* program, the "Use SSL" checkbox in the Mail application's preferences, and so on) where your servers allow them.

a. Wireless networks using the more recent Wi-Fi Protected Access (WPA) protocol, including those made with Apple Airport hardware, are much less crackable than those using the older Wireless Equivalent Privacy (WEP) protocol.

iCab
: This browser, available from *http://www.icab.de*, has a relatively small memory footprint and features built-in HTML validity checking and error-reporting, which can be useful for web designers. (It also may be the only currently popular browser that still offers new versions for ancient, pre-PowerPC Macintoshes running System 7!)

Internet Explorer
: Microsoft's Internet Explorer (IE) comes preinstalled on Mac OS X inside */Applications*. IE is the most popular browser on the Internet and will often be able to handle some sites other browsers can't. Unfortunately, Microsoft has announced that they will not continue with future development of IE for the Macintosh.

Mozilla
: The much-heralded Mozilla is an open source, cross-platform, and very feature-heavy web browser (as well as an email client and Usenet news reader) project originally launched by Netscape in 1998. It hit Version 1.0 in 2002; the latest Carbon version is available from its web site, *http://www.mozilla.org/products/mozilla1.x/*.

Camino

The separate Camino project (*http://www.mozilla.org/products/camino/*) is a true Cocoa port of Mozilla.

Firefox

Firefox (*http://www.mozilla.org/products/firefox/*) is a technology preview of the Mozilla project's next generation standalone browser. It's very fast and supports themes.

OmniWeb

The Omni Group's shareware web browser, which concentrates on having a very streamlined, Cocoa-based interface uses the same KHTML rendering engine as Safari. This is available at *http://www.omnigroup.com/applications/omniweb/*.

Opera

The impressively speedy piece of shareware called Opera (*http://www.opera.com/mac*) has long been a popular alternative browser on Windows machines, and has more recently offered a Carbon version.

Changing the Default Browser

By default, Mac OS X uses Safari to view any URLs you open through other applications (such as Mail). If you find that you prefer a different browser, you'll need to first open Safari one last time, and from its General preferences pane, choose a different default browser to use, as shown in Figure 8-15.

If you wish, you can also choose a separate application for handling local HTML files that you open through the Finder. This involves using any HTML file's Info window to change the file type's default application (as described in the section "The Get Info Window" in Chapter 2). Otherwise, the browser you define in the Internet pane will handle local files, as well.

Browsing in the Terminal

Finally, Lynx deserves special mention. An all-text, console-based web browser, it's one of the first web browsers ever written, in the early 1990s at the University of Kansas. It allows you to surf the Web *very* quickly (if not very prettily) from within the Terminal application (Figure 8-16), using the arrow keys and Return instead of the mouse to follow links, and the space bar to scroll though web pages.

Lynx's home page is at *http://lynx.browser.org*, and you can find an easy-to-install package prepared by the OSXGNU project at *http://www.osxgnu.org/software/Networking/lynx/* or through the Fink system (see Chapter 27).

A more recent text-based browser, *links*, is also worth investigating; it can render HTML tables within a Terminal window and display pages while it loads them, much like a graphical browser.

Figure 8-15. Safari's preferences

Using FTP

The File Transfer Protocol (FTP) is one of the oldest Internet protocols for file sharing that is still in use. It consists of a simple command set for getting lists of available files from servers, as well as for performing file downloads and uploads. (To learn about Mac OS X's more modern and Finder-friendly notions of file sharing, see the earlier section "Mounting Network Disks.")

The most common FTP transactions occur through anonymous, read-only logins to an FTP server, letting you browse through world-readable directories and download the files found therein. Entering a URL with an `ftp` prefix, such as `ftp://ftp.gnome.org` in Safari will pass the request on to the Finder, which will mount the volume as described earlier. Internet Explorer (or any other alternative web browser; see the earlier section "Alternative Browsers") also handles this sort of functionality seamlessly; pointing it at an FTP URL begins an anonymous FTP session with that location, allowing you to browse the directories using the browser window itself. You can also put a username and password into the URL like this: `ftp://`*`username`*`:`*`password`*`@`*`host`* (but see the warning that follows).

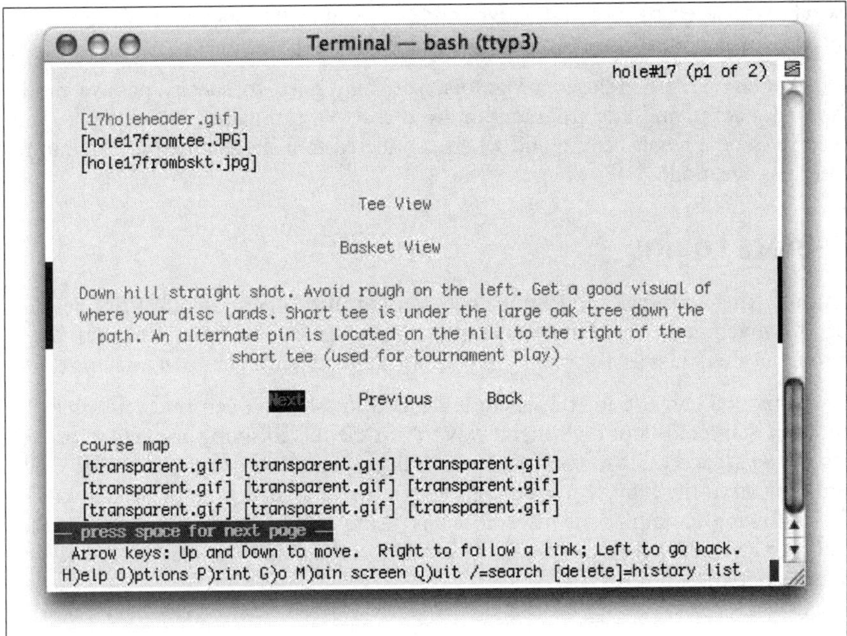

Terminal — bash (ttyp3)
hole#17 (p1 of 2)
[17holeheader.gif]
[hole17fromtee.JPG]
[hole17frombskt.jpg]
Tee View
Basket View
Down hill straight shot. Avoid rough on the left. Get a good visual of
where your disc lands. Short tee is under the large oak tree down the
path. An alternate pin is located on the hill to the right of the
short tee (used for tournament play)
Next
Previous
Back
course map
[transparent.gif] [transparent.gif] [transparent.gif]
[transparent.gif] [transparent.gif] [transparent.gif]
[transparent.gif] [transparent.gif] [transparent.gif]
-- press space for next page --
Arrow keys: Up and Down to move. Right to follow a link; Left to go back.
H)elp O)ptions P)rint G)o M)ain screen Q)uit /=search [delete]=history list

Figure 8-16. Lynx in action

To do anything more sophisticated in an FTP session than merely browsing available files, you have to use an FTP client. Mac OS X doesn't ship with any FTP client Aqua applications, but it does ship with *ftp*, a rather minimalist command-line program (documented in Chapter 28). For a more sophisticated FTP client program, consider the feature-rich, open source Terminal program *ncftp*, available at *http://www.ncftp.com*.

Popular third-party Aqua FTP applications include the shareware programs Fetch (available from *http://fetchsoftworks.com/*), Transmit (available at *http://panic.com/*), FTPeel (*http://www.freshlysqueezedsoftware.com/*), and the open source CyberDuck (*http://icu.unizh.ch/~dkocher/cyberduck/*).

Using FTP non-anonymously represents a security risk because your username and password travel over the network as cleartext, quite visible and vulnerable to eavesdroppers. Consider using the *sftp* or *scp* commands instead, which encrypt your file transfer sessions. See Chapter 28 for more information about them.

Passive FTP Mode

If a firewall lies between you and the Internet, you have to use *passive mode*. Turning on passive mode for Aqua applications is simple: in the Proxies tab of the Network pane (pictured in Figure 8-4), activate the "Use Passive FTP Mode (PASV)" checkbox. Like all settings performed through the Network pane, this state is associated with the current location file, so the FTP mode automatically switches between passive and active modes as you switch locations (once you've specified which locations require passive mode).

When using Terminal-based programs, you may need to specify passive mode through a command-line argument or an interactive command. For example, you need to issue a *passive* command when connected to a site via the *ftp* program to enter passive mode.

Remote Logins

Through the Terminal application, you can log into other (usually Unix or Mac OS X) machines over a network and run command-line programs on them through a shell, just as Terminal lets you normally do with your own machine.

Programs you can use for this include *telnet* and *ssh*. You can find references to both in Chapter 28, but the general way to run them is to simply use *telnet* (or *ssh*) *host*. If *host* accepts the connection, you'll be prompted for a password. Once authenticated, the remote machine greets you with a shell prompt of its own. In the following example, the user `chris` is using *ssh* to connect from his local machine (named `MyPB`) to another Mac OS X machine on his local network (named `natsu`):

```
MyPB:~ chris$ ssh natsu
chris@natsu's password:
Last login: Sat Feb 28 10:08:14 2004 from 192.168.1.9
Welcome to Darwin!
[natsu:~] chris%
```

Note the different prompts, due to different shell configurations this user has on the two machines. Note also that configuring one's shell to display the current hostname within one's prompt can be a good idea, because it acts as a constant reminder as to which machine you're working with!

If your username on the remote machine is not the same as the one you use locally, use the *ssh* command's *ssh username@host* or *ssh –l host* syntax.

If you have X Windows installed on your Mac, you can run other Unix machines' GUI software on your machine, as described in Chapter 26. You can also use VNC to log into other Mac OS X machines and enjoy their full Aqua interfaces; see Chapter 26.

While their basic interfaces are the same, a very important difference lies between the two programs. *telnet* sends and receives all its data as cleartext, while *ssh* works solely with encrypted data. This means that any use of *telnet* can constitute a security risk because network eavesdroppers can capture all your activities, including your username and password. Consider using only *ssh* whenever possible.

Virtual Private Networking

The Internet makes it possible for anyone almost anywhere to access computers across the globe. Of course because access is so easy, LANs need firewalls to prevent unwanted intruders. Such ironclad security, however, can also prove to be a barrier to desired access. A corporate employee on the road, for example, might find it convenient (even necessary) to access the corporate LAN from a hotel room or another LAN to get at internal data. But without a way to get through or bypass the corporate firewall, any access attempts will be futile. Fortunately there are a few ways to access a firewalled LAN, and the best, in most cases, is to use a Virtual Private Network (VPN).

Establishing a VPN connection means creating an encrypted channel, or "tunnel" for all IP traffic between your machine and the corporate VPN server. The VPN server straddles the edge of the corporate LAN, routing the traffic between the LAN and the Internet. Once you've authenticated using the VPN client software built in to Mac OS X, you'll receive an IP on that remote LAN. The VPN server will then pass your data though, decrypting as it sends to the LAN and encrypting as it sends to the Internet. You can then access any IP-based service on that LAN that you could were you physically on-site: Intranet web pages, FTP, IP-based file sharing, etc.

Though all VPN traffic still travels across the Internet to reach the remote LAN, the packets are encrypted well enough to keep any potential eavesdroppers busy for at least several years should they try to decrypt any intercepted data.

Another advantage of a VPN is that, to establish a tunnel, you need only connect to the Internet by the closest available means, thereby saving the expense of a direct dial-up connection to the home office, another method of accessing the LAN remotely.

Mac OS X supports the two most popular VPN protocols, L2TP over IPsec and PPTP. The clients for both are built into the Internet Connect application, found in the Applications folder. Upon opening Internet Connect initially, you'll see a window similar to Figure 8-17.

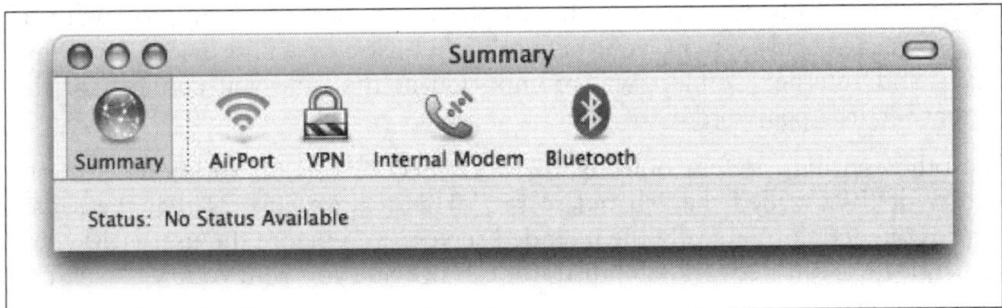

Figure 8-17. The Internet Connect application

Which protocol you use, of course, depends on the type of VPN server you'll be connecting to. If you've not connected to your VPN server before or don't have the information at hand to configure a connection, you'll need to ask your network administrator to provide it.

Establishing a VPN connection with either protocol is a similar procedure. Once a normal Internet connection exists (via broadband, modem, or AirPort, for example), open the Internet Connect application. If it's the first time you've set up a VPN on the computer, you'll find a "VPN" icon on the shelf. Click it, and you'll be prompted to choose either L2TP or PPTP. The icon name will then change to reflect your choice, and the pane will provide fields to enter your account information. If you ever need to use the other protocol, select New VPN connection from the Edit menu, and you'll again be prompted to choose.

To save a configuration, select Edit Configuration from the Configuration pop-up menu (see Figure 8-18). The configuration sheet allows you to add, edit, and remove configurations. It also contains, depending on the protocol, one or two additional settings.

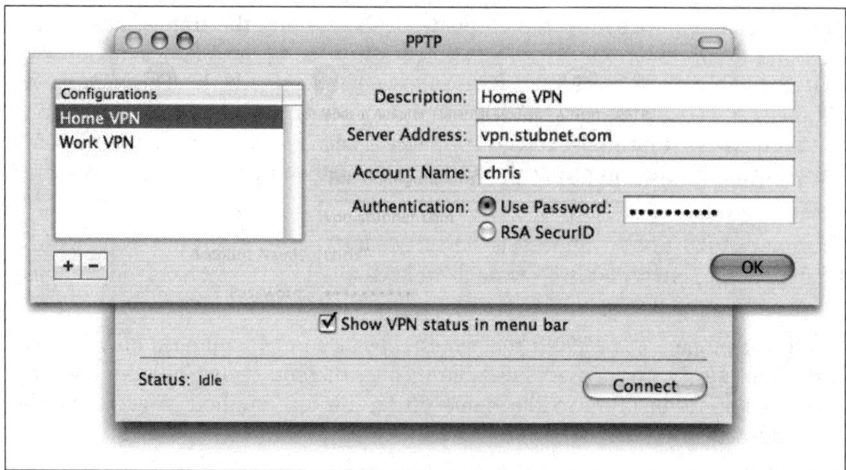

Figure 8-18. Saving a VPN configuration

The first, common to both protocols, is to use an RSA SecurID password instead of a standard password. The RSA SecurID third-party commercial authentication system requires a hardware token that displays a regularly changing password. If your server uses this system, your network administrator will provide you with a token, and Internet Connect will prompt you at the time you connect for the current SecurID password.

The other setting, present only for L2TP connections, is an additional security feature of IPsec called the "shared secret." This feature ensures that the server you're connecting to is really the intended server, even before the user is asked to authenticate. Your network administrator can provide you with your VPN server's shared secret.

Once configuration is complete, click the Connect button to establish the tunnel. You can then use any IP service you'd use on-site—for example, check your email, view Intranet web pages and access internal FTP servers. However, you may not be able to browse services such as file servers from the Network icon or printers in the Printer Setup Utility. To access these services, you need to connect to them using their IP addresses (see Chapter 9).

Once you're finished with the tunnel, it's a good idea to close it. Though you can still access Internet sites outside your LAN while using the VPN, you may find that browsing is not as fast as when you're not tunneling.

If you need to troubleshoot a connection, select Connection Log from the Window menu. Also, checking the box to "Show VPN status in menu bar" provides a quick way to select configurations, and initiate and close subsequent connections.

Rendezvous

Rendezvous is Apple's name for a suite of network technologies that brings to IP networking much of the same ease of configuration and service discovery that AppleTalk brought to Macintosh networking in 1985. Unlike the AppleTalk set of protocols, however, Rendezvous functions fully within the much more common IP networks.

The first piece of Rendezvous, *link-local addressing*, allows your Mac to at least function on the local IP subnet without configuration by you or a DHCP server. Rendezvous does this by assigning to the Mac an unused IP number in the 169.254/16 range when it finds no DHCP server on the network. Thanks to this feature, you can simply plug a number of Macs (or Windows and Linux machines that support link-local addressing) into a hub, turn them on, and have an ad hoc IP network up and running.

Another element of Rendezvous, *multicast-DNS*, provides your Mac with a local hostname (also called a Rendezvous name), allowing any other Rendezvous-enabled computer on the local IP subnet to find it by that name, even when no DNS server exits for that network.

By default, the editable part of your local hostname is the same as your computer name. Your full local hostname name appends that with *.local*. You can change the first part of the name to anything you wish as long as it's unique on your subnet (Rendezvous will check) and contains only upper- or lowercase letters, numbers, hyphens, or periods. To change it, open the Sharing preference pane, and click on the Edit button just below the Computer Name field.

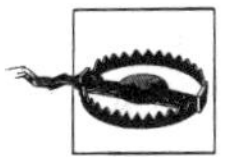

Be careful not to confuse your local hostname with your "Computer Name," which is used instead for AppleTalk and SLP service discovery.

A local hostname gives other users on the network an unchanging, easy-to-remember identifier instead of the numerical IP they would otherwise need when requesting any IP-based services from your computer (for example, web sharing, remote login, FTP), and Rendezvous provides this without the need of a network administrator or DNS server.

If you would like to reach other machines on your subnet by their local hostname without typing *.local* each time, add *local* to the list of search domains in your Network Preference pane. Then, instead of typing *macjon.local*, for example, you can just type `macjon` to reach that computer.

Rendezvous' third piece, *DNS service discovery*, allows your Mac to discover specific services on other Rendezvous-enabled machines. Apple's own applications use this feature in many ways. For example, the Safari web browser, using Rendezvous, lists links to sites hosted on Rendezvous-enabled web servers on the local subnet. Likewise, iTunes lists the play lists of other iTunes users. iChat's Rendezvous messaging, of course, uses this technology as well, automatically discovering and listing for you all other Rendezvous iChatters.

To use some of these services with the firewall turned on, you need to open some specific network ports, as described in Chapter 6 Note that opening network ports can decrease your machine's security.

In fact, a "machine" can be any IP-enabled device. Therefore, Rendezvous-enabled printers, cameras, and other devices can broadcast their services as well. Several such printer models already exist from Brother and Hewlett-Packard. The other major printer vendors have announced future support. Also, television-maker Phillips Electronics has announced it will be supporting Rendezvous in its future products.

Because Rendezvous is Apple's name for the cross-platform technology called "Zeroconf" (for Zero Configuration), you can now use Rendezvous with Zeroconf-enabled Windows and Linux machines, thanks to software products such as Howl (*http://www.swampwolf.com*) and Java Rendezvous (*http://www.strangeberry.com*).

9
Printer Configuration and Printing

From a user's perspective, Mac OS X's printing system contains two major parts: a list of printers your machine knows about, which you can access and modify through the Printer Setup Utility application, and the standard dialog that shows up when you select File→Print (⌘-P) in nearly any application.

How Printing Works

Mac OS X ships with a suite of software known as the Common Unix Printing System (CUPS),* which acts as the operating system's print server. Whenever you ask an application to print a document (using either the Aqua interface described later in the section "The Print Dialog" or the Terminal commands listed later in the section "Command-Line Tools"), it in turn makes a request to the print server. This maintains one or more *queues*, each of which represents a printer device and its first-in, first-out list of *jobs*. Jobs are the documents in the print server's memory, which wait their turn to go to a printer and be made into hardcopy.

Mac OS X's print server is actually a network service that can receive and process print requests from other machines, but its default configuration refuses any request that doesn't come from the same Mac it's running on. In other words, unless you turn on printer sharing (detailed later in the section "Printer Sharing"), printer queues you set up on your Mac through the Printer Setup Utility will be for your machine's own private use. This is probably what most computer users expect.

* You can find information about CUPS, including full user and administrator documentation, at *http://www.cups.org*.

Generally printers come in two varieties:

USB
: Printers directly connected to your Mac via USB cabling are always visible to your machine alone, unless you have printer sharing activated.

Network
: Printers accessible over a network are attached to print servers, which might be (on high-end models) in the printer itself or running on another computer to which that printer is connected. (The computer can be a Mac OS X machine with its own printer-sharing features activated or any other machine running a print server that understands the LPR or IPP printing protocols.)

CUPS handles either case with equal finesse. See the section "Adding and configuring printers," later in this chapter, for more about adding printers to your machine's own list of available printers.

The Print Dialog

Almost every Mac OS X application supports a File→Print (⌘-P) menu command. When selected, a print dialog (Figure 9-1) appears, usually as a sheet attached to the foremost document window.

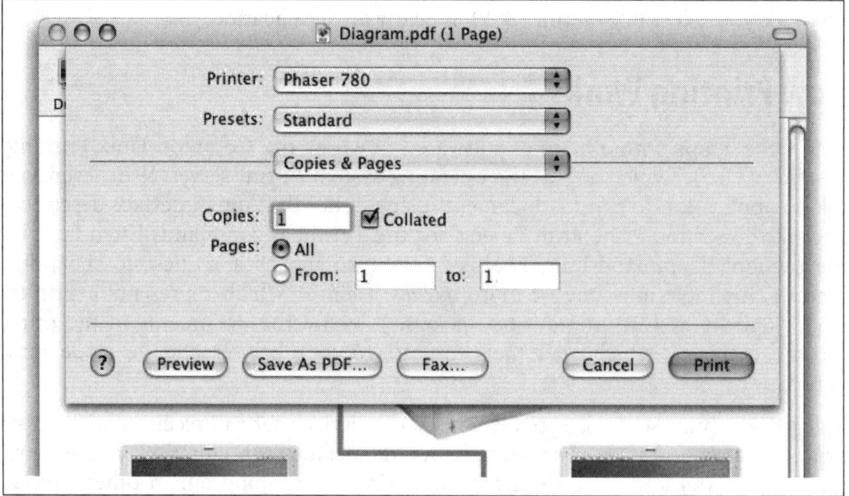

Figure 9-1. The standard Print dialog (as a sheet)

The dialog contains three menus. The first two are always available:

Printer
: This menu, shown in Figure 9-2, contains the name or IP address of every printer you have defined through the Printer Setup Utility (*/Applications/Utilities*). If there are any shared or discovered printers on the local network, they will also appear here, listed under an appropriate submenu. An additional choice, Edit Printer List..., launches the Printer Setup Utility and

summons its printer list editing window for you (see the "The Printer List" section later in this chapter).

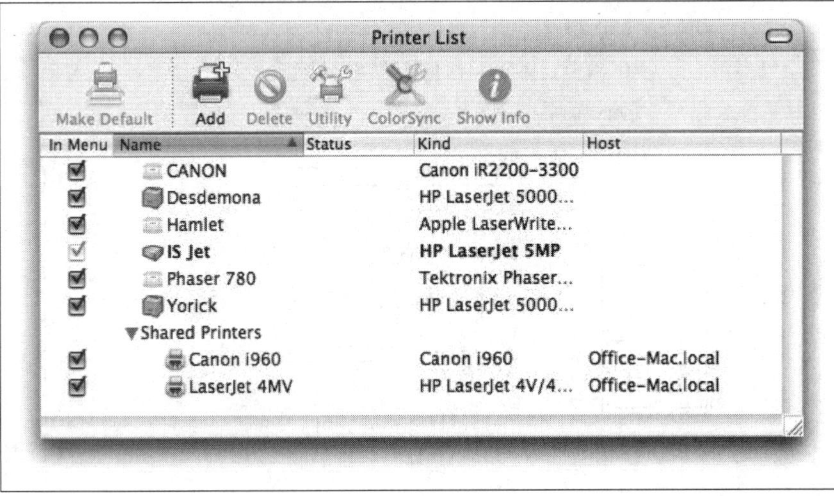

Figure 9-2. Printer Setup Utility's printer list window

The menu's default selection—appearing in the menu after you call up the dialog through File→Print (⌘-P)—is whichever printer you've named as default through Printer Setup Utility.

Presets
: This menu lets you load sets of print settings you've previously used and saved. See the later section "Saving Your Printing Settings" for more information.

Printer Output Menu and Panes
: An unlabeled third menu on the Print dialog lets you navigate between the dialog's various functionality panes (not all of which exist for all applications). When you first open up the dialog, it displays the Copies & Pages pane (which contains the controls you're most likely to adjust from job to job). The panes are described in the following list:

  Copies & Pages
  : This pane lets you specify the number of separate copies of the job that the printer should produce and whether the copies should be collated. By clicking the "From" radio button (see Figure 9-1), you can print a limited range of pages, rather than the entire document. (To print a single page, just enter the same page number in both fields.)

  Layout
  : This pane gives you an easy interface for printing multiple pages, each proportionally scaled down in size, onto a single physical page. As Figure 9-3 shows, you can tile up to 16 logical pages onto a physical page, choose the order in which they appear, and specify a border to put around each. Additionally, if your printer can handle duplex printing,

activating this pane's "Two Sided Printing" checkbox takes advantage of it. You can also use the Binding control to have a page's reverse side be printed upside down, which makes vertical binding feasible.

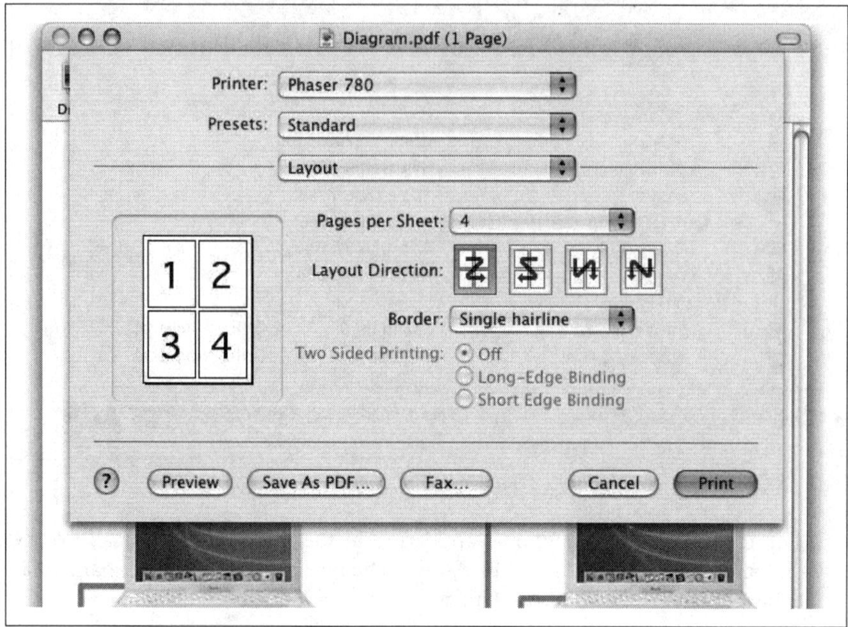

Figure 9-3. The Print dialog's Layout pane

This pane doesn't control the way content is laid out over a single page; see the section "Page Setup," later in this chapter.

Output Options
: Allows you to save the print job to a PDF or raw PostScript file instead of printing it. Choosing to save as a PDF here is equivalent to doing so with the "Save as PDF" button at the bottom of the print dialog box.

Scheduler
: Sets a postponed time, if desired, for the print job to be sent. Also allows you to hold print jobs indefinitely.

Paper Handling
: Specifies reverse order as well as odd- or even-numbered page-only printing.

ColorSync
: Part of the ColorSync color management system. Use this pane to specify whether you want the color conversion processing to take place on the computer (using ColorSync and the printer profile) or for PostScript printers, on the printer itself. This pane also allows you to apply Quartz filters to the printed output. Selecting Add Filters from the Quartz Filter pop-up menu opens a PDF preview of the print job inside the Filters tab of ColorSync Utility, allowing you to preview filters on the fly as you

create and modify them. See the "ColorSync" section later in this chapter for more about ColorSync and Quartz filters.

Cover Page
: Allows you to specify that a cover page be included with the job, and if it should be printed either before or after. The Cover Page Type pop-up menu lists several cover page formats to choose from. An additional Billing Info field allows you to enter a line of additional text to be included on the cover page.

Paper Feed
: Selects which printer paper tray to use for the printout. The default selection, Auto Select, chooses a tray based on the logical page size.

  By selecting the "First page from" radio button, you can split the job's paper source between two trays, both of which you specify separately. This can be useful if, for example, a report's cover page needs to be printed on a heavy stock stored in one tray, and the body pages all use more standard paper that is kept in another.

Error Handling
: This pane, available only with PostScript printers, lets you set the level of error reporting you want to see should a PostScript error occur and specify the system's behavior if the initial paper tray runs out of paper before a job is complete.

Application-specific options
: If the active application offers its own printing options, they will appear in the menu under a heading named after that application. See the "Application-Specific Print Options" section later in this chapter.

Printer Features
: This catch-all pane contains any additional features defined by a PostScript printer's PPD file. Any special printer features not covered by the standard Print dialog controls show up here. If you use a printer with the Generic PPD, you don't get this pane option.

Summary
: This pane simply lists a summary of all current printer settings, including all printer-specific settings found under Printer Features, if any.

Saving Your Printing Settings

The Print dialog's Presets pop-up menu lets you create presets (i.e., "snapshots" of all your chosen printer settings) across all the option panes. In future print jobs, you can recall these settings by selecting them from the same Presets menu.

Selecting Save As from the menu prompts you for a name under which to save the new preset. Once supplied, that name appears permanently under Presets. Selecting that name from the menu later instantly snaps all that preset's settings into place, across all the dialog's panes.

The menu's Save option lets you update the selected preset, modifying it to include all the dialog's current settings. Rename and Delete let you rename and delete presets, respectively.

Application-Specific Print Options

Some applications can specify their own print settings and add them to a pane in the standard Print dialog. This pane shows up as an option in the dialog's navigation pop-up menu. Figure 9-4 shows Internet Explorer's custom Print settings, which contain controls specific to printing web pages.

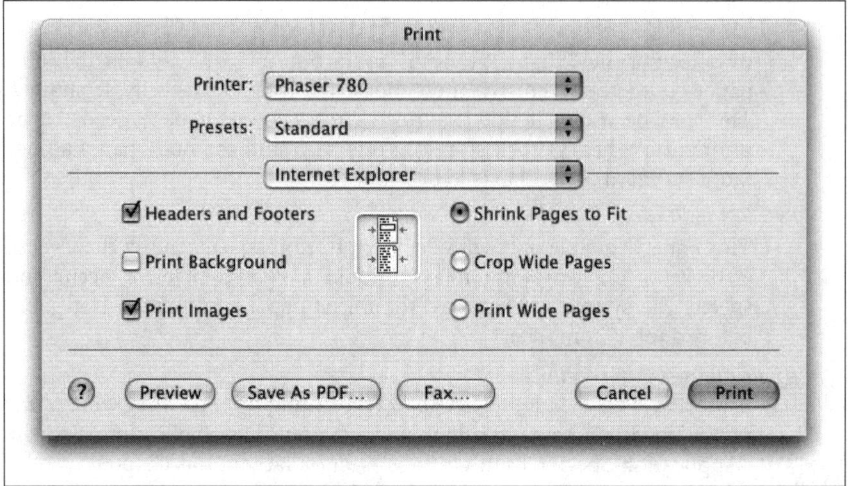

Figure 9-4. Internet Explorer's Print dialog

Preview

Clicking the Preview button opens a print preview (actually a PDF) of the job in the Preview application. There, you can zoom in and out, and use the rest of Preview's tools. Additionally, you can "soft proof" the job by clicking on the lower-left checkbox. Soft proofing simulates the appearance of the printed output on screen by taking into account the effect the printer has on any color information in the document (though it works only with some printers). This would be useful if, for example, you want to preview a color document before it's sent to a monochrome printer.

Save as PDF

Every Mac OS X application that uses the system's standard print system renders its pages via PDF before sending them to the print server. While the most common destination thereafter is a printer (by way of CUPS-defined PDF-to-PostScript and PDF-to-raster filters), you can instead save it to disk in PDF format by clicking this button.

Fax

The Fax button produces a simple interface for sending a print job through your modem as a fax instead of to a printer.

The To field holds the recipient fax machine's telephone number. You can type one in or click on the icon to the right to retrieve a number from your address book.

Enter any text in the Subject field to have it included on the cover page. In the Dialing Prefix field, enter any numbers you need dialed before the fax number (for example, 9 for an outside line).

The Modem pop-up lists the modems found connected to the computer. Use it to select the modem you would like to fax through.

The Presets pop-up menu works similarly to the normal print dialog box, though it allows you to save only those general settings available below the Presets pop-up menu, not those above specific to the fax job.

The unlabeled pop-up menu below Presets is also similar to that in the normal print dialog box, though there are several items that are unique to the fax pane or especially pertinent to faxing:

Fax Cover Page
: Check the Cover page checkbox and, in the field below it, enter any text you would like included on a cover page that will get sent with the fax.

Modem
: Allows you to configure basic modem settings (dialing type, sound on/off, and dial tone) independently of those set in the Network preference pane.

Scheduler
: Just as with printing, you can postpone the fax job for a later time. This could be convenient for faxing at later hours when rates are lower.

Printer Features
: You can specify here whether to send a low-resolution fax, which transmits faster, or a high-resolution fax, which takes longer to send, but looks better.

Once you click the Fax button, you can monitor the job through its queue as with regular print jobs.

To use your computer to receive faxes, you need to configure it with the Print & Fax preference pane, as described later in this chapter.

PDF Workflow

By default, the Save to PDF button at the bottom of the print dialog box really is nothing but a button that saves the job as a PDF. With some simple configuration, however, that button becomes a pop-up menu of items that allow you to further process the generated PDF.

To add this PDF workflow menu, you need only to create a new directory called *PDF Services* inside your user or local Library directory. In other words, once either of these directories exists, the PDF workflow menu will appear in the print dialog box:

/Library/PDF Services
/Users/username/Library/PDF Services

When you first create the menu, it's all but empty; only the normal Print to PDF item exits. However, there are several methods for adding other items, all of which involve placing files or aliases inside either of the PDF Services folder, allowing you to better organize the menu.*

Folder
: Placing a folder inside a PDF Services folder creates a submenu of the PDF Workflow menu, named for that folder. If any other types of items are placed in the folder, they will show up as items of the submenu.

Folder Alias
: Placing an alias to a folder inside a PDF Services folder adds a new item, named for that folder, to the PDF workflow menu. When you select that menu item, the generated PDF goes to that folder without you having to select a location to save it to each time.

Application File
: Placing an application file (or an alias to one) inside a PDF Services folder adds a new item, named for that application, to the PDF workflow menu. When you select that menu item, the generated PDF is then automatically opened by that application.

Unix Tool
: A Unix tool can be a shell, Perl, or Python script, or a script in any other language that can create an executable file. A Unix tool can even be a program written in a compiled language such as C. Placing a Unix tool file (or an alias to one) inside a PDF Services folder adds a new item, named for that tool, to the PDF workflow menu. When you select that menu item, the PDF is generated, and the tool is then executed and handed the following three parameters:

  1. The title of the PDF; originally the printed document's title
  2. The list of the printing options set for that job
  3. The path to the spooled PDF file, by default */tmp/printing.n*, where *n* is the process ID of the application being printed from

  Unix tools used in this way can perform very complex operations on the PDF itself. You could, for example, encrypt the PDF with a password, add a logo to each page, or add pages from other sources.†

* If you have a */Network/Library/PDF Services* directory, adding items to it will work as well, but the existence of this directory, unlike the others, won't force the PDF Workflow menu to be created.

† A Mac OS X technology called Quartz Scripting lets you easily script these kinds of procedures. See *http://developer.apple.com/printing/* for more information.

AppleScript

Placing a compiled AppleScript script file (or an alias to one) inside a PDF Services folder adds a new item, named for that file, to the PDF workflow menu. When you select that menu item, the PDF is generated, and its location sent in an open event to that script. This allows you to not only specify an application to open the PDF but also to further script that application's handling of the PDF. You can, for example, script Mail to email the PDF as an attachment or Photoshop to run its own image processing scripts on the rendered PDF.

Quartz Filter

To add a Quartz filter to the PDF workflow menu, launch the ColorSync Utility and click on its Filters toolbar button. From the pane at right, click the Domains tab. Select a filter from the list at left and check the PDF Workflow checkbox on the Domains tab.

See the "ColorSync" section of this chapter to learn more about the filters themselves.

Deleting the original spooled PDF file, however, isn't always an automatic part of this process; only some applications know to do this. Therefore, any Unix tools or AppleScripts should include code to remove the spooled PDF once it's no longer needed. Also, if you're generating a large number of PDFs by selecting an application from the menu, you should check the */tmp* directory regularly to check that those files aren't accumulating.*

The Simplified Print Sheet

Some applications that aim for an especially easy user interface use a simplified print sheet like that seen in Figure 9-5, which is from iPhoto. It takes several controls from different panes of the standard Print dialog and places them into a single pane.

Clicking a simplified print sheet's Advanced Options button transforms the dialog into the normal print sheet.

Printer Setup Utility

The Printer Setup Utility application (*/Applications/Utilities*) lets you define the list of printers available for use from your machine, as well as obtain queue and status information for each of them. Printer Setup Utility acts as the UI for printing once the application has finished rendering all the pages and sent them off to the print server. The Printer Setup Utility also performs similar functions for faxing, allowing you to view faxes queued for sending.

Printer Setup Utility has two views: an editable list of all the printers the computer knows about and an interactive look into the print queue for each one.

* The daily *cron* job (see Chapter 28) will regularly clear the */tmp* directory, including the spooled PDF files.

Figure 9-5. A simplified print sheet

The Printer List

Figure 9-2 shows a typical Printer List window. The default printer—the one that appears already selected in the standard Print dialog's Printer menu (Figure 9-1)—is in boldface. To change the default printer, select a different one by clicking on its row, then choosing Printers→Make Default (⌘-D), or click the Make Default icon in the toolbar.

The first of the window's five columns holds the In Menu checkbox, which allows you to specify whether you want that printer to show up in the print dialog box's list of printers. Name holds the printer's network name or IP address, Status shows a very brief summary of the printer's current state, with regard to any print jobs you've sent it, Kind shows the model of printer (based on the PPD associated with it), and Host shows the name of the host computer for any shared printer. Double-clicking on any printer's row in this table summons its queue window, which provides much more insight into its current activities, as explained in the later section "Printer Queues."

To remove a printer from the list, select its row, and then hit the Delete button (or select Printers→Delete).

Adding and configuring printers

Clicking Add Printer (or selecting Printers→Add Printer) calls up the lists' Add Printer sheet, seen in Figure 9-6. This dialog contains controls for specifying the new printer's network protocol and location. The sheet contains one pane for each printer communication protocol that Mac OS X can use, and the pop-up menu at the top of the window lets you navigate between these panes:

AppleTalk
: Use this pane to browse and select from the AppleTalk printers on your network. Only the printers on your local subnet will display, unless your LAN's routers are configured to route the AppleTalk protocol.

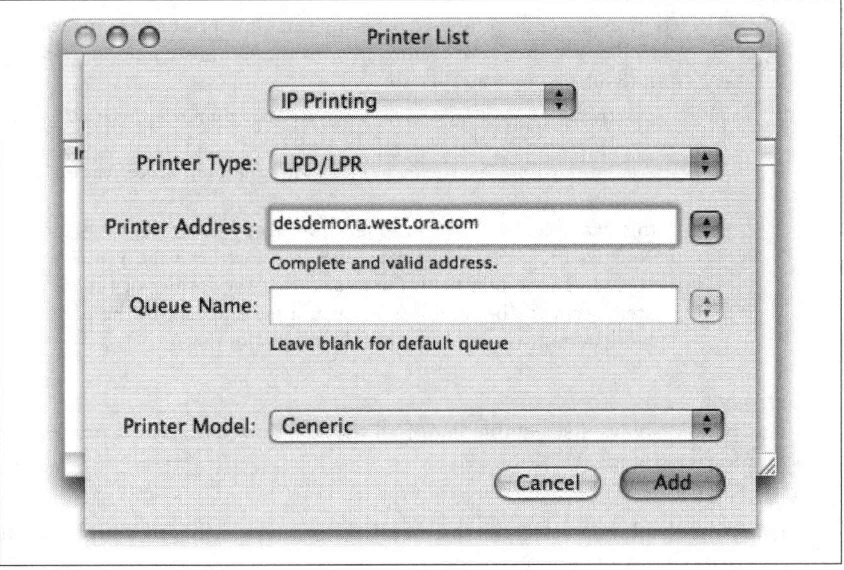

Figure 9-6. Adding a printer queue to the printer list through Printer Setup Utility

This pane gives you another menu to switch between different AppleTalk zones and a column view to browse the currently selected zone (the local one, by default).

IP Printing

This pane lets you set up connections to any Unix (or Mac OS X) print server—LP, LPR, or CUPS—through IP. This server can be another computer running a print server, or it can be a printer itself (very full-featured printer models have an Ethernet card, can take an IP address, and run software to act as their own print servers). Because of TCP/IP's flexibility, this server can be elsewhere on your machine's subnet, or at some antipodal point over the Internet.

Enter the server's Internet hostname or IP address into the Printer's Address text field. (The dialog provides some running commentary below the text field to let you know whether the address is a valid one, even performing DNS lookups while you type.) If you want to use the server's default (or only) printer, leave the Queue Name text field blank. Otherwise, type into it the printer's name.

To complete the setup, choose the name of the printer's manufacturer from the Printer Model pop-up menu, and then the correct driver from the list of models below it.

To investigate the printers queues a given Unix print server makes available, use the *lpstat* command with the *–h* (hostname) and *–p* (printer listing) options, like so:

```
$ lpstat -h my-print-server.my- office.com -p printer room_501_
laserjet disabled since Jan 01 00:00 -
printer color_laser_room_623 is idle.  enabled since Jan 01
00:00
```

In this example, room_501_laserjet and color_ laser_room_623 are the queues the server recognizes, and therefore are valid values in the Queue Name text field. (Note also that the former of the two printers seems to be disabled, but you'd have to talk to the office network administrator to find out the reason for that.)

Rendezvous
This pane displays a selectable list of all the Rendezvous-enabled printers on your local network.

USB
This pane displays a selectable list of all the printers visible to your machine via direct USB connection.

Directory Services
This pane lets you browse and select all the printers defined by the various directory services your computer uses. See Chapter 11.

Windows Printing
This pane allows you to browse and select from the SMB printers on your network. The list displays the computers available through Windows or SMB networking. Double-click a computer in the list to see the printers, if any, that the computer hosts. The pane opens to your local domain or workgroup, but you can browse another by selecting Network Neighborhood from the pop-up menu just above the list.

Additional protocols will also be included in this list if you've installed other printer drivers. Most likely, you'll see items supporting the proprietary discovery protocols from Epson, HP, and Lexmark. Consult the printer's documentation for help with using those.

For cases in which you can't discover your printer using any listed protocol, the Add Printer sheet provides a way to address printers directly. To access the Advanced item that allows this, hold the option key as you click on the Add icon in the Printer List window. You'll then find the additional "Advanced" item at the end of the protocol pop-up menu.

The Advanced pane's Device pop-up menu lists all the printing protocols included with CUPS on Mac OS X. Each type requires a specific Universal Resource Identifier (URI) syntax to address the printer. (Replace any spaces in the required values with the string %20 and any colons with /.) Here are two examples:

AppleTalk Printer Access Protocol

pap://AppleTalk Zone/Printer Name/Protocol

For example:

```
pap://Sales/King%20Lear/LaserWriter
```

Run the *atlookup* command in Terminal to find the printer protocol. See the *atlookup* entry in Chapter 28 for more information.

Windows Printer via Samba

smb://username:password@workgroup/server/printer

For example:

```
smb://chris:gazelle172@seb01/seb01bdc/othello
```

Modifying list entries

Internally, there's not much to a printer list entry; just a network location and (maybe) a printer model type associated with it. Once you've added a printer to the printer list, you can change its settings (such as the PPD it uses) by selecting it, and then choosing Printers → Get Info (⌘-I.) You can also use the CUPS web interface, described in the later section "Web-Based Print Administration."

This is not to be confused with the Utility button (or Configure Printer command, under the Printers menu), which lets you perform remote configuration on the actual printer itself, if that model supports it.

Fax List

The Fax List, available from the View menu, works identically to the Printer List, except you don't need to add fax modems to the list. Instead, any modems connected to the computer, including an internal modem, appears in the list automatically. (The earlier section on faxing describes how to select among the listed modems.)

Printer Queues

The print server maintains a *queue*, a list of pending print jobs, for each printer it knows about. Double-clicking a row in the printer list window reveals that printer's queue window (see Figure 9-7), which lists that printer's queue as well as some basic status information, such as whether the printer is active or idle, or whether or not it is accepting new jobs.

Printer Pools

A *printer pool*, also known in CUPS as a *printer class*, is a single queue configured to send jobs to the first available of the *multiple* printers assigned to that queue. This advanced feature is useful for printing to a bank of printers used by many people, as it ensures that your jobs get printed as soon as possible.

To create a printer pool, select the printers that you want included from the Printer List, using the Shift key to make a contiguous selection and the Command

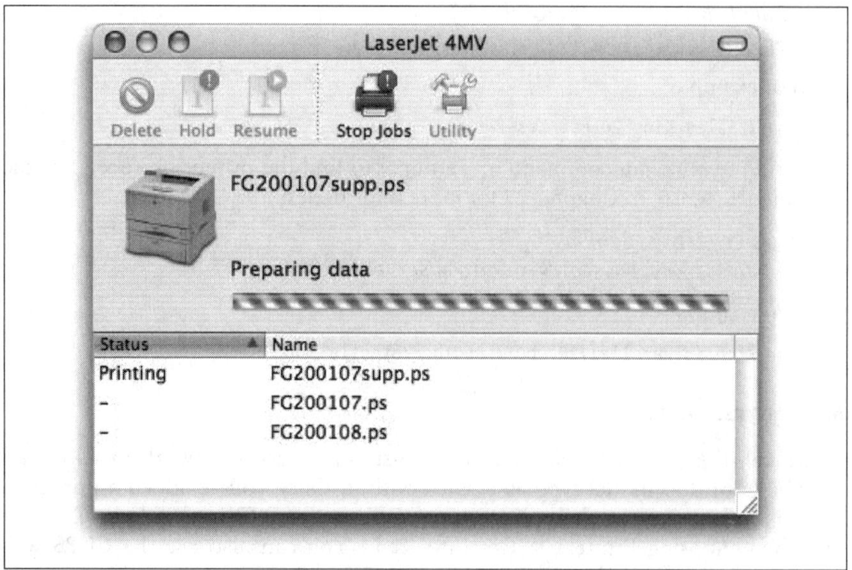

Figure 9-7. A printer queue window

key to make noncontiguous selections. Next, from the Printers menu, select Pool Printers. The resulting sheet allows you to name the pool and arrange the priority of the pool's printers. To rearrange them, simply drag their names in the list into the desired order. Print jobs will go first to the printer at the top of the list. If that printer is busy or offline, the job will go to the next printer down the list, and so on. The printer options available in the print dialog box will come from the first printer in the list.

Desktop Printers

Another timesaving feature is desktop printing. A desktop printer is an icon on your desktop (or wherever you would like, for that matter) that represents any one of your printer queues (Figure 9-8). Printing a document to that queue is as simple as dragging it onto the desktop printer. To create a desktop printer, select a printer from the printer list and choose Printers→Create Desktop Printer. You'll then be prompted to name and save the file.

When you drag some file types to a desktop printer, such as PDFs, JPEGs, TIFFs, and raw PostScript files (*.ps*), the print system itself can send the jobs to the printer. However, dragging and dropping other file types, such as Word and Photoshop documents, causes the creator application of the document to launch with the document and open the print dialog box. After you've clicked Print, the job is sent, and the document window closes.

Regardless of how you send a job to a printer, you can always double-click the desktop printer to monitor its queue.

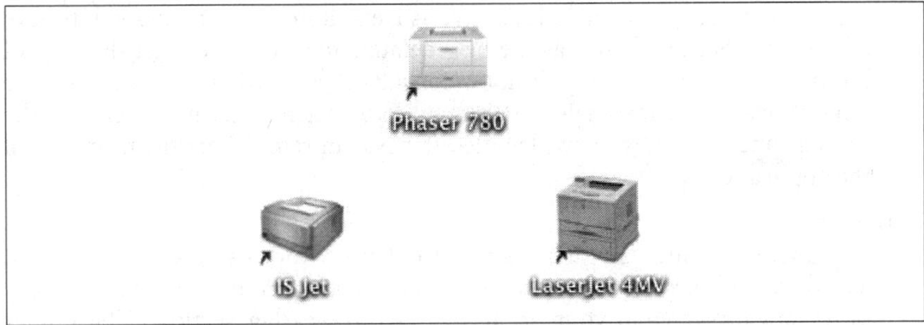

Figure 9-8. Desktop Printer icons

Page Setup

The Page Setup dialog, which you can summon with most applications through File→Page Setup (Shift-⌘-P), lets you define paper size, orientation, and scale options (Figure 9-9).

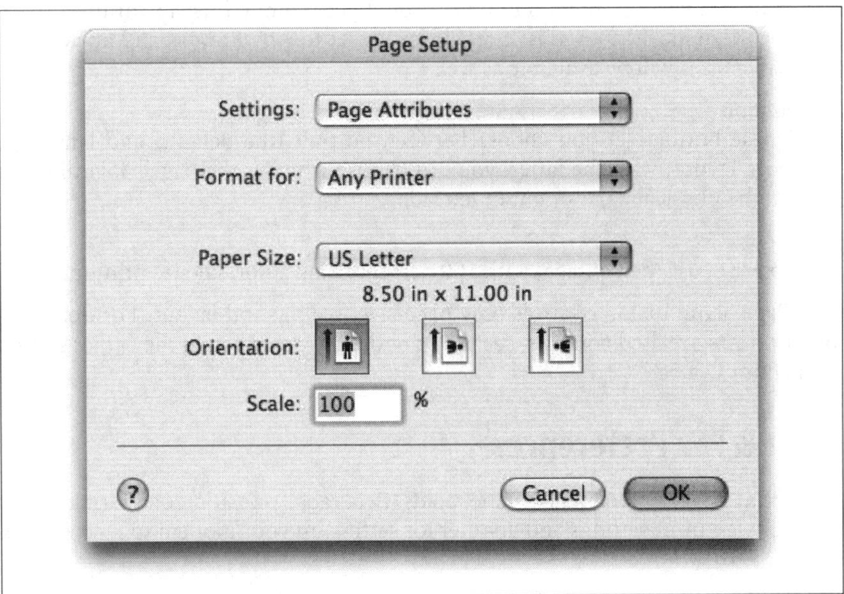

Figure 9-9. The Page Setup dialog

The standard dialog contains the following controls:

Settings
: This pop-up menu switches the dialog's view between the Page Attributes control panel and two other panes: Custom Paper Size, which allows you to configure, name, and save custom paper size settings that then become available for all printers that support custom paper sizes; and Summary, which provides a detailed rundown of the selected paper size's dimensions, including margins.

The pop-up menu also includes a Save as Default item that allows you to save all the Page Setup settings as the new defaults for all printers. At the start of the printing process, an application consults these settings to figure out the dimensions of the rectangle it will draw to for each page. If you change the settings and don't save new defaults, the system remembers them only until the application quits.

Format for
: This menu specifies the printers that the Page Setup dialog's settings affect. The default choice is Any Printer, but you can click on the menu to select any other single printer in your printer list (see the earlier section "The Printer List"). Page Setup can store several sets of options in parallel, one for each printer, as well as the Any Printer set (which acts as default for any printers whose Page Setup options you don't specifically change).

Paper Size
: Clicking this menu reveals all the paper sizes available through the printer selected under the "Format for" menu, including any custom paper sizes (which are grayed-out if not supported by the printer). These sizes are defined by the printers' PPD files; you'll get a limited list for printers using the "Generic" driver or if "Format for" is set to Any Printer, and any custom paper sizes will be available as well.

Orientation
: These buttons let you choose between portrait (the default) and landscape page layout; with the latter, you can choose whether the page's logical top is on the physical page's right or left side.

Scale
: Express, as a percentage, with 100 percent being a normal-size printout.

The Page Setup dialog controls only page-level scaling and layout. For dozens of other printing-related controls, see the Print dialog, described in the earlier section "The Print Dialog."

Print & Fax Preferences

The Print & Fax preference pane holds two tabs, one for configuring a few system-wide print settings and another for setting up your modem to receive faxes (Figure 9-10).

On the Print pane, you'll find:

Set Up Printers
: This button simply opens the Printer Setup Utility.

Selected printer in Print Dialog
: Choose from this pop-up menu the printer you would like selected each time you open the Print dialog box. You can either set it to be the last printer used or choose a specific printer from the list that appears.

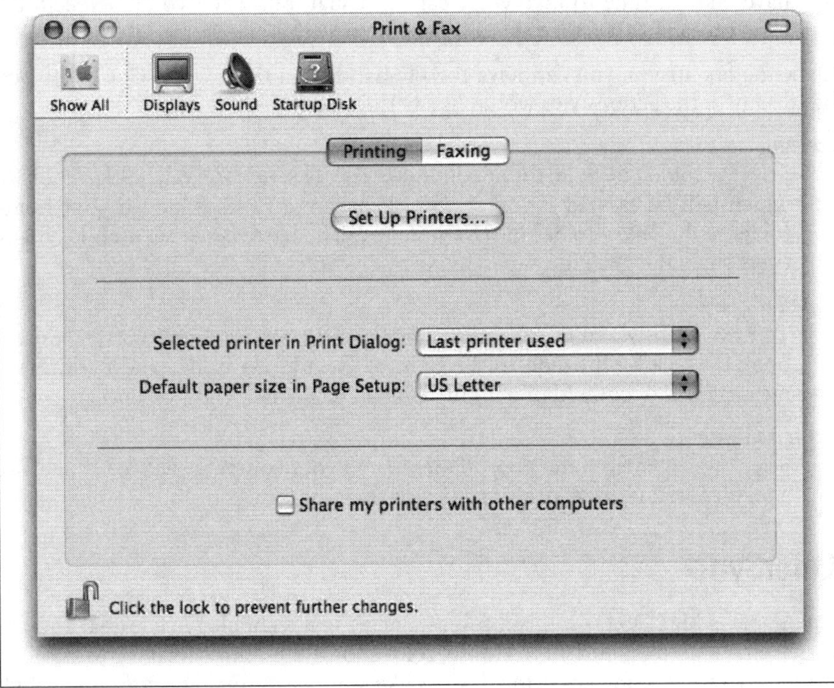

Figure 9-10. The Print & Fax Preference pane

Default paper size in Page Setup
: If you would rather have a different paper size selected in the Page Setup dialog box each time you open it, you can choose one from this pop-up menu.

Share my printers with other computers
: Checking this box is equivalent to turning on Printer Sharing in the Sharing preferences. (See the "Printer Sharing" section later in this chapter.)

The Fax pane (refer to Figure 4-34) provides these settings:

Receive faxes on this computer
: Checking this box allows your computer to receive faxes like a normal fax machine. With a phone line plugged into the modem port, the computer will answer incoming calls and convert each fax into a normal PDF file that can be viewed, printed, or shared.

My Fax Number
: Enter the phone number of the line you have plugged in. This number will be given to the fax machine you're receiving from and will also appear on the top of any faxes you send.

Answer after rings
: Use the arrows to select the number of incoming rings, from 1 to 10, that you want to occur before your modem picks up the call. This is useful with lines that you also share for voice calls. With this number set to a high value, you'll

have enough time to take voice calls as usual, but when you're expecting a fax, you can just wait for the computer to take the call.

Once the fax arrives, you can have the file handled in three ways. Check the box beside any of the actions you would like performed:

Save to
: Select a folder to hold the incoming faxes. The two default folder choices, which will be created if you choose them, are a Faxes folder in your home folder and a Faxes folder in */Users/Shared*. The latter choice is useful if many users share the machine.

Email to
: To have the PDF emailed, enter an address, or choose one from the address book by clicking the icon to the right of the address field. A new addressed message will open in Mail with the PDF attached and ready to send.

Print on printer
: Select a printer from the pop-up menu, and your computer will act much like a regular fax machine, printing faxes as they come in.

ColorSync

ColorSync is Mac OS X's built-in color management technology. The goal of color management is to maintain accurate color along the entire imaging workflow, from the capture of images using devices like scanners or digital cameras, through the output of the images to press, printer, or computer display.

A complete and accurate color management system worthy of a professional design shop requires some additional expense, a bit of work, and a good deal of specialized knowledge. If you intend to go this route and are still new to the process, you should start by talking to a qualified color consultant.

If, on the other hand, you'll be happy enough that your digital snapshots come out close to what you'd expect on an inkjet printer, you can get the job done by yourself. In fact, most of the work is done for you. To begin, it will help to have a basic understanding of why color management is necessary and how it works.

How ColorSync Works

No two color digital devices capture or reproduce the same color in exactly the same way. Too many variables exist in the devices' manufacture, use, and maintenance to expect that one inkjet printer, for example, will put down the exact mixture of ink to produce that blue sky as will another printer, given the exact same data. Color management is necessary to rectify this, translating for one device what another really means by its digital expression of a certain color.

The first key component of color management, then, is the profile, which describes, as a set of numbers in a file, the way a particular device responds to color.

The other key component of color management is the Color Matching Module (CMM)—the computational engine that goes to work when an image moves from one device to the next (for example, from a scanner to a display). In this case, the CMM reads the scanner's profile (which is included with the image file) and the monitor profile (which is stored in the OS), calculates the combined effect they have on color, and provides the display with the adjusted values needed to reproduce the intended color accurately. (Still other scenarios can exist here, depending on the capabilities of the application that's opening the image.)

Using ColorSync

For all this to work properly, the typical user just needs to make sure that ColorSync is using the correct profiles at each step. With Panther, ColorSync has advanced to the point where it can take care of much of this for you.

Device profile registration is a feature of Panther's ColorSync that attempts to automatically assign an accurate, or at least usable profile to each color device that's attached to the computer. For example, when you connect a digital camera, ColorSync can identify any profile the camera provides. If none exists, it chooses a default profile (Camera RGB). This profile is then registered within a ColorSync database so applications that support ColorSync (Image Capture and iPhoto, for example) will know to include it with each image it downloads from the camera.

In many cases these auto-registered profiles will work adequately. However, you might want to go one step further and provide a factory or custom profile. There are several ways to obtain profiles, depending on the device. The first is to check the CD that came with the device or on the manufacturer's web site. Often the profiles are bundled with the device driver's installer. Use the ColorSync Utility, described in the next section, to manually register these profiles.

For display devices, on the other hand, it's best to create your own because the color characteristics of a monitor can vary greatly among units and over time. To create a custom display profile, open the Color tab of the Display preference panel, and click Calibrate. Follow the instructions for calibrating your display, and at the end you'll be asked to name and save its new profile. Choose that profile from the Display Profile list of the Color tab to register it. Display profiles work on everything on the screen, so you'll see their effect immediately.

If your requirements are more demanding, you'll want to have custom profiles generated professionally or purchase the equipment to do it yourself.

With the proper profiles in place, you'll next need to make sure that your editing software, if you're using any, supports ColorSync as well. Popular applications such as Photoshop and iPhoto do, taking into account any embedded profiles in the images they open and adjusting their display accordingly. Consult your application's documentation for information on its ColorSync support.

ColorSync Utility

The ColorSync Utility (*/Applications/Utilities*) holds five panes that allow you to manage your profiles and Quartz filters (Figure 9-11).

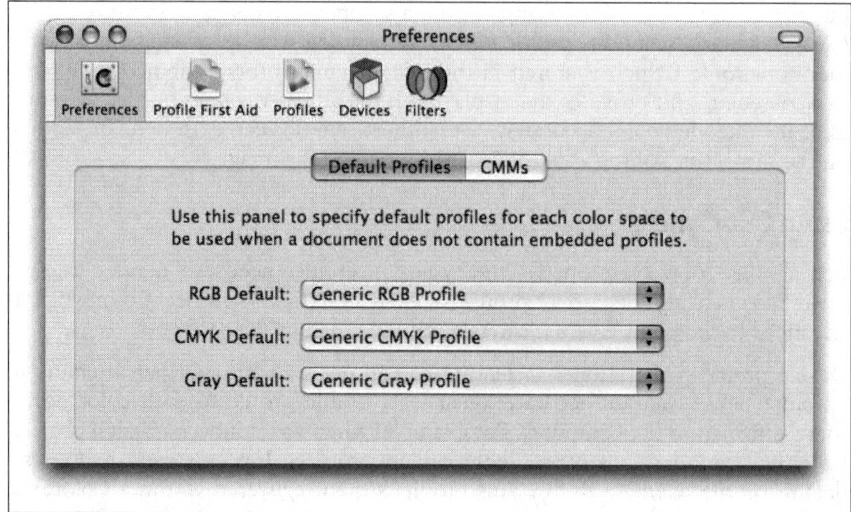

Figure 9-11. The ColorSync Utility window

Preferences
: Not all images ColorSync sees will have a profile embedded. For these "untagged images," you can specify a default profile that supporting applications will use for each image color space (RGB, CMYK, or Gray).

Profile First Aid
: Allows you to verify and repair your installed profiles.

Profiles
: Use this pane to inspect and compare your profiles (Figure 9-12). Clicking the inverted triangle at the top right of the profile list shows a pop-up menu that allows you to sort the profiles by their location on the filesystem by class (input, output, etc.) or by color space.

  This list updates dynamically as new devices are found, and their profiles registered.

  Selecting a profile from the list allows you to view textual information about the profile as well as a three-dimensional plot of its color gamut (the range of colors that profile describes).

  To compare one profile's plot atop another, select the first, click the inverted triangle at the top left of the profile's plot, and select Hold for comparison from the pop-up menu. That plot remains dimmed in the window, allowing you to select other profiles to view over it. Drag over a plot to rotate it in space. Press the option key and drag up and down to zoom out and in, respectively.

Devices
: The Devices pane lists those devices that have profiles registered to them. Selecting a device name from the list allows you to view information about the registered profile as well as select a different profile to register manually.

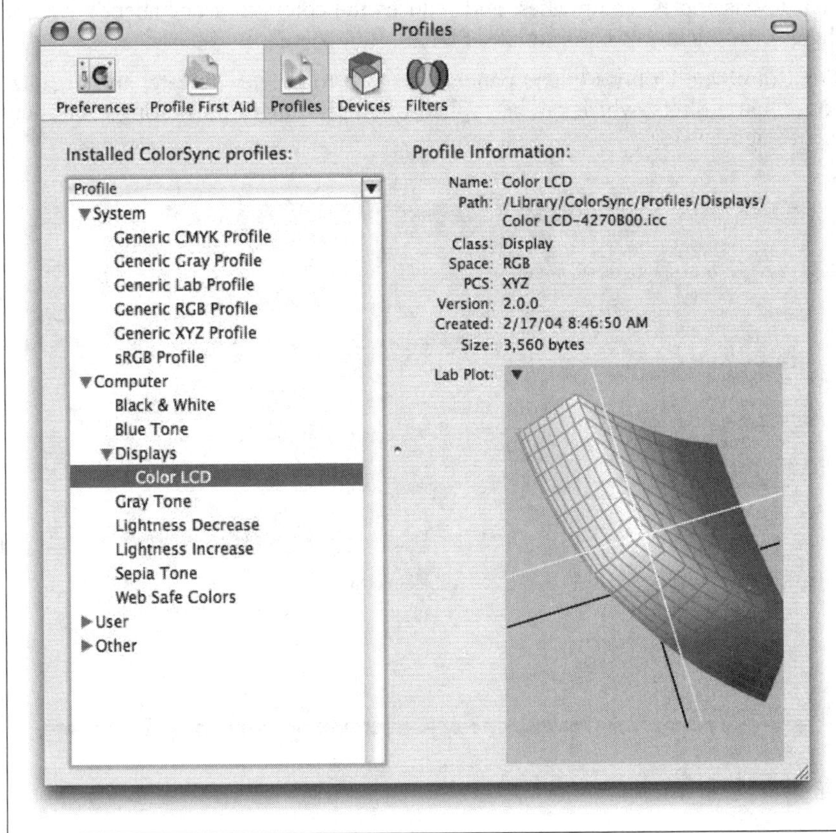

Figure 9-12. ColorSync Utility's Profiles Pane

To do so, click the arrow button beside the words Current Profile. From the button's pop-up menu, choose Other, and navigate to the alternate profile. If you ever need to revert to the original setting, choose Factory from the same menu.

This list also updates dynamically as new devices are found and their profiles registered.

Filters
See the following section, "Quartz Filters."

Quartz Filters

ColorSync profiles have uses that go beyond just color matching. Using Quartz Filters, you can apply profiles that drastically change the colors within a PDF, as well as modify resampling and compression settings.

Quartz filters allow you to keep a single unmodified digital master of your document you can output for multiple purposes. You can, for example, create a filter that downsamples, compresses, and reduces the colors in a document's images, thereby producing a web-optimized PDF.

The ColorSync Utility's Filters pane allows you to preview, create, and organize your Quartz filters, which can be applied when printing or previewing your document (Figure 9-13).

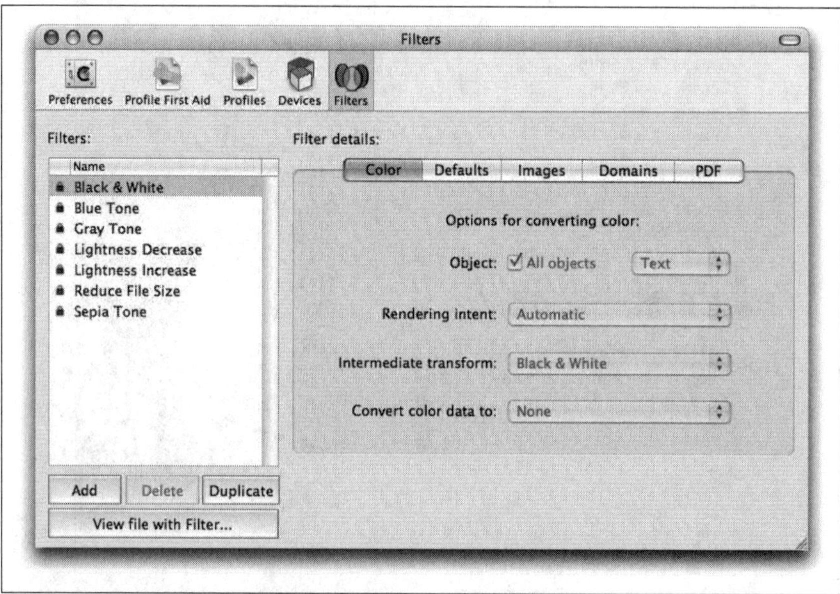

Figure 9-13. ColorSync Utility's Filters Pane

The Filters tab lists several preinstalled locked filters you can apply but not modify. To add your own filters, click the Add button below the list. An untitled item will appear in the list; double-click its name to change it.

With the filter selected in the list, you can set its properties using the five tabs on the right side of the pane. However, if you would like to preview your settings as you adjust them, click the View file with Filter button at the bottom left of Filters window, and choose a PDF to preview when prompted.

Once the PDF is opened in a new window, check the Preview checkbox at top left. The same five tabs from the Filters pane appear here as well, but as items in the unlabeled pop-up menu just below the Details and History tabs. These items work the same whether you choose them from the tabs or from the pop-up menu.

Color

You can apply Quartz filters to all or any one of four types of object in the PDF: text, vector graphics, raster images, or shading. To have the filter effect all types, check the All objects checkbox. Otherwise, uncheck it and choose an object type from the pop-up menu beside it.

From the Rendering intent pop-up menu, you can choose to have the intent determined automatically or select one manually.

The intermediate transform allows you to apply color effects as described in an existing profile or by specifying a custom set. The pop-up menu lists the installed profiles, including those in the abstract group such as Sepia and Lightness Increase. You can choose one of these or choose Custom to define your own. The Custom pane provides sliders to adjust brightness (of dark, medium, or light tones), tint, hue, and saturation.

If you wish to also apply a profile for color matching to the PDF, you can by selecting one from the "Convert color data to" pop-up menu.

Defaults
: Allows you to specify a default color profile to use for untagged images. As with the Color tab, you can apply this setting to all object types or just one.

Images
: Sets the resampling, compression, and convolution (blur and sharpen) options for the filter, which apply only to raster images.

Domains
: Specifies where the filter can be used. For the filter to appear in the ColorSync section of the Print dialog box, check Printing. For it to appear in the PDF workflow pop-up menu, check PDF Workflow. To allow supporting applications to use it, check Applications.

PDF
: Allows you to set several other PDF properties, which appear on a second unlabeled pop-up menu. Choosing Monochrome data lets you convert any such data as specified by a chosen profile. Choosing Image Interpolation lets you enable or disable image smoothing for low-resolution images. Choosing PDF/X-3 lets you save the PDF that's compliant with that standard.*

Once you open a PDF using the View file with Filter button, you can apply *multiple* filters to that document using the Apply button. First, select or create a filter and click Apply. Repeat with as many filters as you would like (even the same filter more than once) and the effects will accumulate each time you click Apply. When you're done, save the file from the File menu.

ColorSync Scripts

Mac OS X comes with several AppleScripts that allow you to perform many profile-related operations. In the */Library/Scripts/ColorSync* directory you'll find scripts to attach profiles to images, remove or rename them, as well change the display profile and many others.

PostScript Converter

Desktop publishing arrived not with the birth of the Macintosh but soon after with the Apple LaserWriter, the first printer to use Adobe's PostScript page

* See *http://www.pdf-x.com/* for more information on the PDF/X standards.

description language, which has became the standard for high-end graphic design applications and the designers, film houses, and print shops who use them.

Also, because PostScript is compact and device-independent (the same PostScript data can print unmodified on most PostScript printers), scientists and engineers have long used raw PostScript as the digital distribution format for their work. Even with the advent of PDF, you'll still find such *.ps* files scattered around the Web.

Both of these uses, however, come with a big caveat, namely that to output PostScript, you need a PostScript printer, which are relatively expensive. The inexpensive color inkjet printers popular in homes and schools don't support PostScript, so their owners have had to go without it, or invest in software (sometimes called a RIP or Raster Image Processor) that converts PostScript to the raster data the printer can handle.

Fortunately, Mac OS X Panther includes software allowing you to print a PostScript job to non-PostScript printer. This capability is built into CUPS, and once you've added your printer to the printer list, you need only drop a PostScript file into the printer's queue window or onto its dock or desktop printer icon. See this chapter's Print dialog section to learn how to generate a PostScript file from any application.

Alternative Printer Interfaces

The Printer Setup Utility is Apple's fully Aqua-integrated print management application, but it's really just one possible frontend to Mac OS X's printing system. CUPS (and therefore Mac OS X) ships with several command-line programs for creating and tracking print jobs, as well as administrating the machine's print server. You can also access the CUPS server through a web browser to track jobs and perform administrative tasks.

Web-Based Print Administration

Because CUPS uses the IPP protocol—an extension of HTTP— it's quite capable of handling ordinary HTTP requests from a web browser. Load *http://localhost:631* in a browser to see your print server's web interface (regardless of your Personal Web Sharing setting). Depending on how permissive you've set CUPS to be (see the section "Sharing Through cupsd.conf" later in this chapter) you may also be able to connect to your machine's CUPS web interface remotely, over the local network, or even the Internet. By default, if Printer Sharing is activated (see the later section "Printer Sharing Through the Sharing Pane"), then any machine that can see your Mac's IP address can also connect to its CUPS server.

The web interface's main page features the following subpages:*

* Those wishing to hack their own CUPS web site may find its document *root* at */usr/share/doc/cups*, and its *cgi-bin* directory at */usr/libexec/cups*. You can modify these files through *cupsd.conf*'s *DocumentRoot* and *ServerBin* directives, respectively. You must have admin privileges to modify any of these files.

Do Administration Tasks
: Provides some simple interfaces for modifying the printer list, managing pending print jobs, and setting up *classes*.

  This is the one part of the site that has any access control set on it by default, allowing connections only from IP 127.0.0.1 (the local machine). See the later section "Sharing Through cupsd.conf" for information on customizing this configuration.

Manage Printer Classes
: Lets you define and manage printer classes (see the earlier section "Printer Pools").

On-Line Help
: Lets you view the CUPS system's documentation as HTML pages or download it as PDF files.

Manage Jobs
: Takes you to a page where you can view and manage pending print jobs in the various print queues on this system.

Manage Printers
: Lets you create, edit, and delete the printer list.

Download the Current CUPS Software
: Whisks you off to the CUPS web site where you can download the most recent CUPS source and binary distributions. (Note that, since CUPS is officially a part of Mac OS X, Apple makes security patches and other important updates to the CUPS software available through Software Update, as they are released.)

Command-Line Tools

While the commands listed next are all part of the CUPS project, several borrow their names and syntax from old-school Unix commands for backwards compatibility (with both existing scripts that might call these commands and Unix-veteran humans who have used these commands for years). This explains, for example, the presence of both *lp* and *lpr*, which do the exact same thing with different syntaxes (see Chapter 28 for detailed descriptions of all of these commands).

lpr
lp
: These commands both create new print jobs and send them to a print server. Along with the *lpoptions*, they serve as the Terminal's equivalents to Aqua's Print dialog.

lpadmin
: An all-around print server administration tool. It lets you modify your machine's printer list, much like Printer Setup Utility but provides even more control through setting user print quotas, individual printer access control, and more.

disable
: Stops a queue. The print server will continue to accept and remember jobs for this printer but won't send them to the printer until the queue is started again.

enable
: Starts a stopped queue.

reject
: Sets a queue to reject all further print jobs.

accept
: Sets a queue to start accepting new print jobs.

lpoptions
: Displays, and lets you set, printer options and defaults. *lpoptions* gives you a command-line interface to the various printer options you set through the Print dialog's various configuration panes (see the section "The Print Dialog" earlier in this chapter).

cancel
lprm
: These commands remove pending jobs from a queue.

lpinfo
: Lists those printer drivers and hardware/network interfaces the current CUPS configurations recognizes.

lpstat
: Lists printer queues currently available to the system, and fetches details about pending print jobs.

Printer Sharing

You can configure your Mac's CUPS print server to listen for incoming print jobs over the network. This lets other computers use your machine as their print server, printing out documents on the printers connected to it, including any network printers in your printer list. These client machines can run any OS that can speak the CUPS, LP, or LPR protocols—e.g., Windows, Unix, or other Mac OS X machines (the latter of which access your printers by adding an IP Printing printer entry into their own printer lists, as described earlier in "Adding and configuring printers," and pointing it at your computer's IP address).

Printer Sharing Through the Sharing Pane

The easiest way to activate this feature involves bringing up the Print & Fax preferences pane (Figure 9-1) and checking the "Share my printers with other computers" checkbox. This automatically modifies the relevant part of the */etc/cups/cupsd.conf* file and restarts the print server for you.

If the Sharing pane finds */etc/cups/cupsd.conf* in an unexpected state (such as the result of your performing manual edits on it), the Sharing pane will refuse to modify the file further; the Printer Sharing checkbox will lock into a checked state, even if you try unchecking it.

Should you find yourself in this situation and wish to make this simple interface available again, remove the existing */etc/cups/cupsd.conf* file (backing it up somewhere first, if you wish), and then copy */etc/cups/cupsd.conf.old* in its place. If *both* files get corrupted somehow, you'll have to fall back to your Mac OS X installation CDs to get fresh copies or download the files anew (along with every other part of CUPS) from *http://www.cups.org*.

This simple interface lets any machine that can see your machine via IP use all the printers attached to it. This may be acceptable behavior if your Mac isn't connected to the Internet or hidden behind a firewall, and therefore has an IP address only other machines on the subnet can see (typically `192.168.X.X` or `10.10.X.X`). However, if your Mac has an IP the whole world can see through the Internet, use this option with care, lest you allow anyone anywhere on Earth to send their documents to your printer! Consider manually configuring your CUPS server instead, as detailed in the next section.

Configuring CUPS

CUPS, an open source project initiated and headed by Easy Software Products, was adopted by Apple as Mac OS X's internal printing system starting with OS Version 10.2.0.

For decades, the majority of Unix systems (including earlier versions of Mac OS X) have used a patchwork of different vendors' printing systems, usually a mix of Berkeley Unix's LPD/LPR and System V's LP, which trace their roots back to the 1970s. As its name suggests, CUPS provides a printing system intended to work on any Unix-based system. It uses more recent technologies, particularly the Internet Printing Protocol (IPP), which layers printing-specific commands onto HTTP.* This allows, among other things, a CUPS-based print server to use HTTP-style authentication and access control, and to accept web client connections (as covered in the earlier section "Web-Based Print Administration").

Sharing Through cupsd.conf

For more sophisticated control and greater security over your computer's role as a network-accessible print server, use a text editor (such as TextEdit, Emacs, or *vi*) to manually modify the CUPS server's configuration file that is found at */etc/cups/cupsd.conf*.

This file purposefully looks and works like Apache's configuration file. Just like */etc/httpd/httpd.conf*, */etc/cups/cupsd.confd* works simply by listing many key/value pairs of server directives, either standing alone (where they affect the

* For another Mac OS X–friendly technology that builds on HTTP, read about WebDAV in Chapter 7.

whole server) or enclosed in XML-like block tags (where they affect a limited scope or location). The default file contains lots of chatty comments to help you figure out which directives belong to what.

Of particular interest are the *Location* directive blocks, which you can find at the end of the file, after the comment that reads *Security Options*. CUPS maps its various features into a directory system accessible by URI, each of which can have its own security settings. Table 9-1 lists these locations.

Table 9-1. Security locations on a CUPS system

Location	Description
/classes	All classes (groups of printers) this system defines
/classes/ *name*	The class named *name*
/printers	All printers this system defines
/printers/ *name*	The printer named *name*
/admin	All this print system's administrative functions

Within each of these locations, you can place authentication and access-control directives, as listed in Table 9-2.

Table 9-2. CUPS access-control directives

Directive	Description
AuthType	HTTP authentication style—can be *None*, *Basic*, or *Digest* (choosing *None* still lets you use address-based authorization)
AuthClass	Authorization class—can be *Anonymous*, *User*, *System* (meaning any user in the group defined by the separate *SystemGroup* directive—*admin* by default), or *Group*
AuthGroup	The group name, if an *AuthClass* of *Group* is used
Order	The order of Deny/Allow processing—either *Deny*, *Allow* or *Allow,Deny*
Allow	An address, domain, or subnet from which connections are allowed
Deny	An address, domain, or subnet from which connections are denied

You can find full documentation for configuring and administering CUPS online at cups.org or by following the *Documentation* link from your machine's own CUPS web interface (see "Web-Based Print Administration").

Printer Drivers

Mac OS X supports PostScript Printer Description (PPD) files for PostScript printers and its own driver format for non-PostScript printers. All these files go into the */Printer* folders of the system-wide *Library* hierarchy, as described in Chapter 7.

Apple chooses to make the Local/System domain difference a little fuzzy with the printer drivers it includes with Mac OS X. Drivers for Apple-branded printers go into */System/Library/Printers*, and other vendors' drivers go into the less-protected */Library/Printers* directory—despite the fact that Apple's installer software puts both kinds of drivers into place, and that Apple itself hasn't sold printers in years.

Generally speaking, you probably don't have to worry too much about having the right printer drivers, because Apple includes hundreds of drivers for several vendors' printer models with Mac OS X and regularly adds to the list (and updates existing drivers) via the System Update application.

Gimp-Print

Among drivers included are those from the Gimp-print package, an open-source project that develops drivers for printers without vendor-supplied Mac OS X–compatible drivers. You'll see the Gimp-Print drivers included in the list of available PPDs when you add a printer with the Printer Setup Utility. Gimp-Print drivers won't always provide the full functionality of every printer, but they will at least allow you to print. For more information about Gimp-Print, visit *http://gimpprint.sourceforge.net*.

10
System Administration Overview

Because Mac OS X has Unix at its heart, performing some system administration tasks is unavoidable, even for the most casual users. For this reason, the system lets you approach many administrative duties from two different angles. Fundamental tasks such as user account management (you'll need at least one user on the system, after all) and network setup may be performed though the friendly frontends of System Preference panes, while a more experienced system administrator can perform more subtle and sophisticated tasks through the Terminal's command line.

As such, much of this chapter assumes knowledge of the Terminal application and Mac OS X's Unix command line; see Chapter 18 first, if necessary. Many administrative tasks also require looking up and modifying information stored in the machine's directory services database. See Chapter 11 for complete coverage of Directory Services and the available user interfaces.

Acting as Root

As with all Unix systems, Mac OS X has a concept of a special user named *root*. The *root* user can read from and modify any part of the filesystem, execute any program, and send signals (including the terminate signal) to all running programs and processes, regardless of who might own them. Root doesn't correspond to any one user; instead, a user with proper access privileges can become root temporarily in order to perform tasks that the Unix file and process permission systems wouldn't otherwise allow, such as launching or reloading system services or installing software on the Unix side of things.

Mac OS X offers a couple of well-known ways to step into root's shoes via the Terminal, and a somewhat obscure way to perform the more dangerous act of logging into the system as the root user.

Using sudo

All admin users who work with the Terminal application (detailed in Chapter 18) should be aware of the *sudo* command (short for "superuser do," and pronounced "sue-doo"), which can precede any Terminal command to run it as root. For example, if you want to copy a file from your current directory to */usr/local/bin*, you could use the following command:

```
natsu:~ chris$ cp my_script.pl /usr/local/bin
cp: /usr/local/bin: Permission denied
natsu:~ chris$
```

A peek at the target directory's permissions reveals the reason:

```
natsu:~ chris$ ls -ld /usr/local/bin
drwxr-xr-x  76 root  wheel  2584 Aug 27 01:18 /usr/ local/bin
natsu:~ chris$
```

The directory is writable by root only. So, here is precisely where *sudo* comes in handy. By preceding the copy command with *sudo*, the system first asks for a password:

```
natsu:~ chris$ sudo cp my_script.pl /usr/local/bin
Password: ********
natsu:~ chris$
```

If the password that's entered is correct for the current user, the system executes the command without complaint.

When performing several root-level commands in a row, you don't need to provide your password each time; *sudo* keeps an internal timer, so running a *sudo* command within a few minutes of a previous one will forgo the password prompt. By using the *–s* flag, you can also run a new shell session under *sudo* in order to make it "sticky," with all subsequent commands run as root:

```
natsu:~ chris$ sudo -s
Password: ********
natsu root#
```

The prompt character changes from $ to #, which tips you off that every command you type now will come from root's mouth. Furthermore, this particular shell, *bash*, is set to show the username within the prompt, making the change more obvious, but not all prompts feature this information; see Chapter 18 to learn more about configuring shell prompts through Terminal. To step back from the ledge and become an ordinary user again, issue the *exit* command, or just hit Ctrl-D, to pop back to your previous shell.

This convenience can go wrong for you if you forget that the root user is all-powerful, turning typos into tragedy. Even though it takes more work, consider making a habit of manually prefacing every root-run command with *sudo*, if only to remind yourself, with each such command, of what you're getting into. See the following section for more about casual root abuse.

The root User Account

Mac OS X lets you log in as root right at the login screen, whereupon you can not only use Terminal commands without any need for further authentication, but you can also do just about anything in the Finder and other system-affecting Aqua applications without any of them complaining about permission problems. As you might imagine, this is somewhat dangerous, so Apple has turned to the security-through-obscurity model, forcing you to follow some very deliberate steps before you can do this.

1. First, you must activate the root user. Launch NetInfo Manager (*/Applications/Utilities*); after authenticating yourself (through either clicking on the window's authentication lock button or selecting Security→Authenticate), select Security→Enable Root User.
2. Now give the root user a password. It should really be something different from your account password, and it should go without saying that it be something very hard to crack. If this is the first time root's been enabled on the system, you'll be prompted automatically to enter a password. Otherwise, you need to manually select Security→Change Root Password to enter it.
3. When you next see the login window, you can log in with username `root`. As Figure 10-1 shows, if you've set the login window to display a list of users rather than a simple pair of username/password text fields (see "Managing Users Through the Accounts Pane," later in this chapter), a mysterious "Other" option rounds out the user list, providing a text entry field. Here, you can type "root."

There are situations in which the "Other" menu doesn't appear even when the root account is enabled (e.g., if NetInfo is turned off in the Directory Access utility). In these cases, you can still get to a username and password prompt at a login window by first pressing an arrow key to select any username in the list, and then pressing Option + Return.

Managing Users and Groups

By default, Mac OS X stores user and group information in the NetInfo database, under */users* and */groups*, respectively. (This is different from how most Unix systems do it; see Chapter 11.)

Managing Users Through the Accounts Pane

While direct manipulation of NetInfo gives you the most control over user accounts, the Accounts preference pane, seen in Figure 10-2, contains controls for creating and deleting user accounts, as well as editing various properties associated with them.

The table on the left side of the pane lists the system's users, showing their names, login pictures, and types (which are either standard or admin). The current user's account is always at top, and the others are listed below it. Clicking on a user's

Figure 10-1. The login window, with the root user enabled

row in this table lets you edit that account's properties using the tabbed section on the right side of the pane. If another user is currently logged in under fast user switching, however, that account name is grayed out in the list, and you'll be unable to modify its properties.

Below the list of accounts is the Login Options button (Figure 10-3), which leads to some controls relevant to the appearance and behavior of the login window:*

Display Login Window as:
: Lets you choose whether the login window displays a list of all the machine's users or simply provides a text field for typing in a username (or a user's full name). In either case, the user logging in must still type in her password.

* The login window is actually an application unto itself, found at */System/Library/CoreServices/loginwindow*. Its *.plist* file, which the Accounts panel lets you modify, is found in */Library/Preferences/com.apple.loginwindow.plist*.

SysAdmin

Figure 10-2. The Accounts preference panel

Automatically log in as
: Sets the user chosen from the pop-up menu to be automatically logged in after the system starts up (provided you can successfully give that user's password here). Only one user on a given Mac can hold this privilege.

  Consider using this feature only if you can control the physical access to the computer.

Hide the Sleep, Restart, and Shut Down buttons
: This checkbox controls whether the Restart and Shut Down buttons appear as part of the login window. (This has no effect on the computer's physical restart button or power switch.)

Enable fast user switching
: Activates the user menu on the right end of the menu bar, allowing you to switch between accounts. See the later section "Fast User Switching" in this chapter.

To create new accounts or remove existing ones, use the + and – buttons near the bottom left of the pane.

Figure 10-3. The Login Options window of the Accounts preference pane

Clicking the add button (+) adds a new unnamed item to the list and displays an empty password tab. This adds the user to the machine's local NetInfo database and creates a new Home folder for him as well. You should use this procedure only when creating accounts intended for use by actual human users. See the later section "Daemons" for information about creating accounts for daemons and other processes. Also, refer to the following section for information on configuring all the tabs.

To remove an account, select its name from the list, and click the minus button (–). Once you do, you'll be prompted with two choices for deleting the account. If you choose Delete Immediately, the system removes the account, its home directory and all files within it.

However, if you would rather keep the account's home folder and delete just the account entry itself, click OK. When you do, that deleted account's entire home folder will be converted into a disk image file and placed in */Users/Deleted Users*. You can then access those files at any time by mounting that image with Disk Utility.

The image and the files it holds are immediately accessible to any administrative user on the machine.

Account configuration

Whether you're configuring a new account or modifying an existing one, the procedure is the same. Clicking a name in the accounts list displays four tabs, which hold the various configuration controls, on the right side of the pane.

Password
: The Name text field holds the user's real, full name. Short Name is for the user's actual username. (Either name will work for most authentication requests.) Enter the same password in both the Password and Verify fields.

  It's permissible to leave the password fields empty, and if you do, you'll not need to enter any password whenever prompted. (Though you will no longer be able to establish a remote login session with this account.) This is obviously a great security risk and not generally recommended. It does, however, keep the login window from appearing during fast user switching

  As you type in your password, you'll see that it's replaced by a series of dots. To increase security, once the password is set, the dot count will stay at seven, regardless of the actual number of characters in the password.

Password Hint
: Enter a phrase here to help you remember your password should you forget it; that hint will appear at the login window after you've tried to log in with an incorrect password three times.

Picture
: By default, a random picture is chosen for use in the login window, your address book record and elsewhere. To use a different picture, click the Edit button, which opens a small palette. You can drag an image file onto the palette, click the Choose button to navigate to one, or, if you have a video camera attached, click the camera icon to capture an image.

  In all cases, once you have an image showing on the palette, position the image in the frame by dragging it, and use the slider to scale it. Click Set when you're done.

Security
: This tab has two sections: one duplicates the FileVault controls found in the Security preference pane (see Chapter 4); another enables administrator privileges for the account.

  The initial account created during the system setup will always have administrator privileges. Also, the system requires that at least one such account always exists. See the later section "Managing Groups" for more about administrator privileges.

The label of the fourth tab differs depending on the account chosen from the list (nonadministrator users can choose only their own account). If it's the account at top, that is, the current user's account, the tab reads Startup Items; otherwise it becomes the Limitations tab.

Startup Items
: Applications added to this list launch automatically whenever that user logs in. To have an application launch in a hidden state (as if you've selected Hide

from its application menu), check the Hide checkbox beside the applications name.

Limitations
: The privileges of nonadministrator accounts can be further constrained using the Limitations tab, which is described next.

Limitations

The Limitations tab of the Accounts Preferences tab lets you define a wide range of usage restrictions for each nonadministrator account on the system (Figure 10-4). Three levels of control are available, each defining one of three corresponding account types. To change levels, click one of the following three buttons on the Limitations tab, specify the desired settings, and leave that button selected as you leave that tab.

No Limits
: Choosing this level defines a Standard account, which has no usage limitations at all. Standard accounts differ from Administrator accounts only by not being in the admin group, and therefore not able to use *sudo* or make changes in the filesystem outside of the User domain.

Some Limits
: This level defines a Managed account, which can have various combinations of usage limitations assigned through this pane. You can specify:

  - Whether the account can use all System Preferences or only Appearance, Desktop & Screen Saver, Dock, Exposé, International, Security, Keyboard & Mouse, Print & Fax, Sound, .Mac, and Universal Access. If you allow all access here, you can then choose whether or not the user can change the account password.
  - Whether the account can modify the dock or burn CDs and DVDs.
  - Which applications the account can and can't use.

Simple Finder
: This level defines a Simplified account, which limits user access to only those applications chosen from this tab. In the Simple Finder, those applications appear in a folder on the dock. That folder opens into a custom, browsable window that holds the icons of the accessible applications.

Nonhuman User Accounts

Some user accounts are intended for use only by programs, for the sake of system security; they typically have no login shell and have permissions limited to the programs they work with, so that if a malicious hacker should compromise the account, the possible damage is minimal. For example, Mac OS X's default Apache configuration has its web server running via the "www" user.

Because a nonhuman user doesn't need such things as a Home folder or a place in the login window's user list, the Accounts pane's New User... might be overkill for creating one. Consider just duplicating and then modifying an existing nonhuman user directory (such as *www*) already in your NetInfo database.

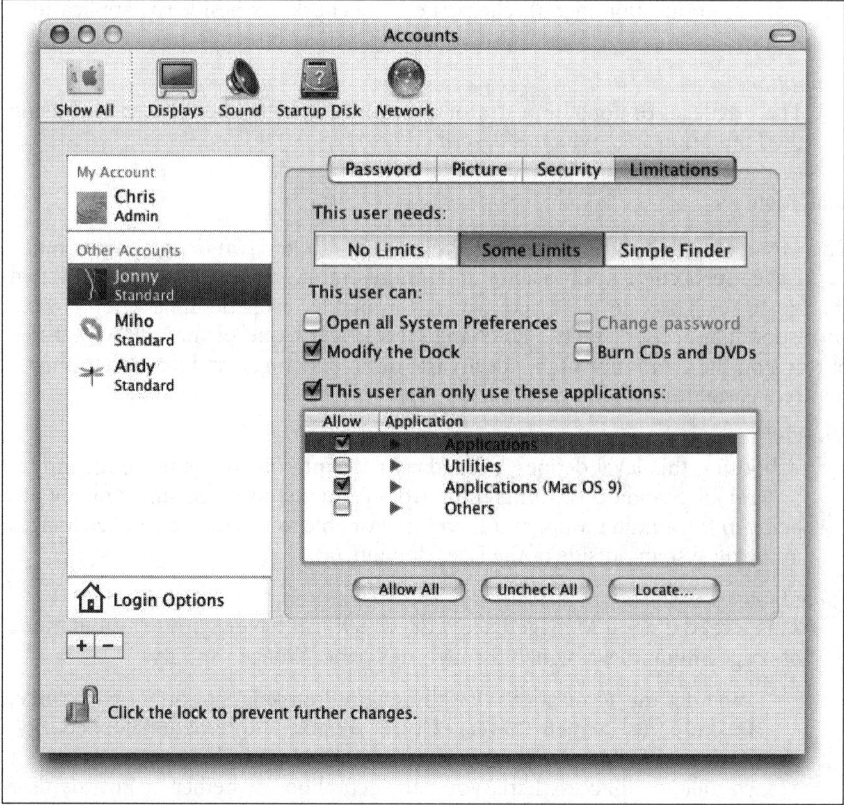

Figure 10-4. The Limitations tab of the Accounts preference pane

Managing Groups

Mac OS X provides no special interface for managing groups; making changes to the machine's groups setup entails using NetInfo Manager or other tools to modify the NetInfo */groups* directory.

You can, however, indirectly control the membership of some groups through the Accounts panel. The real effect of granting a user admin privileges, by checking the Allow user to administer this computer checkbox in the Accounts preference pane (see Chapter 4), is simply to add that user to the *admin* group. Belonging to this group gives users a little more leeway in what the parts of the filesystem they're allowed to read from and write to; for example, the */Applications* folder belongs to the *admin* group and is group-writable (which lets admin users install system-wide Aqua applications). Also, the system logs that you can find in */var/log* are set as readable to *admin* group members.

Furthermore, the *admin* group has global *sudo* privileges, which lets them use the powerful command described in the earlier section "Acting as Root." For this reason, you should check only that checkbox for users you trust with the entire system.

When a human user account is created under Panther, a new group of the same name is created with it, with that account as its only member. This group will likely have its *gid* property set to the same value as its *uid*. The Accounts pane's New User function takes care of this for you. (You can modify *gids* manually through the NetInfo utilities; see Chapter 11.)

Human accounts created under an OS version prior to Panther will instead have a *gid* of `20`, that of the `staff` group. In either case, the group ownership of the items inside a home directory should reflect this as well; they are owned by the user-named group for Panther-created accounts, and by `staff` for older accounts.

Fast User Switching

Fast User Switching provides a quick way to log in to another account while still keeping the original account active, but hidden. During the switch, the display changes from showing the desktop of the first account to showing that of the new one. When performed on Macs that support Quartz Extreme, and when both accounts are using the same display settings, the switch is shown as a rotating cube, with the two desktops on its sides replacing each other (Figure 10-5).

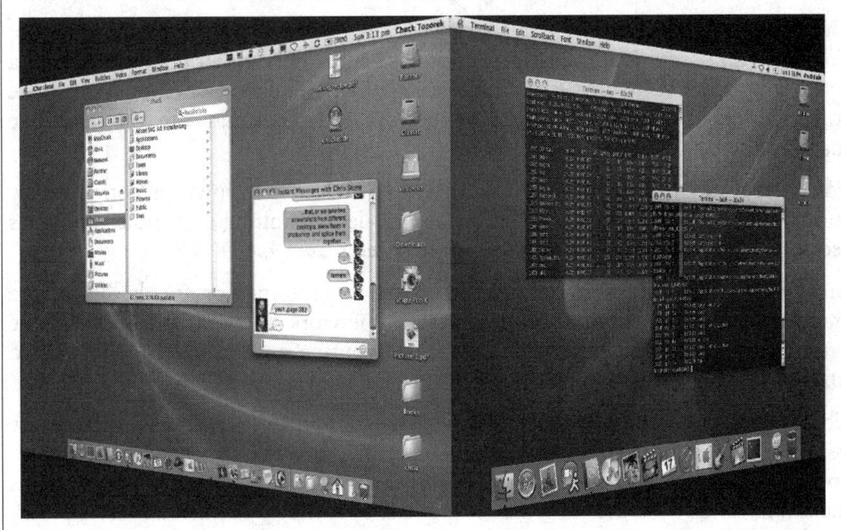

Figure 10-5. Fast User Switching in action

To activate Fast User Switching, open the Accounts preference panel, click the Login Options button, and then select the "Enable fast user switching" checkbox. Once enabled, the Accounts menu item appears at the right end of the menu bar displaying the name of the currently active account. Click the menu to view a list of the other accounts on the machine.

To switch to another user account, simply select its name from the Accounts menu. If that account requires a password, you'll be prompted for it before the switch occurs. Otherwise, the switch occurs immediately. If you have more than two user accounts on your Mac, you can switch to any of them from any other, keeping several logged-in at the same time.

In most cases, when you switch from one account to another, the applications running in the first will continue to run in the background while the second account is displayed. Also, you can usually run the same application in multiple accounts simultaneously. There are some notable exceptions, however; for example, Classic runs for only one account at a time.

Additionally, Fast User Switching can't be used with accounts that have their Home directories mounted over the network.

Alternatively, you can choose to display the Login Window from the menu and keep *all* active accounts active but hidden. You can also get to the Login Window from a button on the authentication dialog box that appears when you attempt to unlock a locked screen or screensaver.

Network Administration

Networks connect computers so that the different systems can share information. For users and system administrators, Unix systems have traditionally provided a set of simple but valuable network services that let you check whether systems are running, refer to files residing on remote systems, communicate via electronic mail, and so on.

For most commands to work over a network, each system must be continuously running a server process in the background, silently waiting to handle the user's request. This kind of process is commonly called a *daemon*.

Most Unix networking commands are based on Internet protocols. These are standardized ways of communicating across a network on hierarchical layers. The protocols range from addressing and packet routing at a relatively low layer to finding users and executing user commands at a higher layer.

The basic user commands that most systems support over Internet protocols are generally called TCP/IP commands, named after the two most common protocols. You can use all of these commands to communicate with other Unix systems including Linux systems. Because all modern operating systems support TCP/IP, commands can also be used to communicate with non-Unix systems.

Mac OS X includes several applications that bring graphical interfaces to these commands. Some, such as Network Utility, are little more than Aqua-window wrappers to the basic command-line tools. Others, like the Network preferences pane, bundle them into programs of their own.

Overview of TCP/IP

TCP/IP is a set of communication protocols that define how different types of computers talk to one another. It's named for its two most common protocols: the Transmission Control Protocol and the Internet Protocol. The Internet

Protocol moves data between hosts; it splits data into packets, which are then forwarded to machines via the network. The Transmission Control Protocol ensures that the packets in a message are reassembled in the correct order at their final destination and that any missing datagrams are re-sent until they are correctly received.

IP addresses

The IP (Internet) address is a 32-bit (or, in the case of IPv6, 128-bit) binary number that differentiates your machine from all others on the network. Each machine on a given network must have a unique IP address.

Gateways and routing

Gateways are hosts responsible for exchanging routing information and forwarding data from one network to another. Each portion of a network that is under a separate local administration is called an *autonomous system* (AS). Autonomous systems connect to one another via exterior gateways. An AS also may contain its own system of networks, linked via interior gateways.

Configuring TCP/IP

Mac OS X expects you to configure your machine's network connection through the Network preference pane, described in "Configuring TCP/IP" in Chapter 8. You can also use traditional Unix command-line tools such as *ifconfig* to view and set the machine's TCP/IP configuration. Any changes you make, however, won't be retained across reboots. To make your changes permanent, you need to add the desired command lines to a startup script.

ifconfig

The network interface represents the way networking software uses the hardware—the driver, the IP address, and so forth. To configure a network interface, use the *ifconfig* command. With *ifconfig*, you can assign an address to a network interface that sets the netmask, broadcast address, and IP address. You can also set network interface parameters that determine ARP, driver-dependent debugging code, and one-packet code as well as the correspondent's address at the other end of a point-to-point link. For more information on *ifconfig*, see Chapter 28.

Troubleshooting TCP/IP

Mac OS X not only includes the standard Unix suite of tools to troubleshoot and diagnose TCP/IP connections, it also gives them a graphic interface through the Network Utility application (Figure 10-6), found in the */Applications/Utilities* folder. You can also run them as command-line tools within the Terminal.

Table 10-1 lists these commands by their Terminal command-line name and their Network Utility name. You can find details of these programs under their respective entries in Chapter 28.

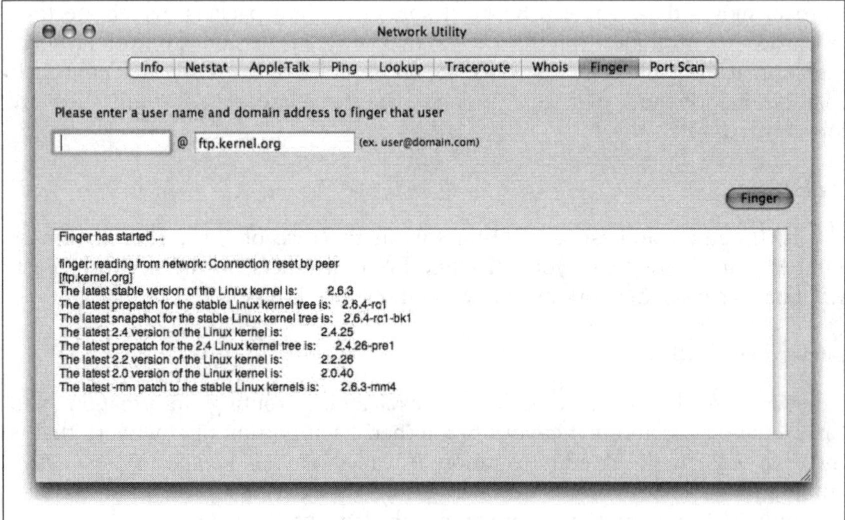

Figure 10-6. Using Network Utility's Finger on a network host

If you're new to system administration (or perhaps just a curious user), feel free to try the various Network Utility tools on different Internet addresses, to see if they lead to machines you control. (Try them on *www.oreilly.com*, for example, or hit your own machine by providing `127.0.0.1` as an address.) Watching the results can show you a lot about how TCP/IP packets behave at the low level.

Table 10-1. TCP/IP troubleshooting tools

Terminal program	Network Utility tab	Purpose
ifconfig	Info	Get information on network interfaces (Ethernet ports, Airport cards, etc.).
netstat		Show general IP data transfer statistics.
netstat	Netstat	Show current IP network status and detailed transfer statistics.
appletalk	*atlookup*AppleTalk	Show AppleTalk Statistics and AppleTalk device information.
ping	Ping	See if a machine at a certain address is alive.
nslookup (or dig)	Lookup	Get DNS information about a domain or host.
traceroute	Traceroute	Details the host-to-host relay route of packets between this and another machine.
whois	Whois	Get administrative DNS information about a domain or host.
finger	Finger	Ask a host for information about one of its users.
portscan[a]	Port Scan	Investigate a host's open TCP/IP ports.

[a] Mac OS X doesn't have a *portscan* command by default; see the "More about port scanning" section later in this chapter.

Some network hosts offer information through *finger* that's not tied to any specific user. For example, Linux hackers know to *finger ftp.kernel.org* to see the latest Linux kernel version numbers.

Unfortunately, the Network Utility's Finger pane doesn't make this possibility obvious; if you fill in its host text field but leave its user field blank, you'll get an error dialog. You can trick the system, however, by typing a space character into the user field. Hitting the Finger at this point performs a *finger* on the machine itself, as shown in Figure 10-7. (Alternatively, you can just use the *finger* Terminal command, documented in Chapter 28.)

More about port scanning

Port scanning is the act of programmatically probing many or all of a machine's TCP/IP ports to determine which ones accept outside network traffic. You can perform this on any machine through Network Utility's Port Scan tab.

It's considered bad form to use the Port Scan tool on hosts without their administrators' knowledge. Because a Port Scan reveals potential weak points in a machine's public network interface, it's both a useful security tool and the first thing black-hat hackers often use to "case the joint," seeing if a machine is an easy target for a break-in. Port Scanning indiscriminately can lead to you or your system administrator receiving accusatory emails from the alarmed owners of these other machines, who have noticed your curiosity in their system logs! Administrative tools such as Snort (*http:// www.snort.org*) can automatically alert system administrators about port scanning attempts on their machines.

Mac OS X doesn't ship with a command-line version of Network Utility's port-scanning tool, but you can create one easily enough, simply by running this command:

```
sudo cp /Applications/Utilities/Network\ Utility.app/Contents/Resources/
stroke /bin/portscan
```

That *stroke* file is a simple program Network Utility uses to perform its port scans, but it works fine all by itself as well. (You don't have to name it *portscan*, but it may make it easier to remember.)

NFS

The Network File System (NFS) is a distributed filesystem that allows users to mount remote filesystems as if they were local. From the Finder's point of view, an NFS-mounted filesystem appears as a disk, usually (but not necessarily) appearing under the special */Network/Servers* folder.

NFS uses a client-server model, in which a server exports directories to be shared, and clients mount the directories to access the files in them. NFS eliminates the need to keep copies of files on several machines by letting the clients all share a single copy of a file on the server. NFS is an RPC-based application-level protocol.

Both mounting and serving filesystems through NFS involve setting up configuration information in NetInfo, and then running command-line programs or launching (or reloading) daemons. For more about NetInfo, see Chapter 11.

You must also have user and group IDs in agreement among all the machines involved in an NFS connection. If your username and UID are `jmac` and `501` on your machine, you should also have UID `501` on any machine whose directories you have mounted. Discrepancies can lead to confusion with filesystem permissions.

> **NFSManager**
>
> Unfortunately, Mac OS X doesn't include any friendly interface to its own NFS abilities; you must manually set NetInfo values and run Terminal commands as this section describes. A third-party alternative solution is NFSManager, a shareware application written by Marcel Bresnik, available at *http://www.bresink.com/osx/NFSManager.html*. It provides a graphical interface to modify the appropriate parts of NetInfo and runs the *mount* and *umount* commands for you.

Mounting NFS

There are two ways to mount NFS filesystems in Mac OS X: static mounting and automounting.

Static NFS mounting

Static mounting simply binds another machine's exported filesystem to a local directory. Depending on the exported system's setup, you might have to be root (or use the *sudo* command) to perform this mount. In any case, use the *mount* command with the *–t* flag set to *nfs*; this directs the *mount* program to use *mount_nfs* to plug the filesystem into the proper place. For example, if the machine `borg` exports its */Users/Shared* directory, and you want it grafted onto your machine's filesystem at */mnt/shared/*, you'd *mkdir* on that directory if it didn't already exist and then run this command:

```
$ mount -t nfs borg:/Users/Shared /mnt/shared
```

To unmount the remote system, simply *umount* the directory:

```
$ umount /mnt/music
```

Use the *showmount* command with the *–e* flag to see what directories a certain host offers for export, as well as the slice of network it exports to. The following example informs you that the host cricket exports two of its directories, */mnt/data* and */home*, but only to the 192.168.2.0 subnet:

```
MyPB:~ chris$ showmount -e cricket
Exports list on cricket:
/mnt/data       192. 168.2.0/255.255.255.0
/home           192. 168.2.0/255.255.255.0
```

SysAdmin

NFS through automount

A daemon named *automount*[*] reads and acts on NFS-mounting information stored in NetInfo. It mounts these remote filesystems whenever the need arises and then unmounts them once they fall idle.

To set up a mount point in this way, create a new directory under the NetInfo */mounts* directory, containing the following properties:

name
: The remote host, followed by a colon, and then the remote directory to mount

vfstype
: The type of filesystem this entry represents; set it to *nfs*

dir
: The local directory to which the remote filesystem should be grafted

opts
: Options passed to *mount_nfs* when mounting.

If you list *net* among the values under the directory's *opts* property, *automount* ignores the value you provided under *dir* and mounts the directory as a disk under *Network/Servers*. Otherwise, it appears under the location you specify with the *dir* property.

Once you set up NetInfo, send a *kill –HUP* to the *automount* process to have it reread the NetInfo database and act accordingly.

Daemons

NFS server daemons, called *nfsd daemons*, run on the server and accept RPC calls from clients. NFS servers also run the *mountd* daemon to handle mount requests. On the client, caching and buffering are handled by *nfsiod*, the NFS I/O daemon, and file locking by *rpc.lockd*, the NFS file locking daemon, in conjunction with *rpc.statd*, the host status-monitoring daemon. The *portmap* daemon maps RPC program numbers to the appropriate TCP/IP port numbers.

[*] With all its options and arguments, it runs as *automount -f -m /automount/Servers -fstab -mnt/private/var/automount/Network/Servers -m /automount/static -static -mnt /private/var/automount.*

> **Viewing Your fstab**
>
> Most Unix systems use a special file known as an *fstab* (short for "filesystem table") to define all the parts of the current filesystem, including known NFS exports originating on other machines. Mac OS X stores this information in NetInfo. Through the *nidump* utility, though, you can view your current filesystem configuration as it appears in an *fstab* file. Just run the *nidump fstab .* command (where "." is an abbreviation for the local NetInfo domain).
>
> Note that Darwin's */etc* directory contains two *fstab* files. These are empty of useful data by default, but any modifications you might make to them are read and acted on during system startup.

Exporting filesystems

Each directory on your machine that you wish to share with other machines via NFS must have its own directory under NetInfo's */exports* directory, as shown in Figure 10-7. (The */exports* directory doesn't exist in a fresh NetInfo distribution, so you may have to create it first.)

Each directory has the following properties:

name
: The local filesystem directory to be exported via NFS.

clients
: A list of hostnames or IP addresses of machines able to mount this directory. If this list has any values, only those machines can NFS-*mount* this directory. Otherwise, *mountd* uses other means (such as the *network* and *mask* options) to determine client eligibility.

opts
: Options read by *mountd*. Each option takes the form of `key=value`. The full list of options appears under the 5 manpage, but here are the more common ones:

  maproot
  : The credential of the specified user is used for remote access by root. The credential includes all the groups to which the user is a member on the local machine. The user may be specified by name or number.

  network
  mask
  : The network subnet and network mask, respectively, that define the network slice you're willing to export this directory to. If you don't have an explicit client list defined under this directory's *clients* property, *mountd* uses these options. If neither the property nor these options are defined, the directory offers itself to worldwide export, which is probably asking for trouble; see the next section.

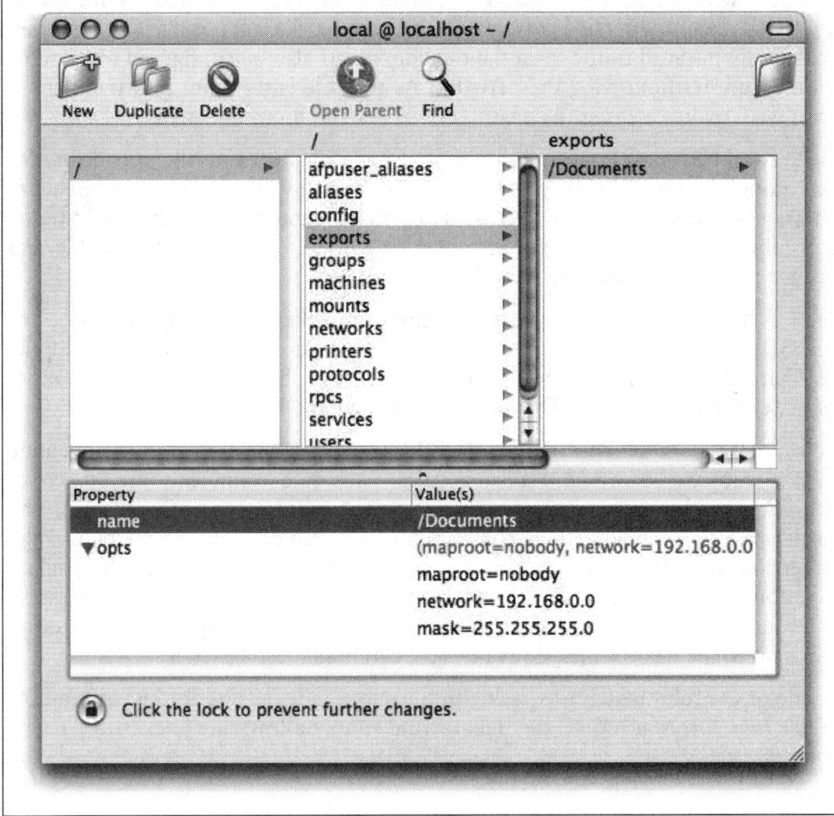

Figure 10-7. Defining an NFS export point through NetInfo

Once you set up NetInfo, send a *kill –HUP* to the *mountd* process to have it reread the NetInfo database and act accordingly.

NFS and network security

NFS offers wonderful convenience and ease of use when properly configured, but all of its traffic is insecure and unencrypted. We recommend that you NFS-export directories only to the local physical subnet, rather than to the whole world. (Also consider not using NFS at all over a wireless (AirPort) connection, which introduces security flaws of its own.)

If you do want to share a filesystem with a broader slice of the Internet, consider setting up a shared disk over AFP or Samba, which at least offer password-based authentication. Also consider sharing the information as a web site through Apache, or an FTP site through *ftpd*, as described in Chapter 28.

Mac OS X's Firewall

A *firewall* is a program running on a system that sits between an internal network and an external network (i.e., the Internet). It is configured with a set of rules that determine what traffic is allowed to pass and what traffic is barred. While a firewall is generally intended to protect the network from malicious or even accidentally harmful traffic from the outside, it can also be configured to monitor and measure traffic leaving the network. As the sole entry point into the system, the firewall makes it easier to construct defenses and monitor activity.

The firewall can also be set up to present a single IP address to the outside world, even though it may use multiple IP addresses internally. This is known as *network address translation (NAT)* or *masquerading*. Masquerading can act as additional protection, hiding the very existence of a network. It also saves the trouble and expense of obtaining multiple IP addresses.

Mac OS X uses *ipfirewall*, a.k.a. *ipfw*, a firewall package originally developed for FreeBSD. Though its traditional user interface is the command-line program *ipfw*, the Sharing preference pane lets you define basic firewall functionality more easily; see the later section "Through the Sharing pane."

Conceptually, *ipfw* is fairly simple: TCP/IP packets passing through the machine are each subjected to a ordered list of rules. Each rule examines some aspects of the packet, such as its point of origin, its direction (incoming or outgoing), and the protocol it uses, and then compares it to a value. If the rule matches the packet, the firewall applies an action—also defined by the rule—to the packet. Common actions include allowing the packet to pass, denying it further passage, or rerouting it to another destination. Once this action happens, the firewall moves on to the next packet. Only one rule can match each packet.

If none of the rules match the packet in question, *ipfw* falls back to its immutable *default rule*. On Mac OS X, the default rule simply allows the packet to pass by unmolested.

Brickhouse, a popular third-party *ipfirewall* frontend for Mac OS X is a shareware application by Brian Hill (*http://personalpages.tds.net/~brian_hill/brickhouse.html*). While the Sharing pane's firewall controls (described later in "Through the Sharing pane") duplicate much of its basic functionality, it does allow more precise editing of the machine's *ipfw* rule set and attempts to simplify the process of IP sharing.

Using the ipfw command

You can view all your machine's current rules by entering *ipfw l* in a Terminal window. For example:

```
MyPB:~ chris$ sudo ipfw l

00100 deny tcp from script.kiddiez.com to localhost 80
01234 deny all from 123.45.67.0/24 to any
65535 allow ip from any to any
```

In this (very) simple configuration, all packets passing through the machine pass through these rules, in this order:

1. (Rule 0100) The firewall turns away TCP connection attempts to port 80 (the web server) on this machine that originate from the host *script.kiddiez.com*.
2. (Rule 01234) The firewall refuses all packets of all kinds originating from the entire `123.45.67.0` subnetwork.
3. (Rule 65535) Finally, the default rule: none of the earlier rules match, so the packet is let through.

Chapter 28 details the *ipfw* command. In brief, you use it to add, edit, and delete rules from the firewall's list. *ipfw* knows where in the list to insert new rules by the number you attach to each one, with lower numbers applying sooner. The default rule, which matches all packets, always has number 65535; no rule can have a higher number (or lower priority) than that.

Through the Sharing pane

Calling up the Sharing pane under System Preferences and then clicking its Firewall tab results in the page shown in Figure 10-8. This control panel gives you a simple way to view and edit *ipfw*'s current *allow* and *deny* rules.

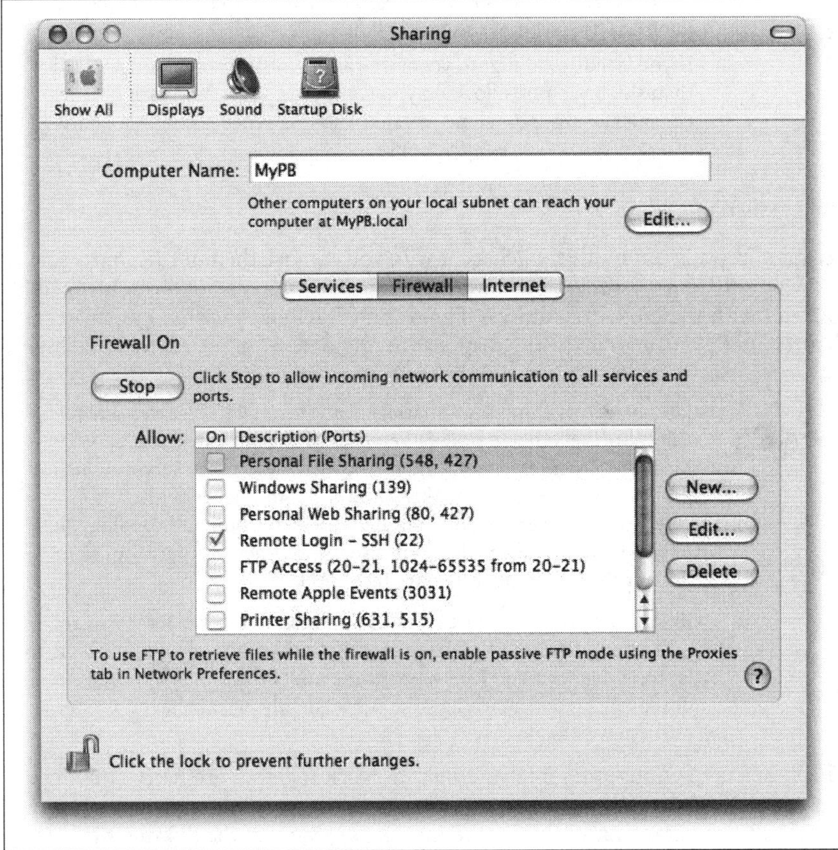

Figure 10-8. The Sharing preference panel's Firewall tab

If the Mac's firewall isn't running—that is, if *ipfw* has no rules defined except for the default *allow ip from any* to *any*—then clicking the Start button immediately applies all the checked rows in the Allow table and ties them off with the penultimate rule *deny tcp from any* to *any*, so that the firewall turns away all TCP traffic outside the specified ports.

If the firewall is running, clicking Stop simply runs *ipfw flush*, removing all the firewall's rules outside of the default. The Allow table remains intact, however, so you can edit rules "offline," and later click the Start button to reapply them all.

If the firewall has been activated by any means other than the Sharing pane (such as by adding rules through the *ipfw* Terminal command), the Sharing pane grays out all these controls and keeps them unavailable until you deactivate the firewall (*ipfw flush* accomplishes this nicely) and restart the System Preferences application.

The Sharing panel's firewall interface uses its own preference file (*/Library/Preferences/com.apple.sharing.firewall.plist*) to keep track of filters you set up. This list can become out of sync with reality if you, for example, set some custom filters in the Sharing pane and then remove them via *ipfw*.

If you need to configure your firewall for tasks more sophisticated than the basic port-blocking you can do through the Sharing pane, consider using *ipfw* alone, or split the difference through a shareware product such as BrickHouse.

Internet sharing

Because firewalls can redirect packets at will, you can use them for *IP sharing*, also known as *IP masquerading*. On Mac OS X, this process involves using *ipfw* together with the Network Address Translation Daemon (*natd*), a system service that rewrites packets to make them appear to originate from the current machine.

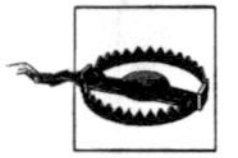

Do *not* activate Internet Sharing if another DHCP server already exists on the subnetwork! Otherwise, confusion can result as your Mac happily intercepts traffic intended for the other server, which probably isn't going to make the other computers (or their users) very happy. Depending on your network's location and topology, it might adversely affect the connectivity of other customers of your ISP or other machines on your office LAN.

In short, don't turn on this feature unless you have total control over your subnetwork. Furthermore, consider not using it at all on laptops that you carry between home and work, lest you forget to deactivate it one morning and subsequently wreak havoc on the office network.

The specifics of configuring *ipfw* and *natd* to work together are hairy and arcane, but Mac OS X provides a one-button interface to set everything up for you—specifically, the Start button inside the Internet tab view of the Sharing preference pane, as shown in Figure 10-9.

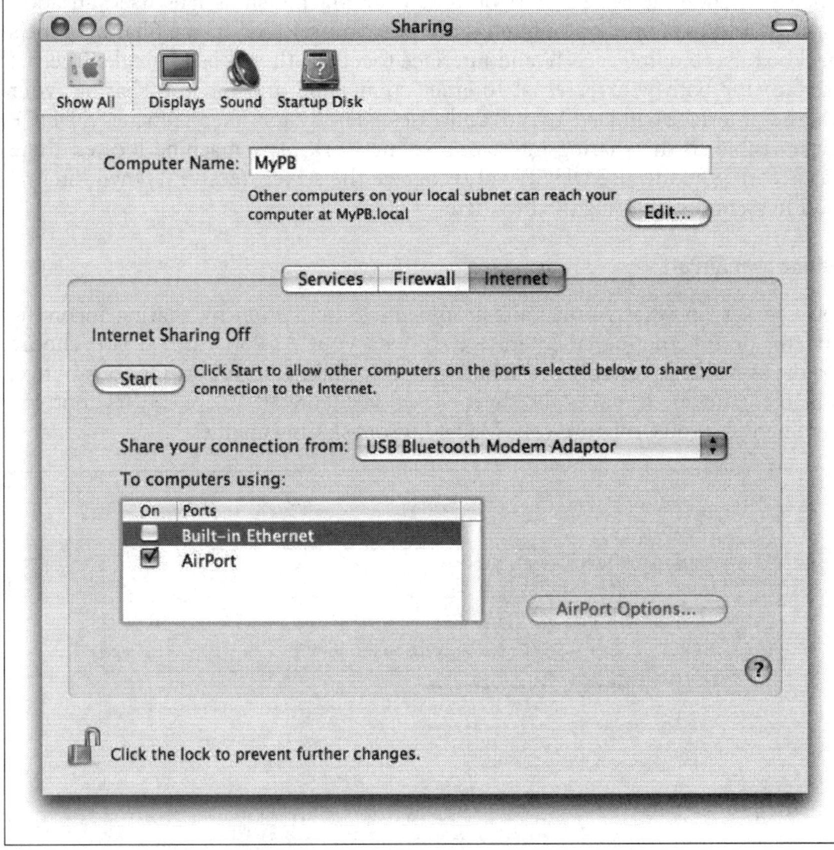

Figure 10-9. The Internet Sharing pane

Before you can activate Internet Sharing, your Mac must have either an Ethernet-based connection to both the Internet and the machines with which it will share its connection (as is the case if your Mac, a cable modem, and the other machines are all connected to the same Ethernet hub), or to two separate network interfaces, one of which is configured to receive Internet traffic in the usual fashion (as described in "The Network Pane" in Chapter 8). The other acts as the interface to all the machines that will use your Mac as their Internet gateway. For example, if you have a modem and an Ethernet port, you can connect to your ISP through dial-up and then share the connection via Ethernet with your local network. Or, if you have Ethernet and an AirPort card, you can share incoming Ethernet-based traffic with nearby machines that also have 802.11b/g wireless capability.

With your machine acting as gateway and firewall, all the computers appear to have the same IP address to the outside world, so all incoming packets will have the same destination address. However, your Mac will know (through binding packets to MAC addresses) which incoming packets are supposed to go to which machines and forward them as appropriate. The whole process works transparently for any Internet task that doesn't require a unique IP address.

When you click the pane's Start button, your Macintosh assigns itself an additional IP address for every outgoing interface you selected in the Sharing pane's checkbox list, binding each IP and interface together. (If you use a single Ethernet interface for both your external Internet connection and internal sharing, your Ethernet interface will have two IP addresses.) The system then launches a DHCP server visible to the sharing interface's subnetwork. Any machine located there that is configured to use DHCP will recognize the server, receive its own internal IP address, and start using the Internet.

Sharing over AirPort

You can set up what Apple calls a *Software Base Station* by sharing incoming modem- or Ethernet-based Internet traffic via your AirPort card. If you choose AirPort as a sharing interface, the Sharing pane makes an AirPort Options button available. Clicking it makes the sheet shown in Figure 10-10 appear. Its controls, listed here, let you configure your Mac's AirPort-sharing abilities.

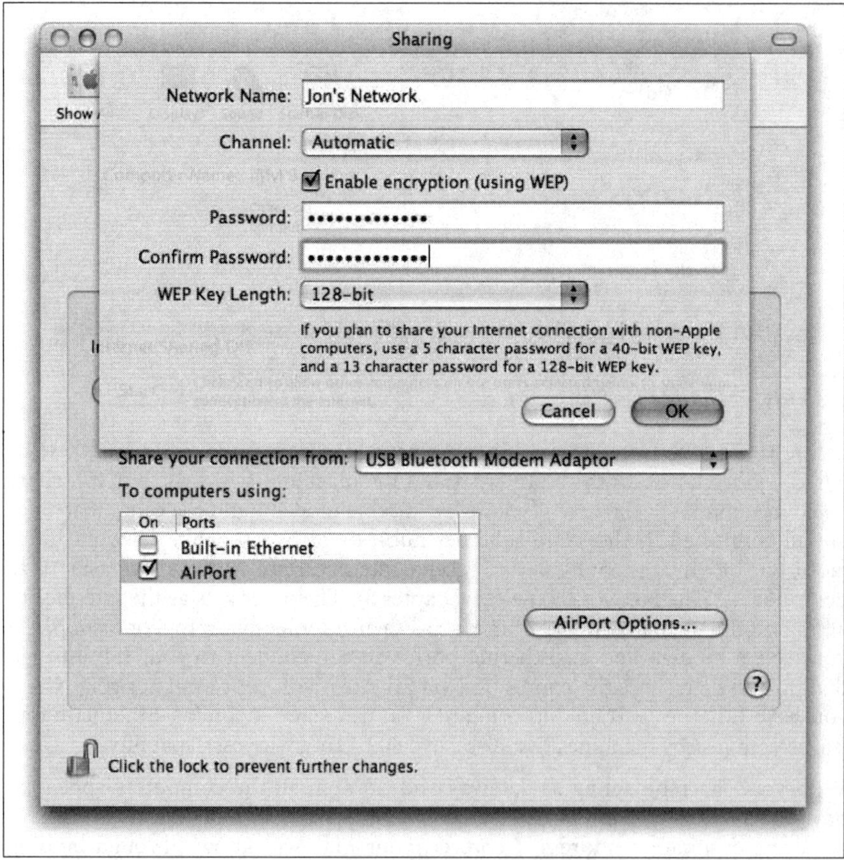

Figure 10-10. The Sharing pane's AirPort configuration options

Network Name

This string will be the network name your Mac will broadcast. Other wireless-equipped computers will see your shared network's presence by this name; Mac OS X users will see it as an option under their AirPort menu extras, for example.

Channel

Select a number to restrict your card's broadcasting to a specific wireless channel. Otherwise, select Automatic (the default option).

Enable encryption

To add a little bit of security to your wireless network, check this box to activate the sheet's remaining controls. (See the warning at the end of this section about AirPort security.)

Password

If you enter (and confirm) a password here, users have to provide the same password in order to share your Internet connection.

WEP key length

You can choose a WEP key length of 40- or 128-bits. (Some client devices might not be able to handle 128-bit encryption.)

One more security note: an AirPort network, like all 802.11b- and 802.11g-based wireless networks, is inherently insecure. Placing WEP encryption or a password on your network stops casual snoopers and would-be freeloaders (respectively), but if a determined outsider really wants to eavesdrop or use your AirPort connection, there's little you can do, short of limiting physical access to the network's covered area. If your network is running from a wireless access point, such as the Apple AirPort Extreme Base Station, however, you can use WPA encryption (Wi-Fi Protected Access), which is more secure than WEP, and 802.1*x* authentication, but neither is available for networks created with Internet sharing.

Single-User Mode

As with other Unix systems, Mac OS X has an unadvertised feature known as *single-user mode*, which lets you boot the system under the most minimal terms. As the name implies, it allows only one user access—that user is whatever human seated at the keyboard directly plugged into the machine. No daemons run, the network interfaces lie dormant, and not even the root filesystem is mounted.

You will seldom, if ever, use your Mac in single-user mode. Some low-level diagnostic activities might require it; this is where you can manually and safely run */sbin/fsck –y* to check and repair filesystem errors on a nonjournaled filesystem, for example, or force one on a journaled filesystem with the *–f* flag.*

* Alhough journaling eliminates most reasons to run *fsck*, doing so can still occasionally reveal filesystem anomalies. However, some errors that can be safely ignored may appear when running *fsck* on a journaled volume. See *http://docs.info.apple.com/article.html?artnum107250* for more information.

Because the one user who logs in during single-user mode happens to be root, you can also change all the system's user passwords, including that of the root account itself. Thus, you can consider single-user mode an emergency back door into the system, should your passwords become lost, and you don't have a system CD available.

Booting into Single-User Mode

You can activate single-user mode only during system startup. To enter single-user mode, hold down ⌘-S during startup, while the Apple logo is displayed. After a moment, instead of the blue Mac OS X startup screen, everything goes black, and startup console messages start spilling down the screen in plain white text, finally ending at a command prompt.

As this point, you can run whatever commands you'd like as root. As the prompt suggests, you can *fsck* the filesystem for problems, and you can *mount* it to work with individual files if you need to. (Specifically, run the command */sbin/mount –uw /* to get the correct permissions and mount point.)

If you want to change any passwords or perform other administrative tasks, you must mount the filesystem and stir up some daemons so that you can access the NetInfo database. Run the following commands, and you'll then be able to, for example, use the *passwd* command at will:

```
#/sbin/mount -uw /
#/usr/libexec/kextd
#/usr/sbin/configd
#/sbin/SystemStarter
```

Wait until you see "Startup Complete," and then start the NetInfo dameon with these commands:

```
#cd /var/db/netinfo
#/usr/sbin/netinfod -s local
```

In this environment, you need to indicate how the passwords are stored, thus the *–i netinfo* argument with *passwd*:

```
#/usr/bin/passwd -i netinfo chris
Changing password for chris.
New password:
```

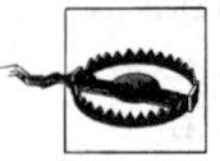

Because the human behind the keyboard during single-user mode is always root, he has power over the entire system. Obviously, you'd prefer that this human is yourself or a trusted ally and not some random interloper who knows about the ⌘-S trick. See the "Open Firmware Password" section in Chapter 13 to learn how to prevent access to single-user mode without a password.

Exiting Single-User Mode

You have three commands to leave single-user mode via various routes:

reboot
: Restarts the computer.

exit
: Continues the normal Mac OS X boot process. If you've manually run *SystemStarter* or otherwise changed or activated features that the system would expect to activate itself during the boot process, consider running *reboot* instead.

shutdown –h now
: Safely shuts down the computer.

SysAdmin

cron Tasks

Through the Unix *cron* utilities, you can have your Macintosh run scripts and other programs at scheduled times or regular intervals. While this is a pretty neat feature that offers convenience to users and crucial maintenance-program scheduling for system administrators, Mac OS X doesn't ship with any friendly GUI frontend to the *cron* utilities. That said, if you can use a text editor (such as any of those described in Chapters 23 or 24), you can set up *cron* tasks for yourself or (if you have the right credentials) the whole machine.

cron works courtesy of a clock-watching daemon named *crond*. When this loads, it reads all the *cron tables* defined in some standard filesystem locations that contain entries representing lists of times or repeating intervals, with a Darwin command to execute for each entry. On Mac OS X, these tables exist in two locations:

/etc/crontab
: This is the *cron* table for the whole system. Each entry in this table represents a command that root runs at the given time. The file is world-readable, but only root may edit it.

/var/cron/tabs/
: This directory contains one file for each user on the machine who uses the *cron* system. You actually don't interact directly with these files (whose permissions prevent it anyway); you must use the *crontab –e* command to edit your own file. You can't read or change other users' *cron* tables.

The *cron* tables' format is tricky and hard to remember (unless you're a system administrator who must update them regularly), but as it happens, the system-wide *crontab* file contains a quick-reference guide to itself. Here's an excerpt from a typical */etc/crontab* file (the beginning numbers are for reference only—see the following list):

```
1           2       3       4        5        6       7
#minute     hour    mday    month    wday     who     command
#
#*/5        *       *       *        *        root    / usr/libexec/atrun
#
# Run daily/weekly/monthly jobs.
```

```
15      3       *       *       *       root    periodic daily
30      4       *       *       6       root    periodic weekly
30      5       1       *       *       root    periodic monthly
10      *       *       *       *       root    / sw/sbin/anacron -s
```

As the commented-out lines at the top suggest, each entry in the table (i.e., each line in the file) is broken up into tab-delineated fields representing time intervals, arranged in this order:

1. Minute.
2. Hour.
3. Day of the month.
4. Month.
5. Day of the week.
6. User to run this command as. (Only for the systemwide *crontab*; an individual user's *crontab* file lacks this field, because all commands are always run as that user.)
7. Command to run.

Each of the first five fields can hold either a number or an asterisk character. Asterisks mean that column doesn't have influence over when the command runs. You can see from this table that the command *periodic monthly* runs at 5:30 A.M. on the first day of every month. If the month (fourth) column held the number 6 instead of an asterisk character, it runs at 5:30 A.M. on June 1st only.

See the *cron(5)* manpage (type *man 5 cron* in the Terminal) for a more exhaustive reference to *cron* table files, which allow for some pretty sophisticated syntax.

cron works great when your computer runs all the time (as *crond*, like all good system daemons, continues to run regardless of which human users—if any—are logged into the machine, as Chapter 1 describes). If you have an iBook or PowerBook, however, its runtimes become less dependable because laptops, like cats, spend much of their lives in sleep mode, and are likely to doze through scheduled tasks. Furthermore, there might be some tasks you wouldn't want a laptop to run when it's on battery, such as the hard-disk-intensive */usr/libexec/locate.updatedb*.

The latter problem is the simpler to solve: if you precede a command with *@AppleNotOnBattery*, the *cron* daemon won't run the command if the machine is running on battery power when the time comes. The following line runs a (notional) *update_all* program every 10 minutes but only when the machine is plugged in:

```
*/10    *    *    *    *    @AppleNotOnBattery /usr/local/bin/update_all
```

If you need your laptop to check its *cron* backlog every time you open it up, so that it executes all the tasks it slept through, investigate *anacron* (*http://sourceforge.net/projects/anacron*), a *cron* replacement, whose main purpose involves this very feature. You can easily install it onto you system via Fink (see Chapter 27).

11 Directory Services

A *directory service* manages information about users and resources such as printers and servers. It can manage this information for anything from a single machine to an entire corporate network. The Directory Service architecture in Mac OS X is called *Open Directory*. Open Directory encompasses flat files (such as */etc/hosts*), NetInfo (the legacy directory service brought over from earlier versions of Mac OS X and NeXTSTEP), LDAPv3, and other services through third-party plug-ins.

This chapter describes how to perform common configuration tasks, such as adding a user or host on Mac OS X with the default configuration. If your system administrator has configured your Macintosh to consult an external directory server, some of these instructions may not work. If that's the case, you should ask your system administrator to make these kinds of changes anyhow!

Understanding Directory Services

In Mac OS X 10.1.*x* and earlier, the system was configured to consult the NetInfo database for all directory information. If you needed to do something simple, such as adding a host, you couldn't just add it to */etc/hosts* and be done with it. Instead, you had to use the NetInfo Manager (or NetInfo's command-line utilities) to add the host to the system.

However, as of Mac OS X 10.2 (Jaguar), NetInfo functions started to become more of a legacy protocol and were reduced to handling the local directory database for machines that didn't participate in a network-wide directory, such as Active Directory or OpenLDAP. NetInfo is still present in Mac OS X Panther, but you can perform many configuration tasks by editing the standard Unix flat files. By default, Panther is configured to consult the local directory (also known as the NetInfo database) for authentication, which corresponds to */etc/passwd* and */etc/group* on other Unix systems. You can override this setting with the Directory

Access application. For more information, see the section "Configuring Directory Services," later in this chapter.

For users whose network configuration consists of an IP address, a default gateway, and some DNS addresses, this default configuration should be fine. You'll need to tap into Open Directory's features for more advanced configurations, such as determining how a user can log into a workstation and find his home directory, even when that directory is hosted on a shared server.

In order to work with Mac OS X's Directory Services, you must first understand the overall architecture, which is known as Open Directory. Directory Services is the part of Mac OS X (and the open source Darwin operating system) that implements this architecture. Figure 11-1 shows the relationship of Directory Services to the rest of the operating system. On the top, server processes, as well as the user's desktop and applications, act as clients to Directory Services, which delegates requests to a directory service plug-in (see the "Configuring Directory Services" section, later in this chapter, for a description of each plug-in).

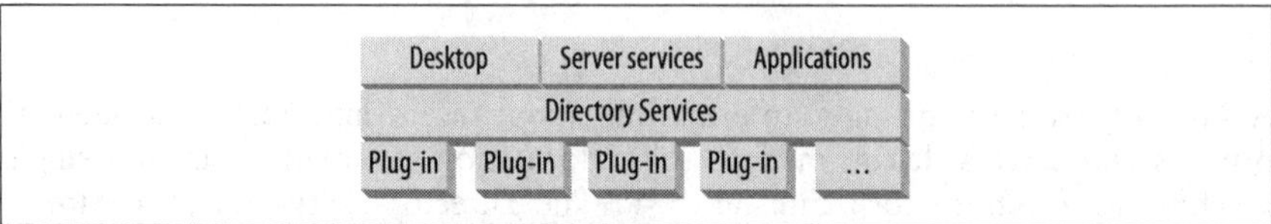

Figure 11-1. The Directory Services architecture

Programming with Directory Services

As a programmer, you frequently need to deal with directory information, whether you realize it or not. Your application uses Directory Services each time it looks up a host entry or authenticates a password. The Open Directory architecture unifies what used to be a random collection of flat files in */etc*. The good news is that the flat files still work. The other good news is that there is a brave new world just beyond those flat files. So, while all your old Unix code should work with the Open Directory architecture, you should look for new ways to accomplish old tasks, especially if you can continue writing portable code.

To get at directory information, Unix applications typically go through the C library using such functions as `gethostent()`. The C library connects to *lookupd*, a thin shim that is the doorway to the *DirectoryService* daemon. The *DirectoryService* daemon consults the available plug-ins until it finds the one that can answer the directory query.

Working with Passwords

One traditional route to user and password information was through the `getpw*` family of functions. However, those functions are not ideal for working with systems that support multiple directories (flat files, NetInfo, LDAP, etc.). Also, in the interest of thwarting dictionary attacks against password files, many operating systems have stopped returning encrypted passwords through those APIs. Many Unix and Linux systems simply return an `"x"` when you invoke a function such as getpwnam( ). However, those systems can return an encrypted password through functions such as getspnam( ), which consult shadow password entries and can generally be invoked by the root user only. Example 11-1 shows the typical usage of such an API, in which the user enters her plaintext password, and the program encrypts it and then compares it against the encrypted password stored in the system.

Example 11-1. Using getpwnam() to retrieve an encrypted password

```
/*
 * getpw* no longer returns a crypted password.
 *
 * Compile with gcc checkpass.c -o checkpass
 * Run with: ./checkpass
 */

#include <pwd.h>
#include <stdio.h>
#include <stdlib.h>

int main(int argc, char *argv[])
{
  const char *user = NULL;
  struct passwd *pwd;

  /* Set the user name if it was supplied on the command
   * line.  Bail out if we don't end up with a user name.
   */
  if (argc == 2)
    user = argv[1];
  if(!user)
  {
    fprintf(stderr, "Usage: checkpass <username>\n");
    exit(1);
  }

  /* Fetch the password entry. */
  if (pwd = getpwnam(user))
  {
    char *password = (char *) getpass("Enter your password: ");

    /* Encrypt the password using the encrypted password as salt.
     * See crypt(3) for complete details.
     */
    char *crypted  = (char *) crypt(password, pwd->pw_passwd);

    /* Are the two encrypted passwords identical? */
    if (strcmp(pwd->pw_passwd, crypted) == 0)
      printf("Success.\n");
    else
    {
      printf("Bad password: %s != %s\n", pwd->pw_passwd, crypted);
      return 1;
```

Example 11-1. Using getpwnam() to retrieve an encrypted password (continued)

```
    }
  }
  else
  {
    fprintf(stderr, "Could not find password for %s.\n", user);
    return 1;
  }
  return 0;

}
```

As of Mac OS X Panther, your code no longer has a chance to look at an encrypted password. There are no functions such as `getspnam( )`, and if you invoke a function such as `getpwnam( )`, you will get one or more asterisks as the result. For example:

```
$ ./checkpass bjepson
Enter your password:
Bad password: ******** != **yRnqib5QSRI
```

There are some circumstances in which you can obtain an encrypted password, but this is not the default behavior of Mac OS X Panther. See the *getpwent(3)* manpage for complete details.

Instead of retrieving and comparing encrypted passwords, you should go through the Linux-PAM APIs. Because Linux-PAM is included with (or available for) many flavors of Unix, you can use it to write portable code. Example 11-2 shows a simple program that uses Linux-PAM to prompt a user for his password.

Example 11-2. Using Linux-PAM to authenticate a user

```
/*
 * Use Linux-PAM to check passwords.
 *
 * Compile with gcc pam_example.c -o pam_example -lpam
 * Run with: ./pam_example <username>
 */
#include <stdio.h>
#include <pam/pam_appl.h>
#include <pam/pam_misc.h>

int main(int argc, char *argv[])
{

  int retval;
  static struct pam_conv pam_conv;
  pam_conv.conv = misc_conv;
  pam_handle_t *pamh = NULL;
  const char *user = NULL;

  /* Set the username if it was supplied on the command
   * line. Bail out if we don't end up with a username.
```

Example 11-2. Using Linux-PAM to authenticate a user (continued)

```
   */
  if (argc == 2)
    user = argv[1];
  if(!user)
  {
    fprintf(stderr, "Usage: pam_example <username>\n");
    exit(1);
  }

  /* Initialize Linux-PAM. */
  retval = pam_start("pam_example", user, &pam_conv, &pamh);
  if (retval != PAM_SUCCESS)
  {
    fprintf(stderr, "Could not start pam: %s\n",
        pam_strerror(pamh, retval));
    exit(1);
  }

  /* Try to authenticate the user. This could cause Linux-PAM
   * to prompt the user for a password.
   */
  retval = pam_authenticate(pamh, 0);
  if (retval == PAM_SUCCESS)
    printf("Success.\n");
  else
    fprintf(stderr, "Failure: %s\n", pam_strerror(pamh, retval));

  /* Shutdown Linux-PAM. Return with an error if
   * something goes wrong.
   */
  return pam_end(pamh, retval) == PAM_SUCCESS ? 0 : 1;
}
```

In order for this to work, you must create a file called *pam_sample* in */etc/pam.d* with the following contents (the filename must match the first argument to `pam_start()`):

```
auth        required  pam_securityserver.so
account     required  pam_permit.so
password    required  pam_deny.so
```

Be careful when making any changes in the */etc/pam.d* directory. If you change one of the files that is consulted for system login, you may lock yourself out of the system. For more information on Linux-PAM, see the *pam(8)* manpage.

Configuring Directory Services

In order to configure Directory Services, use the Directory Access application located in */Applications/Utilities*, shown in Figure 11-2. You can enable or disable various directory service plug-ins, or change their configuration.

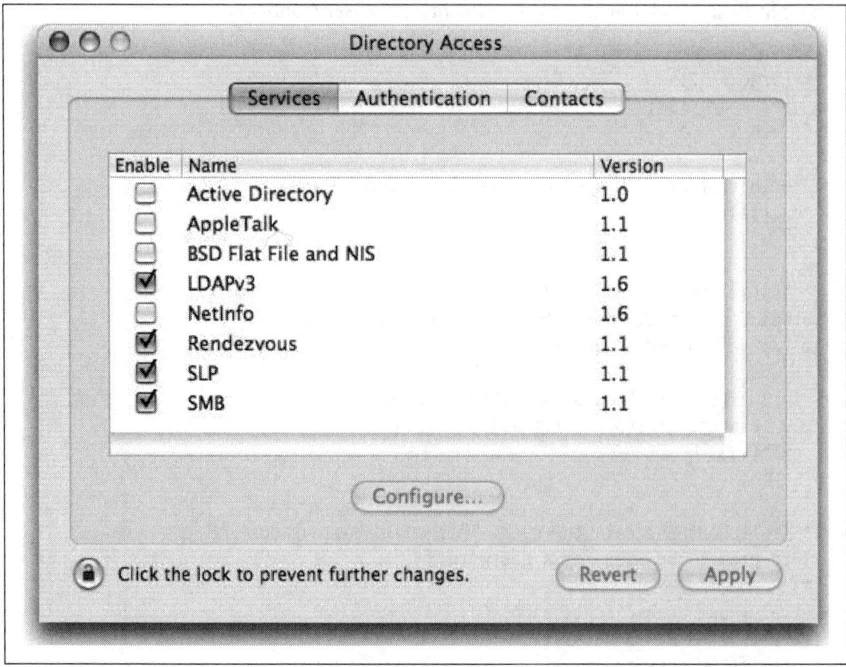

Figure 11-2. The Directory Access application shows the available plug-ins

Directory Access supports the following plug-ins:

Active Directory
: This plug-in lets Mac OS X consult an Active Directory domain on a server running Windows 2000 or Windows 2003.

AppleTalk
: This is the ultimate Mac OS legacy protocol. AppleTalk was the original networking protocol supported by Mac OS versions prior to Mac OS X. Linux and the server editions of Windows also support AppleTalk.

BSD Flat File and NIS
: This includes the Network Information Service (NIS) and the flat files located in the */etc* directory, such as *hosts*, *exports*, and *services*. By default, this option is switched off. After you enable it, click Apply, switch to the Authentication tab, choose Custom Path from the search menu, click the Add button, choose */BSD/Local*, and click Apply again.

LDAPv3
: This is the same version of LDAP used by Microsoft's Active Directory and Novell's NDS. In addition to the client components, Mac OS X includes *slapd*, a standalone LDAP daemon. Mac OS X's LDAP support comes through OpenLDAP (*http://www.openldap.org*), an open source LDAPv3 implementation.

NetInfo
This is a legacy Directory Services protocol introduced in NeXTSTEP. If the checkbox is off (the default), NetInfo uses the local domain but doesn't consult network-based NetInfo domains. If the checkbox is on, NetInfo will also look for and potentially use any network-based domains that it finds.

NetInfo and LDAP both use the same data store, which is contained in */var/db/netinfo/*. The data store is a collection of embedded database files.

Rendezvous
This is Apple's zero-configuration protocol for discovering file sharing, printers, and other network services. It uses a peer-to-peer approach to announce and discover services automatically as devices join a network.

SLP
This is the Service Location Protocol, which supports file and print services over IP.

SMB
This is the Server Message Block protocol, which is Microsoft's protocol for file and print services.

Under the Services tab, everything except NetInfo and BSD Configuration Files is enabled by default. However, if you go to the Authentication tab (Figure 11-3), you'll see that NetInfo is the sole service in charge of authentication (which is handled by */etc/passwd* and */etc/group* on other Unix systems).

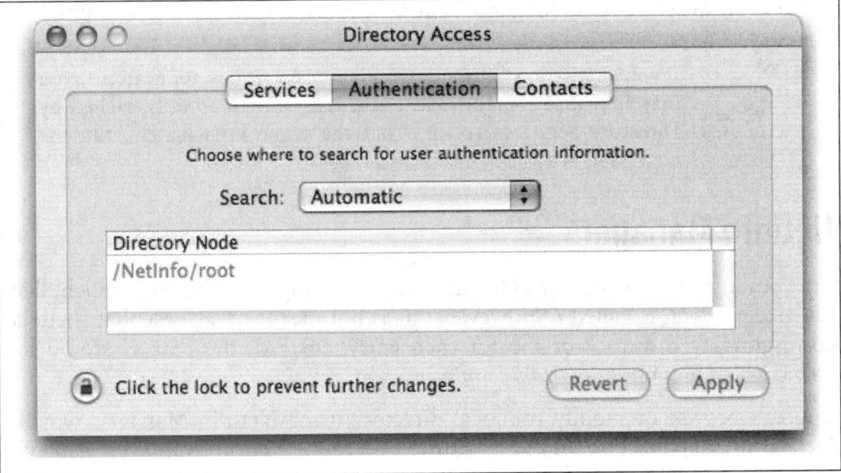

Figure 11-3. The Directory Access Authentication tab

By default, the Authentication tab is set to Automatic. You can set the Search pop up to any of the following:

Automatic
: This is the default, which searches (in order): the local NetInfo directory, a shared NetInfo domain, and a shared LDAPv3 domain.

Local directory
: This searches only the local NetInfo directory.

Custom path
: This allows you to use BSD flat files (*/etc/passwd* and */etc/group*). After you select Custom path from the pop up, click Add and select */BSD/Local* (this option appears in the list only if you have enabled BSD Flat File and NIS on the Services tab and clicked Apply).

After you have changed the Search setting, click Apply. The Contact tab is set up identically to the Authentication tab and is used by programs that search Directory Services for contact information (office locations, phone numbers, full names, etc.).

Enabling BSD flat files doesn't copy or change the information in the local directory (the NetInfo database). If you want to rely only on flat files, you need to find all the user entries from the local directory (use the command *nidump passwd .* to list them all) and add them to the password flat files (*/etc/passwd* and */etc/master.passwd*) with the *vipw* utility (don't edit either file directly). When you're done editing the password file, *vipw* invokes *pwd_mkdb* to rebuild the databases (*/etc/spwd.db* and */etc/pwd.db*) that look up usernames and passwords. Switching to flat files allows you to access encrypted passwords through `getpwnam( )` and friends, but also means you can no longer use the GUI tools to manage user accounts.

If you change any settings in the Directory Access applications, you may find that some invalid credentials are temporarily cached by Directory Services. To clear out the cache immediately, run the command `lookupd -flushcache` as *root*.

NetInfo Manager

The local directory is organized hierarchically, starting from the *root*, which, like a filesystem's *root*, is called */*. However, this is not meant to suggest that there is a corresponding directory or file for each entry. Instead, the data is stored in a collection of files under */var/db/netinfo*.

You can browse or modify the local directory using NetInfo Manager, which is located in */Applications/Utilities*. Figure 11-4 shows NetInfo Manager displaying the properties of the *mysql* user.

Directory Services Utilities

This chapter demonstrates four Directory Services utilities: *dscl*, *nireport*, *nidump*, and *niload*. Table 11-1 describes these and other NetInfo utilities.

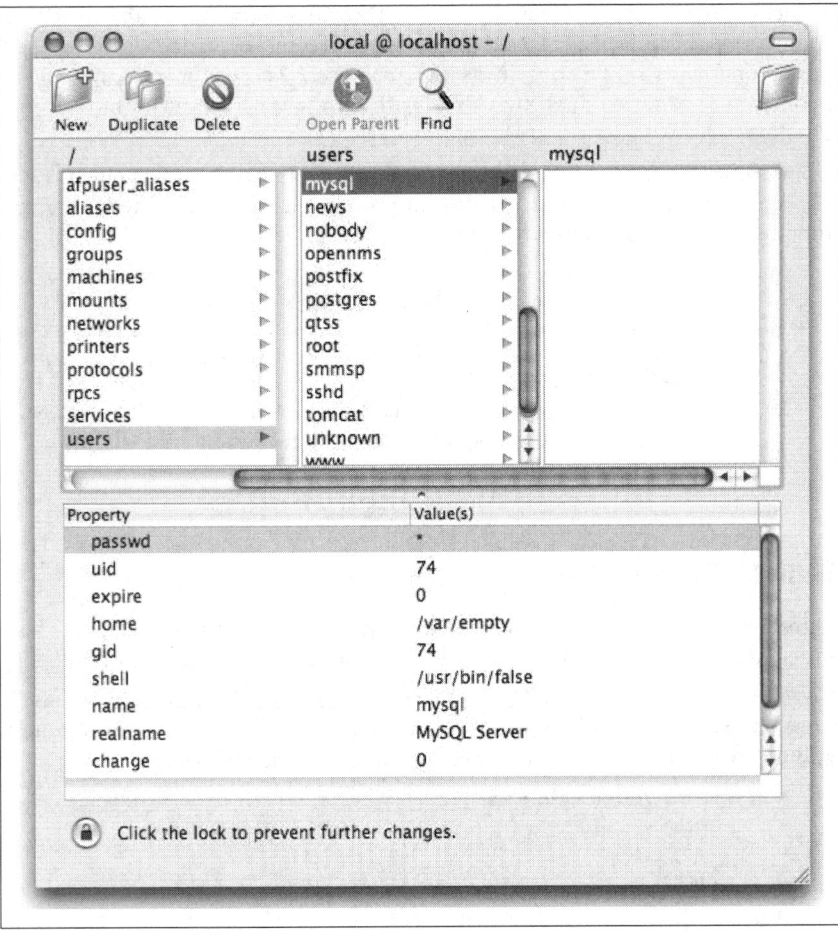

Figure 11-4. Browsing the local directory

Table 11-1. NetInfo tools

Tool	Description
dscl	Provides a command-line interface to Directory Services
nicl	Provides a command-line interface to NetInfo
nidump	Extracts flat file format data (such as */etc/passwd*) from NetInfo
nifind	Finds a NetInfo directory
nigrep	Performs a regular expression search on NetInfo
niload	Loads flat file format data (such as */etc/passwd*) into NetInfo
nireport	Prints tables from NetInfo
niutil	NetInfo utility for manipulating the database

The *nidump* and *nireport* utilities display the contents of the local directory. *niload* loads the contents of flat files (such as */etc/passwd* or */etc/hosts*) into Directory

Services. *niutil* directly manipulates the Directory Services database; it's the command-line equivalent of NetInfo Manager. To make changes, use *sudo* with these commands or first log in as the *root* user. The commands that can be performed as a normal user are shown without the *sudo* command in the examples that follow.

Unlike other *ni** utilities, *nicl* acts directly on the database files. Consequently, you can use *nicl* to modify the local directory even when Directory Services is not running (such as when you boot into single-user mode).

When you use any of these utilities, you are making potentially dangerous changes to your system. However, even if you trash the local directory with reckless usage of these commands, you can restore the NetInfo database from your last backup. For more details, see the "Restoring the Directory Services Database" section, later in this chapter. To back up the local NetInfo database, use the command:

```
nidump -r / -t localhost/local > backup.nidump
```

Managing Groups

Directory Services stores information about groups in its */groups* directory. This is different from the */etc/group* file, which is consulted only in single-user mode.

To list all of the group IDs (GIDs) and group names for the local domain, invoke *nireport* with the NetInfo domain (., the local domain), the directory (*/groups*), and the properties you want to inspect—in this case, *gid* and *name*:

```
$ nireport . /groups gid name
-2      nobody
-1      nogroup
0       wheel
1       daemon
2       kmem
3       sys
4       tty
5       operator
6       mail
7       bin
20      staff
25      smmsp
26      lp
27      postfix
28      postdrop
31      guest
45      utmp
66      uucp
68      dialer
69      network
70      www
74      mysql
75      sshd
```

```
76        qtss
78        mailman
79        appserverusr
80        admin
81        appserveradm
99        unknown
```

Although the flat file format is called *group* (after the */etc/group* file), the group directory is */groups*. If you forget that last *s*, *nireport* will look for the wrong directory. However, if you want to dump the groups directory in the */etc/group* file format, use the command *nidump group .* without that last *s*.

Directory Services

Creating a Group with niload

The *niload* utility can be used to read the flat-file format used by */etc/group* (`name:password:gid:members`). To add a new group, you can create a file that adheres to that format and load it with *niload*. For ad hoc work, you can use a *here* document (an expression that functions as a quoted string, but spans multiple lines) rather than a separate file:

```
$ sudo niload group . <<EOF
> writers:*:1001:
> EOF
```

Creating a Group with dscl

To create a group with *dscl*, you need to create a directory under */groups* and set the *gid* and *passwd* properties. An asterisk (*) specifies no password; be sure to quote it so that the shell doesn't attempt to expand it. The following creates a group named *writers* as GID 5005 with no password and no members:

```
$ sudo dscl . create /groups/writers gid 5005
$ sudo dscl . create /groups/writers passwd '*'
```

Adding Users to a Group

You can add users to the group by appending values to the *users* property with *dscl*'s *merge* command at the command line (or by using the *merge* command interactively; start *dscl* in interactive mode with *sudo dscl .*). If the *users* property doesn't exist, *dscl* creates it. If the users are already part of the group, they aren't added to the list (contrast this with the *-append* command, which can result in the same user being added more than once if the command is invoked multiple times):

```
$ sudo dscl . merge /groups/writers users bjepson rothman
```

Listing Groups with nidump

Use *nidump* to confirm that the new group was created correctly. To list groups with *nidump*, pass in the format (in this case, the *group* file) and the domain (., the local domain):

```
$ nidump group . | grep writers
writers:*:5005:bjepson,rothman
```

Because you can use *nireport* to dump any directory, you can also use it to see this information:

```
$ nireport . /groups name passwd gid users | grep writers
writers *       5005    bjepson,rothman
```

Deleting a Group

To delete a group, use *dscl*'s *delete* command. Be careful with this command, because it will delete everything in and below the specified NetInfo directory:

```
$ sudo dscl / delete /groups/writers
```

Managing Users and Passwords

The Directory Services equivalent of the *passwd* file resides under the */users* portion of the directory. Although Mac OS X includes */etc/passwd* and */etc/master.passwd* files, they are consulted only while the system is in single-user mode, or if the system has been reconfigured to use BSD Flat Files (see the "Configuring Directory Services" section, earlier in this chapter).

To add a normal user to your system, you should use System Preferences→Accounts. However, if you want to bulk-load NetInfo with many users or create a user while logged in over *ssh*, you can use *dscl* or *niload*.

You can list all users with the *nireport* utility. Supply the NetInfo domain (., the local domain), the directory (*/users*), and the properties you want to inspect (*uid*, *name*, *home*, *realname*, and *shell*):

```
$ nireport . /users uid name home realname shell
-2   nobody    /var/empty         Unprivileged User          /usr/bin/false
0    root      /var/root          System Administrator       /bin/sh
1    daemon    /var/root          System Services            /usr/bin/false
99   unknown   /var/empty         Unknown User               /usr/bin/false
25   smmsp     /private/etc/mail  Sendmail User              /usr/bin/false
2    lp        /var/spool/cups    Printing Services          /usr/bin/false
27   postfix   /var/spool/postfix Postfix User               /usr/bin/false
70   www       /Library/WebServer World Wide Web Server      /usr/bin/false
71   eppc      /var/empty         Apple Events User          /usr/bin/false
74   mysql     /var/empty         MySQL Server               /usr/bin/false
75   sshd      /var/empty         sshd Privilege separation  /usr/bin/false
76   qtss      /var/empty         QuickTime Streaming Server /usr/bin/false
77   cyrus     /var/imap          Cyrus User                 /usr/bin/false
78   mailman   /var/empty         Mailman user               /usr/bin/false
79   appserver /var/empty         Application Server         /usr/bin/false
```

Creating a User with niload

The *niload* utility understands the flat-file format used by */etc/passwd* (`name:password:uid:gid:class:change:expire:gecos:home_dir:shell`). See the *passwd(5)* manpage for a description of each field. To add a new user, create a file that adheres to that format, and load it with *niload*. You can use a here document rather than a separate file. This example creates a user for Ernest Rothman with a UID of 701 and membership in the group numbered 701, which you'll create next:

```
$ sudo niload passwd . <<EOF
> rothman:*:701:701::0:0:Ernest Rothman:/Users/rothman:/bin/bash
> EOF
```

Next, create a group with the same name as the new user and a GID that matches his UID (as of Mac OS X 10.3, users are given their own groups):

```
$ sudo niload group . <<EOF
> rothman:*:701:
> EOF
```


As you can see from the example, the user's password field is set to *, which disables logins for that account. To set the password, use the *passwd* command:

```
$ sudo passwd rothman
Changing password for rothman.
New password: ********
Retype new password: ********
```

If you *niload* a user that already exists, that user's entry is updated with the new information. Before the user can log in, you must create her home directory (see the "Creating a User's Home Directory" section, later in this chapter).

Creating a User with dscl

To create a user with *dscl*, you need to create a directory under */users* and set the *uid*, *gid*, *shell*, *realname*, and *home* properties.

The following commands will create the same user shown in the previous section:

```
$ sudo dscl . create /users/rothman uid 701
$ sudo dscl . create /users/rothman gid 701
$ sudo dscl . create /users/rothman shell /bin/bash
$ sudo dscl . create /users/rothman home /Users/rothman
$ sudo dscl . create /users/rothman realname "Ernest Rothman"
$ sudo dscl . create /users/rothman passwd \*
$ sudo dscl . create /groups/rothman gid 701
$ sudo dscl . create /groups/rothman passwd \*
```

Be sure to quote or escape the asterisk (*) in the `passwd` entries. After you create the user, you should set the password as shown in the previous section.

Creating a User's Home Directory

One thing NetInfo can't do for you is create the user's home directory. Mac OS X keeps a skeleton directory under the */System/Library/User Template* directory. If you look in this directory, you'll see localized versions of a user's home directory. To copy the localized English version of the home directory, use the *ditto* command with the *--rsrc* flag to preserve any resource forks that may exist:

```
$ sudo ditto --rsrc \
  /System/Library/User\ Template/English.lproj /Users/rothman
```

Then, use *chown* to recursively set the ownership of the home directory and all its contents (make sure you set the group to a group of which the user is a member):

```
$ sudo chown -R rothman:rothman /Users/rothman
```

This change makes the new user the owner of his home directory and all its contents.

Granting Administrative Privileges

To give someone administrative privileges, add that user to the *admin* group (*/groups/admin*). This gives the user the ability to use *sudo* and run applications (such as software installers) that require such privileges:

```
$ sudo dscl . merge /groups/admin users rothman
```

If you want this setting to take place immediately, you can run the command *sudo lookupd –flushcache* to flush any cached credentials.

Modifying a User

You can change a user's properties using the *create* command, even if that property already exists. For example, to change *rothman*'s shell to *zsh*, use:

```
$ sudo dscl . -create /users/rothman shell /bin/zsh
```

You can also modify most user settings with System Preferences→Accounts. If you want to do things the traditional Unix way, Mac OS X includes *chsh*, *chfn*, and *chpass* as of Version 10.3.

Listing Users with nidump

Use *nidump* to confirm that *rothman* was added successfully. To list users with *nidump*, pass in the format (in this case, the *passwd* file) and the domain (use . for the local domain):

```
$ nidump passwd . | grep rothman
rothman:********:701:701::0:0:Ernest Rothman:/Users/rothman:/bin/zsh
```

Deleting a User

To delete a user, use *dscl*'s *delete* command. Because *delete* recursively deletes everything under the specified directory, use this command with caution:

```
$ sudo dscl . delete /users/rothman
```

If you want to also delete that user's home directory, you have to do it manually.

Managing Hostnames and IP Addresses

Mac OS X consults both the */etc/hosts* file and the */machines* portion of the local directory. For example, the following entry in */etc/hosts* maps the hostname *xyzzy* to 192.168.0.1:

```
192.168.0.1    xyzzy
```

Creating a Host with niload

The *niload* utility understands the flat-file format used by */etc/hosts* (*ip_address name*). See the *hosts(5)* manpage for a description of each field. To add a new host, create a file using that format and load it with *niload*. This example adds the host *xyzzy*:

```
$ sudo niload hosts . <<EOF
> 192.168.0.1 xyzzy
> EOF
```

If you add an entry that already exists, it will be overwritten.

The */etc/hosts* file takes precedence over the local directory, so if you enter the same hostname with different IP addresses in both places, Mac OS X uses the one in */etc/hosts*.

Directory Services

Exporting Directories with NFS

You can use the */etc/exports* file to store folders you want to export over NFS. For example, the following line exports the */Users* directory to two hosts (`192.168.0.134` and `192.168.0.106`):

```
/Users  -ro 192.168.0.134 192.168.0.106
```

The NFS server will start automatically at boot time if there are any exports in that file. After you've set up your exports, you can reboot, and NFS should start automatically. NFS options supported by Mac OS X include the following (see the *exports(5)* manpage for complete details):

`-maproot=`*`user`*
: Specifies that the remote *root* user should be mapped to the specified user. You may specify either a username or numeric UID.

`-maproot=`*`user:`*`[`*`group`*`[`*`:group...`*`]]`
: Specifies that the remote *root* user should be mapped to the specified user with the specified group credentials. If you include the colon with no groups, as in `-maproot=`*`username`*`:`, it means the remote user should have no group credentials. You may specify a username or numeric UID for *user* and a group name or numeric GID for *group*.

`-mapall=`*`user`*
: Specifies that all remote users should be mapped to the specified user.

`-mapall=`*`user`*`:`[*`group`*[`:`*`group`*...]]
: Specifies that all remote users should be mapped to the specified user with the specified group credentials. If you include the colon with no groups, as in `mapall=`*`username`*`:`, it specifies that the remote user should be given no group credentials.

`-kerb`
: Uses a Kerberos authentication server to authenticate and map client credentials.

`-ro` Exports the filesystem as read-only. The synonym `-o` is also supported.

Flat Files and Their Directory Services Counterparts

As mentioned earlier, Directory Services manages information for several flat files in earlier releases of Mac OS X, including */etc/printcap*, */etc/mail/aliases*, */etc/protocols*, and */etc/services*. For a complete list of known flat-file formats, see the *nidump* and *niload* manpages.

Although you can edit these flat files directly as you would on any other Unix system, you can also use Directory Services to manage this information. You can use *niload* with a supported flat-file format to add entries, or you can use *dscl* or NetInfo Manager to directly manipulate the entries. Table 3-2 lists each flat file, the corresponding portion of the directory, and important properties associated with each entry. See the *netinfo(5)* manpage for complete details. Properties marked with (list) can take multiple values. (For an example, see the "Adding Users to a Group" section, earlier in this chapter.)

The "Flat files or local database?" column in Table 11-2 indicates whether Directory Services consults the flat file, the local database, or both. You can use Directory Access to modify the way information is looked up on your Macintosh.

Table 11-2. Flat files and their NetInfo counterparts

Flat file	NetInfo directory	Important properties	Flat files or local database?
/etc/exports	*/exports*	name, clients (list), opts (list)	Flat files
/etc/fstab	*/mounts*	name, dir, type, opts (list), passno, freq	Local database
/etc/group	*/groups*	name, passwd, gid, users (list)	Local database
/etc/hosts	*/machines*	ip_address, name (list)	Both; entries in */etc/hosts* take precedence
/etc/mail/aliases	*/aliases*	name, members (list)	Flat files
/etc/networks	*/networks*	name (list), address	Flat files
/etc/passwd, */etc/master.passwd*	*/users*	name, passwd, uid, gid, realname, home, shell	Local database
/etc/printcap	*/printers*	*name*, and various *printcap* properties (see the *printcap(5)* manpage)	Flat files
/etc/protocols	*/protocols*	name (list), number	Flat files

Table 11-2. Flat files and their NetInfo counterparts (continued)

Flat file	NetInfo directory	Important properties	Flat files or local database?
/etc/rpc	*/rpcs*	name (list), number	Flat files
/etc/services	*/services*	*name* (list), *port*, *protocol* (list)	Flat files

Restoring the Directory Services Database

If the local directory database is damaged, boot into single-user mode by holding down ⌘-S as the system starts up. Next, check to see if you have a backup of the NetInfo database. The */etc/daily cron* job backs up the database each time it is run. You can find the backup in */var/backups/local.nidump*. If you don't have a backup, you won't be able to restore. The *local.nidump* file is overwritten each time the *cron* job runs, so make sure you back it up regularly (preferably to some form of removable media).

Directory Services

If your computer is generally not turned on at 3:15 a.m. (the default time for the *daily cron* job), you'll never get a backup of your local directory. You can solve this problem by editing */etc/crontab* to run this job at a different time, or to run the job periodically with the command *sudo periodic daily*.

After the system boots in single-user mode, you should:

1. Wait for the `root#` prompt to come up.
2. Fix any filesystem errors; if you are using a journaled filesystem, this step won't be necessary (and if you try to run this command, you'll get an error):
```
# /sbin/fsck -y
```
3. Mount the *root* filesystem as read/write:
```
# /sbin/mount -uw /
```
4. Change directories, and go to the NetInfo database directory:
```
# cd /var/db/netinfo/
```
5. Move the database out of the way, and give it a different name:
```
# mv local.nidb/ local.nidb.broken
```
6. Start enough of the system to use NetInfo (each command may take several seconds or more to complete; the last message you see should be "Startup complete."):
```
# /usr/libexec/kextd
# /usr/sbin/configd
# /sbin/SystemStarter
```
7. Create a blank NetInfo database, and start NetInfo (be sure you are still in the */var/db/netinfo* directory from Step 4):
```
# /usr/libexec/create_nidb
# /usr/sbin/netinfod -s local
```

8. Load the backup into NetInfo:

```
# /usr/bin/niload  -d -r / . < /var/backups/local.nidump
```

After you have completed these steps, reboot the system with the *reboot* command.

If you totally mess up and find that you forgot to backup your NetInfo database, you can stop at Step 8, and issue the command *rm /var/db/.AppleSetupDone*. This makes Mac OS X think that it's being booted for the first time next time you reboot. As a result, it will run the setup assistant so you can create the initial user for the system, bringing your system to a usable state for further repairs.

12
Running Network Services

A *network service* is a program running on a local machine that other machines can connect to and use over a network. Common examples include web, email, and file-transfer servers.

This chapter builds on the network administration fundamentals covered in Chapter 10 to describe how network services work in general, and how several of the more popular services work on Mac OS X. For information on using these services client-side, consult Chapter 8.

Network Services Overview

Generally, a network service operates through a *daemon* program that listens for incoming connections on a certain port; web servers usually listen on port 80, for example, and *ssh* connections typically happen on port 22. (The precise way it accomplishes this is implementation-specific; it might choose to handle the whole connection itself or fork off another process to handle it so the daemon can get back to listening.)

Running Services in Mac OS X

Like so many other administrative tasks in Mac OS X, you have two ways to run the network services. The classic Unix way involves invoking the daemon on the command line, either manually through the Terminal or with a script. The Sharing preference pane, though, provides a very simple on/off switch for many network services.

Running Services Through the Sharing Pane

The Sharing pane contains three tabbed panes shown in Figure 12-1.

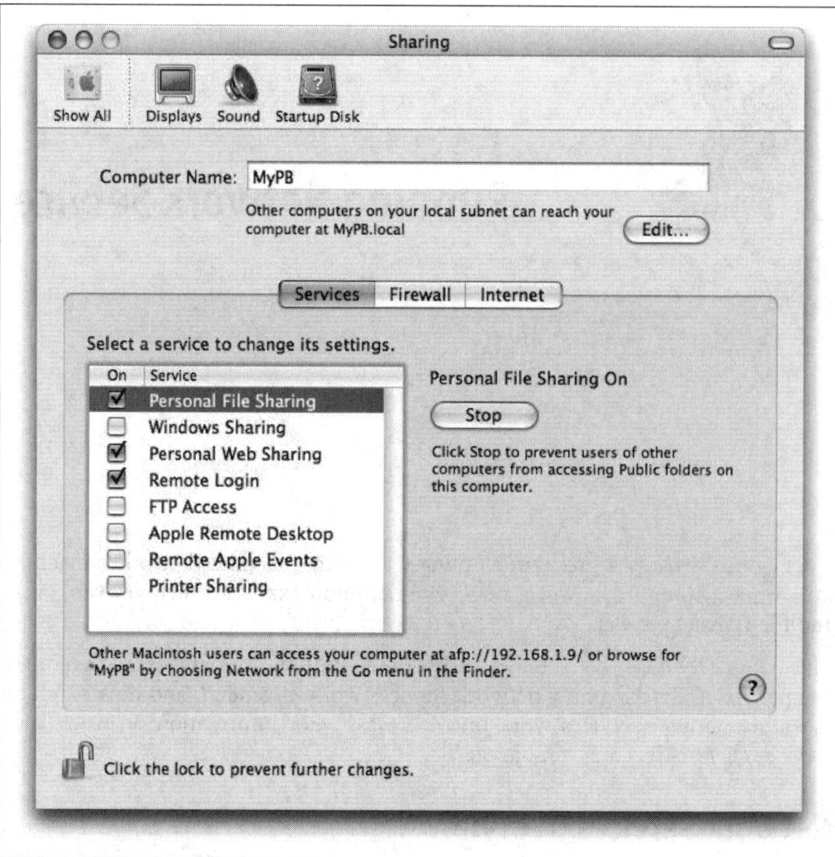

Figure 12-1. The Sharing preference panel's Services pane

Services
: Lists several service daemons you can control.

Firewall
: Contains controls for the system's built-in firewall. (See the section "Mac OS X's Firewall" in Chapter 10.)

Internet
: Lets you enable/disable Internet sharing.

Every item in the Services list is visually paired with an On checkbox and is (behind the scenes) associated with a daemon program. Generally, when you check a checkbox, the related daemon launches; unchecking the checkbox kills the daemon, making the service unavailable. In some cases, the system service remains running in either state, but toggling the checkbox causes the system to rewrite its configuration file and then restart it.

Personal File Sharing
: When active, other computers can mount disks and folders on your filesystem via AFP. See the later section "File Sharing Services."

Windows Sharing
: The same as Personal file sharing but uses the SMB protocol to share disks and folders, making access easier for users of Microsoft Windows machines—though other operating systems, including Mac OS X, can also mount SMB shares easily. See the later section "File Sharing Services."

Personal Web Sharing
: Checking this launches the computer's Apache web server. See the later section "Web Services."

Remote Login
: Launches the Mac's SSH server. See the later section, "The Secure Shell."

FTP Access
: Runs the FTP server, as described later in the section "File Transfer Protocol (FTP)."

Apple Remote Desktop
: Runs the Apple Remote Desktop (ADR) client daemons, which allow a remote machine running the ADR administrations software (available separately) to manage the client machine. A teacher running ADR, for example, can remotely view a student's display, install software, or generate system information reports on any computer running the client. When you click to enable the client, an Access Privileges button on the pane is enabled as well, allowing the client to specify how much access a remote ADR user can have.

Remote Apple Events
: When activated, every active application that responds to Apple Events (i.e., is controllable by AppleScript) also becomes a web service that responds to the SOAP protocol, accessible from anywhere on the Internet. Chapter 14 covers Apple Events in more detail.

Printer Sharing
: Activates printer sharing. See the section "Printer Sharing" in Chapter 9.

Mail Services

Email-related daemons can be put into two categories: *mail transport agents* (MTAs), which send new email messages to their destination machines, and *mail delivery agents* (MDAs), which send mail that's landed in a user's mailbox to that user's personal computer.

Mail Transport Agents (Postfix)

A mail transport agent sends email to other computers, most often via the SMTP protocol. Mac OS X ships with Postfix, a program that aims to be an improved alternative to the still more common *sendmail* program that shipped with previous versions of Mac OS X.

Run Postfix only if you need to provide mail-sending services to yourself or your network. You don't need to run this service to simply send email as long as there is an SMTP server that will accept connections from your machine; most ISPs provide mail services on their own servers, for example.

Using Postfix

You can configure Postfix to work in two ways on your machine. The first, as a local mailer, allows you to send and receive local messages, as well as send messages to external Internet addresses. This mode is useful for receiving the regular *cron* reports that get sent to *root*, for allowing scripts to send mail, and for sending quick messages from the command line using the *mail* command.

Postfix can also run as a standalone mail server, able to exchange mail with other servers on the Internet. Even if you don't need to run your own full-fledged mail server, this mode lets you use your regular GUI email client and send mail directly from your Mac to any Internet address, eliminating the need for you to first relay your mail through an external SMTP server. This option can be very helpful when, for whatever reasons, your ISP's server becomes unreachable.

Configuring a local mailer

Mac OS X has no easy interface for running Postfix, but it doesn't take too much work to get it running as a local mailer because most of the setup has already been done for you. By default, */etc/hostconfig* contains the line `MAILSERVER=-Automatic-`, which causes the Postfix startup script, */System/Library/StartupItems/postfix/postfix*, to launch the *postfix-watch* daemon. (See the section "Configuring Startup Items" later in this chapter for more information on how this works.)

postfix-watch then monitors the mail queue for new local mail and launches the rest of the Postfix system when any arrives. Once Postfix delivers the mail, it continues running for an hour and then, if there's no further mail, dies. Without any configuration, then, Panther will let you send local mail. To confirm, send a message to yourself:

```
ChrisPB:~ chris$ mail chris
Subject: Test
Testing 1,2,3
.
EOT
ChrisPB:~ chris$
```

Check local mail using the *mail* command by itself:

```
ChrisPB:~ chris$ mail
Mail version 8.1 6/6/93.  Type ? for help.
"/var/mail/chris": 1 message 1 new
>N  1 chris@ChrisPB.local   Tue Dec  2 08:55  14/441   "Test"
& (Return)
Message 1:
From chris@ChrisPB.local  Tue Dec  2 08:55:12 2003
X-Original-To: chris
```

```
Delivered-To: chris@ChrisPB.local
To: chris@ChrisPB.local
Subject: Test
Date: Tue,  2 Dec 2003 08:55:12 -0800 (PST)
From: chris@ChrisPB.local (Chris Stone)

Testing 1,2,3

& q
Saved 1 message in mbox
ChrisPB:~ chris$
```

However, even with local mail working, you might still have a problem passing mail to other mail servers because most require that any incoming messages be from a valid domain (one whose name resolves to an IP number). If a valid domain isn't part of your machine's hostname, you need to specify one (your ISP's, for example) in the Postfix configuration file, */etc/postfix/main.cf*. Depending on your situation, you'll need to define up to three parameters. Find each in *main.cf*, and uncomment their lines (remove the #s) before replacing the values with your own:

`#myhostname = host.domain.tld`
: This parameter identifies your machine to other servers. The full hostname doesn't have to be resolvable, but its domain does (e.g., *domain.tld*). You'll need to define at least this parameter.

`#mydomain = domain.tld`
: This parameter identifies the domain you're sending from, which must be resolvable. You need to define this parameter only if you're defining `myorigin` as well.

`#myorigin = $mydomain`
: This parameter serves two purposes. It's used in the *from* header of outgoing messages as the domain part of the sender's address, and it also gets appended to any recipient address that has no domain specified. For the second reason, then, any mail locally addressed to a simple username, such as root, is sent to `root@myorigin` and not the local root account.

  If you use Postfix as more than just a local mailer, and this is the desired behavior, specify a resolvable domain name for `myorigin`. (In most cases, this value is the same used for `mydomain`, so you can instead use `$mydomain` as the value for `myorigin`.)

  If, on the other hand, you want locally addressed mail to stay local, don't define this parameter, and Postfix will use the value set for `myhostname` in the outgoing *from* headers. In that case, you should use only a domain name, and not a full hostname, for `myhostname`'s value.

If you've made your changes while Postfix is running, execute the command `postfix reload` as root, and the changes will take effect without interrupting mail services.

Chapter 28 contains a list of Postfix's command-line arguments. If you need to customize your Mac's Postfix setup, you should read a good reference book on the topic, such as *Postfix: The Definitive Guide* (O'Reilly) or the online materials found at *http://www.postfix.com*.

During installation of Panther, a script is supposed to run that creates the user accounts required by several system daemons, including Postfix. If you've performed an upgrade to Panther, however, it's possible that this didn't happen, so starting Postfix will fail with an `unknown user` error. You can easily fix this by running the script manually as root. You'll find the script at */Library/Receipts/Essentials.pkg/Contents/Resources/CreateSystemUsers*.

Configuring a mail server

Once you have Postfix running as a local mailer, you can then configure it to operate as a standalone mail server, which requires the services of the SMTP daemon, *smtpd*. As a security precaution, Postfix is configured by default with *smtpd* disabled so won't accept incoming mail. However, it's not difficult to enable *smtpd* so Postfix can at least relay messages from a local email client.

To do this, first modify the file */etc/hostconfig* so the line `MAILSERVER=-AUTOMATIC-` instead reads `MAILSERVER=-YES-`. This ensures that Postfix is running at all times to accept mail. Next, uncomment this line from */etc/postfix/master.cf*:

```
#smtpinetn -  n  -  -smtpd
```

You can then start Postfix by running `/System/Library/StartupItems/Postfix/Postfix start` as *root* (or using `restart` if Postfix is already running).

Finally, configure your email client (including Apple's Mail application, Microsoft's Entourage, and Qualcomm's Eudora) to use either `localhost` or `127.0.0.1` as its SMTP server. Once you do, Postfix will deliver outgoing mail from your Mac directly to your recipients' servers.

By default, Postfix is configured to accept only local connections, so you still won't be able to receive mail from the network. Allowing this involves changing the `inet_interfaces` and `mynetworks_style` parameters in *main.cf*. There are several ways to do this, and security considerations are involved as well, so you should have a strong understanding of the issues before putting a mail server on the network. The Postfix references mentioned previously are a good place to start.

Mail Delivery Agents

Most email users don't read mail directly from their mailhosts; instead, they download their mail from the host to their personal computers. A daemon running on the mailhost called a Mail Delivery Agent (MDA) facilitates this by supporting a mail-delivery protocol, and individual mail clients (Apple's Mail, for example) connect to this service to check for and download new messages.

The two most common MDA protocols are the Post Office Protocol (POP) and the Internet Message Access Protocol (IMAP). POP, the older and more commonly supported of the two, comprises a very simple command set, allowing users to do little besides download their mail and delete it from the server. IMAP represents a newer and more sophisticated protocol that lets users store and organize all their mail on the server-side. This offers much greater convenience to users, but at the cost of more server resources; consider using the *quota* command (see Chapter 25) to set users' storage capacities if you support IMAP.

Unfortunately, Mac OS X ships with neither *popd* nor *imapd*, the daemons that give you POP and IMAP services, respectively. You can cover both these bases by installing the UW IMAP server, available as a source code tarball (*http://www.washington.edu/imap*).*

If you would like to forgo compiling UW IMAP altogether, a shareware utility exists that provides a simple GUI interface allowing you to easily enable Postfix as well as the UW IMAP and POP services. Postfix Enabler is available from *http://www.roadstead.com/weblog/Tutorials/PostfixEnabler.html*.

Web Services

Mac OS X comes with Apache, an open source web server responsible for more than half of all the Internet's web sites.† At its most basic level, Apache runs as a daemon named *httpd* that supports the Hypertext Transfer Protocol (HTTP); it listens to web surfers' requests (on port 80, by default) and replies with response codes and web pages.

Apache Configuration

Apache's configuration information lies in the */etc/httpd* directory, mainly in the file */etc/httpd/httpd.conf*. This file sets up options through lists of directives and values, often mapped to filesystem directories and other criteria. Many of its options are highly specific to Mac OS X, so that Apache works "out of the box"; turning on web services with a single click in the Sharing pane (see the earlier section "Running Services Through the Sharing Pane") launches a full-featured web server on a fresh Mac OS X installation. Here are some highlights (and variances from the defaults that are in a platform-independent Apache installation):

- The `DirectoryRoot` directive defines the location of the server's default location for HTML files and other web-servable documents—in other words, what you'd see if you pointed your web browser to *http://localhost/*. Mac OS X sets this directive to */Library/WebServer/Documents/*.
- Following the usual Unix tradition, Mac OS X Apache lets a host's individual users build personal web sites in their own home folders, accessible by pointing a web browser to *http://network_address/~username*. To find your network address, go to the Sharing preferences panel, as shown in Figure 12-1. Most

* At the time of this writing, imap-2002e is the current release version and doesn't fully support Panther. However, the current development snapshot (*imap-2003.DEV.tar.Z*) does, as should any release versions after 2002e.

† Netcraft tracks the changing popularity levels of Apache and other web servers on its web site at *http://www.netcraft.com/survey/*.

Unix systems define users' personal document roots at *~username/public_html*; Mac OS X Apache sets it to *~username/Sites*.

An `Include` directive at the bottom of the file reads in several additional Apache configuration files located in */etc/httpd/users/*. One *username.conf* file exists for every user created through the Accounts pane (see the section "Managing Users Through the Accounts Pane" in Chapter 10). Each one defines Apache options and directives for serving that user's */Sites* folder over the Web, thus allowing an administrator to set different options on different users' personal web sites.

- Apache keeps two log files, *access_log* and *error_log*, in the */var/log/httpd/* directory. The *access_log* file keeps a record of the files served (graphics, web pages, etc.) and to whom the files were served by displaying the IP address of the machine that accessed the server. The *error_log* file reports any errors from people who have attempted to access a file on the web server that doesn't exist.

Apache Modules

Apache modules are code libraries that extend Apache's abilities beyond fundamental HTTP serving. Apache lets you install modules two ways: *static* modules are "baked in" to the *httpd* program at compile time, while *dynamic* modules are separate files that *httpd* can load and include into its functionality without any recompiling needed.

Mac OS X's Apache setup uses the latter of these strategies. To enable an existing but inactive module, simply locate the `LoadModule` and `AddModule` directives within */etc/httpd/httpd.conf* and remove the # characters from the start of both lines, turning the lines from comments into actual directives. To disable an active module, just insert a # at the start of both lines, commenting them out; then restart the web server.

To install new modules, place their *.so* files (compiling them first, if necessary) into the */usr/libexec/httpd/* directory, and then add new `LoadModule` and `AddModule` lines to */etc/httpd/httpd.conf*.

File Transfer Protocol (FTP)

FTP services run courtesy of the *ftpd* daemon. It allows the machine's users to remotely access the filesystem, so that they can browse directory listings and transfer files to and from the machine. Normally, it obeys the filesystem permissions just as a login shell does. However, if you would like to restrict FTP users' access to their respective home directories, simply add the users' names, one per line, to a file named *ftpchroot* and, as root, save it in */etc*.

Enabling Anonymous FTP

First, as described in Chapter 11, use NetInfo Manager to create a group named *ftp*, making sure to give it an unused GID. Next, use NetInfo Manager again to create a nonhuman user also named *ftp*, under which all-anonymous FTP activity will occur. For consistency, use the same number you specified for the *ftp* group's GID as this new account's UID, again making sure that it's not already being used by another account.

Create a home directory for *ftp*. (Be sure that *ftp*'s NetInfo directory correctly refers to this directory as its home.) Whether or not an */etc/ftpchroot* file exists, the FTP server always forbids an anonymous user from accessing anywhere in the filesystem outside the *ftp* user's Home directory.

You can now populate this directory with whatever you wish to permit anonymous users to browse and download. To make a typical FTP site, add a *pub/* folder containing all the downloadables, as well as an introductory blurb in an *ftpwelcome* file in */etc*; upon connection, the FTP server provides the contents of that file to the FTP client to display or record in the session transcript.

For security's sake, consider changing the ownership of all these files and folders to root using the *chown* command and using *chmod* to make them read-only for all users. This will prevent anonymous FTP users from uploading (and perhaps overwriting) files as well as keep the directory safe from tampering by local users. (A */pub/incoming* directory, writeable by the FTP user, is the typical spot for anonymous file uploads, if you'd like to allow that to a limited degree.)

Remote Login Services

There may come a time when you need to log into your Mac from another machine or log into another Mac (or Unix system) from your machine. For this, Mac OS X offers remote login services such as the Secure Shell, Telnet, and the remote shell.

The Secure Shell

The Secure Shell (SSH), is a protocol for using key-based encryption to allow secure communication between machines. As its name suggests, it is most commonly used for interactive sessions with shells on remote machines, so that you can use the *ssh* command as described in "Remote Logins" in Chapter 8.

Mac OS X ships with the OpenSSH (*http://www.openssh.com*) client and server software. This includes the *ssh* command, which you use to open SSH connections to other machines, and the *sshd* daemon program, which you run to allow other machines to SSH into your Mac.

As with FTP (see the earlier section "File Transfer Protocol (FTP)"), running an SSH service (the *sshd* daemon) on Mac OS X is easy: just activate the Remote Login checkbox in the Sharing pane.

Telnet

Mac OS X versions prior to 10.1.0 shipped with *telnetd*, a daemon that runs the Telnet protocol, as its default remote login server. Telnet is a decades-old method for getting a virtual terminal on a remote machine through a network. However, it's inherently insecure, because all its transmissions are *cleartext*, lacking any sort of encryption, and hence easily readable by malevolent entities monitoring the traffic that enters and leaves your network. Use of Telnet has, in recent years, fallen out of favor for Internet-based remote logins now that such tools as SSH are freely available.

If you must, you can run *telnetd* on your Mac OS X machine. You'll find it in */usr/libexec/telnetd* but won't be able to launch it directly from there. *telnetd* is one of several network services, including *ftpd* and *sshd*, controlled by the super-server process *xinetd*, which listens on the network for service requests and launches the proper daemon on-demand.* The easiest way to have *xinetd* begin passing Telnet requests to *telnetd* is to run the *service* command (a script, actually) as root:

```
sudo service telnet start
```

This command modifies the proper *xinet.d* file (*/etc/xinet.d/telnet*) to enable Telnet services and then force *xinetd* to re-read its configuration files. Once the command is performed, any incoming Telnet requests will cause *telnetd* to launch and receive that connection. To turn this off, simply run the similar command:

```
sudo service telnet stop
```

If you do enable *telnetd*, consider carefully configuring your firewall to allow Telnet connections only from other machines on the local subnetwork. Incoming Telnet traffic from the global Internet can be snooped by outside eavesdroppers, even if connections are limited to trusted machines. Logging into a machine through Telnet is tantamount to shouting your password across a crowded roomful of strangers so that your friend down the hall can hear it. Whenever possible, use *ssh* instead of *telnet*.

The Remote Shell

The *remote shell*, or RSH, is used to issue commands on another system. The *rsh* command allows you to quickly log in and execute a command on a remote host; however, like Telnet, *rsh* is insecure and has been disabled under Mac OS X. You should use SSH instead for remote access to other machines.

File Sharing Services

Mac OS X's native file-sharing method is the Apple Filing Protocol (AFP). As with related technologies such as SMB and NFS (see the section "NFS" in Chapter 10), it lets users of other computers (often, but not necessarily, other Macs) mount volumes of your local filesystem onto their own.

Both the command-line and GUI interfaces for administering AFP are very simple. To turn on AFP, activate the Personal File Sharing checkbox in the Sharing preference pane's Services tab. This simply launches the *AppleFileServer* daemon (which resides in */usr/sbin*). *AppleFileServer* takes no arguments; it makes all your machine's volumes and User folders available for mounting on other computers, as described in the section "Browsing Network File Servers" in Chapter 8. The

* See the "xinetd" section later in this chapter.

program stores its configuration information (including the location of log files, whether it allows Guest access, and so on) in the */Library/Preferences/com.apple.AppleFileServer.plist* file.

Toggling this checkbox in the Sharing pane also modifies the `AFPSERVER` line in */etc/hostconfig*, read by the startup script */System/Library /StartupItems/AppleShare/AppleShare* (see the next section).

The AFP server handles user authentication through Directory Services, in most cases referring to NetInfo for the list of volumes it's allowed to provide to the requesting user. This list, of course, varies depending on the type of account that user has on the server.

Users with no accounts can log in as Guest and are allowed only to mount the Public directories (as defined by the `sharedDir` property of each user's NetInfo record) within each home directory on the server. Once the volume is mounted, its permission system applies just as if that same user were logged into the machine and accessing the filesystem directly. Therefore, guest users can copy items from Public and add items to */Public/Drop Box*, as those items' Unix permissions dictate.

Users with Standard accounts on the server can also access the Public folders of the other user accounts, and additionally have access to their own entire home directories. Users with Admin accounts can choose to mount not only their own entire home directory but also any physical partition or mounted volume on the server.

You can specify additional share points by adding a `SharePoints` subdirectory to the */config* directory in NetInfo and for each share point creating a subdirectory to it with these properties:

Name
: Label for the NetInfo subdirectory.

afp_name
: Label to identify the share point on the network.

directory_path
: Absolute path to the local directory to be shared.

afp_shared
: Use a value of `1` to turn on sharing for the share point or `0` to turn it off.

afp_use_parent_owner
: Switches whether items added to the shared directory should inherit their owner and group properties from the parent directory (use a value of `1`) or maintain the default behavior of inheriting ownership from the user (use a value of `0`).

afp_use_parent_privs
: Switches whether items added to the shared directory should inherit their permissions from the parent directory (use a value of `1`), or maintain the default behavior of giving read/write permissions to the owner and read-only permissions to everyone else (use a value of `0`).

You can allow or disallow guest access to the share point by adjusting those permissions locally on the shared directory. Stop and restart Personal File Sharing once you've configured the share point to make it available. Note that Admin users will not see these share points listed when connecting since they already can access all directories on the server.

If you prefer the convenience of an all-in-one GUI application, the donation-ware utility SharePoints (*http://www.hornware.com/sharepoints*) makes adding share points quick and easy.

Daemon Management

Panther relies on the services of a large number of system daemons for its operation, and every network service you enable adds to the count of potential background processes. While it would be easiest to simply have all the daemons launch at startup, it's much more efficient to do this for just the handful that require it and launch the other daemons only as needed. To coordinate this complex task, Panther uses three mechanisms: *bootstrap daemons*, *StartupItems*, and *xinetd*.

Bootstrap Daemons

Introduced with Panther, the *register_mach_bootstrap_servers* tool, provides a way to have system daemons launch on demand (that is, not until they receive their first service request). In fact, this method will eventually take the place of the *StartupItems* (see the following section) as Mac OS X evolves in future releases.

This tool assembles a list of daemons by reading each file in */etc/mach_init.d/* (for system daemons to be run as root) and */etc/mach_init_per_user.d/* (for user daemons to be run under normal user accounts). It then registers each daemon in the list and the service it provides with the *mach_init* daemon, itself launched by the Mach kernel early in the startup.

Once a daemon is registered, *mach_init* waits for requests from other processes for the services the daemon provides, launching (or relaunching) the daemon only when it detects a request. Such daemons, available to the system so early in the startup process, are known as *bootstrap daemons*. For now, only about a dozen system daemons are handled this way, none of which are network services.

StartupItems

The second mechanism, though now legacy, is still responsible for starting many system and network daemons. During system startup, the *SystemStarter* application scans and runs special scripts kept in */Library/StartupItems/*. If you've installed a daemon yourself and wish to have it launch at startup and be owned by the root user (so that it is running when the first user logs in, and continues to run until the machine is shut down or it's explicitly killed), add another item to this collection of startup items or copy or modify an existing one, if applicable. (More startup scripts are in */System/Library/StartupItems/*, but, like everything else in the */System/* folder, are not meant to be messed with.)

Each object under *StartupItems* is a folder named after its function. Inside it are two important files: a parameter list of options in *StartupParameters.plist* (see the later section "StartupParameters.plist") and the script itself, which must have the same name as the folder.

Example 12-1 shows the contents of the Postfix startup item (*/System/Library/StartupItems/Postfix /Postfix*).

Example 12-1. The Postfix startup item

```
❶ #!/bin/sh
❷ . /etc/rc.common
❹ StartService ()
  {
      if [ "${MAILSERVER:=-NO-}" = "-YES-" ]; then
          ConsoleMessage "Starting mail services"
          /usr/sbin/postfix start
     elif [ "${MAILSERVER:=-NO-}" = "-AUTOMATIC-" ]; then
          /usr/sbin/postfix-watch
      fi
  }

❺ StopService ()
  {
      ConsoleMessage "Stopping Postfix mail services"
      /usr/sbin/postfix stop
      killall -1 postfix-watch 2> /dev/null
  }

❻ RestartService ()
  {
      if [ "${MAILSERVER:=-NO-}" = "-YES-" ]; then
          ConsoleMessage "Reloading Postfix configuration"
          /usr/sbin/postfix reload
      else
          StopService
      fi
  }

❸ RunService "$1"
```

Here's what it does, in order:

❶ The "shebang" line (`#!/bin/sh`) marks this file as a shell script.

❷ It uses the shell's dot command (`.`) to execute the shell script at */etc/rc.common*. This script sets up many environment variables useful to startup scripts.

❸ The script's next command actually comes with this last line, which calls one of the three functions* found in the preceding lines. The `RunService` command calls a function (defined by *rc.common*) that tells the script which of its own three functions to call next, based on the argument provided with this script's execution command. Possible arguments are `start`, `stop`, or `restart`.

❹ If the argument is `start`, the script then knows to execute its `StartService ( )` function, which determines what to do next based on what's in the `MAILSERVER` environment variable (set by *rc.common*, after it reads the */etc/hostconfig* file). If its value is `-YES-`, it dumps a status message to the console (which passes it along to the startup screen) and executes the `postfix start` command. If instead the value is `-AUTOMATIC-`, a different message is displayed, and the `postfix-watch` command is executed. In either case, Postfix is now operable on the machine.

❺ If the argument is `stop`, the script executes its `StopService ( )` function, which dumps a status message, stops Postfix and sends a kill signal to *postfix-watch*, which will die if running.

❻ If the argument is `restart`, the script executes its `RestartService ( )` function. If `MAILSERVER`'s value is -YES-, a status message displays, and Postfix is told to re-read its configuration. Otherwise, the `StopService` function is executed.

Manually running StartupItems

Much like their counterparts, the */etc/rc.init* scripts found on Linux and BSD systems, *StartupItems* can also be run on the command line. When available, it's generally a better idea to use a daemon's *StartupItems* rather than invoke it directly (i.e., by using */System/Library/StartupItems/Postfix/Postfix* instead of directly calling */usr/sbin/postfix*) because the script is "safer"; it ensures that the machine's software and network environment is set up correctly for the daemon's use.

Typically, you must run *StartupItems* as *root* (or under the auspices of the *sudo* command), and, as with the Postfix *StartupItem*, provide one of three standard arguments:

start
: Launch the service this *StartupItem* represents. It usually fails if it's already running.

stop
: Kill this service.

restart
: Equivalent to `stop`-ing and then `start`-ing the service; often it actually sends a HUP (hang-up) signal to the service's process. This causes it to reread its

* A *function* is a chunk of code, defined here within curly braces, that works like a script-within-a-script. Functions are read and stored in memory as the script is executed, but aren't themselves executed unless called by name elsewhere in the same script or from within a different script.

configuration files and act appropriately, allowing it to reconfigure itself without suffering any downtime.

The /etc/hostconfig file

Many *StartupItems* (like the one for Postfix) must make a choice about whether they're supposed to perform their stated function. If you don't want your machine to run as a web server, for example, then you won't want the Apache startup script to launch the *httpd* daemon. You could modify or remove the */System/Library/StartupItems/Apache* folder, but that's a messy solution that would probably lead to confusion if you (or, worse, another administrator on the machine) want to activate Apache later on.

A better solution, and the one that Mac OS X intends you to use, involves modifying the */etc/hostconfig* file. This file, which is nothing more than a newline-separated list of key/value pairs (as well as a few comments), is loaded by */etc/rc.common*, a shell script which itself is run as an initial step by most startup scripts. This means that all the variables it sets become accessible to scripts that load *rc.common*, such as the Apache startup item. Thus, if you simply set *hostconfig*'s `WEBSERVER` key to `-NO-`, the Apache startup script deduces that you don't want web services activated on startup and quietly exits rather than launch the *httpd* daemon. (This is, in fact, exactly what happens when you deactivate the Sharing preference pane's Personal Web Sharing checkbox. Many other System Preferences controls can also modif lines in */etc/hostconfig*.

Network Services

StartupParameters.plist

The *StartupParameters.plist* file (an example of a property list XML file, detailed in Chapter 25) can contain the following keys:

Description
: A brief description of this startup item's function, such as "Apache web server" or "Postfix mail server."

Provides
: A list of keywords that name the services this startup item provides, when run.

Requires
: A list of keywords that name the services that must already be running before this startup item can be launched.

Uses
: A list of keywords that names the services this startup item could use, but doesn't absolutely require.

Messages
: A dictionary of status messages that get sent to the console (and the startup screen, if it's visible) when the startup item starts or stops.

OrderPreference

For cases in which the Requires and Uses keys specify the same startup order for multiple items, this key specifies in a relative way when the startup item should launch. Possible values are `First`, `Early`, `None`, `Late`, and `Last`.

The *SystemStarter* program determines the order in which to run all the system's startup items by scanning their *StartupParameters.plist* files and comparing the values of their `Provides`, `Requires`, `Uses`, and `OrderPreference` keys. It then determines which items will provide other items' `Required` service; those run first, so that later items' prerequisites will be met.

xinetd

xinetd, the extended Internet services daemon, is responsible for launching several of Mac OS X's Internet and other IP-based daemons, including *sshd* (for secure shell services), *ftpd* (for FTP services), and *smbd* (for Windows filesharing and printing services). As you can see by looking at the *IPServices* startup script, *xinetd* itself is actually one of the daemons launched by *SystemStarter*.

Also called a *super-server*, *xinetd* launches daemons on-demand, much like *mach_init*. Super-servers—including *xinetd* or its simpler predecessor, *inetd*—are found on most other Unix-like platforms. *xinetd* determines which daemons it's responsible for by reading the files, each named for a service, in */etc/xinetd.d/*. Each file defines a service and series of attributes, including `disable`, which defines whether the service is disabled or not, and `server`, which specifies the daemon to launch when that service is enabled and requested.

Enabling a *xinetd* service typically means setting that service's `disable` attribute to `no` and sending *xinetd* a *kill –HUP* signal so it will reload its configuration files. This can of course be done manually with a text editor, but two easier methods exist that make that rarely necessary. First, for the following items the Sharing preference pane does all you need: Windows Sharing, Remote Login, FTP Access, and Remote Apple Events, since they are all controlled by *xinetd*.

For any other items in */etc/xinetd.d/*, you can use the *service* command, as shown previously in the *telnet* section. To stop or start a service, the command must be run as *root* and takes two arguments: the service name and an action, either `start` or `stop`. To list all *xinetd*-controlled items, run `service --list` as any user.

13 Security Basics

Thanks to the inherent security of its Unix foundation and a secure-by-default configuration, Panther doesn't give its users much to worry about at first boot-up. However, Panther does include several features that help keep out intruders as you accumulate data and customize the default configuration.

Potential threats exist to many elements of an operating system, and, in most cases, Panther's security features address them to a degree greatly surpassing what's required for a typical user. With a bit of additional tightening, Panther can operate with a level of security acceptable for even much more sensitive environments.

General Security

Panther has several general security features that contribute to the protection of the entire system.

Unix Features

As was covered in Chapter 7, Mac OS X's Unix foundation provides for the basic permissions model that keeps system and user files and processes separate and protected. But equally important for security is Panther's open source roots, in the form of Darwin, which allows anyone to scour the source code for potential vulnerabilities and provide (or allow Apple to provide) fixes quickly. Darwin's source code, corresponding with the open source core that ships with Panther, is available freely through *http://developer.apple.com/darwin*. Apple generally makes available new Darwin versions not long after they've been released as part of each new Mac OS X version.

Also, because Mac OS X can run much of the same software available to other Unix platforms, a large amount of additional security-related software is available for it as well. See Chapter 27 to learn more about acquiring and installing Unix software.

Default Security

Panther is arguably the most secure of any operating system upon initial boot-up. This is mostly due to its conservative default system configuration, which ensures that your Mac will be safe from most security threats without additional configuration on your part. Here are a few things that Mac OS X Panther does by default to help make your Mac secure:

Disabled root account
: Typically, an intruder will attempt to access the root account to obtain complete system control, but as long as the root account stays disabled, the attempts will fail. In fact, Panther provides enough alternatives to the legitimate use of the root account that enabling it is usually not necessary even for system administrators. For example, users can instead authenticate in the Finder to access most protected areas or use *sudo* at the command line to run commands requiring root privileges.

Few open communication ports
: A port scan of a new Panther system will find no open TCP ports at all and only two open UDP ports. This makes for a system so secure, in fact, that turning on the firewall at this point adds no further protection (because there are no vulnerable ports that need blocking).

  The two open ports are UDP 123 used by *ntpd* (the Network Time Protocol Daemon), and 5353, used by *mDNSResponder*, which is part of Rendezvous. Though there are no known vulnerabilities to either daemon, you can turn off the first by unchecking "Set Date & Time automatically" in the Date & Time preferences panel. To keep *mDNSResponder* from launching at startup and eliminate most of Rendezvous' functionality, use the *chmod* command to turn off the executable bit of its StartupItems script, */System/Library/StartupItems/mDNSResponder/mDNSResponder*, and then restart your Mac.

No running network services
: With no ports open, then, you'll also find that Panther has none of its network services turned on by default. Furthermore, only administrators can turn on these services, which include all those listed in the Sharing preferences pane.

Software Update

Software Update helps ensure that the latest security updates, as well as the regular OS and application updates, are applied promptly. These updates, typically provided by Apple within days of a vulnerability announcement, can address one or several security issues at a time, involving both Apple software as well any of the included Unix software, such as OpenSSH or Apache. A list of all Mac OS X security updates is kept at *http://www.info.apple.com/usen/security/security_updates.html*.

Installing system software over the Internet has its own security implications, so the Software Update process uses digital signatures to protect against possible deception on the network. Each update package on Apple's Software server contains a digital signature, which when verified by your Software Update client application, guarantees that the source of the update package is indeed Apple Computer and that the package's data hasn't been modified.

Authentication

These authentication-related security features provide additional protection for your computer while still allowing easy and secure verification for authorized users.

Long Passwords

Panther supports account passwords of virtually unlimited length. In practice, however, you shouldn't set a password that's longer than you're willing to type (most authentication windows don't accept pasted text). Also, command-line utilities can have password length limits of their own. For example, the *sudo* utility doesn't accept passwords longer than 256 characters.

Keychain Access

The Keychain Access application (*/Applications/Utilities*) has other security-related features in addition to its primary function as a repository for your passwords.

Menu extra

Keychain Access has its own menu extra, shown in Figure 13-1, which is activated by selecting View→Show Status. From the Keychain menu extra, you can lock and unlock your keychains as well as open Keychain Access and the Security preferences pane.

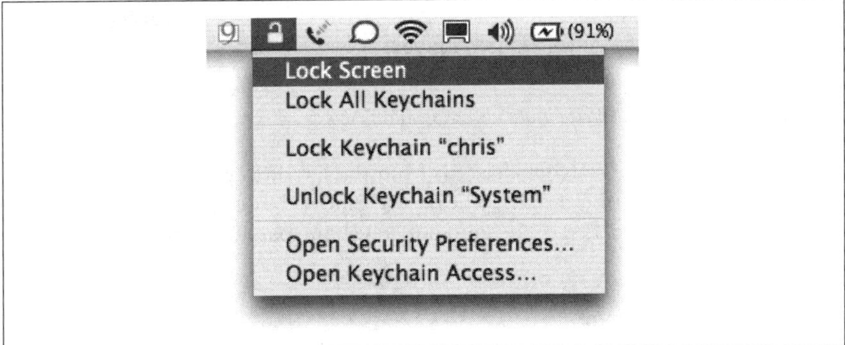

Figure 13-1. The Keychain menu extra

Additionally, by selecting the Lock Screen option from the Keychain menu extra, you can immediately activate a password-protected screensaver. With this option selected, a password is required to disengage the screensaver, even if you haven't selected to always use one in the Security preferences pane (see the "Screen Locking" section of this chapter).

Secure Notes

You can store any text you would like to keep private in a Secure Note. From Keychain Access's File menu, select New Secure Note Item, name the note and add whatever data you want encrypted and password-protected (Figure 13-2). This is a convenient way to store passwords for applications or systems that don't support the keychain, as well as credit-card numbers and PINs.

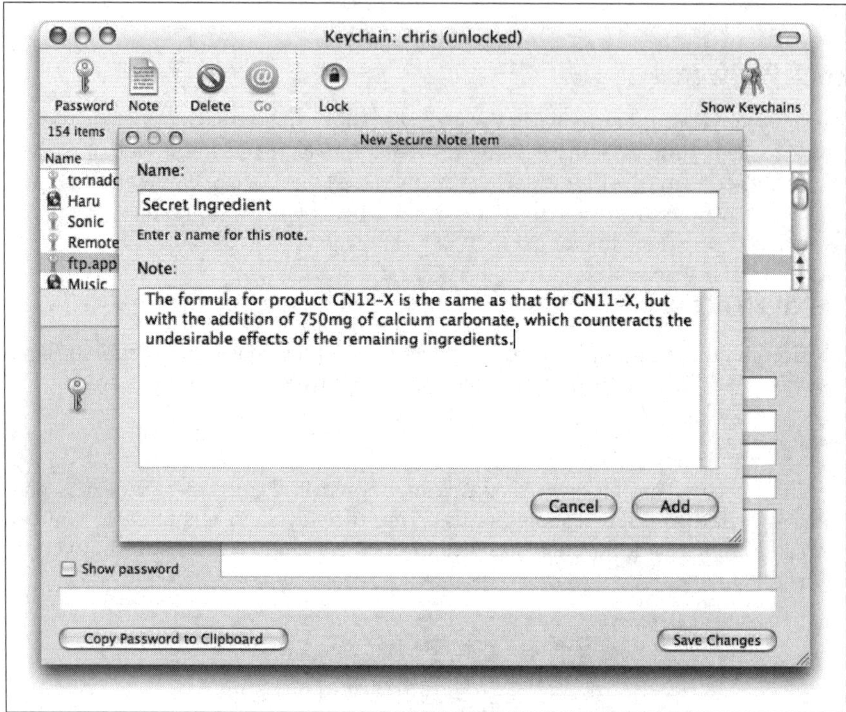

Figure 13-2. Creating a Secure Note with Keychain Access

To access a saved Secure Note, select it from the list of Keychain items, and then from the item's Attributes tab, check the Show Note checkbox. You'll be prompted at least the first time for your keychain password before the text is displayed.

Password Strength Indicator

The keychain is only as secure as the password you set for it, so receiving feedback when choosing a password can help you optimize security greatly. To view this feedback, choose to change your Keychain password from the Edit menu. Click the Info button (the one with the small "i") at the bottom left of the Change

Keychain Password window, and the Password Assistant window will appear, as shown in Figure 13-3.

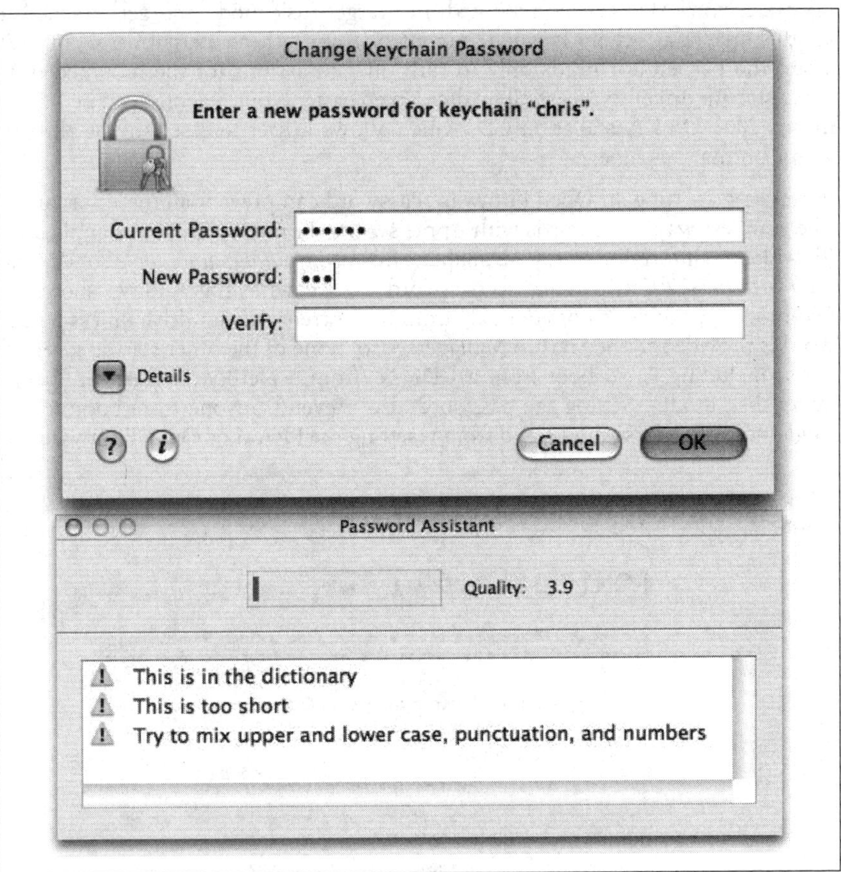

Figure 13-3. Checking password security with the Password Strength Indicator

The Password Assistant's Password Strength Indicator judges your password by several criteria, including length, character variety, and whether it exists in its dictionary (or is close to a word that does), and it alerts you to each issue that applies. A general rating also appears, both as a colored bar gauge running from red to yellow to green (from least to most secure) and as a numerical Quality rating.

Open Firmware Password

Even though Panther's out-of-the-box security protects it well from network attack and casual entry attempts from the keyboard, there are still ways a determined intruder can access your data as long as the computer is physically accessible. For example, someone can simply attach an external FireWire drive and, using the Startup Manager by pressing option during startup, select to boot from it.

Likewise, your Mac can be rebooted into target disk mode and get attached to another machine, where it would mount like any other external drive. In both cases, the perpetrator needs only to turn off permissions for the mounted drive (your startup drive) to access all its data. Even easier, your machine can be booted from a Mac OS X installation CD, which allows a user to reset any or all passwords on that machine.

Fortunately, setting an Open Firmware Password can prevent all these scenarios.* The simplest way to do this is with Apple's Open Firmware Password application (download information is available from *http://docs.info.apple.com/article.html?artnum=120095*). Once a password is set with this utility, shown in Figure 13-4, booting is possible only from the current startup drive unless a password is provided to the Startup Manager. Also, none of the other startup keys will work, including C (to boot from a CD), N (from a NetBoot server), or T (into target disk mode). Setting the password also prevents anyone from booting into single-user or verbose mode, and from resetting the PRAM or Open Firmware.

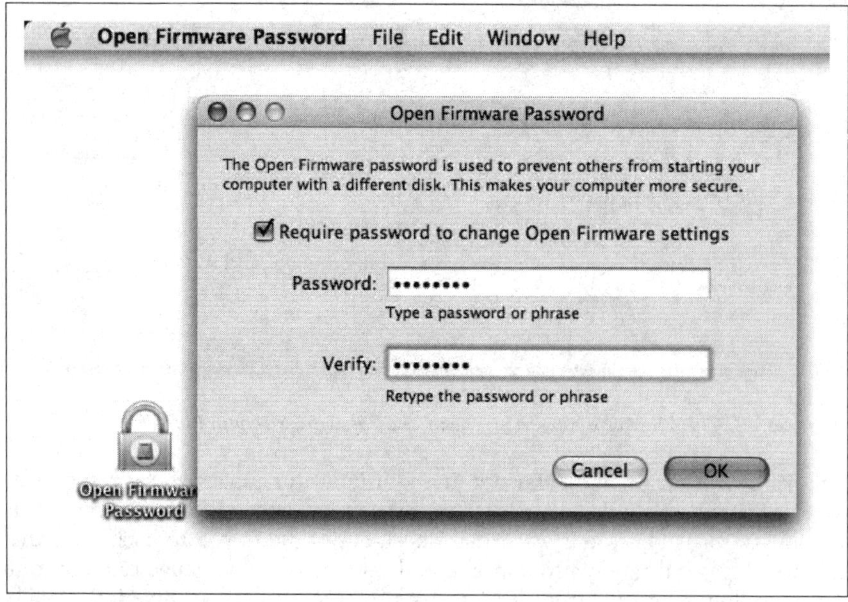

Figure 13-4. Setting the Open Firmware password

For even greater protection, you can configure Open Firmware to not boot the machine without proper authentication; doing so requires several steps:

* This isn't supported by all Macintosh models that can run Panther, for example, tray-loading iMacs or Blue & White G3s. See the article at *http://docs.info.apple.com/article.html/artnum=106482* for more information.

1. Boot your Mac into Open Firmware using the Option-⌘-O-F keyboard shortcut during startup. If you've not yet set an Open Firmware password, you can do so at the Open Firmware prompt by typing `password` and entering a password twice when prompted.
2. Change the value of Open Firmware's *security-mode* variable, which can hold one of three values: `none` (every machine's default value), `command` (the value used by the Open Firmware Password application), or `full`.
3. To prevent booting without a password, set the value to `full` with this command: `security-mode full`.
4. Enter the command `reset-all`, which restarts the computer.

Subsequent startups, then, will only go as far as the open firmware screen until you first press Enter and then type the password when prompted. At the next prompt, enter the `mac-boot` command, and the Mac will continue its startup normally.

To return the machine to its default boot behavior, set Open Firmware's *security-mode* variable back to `none`. If you forget the password and are unable to access Open Firmware, your only resort is to reset Open Firmware by changing the amount of installed memory (either add or remove a memory module), and then resetting the PRAM.

Kerberos and Single Sign-on

Kerberos is a network authentication protocol developed by MIT to allow applications to identify users over open and insecure networks. It's used by governments, large corporations, and higher education. Kerberos is also the native authentication protocol of Active Directory. Since Jaguar, Apple has been moving aggressively to support Kerberos in both Mac OS X Server and Mac OS X, as well as in all the Mac OS X password-using applications, such as Mail, FTP, SSH, and Apple File Sharing. The reason Apple is making this push is to enable single sign-on.

Single sign-on means that after a user enters a name and password in the login window, every application on the system that needs to authenticate itself for a network service can do so automatically without requiring the user to enter a different username and password.

For users of Mac OS X, Kerberos is either configured for your network and just works out of the box, or there is a bit of configuration work to be accomplished. If your network falls into the second category, you need to get some information from your system administrator.

Auto Login

Allowing automatic login at startup is obviously a great security risk, especially if you can't control physical access to the computer. Even a home desktop machine can become portable during a burglary, and allowing auto login makes all your data easily available to the thieves. Because this is Panther's default setting, it's best disabled to ensure even the minimum of protection from unwanted access.

To do so, go to the Security preferences pane, and check the Disable automatic login checkbox.

Filesystem Security

Even with protections in place preventing unauthorized account access, your Mac is still prone to intrusion as long as there's no filesystem protection in place.

FileVault

Your entire filesystem can become accessible to anyone able to mount it as an external drive on a second system. This can occur, for example, if your Mac is put into target disk mode and mounted, or more drastically, if your hard drive is removed and placed in another machine. One way to keep at least your home directory safe from intrusion, even in these cases, is to use FileVault, as discussed in Chapter 4.

FileVault also protects your Home directory from intrusion by other users with admin accounts on the same Mac as yours, who could otherwise use *su* or *sudo* to gain access to any file. As long as you're not logged in, your home directory contents stay encrypted and inaccessible to anyone without your account password or the master password. While a FileVault protected account is logged in, however, its home directory resides unencrypted on the drive, subject to access by anyone with an admin account.

Enabling FileVault does incur some risk, however, because the entire Home directory (when not in use) exists as a single encrypted image file on the hard drive. If that single file becomes corrupted, that image and all the files within can be lost. For this reason, you might want to keep a separate account, used for only sensitive work, with FileVault enabled. Doing so results in a smaller image file that's less prone to corruption and more easily backed up.

Encrypted Images

As an alternative to having FileVault encrypt your entire Home directory, you can instead protect a select group of files by storing them in an encrypted image of your own making. You can do this using either the Disk Utility application or the *hdiutil* command-line utility. Both tools allow you to make sparse image files, which grow as data is added. Normal images, on the other hand, will always use up the amount of space on disk equal to their prespecified capacity.

To create an encrypted disk image, select Images→New→Blank Image from Disk Utility's menus. Name the image file, and specify a save location. Specify in the Size pop-up menu the maximum size to which you would like the image to grow. Select AES-128 from the Encryption pop-up menu and sparse disk image from the Format pop-up, as shown in Figure 13-5. Click OK, and enter a password as prompted. Disk Utility then creates and mounts the image file.

You can create the same image file from the Terminal with the following command:

```
chris$ hdiutil create -type SPARSE  -encryption  -size 1g -fs HFS+ TopSecret
```

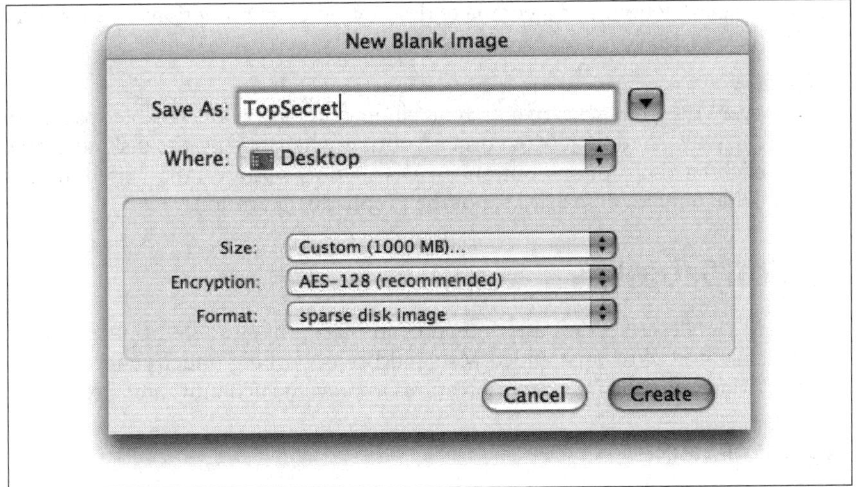

Figure 13-5. Creating an encrypted disk image with Disk Utility

This command creates an encrypted disk image file, named *TopSecret.sparseimage*. Once mounted, the disk image expands to hold up to a gigabyte of data. For more on the *hdiutil* command, see its entry in Chapter 28.

Once you mount an encrypted disk image, you can add data to it like any other volume. When unmounted, however, the disk image stores its data in an encrypted form, accessible only if you can give the appropriate password.

Security

Secure Deletions

Whether you use the Finder's Trash or the *rm* command to delete a file, the only data that is directly changed on the drive is the entry in the filesystem's directory that points to that file; the file's data still remains on the drive. This means that someone with the right tools can still read bits and pieces of those files, if not resurrect the file in its entirety.

Preventing this exposure, then, means overwriting with other data those drive blocks that hold the residual data, ideally not just once, but several times. Panther provides three ways to do this:

Secure Empty Trash
: Choosing this command from the Finder's application menu ensures that all file data in the Trash is overwritten seven times with a mix of specified and random data. This process is compliant with Department of Defense security specifications.

srm
: This Unix utility is the force behind the Finder's Secure Empty Trash feature, which executes *srm* using its *–m* flag. For faster, but less secure deletions, you can run *srm* in the Terminal with its *–s* flag, which overwrites with just one pass. For maximum security, specify neither *–s* nor *–m*, and *srm* will perform

a 35-pass deletion. For a complete description of *srm*'s options, see its entry in Chapter 28.

Disk Utility
: To overwrite all blocks on a drive, including all used and available space, use the "8 Way Random Write Format" option when erasing the disk, available by clicking the Options button on Disk Utility's Erase tab. This option is available only for entire disks, not their individual partitions.

Physical Security

Even with the described security measures in place, they can be of little value if anyone can sit at your unattended Mac and begin working under your logged-in account. Mac OS X includes several features to prevent such unwanted access.

Log Out on Idle

The Security Preferences pane contains a checkbox that enables automatic logout after a specified period of inactivity, from 5 minutes to 16 hours. The behavior of this logout is identical to that of a manual logout, prompting you to save any unsaved documents (the logout stops if you don't answer the prompt).

Screen Locking

Also on the Security Preferences pane is a checkbox to enable screen-locking upon wake from sleep or the screensaver. When enabled, this feature presents an authentication dialog box that prevents display of the desktop until you supply the username and password of any admin user. The dialog box also contains a Switch User button that, when clicked, presents the Login window, allowing other users to log in without disturbing the locked-out account.

Scripting and Development

Mac OS X is a developer's dream come true. On the Unix side, you have access to all the standard programming languages you'd expect to find, such as C/C++, Java, Perl, Python, and Ruby. Mac developers who have installed Apple's Xcode Tools have access to utilities such as Xcode and Interface Builder for building native applications for their Mac, based on Carbon, Cocoa, and even AppleScript.

The chapters in this part include:

- Chapter 14, *AppleScript*
- Chapter 15, *Xcode Tools*
- Chapter 16, *Java on Mac OS X*
- Chapter 17, *CVS*

14
AppleScript

By *scripting*, we mean writing programs that act as "glue"; they pass information between other existing applications to suit some purpose or act as macros, letting a user execute several commands in some program (or across several programs) with a single gesture. In this terminology, scripts are different from full-on applications because they lack a user interface; they just do their job and exit.

The highest-level scripting language on Mac OS X is AppleScript, initially developed by Apple in the early 1990s. AppleScripts enjoy a special dispensation on the Mac because of their native handling of Apple Events, which are simply messages Mac applications pass to one another. The majority of this chapter covers AppleScript, as well as AppleScript Studio, which allows you to use Xcode and Interface Builder to build AppleScript-based GUI applications for Mac OS X.

The Script Menu Extra

Apple's Script menu extra (see Figure 14-1) offers perhaps the most convenient way to run scripts, both of the AppleScript and shell script variety. It doesn't appear in your menu bar by default, but installing it is very easy: just double-click on the *Install Script Menu* program, found in */Applications/AppleScript*. The Script menu extra pops into your menu bar and remains there until you either manually remove it (by command-dragging it off of the menu bar) or run the *Remove Script Menu* program.

This menu extra gets its contents from the */Library/Scripts* folder. As with every other Library-based resource, you add your personal scripts to *~/Library/Scripts*, and administrators can add scripts for all the machine's users to share under */Library/Scripts*.

A new Mac OS X installation actually comes with quite a few scripts already installed into */Library/Scripts*, organized into categorical folders that the script menu extra handles hierarchically. (The folder found at */Applications/AppleScript/*

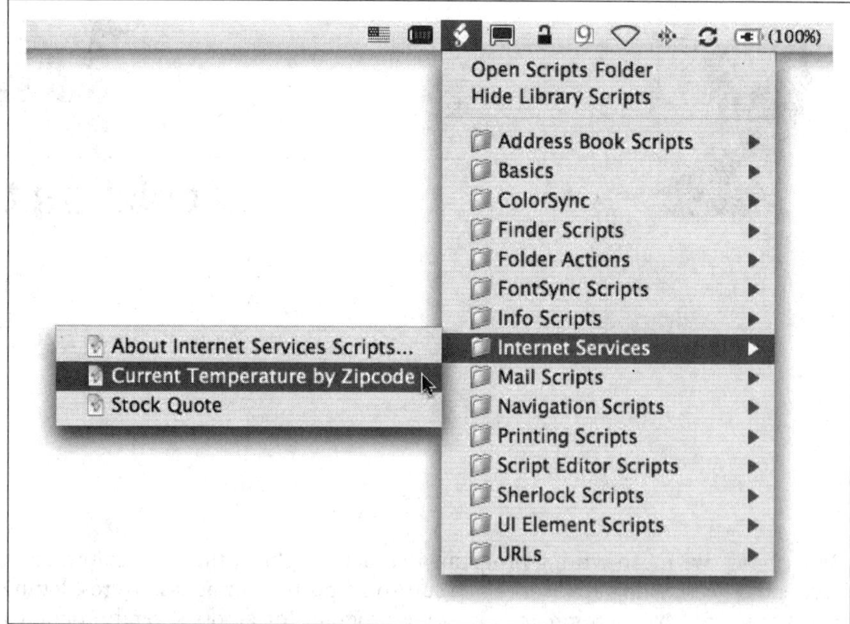

Figure 14-1. The Script menu extra

Example Scripts is actually a symbolic link to this folder.) They are all sample AppleScripts meant to demonstrate some feature of that language; you're free to try running a few (none of them do anything permanent or potentially embarrassing) as well as open any up in Script Editor to view the source code and discover how they work. (In particular, check out the Internet Services scripts, which use SOAP to grab information through web services.)

While all the preinstalled examples are AppleScripts, you can add any kind of interpreted-language program, including Perl programs and shell scripts (as shown in Figure 14-1), into Script menu extra items, just by copying them into a */Library/Scripts* folder, and turning on their executable permission bits (most easily accomplished through the Terminal command *chmod +x `filename`*). When selected from the menu extra, these scripts act as if they were invoked on the command line with no arguments.

Programming AppleScript

AppleScript is a relatively simple programming language with a forté for gluing Macintosh applications together. While you can use it to a limited extent as a general programming language, its real power comes from its native ability to sling Apple Events around, letting even inexperienced programmers create inter-application scripts, as well as programs that drive a single application through a certain multistep task.

About Apple Events

An Apple Event is simply a message that one application running on a Mac OS X system sends to another (or itself), running either on the same computer or on another Macintosh via a network connection. (Technically, the recipient application can even be a program running in a non-Mac OS X environment, if it happens to answer to the Apple Events messaging protocol, but this sort of cross-platform messaging is more often handled by SOAP or XML-RPC.)

On Mac OS X, Apple Events are implemented through Mach kernel messaging, a feature of the operating system's lowest levels. However, for maximum compatibility and maintainability, Apple recommends that developers prefer Apple Events for their software's interapplication functionality. This isn't something you need to think about while writing AppleScripts (which speak strictly in Apple Events), but it is something to keep in mind when writing more sophisticated applications. See "Scripting the Terminal," later in this chapter.

Apple Events don't offer a way to *broadcast* information to other applications, which would let any interested program pick up on its information. Instead, they are always targeted events, with a specific destination application in mind.

To use broadcasting in Cocoa applications, go through the `NSDistributedNotifcationCenter` class; in Carbon code, go through the CoreFoundation's `CFNotificationCenter` class (see "Built-in Documentation" in Chapter 15).

Most useful AppleScripts compile into a list of Apple Event directives; just about every statement in a `tell` block translates into an Apple Event.

The Five-Minute Guide to AppleScript

While AppleScript is sophisticated enough to warrant books unto itself, it is also simple enough to allow you to quickly create programs just by knowing a few tricks and then blundering around from there. For example, if you want to create an AppleScript for mounting your iDisk, you can use the following:

```
tell application "Finder"
    mount volume "http://idisk.mac.com/memberName"
end tell
```

In this script, substitute your .Mac member name for ***`memberName`***. The first time the script is run, you'll be asked to authenticate with your .Mac membership's password (which you can opt to add to your Keychain). Once authenticated, the script mounts your iDisk to your Desktop. It's that easy.

AppleScript uses simple object-oriented notation to describe its environment. Scriptable applications and the things you can manipulate within them are objects (a.k.a. "nouns"); these objects define methods ("verbs") that causes them to perform various actions. For example, just about every scriptable application's AppleScript object recognizes the verb "quit," which, when issued to it by an

Apple Event, causes it to react as if a user had selected the Quit option from an application menu.

The language also includes a small set of built-in keywords to drive these objects around. One of AppleScript's most important keywords is `tell`, which turns a program's focus to a certain object for the length of a code block. Most often, this object is an application that the AppleScript script wishes to control. For example, a block of code that fires Apple Events at the Mail application might look like this:

```
tell application "Mail"
  activate -- brings the application (Mail, in this case) to the front
  (* Other commands that would become Apple Events sent to Mail go here *)
end tell
```

To learn what Apple Event–producing statements you can feed an application while a `tell` block is aimed at it, look at that application's scripting dictionary. Either drag its application icon onto the Script Editor's Finder icon, or choose the application's name from a list after selecting File→Open Dictionary (Shift-⌘-O) in Script Editor. You'll see a window like that shown in Figure 14-2.

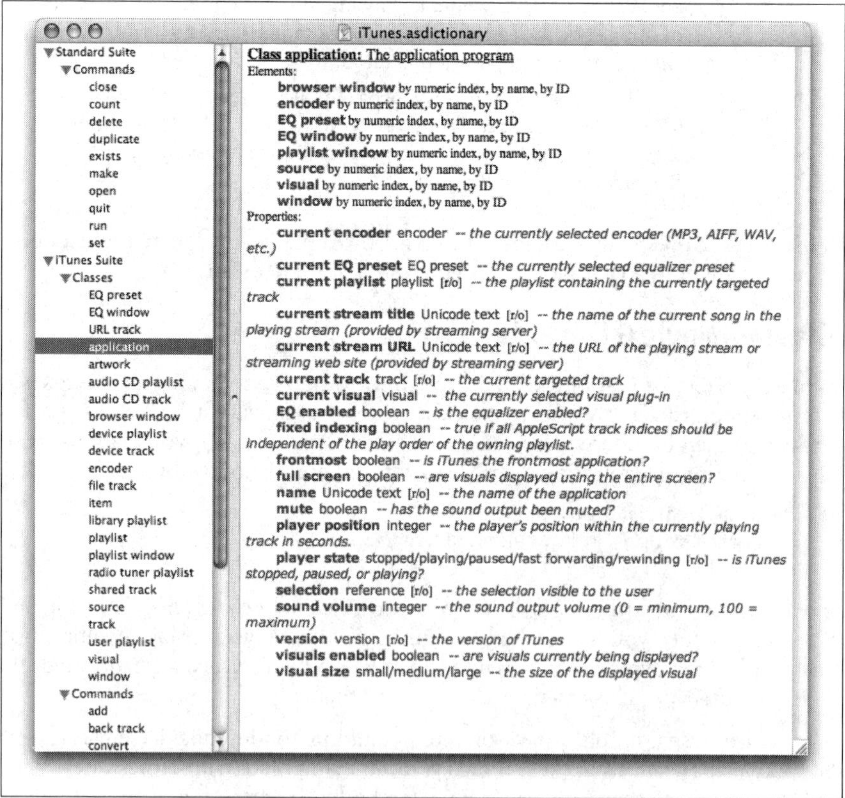

Figure 14-2. iTunes' Dictionary, seen through Script Editor

The list of words and phrases in its left frame shows all the keywords that this application's AppleScript object recognizes: verbs (methods) are in plaintext, and nouns (objects) are in italics. Click on any word to see the dictionary's documentation about its purpose and use, including syntax and return values (for verbs), and available elements and properties (for nouns).

Once you get a feel for AppleScript's syntax and available data types, know how to use `tell`, and can comfortably navigate applications' dictionaries, you're ready to start scripting. For example, let's write a little glue script between iTunes and Mail. The following AppleScript fetches the current track from iTunes and the content of a signature called "Musical Template" from Mail. It then assigns the combination of the two to the signature "Musical," as in the following example:

```
set theTrack to "" -- Declare variable here, to give it global scope
tell application "iTunes"
  set theTrack to current track
end tell

tell application "Mail"
  set theSig to the content of signature "Musical Template"
  set theSig to theSig & (theTrack's name)
  set the content of signature "Musical" to theSig
end tell
```

You can learn about the iTunes `current track` method and the `name` property of the resulting object from iTunes' scripting dictionary; likewise with Mail's `signature` method, with its `content` property.

Of course, the program assumes, perhaps wrongly, that you've set up "Musical" and "Musical Template" signatures already. By modifying Mail's `tell` block and making simple use of AppleScript's built-in *display dialog* function, you can make the script a little more polite:

```
tell application "Mail"
  set requiredSignatures to {"Musical", "Musical Template"}
  repeat with theSignature in requiredSignatures
    if not (exists signature (theSignature as string)) then
      display dialog "Missing signature: " & theSignature
      return
    end if
  end repeat
  set theSig to the content of signature "Musical Template"
  set theSig to theSig & (theTrack's name)
  set the content of signature "Musical" to theSig
end tell
```

Now if either of the script's required signatures fail to exist, Mail will complain with a minimal dialog box, and then the script quietly exits without having any effect. Of course, an even *better* solution creates those signatures if they don't exist already. You might also not rely on a signature-based template and instead place it in a file, which you can access by `tell`ing Finder. You get the idea.

AppleScript syntax summary

Since most of AppleScript's functionality involves controlling objects defined by other applications, its own syntax is fairly small and simple, containing only a handful of keywords and few built-in functions. Tables 14-1 and 14-2 contain its fundamentals.

Table 14-1. AppleScript syntax

Keyword(s)	Purpose	Example
`set`	Value assignment	`set myVar to 4` `set theItem to the first item`
`copy`	Value duplication (objects in the value are duplicated rather than referenced)	`copy myVar to myOtherVar`

The keywords in Table 14-2 can be used in either block style or on one line. For example, a complicated AppleScript `if` structure looks like this:

```
if condition
  (* Statements to execute if the condition is true *)
else
  (* Statements to execute if the condition is false *)
end if
```

A simple `if` statement, however, can fit on one line:

```
if condition then true-condition-statement else false-condition-statement
```

Note that the block-ending `end if` statement becomes unnecessary with this one-line syntax.

Table 14-2. AppleScript flow control keywords

Keyword(s)	Purpose	Example

`if` *`condition`* `[then]` *`true-condition-statements`* `[else` *`false-condition-statements`*`] end if`	Conditionally run statement block. The `else` statement block is optional.	`if my first item exists`
		` return my first item`
		`else`
		`  display dialog "I don't have any items."`
		`end if`

Repeat with *`variable`* in *`list`*	Looping construct. On each iteration, *`variable`* is set to the next value of *`list`*.	`-- tell Mail to synchronize all IMAP accounts`
		`tell application "Mail"`
		`  repeat with theAccount in accounts`
		`if theAccount's account type is imap`
		`  synchronize theAccount`
		`  -- No "else" is needed here;`
		`  -- we ignore other account types.`
		`    end if`
		`  end repeat`
		`end tell`

`try` *`statements`* `[on error` *`statements`*`] end try`	Trap errors, and (optionally) run statements if an error occurs.	`try`
		` set myPath to theDocument's path`
		`on error`
		` display dialog "Uh oh, I couldn't get the path of theDocument."`
		`  return`
		`end try`

And there you have a good idea of AppleScript's fundamentals, without even getting into defining functions or calling other scripts and more advanced magic.

Extending AppleScript

AppleScript is a very extensible language: besides letting applications extend it by defining their own scripting dictionaries, it also recognizes bundles of C or C++ code known as *OSA Extensions*, or, more commonly, *osaxen* (the plural form of *osax*). These software modules extend AppleScript's functionality by defining new functions, which you can invoke at any point.

osaxen take the form of binary files with *.osax* filename extensions. To install an *osax* file, simply add it to an appropriate */Library/ScriptingAdditions* folder. The commands that the *osax* defines become available to users on the machine or network as per the usual Library folder rules (described in the "The Library folder" section in Chapter 7).

For example, the *XML Tools.osax* file available from Late Night Software Ltd. (*http://www.latenightsw.com/freeware/XMLTools2/index.html*), when installed, makes two new functions available: `parse XML`, which turns a string of XML into an AppleScript record structure, and `generate XML`, which performs the opposite transformation.

Online AppleScript and *osaxen* resources include *osaxen.com*, a web site run by MacScripter.net, which hosts hundreds of Mac OS X–compatible *osaxen* packages, and Late Night Software Ltd. (at *http://www.latenightsw.com*), which is home of lots of interesting *osaxen* and other OSA resources.

Script Editor

Apple's Script Editor offers a somewhat atavistic way to create and edit AppleScripts. Script Editor 2 (*/Applications/AppleScript*), shown in Figure 14-3, is the easiest way to write, compile, and run AppleScripts; and applies syntax highlighting when you compile your script.

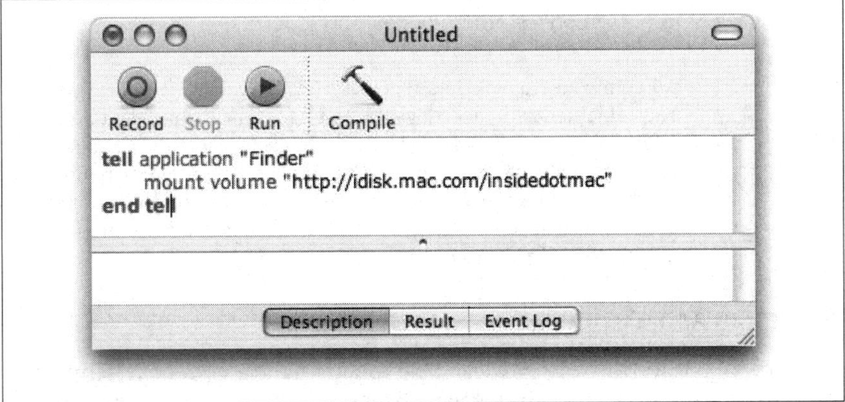

Figure 14-3. The new Script Editor for Panther

Creating, Compiling, and Running AppleScripts

Just start typing into Script Editor's lower text area, or paste or drag text from some other source into it. New text shows up in an orange-colored Courier typeface. While Script Editor features syntax-aware text highlighting and formatting, it doesn't bother applying it until you ask for it by clicking the window's Compile button or selecting Script→Compile (⌘-K). This causes Script Editor to compile (but not run) the script; if successful, it applies syntax highlighting to all that purple text, changing every term's color and text style and every line's indentation level as it sees fit. If it can't compile the script due to a syntax error, it lets you know, by highlighting the point where the compiler got stuck.

The compiler performs application dictionary lookups as necessary to fetch application-specific keywords (which are colored blue by default). Thus, you can get away with referring to `signatures` with a `tell application "Mail"` block, but in other locations—outside of a `tell`, or within a `tell` aimed at the Finder, for example—Script Editor interprets `signatures` as a variable (and colors it green).

To prevent collision with variables and application keywords, consider always using the "studlyCaps" style in your variable names—i.e., preferring variables named `theList` or `myMessages` over `list` or `messages`.

You can modify Script Editor's choice of text-highlighting colors, fonts, and sizes in Script Editor's Formatting preferences (Script Editor→Preferences→Formatting). To change a Font or Color, just double-click on the item, and the appropriate window appears so you can apply the change.

To run a script from Script Editor, click the Run button, or select Script→Run (⌘-R). Script Editor first tries compiling the script if you've made any changes to it since its last compilation or if it hasn't been compiled at all yet and won't run the script if the compiler reports any syntax errors. The script runs until it exits (by finishing execution of all its statements, hitting a `return` statement, or encountering an untrapped runtime error). You can force a script to stop by clicking the Stop button on its window or selecting Script→Stop (⌘-.)

All compiled AppleScripts that you run appear in the system process table under the label `System Events`. If the script falls into an infinite loop or otherwise gets out of hand while you're running a script through the Script menu extra and thus lack Script Editor's handy Stop button, you can just locate and terminate this process, either through the Activity Monitor (*/Applications/Utilities*) or through the Terminal's *ps* and *kill* commands.

Recording AppleScripts

Very few applications are *recordable*, able to automatically generate script statements out of actions that they make. By using Script Editor to record your activities with one of these rare applications, you can quickly generate AppleScript code, either to create a reusable macro or just to investigate the statements needed to produce certain activities with that application.

Saving AppleScripts

In its most raw state, an AppleScript is just a text file, like any other piece of source code. Script Editor's Save dialog offers a Format pop-up menu with the following choices:

Script
: The default option, which causes Script Editor to compile the script and save the file in a binary format with a *.scpt* extension. AppleScripts must be compiled before an application such as Script Editor or the Script menu extra will run them.

The fastest way to start using a new script, once you're happy with how it works, is to save it in compiled form in your *~/Library/Scripts* folder, where it will immediately appear as an option under the Script menu extra (described earlier in "The Script Menu Extra").

Application
: Saves the script as double-clickable application file, complete with a *.app* file extension.

Script Bundle
: Saves the script and any resources as bundled AppleScript. Script Bundles have a *.scptd* file extension. They are new to Mac OS X Panther, and aren't backward compatible with earlier versions of Mac OS X.

Application Bundle
: As with Script Bundles, when you save an AppleScript as an Application Bundle, the script and its resources are bundled together. The compiled script will have a *.app* file extension; however, unlike a Script Bundle, an Application Bundle can be used on earlier versions of Mac OS X because they have a recognized *.app* extension.

Text
: Saves the AppleScript as a plaintext file with a *.applescript* extension.

Testing AppleScripts

Two special windows help you perform simple testing and debugging with your AppleScripts.

If you click on the Result button at the bottom of Script Editor's window (or select View→Show Result, ⌘-2), the return value (if any) of scripts you run in Script Editor appears within this space.

To see a more thorough view of values passing through your script, select View→Show Event Log (⌘-3). When your AppleScript runs, the Event Log displays a line describing every Apple Event generated by your code, interspersed with the events' return values (see Figure 14-4).

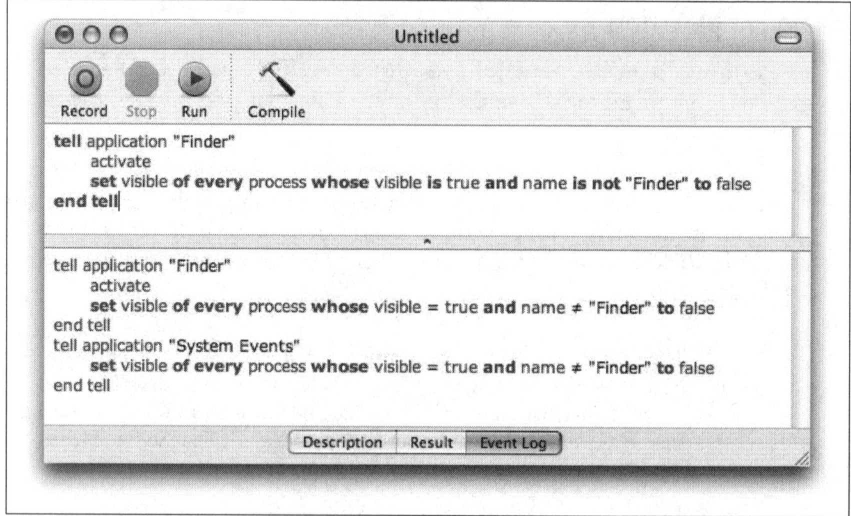

Figure 14-4. A brief AppleScript and its Event Log

Folder Actions

A folder action is a behavior that occurs automatically when certain events take place in a designated folder in the Finder. Folder actions aren't implemented as application, but as scripts with certain handlers which, if present, are called when the corresponding event takes place. For example, when applied to a folder, the following folder action script displays a message whenever files are moved or saved there:

```
on adding folder items to this_folder after receiving these_items
    tell application "Finder"
        set this_name to the name of this_folder
    end tell
    display dialog ((the count of these_items) as string) & ¬
        " items have been added to folder "" & this_name & ¬
        ""." buttons {"OK"} default button 1
end adding folder items to
```

To create a folder action, save the AppleScript as a script file (with a *.scpt*) extension in the *~/Library/Scripts/Folder Action Scripts* folder (or */Library/Scripts/Folder Action Scripts* if you want the script to be available for all users). To apply the folder action script to a folder, Control-click on a folder, and select "Attach a Folder Action" from the context menu, as shown in Figure 14-5.

After selecting this item, the window shown in Figure 14-6 appears, taking you to the *~/Library/Scripts/Folder Action Scripts* folder, from which you can select and choose the folder action script to apply to the folder.

Figure 14-5. Attaching a Folder Action script to a folder

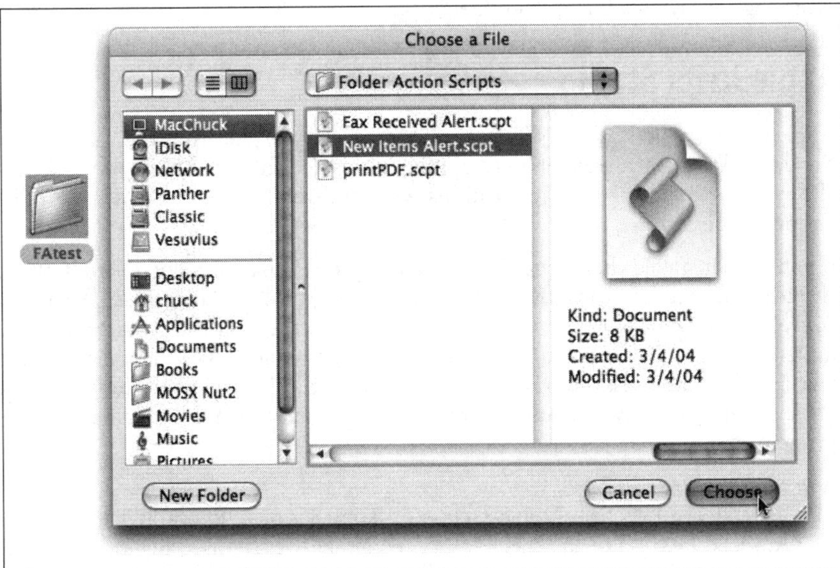

Figure 14-6. Select the folder action script and click on the Choose button to apply the script to a folder

You can also attach multiple folder action scripts to a folder by Control-clicking on a folder and selecting Configure Folder Actions from the context menu. This opens up the Folder Actions Setup window, as shown in Figure 14-7. This window can enable/disable folder actions, as well as add or remove them from the system.

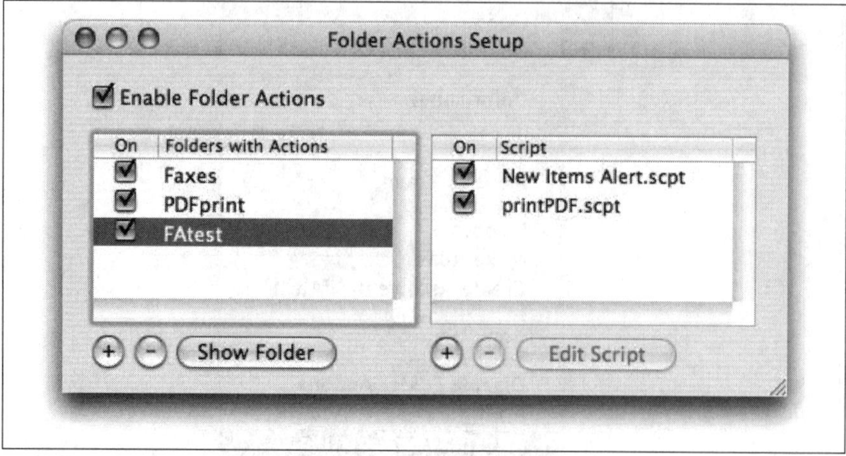

Figure 14-7. The Folder Actions Setup window

Folder actions are really powerful things; you can set one up so that it automatically prints files or uploads them to a web server by simply dragging and dropping, or saving a file into a folder.

AppleScript Studio

AppleScript Studio is a set of software libraries that marries AppleScript with the Xcode and Interface Builder development tools (described in Chapter 15), and allows you to build Cocoa applications with full Aqua interfaces that use AppleScript source code.

If you have installed the Xcode Tools (see Chapter 15), Apple's documentation for AppleScript Studio can be found in */Developer/Documentation/AppleScript/AppleScriptStudioX/index.html*. However, if you already know AppleScript and understand how to program Cocoa or Carbon applications with Xcode and Interface Builder, there isn't a whole lot more to learn. The following describes the basic differences between AppleScript Studio programming and ordinary Cocoa programming:

AppleScript source
: Instead of Objective-C object classes, AppleScript Studio applications have AppleScripts make up their source code. However, like any other Cocoa application's sources, these script files aren't programs unto themselves; they instead define methods (verbs, through AppleScript's `on` *`verbname`* syntax), some of which must bear the responsibility for UI event handlers. As with any Aqua application, a typical AppleScript Studio application spends most of its time in an idle loop, running its methods only when some user-directed event occurs.

Scripts in the source can use AppleScript's `script` *`scriptname`* syntax to define subscripts that play the same role as object classes in other Cocoa applications.

Note that there's still a *main.m* file, written in Objective-C; as with ordinary Cocoa development, you can almost always get away with using the *main.m* that Xcode provides for you, unmodified.

Interface connections
In Interface Builder, you build connections between message-sending interface objects (such as buttons) and the AppleScript handlers they trigger.

However, AppleScript Studio doesn't use the concept of outlets the same way Objective-C Cocoa applications do. Instead of defining outlet objects in the window controller class that represent interface elements (such as a pop-up menu it may wish to get information from when the user clicks a button), AppleScript Studio window controllers simply give you access to an entire `window` object, from which you can access any contained element through the usual AppleScript syntax.

Scripting the Terminal

As Chapter 18 describes, the Terminal application provides a command-line interface to the Unix system running underneath Mac OS X's GUI layers. AppleScript reflects this by offering only one real Terminal-scripting command: `do script`. If you `tell` the Terminal application *do script some_command*, the Terminal acts as if you had invoked *some_command* by typing it on the command line.

Apple provides an excellent TechNote on the `do shell script` command, which can be found at *http://developer.apple.com/technotes/tn2002/tn2065.html*.

For example, if you want the Terminal to display your shell's command path, you can use the following:

```
tell application "Terminal"
    do script "echo $PATH"
end tell
```

When run, this script launches the Terminal (or opens a new Terminal window if the application is already running) and issues the *echo $PATH* command. The result looks something like this:

```
MacChuck:~ chuck$ echo $PATH
/bin:/sbin:/usr/bin:/usr/sbin:/usr/local/vscan:/usr/libexec:/Developer/Tools
MacChuck:~ chuck$
```

Another level of scripting the Terminal uses involves any of the Unix scripting languages that ship with Mac OS X, including Perl, Python, and Ruby. These languages can perform tasks ranging from simple glue between Mac OS X's Unix programs to acting as full-fledged applications in their own right.

Unfortunately, you can't learn these languages by a little bit of guided stumbling, as you can with AppleScript (see the "The Five-Minute Guide to AppleScript" section earlier in this chapter). That said, they're high-level languages that aren't very difficult to pick up, and your Mac includes full documentation for each by way of the Terminal's *man* command; for example, *man perl*. It's likely worth your while to gain some fluency in at least one of these interpreted, Darwin-level languages (see the section "Programming Languages" in Chapter 15 for a little bit of comparative analysis) because they enable you write very powerful and general-purpose programs in very little time. (They aren't geared toward writing Aqua applications, though; for that, turn to Xcode, and the languages it uses, particularly Objective-C. See Chapter 15.)

Note that you can use both kinds of Terminal scripting together. If you write a Perl program to accomplish some task, for example, you can then call it as part of a larger AppleScript script through the Terminal's *do shell script* function.

AppleScript Resources

To continue your path into AppleScript wizardry, here are some resources you'll find quite useful:

- *AppleScript: The Definitive Guide*, by Matt Neuburg (O'Reilly)
- Apple's AppleScript web site (*http://www.apple.com/applescript*)
- Apple's AppleScript mailing list for users (*http://www.lists.apple.com/mailman/listinfo/applescript-users*)
- *The AppleScript Sourcebook*, by Bill Cheeseman (*http://www.applescriptsourcebook.com*)
- Jon Pugh's home page (*http://www.seanet.com/~jonpugh/*)
- MacScripter (*http://www.macscripter.net*)

15

Xcode Tools

Macintosh software development is far easier than ever before. Not only does Mac OS X ship with a large variety of development tools for free, but the tools themselves—especially the integrated development environment applications Xcode and Interface Builder—are beautiful pieces of work that help even newcomers start writing Mac OS X applications quickly.

This chapter outlines the Xcode Tools that ship with Mac OS X Panther and touches on the system resources that make Unix development possible on a Mac.

Getting the Xcode Tools

When first installed onto a machine, Mac OS X actually lacks all the development tools mentioned in this chapter (as well crucial BSD-layer development tools such as gcc 3.3). You have to take a few extra steps to install them.

The fastest way into the Xcode Tools simply involves inserting the Xcode Tools CD that ships with every boxed set of Mac OS X Panther and double-clicking its installer icon. This installs the whole */Developer* hierarchy and various Unix libraries and executables that make software development (or even just compiling programs from downloaded source code) possible.

If you purchased new hardware, you may not have the Xcode Tools CD. Instead, you can install the Xcode Tools by double-clicking on *Developer.mpkg*, found in */Applications/Installers/Developer Tools*.

We recommend that you follow up by joining the Apple Developer Connection (ADC), at *http://connect.apple.com*, which offers a free, online membership. Through the ADC's web site, you can download updates to the Xcode Tools, and also gain access to a searchable, up-to-date archive of documentation and other media (such as QuickTime movies of recent conference presentations) relevant to developing on a Mac.

That said, some of the topics this chapter mentions, in particular, AppleScript, come as part of Mac OS X's distribution, as does the Perl programming language (because many bits and pieces of the underlying system rely on its presence).

The Developer Folder

After installing the Xcode Tools, a Developer folder is placed at the root level of Mac OS X (*/Developer*). Inside the Developer folder, you'll find a host of other folders that contain applications, documentation, sample applications (including their source code), and a suite of command-line utilities for development.

Applications
: This folder contains everything a developer needs to build an application for Mac OS X. The two main applications within this folder are Apple's integrated development environment (IDE), consisting of:

  Interface Builder
  : A tool used to construct the graphical user interfaces (GUIs) for Carbon or Cocoa applications. It's intended for use alongside Xcode, as described later.

  Xcode
  : Formerly known as Project Builder, Xcode is the central development environment for all Mac OS X applications.

Documentation
: This folder holds an immense amount of system documentation in HTML and PDF format, covering the entirety of Mac OS X from a developer's point of view. Topics range from general descriptions of system functionality to highly specific reference manuals, to the Cocoa and Carbon programming APIs. For more about the documentation the Xcode Tools offer, see the later section "Built-in Documentation."

  All the documentation found in this folder also exists on the ADC web site, *http://developer.apple.com*.

Examples
: The */Examples* folder contains a variety of application project folders, organized by category. Some are *.pbproj* files and related Aqua interface and localization resources all ready for opening in Xcode, while others are simple shell scripts or AppleScripts that demonstrate various concepts.

  The */Examples/Web Services* folder, for example, contains a source to an application called *XMethodsInspector*, a couple of AppleScripts (embedded in shell scripts), and a couple of C++ source files. All show different ways of invoking SOAP and XML-RPC web services from your software.

Extras
: This folder contains a set of palettes and index templates you can use with Xcode.

Headers
: This folder contains *FlatCarbon* flat header files, which help developers port applications from Mac OS 9 (which had no concept of Frameworks—see the section "Libraries and Frameworks" later in this chapter, for the difference). The *FlatHeaderConversion* folder holds *tops* and *perl* scripts to help you convert existing legacy source files' header invocations into Mac OS X–style `#include` directives. Either method will help you migrate older Macintosh codebases to Mac OS X, but the latter method results in code that compiles faster.

Java
: Headers and other resources used by Xcode's Cocoa-Java bridge (see the Java entry in the later section, "Programming Languages").

Makefiles
: Makefiles that Xcode transparently uses when building applications. Generally speaking, you can leave these as is.

Palettes
: Interface Builder (described in the later section in this chapter in "Interface Builder") uses *palettes* to hold the basic elements of GUI application interfaces: windows, controls, and views. When designing interfaces with Interface Builder, drag these controls off the available palettes and into the interface that you're designing.

  This folder contains extra palettes beyond those built into Interface Builder.

Private
: This folder contains two command-line utilities, *jam* and *pbhelpindexloader*, which Xcode uses to perform different tasks when compiling code.

Tools
: Command-line tools from Apple, useful for development or working with HFS+ filesystems.

Developer Applications

These Aqua applications all exist within */Developer/Applications*:

Graphics Tools
: This folder contains tools for use with OpenGL programming:

  OpenGL Driver Monitor
  : Displays information about the current machine's graphics card and its OpenGL capabilities.

  OpenGL Profiler
  : Analyzes running OpenGL programs.

  OpenGL Shader Builder
  : A shader tool for use with OpenGL development.

Pixie

Presents you with a magnified view of the pixels directly underneath the mouse pointer, which can serve as an aid in designing custom GUI elements.

Java Tools

This folder contains useful tools for Java developers:

Jar Bundler

This utility allows Java developers to package their program's files and resources into a single double-clickable application.

JavaBrowser

A simple, column-view browser that lets you navigate through the various Java classes installed on your machine. You can view their APIs (including methods, fields, and constructors) as well as their documentation and source code, if available.

By default, the browser knows about several dozen class paths across your filesystem (largely in the */System* domain). Select JavaBrowser→Preferences to add more class paths.

Performance Tools

Here you'll find a suite of applications you can use to help optimize and debug your code, including the CHUD Tools and benchmark software.

MallocDebug

Named after C's `malloc` (memory allocation) function, this application lets you browse the sizes of memory structures within a running application. This can be a great help in detecting memory leaks—the sad state that a program can enter if it allocates more memory than it releases. (Since Objective-C, Mac OS X's *lingua franca*, doesn't feature automatic garbage collection, this can come in quite handy for Cocoa developers.)

ObjectAlloc

Lets you spy on the memory allocation of a running application, much like the *MemoryAlloc* program, but focuses on the higher-level object allocations: Cocoa and Core Foundation. It contains comprehensive documentation under ObjectAlloc→About ObjectAlloc.

Quartz Debug

An analysis and debugging tool for Quartz, the PDF-based, 2D graphics rendering engine that makes Aqua possible. Useful if you're involved in low-level Aqua display hacking, or if you're simply curious as to various application window attributes that the system keeps track of.

Sampler

Another application runtime analysis tool like MallocDebug or ObjectAlloc, except with an emphasis on time, rather than space; it helps you determine which internal functions and routines an application spends its time on while executing and lets you view and pull apart these call stacks in various ways. This makes it a great tool for analyzing and improving application performance.

Spin Control
: This application can help you track down code that causes the spinning rainbow wait cursor to appear so you can rewrite or optimize the code.

Thread Viewer
: Displays parallel threads running within a given application as colorful graphs, displaying their relative levels of activity at a glance, and whether any are in loops, locked, or stopped altogether.

Utilities

This folder contains useful utilities developers need to help make their software more complete:

Bluetooth
: This folder contains the Bluetooth Monitor and PacketDecoder2 applications.

Built Examples
: This folder contains builds of some of the application examples (samples in */Developer/Examples*), including AppearanceSample, BlastApp, a Mac OS X port of Mac OS 9's SimpleText, Sketch, and WorldText.

FileMerge
: A GUI for the *diff* and *merge* command-line tools, which helps you analyze the differences between two text files and merge them into one. It can be especially useful within a CVS context, as described in Chapter 17.

icns Browser
: Lets you view the contents of *icns* resource files, which contain the images and bitmasks that make up Aqua icons. (A single *icns* file can hold several different images, specifying what the icon should look like at various sizes in color depths.)

Icon Composer
: A tool for building *icns* icon files. You don't actually construct the icons with this application; it just binds images you have made through other means into a Mac OS X–friendly format.

IORegistryExplorer
: A graphical browser to the computer's IO Registry system, which is organized like a standard Mac OS X property list, letting you tour the hierarchy of I/O devices available to the OS.

MacPython-2.3
: This folder contains the lone BuildApplet application, which can be used to build an applet from Python script by simply dropping the script file on the application.

PackageMaker
: This application lets you create installer packages, of the sort described in "Software Installers" in Chapter 5. This is useful for distributing software that involves more than a single application bundle.

: Command-line (Darwin) programs often ship as an installer package, usable from Aqua, though they themselves aren't Aqua applications.

PEFViewer

Lets you browse PEF (Preferred Executable Format) files, a kind of shared library format. (You can find examples in */System/Library/CFMSupport*.)

Property List Editor

While you can create Property List files in any text editor, this application eases the process (and removes any XML-related hassles you may have) by letting you build *.plist* files through a graphical, hierarchical-display format. Buttons and pop-up menus control the adding, modification, and deletion of *.plist* elements.

This application doubles as a browser for existing property lists, serving as Mac OS X's default handler for opening *.plist* files from the Finder. For more information on using the Property List Editor, see Chapter 25.

Repeat After Me

Repeat After Me is a tool that is designed to improve the pronunciation of text generated by the Text-To-Speech (TTS) system, by means of editing the pitch and duration of phonemes.

SRLanguageModeler

This application helps developers create, test, and save SRLanguageModel objects. It can parse language model descriptions that have been written out in a special Backus-Naur Form (BNF) and produce SRLanguageModel objects. These can then be tested using the Speech Recognition Manager to determine how well different utterances in the language model can be recognized and distinguished from one another. The SRLanguageModels can be saved to disk in either the data or resource forks of a file so they can be used by an application.

USB Prober

This application can detect and report information about any devices connected to the USB ports, as well as find out which *kexts* are being used by the devices.

Another useful development tool is the Apple Help Indexing Tool, which is located in */Developer/Documentation/AppleHelp*. The Apple Help Indexing Tool is a front-end to the system's content indexer, tuned especially for making Apple Help web sites. To use it, drag and drop a folder filled with HTML onto this application's icon; it automatically generates index files and inserts them into the target folder.

Through this tool, you can also specify an HTTP-based remote root, from which the Apple Help application will try to fetch help files that your other help pages reference, but that aren't present. These pages have a three-day time out on the user's machine. In this way, you can transparently give an application's users the most up-to-date Apple Help-based documentation.

Xcode

Xcode is the centerpiece for all Cocoa and Carbon application development. It lets you construct and manage *projects*, which it defines as collections of files (source code, libraries, and resource files) that go into an application. Included in Xcode are context-aware text editors (featuring syntax highlighting and "smart" indentation), and frontends to the GNU project's *gcc* compiler and *gdb* debugger.

Some of the new features that have been added to Xcode include:

- Code completion
- Built-in API reference documentation
- Distributed builds via Rendezvous
- The ability to import projects from CodeWarrior
- Integrated support for CVS and Perforce source control systems

Xcode's window has two main sections:

- The Groups & Files pane on the left, lists all the files a project uses, including Classes, Targets, Executables, Bookmarks, and NIB files.
- The View on the right lists the files associated with the items you select in the Groups & Files pane. If you click on the Show/Hide Editor button (the one to the left of the Search icon in the toolbar), the view on the right splits in half, revealing the contents of the file selected in the upper half, as shown in Figure 15-1.

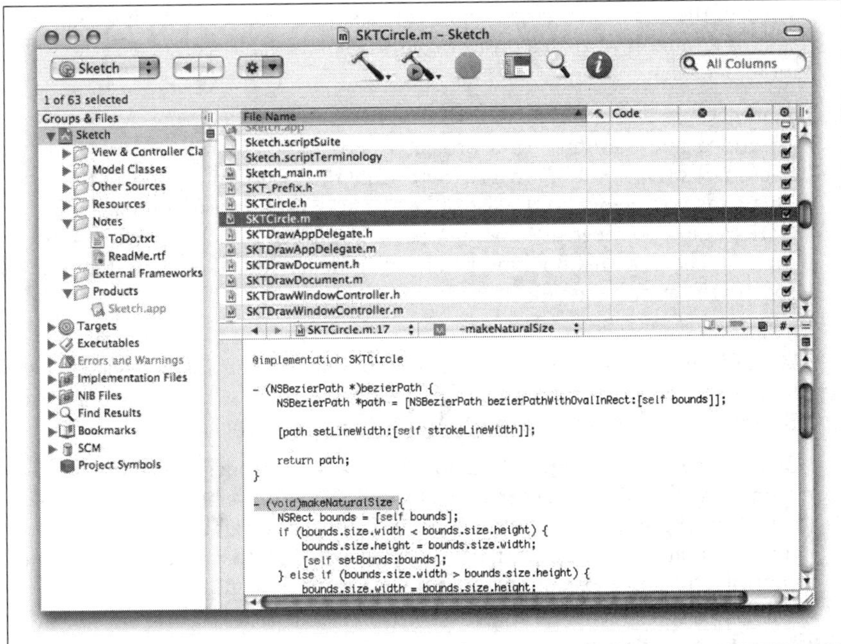

Figure 15-1. The main Xcode window

Items you'll find in the Groups & Files pane include:

Files and Classes
: This view displays, in the left frame, a list of all files a project uses. They are arranged *logically*, not necessarily adhering to the reality of the filesystem; you can create folders (through Group→New Group, or Option-⌘-N) and arrange the list's files within them however you like, without affecting their true filesystem locations.

Furthermore, while many of the files (especially source code specific to this project alone) will reside in the project's real folder, others (such as shared frameworks) are merely present by reference, residing elsewhere on the filesystem. Xcode remembers where all the files actually are, but if you would like to know, simply select one, and choose Project→Get Info (⌘-I).

All the object classes for your project can be browsed as a flat list or as a collapsible hierarchy that displays inheritance. The list visually differentiates between classes defined by linked-in frameworks and those you define yourself (by default, classes defined by the project are blue, and imported ones are black).

Targets
: The list under this tab details the project's *targets*, in the *make* command's sense of the term: each target represents a single product (such as an application or a plug-in) that this project creates. See the later section, "Targets" for more details.

Bookmarks
: To add a line of source to a project's bookmark list, select Find→Add to Bookmarks (Option-⌘-Down Arrow) while the insertion point is in that line. This adds a reference to the list of bookmarks that appears under the Bookmarks item. To view the Bookmarks for a project, click on the disclosure triangle; clicking on a Bookmarked item immediately takes you to that line of code in the appropriate file.

Breakpoints
: While browsing your source code, you can set *breakpoints* by selecting the line of code where you want the breakpoint and selecting Debug→Add Breakpoint at Current Line (⌘-\). A little blue arrow appears at that point.

Breakpoints are a central function of Xcode's debugger. An application running within the debugger pauses in its execution when it encounters an active breakpoint, letting you view the values of variables and other structures at that frozen moment of runtime. You can then use the debugging controls to resume execution as if it hadn't stopped at all.

Built-in Documentation

Once upon a time, developers usually had to sift through different HTML or PDF documentation files on their system to find the information they were looking for. But not anymore. With Xcode, all of Apple's reference documentation has been built-in, making it wildly easy for you to find the information you need without ever leaving Xcode itself.

To launch the documentation viewer, select Help→Show Documentation Window (Option-⌘-?), as shown in Figure 15-2. Use the left pane to select a category you'd like to search, and then enter your query in the Search field. As you type, the window displays your search results in the top half of the window; each character you enter narrows the search down a little more.

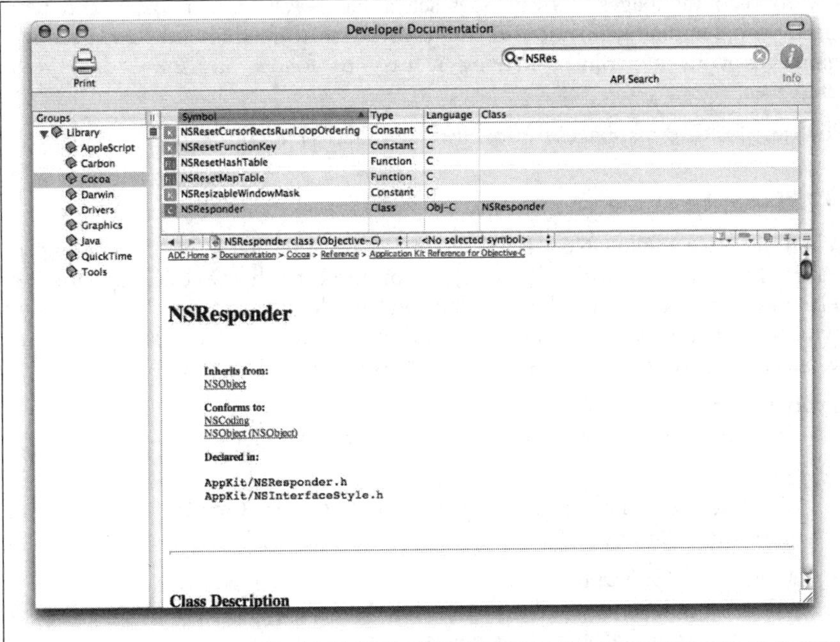

Figure 15-2. Xcode's Documentation Window

While you're editing code, you can Option-double-click any class or method name within the editing window to have Xcode look up its documentation and display any that it finds. (If it finds multiple matches, all the results will show up in the top half of the Documentation Window, letting you narrow the choices.)

To browse available documentation for the classes you're using, click the window's Groups pane. As Figure 15-2 shows, every class in the hierarchy with attached documentation has a little blue book icon beside it. Clicking a book displays the class's HTML documentation in the window's content frame and places a list of all that class's methods into the Members frame, giving another book icon to each one with its own section within the class's documentation.

You can also dig manually into the Framework's contents through the Finder and open up the reference files in a web browser. The */Developer/Documentation* folder contains aliases into the documentation folders of the frameworks you'll probably use the most often, such as the Foundation and Application Kit frameworks.

Manual pages

Like any good Unix system, Mac OS X stores much of its documentation in Unix manual page (or manpage) format. Since manpages tend to deal mainly with C functions and command-line tools, their information isn't always of immediate relevance to most development projects. However, Xcode gives you a convenient way to read manpages anyway: just select Help→Open man page, and then specify the command, function, or topic you wish to read about. Xcode renders manpages with hyperlinks, making it easy to follow any embedded cross-references.

You can also read manpages through the Terminal's *man* program.

Project Types

When you select File→New Project (Shift-⌘-N), the dialog window shown in Figure 15-3 appears with all the types of projects that Xcode supports. By selecting one and clicking the Next button, Xcode creates a new project folder (writing it to the path you specify in the next window) that's preloaded with resource files, NIB files, and frameworks appropriate to the project's type.

Empty Project
: This starts a new project tied (at first) to an empty folder.

Application
: This folder contains projects that help build Cocoa, Carbon, or AppleScript Studio applications.

  AppleScript Application
  : An AppleScript Studio application (see Chapter 14), written primarily with AppleScript (and the merest hint of Objective-C).

  AppleScript Document-based Application
  : Builds a Cocoa application, written in AppleScript, that supports documents.

  AppleScript Droplet
  : Creates a Cocoa application written in AppleScript, that's configured to support files being dropped upon it.

  Carbon Application
  : A Carbon application, authored in C++, that uses *.nib* files for its resources.

  Cocoa Application
  : A Cocoa-based application, written in Objective-C.

  Cocoa Document-based Application
  : A Cocoa-based application, written in Objective-C, that supports documents via NSDocument.

  Cocoa-Java Application
  : Builds a Cocoa application written in Java.

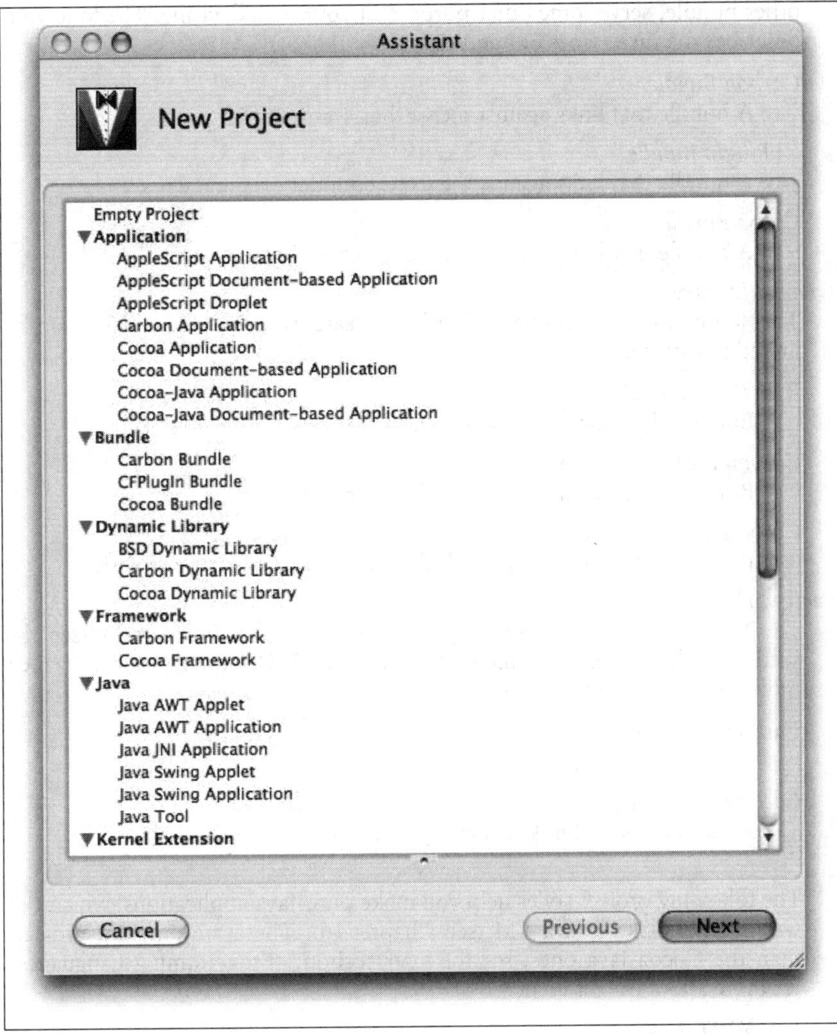

Figure 15-3. Xcode's New Project window

Cocoa-Java Document-based Application
: Builds a Cocoa application written in Java that supports documents via NSDocument.

Bundle
: While Applications and Frameworks are also bundles (as described in the section "Bundles" in Chapter 2), Xcode lets you build "generic" bundles that, while containing executable code and its associated resources just like any

other bundle, serve some other purpose of your own devising. The following describes the three types of bundles:

Carbon Bundle
: A bundle that links against the Carbon framework.

CFPlugIn Bundle
: A bundle that links against the Core Foundation framework.

Cocoa Bundle
: A bundle that links against the Cocoa framework.

Dynamic Library

This folder contains templates that help create dynamic libraries that can be linked to a project:

BSD Dynamic Library
: Builds a dynamic library written in C.

Carbon Dynamic Library
: Builds a dynamic library that links against the Carbon framework.

Cocoa Dynamic Library
: Builds a dynamic library that links against the Cocoa framework.

Framework

The following project types let you create your own frameworks (see the section "Libraries and Frameworks" later in this chapter), against which future projects can link in turn.

Carbon Framework
: A framework that links against Carbon.

Cocoa Framework
: A framework that links against Cocoa.

Java

The following project styles help you make pure-Java applications, which run within Mac OS X's Java VM (see Chapter 16). These are different projects than the Cocoa-Java ones; see the later section, "Programming Languages" for more about the difference.

Java AWT Applet
: An AWT-based Java applet that is built as a Jar* file and run using *appletviewer* or Applet Launcher (see "Java Applets" in Chapter 16).

Java AWT Application
: An AWT-based Java application built as an application bundle.

Java JNI Application
: Builds a Jar file-based JNI application.

* *jar* (Java Archive) files are created through the *jar* utility, one of several standard Java tools that come with Mac OS X; see Chapter 25.

Java Swing Applet
Builds a Swing-based Java applet as a JAR file; the applet can then be run using *appletviewer*.

Java Swing Application
A Swing-based Java applet built as a Jar file and run using *appletviewer* or Applet Launcher (see "Java Applets" in Chapter 16)

Java Tool
A library or application built as a Jar file.

Kernel Extension
The following project templates create kernel extensions (MACH extensions that load at boot time and live in */System/Library/Extensions*).

Generic Kernel Extension
Used for building kernel extensions (kexts).

IOKit Driver
Used for building IOKit drivers for external devices and such.

Standard Apple Plug-ins
The following templates help you create specific types of plug-ins, i.e., bundles meant for loading into a running application. (You can create other sorts of plug-ins through the generic Cocoa or Carbon Bundle templates.)

AB Action Plug-in for C
Builds a C-based Address Book Action.

AB Action Plug-in for Objective-C
Builds a Cocoa-based Address Book Action.

AppleScript Xcode Plugin
Builds a plugin for Xcode using AppleScript.

IBPalette
A custom palette that lets you use Aqua GUI widgets of your own design with Interface Builder (see the section "Interface Builder).

PreferencePane
A plug-in for the System Preferences application.

Screen Saver
A screensaver module for the Desktop & Screen Saver preference panel; see Chapter 4. (Interestingly, this is an example of a plug-in that works with a plug-in.)

Sherlock Channel
Builds a Sherlock Channel that can be used with the Sherlock application.

Static Library
This folder contains templates used to help build the following three types of static libraries:

BSD Static Library
Builds a static library written in C.

Carbon Static Library
: Builds a static library that links against the Carbon framework.

Cocoa Static Library
: Builds a static library that links against the Cocoa framework.

Tool
: This final category of project templates helps you create command-line (Terminal) programs with Xcode:

  C++ Tool
  : A command-line tool that links against the stdc++ library.

  CoreFoundation Tool
  : A command-line tool that links against the Core Foundation framework.

  CoreServices Tool
  : A command-line tool that links against the Core Services framework.

  Foundation Tool
  : A command-line tool that links against the Foundation framework.

  Standard Tool
  : A command-line tool that uses C.

Document-based applications

Some things in the list make a distinction between applications and *document-based applications*. In Mac OS X development terms, a document-based application's prime function involves the creation and editing of individual documents, each of which can be saved to, or loaded from, disk. Such an application uses, along with an application controller and window controllers, a *document controller* class that inherits from the *NSDocument* class and manages these user-editable documents.

Starting a document-based project though Project Builder gives you (among other things) a *MainMenu.nib* NIB file whose File menu is already linked to Open, Save, and Save As actions that do exactly what you'd expect: opening up the dialogs described in the section "Opening and Saving Documents" in Chapter 1. It also creates a document controller class named *MyDocument* that's primed with skeletal methods that save and load the document's data.

One example of a document-based application is Mac OS X's TextEdit. An "ordinary" application doesn't use documents. Instead, it serves some self-contained purpose and in many cases, has only a single interface window, such as with the Address Book or the Property List Editor.

Building Projects

Building a project is as easy as clicking the Build (hammer) button or selecting Build→Build (⌘-B), but Xcode takes a lot of information into account when you do so. It looks for new library dependencies that need to be fulfilled and new code to compile or recompile; it also examines the project's current *target* and *build style* settings to determine what sort of thing it should produce.

Targets

Every Xcode project has at least one target that represents a "deliverable"—something that your project produces. The majority of projects produce only a single executable (either a file or a bundle) and hence have just one target. However, some software projects may find it useful to have more than one target; you may want to build the client and server ends of a client-server package under a single project, for example, or produce a command-line tool that somehow complements your project's main Aqua-application product.

You can add targets to your project through Project→New Target, and edit the settings and *Info.plist* meta-information of any target (including the one you start a new project with) through Project→Edit Active Target (Option-⌘-E). You can view all the targets for a project by clicking on the disclosure triangle next to Targets in the Groups & Files pane.

The Target disclosure displays the current active target and lets you quickly switch to another. While the project window's Files tab lists all the files the project refers to, only the ones with active checkboxes beside them are linked the current target.

Build phases

As with targets, a project has one active build phase at any given time. A build phase is simply a list of arguments Xcode takes into account when compiling the project's targets during as it builds the application. You can view and edit build phases by selecting them under the Targets tab, and you can add new build styles through Project→New Build Phase.

A new project defines two build styles: *Development* and *Deployment*, with the former as the default. When you're ready to release a project, select Deployment as the build style, and then build the project; the products it builds will undergo optimization, which removes all debugging symbols and other bits of binary that make Development-style builds easier to diagnose but slower to run.

Using the Debugger

When you build and run a project in Debug mode (by selecting Build→Build and Debug, or ⌘-Y), you get access to Xcode's Debug window, shown in Figure 15-4. The window's toolbar includes a set of runtime control buttons that lets you pause and restart the debugger. You can also view console messages (including *gdb*'s raw output, which Xcode parses and arranges into the Debug window for you) and anything that the program might send to the Unix Standard Output filehandle.

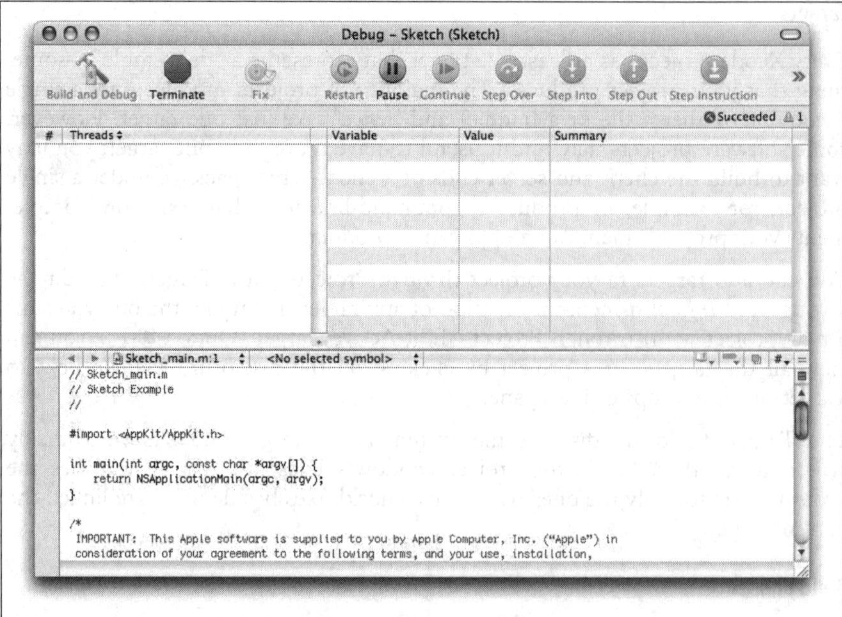

Figure 15-4. Xcode's Debug frame

Programming Languages

As with every operating system, Mac OS X supports as many languages as it has compatible compilers.* Some are described in the following list. Its status as a Unix-flavored system, arguably the most flexible platform for programming, means that it already has a wide support base.

Objective-C

As C is to a "generic" Unix system, and as C++ is to Mac OS 9, one language lies closest to Mac OS X's heart, in terms of support and programming ease: Objective-C. This elegant, object-oriented language, which adds a handful of syntax rules onto plain-vanilla C, is the *lingua franca* of Cocoa development.

In order to better support legacy code, Mac OS X also supports strange notions such as Objective-C++, which allows you to invoke and work with C++ object classes from Objective-C code, and vice versa.

One important downside to Objective-C programming is the fact that most newcomers to Mac OS X programming have likely never used or even seen it before; in fact, it's hard to find any application of it outside of Mac OS X. The developers most likely to already know Objective-C are those who already have programming experience with NeXTSTEP (Mac OS X's predecessor,

* Or compatible virtual machines, in the case of such machine-independent languages as Java (see Chapter 16) or Squeak (a Smalltalk-based programming environment found at *http://www.squeak.org*).

whose OpenStep libraries evolved into the Cocoa frameworks we have today). Fortunately, Objective-C doesn't present large barriers to entry; people with any programming experience can start down this path by reading *The Objective-C Programming Language*, a concise, excellent, and free book found in */Developer/Documentation/Cocoa/Conceptual/ObjectiveC/*.

Java

Java has a dual-faced nature on Mac OS X. Through the Java Bridge software that lurks among the system's Xcode Tools, programmers more familiar with Java than with Objective-C can use it to develop Cocoa applications through the Xcode environment; all the Cocoa and Foundation classes have Java APIs identical in spirit (if not in syntax) to their Objective-C interfaces. You can find these documented in the *Java* folders of */Developer/Documentation/Cocoa/Reference/ApplicationKit* and */Developer/Documentation/Cocoa/Reference/Foundation*, or by browsing class documentation in a Cocoa-Java project as described earlier in "Built-in Documentation."

However, the resulting Cocoa applications will *not* be Java applications! They'll run solely on Mac OS X, just like any other Cocoa program. Xcode's Java Bridge exists solely as a convenience for new developers who know Java but not Objective-C (a situation far more likely than the opposite). We recommend that Cocoa programmers who do know Java consider learning Objective-C anyway.

Mac OS X also supports pure Java applications, which really do run within the Java VM, as described in Chapter 16. The trade-off is that they don't really use Aqua interface; instead, they must provide a UI of their own. Fortunately, Mac OS X ships with an Aqua-like PLAF (pluggable look-and-feel) plug-in for Java Swing, and even makes it the default swing interface, as predefined in the */Library/Java/Home/lib/swing.properties* file.

While Xcode bends over backwards to accommodate Java-Cocoa development, it can only do so much with pure Java programming; you can't use Interface Builder at all to help you create Swing UIs, for example. Pure Java developers may wish to also investigate Emacs (see Chapter 24) or third-party solutions such as the Java-based, open source NetBeans (*http://www.netbeans.org*).

AppleScript

This scripting language has been a part of Mac OS since System 7.1. It's a rich language tuned specifically to act as the glue between applications.

Historically, AppleScript programs run in their own environment, doing whatever they do and then quitting, without any fancy UI. Mac OS X's Xcode Tools lets you build Cocoa-based applications using AppleScript Studio, which allows your AppleScripts to hook into Cocoa interface APIs. See Chapter 14 for more information on AppleScript.

Perl

Perl is a powerful, general-purpose language with a special knack for text processing that can be used for either simple cross-application scripting, high-level object-oriented application development, CGI programming, and just about anything else. Unlike AppleScript or Objective-C, Perl speaks expressly to Mac OS X's Unix side, so you'll probably find Perl programming most comfortable in a text editor such as Emacs (see Chapter 24); Mac OS X includes two Emacs modes for editing Perl code (the simple `perl-mode` and the highly configurable `cperl-mode`).

While Mac OS X ships with Perl (out of necessity, since so much of the distribution depends on Perl to install and run correctly), it doesn't include any connection between it and Aqua; you can write only non-Aqua applications, such as Darwin-based Terminal applications or system daemons, or use Perl/Tk to make GUI programs if you have X Windows installed (as described in Chapter 26). However, the infant CamelBones project (found at *http://camelbones.sourceforge.net*) aims to bridge the worlds of Perl and Cocoa programming.

Python

Python is another open source, Unix-grounded, all-purpose programming language. Boasting a cleaner syntax and a sizeable support community of its own, Python proves an attractive alternative to Perl for many programmers. With Panther, Apple has added Python bindings to Quartz, making it possible for Python scripts to make calls to the CoreGraphics libraries.

Interface Builder

Because it is so graphically oriented, Aqua applications adhere to a very passive runtime model. In fact, a typical Mac OS X application spends most of its time running in an idle loop, waiting for some sort of user input, such as a keypress or a mouseclick onto one of its buttons. Through the Interface Builder application, you specify the onscreen controls that your application will have and tie these into handler methods within your code.

Interface Builder helps you generate *.nib* files, which are serialized versions of Cocoa application elements. Typically, an application has one *.nib* file for every window that its interface contains. A very simple text-editing application, for example, might have one such file for its document window (containing the text view in which the user actually types), another for the application's Preferences window, and a third for its About panel. All but the most minimal applications also contain a *.nib* that holds its menu-bar menus (including its application menu and everything to the right of it, as described in the section "The Menu Bar" in Chapter 1).

Through Interface Builder, you can build these windows by dragging template windows, controls, and views off of palettes, as shown in Figure 15-5. You can then establish connections between parts of the window and classes belonging to your application.

Normally, you define a special class known as a *Window Controller* for every window (and therefore every *.nib* file), and supply it with two types of data: *outlets*, which are pointers to things existing on the window, and *actions*, which are pointers that connect window controls back to methods in the project's source.

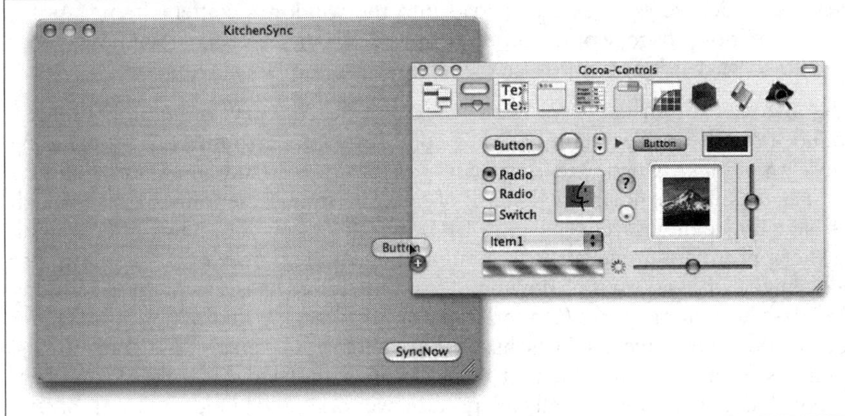

Figure 15-5. Building a window with Interface Builder

To learn more about creating applications for Mac OS X, see *Learning Cocoa with Objective-C* (O'Reilly).

Libraries and Frameworks

Projects you build with Project Builder link against Mach-style dynamic libraries. Rather than `#include`-ing flat header files, though, projects usually link against frameworks, which include both libraries and related resources.* (See the */Developer/Headers* folder, described earlier in the section "The Developer Folder," for a fast way to port flat-library-linking legacy code.)

Frameworks

Frameworks are simply dynamic libraries packaged into bundles. Along with the library file itself lives its related resources. Like all bundles, frameworks use a consistently named internal structure of folders, so that programs can easily find what they need within. These resources can include images, plists, and NIB files, just like an application bundle. This not only makes shared code libraries possible but also complete shared interface libraries. The standard spell checker interface, for example, actually lives as a NIB file within the Application Kit (or AppKit) framework's resources.

Resources particular to framework bundles—and of interest to developers wishing to use them in their software projects—include the library's header files and class documentation. You can navigate to and open these from the Finder if you'd like, but Project Builder gives you easier ways to browse these framework resources if you've loaded a reference to the framework into your project. Clicking the disclosure triangle next to a framework icon in the Files tab reveals that framework's

* Unix emigres looking for a lengthy discussion about Darwin's dynamic libraries versus ELF libraries may wish to reference *Mac OS X Panther for Unix Geeks* (O'Reilly).

headers, which you can select to load into the window's content frame. As for documentation, frameworks automatically add any HTML documents they provide to the Class browser—see the section "Built-in Documentation."

The system's search paths for frameworks are the */Library/ Frameworks* folders found around the filesystem; Apple's core development frameworks (including those that make Cocoa development possible) are found in */System/Library/Frameworks*. Xcode abstracts the task of selecting from these frameworks through its New Project interface (see Figure 15-3), which sets up your new project to link to the appropriate frameworks. Linking in non-Apple frameworks (such as those your might write yourself or download from the Internet) is as simple as selecting Project→Add Frameworks (Option-⌘-A) or just dragging the frameworks' Finder icons into your project's Files list. From there, you can use the frameworks' methods from any source file that `#includes` its main header file; the documentation included with more socially adept frameworks should guide you from there.

The Info.plist File

Metainformation about your project, which you usually define through Xcode's Project→Edit Active Target (Option-⌘-E) dialog, is stored in a special *Info.plist* file, which Xcode writes to the application's */Contents* folder upon building. Every Bundle-style application on your system (that is, every Cocoa application and every Bundle-style Carbon or Java application as well) has one of these files, which are, like all *.plist* files, in Property List XML format (described in Chapter 25).

Taken together, all the */Applications/AppName.app/Contents/Info.plist* files installed in all the filesystem's domain-level Applications folders compose a registry of all applications available to the machine. This lets the system build a database of application information, which lets the Finder assign the correct `Kind` to application-specific files under its List view and Info windows, the *defaults* program pair preference domains to applications (see Chapter 25), and more. The application itself can also pull information from this file to help build its About dialog, for example, as well as to find out what file format its own documents use.

A related file, *version.plist*, can exist in the same directory as *Info.plist*. As its name suggests, it contains information about the applications' version and build numbers, as well as release status.

16
Java on Mac OS X

Mac OS X has always shipped with a Java runtime included. Panther includes two versions of the Java 2 Standard Edition virtual machine (JVM): J2SE 1.3.1 and J2SE 1.4.1. In the days of Classic, there were different virtual machines available from different vendors and different versions for each release or update. Before Mac OS X was released, however, Apple decided that a single JVM would provide a consistent user experience and that it was their responsibility to provide the JVM.

With the first release of Mac OS X, Apple drew a line in the sand. They would support Java 2 on Mac OS X and not on any previous version of their operating system. Similarly, when Apple released their version of J2SE 1.4.1 in early 2003, they announced that they would support only Jaguar and beyond. Panther includes both versions of the JVM to support legacy programs that require J2SE 1.3.1. J2SE 1.4.2 will likely be released before this book is available and will be supported in Panther and higher.

This chapter provides an overview of the tools available for developing and running Java applets and applications on Mac OS X. All of the standard command-line tools, such as *java*, *jar*, and *javadoc* are available. Much of Apple's added value, though, lies mostly in the user-friendly enhancements for running Java applications that look and feel like double-clickable native applications.

Java Tools and Applications

You will find the most commonly used preinstalled Java tools and applications in three places: */Applications/Utilities*, */Developer*, and */Library/Java/Home*. This section provides you with a quick look at what is available.

/Applications/Utilities

All end users can find a core set of Java applications in */Applications/Utilities/Java*, which includes the following:

Applet Launcher
: The AppletLauncher application can be used in place of a browser to launch and test Java applets.

Input Method HotKey
: Used to set a keyboard combination that involves the input method dialog in applications with multiple input methods.

Java 1.3.1 Plugin Settings
Java 1.4.1 Plugin Settings
: The Java Plugin Settings set the preferences used for running browser-based Java applets. Depending on which version of Mac OS X you are running, you may see this available for Version 1.3.1, 1.4.1, and/or 1.4.2.

Java Web Start
: Java Web Start files are downloaded from a web page and then run locally in a richer, nonbrowser–based client.

Two other applications you'll find useful for working with Java in the */Applications/Utilities* directory include the Terminal and Console applications. The Terminal can be used to compile and execute Java applications, as well as for bundling the application as a *jar* file for easy distribution. Messages and some output from non-command-line Java applications won't be seen in the Terminal. You will have to consult the Console for a record of what might have gone wrong with a GUI application.

/Developer

If you are interested in doing any development on your Mac, you should install the Xcode Tools from the CD that Apple distributes with Panther. You should also join the Apple Developer Connection (ADC) for the free Online ADC Membership. The Java team at Apple has previewed most of their recent releases for free through the ADC, including the J2SE 1.4.1 and 1.4.2 releases, Java3D, and JAI (Java Advanced Imaging). The QuickTime team also made the QuickTime Java release available ahead of time to ADC members.

In the */Developer/Java* subdirectory you will find all the documentation you need in the form of header and *job* files. The first time you try to access them with your browser, you are given directions on how to unpack them from the Terminal.

Inside of */Developer/Applications/Java Tools* you will find the Jar Bundler tool that we'll discuss later in this chapter. It enables you to wrap one or more *jar* files together with other resources in a double-clickable native Mac OS X application bundle. The JavaBrowser is a simple application for browsing the Java documentation from Apple and Sun.

The */Developer/Applications* directory also contains Xcode. This is Apple's free IDE that is very useful for developing Cocoa applications. For Cocoa applications, you can use Interface Builder to cleanly design your GUI and then tie it to the controllers you code up. There is no analogous facility for Swing-based Java applications. Further, Xcode doesn't work in a natural way for Java developers, because packaging is not mapped in an obvious way to the directory structure.

/Library/Java/Home

The */Library/Java/Home/bin* directory contains the command-line executables you will most often use in your Java development. You will compile your code using *javac* and run it using *java*. For example, if you create a Java source file named *example.java*, you can compile it with *javac example.java*. You can later run the Java application using the command *java example*. Even though the *example.java* file is compiled into the file *example.class*, you don't have to type *java example.class*.

The *jar* tool can create and expand Java archives, and the *javadoc* tool is provided to generate documentation from Java source files. For securing code, you can use the *policytool*, *jarsigner*, and *keytool*. For working with objects distributed across the network, you can use the *rmi* tools. This includes *rmic* for generating stubs and skeletons; *rmid* and *rmiregistry* persist the *rmi* bootstrap and persist the data if your computer needs to be restarted. Details about these standard tools are beyond the scope of this book. The main point is that the standard command-line Java tools are available to you in Mac OS X.

Running Mac-Friendly Java Programs

There are two worlds of Mac OS X: the Unix side and the GUI side. On the one hand, there is the Unix side that has you popping open a Terminal window and typing *sed*, *sudo*, or *ls*. The typical Mac OS X user doesn't spend much time in that world, mainly because the more public side of Mac OS X is the bright, shiny Aqua interface. Fortunately, you can run many Java programs by double-clicking on an icon or navigating to a web page.

There are many Java programs that fall into this category. The first type involves desktop applications written in Java, but installed and run just like any other native Mac OS X application. The second type is a Java applet, which typically runs within a web browser. When you open a web page that contains an applet, Java code is downloaded to your machine and run inside a restricted part of your disk called a *sandbox*. The sandbox approach is dependent on browsers to support Java from within. A third approach is a hybrid called *Java Web Start* (JWS). In this case you download a small piece of code in the browser, and a helper application takes over, allowing you to run the application independent from the browser. You can even choose to transform a JWS application into a standalone, double-clickable application.

In each case, Java code is executing on your machine using your instance of the Java Virtual Machine (JVM). There are other times you may be depending on Java code without knowing it. As you access web sites and use applications on your Desktop, you might also be interacting with remote Java applications. These can be in the form of Java ServerPages (JSP), servlets, or a Java application serving up content or providing you with web services. In these cases, you generally don't care what language the remote server is using. A third category includes Java programs that require a JVM on your computer and another JVM on the server. The two programs communicate by transforming objects, sending them over the network, and then reconstituting them on the client side.

A description of RMI, Jini, or other such technologies is well beyond the scope of this chapter. For additional information about these and other Java technologies, see *Mac OS X for Java Geeks* (O'Reilly)

Desktop Java Applications

Apple has made it easy for Java developers to produce native-looking double-clickable applications. In the final section of this chapter you will see that it doesn't require much work for a developer to package a Java application so that starting it up and using it has the same feel as an application written in Cocoa or Carbon.

For much of the rest of this chapter you will experiment with the Jar Bundler application, which is included with Panther as part of the Xcode Tools suite. You can find this application in */Developer/Applications/Java Tools/Jar Bundler*. Make a copy of this application so that you don't risk damaging the original.

In the ideal case, it should not matter to you which language an application is written in. There is nothing special for you to do; just double-click and go. If you are curious, make a copy of the application and examine the package contents by right-clicking on the copy and selecting *Show Package Contents*. For example, Figure 16-1 shows the contents of the Jar Bundler application.

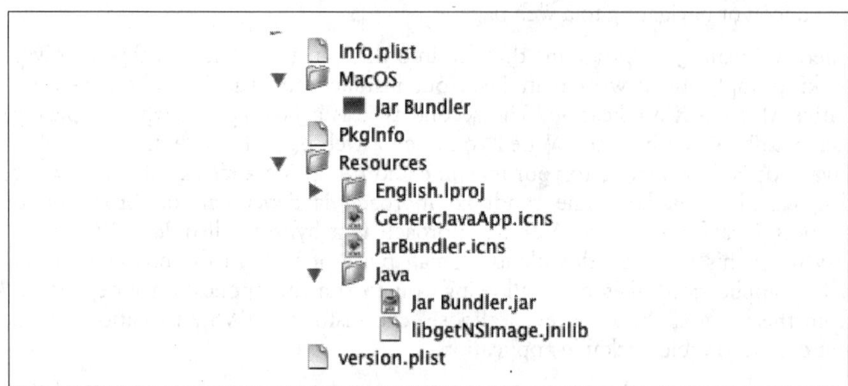

Figure 16-1. The contents of the Jar Bundler application

What identifies this as a Java application is the *jar* file, located in *Resources/Java/Jar Bundler.jar*. You can inspect your favorite applications to see which are Java applications.

As you will see later, a *jar* file is basically a *zip* file with some extra information. This particular *jar* file contains 47 items. You can use the *jar* utility from the command line to show the contents of this *jar* file; for example: *jar -tf Jar\ Bundler.jar*. To run the application, you first need to identify the class file. Double-click on *Info.plist*, and the Property List Editor displays the name value pairs. Scroll down and open up the Java related dictionaries, and you should see something similar to what is shown in Figure 16-2.

Property List	Class	Value
▼Java	Dictionary	5 key/value pairs
▼ClassPath	Array	1 ordered object
0	String	$JAVAROOT/Jar Bundler.jar
JVMVersion	String	1.4+
MainClass	String	JarBundler
▼Properties	Dictionary	1 key/value pair
apple.laf.useScreenMenuBar	String	true
WorkingDirectory	String	$APP_PACKAGE/Contents/Resources/Java
▼NSJavaPath	Array	1 ordered object
0	String	Jar Bundler.jar
NSJavaRoot	String	Contents/Resources/Java

Figure 16-2. The Jar Bundler Java Properties from Info.plist

The *MainClass* property has the value *JarBundler*. The *JVMVersion* indicates which version of the JVM is required. The *apple.laf.useScreenMenuBar* property indicates whether the menu for your Java application displays at the top of the containing JFrame as it does in native Windows applications or at the top of the screen as it does in native Macintosh applications.

Java Applets

The most common way to know you are running a Java applet is when something goes wrong. For the most part, when you navigate to a web page containing a Java applet, it should just load and run. You fill find many examples in */Developer/Examples/Java*. The Applets folder contains a classic set of applets that is older than Mac OS X. If you double-click on any of the HTML files in the *Applets/MoleculeViewer* directory, your default browser should open, and you should see molecules that rotate when you click and drag them in any direction. These examples display and work correctly in Apple's Safari browser. You will find more recent applets that show off various Swing and sound capabilities in the *JFC* and *Sound* directories.

Before Apple released Safari, they provided a browser-independent method for viewing applets called *AppletLauncher*, and Panther still ships with *AppletLauncher* (*/Applications/Utilities/Java*). Double-click *AppletLauncher* to start it, and then navigate to an HTML page that contains an applet. For example, choose *example3.html* from the *MoleculeViewer* directory; each applet opens and runs in a new window, as shown in Figure 16-3.

You can also select from the Applet menu to view the contents of the Applet tag, the Applet Info, and the Character encoding. Other menu items allow you to

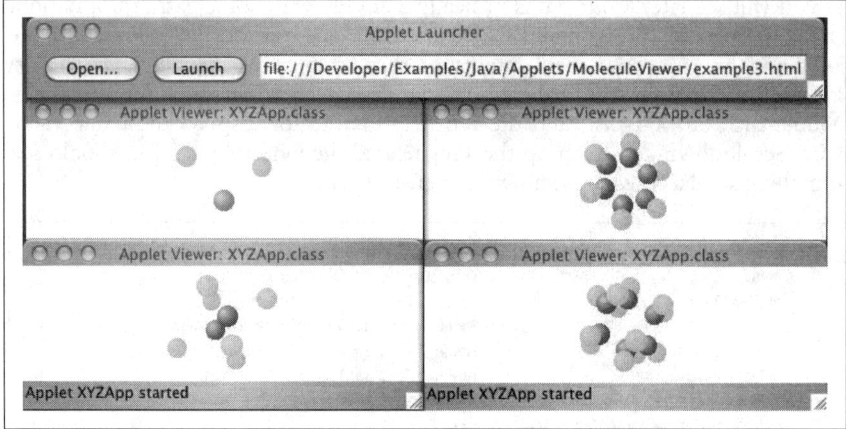

Figure 16-3. MoleculeViewer example 3 in the Applet Launcher

Restart, Stop, Start, Save, and Clone the Applet. Cloning an applet results in a second instance of the same applet.

You can further tune how applets are run in the browser using the Java Plugin Settings applications for J2SE 1.3.1 and J2SE 1.4.1 (*/Applications/Utilities/Java*); however, you typically won't need to make adjustments to these settings. The Java 1.4.1 Plugin Settings application has the Panther look and feel and offers more sophisticated setting controls than the Java 1.3.1 version. Both allow you to indicate whether or not the Java Console is visible and whether an exception dialog box is displayed. With the J2SE 1.3.1 version, you can clear the JAR Cache to prevent you from using a previously downloaded *jar* file. For applets that seldom change, caching improves the user experience. There is a danger, however, that a user won't be running the most recent version of your applet. In the J2SE 1. 4.1 version, you can also enable or disable caching, set the location and size of the cache, and set the amount of compression to be applied to *jar* files. Each version also allows you a different amount of control over the certificates that indicate the trustworthiness of the applet being run.

Java Web Start Applications

Java Web Start provides a means of easily deploying a Java application. In a way, it is somewhere between an applet and an application. You start up a JWS application by clicking on a web page link. A file with the extension *.jnlp* is then downloaded to your Mac. The JWS application included in Panther (*/Applications/Utilities/Java*) launches, opens the file, and downloads the necessary resources to a special location on your machine. For Panther, the default location is in *~/Library/Caches/Java Web Start/cache*.

To get a better idea of what is going on, go to Apple's home page for JWS (*http://developer.apple.com/java/javawebstart/*), and click on the link labeled "Welcome to Web Start". The file *JWS_demo.jnlp* (shown in Example 16-1) is automatically downloaded. This is not a working Java application but is a special XML file that contains much of the information you would find in an applet tag. As you can see in the example, the *.jnlp* file specifies which Java archive files to download, which version of the JVM will run the application, and which class is the Main class that will start the application.

Example 16-1. JNLP file for Java Web Start demo

```
<?xml version="1.0" encoding="UTF-8"?>

<jnlp spec="1.0+" codebase="http://developer.apple.com/java/ ↵
javawebstart/apps/welcome" href="JWS_Demo.jnlp">
  <information>
    <title>Welcome to Web Start!</title>
    <vendor>Apple Computer, Inc.</vendor>
    <homepage href="http://developer.apple.com/java/ javawebstart" />
    <offline-allowed />
  </information>
  <resources>
    <j2se version="1.3+" />
    <jar href="WebStartDemo.jar" />
  </resources>
  <application-desc main-class="com.apple.mrj.javawebstart.DemoMain" />
</jnlp>
```

Double-click on the *.jnlp* file to start the application. The second time you start the application, you will be prompted to create a standalone application. You can configure the standalone application and where its cache will be stored, along with other properties using the Preferences menu item in the JWS application.

If you choose, an application is created with the name *Welcome to Web Start!* Reveal the package contents, and double-click on *info.plist* to see the details shown in Figure 16-4.

Property List	Class	Value
▼Root	Dictionary	7 key/value pairs
CFBundleExecutable	String	Welcome to Web Start!
CFBundleIconFile	String	icon.icns
CFBundleIdentifier	String	com.apple.jnlp-http___developer.apple.com_java_javawebstart_apps_welcome_JWS_Demo.jnlp
CFBundleName	String	Welcome to Web Start!
CFBundlePackageType	String	APPL
CFBundleSignature	String	????
▼Java	Dictionary	2 key/value pairs
JNLP	String	http://developer.apple.com/java/javawebstart/apps/welcome/JWS_Demo.jnlp
JVMVersion	String	1.4*

Figure 16-4. Info.plist for "Welcome to Web Start!"

You can create a different icon and place it inside the Resources folder in place of *icon.icns*, and then change the `CFBundleIconFile` entry to match the name of the new icon. The String value for the JNLP variable is the URL pointing to the original *.jnlp* file (*http://developer.apple.com/java/javawebstart/apps/welcome/JWS_Demo.jnlp*). On startup, the application checks to make sure you are running the most recent version of the application.

Running Generic Java Applications

There are many Java developers who write code and never consider that their application might someday run on a Mac. After all, the whole concept behind Java is that the code can be written once and run anywhere. In many cases, these programs will run fine on Mac OS X. One of the biggest advantages of including a JVM with every Mac is the large number of programs that are enabled on the platform. In this section you will see how to run Java programs that aren't specifically packaged for use on a Mac.

Running from jar Files

You have seen that a *jar* file is a Java archive much like a *zip* or *tar* file. Try this out:

- Make a copy of the file *Jar Bundler.jar* that you found inside the JarBundler application.
- Make a copy of *Jar Bundler.jar* with the name *JarBundler.zip*.
- Expand the *JarBundler.zip* file using the version of StuffIt Expander included with Panther.

When you do, you end up with a folder containing many class files and two subdirectories. The *META-INF* folder contains a single file named, *MANIFEST.MF*. This directory and file are what differentiates a *jar* file from a *zip* file. The *MANIFEST.MF* file may contain the name of the Java class file intended to initiate the application; this makes the *jar* file double-clickable.

There are many advantages to working with *jar* files instead of the individual class files. When you zip up a bunch of files scattered across directories, not only is the result compressed and smaller than the sum of the individual files, you are also left with only one file to keep track of.

You can also run an application from a *jar* file; you just need to make sure the *jar* file is in the *classpath*. You can think of the classpath as the locations in which the Java runtime looks for class files that are part of the application. You also need to pass in the name of the class file that is considered the *main class*; this is the class that starts the application. You can obtain this information from the *Info.plist* file you looked at earlier. Copy the files *Jar Bundler.jar* and *libgetNSImage.jni* from the */Contents/Resources/Java* directory to your Desktop. The *.jni* file is needed for this application to access native Mac OS X resources. Launch the Terminal application (*/Applications/Utilities*) and change directories to your user directory (*cd ~/*). You can start JarBundler application with this command:

```
$ java -classpath .:"Jar Bundler.jar" JarBundler
```

The *jar* tool is part of the standard Java distribution. You can use it to expand a *jar* file or to archive class files into a Java archive. You can also use it to update the manifest to add information on resources or on the main class to be executed. Assuming you are still in the directory containing *Jar Builder.jar*, enter the following command into the Terminal window to expand the *jar* file:

```
$ jar xvf "Jar Bundler.jar"
```

Here's what this command means:

- The *x* indicates that you are expanding a file.
- The *v* signals that you want the output to be verbose so that you can view the results of what is being done.
- The *f* flag specifies the *jar* file, in this case, *Jar Bundler.jar*.

You can use the *jar* tool with these same options to expand any *zip* file as well. To create a *jar* file, use the *c* flag in place of *x*, and specify the name of the file being created and the files being included. For Panther and earlier, this was a nice way to zip up files. With Panther, you can now Control-click (or right-click) on a file and choose the *Create Archive of* option from the contextual menu.

To make the *Jar Bundler.jar* file double-clickable, you need to add information about the main class to the manifest. Add the highlighted line to *MANIFEST.MF* using TextEdit, as follows:

```
Manifest-Version: 1.0
Main-class: JarBundler
Created-By: 1.4.1_01 (Apple Computer, Inc.)
```

Save this as *MANIFEST.MF* in your Desktop folder along with the existing *Jar Bundler.jar* file. Now use the *jar* command with the *u* and *m* flags that indicate you are updating the indicated manifest file using the one specified. In this case, type this command:

```
$ jar uvmf MANIFEST.MF "Jar Bundler.jar"
```

You should get the response "updated manifest" to indicate that the manifest for *Jar Bundler.jar* was updated with the information in *MANIFEST.MF*. Now you can double-click on *Jar Bundler.jar* to launch the application. This is a nice technique for creating cross-platform applications with very little effort.

Running from class Files

Look at the contents of the Jar Bundler folder that was created when you expanded the *zip* or *jar* versions of *Jar Bundler.jar*. There is a mass of class files at the top level and in subdirectories of the *com* folder. You may get a Java application as a collection of class files. As long as you can determine the location of the main class file and have some understanding of the intended classpath you can run this application from the command line. For an application you find online, there should be a *README* file or other instructions containing this information.

In the Jar Bundler example, you know that the name of the main class is *JarBundler*. One of the issues that trips up end users with Java applications is that files being referenced need to be in the classpath or in some fixed location. In the current case, your class files are inside the Jar Bundler folder, and the *libgetNSImage.jni* file is outside of the folder and not visible to the application. Make a copy of *libgetNSImage.jni* and copy it into the Jar Bundler folder. From the Terminal, execute the following two commands:

```
$ cd "Jar Bundler Folder"/
$ java JarBundler
```

The first command puts you inside the Jar Bundler folder, and the second runs the application.

Running from a Shell Script

Many open source projects are distributed with scripts for setting variables and easily starting the application. The contents of the script can be entered line-by-line from the command line, but this makes the application difficult to run. The Windows version is usually a file with the suffix *.bat*, and the Unix version is usually a file with the suffix *.sh*. If the script is written without Mac OS X in mind, you may need to customize the values of some of the variables. For instance, the JavaHome variable should be set to */Library/Java/Home*.

Consider the Jar Bundler example. Open TextEdit, create a new document, and then select the menu item Format→Make Plain Text. Because the Jar Bundler folder is in the Desktop folder of your Home directory, the shell script needs only the following information:

```
cd ~/Desktop/"Jar Bundler Folder"/
java JarBundler
```

Choose an appropriate name for this script, such as *run.sh*, and save the file. To run it, open the Terminal application, and navigate to the directory where you saved the shell script. Execute the script as follows:

```
sh run.sh
```

You can also create your own AppleScript application to execute this series of commands. Launch the ScriptEditor application (*/Applications/AppleScript*), and enter the code shown in Figure 16-5.

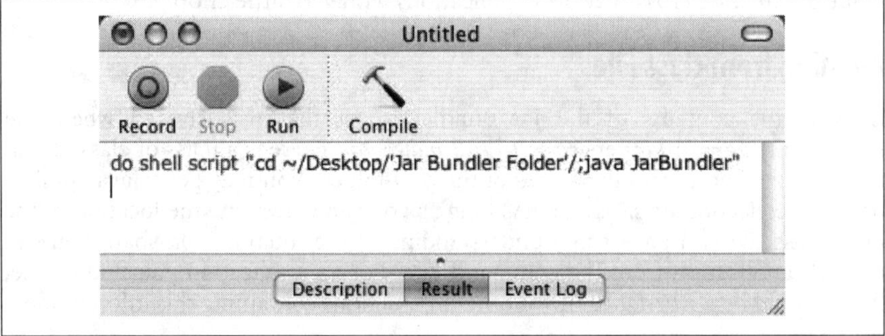

Figure 16-5. AppleScript for Jar Bundler

You can test this script by clicking on the Run button. You can also save the script as an application and then run it by double-clicking it.

Java on the Command Line

You can run Java programs from the command line using the *java* command. Generally, you invoke it in one of two ways:

java [options] [class] argument1 argument2...
: Loads the specified class, and runs its main method. If it has no such method, or if it's in the wrong format, the class will fail to launch. To be invokable like this, a Java class's main method must have the signature:

```
public static void main(String[] args).
```

You should have a class path defined so that the Java interpreter will know where on the filesystem to search for the specified class. See the next section.

java [options] –jar jarfile arguments
: In this case, the *–jar* option tells the Java interpreter to launch a program encapsulated in a *jar* file. This works only if the *jar* file knows its own *Main-class*, which defines the *main* method.

jar files, like Mac OS X applications, are self-contained and ignore the user's class path definitions.

This section involves using the Terminal. If you are completely unfamiliar with this application or with using a Unix command line in general, you may want to skip ahead to Chapter 18 first.

You can find a full list of Java's options under its manpage, but here are some of the more useful ones:

`-cp`
: Lets you define the class path for one command invocation. See the next section.

-property=value
: Sets a system property value.

`-verbose`
: Displays information about each loaded class.

If the Java program you want to run from the command line is a self-contained Mac OS X application, you can simply run the command *open Application*, just as you would with any Cocoa, Carbon, or Classic application.

Class Paths

When you launch a Java program from the command line by invoking its class, you must have class paths defined. This is a list of filesystem paths pointing to directories and *jar* files that the Java interpreter can search in order to locate the referenced class definition, as well as any classes that it might reference in turn.

There are two ways you can set class paths. If you're using the *java* command in the Terminal, you can feed it the *–cp* flag followed by a colon-delimited list of paths. For example, this command includes both the current directory (abbreviated as ".") and the */Library/Java* folder located in your Home folder in the class path while invoking the *MyClass* class:

```
$ java -cp .:~/Library/Java/ MyClass
```

You can set class paths in a more permanent fashion through the `CLASSPATH` environment variable (see the section "Environment Variables" in Chapter 21).

Some Java programs intended to run on the command line make things easier for users by including a shell or Perl script that acts as its frontend. Quite often, this script's job involves setting up class paths properly before running the Java interpreter on the program's main class.

Other applications' Java-related configuration might also deal with class paths. Internet Explorer, for example, lets you specify additional class paths that Java applets can use.

Other Command-Line Tools

Mac OS X ships with Sun's full suite of Unix command-line Java tools, which includes the *java* command. However, the rest—such as *javac*, the Java compiler, and the documentation browser *javadoc*—are of interest to Java developers. To learn more about these commands, view their respective manpages.

Customizing Java Applications

If you have some individual class files, you can use the *jar* tool to package them up into one or more *jar* files. Once you have *jar* files, you can transform them to double-clickable *jar* files, or wrap them in shell scripts or AppleScripts.

This section shows you how use the Jar Bundler tool (*/Developer/Applications/Java Tools*) that you used earlier to customize a Java application.

Start the Jar Bundler, and then click the Choose button and navigate to the *Jar Bundler.jar* file that you copied to the Desktop. The next step is to select the Main class, as shown in Figure 16-6.

It may surprise you to find that there is more than one choice. The application can be started using the *JarBundler* class as we have done, or the *JarInspector* class. The technical reason is that they each contain a method with this signature:

```
public static void main(String[] args)
```

Choose *JarBundler*, and leave the rest of the options set to their default values. Select the Classpath and Files tab, and you will see the *jar* file already included in both headings. You also need to add *libgetNSImage.jnilib* to the Files and Resources section, as shown in Figure 16-7.

For now, we won't set any properties, so click the Create Application button. The dialog prompts you for where you want to save the application and what you want to call it. Choose a name and save it in your */Applications* directory.

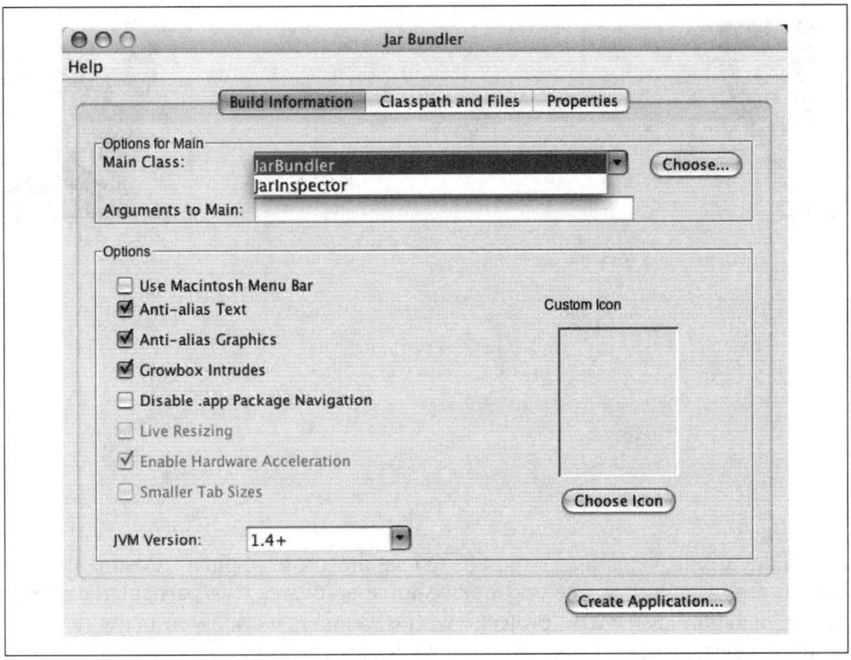

Figure 16-6. The Jar Bundler tool

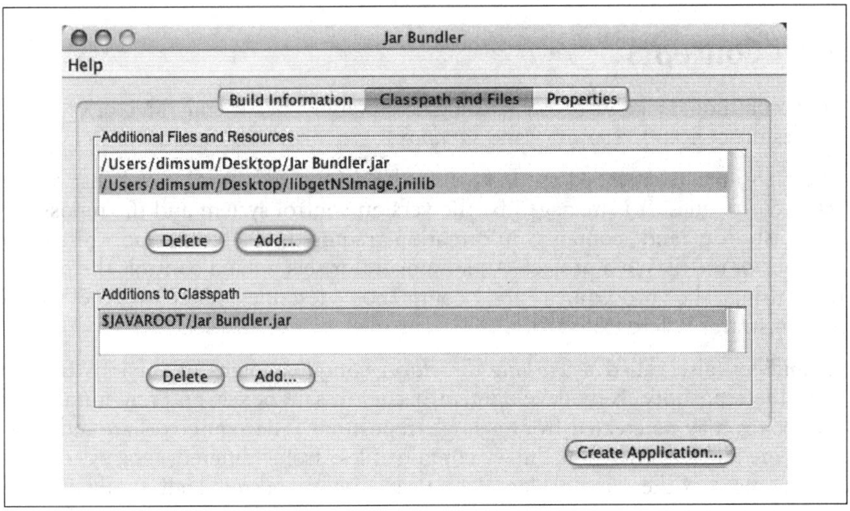

Figure 16-7. The classpaths and Files tab

Java

17
CVS

The Concurrent Versions System (CVS) is the most popular revision control system among users of free and open source software. It is particularly appropriate for highly distributed projects, with developers working on many different computer systems and even in different parts of the world.

This chapter is based on CVS Version 1.11.2.

Basic Concepts

To accommodate large projects using a hierarchy of several directories, CVS defines the concepts *repository* and *sandbox*.

The *repository* (also called an *archive*) is the centralized storage area that stores the projects' files. It is managed by the version control system and the repository administrator, and contains information required to reconstruct historical versions of the files in a project. An administrator sets up and controls the repository using the procedures and commands described later in the "CVS Administrator Reference" section.

A *sandbox* (also called a *working directory*) contains copies of versions of files from the repository. New development occurs in sandboxes, and any number of sandboxes may be created from a single repository. The sandboxes are independent of one another and may contain files from different stages of the development of the same project. Users set up and control sandboxes using the procedures and commands found in the later section "CVS User Reference."

In a typical interaction with CVS, a developer checks out the most current code from the repository, makes changes, tests the results, and then commits those changes back to the repository when they are deemed satisfactory.

Locking and Merging

Some systems, such as RCS (Revision Control System) and the older SCCS (Source Code Control System), use a *locking model* that coordinates the efforts of multiple developers by serializing file modifications. The locking model is pessimistic: it assumes that conflicts must be avoided. Serialization of file modifications through locks prevents conflicts, but it is cumbersome to have to lock files for editing when bug-hunting. Often, developers will circumvent the lock mechanism to keep working, which is an invitation to trouble.

To handle work by multiple developers on a single file, CVS uses a *merging model* that allows everyone to have access to the files at all times and supports concurrent development. The merging model is optimistic: it assumes that conflicts are not common and that when they do occur, it usually isn't difficult to resolve them.

CVS can operate under a locking model via the *-L* and *-l* options to the *admin* command. Also, CVS has special commands (*edit* and *watch*) for those who want additional development coordination support. CVS uses locks internally to prevent corruption when multiple people are accessing the repository simultaneously, but this is different from the user-visible locks of the locking model.

Conflicts and Merging

In the event that two developers commit changes to the same version of a file, CVS automatically defers the commit of the second committer's file. The second committer then issues the *cvs update* command, which merges the first committer's changes into the local file. In many cases, the changes are in different areas of the file, and the merge is successful. However, if both developers have made changes to the same area of the file, the second to commit will have to resolve the conflict. This involves examining the problematic areas of the file and selecting among the multiple versions or making changes that resolve the conflict.

CVS detects only textual conflicts, but conflict resolution is concerned with keeping the project as a whole logically consistent. Therefore, conflict resolution sometimes involves changing files other than the one CVS complained about.

For example, if one developer adds a parameter to a function definition, it may be necessary for all the calls to that function to be modified to pass the additional parameter. This is a logical conflict, so its detection and resolution is the job of the developers (with support from tools, such as compilers and debuggers); CVS won't notice the problem.

In any merge situation, whether or not there was a conflict, the second developer to commit will often want to retest the resulting version of the project because it has changed since the original commit. Once it passes the test, the developer will need to recommit the file.

Tagging

CVS tracks file versions by revision number, which can be used to retrieve a particular revision from the repository. In addition, it is possible to create symbolic tags so that a group of files (or an entire project) can be referred to by a single identifier even when the revision numbers of the files aren't the same (which is most often the case). This capability is often used to keep track of released versions or other important project milestones.

For example, the symbolic tag *hello-1_0* might refer to revision number 1.3 of *hello.c* and revision number 1.1 of *Makefile* (symbolic tags are created with the *tag* and *rtag* commands).

Branching

The simplest form of development is *linear* development, in which there is a succession of revisions to a file, each derived from the prior revision. Many projects can get by with a completely linear development process, but larger projects (as measured by number of files, number of developers, and/or size of the user community) often run into maintenance issues that require additional capabilities. Sometimes it is desirable to do some speculative development while the main line of development continues uninterrupted. Other times, bugs in the currently released version must be fixed while work on the next version is already underway. In both of these cases, the solution is to create a *branch* (or *fork*) from an appropriate point in the development of the project. If, at a future point, some or all of the changes on the branch are needed on the main line of development (or elsewhere), they can be *merged* together (*joined*).

Branches are forked with the *tag -b* command; they are joined with the *update -j* command.

CVS Command Format

CVS commands are of the form:

```
cvs global_options command command_options
```

For example, here is a simple sequence of commands showing both kinds of options in the context of creating a repository, importing existing files, and performing a few common operations on them:

```
$ cvs -d /usr/local/cvsrep init
$ cd ~/work/hello
$ cvs -d /usr/local/cvsrep import -m 'Import' hello vendor start
$ cd ..
$ mv hello hello.bak
$ cvs -d /usr/local/cvsrep checkout hello
$ cd hello
$ vi hello.c
$ cvs commit -m 'Fixed a typo'
$ cvs tag hello-1_0
$ cvs remove -f Makefile
$ cvs commit -m 'Removed old Makefile'
$ cvs upd -r hello-1_0
$ cvs upd -A
```

Some global options are common to both user and administrator commands, and some are specific to each. The common global options are described in the next section, and the administrator and user options are described in the sections "CVS Administrator Reference" and "CVS User Reference," respectively.

Common Global Options

Table 17-1 lists the global options that apply to both user and administrator commands.

Table 17-1. Common global options

Option	Description
-b *bindir*	Location of external RCS programs. This option is obsolete, having been deprecated at CVS versions above 1.9.18.
-T *tempdir*	Absolute path for temporary files. Overrides the setting of *$TMPDIR*.
-v, --version	Display version and copyright information.

Gotchas

The following list clarifies a few aspects of CVS that can sometimes cause confusion:

File orientation
: While directories are supported, they aren't versioned in the same way traditional files are. This is particularly important in the early evolutionary stages of a project, when the structure may be in flux. Also, if the project is undergoing major changes, the structure is likely to change. See the later section "Hacking the Repository."

Text orientation
: There is no equivalent to *diff* for binary files, although CVS's support for binary files is usually sufficient. Use *admin -kb* to tell CVS a file is binary.

Line orientation
: Moving a segment of code from one place in a file to another is seen as a delete (from the old location) and an unrelated add (to the new location).

CVS is not syntax-aware
: As far as CVS is concerned, small formatting changes are equivalent to sweeping logic changes in the same line ranges.

CVS Administrator Reference

This section provides details on creating and configuring repositories and performing other CVS administrative tasks. A single computer can run multiple copies of the CVS server, and each server can serve multiple repositories.

Creating a Repository

Select a directory that will contain the repository files (*/usr/local/cvsrep* is used in the following examples). Use the *init* command to initialize the repository. Either set the $CVSROOT environment variable to the absolute path of the repository:

```
$ export CVSROOT=/usr/local/cvsrep
$ cvs init
```

or use the *-d* option to specify the absolute path to the repository:

```
$ cvs -d /usr/local/cvsrep init
```

For information on importing code, see the section "CVS User Reference," especially *import* and *add*.

Setting up the password server with inetd

If your server uses *inetd* to control services and you want users to access the repository from other computers, configure the *pserver* by doing the following as root:

- Make sure there is an entry in */etc/services* similar to the following:

  ```
  cvspserver 2401/tcp
  ```

- If you aren't using *tcpwrappers*, place a line like this in */etc/inetd.conf*:

  ```
  cvspserver stream tcp nowait root /usr/bin/cvs cvs --allow-root=/usr/
  local/cvsroot pserver
  ```

- If you *are* using *tcpwrappers*, use a line like this:

  ```
  cvspserver stream tcp nowait root /usr/sbin/tcpd /usr/bin/cvs
  --allow-root=/usr/local/cvsroot pserver
  ```

- Once these changes are in place, restart *inetd* (or send it the appropriate signal to cause it to reread *inetd.conf*).

Setting up the password server with xinetd

If your server uses *xinetd* to control services and you want users to access the repository from other computers, configure the *pserver* by doing the following as root:

- Make sure there is a file */etc/xinetd.d/cvspserver* similar to the following:

  ```
  service cvspserver
  {
    port        = 2401
    socket_type = stream
    protocol    = tcp
    wait        = no
    user        = root
    passenv     = PATH
    server      = /usr/local/bin/cvs
    server_args = -f --allow-root=/usr/local/cvsroot pserver
  }
  ```

- Once these changes are in place, restart *xinetd* (or send it the appropriate signal to cause it to reread its configuration.

Security Issues

The following security issues need to be considered when working with CVS:

- The contents of files will be transmitted in the open over the network with *pserver* and *rsh*. With *pserver*, passwords are transmitted in the open as well.
- When using a local repository (i.e., when CVS is not being used in client/server mode), developers need write access to the repository, which means they can hack it.
- The CVS server runs as root briefly before changing its UID.
- The *~/.cvspass* file must be kept unreadable by all users except the owner to prevent passwords from being accessible.
- A user who has authority to make changes to the files in the *CVSROOT* module can run arbitrary programs.
- Some of the options to the *admin* command are very dangerous, so it is advisable to restrict its use. This can be accomplished by creating a user group named *cvsadmin*. If this user group exists, only users in that group can run the *admin* command (except *admin -kkflag*, which is available to everyone).

Repository Structure

The CVS repository is implemented as a normal directory with special contents. This section describes the contents of the repository directory.

The CVSROOT directory

The *CVSROOT* directory contains the administrative files for the repository; other directories in the repository contain the modules. The administrative files permit (and ignore) blank lines and comment lines in addition to the lines containing real configuration information. Comment lines start with a hash mark (#).

Some of the administrative files contain filename patterns to match file and directory names. These patterns are regular expressions like those used in GNU Emacs. Table 17-2 contains the special constructions used most often.

Table 17-2. Filename pattern special constructions

Construction	Description
^	Matches the beginning of the string
$	Matches the end of the string
.	Matches any single character
*	Modifies the preceding construct to match zero or more repetitions

CVS will perform a few important expansions in the contents of the administrative files before interpreting the results. First, the typical shell syntax for referring to a home directory is ~/, which expands to the home directory of the user running CVS; *~user* expands to the home directory of the specified user.

In addition, CVS provides a mechanism similar to the shell's environment variable expansion capability. Constructs such as *${variable}* are replaced by the value of the named variable. Variable names start with letters and consist entirely of letters, numbers, and underscores. Curly brackets may be omitted if the character immediately following the variable reference is not a valid variable name character. While this construct looks like a shell environment variable reference, the full environment is not available. Table 17-3 contains the built-in variables.

Table 17-3. Administrative file variables

Variable	Description
CVSEDITOR EDITOR VISUAL	The editor CVS uses for log-file editing.
CVSROOT	The repository locator in use.
USER	The name of the user (on the server, if using a remote repository) running CVS.
=*var*	The value of a user-defined variable named *var*. Values for these variables are provided by the global *-s* option.

To edit these files, check out the *CVSROOT* module from the repository, edit the files, and commit them back to the repository. You must commit the changes for them to affect CVS's behavior.

Table 17-4 describes the administrative files and their functions.

Table 17-4. CVSROOT files

File	Description
checkoutlist	Extra files to be maintained in *CVSROOT*
commitinfo	Specifications for commit governors
config	Settings to affect the behavior of CVS
cvsignore	Filename patterns of files to ignore
cvswrappers	Specifications for *checkout* and *commit* filters
editinfo	Specifications for log editors (obsolete)
history	Logs information for the *history* command
loginfo	Specifies *commit* notifier program(s)
modules	Module definitions
notify	Notification processing specifications
passwd	A list of users and their CVS-specific passwords
rcsinfo	Template form for log messages
readers	A list of users having read-only access
taginfo	Tag processing specifications
users	Alternate user email addresses for use with *notify*
verifymsg	Specifies log message evaluator program
writers	A list of users having read/write access

Because the *editinfo* file is obsolete, use the `$EDITOR` environment variable (or the *-e* option) to specify the editor and the *verifymsg* file to specify an evaluator.

Each line of the *taginfo* file contains a filename pattern and a command line to execute when files with matching names are tagged.

The checkoutlist file

Whenever changes to files in the *CVSROOT* module are committed, CVS prints the message:

```
cvs commit: Rebuilding administrative file database
```

This informs you that the checked-out copy in the repository has been updated to reflect any changes just committed. As with any other module directory in the repository, the *CVSROOT* directory contains RCS (**,v*) files that retain the history of the files. However, to use the files, CVS needs a copy of the latest revision. So, when CVS prints this message, it is checking out the latest revisions of the administrative files.

If you have added files to the *CVSROOT* module (such as scripts to be called via entries in the *loginfo* file), you need to list them in the *checkoutlist* file. This makes CVS treat them the same way it treats the standard set of *CVSROOT* files.

Each line in this file consists of a filename and an optional error message that is displayed in case there is trouble checking out the file.

The commitinfo file

Whenever a *commit* is being processed, CVS consults this file to determine whether or not any precommit checking of the file is required. Each line of the file contains a directory name pattern, followed by the path of a program to invoke when files are committed in directories with matching names.

Aside from the usual filename-pattern syntax, there are two special patterns:

ALL
: If this pattern is present in the file, all files are passed to the specified checking program. CVS then looks for a pattern that matches the name of each particular file and runs the additional checks found, if any.

DEFAULT
: If this pattern is present in the file, all files for which there was no pattern match are sent to the specified checking program. The automatic match of every file to the *ALL* entry, if any, doesn't count as a match when determining whether or not to send the file to the *DEFAULT* checking program.

CVS constructs the command line for the checking program by appending the full path to the directory within the repository and the list of files being committed (this means you can specify the first few command-line arguments to the program, if necessary). If the checking program exits with a nonzero status, the *commit* is aborted.

The programs that run via this mechanism run on the server computer when a remote repository is used. Here is an example of a *commitinfo* file:

```
ALL $CVSROOT/CVSROOT/commit-ALL.pl
DEFAULT $CVSROOT/CVSROOT/commit-DEFAULT.pl
CVSROOT$ $CVSROOT/CVSROOT/commit-CVSROOT.pl
```

This example assumes you will create the script files in the *CVSROOT* module and add them to the *checkoutlist* file.

The config file

Repository configuration is specified in the *config* administrative file:

LockDir=`dir`
: Directs CVS to put its lock files in the alternate directory given instead of in the repository itself, allowing users without write access to the repository (but with write access to `dir`) to read from the repository.

  Version 1.11 supports this option. Version 1.10 doesn't support alternate directories for lock files and reports an error if this option is set. Older versions of CVS (1.9 and previous) don't support this option either and will not report an error. Don't mix versions that support alternate directories for lock files with versions that don't because lock files in both places defeat the purpose of having them.

LogHistory=`types`
: Determines the types of activities that are logged to the *history* administrative file. The special value *all* implies all the record types listed in Tables 17-19, 17-20, and 17-21. Any subset of those record types can be specified by listing them. For example, the line *LogHistory=*`MAR` logs commit-related events only.

SystemAuth=`value`
: CVS tries to authenticate users via the *CVSROOT/passwd* file first; if that fails, and this option is set to *yes*, CVS tries to authenticate via the system's user database. This option is used with the password server. The default is *yes*.

TopLevelAdmin=`value`
: If this option is set to *yes*, an additional *CVS* directory is created at the top-level directory when *checkout* is run. This allows the client software to detect the repository locator in that directory (see the section "Repository Locators"). The default is *no*.

  This option is useful if you check out multiple modules to the same sandbox directory. If it is enabled, you won't have to provide a repository locator after the first checkout; CVS infers it from the information in the top-level *CVS* directory created during the first checkout.

The cvsignore file

The *cvsignore* administrative file contains a list of filename patterns to ignore, just like the *.cvsignore* files that can appear in sandboxes and user home directories. Unlike the filename patterns in other administrative files, these patterns are in *sh* syntax; they aren't GNU Emacs-style regular expressions. There can be multiple patterns on a line, separated by whitespace (consequently, the patterns themselves can't contain whitespace).

There is a slight difference between filename patterns in *sh* and CVS. Because the CVS patterns aren't subject to variable interpolation, a pattern such as _$* (which is one of the patterns built into CVS) will match a file named *_$foo* but not one named _. But, if you present the same pattern to *sh*, the $* part is interpolated resulting in an effective pattern of just _, which then matches the file _, but not *_$foo*. This becomes particularly important if you are writing your own utilities to work with CVS, and you need to implement the same policy for ignoring files.

Table 17-5 shows the most commonly used *sh*-style pattern constructs.

Table 17-5. Filename patterns for cvsignore

Construct	Description
?	Any one character
*	Any sequence of zero or more characters

Again, diverging from the standards used by the rest of the administrative files, the *cvsignore* file doesn't support comments.

The cvswrappers file

While the *cvsignore* file allows CVS to ignore certain files, the *cvswrappers* file allows you to give CVS default options for commands that work with files. Lines in this file consist of a *sh*-style filename pattern followed by a *-k* (keyword substitution mode) option and/or an *-m* (update method) option. The legal values for *-k* are described in Table 17-17. The legal values for *-m* are *COPY* and *MERGE*.

If *-m COPY* is specified, CVS won't attempt to merge the files. Instead, it presents the user with conflicting versions of the file, and the user can choose one or the other or resolve the conflict manually.

For example, to treat all files ending in *.jpg* as binary, add this line to the file:

```
*.jpg -k b
```

The history file

If this file exists, CVS inserts records of activity against the repository. This information produces displays of the *cvs history* command. The history file is not intended for direct reading or writing by programs other than CVS.

A repository set up with *cvs init* automatically has a *history* file.

The loginfo file

The *loginfo* administrative file works much like the *commitinfo* file and can use the special patterns *ALL* and *DEFAULT*. This file allows you to do something with *commit* log messages and related information.

The programs called during *loginfo* processing receive the log message on standard input. Table 17-6 shows the three codes that can pass additional information to the called programs via command-line arguments.

Table 17-6. Special loginfo variables

Variable	Description
s	Filename
V	Pre-commit revision number
v	Post-commit revision number

If a percent sign (%) followed by the desired variable is placed after the command path, CVS inserts the corresponding information as a whitespace-separated list with one entry for each file, preceded by the repository path (as with *commitinfo*). There can be only one percent sign on the command line, so if you want information from more than one variable, place the variable names inside curly brackets: `%{...}`. In this case, each file-specific entry has one field for each variable, separated by commas. For example, the code `%{sVv}` expands into a list like this:

```
/usr/local/cvsrep/hello Makefile,1.1,1.2 hello.c,1.8,1.9
```

It can be helpful to send email notifications each time someone commits a file to the repository. Developers can monitor this stream of notices to determine when they should pull the latest development code into their private sandboxes. For example, consider a developer doing some preparatory work in his sandbox while he awaits stabilization and addition of another developer's new library. As soon as the new library is added and committed, email notification goes out, and the waiting developer sees that the code is ready to use. So, he runs *cvs upd -d* in the appropriate directory to pull in the new library code and then sets about integrating it with his work.

It is simple to set up this kind of notification. Just add a line like this to the *CVSROOT/loginfo* file:

```
DEFAULT mail -s %s developers@company.com
```

Often, the email address is a mailing list, which has all the interested parties (developers or otherwise) on the distribution list. If you want to send messages to multiple email addresses, you can write a script to do that and have that script called via this file. Alternatively, you can use the *log.pl* program that comes as part of the CVS source distribution (located at */usr/local/src/cvs-1.11/contrib/log.pl*, assuming CVS was unpacked into */usr/local/src*). Instructions for its use are provided as comments in the file.

The modules file

The top-level directories in a repository are called *modules*. In addition to these physical modules, CVS provides a mechanism to create logical modules through the *modules* administrative file. Here are the three kinds of logical modules:

Alias

Alias modules are defined by lines of the form:

```
module_name -a alias_module ...
```

Using an alias module name in a CVS command is equivalent to using its component modules (after the *-a* option) directly.

Regular

Regular modules are defined by lines of the form:

```
module_name [options] directory file ...
```

Checking out `module_name` results in the specified files from `directory` being checked out into a directory named `module_name`. The intervening directories (if any) aren't reflected in the sandbox.

Ampersand

Ampersand modules are defined by lines of the form:

```
module_name [options] &other_module ...
```

Checking out such a module results in a directory named `module_name`, which in turn contains copies of the `other_module` modules.

Table 17-7 shows the options that can define modules.

Table 17-7. Module options

Option	Description
-d name	Overrides the default working directory name for the module.
-e prog	Runs the program *prog* when files are exported from the module; the module name is passed in to *prog* as the sole argument.
-i prog	Runs the program *prog* when files are committed to the module; the repository directory of the committed files is passed in to *prog* as the sole argument.
-i prog	Runs the program *prog* when files are checked out from the module; the module name is passed in to *prog* as the sole argument.
-s status	Assigns a status descriptor to the module.
-t prog	Runs the program *prog* when files are tagged in the module using *rtag*; the module name and the symbolic tag are passed in to *prog*.
-u prog	Runs the program *prog* when files are updated in the module's top-level directory; the full path to the module within the repository is passed in to *prog* as the sole argument.

Alias modules provide alternative names for other modules or shortcuts for referring to collections or subdirectories of other modules. Alias module definitions function like macro definitions in that they cause commands to run as if the expanded list of modules and directories were on the command line. Alias modules don't cause the modules of their definition to be grouped together under the alias name (use ampersand modules for that). For example, the definition:

```
h -a hello
```

makes the name *h* a synonym for the *hello* module. This definition:

```
project -a library client server
```

allows you to check out all three modules of the project as a unit. If an entry in the definition of an alias module is preceded by an exclamation point (!), the named directory is excluded from the module.

Regular modules allow you to create modules that are subsets of other modules. For example, the definition:

```
header library library.h
```

creates the *header* module, which consists of only the *library.h* file from the *library* module.

Ampersand modules are true logical modules. There are no top-level directories for them in the repository, but you can check them out to sandboxes, and directories with their names will then appear. The modules listed in the definition are below that directory. For example:

```
project &library &client &server
```

is almost the same as the alias module example given earlier, except that the submodules are checked out inside a subdirectory named *project*.

In this file, long definitions may be split across multiple lines by terminating all but the last line with backslashes (\).

The notify file

This file is used in conjunction with the *watch* command. When notifications are appropriate, this file is consulted to determine how to do the notification.

Each line of the *notify* file contains a filename pattern and a command line. CVS' notification mechanism uses the command line specified to perform notifications for files with names that match the corresponding pattern.

There is a single special-purpose variable, *%s*, that can appear in the command specification. When the command is executed, the name of the user to notify replaces the variable name. If the *users* administrative file exists, the usernames are looked up there, and the resulting values are used for *%s* instead. This allows email to be sent to accounts other than those on the local machine. Details are sent to the notification program via standard input.

Typical usage of this feature is the single entry:

```
ALL mail %s -s "CVS notification"
```

In fact, this entry is present in the default *notify* file that's created when you run *cvs init* to create a repository (although it is initially commented out).

The passwd file

If you access the repository via a *pserver* repository locator (see the section "Repository Locators"), CVS can have its own private authentication information, separate from the system's user database. This information is stored in the *CVSROOT/passwd* administrative file.

This feature provides anonymous CVS access over the Internet. By creating an entry for a public user (usually *anoncvs* or *anonymous*), the *pserver* can be used by many people sharing the public account. If you don't want to create a system user with the same name as the public user, or if you have such a user but it has a different purpose, you can employ a user alias to map it to something else:

```
anonymous:TY7QWpLw8bvus:cvsnoname
```

You should then make sure to create the *cvsnoname* user on the system. You can use */bin/false* as the login shell, and the repository's root directory as the home directory for the user.

If you leave the password field empty for the anonymous user, CVS will accept any password (as of Version 1.11). To restrict the public user to read-only access, list it in the *CVSROOT/readers* administrative file.

Additionally, CVS' private user database is useful even if you don't want to set up anonymous CVS access. You can restrict access to a subset of the system's users, provide remote access to users who don't have general system access, or prevent a user's normal system password from being transmitted in the clear over the network (see the section "Security Issues").

There is no *cvs passwd* command for setting CVS-specific passwords (located in the repository file *CVSROOT/passwd*). CVS-specific user and password management is a manual task.

The rcsinfo file

CVS consults this file when doing a *commit* or *import* to determine the log message editor template. Each entry in the file consists of a filename pattern and the name of the file to use as the template for module directories with matching names.

The *ALL* and *DEFAULT* special patterns apply to this file.

The readers file

If this file exists, users listed in it have read-only access.

The taginfo file

CVS consults this file whenever the *tag* or *rtag* commands are used. Entries in this file are filename patterns and program specifications. The *ALL* special pattern applies to this file.

The *taginfo* file is called with the tag, the operation being performed, the module directory name (relative to the repository root), and the filename and revision number for each affected file. The valid operations are *add* (for *tag*), *del* (for *tag -d*), and *mov* (for *tag -F*).

If the *taginfo* program returns a nonzero status, the *tag* or *rtag* command that caused its execution is aborted.

The users file

If this file exists, it is consulted during processing of the *notify* administrative file's contents. Entries in this file consist of two colon-separated fields on a single line.

The first field is the name of a user, and the second field is a value (normally the user's email address on another machine). For example:

```
john:john@somecompany.com
jane:jane@anothercompany.com
```

The verifymsg file

CVS consults this file to determine if log messages should be validated. If the program returns a nonzero status, the commit is aborted. The *verifymsg* file is called with the full path to a file containing the log message to be verified.

The *ALL* special pattern is not supported for this file, although *DEFAULT* is. If more than one pattern matches, the first match is used.

The writers file

If this file exists, users listed in it have read/write access (unless they are also listed in the *readers* file, in which case they have read-only access).

Hacking the Repository

Because the repository is a normal directory, albeit one with special contents, it is possible to *cd* into the directory and examine its contents and/or make changes to the files and directories there. For each file that has been added, there is a file with the same name followed by *,v* in a corresponding directory in the repository. These are RCS (the format, not the program) files that contain multiple versions of the file.

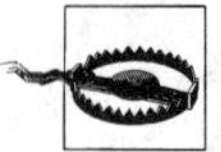

Because the activities discussed in this section involve making changes directly to the repository instead of working through CVS commands, you should exercise extreme caution and have current backups when following these instructions.

Restructuring a project

Restructuring the project by moving files and directories around (and possibly renaming them) in the repository allows the files to retain their history. The standard way to rename a file when using CVS is to rename the file in the sandbox and do a *cvs remove* on the old name and a *cvs add* on the new name. This results in the file being disconnected from its history under the new name, so sometimes it is better to do the renaming directly in the repository. However, doing this while people have active sandboxes is dangerous because the sandboxes will contain information about a file that is no longer in the repository.

Obsolete and temporary files

When importing an entire project, all the project's files are added to the repository; however, if some files shouldn't be added, you'll want to remove them. Doing a *cvs remove* accomplishes this, but copies of those files will remain in the repository's *.Attic* directory forever. To avoid this, you can delete the files from the repository directly before checking out sandboxes from it.

Importing

If you have an existing code base, you should import it into CVS in a way that preserves the most historical information. This section provides instructions for importing projects into CVS from code snapshots or other version-control systems. Except for the code-snapshot import procedure, all are based on conversion to RCS files, followed by placing the RCS files in the proper location in the CVS repository.

Importing code snapshots

If you have maintained project history archives manually by taking periodic snapshots of the code, you can import the first snapshot, tag it with the date or version number, and then successively overlay the updated files from later archives. Each set can then be committed and tagged in order to bootstrap a repository that maintains the prior history.

For example, first unpack the distributions (this assumes they unpack to directories containing the version numbers):

```
$ tar xvzf foo-1.0.tar.gz
$ tar xvzf foo-1.1.tar.gz
$ tar xvzf foo-2.0.tar.gz
```

Next, make a copy of the first version, import it into the CVS repository, check it out to make a sandbox (because importing doesn't convert the source directory into a sandbox), and use *cvs tag* to give it a symbolic name reflecting the project version:

```
$ mkdir foo
$ cp -R -p foo-1.0/* foo
$ cd foo
$ cvs import -m 'Imported version 1.0' foo vendor start
$ cd ..
$ mv foo foo.bak
$ cvs checkout foo
$ cd foo
$ cvs tag foo-1_0
$ cd ..
```

Now, apply the differences between Version 1.0 and 1.1 to the sandbox, commit the changes, and create a tag:

```
$ diff -Naur foo-1.0 foo-1.1 | (cd foo; patch -Np1)
$ cd foo
$ cvs commit -m 'Imported version 1.1'
$ cvs tag foo-1_1
$ cd ..
```

Apply the differences between Version 1.1 and 2.0 to the sandbox, commit the changes, and create a tag:

```
$ diff -Naur foo-1.1 foo-2.0 | (cd foo; patch -Np1)
$ cd foo
$ cvs commit -m 'Imported version 2.0'
$ cvs tag foo-2_0
```

You can now use the *log* command to view the history of the files, browse past versions of the files, and continue development under version control.

Importing from RCS

If you are migrating from RCS to CVS, following these instructions will result in a usable CVS repository. This procedure involves direct modification of the CVS repository, so it should be undertaken with caution.

Before beginning, make sure none of the files to be imported into CVS is locked by RCS. Then, create a new CVS repository and module (or a new module within an existing repository). Next, create directories in the CVS repository to mirror the project's directory structure. Finally, copy all the version files (*,v*) from the project (which may be in *RCS* subdirectories) into the appropriate directories in the repository (without *RCS* subdirectories).

For example, first move aside the directory under RCS control, create an empty directory to build the new CVS structure, import the directory, and then check it out to make a sandbox:

```
$ mv foo foo-rcs
$ mkdir foo
$ cd foo
$ cvs import -m 'New empty project' foo vendor start
$ cd ..
$ mv foo foo.bak
$ cvs checkout foo
```

Next, make directories and add them to the repository to match the structure in the RCS project:

```
$ cd foo
$ mkdir dir
$ cvs add dir
$ cd ..
```

Now, copy the *,v* files from the RCS project into the repository for the CVS project:

```
$ cp -p foo-rcs/*,v $CVSROOT/foo
$ cp -p foo-rcs/dir/*,v $CVSROOT/foo/dir
```

Finally, issue the *cvs update* command in the sandbox directory to bring in the latest versions of all the files:

```
$ cd foo
$ cvs upd
```

Importing from SCCS

To import from SCCS, use the *sccs2rcs* script located in the *contrib* directory of the CVS distribution to convert the files to RCS format, and then follow the preceding RCS procedure. You must have both CVS and SCCS installed for this to work. The script's comments contain additional instructions.

Importing from PVCS

To import from PVCS, use the *pvcs_to_rcs* script located in the *contrib* directory of the CVS distribution to convert the files to RCS format, and then follow the preceding RCS procedure. You must have both CVS and PVCS installed for this to work. The script's comments contain additional instructions.

Using an Interim Shared Sandbox

Projects will sometimes develop unintended environmental dependencies over time, especially when there is no pressure for the code to be relocatable. A project developed outside version control may even be initially developed in place (at its intended installation location). While these practices are not recommended, they do occur in real-world situations. CVS can help to improve the situation by encouraging relocatability from the beginning of a project.

The default mode of operation for CVS is multiple independent sandboxes, all coordinated with a central shared repository. Code that runs in this environment is necessarily (at least partially) relocatable. So, using CVS from the beginning of a project helps ensure flexibility.

However, if a project is already well underway, an interim approach can be used. For example, you can convert the development area to a single shared sandbox by importing the code into CVS and checking it back out again:

```
$ cd /usr/local/bar
$ cvs import bar vendor start
$ cd ..
$ mv bar bar.bak
$ cvs checkout bar
```

Chances are good that this approach is too aggressive and will check in more files than absolutely necessary. You can either go back and hack the repository to remove the files that shouldn't be there or just issue the *cvs remove* command to delete them as you discover them.

In addition, there will probably be some binary files in the sandbox that were imported as text files. Wherever you see a binary file that needs to remain in the repository, you should issue the command *cvs admin -kb `file`*, then make a fresh copy from the project backup. Finally, issue the command *cvs commit `file`* to commit the fixed file back to the repository.

Having version control in place before making flexibility enhancements is a good idea, because it makes it easier to find (and possibly reverse) changes that cause trouble.

The repository locator (see the section "Repository Locators") is specified via the -*d* option or the `$CVSROOT` environment variable. It is stored in the various *CVS/root* sandbox files. If you use the password server (*pserver*), the UID of the person checking out the sandbox will be remembered. If more than one person is working with a particular sandbox, they will have to share an account for CVS access.

One way to share accounts is to have a neutral user account with a password known by everyone with CVS access. One person then issues the *cvs login* command with that UID and password. Once you are no longer using a shared sandbox, this workaround won't be necessary. However, during the time you use a shared sandbox, it is important that the developers type their real UIDs into their log messages because all the changes will appear to have been made by the common user.

Global Server Option

The server has one global option: *--allow-root=`rootdir`*. This option tells the CVS server to accept and process requests for the specified repository.

Administrator Commands

Table 17-8 lists the commands CVS administrators can use to manage their repositories.

Table 17-8. Administrator commands

Command	Description
admin, adm, rcs	Perform administrative functions
init	Create a new repository
kserver	Run in Kerberos server mode
pserver	Run in password server mode
server	Run in remote server mode

admin

```
admin
 [ -b[rev] ]
 [ -cstring ]
 [ -kkflag ]
 [ -l[rev] ]
 [ -L ]
 [ -mrev:msg ]
 [ -nname[:[rev]] ]
 [ -Nname[:[rev]] ]
 [ -orange ]
 [ -q ]
 [ -sstate[:rev]
 [ -t[file] ]
```

```
[ -t-string ]
[ -u[rev] ]
[ -U ]
[ files ... ]
```

The *admin* command performs administrative functions. If a *cvsadmin* user group exists, only the users in that group will be able to run *admin* with options other than *-k*. Options that may be used with the *admin* command are listed here:

-b[rev]
: Set the default branch.

-cstring
: Obsolete. Set the comment leader.

-kkflag
: Set the default keyword substitution mode.

-l[rev]
: Lock the specified revision.

-L
: Enable strict locking.

-mrev:msg
: Change the revision's log message.

-nname[:[rev]]
: Give the specified branch or revision the symbolic name *name*.

-Nname[:[rev]]
: The same as *-n*, except that if *name* is already in use, it is moved.

-orange
: Delete revisions permanently.

-q
: Don't print diagnostics.

-sstate[:rev]
: Change the state of a revision.

-t[file]
: Set the descriptive text in the RCS file.

-t-string
: Set the descriptive text in the RCS file to *string*.

-u[rev]
: Unlock the specified revision.

-U
: Disable strict locking.

If the revision specified for *-l* is a branch, the latest revision on that branch is used. If no revision is given, the latest revision on the default branch is used.

If the name given for *-n* is already in use, an error is generated. You can use *-N* to move a tag (change the revision associated with the tag); however, you should normally use *cvs tag* or *cvs rtag* instead.

The *-o* option is very dangerous and results in a permanent loss of information from the repository. Use it with extreme caution and only after careful consideration. See Table 17-9 for the various ways to specify ranges. There must not be any branches or locks on the revisions to be removed. Beware of interactions between this command and symbolic names.

If no *file* is specified for the *-t* option, CVS reads from standard input until it reaches the end of the file or a period on a line by itself.

The determination of the target revision for the *-u* option is the same as for *-l*.

Table 17-9. Range formats

Format	Description
rev1::rev2	Eliminate versions between *rev1* and *rev2*, retaining only enough information to go directly from *rev1* to *rev2*. The two specified versions are retained.
::rev2	The same as *rev1::rev2*, except the first revision is the branchpoint revision.
rev1::	The same as *rev1::rev2*, except the second revision is the end of the branch, and it is deleted instead of retained.
rev	Delete the specified revision.
rev1:rev2	The same as *rev1::rev2*, except the two named revisions are deleted as well.
:rev2	The same as *::rev2*, except the named revision is deleted as well.
rev1:	The same as *rev1::*, except the named revision is deleted as well.

The following options are present in CVS for historical reasons and should not be used. (Using these options may corrupt the repository.)

-alogins
: Append the logins to the RCS file's access list.

-Aoldfile
: Append the access list of oldfile to the access list of the RCS file.

-e[logins]
: Erase logins from the RCS file's access list, or erase all if a list is not provided.

-i
: Create and initialize a new RCS file. Don't use this option; instead, use *add* to add files to a CVS repository.

-I
: Run interactively. This option doesn't work with client/server CVS and is likely to be removed in a future version.

-Vn
: This option specified that the RCS files used by CVS should be made compatible with a specific version of RCS.

-xsuffixes
: This option used to be described as determining the filename suffix for RCS files, but CVS has always used only *,v* as the RCS file suffix.

init

```
init
```

Initializes the repository. Use the global *-d* option to specify the repository's directory if $CVSROOT isn't set appropriately.

The newly initialized repository contains a *CVSROOT* module and nothing else. Once the repository is initialized, use other CVS commands to add files to it or to check out the *CVSROOT* module to make changes to the administrative files.

kserver

`kserver`

Operate as a server with Kerberos authentication, providing access to the repositories specified before the command with the *--allow-root* option. This command is used in the *inetd.conf* file, not on the command line. Another global option frequently used with this command is *-T* (see Table 17-1).

pserver

`pserver`

Operate as a password-authenticated server, providing access to the repositories specified before the command with the *--allow-root* option. This command is used in the *inetd.conf* file, not on the command line. Another global option frequently used with this command is *-T* (see Table 17-1).

server

`server`

The CVS client runs this command on the remote machine when connecting to a repository specified by an *:ext:* repository locator (usually via RSH or SSH).

CVS User Reference

This section provides details on connecting to a repository, the structure of sandboxes, and using the CVS commands.

Repository Locators

CVS currently supports six methods for the client to access the repository: local, forked, external, a password server, a GSS-API (Generic Security Services API) server, and a Kerberos 4 server (most Kerberos users will want to use GSS-API). Table 17-10 describes the various repository locator types and their respective access methods.

Table 17-10. Repository access types and methods

Method	Locator format	Description
Local	*path* *:local:path*	If the repository directory is local to the computer from which you will access it (or appears local, such as an NFS or Samba mounted filesystem), the repository string is just the pathname of the repository directory, such as */usr/local/cvsrep*, or it can use the *:local:* prefix.

Table 17-10. Repository access types and methods (continued)

Method	Locator format	Description
Forked local	*:fork:path*	This type of locator is used primarily for debugging the CVS protocol code; it causes CVS to start (fork) a separate process to work with the repository and communicates with it using the CVS remote protocol.
External	*:ext:user@host:path*	External repositories are accessed via a remote shell utility, usually *rsh* (the default) or *ssh*. The environment variable $CVS_RSH is used to specify the remote shell program.
Password server	*:pserver:user@host:path*	Password server repositories require authentication to a user account before allowing use of the repository. Public CVS servers are commonly configured this way so they can provide anonymous CVS access. See the section "The passwd file" earlier in this chapter for more information on anonymous CVS.
GSS-API server	*:gserver:*	This locator type is used for servers accessible via Kerberos 5 or other authentication mechanisms supported by GSS-API.
Kerberos server	*:kserver:*	This locator type is used for servers accessible via Kerberos 4.

Configuring CVS

CVS's behavior can be influenced by two classes of settings other than the command-line arguments: *environment variables* (see Table 17-11) and *special files* (see Table 17-12).

Table 17-11. Environment variables

Variable	Description
$CVS_CLIENT_LOG	Client-side debugging file specification for client/server connections. $CVS_CLIENT_LOG is the basename for the *$CVS_CLIENT_LOG.in* and *$CVS_CLIENT_LOG.out* files, which are written in the current working directory at the time a command is executed.
$CVS_CLIENT_PORT	The port number for *:kserver:* locators. $CVS_CLIENT_PORT doesn't need to be set if the *kserver* is listening on port 1999 (the default).
$CVS_IGNORE_REMOTE_ROOT	According to the *change log*, this variable was removed from CVS with Version 1.10.3.
$CVS_PASSFILE	Password file for *:pserver:* locators. This variable must be set before issuing the *cvs login* to have the desired effect. Defaults to *$HOME/.cvspass*.
$CVS_RCMD_PORT	For non-Unix clients, the port for connecting to the server's *rcmd* daemon.
$CVS_RSH	Remote shell for *:ext:* locators, if not *rsh*.
$CVS_SERVER	Remote server program for *:ext:* locators, if not *cvs*.
$CVS_SERVER_SLEEP	Server-side execution delay (in seconds) to allow time to attach a debugger.
$CVSEDITOR	Editor used for log messages; overrides $EDITOR.
$CVSIGNORE	A list of filename patterns to ignore, separated by whitespace. (See also *cvsignore* in Table 17-4 and *.cvsignore* in Table 17-12.)
$CVSREAD	Determines read-only (if the variable is set) or read/write (if the variable is not set) for *checkout* and *update*.
$CVSROOT	Default repository locator.
$CVSUMASK	Used to determine permissions for (local) repository files.

Table 17-11. Environment variables (continued)

Variable	Description
`$CVSWRAPPERS`	A list of filename patterns for the *cvswrappers* function. See also the "Repository Structure" section.
`$EDITOR`	Specifies the editor to use for log messages; see notes for $CVSEDITOR.
`$HOME`	On Unix, used to find the *.cvsrc* file.
`$HOMEDRIVE, $HOMEPATH`	On Windows NT, used to find the *.cvsrc* file.
`$PATH`	Used to locate programs to run.

`$TEMP`
`$TMP`
`$TMPDIR`
	Location for temporary files. $TMPDIR is used by the server. On Unix, */tmp* (and *TMP* on Windows NT) may not be overridden for some functions of CVS due to reliance on the system's *tmpnam()* function.

`$VISUAL`	Specifies the editor to use for log messages; see notes for $CVSEDITOR.

Despite the similarity in names, the `$CVSROOT` environment variable and the *CVSROOT* directory in a repository are not related to each other.

The "RSH" in the name of the `$CVS_RSH` environment variable doesn't refer to the particular program (*rsh*), but rather to the program CVS is supposed to use for creating remote shell connections (which could be some program other than *rsh*, such as *ssh*).

Because there is only one way to specify the remote shell program to use ($CVS_RSH) and because this is a global setting, users that commonly access multiple repositories may need to pay close attention to which repository they are using. If one repository requires one setting of this variable and another requires a different setting, you will have to change this variable between accesses to repositories requiring different settings. This aspect of the repository access method is not stored in the *CVS/Root* file in the sandbox (see the section "CVS directories," later in this chapter). For example, if you access some repositories via *rsh* and some via *ssh*, you can create the following two utility aliases (*bash* syntax):

```
$ alias cvs="export CVS_RSH=ssh; cvs"
$ alias cvr="export CVS_RSH=rsh; cvs"
```

Table 17-12 shows the files used by the CVS command-line client for server connection and client configuration information. These files reside in the user's home directory.

Table 17-12. Client configuration files

Option	Description
~/.cvsignore	Filename patterns of files to ignore
~/.cvspass	Passwords cached by *cvs login*
~/.cvsrc	Default command options
~/.cvswrappers	User-specific *checkout* and *commit* filters

The *~/.cvspass* file is really an operational file, not a configuration file. It is used by the *cvs* client program to store the repository user account password between *cvs login* and *cvs logoff*.

Here are some common *.cvsrc* settings:

update -dP
: Bring in new directories and prune empty directories on *cvs update*.

diff -c
: Give output in context *diff* format.

Creating a Sandbox

In order to use CVS, you must create a sandbox or have one created for you. This section describes sandbox creation, assuming there is already a module in the repository you want to work with. See the *import* command for information on importing a new module into the repository.

1. Determine the repository locator. Talk to the repository administrator if you need help finding the repository or getting the locator syntax right.
2. If this will be your main repository, set $CVSROOT; otherwise, use the *-d* option when running CVS commands that don't infer the repository from the sandbox files.
3. Pick a module to check out.
4. Pick a sandbox location, and *cd* to the parent directory.
5. If the repository requires login, do *cvs login*.
6. Run *cvs checkout* `module`.

For example:

```
$ export CVSROOT=/usr/local/cvsroot
$ cd ~/work
$ cvs checkout hello
```

Sandbox Structure

This section describes the files and directories that may be encountered in sandboxes.

.cvsignore files

Sandboxes may contain *.cvsignore* files. These files specify filename patterns for files that may exist in the sandbox but that normally won't be checked into CVS. This is commonly used to cause CVS to bypass derived files.

.cvswrappers files

Sandboxes may contain *.cvswrappers* files, which provide directory-specific file handling information like that in the repository configuration file *cvswrappers* (see the section "The cvswrappers file" earlier in this chapter).

CVS directories

Each directory in a sandbox contains a *CVS* directory. The files in this directory (see Table 17-13) contain metadata used by CVS to locate the repository and track which file versions have been copied into the sandbox.

Table 17-13. Files in the CVS directories

File	Description
Base *Baserev* *Baserev.tmp*	The *Base* directory stores copies of files when the *edit* command is used. The *Baserev* file contains the revision numbers of the files in *Base*. The *Baserev.tmp* file is used to update the *Baserev* file.
Checkin.prog *Update.prog*	The programs specified in the *modules* file for options *-i* and *-u*, respectively (if any).
Entries	Version numbers and timestamps for the files as they were copied from the repository when checked out or updated.
Entries.Backup *Entries.Log* *Entries.Static*	Temporary and intermediate files used by CVS.
Notify *Notify.tmp*	Temporary files used by CVS to deal with notifications for commands such as *edit* and *unedit*.
Repository	The name by which the directory is known in the repository.
Root	The repository locator in effect when the sandbox was created (via *cvs checkout*).
Tag	Information about sticky tags and dates for files in the directory.
Template	Stores the contents of the *rcsinfo* administrative file from the repository for remote repositories.

Because each sandbox directory has one *CVS/Root* file, a sandbox directory corresponds to exactly one repository. You can't check out some files from one repository and some from another into a single sandbox directory.

Client Global Options

Table 17-14 lists the global options that control the operation of the CVS client program.

Table 17-14. Client global options

Option	Description
-a	Authenticate (*gserver* only).
-d root	Locate the repository. Overrides the setting of $CVSROOT.
-e editor	Specify message editor. Overrides the settings of $CVSEDITOR and $EDITOR.
-f	Don't read *~/.cvsrc*. Useful when you have *.cvsrc* settings that you want to forgo for a particular command.
-H [command] *--help [command]*	Display help. If no command is specified, displays general CVS help, including a list of other help options.
-l	Don't log command in history.
-n	Don't change any files. Useful when you want to know ahead of time which files will be affected by a particular command.
-q	Be quiet.

Table 17-14. Client global options (continued)

Option	Description
-Q	Be very quiet. Print messages for serious problems only.
-r	Make new working files read-only.
-s *variable=value*	Set the value of a user variable to a given value. User variables can be used in the contents of administrative files.
-t	Trace execution. Helpful in debugging remote repository connection problems and, in conjunction with *-n*, in determining the effect of an unfamiliar command.
-w	Make new working files read/write. Overrides $CVSREAD. Files are read/write unless $CVSREAD is set or *-r* is specified.
-x	Encrypt. (Introduced in Version 1.10.)
-z gzip_level	Set the compression level. Useful when using CVS in client/server mode across slow connections.

Common Client Options

Tables 17-15 and 17-16 describe options common to many CVS commands. Table 17-15 lists the common options with a description of their function, while Table 17-16 lists which options can be used with the user commands. In the sections that follow, details are provided only for options that aren't listed here or that don't function as described here.

Table 17-15. Common options

Option	Description
-D date	Use the most recent revision no later than *date* (see the next section for supported date formats).
-f	For commands that involve tags (via *-r*) or dates (via *-D*), include files not tagged with the specified tag or not present on the specified date. The most recent revision is included.
-k kflag	Determine how keyword substitution is performed. The space between *-k* and *kflag* is optional. See Table 17-17 for the list of keyword substitution modes.
-l	Don't recurse into subdirectories.
-n	Don't run module programs.
-R	Do recurse into subdirectories (the default). As of Version 1.11, CVS can work in sandboxes with directories checked out from different repositories.
-r rev	Use a particular revision number or symbolic tag.

Table 17-16 shows which common options are applicable to each user command.

Table 17-16. Common client option applicability

Command	-D	-f	-k	-l	-n	-R	-r
add			✓				
annotate	✓	✓		✓		✓	✓
checkout	✓	✓	✓	✓	✓	✓	✓
commit				✓	✓	✓	✓
diff	✓		✓	✓		✓	✓
edit				✓		✓	

Table 17-16. Common client option applicability (continued)

Command	-D	-f	-k	-l	-n	-R	-r
editors				✓		✓	
export	✓	✓	✓	✓	✓	✓	✓
help							
history	✓						✓
import			✓				
log				✓		✓	
login							
logout							
rannotate	✓	✓		✓		✓	✓
rdiff	✓	✓		✓		✓	✓
release							
remove				✓		✓	
rlog				✓		✓	
rtag	✓	✓		✓		✓	✓
status				✓		✓	
tag				✓		✓	
unedit				✓		✓	
update	✓	✓	✓	✓		✓	✓
version							
watch				✓		✓	
watchers				✓		✓	

Date formats

CVS can understand dates in a variety of formats, including:

ISO standard
: The preferred format is *YYYY-MM-DD HH:MM*, which would read as 2000-05-17, or 2000-05-17 22:00. The technical details of the format are defined in the ISO 8601 standard.

Email standard
: For example: 17 May 2000. The technical details of the format are defined in the RFC 822 and RFC 1123 standards.

Relative
: For example:10 days ago, 4 years ago.

Common
: *month/day/year*. This form can cause confusion because not all cultures use the first two fields in this order (e.g., 1/2/2000 is ambiguous).

Other
: Other formats are accepted, including *YYYY/MM/DD* and those omitting the year (which is assumed to be the current year).

Keyword substitutions

Table 17-17 describes the keyword substitution modes that can be selected with the *-k* option. CVS uses keyword substitutions to insert revision information into files when they are checked out or updated.

Table 17-17. Keyword substitution modes

Mode	Description
b	Binary mode. Treat the file the same as with mode *o*, but also avoid newline conversion.
k	Keyword-only mode. Flatten all keywords to just the keyword name. Use this mode if you want to compare two revisions of a file without seeing the keyword substitution differences.
kv	Keyword-value mode. The keyword and the corresponding value are substituted. This is the default mode.
kvl	Keyword-value-locker mode. This mode is the same as *kv* mode, except it always adds the lock holder's user ID if the revision is locked. The lock is obtained via the *cvs admin -l* command.
o	Old-contents mode. Use the keyword values as they appear in the repository rather than generate new values.
v	Value-only mode. Substitute the value of each keyword for the entire keyword field, omitting even the *$* delimiters. This mode destroys the field in the process, so use it cautiously.

Keyword substitution fields are strings of the form `$Keyword ...$`. These are the valid keywords:

Author
: The UID of the person who committed the revision.

Date
: The date and time (in standard UTC format) the revision was committed.

Header
: The full path of the repository RCS file; the revision number; the commit date, time, and UID; the file's state; and the lock holder's UID if the file is locked.

Id
: A shorter form of *Header*, omitting the leading directory name(s) from the RCS file's path, leaving only the filename.

Name
: The tag name that retrieves the file, or empty if no explicit tag is given when the file was retrieved.

Locker
: The UID of the user holding a lock on the file, or empty if the file isn't locked.

Log
: The RCS filename. In addition to keyword expansion in the keyword field, each commit adds additional lines in the file immediately following the line containing this keyword. The first such line contains the revision number and the commit date, time, and UID. Subsequent lines are the contents of the commit log message. The result over time is a reverse-chronological list of log entries for the file. Each additional line is preceded by the same characters that precede the keyword field on its line. This allows the log information to be formatted in a comment for most languages. For example:

```
#
# foo.pl
#
# $Log: ch15,v $
#
# Revision 1.2  2000/06/09 22:10:23  me
# Fixed the new bug introduced when the last one was fixed.
#
# Revision 1.1  2000/06/09 18:07:51  me
# Fixed the last remaining bug in the system.
#
```

Don't place any keyword fields in your log messages if you use this keyword because they will get expanded.

RCSfile
: The name of the RCS file (without any leading directories).

Revision
: The revision number of the file.

Source
: The full path of the RCS file.

State
: The file's state, as assigned by *cvs admin -s* (if you don't set the state explicitly, it will be set to `Exp` by default).

User Commands

The CVS client program provides the user commands defined in Table 17-18.

Table 17-18. User commands

Command	Description
ad, add, new	Indicate that files/directories should be added to the repository.
ann, annotate	Display contents of the head revision of a file, annotated with the revision number, user, and date of the last change for each line.
checkout, co, get	Create a sandbox for a module.
ci, com, commit	Commit changes from the sandbox back to the repository.
di, dif, diff	View differences between file versions.
edit	Prepare to edit files. This is used to enhance developer coordination.
editors	Display a list of users working on the files. This is used to enhance developer coordination.
ex, exp, export	Retrieve a module, but don't make the result a sandbox.
help	Get help.
hi, his, history	Display the log information for files.
im, imp, import	Import new modules into the repository.
lgn, login, logon	Log into (cache the password for) a remote CVS server.
lo, log	Show the activity log for the file(s).
logout	Log off from (flush the password for) a remote CVS server.
pa, patch ,rdiff	Release *diff*. The output is the format of input to Larry Wall's *patch* command. Doesn't have to run from within a sandbox.

Table 17-18. User commands (continued)

Command	Description
rannotate	Display contents of the head revision of a module, annotated with the revision number, user, and date of the last change for each line.
re ,rel, release	Perform a logged delete on a sandbox.
rlog	Show the activity log for the module(s).
remove, rm, delete	Remove a file or directory from the repository.
rt, rtag, rfreeze	Tag a particular revision.
st, stat, status	Show detailed status for files.
ta, tag, freeze	Attach a tag to files in the repository.
unedit	Abandon file modifications and make read-only again.
up, upd, update	Synchronize sandbox to repository.
version	Display the version of the CVS client (and server, if appropriate) being used.
watch	Manage the watch settings. This is used to enhance developer coordination.
watchers	Display the list of users watching for changes to the files. This is used to enhance developer coordination.

add

```
add
 [ -k kflag ]
 [ -m message ]
 file ...
```

Indicate that files/directories should be added to the repository. They aren't actually added until they are committed via *cvs commit*. This command is also used to resurrect files that have been deleted with *cvs remove*.

The standard meaning of the common client option *-k* applies. The only additional option that can be used with the *add* command is *-m message*. This option is used to provide a description of the file (which appears in the output of the *log* command).

annotate

```
annotate
 [ [ -D date | -r rev ] -f ]
 [ -F ]
 [ -l | -R ]
 file ...
```

CVS prints a report showing each line of the specified file. Each line is prefixed by information about the most recent change to the line, including the revision number, user, and date. If no revision is specified, the head of the trunk is used.

The standard meanings of the common client options *-D*, *-f*, *-l*, *-r*, and *-R* apply. There is one additional option:

-F Annotate binary files. CVS normally skips binary files.

checkout

```
checkout
 [ -A ]
 [ -c | -s ]
 [ -d dir [ -N ] ]
 [ [ -D date | -r rev ] -f ]
 [ -j rev1 [ -j rev2 ] ]
 [ -k kflag ]
 [ -l | -R ]
 [ -n ]
 [ -p ]
 [ -P ]
 module ...
```

Copy files from the repository to the sandbox.

The standard meanings of the common client options *-D*, *-f*, *-k*, *-l*, *-n*, *-r*, and *-R* apply. Additional options are:

-A Reset any sticky tags or dates.

-c Copy the *module* file to standard output.

-d dir
: Override the default directory name.

-j rev
: Join branches together.

-N Don't shorten module paths.

-p Pipe the files to standard output, with header lines between them showing the filename, RCS filename, and version.

-P Prune empty directories.

-s Show status for each module from the *modules* file.

commit

```
commit
 [ -f | [ -l | -R ] ]
 [ -F file | -m message ]
 [ -n ]
 [ -r revision ]
 [ file ... ]
```

Commit the changes (if any) made to the specified files in the sandbox to the repository. If no files are specified, commit all modified files.

The standard meanings of the common client options *-l*, *-n*, *-r*, and *-R* apply. Use of the *-r* option causes the revision to be sticky, requiring the use of *admin -A* to continue to use the sandbox. Additional options are:

-f Force commit, even if no changes were made.

-F file
: Use the contents of the file as the message.

-m message
: Use the message specified.

diff

```
diff
 [ -k kflag ]
 [ -l | -R ]
 [ format ]
 [ [ -r rev1 | -D date1 ] [ -r rev2 | -D date2 ] ]
 [ file ... ]
```

Compare two versions of a file, and display the differences in a format determined by the options. By default, the sandbox version of the file is compared to the repository version it was originally copied from.

The standard meanings of the common client options *-D*, *-k*, *-l*, *-r*, and *-R* apply. All options for the *diff* command can also be used.

edit

```
edit
 [ -a action ]
 [ -l | -R ]
 [ file ... ]
```

The *edit* command is used in conjunction with *watch* to permit a more coordinated (serialized) development process. It makes the file writable and sends out an advisory to any users that have requested them. A temporary *watch* is established that's removed automatically when either the *unedit* or the *commit* command is issued.

The standard meanings of the common client options *-l* and *-R* apply. The only additional option that can be used with the *edit* command is *-a actions*. This option is used to specify the actions to watch. The legal values for actions are described in the entry for the *watch* command.

editors

```
editors
 [ -l | -R ]
 [ file ... ]
```

Display a list of users working on the files specified. This is determined by checking which users have run the *edit* command on those files. If the *edit* command isn't used, no results are displayed.

The standard meanings of the common client options *-l* and *-R* apply.

See also *watch*.

export

```
export
 [ -d dir [ -N ] ]
 [ -D date | -r rev ]
 [ -f ]
```

```
[ -k kflag ]
[ -l | -R ]
[ -n ]
[ -P ]
module ...
```

Export files from the repository, much like the *checkout* command, except that the result is not a sandbox (i.e., *CVS* subdirectories aren't created). This can be used to prepare a directory for distribution. For example:

```
$ cvs export -r foo-1_0 -d foo-1.0 foo
$ tar czf foo-1.0.tar.gz foo-1.0
```

The standard meanings of the common client options *-D*, *-f*, *-k*, *-l*, *-n*, *-r*, and *-R* apply. Additional options are:

-d dir
: Use *dir* as the directory name instead of using the module name.

-n
: Don't run any checkout programs.

-N
: Don't shorten paths.

When checking out a single file located one or more directories down in a module's directory structure, the *-N* option can be used with *-d* to prevent the creation of intermediate directories.

help

```
help
```

Display helpful information about using the *cvs* program.

history

```
history
 [ -a | -u user ]
 [ -b string ]
 [ -c ]
 [ -D date ]
 [ -e | -x type ]
 [ -f file | -m module | -n module | -p repository ]...
 [ -l ]
 [ -o ]
 [ -r rev ]
 [ -t tag ]
 [ -T ]
 [ -w ]
 [ -x types ]
 [ -z zone ]
 [ file ... ]
```

Display historical information. To use the *history* command, you must first set up the *history* file in the repository. See the section "Repository Structure" for more information on this file.

When used with the *history* command, the functions *-f*, *-l*, *-n*, and *-p* aren't the same as elsewhere in CVS.

The standard meanings of the common client options *-D* and *-r* apply. History is reported for activity subsequent to the date or revision indicated. Here are additional options:

-a Show history for all users (default is current user).

-b *str*
: Show history back to the first record containing *str* in the module name, filename, or repository path.

-c Report each *commit*.

-e Report everything.

-f *file*
: Show the most recent event for *file*.

-l Show last event only.

-m *module*
: Produce a full report on *module*.

-n *module*
: Report the last event for *module*.

-o Report on modules that have been checked out.

-p *repository*
: Show history for a particular repository directory.

-t *tag*
: Show history since *tag* was last added to the history file.

-T Report on all tags.

-u *name*
: Show history for a particular user.

-w Show history only for the current working directory.

-x *types*
: Report on specific types of activity. See Table 17-19.

-z *zone*
: Display times according to the specified time zone.

The *-p* option should limit the *history* report to entries for the directory or directories (if multiple *-p* options are specified) given, but as of Version 1.10.8, it doesn't seem to affect the output. For example, to report history for the CVSROOT and *hello* modules, run the command:

```
cvs history -p CVSROOT -p hello
```

Using *-t* is faster than using *-r* because it needs to search only through the history file, not all of the RCS files.

The record types shown in Table 17-19 are generated by *update* commands.

Table 17-19. Update-related history record types

Type	Description
C	Merge was necessary, but conflicts requiring manual intervention occurred
G	Successful automatic merge
U	Working file copied from repository
W	Working copy deleted

The record types shown in Table 17-20 are generated by *commit* commands.

Table 17-20. Commit-related history record types

Type	Description
A	Added for the first time
M	Modified
R	Removed

Each record type shown in Table 17-21 is generated by a different command.

Table 17-21. Other history record types

Type	Command
E	*export*
F	*release*
O	*checkout*
T	*rtag*

import

```
import
 [ -b branch ]
 [ -d ]
 [ -I pattern ]
 [ -k kflag ]
 [ -m message ]
 [ -W spec ]
 module
 vendor_tag
 release_tag ...
```

Import an entire directory into the repository as a new module. Used to incorporate code from outside sources or other code that was initially created outside the control of the CVS repository. More than one `release_tag` may be specified, in which case multiple symbolic tags are created for the initial revision.

The *vendor_tag* argument tracks third-party code that may be used in your project. By using different values for this argument, you can track the third-party code separately and upgrade that portion of your code to a new release with a subsequent *cvs import* command. Because the argument is not optional, use some conventional value such as "vendor" whenever the code being imported shouldn't be tracked separately.

The *release_tag* argument associates a symbolic tag with the initial version of every file being imported. Because this argument is not optional, use some conventional value such as "start" whenever you don't have a more meaningful value to provide.

The standard meaning of the common client option *-k* applies. Additional options are:

-b branch
: Import to a vendor branch.

-d
: Use the modification date and time of the file instead of the current date and time as the import date and time. For local repository locators only.

-I pattern
: Filename patterns for files to ignore.

-m message
: Use *message* as the log message instead of invoking the editor.

-W spec
: Wrapper specification.

The *-k* setting applies only to files imported during this execution of the command. The keyword substitution modes of files already in the repository aren't modified.

When used with -W, the *spec* variable is in the same format as entries in the *cvswrappers* administrative file (see the section "The cvswrappers file").

Table 17-22 describes the status codes displayed by the *import* command.

Table 17-22. import status codes

Status	Description
C	Changed. The file is in the repository, and the sandbox version is different; a merge is required.
I	Ignored. The *.cvsignore* file is causing CVS to ignore the file.
L	Link. Symbolic links are ignored by CVS.
N	New. The file is new; it has been added to the repository.
U	Update. The file is in the repository, and the sandbox version is not different.

log

```
log
 [ -b ]
 [ -d dates ]
 [ -h ]
 [ -N ]
 [ -rrevisions ]
 [ -R ]
 [ -s states ]
 [ -t ]
 [ -wlogins ]
 [ file ... ]
```

Print an activity log for the files.

The standard meaning of the common client option *-l* applies. Additional options are:

-b List revisions on default branch.

-d dates
Report on these dates.

-h Print header only.

-N Don't print tags.

-r[revisions]
Report on the listed revisions. There is no space between *-r* and its argument. Without an argument, the latest revision of the default branch is used.

-R Print RCS filename only. The usage of *-R* here is different from elsewhere in CVS (*-R* usually causes CVS to operate recursively).

-s states
Print only those revisions having one of the specified states.

-S Don't print the header if the output would otherwise be empty.

-t Print only header and descriptive text.

-wlogins
Report on checkins by the listed logins. There is no space between *-w* and its argument.

For *-d*, use the date specifications in Table 17-23. Multiple specifications separated by semicolons may be provided. For *-s*, separate multiple states with commas.

Table 17-23. log date range specifications

Specification	Description
d1<*d2* or *d2*>*d1*	The revisions dated between *d1* and *d2*, exclusive
d1<=*d2* or *d2*>=*d1*	The revisions dated between *d1* and *d2*, inclusive
<*d* or *d*>	The revisions dated before *d*
<=*d* or *d*>=	The revisions dated on or before *d*
d< or >*d*	The revisions dated after *d*
d<= or >=*d*	The revisions dated on or after *d*
d	The most recent revision dated *d* or earlier

For *-r*, use the revision specifications in Table 17-24.

Table 17-24. log revision specifications

Specification	Description
rev1: *rev2*	The revisions between *rev1* and *rev2*, inclusive.
:rev	The revisions from the beginning of the branch to *rev*, inclusive.
rev:	The revisions from *rev* to the end of the branch, inclusive.
branch	All revisions on the branch.
branch1: *branch2*	All revisions on all branches between *branch1* and *branch2*, inclusive.
branch.	The latest revision on the branch.

For *rev1:rev2*, it is an error if the revisions aren't on the same branch.

login

```
login
```

Log into a remote repository. The password entered is cached in the *~/.cvspass* file because a connection to the server is not maintained across invocations.

logout

```
logout
```

Log out of a remote repository. The password cached in the *~/.cvspass* file is then deleted.

rannotate

```
rannotate
 [ [ -D date | -r rev ] -f ]
 [ -F ]
 [ -l | -R ]
 module ...
```

CVS prints a report showing each line of the specified module or module file. Each line is prefixed by information about the most recent change to the line, including the revision number, user, and date. If no revision is specified, the head of the trunk is used.

The *rannotate* command differs from the *annotate* command in that it refers directly to modules (and their files) in the repository rather than inferring the module based on the sandbox from which it is run. The first path component of each `module` argument must be a valid module for the repository.

The standard meanings of the common client options *-D*, *-f*, *-l*, *-r*, and *-R* apply. There is one additional option:

-F Annotate binary files. CVS normally skips binary files.

rdiff

```
rdiff
 [ -c | -s | -u ]
 [ { { -D date1 | -r rev1 } [ -D date2 | -r rev2 ] } | -t ]
 [ -f ]
 [ -l | -R ]
 [-V vn]
 file ...
```

Create a *patch* file that can convert a directory containing one release into a different release.

The standard meanings of the common client options *-D*, *-f*, *-l*, *-r*, and *-R* apply. Here are additional options:

-c Use *context diff* format (the default).

-s Output a summary of changed files instead of a *patch* file.

-t Show the differences between the two most recent revisions.

-u Use *unidiff* format.

-V `rcsver`
Obsolete. Used to specify version of RCS to emulate for keyword expansion. (Keyword expansion emulates RCS Version 5.)

release

```
release
 [ -d ]
 directory ...
```

Sandboxes can be abandoned or deleted without using *cvs release*, but using the *release* command logs an entry to the history file (if this mechanism is configured) about the sandbox being destroyed. In addition, it checks the disposition (recursively) of each sandbox file before deleting anything. This can prevent destroying work that has not yet been committed.

There is only one option that can be used with the *release* command: the *-d* option deletes the sandbox copy if no uncommitted changes are present.

New directories (including any files in them) in the sandbox will be deleted if the *-d* option is used with *release*.

The status codes listed in Table 17-25 describe the disposition of each file encountered in the repository and the sandbox.

Table 17-25. release status codes

Status	Description
A	The sandbox file has been added (the file was created, and *cvs add* was run), but the addition has not been committed.
M	The sandbox copy of the file has been modified.
P U	Update available. There is a newer version of the file in the repository, and the copy in the sandbox has not been modified.
R	The sandbox copy was removed (the file was deleted, and *cvs remove* was run), but the removal was not committed.
?	The file is present in the sandbox but not in the repository.

remove

```
remove
 [ -f ]
 [ -l | -R ]
 [ file ... ]
```

Indicate that files should be removed from the repository. The files aren't actually removed until they are committed. Use *cvs add* to resurrect files that have been removed if you change your mind later.

The standard meanings of the common client options *-l* and *-R* apply. Only one other option may be used with the *remove* command: the *-f* option deletes the file from the sandbox first.

rlog

```
rlog
 [ -b ]
 [ -d dates ]
 [ -h ]
 [ -N ]
 [ -rrevisions ]
 [ -R ]
 [ -s state ]
 [ -t ]
 [ -wlogins ]
 [ module ... ]
```

Print an activity log for the modules.

The standard meaning of the common client option *-l* applies. Additional options are:

-b List revisions on default branch.

-d dates
: Report on these dates.

-h Print header only.

-N Don't print tags.

-r[revisions]
: Report on the listed revisions. There is no space between *-r* and its argument. Without an argument, the latest revision of the default branch is used.

-R Print RCS filename only. The usage of *-R* here is different from elsewhere in CVS (*-R* usually causes CVS to operate recursively).

-s state
: Print only those revisions having the specified state.

-t Print only header and descriptive text.

-wlogins
: Report on checkins by the listed logins. There is no space between *-w* and its argument.

For *-d*, use the date specifications in Table 17-23. Multiple specifications separated by semicolons may be provided.

For *-r*, use the revision specifications in Table 17-24.

rtag

```
rtag
 [ -a ]
 [ -b ]
 [ -B ]
 [ -d ]
 [ -D date | -r rev ]
 [ -f ]
 [ -F ]
 [ -l | - R ]
 [ -n ]
 tag
 file ...
```

Assign a tag to a particular revision of a set of files. If the file already uses the tag for a different revision, *cvs rtag* will complain unless the *-F* option is used. This command doesn't refer to the sandbox file revisions (use *cvs tag* for that), so it can be run outside a sandbox if desired.

The standard meanings of the common client options *-D*, *-f*, *-l*, *-r*, and *-R* apply. Additional options are:

-a Search the attic for removed files containing the tag.

-b Make it a branch tag.

-B Allow movement or deletion of branch tags (used with *-d* or *-F*.)

-d Delete the tag.

-F Force. Move the tag from its current revision to the one specified.

-n Don't run any tag program from the modules file.

status

```
status
 [ -l | -R ]
 [ -v ]
 [ file ... ]
```

Display the status of the files.

The standard meanings of the common client options *-l* and *-R* apply. You can use `status -v` to include tag information.

tag

```
tag
 [ -b ]
 [ -c ]
```

```
[ -d ]
[ -D date | -r rev ]
[ -f ]
[ -F ]
[ -l | R ]
tag
[ file ... ]
```

Assign a tag to the sandbox revisions of a set of files. You can use the *status -v* command to list the existing tags for a file.

The *tag* must start with a letter and consist entirely of letters, numbers, dashes, and underscores. Therefore, while you might want to tag your *hello* project with *1.0* when you release Version 1.0, you'll need to tag it with something like *hello-1_0* instead.

The standard meanings of the common client options *-D*, *-f*, *-l*, *-r*, and *-R* apply. Additional options are:

-b Make a branch.

-c Check for changes. Make sure the files aren't locally modified before tagging.

-d Delete the tag.

-F Force. Move the tag from its current revision to the one specified.

Because the *-d* option throws away information that might be important, you should use it only when absolutely necessary. It is usually better to create a different tag with a similar name.

unedit

```
unedit
 [ -l | -R ]
 [ file ... ]
```

Abandon file modifications and make the file read-only again. Watchers will be notified.

The standard meanings of the common client options *-l* and *-R* apply.

update

```
update
 [ -A ]
 [ -C ]
 [ -d ]
 [ -D date | -r rev ]
 [ -f ]
 [ -I pattern ]
 [ -j rev1 [ -j rev2 ] ]
 [ -k kflag ]
 [ -l | -R ]
 [ -p ]
 [ -P ]
```

```
[ -W spec ]
[ file ... ]
```

Update the sandbox, merging in any changes from the repository. For example:

```
cvs -n -q update -AdP
```

can do a quick status check of the current sandbox versus the head of the trunk of development.

The standard meanings of the common client options *-D*, *-f*, *-k*, *-l*, *-r*, and *-R* apply. Additional options are:

-A Reset sticky tags.

-C Replace modified files with clean copies.

-d Create and update new directories.

-I pattern
Provide filename patterns for files to ignore.

-j revision
Merge in (join) changes between two revisions.

-p Check out files to standard output.

-P Prune empty directories.

-W spec
Provide wrapper specification.

When using *-C*, CVS makes backups of modified files before copying the clean version. The backup files are named *.#file.revision*.

Using *-D* or *-r* results in sticky dates or tags, respectively, on the affected files (using *-p* along with these prevents stickiness). Use *-A* to reset any sticky tags or dates.

If two *-j* specifications are made, the differences between them are computed and applied to the current file. If only one is given, the common ancestor of the sandbox revision and the specified revision is used as a basis for computing differences to be merged. For example, suppose a project has an experimental branch, and important changes to the file *foo.c* were introduced between revisions 1.2.2.1 and 1.2.2.2. Once those changes have proven stable, you want them reflected in the main line of development. From a sandbox with the head revisions checked out, run:

```
$ cvs update -j 1.2.2.1 -j 1.2.2.2 foo.c
```

CVS finds the differences between the two revisions and applies those differences to the file in your sandbox.

The *spec* used with *-W* is in the same format as entries in the *cvswrappers* administrative file (see the section "The cvswrappers file").

The status codes listed in Table 17-26 describe the action taken on each file encountered in the repository and the sandbox.

Table 17-26. update status codes

Status	Description
A	Added. Server took no action because there was no repository file. Indicates that *cvs add*, but not *cvs commit*, has been run.
C	Conflict. Sandbox copy is modified (it has been edited since it was checked out or last committed). There was a new revision in the repository, and there were conflicts when CVS merged its changes into the sandbox version.

Table 17-26. update status codes (continued)

Status	Description
M	Modified. Sandbox copy is modified (it has been edited since it was checked out or last committed). If there was a new revision in the repository, its changes were successfully merged into the file (no conflicts).
P	Patched. Same as *U*, but indicates the server used a *patch*.
R	Removed. Server took no action. Indicates that *cvs remove*, but not *cvs commit*, has been run.
U	Updated. The file was brought up to date.
?	File is present in sandbox but not in repository.

version

```
version
```

Display the version of the CVS client (and server, if appropriate) being used.

watch

```
watch
 { { on | off } | { add | remove } [ -a action ] }
 [ -l | -R ]
 file ...
```

The *watch* command controls CVS's edit tracking mechanism. By default, CVS operates in its concurrent development mode, allowing any user to edit any file at any time. CVS includes this *watch* mechanism to support developers who would rather be notified of edits made by others proactively than discover them when doing an *update*. The *CVSROOT/notify* file determines how notifications are performed.

Table 17-27 shows the *watch* subcommands and their uses.

Table 17-27. watch subcommands

Subcommand	Description
add	Start watching files
off	Turn off watching
on	Turn on watching
remove	Stop watching files

The standard meanings of the common client options *-l* and *-R* apply. The only other option that can be used with the *watch* command is *-a action*. The *-a* option is used in conjunction with one of the actions listed in Table 17-28.

Table 17-28. watch Actions

Action	Description
all	All of the following.
commit	A user has committed changes.
edit	A user ran *cvs edit*.

Table 17-28. watch Actions (continued)

Action	Description
none	Don't watch. Used by the *edit* command.
unedit	A user ran *cvs unedit*, *cvs release*, or deleted the file and ran *cvs update*, re-creating it.

See also *edit*, *editors*, *unedit*, and *watchers*.

watchers

```
watchers
 [ -l | -R ]
 [ file ... ]
```

Display a list of users watching the specified files. This is determined by checking which users have run the *watch* command on a particular file (or set of files). If the *watch* command has not been used, no results are displayed.

The standard meanings of the common client options *-l* and *-R* apply.

See also *watch*.

Under Mac OS X's Hood

Now it's time to roll up your sleeves. This part of the book goes deeper into the BSD Unix side of Mac OS X: it introduces the Terminal application (your interface to Darwin) and covers topics on pattern matching, shells, using the defaults command, using Apple's X11 distribution of the X Window System, and installing Unix applications on your Mac.

This part wraps up with the most complete Unix command reference you'll find in print for Mac OS X. Every command and option has been verified against Panther; in many cases, this reference is more accurate than the manpages installed on your system.

The chapters in this part include:

- Chapter 18, *Using the Terminal*
- Chapter 19, *Shell Overview*
- Chapter 20, *bash: The Bourne-Again Shell*
- Chapter 21, *tcsh: An Extended C Shell*
- Chapter 22, *Pattern Matching*
- Chapter 23, *The vi Editor*
- Chapter 24, *The Emacs Editor*
- Chapter 25, *The Defaults System*
- Chapter 26, *The X Window System*
- Chapter 27, *Installing Unix Software*
- Chapter 28, *Unix Command Reference*

18
Using the Terminal

The Terminal application (*/Applications/Utilities*) is your gateway between the candy-coated Aqua graphical interface and the no-nonsense command-line interface that Darwin uses. This book (as well as a lot of Apple documentation) tends to use the terms *command line* and *Terminal* interchangeably because, with Mac OS X, to get to the former you must go through the latter.

Using the Terminal

Each window in the Terminal represents a separate *shell* process—a command-line interpreter ready to accept your instructions, as described in the section "Introduction to the Shell" in Chapter 19.

Terminal Preferences

The Terminal application's user settings control not just the application's look and feel, but the ways you interact with your shells. This section covers the more important application preferences to know about.

Setting a default shell

There are two ways to set a default shell when using your system, which are suggested by the "When creating a new Terminal window" radio buttons found in Terminal's Preferences window (Terminal→Preferences, ⌘-,), seen in Figure 18-1.

The lazier way involves activating the "Execute this command" button and typing a shell's path into the neighboring text field. Henceforth, whenever you open a new Terminal window, that shell will launch in place of your default login shell. This is a nice solution if you use only Terminal as a command line and never log in remotely to your machine, or if you're not a member of the machine's `admin` group and hence can't set your login shell to something else.

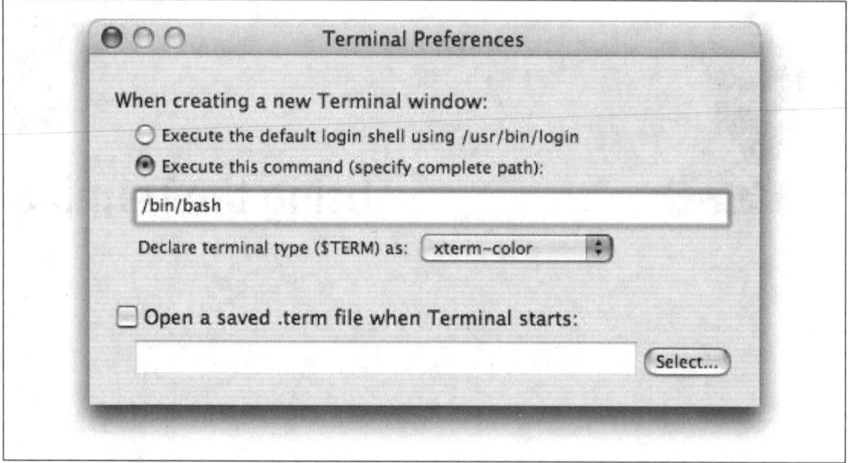

Figure 18-1. The Terminal Preferences dialog

A more permanent, but less obvious, way involves changing your account's default shell. This affects not just the shell Terminal opens by default but the shell that appears when you use a different command-line access application or log in to your machine from some other location via *ssh* (described in "The Secure Shell" in Chapter 12). If you have admin privileges, you can do this through the NetInfo database by adjusting your user account's low-level preferences. Launch NetInfo Manager and navigate to its */users/your-username* directory. (For a complete review of NetInfo, see Chapter 11.) Locate the *shell* property, double-click its value, and type some other shell's path in its place, as shown in Figure 18-2.

If you don't have admin access, you can ask someone who does to take these steps for you. Once your *shell* property under NetInfo has been reset one way or another, select the Terminal preferences' "Execute the default login shell using /usr/bin/login" radio button.

You can always change your shell on the fly by invoking it as a command. If you're running *zsh* and wish to temporarily drop into *tcsh* for some reason (perhaps you're following some Unix program's arcane installation instructions, which are written only in *tcsh*-ese), you can just type *tcsh* (or the full path, */bin/tcsh*) at the command prompt.

A shell launched in this manner runs as a child to the Terminal window's main shell, so when you exit the second shell you'll pop safely back out to the first shell's command prompt.

For a *really* lazy way to change your shell, you can make the first line of your default shell's *rc* file a command to switch to your shell of choice! This is a rather slovenly solution and will probably cause you (or others) confusion later. Use one of the other solutions that this section presents, if at all possible.

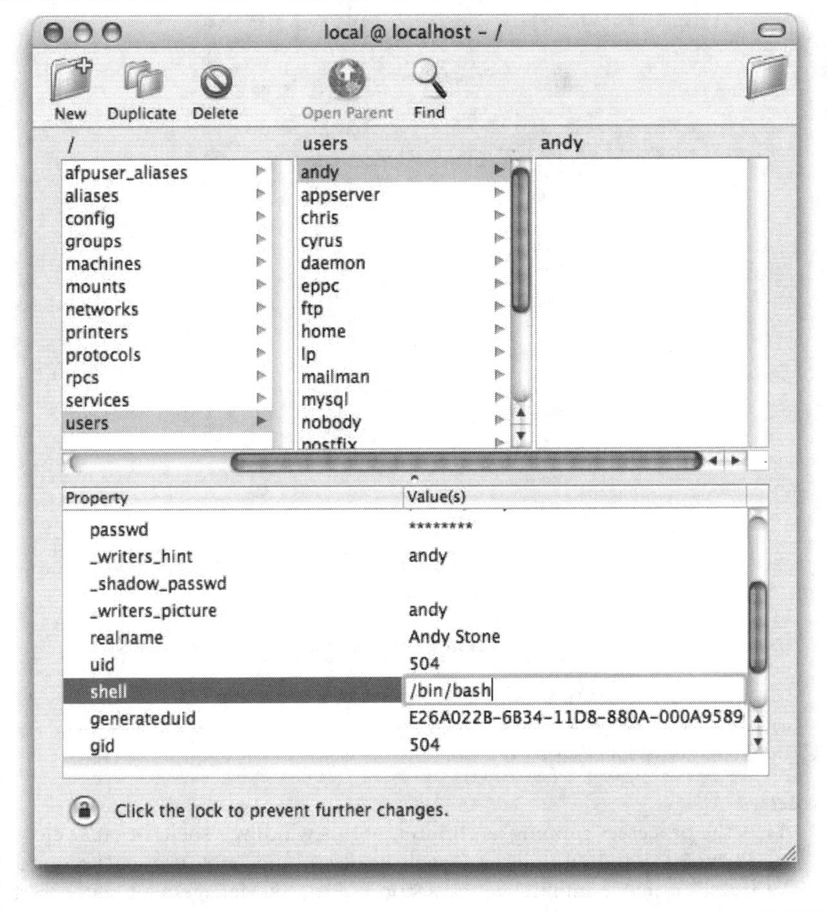

Figure 18-2. Changing a user's default shell through NetInfo Manager

The Terminal Inspector

If you select File→Show Info (⌘-I) or Terminal→Window Settings, the Terminal Inspector window (shown in Figure 18-3) will appear. This window lets you set a variety of visual and shell-interaction options affecting the front-most Terminal window.

The pop-up menu at the top of the window lets you navigate between its many panes, summarized in the following list:

Shell
: Lists the shell tied to this Terminal window, and lets you define the application's behavior when you exit a shell (through the *logout* or *exit* commands, or sending an EOF signal to the main shell through Control-D). See the earlier section "Setting a default shell" for information about changing shells.

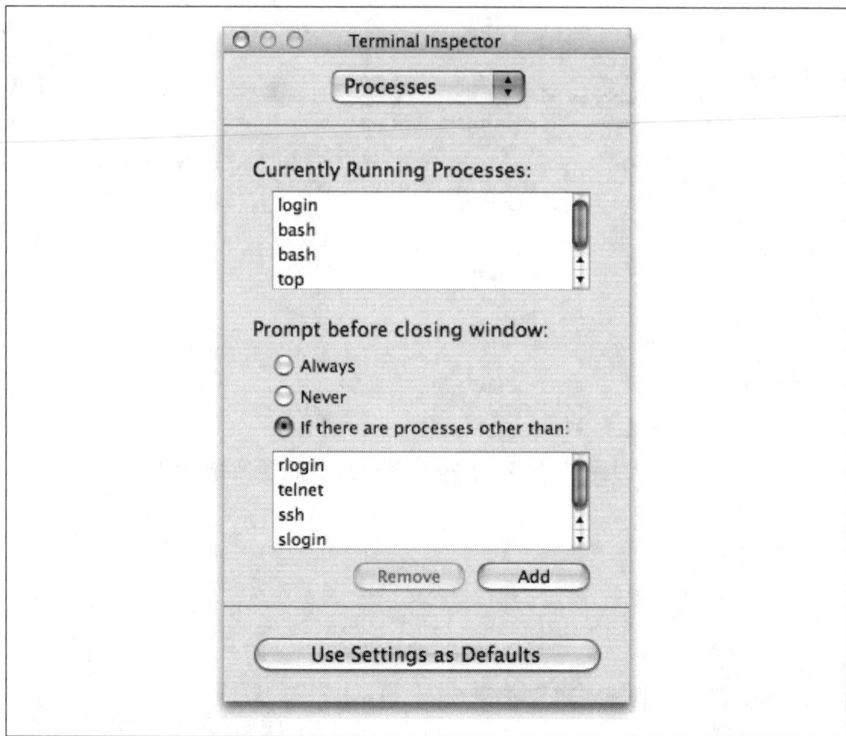

Figure 18-3. The Terminal Inspector window

Processes

Lists the processes running as children of this window's shell. Because closing a Terminal window kills its shell process and any non-backgrounded processes it may contain (see the section "Process Management" later in this chapter), this pane lets you specify the Terminal's behavior if some processes are still running when you close a window. As Figure 18-3 shows, you can have Terminal always prompt you to confirm a window's closure, never prompt you, or prompt you only when processes other than those in the given list exist among the shell's children (use the Remove and Add buttons to modify the list)

Emulation

Terminal is a VT100 emulation program, meaning that it speaks a protocol originally conceived for a certain class of terminals made by (the now-defunct) Digital Equipment Corporation in the late 1970s and early 1980s. The Terminal's Emulation preferences pane gives you a list of checkboxes that control high-level mapping between your Mac's keyboard and the underlying terminal protocol, as follows:

Escape non-ASCII characters

If you use either the *bash* or *tcsh* shells, checking this box allows you to enter characters outside those in the standard ASCII set on the command line. Terminal translates the non-ASCII characters into octal ASCII character codes that the shell can interpret properly. (This works as long as character set encoding is set to Unicode in the Display section of the Terminal Inspector.)

Option click to position cursor
: Though it may resemble an Aqua text view in some ways, a Terminal window is normally unresponsive to mouse clicks, making you use keyboard commands to move the cursor around. If you check this box, however, you can option-click a Terminal window to automatically reposition the cursor to that point. This can be a handy function when using Terminal-based text editors, such as Emacs or vi.

Paste newlines as carriage returns
: When this checkbox is active, any newline characters within text that you paste into a Terminal window through the standard Edit→Paste (⌘-V) command are automatically converted to carriage return characters.

Strict VT-100 keypad behavior
: When checked, the number keypad functions according to the VT-100 protocol.

Reverse linewrap
: In most cases when you move the cursor right to left to the beginning of a wrapped line, it will continue up through the wrap to the end of the previous line. When using some older applications or remote systems, however, you might find that the cursor won't wrap unless this feature is enabled.

Audible bell
: Bell characters cause the Mac to sound its system beep.

Visual bell
: Bell characters cause the Mac's screen to pulse.

Buffer
: Lets you set how many lines of history the Terminal window remembers (and lets you scroll back to via the window's scrollbar), and how it handles line wrapping.

Display
: Contains general display options for Terminal's windows, including:

  Cursor Style
  : Sets the cursor's shape and blinking pattern.

  Text
  : Sets the font as well as several font properties, including anti-aliasing and spacing. Also includes a setting that allows you to select and drag text from anywhere in a Terminal window and drop it into the command line or onto the desktop to create a clip file.

  Character set encoding
  : Terminal uses Unicode UTF-8 as its default, but that can be changed here for compatibility with remote systems using other encodings.

Color

Lets you set the window's text, background, cursor and text- selection colors. You can either select from one of the prespecified combinations or create your own. You can also use an image file instead of a color for window backgrounds. The Transparency slider sets the background's opacity level; setting it to something less than full opacity (by dragging the slider to the right) lets you work with a Terminal window while keeping things behind it visible. This can prove useful when following instructions contained in another window without having to resize either.

Activating the pane's "Disable ANSI color" checkbox prevents your color choices from being overridden by ANSI color-setting instructions the terminal might receive.

Window

Lets you set the window's dimensions in terms of rows and columns of text, and assign it a title based on a number of checkbox-based criteria, as Figure 18-4 shows.

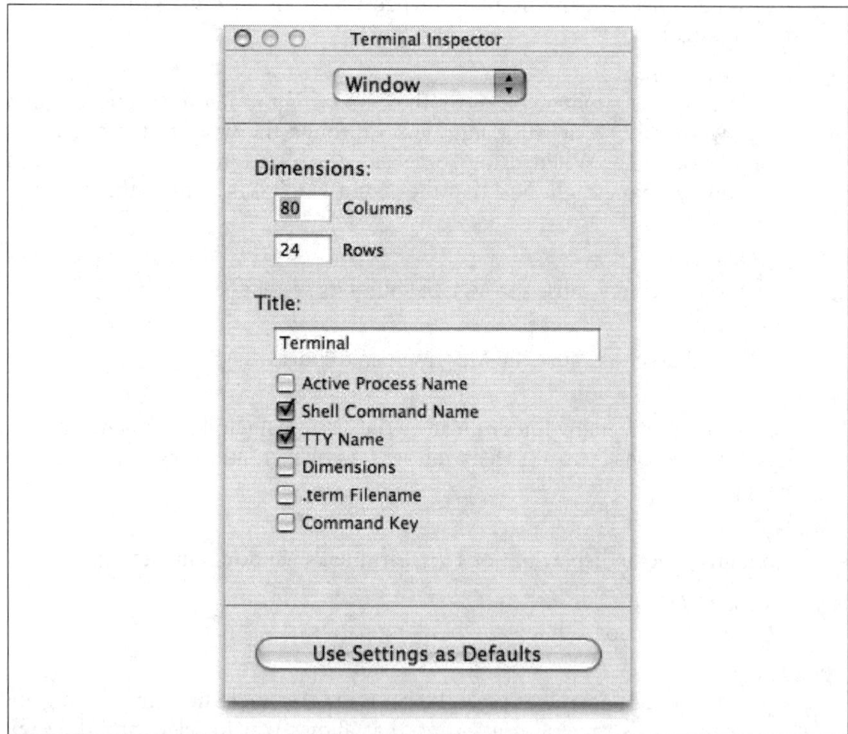

Figure 18-4. The terminal inspector's Window pane

Keyboard

The following options are available for configuring how the Terminal interacts with the keyboard:

Key Mappings

Some Terminal programs, run locally or from a remote machine, allow or even require you to use function keys to issue commands. Key Mappings allows you to add and edit custom key and command pairs using the function, arrow, Home, End, and Page keys.

Delete key sends backspace

Some Terminal programs make a distinction between the delete character (which your Delete key normally sends) and a backspace character. Try checking this box if you find the Delete key is not doing what you expect.

Use option key as meta key

Some Terminal programs (such as the Emacs text editor) define a "Meta" key for certain keystrokes. Because your Mac keyboard lacks such a thing, checking this box will have your Option key stand in for it.

Clicking on the "Use Settings as Defaults" button at the bottom of the inspector window saves all the panes' settings as your Terminal application defaults. This means that all future Terminal windows you open, either by launching the Terminal or by selecting File→New Shell (⌘-N) will use the settings you've just configured. See the next section.

Saving and Loading Terminals

After you set up a Terminal window and shell via the Terminal Inspector window (see the section "The Terminal Inspector" later in this chapter), you have two ways to save these settings for future Terminal sessions: either click the "Use Settings as Defaults" button to make them the Terminal applications' overall default settings, or save the front-most window's settings to a file through File→Save (⌘-S). This creates a *.term* file that stores all the window's settings. (The *.term* file uses the standard XML property list format described in the section "Property Lists" in Chapter 25, so you can manually browse these files if you wish.) It's most convenient to save *.term* files in *~/Library/Application Support/Terminal*, a directory you might need to create initially. You can then access any *.term* files placed in that directory by choosing one from the File→Library menu. You can also open *.term* files using the File→Open (⌘-O) menu command.

One useful utility for managing *.term* files is Terminal Pal from Freshly Squeezed Software (*http://www.freshlysqueezedsoftware.com/products/freeware*). When installed, Terminal Pal provides quick access to *.term* files you've saved, allowing you to quickly launch Terminal windows with different settings.

As Figure 18-5 shows, the dialog has an extra set of controls. If you select All Windows (rather than the default Main Window) from the "What to save" pop-up menu, then all the Terminal's open windows, including their onscreen positions, get stored to the resulting *.term* file. This is the option to choose if you like to arrange multiple Terminal windows, perhaps with different properties, in a "just-right" arrangement for a certain task.

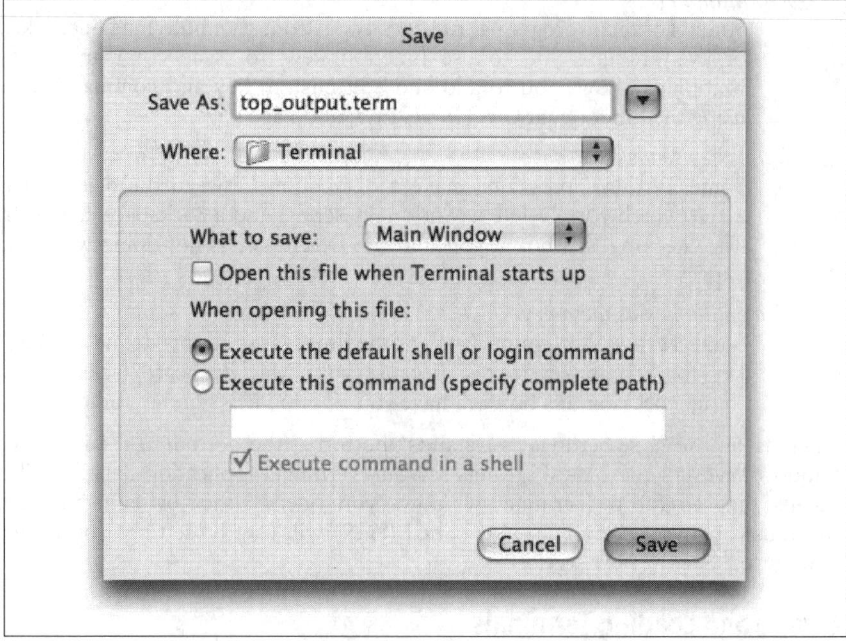

Figure 18-5. The Terminal's Save dialog

Activating the "Open this file when Terminal starts up" checkbox will do just what it says. Note that you can set several *.term* files with this function; if you wish to have a single such file as your default and later change your mind about which *.term* file to use, you have to re-save the original window settings with File→Save As (Shift- ⌘-S) and deactivate that checkbox.

Using the final controls, you can choose to attach to the *.term* file a command that executes each time you open that file. Configure this by selecting the "Execute this command" checkbox and entering the command in the field below it. If you want Terminal to also execute the default shell or login command as specified in the Terminal Preferences dialog, check the "Execute command in a shell" checkbox. With the box unchecked, Terminal will execute only your specified command and close the window once the command is complete.

Connect to Server

Several of Panther's network daemons advertise their services on the local network using Rendezvous' discovery protocol. Terminal's Connect to Server window (File→Connect to Server) allows you to browse and contact these remote *ssh*, *sftp*, *telnet*, and *http* servers without needing to provide a hostname or IP address (Figure 18-6).

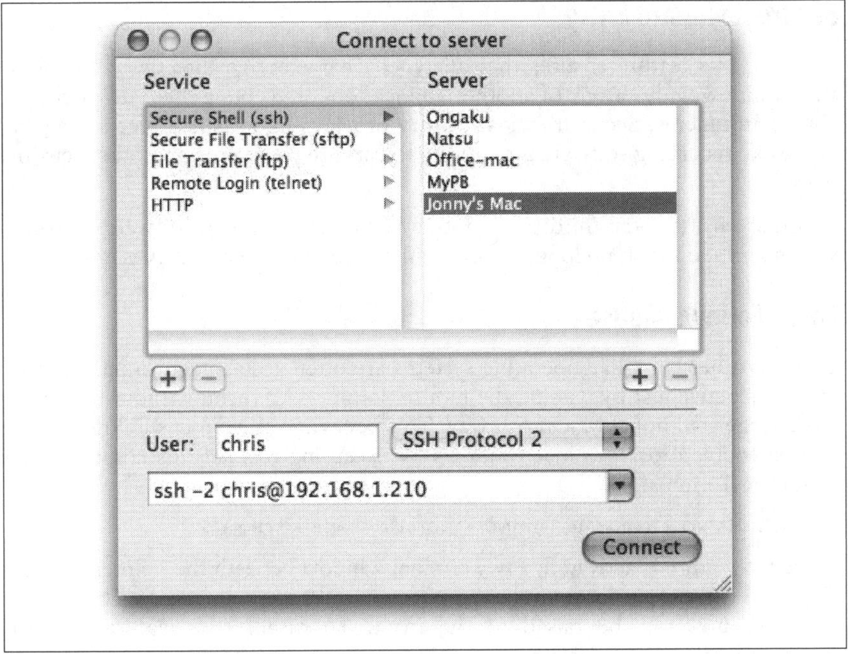

Figure 18-6. The Terminal's Save dialog

Clicking on an item in the Service column shows all remote, Rendezvous-enabled daemons of the selected type in the Server column. When you click on a server name, an appropriate connection command appears in the field at the bottom of the window. Above that field are optional settings specific to the chosen service. You can specify an alternate login name, for example, or choose to use SSH 1 instead of the default SSH 2 protocol for a secure shell connection, and the appropriate change will be made to the command.

Clicking the HTTP service will list all user web sites found on each of the supported servers. When you select a site, an appropriate *ping* command appears in the command field (the command will actually be the same, *ping hostname*, for each server, regardless of the chosen site).

Each connection command that you use is permanently added to the command field's pop-up list, thereby building a list of connection bookmarks for you.

You can manually add other Rendezvous-enabled services (as they become available) to the Services list using the add button (+) below it. To contact a server without Rendezvous-enabled services, you can manually add that server to the Server list using its add button. That way, even without using Rendezvous, you can still keep bookmarks of commonly used connections.

A Connect to Server command also exists on the pop-up menu for Terminal's dock icon. Selecting it opens the same Connect to Server browse window.

Secure Keyboard Entry

Enabling this feature ensures that all typed characters go directly to the active shell window without risk of another application intercepting them. In high-security environments, Secure Keyboard Entry provides important protection against keystroke recording software attempting to capture passwords and other sensitive data.

If you are using some third-party hot-key or macro-enabling software, however, you might find that it no longer works while Secure Keyboard Entry is enabled.

Focus Follows Mouse

Users of other Unix-like operating systems are often accustomed to making their windows active just by passing the mouse pointer over them, without needing to click in the traditional Macintosh way. This behavior, called focus follows mouse, can be enabled for Terminal windows by executing this *defaults* command and restarting Terminal:

```
defaults write com.apple.Terminal FocusFollowsMouse -string YES
```

Once the feature is activated, any Terminal window beneath the pointer, whether Terminal is the front-most application or not, will accept text entry. The window will not, however, be raised to the front. To disable the feature, run this command, and restart Terminal:

```
defaults write com.apple.Terminal FocusFollowsMouse -string NO
```

Split-View Scrollback

Split-view windows are nothing new to users of most word-processing software, and Terminal windows provide the same convenience. To split a Terminal window, click the small box just below the right end of the window's titlebar (Figure 18-7). A horizontal dividing bar will appear, which you can drag up and down to resize the height of the two panels. The top panel keeps the scroll bar, allowing you to scroll back up through your entire buffer, while keeping the prompt visible in the other panel. To return to a single pane, click the small box again.

Process Management

Each command you invoke or program that you run from a Terminal window becomes a child of that terminal's shell. The Terminal window can juggle many child processes at once, but only one at a time is brought to the foreground, writing its output (through the Unix standard output file handle) to the Terminal, and accepting keyboard input (via Unix standard input) from the user. Any other processes are either placed in the background—running but not displaying any interface or accepting input—or suspended (paused) in the process of execution.

You can control the application in the foreground by sending it Unix signals via the keystrokes listed in Table 18-1. Programs usually respond to them as listed,

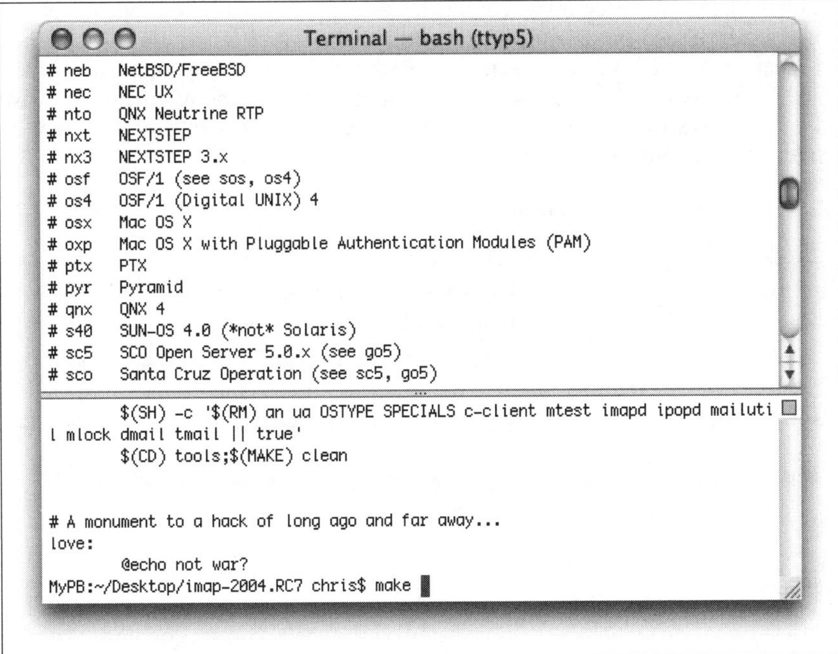

Figure 18-7. A split-view Terminal window

though individual programs may interpret them differently. (The Emacs text editor, for example, ties a text-searching function to the Control-S keystroke.)

Table 18-1. Foreground process control keystrokes

Keystroke	Description
Control-C	Sends an interrupt signal, which usually causes the program to exit.
Control-D	Sends an end-of-file signal. If a program is accepting multiple lines of input from you, this signals that you're finished providing it.
Control-Z	Suspends the process in the foreground, and returns you to the command line.
Control-S	Suspends the process in the foreground, but keeps it in the foreground.
Control-Q	Resumes a suspended process, and brings it to the foreground.

Control-Q is a good keystroke to try if a Terminal window ceases to update or accept input for no obvious reason, while other Terminal windows continue behaving normally. You may have hit Control-S by mistake.

Terminal aliases Control-C to the File→Send break (Control-C or ⌘-.) menu selection. ⌘-. is a legacy Mac keyboard shortcut for interrupting programs; it's often used to quickly invoke the Cancel button in dialog windows.

Table 18-2 lists some Terminal commands that are useful for viewing and controlling backgrounded processes. You can find complete references for most of them in Chapter 28. See the next section to find out a process's process ID number (PID), which many of these commands require. (You can also use the more convenient `%N` syntax described by that section when working with processes that are children of the current Terminal window's shell.)

Table 18-2. Process control commands

Command	Description
ps	Lists Terminal-based processes belonging to you.
jobs	Lists processes that are children of this terminal's shell process.
fg *`pid`*	Foregrounds (and resumes, if suspended) the process with that *`pid`*.
bg *`pid`*	Backgrounds (and resumes, if suspended) the process with that *`pid`*.
kill *`-signal pid`*	Sends a *`signal`* (the terminate signal, by default) to the process with that *`pid`*.
killall *`-signal process-name`*	Sends a *`signal`* (the terminate signal, by default) to all processes with that name.

Seeing processes

Typing *ps* by itself displays a simple list of all the shells you are running, as well as all their child processes:

```
MyPB:~ chris$ ps
  PID  TT  STAT      TIME COMMAND
 4295  p1  S+     0:00.03 vi /etc/hostconfig
 4299  p2  Ss     0:00.04 -bin/tcsh -i
 4286  p2  Ss     0:00.03 -bash
 4293  p2  S+     0:18.11 tail -f /var/log/httpd/error_log
 4297  p3  Ss     0:00.04 -bash
 4366  p3  S+     0:00.01 vi README
 4250 std  S      0:00.10 -bash
MyPB:~ chris$
```

Here you can see that the user `chris` owns four shell processes: three instances of the *bash* shell, and one *tcsh*. (As it happens, there are three Terminal windows open and running the shell of choice, *bash*, while in the background, a shell script that invokes *tcsh* is running; see Chapters 20 and 21.) Within these shells, there are two *vi* sessions active, and a *tail* program is dutifully running on the Apache web server's error log.

The numbers in the first column of the table show the PID number of each process. These are what you can feed to the commands listed in Table 18-2 in order to foreground, background, or send signals to them.

Alternatively, you can use shell-relative PIDs with these commands. Invoking *jobs* lists only those the processes running as children to the current shell:

```
MyPB:~ chris$ jobs
[1]    running    sudo bin/safe_mysqld
```

```
[2]  + vi README
MyPB:~ chris$
```

The bracketed numbers leading each row of this output table can be used instead of PIDs when issuing process-control commands. The number can be prefaced with a percentage sign (%) to show that you're using a relative PID. So, to foreground that *vi* process, type *fg %2*. In this particular instance, you can also type *fg* for the same effect; the plus-sign symbol next to the number says it's a child process, and hence the default target for commands like *fg* and *bg*.

For another view of a Terminal window's child processes, select File→Get Info (⌘-I) and select the Processes choice from the resulting window's pop-up menu. See the section "The Terminal Inspector," earlier in this chapter, for more about this window's views and options.

To see a list of all the processes you're running on this machine, use *ps x*:

```
MyPB:~ chris$ ps x
  PID  TT  STAT      TIME COMMAND
  212  ??  Ss    9:17.40 /System/Library/Frameworks/ApplicationServices.framew
  229  ??  Rs    3:15.03 /System/Library/Frameworks/ApplicationServices.framew
  232  ??  Ss    0:01.31 /System/Library/CoreServices/loginwindow.app/Contents
  410  ??  Ss    0:00.70 /System/Library/CoreServices/pbs
  417  ??  S     0:05.70 /System/Library/CoreServices/Dock.app/Contents/MacOS/
  423  ??  S     1:10.17 /System/Library/CoreServices/SystemUIServer.app/Conte
  424  ??  S     3:12.61 /System/Library/CoreServices/Finder.app/Contents/MacO
  451  ??  S     0:07.94 /Users/chris/Library/PreferencePanes/iChatStatus.pref
  474  ??  Ss    0:01.20 /System/Library/PrivateFrameworks/InstantMessage.fram
  517  ??  S     1:31.56 /Applications/Mail.app/Contents/MacOS/Mail -psn_0_196
  518  ??  S     4:52.70 /Applications/Safari.app/Contents/MacOS/Safari -psn_0
  519  ??  S     0:24.25 /Applications/iChat.app/Contents/MacOS/iChat -psn_0_2
  520  ??  S     0:15.66 /Applications/JabberFoX.app/Contents/MacOS/JabberFoX
  522  ??  S     0:15.81 /System/Library/CoreServices/System Events.app/Conten
  524  ??  S     0:00.04 /Applications/Utilities/X11.app/Contents/MacOS/X11 -p
  536  ??  S     1:41.81 /Applications/Mozilla Firebird.app/Contents/MacOS/Moz
  558  ??  S     0:26.15 /Applications/Utilities/Terminal.app/Contents/MacOS/T
  595  ??  S     9:37.66 /Applications/Microsoft Office X/Microsoft Word /Appl
  596  ??  S     0:04.89 /Applications/Microsoft Office X/Office/Microsoft Dat
  602  ??  S     0:00.09 /System/Library/Services/AppleSpell.service/Contents/
  604  ??  S     0:52.12 /Applications/TextEdit.app/Contents/MacOS/TextEdit -p
  614  ??  S     0:00.32 /System/Library/CoreServices/SecurityAgent.app/Conten
  684  ??  S     3:41.83 /Applications/iTunes.app/Contents/MacOS/iTunes -psn_0
  746 std  Ss    0:00.06 -bash
  559  p3  Ss+   0:00.04 -bash
MyPB:~ chris$
```

This lists both the Terminal-controlled programs and the Aqua applications that are running, as well as the frameworks, system services, and plug-ins used by those applications. They are, after all, just Unix programs, all with their own PIDs.

Running *ps* with the *aux* options lists every single process running on the machine, regardless of context or user. This would, at a typical moment in any

Mac OS X machine's life, be enough to fill a couple of pages of this book. You can pipe this output through the *grep* command to automatically filter the results: *ps ax | grep bash* shows a table describing all the *bash* processes every user is currently running, for example.

For a friendlier interface to browsing active processes, see the Activity Monitor (*/Applications/Utilities*).

Sending signals with kill and killall

As its name suggests, *kill*'s most common function involves terminating programs, through its default usage: *kill* `pid`. Actually, *kill* sends a Unix signal of some kind to the program, and the default happens to be the terminate (TERM) signal. You can send different signals through the *kill* `-signal pid` syntax, where `signal` is a signal name or number.

The even more violent-sounding *killall* is often more convenient than *kill* is. This really just lets you refer to processes by their name, saving you from having to look up their PIDs first. For example, *killall tail* sends the TERM signal to all *tail* processes running under one name.

killall –HUP `process` is a traditional Unix idiom for having a continually running process, such as a network daemon, reload its configuration information. However, if a Startup Script is available for this service, you should favor running that instead, even if they both ultimately have a similar effect; see the section "StartupItems" in Chapter 12.

xterm

If you've installed the X Windows system on your Mac, you can use the *xterm* program that comes with it, as well as a variety of alternative terminals available for this windowing system. Consult Chapter 26 for full details.

Mac OS X's Console Mode

While not quite a Terminal alternative *per se*, Mac OS X's built-in console login mode lets you choose to use Darwin's command-line interface instead of the Aqua GUI for the length of a login session.

To enter console mode, you first need to have the Mac OS X login window display only name and passwords fields (see Chapter 4). Next, at the login window, identify yourself as `>console` and click Log In (or press Return) without providing a password. The Aqua interface vanishes, replaced by a standard Unix login prompt. Despite the vastly different appearance, it's the same old Mac OS X login procedure: type in your username and password as directed, and you're in.

Once you log out (through the *logout* command or by *exit*ing your shell program), the Aqua's login window will appear once more. You need to pull the `>console` trick again in order to reenter console mode; otherwise, subsequent logins will launch the Finder, as usual.

See the section "Single-User Mode" in Chapter 10.

19 Shell Overview

The shell is a program that acts as a buffer between you and the operating system. In its role as a command interpreter, it should (for the most part) act invisibly. It can also be used for simple programming. The shell receives the commands you enter using the Terminal (or a similar program), and decides what to do with it.

This chapter provides a basic overview of the shells included with Mac OS X. Refer to Chapters 20 and 21 for specific information about Mac OS X's two most-used shells, *bash* and *tcsh*, respectively.

Introduction to the Shell

The shell is the user interface to Unix, and by the same token, several shells are available in Unix. Mac OS X provides you with more than one shell to choose from. Each shell has different features, but all of them affect how commands will be interpreted and provide tools to create your Unix environment.

Let's suppose that the Unix operating system is a car. When you drive, you issue a variety of "commands": you turn the steering wheel, press the accelerator, or step on the brake. But how does the car translate your commands into the action you want? The car's drive mechanism, which can be thought of as the car's user interface, is responsible. Cars can be equipped with front-wheel drive, rear-wheel drive, four-wheel drive, and sometimes combinations of these.

The shell is simply a program that allows the system to understand your commands. (That's why the shell is often called a *command interpreter*.) For many users, the shell works invisibly behind the scenes. Your only concern is that the system does what you tell it to; you don't care about the inner workings. In the car analogy, this is comparable to pressing the brake. Most of us don't care whether the user interface involves disk brakes, drum brakes, or antilock brakes, as long as the car stops when you tell it to.

There are three main uses for the shell:

- Interactive use
- Customization of your Unix session
- Programming

Interactive use
: When the shell is used interactively, it waits for you to issue commands, processes them (to interpret special characters such as wildcards), and executes them. Shells also provide a set of commands, known as *built-ins*, to supplement Unix commands.

Customization of your Unix session
: A Unix shell defines *variables*, such as the location of your *Home* directory, to control the behavior of your Unix session. Some variables are preset by the system; you can define others in startup files that are read when you log in or interactively for a single session. Startup files can also contain Unix commands or special shell commands, that are executed every time you log in.

Programming
: A series of individual commands (be they shell commands or other Unix commands available on the system) combined into one executable file is called a *shell script*. Scripts are useful for executing a series of individual commands, but they can also execute commands repeatedly (in a loop) or conditionally (`if-else`), as in many high-level programming languages.

  bash, which is Mac OS X Panther's default user shell, is considered a powerful programming shell, while scripting in *tcsh* (the default user shell for earlier versions of Mac OS X) is rumored to be hazardous to your health.

Shell Flavors

Many different Unix shells are available on Mac OS X Panther. This book describes the two most popular shells:

- The Bourne-Again shell (*bash*), which is based on the Bourne shell (*sh*). *bash* is the default Unix shell in Mac OS X Panther and is the most commonly used shell for other Unix-variants, including most Linux distributions and FreeBSD.
- *tcsh*, an extension of the C shell, *csh*, that is included instead of *csh* on Mac OS X.

Most Unix systems have more than one shell, and it's not uncommon for people to use one shell for writing scripts and another for interactive use. Other popular shells included with Mac OS X Panther can be found in the */bin* directory and are available to all users on the system.

You can change to another shell by typing the program name at the command line. For example, to change from *bash* to *tcsh*, type:

```
$ exec tcsh
```

Common Features

Table 19-1 is a sampling of features that are common to *bash* and *tcsh*.

Table 19-1. Common shell features

Symbol/command	Meaning/action
>	Redirect output
>>	Append to file
<	Redirect input
<<	Here document (redirect input)
|	Pipe output
&	Run process in background
;	Separate commands on same line
*	Match any character(s) in filename
?	Match single character in filename
!*n*	Repeat command number *n*
[ ]	Match any characters enclosed
( )	Execute in subshell
``	Substitute output of enclosed command
" "	Partial quote (allows variable and command expansion)
' `	Full quote (no expansion)
\	Quote following character
$*var*	Use value for variable
$$	Process ID
$0	Command name
$*n*	*n*th argument (0<*n*_9)
$*	All arguments as simple words
#	Begin comment
Tab	Complete current word
bg	Background execution
break	Break from loop statements
cd	Change directory
continue	Resume a program loop
echo	Display output
eval	Evaluate arguments
exec	Execute a new shell
fg	Foreground execution
jobs	Show active jobs
kill	Terminate running jobs
newgrp	Change to a new group
shift	Shift positional parameters
stop	Suspend a background job
suspend	Suspend a foreground job (such as a shell created by *su*)

Table 19-1. Common shell features (continued)

Symbol/command	Meaning/action
`time`	Time a command
`umask`	Set default file permissions for new files
`unset`	Erase variable or function definitions
`wait`	Wait for a background job to finish

Differing Features

Table 19-2 is a sampling of features that differ between the two shells.

Table 19-2. Differences between the bash and tcsh shells

Meaning/action	bash	tcsh
Default prompt	`$`	`%`
Force redirection	`>|`	`>!`
Force append		`>>!`
Variable assignment	*var=val*	`set` *var=val*
Set environment variable	`export` *var=val*	`setenv` *var val*
Command substitution	`$(`*command*`)`, ` `` `	` `` `
Number of arguments	`$#`	`$#argv`
Execute commands in *file*	`.` *file*	`source` *file*
End a loop statement	`done`	`end`
End *case* or *switch*	`esac`	`endsw`
Loop through variables	`for/do`	`foreach`
Sample `if` statement	`if [$i -eq 5]`	`if ($i==5)`
End `if` statement	`fi`	`endif`
Set resource limits	`ulimit`	`limit`
Read from terminal	`read`	`$<`
Make a variable read-only	`readonly`	`set -r`
Show possible completions	Tab Tab	
Ignore interrupts	`trap 2`	`onintr`
Begin `until` loop	`until/do`	`until`
Begin `while` loop	`while/do`	`while`

20
bash: The Bourne-Again Shell

bash is the GNU version of the standard Bourne shell—the original Unix shell—and incorporates many popular features from other shells such as *csh*, *tcsh*, and the Korn shell (*ksh*). *tcsh*, which is described in the following chapter, offers many of the features in this chapter, and is also available on most distributions of Linux. However, *bash* is the default user shell for Mac OS X Panther.

If executed as part of the user's login, *bash* starts by executing any commands found in */etc/profile*. It executes the commands found in *~/.bash_profile*, *~/.bash_login*, or *~/.profile* (searching for each file only if the previous file is not found).

In addition, every time it starts (as a subshell or a login shell), *bash* looks for a file named *~/.bashrc*. Many system administration utilities create a small *~/.bashrc* automatically, and many users create quite large startup files. Any commands that can be executed from the shell can be included. Here's a small sample file:

```
# Set bash variable to keep 50 commands in history.
HSTSIZE=50
#
# Set prompt to show current working directory and history number of
# command.
PS1='\w: Command \!$ '
#
# Set path to search for commands in my directories, then standard ones.
PATH=~/bin:~/scripts:$PATH
#
# Keep group and others from writing my newly created files.
umask 022
#
# Show color-coded file types.
alias ls='ls --color=yes'
#
# Make executable and .o files ugly yellow so I can find and delete them.
export LS_COLORS="ex=43:*.o=43"
```

```
#
# Quick and dirty test of a single-file program.
function gtst () {
    g++ -o $1 $1.C && ./$1
}
#
# Remove .o files.
alias clean='find ~ -name \*.o -exec rm {} \;'
```

bash provides the following features:

- Input/output redirection
- Wildcard characters (metacharacters) for filename abbreviation
- Shell variables for customizing your environment
- Powerful programming capabilities
- Command-line editing (using *vi*- or Emacs-style editing commands)
- Access to previous commands (command history)
- Integer arithmetic
- Arithmetic expressions
- Command name abbreviation (aliasing)
- Job control
- Integrated programming features
- Control structures
- Directory stacking (using *pushd* and *popd*)
- Brace/tilde expansion
- Key bindings

Invoking the Shell

The command interpreter for *bash* can be invoked as follows:

bash [*options*] [*arguments*]

bash can execute commands from a terminal (when *-i* is specified), from a file (when the first *argument* is an executable script), or from standard input (if no arguments remain or if *-s* is specified).

Options

Options that appear here with double hyphens also work when entered with single hyphens, but using double hyphens is standard coding procedure.

-, --
: Treat all subsequent strings as arguments, not options.

-D, --dump-strings
: For execution in non-English locales, dump all strings that *bash* translates.

--dump-po-strings
  Same as *--dump-strings*, but uses the GNU *gettext* po (portable object) format suitable for scripting.

-c `str`
  Read commands from string `str`.

--help
  Print usage information and exit.

-i Create an interactive shell (prompt for input).

-l, --login
  Behave like a login shell; try to process */etc/profile* on startup. Then process *~/.bash_profile*, *~/.bash_login*, or *~/.profile* (searching for each file only if the previous file is not found).

--noediting
  Disable line editing with arrow and control keys.

--noprofile
  Don't process */etc/profile*, *~/.bash_profile*, *~/.bash_login*, or *~/.profile* on startup.

--norc
  Don't process *~/.bashrc* on startup.

--posix
  Conform to POSIX standard.

-r, --restricted
  Restrict users to a very secure, limited environment; for instance, they can't change out of the startup directory or use the > sign to redirect output.

--rcfile `file`
  Substitute `file` for *.bashrc* on startup.

-s Read commands from standard input. Output from built-in commands goes to file descriptor 1; all other shell output goes to file descriptor 2.

-v, --verbose
  Print each line as it is executed (useful for tracing scripts).

--version
  Print information about which version of *bash* is installed.

-x Turn on debugging, as described under the *-x* option to the *set* built-in command later in this chapter.

The remaining options to *bash* are listed under the *set* built-in command.

Arguments

Arguments are assigned, in order, to the positional parameters `$1`, `$2`, and so forth. If the first argument is an executable script, it is assigned to `$0`; then commands are read from it, and remaining arguments are assigned to `$1`, `$2`, and so on.

Syntax

This subsection describes the many symbols peculiar to *bash*. The topics are arranged as follows:

- Special files
- Filename metacharacters
- Command-line editing
- Quoting
- Command forms
- Redirection forms
- Coprocesses

Special Files

File	Purpose
/etc/profile	Executed automatically at login.
$HOME/.bash_profile	Executed automatically at login.
$HOME/.bashrc	Executed automatically at shell startup.
$HOME/.bash_logout	Executed automatically at logout.
$HOME/.bash_history	Record of last session's commands.
$HOME/.inputrc	Initialization file for reading input in an interactive shell.
/etc/passwd	Source of home directories for ~*name* abbreviations.

Filename Metacharacters

Characters	Meaning
*	Match any string of zero or more characters.
?	Match any single character.
[*abc*...]	Match any one of the enclosed characters; a hyphen can be used to specify a range (e.g., a–z, A–Z, 0–9).
[!*abc*...]	Match any character *not* among the enclosed characters.
[^*abc*...]	Same as [!*abc*...].
{*str1*,...}	Brace expansion: match any of the enclosed strings.
~*name*	Home directory of user *name*. With no *name*, Home directory of current user.
~+	Current working directory (PWD).
~-	Previous working directory from directory stack (OLDPWD; see also the *pushd* built-in command).
~+*n*	The *n*th entry in the directory stack, counting from the start of the list with the first entry being 0.
~-*n*	The *n*th entry in the directory stack, counting from the end of the list with the last entry being 0.

Patterns can be a sequence of patterns separated by |. If any subpatterns match, the entire sequence is considered matching. This extended syntax resembles that of *egrep* and *awk*.

Examples

```
$ ls new*          List new and new.1
$ cat ch?          Match ch9 but not ch10
$ vi [D-R]*        Match files that begin with uppercase D through R
```

Command-Line Editing

Command lines can be edited like lines in either Emacs or *vi*. Emacs is the default. See "Line-Edit Mode" later in this chapter for more information.

vi mode has two submodes, input mode and command mode. The default is input mode; you can go to command mode by pressing Esc. In command mode, typing *a* (append) or *i* (insert) returns you to input mode.

Some users discover that the Del or Backspace key on the terminal doesn't delete the character before the cursor, as it should. Sometimes this problem can be solved by issuing one of the following commands (or placing it in your *.bashrc* file):

```
stty erase ^?
stty erase ^H
```

See the *stty* command in Chapter 28 for more information.

Tables 20-1 through 20-14 show various Emacs and *vi* commands.

Table 20-1. Basic Emacs-mode commands

Command	Description
Ctrl-b	Move backward one character (without deleting).
Ctrl-f	Move forward one character.
Del	Delete one character backward.
Ctrl-d	Delete one character forward.

Table 20-2. Emacs-mode word commands

Command	Description
M-b	Move one word backward.
M-f	Move one word forward.
M-Del	Kill one word backward.
M-d	Kill one word forward.
Ctrl-y	Retrieve (*yank*) last item killed.

Table 20-3. Emacs-mode line commands

Command	Description
Ctrl-a	Move to beginning of line.
Ctrl-e	Move to end of line.
Ctrl-k	Kill forward to end of line.

Table 20-4. Emacs-mode commands for moving through the history file

Command	Description
Ctrl-p	Move to previous command.
Ctrl-n	Move to next command.
Ctrl-r	Search backward.
M-<	Move to first line of history file.
M->	Move to last line of history file.

Table 20-5. Emacs-mode completion commands

Command	Description
Tab	Attempt to perform general completion of the text.
M-?	List the possible completions.
M-/	Attempt filename completion.
Ctrl-x /	List the possible filename completions.
M-~	Attempt username completion.
Ctrl-x ~	List the possible username completions.
M-$	Attempt variable completion.
Ctrl-x $	List the possible variable completions.
M-@	Attempt hostname completion.
Ctrl-x @	List the possible hostname completions.
M-!	Attempt command completion.
Ctrl-x !	List the possible command completions.
M-Tab	Attempt completion from previous commands in the history list.

Table 20-6. Miscellaneous Emacs-mode commands

Command	Description
Ctrl-j	Same as Return.
Ctrl-l	Clear the screen, placing the current line at the top of the screen.
Ctrl-m	Same as Return.
Ctrl-o	Same as Return, then display next line in command history.
Ctrl-t	Transpose character left of and under the cursor.
Ctrl-u	Kill the line from the beginning to point.
Ctrl-v	Insert keypress instead of interpreting it as a command.
Ctrl-[	Same as Esc (most keyboards).
M-c	Capitalize word under or after cursor.
M-u	Change word under or after cursor to all capital letters.
M-l	Change word under or after cursor to all lowercase letters.
M-.	Insert last word in previous command line after point.
M-_	Same as *M-.* .

Table 20-7. Editing commands in vi input mode

Command	Description
Del	Delete previous character.
Ctrl-W	Erase previous word (i.e., erase until a blank).
Ctrl-V	Insert next keypress instead of interpreting it as a command.
Esc	Enter command mode (see Table 20-8).

Table 20-8. Basic vi command-mode commands

Command	Description
h	Move left one character.
l	Move right one character.
b	Move left one word.
w	Move right one word.
B	Move to beginning of preceding nonblank word.
W	Move to beginning of next nonblank word.
e	Move to end of current word.
E	Move to end of current nonblank word.
0	Move to beginning of line.
^	Move to first nonblank character in line.
$	Move to end of line.

Table 20-9. Commands for entering vi input mode

Command	Description
i	Insert text before current character (insert).
a	Insert text after current character (append).
I	Insert text at beginning of line.
A	Insert text at end of line.
r	Replace current character with next keypress.
R	Overwrite existing text.

Table 20-10. Some vi-mode delete commands

Command	Description
dh	Delete one character backward.
dl	Delete the current character.
db	Delete one word backward.
dw	Delete one word forward.
dB	Delete one nonblank word backward.
dW	Delete one nonblank word forward.
d$	Delete to end-of-line.
d0	Delete to beginning of line.

Table 20-11. Abbreviations for vi-mode delete commands

Command	Description
D	Delete to end of line (equivalent to *d$*).
dd	Delete entire line (equivalent to *0d$*).
C	Delete to end of line; enter input mode (equivalent to *c$*).
cc	Delete entire line; enter input mode (equivalent to *0c$*).
X	Delete character backward (equivalent to *dh*).
x	Delete the current character (equivalent to *dl*).

Table 20-12. vi-mode commands for searching the command history

Command	Description
k or -	Move backward one line.
j or +	Move forward one line.
G	Move to first line in history.
/*string*	Search backward for *string*.
?*string*	Search forward for *string*.
n	Repeat search in same direction as previous.
N	Repeat search in opposite direction of previous.

Table 20-13. vi-mode character-finding commands

Command	Description
f*x*	Move right to next occurrence of *x*.
F*x*	Move left to previous occurrence of *x*.
t*x*	Move right to next occurrence of *x*, then back one space.
T*x*	Move left to previous occurrence of *x*, then forward one space.
;	Redo last character-finding command.
,	Redo last character-finding command in opposite direction.

Table 20-14. Miscellaneous vi-mode commands

Command	Description
~	Invert (toggle) case of current character(s).
_	Insert last word of previous command after cursor; enter input mode.
Ctrl-L	Clear the screen and redraw the current line on it; good for when your screen becomes garbled.
#	Prepend # (comment character) to the line and send it to the history file; useful for saving a command to be executed later, without having to retype it.

Quoting

Quoting disables a character's special meaning and allows it to be used literally, as itself. The following characters have special meaning to *bash*:

<table>
<tr><th>Character</th><th>Meaning</th></tr>
<tr><td>;</td><td>Command separator</td></tr>
<tr><td>&</td><td>Background execution</td></tr>
<tr><td>()</td><td>Command grouping (enter a subshell)</td></tr>
<tr><td>{}</td><td>Command block</td></tr>
<tr><td>|</td><td>Pipe</td></tr>
<tr><td>> < &</td><td>Redirection symbols</td></tr>
<tr><td>* ? [ ] ~ !</td><td>Filename metacharacters</td></tr>
<tr><td>" ' \</td><td>Used in quoting other characters</td></tr>
<tr><td>`</td><td>Command substitution</td></tr>
<tr><td>$</td><td>Variable substitution (or command substitution)</td></tr>
<tr><td>newline space tab</td><td>Word separators</td></tr>
<tr><td>#</td><td>Comment</td></tr>
</table>

The following characters can be used for quoting:

Character	Action
""	Everything between " and " is taken literally, except for the following characters that keep their special meaning:
	$ Variable substitution will occur.
	` Command substitution will occur.
	" This marks the end of the double quote.
''	Everything between ' and ' is taken literally, except for another '.
\	The character following \ is taken literally. Use within "" to escape ", $, and '. Often used to escape itself, spaces, or newlines.

Examples

```
$ echo 'Single quotes "protect" double quotes'
Single quotes "protect" double quotes

$ echo "Well, isn't that \"special\"?"
Well, isn't that "special"?

$ echo "You have `ls|wc -l` files in `pwd`"
You have  43 files in /home/bob

$ echo "The value of \$x is $x"
The value of $x is 100
```

Command Forms

Syntax	Effect
cmd &	Execute *cmd* in background.
cmd1 ; *cmd2*	Command sequence; execute multiple *cmds* on the same line.
(*cmd1* ; *cmd2*)	Subshell; treat *cmd1* and *cmd2* as a command group.

Syntax	Effect
cmd1 | *cmd2*	Pipe; use output from *cmd1* as input to *cmd2*.
cmd1 \`*cmd2*\`	Command substitution; use *cmd2* output as arguments to *cmd1*.
cmd1 $(*cmd2*)	Command substitution; nesting is allowed.
cmd1 && *cmd2*	AND; execute *cmd2* only if *cmd1* succeeds.
cmd1 || *cmd2*	OR; execute *cmd2* only if *cmd1* fails.
{ *cmd1* ; *cmd2* }	Execute commands in the current shell.

Examples

```
$ cd; ls                                Execute sequentially
$ (date; who; pwd) > logfile            All output is redirected
$ sort file | pr -3 | lp                Sort file, page output, then print
$ vi `grep -l ifdef *.c`                Edit files found by grep
$ egrep '(yes|no)' `cat list`           Specify a list of files to search
$ egrep '(yes|no)' $(cat list)          Same as previous using bash command
                                        substitution
$ egrep '(yes|no)' $(<list)             Same, but faster
$ grep XX file && lp file               Print file if it contains the pattern
$ grep XX file || echo "XX not found"   Echo an error message if pattern
                                        not found
```

Redirection Forms

File descriptor	Name	Common abbreviation	Typical default
0	Standard input	stdin	Keyboard
1	Standard output	stdout	Screen
2	Standard error	stderr	Screen

The usual input source or output destination can be changed as shown in Table 20-15.

Table 20-15. I/O redirectors

Redirector	Function
> `file`	Direct standard output to `file`.
< `file`	Take standard input from `file`.
cmd1 | *cmd2*	Pipe; take standard output of *cmd1* as standard input to *cmd2*.
>> `file`	Direct standard output to `file`; append to `file` if it already exists.
>| `file`	Force standard output to `file` even if *noclobber* is set.
n>| `file`	Force output from the file descriptor *n* to `file` even if *noclobber* is set.
<> `file`	Use `file` as both standard input and standard output.
<< `text`	Read standard input up to a line identical to `text` (`text` can be stored in a shell variable). Input is usually typed on the screen or in the shell program. Commands that typically use this syntax include *cat*, *echo*, *ex*, and *sed*. If `text` is enclosed in quotes, standard input will not undergo variable substitution, command substitution, etc.
n> `file`	Direct file descriptor *n* to `file`.
n< `file`	Set `file` as file descriptor *n*.

Table 20-15. I/O redirectors (continued)

Redirector	Function
>&*n*	Duplicate standard output to file descriptor *n*.
<&*n*	Duplicate standard input from file descriptor *n*.
&>*file*	Direct standard output and standard error to *file*.
<&-	Close the standard input.
>&-	Close the standard output.
n>&-	Close the output from file descriptor *n*.
n<&-	Close the input from file descriptor *n*.

Examples

```
$ cat part1 > book
$ cat part2 part3 >> book
$ mail tim < report
$ grep Chapter part* 2> error_file

$ sed 's/^/XX /' << END_ARCHIVE
> This is often how a shell archive is "wrapped",
> bundling text for distribution. You would normally
> run sed from a shell program, not from the command line.
> END_ARCHIVE
XX This is often how a shell archive is "wrapped",
XX bundling text for distribution. You would normally
XX run sed from a shell program, not from the command line.
```

To redirect standard output to standard error:

```
$ echo "Usage error:  see administrator" 1>&2
```

The following command sends output (files found) to *filelist* and sends error messages (inaccessible files) to file *no_access*:

```
$ find / -print > filelist 2>no_access
```

Variables

Preface a variable by a dollar sign ($) to reference its value. You can also optionally enclose it in braces ({ }). You can assign a value to a variable through an equals sign (=) with no whitespace on either side of it:

```
$ TMP=temp.file
```

By default, variables are seen only within the shell itself; to pass variables to other programs invoked within the shell, see the *export* built-in command.

If enclosed by brackets ([ ]), the variable is considered an array variable. For instance:

```
$ DIR_LIST[0]=src
$ DIR_LIST[1]=headers
$ ls ${DIR_LIST[1]}
```

The contents of headers are listed. Many substitutions and commands in this chapter handle arrays by operating on each element separately.

Variable Substitution

In the following substitutions, braces ({ }) are optional, except when needed to separate a variable name from following characters that would otherwise be considered part of the name.

Variable	Meaning
${*var*}	Value of variable *var*.
$0	Name of the program.
${*n*}	Individual arguments on command line (positional parameters); 1 ≤ *n* ≤ 9.
$#	Number of arguments on command line.
$*	All arguments on command line.
$@	Same as $*, but contents are split into words when the variable is enclosed in double quotes.
$$	Process number of current shell; useful as part of a filename for creating temporary files with unique names.
$?	Exit status of last command (normally 0 for success).
$!	Process number of most recently issued background command.
$-	Current execution options (see the *set* built-in command). By default, *hB* for scripts and *himBH* for interactive shells.
$_	Initially set to name of file invoked for this shell, then set for each command to the last word of the previous command.

Tables 20-16 through 20-18 show various types of operators that can be used with *bash* variables.

Table 20-16. Substitution operators

Operator	Substitution
${*varname*:-*word*}	If *varname* exists and isn't null, return its value; otherwise, return *word*.
Purpose:	Returning a default value if the variable is undefined.
Example:	`${count:-0}` evaluates to 0 if `count` is undefined.
${*varname*:=*word*}	If *varname* exists and isn't null, return its value; otherwise set it to *word* and then return its value. Positional and special parameters cannot be assigned this way.
Purpose:	Setting a variable to a default value if it is undefined.
Example:	`${count:=0}` sets `count` to 0 if it is undefined.
${*varname*:?*message*}	If *varname* exists and isn't null, return its value; otherwise, print *varname*: followed by *message*, and abort the current command or script (noninteractive shells only). Omitting *message* produces the default message "parameter null or not set."
Purpose:	Catching errors that result from variables being undefined.
Example:	`{count:?"undefined"}` prints "count: undefined" and exits if `count` is undefined.
${*varname*:+*word*}	If *varname* exists and isn't null, return *word*; otherwise, return null.
Purpose:	Testing for the existence of a variable.
Example:	`${count:+1}` returns 1 (which could mean true) if `count` is defined.

Table 20-16. Substitution operators (continued)

Operator	Substitution
${#*varname*}	Return the number of characters in the value of *varname*.
Purpose:	Preparing for substitution or extraction of substrings.
Example:	If `${USER}` currently expands to `root`, `${#USER}` expands to 4.

Table 20-17. Pattern-matching operators

Operator	Meaning
${*variable#pattern*}	If the pattern matches the beginning of the variable's value, delete the shortest part that matches and return the rest.
${*variable##pattern*}	If the pattern matches the beginning of the variable's value, delete the longest part that matches and return the rest.
${*variable%pattern*}	If the pattern matches the end of the variable's value, delete the shortest part that matches and return the rest.
${*variable%%pattern*}	If the pattern matches the end of the variable's value, delete the longest part that matches and return the rest.
${*var*/*pat*/*sub*}	Return *var* with the first occurrence of *pat* replaced by *sub*. Can be applied to $* or $@, in which case each word is treated separately. If *pat* starts with #, it can match only the start of *var*; if *pat* ends with %, it can match only the end of *var*.
${*var*//*pat*/*sub*}	Return *var* with every occurrence of *pat* replaced by *sub*.
${*variable*:*n*}	Truncate the beginning of the variable and return the part starting with character number *n*, where the first character is 0.
${*variable*:*n*:*l*}	Starting with character number *n*, where the first character is 0, return a substring of length *l* from the variable.

Table 20-18. Expression evaluation

Operator	Meaning
$((*arithmetic-expression*))	Return the result of the expression. Arithmetic operators are described in the section "Arithmetic Expressions."
Example:	`TODAY='date +%-d'; echo $(($TODAY+7))` stores the number of the current day in `$TODAY` and then prints that number plus 7 (the number of the same day next week).
[[$*condition*]]	Return 1 if *condition* is true and 0 if it is false. Conditions are described under the *test* built-in command.

Built-in Shell Variables

Built-in variables are set automatically by the shell and are typically used inside shell scripts. Built-in variables can use the variable substitution patterns shown earlier. When setting variables, you don't include dollar signs, but when referencing their values later, the dollar signs are necessary.

Tables 20-19 through 20-22 show the commonly used built-in variables in *bash*.

Table 20-19. Behavior-altering variables

Variable	Meaning
auto_resume	Allows a background job to be brought to the foreground simply by entering a substring of the job's command line. Values can be `substring` (resume if the user's string matches part of the command), `exact` (string must exactly match command), or another value (string must match at beginning of command).
BASH_ENV	Startup file of commands to execute, if *bash* is invoked to run a script.
CDPATH	Colon-separated list of directories to search for the directory passed in a *cd* command.
EDITOR	Pathname of your preferred text editor.
IFS	Word separator; used by shell to parse commands into their elements. The default separators are space, tab, and newline.
IGNOREEOF	If nonzero, don't allow use of a single Ctrl-D (the end-of-file or EOF character) to log off; use the *exit* command to log off.
PATH	Colon-separated list of directories to search for each command.
PROMPT_COMMAND	Command that *bash* executes before issuing a prompt for a new command.
PS1	Prompt displayed before each new command; see the later section "Variables in Prompt" for ways to introduce into the prompt dynamically changing information such as the current working directory or command history number.
PS2	Prompt displayed before a new line if a command is not finished.
PS3	Prompt displayed by *select* built-in command.
PS4	Prompt displayed by *-x* debugging (see the section "Invoking the Shell") and the *set* built-in command).

Table 20-20. History variables

Variable	Meaning
FCEDIT	Pathname of editor to use with the *fc* command.
HISTCMD	History number of the current command.
HISTCONTROL	If `HISTCONTROL` is set to the value of `ignorespace`, lines beginning with a space are not entered into the history list. If set to `ignoredups`, lines matching the last history line are not entered. Setting it to `ignoreboth` enables both options.
HISTFILE	Name of history file on which the editing modes operate.
HISTFILESIZE	Maximum number of lines to store in the history file. The default is 500.
HISTSIZE	Maximum number of commands to remember in the command history. The default is 500.

Table 20-21. Mail variables

Variable	Meaning
MAIL	Name of file to check for incoming mail.
MAILCHECK	How often, in seconds, to check for new mail (default is 60 seconds).
MAILPATH	List of filenames, separated by colons (:), to check for incoming mail.

Table 20-22. Status variables

Variable	Meaning
BASH	Pathname of this instance of the shell you are running.
BASH_VERSION	Version number of the shell you are running.

Table 20-22. Status variables (continued)

Variable	Meaning
COLUMNS	Number of columns your display has.
DIRSTACK	List of directories manipulated by *pushd* and *popd* commands.
EUID	Effective UID of process running this shell, in the form of the number recognized by the system.
GROUPS	Groups to which user belongs, in the form of the numbers recognized by the system.
HOME	Name of your home (login) directory.
HOSTNAME	Host the shell is running on.
HOSTTYPE	Short name indicating the type of machine the shell is running on; for instance, *i486*.
LINES	The number of lines your display has.
MACHTYPE	Long string indicating the machine the shell is running on; for instance, *i486-pc-linux-gnu*.
OLDPWD	Previous directory before the last *cd* command.
OSTYPE	Short string indicating the operating system; for instance, *linux-gnu*.
PPID	PID of parent process that invoked this shell.
PWD	Current directory.
SECONDS	Number of seconds since the shell was invoked.
SHELL	Pathname of the shell you are running.
SHLVL	Depth to which running shells are nested.
TERM	The type of terminal that you are using.
UID	Real UID of process running this shell, in the form of the number recognized by the system.

Arithmetic Expressions

The *let* command performs integer arithmetic. *bash* provides a way to substitute integer values (for use as command arguments or in variables); base conversion is also possible.

Expression	Meaning
((*expr*))	Use the value of the enclosed arithmetic expression.

Operators

bash uses arithmetic operators from the C programming language; the following list is in decreasing order of precedence. Use parentheses to override precedence.

Operator	Meaning
-	Unary minus
! ~	Logical negation; binary inversion (one's complement)
* / %	Multiplication; division; modulus (remainder)
+ -	Addition; subtraction
<< >>	Bitwise left shift; bitwise right shift
<= >=	Less than or equal to; greater than or equal to
< >	Less than; greater than

Operator	Meaning
== !=	Equality; inequality (both evaluated left to right)
&	Bitwise AND
^	Bitwise exclusive OR
|	Bitwise OR
&&	Logical AND
||	Logical OR
=	Assign value
+= -=	Reassign after addition/subtraction
*= /= %=	Reassign after multiplication/division/remainder
&= ^= |=	Reassign after bitwise AND/XOR/OR
<<= >>=	Reassign after bitwise shift left/right

Examples

See the *let* built-in command for more information and examples.

```
let "count=0" "i = i + 1"          Assign i and count
let "num % 2"; echo $?             Test for an even number
```

Command History

bash lets you display or modify previous commands. Commands in the history list can be modified using:

- Line-edit mode
- The *fc* command

Line-Edit Mode

Line-edit mode lets you emulate many features of the *vi* and Emacs editors. The history list is treated like a file. When the editor is invoked, you type editing keystrokes to move to the command line you want to execute. On most terminals, arrow keys work in both Emacs mode and *vi* command mode. You can also change the line before executing it. See Table 20-23 for some examples of common line-edit commands. When you're ready to issue the command, press Return.

The default line-edit mode is Emacs. To enable *vi* mode, enter:

```
$ set -o vi
```

Note that *vi* starts in input mode; to type a *vi* command, press Esc first.

The mode you use for editing *bash* commands is entirely separate from the editor that is invoked for you automatically within many commands (for instance, the editor invoked by mail readers when you ask them to create a new mail message). To change the default editor, set the VISUAL or EDITOR variable to the filename or full pathname of your favorite editor:

```
$ export EDITOR=emacs
```

Table 20-23. Common editing keystrokes

vi	Emacs	Result
k	Ctrl-p	Get previous command.
j	Ctrl-n	Get next command.
/*string*	Ctrl-r *string*	Get previous command containing *string*.
h	Ctrl-b	Move back one character.
l	Ctrl-f	Move forward one character.
b	M-b	Move back one word.
w	M-f	Move forward one word.
X	Del	Delete previous character.
x	Ctrl-d	Delete one character.
dw	M-d	Delete word forward.
db	M-Ctrl-h	Delete word back.
xp	Ctrl-t	Transpose two characters.

bash

The fc Command

Use *fc -l* to list history commands, and *fc -e* to edit them. See the *fc* built-in command for more information.

Examples

```
$ history            Display the command history list
$ fc -l 20 30        List commands 20 through 30
$ fc -l -5           List the last five commands
$ fc -l cat          List the last command beginning with cat
$ fc -ln 5 > doit    Save command 5 to file doit
$ fc -e vi 5 20      Edit commands 5 through 20 using vi
$ fc -e emacs        Edit previous command using Emacs
$ !!                 Reexecute previous command
$ !cat               Reexecute last cat command
$ !cat foo-file      Reexecute last command, adding foo-file to the end of the argument list
```

Command Substitution

Syntax	Meaning
!	Begin a history substitution.
!!	Previous command.
!*N*	Command number *N* in history list.
!-*N*	*N*th command back from current command.
!*string*	Most recent command that starts with *string*.
!?*string*?	Most recent command that contains *string*.
!?*string*?%	Most recent command argument that contains *string*.
!$	Last argument of previous command.
!#	The current command up to this point.

Syntax	Meaning
!!*string*	Previous command, then append *string*.
!*N string*	Command *N*, then append *string*.
!{*s1*}*s2*	Most recent command starting with string *s1*, then append string *s2*.
^*old*^new^	Quick substitution; change string *old* to *new* in previous command, and execute modified command.

Variables in Prompt

Using the following variables, you can display information about the current state of the shell or the system in your *bash* prompt. Set the PS1 variable to a string including the desired variables. For instance, the following command sets PS1 to a string that includes the \w variable to display the current working directory and the \! variable to display the number of the current command. The next line is the prompt displayed by the change.

```
$ PS1='\w: Command \!$ '
~/book/linux: Command 504$
```

Variable	Meaning
\a	Alarm (bell).
\d	Date in the format "Mon May 8".
\e	Escape character (terminal escape, not backslash).
\h	Hostname.
\j	Number of background jobs (active or stopped).
\l	Current terminal name.
\n	Newline inserted in the prompt.
\r	Carriage return inserted in the prompt.
\s	Current shell.
\t	Time in 24-hour format, where 3:30 p.m. appears as 15:30:00.
\u	User's account name.
\v	Version and release of *bash*.
\w	Current working directory.
\A	Time in 24-hour format, where 3:30 p.m. appears as 15:30.
\D{*format*}	Time in the specified format interpreted by *strftime*; an empty format displays the locale-specific current time.
\H	Like *\h*.
\T	Time in 12-hour format, where 3:30 p.m. appears as 03:30:00.
\V	Version, release, and patch level of *bash*.
\W	Last element (following last slash) of current working directory.
\\	Single backslash inserted in the prompt.
\!	Number of current command in the command history.
\#	Number of current command, where numbers start at 1 when the shell starts.
\@	Time in 12-hour format, where 3:30 p.m. appears as 03:30 p.m.
\$	Indicates whether you are *root*: displays # for *root*, $ for other users.
\[	Starts a sequence of nonprinting characters, to be ended by *\]*.

Variable	Meaning
\]	Ends the sequence of nonprinting characters started by \[.
nnn	The character in the ASCII set corresponding to the octal number *nnn* inserted into the prompt.

Job Control

Job control lets you place foreground jobs in the background, bring background jobs to the foreground, or suspend (temporarily stop) running jobs. Job control is enabled by default. Once disabled, it can be reenabled by any of the following commands:

```
bash -m -i
set -m
set -o monitor
```

Many job control commands take *jobID* as an argument. This argument can be specified as follows:

%n Job number *n*

%s Job whose command line starts with string *s*

%?s
Job whose command line contains string *s*

%% Current job

%+ Current job (same as preceding)

%- Previous job

bash provides the following job control commands. For more information on these commands, see the upcoming section "Built-in Commands."

bg Put a job in the background.

fg Put a job in the foreground.

jobs
List active jobs.

kill Terminate a job.

stop
Suspend a background job.

stty tostop
Stop background jobs if they try to send output to the terminal.

wait
Wait for background jobs to finish.

Ctrl-Z
Suspend a foreground job, and use *bg* or *fg* to restart it in the background or foreground. (Your terminal may use something other than *Ctrl-Z* as the suspend character.)

Built-in Commands

Examples to be entered as a command line are shown with the $ prompt. Otherwise, examples should be treated as code fragments that might be included in a shell script. For convenience, some of the reserved words used by multiline commands also are included.

#

#

Ignore all text that follows on the same line. # is used in shell scripts as the comment character and is not really a command.

#!

#!*shell*

Used as the first line of a script to invoke the named *shell* (with optional arguments) or other program. For example:

```
#!/bin/bash
```

:

:

Null command. Returns an exit status of 0. Sometimes used as the first character in a file to denote a *bash* script. Shell variables can be placed after the : to expand them to their values.

Example

To check whether someone is logged in:

```
if who | grep -w $1 > /dev/null
   then :      # do nothing
   # if pattern is found
   else echo "User $1 is not logged in"
fi
```

.

. *file* [*arguments*]

Same as *source*.

alias

alias [**-p**] [*name*[=*cmd*]]

Assign a shorthand *name* as a synonym for *cmd*. If *=cmd* is omitted, print the alias for *name*; if *name* is also omitted or if *-p* is specified, print all aliases. See also *unalias*.

bg

bg [*jobIDs*]

Put current job or *jobIDs* in the background. See the earlier section "Job Control."

bash

bind

bind [*options*]
bind [*options*] *key*:*function*

Print or set the bindings that allow keys to invoke functions such as cursor movement and line editing. Typical syntax choices for *keys* are "\C-t" for Ctrl-T and "\M-t" or "\et" for Esc-T (quoting is needed to escape the sequences from the shell). Function names can be seen though the *-l* option.

Options

-f filename
: Consult *filename* for bindings, which should be in the same format as on the *bind* command line.

-l
: Print all Readline functions, which are functions that can be bound to keys.

-m keymap
: Specify a keymap for this and further bindings. Possible keymaps are emacs, emacs-standard, emacs-meta, emacs-ctlx, vi, vi-move, vi-command, and vi-insert.

-p
: Display all functions and the keys that invoke them, in the format by which keys can be set.

-q function
: Display the key bindings that invoke *function*.

-r key
: Remove the binding attached to *key* so that it no longer works.

-s
: Display all macros and the keys that invoke them, in the format by which keys can be set.

-u function
: Remove all the bindings attached to *function* so that no keys will invoke it.

-v
: Display all Readline variables (settings that affect history and line editing) and their current settings, in the format by which variables can be set.

-x key:command
: Bind key to a shell command.

-P
: Display all bound keys and the functions they invoke.

-S
: Display all macros and the keys that invoke them.

-V Display all Readline variables (settings that affect history and line editing) and their current settings.

Example

Bind Ctrl-T to `copy-forward-word`, the function that copies the part of the word following the cursor so it can be repasted:

```
$ bind "\C-t":copy-forward-word
```

break

`break` `[`*`n`*`]`

Exit from the innermost (most deeply nested) *for*, *while*, or *until* loop, or from the *n*th innermost level of the loop. Also exits from a *select* list.

builtin

`builtin` *`command`* `[`*`arguments`*`]`

Execute *command*, which must be a shell built-in. Useful for invoking built-ins within scripts of the same name.

case

```
case string
 in
 regex)
 commands
 ;;
 ...
 esac
```

If *`string`* matches regular expression *regex*, perform the following *commands*. Proceed down the list of regular expressions until one is found. (To catch all remaining strings, use * as *regex* at the end.)

cd

`cd` `[`*`options`*`] [`*`dir`*`]`

With no arguments, change to user's home directory. Otherwise, change working directory to *`dir`*. If *dir* is a relative pathname but is not in the current directory, search the CDPATH variable.

Options

-L Force symbolic links to be followed.

-P Don't follow symbolic links, but use the physical directory structure.

command

command [*options*] *command* [*arguments*]

Execute *command*, but don't perform function lookup (i.e., refuse to run any command that is neither in PATH nor a built-in). Set exit status to that returned by *command* unless *command* cannot be found, in which case exit with a status of 127.

Options

-p Search default path, ignoring the PATH variable's value.

-v Print the command or filename that invokes the command.

-V Like *-v*, but also print a description of the command.

-- Treat everything that follows as an argument, not an option.

bash

compgen

compgen [*options*] [*word*]

Generate possible completion matches for *word* for use with *bash*'s programmable completion feature, and write the matches to standard output. If *word* is not specified, display all completions. See *complete* for the options; any except *-p* and *-r* can be used with *compgen*.

complete

complete [*options*] *names*

Specify completions for arguments to each *name*, for use with *bash*'s programmable completion feature. With no options or with *-p*, print all completion specifications such that they can be reused as input.

Options

-o comp-option
: Specify other aspects of the completion specification's behavior besides generating a completion. Possible values of *comp-option* are:

  default
  : Use *readline*'s default filename completion if the completion specification generates no matches.

  dirnames
  : Use directory name completion if the completion specification generates no matches.

  filenames
  : Tell *readline* that the completion specification generates filenames so that it can process them accordingly. For use with shell functions.

  nospace
  : Tell *readline* not to append a space to completions at the end of the line. This is the default.

-p Print all completion specifications.

-r Remove completion specification for each *name*, or all specifications if no names are given.

-A action
: Specify an action to generate a list of completions. Possible actions are:

alias
: Alias names. May be specified as *-a*.

arrayvar
: Array variable names.

binding
: *readline* key binding names.

builtin
: Shell built-in command names. May be specified as *-b*.

command
: Command names. May be specified as *-c*.

directory
: Directory names. May be specified as *-d*.

disabled
: Disabled shell built-in command names.

enabled
: Enabled shell built-in command names.

export
: Exported shell variable names. May be specified as *-e*.

file
: Filenames. May be specified as *-f*.

function
: Shell function names.

group
: Group names. May be specified as *-g*.

helptopic
: Help topic names accepted by the *help* built-in command.

hostname
: Hostnames, from the file specified by `HOSTFILE`.

job
: Job names, if job control is active. May be specified as *-j*.

keyword
: Shell reserved words. May be specified as *-k*.

running
: Names of running jobs, if job control is active.

service
: Service names. May be specified as *-s*.

setopt
: Valid arguments for the *-o* option to the *set* built-in command.

shopt
: Valid shell option names for the *shopt* built-in command.

signal
: Signal names.

stopped
: Names of stopped jobs, if job control is active.

user
: Usernames. May be specified as *-u*.

variable
: Shell variable names. May be specified as *-v*.

-C *command*
: Execute the specified command in a subshell and use the output as possible completions.

-F *function*
: Execute the specified function in the current shell and take the possible completions from the COMPREPLY array variable.

-G *globpat*
: Expand the specified filename expansion pattern to generate the possible completions.

-P *prefix*
: Prepend the specified prefix to each possible completion after all other options have been applied.

-S *suffix*
: Append the specified suffix to each possible completion after all other options have been applied.

-W *list*
: Split the specified word list and expand each resulting word. The possible completions are the members of the resulting list that match the word being completed.

-X *pattern*
: Use the specified pattern as a filter and apply it to the list of possible completions generated by all the other options except *-P* and *-S*, removing all matches from the list. A leading ! in the *pattern* negates it so that any completion that doesn't match the pattern is removed.

continue

continue [*n*]

Skip remaining commands in a *for*, *while*, or *until* loop, resuming with the next iteration of the loop (or skipping *n* loops).

declare

declare [*options*] [*name*[=*value*]]
typeset [*options*] [*name*[=*value*]]

Print or set variables. Options prefaced by + instead of - are inverted in meaning.

Options

-a Treat the following names as array variables.

-f Treat the following names as functions.

-i Expect variable to be an integer, and evaluate its assigned value.

-p Print names and settings of all shell variables and functions; take no other action.

-r Don't allow variables to be reset later.

-x Mark variables for subsequent export.

-F Print names of all shell functions; take no other action.

---

dirs

dirs [*options*]

Print directories currently remembered for *pushd/popd* operations.

Options

+entry
Print *entry*th entry from start of list (list starts at 0).

-entry
Print *entry*th entry from end of list.

-c Clear the directory stack.

-l Long listing.

-p Print the directory stack, one entry per line.

-v Like *-p*, but prefix each entry with its position in the stack.

---

disown

disown [*options*] [*jobIDs*]

Let job run, but disassociate it from the shell. By default, does not even list the job as an active job; commands like *jobs* and *fg* will no longer recognize it. When *-h* is specified, the job is recognized but is kept from being killed when the shell dies.

Options

-a Act on all jobs.

-h Do not pass a SIGHUP signal received by the shell on to the job.

---

echo

echo [*options*] [*strings*]

Write each *string* to standard output, separated by spaces and terminated by a newline. If no strings are supplied, echo a newline. (See also *echo* in Chapter 28.)

Options

-e Enable interpretation of escape characters:

- *\a* Audible alert
- *\b* Backspace
- *\c* Suppress the terminating newline (same as *-n*)
- *\e* Escape character
- *\f* Form feed
- *\n* Newline
- *\r* Carriage return
- *\t* Horizontal tab
- *\v* Vertical tab
- \\ Backslash
- *\nnn*
  The character in the ASCII set corresponding to the octal number *nnn*.
- *\xnn*
  The character in the ASCII set corresponding to the hexadecimal number *nn* (1 or 2 hex digits).

-n Don't append a newline to the output.

-E Disable interpretation of escape characters.

---

enable

enable [*options*] [*built-in* ...]

Enable (or when *-n* is specified, disable) built-in shell commands. Without *built-in* argument or with *-p* option, print enabled built-ins. With *-a*, print the status of all built-ins. You can disable shell commands in order to define your own functions with the same names.

Options

-a Display all built-ins, both enabled and disabled.

-d Delete a built-in command that was previously loaded with *-f*.

-f filename
On systems that support dynamic loading, load the new built-in command *built-in* from the shared object *filename*.

-n Disable each specified *built-in*.

-p Display enabled built-ins.

-s Restrict display to special built-ins defined by the POSIX standard.

---

eval

eval [*command args...*]

Perform *command*, passing *args*.

exec

exec [*options*] [*command*]

Execute *command* in place of the current shell (instead of creating a new process). *exec* is also useful for opening, closing, or copying file descriptors.

Options

-a name
: Tell *command* that it was invoked as *name*.

-c
: Remove all environment variables from the process when the new command runs.

-l
: Treat the new process as if the user were logging in.

Examples

`$ trap 'exec 2>&-' 0`	*Close standard error when shell script exits (signal 0)*
`$ exec /bin/tcsh`	*Replace current shell with extended C shell*
`$ exec < infile`	*Reassign standard input to infile*

exit

exit [*n*]

Exit a shell script with status *n* (e.g., *exit 1*). *n* can be zero (success) or nonzero (failure). If *n* is not given, exit status will be that of the most recent command. *exit* can be issued at the command line to close a window (log out).

Example

```
if [ $# -eq 0 ]; then
   echo "Usage:  $0 [-c] [-d] file(s)"
   exit 1     # Error status
fi
```

export

export [*options*] [*variables*]
export [*options*] [*name*=[*value*]]...

Pass (export) the value of one or more shell *variables*, giving global meaning to the variables (which are local by default). For example, a variable defined in one shell script must be exported if its value will be used in other programs called by the script. When a shell variable has been exported, you can access its value by referencing the equivalent environment variable. If no *variables* are given, *export* lists the variables exported by the current shell. If *name* and *value* are specified, *export* assigns *value* to a variable *name* and exports it.

Options

--
: Treat all subsequent strings as arguments, not options.

-f
: Expect *variables* to be functions.

-n Unexport variable.

-p List variables exported by current shell.

fc

fc [*options*] [*first*] [*last*]
fc -s [*oldpattern=newpattern*] [*command*]

Display or edit commands in the history list. (Use only one of *-l* or *-e*.) *fc* provides capabilities similar to the C shell's *history* and ! syntax. *first* and *last* are numbers or strings specifying the range of commands to display or edit. If *last* is omitted, *fc* applies to a single command (specified by *first*). If both *first* and *last* are omitted, *fc* edits the previous command or lists the last 16. A negative number is treated as an offset from the current command. The second form of *fc* takes a history *command*, replaces *old* string with *new* string, and executes the modified command. If no strings are specified, *command* is reexecuted. If no *command* is given either, the previous command is reexecuted. *command* is a number or string like *first*. See earlier examples under the section "Command History."

Options

-e [editor]
Invoke *editor* to edit the specified history commands. The default *editor* is set by the shell variable FCEDIT. If FCEDIT is not set, the value of EDITOR is used, or *vi* if neither is set.

-l [first last]
List the specified command or range of commands, or list the last 16.

-n Suppress command numbering from the *-l* listing.

-r Reverse the order of the *-l* listing.

-s oldpattern=newpattern
Edit command(s), replacing all occurrences of the specified old pattern with the new pattern. Then reexecute.

fg

fg [*jobIDs*]

Bring current job or *jobIDs* to the foreground. See the section "Job Control."

for

for *x* [**in** *list*]
 do
 commands
 done

Assign each word in *list* to *x* in turn and execute commands. If *list* is omitted, $@ (positional parameters) is assumed.

bash

Examples

Paginate all files in the current directory and save each result:

```
for file in *
do
     pr $file > $file.tmp
done
```

Search chapters for a list of words (like *fgrep -f*):

```
for item in `cat program_list`
do
     echo "Checking chapters for"
     echo "references to program $item..."
     grep -c "$item.[co]" chap*
done
```

function

```
function command
{
 ...
}
```

Define a function. Refer to arguments the same way as positional parameters in a shell script ($1, etc.) and terminate with }.

getopts

getopts *string name* [*args*]

Process command-line arguments (or *args*, if specified) and check for legal options. *getopts* is used in shell script loops and is intended to ensure standard syntax for command-line options. *string* contains the option letters to be recognized by *getopts* when running the shell script. Valid options are processed in turn and stored in the shell variable *name*. If an option letter is followed by a colon, the option must be followed by one or more arguments.

hash

hash [*options*] [*commands*]

Search for *commands* and remember the directory in which each command resides. Hashing causes the shell to remember the association between a name and the absolute pathname of an executable, so that future executions don't require a search of PATH. With no arguments or only *-l*, *hash* lists the current hashed commands. The display shows *hits* (the number of times the command is called by the shell) and *command* (the full pathname).

Options

-d Forget the remembered location of each specified command.

-l Display the output in a format that can be reused as input.

-p filename
: Assume *filename* is the full path to the command and don't do a path search.

-r
: Forget the locations of all remembered commands.

-t
: Print the full pathname for each command. With more than one command, print the command before each full path.

help

help [**-s**] [*string*]

Print help text on all built-in commands or those matching *string*. With *-s*, display only brief syntax; otherwise display summary paragraph also.

history

history [*options*]
history [*lines*]

Print a numbered command history, denoting modified commands with *. Include commands from previous sessions. You may specify how many lines of history to print.

Options

-a [file]
: *bash* maintains a file called *.bash_history* in the user's home directory, a record of previous sessions' commands. Ask *bash* to append the current session's commands to *.bash_history* or to *file*.

-c
: Clear history list: remove all previously entered commands from the list remembered by the shell.

-d offset
: Delete the history entry at the specified offset from the beginning of the history list.

-n [file]
: Append to the history list those lines in *.bash_history* or in *file* that haven't yet been included.

-p args
: Perform history substitution on the specified arguments, and display the result on standard output. The results aren't stored in the history list. Each argument must be quoted to disable normal history expansion.

-r [file]
: Use *.bash_history* or *file* as the history list, instead of the working history list.

-s args
: Remove the last command in the history list, and then add the specified arguments to the list as a single entry (but don't execute the entry).

-w [file]
: Overwrite *.bash_history* or *file* with the working history list.

if

if *test-cmds*

Begin a conditional statement. The possible formats, shown here side by side, are:

```
if test-cmds     if test-cmds      if test-cmds
   then             then              then
      cmds1            cmds1             cmds1
fi                  else              elif test-cmds
                       cmds2             then
                 fi                         cmds2
                                            ...
                                      else
                                         cmdsn
                                   fi
```

Usually, the initial *if* and any *elif* lines execute one *test* or [] command (although any series of commands is permitted). When *if* succeeds (that is, the last of its *test-cmds* returns 0), *cmds1* are performed; otherwise, each succeeding *elif* or *else* line is tried.

jobs

jobs [*options*] [*jobIDs*]

List all running or stopped jobs, or those specified by *jobIDs*. For example, you can check whether a long compilation or text format is still running. Also useful before logging out. See also the earlier section"Job Control."

Options

-l List job IDs and process GIDs.

-n List only jobs whose status has changed since last notification.

-p List process GIDs only.

-r List active, running jobs only.

-s List stopped jobs only.

-x command [arguments]
: Execute *command*. If *jobIDs* are specified, replace them with *command*.

kill

kill [*options*] *IDs*

Terminate each specified PID or job ID. You must own the process or be a privileged user. See also the section "Job Control" and the *killall* command in Chapter 28.

Options

-signal
: The signal number (from *ps -f*) or name (from *kill -l*). The default is TERM (signal number 15). With a signal number of 9, the kill is unconditional. If nothing else works to kill a process, *kill -9* almost always kills it, but it doesn't allow the process any time to clean up.

`--` Consider all subsequent strings to be arguments, not options.

-l [arg]
: With no argument, list the signal names. (Used by itself.) The argument can be a signal name or a number representing either the signal number or the exit status of a process terminated by a signal. If it is a name, the corresponding number is returned; otherwise, the corresponding name is returned.

-n signum
: Specify the signal number to send.

-s signal
: Specify *signal*. May be a signal name or number.

let

let *expressions*

Perform arithmetic as specified by one or more integer *expressions*. *expressions* consist of numbers, operators, and shell variables (which don't need a preceding $), and must be quoted if they contain spaces or other special characters. For more information and examples, see the earlier section "Arithmetic Expressions." See also *expr* in Chapter 28.

Examples

Both of the following examples add 1 to variable `i`:

```
let i=i+1
let "i = i + 1"
```

local

local [*options*] [*variable*[=*value*]] [*variable2*[=*value*]] ...

Without arguments, print all local variables. Otherwise, create (and set, if specified) one or more local variables. See the *declare* built-in command for options. Must be used within a function.

logout

logout [*status*]

Exit the shell, returning *status* as exit status to invoking program if specified. Can be used only in a login shell. Otherwise, use *exit*.

popd

popd [*options*]

Manipulate the directory stack. By default, remove the top directory, and *cd* to it. If successful, run *dirs* to show the new directory stack.

Options

+n Remove the *n*th directory in the stack, counting from 0.

-n Remove the *n*th entry from the bottom of the stack, counting from 0.

-n Don't do a *cd* when removing directories from the stack.

---

printf

printf *string* [*arguments*]

Format the *arguments* according to *string*. Works like the C library *printf* function. Standard *printf* percent-sign formats are recognized in *string*, such as %i for integer. Escape sequences such as *\n* can be included in *string* and are automatically recognized; if you want to include them in *arguments*, specify a *string* of %b. You can escape characters in *arguments* to output a string suitable for input to other commands by specifying a *string* of %q.

Examples

```
$ printf "Previous command: %i\n" "$(($HISTCMD-1))"
Previous command: 534
$ echo $PAGER
less -E
$ printf "%q\n" "\t$PAGER"
\\tless\ -E
```

The last command would probably be used to record a setting in a file where it could be read and assigned by another shell script.

---

pushd

pushd [*directory*]
pushd [*options*]

By default, switch top two directories on stack. If specified, add a new directory to the top of the stack instead, and *cd* to it.

Options

+n Rotate the stack to place the *n*th (counting from 0) directory at the top.

-n Rotate the stack to place the *n*th directory from the bottom of the stack at the top.

-n Don't do a *cd* when adding directories to the stack.

---

pwd

pwd [**option**]

Display the current working directory's absolute pathname. By default, any symbolic directories used when reaching the current directory are displayed, but with *-P*, or if the *-o* option to the *set* built-in is set, the real names are displayed instead.

Options

-L Include any symbolic links in the pathname.

-P Don't include symbolic links in the pathname.

read

read [*options*] [*variable1 variable2* ...]

Read one line of standard input and assign each word (as defined by IFS) to the corresponding *variable*, with all leftover words assigned to the last variable. If only one variable is specified, the entire line is assigned to that variable. The return status is 0 unless EOF is reached, a distinction that is useful for running loops over input files. If no variable names are provided, read the entire string into the environment variable REPLY.

bash

Options

-a var
: Read each word into an element of *var*, which is treated as an array variable.

-d char
: Stop reading the line at *char* instead of at the newline.

-e Line editing and command history are enabled during input.

-n num
: Read only *num* characters from the line.

-p string
: Display the prompt *string* to the user before reading each line, if input is interactive.

-r Raw mode; ignore \ as a line continuation character.

-s Don't echo the characters entered by the user (useful for reading a password).

-t seconds
: Time out and return without setting any variables if input is interactive and no input has been entered for *seconds* seconds.

-u fd
: Read input from specified file descriptor *fd* instead of standard input.

Examples

```
$ read first last address
Sarah Caldwell 123 Main Street
$ echo "$last, $first\n$address"
Caldwell, Sarah
123 Main Street
```

The following commands, which read a password into the variable $user_pw and then display its value, use recently added options that are not in all versions of *bash* in current use.

```
$ read -sp "Enter password (will not appear on screen)" user_pw
Enter password (will not appear on screen)
$ echo $user_pw
You weren't supposed to know!
```

The following script reads input from the system's password file, which uses colons to delimit fields (making it a popular subject for examples of input parsing):

```
IFS=:
cat /etc/passwd |
while
read account pw user group gecos home shell
do
echo "Account name $account has user info: $gecos"
done
```

readonly

readonly [*options*] [*variable1 variable2...*]

Prevent the specified shell variables from being assigned new values. Variables can be accessed (read) but not overwritten.

Options

-a Treat the following names as array variables.

-f Treat the following names as functions and set them read-only so that they can't be changed.

-p Display all read-only variables (default).

return

return [*n*]

Normally used inside a function to exit the function with status *n* or with the exit status of the previously executed command. Can be used outside a function during execution of a script by the . command to cause the shell to stop execution of the script. The return status is *n* or the script's exit status.

select

select *name* [**in** *wordlist* **;**]
do
commands
done

Choose a value for *name* by displaying the words in *wordlist* to the user and prompting for a choice. Store user input in the variable REPLY and the chosen word in *name*. Then execute *commands* repeatedly until they execute a *break* or *return*. The default prompt can be changed by setting the PS3 shell variable.

set

set [*options*] [*arg1 arg2* ...]

With no arguments, *set* prints the values of all variables known to the current shell. Options can be enabled (*-option*) or disabled (*+option*). Options can also be set when the shell is invoked, via *bash*. Arguments are assigned in order to $1, $2, and so on.

Options

- Turn off *-v* and *-x*, and turn off option processing.

-- Used as the last option; turn off option processing so that arguments beginning with - are not misinterpreted as options. (For example, you can set $1 to -1.) If no arguments are given after --, unset the positional parameters.

-a From now on, automatically mark variables for export after defining or changing them.

-b Report background job status at termination instead of waiting for next shell prompt.

-e Exit if a command yields a nonzero exit status.

-f Don't expand filename metacharacters (e.g., * ? [ ]). Wildcard expansion is sometimes called *globbing*.

-h Locate and remember commands as they are defined.

-k Assignment of environment variables (*var=value*) will take effect regardless of where they appear on the command line. Normally, assignments must precede the command name.

-m Monitor mode. Enable job control; background jobs execute in a separate process group. *-m* usually is set automatically.

-n Read commands, but don't execute. Useful for checking errors, particularly for shell scripts.

-o [m]
: List shell modes, or turn on mode *m*. Many modes can be set by other options. The modes can be turned off through the *+o* option. Modes are:

allexport
: Same as *-a*.

braceexpand
: Same as *-B*.

emacs
: Enter Emacs editing mode (on by default).

errexit
: Same as *-e*.

hashall
: Same as *-h*.

histexpand
: Same as *-H*.

history
: Default. Preserve command history.

bash

ignoreeof
Don't allow use of a single Ctrl-D (the end-of-file or EOF character) to log off; use the *exit* command to log off. This has the same effect as setting the shell variable `IGNOREEOF=1`.

interactive-comments
Allow comments to appear in interactive commands.

keyword
Same as *-k*.

monitor
Same as *-m*.

noclobber
Same as *-C*.

noexec
Same as *-n*.

noglob
Same as *-f*.

notify
Same as *-b*.

nounset
Same as *-u*.

onecmd
Same as *-t*.

physical
Same as *-P*.

posix
Match POSIX standard.

privileged
Same as *-p*.

verbose
Same as *-v*.

vi
Enable *vi*-style command-line editing.

xtrace
Same as *-x*.

+o [m]
Display the *set* commands that recreate the current mode settings or turn off mode *m*. See the *-o* option for a list of modes.

-p Start up as a privileged user; don't process *$HOME/.profile*.

-t Exit after one command is executed.

-u Indicate an error when user tries to use a variable that is undefined.

-v Show each shell command line when read.

-x Show commands and arguments when executed, preceded by a + or the prompt defined by the `PS4` shell variable. This provides step-by-step debugging of shell scripts. (Same as *-o xtrace*.)

-B Default. Enable brace expansion.

-C Don't allow output redirection (>) to overwrite an existing file.

-H Default. Enable ! and !! commands.

-P Print absolute pathnames in response to *pwd*. By default, *bash* includes symbolic links in its response to *pwd*.

Examples

`set -- "$num" -20 -30`	*Set $1 to $num, $2 to -20, $3 to -30*
`set -vx`	*Read each command line; show it; execute it; how it again (with arguments)*
`set +x`	*Stop command tracing*
`set -o noclobber`	*Prevent file overwriting*
`set +o noclobber`	*Allow file overwriting again*

bash

---

shift

shift [*n*]

Shift positional arguments (e.g., `$2` becomes `$1`). If *n* is given, shift to the left *n* places.

---

shopt

shopt [*options*] [*optnames*]

Set or unset variables that control optional shell behavior. With no options or with *-p*, display the settable *optnames*.

Options

-o Allow only options defined for the *set -o* built-in to be set or unset.

-p Display output in a form that can be reused as input.

-q Quiet mode. Suppress normal output.

-s Set (enable) each specified option. With no *optname*, list all set options.

-u Unset (disable) each specified option. With no *optname*, list all unset options.

Settable shell options

Unless otherwise noted, options are disabled by default.

cdable_vars
If an argument to the *cd* built-in is not a directory, assume that it's a variable containing the name of the directory to change to.

cdspell
For interactive shells, check for minor errors in the name of a directory component (transposed characters, a missing character, or an extra character). Print the corrected name and proceed.

checkhash
Check that a command found in the hash table actually exists before trying to execute it; if it is not found, do a path search.

checkwinsize
: Check the window size after each command, and update `LINES` and `COLUMNS` as necessary.

cmdhist
: Attempt to save all lines of a multiline command in one history entry to facilitate re-editing.

dotglob
: Include filenames beginning with . in the results of pathname expansion.

execfail
: For a noninteractive shell, don't exit if the file specified as an argument to *exec* cannot be executed. For an interactive shell, don't exit from the shell if *exec* fails.

expand_aliases
: Expand aliases. Enabled by default for interactive shells.

extglob
: Enable the shell's extended pattern-matching features for pathname expansion.

histappend
: Append the history list to the file specified by `HISTFILE` when the shell exits, instead of overwriting the file.

histreedit
: Give the user a chance to re-edit a failed history substitution.

histverify
: Load a history substitution into the *readline* editing buffer so it can be further edited, instead of immediately passing it to the shell parser.

hostcomplete
: Try to provide hostname completion when a word containing @ is being completed. Set by default.

huponexit
: Send `SIGHUP` to all jobs when an interactive login shell exits.

interactive_comments
: In an interactive shell, treat any word beginning with a #, and any subsequent characters, as a comment. Set by default.

lithist
: If *cmdhist* is also enabled, save multiline commands to the history file separated by embedded newlines rather than semicolons (;) when possible.

login_shell
: Set by the shell if it is started as a login shell. Can't be changed by the user.

mailwarn
: Warn if a mail file has been accessed since the last time *bash* checked it.

no_empty_cmd_completion
: Don't attempt to search the `PATH` for possible completions when completion is attempted on an empty line.

nocaseglob
: Use case-insensitive filename matching during pathname expansion.

nullglob
: Allow patterns that don't match any files to expand to a null string.

progcomp
Enable the programmable completion facilities. Set by default.

promptvars
Perform variable and parameter expansion on prompt strings after performing normal expansion. Set by default.

restricted_shell
Set by the shell if started in restricted mode. This option can't be changed by the user and is not reset when the startup files are executed.

shift_verbose
Cause the *shift* built-in to print an error message when the shift count is greater than the number of positional parameters.

sourcepath
Cause the *source* built-in (.) to search the PATH to find the directory containing a file supplied as an argument. Set by default.

xpg_echo
Cause the *echo* built-in to expand backslash-escape sequences by default.

bash

---

source

source *file* [*arguments*]

Read and execute lines in *file*. *file* doesn't have to be executable but must reside in a directory searched by PATH. Any *arguments* are passed as positional parameters to the file when it is executed.

---

suspend

suspend [-f]

Same as Ctrl-Z.

Option

-f Force suspend, even if shell is a login shell.

---

test

test *condition*
[*condition* **]**

Evaluate a *condition* and, if its value is true, return a zero exit status; otherwise, return a nonzero exit status. An alternate form of the command uses [ ] rather than the word *test*. *condition* is constructed using the following expressions. Conditions are true if the description holds true.

File conditions

-a file
file exists.

-b file
: *file* is a block special file.

-c file
: *file* is a character special file.

-d file
: *file* is a directory.

-e file
: *file* exists.

-f file
: *file* is a regular file.

-g file
: *file* has the `set-group-ID` bit set.

-h file
: *file* is a symbolic link.

-k file
: *file* has its sticky bit (no longer used) set.

-p file
: *file* is a named pipe (FIFO).

-r file
: *file* is readable.

-s file
: *file* has a size greater than 0.

-t [n]
: The open file descriptor *n* is associated with a terminal device (default *n* is 1).

-u file
: *file* has its `set-user-ID` bit set.

-w file
: *file* is writable.

-x file
: *file* is executable.

-G file
: *file*'s group is the process's effective GID.

-L file
: *file* is a symbolic link.

-N file
: *file* has been modified since its last time of access.

-O file
: *file*'s owner is the process's effective UID.

-S file
: *file* is a socket.

f1 -ef f2
: Files *f1* and *f2* are linked (refer to the same file through a hard link).

f1 -nt f2
: File *f1* is newer than *f2*.

f1 -ot *f2*
  File *f1* is older than *f2*.

String conditions

-n *s1*
  String *s1* has nonzero length.

-o *s1*
  Shell option *s1* is set. Shell options are described under the *set* built-in command.

-z *s1*
  String *s1* has 0 length.

s1 = *s2*
  Strings *s1* and *s2* are identical.

s1 == *s2*
  Strings *s1* and *s2* are identical.

s1 != *s2*
  Strings *s1* and *s2* aren't identical.

s1 < *s2*
  String *s1* is lower in the alphabet (or other sort in use) than *s2*. By default, the check is performed character-by-character against the ASCII character set.

s1 > *s2*
  String *s1* is higher in the alphabet (or other sort in use) than *s2*.

string
  string is not null.

Integer comparisons

n1 -eq *n2*
  n1 equals *n2*.

n1 -ge *n2*
  n1 is greater than or equal to *n2*.

n1 -gt *n2*
  n1 is greater than *n2*.

n1 -le *n2*
  n1 is less than or equal to *n2*.

n1 -lt *n2*
  n1 is less than *n2*.

n1 -ne *n2*
  n1 does not equal *n2*.

Combined forms

! *condition*
  True if *condition* is false.

condition1 -a *condition2*
  True if both conditions are true.

condition1 -o *condition2*
  True if either condition is true.

Examples

Each of the following examples shows the first line of various statements that might use a test condition:

`while test $# -gt 0`	*While there are arguments ...*
`while [ -n "$1" ]`	*While the first argument is nonempty ...*
`if [ $count -lt 10 ]`	*If $count is less than 10 ...*
`if [ -d RCS ]`	*If the RCS directory exists ...*
`if [ "$answer" != "y" ]`	*If the answer is not y ...*
`if [ ! -r "$1" -o ! -f "$1" ]`	*If the first argument is not a readable file or a regular file ...*

times

times

Print accumulated process times for user and system.

trap

trap [*option*] [*commands*] [*signals*]

Execute *commands* if any of *signals* is received. Each *signal* can be a signal name or number. Common signals include 0, 1, 2, and 15. Multiple commands should be quoted as a group and separated by semicolons internally. If *commands* is the null string (e.g., *trap* "" *signals*), then *signals* is ignored by the shell. If *commands* is omitted entirely, reset processing of specified signals to the default action. If both *commands* and *signals* are omitted, list current trap assignments. See the examples at the end of this entry and under *exec*.

Options

-*l* List signal names and numbers.

-p Used with no *commands* to print the trap commands associated with each *signal*, or all signals if none is specified.

Signals

Signals are listed along with what triggers them.

0 Exit from shell (usually when shell script finishes).

1 Hang up (usually logout).

2 Interrupt (usually through Ctrl-C).

3 Quit.

4 Illegal instruction.

5 Trace trap.

6 Abort.

7 Unused.

8 Floating-point exception.

9 Termination.

10 User-defined.

11 Reference to invalid memory.

12 User-defined.

13 Write to a pipe without a process to read it.

14 Alarm timeout.

15 Software termination (usually via *kill*).

16 Unused.

17 Termination of child process.

18 Continue (if stopped).

19 Stop process.

20 Process suspended (usually through Ctrl-Z).

21 Background process has tty input.

22 Background process has tty output.

23–28
Unused.

29 I/O possible on a channel.

Examples

```
trap "" 2        Ignore signal 2 (interrupts)
trap 2           Obey interrupts again
```

Remove a *$tmp* file when the shell program exits or if the user logs out, presses Ctrl-C, or does a *kill*:

```
trap "rm -f $tmp; exit" 0 1 2 15
```

---

type

type [*options*] *commands*

Report absolute pathname of programs invoked for *commands* and whether or not they are hashed.

Options

-- Consider all subsequent strings to be arguments, not options.

-a, -all
Print all occurrences of *command*, not just that which would be invoked.

-f Suppress shell function lookup.

-p, -path
Print the hashed value of *command*, which may differ from the first appearance of *command* in the PATH.

-t, -type
Determine and state if *command* is an alias, keyword, function, built-in, or file.

-P Force a PATH search for each name, even if *-t* would not return a value of "file" for the name.

Example

```
$ type mv read
mv is /bin/mv
read is a shell built-in
```

typeset

typeset

Obsolete. See *declare*.

ulimit

ulimit [*options*] [*n*]

Print the value of one or more resource limits or, if *n* is specified, set a resource limit to *n*. Resource limits can be either hard (*-H*) or soft (*-S*). By default, *ulimit* sets both limits or prints the soft limit. The options determine which resource is acted on. Values are in 1024-byte increments unless otherwise indicated.

Options

-- Consider all subsequent strings to be arguments, not options.

-a Print all current limits.

-H Hard resource limit.

-S Soft resource limit.

Specific limits

These options limit specific resource sizes.

-c Core files.

-d Size of processes' data segments.

-f Size of shell-created files.

-l Size of memory that the process can lock.

-m Resident set size.

-n Number of file descriptors. On many systems, this can't be set.

-p Pipe size, measured in blocks of 512 bytes.

-s Stack size.

-t Amount of CPU time, counted in seconds.

-u Number of processes per user.

-v Virtual memory used by shell.

umask

umask [*options*] [*nnn*]

Display file creation mask or set file creation mask to octal value *nnn*. The file creation mask determines which permission bits are turned off (e.g., *umask 002* produces *rw-rw-r--*).

Options

-p Display mask within a *umask* command so that a caller can read and execute it.

-S Display *umask* symbolically rather than in octal.

bash

unalias

unalias [-a] *names*

Remove *names* from the alias list. See also *alias*.

Option

-a Remove all aliases.

unset

unset [*options*] *names*

Erase definitions of functions or variables listed in *names*.

Options

-f Expect *name* to refer to a function.

-v Expect *name* to refer to a variable (default).

until

```
until
 test-commands
 do
 commands
 done
```

Execute *test-commands* (usually a test or [ ] command); if the exit status is nonzero (that is, the test fails), perform *commands*. Repeat.

wait

wait [*ID*]

Pause in execution until all background jobs complete (exit status 0 will be returned), or until the specified background PID or job ID completes (exit status of *ID* is returned). Note that the shell variable $! contains the PID of the most recent background process. If job control is not in effect, *ID* can only be a PID number. See the section “Job Control.”

Example

```
wait $!      Wait for last background process to finish
```

while

```
while
 test-commands
 do
 commands
 done
```

Execute *test-commands* (usually a `test` or `[ ]` command); if the exit status is 0, perform *commands*. Repeat.

21
tcsh: An Extended C Shell

This chapter describes *tcsh*, an enhanced version of the C shell. *tcsh* is also used as the C shell; in that case, the *tcsh* features described in this chapter work even when you run *csh*. The C shell was so named because many of its programming constructs and symbols resemble those of the C programming language.

The default shell is *bash*. However, earlier versions of Mac OS X used *tcsh* as the default shell. If you want to use *tcsh*, you first need to change your default. To change your default shell, launch the Terminal application (*/Applications/Utilities*), and then change the shell to */bin/tcsh* in the Terminal's Preferences (Terminal→Preferences).

Overview of Features

Features of *tcsh* include:

- Input/output redirection
- Wildcard characters (metacharacters) for filename abbreviation
- Shell variables for customizing your environment
- Integer arithmetic
- Access to previous commands (command history)
- Command-name abbreviation (aliasing)
- A built-in command set for writing shell programs
- Job control
- Command-line editing and editor commands
- Word completion (tab completion)
- Spellchecking
- Scheduled events, such as logout or terminal locking after a set idle period and delayed commands

- Read-only variables

Invoking the Shell

The shell command interpreter can be invoked as follows:

```
tcsh [options] [arguments]
```

tcsh uses syntax resembling C and executes commands from a terminal or a file. The options *-n*, *-v*, and *-x* are useful when debugging scripts.

Options

-b
: Allow the remaining command-line options to be interpreted as options to a specified command rather than as options to *tcsh*.

-c
: Read and execute commands specified from the argument that follows and place any remaining arguments in the argv shell variable.

-d
: Load directory stack from *~/.cshdirs* even if not a login shell.

-e
: Exit if a command produces errors.

-f
: Fast startup; start without executing *.tcshrc*.

-i
: Invoke interactive shell (prompt for input) even if not on a terminal.

-l
: Login shell (must be the only option specified).

-m
: Load *~/.tcshrc* even if effective user is not the owner of the file.

-n
: Parse commands, but don't execute.

-q
: Accept `SIGQUIT` when used under a debugger. Disables job control.

-s
: Read commands from the standard input.

-t
: Exit after executing one line of input (which may be continued with a \ to escape the newline).

-v
: Display commands before executing them; expand history substitutions, but not other substitutions (e.g., filename, variable, and command). Same as setting *verbose*.

-V
: Same as *-v*, but also display *.tcshrc*.

-x
: Display commands before executing them, but expand all substitutions. Same as setting *echo*.

-X
: Same as *-x*, but also display *.tcshrc*.

Arguments

Arguments are assigned, in order, to the positional parameters `$1`, `$2`, and so on. If the first argument is an executable script, commands are read from it, and remaining arguments are assigned to `$1`, `$2`, and so forth.

Syntax

This section describes the many symbols used by *tcsh*. The topics are arranged as follows:

- Special files
- Filename metacharacters
- Quoting
- Command forms
- Redirection forms

Special Files

Filename	Description
~/.tcshrc or *~/.cshrc*	Executed at each instance of shell startup. If no *~/.tcshrc* is found, *tcsh* uses *~/.cshrc* if present.
~/.login	Executed by login shell after *.tcshrc* at login.
~/.cshdirs	Executed by login shell after *.login*.
~/.logout	Executed by login shell at logout.
/etc/passwd	Source of home directories for ~*name* abbreviations.

tcsh

Filename Metacharacters

Characters	Meaning
*	Match any string of 0 or more characters.
?	Match any single character.
[*abc*...]	Match any one of the enclosed characters; a hyphen can specify a range (e.g., a-z, A-Z, 0-9).
{*abc*,*xxx*,...}	Expand each comma-separated string inside braces.
~	Home directory for the current user.
~*name*	Home directory of user *name*.

Examples

```
% ls new*           Match new and new.1
% cat ch?           Match ch9 but not ch10
% vi [D-R]*         Match files that begin with uppercase D through R
% ls {ch,app}?      Expand, then match ch1, ch2, app1, app2
% cd ~tom           Change to tom's home directory
```

Quoting

Quoting disables a character's special meaning and allows it to be used literally, as itself. The characters in the following table have special meaning to *tcsh*.

Characters	Description
;	Command separator
&	Background execution
( )	Command grouping
		Pipe
* ? [ ] ~	Filename metacharacters
{ }	String expansion characters (usually don't require quoting)
> < & !	Redirection symbols
! ^	History substitution, quick substitution
" ' \	Used in quoting other characters
`	Command substitution
$	Variable substitution
newline space tab	Word separators

The characters that follow can be used for quoting:

`""`
: Everything between " and " is taken literally except for the following characters, which keep their special meaning:

  `$` Variable substitution will occur.

  `` ` `` Command substitution will occur.

  `"` The end of the double quote.

  `\` Escape next character.

  `!` The history character.

  newline
  The newline character.

`''`
: Everything between ' and ' is taken literally except for ! (history).

`\`
: The character following a \ is taken literally. Use within "" to escape ", $, and `. Often used to escape itself, spaces, or newlines. Always needed to escape a history character (usually !).

Examples

```
% echo 'Single quotes "protect" double quotes'
Single quotes "protect" double quotes

% echo "Well, isn't that "\""special?"\"
Well, isn't that "special?"

% echo "You have `ls|wc -l` files in `pwd`"
You have 43 files in /home/bob

% echo The value of \$x is $x
The value of $x is 100
```

Command Forms

Command	Action
cmd &	Execute *cmd* in background.
cmd1 ; *cmd2*	Command sequence; execute multiple *cmds* on the same line.
(*cmd1* ; *cmd2*)	Subshell; treat *cmd1* and *cmd2* as a command group.
cmd1 | *cmd2*	Pipe; use output from *cmd1* as input to *cmd2*.
cmd1 \`*cmd2*\`	Command substitution; run *cmd2* first and use its output as arguments to *cmd1*.
cmd1 || *cmd2*	OR; execute either *cmd1* or (if *cmd1* fails) *cmd2*.
cmd1 && *cmd2*	AND; execute *cmd1* and then (if *cmd1* succeeds) *cmd2*.

Examples

```
% cd; ls                               Execute sequentially
% (date; who; pwd) > logfile           All output is redirected
% sort file | pr -3 | lp               Sort file, page output, then print
% vi `grep -l ifdef *.c`               Edit files found by grep
% egrep '(yes|no)' `cat list`          Specify a list of files to search
% grep XX file && lp file              Print file if it contains the pattern
% grep XX file || echo XX not found    Echo an error message if XX not found
```

tcsh

Redirection Forms

File descriptor	Name	Common abbreviation	Typical default
0	Standard input	stdin	Keyboard
1	Standard output	stdout	Screen
2	Standard error	stderr	Screen

The usual input source or output destination can be changed with redirection commands listed in the following sections.

Simple redirection

Command	Action
cmd > *file*	Send output of *cmd* to *file* (overwrite).
cmd >! *file*	Same as preceding, even if *noclobber* is set.
cmd >> *file*	Send output of *cmd* to *file* (append).
cmd>>! *file*	Same as preceding, even if *noclobber* is set.
cmd < *file*	Take input for *cmd* from *file*.
cmd << *text*	Read standard input up to a line identical to *text* (*text* can be stored in a shell variable). Input usually is typed on the screen or in the shell program. Commands that typically use this syntax include *cat*, *echo*, *ex*, and *sed*. If *text* is enclosed in quotes, standard input will not undergo variable substitution, command substitution, etc.

Multiple redirection

Command	Action
cmd >& *file*	Send both standard output and standard error to *file*.
cmd >&! *file*	Same as preceding, even if *noclobber* is set.
cmd >>& *file*	Append standard output and standard error to end of *file*.
cmd >>&! *file*	Same as preceding, even if *noclobber* is set.
cmd1 |& *cmd2*	Pipe standard error together with standard output.
(*cmd*> *f1*) >& *f2*	Send standard output to file *f1* and standard error to file *f2*.
cmd | tee *files*	Send output of *cmd* to standard output (usually the screen) and to *files*.

Examples

```
% cat part1 > book                          Copy part1 to book
% cat part2 part3 >> book                   Append parts 2 and 3 to same file as part1
% mail tim < report                         Take input to message from report
% cc calc.c >& error_out                    Store all messages, including errors
% cc newcalc.c >&! error_out                Overwrite old file
% grep Unix ch* |& pr                       Pipe all messages, including errors
% (find / -print > filelist) >& no_access   Separate error messages from list of files
% sed 's/^/XX /' << "END_ARCHIVE"           Supply text right after command
This is often how a shell archive is "wrapped",
bundling text for distribution. You would normally
run sed from a shell program, not from the command line.
"END_ARCHIVE"
```

Variables

This subsection describes the following:

- Variable substitution
- Variable modifiers
- Predefined shell variables
- Formatting for the prompt variable
- Sample *.tcshrc* file
- Environment variables

Variable Substitution

In the following substitutions, braces ({ }) are optional, except when needed to separate a variable name from following characters that would otherwise be considered part of the name.

Variable	Description
${*var*}	The value of variable *var*.
${*var*[*i*]}	Select word or words in position *i* of *var*. *i* can be a single number, a range *m*-*n*, a range -*n* (missing *m* implies 1), a range *m*- (missing *n* implies all remaining words), or * (select all words). *i* also can be a variable that expands to one of these values.

Variable	Description
`${#var}`	The number of words in *var*.
`${#argv}`	The number of arguments.
`$0`	Name of the program.
`${argv[n]}`	Individual arguments on command line (positional parameters); $1 \leq n \leq 9$.
`${n}`	Same as `${argv[n]}`.
`${argv[*]}`	All arguments on command line.
`$*`	Same as `{$argv[*]}`.
`$argv[$#argv]`	The last argument.
`${?var}`	Return 1 if *var* is set, 0 if not.
`$$`	Process number of current shell; useful as part of a filename for creating temporary files with unique names.
`${?name}`	Return 1 if *name* is set, 0 if not.
`$?0`	Return 1 if input filename is known, 0 if not.

Examples

Sort the third through last arguments, and save the output in a file whose name is unique to this process:

```
sort $argv[3-] > tmp.$$
```

Process *.tcshrc* commands only if the shell is interactive (i.e., the `prompt` variable must be set):

```
if ($?prompt) then
   set commands,
   alias commands,
   etc.
endif
```

Variable Modifiers

Except for `$?var`, `$$`, and `$?0`, the variable substitutions in the preceding section may be followed by one of these modifiers (when braces are used, the modifier goes inside them):

`:r` Return the variable's root (the portion before the last dot).

`:e` Return the variable's extension.

`:h` Return the variable's header (the directory portion).

`:t` Return the variable's tail (the portion after the last slash).

`:gr` Return all roots.

`:ge` Return all extensions.

`:gh` Return all headers.

`:gt` Return all tails.

:q Quote a wordlist variable, keeping the items separate. Prevents further substitution. Useful when the variable contains filename metacharacters that shouldn't be expanded.

:x Quote a pattern, expanding it into a wordlist.

Examples using pathname modifiers

The following table shows the effect of pathname modifiers if the aa variable is set as follows:

```
set aa=(/progs/num.c /book/chap.ps)
```

Variable portion	Specification	Output result
Normal variable	`echo $aa`	*/progs/num.c /book/chap.ps*
Second root	`echo $aa[2]:r`	*/book/chap*
Second header	`echo $aa[2]:h`	*/book*
Second tail	`echo $aa[2]:t`	*chap.ps*
Second extension	`echo $aa[2]:e`	*ps*
Root	`echo $aa:r`	*/progs/num /book/chap.ps*
Global root	`echo $aa:gr`	*/progs/num /book/chap*
Header	`echo $aa:h`	*/progs /book/chap.ps*
Global header	`echo $aa:gh`	*/progs /book*
Tail	`echo $aa:t`	*num.c /book/chap.ps*
Global tail	`echo $aa:gt`	*num.c chap.ps*
Extension	`echo $aa:e`	*c /book/chap.ps*
Global extension	`echo $aa:ge`	*c ps*

Examples using quoting modifiers

Unless quoted, the shell expands variables to represent files in the current directory:

```
% set a="[a-z]*" A="[A-Z]*"
% echo "$a" "$A"
[a-z]* [A-Z]*

% echo $a $A
at cc m4 Book Doc

% echo $a:x $A
[a-z]* Book Doc

% set d=($a:q $A:q)
% echo $d
at cc m4 Book Doc

% echo $d:q
[a-z]* [A-Z]*
```

```
% echo $d[1] +++ $d[2]
at cc m4 +++ Book Doc

% echo $d[1]:q
[a-z]*
```

Predefined Shell Variables

Variables can be set in one of two ways; by assigning a value:

```
set var=value
```

or by simply turning the variable on:

```
set var
```

In the following table, variables that accept values are shown with the equals sign followed by the type of value they accept; the value is then described (note, however, that variables such as `argv`, `cwd`, and `status` are never explicitly assigned). For variables that are turned on or off, the table describes what they do when set. `tcsh` automatically sets (and, in some cases, updates) the variables `addsuffix`, `argv`, `autologout`, `command`, `cwd`, `dirstack`, `echo-style`, `edit`, `gid`, `home`, `loginsh`, `logout`, `oid`, `owd`, `path`, `prompt`, `prompt2`, `prompt3`, `shell`, `shlvl`, `status`, `tcsh`, `term`, `tty`, `uid`, `user`, and `version`.

tcsh

Variable	Description
`addsuffix`	Append / to directories and a space to files during tab completion to indicate a precise match.
`afsuser`	Set value to be used instead of the local username for Kerberos authentication with the `autologout` locking feature.
`ampm`	Display all times in 12-hour format.
`argv=(`*`args`*`)`	List of arguments passed to current command; default is ( ).
`autocorrect`	Check spelling before attempting to complete commands.
`autoexpand`	Expand history (such as ! references) during command completion.
`autolist[=ambiguous]`	Print possible completions when correct one is ambiguous. If `ambiguous` is specified, print possible completions only when completion adds no new characters.
`autologout=` *`logout-minutes`* `[`*`locking-minutes`*`]`	Log out after *`logout-minutes`* of idle time. Lock the terminal after *`locking-minutes`* of idle time, requiring a password before continuing. Not used if the `DISPLAY` environment variable is set.
`backslash_quote`	Always allow backslashes to quote \, ', and ".
`catalog`	Use *tcsh.${catalog}* as the filename of the message catalog. The default is *tcsh*.
`cdpath=`*`dirs`*	List of alternate directories to search when locating arguments for *cd*, *popd*, or *pushd*.
`color`	Turn on color for *ls-F*, *ls*, or both. Setting to nothing is equivalent to setting for both.
`colorcat`	Enable color escape sequence for Native Language System (NLS) support and display NLS messages in color.
`command`	If set, hold the command passed to the shell with the *-c* option.
`complete=enhance`	When enhance, ignore case in completion, treat `.`, `-`, and `_` as word separators, and consider `_` and `-` to be the same.

Variable	Description
continue=*cmdlist*	If set to a list of commands, continue those commands instead of starting new ones.
continue_args=*cmdlist*	Like continue, but execute the following: echo \`pwd\` $argv > ~/.*cmd*_pause; %*cmd*
correct={cmd|complete|all}	When cmd, spell check commands. When complete, complete commands. When all, spell lcheck whole command line.
cwd=*dir*	Full pathname of current directory.
dextract	When set, the *pushd* command extracts the desired directory and puts it at the top of the stack instead of rotating the stack.
dirsfile=*file*	History file consulted by *dirs -S* and *dirs -L*. Default is *~/.cshdirs*.
dirstack	Directory stack, in array format. dirstack[0] is always equivalent to cwd. The other elements can be artificially changed.
dspmbyte=*code*	Enable use of multibyte code; for use with Kanji. See the *tcsh* manpage for details.
dunique	Make sure that each directory exists only once in the stack.
echo	Redisplay each command line before execution; same as *csh -x* command.
echo_style={bsd|sysv|both|none}	Don't echo a newline with *-n* option (bsd), parse escaped characters (sysv), do both, or do neither.
edit	Enable command-line editor. Set by default for interactive shells.
ellipsis	For use with prompt variable. Use ... to represent skipped directories.
fignore=*suffs*	List of filename suffixes to ignore during filename completion.
gid	User's GID.
group	User's group name.
histchars=*ab*	A two-character string that sets the characters to use in history substitution and quick substitution (default is !^).
histdup={all|prev|erase}	Maintain a record only of unique history events (all); don't enter a new event when it is the same as the previous one (prev) or remove an old event that is the same as the new one (erase).
histfile=*file*	History file consulted by *history -S* and *history -L*. Default is *~/.history*.
histlit	Don't expand history lines when recalling them.
history=*n format*	The first word indicates the number of commands to save in the history list. The second indicates the format with which to display that list (see the "Formatting for the Prompt Variable" section for possible formats).
home=*dir*	Home directory of user, initialized from HOME. The ~ character is shorthand for this value.
ignoreeof	Ignore an end-of-file (EOF) from terminals; prevents accidental logout.
implicitcd	If directory name is entered as a command, *cd* to that directory. Can be set to verbose to echo the *cd* to standard output.
inputmode={insert|overwrite}	Control editor's mode.
killdup={all|prev|erase}	Enter only unique strings in the kill ring (all); don't enter new string when it is the same as the current killed string (prev) or erase from the kill ring an old string that is the same as the current string (erase).
killring=*num*	Set the number of killed strings to keep in memory to *num*. The default is 30. If unset or set to a number less than 2, keep only the most recent killed string.
listflags=*flags*	One or more of the *x*, *a*, or *A* options for the *ls-F* built-in command. Second word can be set to path for *ls* command.
listjobs[=long]	When a job is suspended, list all jobs (in long format, if specified).

Variable	Description
`listlinks`	In *ls -F* command, include type of file to which links point.
`listmax=`*num*	Don't allow `list-choices` to print more than *num* choices before prompting.
`listmaxrows=`*num*	Don't allow `list-choices` to print more than *num* rows of choices before prompting.
`loginsh`	Set if shell is a login shell.
`logout`	Indicates status of an imminent logout (`normal`, `automatic`, or `hangup`).
`mail=(`*n files*`)`	One or more files checked for new mail every 5 minutes or (if *n* is supplied) every *n* seconds.
`matchbeep= {never|nomatch| ambiguous|notunique}`	Specifies circumstances under which completion should beep: never, if no match exists, if multiple matches exist, or if multiple matches exist and one is exact. If unset, `ambiguous` is used.
`nobeep`	Disable beeping.
`noclobber`	Don't redirect output to an existing file; prevents accidental destruction of files.
`noding`	Don't print "DING!" in prompt time specifiers when the hour changes.
`noglob`	Turn off filename expansion; useful in shell scripts.
`nokanji`	Disable Kanji (if supported).
`nonomatch`	Treat filename metacharacters as literal characters if no match exists (e.g., *vi ch** creates new file *ch** instead of printing "No match").
`nostat=`*directory-list*	Don't stat *directory-list* during completion.
`notify`	Declare job completions when they occur.
`owd`	Old working directory.
`path=(`*dirs*`)`	List of pathnames in which to search for commands to execute. Initialized from `PATH`; the default is *. /usr/ucb /usr/bin*.
`printexitvalue`	Print all nonzero exit values.
`prompt='`*str*`'`	String that prompts for interactive input; default is %. See the later section "Formatting for the Prompt Variable" for formatting information.
`prompt2='`*str*`'`	String that prompts for interactive input in `foreach` and `while` loops and continued lines (those with escaped newlines). See the section "Formatting for the Prompt Variable" for formatting information.
`prompt3='`*str*`'`	String that prompts for interactive input in automatic spelling correction. See the section "Formatting for the Prompt Variable" for formatting information.
`promptchars=`*cc*	Use the two characters specified as *cc* with the `%# prompt` sequence to indicate normal users and the superuser, respectively.
`pushdsilent`	Don't print directory stack when *pushd* and *popd* are invoked.
`pushdtohome`	Change to home directory when *pushd* is invoked without arguments.
`recexact`	Consider completion to be concluded on first exact match.
`recognize_only_ executables`	When command completion is invoked, print only executable files.
`rmstar`	Prompt before executing the command *rm **.
`rprompt=`*string*	The string to print on the right side of the screen while the prompt is displayed on the left. Specify as for `prompt`.
`savedirs`	Execute *dirs -S* before exiting.
`savehist=`*max* [merge]	Execute *history -S* before exiting. Save no more than *max* lines of history. If specified, merge those lines with previous history saves, and sort by time.
`sched=`*string*	Format for `sched`'s printing of events. See the section "Formatting for the Prompt Variable" for formatting information.
`shell=`*file*	Pathname of the shell program.

tcsh

Variable	Description
`shlvl`	Number of nested shells.
`status=`*n*	Exit status of last command. Built-in commands return 0 (success) or 1 (failure).
`symlinks={chase|ignore|expand}`	Specify manner in which to deal with symbolic links. Expand them to real directory name in *cwd* (`chase`), treat them as real directories (`ignore`), or expand arguments that resemble pathnames (`expand`).
`tcsh`	Version of *tcsh*.
`term`	Terminal type.
`time='`*n %c*`'`	If command execution takes more than *n* CPU seconds, report user time, system time, elapsed time, and CPU percentage. Supply optional *%c* flags to show other data.
`tperiod`	Number of minutes between executions of `periodic` alias.
`tty`	Name of tty, if applicable.
`uid`	User ID.
`user`	Username.
`verbose`	Display a command after history substitution; same as *tcsh -v*.
`version`	Shell's version and additional information, including options set at compile time.
`visiblebell`	Flash screen instead of beeping.
`watch=(`[*n*] *`user terminal...`*`)`	Watch for *`user`* logging in at *`terminal`*, where *`terminal`* can be a *tty* name or any. Check every *n* minutes, or 10 by default.
`who=`*`string`*	Specify information to be printed by `watch`.
`wordchars=`*chars*	List of all nonalphanumeric characters that may be part of a word. Default is `*?_-.[]~=`.

Formatting for the Prompt Variable

tcsh provides a list of substitutions that can be used in formatting the prompt. The list of available substitutions includes:

%% Literal %.

%/ The present working directory

%~ The present working directory, in ~ notation.

%# # for the superuser, > for others.

%? Previous command's exit status.

%$*var*
: The value of the shell or environment variable *var*.

%{*string*%}
: Include *string* as a literal escape sequence to change terminal attributes (but shouldn't move the cursor location); can't be the last sequence in the prompt.

\c, ^c
: Parse c as in the *bindkey* built-in command.

%b End boldfacing.

%c[*[0]n*], %.[[0]*n*]
: The last *n* (default 1) components of the present working directory; if 0 is specified, replace removed components with /<skipped>.

%d Day of the week (e.g., Mon, Tue).

%h, %!, !
: Number of current history event.

%j The number of jobs.

%l Current tty.

%m First component of hostname.

%n Username.

%p Current time, with seconds (12-hour mode).

%s End standout mode (reverse video).

%t, %@
: Current time (12-hour format).

%u End underlining.

%w Month (e.g., Jan, Feb).

%y Year (e.g., 99, 00).

%B Begin boldfacing.

%C Similar to %c, but use full pathnames instead of ~ notation.

%D Day of month (e.g., 09, 10).

%L Clear from the end of the prompt to the end of the display or the line.

%M Fully qualified hostname.

%P Current time, with seconds (24-hour format).

%R In prompt2, the parser status; in prompt3, the corrected string; and in history, the history string.

%S Begin standout mode (reverse video).

%T Current time (24-hour format).

%U Begin underlining.

%W Month (e.g., 09, 10).

%Y Year (e.g., 1999, 2000).

Sample .tcshrc File

```
# PREDEFINED VARIABLES

set path=(~ ~/bin /usr/ucb /bin /usr/bin . )
set mail=(/usr/mail/tom)
```

```
if ($?prompt) then              # settings for interactive use
  set echo
  set noclobber ignoreeof

  set cdpath=(/usr/lib /usr/spool/uucp)
# Now I can type cd macros
# instead of cd /usr/lib/macros

  set history=100
  set prompt='tom \!% '          # includes history number
  set time=3

# MY VARIABLES

  set man1="/usr/man/man1"      # lets me do   cd $man1, ls $man1
  set a="[a-z]*"                # lets me do   vi $a
  set A="[A-Z]*"                # or           grep string $A

# ALIASES

  alias c "clear; dirs"         # use quotes to protect ; or |
  alias h "history|more"
  alias j jobs -l
  alias ls ls -sFC              # redefine ls command
  alias del 'mv \!* ~/tmp_dir' # a safe alternative to rm
endif
```

Environment Variables

tcsh maintains a set of *environment variables*, which are distinct from shell variables and aren't really part of the shell. Shell variables are meaningful only within the current shell, but environment variables are exported automatically, making them available globally. For example, shell variables are accessible only to a particular script in which they're defined, whereas environment variables can be used by any shell scripts, mail utilities, or editors you might invoke.

Environment variables are assigned as follows:

```
setenv VAR value
```

By convention, environment variable names are all uppercase. You can create your own environment variables, or you can use the predefined environment variables that follow.

The following environment variables have corresponding *tcsh* shell variables. When either one changes, the value is copied to the other.

`AFSUSER`
: Alternative to local user for Kerberos authentication with `autologout` locking; same as `afsuser`.

`GROUP`
: User's group name; same as `group`.

`HOME`
: Home directory; same as `home`.

`PATH`
: Search path for commands; same as `path`.

`SHLVL`
: Number of nested shell levels; same as `shlvl`.

`TERM`
: Terminal type; same as `term`.

`USER`
: User's login name; same as `user`.

Other environment variables, which don't have corresponding shell variables, include the following:

`COLUMNS`
: Number of columns on terminal.

`DISPLAY`
: Identifies user's display for the X Window System. If set, the shell doesn't set `autologout`.

`EDITOR`
: Pathname to default editor. See also `VISUAL`.

`HOST`
: Name of machine.

`HOSTTYPE`
: Type of machine. Obsolete; will be removed eventually.

`HPATH`
: Colon-separated list of directories to search for documentation.

`LANG`
: Preferred language. Used for native language support.

`LC_CTYPE`
: The locale, as it affects character handling. Used for native language support.

`LINES`
: Number of lines on the screen.

`LOGNAME`
: Another name for the `USER` variable.

`LS_COLORS`
: Colors for use with the *ls* command. See the *tcsh* manpage for detailed information.

`MACHTYPE`
: Type of machine.

`MAIL`
: The file that holds mail. Used by mail programs. This isn't the same as the shell variable `mail`, which only checks for new mail.

`NOREBIND`
: Printable characters not rebound. Used for native language support.

`OSTYPE`
: Operating system.

`PWD`
: The current directory; the value is copied from *cwd*.

`REMOTEHOST`
: Machine name of remote host.

`SHELL`
: Undefined by default; once initialized to `shell`, the two are identical.

`TERMCAP`
: The file that holds the cursor-positioning codes for your terminal type. Default is */etc/termcap*.

`VENDOR`
: System vendor.

`VISUAL`
: Pathname to default full-screen editor. See also `EDITOR`.

Expressions

Expressions are used in `@`, `if`, and `while` statements to perform arithmetic, string comparisons, file testing, and so on. `exit` and `set` also specify expressions, as can the *tcsh* built-in command *filetest*. Expressions are formed by combining variables and constants with operators that resemble those in the C programming language. Operator precedence is the same as in C and can be remembered as follows:

1. `* / %`
2. `+ -`

Group all other expressions inside parentheses. Parentheses are required if the expression contains <, >, &, or |.

Operators

Operators can be one of the following types.

Assignment operators

Operator	Description
`=`	Assign value.
`+= -=`	Reassign after addition/subtraction.
`*= /= %=`	Reassign after multiplication/division/remainder.
`&= ^= |=`	Reassign after bitwise AND/XOR/OR.
`++`	Increment.
`--`	Decrement.

Arithmetic operators

Operator	Description
`* / %`	Multiplication; integer division; modulus (remainder).
`+ -`	Addition; subtraction.

Bitwise and logical operators

<table>
<tr><th>Operator</th><th>Description</th></tr>
<tr><td><code>~</code></td><td>Binary inversion (one's complement).</td></tr>
<tr><td><code>!</code></td><td>Logical negation.</td></tr>
<tr><td><code><< >></code></td><td>Bitwise left shift; bitwise right shift.</td></tr>
<tr><td><code>&</code></td><td>Bitwise AND.</td></tr>
<tr><td><code>^</code></td><td>Bitwise exclusive OR.</td></tr>
<tr><td><code>|</code></td><td>Bitwise OR.</td></tr>
<tr><td><code>&&</code></td><td>Logical AND.</td></tr>
<tr><td><code>||</code></td><td>Logical OR.</td></tr>
<tr><td><code>{ </code>command<code> }</code></td><td>Return 1 if command is successful, 0 otherwise. Note that this is the opposite of command's normal return code. The <code>$status</code> variable may be more practical.</td></tr>
</table>

Comparison operators

Operator	Description
`== !=`	Equality; inequality.
`<= >=`	Less than or equal to; greater than or equal to.
`< >`	Less than; greater than.

File inquiry operators

Command substitution and filename expansion are performed on *file* before the test is performed. Operators can be combined (e.g., `-ef`). The following is a list of the valid file inquiry operators:

Operator	Description
`-b` *file*	The file is a block special file.
`-c` *file*	The file is a character special file.
`-d` *file*	The file is a directory.
`-e` *file*	The file exists.
`-f` *file*	The file is a plain file.
`-g` *file*	The file's `set-group-ID` bit is set.
`-k` *file*	The file's sticky bit is set.
`-l` *file*	The file is a symbolic link.
`-L` *file*	Apply any remaining operators to symbolic link, not the file it points to.
`-o` *file*	The user owns the file.

Operator	Description
`-p` *file*	The file is a named pipe (FIFO).
`-r` *file*	The user has read permission.
`-s` *file*	The file has nonzero size.
`-S` *file*	The file is a socket special file.
`-t` *file*	*file* is a digit and is an open file descriptor for a terminal device.
`-u` *file*	The file's `set-user-ID` bit is set.
`-w` *file*	The user has write permission.
`-x` *file*	The user has execute permission.
`-X` *file*	The file is executable and is in the path, or is a shell built-in.
`-z` *file*	The file has 0 size.
`!`	Reverse the sense of any preceding inquiry.

Finally, *tcsh* provides the following operators, which return other kinds of information:

Operator	Description
`-A[:]` *file*	Last time *file* was accessed, as the number of seconds since the epoch. With a colon (:), the result is in timestamp format.
`-C[:]` *file*	Last time inode was modified. With a colon (:), the result is in timestamp format.
`-D` *file*	Device number.
`-F` *file*	Composite file identifier, in the form *device:inode*.
`-G[:]` *file*	Numeric GID for the file. With a colon (:), the result is the group name if known, otherwise the numeric GID.
-I *file*	Inode number.
`-L` *file*	The name of the file pointed to by symbolic link *file*.
`-M[:]` *file*	Last time file was modified. With a colon (:), the result is in timestamp format.
`-N` *file*	Number of hard links.
`-P[:]` *file*	Permissions in octal, without leading 0. With a colon (:), the result includes a leading 0.
`-P`*mode*`[:]` *file*	Equivalent to `-P` *file* ANDed to *mode*. With a colon (:), the result includes a leading 0.
`-U[:]` *file*	Numeric UID of the file's owner. With a colon (:), the result is the username if known, otherwise the numeric UID.
`-Z` *file*	The file's size, in bytes.

Examples

The following examples show `@` commands and assume *n* = 4:

Expression	Value of $x
`@ x = ($n > 10 || $n < 5)`	1
`@ x = ($n >= 0 && $n < 3)`	0
`@ x = ($n << 2)`	16
`@ x = ($n >> 2)`	1
`@ x = $n % 2`	0
`@ x = $n % 3`	1

The following examples show the first line of `if` or `while` statements:

Expression	Meaning
`while ($#argv != 0)`	While there are arguments...
`if ($today[1] == "Fri")`	If the first word is "Fri"...
`if (-f $argv[1])`	If the first argument is a plain file...
`if (! -d $tmpdir)`	If `tmpdir` is not a directory...

Command History

Previously executed commands are stored in a history list. You can access this list to verify commands, repeat them, or execute modified versions of them. The *history* built-in command displays the history list; the predefined variables `histchars` and `history` also affect the history mechanism. There are a number of ways to use the history list:

- Rerun a previous command
- Edit a previous command
- Make command substitutions
- Make argument substitutions (replace specific words in a command)
- Extract or replace parts of a command or word

The easiest way to take advantage of the command history is to use the arrow keys to move around in the history, select the command you want, and then rerun it or use the editing features described in the section "Command-Line Editing," later in this chapter, to modify the command. The arrow keys are:

Key	Description
Up arrow	Previous command.
Down arrow	Next command.
Left arrow	Move left in command line.
Right arrow	Move right in command line.

The next sections describe some tools for editing and rerunning commands. With the C shell, which doesn't have the command-line editing features of *tcsh*, these tools are important for rerunning commands. With *tcsh*, they are less often used, but they still work.

Command Substitution

Command	Description
`!`	Begin a history substitution.
`!!`	Previous command.
`!N`	Command number *N* in history list.
`!-N`	*N*th command back from current command.

Command	Description
!*string*	Most recent command that starts with *string*.
!?*string*?	Most recent command that contains *string*.
!?*string*?%	Most recent command argument that contains *string*.
!$	Last argument of previous command.
!!*string*	Previous command, then append *string*.
!*N string*	Command *N*, then append *string*.
!{*s1*}*s2*	Most recent command starting with string *s1*, then append string *s2*.
^*old*^*new*^	Quick substitution; change string *old* to *new* in previous command, and execute modified command.

Command Substitution Examples

The following command is assumed:

```
%3 vi cprogs/01.c ch002 ch03
```

Event number	Command typed	Command executed
4	`^00^0`	`vi cprogs/01.c ch02 ch03`
5	`nroff !*`	`nroff cprogs/01.c ch02 ch03`
6	`nroff !$`	`nroff ch03`
7	`!vi`	`vi cprogs/01.c ch02 ch03`
8	`!6`	`nroff ch03`
9	`!?01`	`vi cprogs/01.c ch02 ch03`
10	`!{nr}.new`	`nroff ch03.new`
11	`!!|lp`	`nroff ch03.new | lp`
12	`more !?pr?%`	`more cprogs/01.c`

Word Substitution

Colons may precede any word specifier.

Specifier	Description
:0	Command name
:*n*	Argument number *n*
^	First argument
$	Last argument
:*n*-*m*	Arguments *n* through *m*
-*m*	Words 0 through *m*; same as :0-*m*
:*n*-	Arguments *n* through next-to-last
:*n**	Arguments *n* through last; same as *n*-$
*	All arguments; same as ^-$ or 1-$
#	Current command line up to this point; fairly useless

Word Substitution Examples

The following command is assumed:

```
%13 cat ch01 ch02 ch03 biblio back
```

Event number	Command typed	Command executed
14	`ls !13^`	`ls ch01`
15	`sort !13:*`	`sort ch01 ch02 ch03 biblio back`
16	`lp !cat:3*`	`more ch03 biblio back`
17	`!cat:0-3`	`cat ch01 ch02 ch03`
18	`vi !-5:4`	`vi biblio`

History Modifiers

Command and word substitutions can be modified by one or more of the following modifiers:

Printing, substitution, and quoting

Modifier	Description
`:p`	Display command, but don't execute.
`:s/`*old*`/`*new*	Substitute string *new* for *old*, first instance only.
`:gs/`*old*`/`*new*	Substitute string *new* for *old*, all instances.
`:&`	Repeat previous substitution (`:s` or `^` command), first instance only.
`:g&`	Repeat previous substitution, all instances.
`:q`	Quote a wordlist.
`:x`	Quote separate words.

Truncation

Modifier	Description
`:r`	Extract the first available pathname root (the portion before the last period).
`:gr`	Extract all pathname roots.
`:e`	Extract the first available pathname extension (the portion after the last period).
`:ge`	Extract all pathname extensions.
`:h`	Extract the first available pathname header (the portion before the last slash).
`:gh`	Extract all pathname headers.
`:t`	Extract the first available pathname tail (the portion after the last slash).
`:gt`	Extract all pathname tails.
`:u`	Make first lowercase letter uppercase.
`:l`	Make first uppercase letter lowercase.
`:a`	Apply modifier(s) following `a` as many times as possible to a word. If used with `g`, `a` is applied to all words.

History Modifier Examples

From the preceding, command number 17 is:

```
%17 cat ch01 ch02 ch03
```

Event number	Command typed	Command executed
19	`!17:s/ch/CH/`	`cat CH01 ch02 ch03`
20	`!17g&`	`cat CH01 CH02 CH03`
21	`!more:p`	`more cprogs/01.c` *(displayed only)*
22	`cd !$:h`	`cd cprogs`
23	`vi !mo:$:t`	`vi 01.c`
24	`grep stdio !$`	`grep stdio 01.c`
25	`^stdio^include stdio^:q`	`grep "include stdio" 01.c`
26	`nroff !21:t:p`	`nroff 01.c` *(is that what I wanted?)*
27	`!!`	`nroff 01.c` *(execute it)*

Special Aliases

Certain special aliases can be set in *tcsh*. The aliases are initially undefined. Once set, the commands they specify are executed when specific events occur. The following is a list of the special aliases and when they are executed:

`beepcmd`
: At beep.

`cwdcmd`
: When the current working directory changes.

`jobcmd`
: Before running a command or before its state changes. Like `postcmd`, but doesn't print built-ins.

`helpcommand`
: Invoked by the *run-help* editor command.

`periodic`
: Every few minutes. The exact amount of time is set by the `tperiod` shell variable.

`precmd`
: Before printing a new prompt.

`postcmd`
: Before running a command.

`shell` *`shell`*
: If a script doesn't specify a shell, interpret it with *`shell`*, which should be a full pathname.

Command-Line Manipulation

tcsh offers a certain amount of functionality in manipulating the command line, including word or command completion and the ability to edit a command line.

Completion

The shell automatically completes words and commands when you press the Tab key and notifies you when a completion is finished by appending a space to complete filenames or commands and a / to complete directories.

In addition, *tcsh* recognizes ~ notation for home directories; it assumes that words at the beginning of a line and subsequent to |, &, ;, ||, or && are commands and modifies the search path appropriately. Completion can be done midword; only the letters to the left of the prompt are checked for completion.

Related Shell Variables

- `autolist`
- `fignore`
- `listmax`
- `listmaxrows`

Related Command-Line Editor Commands

- `complete-word-back`
- `complete-word-forward`
- `expand-glob`
- `list-glob`

Related Shell Built-ins

- `complete`
- `uncomplete`

Command-Line Editing

tcsh lets you move your cursor around in the command line, editing the line as you type. There are two main modes for editing the command line, based on the two most common text editors: Emacs and *vi*. Emacs mode is the default; you can switch between the modes with:

`bindkey -e`	*Select Emacs bindings*
`bindkey -v`	*Select vi bindings*

The main difference between the Emacs and *vi* bindings is that the Emacs bindings are modeless (i.e., they always work). With the *vi* bindings, you must switch between input and command modes; different commands are useful in each mode. Here are some additional differences:

- Emacs mode is simpler; *vi* mode allows finer control.
- Emacs mode allows you to yank cut text and set a mark; *vi* mode doesn't.
- The command-history searching capabilities differ.

Emacs mode

Tables 21-1 through 21-3 describe the various editing keystrokes available in Emacs mode.

Table 21-1. Cursor positioning (Emacs mode)

Command	Description
Ctrl-B	Move cursor back (left) one character.
Ctrl-F	Move cursor forward (right) one character.
M-b	Move cursor back one word.
M-f	Move cursor forward one word.
Ctrl-A	Move cursor to beginning of line.
Ctrl-E	Move cursor to end of line.

Table 21-2. Text deletion (Emacs mode)

Command	Description
Del or Ctrl-H	Delete character to left of cursor.
Ctrl-D	Delete character under cursor.
M-d	Delete word.
M-Del or M-Ctrl-H	Delete word backward.
Ctrl-K	Delete from cursor to end of line.
Ctrl-U	Delete entire line.

Table 21-3. Command history (Emacs mode)

Command	Description
Ctrl-P	Previous command.
Ctrl-N	Next command.
Up arrow	Previous command.
Down arrow	Next command.
cmd-fragment M-p	Search history for *cmd-fragment*, which must be the beginning of a command.
cmd-fragment M-n	Like *M-p*, but search forward.
M-*num*	Repeat next command *num* times.
Ctrl-Y	Yank previously deleted string.

vi mode

vi mode has two submodes, input mode and command mode. The default mode is input. You can toggle modes by pressing Esc; alternatively, in command mode, typing *a* (append) or *i* (insert) returns you to input mode.

Tables 21-4 through 21-10 describe the editing keystrokes available in *vi* mode.

Table 21-4. Command history (vi input and command modes)

Command	Description
Ctrl-P	Previous command
Ctrl-N	Next command
Up arrow	Previous command
Down arrow	Next command
Esc	Toggle mode

Table 21-5. Editing (vi input mode)

Command	Description
Ctrl-B	Move cursor back (left) one character.
Ctrl-F	Move cursor forward (right) one character.
Ctrl-A	Move cursor to beginning of line.
Ctrl-E	Move cursor to end of line.
DEL or Ctrl-H	Delete character to left of cursor.
Ctrl-W	Delete word backward.
Ctrl-U	Delete from beginning of line to cursor.
Ctrl-K	Delete from cursor to end of line.

Table 21-6. Cursor positioning (vi command mode)

Command	Description
h or Ctrl-H	Move cursor back (left) one character.
l or SPACE	Move cursor forward (right) one character.
w	Move cursor forward one word.
b	Move cursor back one word.
e	Move cursor to next word ending.
W, B, E	Like *w*, *b*, and *e*, but treat only whitespace as word separator instead of any nonalphanumeric character.
^ or Ctrl-A	Move cursor to beginning of line (first nonwhitespace character).
0	Move cursor to beginning of line.
$ or Ctrl-E	Move cursor to end of line.

tcsh

Table 21-7. Text insertion (vi command mode)

Command	Description
a	Append new text after cursor until *Esc*.
i	Insert new text before cursor until *Esc*.
A	Append new text after end of line until *Esc*.
I	Insert new text before beginning of line until *Esc*.

Table 21-8. Text deletion (vi command mode)

Command	Description
x	Delete character under cursor.
X or Del	Delete character to left of cursor.
dm	Delete from cursor to end of motion command *m*.
D	Same as *d$*.
Ctrl-W	Delete word backward.
Ctrl-U	Delete from beginning of line to cursor.
Ctrl-K	Delete from cursor to end of line.

Table 21-9. Text replacement (vi command mode)

Command	Description
c*m*	Change characters from cursor to end of motion command *m* until *Esc*.
C	Same as *c$*.
r*c*	Replace character under cursor with character *c*.
R	Replace multiple characters until *Esc*.
s	Substitute character under cursor with characters typed until *Esc*.

Table 21-10. Character-seeking motion (vi command mode)

Command	Description
f*c*	Move cursor to next instance of *c* in line.
F*c*	Move cursor to previous instance of *c* in line.
t*c*	Move cursor just before next instance of *c* in line.
T*c*	Move cursor just after previous instance of *c* in line.
;	Repeat previous *f* or *F* command.
,	Repeat previous *f* or *F* command in opposite direction.

Job Control

Job control lets you place foreground jobs in the background, bring background jobs to the foreground, or suspend (temporarily stop) running jobs. The shell provides the following commands for job control. For more information on these commands, see the section "Built-in Commands."

bg Put a job in the background.

fg Put a job in the foreground.

jobs
List active jobs.

kill
Terminate a job.

notify
Notify when a background job finishes.

stop
Suspend a background job.

Ctrl-Z
Suspend the foreground job.

Many job control commands take *jobID* as an argument. This argument can be specified as follows:

%*n* Job number *n*.

%*s* Job whose command line starts with string *s*.

%?*s*
Job whose command line contains string *s*.

%% Current job.

% Current job (same as preceding).

%+ Current job (same as preceding).

%- Previous job.

tcsh

Built-in Commands

@

@ [*variable*[*n*]=*expression*]

Assign the value of the arithmetic *expression* to *variable*, or to the *n*th element of *variable* if the index *n* is specified. With no *variable* or *expression* specified, print the values of all shell variables (same as *set*). Expression operators as well as examples are listed under the earlier section"Expressions.". Two special forms are also valid:

@ *variable*++
Increment *variable* by 1.

@ *variable*--
Decrement *variable* by 1.

#

#

Ignore all text that follows on the same line. # is used in shell scripts as the comment character and is not really a command.

#!

#!*shell*

Used as the first line of a script to invoke the named *shell* (with optional arguments) or other program. For example:

```
#!/bin/tcsh -f
```

:

:

Null command. Returns an exit status of 0. The colon command is often put as the first character of a Bourne or Korn shell script to act as a place holder to keep a # (hash) from accidentally becoming the first character.

alias

alias [*name* [*command*]]

Assign *name* as the shorthand name, or alias, for *command*. If *command* is omitted, print the alias for *name*; if *name* also is omitted, print all aliases. Aliases can be defined on the command line, but more often they are stored in *.tcshrc* so that they take effect upon logging in. (See the sample *.tcshrc* file earlier in this chapter.) Alias definitions can reference command-line arguments, much like the history list. Use `\!*` to refer to all command-line arguments, `\!^` for the first argument, `\!\!:2` for the second, `\!$` for the last, and so on. An alias *name* can be any valid Unix command except *alias* or *unalias*; however, you lose the original command's meaning unless you type *name*. See also *unalias* and the section "Special Aliases."

Examples

Set the size for windows under the X Window System:

```
alias R 'set noglob; eval `resize` unset noglob'
```

Show aliases that contain the string *ls*:

```
alias | grep ls
```

Run *nroff* on all command-line arguments:

```
alias ms 'nroff -ms \!*'
```

Copy the file that is named as the first argument:

```
alias back 'cp \!^ \!^.old'
```

Use the regular *ls*, not its alias:

```
% \ls
```

alloc

alloc

Print totals of used and free memory.

bg

bg [*jobIDs*]

Put the current job or the jobIDs in the background.

Example

To place a time-consuming process in the background, you might begin with:

```
4% nroff -ms report Ctrl-Z
```

and then issue any one of the following:

```
5% bg
5% bg %         Current job
5% bg %1        Job number 1
5% bg %nr       Match initial string nroff
5% % &
```

tcsh

bindkey

bindkey [*options*] [*key*] [*command*]

Display all key bindings, or bind a key to a command.

Options

-a List standard and alternate key bindings.

-b key
: Expect *key* to be one of the following: a control character (in hat notation, e.g., `^B`, or C notation, e.g., `C-B`); a metacharacter (e.g., `M-B`); a function key (e.g., `F-`*`string`*); or an extended prefix key (e.g., `X-B`).

-c command
: Interpret *command* as a shell, not editor, command.

-d key
: Bind key to its original binding.

-e Bind to standard Emacs bindings.

-k key
: Expect *key* to refer to an arrow (`left`, `right`, `up`, or `down`).

-l List and describe all editor commands.

-r key
: Completely unbind *key*.

-s Interpret *command* as a literal string and treat as terminal input.

-u Print usage message.

-v Bind to standard *vi* bindings.

break

break

Resume execution following the *end* command of the nearest enclosing *while* or *foreach*.

breaksw

breaksw

Break from a `switch`; continue execution after the `endsw`.

built-ins

built-ins

Print all built-in shell commands.

bye

bye

Same as *logout*.

case

case *pattern* :

Identify a *pattern* in a *switch*.

cd

cd [*options*] [*dir*]

Change working directory to *dir*. Default is user's home directory. If *dir* is a relative pathname but is not in the current directory, the `cdpath` variable is searched. See the sample *.tcshrc* file earlier in this chapter.

Options

- \- Change to previous directory.
- *-l* Explicitly expand ~ notation; implies *-p*.
- *-n* Wrap entries before end-of-line; implies *-p*.
- *-p* Print directory stack.
- *-v* Print entries one per line; implies *-p*.

chdir

chdir [*dir*]

Same as *cd*. Useful if you are redefining *cd*.

complete

complete [*string* [*word/pattern/list*[:*select*]/[*suffix*]]]

List all completions, or, if specified, all completions for *string* (which may be a pattern). Further options can be specified.

Options for word

c Complete current word only, without referring to *pattern*.

C Complete current word only, referring to *pattern*.

n Complete previous word.

N Complete word before previous word.

p Expect *pattern* to be a range of numbers. Perform completion within that range.

tcsh

Options for list

Various *lists* of strings can be searched for possible completions. Some *list* options include:

(*string*)
: Members of the list *string*

$*variable*
: Words from *variable*

`*command*`
: Output from *command*

a Aliases

b Bindings

c Commands

C External (not built-in) commands

d Directories

D Directories whose names begin with *string*

e Environment variables

f Filenames

F Filenames that begin with *string*

g Groups

j Jobs

l Limits

n Nothing

s Shell variables

S Signals

t Text files

T Text files whose names begin with *string*

u Users

v Any variables

x Like *n*, but prints *select* as an explanation with the editor command `list-choices`

X Completions

select

select should be a glob pattern. Completions are limited to words that match this pattern. *suffix* is appended to all completions.

---

continue

continue

Resume execution of nearest enclosing *while* or *foreach*.

---

default

default :

Label the default case (typically last) in a *switch*.

---

dirs

dirs [*options*]

Print the directory stack, showing the current directory first. See also *popd* and *pushd*.

Options

-c Clear the directory stack.

-l Expand the home directory symbol (~) to the actual directory name.

-n Wrap output.

-v Print one directory per line.

-L file
: Re-create stack from *file*, which should have been created by *dirs -S file*.

-S file
: Print to *file* a series of *pushd* and *popd* commands that can be invoked to replicate the stack.

---

echo

echo [**-n**] *string*

Write *string* to standard output; if *-n* is specified, the output is not terminated by a newline. Set the `echo_style` shell variable to emulate BSD and/or System V *echo* flags and escape sequences. See also *echo* in Chapter 28.

echotc

echotc [*options*] *arguments*

Display terminal capabilities or move cursor on screen, depending on the argument.

Options

-s Return empty string, not error, if capability doesn't exist.

-v Display verbose messages.

Arguments

`baud`
: Display current baud rate.

`cols`
: Display current column.

`cm column row`
: Move cursor to specified coordinates.

`home`
: Move cursor to home position.

`lines`
: Print number of lines per screen.

`meta`
: Does this terminal have meta capacity (usually the Alt key)?

`tabs`
: Does this terminal have tab capacity?

else

else

Reserved word for interior of *if* ... *endif* statement.

end

end

Reserved word that ends a *foreach* or *switch* statement.

endif

endif

Reserved word that ends an *if* statement.

endsw

endsw

Reserved word that ends a *switch* statement.

eval

eval *args*

Typically, *eval* is used in shell scripts, and *args* is a line of code that may contain shell variables. *eval* forces variable expansion to happen first and then runs the resulting command. This "double scanning" is useful any time shell variables contain I/O redirection symbols, aliases, or other shell variables. (For example, redirection normally happens before variable expansion, so a variable containing redirection symbols must be expanded first using *eval*; otherwise, the redirection symbols remain uninterpreted.)

Examples

The following line can be placed in the *.login* file to set up terminal characteristics:

```
set noglob eval `tset -s xterm` unset noglob
```

The following commands show the effect of *eval*:

```
% set b='$a'
% set a=hello
% echo $b              Read the command line once
$a
% eval echo $b         Read the command line twice
hello
```

Another example of *eval* can be found under *alias*.

exec

exec *command*

Execute *command* in place of current shell. This terminates the current shell, rather than creating a new process under it.

exit

exit [(*expr*)]

Exit a shell script with the status given by *expr*. A status of zero means success; nonzero means failure. If *expr* is not specified, the exit value is that of the *status* variable. *exit* can be issued at the command line to close a window (log out).

fg

fg [*jobIDs*]

Bring the current job or the jobIDs to the foreground. *jobID* can be `%job-number`.

Example

If you suspend a *vi* editing session (by pressing Ctrl-Z), you might resume *vi* using any of these commands:

```
% %
% fg
% fg %
% fg %vi        Match initial string
```

filetest

filetest *-op files*

Apply *op* file-test operator to *files*. Print results in a list. See the earlier section "File inquiry operators" for the list of file-test operators.

foreach

foreach *name* (*wordlist*)
 commands
end

Assign variable *name* to each value in *wordlist* and execute *commands* between *foreach* and *end*. You can use *foreach* as a multiline command issued at the shell prompt (first of the following examples), or you can use it in a shell script (second example).

Examples

Rename all files that begin with a capital letter:

```
% foreach i ([A-Z]*)
? mv $i $i.new
? end
```

Check whether each command-line argument is an option or not:

```
foreach arg ($argv)
   # does it begin with - ?
   if ("$arg" =~ -*) then
      echo "Argument is an option"
   else
      echo "Argument is a filename"
   endif
end
```

glob

glob *wordlist*

Do filename, variable, and history substitutions on *wordlist*. No \ escapes are recognized in its expansion, and words are delimited by null characters. *glob* is typically used in shell scripts to hardcode a value so that it remains the same for the rest of the script.

tcsh

goto

goto *string*

Skip to a line whose first nonblank character is *string* followed by a colon, and continue execution below that line. On the *goto* line, *string* can be a variable or filename pattern, but the label branched to must be a literal, expanded value and must not occur within a *foreach* or *while*.

hashstat

hashstat

Display statistics that show the hash table's level of success at locating commands via the path variable.

history

history [*options*]

Display the list of history events. (History syntax is discussed in the earlier section "Command History.")

Options

-c Clear history list.

-h Print history list without event numbers.

-r Print in reverse order; show oldest commands last.

n Display only the last *n* history commands, instead of the number set by the history shell variable.

-L file
Load series of *pushd* and *popd* commands from *file* in order to re-create a saved stack.

-M file
Merge the current directory stack and the stack saved in *file*. Save both, sorted by time, in *file* as a series of *pushd* and *popd* commands.

-S file
Print to *file* a series of *pushd* and *popd* commands that can be invoked to replicate the stack.

-T Print with timestamp.

Example

To save and execute the last five commands:

```
history -h 5 > do_it
source do_it
```

hup

hup [*command*]

Start *command*, but make it exit when sent a hangup signal, which is sent when shell exits. By default, configure shell script to exit on hangup signal.

if

`if`

Begin a conditional statement. The simple format is:

```
if (expr) cmd
```

There are three other possible formats, shown side by side:

```
if (expr) then    if (expr) then    if (expr) then
   cmds               cmds1             cmds1
endif             else              else if (expr) then
                      cmds2             cmds2
                  endif             else
                                        cmds3
                                    endif
```

In the simplest form, execute *cmds* if *expr* is true, otherwise do nothing. (Redirection still occurs; this is a bug.) In the other forms, execute one or more commands. If *expr* is true, continue with the commands after *then*; if *expr* is false, branch to the commands after *else* or *else if* and continue checking. For more examples, see the earlier section "Expressions" or the *shift* or *while* commands.

Example

Take a default action if no command-line arguments are given:

```
if ($#argv == 0) then
   echo "No filename given. Sending to Report."
   set outfile = Report
else
   set outfile = $argv[1]
endif
```

jobs

`jobs [-l]`

List all running or stopped jobs; *-l* includes PIDs. For example, you can check whether a long compilation or text format is still running. Also useful before logging out.

kill

kill [*options*] *IDs*

Terminate each specified process ID or job ID. You must own the process or be a privileged user. This built-in is similar to */bin/kill* described in Chapter 28 but also allows symbolic job names. Stubborn processes can be killed using `signal 9`.

Options

-l List the signal names. (Used by itself.)

-signal, -s signal
The signal number or name without the SIG prefix (e.g., HUP, not SIGHUP). The command *kill -l* prints a list of the available signal names. The list varies by system architecture; for a PC-based system, it looks like this:

```
% kill -l
HUP INT QUIT ILL TRAP ABRT BUS FPE KILL USR1 SEGV USR2
PIPE ALRM TERM STKFLT CHLD CONT STOP TSTP TTIN TTOU URG
XCPU XFSZ VTALRM PROF WINCH POLL PWR SYS RTMIN RTMIN+1
RTMIN+2 RTMIN+3 RTMAX-3 RTMAX-2 RTMAX-1 RTMAX
```

The signals and their numbers are defined in */usr/include/asm/signal.h*; look in that file to find the signals that apply to your system.

Examples

If you've issued the following command:

```
44% nroff -ms report &
```

you can terminate it in any of the following ways:

```
45% kill 19536      PID
45% kill %          Current job
45% kill %1         Job number 1
45% kill %nr        Initial string
45% kill %?report   Matching string
```

limit

limit [**-h**] [*resource* [*limit*]]

Display limits or set a *limit* on resources used by the current process and by each process it creates. If no *limit* is given, the current limit is printed for *resource*. If *resource* also is omitted, all limits are printed. By default, the current limits are shown or set; with *-h*, hard limits are used. A hard limit imposes an absolute limit that can't be exceeded. Only a privileged user may raise it. See also *unlimit*.

Option

-h Use hard, not current, limits.

Resources

`coredumpsize`
    Maximum size of a core dump file.

`cputime`
    Maximum number of seconds the CPU can spend; can be abbreviated as *cpu*.

`datasize`
    Maximum size of data (including stack).

`descriptors`
    Maximum number of open files.

`filesize`
    Maximum size of any one file.

`maxproc`
    Maximum number of processes.

`memorylocked`
    Maximum size a process can lock into memory.

`memoryuse`
    Maximum amount of physical memory that can be allocated to a process.

`vmemoryuse`
    Maximum amount of virtual memory that can be allocated to a process.

`stacksize`
    Maximum size of stack.

Limit

A number followed by an optional character (a unit specifier).

For `cputime`:	*n*h (for *n* hours)
	*n*m (for *n* minutes)
	mm:*ss* (minutes and seconds)
For others:	*n*k (for *n* kilobytes, the default)
	*n*m (for *n* megabytes)

log

`log`

Consult the *watch* variable for list of users being watched. Print list of those who are presently logged in.

login

`login` [*user*|**`-p`**]

Replace *user*'s login shell with */bin/login*. *-p* is used to preserve environment variables.

logout

logout

Terminate the login shell.

ls-F

ls-F [*options*] [*files*]

Faster alternative to *ls -F*. If given any options, invokes *ls*.

newgrp

newgrp [-] [*group*]

Change user's GID to specified GID or, if none is specified, to original GID. If - is entered as an option, reset environment as if user had logged in with new group.

nice

nice [+*n*] *command*

Change the execution priority for *command* or, if none is given, change priority for the current shell. (See also *nice* in Chapter 28.) The priority range is -20 to 20, with a default of 4. The range seems backward: -20 gives the highest priority (fastest execution); 20 gives the lowest. Only a privileged user may specify a negative number.

+*n* Add *n* to the priority value (lower job priority).

-*n* Subtract *n* from the priority value (raise job priority). Privileged users only.

nohup

nohup [*command*]

"No hangup signals." Don't terminate *command* after terminal line is closed (i.e., when you hang up from a phone or log out). Use without *command* in shell scripts to keep script from being terminated. (See also *nohup* in Chapter 3.)

notify

notify [*jobID*]

Report immediately when a background job finishes (instead of waiting for you to exit a long editing session, for example). If no *jobID* is given, the current background job is assumed.

onintr

onintr *label*
onintr -
onintr

"On interrupt." Used in shell scripts to handle interrupt signals (similar to *bash*'s *trap* 2 and *trap* "" 2 commands). The first form is like a *goto label*. The script will branch to label: if it catches an interrupt signal (e.g., Ctrl-C). The second form lets the script ignore interrupts. This is useful at the beginning of a script or before any code segment that needs to run unhindered (e.g., when moving files). The third form restores interrupt handling previously disabled with *onintr -*.

Example

```
onintr cleanup          Go to "cleanup" on interrupt
  .
  .                     Shell script commands
  .
cleanup:                Label for interrupts
  onintr -              Ignore additional interrupts
  rm -f $tmpfiles       Remove any files created
  exit 2                Exit with an error status
```

popd

popd [*options*]

Remove the current entry (or the *n*th entry) from the directory stack and print the stack that remains. The current entry has number 0 and appears on the left. See also *dirs* and *pushd*.

Options

+n Specify *n*th entry.

-l Expand ~ notation.

-n Wrap long lines.

-p Override the pushdsilent shell variable, which otherwise prevents the printing of the final stack.

-v Print precisely one directory per line.

printenv

printenv [*variable*]

Print all (or one specified) environment variables and their values.

pushd

pushd *name*
pushd [*options*]
pushd

The first form changes the working directory to *name* and adds it to the directory stack. The second form rotates the *n*th entry to the beginning, making it the working directory. (Entry numbers begin at 0.) With no arguments, *pushd* switches the first two entries and changes to the new current directory. The *+n*, ***-l***, ***-n***, and ***-v*** options behave the same as in *popd*. See also *dirs* and *popd*.

Examples

```
% dirs
/home/bob /usr
% pushd /etc                  Add /etc to directory stack
/etc /home/bob /usr
% pushd +2                    Switch to third directory
/usr /etc /home/bob
% pushd                       Switch top two directories
/etc /usr /home/bob
% popd                        Discard current entry; go to next
/usr /home/bob
```

rehash

rehash

Recompute the internal hash table for the PATH variable. Use *rehash* whenever a new command is created during the current session. This allows the PATH variable to locate and execute the command. (If the new command resides in a directory not listed in PATH, add directory to PATH before rehashing.) See also *unhash*.

repeat

repeat *n command*

Execute *n* instances of *command*.

Examples

Print three copies of memo:

```
% repeat 3 pr memo | lp
```

Read 10 lines from the terminal and store in item_list:

```
% repeat 10 line > item_list
```

Append 50 boilerplate files to report:

```
% repeat 50 cat template >> report
```

sched

sched [*options*]
sched *time command*

Without options, print all scheduled events. The second form schedules an event. *time* should be specified in *hh:mm* form (e.g., 13:00).

Options

+hh:mm
Schedule event to take place *hh:mm* from now.

-n Remove *n*th item from schedule.

set

set *variable=value*
set [*options*] *variable*[*n*]=*value*
set *variable*
set

Set *variable* to *value* or, if multiple values are specified, set the variable to the list of words in the value list. If an index *n* is specified, set the *n*th word in the variable to *value*. (The variable must already contain at least that number of words.) If only *variable* is specified, set the variable to null. With no arguments, display the names and values of all set variables. See also the earlier section "Predefined Shell Variables." Only one of *-f* or *-l* can be given.

tcsh

Options

-f Set only the first occurrence of a variable to keep it unique.

-l Set only the last occurrence of a variable to keep it unique.

-r List only read-only variables, or set specified variable to read-only.

Examples

```
% set list=(yes no maybe)        Assign a wordlist
% set list[3]=maybe              Assign an item in existing wordlist
% set quote="Make my day"        Assign a variable
% set x=5 y=10 history=100       Assign several variables
% set blank                      Assign a null value to blank
```

setenv

setenv [*name* [*value*]]

Assign a *value* to an environment variable *name*. By convention, *name* is uppercase. *value* can be a single word or a quoted string. If no *value* is given, the null value is assigned. With no arguments, display the names and values of all environment variables. *setenv* is not necessary for the PATH variable, which is automatically exported from *path*.

settc

settc *capability value*

Set terminal *capability* to *value*.

setty

setty [*options*] [**+**|**-***mode*]

Don't allow shell to change specified tty modes. By default, act on the execute set.

Options

+mode
: Without arguments, list all modes in specified set that are on. Otherwise, turn on specified mode.

-mode
: Without arguments, list all modes in specified set that are off. Otherwise, turn off specified mode.

-a List all modes in specified set.

-d Act on the edit set of modes (used when editing commands).

-q Act on the quote set of modes (used when entering characters verbatim).

-x Act on the execute set of modes (used when executing examples). This is the default.

shift

shift [*variable*]

If *variable* is given, shift the words in a wordlist variable; i.e., *name*[2] becomes *name*[1]. With no argument, shift the positional parameters (command-line arguments; i.e., $2 becomes $1. *shift* is typically used in a while loop. See additional example under *while*.

Example

```
while ($#argv)          While there are arguments
    if (-f $argv[1])
       wc -l $argv[1]
    else
       echo "$argv[1] is not a regular file"
    endif
    shift               Get the next argument
end
```

source

source [**-h**] *script* [*args*]

Read and execute commands from a shell script. With *-h*, the commands are added to the history list but aren't executed. Arguments can be passed to the script and are put in argv.

Example

```
source ~/.cshrc
```

stop

stop *jobIDs*

Stop the background jobs specified by *jobIDs*; this is the complement of Ctrl-Z or *suspend*.

suspend

suspend

Suspend the current foreground job; same as Ctrl-Z. Often used to stop an su command.

switch

switch

Process commands depending on the value of a variable. When you need to handle more than three choices, *switch* is a useful alternative to an *if-then-else* statement. If the *string* variable matches *pattern1*, the first set of *commands* is executed; if *string* matches *pattern2*, the second set of *commands* is executed; and so on. If no patterns match, execute commands under the *default* case. *string* can be specified using command substitution, variable substitution, or filename expansion. Patterns can be specified using the pattern matching symbols *, ?, and [ ]. *breaksw* is used to exit the *switch*. If *breaksw* is omitted (which is rarely done), the *switch* continues to execute another set of commands until it reaches a *breaksw* or *endsw*. Following is the general syntax of *switch*, side by side with an example that processes the first command-line argument:

```
switch (string)           switch ($argv[1])
  case pattern1:          case -[nN]:
      commands            nroff $file | lp
      breaksw             breaksw
  case pattern2:          case -[Pp]:
      commands            pr $file | lp
      breaksw             breaksw
  case pattern3:          case -[Mm]:
      commands            more $file
```

tcsh

```
        breaksw           breaksw
        .                 case -[Ss]:
        .                 sort $file
        .                 breaksw
    default:              default:
        commands          echo "Error-no such option"
                          exit 1
        breaksw           breaksw
endsw                     endsw
```

telltc

telltc

Print all terminal capabilities and their values.

time

time [*command*]

Execute a *command* and show how much time it uses. With no argument, *time* can be used in a shell script to time the script.

umask

umask [*nnn*]

Display file creation mask or set file creation mask to octal *nnn*. The file creation mask determines which permission bits are turned off. With no *nnn*, print the current mask.

unalias

unalias *pattern*

Remove all aliases whose names match *pattern* from the alias list. See *alias* for more information.

uncomplete

uncomplete *pattern*

Remove completions (specified by *complete*) whose names match *pattern*.

unhash

unhash

Stop using the internal hash table. The shell stops using hashed values and searches the path directories to locate a command. See also *rehash*.

unlimit

unlimit [**-h**] [*resource*]

Remove the allocation limits on *resource*. If *resource* is not specified, remove limits for all resources. See *limit* for more information. With *-h*, remove hard limits. This command can be run only by a privileged user.

unset

unset *variables*

Remove one or more *variables*. Variable names may be specified as a pattern, using filename metacharacters. Does not remove read-only variables. See *set*.

unsetenv

unsetenv *variable*

Remove an environment variable. Filename matching is not valid. See *setenv*.

wait

wait

Pause in execution until all child processes complete, or until an interrupt signal is received.

watchlog

watchlog

Same as *log*. Must have been compiled into the shell; see the `version` shell variable.

where

where *command*

Display all aliases, built-ins, and executables named *command* found in the path.

which

which *command*

Report which version of command will be executed. Same as the executable *which*, but faster, and checks *tcsh* built-ins.

while

while (*expression*)
  commands
end

As long as *expression* is true (evaluates to nonzero), evaluate *commands* between *while* and *end*. *break* and *continue* can terminate or continue the loop.

Example

```
set user = (alice bob carol ted)
while ($argv[1] != $user[1])      Cycle through each user, checking for a match
   shift user                     If we cycled through with no match...
   if ($#user == 0) then
     echo "$argv[1] is not on the list of users"
     exit 1
   endif
end
```

22 Pattern Matching

A number of Unix text-processing utilities let you search for, and in some cases change, text patterns rather than fixed strings. These utilities include the editing programs *ed*, *ex*, *vi*, Emacs, and *sed*, the *gawk* scripting language, and the commands *grep* and *egrep*. Text patterns (also called *regular expressions*) contain normal characters mixed with special characters (called *metacharacters*).

Perl's regular expression support is so rich that it does not fit into this book; you can find a description in the O'Reilly books *Mastering Regular Expressions*, *Perl in a Nutshell*, *Perl 5 Pocket Reference*, or *Programming Perl*. The Emacs editor also provides regular expressions similar to those shown in this chapter.

ed and *ex* are hardly ever used as standalone, interactive editors nowadays. But *ed* can be found as a batch processor invoked from shell scripts, and *ex* commands are often invoked within *vi* through the colon (:) command. We use *vi* in this chapter to refer to the regular expression features supported by both *vi* and the *ex* editor on which it is based. *sed* and *gawk* are widely used in shell scripts and elsewhere as filters to alter text.

Filenames Versus Patterns

When you issue a command on the command line, special characters are seen first by the shell, and then by the program; therefore, unquoted metacharacters are interpreted by the shell for filename expansion. The command:

```
$ grep [A-Z]* chap[12]
```

can, for example, be transformed by the shell into:

```
$ grep Array.c Bug.c Comp.c chap1 chap2
```

and can then try to find the pattern `Array.c` in files `Bug.c`, `Comp.c`, `chap1`, and `chap2`. To bypass the shell and pass the special characters to *grep*, use quotes:

```
$ grep "[A-Z]*" chap[12]
```

Double quotes suffice in most cases, but single quotes are the safest bet.

Note also that in pattern matching, ? matches zero or one instance of a regular expression; in filename expansion, ? matches a single character.

Metacharacters, Listed by Unix Program

Some metacharacters are valid for one program but not for another. Those that are available to a Unix program are marked by a checkmark (✓) in Table 22-1. Items marked with a P are specified by POSIX; double-check your system's version. Full descriptions are provided after the table.

Table 22-1. Unix metacharacters

Symbol	ed	ex	vi	sed	awk	grep	egrep	Action
.	✓	✓	✓	✓	✓	✓	✓	Match any character.
*	✓	✓	✓	✓	✓	✓	✓	Match zero or more preceding.
^	✓	✓	✓	✓	✓	✓	✓	Match beginning of line/string.
$	✓	✓	✓	✓	✓	✓	✓	Match end of line/string.
\	✓	✓	✓	✓	✓	✓	✓	Escape following character.
[ ]	✓	✓	✓	✓	✓	✓	✓	Match one from a set.
(\)	✓	✓	✓	✓		✓		Store pattern for later replay.[a]
\n	✓	✓	✓	✓		✓		Replay subpattern in match.
{ }					✓P		✓P	Match a range of instances.
\{ \}	✓			✓		✓		Match a range of instances.
\< \>	✓	✓	✓					Match word's beginning or end.
+					✓		✓	Match one or more preceding.
?					✓		✓	Match zero or one preceding.
|					✓		✓	Separate choices to match.
( )					✓		✓	Group expressions to match.

[a] Stored subpatterns can be replayed during matching. See Table 22-2.

Note that in *ed*, *ex*, *vi*, and *sed*, you specify both a search pattern (on the left) and a replacement pattern (on the right). The metacharacters in Table 22-1 are meaningful only in a search pattern.

In *ed*, *ex*, *vi*, and *sed*, the metacharacters in Table 22-2 are valid only in a replacement pattern.

Table 22-2. Metacharacters in replacement patterns

Symbol	ex	vi	sed	ed	Action
\	✓	✓	✓	✓	Escape following character.
\n	✓	✓	✓	✓	Text matching pattern stored in \(\).
&	✓	✓	✓	✓	Text matching search pattern.
~	✓	✓			Reuse previous replacement pattern.

Table 22-2. Metacharacters in replacement patterns (continued)

Symbol	ex	vi	sed	ed	Action
%				✓	Reuse previous replacement pattern.
\u \U	✓	✓			Change character(s) to uppercase.
\l \L	✓	✓			Change character(s) to lowercase.
\E	✓	✓			Turn off previous \U or \L.
\e	✓				Turn off previous \u or \l.

Metacharacters

The characters in Table 22-3 have special meaning only in search patterns.

Table 22-3. Metacharacters used in search patterns

Character	Pattern
.	Match any single character except newline. Can match newline in *awk*.
*	Match any number (or none) of the single character that immediately precedes it. The preceding character can also be a regular expression; e.g., since . (dot) means any character, .* means match any number of any character.
^	Match the following regular expression at the beginning of the line or string.
$	Match the preceding regular expression at the end of the line or string.
[ ]	Match any one of the enclosed characters. A hyphen (-) indicates a range of consecutive characters. A circumflex (^) as the first character in the brackets reverses the sense: it matches any one character not in the list. A hyphen or close bracket (]) as the first character is treated as a member of the list. All other metacharacters are treated as members of the list (i.e., literally).
{*n*,*m*}	Match a range of occurrences of the single character that immediately precedes it. The preceding character can also be a metacharacter. {*n*} matches exactly *n* occurrences, {*n*,} matches at least *n* occurrences, and {*n*,*m*} matches any number of occurrences between *n* and *m*. *n* and *m* must be between 0 and 255, inclusive.
\\{*n*,*m*\\}	Just like {*n*,*m*}, above, but with backslashes in front of the braces.
	Turn off the special meaning of the character that follows.
\(\)	Save the pattern enclosed between \(and \) into a special holding space. Up to nine patterns can be saved on a single line. The text matched by the subpatterns can be replayed in substitutions by the escape sequences \1 to \9.
\n	Replay the *n*th subpattern enclosed in \(and \) into the pattern at this point. *n* is a number from 1 to 9, with 1 starting on the left. See the section "Examples of Searching" later in this chapter.
\< \>	Match characters at beginning (\<) or end (\>) of a word.
+	Match one or more instances of preceding regular expression.
?	Match zero or one instances of preceding regular expression.
|	Match the regular expression specified before or after.
( )	Apply a match to the enclosed group of regular expressions.

Many Unix systems allow the use of POSIX character classes within the square brackets that enclose a group of characters. These classes, listed in Table 22-4, are typed enclosed in [: and :]. For example, [[:alnum:]] matches a single alphanumeric character.

Table 22-4. Character classes

Class	Characters matched
`alnum`	Alphanumeric characters
`alpha`	Alphabetic characters
`blank`	Space or tab
`cntrl`	Control characters
`digit`	Decimal digits
`graph`	Nonspace characters
`lower`	Lowercase characters
`print`	Printable characters
`space`	Whitespace characters
`upper`	Uppercase characters
`xdigit`	Hexadecimal digits

The characters in Table 22-5 have special meaning only in replacement patterns.

Table 22-5. Metacharacters used in replacement patterns

Character	Pattern
`\`	Turn off the special meaning of the character that follows.
`\`*n*	Restore the text matched by the nth pattern previously saved by `\(` and `\)`. *n* is a number from 1 to 9, with 1 starting on the left.
`&`	Reuse the text matched by the search pattern as part of the replacement pattern.
`~`	Reuse the previous replacement pattern in the current replacement pattern. Must be the only character in the replacement pattern. (*ex* and *vi*)
`%`	Reuse the previous replacement pattern in the current replacement pattern. Must be the only character in the replacement pattern. (*ed*)
`\u`	Convert first character of replacement pattern to uppercase.
`\U`	Convert entire replacement pattern to uppercase.
`\l`	Convert first character of replacement pattern to lowercase.
`\L`	Convert entire replacement pattern to lowercase.
`\e, \E`	Turn off previous `\u`, `\U`, `\l`, and `\L`.

Examples of Searching

When used with *grep* or *egrep*, regular expressions should be surrounded by quotes. (If the pattern contains a `$`, you must use single quotes; e.g., '*pattern*'.) When used with *ed*, *ex*, *sed*, and *awk*, regular expressions are usually surrounded by `/`, although (except for `awk`) any delimiter works. Tables 22-6 through Table 22-9 show some example patterns.

Table 22-6. General search patterns

Pattern	What does it match?
bag	The string *bag*.
^bag	*bag* at the beginning of the line.
bag$	*bag* at the end of the line.
^bag$	*bag* as the only word on the line.
[Bb]ag	Bag or bag.
b[aeiou]g	Second letter is a vowel.
b[^aeiou] g	Second letter is a consonant (or uppercase or symbol).
b.g	Second letter is any character.
^...$	Any line containing exactly three characters.
^.	Any line that begins with a dot.
^\.[a- z][a-z]	Same, followed by two lowercase letters (e.g., *troff* requests).
^\.[a-z]\ {2\}	Same as previous; *ed*, *grep*, and *sed* only.
^\[^.]	Any line that doesn't begin with a dot.
bugs*	bug, bugs, bugss, etc.
"word"	A word in quotes.
"*word"*	A word, with or without quotes.
[A-Z][A- Z]*	One or more uppercase letters.
[A-Z]+	Same; *egrep* or *awk* only.
[[:upper:]]+	Same; POSIX *egrep* or *awk*.
[A-Z].*	An uppercase letter, followed by zero or more characters.
[A-Z]*	Zero or more uppercase letters.
[a-zA-Z]	Any letter.
[^0-9A- Za-z]	Any symbol or space (not a letter or a number).
[^[:alnum :]]	Same, using POSIX character class.

Table 22-7. egrep and awk search patterns

<table>
<tr><th>egrep or awk pattern</th><th>What does it match?</th></tr>
<tr><td>[567]</td><td>One of the numbers 5, 6, or 7.</td></tr>
<tr><td>five|six|seven</td><td>One of the words five, six, or seven.</td></tr>
<tr><td>80[2-4]?86</td><td>8086, 80286, 80386, or 80486.</td></tr>
<tr><td>80[2-4]?86|(Pentium(- II)?)</td><td>8086, 80286, 80386, 80486, Pentium, or Pentium-II.</td></tr>
<tr><td>compan(y|ies)</td><td>Company or companies.</td></tr>
</table>

Table 22-8. ex and vi search patterns

ex or vi pattern	What does it match?
\<the	Words like *theater* or *the*.
the\>	Words like *breathe* or *the*.
\<the\>	The word *the*.

Table 22-9. ed, sed and grep search patterns

ed, sed or grep pattern	What does it match?
`0\{5,\}`	Five or more zeros in a row.
`[0-9]\{3\}-[0-9]\{2\}-[0-9]{4\ }`	U.S. Social Security number (*nnn-nn-nnnn*).
`\(`*why*`\).*\1`	A line with two occurrences of *why*.
`\([[:alpha:]_][[:alnum:]_.]*\) = \1;`	C/C++ simple assignment statements.

Examples of Searching and Replacing

The examples in Table 22-10 show the metacharacters available to *sed* and *vi*. We have shown *vi* commands with an initial colon because that is how they are invoked with *vi*. A space is marked by a ❒; a tab is marked by *tab*.

Table 22-10. Searching and replacing

Command	Result
`s/.*/( & )/`	Redo the entire line, but add parentheses.
`s/.*/mv & &.old/`	Change a word list (one word per line) into *mv* commands.
`/^$/d`	Delete blank lines.
`:g/^$/d`	Same as previous, in *vi* editor.
`/^[❒`*tab*`]*$/d`	Delete blank lines, plus lines containing only spaces or tabs.
`:g/^[❒`*tab*`]*$/d`	Same as previous, in *vi* editor.
`s/❒❒*/❒/g`	Turn one or more spaces into one space.
`:%s/❒❒*/❒/g`	Same as previous, in *ex* editor.
`:s/[0-9]/Item &:/`	Turn a number into an item label (on the current line).
`:s`	Repeat the substitution on the first occurrence.
`:&`	Same as previous.
`:sg`	Same, but for all occurrences on the line.
`:&g`	Same as previous.
`:%&g`	Repeat the substitution globally (i.e., on all lines).
`:.,$s/Fortran/\ U&/g`	On current line to last line, change word to uppercase.
`:%s/.*/\L&/`	Lowercase entire file.
`:s/\<./\u&/g`	Uppercase first letter of each word on current line (useful for titles).
`:%s/yes/No/g`	Globally change a word to *No*.
`:%s/Yes/~/g`	Globally change a different word to *No* (previous replacement).

Finally, here are some *sed* examples for transposing words. A simple transposition of two words might look like this:

```
s/die or do/do or die/                  Transpose words
```

The real trick is to use hold buffers to transpose variable patterns. For example:

```
s/\([Dd]ie\) or \([Dd]o\)/\2 or \1/    Transpose, using hold buffers
```

23 The vi Editor

vi is the classic screen-editing program for Unix. A number of enhanced versions exist, including *nvi*, *vim*, *vile*, and *elvis*. On Mac OS X Panther, the *vi* command is linked to *vim*. The Emacs editor, covered in Chapter 24, has several *vi* modes that allow you to use the same commands covered in this chapter.

The *vi* editor operates in two modes, *command mode* and *insert mode*. The dual mode makes *vi* an attractive editor for users who separate text entry from editing. For users who edit as they type, Emacs modeless editing can be more comfortable.

vi is based on an older line editor called *ex*. A user can invoke powerful editing capabilities within *vi* by typing a colon (:), entering an *ex* command, and pressing the Return key. Furthermore, you can place *ex* commands in a startup file called *~/.exrc*, which *vi* reads at the beginning of your editing session. Because *ex* commands are still an important part of *vi*, they are also described in this chapter.

One of the most common versions of *vi* is Bram Moolenaar's Vi IMproved, or *vim*. On Mac OS X Panther, *vim* is the default version of *vi* and runs when you invoke *vi*. *vim* changes some of the basic features of *vi*, most notoriously changing the undo key to support multiple levels of undo. While seasoned users of *vi* find *vim*'s changes disturbing, those new to *vi* find *vim*'s extensive features attractive.

Wherever a command or option applies to *vim* only, those items are flagged in this chapter with (**vim**) after their description.

Fully documenting *vim* is beyond the scope of this chapter, but we do cover some of its most commonly used options and features. Beyond what we cover here, *vim* offers enhanced support to programmers through an integrated build and debugging process, syntax highlighting, extended *ctags* support, and support for Perl and Python, as well as GUI fonts and menus, function key mapping, independent mapping for each mode, and more. Fortunately, *vim* comes with a powerful help program you can use to learn more about the things we just couldn't fit into this chapter.

For more information, see the O'Reilly book *Learning the vi Editor*.

Review of vi Operations

This section provides a review of the following:

- Command-line options
- *vi* modes
- Syntax of *vi* commands
- Status-line commands

Command Mode

Once the file is opened, you are in command mode. From command mode, you can:

- Invoke insert mode.
- Issue editing commands.
- Move the cursor to a different position in the file.
- Invoke ex commands.
- Invoke a Linux shell.
- Save or exit the current version of the file.

Insert Mode

In insert mode, you can enter new text in the file. Press the Esc or Ctrl-[keys to exit insert mode and return to command mode. The following commands invoke insert mode:

a Append after cursor.

A Append at end of line.

c Begin change operation (must be followed by a movement command).

C Change to end of line.

i Insert before cursor.

I Insert at beginning of line.

o Open a line below current line.

O Open a line above current line.

r Replace character under cursor.

R Begin overwriting text.

s Substitute a character.

S Substitute entire line.

Syntax of vi Commands

In *vi*, commands have the following general form:

```
[n] operator [m] object
```

Here are the basic editing operators:

c Begin a change.

d Begin a deletion.

y Begin a yank (or copy).

If the current line is the object of the operation, the operator is the same as the object: `cc`, `dd`, `yy`. Otherwise, the editing operators act on objects specified by cursor-movement commands or pattern-matching commands. *n* and *m* are the number of times the operation is performed or the number of objects the operation is performed on. If both *n* and *m* are specified, the effect is *n* × *m*.

An object can represent any of the following text blocks:

Word
: Includes characters up to a space or punctuation mark. A capitalized object is a variant form that recognizes only blank spaces.

Sentence
: Extends to `.`, `!`, or `?` followed by two spaces.

Paragraph
: Extends to next blank line or *nroff/troff* paragraph macro (defined by *para=* `option`).

Section
: Extends to next *nroff/troff* section heading (defined by *sect=*`option`).

Examples

`2cw`
: Change the next two words

`d}` Delete up to next paragraph

`d^` Delete back to beginning of line

`5yy`
: Copy the next five lines into temporary buffer (for future pasting)

`y]]`
: Copy up to the next section into temporary buffer (for future pasting)

Status-Line Commands

Most commands aren't echoed on the screen as you input them. However, the status line at the bottom of the screen is used to echo input for the following commands:

`/` Search forward for a pattern

`?` Search backward for a pattern

vi

: Invoke an *ex* command

! Pipe the text indicated by a subsequent movement command through the following shell command, and replace the text with the output of the shell command

Commands that are input on the status line must be entered by pressing the Return key. In addition, error messages and output from the Ctrl-G command are displayed on the status line.

vi Command-Line Options

Here are the three most common ways to start a *vi* session:

```
vi file
vi +n file
vi +/ pattern file
```

You can open *file* for editing, optionally at line *n* or at the first line matching *pattern*. If no *file* is specified, *vi* opens with an empty buffer. The command-line options that can be used with *vi* are as follows (*vim*-only options are labeled):

+[*num*]
: Start editing at line number *num*, or the last line of the file if *num* is omitted.

+/pattern
: Start editing at the first line matching *pattern*. (Fails if *nowrapscan* is set in your *.exrc* startup file.)

-b Edit the file in binary mode. (**vim**)

-c command
: Run the given *vi* command upon startup. Only one *-c* option is permitted. *ex* commands can be invoked by prefixing them with a colon. An older form of this option, *+command*, is still supported.

--cmd command
: Like *-c*, but execute the command before any resource files are read. (**vim**)

-d Run in diff mode. Works like *vimdiff*. (**vim**)

-e Run as *ex* (line editing rather than full-screen mode).

-h Print help message, then exit.

-i file
: Use the specified *file* instead of the default *.viminfo* to save or restore *vim*'s state. (**vim**)

-l Enter LISP mode for running LISP programs (not supported in all versions).

-m Start the editor with the write option turned off so the user can't write to files. (**vim**)

-n Don't use a swap file; record changes in memory only. (**vim**)

--noplugin
: Don't load any plug-ins. (**vim**)

-o[n]
Start *vim* with *n* open windows. The default is to open one window for each file. (**vim**)

-r [file]
Recovery mode; recover and resume editing on *file* after an aborted editor session or system crash. Without *file*, list files available for recovery.

-s, -s scriptfile
When running in *ex* mode (*-e*), suppress prompts or informative messages sent to the console. Otherwise, read and execute commands given in the specified *scriptfile* as if they were typed in from the keyboard. (**vim**)

-t tag
Edit the file containing *tag* and position the cursor at its definition. (See *ctags* in Chapter 28 for more information.)

-u file
Read configuration information from the specified resource file instead of default *.vimrc* resource files. If the *file* argument is NONE, *vim* will read no resource files, load no plug-ins, and run in compatible mode. If the argument is NORC, it will read no resource files but it will load plug-ins. (**vim**)

-v Run in full-screen mode (default).

--version
Print version information, then exit.

-w rows
Set the window size so *rows* lines at a time are displayed; useful when editing over a slow dial-up line.

-x Prompt for a key that will be used to try to encrypt or decrypt a file using *crypt* (not supported in all versions).

-y Modeless *vi*; run *vim* in insert mode only, without a command mode. This is the same as invoking *vim* as *evim*. (**vim**)

-C Same as *-x*, but assume the file is encrypted already (not supported in all versions). For *vim*, this option starts the editor in *vi*-compatible mode.

-D Debugging mode for use with scripts. (**vim**)

-L List files that were saved due to an aborted editor session or system crash (not supported in all versions). For *vim* this option is the same as *-r*.

-M Don't allow text in files to be modified. (**vim**)

-N Run *vim* in a non-*vi*-compatible mode. (**vim**)

-O[n]
Start *vim* with *n* open windows arranged vertically on the screen. (**vim**)

-R Edit files read-only.

-S commandfile
Source commands given in *commandfile* after loading any files for editing specified on the command line. Shorthand for the option *-c source*. (**vim**)

-T type

Set the terminal type. This value overrides the `$TERM` environment variable. (**vim**)

-V[n]

Verbose mode; print messages about what options are being set and what files are being read or written. You can set a level of verbosity to increase or decrease the number of messages received. The default value is 10 for high verbosity. (**vim**)

-W *`scriptfile`*

Write all typed commands from the current session to the specified *`scriptfile`*. The file created can be used with the **-s** command. (**vim**)

-Z Start *vim* in restricted mode. Don't allow shell commands or suspension of the editor. (**vim**)

ex Command-Line Options

While most people know *ex* commands only by their use within *vi*, the editor also exists as a separate program and can be invoked from the shell (for instance, to edit files as part of a script). Within *ex*, you can enter the *vi* or *visual* command to start *vi*. Similarly, within *vi*, you can enter Q to quit the *vi* editor and enter *ex*.

If you invoke *ex* as a standalone editor, you can include the following options:

+[num]

Start editing at line number *num*, or the last line of the file if *num* is omitted.

`+/pattern`

Start editing at the first line matching *`pattern`*. (Fails if *nowrapscan* is set in your *.exrc* startup file.)

-c command

Run the given *ex* command at startup. Only one *-c* option is permitted. An older form of this option, *+command*, is still supported.

-e Run as a line editor rather than full-screen *vi* mode (default).

-l Enter LISP mode for running LISP programs (not supported in all versions).

-r [*`file`*]

Recover and resume editing on *`file`* after an aborted editor session or system crash. Without *`file`*, list files available for recovery.

-s Silent; don't display prompts. Useful when running a script. This behavior also can be set through the older - option.

-t tag

Edit the file containing *tag* and position the cursor at its definition (see *ctags* in Chapter 28 for more information).

-v Run in full-screen mode (same as invoking *vi*).

-w rows
: Set the window size so *rows* lines at a time are displayed; useful when editing by a slow dial-up line.

-x Prompt for a key that will try to encrypt or decrypt a file using *crypt* (not supported in all versions).

-C Same as *-x*, but assume the file is encrypted already (not supported in all versions).

-L List files that were saved due to an editor or system crash (not supported in all versions).

-R Edit files read-only; don't allow changes to be saved.

You can exit *ex* in several ways:

:x Exit (save changes and quit).

:q! Quit without saving changes.

:vi Enter the *vi* editor.

Movement Commands

Some versions of *vi* don't recognize extended keyboard keys (e.g., arrow keys, Page Up, Page Down, Home, Insert, and Delete); some do. All, however, recognize the keys in this section. Many users of *vi* prefer to use these keys, because it helps them keep their fingers on the home row of the keyboard. A number preceding a command repeats the movement. Movement commands are also objects for change, delete, and yank operations.

Character

Command	Action
h, j, k, l	Left, down, up, right (←, ↓, ↑, →)
Spacebar	Right
Backspace	Left
Ctrl-H	Left

Text

Command	Action
w, b	Forward, backward by word (treating punctuation marks as words).
W, B	Forward, backward by word (recognizing only whitespace, not punctuation, as separators).
e	End of word (treating a punctuation mark as the end of a word).
E	End of word (recognizing only whitespace as the end of a word).
ge	End of previous word (treating a punctuation mark as the end of a word). (vim)
gE	End of previous word (recognizing only whitespace as the end of a word). (vim)
), (	Beginning of next, current sentence.

vi

Command	Action
},{	Beginning of next, current paragraph.
]],[[	Beginning of next, current section.
][, []	End of next, current section. (vim)

Lines

Long lines in a file may show up on the screen as multiple lines. While most commands work on the lines as defined in the file, a few commands work on lines as they appear on the screen.

Command	Action
0, $	First, last position of current line.
^, _	First nonblank character of current line.
+, -	First character of next, previous line.
Return	First nonblank character of next line.
n|	Column *n* of current line.
g0, g$	First, last position of screen line. (vim)
g^	First nonblank character of screen line. (vim)
gm	Middle of screen line. (vim)
gk, gj	Move up, down one screen line. (vim)
H	Top line of screen.
M	Middle line of screen.
L	Last line of screen.
nH	*n* lines after top line of screen.
nL	*n* lines before last line of screen.

Screens

Command	Action
Ctrl-F, Ctrl-B	Scroll forward, backward one screen.
Ctrl-D, Ctrl-U	Scroll down, up one-half screen.
Ctrl-E, Ctrl-Y	Show one more line at bottom, top of window.
z Return	Reposition line with cursor to top of screen.
z.	Reposition line with cursor to middle of screen.
z-	Reposition line with cursor to bottom of screen.
Ctrl-L	Redraw screen (without scrolling).

Searches

Command	Action
/pattern	Search forward for *pattern*.
/	Repeat previous search forward.

Command	Action
/*pattern*/+*n*	Go to line *n* after *pattern*.
?*pattern*	Search backward for *pattern*.
?	Repeat previous search backward.
?*pattern*?-n	Go to line *n* before *pattern*.
n	Repeat previous search.
N	Repeat previous search in opposite direction.
%	Find match of current parenthesis, brace, or bracket.
*	Search forward for word under cursor. Matches only exact words. (**vim**)
#	Search backward for word under cursor. Matches only exact words. (**vim**)
g*	Search backward for word under cursor. Matches the characters of this word when embedded in a longer word. (**vim**)
g#	Search backward for word under cursor. Matches the characters of this word when embedded in a longer word. (**vim**)
fx	Move forward to *x* on current line.
Fx	Move backward to *x* on current line.
tx	Move forward to just before *x* in current line.
Tx	Move backward to just after *x* in current line.
,	Reverse search direction of last f, F, t, or T.
;	Repeat last character search (f, F, t, or T).
:noh	Suspend search highlighting until next search. (**vim**).

Line numbering

Command	Action
Ctrl-G	Display current filename and line number.
gg	Move to first line in file. (**vim**)
*n*G	Move to line number *n*.
G	Move to last line in file.
:*n*	Move to line number *n*.

Marking position

Command	Action
mx	Mark current position with character *x*.
`x	(backquote) Move cursor to mark *x*.
'x	(apostrophe) Move to start of line containing *x*.
``	(backquotes) Return to previous mark (or location prior to search).
''	(apostrophes) Like preceding, but return to start of line.
'"	(apostrophe quote) Move to position when last editing the file. (**vim**)
`[, `]	(backquote bracket) Move to beginning/end of previous text operation. (**vim**)
'[, ']	(apostrophe bracket) Like preceding, but return to start of line where operation occurred. (**vim**)
`.	(backquote period) Move to last change in file. (**vim**)

Command	Action
'.	(apostrophe period) Like preceding, but return to start of line. (**vim**)
:marks	List active marks. (**vim**)

Edit Commands

Recall that c, d, and y are the basic editing operators.

Inserting New Text

Command	Action
a	Append after cursor.
A	Append to end of line.
i	Insert before cursor.
I	Insert at first nonblank character of line.
gI	Insert at beginning of line. (**vim**)
o	Open a line below cursor.
O	Open a line above cursor.
Esc	Terminate insert mode.

The following commands work in insert mode.

Command	Action
Tab	Insert a tab.
Backspace	Delete previous character.
Ctrl-E	Insert character found just below cursor. (**vim**)
Ctrl-Y	Insert character found just above cursor. (**vim**)
Ctrl-H	Delete previous character (same as Backspace).
Delete	Delete current character.
Ctrl-W	Delete previous word. (**vim**)
Ctrl-A	Repeat last insertion. (**vim**)
Ctrl-I	Insert a tab.
Ctrl-N	Insert next completion of the pattern to the left of the cursor. (**vim**)
Ctrl-P	Insert previous completion of the pattern to the left of the cursor. (**vim**)
Ctrl-T	Shift line right to next shift width. (**vim**)
Ctrl-D	Shift line left to previous shift width. (**vim**)
Ctrl-U	Delete current line.
Ctrl-V	Insert next character verbatim.
Ctrl-[	Terminate insert mode.

Some of the control characters listed in the previous table are set by *stty*. Your terminal settings may differ.

Changing and Deleting Text

The following table isn't exhaustive but illustrates the most common operations.

Command	Action
cw	Change through end of current word.
cc	Change line.
c$	Change text from current position to end of line.
C	Same as c$.
dd	Delete current line.
d$	Delete remainder of line.
D	Same as d$.
*n*dd	Delete *n* lines.
dw	Delete a word.
d}	Delete up to next paragraph.
d^	Delete back to beginning of line.
d/*pattern*	Delete up to first occurrence of *pattern*.
dn	Delete up to next occurrence of pattern.
df*a*	Delete up to and including *a* on current line.
dt*a*	Delete up to (not including) *a* on current line.
dL	Delete up to last line on screen.
dG	Delete to end of file.
gqap	Reformat current paragraph to *textwidth*. (**vim**)
g~w	Switch case of word. (**vim**)
guw	Change word to lowercase. (**vim**)
gUw	Change word to uppercase. (**vim**)
p	Insert last deleted or yanked text after cursor.
gp	Same as p, but leave cursor at end of inserted text. (**vim**)
]p	Same as p, but match current indention. (**vim**)
[p	Same as P, but match current indention. (**vim**)
P	Insert last deleted or yanked text before cursor.
gP	Same as P, but leave cursor at end of inserted text. (**vim**)
r*x*	Replace character with *x*.
R*text*	Replace *text* beginning at cursor.
s	Substitute character.
*n*s	Substitute *n* characters.
S	Substitute entire line.
u	Undo last change.
Ctrl-R	Redo last change. (**vim**)
U	Restore current line.
x	Delete current character.
X	Delete back one character.
*n*X	Delete previous *n* characters.

Command	Action
.	Repeat last change.
~	Reverse case.
&	Repeat last substitution.
Y	Copy (yank) current line to temporary buffer.
yy	Same as Y.
"*x*yy	Copy current line to buffer *x*.
ye	Copy text to end of word into temporary buffer.
yw	Same as ye.
y$	Copy rest of line into temporary buffer.
"*x*dd	Delete current line into buffer *x*.
"*X*dd	Delete current line and append to buffer *x*.
"*x*p	Put contents of buffer *x*.
J	Join previous line to current line.
gJ	Same as J, but without inserting a space. (**vim**)
:j!	Same as J.
Ctrl-A	Increment number under cursor. (**vim**)
Ctrl-X	Decrement number under cursor. (**vim**)

Saving and Exiting

Writing a file means saving the edits and updating the file's modification time.

Command	Action
ZZ	Quit vi, writing the file only if changes were made.
:x	Same as ZZ.
:wq	Write and quit file.
:w	Write file.
:w *file*	Save copy to *file*.
:n1,n2w *file*	Write lines *n1* to *n2* to new *file*.
:n1,n2w >> *file*	Append lines *n1* to *n2* to existing *file*.
:w!	Write file (overriding protection).
:w! *file*	Overwrite *file* with current buffer.
:w %.*new*	Write current buffer named *file* as *file.new*.
:q	Quit file.
:q!	Quit file (discarding edits).
Q	Quit vi and invoke ex.
:vi	Return to vi after Q command.
%	Current filename.
#	Alternate filename.

Accessing Multiple Files

Command	Action
:e *file*	Edit *file*; current file becomes the alternate file.
:e!	Restore last saved version of current file.
:e+ *file*	Begin editing at end of new *file*.
:e+ n file	Open new *file* at line *n*.
:e#	Open to previous position in alternate (previously edited) file.
:ta *tag*	Edit file containing *tag* at the location of the tag.
:n	Edit next file.
:n!	Force next file into buffer (don't save changes to current file).
:n *files*	Specify new list of *files*.
:args	Display multiple files to be edited.
:rew	Rewind list of multiple files to top.

Window Commands

The following table lists common commands for controlling windows in *vim*. See also the *split*, *vsplit*, and *resize* commands in Chapter 28. For brevity, control characters are marked in the following list by ^.

Command	Action
:new	Open a new window.
:new *file*	Open *file* in a new window.
:sp *file*	Split the current window.
:sv*file*	Same as :sp, but make new window read-only.
:sn*file*	Edit next file in new window.
:clo	Close current window.
:hid	Hide current window, unless it is the only visible window.
:on	Make current window the only visible one.
:res *n*	Resize window to *n* lines.
:wa	Write all changed buffers to file.
:qa	Close all buffers and exit.
^W s	Same as :sp.
^W n	Same as :new.
^W ^	Open new window with alternate (previously edited) file.
^W c	Same as :clo.
^W o	Same as :only.
^W j, ^W k	Move cursor to next/previous window.
^W p	Move cursor to previous window.
^W h, ^W l	Move cursor to window on left/right.
^W t, ^W b	Move cursor to window on top/bottom of screen.
^W K, ^W B	Move current window to top/bottom of screen.

Command	Action
^W H, ^W L	Move current window to far left/right of screen.
^W r, ^W R	Rotate windows down/up.
^W +, ^W -	Increase/decrease current window size.
^W =	Make all windows same height.

Interacting with the Shell

Command	Action
:r *file*	Read in contents of *file* after cursor.
:r !*command*	Read in output from *command* after current line.
:nr !*command*	Like preceding, but place after line *n* (0 for top of file).
:!*command*	Run *command*, then return.
!*object command*	Send *object*, indicated by a movement command, as input to shell command *command*; replace *object* with command output.
:*n1*,*n2*! *command*	Send lines *n1* through *n2* to *command*; replace with output.
n!!*command*	Send *n* lines to *command*; replace with output.
!!	Repeat last system command.
!!*command*	Replace current line with output of *command*.
:sh	Create subshell; return to file with EOF.
Ctrl-Z	Suspend editor; resume with fg.
:so *file*	Read and execute *ex* commands from *file*.

Macros

Command	Action
:ab in out	Use *in* as abbreviation for *out*.
:unab in	Remove abbreviation for *in*.
:ab	List abbreviations.
:map c *sequence*	Map character *c* as *sequence* of commands.
:unmap c	Disable map for character *c*.
:map	List characters that are mapped.
:map! c *sequence*	Map character *c* to input mode *sequence*.
:unmap! c	Disable input mode map (you may need to quote the character with Ctrl-V).
:map!	List characters that are mapped to input mode.
qx	Record typed characters into register specified by letter *x*. If letter is uppercase, append to register. (**vim**)
q	Stop recording. (**vim**)
@x	Execute the register specified by letter *x*. (**vim**)

In *vi*, the following characters are unused in command mode and can be mapped as user-defined commands:

Letters

  `g K q V v`

Control keys

  `^K ^O ^T ^W ^X`

Symbols

  `_ * \ =`

The = is used by *vi* if LISP mode is set. *vim* uses all of these characters, but you can create macros for function keys and multiple character commands. See `:help :map` for details. Other versions of *vi* may use some of these characters as well, so test them before using them.

Miscellaneous Commands

Command	Action
<	Shift line left to position indicated by following movement command.
>	Shift line right to position indicated by following movement command.
<<	Shift line left one shift width (default is eight spaces).
>>	Shift line right one shift width (default is eight spaces).
>}	Shift right to end of paragraph.
<%	Shift left until matching parenthesis, brace, bracket, etc. (Cursor must be on the matching symbol.)
=	Indent line in C-style, or using program specified in *equalprg* option. (**vim**)
K	Look up word under cursor in manpages (or program defined in *keywordprg*). (**vim**)
^[	Abort command or end input mode.
^]	Perform a tag lookup on the text under the cursor.
^\	Enter *ex* line-editing mode.
^^	(Caret key with Ctrl key pressed) Return to previously edited file.

Alphabetical List of Keys in Command Mode

For brevity, control characters are marked by ^.

Command	Action
a	Append text after cursor.
A	Append text at end-of-line.
^A	Search for next occurrence of word under cursor. Increment number in *vim* when cursor is on a number.
b	Back up to beginning of word in current line.
B	Back up one word, treating punctuation marks as words.
^B	Scroll backward one window.
c	Change text up to target of next movement command.
C	Change to end of current line.
^C	End insert mode; interrupts a long operation.

Command	Action
d	Delete up to target of next movement command.
D	Delete to end of current line.
^D	Scroll down half-window; in insert mode, unindent to *shiftwidth* if *autoindent* is set (or when using *vim*).
e	Move to end of word.
E	Move to end of word, treating punctuation as part of word.
^E	Show one more line at bottom of window.
f	Find next character typed forward on current line.
F	Find next character typed backward on current line.
^F	Scroll forward one window.
g	Unused in *vi*. Begins many multiple-character commands in *vim*.
G	Go to specified line or end of file.
^G	Print information about file on status line.
h	Left arrow cursor key.
H	Move cursor to home position.
^H	Left arrow cursor key; backspace key in insert mode.
i	Insert text before cursor.
I	Insert text before first nonblank character on line.
^I	Unused in command mode; in insert mode, same as Tab key.
j	Down arrow cursor key.
J	Join previous line to current line.
^J	Down arrow cursor key; in insert mode, move down a line.
k	Up arrow cursor key.
K	Unused in *vi*. Look up word using *keywordprg* in *vim*.
^K	Unused in *vi*. Insert multiple-keystroke character in *vim*.
l	Right arrow cursor key.
L	Move cursor to last position in window.
^L	Redraw screen.
m	Mark the current cursor position in register (a–z).
M	Move cursor to middle position in window.
^M	Move to beginning of next line.
n	Repeat the last search command.
N	Repeat the last search command in reverse direction.
^N	Down arrow cursor key.
o	Open line below current line.
O	Open line above current line.
^O	Unused in *vi*. Return to previous jump position in *vim*.
p	Put yanked or deleted text after or below cursor.
P	Put yanked or deleted text before or above cursor.
^P	Up arrow cursor key.
q	Unused in *vi*. Record keystrokes in *vim*.
Q	Quit *vi* and enter *ex* line-editing mode.
^Q	Unused in *vi*. Same as ^V in *vim* (On some terminals, resume data flow.)

Command	Action
r	Replace character at cursor with the next character you type.
R	Replace characters.
^R	Redraw the screen.
s	Change the character under the cursor to typed characters.
S	Change entire line.
^S	Unused. (On some terminals, stop data flow.)
t	Find next character typed forward on current line and position cursor before it.
T	Find next character typed backward on current line and position cursor after it.
^T	Unused in command mode for *vi*. Pop tag from tagstack in *vim*. In insert mode, move to next tab setting.
u	Undo the last change made. In *vi*, a second undo redoes an undone command. *vim* supports multiple levels of undo. To redo, use Ctrl-R.
U	Restore current line, discarding changes.
^U	Scroll the screen upward a half-window.
v	Unused in *vi*. Enter visual mode in *vim*.
V	Unused in *vi*. Enter linewise visual mode in *vim*.
^V	Unused in command mode for *vi*. Enter blockwise visual mode in *vim*. In insert mode, insert next character verbatim.
w	Move to beginning of next word.
W	Move to beginning of next word, treating punctuation marks as words.
^W	Unused in command mode in *vi*. Begins window commands in *vim*. In insert mode, back up to beginning of word.
x	Delete character under cursor.
X	Delete character before cursor.
^X	Unused in *vi*. Decrement number in *vim* when cursor is on a number. In insert mode in *vim*, begins several commands.
y	Yank or copy text up to target of following movement command into temporary buffer.
Y	Make copy of current line.
^Y	Show one more line at top of window.
z	Reposition line containing cursor. z must be followed by Return (reposition line to top of screen), . (reposition line to middle of screen), or - (reposition line to bottom of screen).
ZZ	Exit the editor, saving changes.

vi

Syntax of ex Commands

To enter an *ex* command from *vi*, type:

```
:[address] command [options]
```

An initial : indicates an *ex* command. As you type the command, it is echoed on the status line. Enter the command by pressing Return. *address* is the line number or range of lines that are the object of *command*. *options* and *addresses* are described in the following sections. *ex* commands are described in the section "Alphabetical Summary of ex Commands."

Options

! Indicates a variant command form, overriding the normal behavior.

count

The number of times the command is to be repeated. Unlike *vi* commands, the *count* comes after the command, not before it. Numbers preceding an *ex* command are considered to be part of the *address*. For example, 3d deletes line 3; d3 deletes 3 lines beginning with the current line.

file

The name of a file that is affected by the command. % stands for current file; # stands for previous file.

Addresses

If no address is given, the current line is the object of the command. If the address specifies a range of lines, the format is:

x,*y*

where *x* and *y* are the first and last addressed lines (*x* must precede *y* in the buffer). *x* and *y* may be line numbers or symbols. Using ; instead of , sets the current line to *x* before interpreting *y*.

Address Symbols

Symbol	Meaning
1,$	All lines in the file
%	All lines; same as 1,$
x,*y*	Lines *x* through *y*
x;*y*	Lines *x* through *y*, with current line reset to *x*
0	Top of file
.	Current line
n	Absolute line number *n*
$	Last line
x-*n*	*n* lines before *x*
x+n	*n* lines after *x*
-[*n*]	One or *n* lines previous
+[*n*]	One or *n* lines ahead
'*x*	Line marked with *x*
''	Previous mark
/*pattern*/	Forward to line matching *pattern*
?*pattern*?	Backward to line matching *pattern*

Alphabetical Summary of ex Commands

ex commands can be entered by specifying any unique abbreviation. In this listing, the full name appears in the margin, and the shortest possible abbreviation is used in the syntax line. Examples are assumed to be typed from *vi*, so they include the : prompt.

abbrev

ab [*string text*]

Define *string* when typed to be translated into *text*. If *string* and *text* aren't specified, list all current abbreviations.

Examples

Note: ^M appears when you type Ctrl-V followed by Return.

```
:ab ora O'Reilly & Associates, Inc.
:ab id Name:^MRank:^MPhone:
```

append

[*address*] **a**[**!**]

Append new text at specified *address*, or at present address if none is specified. Add a ! to switch the *autoindent* setting that will be used during input (e.g., if *autoindent* is enabled, ! disables it). Enter new text after entering the command. Terminate input of new text by entering a line consisting of just a period.

Example

```
:a        Begin appending to current line
Append this line
and this line too.
.         Terminate input of text to append
```

args

ar

Print filename arguments (the list of files to edit). The current argument is shown in brackets ([ ]).

cd

cd *dir*
chdir *dir*

Change current directory within the editor to *dir*.

bdelete

[*n*] **bd**[**!**] [*n*]

Unload buffer *n* and remove it from the buffer list. Add a ! to force removal of an unsaved buffer. The buffer may also be specified by filename. If no buffer is specified, remove the current buffer. (**vim**)

buffer

[*n*] **b**[**!**] [*n*]

Begin editing buffer *n* in the buffer list. Add a ! to force a switch from an unsaved buffer. The buffer may also be specified by filename. If no buffer is specified, continue editing the current buffer. (**vim**)

buffers

buffers[**!**]

Print the listed members of the buffer list. Some buffers (e.g., deleted buffers) won't be listed. Add ! to show unlisted buffers. *ls* is another abbreviation for this command. (**vim**)

center

[*address*] **ce** [*width*]

Center line within the specified *width*. If *width* is not specified, use *textwidth*. (**vim**)

change

[*address*] **c**[**!**] *text*

Replace the specified lines with *text*. Add a ! to switch the *autoindent* setting during input of *text*. Terminate input by entering a line consisting of just a period.

close

clo[**!**]

Close current window unless it is the last window. If buffer in window is not open in another window, unload it from memory. This command won't close a buffer with unsaved changes, but you can add ! to hide it instead. (**vim**)

copy

[*address*] **co** *destination*

Copy the lines included in *address* to the specified *destination* address. The command *t* is the same as *copy*.

Example

:1,10 co 50	*Copy first 10 lines to just after line 50*

delete

[*address*] **d** [*buffer*]

Delete the lines included in *address*. If *buffer* is specified, save or append the text to the named buffer.

Examples

:/Part I/,/Part II/-1d	*Delete to line above "Part II"*
:/main/+d	*Delete line below "main"*
:.,$d	*Delete from this line to last line*

edit

e[**!**] [**+***n*] [*file*]

Begin editing *file*. Add a ! to discard any changes to the current file. If no *file* is given, edit another copy of the current file. With the +*n* argument, begin editing on line *n*.

Examples

:e file	
:e#	*Return to editing the previous file*
:e!	*Discard edits since last save*

vi

exusage

exu [*command*]

Print a brief usage message describing *command* or a list of available commands if *command* is omitted. (In *vim*, use the *help* command instead.)

file

f [*filename*]

Change the filename for the current buffer to *filename*. The next time the buffer is written, it will be written to file *filename*. When the name is changed, the buffer's *notedited* flag is set, to indicate you aren't editing an existing file. If the new filename is the same as a file that already exists on the disk, you need to use :w! to overwrite the existing file. When specifying a filename, the % character indicates the current filename. If no *filename* is specified, print the current name and status of the buffer.

Example

```
:f %.new
```

fold

address **fo**

Fold the lines specified by *address*. A fold collapses several lines on the screen into one line, which can later be unfolded. It doesn't affect the text of the file. (**vim**)

foldclose

[*address*] **foldc**[**!**]

Close folds in specified *address* or at present address if none is specified. Add a ! to close more than one level of folds. (**vim**)

foldopen

[*address*] **foldo**[**!**]

Open folds in specified *address*, or at present address if none is specified. Add a ! to open more than one level of folds. (**vim**)

global

[*address*] **g**[**!**]**/***pattern***/**[*commands*]

Execute *commands* on all lines that contain *pattern* or, if *address* is specified, on all lines within that range. If *commands* aren't specified, print all such lines. If ! is used, execute *commands* on all lines that don't contain *pattern*. See *v*.

Examples

:g/Unix/p	*Print all lines containing "Unix"*
:g/Name:/s/tom/Tom/	*Change "tom" to "Tom" on all lines containing "Name:"*

help

h

Print a brief help message. Information on particular commands can be obtained through the *exusage* and *viusage* commands. (In *vim* this command provides extensive information for all commands, and neither *exusage* nor *viusage* is used.)

hide

hid

Close current window unless it is the last window, but don't remove the buffer from memory. This is a safe command to use on an unsaved buffer. (**vim**)

insert

address **i[!]**

Insert new text at line before the specified *address*, or at present address if none is specified. Add a ! to switch the *autoindent* setting during input of text. Enter new text after entering the command. Terminate input of new text by entering a line consisting of just a period.

join

[*address*] **j[!]** [*count*]

Place the text in the specified *address* on one line, with whitespace adjusted to provide two blank characters after a period, no blank characters after a), and one blank character otherwise. Add a ! to prevent whitespace adjustment.

Example

:1,5j! *Join first five lines, preserving whitespace*

jumps

ju

Print jump list used with Ctrl-I and Ctrl-O commands. The jump list is a record of most movement commands that skip over multiple lines. It records the position of the cursor before each jump. (**vim**)

k

[*address*] **k** *char*

Mark the given *address* with *char*. Return later to the line with '*char*.

list

[*address*] **l** [*count*]

Print the specified lines so that tabs display as ^I, and the ends of lines display as $. The *l* command is a temporary version of `:set list`.

left

[*address*] **le** [*count*]

Left-align lines specified by *address*, or current line if no address is specified. Indent lines by *count* spaces. (**vim**)

map

map[**!**] [*char commands*]

Define a keyboard macro named *char* as the specified sequence of *commands*. *char* is usually a single character, or the sequence #*n*, representing a function key on the keyboard. Use a ! to create a macro for input mode. With no arguments, list the currently defined macros.

Examples

:map K dwwP	*Transpose two words*
:map q :w^M:n^M	*Write current file; go to next*
:map! + ^[bi(^[ea)	*Enclose previous word in parentheses*

mark

[*address*] **ma** *char*

Mark the specified line with *char*, a single lowercase letter. Return later to the line with '*char*. *vim* also uses uppercase and numeric characters for marks. Lowercase letters work the same as in *vi*. Uppercase letters are associated with filenames and can be used between multiple files. Numbered marks, however, are maintained in a special *viminfo* file and can't be set using this command. Same as ***k***.

marks

marks [*chars*]

Print list of marks specified by *chars* or all current marks if no *chars* specified. (**vim**)

Example

:marks abc	*Print marks a, b and c.*

mkexrc

mk[**!**] *file*

Create an *.exrc* file containing a *set* command for every *ex* option, set to defaults.

move

[*address*] **m** *destination*

Move the lines specified by *address* to the *destination* address.

Example

:.,/Note/m /END/	*Move text block after line containing "END"*

new

[*count*]**new**

Create a new window *count* lines high with an empty buffer. (**vim**)

next

n[!] [[**+***command*] *filelist*]

Edit the next file from the command-line argument list. Use *args* to list these files. If *filelist* is provided, replace the current argument list with *filelist* and begin editing on the first file; if *command* is given (containing no spaces), execute *command* after editing the first such file. Add a ! to discard any changes to the current file.

Example

:n chap*	*Start editing all "chapter" files*

nohlsearch

noh

Temporarily stop highlighting all matches to a search when using the *hlsearch* option. Highlighting is resumed with the next search. (**vim**)

number

[*address*] **nu** [*count*]

Print each line specified by *address*, preceded by its buffer line number. Use # as an alternate abbreviation for *number*. *count* specifies the number of lines to show, starting with *address*.

open

[*address*] **o** [**/***pattern***/**]

Enter *vi*'s open mode at the lines specified by *address* or at the lines matching *pattern*. Enter and exit open mode with Q. Open mode lets you use the regular *vi* commands, but only one line at a time. May be useful on slow dial-up lines.

preserve

pre

Save the current editor buffer as though the system had crashed.

previous

prev[**!**]

Edit the previous file from the command-line argument list.

print

[*address*] **p** [*count*]
[*address*] **P** [*count*]

Print the lines specified by *address*. *count* specifies the number of lines to print, starting with *address*. Add a ! to discard any changes to the current file.

Example

:100;+5p *Show line 100 and the next 5 lines*

put

[*address*] **pu** [*char*]

Restore the lines that were previously deleted or yanked from named buffer *char*, and put them after the line specified by *address*. If *char* is not specified, restore the last deleted or yanked text.

qall

qa[**!**]

Close all windows and terminate current editing session. Use ! to discard changes made since the last save. (**vim**)

quit

q[**!**]

Terminate current editing session. Use ! to discard changes made since the last save. If the editing session includes additional files in the argument list that were never accessed, quit by typing q! or by typing q twice. (In *vim*, if multiple windows are open, this command will close only the current window; use qall to quit multiple windows.)

read

[*address*] **r** *file*

Copy in the text from *file* on the line below the specified *address*. If *file* is not specified, the current filename is used.

Example

:0r $HOME/data *Read file in at top of current file*

read

[*address*] **r** !*command*

Read the output of Linux *command* into the text after the line specified by *address*.

Example

```
:$r !cal        Place a calendar at end of file
```

recover

rec [*file*]

Recover *file* from system save area.

redo

red

Restore last undone change. Same as Ctrl-R. (**vim**)

resize

res [[+|-]*n*]

Resize current window to be *n* lines high. If + or - is specified, increase or decrease the current window height by *n* lines. (**vim**)

rewind

rew[!]

Rewind argument list and begin editing the first file in the list. The ! flag rewinds, discarding any changes to the current file that haven't been saved.

right

[*address*] **le** [*width*]

Right-align lines specified by *address*, or current line if no address is specified, to column *width*. Use *textwidth* option if no *width* is specified. (**vim**)

sbuffer

[*n*] **sb** [*n*]

Split the current window and begin editing buffer *n* from the buffer list in the new window. The buffer to be edited may also be specified by filename. If no buffer is specified, open the current buffer in the new window. (**vim**)

sbnext

[*count*] **sbn** [*count*]

Split the current window and begin editing the *count* next buffer from the buffer list. If no count is specified, edit the next buffer in the buffer list. (vim)

snext

[*count*] **sn** [[+*n*] *filelist*]

Split the current window and begin editing the next file from the command-line argument list. If *count* is provided, edit the *count* next file. If *filelist* is provided, replace the current argument list with *filelist* and begin editing the first file. With the +*n* argument, begin editing on line *n*. Alternately, *n* may be a pattern of the form /*pattern*. (vim)

split

[*count*] **sp** [+*n*] [*filename*]

Split the current window and load *filename* in the new window, or the same buffer in both windows if no file is specified. Make the new window *count* lines high, or if *count* is not specified, split the window into equal parts. With the +*n* argument, begin editing on line *n*. *n* may also be a pattern of the form /*pattern*. (vim)

sprevious

[*count*] **spr** [+*n*]

Split the current window and begin editing the previous file from the command-line argument list in the new window. If *count* is specified, edit the *count* previous file. With the +*n* argument, begin editing on line *n*. *n* may also be a pattern of the form /*pattern*. (vim)

script

sc[**!**] [*file*]

Create a new shell in a buffer that can be saved, optionally specifying *file* where the buffer can be saved. Can be used only in *vi*.

set

se *parameter1 parameter2* ...

Set a value to an option with each *parameter*, or if no *parameter* is supplied, print all options that have been changed from their defaults. For Boolean-valued options, each *parameter* can be phrased as *option* or *nooption*; other options can be assigned with the syntax *option=value*. Specify *all* to list current settings.

Examples

```
:set nows wm=10
:set all
```

shell

sh

Create a new shell. Resume editing when the shell is terminated.

source

so *file*

Read and execute *ex* commands from *file*.

Example

```
:so $HOME/.exrc
```

stop

st

Suspend the editing session. Same as Ctrl-Z. Use *fg* to resume session.

substitute

[*address*] **s** [/*pattern*/*replacement*/] [*options*] [*count*]

Replace each instance of *pattern* on the specified lines with *replacement*. If *pattern* and *replacement* are omitted, repeat last substitution. *count* specifies the number of lines on which to substitute, starting with *address*. When preceded by the *global* (*g*) or *v* command, this command can be specified with a blank *pattern*, in which case the pattern from the *g* or *v* command is used.

Options

c Prompt for confirmation before each change.

g Substitute all instances of *pattern* on each line.

p Print the last line on which a substitution was made.

Examples

`:1,10s/yes/no/g`	*Substitute on first 10 lines*
`:%s/[Hh]ello/Hi/gc`	*Confirm global substitutions*
`:s/Fortran/\U&/ 3`	*Uppercase first instance of "Fortran" on next three lines*
`:g/^[0-9][0-9]*/s//Line &:/`	*For every line beginning with one or more digits, add the "Line" and a colon*

vi

suspend

su

Suspend the editing session. Same as Ctrl-Z. Use *fg* to resume session.

sview

[*count*] **sv** [+*n*] [*filename*

Same as the *split* command, but set the *readonly* option for the new buffer. (**vim**)

t

[*address*] **t** *destination*

Copy the lines included in *address* to the specified *destination*. *t* is an alias for *copy*.

Example

:%t$ *Copy the file and add it to the end*

tag

[*address*] **ta[!]** *tag*

Switch the editing session to the file containing *tag*.

Example

Run *ctags*, then switch to the file containing *myfunction*:

```
:!ctags *.c
:tag myfunction
```

tags

tags

Print list of tags in the tag stack. (**vim**)

unabbreviate

una *word*

Remove *word* from the list of abbreviations.

undo

u

Reverse the changes made by the last editing command. In *vi* the undo command will undo itself, redoing what you undid. *vim* supports multiple levels of undo. Use *redo* to redo an undone change in *vim*.

unhide

[*count*] **unh**

Split screen to show one window for each active buffer in the buffer list. If specified, limit the number of windows to *count*. (vim)

unmap

unm[**!**] *char*

Remove *char* from the list of keyboard macros. Use ! to remove a macro for input mode.

v

[*address*] **v/***pattern***/**[*commands*]

Execute *commands* on all lines not containing *pattern*. If *commands* aren't specified, print all such lines. *v* is equivalent to g!. See *global*.

Example

:v/#include/d	*Delete all lines except "#include" lines*

version

ve

Print the editor's current version number.

vi

vi [**+***n*] *file*

Begin editing *file*, optionally at line *n*. Can be used only in *vi*.

view

vie[[**+***n*] *filename*]

Same as *edit*, but set file to *readonly*. When executed in *ex* mode, return to normal or visual mode. (**vim**)

visual

[*address*] **vi** [*type*] [*count*]

Enter visual mode (*vi*) at the line specified by *address*. Exit with Q. *type* can be either -, ^, or . . (See the *z* command.) *count* specifies an initial window size.

viusage

viu [*key*]

Print a brief usage message describing the operation of *key*, or a list of defined keys if *key* is omitted. (In *vim* use the *help* command instead.)

vsplit

[*count*] **vs** [+*n*] [*filename*]

Same as the *split* command but split the screen vertically. The *count* argument can specify a width for the new window. (**vim**)

wall

wa[!]

Write all changed buffers with filenames. Add ! to force writing of any buffers marked *readonly*. (**vim**)

wnext

[*count*] **wn**[!] [[+*n*] *filename*]

Write current buffer and open next file in argument list, or the *count* next file if specified. If *filename* is specified, edit it next. With the +*n* argument, begin editing on line *n*. *n* may also be a pattern of the form /*pattern*. (**vim**)

wq

wq[!]

Write and quit the file in one command. The ! flag forces the editor to write over any current contents of *file*.

wqall

wqa[!]

Write all changed buffers and quit the editor. Add ! to force writing of any buffers marked *readonly*. *xall* is another alias for this command. (**vim**)

write

[*address*] **w**[**!**] [[**>>**] *file*]

Write lines specified by *address* to *file*, or write full contents of buffer if *address* is not specified. If *file* is also omitted, save the contents of the buffer to the current filename. If >>*file* is used, write contents to the end of an existing *file*. The ! flag forces the editor to write over any current contents of *file*.

write

[*address*] **w !***command*

Write lines specified by *address* to *command*.

Examples

:1,10w name_list	*Copy first 10 lines to name_list*
:50w >> name_list	*Now append line 50*

X

X

Prompt for an encryption key. This can be preferable to *:set key* as typing the key is not echoed to the console. To remove an encryption key, just reset the *key* option to an empty value. (**vim**)

xit

x

Write the file if it was changed since the last write, then quit.

yank

[*address*] **ya** [*char*] [*count*]

Place lines specified by *address* in named buffer *char*. If no *char* is given, place lines in general buffer. *count* specifies the number of lines to yank, starting with *address*.

Example

```
:101,200 ya a
```

z

[*address*] **z** [*type*] [*count*]

Print a window of text, with the line specified by *address* at the top. *count* specifies the number of lines to be displayed.

Type

- `+` Place specified line at top of window (the default).
- `-` Place specified line at bottom of window.
- `.` Place specified line in center of window.
- `^` Move up one window.
- `=` Place specified line in center of window, and leave as the current line.

!

[*address*] **!***command*

Execute Linux *command* in a shell. If *address* is specified, apply the lines contained in *address* as standard input to *command*, and replace the lines with the output.

Examples

:!ls	*List files in the current directory*
:11,20!sort -f	*Sort lines 11-20 of current file*

=

[*address*] =

Print the line number of the next line matching *address*. If no address is given, print the number of the last line.

< >

[*address*]**<**[*count*]
[*address*]**>**[*count*]

Shift lines specified by *address* either left (<) or right (>). Only blanks and tabs are removed in a left shift. *count* specifies the number of lines to shift, starting with *address*.

---

address

address

Print the line specified in *address*.

Return

Return

Print the next line in the file.

@

`[address] @ [char]`

Execute contents of register specified by *char*. If *address* is given, move cursor to the specified address first. Both *star* and * are aliases for this command. (**vim**)

@@

`[address] @`

Repeat the last `@` command. If *address* is given, move cursor to the specified address first. (vim)

&

`& [options] [count]`

Repeat the previous substitution (*s*) command. *count* specifies the number of lines on which to substitute, starting with *address*.

Examples

`:s/Overdue/Paid/`	*Substitute once on current line*
`:g/Status/&`	*Redo substitution on all "Status" lines*

~

`[address] ~ [count]`

Replace the previous regular expression with the previous replacement pattern from a *substitute* (*s*) command.

vi Configuration

This section describes the following:

- The *:set* command
- Options available with *:set*
- Sample *~/.exrc* file

The :set Command

The *:set* command lets you specify options that change characteristics of your editing environment. Options may be put in the *~/.exrc* file or set during a *vi* session.

The colon shouldn't be typed if the command is put in *~/.exrc*.

Command	Action
`:set` *x*	Enable option *x*.
`:set no`*x*	Disable option *x*.
`:set` *x=val*	Give *value* to option *x*.
`:set`	Show changed options.
`:set all`	Show all options.
`:set` *x?*	Show value of option *x*.

Options Used by :set

The following table describes the options to *:set*. The first column includes the optional abbreviation, if there is one, and uses an equals sign to show that the option takes a value. The second column gives the default, and the third column describes the behavior of the enabled option.

Option	Default	Description
`autoindent (ai)`	`noai`	In insert mode, indent each line to the same level as the line above or below.
`autoprint (ap)`	`ap`	Display changes after each editor command. (For global replacement, display last replacement.)
`autowrite (aw)`	`noaw`	Automatically write (save) file if changed, before opening another file with *:n* or before giving a Linux command with `:!`.
`background (bg)`		Describe the background so the editor can choose appropriate highlighting colors. Default value of `dark` or `light` depends on the environment in which the editor is invoked. (**vim**)
`backup (bk)`	`nobackup`	Create a backup file when overwriting an existing file. (**vim**)
`backupdir= (bdir)`	`.,~/tmp/,~/`	Name directories in which to store backup files if possible. The list of directories is comma-separated and in order of preference. (**vim**)
`backupext= (bex)`	`~`	String to append to filenames for backup files. (**vim**)
`beautify (bf)`	`nobf`	Ignore all control characters during input (except tab, newline, or formfeed).
`cindent (cin)`	`nocindent`	Insert indents in appropriate C format. (**vim**)
`compatible (cp)`	`cp`	Make *vim* behave more like *vi*. Default is `nocp` when a *~/.vimrc* file is found. (**vim**)
`directory= (dir)`	`/tmp`	Name the directory in which *ex* stores buffer files. (Directory must be writable.)
`edcompatible`	`noed-compatible`	Use *ed*-like features on substitute commands.
`equalprg= (ep)`		Use the specified program for the = command. When the option is blank (the default), the key invokes the internal C indention function or the value of the *indentexpr* option. (**vim**)
`errorbells (eb)`	`errorbells`	Sound bell when an error occurs.
`exrc (ex)`	`noexrc`	Allow the execution of *~/.exrc* files that reside outside the user's home directory.

Option	Default	Description
`formatprg= (fp)`		The *gq* command will invoke the named external program to format text. It will call internal formatting functions when this option is blank (the default). (**vim**)
`gdefault (gd)`	`nogdefault`	Set the *g* flag on for substitutions by default. (**vim**)
`hardtabs= (ht)`	`8`	Define boundaries for terminal hardware tabs.
`hidden (hid)`	`nohidden`	Hide buffers rather than unload them when they are abandoned. (**vim**)
`hlsearch (hls)`	`hlsearch`	Highlight all matches of most recent search.
`history= (hi)`	`20`	Number of *ex* commands to store in the history table. (**vim**)
`ignorecase (ic)`	`noic`	Disregard case during a search.
`incsearch (is)`	`noincsearch`	Highlight matches to a search pattern as it is typed. (**vim**)
`lisp`	`nolisp`	Insert indents in appropriate LISP format. ( ), { }, [[, and]] are modified to have meaning for LISP.
`list`	`nolist`	Print tabs as `^I`; mark ends of lines with `$`. (Use *list* to tell if tabs or spaces are at the end of a line.)
`magic`	`magic`	Wildcard characters . (dot), * (asterisk), and [ ] (brackets) have special meaning in patterns.
`mesg`	`mesg`	Permit system messages to display on terminal while editing in *vi*.
`mousehide (mh)`	`mousehide`	When characters are typed, hide the mouse pointer. (**vim**)
`number (nu)`	`nonu`	Display line numbers on left of screen during editing session.
`paste`	`nopaste`	Change the defaults of various options to make pasting text into a terminal window work better. All options are returned to their original value when the *paste* option is reset. (**vim**)
`redraw (re)`	`noredraw`	Terminal redraws screen whenever edits are made (in other words, insert mode pushes over existing characters, and deleted lines immediately close up). Default depends on line speed and terminal type. *noredraw* is useful at slow speeds on a dumb terminal: deleted lines show up as @, and inserted text appears to overwrite existing text until you press Esc.
`remap`	`remap`	Allow nested map sequences.
`report=`	`5`	Display a message on the prompt line whenever you make an edit that affects at least a certain number of lines. For example, `6dd` reports the message "6 lines deleted."
`ruler (ru)`	`ruler`	Show line and column numbers for the current cursor position. (**vim**)
`scroll=`	`<1/2 window>`	Amount of screen to scroll.
`sections= (sect)`	`SHNHH HUnhsh`	Define section delimiters for [[ ]] movement. The pairs of characters in the value are the names of *nroff*/*troff* macros that begin sections.
`shell= (sh)`	`/bin/sh`	Pathname of shell used for shell escape (*:!*) and shell command (*:sh*). Default value is derived from `SHELL` variable.
`shiftwidth= (sw)`	`8`	Define number of spaces used by the indent commands (^T, ^D, >>, and <<).

Option	Default	Description
`showmatch (sm)`	`nosm`	In *vi*, when) or } is entered, cursor moves briefly to matching (or {. (If the match is not on the screen, rings the error message bell.) Very useful for programming.
`showmode`	`noshowmode`	In insert mode, displays a message on the prompt line indicating the type of insert you are making, such as "Open Mode" or "Append Mode."
`slowopen (slow)`		Hold off display during insert. Default depends on line speed and terminal type.
`smartcase (scs)`	`nosmartcase`	Override the *ignorecase* option when a search pattern contains uppercase characters. (**vim**)
`tabstop= (ts)`	`8`	Define number of spaces that a tab indents during editing session. (Printer still uses system tab of 8.)
`taglength= (tl)`	`0`	Define number of characters that are significant for tags. Default (0) means that all characters are significant.
`tags=`	`tags /usr/lib/tags`	Define pathname of files containing tags (see the *ctags* command in Chapter 28). By default, the system looks for files *tags* (in the current directory) and */usr/lib/tags*.
`term=`		Set terminal type.
`terse`	`noterse`	Display shorter error messages.
`timeout (to)`	`timeout`	Keyboard maps timeout after 1 second.
`ttytype=`		Set terminal type. Default is inherited from `TERM` environment variable.
`undolevels= (ul)`	`1000`	Number of changes that can be undone. (**vim**)
`warn`	`warn`	Display the message "No write since last change."
`window= (w)`		Show a certain number of lines of the file on the screen. Default depends on line speed and terminal type.
`wrapmargin= (wm)`	`0`	Define right margin. If greater than 0, automatically insert carriage returns to break lines.
`wrapscan (ws)`	`ws`	Searches wrap around either end of file.
`writeany (wa)`	`nowa`	Allow saving to any file.
`writebackup (wb)`	`wb`	Back up files before attempting to overwrite them. Remove the backup when the file has been successfully written.

Sample ~/.exrc File

The following lines of code are an example of a customized *.exrc* file:

```
set nowrapscan wrapmargin=7
set sections=SeAhBhChDh nomesg
map q :w^M:n^M
map v dwElp
ab ORA O'Reilly & Associates, Inc.
```

24 The Emacs Editor

The Emacs editor is found on many Unix systems, including Mac OS X Panther, because it is a popular alternative to *vi*. Many versions are available. This book documents GNU Emacs. For more information, see the O'Reilly book *Learning GNU Emacs*.

Emacs is much more than "just an editor"; in fact, it provides a fully integrated user environment. From within Emacs you can issue individual shell commands, or open a window where you can work in the shell, read and send mail, read news, access the Internet, write and test programs, and maintain a calendar. To fully describe Emacs would require more space than we have available. In this chapter, therefore, we focus on the editing capabilities of Emacs.

To start an Emacs editing session, type:

```
emacs
```

You can also specify one or more files for Emacs to open when it starts:

```
emacs files
```

Emacs Concepts

This section describes some Emacs terminology that may be unfamiliar if you haven't used Emacs before.

Modes

One of the features that makes Emacs popular is its editing modes. The modes set up an environment designed for the type of editing you are doing, with features such as having appropriate key bindings available and automatically indenting according to standard conventions for that type of document. There are two types of modes—major and minor. The major modes include modes for various programming languages such as C or Perl, for text processing (e.g., SGML or even straight text), and many more. One particularly useful major mode is Dired (Directory Editor), which has commands that let you manage directories. Minor modes set or unset features that are independent of the major mode, such as auto-fill (which controls word wrapping), insert versus overwrite, and auto-save. For a full discussion of modes, see *Learning GNU Emacs* or the Emacs Info documentation system (C-h i).

Buffer and Window

When you open a file in Emacs, the file is put into a buffer so you can edit it. If you open another file, that file goes into another buffer. The view of the buffer contents that you have at any point in time is called a *window*. For a small file, the window might show the entire file; for a large file, it shows only a portion of a file. Emacs allows multiple windows to be open at the same time to display the contents of different buffers or different portions of a single buffer.

Point and Mark

When you are editing in Emacs, the position of the cursor is known as *point*. You can set a *mark* at another place in the text to operate on the region between point and mark. This is a very useful feature for such operations as deleting or moving an area of text.

Kill and Yank

Emacs uses the terms *kill* and *yank* for the concepts more commonly known today as cut and paste. You cut text in Emacs by killing it, and paste it by yanking it back. If you do multiple kills in a row, you can yank them back all at once.

Typical Problems

A common problem with Emacs is that the Del or Backspace key doesn't delete the character before the cursor, as it should, but instead invokes a help prompt. This problem is caused by an incompatible terminal setup file. A fairly robust fix is to create a file named *.emacs* in your home directory (or edit one that's already there) and add the following lines:

```
(keyboard-translate ?\C-h ?\C-?)
(keyboard-translate ?\C-\\ ?\C-h)
```

Now the Del or Backspace kill should work, and you can invoke help by pressing C-\ (an arbitrarily chosen key sequence).

Another potential problem is that on some systems, C-s causes the terminal to hang. This is due to an old-fashioned handshake protocol between the terminal and the system. You can restart the terminal by pressing C-q, but that doesn't help you enter commands that contain the sequence C-s. The solution (aside from using a more modern dial-in protocol) is to create new key bindings that replace C-s or to enter those commands as M-x *command-name*. This isn't specifically an Emacs problem, but it can cause problems when you run Emacs in a terminal window because C-s and C-q are commonly used Emacs key sequences.

Notes on the Tables

Emacs commands use the Control key and the Meta key—a system-neutral way to describe a function-changing modifier key. On a Mac, this corresponds to the Option key. (This behavior is set through the Terminal applications' preferences—see Chapter 18.)

In this chapter, the notation C- indicates that the Control key is pressed at the same time as the character that follows. Similarly, M- indicates the use of the Meta, or Option key on Mac OS X: either hold Option while typing the next character, *or* press and release the Escape key followed by the next character.

Absolutely Essential Commands

If you're just getting started with Emacs, here's a short list of the most important commands to know:

Binding	Action
C-h	Enter the online help system.
C-x C-s	Save the file.
C-x C-c	Exit Emacs.
C-x u	Undo last edit (can be repeated).
C-g	Get out of current command operation.
C-p	Up by one line.
C-n	Down by one line.
C-f	Forward by one character.
C-b	Back by one character.
C-v	Forward by one screen.
M-v	Backward by one screen.
C-s	Search forward for characters.
C-r	Search backward for characters.
C-d	Delete current character.
Del	Delete previous character.
Backspace	Delete previous character.

Summary of Commands by Group

Tables list keystrokes, command name, and description. C- indicates the Ctrl key; M- indicates the Meta key.

File Handling Commands

Binding	Command	Action
C-x C-f	find-file	Find file and read it.
C-x C-v	find-alternate-file	Read another file; replace the one read currently in the buffer.
C-x i	insert-file	Insert file at cursor position.

Binding	Command	Action
C-x C-s	save-buffer	Save file. (If terminal hangs, C-q restarts.)
C-x C-w	write-file	Write buffer contents to file.
C-x C-c	save-buffers-kill-emacs	Exit Emacs.
C-z	suspend-emacs	Suspend Emacs (use *exit* or *fg* to restart).

Cursor Movement Commands

In addition to the key bindings shown in this table, you can use the arrow keys to move around in Emacs. When you run Emacs in a graphical display environment (e.g., in the X Window System), you can also use the mouse for operations such as moving the cursor or selecting text.

Binding	Command	Action
C-f	forward-char	Move forward one character (right).
C-b	backward-char	Move backward one character (left).
C-p	previous-line	Move to previous line (up).
C-n	next-line	Move to next line (down).
M-f	forward-word	Move one word forward.
M-b	backward-word	Move one word backward.
C-a	beginning-of-line	Move to beginning of line.
C-e	end-of-line	Move to end-of-line.
M-a	backward-sentence	Move backward one sentence.
M-e	forward-sentence	Move forward one sentence.
M-{	backward-paragraph	Move backward one paragraph.
M-}	forward-paragraph	Move forward one paragraph.
C-v	scroll-up	Move forward one screen.
M-v	scroll-down	Move backward one screen.
C-x [	backward-page	Move backward one page.
C-x]	forward-page	Move forward one page.
M->	end-of-buffer	Move to end-of-file.
M-<	beginning-of-buffer	Move to beginning of file.
(none)	goto-line	Go to line *n* of file.
(none)	goto-char	Go to character *n* of file.
C-l	recenter	Redraw screen with current line in the center.
M-*n*	digit-argument	Repeat the next command *n* times.
C-u *n*	universal-argument	Repeat the next command *n* times.

Deletion Commands

Binding	Command	Action
Del	backward-delete-char	Delete previous character.
C-d	delete-char	Delete character under cursor.
M-Del	backward-kill-word	Delete previous word.

Binding	Command	Action
M-d	kill-word	Delete the word the cursor is on.
C-k	kill-line	Delete from cursor to end-of-line.
M-k	kill-sentence	Delete sentence the cursor is on.
C-x Del	backward-kill-sentence	Delete previous sentence.
C-y	yank	Restore what you've deleted.
C-w	kill-region	Delete a marked region (see the next section "Paragraphs and Regions").
(none)	backward-kill-paragraph	Delete previous paragraph.
(none)	kill-paragraph	Delete from the cursor to the end of the paragraph.

Paragraphs and Regions

Binding	Command	Action
C-@	set-mark-command	Mark the beginning (or end) of a region.
C-Space	(Same as preceding)	(Same as preceding)
C-x C-p	mark-page	Mark page.
C-x C-x	exchange-point-and-mark	Exchange location of cursor and mark.
C-x h	mark-whole-buffer	Mark buffer.
M-q	fill-paragraph	Reformat paragraph.
(none)	fill-region	Reformat individual paragraphs within a region.
M-h	mark-paragraph	Mark paragraph.
M-{	backward-paragraph	Move backward one paragraph.
M-}	forward-paragraph	Move forward one paragraph.
(none)	backward-kill-paragraph	Delete previous paragraph.
(none)	kill-paragraph	Delete from the cursor to the end of the paragraph.

Stopping and Undoing Commands

Binding	Command	Action
C-g	keyboard-quit	Abort current command.
C-x u	advertised-undo	Undo last edit (can be done repeatedly).
(none)	revert-buffer	Restore buffer to the state it was in when the file was last saved (or auto-saved).

Transposition Commands

Binding	Command	Action
C-t	transpose-chars	Transpose two letters.
M-t	transpose-words	Transpose two words.
C-x C-t	transpose-lines	Transpose two lines.
(none)	transpose-sentences	Transpose two sentences.
(none)	transpose-paragraphs	Transpose two paragraphs.

Capitalization Commands

Binding	Command	Action
M-c	capitalize-word	Capitalize first letter of word.
M-u	upcase-word	Uppercase word.
M-l	downcase-word	Lowercase word.
M- - M-c	negative-argument; capitalize-word	Capitalize previous word.
M- - M-u	negative-argument; upcase-word	Uppercase previous word.
M- - M-l	negative-argument; downcase-word	Lowercase previous word.
(none)	capitalize-region	Capitalize initial letters in region.
C-x C-u	upcase-region	Uppercase region.
C-x C-l	downcase-region	Lowercase region.

Incremental Search Commands

Binding	Command	Action
C-s	isearch-forward	Start or repeat incremental search forward.
C-r	isearch-backward	Start or repeat incremental search backward.
Return	(none)	Exit a successful search.
C-g	keyboard-quit	Cancel incremental search; return to starting point.
Del	(none)	Delete incorrect character of search string.
M-C-r	isearch-backward-regexp	Incremental search backward for regular expression.
M-C-s	isearch-forward-regexp	Incremental search forward for regular expression.

Word Abbreviation Commands

Binding	Command	Action
(none)	abbrev-mode	Enter (or exit) word abbreviation mode.
C-x a -	inverse-add-global-abbrev	Define previous word as global (mode-independent) abbreviation.
C-x a i l	inverse-add-mode-abbrev	Define previous word as mode-specific abbreviation.
(none)	unexpand-abbrev	Undo the last word abbreviation.
(none)	write-abbrev-file	Write the word abbreviation file.
(none)	edit-abbrevs	Edit the word abbreviations.
(none)	list-abbrevs	View the word abbreviations.
(none)	kill-all-abbrevs	Kill abbreviations for this session.

Buffer Manipulation Commands

Binding	Command	Action
C-x b	switch-to-buffer	Move to specified buffer.
C-x C-b	list-buffers	Display buffer list.
C-x k	kill-buffer	Delete specified buffer.

Binding	Command	Action
(none)	kill-some-buffers	Ask about deleting each buffer.
(none)	rename-buffer	Change buffer name to specified name.
C-x s	save-some-buffers	Ask whether to save each modified buffer.

Window Commands

Binding	Command	Action
C-x 2	split-window-vertically	Divide the current window in two vertically, resulting in one window on top of the other.
C-x 3	split-window-horizontally	Divide the current window in two horizontally, resulting in two side-by-side windows.
C-x >	scroll-right	Scroll the window right.
C-x <	scroll-left	Scroll the window left.
C-x o	other-window	Move to the other window.
C-x 0	delete-window	Delete current window.
C-x 1	delete-other-windows	Delete all windows but this one.
(none)	delete-windows-on	Delete all windows on a given buffer.
C-x ^	enlarge-window	Make window taller.
(none)	shrink-window	Make window shorter.
C-x }	enlarge-window- horizontally	Make window wider.
C-x {	shrink-window- horizontally	Make window narrower.
M-C-v	scroll-other-window	Scroll other window.
C-x 4 f	find-file-other-window	Find a file in the other window.
C-x 4 b	switch-to-buffer-other-window	Select a buffer in the other window.
C-x 5 f	find-file-other-frame	Find a file in a new frame.
C-x 5 b	switch-to-buffer-other-frame	Select a buffer in another frame.
(none)	compare-windows	Compare two buffers; show first difference.

Special Shell Mode Characters

The following table shows commands that can be used in Shell mode. To enter Shell mode, run the command M-x shell.

Binding	Command	Action
C-c C-c	interrupt-shell-subjob	Terminate the current job.
C-c C-d	shell-send-eof	End-of-file character.
C-c C-u	kill-shell-input	Erase current line.
C-c C-w	backward-kill-word	Erase the previous word.
C-c C-z	stop-shell-subjob	Suspend the current job.

Indentation Commands

Binding	Command	Action
C-x .	set-fill-prefix	Prepend each line in paragraph with characters from beginning of line up to cursor column; cancel prefix by typing this command in column 1.
(none)	indented-text-mode	Major mode: each tab defines a new indent for subsequent lines.
(none)	text-mode	Exit indented text mode; return to text mode.
M-C-\	indent-region	Indent a region to match first line in region.
M-m	back-to-indentation	Move cursor to first character on line.
M-^	delete-indentation	Join this line to the previous line.
M-C-o	split-line	Split line at cursor; indent to column of cursor.
(none)	fill-individual- paragraphs	Reformat indented paragraphs, keeping indentation.

Centering Commands

Binding	Command	Action
(none)	center-line	Center line that cursor is on.
(none)	center-paragraph	Center paragraph that cursor is on.
(none)	center-region	Center currently defined region.

Macro Commands

Binding	Command	Action
C-x (	start-kbd-macro	Start macro definition.
C-x)	end-kbd-macro	End macro definition.
C-x e	call-last-kbd-macro	Execute last macro defined.
M-*n* C-x e	digit-argument and call-last-kbd-macro	Execute last macro defined *n* times.
C-u C-x (	start-kbd-macro	Execute last macro defined, then add keystrokes.
(none)	name-last-kbd-macro	Name last macro you created (before saving it).
(none)	insert-last-keyboard- macro	Insert the macro you named into a file.
(none)	load-file	Load macro files you've saved.
(none)	*macroname*	Execute a keyboard macro you've saved.
C-x q	kbd-macro-query	Insert a query in a macro definition.
C-u C-x q	(none)	Insert a recursive edit in a macro definition.
M-C-c	exit-recursive-edit	Exit a recursive edit.

Detail Information Help Commands

Binding	Command	Action
C-h a	command-apropos	What commands involve this concept?
(none)	apropos	What commands, functions, and variables involve this concept?
C-h c	describe-key-briefly	What command does this keystroke sequence run?

Binding	Command	Action
C-h b	describe-bindings	What are all the key bindings for this buffer?
C-h k	describe-key	What command does this keystroke sequence run, and what does it do?
C-h l	view-lossage	What are the last 100 characters I typed?
C-h w	where-is	What is the key binding for this command?
C-h f	describe-function	What does this function do?
C-h v	describe-variable	What does this variable mean, and what is its value?
C-h m	describe-mode	Tell me about the mode the current buffer is in.
C-h s	describe-syntax	What is the syntax table for this buffer?

Help Commands

Binding	Command	Action
C-h t	help-with-tutorial	Run the Emacs tutorial.
C-h i	info	Start the Info documentation reader.
C-h n	view-emacs-news	View news about updates to Emacs.
C-h C-c	describe-copying	View the Emacs General Public License.
C-h C-d	describe-distribution	View information on ordering Emacs from the FSF.
C-h C-w	describe-no-warranty	View the (non)warranty for Emacs.

Summary of Commands by Key

Emacs commands are presented next in two alphabetical lists. Tables list keystrokes, command name, and description. C- indicates the Ctrl key; M- indicates the Meta key.

Control-Key Sequences

Binding	Command	Action
C-@	set-mark-command	Mark the beginning (or end) of a region.
C-Space	(Same as preceding)	(Same as preceding)
C-]	abort-recursive-edit	Exit recursive edit and exit query-replace.
C-a	beginning-of-line	Move to beginning of line.
C-b	backward-char	Move backward one character (left).
C-c C-c	interrupt-shell-subjob	Terminate the current job.
C-c C-d	shell-send-eof	End-of-file character.
C-c C-u	kill-shell-input	Erase current line.
C-c C-w	backward-kill-word	Erase previous word.
C-c C-z	stop-shell-subjob	Suspend current job.
C-d	delete-char	Delete character under cursor.
C-e	end-of-line	Move to end-of-line.
C-f	forward-char	Move forward one character (right).
C-g	keyboard-quit	Abort current command.

Binding	Command	Action
C-h	help-command	Enter the online help system.
C-h a	command-apropos	What commands involve this concept?
C-h b	describe-bindings	What are all the key bindings for this buffer?
C-h c	describe-key-briefly	What command does this keystroke sequence run?
C-h C-c	describe-copying	View the Emacs General Public License.
C-h C-d	describe-distribution	View information on ordering Emacs from the FSF.
C-h C-w	describe-no-warranty	View the (non)warranty for Emacs.
C-h f	describe-function	What does this function do?
C-h i	info	Start the Info documentation reader.
C-h k	describe-key	What command does this keystroke sequence run, and what does it do?
C-h l	view-lossage	What are the last 100 characters I typed?
C-h m	describe-mode	Tell me about the mode the current buffer is in.
C-h n	view-emacs-news	View news about updates to Emacs.
C-h s	describe-syntax	What is the syntax table for this buffer?
C-h t	help-with-tutorial	Run the Emacs tutorial.
C-h v	describe-variable	What does this variable mean, and what is its value?
C-h w	where-is	What is the key binding for this command?
C-k	kill-line	Delete from cursor to end-of-line.
C-l	recenter	Redraw screen with current line in the center.
C-n	next-line	Move to next line (down).
C-p	previous-line	Move to previous line (up).
C-q	quoted-insert	Insert next character typed. Useful for inserting a control character.
C-r	isearch-backward	Start or repeat nonincremental search backward.
C-r	(none)	Enter recursive edit (during query replace).
C-s	isearch-forward	Start or repeat nonincremental search forward.
C-t	transpose-chars	Transpose two letters.
C-u *n*	universal-argument	Repeat the next command *n* times.
C-u C-x (	start-kbd-macro	Execute last macro defined, then add keystrokes.
C-u C-x q	(none)	Insert recursive edit in a macro definition.
C-v	scroll-up	Move forward one screen.
C-w	kill-region	Delete a marked region.
C-x (	start-kbd-macro	Start macro definition.
C-x)	end-kbd-macro	End macro definition.
C-x [	backward-page	Move backward one page.
C-x]	forward-page	Move forward one page.
C-x ^	enlarge-window	Make window taller.
C-x {	shrink-window-horizontally	Make window narrower.
C-x }	enlarge-window-horizontally	Make window wider.
C-x <	scroll-left	Scroll the window left.
C-x >	scroll-right	Scroll the window right.

Binding	Command	Action
C-x .	set-fill-prefix	Prepend each line in paragraph with characters from beginning of line up to cursor column; cancel prefix by typing this command in column 1.
C-x 0	delete-window	Delete current window.
C-x 1	delete-other-windows	Delete all windows but this one.
C-x 2	split-window-vertically	Divide current window in two vertically, resulting in one window on top of the other.
C-x 3	split-window-horizontally	Divide current window in two horizontally, resulting in two side-by-side windows.
C-x 4 b	switch-to-buffer-other-window	Select a buffer in the other window.
C-x 4 f	find-file-other-window	Find a file in the other window.
C-x 5 b	switch-to-buffer-other-frame	Select a buffer in another frame.
C-x 5 f	find-file-other-frame	Find a file in another frame.
C-x a -	inverse-add-global-abbrev	Define previous word as global (mode-independent) abbreviation.
C-x a i l	inverse-add-mode-abbrev	Define previous word as mode-specific abbreviation.
C-x b	switch-to-buffer	Move to the buffer specified.
C-x C-b	list-buffers	Display the buffer list.
C-x C-c	save-buffers-kill-emacs	Exit Emacs.
C-x C-f	find-file	Find file and read it.
C-x C-l	downcase-region	Lowercase region.
C-x C-p	mark-page	Place cursor and mark around whole page.
C-x C-q	(none)	Toggle read-only status of buffer.
C-x C-s	save-buffer	Save file. (If terminal hangs, C-q restarts.)
C-x C-t	transpose-lines	Transpose two lines.
C-x C-u	upcase-region	Uppercase region.
C-x C-v	find-alternate-file	Read an alternate file, replacing the one currently in the buffer.
C-x C-w	write-file	Write buffer contents to file.
C-x C-x	exchange-point-and-mark	Exchange location of cursor and mark.
C-x Del	backward-kill- sentence	Delete previous sentence.
C-x e	call-last-kbd-macro	Execute last macro defined.
C-x h	mark-whole-buffer	Place cursor and mark around whole buffer.
C-x i	insert-file	Insert file at cursor position.
C-x k	kill-buffer	Delete the buffer specified.
C-x o	other-window	Move to the other window.
C-x q	kbd-macro-query	Insert a query in a macro definition.
C-x s	save-some-buffers	Ask whether to save each modified buffer.
C-x u	advertised-undo	Undo last edit (can be done repeatedly).
C-y	yank	Restore killed text.
C-z	suspend-emacs	Suspend Emacs (use *exit* or *fg* to restart).

Emacs

Meta-Key Sequences

Binding	Command	Action
M-- M-c	negative-argument; capitalize-word	Capitalize previous word.
M-- M-l	negative-argument; downcase-word	Lowercase previous word.
M-- M-u	negative-argument; upcase-word	Uppercase previous word.
M-$	spell-word	Check spelling of word after cursor.
M-%	query-replace	Search for and replace a string.
M-!	shell-command	Prompt for a shell command and run it.
M-<	beginning-of-buffer	Move to beginning of file.
M->	end-of-buffer	Move to end-of-file.
M-{	backward-paragraph	Move backward one paragraph.
M-}	forward-paragraph	Move forward one paragraph.
M-^	delete-indentation	Join this line to the previous one.
M-*n*	digit-argument	Repeat the next command *n* times.
M-*n* C-x e	digit-argument; call-last-kbd-macro	Execute the last defined macro *n* times.
M-a	backward-sentence	Move backward one sentence.
M-b	backward-word	Move one word backward.
M-c	capitalize-word	Capitalize first letter of word.
M-C-\	indent-region	Indent a region to match first line in region.
M-C-c	exit-recursive-edit	Exit a recursive edit.
M-C-o	split-line	Split line at cursor; indent to column of cursor.
M-C-r	isearch-backward-regexp	Incremental search backward for regular expression.
M-C-s	isearch-forward-regexp	Incremental search forward for regular expression.
M-C-v	scroll-other-window	Scroll other window.
M-d	kill-word	Delete word that cursor is on.
M-Del	backward-kill-word	Delete previous word.
M-e	forward-sentence	Move forward one sentence.
M-f	forward-word	Move one word forward.
(none)	fill-region	Reformat individual paragraphs within a region.
M-h	mark-paragraph	Place cursor and mark around whole paragraph.
M-k	kill-sentence	Delete sentence that cursor is on.
M-l	downcase-word	Lowercase word.
M-m	back-to-indentation	Move cursor to first nonblank character on line.
M-q	fill-paragraph	Reformat paragraph.
M-t	transpose-words	Transpose two words.
M-u	upcase-word	Uppercase word.
M-v	scroll-down	Move backward one screen.
M-x	(none)	Execute a command by typing its name.

Summary of Commands by Name

The following Emacs commands are presented alphabetically by command name. Use M-x to access the command name. Tables list command name, keystroke, and description. C- indicates the Ctrl key; M- indicates the Meta key.

Command	Binding	Action
macroname	(none)	Execute a keyboard macro you've saved.
abbrev-mode	(none)	Enter (or exit) word abbreviation mode.
abort-recursive-edit	C-]	Exit recursive edit and query replace.
advertised-undo	C-x u	Undo last edit (can be done repeatedly).
apropos	(none)	What functions and variables involve this concept?
back-to-indentation	M-m	Move cursor to first nonblank character on line.
backward-char	C-b	Move backward one character (left).
backward-delete-char	Del	Delete previous character.
backward-kill-paragraph	(none)	Delete previous paragraph.
backward-kill-sentence	C-x Del	Delete previous sentence.
backward-kill-word	C-c C-w	Delete previous word.
backward-kill-word	M-Del	Delete previous word.
backward-page	C-x [	Move backward one page.
backward-paragraph	M-{	Move backward one paragraph.
backward-sentence	M-a	Move backward one sentence.
backward-word	M-b	Move backward one word.
beginning-of-buffer	M-<	Move to beginning of file.
beginning-of-line	C-a	Move to beginning of line.
call-last-kbd-macro	C-x e	Execute last macro defined.
capitalize-region	(none)	Capitalize region.
capitalize-word	M-c	Capitalize first letter of word.
center-line	(none)	Center line that cursor is on.
center-paragraph	(none)	Center paragraph that cursor is on.
center-region	(none)	Center currently defined region.
command-apropos	C-h a	What commands involve this concept?
compare-windows	(none)	Compare two buffers; show first difference.
delete-char	C-d	Delete character under cursor.
delete-indentation	M-^	Join this line to previous one.
delete-other-windows	C-x 1	Delete all windows but this one.
delete-window	C-x 0	Delete current window.
delete-windows-on	(none)	Delete all windows on a given buffer.
describe-bindings	C-h b	What are all the key bindings for in this buffer?
describe-copying	C-h C-c	View the Emacs General Public License.
describe-distribution	C-h C-d	View information on ordering Emacs from the FSF.
describe-function	C-h f	What does this function do?
describe-key	C-h k	What command does this keystroke sequence run, and what does it do?

Emacs

Command	Binding	Action
describe-key-briefly	C-h c	What command does this keystroke sequence run?
describe-mode	C-h m	Tell me about the mode the current buffer is in.
describe-no-warranty	C-h C-w	View the (non)warranty for Emacs.
describe-syntax	C-h s	What is the syntax table for this buffer?
describe-variable	C-h v	What does this variable mean, and what is its value?
digit-argument	M-*n*	Repeat next command *n* times.
downcase-region	C-x C-l	Lowercase region.
downcase-word	M-l	Lowercase word.
edit-abbrevs	(none)	Edit word abbreviations.
end-kbd-macro	C-x)	End macro definition.
end-of-buffer	M->	Move to end-of-file.
end-of-line	C-e	Move to end-of-line.
enlarge-window	C-x ^	Make window taller.
enlarge-window-horizontally	C-x }	Make window wider.
exchange-point-and-mark	C-x C-x	Exchange location of cursor and mark.
exit-recursive-edit	M-C-c	Exit a recursive edit.
fill-individual-paragraphs	(none)	Reformat indented paragraphs, keeping indentation.
fill-paragraph	M-q	Reformat paragraph.
fill-region	(none)	Reformat individual paragraphs within a region.
find-alternate-file	C-x C-v	Read an alternate file, replacing the one currently in the buffer.
find-file	C-x C-f	Find file and read it.
find-file-other-frame	C-x 5 f	Find a file in another frame.
find-file-other-window	C-x 4 f	Find a file in another window.
forward-char	C-f	Move forward one character (right).
forward-page	C-x]	Move forward one page.
forward-paragraph	M-}	Move forward one paragraph.
forward-sentence	M-e	Move forward one sentence.
forward-word	M-f	Move forward one word.
goto-char	(none)	Go to character *n* of file.
goto-line	(none)	Go to line *n* of file.
help-command	C-h	Enter the online help system.
help-with-tutorial	C-h t	Run the Emacs tutorial.
indent-region	M-C-\	Indent a region to match first line in region.
indented-text-mode	(none)	Major mode: each tab defines a new indent for subsequent lines.
info	C-h i	Start the Info documentation reader.
insert-file	C-x i	Insert file at cursor position.
insert-last-keyboard-macro	(none)	Insert the macro you named into a file.
interrupt-shell-subjob	C-c C-c	Terminate the current job (shell mode).
inverse-add-global-abbrev	C-x a -	Define previous word as global (mode-independent) abbreviation.
inverse-add-mode-abbrev	C-x a i l	Define previous word as mode-specific abbreviation.
isearch-backward	C-r	Start incremental search backward.
isearch-backward-regexp	M-C-r	Same, but search for regular expression.

Command	Binding	Action
isearch-forward	C-s	Start incremental search forward.
isearch-forward-regexp	M-C-s	Same, but search for regular expression.
kbd-macro-query	C-x q	Insert a query in a macro definition.
keyboard-quit	C-g	Abort current command.
kill-all-abbrevs	(none)	Kill abbreviations for this session.
kill-buffer	C-x k	Delete the buffer specified.
kill-line	C-k	Delete from cursor to end-of-line.
kill-paragraph	(none)	Delete from cursor to end of paragraph.
kill-region	C-w	Delete a marked region.
kill-sentence	M-k	Delete sentence the cursor is on.
kill-shell-input	C-c C-u	Delete current line.
kill-some-buffers	(none)	Ask about deleting each buffer.
kill-word	M-d	Delete word the cursor is on.
list-abbrevs	(none)	View word abbreviations.
list-buffers	C-x C-b	Display buffer list.
load-file	(none)	Load macro files you've saved.
mark-page	C-x C-p	Place cursor and mark around whole page.
mark-paragraph	M-h	Place cursor and mark around whole paragraph.
mark-whole-buffer	C-x h	Place cursor and mark around whole buffer.
name-last-kbd-macro	(none)	Name last macro you created (before saving it).
negative-argument; capitalize-word	M-- M-c	Capitalize previous word.
negative-argument; downcase-word	M-- M-l	Lowercase previous word.
negative-argument; upcase-word	M-- M-u	Uppercase previous word.
next-line	C-n	Move to next line (down).
other-window	C-x o	Move to the other window.
previous-line	C-p	Move to previous line (up).
query-replace	M-%	Search for and replace a string.
query-replace-regexp	(none)	Query-replace a regular expression.
quoted-insert	C-q	Insert next character typed. Useful for inserting a control character.
recenter	C-l	Redraw screen, with current line in center.
rename-buffer	(none)	Change buffer name to specified name.
replace-regexp	(none)	Replace a regular expression unconditionally.
re-search-backward	(none)	Simple regular-expression search backward.
re-search-forward	(none)	Simple regular-expression search forward.
revert-buffer	(none)	Restore buffer to the state it was in when the file was last saved (or auto-saved).
save-buffer	C-x C-s	Save file. (If terminal hangs, C-q restarts.)
save-buffers-kill-emacs	C-x C-c	Exit Emacs.
save-some-buffers	C-x s	Ask whether to save each modified buffer.
scroll-down	M-v	Move backward one screen.

Command	Binding	Action
scroll-left	C-x <	Scroll the window left.
scroll-other-window	M-C-v	Scroll other window.
scroll-right	C-x >	Scroll the window right.
scroll-up	C-v	Move forward one screen.
set-fill-prefix	C-x .	Prepend each line in paragraph with characters from beginning of line up to cursor column; cancel prefix by typing this command in column 1.
set-mark-command	C-@ or C-Space	Mark the beginning (or end) of a region.
shell-command	M-!	Prompt for a shell command and run it.
shell-send-eof	C-c C-d	End-of-file character (shell mode).
shrink-window	(none)	Make window shorter.
shrink-window-horizontally	C-x {	Make window narrower.
spell-buffer	(none)	Check spelling of current buffer.
spell-region	(none)	Check spelling of current region.
spell-string	(none)	Check spelling of string typed in minibuffer.
spell-word	M-$	Check spelling of word after cursor.
split-line	M-C-o	Split line at cursor; indent to column of cursor.
split-window-horizontally	C-x 3	Divide current window horizontally into two.
split-window-vertically	C-x 2	Divide current window vertically into two.
start-kbd-macro	C-x (	Start macro definition.
stop-shell-subjob	C-c C-z	Suspend current job.
suspend-emacs	C-z	Suspend Emacs (use *fg* to restart).
switch-to-buffer	C-x b	Move to the buffer specified.
switch-to-buffer-other-frame	C-x 5 b	Select a buffer in another frame.
switch-to-buffer-other-window	C-x 4 b	Select a buffer in another window.
text-mode	(none)	Enter text mode.
transpose-chars	C-t	Transpose two characters.
transpose-lines	C-x C-t	Transpose two lines.
transpose-paragraphs	(none)	Transpose two paragraphs.
transpose-sentences	(none)	Transpose two sentences.
transpose-words	M-t	Transpose two words.
unexpand-abbrev	(none)	Undo the last word abbreviation.
universal-argument	C-u *n*	Repeat the next command *n* times.
upcase-region	C-x C-u	Uppercase region.
upcase-word	M-u	Uppercase word.
view-emacs-news	C-h n	View news about updates to Emacs.
view-lossage	C-h l	What are the last 100 characters I typed?
where-is	C-h w	What is the key binding for this command?
write-abbrev-file	(none)	Write the word abbreviation file.
write-file	C-x C-w	Write buffer contents to file.
yank	C-y	Restore what you've deleted.

Extending Emacs

Emacs' many modes come courtesy of *elisp* files, programs written in Emacs' own LISP-based language and stored in *.el* and *.elc* files (the latter for compiled files). Getting into the Elisp language is outside the topic of this book,* but be aware that all the modes you're working with are written in *elisp*.

Darwin's directory for Emacs extensions is */usr/share/emacs/emacs-version-numberlisp*. Generally speaking, installing Emacs extensions that you download is as simple as moving them into this folder or into the neighboring *site-lisp* directory. Some *.el* files need to be compiled in order to work; this involves using the *M-x byte-compile-file* command from within Emacs. Packages that contain many interdependent files, such as the PSGML extension for editing SGML and XML files (*http://www.lysator.liu.se/projects/about_psgml.html*), may make this process easier by including standard Unix *configure* and *Makefile* files, which often just run Emacs in batch mode to compile the files in the right order.

Many modes require you to activate various Emacs variables and settings before they'll work. This usually involves editing your *.emacs* file (see the next section) in some way and is usually described in the extension's *README* file, or perhaps in the comment section of the *elisp* file itself.

Many Emacs modes and main functions are centered around programming. The *elisp* files that ship with Mac OS X include full-featured (which is to say, many-variabled) major modes for C, Java, Perl, and many other languages. Through Meta-X commands such as *compile*, *debug*, and the *compilation-mode* major mode, you can even use Emacs as a complete build-and-debug environment.

That said, there's not much reason to use Emacs as your IDE, unless you're working with a very obscure language that lacks editor support outside of Emacs modes (such as *elisp*!) or with a rapid-development language with a console-based interface that doesn't really need an IDE, such as Perl or shell scripting. For all other Mac OS X programming, investigate what Project Builder can do.

The .emacs File

You can configure Emacs' default behavior by creating and editing a special *elisp* file called *.emacs* in your Home folder. (As with all dotfiles, the Finder hides *.emacs* from sight; see the section "Hidden Files" in Chapter 7.) Emacs executes all the commands in this file whenever you launch the program, so it's a great place to set variables, activate and customize major mode options, and so on.

Even if you don't know *elisp*, it's good to know about *.emacs* because Emacs extensions that you download from the Internet often require it. If you use Emacs a lot, you may find your *.emacs* file growing over time. A well-organized *elisp* file maintains scalability through grouping similar commands together into well-

* However, there are books on this topic alone, such as *Writing GNU Emacs Extensions* (O'Reilly).

commented blocks, so that you know what everything does each time you return to add to (or debug) the file.

As an example, here's part of the *.emacs* file on a Mac OS X system:

```
; First, adjust my loadpath so I can see me own .el files
(setq load-path (cons (expand-file-name "/Users/jmac/emacs-lisp/") load-
path)
)
; Activate and configure PSGML mode

(autoload 'sgml-mode "psgml" "Major mode to edit SGML files." t )
(custom-set-variables)
(custom-set-faces
 '(font-lock-comment-face ((((class color) (background dark)) (:foreground
"orchid1")))))
;; required for Emacs 21
(setq after-change-function nil)


;; Activate XSL-editing mode
(autoload 'xsl-mode "xslide" "Major mode for XSL stylesheets." t)

;; Turn on font lock when in XSL mode
(add-hook 'xsl-mode-hook
          'turn-on-font-lock)

(setq auto-mode-alist
      (append
       (list
        '("\\.xsl" . xsl-mode))
       auto-mode-alist))

;; Activate the 'time-clock' minor mode, which adds time-tracking
functionality.

   (require 'timeclock)

;; Define some keystrokes to trigger timeclock functions quickly.
   (define-key ctl-x-map "ti" 'timeclock-in)
   (define-key ctl-x-map "to" 'timeclock-out)
   (define-key ctl-x-map "tc" 'timeclock-change)
   (define-key ctl-x-map "tr" 'timeclock-reread-log)
   (define-key ctl-x-map "tu" 'timeclock-update-modeline)
   (define-key ctl-x-map "tw" 'timeclock-when-to-leave-string)

;; The M-x-erase-buffer command will warn you about your rash deed unless
;; you have the following variable set:
(put 'erase-buffer 'disabled nil)
```

You can find plenty of other *.emacs* examples online, including a whole repository just for them at *http://www.dotfiles.com*.

Note the path-extending command, *(setq load-path ...)*, at the top of the previous example. If you're not a member of the machine's *admin* group, and thus lack the *sudo* powers necessary to write to the */usr/share/emacs/21.1/* directory, you can define your own space to place *elisp* files, just as we have here with the directory */Users/jmac/emacs-lisp*. This tells Emacs to add that directory to the paths it scans when it seeks extension files.

GUI Emacs

Various solutions exist for running Emacs outside of the Terminal. Unfortunately, none of them are very obvious:

Through X Windows
: If you're running X Windows on your Macintosh, you can compile Emacs and run it with X support.

XEmacs
: XEmacs (*http://www.xemacs.org*) is a separate project in the Unix world, aiming to maintain a version of Emacs more suited to use in a GUI environment than GNU Emacs. A Carbon version of XEmacs has existed for about as long as Mac OS X has, thanks to the efforts of Pitts Jarvis; see *http://homepage.mac.com/pjarvis/xemacs.html*.

Mac-patched Emacs
: Finally, you can try using a version of GNU Emacs that's been patched to play nicer with the Aqua interface, such as the one available at this site, *http://www.porkrind.org/emacs/*, courtesy of Andrew Choi and David Caldwell.

25

The Defaults System

Native Mac OS X applications store their preferences in the *defaults database*. This is made up of each application's property list (*plist*) file, which is an XML file consisting of key/value pairs that define the preferences for an application or service of the operating system.

If an application has a *plist* file, every time you change its preferences, the changes are saved back to the *plist* file. Also included in the defaults database system are the changes you make to your system via the panels found in System Preferences (*/Applications*).

As an administrator, you may need to access your or another user's preferences. This is done from the Terminal using the *defaults* command. This chapter covers Mac OS X's preferences system, including the format and location of application and system preference files, how they work, and how to view and adjust their settings using the Property List Editor (*/Developer/Applications/Utilities*) and the Terminal.

Property Lists

User-defined property lists are stored in *~/Library/Preferences*, and the appropriate *plist* is called up when an application launches. Property lists can contain literal preferences set through the application's Application→Preferences dialog, or subtler things such as window coordinates or the state of an option (such as whether to display the battery menu extra in the menu bar, as shown in Example 25-1).

Example 25-1. The com.apple.menuextra.battery.plist file

```
<?xml version="1.0" encoding="UTF-8"?>
<!DOCTYPE plist PUBLIC "-//Apple Computer//DTD PLIST 1.0//EN" "http://www.apple.
com/DTDs/PropertyList-1.0.dtd">
<plist version="1.0">
```

Example 25-1. The com.apple.menuextra.battery.plist file (continued)

```
<dict>
        <key>ShowPercent</key>
        <string>YES</string>
        <key>ShowTime</key>
        <string>NO</string>
</dict>
</plist>
```

Each property list is named after its *domain*, the unique namespace that an application uses when working with its preference files. Domains can look like any string, but the Apple-recommended format is similar to a URL, just in reverse. The naming convention is based on the developer's company or organization's name, using the application's name as the domain. All of the *plist* files for the System Preferences and other iApps use the syntax *com.apple.domain.plist*, where *domain* is the name of the service or application. For example, the *plist* file for the Dock's preferences is *com.apple.dock.plist*, while the preferences file for OmniGraffle (if you have it installed) is *com.omnigroup.OmniGraffle.plist*.

Not all application preference files are part of the preferences system. Some applications may write their user preference files in a proprietary format to *~/Library/Preferences*. These are typically Carbon applications not packaged into bundles, and hence lacking the *Info.plist* files they need to claim a preferences domain. As such, these preference files can't be read or altered by the *defaults* command (described later), even though they are stored in *~/Library/Preferences*.

Classic applications, on the other hand, are even more antisocial, always writing their preference files in opaque formats in Mac OS 9's */System Folder/Preferences* folder.

To get a list of the *com.apple.*`domain` *plist* files in the *~/Library/Preferences* directory, issue the following commands:

```
$ cd ~/Library/Preferences
$ ls com.apple.* > ~/Desktop/plists.txt
```

The first command places you in the *~/Library/Preferences* directory; the second gives a wildcard search for all files that begin with *com.apple*, and then redirects that listing to a file named *plists.txt* and saves that file on your Desktop. Because each application (including the menu extras, described in Chapter 1) creates its own *plist* file, this listing can be long.

Looking at Example 25-1, you can see the basic structure of a *plist* file. At the most basic level, a *plist* file can be broken down into three parts: dictionaries, keys, and values for the keys. The dictionary sections, denoted with `<dict/>`, set the structure; keys (`<key/>`) define an available preference, and the values for the keys in this example are strings (`<string/>`).

The values for a key are defined within either a `<data/>`, `<date/>`, `<boolean/>`, `<string/>`, or `<integer/>` tag. Keys can also contain nested dictionary sections or

NSGlobalDomain, the Master Domain

One special domain named `NSGlobalDomain` acts as a parent to all the other preferences domains on the system. They inherit its settings, which are all related to system-wide preferences that applications access frequently, such as localized time-format information and the currently selected system beep.

Run *defaults read NSGlobalDomain* or simply *defaults read –g* within the Terminal to see `NSGlobalDomain`'s current settings.

arrays (`<array/>`) sections for holding encoded values or a series of strings. Nested dictionaries are referred to as children of the parent dictionary. For example, *com.apple.dock.plist* has a *persistent-apps* key, which contains an array for all of the applications in the Dock (to the left of the divider bar). Within the array, you'll see a number of nested dictionaries that define the parameters for the application's icon in the Dock. Example 25-2 shows the array item for *Mail.app*'s Dock icon.

Example 25-2. Mail.app's array in com.apple.dock.plist

```
<key>persistent-apps</key>
<array>
....
        <dict>
            <key>GUID</key>
            <integer>1871630911</integer>
            <key>tile-data</key>
            <dict>
                <key>file-data</key>
                <dict>
                    <key>_CFURLAliasData</key>
                    <data>
                    AAAAAACQAAMAAQAAu77rNQAASCsAAAAAAAD
                    KgAARrIAALthjLAAAAAACSD//gAAAAAAAAA
                    /////wABAAQAAAMqAA4AEgAIAEOAYQBpAGwA
                    LgBhAHAAcAAPABAABwBQAGEAbgBOAGgAZQBy
                    ABIAFUFwcGxpY2F0aW9ucy9NYWlsLmFwcAAA
                    EwABLwD//wAA
                    </data>
                    <key>_CFURLString</key>
                    <string>/Applications/Mail.app</string>
                    <key>_CFURLStringType</key>
                    <integer>0</integer>
                </dict>
                <key>file-label</key>
                <string>Mail</string>
                <key>file-mod-date</key>
                <integer>-1136549615</integer>
                <key>file-type</key>
                <integer>9</integer>
```

Example 25-2. Mail.app's array in com.apple.dock.plist (continued)

```
                <key>parent-mod-date</key>
                <integer>-1134631645</integer>
            </dict>
            <key>tile-type</key>
            <string>file-tile</string>
        </dict>
...
</array>
```

Because a *plist* file is nothing more than text, you can use any text editor (such as TextEdit, BBEdit, *vi*, or Emacs) to view and edit its contents; however, the preferred method is to use the Property List Editor (*/Developer/Applications/Utilities*), described later. The Property List Editor application is installed when you install the Xcode Tools. See Chapter 15 for details on how to install or obtain the Xcode Tools.

Viewing and Editing Property Lists

There are two ways you can view and edit the contents of an application's preferences file:

- With the Property List Editor (*/Developer/Applications/Utilities*)
- From the command line, using the *defaults* command

The Property List Editor is available on your system only after installing the Xcode Tools; however, the *defaults* command is available with the base installation of Mac OS X, and doesn't require you to install any additional software.

Viewing is one thing, but knowing what you can enter into a *plist* file requires a bit of investigative work. An application asserts its domain through the *CFBundleIdentifier* key in its internal *Info.plist* file, which is stored in an application's */Contents* directory. For example, the *Info.plist* file for the Dock can be found in */System/Library/CoreServices/Dock.app/Contents*.

The preferences available to an application are defined via the *CFBundleExecutable* key in the *Info.plist* file. Typically, the string for *CFBundleExecutable* is the short name for the application (e.g., Dock). This executable can be found in an application's */Contents/MacOS* directory; e.g., the Dock executable is located in */System/Library/CoreServices/Dock.app/Contents/MacOS*.

To see a listing of available keys and strings for an application, use the *strings* command in the Terminal, followed by the path to the application's short name as defined by *CFBundleExecutable*:

```
$ strings /System/Library/CoreServices/Dock.app/Contents/MacOS/Dock
```

Unfortunately, the output from *strings* doesn't have a discernible structure. You'll need to sift through the output to find hints about the preferences you can set and alter using the Property List Editor or the *defaults* command, defined in the following sections.

Using the Property List Editor

The Property List Editor, shown in Figure 25-1, is a GUI tool that lets you view and edit property list files.

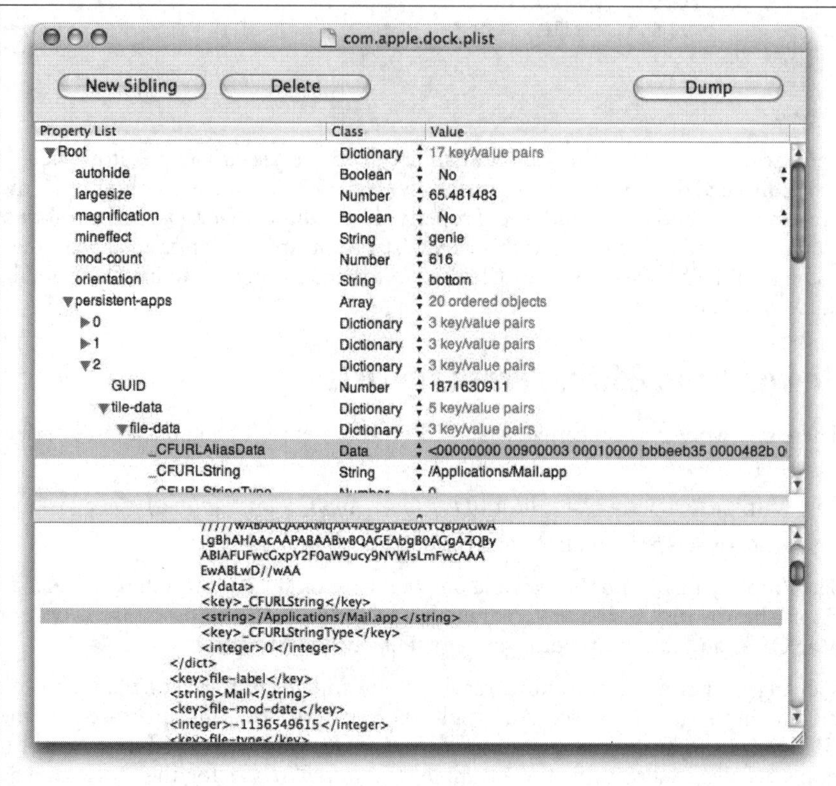

Figure 25-1. The Property List Editor

At their base, every *plist* has a Root item, which contains all the dictionaries, arrays, keys, and values that define the preferences for an application. When you initially open a *plist* file, all its elements are hidden inside the Root item. If you click on the disclosure triangle next to Root (this is similar to the List View of the Finder), the keys of the *plist* are revealed in the first column.

If you select a Dictionary or Array item in the Property List column that has a disclosure triangle next to it, you can use ⌘-right (or left) arrow to respectively open or close a disclosure triangle. Likewise, Option-⌘-right (or left) Arrow respectively opens or closes all of the disclosure triangles in the Property List Editor. For example, if you select Root and hit Option-⌘-right arrow, all of the contents of that *plist* file are shown in the upper display; Option-⌘-left arrow closes them again.

As shown in Figure 25-1, there are three columns in the Property List Editor's display:

Property List
: The Property List column lists the items seen in the `<key/>` tags of a *plist*'s XML file.

Class
: The Class column lists the classes available for each key definition. Clicking on the set of up/down arrows next to a class reveals a pop-up menu, from which you can select from one of seven possible classes including:

  String
  : A string can contain alphanumeric text, such as an application path (e.g., */Applications/Mail.app/*), a single-word response that defines the action of a key, or the default position of the application's window (e.g., `{{125, 0}, {205, 413}}`).

  Dictionary
  : Dictionary items are grayed out in the Property List Editor's display and give you details on the number of key/value pairs listed in that dictionary item. Dictionaries are tagged as `<dict/>` in the XML file.

  Array
  : Like dictionaries, the Value column is grayed out for an Array, showing you the number of ordered objects available in that array. Within each array, you will find another Dictionary item listing its key/value pairs. Arrays are tagged as `<array/>` in the XML file.

  Boolean
  : Contains YES or NO responses as its value, and are tagged as `<true/>` or `</false>`, respectively, as the value in the XML file.

  Number
  : Contains a floating-point value for the key, such as a percentage value for the opaqueness of the Terminal application (e.g., 0.750000 for 75 percent) or the version number for an application. Values in the Number class are tagged in the *plist* file using `<integer/>`.

  Date
  : Contains the date in MM/DD/YY format. The Date Value can also include a time, in HH:MM:SS format.

  Data
  : Data information is stored as a string of encoded alphanumeric data, inside a set of opening and closing angle brackets. If you look closely at the Value, you'll see that the numbers are in blocks of eight characters (numbers and/or letters), which reveal its form as binary data. Example 25-3 shows the Data Value for *Mail.app*'s icon alias in the Dock.

Example 25-3. The Data Value for _CFURLAliasData as binary data

```
<00000000 00900003 00010000 bbbeeb35 0000482b 00000000 0000032a
000046b2 0000bb61 8cb00000 00000920 fffe0000 00000000 0000ffff
ffff0001 00040000 032a000e 00120008 004d0061 0069006c 002e0061
00700070 000f0010 00070050 0061006e 00740068 00650072 00120015
4170706c 69636174 696f6e73 2f4d6169 6c2e6170 70000013 00012f00
ffff0000 >
```

Value
: Contains the value for the Class.

To view the XML source for the *plist* file, click on the Dump button in the upper-right corner of the Property List Editor's window. You can't edit the XML source in the Property List Editor; edits to the *plist* file are made in the upper portion of the window.

You should avoid changing a *plist* file used by an application that's currently in use, because it can crash the application or cause it and your system to behave strangely.

To edit an item, double-click on the item you want to edit to select it, type in the new value, and then hit Return to accept the new value. If you want to see the change in the XML source, hit the Dump button again. After the changes have been entered, save the file before closing (File→Save, or ⌘-S).

The defaults Command

Another way to view and change the contents of a *plist* file is with the *defaults* command from the Terminal. The *defaults* command gives you an abstract way to read from and write to the preferences system. It lets you quickly modify any or all of an application's saved-state settings, which can prove quite handy when debugging your own applications. As with any command-line program, you can write shell scripts to run several invocations of *defaults* with a single command, letting you set the application's stage however you like in an instant.

If the preferences domain is bound to a specific host, you must specify a host with the *–host* option or refer to the current machine with the *–currentHost* option.

The following section contains a complete reference for the *defaults* command.

defaults

```
defaults [host] subcommand domain [option] [key]
defaults [-currentHost | -host hostname ] read [domain [key]]
defaults [-currentHost | -host hostname ] read-type domain key
defaults [-currentHost | -host hostname ] write domain { 'plist' | domain key '
value ' }
defaults [-currentHost | -host hostname ] rename domain old_key new_key
defaults [-currentHost | -host hostname ] delete [ domain [ key ]]
defaults [-currentHost | -host hostname ] { domains | find word | help }
```

Used to access Mac OS X's user defaults database to read, write (set or change), and delete system and application preferences.

The *defaults* command allows users and administrators to read, write, and delete Mac OS X user defaults from a command-line shell. An application's defaults belong to a *domain*, which typically correspond to individual applications; however, they can apply to system settings made via the System Preferences panels. Each domain has a dictionary of keys and values representing its defaults. Keys are always strings, but values can be complex data structures comprising arrays, dictionaries, strings, and binary data. These data structures are stored as XML property lists.

Though all applications, system services, and other programs have their own domains, they also share a domain named `NSGlobalDomain`. If a default isn't specified in the application's domain but is specified in `NSGlobalDomain`, the application uses the value in that domain.

Host

-currentHost
: Restricts the actions of the *defaults* command to the domains listed in *~/Library/Preferences/ByHost*.

-host hostname
: Used to specify the *hostname*, based on the Ethernet MAC address of the system the user is logged in to.

Subcommands

read
: Prints all the user's defaults, for every domain, to standard output.

read domain
: Prints all the user's defaults for *domain* to standard output.

read-type domain key
: Prints the type of *key* for the given *domain*.

read domain key
: Prints the value for the default of *domain* identified by *key*.

write domain key 'value'
: Writes value as the value for *key* in *domain*. The *value* must be a property list and must be enclosed in single quotes. For example:

```
defaults write com.companyname.appname "Default Color" '(255, 0, 0)'
```

sets the application's *value* for the *key* (`Default Color`) to an array, which contains the string `255, 0, 0` (for the RGB values). Note that the *key* is enclosed in quotation marks because it contains a space.

write domain plist
: Overwrites the defaults information in a domain with that given as *plist*. *plist* must be a property list representation of a dictionary and must be enclosed in single quotes. For example:

```
defaults write com.companyname.appname '{ "Default Color" = (255, 0, 0);
"Default Font" = Helvetica; }';
```

erases any previous defaults for *com.companyname.appname* and writes the values for the two names into the defaults system.

delete `domain`
: Removes all default information for *`domain`*.

delete `domain key`
: Removes the default named *`key`* from *`domain`*.

`domains`
: Prints the names of all defaults *`domains`* on the user's system.

find `word`
: Searches for *`word`* in the domain names, keys, and values of the user's defaults, and prints the results to standard output.

help
: Prints a list of possible command formats.

–h Prints an abbreviated list of possible command formats.

Options

–g Used as a synonym for the domain `NSGlobalDomain`. You can also use *"Apple Global Domain"* (including the quotation marks) as a synonym for the domain `NSGlobalDomain`. For example:

```
$ defaults read "Apple Global Domain"
```

displays the same thing as:

```
$ defaults read -g
```

or:

```
$ defaults read NSGlobalDomain
```

or:

```
$ defaults read -globalDomain
```

The following list specifies values for preference keys:

–app
: Specifies an application found in the */Applications* directory, rather than using its domain. For example:

```
$ defaults read -app Mail
```

outputs the defaults data for the Mail application.

–array
: Allows the user to specify an array as the value for the given preference key:

```
defaults write somedomain preferenceKey -array element1 element2 element3
```

The specified array overwrites the value of the *key* if the *key* is present at the time of the `write`. If the *key* isn't present, it's created with the new value.

–array-add
: Allows the user to add new elements to the end of an array for a *key*, which has an array as its value. Usage is the same as *–array*. If the *key* isn't present at the time of the `write`, it's created with the specified array as its value.

–dict
: Allows the user to add a dictionary to the defaults database for a domain. Keys and values are specified in order:

```
defaults write somedomain preferenceKey -dict key1 value1 key2 value2
```

The specified dictionary overwrites the *value* of the *key* if the *key* is present at the time of the `write`. If the *key* isn't present, it's created with the new *value*.

–dict-add

Allows the user to add new key/value pairs to a dictionary for a *key* that has a dictionary as its value. Usage is the same as *–dict*. If the *key* isn't present at the time of the `write`, it is created with the specified dictionary as its value.

Host-Specific Preferences

A folder called *ByHost* can exist within *~/Library/Preferences*. *ByHost* contains property list files defining preferences specific to an application on a certain host. These files have filenames following the format of *com.apple.address.plist*, in which *address* is the Ethernet MAC address associated with the *–currentHost*.

To read the *plist* files located in the *ByHost* directory, you need to specify the *–currentHost* option, as follows:

```
$ defaults -currentHost read com.apple.screensaver
```

Notice that you don't need to specify the Ethernet address that's part of the filename. The *–currentHost* option tells the *defaults* command to read the specified domain from the *ByHost* directory.

26

The X Window System

Although the X in "Mac OS X" is not the same X as in "The X Window System," you can get them to play nice together.

Most Unix systems use the X Window System as their default GUI. (We'll refer to the X Window System as X11 instead of X, to avoid confusion with Mac OS X.) X11 includes development tools and libraries for creating graphical applications for Unix-based systems. Mac OS X doesn't use X11 as its GUI, relying instead on Quartz (and, on compatible hardware, Quartz Extreme), a completely different graphics system. However, Apple's own implementation of X11 for Mac OS X, based on the open source XFree86 Project's X11 (*http://www.xfree86.org/*), was initially released as a beta for Jaguar and is now bundled with Mac OS X Panther as an optional installation. Apple also provides an X11 software development kit (the X11 SDK) on the Xcode Tools CD that ships with Panther.

This chapter highlights some of the key features of Apple's X11 distribution and explains how to install Apple's X11 and the X11 SDK. It also explains how to use X11 in both rootless and full-screen modes (using the GNOME and KDE desktops). You'll also learn how to connect to other X Window systems using Virtual Network Computer (VNC), as well as how to remotely control the Mac OS X Aqua desktop from other X11 systems.

From Aqua to X11, there's no shortage of graphical environments for Mac OS X. The operating system's solid Unix underpinnings and powerful graphics subsystem make it possible for developers to support alternative graphical environments. For this reason, a humble iBook can make a fine cockpit for a network of heterogeneous machines!

About Apple's X11

As noted earlier, Apple's X11 distribution is based on the open source XFree86 Project's XFree86, Version 4.3. The X11 package has been optimized for Mac OS X and has the following features:

- X11R6.6 window server
- Support for the RandR (Resize and Rotate) extension
- Strong integration with Mac OS X environment
- A Quartz window manager that provides Aqua window decorations, ability to minimize windows to the Dock, and pasteboard integration
- Can use other window managers
- Compatible with Expose
- Supports rootless and full-screen modes
- Customizable Application menu, which allows you to add applications for easy launching and to map keyboard shortcuts
- Customizable Dock menu, which allows you to add applications for easy launching, to map keyboard shortcuts, and to list all open windows
- Finder integration, which supports auto-detection of X11 binaries and double-clicking to launch X11 binaries, starting the X server if it is not already running
- Preference settings for system color map, key equivalents, system alerts, keyboard mapping, and multi-button mouse emulation
- Hardware acceleration support for OpenGL (GLX) and Direct CG (AIPI)

Installing X11

Apple's X11 for Mac OS X is available as an optional installation bundled with Mac OS X. To install it when you first install (or upgrade an existing installation of) Mac OS X Panther, you must customize the installation (in the Selection Type phase) and select the X11 checkbox. If you don't install X11 during the Mac OS X installation, you can install it later by inserting the Install Mac OS X Disc 3 CD, then finding and double-clicking the *X11User.pkg* package in the Packages folder.

The installation places the double-clickable X11 application in the */Applications/Utilities* folder. If you want to build X11-based applications, you need to install the X11SDK, which is located as an optional package on the Xcode Tools CD (*/Developer Tools/Packages/X11SDK.pkg*).

Running X11

X11 can be run in two modes: *full screen* or *rootless* (the default). Both modes run side by side with Aqua, although full-screen mode hides the Finder and Mac OS X's desktop (to hide X11 and return to the Finder, press Option-⌘-A).

To launch the X server, double-click the X11 application (in */Applications/Utilities*). An *xterm* window that looks similar to a Mac OS X Terminal window opens, sporting Aqua-like buttons for closing, minimizing, and maximizing the window. Also, X11 windows minimize to the Dock, just like other Aqua windows. Figure 26-1 shows a Terminal window and an *xterm* window side by side.

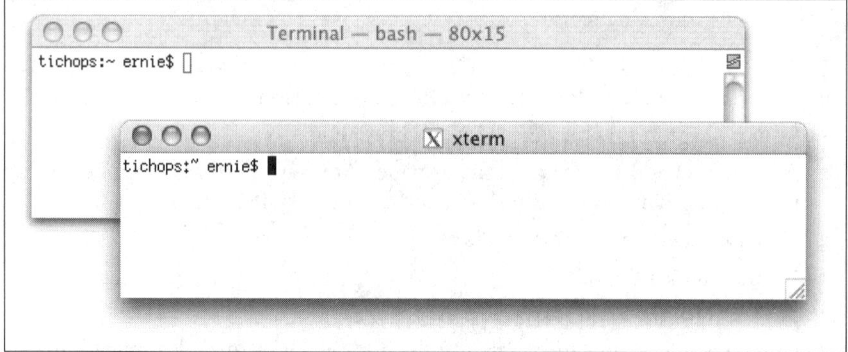

Figure 26-1. A Terminal and an xterm sporting the Aqua look

If you're using the default configuration, you'll also notice three obvious differences from a Terminal window. In particular:

- The *xterm* window has a titlebar that reads "xterm."
- The *xterm* window doesn't have vertical and horizontal scrollers.
- The *xterm* window doesn't have a split-window option.

A less obvious difference between a Terminal window and an X11 *xterm* window is that Control-clicking (or right-clicking) in an *xterm* window doesn't invoke the same contextual menu it does in a Terminal window. Control-clicking, Control-Option-clicking, and Control-⌘-clicking in an *xterm* invokes *xterm*-specific contextual menus, as shown in Figures 26-2, 26-3, and 26-4. If you have a three-button mouse, Control-clicking with the right mouse button does the same thing as Control-⌘-clicking; Control-clicking with the middle button does the same thing as Control-Option-clicking.

You can use Fink to install an *xterm* replacement such as *rxvt* or *eterm*. See Chapter 27 for more information on Fink.

Mac OS X emulates right-mouse clicks with Control-click. In X11, you can configure key combinations that simulate two- and three-button mice.

By default, Option-click simulates the middle mouse button, and ⌘-click simulates the right mouse button. You can use X11→Preferences to enable or disable this, but you can't change which key combinations are used (although you can use *xmodmap* as you would under other X11 systems to remap pointer buttons).

In rootless mode, X11 applications take up their own window on your Mac OS X desktop. In full-screen mode, X11 takes over the entire screen and is suitable for running an X11 desktop environment (DTE) such as GNOME, KDE, or Xfce. If

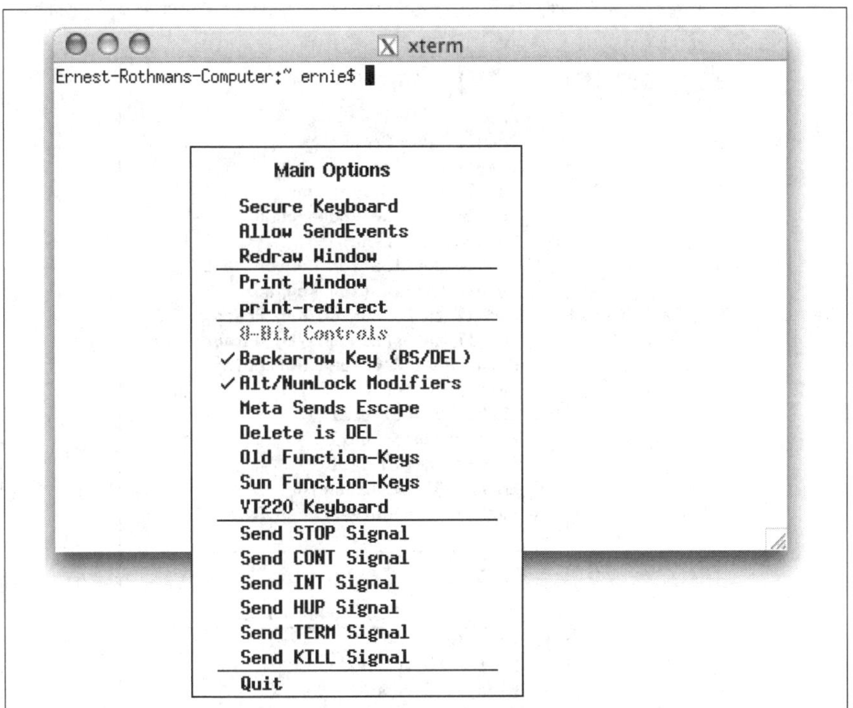

Figure 26-2. Control-click (or Control-left-click) in an xterm window

you want to run X11 in full-screen mode, you have to enable this mode in the X11 Preferences by clicking the Output tab and selecting the full-screen mode checkbox.

You can still access your Mac OS X desktop while in full-screen mode by pressing Option-⌘-A. To go back to the X11 desktop, bring X11 to the front by clicking its icon in the Dock or using ⌘-Tab, and press Option-⌘-A.

Customizing X11

There are a number of things you can customize in X11. For example, you can customize your *xterm* window, set X11 application preferences, customize the X11 application and Dock menus, and specify which window manager to use.

Dotfiles, Desktops, and Window Managers

To customize X11, you can create an *.xinitrc* script in your home directory. A sample *.xinitrc* script is provided in */etc/X11/xinit/xinitrc*.

Using the script as a starting point, you can specify which X11-based applications to start when X11 is launched, including which window manager you'd like to use as your default. The default window manager for X11 is the Quartz window

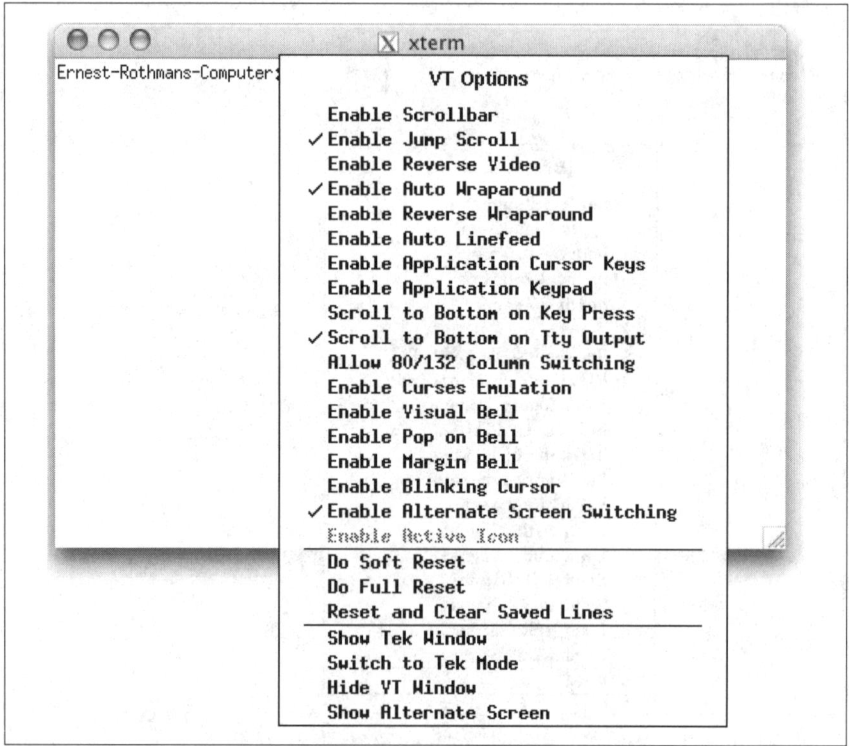

Figure 26-3. Control-Option-click (or Control-middle-click) in an xterm window

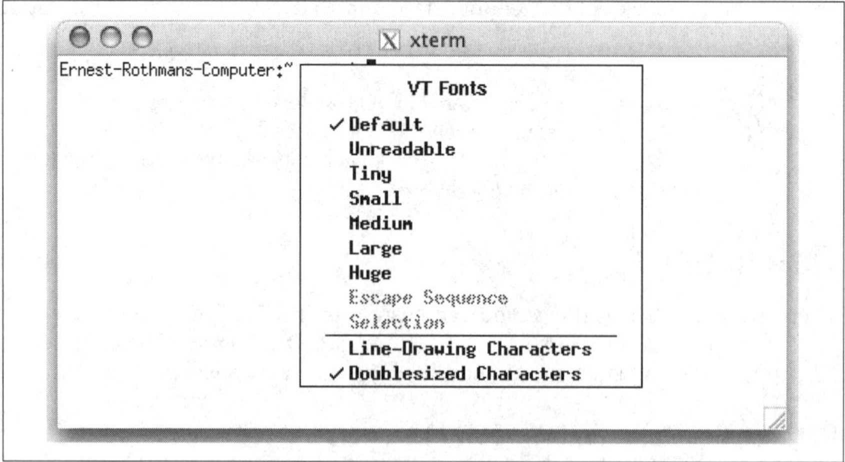

Figure 26-4. Control-⌘-click (or Control-right-click) in an xterm window

manager (or *quartz-wm*). The tab window manager (or *twm*) is also bundled with X11, but many other window managers are available. You can visit the following web sites to get instructions and binaries for a variety of window managers and DTEs:

Fink
: *http://fink.sourceforge.net*

DarwinPorts
: *http://darwinports.opendarwin.org*

GNU-Darwin
: *http://gnu-darwin.sourceforge.net*

OroborOSX
: *http://oroborosx.sourceforge.net*

If you're going to use your own *.xinitrc* file and want to use the Quartz window manager, make sure you start the Quartz window manager with the command:

```
exec /usr/X11R6/bin/quartz-wm &
```

Once you've installed X11, you will probably want to install additional X11 applications, window managers, and perhaps other DTEs (even if you are using Apple's window manager, you can still run most binaries from other DTEs such as GNOME and KDE even without using that DTE as your desktop). One of the easiest ways to install additional window managers is to use Fink. Table 26-1 lists some of the window managers and desktops that can be installed via Fink. (For information on installing and updating Fink, see Chapter 27.)

Table 26-1. Window managers available for Fink

Window manager/desktop	Fink package name
Blackbox	*blackbox*
Enlightenment	*enlightenment*
FVWM	*fvwm, fvwm2*
GNOME	*bundle-gnome*
IceWM	*icewm*
KDE	*bundle-kde*
mwm	*lesstif*
Oroborus	*oroborus, oroborus2*
PWM	*pwm*
Sawfish	*sawfish*
Window Maker	*windowmaker*
XFce	*xfce*

Fink has entire sections (*http://fink.sourceforge.net/pdb/sections.php*) devoted to GNOME and KDE, where you will find an extensive set of libraries, utilities, and plug-ins. Also included in the GNOME section are GTK+, *glib*, and Glade. Installing GNOME and KDE may be especially useful if you want to develop software for these desktops.

Fink installs everything in its */sw* directory. So, for example, if you've installed *lesstif* and want to use the *mwm* window manager, you must include */sw/bin* in your path or include */sw/bin/mwm &* in your *.xinitrc* file to start the Motif window manager. However, if you've installed Fink according to its instructions, */sw/bin* will already be in your path (see Chapter 27).

You can customize the *xterm* window in Apple's X11 the same way you customize *xterm* on any other system running X11. You can, for example, set resources in an *.Xdefaults* file in your home directory or use escape sequences to set the title bar (see "Customizing the Terminal on the Fly" in Chapter 1).

X11 Preferences, Application Menu, and Dock Menu

You can also customize your X11 environment by setting X11's preferences via the X11→Preferences window (⌘-,) and adding programs to its Application menu. X11's preferences are organized into three categories: Input, Output, and Security. X11's options are detailed in the following sections.

Input

The following options control how X11 interacts with input devices:

Emulate three-button mouse
: Determines whether Option-click and ⌘-click mimic the middle and right buttons.

Follow system keyboard layout
: Allows input menu changes to overwrite the current X11 keymap.

Enable key equivalents under X11
: Enabled menu bar key equivalents, which may interfere with X11 applications that use the Meta modifier.

By default, all three options are enabled.

Output

The following options configure X11's look and feel:

Colors
: This pop-up menu offers the following options:

- From Display
- 256 Colors
- Thousands
- Millions

By default, the Color pop-up is set to "From Display"; if you change this setting to something else, you need to relaunch X11 for the change to take effect.

Full-screen mode
: This option is unchecked by default. When unchecked, X11 runs in rootless mode, which means that X11 windows can reside side by side with Aqua

windows. In full-screen mode, use Option-⌘-A to toggle full-screen X11 and Aqua.

Use system alert effect
Determines whether X11's beeps use the system alert, as specified in the Sound Effects System Preference. If unchecked, X11 windows use a standard Unix system beep to sound an alert.

Security

The following options configure X11's security features:

Authenticate connections
Determines whether X11 creates Xauthority access-control keys. If the system's IP address changes, you should relaunch X11 because the old keys will become invalid.

Allow connections from network clients
If you use this option, be sure to select Authenticate connections to ensure the security of your system. If this is disabled, remote applications won't be able to connect.

Both settings are checked by default. If you make any changes to these settings, you must quit and restart X11 for the change to take effect.

Customizing X11's Applications menu

X11's Applications menu can be used to quickly launch X11 applications, so you don't have to enter their command path. You can add other X11 applications to this menu and assign keyboard shortcuts by selecting Applications→Customize to bring up the X11 Application Menu dialog window, shown in Figure 26-5.

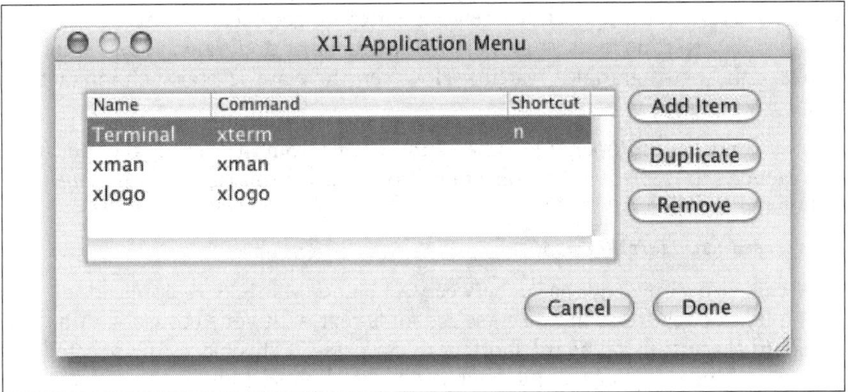

Figure 26-5. X11 Application Menu customization window

The same X11 Application Menu customization window can be opened by Control-clicking on X11's Dock icon and selecting Customize from the contextual menu. When you Control-click on X11's Dock icon, you will see that the applications shown in Figure 26-5 are listed there as well. X11's context menu allows you to quickly launch other X11 applications and to switch between windows of currently running X11 applications.

X11-Based Applications and Libraries

You can use Fink to install many X11-based applications, such as the GNU Image Manipulation Program (GIMP), *xfig/transfig*, ImageMagick, *nedit*, and many others. Because Fink understands dependencies, installing some of these applications will cause Fink to first install several other packages. For example, because the text editor *nedit* depends on Motif libraries, Fink will first install *lesstif*. (This also gives you the Motif window manager, *mwm*.) Similarly, when you install the GIMP via Fink, you will also install the packages for GNOME, GTK+, and *glib* because Fink handles any package dependencies you might encounter.

You can also use Fink (see Chapter 27) to install libraries directly. For example, the following command can install the X11-based Qt libraries:

```
$ fink install qt
```

This is an Aqua version of Qt for Mac OS X (available from Trolltech, *http://www.trolltech.com*); however, Qt applications don't automatically use the library. Instead, you need to recompile and link the application against the Aqua version of Qt, which may not always be a trivial task.

Another interesting development is the port of KDE to Mac OS X. As of this writing, Konqueror had been ported, and a port of Koffice was underway. To keep abreast of developments pertaining to KDE on Mac OS X, see *http://ranger.befunk.com/blog/*.

Aqua-X11 Interactions

Because X11-based applications rely on different graphics systems, even when running XDarwin in rootless mode, GUI interactions don't always run smoothly between these two graphics systems. However, there are several such interactions that run very well.

First, it is possible to open X11-based applications from the Terminal application. To launch an X11-based application from the Terminal, use the *open-x11* command as follows:

```
$ open-x11 /sw/bin/gimp
```

You can also copy and paste between X11 and Mac OS X applications. For example, to copy from an *xterm*, select some text with your mouse, and use the standard Macintosh keyboard shortcut to copy, ⌘-C. This places the selected text into the clipboard. To paste the contents of the clipboard into a Mac OS X application (such as the Terminal), simply press ⌘-V.

To copy from a Mac OS X application, highlight some text and press ⌘-C. The copied text can be pasted into an *xterm* window by pressing the middle button of a three-button mouse or by Command-clicking in the X11 application.

Connecting to Other X Window Systems

You can connect from Mac OS X to other X Window systems using *ssh* with X11 forwarding. If you use OpenSSH (which is included with Mac OS X), you must use the *–X* option to request X11 forwarding (the –2 option specifies the SSH Version 2 protocol, as opposed to the older Version 1 protocol). For example:

```
$ ssh -2 -X remotemachine -l username
```

As long as X11 is running, this can be entered in either an *xterm* window or in the Terminal. To have the X11 forwarding enabled in Terminal, you must have the `DISPLAY` variable set prior to making the connection. Under the *bash* shell (and other Bourne-compatible shells) use:

```
DISPLAY=:0.0; export DISPLAY
```

Under *csh* and *tcsh*, use:

```
setenv DISPLAY :0.0
```

It's also possible to create a double-clickable application that connects to a remote machine via SSH 2, with X11 forwarding enabled. For example, you can use the following script for this purpose:

```
#!/bin/sh
DISPLAY=:0.0; export DISPLAY
/usr/X11R6/bin/xterm -e ssh -2 -X remotemachine -l username
```

If you've installed the commercial version of SSH from *http://www.ssh.com*, the equivalent of the preceding script is as follows:

```
#!/bin/sh
DISPLAY=:0.0; export DISPLAY
/usr/X11R6/bin/xterm -e ssh2 remotemachine -l username
```

The X11 forwarding flag is *+x* with the commercial SSH, but it is enabled by default, so that you need not include it in the command.

Using Apple's X11, you can add an Application menu item to accomplish the same task. To do this, start by saving the previous script to whatever you'd like to call this application. For example, suppose you want to connect to a remote machine named *mrchops* with a username of *eer*. You can name the application *sshmrchops* and save it as *~/bin/sshmrchops.sh*. In X11, select Applications→Customize, and then click the Add Item button, as shown in Figure 26-6.

That's it! Now you can launch the connection to the remote machine via the menu bar and the Dock. Once you connect to a machine running X11, you can start X11-based applications on the remote machine and display them on your Mac OS X machine.

You can also do the reverse (SSH to your Mac and run X11 applications on the Mac, but display them on the local machine), but be sure to edit */etc/sshd_config* and change this line:

```
#X11Forwarding no
```

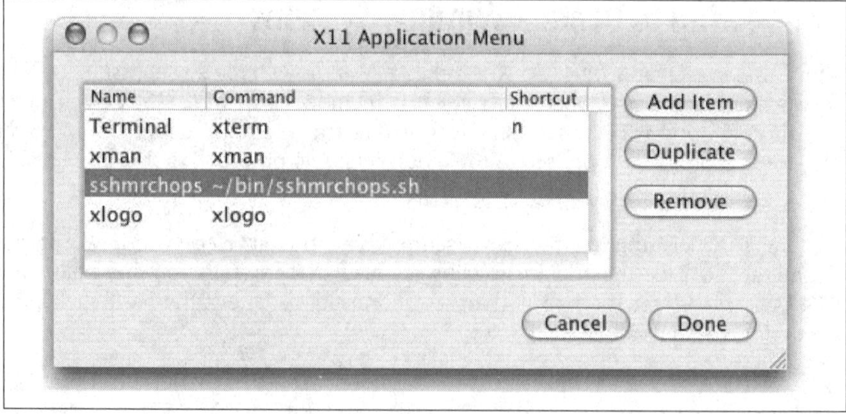

Figure 26-6. Adding an item to the X11 application menu

to this:

```
X11Forwarding yes
```

You will also need to stop and restart Remote Login using System Preferences→Sharing for this change to take effect.

osx2x

These days, it's fairly common to find a Mac sitting next to as many as four Linux or Unix systems, each running an X11-based desktop. You may also have more than one Mac on your desk. In such situations, it's convenient to use only one keyboard and mouse to control all your Mac OS X and X11-based desktops, saving valuable desktop space. Enter Michael Dales' free BSD-licensed application *osx2x* (*http://opendarwin.org/projects/osx2x/*).

To use this handy little application, log into your Linux/Unix box running an X11 server, and enter the command:

```
xhost + mymachost
```

Then, double-click the *osx2x* application, and once the main window appears, click New Connection to open a drop-down window. In the drop-down window's Hostname field, supply the hostname or IP address of the Unix box running the X11 desktop, followed by either `:0` or `:0.0` (without any spaces), as in `myhost:0.0`. Next, select the Edge detection (East, West, North, or South), and the connection type X11. If, on the other hand, you are connecting your Mac to a machine running a VNC (Virtual Network Computer, described in the next section) server (for example, another Mac), select VNC as the Connection type rather than X11, and enter the VNC server password. You can switch back and forth between the Mac and the remote machine with Control-T, or you can enable edge detection and choose the position of your X11 system relative to your Mac. For example, if your Mac is to the left of your destination X11 machine, select East as illustrated in Figure 26-7.

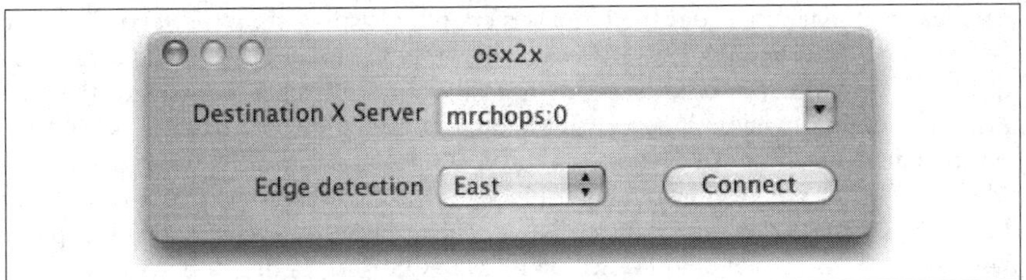

Figure 26-7. Controlling a neighboring X11 desktop with osx2x

In addition to using one keyboard and mouse to control up to four systems, you can use *osx2x* to copy text from an x11 clipboard using ⌘-C and paste on the Mac OS X side using ⌘-V.

Virtual Network Computer

One of the attractive features of Mac OS X is the ease with which you can integrate a Mac OS X system into a Unix environment consisting of multiple Unix workstations that typically rely on X11 for their GUI. In the previous section, for example, we explained how to log in to a remote Unix machine, launch an X11 application, and display the application on your Mac. The reverse process is also possible. You can log into a remote Mac OS X machine from another computer, launch an application on the remote Mac OS X machine, and have the application display on your local machine. The local machine, meanwhile, can be running the X Window System, Microsoft Windows, or any another platform supported by Virtual Network Computer (VNC).

VNC consists of two components:

- A VNC server, which must be installed on the remote machine
- A VNC viewer, which is used on the local machine to view and control applications running on the remote machine

The VNC connection is made through a TCP/IP connection.

The VNC server and viewer may not only be on different machines, but they can also be installed on different operating systems. This allows you to, for example, connect from Solaris to Mac OS X. Using VNC, you can launch and run both X11 and Aqua applications on Mac OS X, but view and control them from your Solaris box.

VNC can be installed on Mac OS X with the Fink package manager (look for the *vnc* package), but that version (the standard Unix version of the VNC server) supports only X11 programs, not Aqua applications. This standard Unix version of VNC translates X11 calls into the VNC protocol. All you need on the client machine is a VNC viewer. An attractive Mac-friendly alternative to the strictly X11-based VNC server is OSXvnc (*http://www.redstonesoftware.com/vnc.html*).

The standard Unix version of the VNC server is quite robust. Rather than interacting with your display, it intercepts and translates the X11 network protocol. (In fact, the Unix version of the server is based on the XFree86 source code.)

Applications that run under the Unix server aren't displayed on the server's screen (unless you set the DISPLAY environment variable to :0.0, in which case it's displayed only on the remote server, not on your VNC client). Instead, they are displayed on an invisible X server that relays its virtual display to the VNC viewer on the client machine. OSXvnc works in a similar manner except it supports the Mac OS X Aqua desktop instead of X11. With the OSXvnc server running on your Mac OS X system, you can use a VNC client on another system, for example, a Unix system, to display and control your Mac OS X Aqua desktop. You can even tunnel these VNC connections (both X11 and Aqua) through SSH.

Launching VNC

If you installed VNC on your Mac OS X system via Fink (or on any Unix system for that matter), you can start the VNC server by issuing the following command:

```
vncserver
```

If you don't have physical access to the system on which you want to run the VNC server, you can log in into it remotely and enter the command before logging out:

```
nohup vncserver
```

This starts the VNC server, and *nohup* makes sure that it continues to run after you log out. In either case, the first time you start *vncserver*, you need to supply a password, which you need anyway when connecting from a remote machine. (This password can be changed using the command *vncpasswd*.) You can run several servers; each server is identified by its hostname with a *:number* appended. For example, suppose you start the VNC server twice on a machine named *abbott*; the first server will be identified as *abbott:1* and the second as *abbott:2*. You will need to supply this identifier when you connect from a client machine.

By default, the VNC server runs *twm*. So, when you connect, you will see an X11 desktop instead of the Mac OS X desktop. You can specify a different window manager in *~/.vnc/xstartup*. To terminate the VNC server, use the following command syntax:

```
vncserver -kill :display
```

For example, to terminate *abbott:1*, you would issue the following command while logged into *abbott* as the user who started the VNC server:

```
vncserver -kill :1.
```

VNC and SSH

VNC passwords and network traffic are sent over the wire as plaintext. However, you can use SSH with VNC to encrypt this traffic.

There is a derivative of VNC, called TightVNC, which is optimized for bandwidth conservations. (If you are using Fink, you can install it with the command *fink install tightvnc*). TightVNC also offers automatic SSH tunneling on Unix and backward compatibility with the standard VNC.

If you want to tunnel your VNC connection through SSH, you can do it even without TightVNC. To illustrate this process, let's consider an example using a Sun workstation running Solaris named *mrchops* and a PowerBook G4 named *tichops* running Panther. In the following example, the VNC server is running on the Solaris machine and a VNC client on the Mac OS X machine. To display and control the remote Solaris GNOME desktop on your local Mac OS X system, do the following:

1. Log in to the Solaris machine, *mrchops*, via SSH if you need login remotely.
2. On *mrchops*, enter this command to start the VNC server on *display :1*:

   ```
   nohup vncserver :1
   ```

3. In your *~/.vnc* directory, edit the *xstartup* file so that the *gnome* will start when you connect to the VNC server with a VNC client. In particular, your *xstartup* file should look like this:

   ```
   #!/bin/sh
   xrdb $HOME/.Xresources
   xterm  -geometry 80x24+10+10 -ls -title "$VNCDESKTOP Desktop" &

   exec /usr/bin/gnome-session &
   ```

4. Log out from the Solaris box, *mrchops*.
5. From a Terminal window (or *xterm*) on your Mac OS X machine, log in to *mrchops* via *ssh:*

   ```
   ssh -L 5902:localhost:5901 mrchops
   ```

   Any references to *display :2* on your Mac will connect to the Solaris machine's *display :1* through an SSH tunnel (*display :1* uses port 5901, *display :2* uses 5902). You may need to add the *–l* option to this command if your username on the Solaris machine is different from the one you're using on your Mac OS X machine. For example, say your username on *mrchops* is *brian,* but on *tichops* it's *ernie;* the following command would be issued instead of the previous:

   ```
   ssh -L 5902:localhost:5901 mrchops -l brian
   ```

   Additionally, you may need to open ports through any firewalls you may have running. Open ports 5900-5902 for VNC, and 22 for *ssh*.

6. On your Mac, you can start X11 or run *vncviewer* from the command line:

   ```
   vncviewer localhost:2
   ```

   You can also run an Aqua VNC client such as *VNCDimension* (*http://www.mdimension.com/*) or *Chicken of the VNC* (*http://sourceforge.net/projects/cotvnc/*). Figure 26-8 shows a *VNCDimension* connection to a Solaris GNOME desktop.

Connecting to the Mac OS X VNC Server

To connect to a Mac OS X machine that is running a VNC server, you will need a VNC viewer. We mentioned two Mac OS X viewers (*VNCDimension* and *Chicken of the VNC*) earlier, and additional Mac OS X viewers can be found on Version Tracker or MacUpdate (*http://www.versiontracker.com/macosx/* or *http://www.*

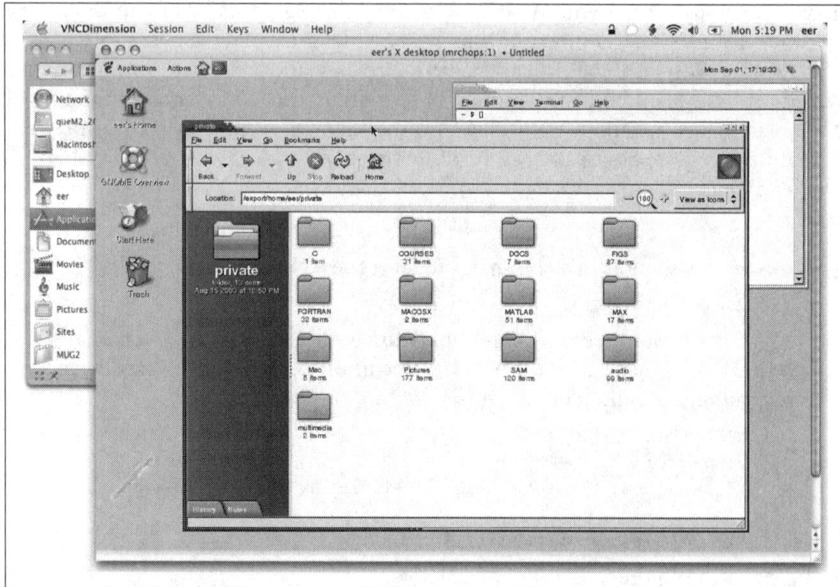

Figure 26-8. VNCDimension displaying a remote GNOME desktop

macupdate.com) by searching for "VNC". VNC or TightVNC provide viewers for Unix systems, which can be used to display and control the Mac OS X Aqua desktop.

To connect, start your viewer and specify the hostname and display number, such as *chops:1* or *chops:2*. If all goes well, you'll be asked for your password and then be connected to the remote Mac OS X desktop. VNC connections to Mac OS X Aqua desktops can be established through SSH tunnels.

To illustrate this process, let's do the reverse of what we did in our last example; let's make an SSH-secured connection from a Solaris machine to the Mac OS X machine running the VNC server. Again, let's assume that the name of the Solaris machine is *mrchops,* and the Mac OS X machine has a hostname of *tichops.*

1. On *tichops,* double-click the OSXvnc application. Select a display number (we've selected 1 in this example). The port number will be filled in automatically once you've selected the display number. Next, enter a password that can connect to the VNC server, and click the Start Server button. This step is illustrated in Figure 26-9.

   You can also *ssh* to *tichops* and start OSXvnc from the command line. For a list of command-line options enter:

   ```
   /Applications/OSXvnc.app/OSXvnc-server -help
   ```

2. On the Solaris machine, *mrchops*, enter:

   ```
   ssh -L 5902:localhost:5901 tichops
   ```

3. In another *xterm* window on *mrchops,* enter:

   ```
   vncviewer localhost:2
   ```

4. The resulting VNC connection is shown in shown in Figure 26-10.

Figure 26-9. Starting the OSXvnc server

Figure 26-10. Mac OS X desktop displayed and controlled on a Solaris GNOME desktop

Although we could control the Mac OS X desktop from the Sun Solaris machine, the image quality of the Mac OS X desktop shown in Figure 26-10 is rather poor on the systems we used (Sun Ultra 10-440 running Solaris 8 and a PowerBook G4 running Mac OS X Panther).

A wrapper application for OSXvnc, Share My Desktop (SMD), is available from Bombich Software (*http://www.bombich.com/software/smd.html*) and is licensed under the GNU General Public License. This handy little application reduces the process of launching the OSXvnc server to a one-click operation. To start the VNC server, just launch the SMD application and click the "Start Sharing" button as shown in Figure 26-11. A random password and port for the VNC server is automatically chosen. You can modify the default setting in SMD's Preferences. In particular, you can keep the password private (it is displayed as asterisks in the SMD main window), and either generate a random password (default) or specify your own password. Additionally, you can select two energy saving settings: allow the screen to dim, and allow the computer to sleep.

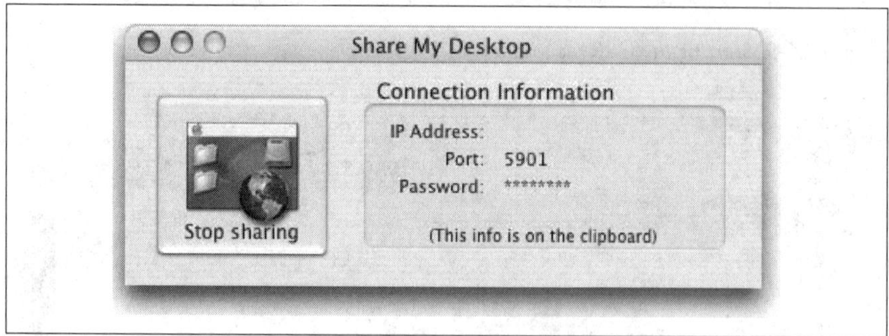

Figure 26-11. Share My Desktop's one click to start/stop the VNC server

If you want the VNC server to run whenever the Mac OS X system is running, SMD provides a way to install and configure a systemwide VNC server that will, optionally, start when you boot up your Mac OS X system. To take advantage of this feature, you need to be logged in as an administrative user. Assuming this is the case, open the SMD application, and select File→Manage System VNC Server to open the dialog window as shown in Figure 26-12.

Click the lock to make changes and supply your administrative password (you must be an administrative user to do this). This pop-up window will allow you to install the VNC server and startup item, configure settings (password, port, display name, start VNC server on startup, allow the screen to dim, allow the computer to sleep), and to turn on/off the System VNC Server. If you click the Install System VNC button, the *OSXvnc-server* and *storepasswd* binaries will be installed in */usr/local/bin* and a startup item in */Library/StartupItems/*. A backup of the */etc/hostconfig* file is also made, in case you later want to uninstall the systemwide VNC server and return to the settings you had prior to the installation of the system VNC.

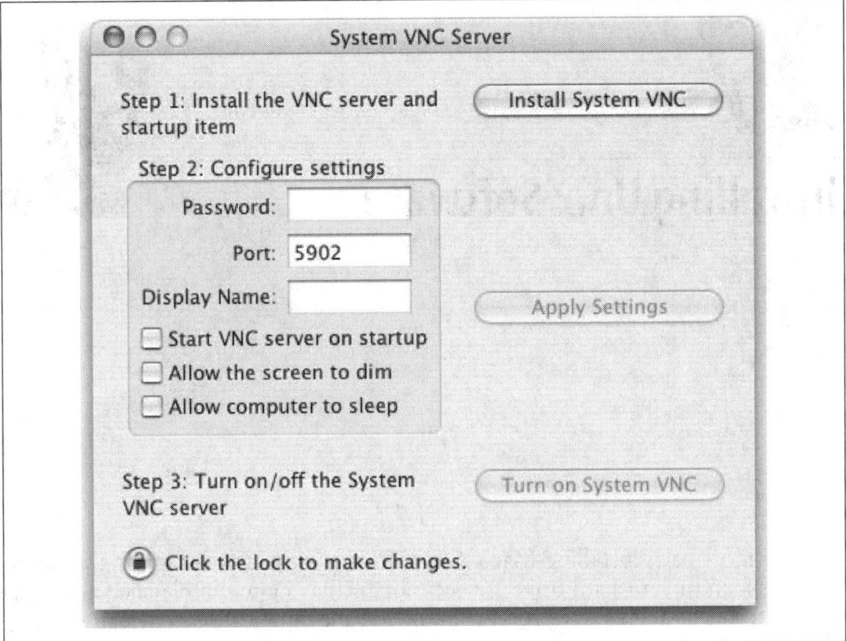

Figure 26-12. Installing a System VNC Server with Share My Desktop

The settings for the systemwide VNC server are stored in */etc/vnc_settings*, and the password is stored in */etc/vnc_pass*. Changing the "Start VNC server on startup" option resets the value of VNCSERVER in the */etc/hostconfig* file. If you've installed the systemwide VNC server using this procedure, you can uninstall it (along with its configuration files) by clicking the "Uninstall System VNC" button in the same Manage System VNC Server pop-up window. This uninstall procedure also restores the */etc/hostconfig*, which was backed up when you installed VNC server. Since this can overwrite system configuration changes you've made since installing VNC, we suggest that you instead edit the VNCSERVER line so that it is set to `-NO-` instead of `-YES-` and restart.

VNC clients and servers are available for Windows machines, so Windows clients can connect to Mac OS X and other Unix VNC servers. Mac OS X clients can also connect to and control Windows VNC servers (see *http://www.realvnc.com/*). As an alternative to VNC, you can use Microsoft's free Remote Desktop Client (RDC, available at *http://www.microsoft.com/mac/otherproducts/otherproducts.aspx?pid=remotedesktopclient*) to remotely control a Windows desktop from a Mac OS X machine.

27
Installing Unix Software

For the most part, installing Mac OS X software is as easy as dragging an application's icon to your hard drive, or occasionally having to double-click a package icon and run through a few prompts in the Installer application. Thereafter, everything Just Works.

Installing software for Darwin, the Unix side of Mac OS X, is not always so easy. Because Mac OS X's graphical interface tends to keep Darwin and its activities invisible in the background, many Mac OS X users never need to worry about this. However, through Darwin, you have access to a whole world of largely open source software written for the Unix operating system. In Mac OS X's "factory" state (with the Xcode Tools installed), you can immediately start installing and using Unix software that uses a command-line interface (or has no interface at all, as with system daemons). If you install the X Window System (as described in Chapter 26), you can start using all manner of GUI-using Unix software as well.

This chapter discusses the various strategies you have for Darwin-side software installation, including DIY-style compiling from raw source code and the rather friendlier use of package managers.

Package Managers

A *package management system* uses a local database to keep track of software packages installed on the machine and the dependencies that run among them. New packages consult this database to see if other packages whose presence they depend upon are already installed, and they assist with package uninstalls by remembering the location of all the files and directories involved during installation (as well as alerting you in case other installed packages depend on this one, so that removing it would break all of them).

At the time of this writing, Mac OS X is still quite a young OS (despite its ancient Unix roots), so what few package management systems exist are still struggling down the road toward maturity. That said, users willing to spend a little extra time behind the Terminal can expand their Mac's software repertoire safely.

Mac OS X has a native but rudimentary package management system, that uses a filesystem-based database stored in */Library/Receipts*. See the section "Uninstalling applications" in Chapter 5.

Fink

Fink is a package management system based on Debian GNU/Linux's (*http://www.debian.org*) popular *dpkg* and *apt- get* utilities, which let you easily sync a local package-information database with that of a central, Internet-based repository, as well as search for, install, and uninstall packages of ready-to-go binaries with single commands.

You can download Fink's essential command-line tools as a standard Mac OS X package by pointing your web browser to *http://fink.sourceforge.net* and following the instructions contained therein. (This book has left instructions purposefully vague to let the good Fink maintainers modify their online instructions with future releases.)

At the time of this writing, Fink installs all of its packages (including *dpkg* and other essential tools) in a directory called */sw*, creating it in the (likely) event that it doesn't already exist. This is Fink's way of preventing any possible conflicts with software that you (or Mac OS X system CDs and upgrades) might install in more traditional Unix directories.

You can take the road between caution and convenience by telling Fink to install its goodies into */usr/local*, the traditional Unix location for software accessible to all the system's users but not crucial to the system itself. (The distinction is similar between Mac OS X's demarcation of the */System/Library* and */Library* folders.)

Once Fink is installed, the following command-line programs becomes available to you. Consult their respective manpages for a full usage guide to each.

fink
: This command works as an abstract frontend to many of the following commands, including *apt-get* and *apt-cache*.

dpkg
: A lower-level interface to the package manager. You'll likely use *dselect* or *apt-get* more often, but this command gives you some functionality those programs don't. For example, you can see a list of what files a package installs by running *dpkg –L package-name*.

dselect
: A console-based browser of the Fink database and the system's installed and available packages.

apt-get command package

This very handy utility lets you install and modify packages through single commands, including the following:

apt-get install package

Install the named package.

apt-get remove package

Uninstall the named package.

apt-get update

Resynchronize the local Fink database with the central Fink repository via the Internet.

apt-cache

You can use this program to comb through your local Fink database without changing or installing anything. With its *search* command, you can send keyword queries to the database. For example, to see all packages that might deal with XML:

```
[jmac@Jason-McIntoshs-Computer jmac]$ apt-cache search xml
ant - Java based build tool.
dia - Diagram drawing program
expat - C library for parsing XML
gnumeric - Spreadsheet program for gnome, reads many formats
imagemagick - Tools and libs manipulate images in many formats.
libxml - XML parsing library
libxml2 - XML parsing library, version 2
neon - HTTP/WebDAV client library with a C API
[jmac@Jason-McIntoshs-Computer jmac]%
```

You can then, for example, run *apt-get install expat* and suddenly have the expat XML libraries installed on your machine.

Fink Commander, a open source project led by Steve Burr, provides an Aqua-level GUI into your machine's Fink installation. Through this application, you can easily browse and search through Fink's available packages, see which packages you have installed, and install or remove packages with one click.

You can download Fink Commander from *http://finkcommander.sourceforge.net*.

GNU Mac OS X Packages

The GNU Mac OS X Public Archive (*http://www.osxgnu.org*) aims to create standard Mac OS X installer packages (of the sort described in the section "Software Installers" in Chapter 5) for the ever-growing wealth of software under the GNU open source license, a staple of the Unix world. Unlike Fink, it doesn't provide its own package management framework, instead using and extending the bare-bones package management utilities that already ship as part of Mac OS X. In other words, you can install and manage packages without having to drop into the Terminal.

Where Fink has Fink Commander, the GNU Mac OS X archive has Mac OS X's Package Manager, an Aqua application that lets you view the packages you have installed on your Mac and gives you an easy way to delete any you no longer need. (It also provides assistance in creating packages of your own, in keeping with the GNU Mac OS X project's goals.)

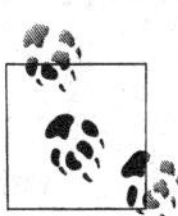

Unlike Fink Commander, the Mac OS X Package Manager won't version-track and download packages for you; you've got to do that yourself, via the project's web site. Mac OS X's package manager just isn't as intertwined with the Internet as is the Debian package manager Fink employs.

Installing from Source

Open source Unix software not available as Mac OS X packages exists as bundles of raw (usually C) source code and helper files. Fortunately, there are some long-standing traditions and idioms with Unix source installation that make this process somewhat easier, but there also remain many places to get stuck, which can bewilder those without C-programming experience (and bewilder those *with* experience if the source is messy enough).

The usual idiom for installing software from source runs as follows.

1. Obtain the source code as a *.tar.gz* file (a.k.a. a *tarball*). If you download it through a web browser, StuffIt Expander automatically inflates it into a folder within your browser's download folder (see "File Compression" in Chapter 5); otherwise, manually use StuffIt Expander or (since you're probably in the Terminal already) the *tar* command, with its *xzvf* (*tar*-extract, *gzip*-extract, verbose-mode, file-based) options, like so:

   ```
   [jmac]$ tar xvzf something-i-just-downloaded.tar. gz
   ...output of list of files and directories extracted...
   [jmac]$
   ```

2. *cd* into the directory created through the previous step, and read the *README* and *INSTALL* files (and generally anything else with an all-caps filename), if they exist. These provide important information, including hints for installing the software on various systems—if Darwin or Mac OS X appear here, you're in luck. Also consult any information found on the web site for the *ftp* directory from which you obtained the source. Be generally suspicious of tarballs that don't contain any of this documentation.

3. Run the software's *configure* script (by typing **./configure**). This script examines your computer, noting its processor type and the operating system that it runs, and tries to build a *Makefile* with commands and settings that will help the software compile correctly on it.

   You can feed the *configure* script some arguments to give it hints or force some of its settings. If it can't figure out what kind of OS you have (it will tell you as much, if so), you can help it out a little by copying the files */usr/share/libtool/config. guess* and */usr/share/libtool/config.sub* into the current directory and running *./configure* again. These two files, kindly provided by Apple, can give a helpful nudge to a Unix source that has never seen Darwin before, providing it with some introductory configuration information. (Alternately, you can try running it again, this time typing:

```
./configure --with-host-type=powerpc-apple-darwinversion-number
```

where *version-number* is the number you see when you run *uname -v*.)

4. Run the system's *make* command. This will try building the software, based on the *Makefile* generated through the previous step.

   This is the do-or-die step of attempting to build from source. As the build process advances step by step, it echoes every compiler or shell command that it attempts to run. If everything compiles smoothly, the process silently exits, leaving the software ready to test and install. Otherwise, it will spew asterisk-studded error messages at you, leaving you to puzzle out what to do next.

   If the latter situation occurs, you have a few options. First, look at the first error message. If it complains about something obvious, like a missing file or directory, see if you can satisfy the problem by building symlinks, changing your working directory, or adjusting the *Makefile* and running *make* again. (Subsequent invocations of *make* will resume the build where it left off, unless you run *make clean* at some point to delete all the interim files and directories.) If it can't find a library, confirm that you have the library it's seeking, then try giving it a hint as to where it can find the library, either by manually re-running the last echoed compiler command with an additional *-L* argument, or by adjusting the *Makefile* to change or expand its library-path variables. If all else fails (which it often will), turn to a web-searching resource such as Google.com, running a search query such as:

   ```
   "mac os x" "software-name" "error-message"
   ```

   and seek wisdom from those who may have traveled this path before you.

   All this explains why prepackaged software is a good thing.

5. If you survived the *make* ordeal, congratulations. Try running *make test*. Not all source distributions include a test suite (ones that don't just return a message such as `Unable to make target "test"`) here, but if they do, it's worth running to see if everything works as it should.

6. Finally, run *make install*. This copies all the build binaries, libraries, and manpages into their permanent homes across the filesystem. In the likely event that the software in question installs in some place other than your home directory, you'll need to run *sudo make install*. Depending on the software, you may be able to get away with a home-directory installation, but often you have to provide the *configure* script with an argument such as *--prefix=/Users/username*. Consult the software's *README* file.

You should now be able to *cd* to some location other than the source directory (such as your home directory) and, if the freshly installed software included executables, invoke them from the command line.

28
Unix Command Reference

This chapter presents the Mac OS X user, programmer, and system administration commands available through the Terminal (see Chapter 18). Each entry is labeled with the command name on the outer edge of the page. The syntax line is followed by a brief description and a list of available options. Many commands come with examples at the end of the entry. If you need only a quick reminder or suggestion about a command, you can skip directly to the examples.

Typographic conventions for describing command syntax are in the Preface. For help in locating commands, see the Index at the back of this book.

We've tried to be as thorough as possible in listing the options. Basic command information and most options should be correct; however, new options are added, and sometimes older options may have been dropped. You may, therefore, find some differences between the options you find described here and the ones on your system. When there seems to be a discrepancy, check the manpage (by way of the `man` command). For most commands, you can also use the `--help` option to get a brief usage message. (Even when it isn't a valid option, it usually results in an "invalid option" error message, along with the usage message.)

Traditionally, commands take single-letter options preceded by a single hyphen, like `-d`. A more recent Unix convention allows long options preceded by two hyphens, like `--debug`. Often, a feature can be invoked through either the old style or the new style of options.

Some options can be invoked only by a user with root (superuser) privileges (see the section "Acting as Root" in Chapter 10).

There are 309 Unix commands listed in this chapter, many of which don't have manpages, or worse—inaccurate manpages—on the system. These commands give you the basics of what you need to know to get under the hood of your Mac OS X system ... and more.

Alphabetical Summary of Commands

The sections that follow list the more commonly used Unix commands in alphabetical order. The page footer on right-hand pages references the last command listed on that page.

ac

```
ac [options] [users]
```

Displays accumulative Aqua and shell login times for *users*, or for all users if none is specified. By default, ac reads from */var/log/wtmp* (see also `last`).

Options

`-d` Show totals for each day.

`-p` Show totals for each user.

`-w` *file*
: Read accounting data from *file* instead of */var/log/wtmp*.

appleping

```
appleping host [ packet-size [ npackets ]]
```

Sends AppleTalk Echo Protocol (AEP) request packets to *host* and displays transmission statistics if successful. The AppleTalk *host* is specified in either of the following ways:

name:type[@zone]
: The host's *name* and *type*, as shown by the `atlookup` command. If *zone* isn't specified, the current zone is used.

`network-node`
: The host's network and node number in hexadecimal, as shown by the `atlookup` command.

Options

packet-size
: Send packets of *packet-size* bytes (a value between 14 and 599). The default value is 64.

npackets
: Send *npackets* number of packets before stopping. If *npackets* is not specified, `appleping` continues until you've sent an interrupt (using Control-C, for example).

appletalk

```
appletalk options
```

Displays or configures AppleTalk network interfaces. Any user may display settings, but only the superuser may change them. `appletalk` allows you to start and stop AppleTalk on a single port (network interface), or configure AppleTalk routing or multihoming on multiple ports.

General options

`-d` Deactivate AppleTalk.

`-n` Show current AppleTalk interface, network number, node ID, and zone name.

`-p` Show AppleTalk information stored in parameter RAM (PRAM).

`-s` Show AppleTalk statistics.

Single port options

`-h` *[zone]*
: Change the default AppleTalk zone to *zone*, or if *zone* isn't specified, display the current zone.

`-q` Use with `-u` to start AppleTalk in quiet mode; doesn't prompt for zone selection.

`-u` *port*
: Start AppleTalk on the network interface *port* (`en0`, for example).

Multiple port options

`-c` Verify the AppleTalk configuration file, */etc/appletalk.cfg*, without starting AppleTalk. Use with `-r` or `-x`.

`-e` Same as `-c`, but also display the AppleTalk configuration.

`-f` *file*
: Use *file* instead of the default */etc/appletalk.cfg* to start AppleTalk. Use with `-r` or `-x`.

`-j` Display AppleTalk router status.

`-m` *n* Limit routing speed to a maximum *n* packets per second.

`-q` Use with `-r` or `-x` to start AppleTalk in quiet mode; doesn't prompt for zone selection.

`-r` Start AppleTalk in routing mode.

`-t` Show the AppleTalk routing table.

`-v` *n* Set the maximum number of entries in the AppleTalk routing table to *n*. Use with `-r` or `-x`. Useful with large AppleTalk networks.

`-w` *n* Set the maximum number of entries in the Zone Information Protocol (ZIP) table to *n*. Use with `-r` or `-x`. Useful with large AppleTalk networks.

-x Start AppleTalk in multihoming mode.

-z List all AppleTalk zones.

Examples

Stop AppleTalk, using sudo to gain superuser privileges:

```
$ sudo appletalk -d
```

Start AppleTalk on the en1 interface:

```
$ sudo appletalk -u en1
```

Start an AppleTalk router in quiet mode:

```
$ sudo appletalk -q -r
```

---

appletviewer

appletviewer [*options*] *urls*

Connects to the specified *urls* and runs any Java applets they specify in their own windows, outside the context of a web browser.

Options

-debug
: Run the applet viewer from within the Java debugger, *jdb*.

-encoding *name*
: Specify the input HTML file encoding.

-J *opt*
: Pass *opt* on to the java command. *opt* shouldn't contain spaces; use multiple -J options if necessary.

---

apply

apply [*options*] *command arguments*

Allows you to run a given command multiple times, each time with a different argument. By default, apply pairs and runs *command* followed by each argument listed in *arguments*. To place the argument elsewhere in *command*, mark that location in *command* with %*n*, where *n* is the *n*th unused item listed in *arguments* (see examples).

Options

-a*character*
: Use *character* instead of %.

-*number*
: Instead of pairing arguments one at a time with *command*, use them *number* at a time with *command*. If *number* is 0, none of the arguments will be used with

command, but *command* will still run once for each item listed in *arguments*. If *command* contains %n, *number* is ignored.

Examples

Ping three different hosts, sending three packets to each:

```
$ apply 'ping -c3' host1.com host2.com host3.com
```

Ping three different hosts, sending a different number of packets to each:

```
$ apply -2 'ping -c' 3 host1.com 4 host2.com 5 host3.com
```

Ping three different hosts, and write output to file *pinglog*:

```
$ apply 'ping -c3 %1 >> pinglog' host1.com  host2. comø
host3.com
```


---

apropos

```
apropos keywords
```

Looks up one or more keywords in the online manpages. Same as `man -k`. See also `whatis`.

---

asr

```
asr -source sourcepath -target targetpath [options] asr
-imagescan imagepath
```

Copies the contents of a disk image or source volume onto a target volume. `asr` (Apple Software Restore) can also scan and prepare disk images when given the `-imagescan` option, allowing the images to be restored from more efficiently. `asr` usually needs to run as root.

sourcepath can be the pathname of either a disk image or a volume, while *targetpath* can specify only a volume. Volumes can be specified by either their */dev* entries (e.g., */dev/disk0s10*) or mountpoints (e.g., */Volumes/Disk 2*).

For disk image creation, use either Disk Copy or the command line utility `hdiutil`. Once a volume has been restored, it might be necessary to use the bless utility to make it bootable. (See `hdiutil` and `bless`).

For a complete description of the imaging and restoration process, as well as tips on optimizing restores using the buffer settings, see the `asr` manpage.

Options

`-buffers` *n*
: During block-copies, use *n* number of buffers instead of the default eight.

`-blockonly`
: When used with `–imagescan`, insert only information relevant to block-copies. This makes the scan much faster, but an image scanned with `–blockonly` can't be block-copied; an error will occur.

`-buffersize` *n*
: During block-copies, use buffers of size *n* bytes instead of the default 1000. *n* can also be specified in bytes, kilobytes, megabytes, or gigabytes by appending it with `b`, `k`, `m`, or `g`, respectively.

`-csumbuffers` *n*
: Use *n* number of buffers specifically for checksumming. By default, checksumming is performed with the same buffers used for copying.

`-csumbuffersize` *n*
: Use checksum buffers of size *n* bytes. *n* can also be specified in bytes, kilobytes, megabytes, or gigabytes by appending it with `b`, `k`, `m`, or `g`, respectively.

`-debug`
: Print additional information during operation to assist in troubleshooting.

`-disableOwners`
: Don't enable the owners for the source and target. By default, `asr` ensures that all owners are enabled, allowing for more accurate file-by-file copying. If given, this option is ignored during block-copies.

As of `asr` Version 14.4, this option doesn't function as described; if given, `-disableOwners` behaves as if the `-debug` option were given instead.

`-erase`
: Erase the target volume before copying to it. If this option is not used, `asr` will instead restores in-place, overwriting only those files having the same name and location in both *sourcepath* and *targetpath* and copying from *sourcepath* anything not already in *targetpath*. Using the `-erase` option allows `asr` to perform a block-copy restore, which can be faster than the file-by-file copying procedure used when restoring in place.

`-h` Print a brief help message. This option can only be used by itself.

`-imagescan` *imagepath*
: Scan disk image *imagepath* and generate checksums. Scanning optimizes images that `asr` will use as source images for restores. This option can only be used by itself.

`-nocheck`
: Don't verify copied data. By default, `asr` uses checksums generated during the image scan for verification. This option will bypass that verification, allowing `asr` to restore from images that haven't first been scanned.

`-noprompt`
: Don't prompt before erasing *targetpath* when the `-erase` option is used.

`-nowrapper`
: Force an HFS wrapper to not be created on the target volume if the `-erase` option is used.

`-rebuild`
: Rebuild the Classic system's desktop database on *targetpath*.

-wrapper
: Create an HFS wrapper on the target volume if the -erase option is used.

-v
: Print version information. This option can only be used by itself.

-verbose
: Print verbose progress and error messages.

Examples

Typically, asr requires root privileges, provided by the sudo command in these examples:

Clone one volume to another:

```
$ sudo asr -source /Volumes/Mac\HD -target /Volumes/Disk\ ↵
2 -erase
```

Restore-in-place from a disk image:

```
$ sudo asr -source /Volumes/Images/image1.dmg - target ↵
/Volumes/Disk\ 2
```

---

at

at [*options*] [*time*] [*date*] [+ *increment*]

Executes commands entered on standard input at a specified *time* and optional *date*. (See also batch and crontab.) End input with EOF. *time* can be formed either as a numeric hour (with optional minutes and modifiers) or as a keyword. *date* can be formed either as a month and date, a day of the week, or a special keyword. *increment* is a positive integer followed by a keyword. See the following lists for details.

at won't run until you first enable atrun by uncommenting its line in */etc/crontab*.

Options

-f *file*
: Execute commands listed in *file*.

-m
: Send mail to user after job is completed (if an MTA such as *sendmail* is configured to run).

-q *queuename*
: Schedule the job in *queuename*. Values for *queuename* are the lowercase letters a through l. Queue a is the default queue for at jobs. Queue b is the queue for batch jobs. Queues with higher letters run with increased niceness (receive less priority).

Time

hh:mm [modifiers]
: Hours can have one or two digits (a 24-hour clock is assumed by default); optional minutes can be given as one or two digits; the colon can be omitted if the format is *h*, *hh*, or *hhmm*; e.g., valid times are 5, 5:30, 0530, and 19:45. If modifier am or pm is added, *time* is based on a 12-hour clock.

`midnight` | `noon` | `now` | `teatime`
: Use any one of these keywords in place of a numeric time. `now` must be followed by an *`increment`*. `teatime` is 4:00 P.M.

Date

`month num [year]` | *`MM/DD/YY`* | *`DD.MM.YY`*
: *`month`* is one of the 12 months, abbreviated to their first three letters; *`num`* is the calendar day of the month; *`year`* is the four- digit year. If the given *`month`* occurs before the current month, `at` schedules that month next year.

`today` | `tomorrow`
: Indicate the current day or the next day. If *`date`* is omitted, `at` schedules `today` when the specified *`time`* occurs later than the current time; otherwise, `at` schedules `tomorrow`.

Increment

Supply a numeric increment if you want to specify an execution time or day relative to the current time. The number should precede any of the keywords `minute`, `hour`, `day`, or `week` (or their plural forms).

Examples

Note that the first two commands are equivalent:

```
$ at 1945 Dec 9
$ at 7:45pm Dec 9
$ at now + 5 hours
$ at noon tomorrow
```

---

at_cho_prn

```
at_cho_prn [type[@zone]]
```

Specifies the default AppleTalk printer be used with `atprint`. With no arguments, `at_cho_prn` prompts you to choose from the list of zones, and then from the list of network-visible entities (NVEs) of type `LaserWriter` and `ImageWriter` in the chosen zone. Use *type* to specify a different type of NVE to list. Use *zone* to specify a zone to search, bypassing the zone selection prompt. `at_cho_prn` requires superuser privileges to run.

---

atlookup

```
atlookup [options] [scope]
```

Lists network-visible entities (NVEs) on the AppleTalk network. If *scope* isn't specified, `atlookup` lists all NVEs in the current zone.

Options

`-a`
: Show only NVE names and types in the list; don't include network numbers.

`-C`
: When used with `-z`, display zones in several columns instead of one.

-d Print network numbers in decimal format instead of the default hexadecimal.

-r *n* Retry unsuccessful lookups *n* times. The default is 8.

-s *n* Retry unsuccessful lookups *n* seconds apart. The default is one second.

-x Convert nonprintable characters in lists to their hexadecimal equivalents, prefaced with /.

-z List all zones on the network. Used alone or with -C.

Scope

Specify the scope of the lookup by NVE *name*, *type*, and *zone* using this syntax:

```
[name[:type[@zone]]]
```

You can use the = wildcard anywhere in *name* or *type* to match zero or more characters, except with older AppleTalk Phase 1 nodes, which ignore such lookups. The = wildcard works with all AppleTalk nodes, however, when used by itself to match all names or types. Lookups are not case-sensitive.

Examples

Display all NVEs of type darwin in the current zone:

```
$ atlookup =:darwin
```

Display all NVEs on printers named with sales in the current zone (not AppleTalk Phase 1 compliant):

```
$ atlookup sales=:=
```

---

atprint

```
atprint [printer]
```

Sends data from standard input to AppleTalk printer *printer*, or the printer chosen with at_cho_prn if no printer is specified. Specify *printer* using the [*name*[:*type*[@*zone*]]] syntax as described for atlookup. If the printer is a PostScript device, you must first reformat non-PostScript data, such as plaintext, to PostScript before printing with atprint. You can do this easily using enscript, as shown in the first example.

Examples

Print text file *addresslist* to the AppleTalk PostScript printer sales:

```
$ enscript -p- | atprint addresslist | sales
```

Print grep's manpage to the at_cho_prn chosen printer, using man's -t option to format it for PostScript printing:

```
$ man -t grep| atprint
```

atq

```
atq [options]
```

Lists jobs created by the `at` command that are still in the queue. Normally, jobs are sorted by the order in which they execute.

Options

`-q` *queuename*
: Show jobs pending in queue *queuename*.

`-v` Show jobs that have completed but not yet been deleted.

atrm

```
atrm jobIDs
```

Removes jobs queued with `at` that match the specified *jobIDs*.

atstatus

```
atstatus [printer]
```

Displays the status of AppleTalk printer *printer* or the printer chosen with `at_cho_prn` if no printer is specified. Specify *printer* using the [*name*[:*type*[@*zone*]]] syntax as described for `atlookup`.

AuthorizationTrampoline

```
AuthorizationTrampoline command filedesc argument...
```

An SUID *root* program that invokes actions with superuser privileges on behalf of applications calling the *AuthorizationExecuteWithPrivileges* routine (part of the Security framework's Authorization Services API). Successful use of this routine requires authorization against the `system.privilege.admin` right defined in */etc/authorization*, meaning that it's limited to *root* and to those in the *admin* group.

Options/Usage

argument
: A list of arguments to be passed to *command*.

command
: The path to the program to be executed with superuser privileges.

filedesc
: A file descriptor for a temporary file containing the authorization reference obtained by the application calling *AuthorizationExecuteWithPrivileges*. The reference is used by `AuthorizationTrampoline` to determine if the request should be allowed.

autodiskmount

```
autodiskmount [-d] [-v] [-a] [-F [-V vol_name]]
```

Automatically discovers and mounts disk volumes.

Options/Usage

-a Mount removable disk volumes, as well as volumes on fixed disks.

-d Print debugging information to standard output.

-F Print the device name and filesystem type of the largest unmounted HFS+ or UFS volume on an internal fixed disk to standard output. If all volumes are the same size, prints information for the first one found. If -a is specified, prints information for all such volumes.

-v Should print a list of mounted volumes to standard error after it's finished working, but this doesn't work in Panther.

-V Print information only for the specified volume, if found.

automount

```
automount -help
automount -V
automount [-m map_directory map [-mnt mount_directory] [-1]]... [-a mount_
directory] [-d] [-D { mount | nsl | options | proc | select | all }]... [-f]
[-s] [-tcp] [-tl timeout] [-tm timeout]
```

Provides transparent, automated access to NFS and AFP shares. When running, any filesystem access to *map_directory* is intercepted by automount. Typically, automount will then set up a symbolic link from *map_directory* or one of its subdirectories to a mount point under *mount_directory*, automatically creating directories and mounting remote volumes as needed. It will also unmount remote volumes that have been idle for too long. Directories or mounts set up by automount are removed when automount exits.

automount makes use of *maps* to determine how to mount volumes. When using a file as a map, the format is similar to that used by NFS automounters on other Unix platforms. Each entry in the file consists of a single line, either a comment beginning with a hash mark (#) or a mount directive of the form:

```
subdirectory server:/pathname
```

If this line were included in a file named */etc/mountmaps*, and automount were called like so:

```
# automount -m /mount_directory /etc/mountmaps
```

upon accessing */mount_directory*, automount would mount the NFS-exported *server:/pathname* on */private/mount_directory/subdirectory* and create a symlink to that mount point from */mount_directory/subdirectory*.

At one time it was also possible to use a map stored in a NetInfo database under */mountmaps/*, but that functionality has been deprecated in future versions of Mac OS X.

In addition to map files, there are several special maps available. Foremost among them are those used by default on Mac OS X systems, `-fstab`, `-static`, and `-nsl`. The following commands are run from the *NFS* startup item:

```
automount -m /Network -nsl
automount -m /automount/Servers -fstab -mnt /private/var/automount/↵
Network/Servers -m /automount/static -static -mnt /private/var/automount
```

Both `-fstab` and `-static` maps use similar configuration formats, stored in an Open Directory database under */mounts/*. The following configuration line will trigger *automount* when using the `-fstab` map:

```
server:/subdirectory /mount_point url↵
  net,url==afp://;AUTH=NO%20USER%20AUTHENT@server/share_name 0 0
```

The AFP mount will be the example used for the remainder of this section, but an equivalent NFS configuration looks like this:

```
server:/subdirectory /mount_point nfs net 0 0
```

There are several options for getting this configuration into Open Directory; one is to use `niload fstab` *`domain`*, then enter the configuration line, followed by Ctrl-D. It's stored in Open Directory like this (as displayed by `nidump -r /mounts` *`domain`*):

```
{
  "name" = ( "mounts" );
  CHILDREN = (
    {
      "dir" = ( "/mount_point" );
      "dump_freq" = ( "0" );
      "name" = ( "server:/subdirectory" );
      "opts" = ( "net", "url==afp://;
                        AUTH=NO%20USER%20AUTHENT@server/share_name" );
      "passno" = ( "0" );
      "vfstype" = ( "url" );
    }
  )
}
```

The `net` option is the signal for this configuration line to be used by `automount` with the `-fstab` map. Without the `net` option, this configuration line is picked up by the `-static` map.

With this configuration, and `automount` called like so:

```
# automount -m /automount/Servers -fstabø
  -mnt /private/var/automount/Network/Servers
```

upon accessing */automount/Servers*, *automount* would mount *`share_name`* from *server* on */private/var/automount/Network/Servers/server/*`subdirectory`, and create a symlink from */automount/Servers/*`server`. (Alternatively, the mount may be accessed via */Network/Servers/*`server`, thanks to a symlink created by the NFS startup item.) The configured mount point (the value of the *dir* property) is ignored by the `-fstab` map.

Don't use a map_*directory* argument to -m that traverses a symlink, or any accesses to the mount will hang. For example, it's OK to do this:

```
# automount -m /private/tmp/map_dir -fstab
```

but not this:

```
# automount -m /tmp/map_dir -fstab
```

because */tmp* is a symlink to */private/tmp*.

While the -static map uses a configuration very much like that for -fstab, its mounting and linking behavior is significantly different. With a configuration like this (viewed as the output of nidump fstab *domain*):

```
server:/subdirectory /mount_point url ↵
  url==afp://;AUTH=NO%20USER%20AUTHENT@server/share_name 0 0
```

and automount called like so:

```
# automount -m /automount/static -static -mnt /private/var/automount
```

upon accessing */mount_point*, automount would mount *share_name* from *server* on */private/var/automount/mount_point*, create a symlink to this from */automount/static/mount_point*, and then another from */mount_point* to */automount/static/mount_point*. The configured *server:/subdirectory* (the value of the *name* property) is ignored by the -static map for AFP shares. (Incidentally, the term "static" is a misnomer. Mounts are made dynamically when they're accessed, just as with the -fstab map.)

The -nsl map uses the Network Services Location service discovery API to automatically find available shares on the network (just as the Finder's Connect to Server... menu item does) and create mounts for them. With automount invoked like this:

```
# automount -m /Network -nsl
```

discovered shares are mounted on subdirectories of */private/var/automount/Network/server*, with a symlink created from */Network/server*.

Before version 10.3, the -nsl map didn't really work, and generated I/O errors when access to a mount was attempted. The automount command, which uses the -nsl map in the NFS startup item, was added in Panther.

Another special map is the -user map. It doesn't actually cause any remote filesystems to be mounted on its own; it merely sets up symlinks to every user account's home directory from the *map_directory*, which may be useful if you want a single place to look in for everyone's home directory. But proceed cautiously if you have a very large number of user accounts.

The -host map is meant to automatically mount NFS exports from hosts listed in a NIS hosts map, when accessing a subdirectory of the *map_directory* with the same name as the host. For example, accessing */net/hostname/export* should mount *hostname:/export*, if */net* is the *map_directory*. This is similar to the -hosts map of other NFS automounters.

AFP URLs

The format of the AFP URLs in the `automount` examples is described in the manpage for `mount_afp`, but there are constraints you should be aware of:

- First, *server* must be a valid TCP/IP hostname or IP address, which may be different than the AFP name that shows up, for example, in a Connect to Server... dialog window.
- Second, *share_name* is the AFP name for the share point, which is not necessarily the same as the full pathname to the share point on the server.
- Finally, there are a few ways to handle authentication to the AFP server. If guest access to the share is allowed, you may use a URL like those in the examples for `automount`:

```
afp://;AUTH=NO%20USER%20AUTHENT@server/share_name
```

If user authentication is required, you have two options. The first is to specify the necessary authentication information in the URL like so:

```
afp://username:password@server/share_name
```

However, this makes the authentication password available to anyone with access to the configuration stored in Open Directory. The other option is to leave out the authentication parameters:

```
afp://server/share_name
```

In this case, the user logged into the graphical console is presented with an authentication dialog to enable access to the share. Of course, if no one is logged into the GUI, this won't work, and the mount attempt will fail.

The `-null` map mounts... well, nothing. It will, however, intercept filesystem calls for the *map_directory*, thus effectively mounting an empty directory over whatever might have been there before. In the original `automount`, from which NeXT's and Apple's versions are descended, this was meant to nullify configuration entries included from a network-wide NIS map.

When running in daemon mode, `automount` stores its PID in */var/run/automount.pid* and responds to SIGHUP by reloading its configuration.

Options

`-1`
: Create directories on the path to a `-fstab` mount point one at a time, as they're traversed, rather than creating the entire path to a mount point when the mount is accessed. However, using this option leads to I/O errors when trying to access the mount.

`-a`
: Specify the directory in which mounts are made. Symbolic links from the directory specified in the `-m` option are used to access these mounts. The default is */private/var/automount*.

`-d`
: Send debugging output to standard error, and prevents daemonization.

-D Output debugging messages of the specified type. If the -d option is used, output is to standard error; otherwise it's via *syslog*. Multiple occurrences of this option may be used to specify multiple types.

-f Used internally by *automount* to indicate that the process has already forked during daemonization. (You can see in the output of ps -ax that the automount daemon runs with the -f flag, even though it isn't invoked that way from the NFS startup item.)

-help
: Print a usage statement to standard output.

-m Use the specified map to mount shares and create symlinks from the specified directory to the mount points. The map argument can be an absolute pathname to a file, a map in the */mountmaps/* directory of an Open Directory domain, or one of the special values -fstab, -host, -nsl, -null, -static, or -user. Multiple -m options enable the use of multiple maps. In the absence of a -m option, automount attempts to find maps in Open Directory.

-mnt
: Like *–a*, but specific to a single map.

-s Supposedly create all mounts at startup and never unmount them. However, mounts are still only attempted upon access, at which point automount prints a bus error and dumps core when using this option.

-tcp
: Attempt to mount NFS volumes over TCP, instead of the default UDP.

-tl Specify a time-to-live for mount names, in seconds. After the timeout expires, mounts are rechecked. A timeout of 0 sets an infinite TTL. The default is 10000.

-tm Specify a timeout to retry failing mounts, in seconds. The timeout roughly doubles with each mount attempt, until giving up after a few tries. The default is 20.

-V Print version number and host information to standard output.

banner

banner [-w *width*] *message*

Prints *message* as a poster on the standard output.

Options

-w *width*
: Specify the maximum width of the poster. Default is 132.

basename

```
basename pathname [suffix]
```

Given a *pathname*, strips the path prefix and leaves just the filename, which is printed on standard output. If specified, a filename *suffix* (e.g., *.c*) is removed also. basename is typically invoked via command substitution ('...') to generate a filename. See also dirname.

Example

Given the following fragment from a Bourne shell script:

```
ofile=output_file
myname="`basename $0`"
echo "$myname: QUITTING: can't open $ofile" 1>&2
exit 1
```

If the script is called do_it, the following message is printed on standard error:

```
do_it: QUITTING: can't open output_file
```

batch

```
batch [options]
```

Executes commands entered on standard input. Ends with EOF. Unlike at, which executes commands at a specific time, batch executes commands one after another (waiting for each one to complete). This avoids the potentially high system load caused by running several background jobs at once. See also at.

batch is equivalent to issuing the command at -q b now.

Options

-f *file*
: Execute commands listed in *file*.

-m
: Send mail to user after job is completed (if an MTA such as *sendmail* is configured to run).

Example

```
% batch
sort in > out
troff -ms bigfile > bigfile.ps
EOF
```

bc

```
bc [options] [files]
```

Interactively performs arbitrary-precision arithmetic or converts numbers from one base to another. Input can be taken from *files* or read from the standard input. To exit, type quit or EOF.

Options

-c Don't invoke dc; compile only. (Because bc is a preprocessor for dc, bc normally invokes dc.)

-l Make available functions from the math library.

-q Quiet, don't print welcome message.

-s Don't use extensions to POSIX bc.

-v Print version number.

-w Warn if extensions are used.

bc is a language (and compiler) whose syntax resembles that of C. bc consists of identifiers, keywords, and symbols, which are briefly described here. Examples follow at the end of this section.

Identifiers

An identifier is a single character, consisting of the lowercase letters a–z. Identifiers are used as names for variables, arrays, and functions. Within the same program, you may name a variable, an array, and a function using the same letter. The following identifiers would not conflict:

x Variable *x*.

x[i]
: Element *i* of array *x*. *i* can range from 0 to 2047 and can also be an expression.

x(y,z)
: Call function *x* with parameters *y* and *z*.

Input/output keywords

ibase, obase, and scale each store a value. Typing them on a line by themselves displays their current value. More commonly, you would change their values through assignment. Letters A–F are treated as digits whose values are 10–15.

ibase = *n*
: Numbers that are input (e.g., typed) are read as base *n* (default is 10).

obase = *n*
: Numbers displayed are in base *n* (default is 10). Note: once ibase has been changed from 10, use digit "A" to restore ibase or obase to decimal.

scale = *n*
: Display computations using *n* decimal places (default is 0, meaning that results are truncated to integers). scale is normally used only for base-10 computations.

Statement keywords

A semicolon or a newline separates one statement from another. Curly braces are needed only when grouping multiple statements.

`if` *(rel-expr) {statements}*
: Do one or more *statements* if relational expression *rel-expr* is true; for example:

```
if (x == y) i = i + 1
```

`while` *(rel-expr) {statements}*
: Repeat one or more *statements* while *rel-expr* is true; for example:

```
while (i > 0) {p = p*n; q = a/b; i = i-1}
```

`for` *(expr1; rel-expr; expr2) {statements}*
: Similar to `while`; for example, to print the first 10 multiples of 5, you can type:

```
for (i = 1; i <= 10; i++) i*5
```

`break`
: Terminate a `while` or `for` statement.

`quit`
: Exit `bc`.

Function keywords

`define` *j (k) {*
: Begin the definition of function *j* having a single argument *k*. Additional arguments are allowed, separated by commas. Statements follow on successive lines. End with a }.

`auto` *x , y*
: Set up *x* and *y* as variables local to a function definition, initialized to 0 and meaningless outside the function. Must appear first.

`return`*(expr)*
: Pass the value of expression *expr* back to the program. Return 0 if (*expr*) is left off. Used in function definitions.

`sqrt`*(expr)*
: Compute the square root of expression *expr*.

`length`*(expr)*
: Compute how many digits are in *expr*.

`scale`*(expr)*
: Same as previous, but count only digits to the right of the decimal point.

Math library functions

These are available when `bc` is invoked with `-l`. Library functions set `scale` to 20.

`s`*(angle)*
: Compute the sine of *angle*, a constant or expression in radians.

`c`*(angle)*
: Compute the cosine of *angle*, a constant or expression in radians.

`a`*(n)*
: Compute the arctangent of *n*, returning an angle in radians.

e(*expr*)
: Compute e to the power of *expr*.

l(*expr*)
: Compute natural log of *expr*.

j(*n, x*)
: Compute Bessel function of integer order *n*.

Operators

These consist of operators and other symbols. Operators can be arithmetic, unary, assignment, or relational.

Arithmetic	`+ - * / % ^`
Unary	`- ++ --`
Assignment	`=+ =- =* =/ =% =^ =`
Relational	`< <= > >= == !=`

Other symbols

/* */
: Enclose comments.

() Control the evaluation of expressions (change precedence). Can also be used around assignment statements to force the result to print.

{} Used to group statements.

[] Array index.

"*text*"
: Use as a statement to print *text*.

Examples

Note that when you type some quantity (a number or expression), it is evaluated and printed, but assignment statements produce no display:

```
ibase = 8          Octal input
20                 Evaluate this octal number
16                 Terminal displays decimal value
obase = 2          Display output in base 2 instead of base 10
20                 Octal input
10000              Terminal now displays binary value
ibase = A          Restore base 10 input
scale = 3          Truncate results to three places
8/7                Evaluate a division
1.001001000        Oops! Forgot to reset output base to 10
obase = 10         Input is decimal now, so "A" isn't needed
8/7
1.142              The Terminal displays result (truncated)
```

The following lines show the use of functions:

```
define p(r,n){     Function p uses two argument
  auto v           v is a local variable
  v = r^n          r raised to the n power
```

```
  return(v)}        Value returned
scale = 5
x = p(2.5,2)        x = 2.5 ^ 2
x                   Print value of x
6.25
length(x)           Number of digits
3
scale(x)            Number of places to right of decimal point
2
```

biff

```
biff [y | n | b]
```

Turns mail notification on or off. With no arguments, `biff` indicates the current status.

When mail notification is turned on, each time you get incoming mail, the bell rings, and the first few lines of each message are displayed. `biff` depends on the `comsat` daemon to be running. If the `b` option is specified, incoming mail rings the bell but doesn't print any lines of the message.

bless

```
bless [folder options | device options | info options]
```

Enables a device containing a Mac OS 9, Darwin, or Mac OS X system folder to be bootable and selects an enabled device or system folder to be the default boot system. `bless` can also report the current boot settings.

Folder options

Use `bless`'s folder options to enable and select system folders.

`-bootinfo` *pathname*
: Enable a volume on New World Macintoshes to boot into Mac OS X by copying file *pathname* into the Mac OS X system folder (specified with `-folder`) to use as the BootX file. *pathname* is typically */usr/standalone/ppc/bootx.bootinfo*.

`-bootBlocks`
: Enable a volume to boot into Mac OS 9 by setting the required boot blocks.

`-bootBlockFile` *pathname*
: Enable a volume to boot into Mac OS 9 by setting the required boot blocks, which are extracted from the data fork of file *pathname*.

`-folder` *pathname*
: Bless a Mac OS X system for booting, identified by its CoreServices directory *pathname*. (See example.)

`-folder9` *pathname*
: Bless a Mac OS 9 folder for booting or use by Classic, identified by its system folder *pathname*. (See example.)

`-label` *name*
: Use *name* as the system volume label used by the OS Picker, which appears when the Option key is held during startup.

`-labelfile` *file*
: Use *file* as an existing, pre-rendered label for the OS picker.

`-mount` *pathname*
: Select to boot from volume *pathname* using its already blessed system folder, instead of selecting a specific folder. Specify a volume by its mount point pathname, such as */Volumes/Macintosh HD*.

`-openfolder` *directory*
: Open *directory* when the volume is attached.

`-save9`
: Retain the blessing of the blessed Mac OS 9 system folder when the `-folder` or `-mount` option is used, but the `-folder9` option is not.

`-saveX`
: Retain the blessing of the blessed Mac OS X system folder when the `-folder` or `-mount` option is used, but the `-folder` option is not.

`-setBoot`
: Set the specified partition as the boot partition.

`-setOF`
: Set the computer to boot at next startup from the system specified by the `-folder` or `-folder9` option. `bless` writes to Open Firmware's `boot-device` variable.

`-system` *pathname*
: Enable a volume to boot into Mac OS 9 by setting the required boot blocks, which are extracted from the System file *pathname*.

`-systemfile` *pathname*
: Insert the data fork of System file *pathname* into the System file of the Mac OS 9 system folder specified by the `-folder9` option.

`-use9`
: When both the `-folder` and `-folder9` options are given, use the Mac OS 9 system as the default system for that volume.

Device options

Use `bless`'s device options to set up new boot devices.

`-bootBlockFile` *pathname*
: Enable the volume specified by `-device` to boot into Mac OS 9 by setting the required boot blocks, which are extracted from the data fork of file *pathname*.

`-device` *pathname*
: Select an unmounted device for setup by opening its block file *pathname*

`-format [fstype]`
: Use filesystem type *fstype* to format the device specified by the `-device` option. If *fstype* isn't specified, `bless` format the device using HFS+ with an HFS wrapper.

`-fsargs arguments`
: Apply additional *arguments* when preparing the device specified by the `-device` option. *arguments* can be any options that exist for the `newfs` command.

`-label name`
: Use *name* as the label for the new filesystem specified by the `-device` option.

`-mount pathname`
: Use *pathname* as the temporary mount point for the HFS wrapper.

`-setOF`
: Set the computer to boot at next startup from the device specified by the `-device` option. `bless` sets this by writing to Open Firmware's `boot-device` variable.

`-system pathname`
: Use the file specifications from file *pathname* instead of from both the files specified by the `-bootBlockFile` and `-wrapper` options.

`-wrapper pathname`
: Mount the HFS wrapper on the mount point specified by `-mount` and insert the System file *pathname* into the wrapper, making it the default System file.

`-xcoff pathname`
: Enable a volume on Old World Macintoshes to boot into Mac OS X using file *pathname* as the HFS+ StartupFile. *pathname* is typically */usr/standalone/ppc/bootx.xcoff*.

Info options

`-bootBlocks`
: Display fields from the boot blocks of volume specified by `-info`.

`-info [pathname]`
: Display the blessed system folder(s) on volume *pathname* or the default startup volume as set in Open Firmware if *pathname* isn't specified.

`-plist`
: Provide all information in *plist* format; used with `-info`.

General options

`-quiet`
: Operate in quiet mode; don't produce any output.

`-verbose`
: Be verbose; print extra output.

Examples

Bless a Mac OS X–only volume, and have it boot at next restart:

```
$ bless -folder "/Volumes/Mac  OS X/System/ Library/ø
CoreServices" -setOF
```

Set a current system volume that holds both a Mac OS X and a Mac OS 9 system to boot Mac OS 9 at next restart:

```
$ bless -folder9 "/Volumes/Mac  OS 9/System Folder" -saveXø
-use9 -setOF
```

See the bless manpage for more examples.

---

cal

```
cal [options] [[month] year]
```

With no arguments, prints a calendar for the current month. Otherwise, prints either a 12-month calendar (beginning with January) for the given *year* or a one-month calendar of the given *month* and *year*. *month* ranges from 1 to 12; *year* ranges from 1 to 9999.

Options

-j
: Print all days with Julian dates, which number from 1 (for January 1) to the last day of the year.

-y
: Print the entire calendar for the current year.

Examples

```
$ cal -j 12 2003
$ cal 2003 > year_file
```

---

calendar

```
calendar [option]
```

Reads your *calendar* file and displays all lines that contain the current date. The *calendar* file is like a memo board. You create the file and add entries such as the following:

```
5/4     meeting with design group at 2 pm
may 6   pick up anniversary card on way home
```

When you run calendar on May 4, the first line is displayed. calendar can be automated by using crontab or at, or by including it in your startup files *.profile* or *. login*.

Options

-A *num*
: Print the next *num* days in the future, including today.

-a
: Allow a privileged user to invoke calendar for all users, searching each user's login directory for a file named calendar. Entries that match are sent to a user via mail. This feature is intended for use via cron. It isn't recommended in networked environments with large user bases.

-B *num*
: Print the previous *num* days in the past, including today.

-d *MMDD [[YY]YY]*
: Display lines for the given date.

-F *daynum*
: Specify "virtual Friday," the last day before the weekend.

-f *filename*
: Display calendar items from file *filename* instead of the default *calendar* file in your home directory.

-l *n*
: Display calendar items up to *n* days ahead from the current date as well.

-W *num*
: Print the next *num* days in the future, including today, but not counting weekend days in the count.

-w *n* Force calendar to skip over weekends. Display calendar items up to *n* days ahead from the current date only when the current day is a Friday. The default for *n* is 2.

---

cancel

```
cancel [options] [printer]
```

Cancels print requests made with `lp`. The request can be specified by its ID, by the *printer* on which it is currently printing, or by the username associated with the request (only privileged users can cancel another user's print requests). Use `lpstat` to determine either the *id* or the *printer* to cancel.

Options

-a Cancel all queued requests to the specified *printer*.

-h Specify the hostname of the print server hostname, "localhost" by default.

-u *username*
: Cancel jobs for user *username*.

id Cancel print request *id*.

---

cat

```
cat [options] [files]
```

Reads one or more files and print them on standard output. Reads standard input if no files are specified or if – is specified as one of the files; end input with EOF. Use the > shell operator to combine several files into a new file; >> appends files to an existing file.

Options

-b Like -n, but don't number blank lines.

-e Print a $ to mark the end of each line. Implies the -v option.

-n Number lines.

-s Squeeze out extra blank lines.

-t Print each tab as ^I. Implies the -v option.

-u Print output as unbuffered (default is buffered in blocks or screen lines).

-v Display control characters and other nonprinting characters.

Examples

Display a file:

```
$ cat ch1
```

Combine files:

```
$ cat ch1 ch2 ch3 > all
```

Append to a file:

```
$ cat note5 >> notes
```

Create file at terminal; end with EOF:

```
$ cat > temp1
```

Create file at terminal; end with STOP:

```
$ cat > temp2 << STOP
```

CCLEngine

CCLEngine -l *integer* -f *filename* -s { 0 | 1 } -e { 0 | 1 } -c { 0 | 1 } -p { 0 | 1 } -d { 0 | 1 } -m { 0 | 1 | 2 } [-v] [-E] -S *octal_integer* -I *string* -i *URL* -C *string* -T *phone_num* -U *username* -P *password*

Parses a modem script and initiates a PPP dialout. When a PPP connection is attempted, pppd starts up, parses */Library/Preferences/SystemConfiguration/preferences.plist*, and calls CCLEngine with the appropriate arguments.

Options

-c If set to 1, enable Van Jacobson TCP/IP header compression. This is the opposite of the novj option to pppd, and is obtained from the IPCPCompressionVJ parameter in */Library/Preferences/SystemConfiguration/preferences.plist*.

-C If the modem script asks for input, this option provides the label for the alternate button (i.e., the one that's not labeled "OK") on the dialog that pops up. Normally this is set to "Cancel."

-d If set to 1, start dialing the modem without waiting for a dial tone. This corresponds to the modemdialmode option to pppd and is obtained from the DialMode parameter in */Library/Preferences/SystemConfiguration/preferences.plist*.

-e If set to 1, enable compression and error correction in the modem. This corresponds to the modemcompress and modemreliable options to pppd, and is obtained from the ErrorCorrection parameter in */Library/Preferences/SystemConfiguration/preferences.plist*.

`-E` Print output to standard error.

`-f` Provide the name of a modem script, normally in */System/Library/Modem Scripts/*. This corresponds to the `modemscript` option to `pppd` and is obtained from the `ConnectionScript` parameter in */Library/Preferences/SystemConfiguration/preferences.plist*.

`-i` If the modem script asks for input, this option provides a URL for the icon on the dialog that pops up. Normally this is set to *file://localhost/System/Library/Extensions/PPPSerial.ppp/Contents/Resources/NetworkConnect.icns*.

`-I` If the modem script asks for input, this option provides the title for the dialog that pops up. Normally this is set to "Internet Connect."

`-l` Specify the service ID for the network configuration to use from */Library/Preferences/SystemConfiguration/preferences.plist*. This corresponds to the *serviceid* option to *pppd*.

`-m` Determine whether the modem should try to connect (`0`), disconnect (`1`), or be set up to answer calls (`2`).

`-p` If set to `1`, the modem uses pulse dialing. This corresponds to the `modempulse` and `modemtone` options to `pppd`, and is obtained from the `PulseDial` parameter in */Library/Preferences/SystemConfiguration/preferences.plist*.

`-P` Specify the password to use for PPP authentication.

`-s` If set to `1`, enable sound output from the modem through the computer speakers. This corresponds to the `modemsound` option to `pppd`, and is obtained from the `Speaker` parameter in */Library/Preferences/SystemConfiguration/preferences.plist*.

`-S` Specify the *syslog* priority level and facility to use for logging errors. The argument is an octal integer that serves as the first argument to a *syslog* system call, as described in the *syslog* manpage and in */usr/include/sys/syslog.h*. The low-order digit specifies priority level from `0` (*emerg*) to `7` (*debug*), while the higher-order digits specify facility. The default is `150`, which logs to the *`remoteauth`* facility at *emerg* level.

`-T` Specify the telephone number to dial. This corresponds to the `remoteaddress` and `altremoteaddress` options to `pppd`, and is obtained from the `CommRemoteAddress` and `CommAlternateRemoteAddress` parameters in */Library/Preferences/SystemConfiguration/preferences.plist*.

`-U` Specify the username to use for PPP authentication. This corresponds to the `user` option to `pppd` and is obtained from the `AuthName` parameter in */Library/Preferences/SystemConfiguration/preferences.plist*.

`-v` If set to `1`, enable verbose logging to */tmp/ppp.log*. Taken from the `VerboseLogging` parameter in */Library/Preferences/SystemConfiguration/preferences.plist*.

cd9660.util

```
cd9660.util { -m | -M } device mount_point
cd9660.util { -p | -u } device
```

Mounts ISO-9660 (CD-ROM) filesystems into the directory hierarchy.

Options

-m
: Mount the device.

-M
: Attempt to force the mount.

-p
: Probe the device and print the volume name to standard output.

-u
: Unmount the device. This function doesn't appear to work.

device
: The CD device filename, e.g., *disk1s2*.

mount_point
: The directory on which the CD filesystem is mounted.

certtool

```
certtool { v | d | D } filename [h] [v] [d]
certtool y [h] [v] [k=keychain [c [p=password]]]
certtool c [h] [v] [a] [k=keychain [c [p=password]]]
certtool { r | I } filename [h] [v] [d] [a] [k=keychain [c [p=password]]]
certtool i filename [h] [v] [d] [a] [k=keychain [c [p=password]]] [r=filename
[f={ 1 | 8 | f }]]
```

Manages X.509 SSL/TLS certificates. It uses the Common Data Security Architecture (CDSA) in much the same way that */System/Library/OpenSSL/misc/CA.pl* uses OpenSSL to ease the process of managing certificates.

As arguments it takes a single-letter command, often followed by a filename, and possibly some options.

Options

a
: When adding an item to a keychain, create a key pair including a private key with a more restrictive ACL than usual. (The default behavior creates a private key with no additional access restrictions, while specifying this option adds a confirmation requirement to access the private key which only `certtool` is allowed to bypass.)

c
: As a command, walks you through a series of interactive prompts to create a certificate and a public/private key pair to sign and possibly encrypt it. The resulting certificate (in DER format) is stored in your default keychain. (Note that the first prompt, for a `key and certificate label`, is asking for two space-separated items. Common choices are an organization name for the key and a label designating the purpose of the certificate.)

  As an option, instructs `certtool` to create a new keychain by the name given in the `k` option.

`d` As a command, display the certificate contained in *filename*.

As an option, indicates that the format of the CSR or CRL contained in *filename* is DER (a binary format), instead of the default PEM (an ASCII format, which is essentially a DER certificate with Base64 encoding).

`D` Display the certificate revocation list (CRL) contained in *filename*.

`f` Specify the format of the private key in the file specified with the `r` option. The format is specified by a single character, either `1` (for OpenSSL's PKCS1, the default), `8` (PKCS8), or `f` (FIPS186, or BSAFE).

`h` Print a usage statement to standard output, negating whichever command was given.

`i` Import the certificate contained in *filename* into the default keychain.

`I` Import the CRL contained in *filename* into the default keychain.

`k` Specify the name of a keychain (in *~/Library/Keychains*) to use other than the default.

`p` Specify the keychain password on the command line. To avoid password exposure, it's better to let `certtool` prompt for it.

`r` As a command, walks you through a series of interactive prompts to create a certificate-signing request (CSR) and a public/private key pair to sign and possibly encrypt it. The resulting CSR is stored in *filename*.

As an option, specifies the file containing a private key for the certificate being imported. This is useful if you've used OpenSSL to generate a certificate, instead of `certtool`.

`v` As a command, verifies the CSR contained in *filename*.

As an option, should enable verbose output, but it doesn't actually seem to make a difference.

`y` As a command, displays the certificates and CRLs in the specified keychain.

checkgid

```
checkgid group_name...
```

Checks for the existence of the specified groups. If all groups exist, the return value is 0, and nothing is printed. If any groups don't exist, the return value is 255, and the following is printed to standard error for each nonexistent *group_name*:

```
checkgid: group 'group_name' not found
```

`checkgid` should be run with superuser privileges.

This tool is part of the Apache distribution.

Options

group_name
: Take a list of group names as arguments. It should also be able to take numeric GIDs as *#groupID*, but checkgid always returns successful for arguments of that form.

chflags

```
chflags [options] flags files
```

Changes the file flags of one or more *files*. *flags* is a comma-separated list of file flags, described later. To unset a flag, use the same command but with no added to the front of the flag's name. To view a file's current flags, use the ls -lo command.

Options

-H
: If any of the pathnames given in the command line are symbolic links, follow only those links during recursive operation. Works only with the -R option.

-L
: Follow all symbolic links during recursive operation. Works only with the -R option.

-P
: Follow no symbolic links during recursive operation. Works only with the -R option (the default).

-R
: Recursively descend through the directory, including subdirectories and symbolic links, changing the specified file flags as it proceeds.

Flags

Flag name	Flag set	Who can change
arch	archived	Superuser only
opaque	opaque	Owner or superuser only
nodump	nodump	Owner or superuser only
sappnd	system append-only	Superuser only
schg	system immutable	Superuser only
uappnd	user append-only	Owner or superuser only
uchg	user immutable	Owner or superuser only

Though the system append-only (sappend) and system immutable (schg) flags can be set by the superuser in normal system mode, you can only *unset* them while in single-user mode.

Examples

Setting the user immutable (uchg) flag for a file prevents it from being deleted, changed, or moved. By locking a file in the Finder, you're actually setting its user immutable flag. Therefore, this command locks the file as well:

```
$ chflags uchg importantfile.doc
```

Unset the user immutable flag and thus unlock the file:

```
$ chflags nouchg importantfile.doc
```

chgrp

```
chgrp [options] newgroup files
```

Changes the ownership of one or more *files* to *newgroup*. *newgroup* is either a GID number or a group name known to directory services. You must own the file or be a privileged user to succeed with this command.

Options

`-f` Force error messages to be suppressed.

`-h` Change the permissions of the link, rather than the referent.

`-H` If any of the pathnames given in the command line are symbolic links, follow only those links during recursive operation. Works only with the `-R` option.

`-L` Follow all symbolic links during recursive operation. Works only with the `-R` option.

`-P` Follow no symbolic links during recursive operation. Works only with the `-R` option (the default).

`-R` Recursively descend through the directory, including subdirectories and symbolic links, setting the specified GID as it proceeds.

`-v` Verbose output, showing files as they are changed.

chkpasswd

```
chkpasswd [-c] [-i infosystem] [-l location] [username]
```

Useful for scripts, this prompts for a password which is then compared against the appropriate directory service for the user specified. If the password is correct, `chkpasswd` returns 0; otherwise, it returns 1, and the string `Sorry` is printed to standard error.

Options

`-c` Compare user input with the password hash directly, rather than running it through the *crypt* algorithm first.

`-i` Specify the directory service to use, which may be `file`, `netinfo`, `nis`, or `opendirectory`.

`-l` Depending on the directory service being used, it's either a file (defaults to */etc/master.passwd*), a NetInfo domain or server/tag combo, a NIS domain, or an Open Directory node (like */NetInfo/root*).

username
: Designate whose password is checked. It defaults to that of the user running the command.

chmod

`chmod [option] mode files`

Changes the access *mode* of one or more *files*. Only the owner of a file or a privileged user may change its mode. Create *mode* by concatenating the characters from `who`, `opcode`, and `permission`. `who` is optional (if omitted, default is `a`); choose only one `opcode`.

Options

`-f`
: Suppress error message upon failure to change a file's mode.

`-h`
: Change the permissions of the link, rather than the referent.

`-H`
: If any of the pathnames given in the command line are symbolic links, follow only those links during recursive operation. Works only with the `-R` option.

`-L`
: Follow all symbolic links during recursive operation. Works only with the `-R` option.

`-P`
: Follow no symbolic links during recursive operation. Works only with the `-R` option (the default).

`-R`
: Recursively descend directory arguments while setting modes.

`-v`
: Verbose output, showing files as they are changed. If `-v` appears more than once, the old and new permissions are shown as well.

Who

`u`
: User

`g`
: Group

`o`
: Other

`a`
: All (default)

Opcode

`+`
: Add permission

`-`
: Remove permission

`=`
: Assign permission (and remove permission of the unspecified fields)

Permission

`r`
: Read

`w`
: Write

`x`
: Execute (file) or search (directory)

`X`
: Set the execute bit for all *who* values if any of the execute bits are already set in the specified file; meaningful only in conjunction with the *op* symbol `+`

`s`
: Set user (or group) ID

`t`
: Sticky bit; save text mode (file) or prevent removal of files by nonowners (directory)

`u` User's present permission

`g` Group's present permission

`o` Other's present permission

Alternatively, specify permissions by a three-digit sequence. The first digit designates owner permission; the second, group permission; and the third, others permission. Permissions are calculated by adding the following octal values:

`4` Read

`2` Write

`1` Execute

A fourth digit may precede this sequence. This digit assigns the following modes:

`4` Set UID on execution

`2` Set GID on execution or set mandatory locking

`1` Sticky bit

Examples

Add execute-by-user permission to *file*:

```
$ chmod u+x file
```

Either of the following assigns read-write-execute permission by owner (7), read-execute permission by group (5), and execute-only permission by others (1) to *file*:

```
$ chmod 751 file
$ chmod u=rwx,g=rx,o=x file
```

Any one of the following assigns read-only permission to *file* for everyone:

```
$ chmod =r file
$ chmod 444 file
$ chmod a-wx,a+r file
```

Set the UID, assign read-write-execute permission by owner, and assign read-execute permission by group and others:

```
$ chmod 4755 file
```

chown

```
chown [options] newowner[:newgroup] files
```

Changes the ownership of one or more *files* to *newowner*. *newowner* is either a UID number or a login name known to directory services. The optional *newgroup* is either a GID number or a group name known to directory services. When *newgroup* is supplied, the behavior is to change the ownership of one or more *files* to *newowner* and make it belong to *newgroup*.

Options

-f Force error messages to be suppressed.

-h Change the ownership of the link, rather than the referent.

-H If any of the pathnames given in the command line are symbolic links, follow only those links during recursive operation. Works only with the -R option.

-L Follow all symbolic links during recursive operation. Works only with the -R option.

-P Follow no symbolic links during recursive operation. Works only with the -R option (the default).

-R Recursively descend through the directory, including subdirectories, resetting the ownership ID.

-v Verbose output, showing files as they are changed. If -v appears more than once, the old and new permissions will be shown as well.

---

cksum

cksum [*files*]

Calculates and prints a cyclic redundancy check (CRC) for each file. The CRC algorithm is based on the polynomial used for Ethernet packets. For each file, cksum prints a line of the form:

sum *count filename*

Here, sum is the CRC, *count* is the number of bytes in the file, and *filename* is the file's name. The name is omitted if standard input is used.

---

clear

clear

Clear the Terminal display.

---

cmp

cmp [*options*] *file file2* [*skip1* [*skip2*]]

Compares *file1* with *file2*. Use standard input if *file1* or *file2* is – . To begin the comparison from byte offsets other than at the beginning of the files, use the optional arguments *skip1* and *skip2*, which specify the byte offsets from the beginning of each file. By default, the value is decimal. To use hexadecimal or octal values, precede them with a leading 0x or 0, respectively. See also comm and diff. The exit codes are as follows:

0 Files are identical.

1 Files are different.

2 Files are inaccessible.

Options

`-c, --print-chars`
: Print differing bytes as characters.

`-i N, --ignore-initial= N`
: Ignore differences in the first *N* bytes of input.

`-l`
: For each difference, print the byte number in decimal and the differing bytes in octal.

`-s`
: Work silently; print nothing, but return exit codes.

`-v, --version`
: Output version info.

Example

Print a message if two files are the same (exit code is 0):

```
$ cmp -s old new && echo 'no changes'
```

colcrt

`colcrt [options] [files]`

A postprocessing filter that handles reverse linefeeds and escape characters, allowing output from `tbl` or `nroff` to appear in reasonable form on a terminal. Puts half-line characters (e.g., subscripts or superscripts) and underlining (changed to dashes) on a new line between output lines.

Options

`-`
: Don't underline.

`-2`
: Double space by printing all half lines.

colrm

`colrm [start [stop]]`

Removes specified columns from a file, where a column is a single character in a line. Reads from standard input, and writes to standard output. Columns are numbered starting with 1; begin deleting columns at (including) the *start* column, and stop at (including) the *stop* column. Entering a tab increments the column count to the next multiple of either the *start* or *stop* column; entering a backspace decrements it by 1.

Example

List all of the contents of a directory and remove the permissions, UID and GID, file size, and the date/time information, leaving just the filenames:

```
$ ls -la | colrm 1 50
```

column

```
column [options] [files]
```

Formats input from one or more *files* into columns, filling rows first. Reads from standard input if no files are specified. Checks the COLUMNS environment variable for the current terminal width if necessary.

Options

-c *num*
: Format output into *num* columns.

-s *char*
: Delimit table columns with *char*. Meaningful only with -t.

-t
: Format input into a table. Delimit with whitespace, unless an alternate delimiter has been provided with -s.

-x
: Fill columns before filling rows.

comm

```
comm [options] file1 file2
```

Compares lines common to the sorted files *file1* and *file2*. Three-column output is produced: lines unique to *file1*, lines unique to *file2*, and lines common to both *files*. comm is similar to diff in that both commands compare two files. In addition, comm can be used like uniq; that is, comm selects duplicate or unique lines between two sorted files, whereas uniq selects duplicate or unique lines within the same sorted file.

Options

-
: Read the standard input.

-1
: Suppress printing of Column 1.

-2
: Suppress printing of Column 2.

-3
: Suppress printing of Column 3.

-12
: Print only lines in Column 3 (lines common to *file1* and *file2*).

-13
: Print only lines in Column 2 (lines unique to *file2*).

-23
: Print only lines in Column 1 (lines unique to *file1*).

Example

Compare two lists of top 10 movies and display items that appear in both lists:

```
$ comm -12 shalit_top10 maltin_top10
```

compress

```
compress [options] [files]
```

Reduces the size of one or more *files* using adaptive Lempel- Ziv coding and move to *file.Z*. Restore with uncompress or zcat.

With a filename of -, or with no *files*, compress reads standard input.

Unisys claims a patent on the algorithm used by compress. Today, gzip is generally preferred for file compression.

compress doesn't preserve resource forks or HFS metadata when compressing files that contain them.

Options

-b*n* Limit the number of bits in coding to *n*; *n* is 9–16; 16 is the default. A lower *n* produces a larger, less densely compressed file.

-c Write to the standard output (don't change files).

-f Compress unconditionally; i.e., don't prompt before overwriting files. Also, compress files even if the resulting file would actually be larger.

-v Print the resulting percentage of reduction for *files*.

configd

```
configd [-b] [-B bundle_ID] [-d] [-t pathname] [-v] [-V bundle_ID]
```

The System Configuration Server monitors changes to network-related items such as link status, DHCP assignments, PPP connections, and IP configuration, and provides an API for applications to be notified of these changes. To monitor various items, it uses a set of plug-in configuration agents, including the Preferences Monitor, the Kernel Event Monitor, the PPP Controller Agent, the IP Configuration Agent, and the IP Monitor Agent. The agent plug-ins are located in */System/Library/SystemConfiguration/*. More information on the System Configuration framework can be found at *http://developer.apple.com/techpubs/macosx/Networking/SysConfigOverview926/*.

It's started as a bootstrap daemon, from */etc/mach_init.d/configd.plist* (processed by *register_mach_bootstrap_servers*). When running in daemon mode, configd stores its PID in */var/run/configd.pid*.

Options

-b Disable loading of all agents.

-B Disable loading of the specified agent.

-d Run the process in the foreground, preventing daemonization.

-t Load the agent specified by *pathname*.

-v Enable verbose logging.

-V Enable verbose logging for the specified agent.

cp

```
cp [options] file1 file
cp [options] files directory
```

Copies *file1* to *file2*, or copies one or more *files* to the same names under *directory*. If the destination is an existing file, the file is overwritten; if the destination is an existing directory, the file is copied into the directory (the directory is not overwritten). If one of the inputs is a directory, uses the `-R` option.

`cp` doesn't preserve resource forks or HFS metadata when copying files that contain them. For such files, use `CpMac` or `ditto` instead.

Options

`-f` Remove the target file, if it exists, before creating the new copy. Also, don't prompt for confirmation of overwrites. Overrides previous `-i` or `-n` options.

`-H` If any of the pathnames given in the command line are symbolic links, follow only those links during recursive operation. Works only with the `-R` option.

`-i` Prompt for confirmation (`y` for yes) before overwriting an existing file.

`-L` Follow all symbolic links during recursive operation. Works only with the `-R` option.

`-n` Doesn't overwrite existing target file. Overrides previous `-f` or `-i` options.

`-p` Preserve the modification time and permission modes for the copied file. (Normally `cp` supplies the permissions of the invoking user.)

`-P` Follow no symbolic links during recursive operation. Works only with the `-R` option (the default).

`-R` Recursively copy a directory, its files, and its subdirectories to a destination *directory*, duplicating the tree structure. (This option is used with the second command-line format when at least one of the source *file* arguments is a directory.)

Example

Copy two files to their parent directory (keep the same names):

```
$ cp outline memo ..
```

cpio

```
cpio control_options [options]
```

Copies file archives in from or out to disk or to another location on the local machine. Note that until native drivers for tape drives exist for Mac OS X, `cpio` can't write to tape. Each of the three control options, `-i`, `-o`, or `-p`, accepts different options. (See also `ditto`, `pax`, and `tar`.)

`cpio` doesn't preserve resource forks or metadata when copying files that contain them. For such files, use `ditto` instead.

cpio -i *[options] [patterns]*

Copy in (extract) files whose names match selected *patterns*. Each pattern can include filename metacharacters from the Bourne shell. (Patterns should be quoted or escaped so they are interpreted by cpio, not by the shell.) If no pattern is used, all files are copied in. During extraction, existing files aren't overwritten by older versions in the archive (unless -u is specified).

cpio -o *[options]*

Copy out a list of files whose names are given on the standard input.

cpio -p *[options] directory*

Copy files to another directory on the same system. Destination pathnames are interpreted relative to the named *directory*.

Comparison of valid options

Options available to the -i, -o, and -p options are shown respectively in the first, second, and third row below. (The – is omitted for clarity.)

```
i:     b B c C d E f H I   m  r s S t u v 6
o: a A   B c C       H   L  O           v
p: a           d       l L m          u v
```

Options

-a Reset access times of input files.

-A Append files to an archive (must use with -O).

-b Swap bytes and half-words. Words are 4 bytes.

-B Block input or output using 5120 bytes per record (default is 512 bytes per record).

-c Read or write header information as ASCII characters; useful when source and destination machines are different types.

-C *n* Like -B, but block size can be any positive integer *n*.

-d Create directories as needed.

-E *file*

Extract filenames listed in *file* from the archive.

-f Reverse the sense of copying; copy all files except those that match *patterns*.

-H *format*

Read or write header information according to *format*. Values for *format* are ustar (IEEE/P1003 Data Interchange Standard header) or tar (tar header).

-I *file*

Read *file* as an input archive.

-l Link files instead of copying. Can be used only with -p.

-L Follow symbolic links.

-m Retain previous file-modification time.

`-O file`
: Direct the output to *file*.

`-r` Rename files interactively.

`-s` Swap bytes.

`-S` Swap half-words.

`-t` Print a table of contents of the input (create no files). When used with the `-v` option, resembles output of `ls -l`.

`-u` Unconditional copy; old files can overwrite new ones.

`-v` Print a list of filenames.

`-6` Process a PWB Unix 6th Edition archive format file. Useful only with the `-i` option, mutually exclusive with `-c` and `-H`.

Examples

Generate a list of old files using `find`; use list as input to `cpio`:

```
$ find . -name "*.old" -print | cpio -ocBvO ~/archive
```

Restore from a tape drive (if supported) all files whose name contains "save" (subdirectories are created if needed):

```
$ cpio -icdv "*save*" < /dev/rmt/0
```

To move a directory tree:

```
$ find . -depth -print | cpio -padml /mydir
```

CpMac

`CpMac [-mac] [-p] [-r] source_path [source_path...] dest_path`

Copies files, keeping multiple forks and HFS attributes intact.

Options

`-mac`
: Arguments use legacy Mac OS pathname syntax (i.e., colons as path separators, paths as viewed from the Finder).

`-p` Preserve file attributes.

`-r` Recursively copy directory contents.

---

create_nidb

`create_nidb [tag [master_hostname [root_dir]]`

A Perl script that creates and populates an Open Directory database from the contents of flat files in */etc/*. This may be especially useful if you have configuration information you wish to carry over from another Unix system. Currently *create_nidb* uses the following files:

> */etc/master.passwd*
> */etc/group*
> */etc/hosts*
> */etc/networks*

create_nidb should be run with superuser privileges.

Options

master_hostname
: The name of the host serving the master copy of the Open Directory database. The default is `localhost` if the tag is `local`, otherwise it's the hostname of the system on which *create_nidb* is run.

root_dir
: The directory in which *var/db/netinfo/tag.nidb* is created. The default is `/`.

tag The tag of the Open Directory database. The default is `local`.

---

crontab

```
crontab [-u user] [file]
crontab [-u user] options
```

Runs `crontab` on your current crontab file, or specifies a crontab *`file`* to add to the crontab directory. A privileged user can run `crontab` for another user by supplying `-u` *`user`* before any of the other options.

A crontab file is a list of commands, one per line, that executes automatically at a given time. Numbers are supplied before each command to specify the execution time. The numbers appear in five fields, as follows:

```
Minute        0-59
Hour          0-23
Day of month  1-31
Month         1-12
Day of week   0-6, with 0 = Sunday
```

Use a comma between multiple values, a hyphen to indicate a range, and an asterisk to indicate all possible values. For example, assuming the following crontab entries below:

```
59 3 * * 5        find / -print | backup_program
0 0 1,15 * *      echo "Timesheets due" | mail user
```

The first command backs up the system files every Friday at 3:59 a.m., and the second command mails a reminder on the 1st and 15th of each month.

Options

`-e` Edit the user's current crontab file (or create one).

`-l` List the user's file in the crontab directory.

`-r` Delete the user's file in the crontab directory.

curl

```
curl [options] [URL...]
```

Transfers files to and from servers using one or more URLs. `curl` supports several common protocols specified in *URL*: HTTP, HTTPS, FTP, GOPHER, DICT, TELNET, LDAP, and FILE. The following descriptions and examples cover `curl`'s basic operation; for a complete description, refer to `curl`'s manpage.

The version of `curl` included with versions of Mac OS X at least up to 10.2.1 can cause `curl` to display a "malloc" error after transfers finish. This error doesn't affect the success of the transfers, however, and in most cases can be ignored.

URL expressions

{a, b, c, ...}
: Form multiple URLs, each using one of the alternate variables specified within the braces as part of its string. For example, this string expands into three different URLs: *http://www. somesite.com/~{jonny,andy,miho}*.

[n1–n2]
: Form multiple URLs, each using one of the letters or numbers in the range specified within the brackets as part of its string. For example, this string expands into five different URLs: *http://www[1-5].somesite.com/*. Note that brackets need to be escaped from the shell (i.e., preceded with a backslash or surrounded in quotes).

Selected options

`-C` *offset*, `--continue-at` *offset*
: Resume transfer after skipping the first *offset* bytes of the source file, for cases when the previous transfer attempt was interrupted.

`-M`, `--manual`
: Display a detailed usage manual.

`-o` *filename*, `--output` *filename*
: Save downloaded data to *filename* instead of standard output. If you specify multiple URLs using braces or brackets and use `#`*n* within *filename*, it is replaced in each new filename by each of the multiple values inside the *n*th braces or brackets in the URL (see example).

`-O`, `--remote-name`
: Save downloaded data to a local file of the same name as the remote file, instead of standard output.

`-T` *filename*, `--upload-file` *filename*
: Upload local file *filename* to *URL*. If *URL* ends with a slash, `curl` uses the local filename for the uploaded copy. Otherwise, the name at the end of *URL* is used.

`-#`, `--progress-bar`
: Display a progress bar instead of the default statistics during transfers.

Examples

Perform an anonymous FTP download into the working directory:

```
$ curl -O ftp://ftp.xyzsite.com/installer.sit
```

Download three sequentially named files from two different servers as user *jon*:

```
$ curl "ftp://jon@ftp.{abc,xyz}site.com/ installer[1-3].sit" ↵
-o "#1_installer#2.sit
```

Upload a file to an iDisk's Public folder:

```
$ curl -T archive.tar http://idisk.mac.com/jon4738/Public/
```

---

cut

`cut options [files]`

Selects a list of columns or fields from one or more files. Either `-c` or `-f` must be specified. *list* is a sequence of integers. Use a comma between separate values and a hyphen to specify a range (e.g., `1-10,15,20` or `50-`). See also `paste` and `join`.

Options

`-b list`
: This *list* specifies byte positions, not character positions. This is important when multibyte characters are used. With this option, lines should be 1023 bytes or less in size.

`-c list`
: Cut the character positions identified in *list*.

`-d c`
: Use with `-f` to specify field delimiter as character *c* (default is tab); special characters (e.g., a space) must be quoted.

`-f list`
: Cut the fields identified in *list*.

`-n` Don't split characters. When used with `-b`, `cut` doesn't split multibyte characters.

`-s` Use with `-f` to suppress lines without delimiters.

Examples

Display only `ping` times while pinging a host:

```
$ ping 192.168.10.58 | cut -sd= -f4
```

Find out who is logged on, but list only login names:

```
$ who | cut -d" " -f1
```

Cut characters in the fourth column of *file*, and paste them back as the first column in the same file. Send the results to standard output:

```
$ cut -c4 file | paste - file
```

date

```
date [option] [+format]
date [options] [string]
```

In the first form, prints the current date and time, specifying an optional display *format*. In the second form, a privileged user can set the current date by supplying a numeric *string*. *format* can consist of literal text strings (blanks must be quoted) as well as field descriptors, whose values will appear as described next (the listing shows some logical groupings).

Format

`%n` Insert a newline.

`%t` Insert a tab.

`%m` Month of year (01–12).

`%d` Day of month (01–31).

`%y` Last two digits of year (00–99).

`%D` Date in `%m/%d/%y` format.

`%b` Abbreviated month name.

`%e` Day of month (1–31); pad single digits with a space.

`%Y` Four-digit year (e.g., 2004).

`%C` "Century," or year/1000, as an integer.

`%g` Week-based year within century (00–99).

`%G` Week-based year, including the century (0000–9999).

`%h` Same as `%b`.

`%B` Full-month name.

`%H` Hour in 24-hour format (00–23).

`%M` Minute (00–59).

`%S` Second (00–61); 61 permits leap seconds and double-leap seconds.

`%R` Time in `%H:%M` format.

`%T` Time in `%H:%M:%S` format.

`%k` Hour (24-hour clock; 0–23); single digits are preceded by a space.

`%l` Hour (12-hour clock; 1–12); single digits are preceded by a space.

`%I` Hour in 12-hour format (01–12).

`%p` String to indicate a.m. or p.m. (default is `AM` or `PM`).

`%r` Time in `%I:%M:%S %p` format.

`%a` Abbreviated weekday.

`%A` Full weekday.

%w Day of week (Sunday = 0).

%u Weekday as a decimal number (1–7), Sunday = 1.

%U Week number in year (00–53); start week on Sunday.

%W Week number in year (00–53); start week on Monday.

%V The ISO-8601 week number (01–53). In ISO-8601, weeks begin on a Monday, and week 1 of the year is the one that includes both January 4th and the first Thursday of the year. If the first Monday of January is the 2nd, 3rd, or 4th, the preceding days are part of the last week of the previous year.

%j Julian day of year (001–366).

%Z Time-zone name.

%x Country-specific date format.

%X Country-specific time format.

%c Country-specific date and time format (default is %a %b %e %T %Z %Y; e.g., Mon Feb 23 14:30:59 PST 2004).

The actual formatting is done by the `strftime(3)` library routine.

Options

`-r` *seconds*
: Print the date and time that is *seconds* from the Epoch (00:00:00 UTC, January 1, 1970).

`-u` Display or set the time using Greenwich Mean Time (UTC).

Strings for setting the date

A privileged user can set the date by supplying a numeric *string*. *string* consists of time, day, and year concatenated in one of three ways: *time* or [*day*]*time* or [*day*]*time*[*year*]. Note: don't type the brackets.

time
: A two-digit hour and two-digit minute (*HHMM*); *HH* uses 24- hour format.

day
: A two-digit month and two-digit day of month (*mmdd*); the default is current day and month.

year
: The year specified as either the full four digits or just the last two digits; the default is current year.

Examples

Set the date to February 23 (0223), 4 a.m. (0400), 2004 (04):

```
$ date 0223040004
```

The following command:

```
$ date +"Hello%t Date is %D %n%t Time is %T"
```

produces a formatted date as follows:

```
Hello         Date is 02/23/04
              Time is 17:53:39
```

dc

```
dc [file]
```

An interactive desk calculator program that performs arbitrary-precision integer arithmetic (input may be taken from a *file*). Normally you don't run dc directly because it's invoked by bc (see bc). dc provides a variety of one-character commands and operators that perform arithmetic; dc works like a Reverse Polish calculator; therefore, operators and commands follow the numbers they affect. Operators include + - / * % ^ (as in C, although ^ means exponentiation); some simple commands include:

p
: Print current result.

q
: Quit dc.

c
: Clear all values on the stack.

v
: Take square root.

i
: Change input base; similar to bc's ibase.

o
: Change output base; similar to bc's obase.

k
: Set scale factor (number of digits after decimal); similar to bc's scale.

!
: Remainder of line is a Unix command.

Examples

```
3 2 ^ p     Evaluate 3 squared, then print result
9

8 * p       Current value (9) times 8, then print result
72

47 - p      Subtract 47 from 72, then print result
25

v p         Square root of 25, then print result
5

2 o p       Display current result in base 2
101
```

Spaces aren't needed except between numbers.

Unix Command Reference

dd

```
dd [option = value]
```

Makes a copy of an input file (`if=`) or standard input if there's no named input file, using the specified conditions, and sends the results to the output file (or standard output if `of` isn't specified). Any number of options can be supplied, although `if` and `of` are the most common and are usually specified first. Because `dd` can handle arbitrary block sizes, it is useful when converting between raw physical devices.

`dd` doesn't preserve resource forks or HFS metadata when copying files that contain them.

Options

`bs=`*n*
: Set input and output block size to *n* bytes; this option supersedes `ibs` and `obs`.

`cbs=`*n*
: Set the size of the conversion buffer (logical record length) to *n* bytes. Use only if the conversion *flag* is `ascii`, `asciib`, `ebcdic`, `ebcdicb`, `ibm`, `ibmb`, `block`, or `unblock`.

`conv=`*flags*
: Convert the input according to one or more (comma-separated) *flags* listed next. The first six *flags* are mutually exclusive. The next two are mutually exclusive with each other, as are the following two.

`ascii`
: EBCDIC to ASCII.

`asciib`
: EBCDIC to ASCII, using BSD-compatible conversions.

`ebcdic`
: ASCII to EBCDIC.

`ebcdicb`
: ASCII to EBCDIC, using BSD-compatible conversions.

`ibm`
: ASCII to EBCDIC with IBM conventions.

`ibmb`
: ASCII to EBCDIC with IBM conventions, using BSD-compatible conversions.

`block`
: Variable-length records (i.e., those terminated by a newline) to fixed-length records.

`unblock`
: Fixed-length records to variable length.

`lcase`
: Uppercase to lowercase.

`ucase`
: Lowercase to uppercase.

`noerror`
: Continue processing when errors occur (up to five in a row).

`notrunc`
: Don't truncate the output file. This preserves blocks in the output file that this invocation of `dd` didn't write.

`swab`
: Swap all pairs of bytes.

`sync`
: Pad input blocks to `ibs`.

`count=`*n*
: Copy only *n* input blocks.

`files=`*n*
: Copy *n* input files (e.g., from magnetic tape), then quit.

`ibs=`*n*
: Set input block size to *n* bytes (default is 512).

`if=`*file*
: Read input from *file* (default is standard input).

`obs=`*n*
: Set output block size to *n* bytes (default is 512).

`of=`*file*
: Write output to *file* (default is standard output).

`iseek=`*n*
: Seek *n* blocks from start of input file (like `skip`, but more efficient for disk file input).

`oseek=`*n*
: Seek *n* blocks from start of output file.

`seek=`*n*
: Same as `oseek` (retained for compatibility).

`skip=`*n*
: Skip *n* input blocks; useful with magnetic tape.

You can multiply size values (*n*) by a factor of 1024, 512, or 2 by appending the letters `k`, `b`, or `w`, respectively. You can use the letter `x` as a multiplication operator between two numbers.

Examples

Convert an input file to all lowercase:

```
$ dd if=caps_file of=small_file conv=lcase
```

Retrieve variable-length data; write it as fixed-length to out:

```
$ data_retrieval_cmd | dd of=out conv=sync,block
```

defaults

```
defaults [-currentHost | -host name] command
```

Modifies the defaults system. When you customize your Mac using the System Preferences, all those changes and settings are stored in the defaults system. Everything that you've done to make your Mac your own is stored as XML data in the form of a property list (or *plist*). This property list is, in turn, stored in *~/Library/Preferences*.

Every time you change one of those settings, that particular property list is updated. There are two other ways to alter the property lists: using the Property List Editor application (*/Developer/Applications*) or using the `defaults` command in the Terminal. Whether you use System Preferences, Property List Editor, or the `defaults` command, any changes you make affect the current user.

Options

`-currentHost`
: Perform operations on the local machine.

`-host` *name*
: Perform operations on the specified host.

Commands

`read`
: Print all your current settings.

`read` *domain*
: Print your settings for the specified domain, such as *com. apple.dock*.

`read` *domain key*
: Print the value of the specified key. For example, to see the current Dock orientation, use: `defaults read com.apple.dock orientation`

`read-type` *domain key*
: Print the datatype of the specified key. For example, `defaults read-type com.apple.dock orientation` tells you that the type of the orientation key is *string*.

`write` *domain key value*
: Write a value to the specified key.

`rename` *domain old_key new_key*
: Rename the specified key.

`delete` *domain*
: Delete the specified domain. So, if you issue the command `defaults delete com.apple.dock`, the Dock forgets everything. The next time you log in, the Dock's settings are set to the system default.

`delete` *domain key*
: Delete the specified key. So, if you issue the command `defaults delete com.apple.dock orientation`, the Dock forgets its orientation. The next time you log in, the Dock's settings are set to the system default.

`domains`
: List all the domains in your defaults.

`find` *`string`*
: Search all defaults for the specified string.

`help`
: Print a list of options.

Values

A value may take one of the following forms:

`string`
: Specify a string value. For example: `defaults write com.apple.dock orientation right`.

`-type` *`value`*
: Specify a value of the specified type. The type may be *`string`*, *`float`*, or *`boolean`*. For example, `defaults write com.apple.dock autohide -boolean true`.

`-array` *`[-add] value [value...]`*
: Create or add to a list of defaults. For example, you can create a list of your favorite colors with `defaults write personal.favorites colors -array red, blue`. Use `-add` to add values to an existing array.

`-dict` *`[-add] key value [key value...]`*
: Create or add to a dictionary list. For example, you can create a dictionary of preferred pet foods with `defaults write personal.pets food -dict cat salmon dog steak`.

Using the `defaults` command is not for the foolhardy. If you manage to mangle your settings, the easiest way to correct the problem is to go back to that application's Preferences pane and reset your preferences. In some cases, you can use `defaults delete`, which will be reset to the same defaults when you next log in. Because the `defaults` command affects only the current user, you can also create a user just for testing random `defaults` tips you pick up on the Internet.

Examples

View all the user defaults on your system:

```
$ defaults domains
```

This prints a listing of all the domains in the user's defaults system. The list you see is run together with spaces in between—not quite the prettiest way to view the information.

View the settings for your Terminal:

```
$ defaults read com.apple.Terminal
```

This command reads the settings from the *com.apple.Terminal.plist* file, found in *~/Library/Preferences*. This listing is rather long, so you might want to pipe the output to `less` or `more` to view the contents one screen at a time:

```
$ defaults read com.apple.Terminal | more
```

Change your Dock's default location to the top of the screen:

```
$ defaults write com.apple.Dock orientation top
```

This moves the Dock to the top of the screen underneath the menu bar. After changing that setting, youl need to log out from the system and then log back in to see the Dock under the menu bar.

df

`df [options] [name]`

Reports the number of free disk blocks and inodes available on all mounted filesystems or on the given *name*. (Unmounted filesystems are checked with `-F`.) *name* can be a device name (e.g., */dev/disk0s9*), the directory name of a mount point (e.g., */Volumes/Drive2*), a directory name, or a remote filesystem name (e.g., an NFS filesystem). Besides the options listed, there are additional options specific to different filesystem types or `df` modules.

Options

`-a` Show all mount points, even if mounted with `MNT_IGNORE`.

`-b` Print sizes in 512-byte blocks.

`-g` Print sizes in gigabytes.

`-i` Report free, used, and percent-used inodes.

`-k` Print sizes in kilobytes.

`-l` Show local filesystems only.

`-m` Print sizes in megabytes.

`-n` Print already known, potentially stale statistics about the filesystems, without requesting or calculating new statistics. This should be used only when requesting statistics would cause a large delay.

`-t` *type1 [, type2 , ...]*
Show only filesystem types specified.

diff

`diff [options] [diroptions] file1 file2`

Compares two text files. `diff` reports lines that differ between *file1* and *file2*. Output consists of lines of context from each file, with *file1* text flagged by a < symbol, and *file2* text by a > symbol. Context lines are preceded by the `ed` command (`a`, `c`, or `d`) that convert *file1* to *file2*. If one of the files is `-`, standard input is read. If one of the files is a directory, `diff` locates the filename in that directory corresponding to the other argument (e.g., `diff my_ dir junk` is the same as `diff my dir/junk junk`). If both arguments are directories, `diff` reports lines that differ between all pairs of files having equivalent names (e.g., `olddir/program` and newdir/program); in addition, diff lists filenames unique to one directory, as well as subdirectories common to both. See also cmp.

Options

Options -c, -C, -D, -e, -f, -h, and -n can't be combined with one another (they are mutually exclusive).

-a, --text
: Treat all files as text files. Useful for checking to see if binary files are identical.

-b, --ignore-space-change
: Ignore repeating blanks and end-of-line blanks; treat successive blanks as one.

-B, --ignore-blank-lines
: Ignore blank lines in files.

-c
: Context diff: print three lines surrounding each changed line.

-C *n*, --context*[=n]*
: Context diff: print *n* lines surrounding each changed line. The default context is three lines.

--changed-group-format=*format*
: Use *format* to output a line group containing differing lines from both files in if-then-else format.

-d, --minimal
: Ignore segments of numerous changes and output a smaller set of changes. This may cause a significant slowdown in diff.

-D *symbol*, --ifdef=*symbol*
: When handling C files, create an output file that contains the contents of both input files, including #ifdef and #ifndef directives that reflect the directives in both files.

-e, --ed
: Produce a script of commands (a, c, d) to recreate *file2* from *file1* using the ed editor.

-f
: Produce a script to recreate *file1* from *file2*; the script is in the opposite order, so it isn't useful to ed.

-F *regexp*, --show-function-line*[=regexp]*
: For context and unified diff, show the most recent line containing *regexp* before each block of changed lines.

--forward-ed
: Make output that looks vaguely like an ed script but has changes in the order they appear in the file.

-H
: Speed output of large files by scanning for scattered small changes; long stretches with many changes may not show up.

`-help`
: Print brief usage message.

`--horizon-lines=`*`n`*
: In an attempt to find a more compact listing, keep *n* lines on both sides of the changed lines when performing the comparison.

`-i, --ignore-case`
: Ignore case in text comparison. Uppercase and lowercase are considered the same.

`-I` *regexp*, `--ignore-matching-lines=`*regexp*
: Ignore lines in files that match the regular expression *regexp*.

`--ifdef=`*name*
: Make merged if-then-else format output, conditional on the preprocessor macro *name*.

`-L` *label*, `--label` *label*, `--label=`*label*
: For context and unified `diff`, print *label* in place of the filename being compared. The first such option applies to the first filename and the second option to the second filename.

`--left-column`
: For two-column output (-y), show only left column of common lines.

`--line-format=`*format*
: Use *format* to output all input lines in if-then-else format.

`-n, -rcs`
: Produce output in RCS `diff` format.

`-N, --new-file`
: Treat nonexistent files as empty.

`--new-group-format=`*format*
: Use *format* to output a group of lines taken from just the second file in if-then-else format.

`--new-line-format=`*format*
: Use *format* to output a line taken from just the second file in if-then-else format.

`--old-group-format=`*format*
: Use *format* to output a group of lines taken from just the first file in if-then-else format.

`--old-line-format=`*format*
: Use *format* to output a line taken from just the first file in if-then-else format.

`-p, --show-c-function`
: When handling files in C or C-like languages such as Java, show the function containing each block of changed lines. Assumes `-c`, but can also be used with a unified `diff`.

`-P, --unidirectional-new-file`
: If two directories are being compared, and the first lacks a file that is in the second, pretend that an empty file of that name exists in the first directory.

`-q, --brief`
: Output only whether files differ.

`--sdiff-merge-assist`
: Print extra information to help `sdiff`. `sdiff` uses this option when it runs `diff`.

`--suppress-common-lines`
: Don't print common lines in side-by-side format.

`-t, --expand-tabs`
: Produce output with tabs expanded to spaces.

`-T, --initial-tab`
: Insert initial tabs into output to line up tabs properly.

`--unchanged-group-format=`*`format`*
: Use *`format`* to output a group of common lines taken from both files in if-then-else format.

`-u`
: Unified `diff`; print old and new versions of lines in a single block, with three lines surrounding each block of changed lines.

`-U` *`n`*`, --unified`*`[=n]`*
: Unified `diff`; print old and new versions of lines in a single block, with *n* lines surrounding each block of changed lines. The default context is 3 lines.

`-v, --version`
: Print version number of this version of `diff`.

`-w, --ignore-all-space`
: Ignore all whitespace in files for comparisons.

`-W` *`n`*`, --width=`*`n`*
: For two-column output (-y), produce columns with a maximum width of *n* characters. Default is 130.

`-x` *`regexp`*`, --exclude=`*`regexp`*
: Don't compare files in a directory whose names match *`regexp`*.

`-X` *`filename`*`, --exclude-from=`*`filename`*
: Don't compare files in a directory whose names match patterns described in the file *`filename`*.

`-y, --side-by-side`
: Produce two-column output.

`-`*`n`*
: For context and unified `diff`, print *n* lines of context. Same as specifying a number with `-C` or `-U`.

Diroptions

The following diroptions are valid only when both file arguments are directories.

`-l, --paginate`
: Paginate output by passing it to `pr`.

`-r, --recursive`
: Compare subdirectories recursively.

`-s, --report-identical-files`
: Indicate when files don't differ.

`-S` *`filename`*, `--starting-file=`*`filename`*
: For directory comparisons, begin with the file *`filename`*, skipping files that come earlier in the standard list order.

---

diff3

```
diff3 [options] file1 file2 file3
```

Compares three files and reports the differences. No more than one of the files may be given as – (indicating that it is to be read from standard input). The output is displayed with the following codes:

`====`
: All three files differ.

`====1`
: *`file1`* is different.

`====2`
: *`file2`* is different.

`====3`
: *`file3`* is different.

`diff3` is also designed to merge changes in two differing files based on a common ancestor file (i.e., when two people have made their own set of changes to the same file). `diff3` can find changes between the ancestor and one of the newer files and generate output that adds those differences to the other new file. Unmerged changes are places where both newer files differ from each other and at least one of them is from the ancestor. Changes from the ancestor that are the same in both of the newer files are called *merged changes*. If all three files differ in the same place, it is called an *overlapping change*.

This scheme is used on the command line with the ancestor being *`file2`*, the second filename. Comparison is made between *`file2`* and *`file3`*, with those differences then applied to *`file1`*.

Options

`-3, --easy-only`
: Create an `ed` script to incorporate into *`file1`* unmerged, non-overlapping differences between *`file1`* and *`file3`*.

-a, --text
: Treat files as text.

-A, --show-all
: Create an ed script to incorporate all changes, showing conflicts in bracketed format.

-e, --ed
: Create an ed script to incorporate into *file1* all unmerged differences between *file2* and *file3*.

-E, --show-overlap
: Create an ed script to incorporate unmerged changes, showing conflicts in bracketed format.

-i
: Append the w (save) and q (quit) commands to ed script output.

-L *label*, --label=*label*
: Use *label* to replace filename in output.

-m, --merge
: Create file with changes merged (not an ed script).

-T, --initial-tab
: Begin lines with a tab instead of two spaces in output to line tabs up properly.

-v, --version
: Print version information, and then exit.

-x, --overlap-only
: Create an ed script to incorporate into *file1* all differences in which all three files differ (overlapping changes).

-X
: Same as -x, but show only overlapping changes, in bracketed format.

---

dig

dig [@*server*] *host* [*querytype*] [*queryclass*] [*options*]

Queries Internet domain name servers. Like the nslookup command, dig displays information about *host* as returned by the default or a specified name server. With dig, you specify all aspects of the query on the command line; there's no interactive mode as with nslookup.

Specify the name server to query with @*server*, using either a domain name or an IP in *server*. The default is to query the name servers in *resolv.conf*. Specify the type of query in *querytype*; the default is to look up address records. The supported types are:

A
: Host's Internet address

ANY
: Any available information (default)

AXFR
: Request zone transfer

HINFO
: Host CPU and operating system type

MX
: Mail exchanger

NS
: Nameserver for the named zone

SOA
: Domain start-of-authority

Use *queryclass* to specify query class of either `IN` (Internet) or `ANY`. Default is `IN`.

Options

The following descriptions cover `dig`'s basic operation; for a complete description, refer to `dig`'s manpage.

`-x` *address*
: Reverse map *address*, which allows you to locate a hostname when only an IP number is available. Implies ANY as the query type.

`-p` *port*
: Send queries to the specified port instead of port 53, the default.

`+norec`*[urse]*
: Turn off recursion (on by default).

`+vc`
: Send TCP-based queries (queries are UDP by default).

DirectoryService

```
DirectoryService [-h | -v]
DirectoryService [-appledebug | -appleframework | -applenodaemon |
-appleoptions | -appleperformance | -appleversion]
```

The server process for the Directory Service framework. It's started as a bootstrap daemon, from */etc/mach_init.d/DirectoryService.plist* (processed by *register_mach_bootstrap_servers*).

The manpage for *DirectoryService* on Panther is very good, but this entry details the additional `-apple` options.

Options

`-appledebug`
: Run the service in debug mode, disabling daemonization and logging to */Library/Logs/DirectoryService/DirectoryService.debug.log*.

`-appleoptions`
: Print a usage statement for the second form of command invocation to standard output.

`-appleperformance`
: Run the service in the foreground and log extensively.

`-appleversion`
: Print software build version to standard output.

-h Print a usage statement for the first form of command invocation to standard output.

-v Print software release version to standard output.

dirname

```
dirname pathname
```

Prints *pathname*, excluding the last level. Useful for stripping the actual filename from a pathname. If there are no slashes (no directory levels) in *pathname*, `dirname` prints . to indicate the current directory. See also `basename`.

diskarbitrationd

```
diskarbitrationd [-d]
```

Manages communication between processes about the mounting and unmounting of disk volumes. On Panther, this takes on part of the role formerly held by `autodiskmount` in Jaguar.

`diskarbitrationd` starts as a bootstrap daemon, from */etc/mach_init.d/diskarbitrationd.plist* (processed by *register_mach_bootstrap_servers*), and stores its PID in */var/run/diskarbitrationd.pid*.

Options

-d Run in debug mode, preventing daemonization.

disktool

```
disktool [-l | -r | -x | -y]
disktool [-d | -e | -g | -m | -p | -u | -A | -D | -S] device
disktool -s device integer_flag
disktool -n device vol_name
disktool -a device vol_name vol_flags
disktool -c userID
```

Controls disks, including mounting, unmounting, ejecting, enabling permissions, and volume naming. Most options require a device name argument (e.g., `disk0`), and some require additional parameters.

Options

-a Add disk to Disk Arbitration tables to notify applications of a mounted volume. This is useful if you have forced a mount, thus bypassing standard notification.

-A Activate permissions on the volume, adding an entry to */var/db/volinfo.database* if one doesn't already exist.

-c Specify UID of account to use when mounting disks.

-d Remove disk from Disk Arbitration tables, to notify applications of a dismount. This is useful if you have forced a dismount, thus bypassing standard notification.

-D Deactivate permissions on the volume.

-e Eject disk.

-g Print HFS encoding on a volume to standard output.

-l List disk volumes to standard output.

-m Mount disk.

-n Give the device a new volume name. For HFS, HFS+, and UFS partitions only.

-p Unmount partition. Device name is that of a partition (e.g., `disk0s5`).

-r Refresh Disk Arbitration tables.

-s Set HFS encoding on a volume. Takes encoding as additional integer argument.

-S Print status of volume in */var/db/volinfo.database* to standard output.

-u Unmount disk.

-x Disallow dismounts and ejects.

-y Allow dismounts and ejects.

diskutil

```
diskutil list [device]
diskutil mount[Disk] device
diskutil { info[rmation] | unmount[Disk] | eject | verifyDisk | repairDisk |
enableJournal | disableJournal | verifyPermissions | repairPermissions |
eraseOptical [quick] | zeroDisk | randomDisk [integer] } { mount_point |
device }
diskutil repairOS9Permissions
diskutil rename { mount_point | device } vol_name
diskutil eraseVolume format vol_name { mount_point | device }
diskutil eraseDisk format vol_name [OS9Drivers] { mount_point | device }
diskutil partitionDisk device num_partitions [OS9Drivers | MBRFormat] part1_
format part1_name part1_size [part2_format part2_name part2_size ...]
diskutil checkRAID
diskutil createRAID { mirror | stripe } set_name format device1 device2
[device3...]
diskutil enableRAID mirror device
diskutil destroyRAID { set_UUID | device }
diskutil repairMirror { set_UUID | device } partition_num from_device to_device
```

Controls disk volumes, including mounting, unmounting, ejecting, erasing, journaling, partitioning, fixing permissions, and setting up RAIDs. This is a command-line analog of the Disk Utility application and contains functionality beyond the somewhat less user-friendly `disktool`.

Volumes are specified by mount point (directory on which the volume is mounted) or device name (e.g., `disk0s1`). Filesystem types specified by *format* arguments may be `HFS+`, `JournaledHFS+`, `HFS`, `UFS`, or `MS-DOS`.

Options

`checkRAID`
: Check the status of RAID sets. Requires privileged access.

`createRAID`
: Create a mirror (RAID 1) or a stripe (RAID 0) on a set of devices. Requires privileged access.

`destroyRAID`
: Destroy an existing mirrored or striped RAID set. Requires privileged access.

`disableJournal`
: Disable journaling on an HFS+ volume. Requires privileged access.

`eject`
: If a disk is ejectable, unmount and eject the disk. Requires privileged access, unless the user running `diskutil` is logged into the graphical console.

`enableJournal`
: Enable journaling on an HFS+ volume. The journal keeps a record of all filesystem operations, which allows the system to roll back to a consistent filesystem state in the event of a crash. This eliminates the need for disk verification after a crash. Requires privileged access.

`enableRAID`
: Convert a single disk into an unpaired member of a mirrored RAID set. Requires privileged access.

`eraseDisk`
: Unmount and reformat an entire disk. Requires privileged access.

`eraseOptical`
: Unmount and erase a read/write optical disk. Requires privileged access.

`eraseVolume`
: Unmount and reformat a disk partition. Requires privileged access.

`information`
: Prints data about the device to standard output, including device name, volume name and mount point, filesystem format, disk hardware access protocol, total and free diskspace, and whether the device is read-only or ejectable.

`list`
: List partitions on the system or just on the specified disk device, including device names, volume names, and sizes.

`mount`
: Mount the specified partition. Requires privileged access, unless the user running `diskutil` is logged into the graphical console.

`mountDisk`
: Mount all partitions on the specified disk. Requires privileged access, unless the user running `diskutil` is logged into the graphical console.

`partitionDisk`
: Repartition the specified disk. The `MBRFormat` flag causes the partition map to be DOS-compatible, with a Master Boot Record (MBR). The number of partitions (*`num_partitions`*) is limited to 8. Partition sizes are given as a number concatenated with a letter, where the letter is `B` (for bytes), `K` (for kilobytes), `M` (for megabytes), `G` (for gigabytes), or `T` (for terabytes). The current boot disk can't be repartitioned. Requires privileged access.

`randomDisk`
: Erase a disk while overwriting its contents with random data (optionally, more than once, as specified by an additional argument). Requires privileged access.

`rename`
: Give the device a new volume name. For HFS, HFS+, and UFS partitions only.

`repairDisk`
: Unmount the device, attempt to repair any filesystem inconsistencies it finds, and remount the device. Requires privileged access.

`repairMirror`
: Repair a mirrored RAID set. If `checkRAID` reports a problem with a mirrored partition, this lets you sync the data for that partition from the good copy to the bad copy. Requires privileged access.

`repairOS9Permissions`
: Reset file permissions on the System and Applications folders associated with a user's Classic environment.

`repairPermissions`
: Scan the *Archive.bom* files in */Library/Receipts* for installed software packages and reset file permissions according to what they should have been upon installation. Requires privileged access.

`unmount`
: Unmount the specified partition. Requires privileged access, unless the user running `diskutil` is logged into the graphical console.

`unmountDisk`
: Unmount all partitions on the specified disk. Requires privileged access, unless the user running `diskutil` is logged into the graphical console.

`verifyDisk`
: Unmount the device, scan it for filesystem inconsistencies, and remount the device. Requires privileged access.

`verifyPermissions`
: Scan the *Archive.bom* files in */Library/Receipts* for installed software packages and verify whether file permissions are set according to what they should have been upon installation. Requires privileged access.

`zeroDisk`
: Erase a disk while overwriting its contents with zeros. Requires privileged access.

---

ditto

```
ditto [options] files directory
ditto [options] directory1 directory2
```

Copies files and directories while preserving most file information, including resource fork and HFS metadata information when desired. `ditto` preserves the permissions, ownership, and timestamp of the source files in the copies. `ditto` overwrites identically named files in the target directory without prompting for confirmation.

`ditto` works like `cp` in the first synopsis form. However, the second form differs in that `cp -r` copies the entire *directory1* into an existing *directory2*, while `ditto` copies the contents of *directory1* into *directory2*, creating *directory2* if it doesn't already exist.

Options

`-arch` *arch*
: When copying fat binary files, copy only the code for chip type *arch*. Fat binary files contain different code for different chip architectures. The `-arch` flag allows you to "thin" the binary by copying only the code for the specified chip. Possible values for *arch* include `ppc`, `m68k`, `i386`, `hppa`, and `sparc`.

`-bom` *pathname*
: When copying a directory, include in the copy only those items listed in *BOM* file *pathname*. See also `mkbom` for information on making a *BOM* file.

`-c` Create a CPIO archive at *directory2*.

`-k` Specify that archives are in PKZip format.

`--keepParent`
: Embed *directory1*'s parent directory in *directory2*.

`-rsrcFork`, `-rsrc`
: When copying files, include any resource fork and HFS metadata information.

`-v` Be verbose; report each directory copied.

`-V` Be very verbose; report each file, symlink and device copied.

`-x` Unpack the CPIO archives at *directory1*.

`-X` Don't descend into directories on another device.

`-z` Specify compressed CPIO archives.

Example

Duplicate an entire home directory, copying the contents of directory */Users/chris* into the directory */Volumes/Drive 2/Users/chris* and preserving resource forks and HFS metadata:

```
$ ditto -rsrc /Users/chris "/Volumes/Drive 2/Users/chris"
```

dmesg

`dmesg [options]`

Displays the system control messages from the kernel ring buffer. This buffer stores all messages since the last system boot or the most recent ones, if the buffer has been filled.

Options

`-M` *core*
: Use the specified *core* file from which to extract messages instead of */dev/kmem*.

`-N` *system*
: Use the specified *system* instead of the default */mach_kernel*.

dnsquery

`dnsquery [options] host`

Queries Internet domain name servers. A simpler alternative to `nslookup`, `dnsquery` displays information about *host* as returned by the default or a specified name server.

Options

`-n` *nameserver*
: Query server *namerserver* instead of the default name server specified in */etc/resolve.conf*.

`-t` *type*
: Change type of information returned from a query to one of the following:

  `A` Host's Internet address

  `AFSDB`
  DCE or AFS server

  `ANY` Any available information (default)

  `CNAME`
  Canonical name for an alias

  `HINFO`
  Host CPU and operating system type

  `MG` Mail group member

MINFO
: Mailbox or mail list information

MX
: Mail exchanger

NS
: Nameserver for the named zone

PTR
: Hostname or pointer to other information

RP
: Responsible person

SOA
: Domain start-of-authority

WKS
: Supported well-known services

-c *class*
: Set query class to IN (Internet), CHAOS, HESIOD, or ANY. Default is IN.

-r *number*
: Set number of retries to *number*.

-p *period*
: Set seconds to wait before retries to *period*.

-d
: Turn on debugging mode.

-s, -v
: Connect with the name server using a TCP stream rather than a UDP datagram, the default.

---

drutil

```
drutil help [subcommand]
drutil { version | list | poll }
drutil { info | discinfo | trackinfo | status | cdtext | subchannel | eject
} [-drive drive_spec]
drutil { erase | bulkerase } { full | quick } [-drive drive_spec]
drutil tray { eject | open | close } [-drive drive_spec]
drutil getconfig { current | supported } [-drive drive_spec]
drutil filename filename
drutil dumpiso device block_num [format]
```

Manages disk drives that can write to optical media, using the Disc Recording framework.

Options

bulkerase
: Erase an optical disk as the erase subcommand, then prompt for another disk to erase. This repeats until the process is killed.

cdtext
: Display CD-Text data contained on an audio CD.

discinfo
: Print information about the optical disk in the drive to standard output.

`dumpiso`
: Dump ISO-9660 and Joliet formatting data from an optical disk. The *device* argument is a disk device filename, such as */dev/disk1*. The *block_num* argument specifies the block to dump. The *format* argument is one of `None`, `Boot`, `Dir`, `HFSPlusVH`, `LPath`, `MPath`, `PVD`, `SVD`, `VDST`, or `VPD`.

`eject`
: Unmount and eject an optical disk. Same as `drutil tray eject`.

`erase`
: Erase a rewritable optical disk and eject it. A `quick` erasure removes only formatting information so that the disk appears to be blank; a `full` erasure overwrites the entire disk but takes considerably longer.

filename
: Show how the given filename is converted when burning to an optical disk, given the support available with different formats, including ISO-9660 levels 1 and 2, ISO-9660 with Joliet extensions, and HFS+.

`getconfig`
: Print the features supported by an optical disk drive to standard output. Using `current` lists enabled features, while `supported` lists all possible features. Features include audio CD support, DVD support, power management, and real-time streaming.

`help`
: Print a usage statement to standard output, either for the specified subcommand or for `drutil` as a whole.

`info`
: Print information about drives to standard output, such as vendor, hardware interface, cache size, and write capabilities.

`list`
: Print a list of all disk drives attached to the system that can burn optical disks.

`poll`
: Repeatedly poll an optical drive for information until terminated.

`status`
: Print status information about an optical disk to standard output, such as disk type, number of sessions and tracks, and remaining disk space.

`subchannel`
: Unmount a CD and print subchannel information to standard output, including the CD's media catalog number (MCN) and each track's International Standard Recording Code (ISRC).

`trackinfo`
: Print information about tracks on an optical disk to standard output.

`tray`
: Manipulate drives with motorized trays. Some optical disk drives have trays that can be automatically opened and closed; some can only be opened (and

must be closed) manually; some have nonmotorized trays; and slot-loading drives have no trays. The `eject` argument unmounts a disk and opens the tray, the `open` argument opens a tray only if the drive is empty, and the `close` argument closes the tray.

`version`
: Print the operating system and version, and version identifiers for the Disc Recording framework and I/O Kit to standard output.

`-drive`
: Some systems have multiple writable optical drives. The `-drive` option lets you manipulate a drive other than the one chosen automatically by system. The *`drive_spec`* argument may be one of the following: an integer used to select a particular drive (according the numbering produced by `drutil list`), a string used to match a drive's vendor or product name, or a keyword used to restrict the list of drives that may be manipulated. The keyword is one of `internal`, `external`, `atapi`, `firewire`, `scsi`, or `usb`.

---

du

`du [`*`options`*`] [`*`directories`*`]`

Prints disk usage (as the number of 512-byte blocks used by each named directory and its subdirectories; default is current directory).

Options

`-a` Print usage for all files, not just subdirectories.

`-c` In addition to normal output, print grand total of all arguments.

`-H` Follow symbolic links, but only if they are command-line arguments.

`-h` Human-readable output, with units spelled out: bytes, kilobytes, etc.

`-I` *`mask`*
: Ignore entries matching *`mask`*.

`-k` Print sizes in kilobytes.

`-L` Follow symbolic links.

`-P` Don't follow any symbolic links.

`-s` Print a total for each file specified.

`-x, --one-file-system`
: Display usage of files in current filesystem only.

---

dynamic_pager

`dynamic_pager [-F `*`filename`*`] [-H `*`hire_point`*`] [-L `*`layoff_ point`*`] [-P `*`priority`*`] [-S `*`file_size`*`]`

Manages virtual memory swap files. This tool is started from */etc/rc* during the boot process.

Starting with Panther, when `dynamic_pager` is invoked without `-H`, `-L`, or `-S` options, it creates swap files that are sized dynamically according to paging needs and available disk space.

Options

`-F` Specify the base absolute pathname for swap files. Swap filenames consist of this base and a whole number suffix, starting at `0`. The default is */private/var/vm/swapfile*.

`-H` Create an additional swap file when free swap space drops below the *`hire_point`* in bytes. The default is `0`, which disables the use of this swap space.

`-L` Attempt to consolidate memory and remove a swap file when free swap space rises above the *`layoff_point`* in bytes. The *`layoff_point`* must be set higher than the sum of the swap file size and the *`hire_point`*, unless it is set to `0` (the default), which disables layoffs.

`-P` Determine the priority of this swap space. The default is `0`.

`-S` Determine the size of swap files created, in bytes. The default is `20000000`.

---

echo

```
echo [-n] [string]
```

Echoes arguments to standard output. Often used for producing prompts from shell scripts.

Option

`-n` Suppress printing of newline after text.

Example

```
$ echo "testing printer" | lp
```

---

egrep

```
egrep [options] [regexp] [files]
```

Searches one or more *`files`* for lines that match an extended regular expression *`regexp`*. `egrep` doesn't support the regular expressions \(, \), \n, \<, \>, \{, or \}, but does support the other expressions, as well as the extended set +, ?, |, and ( ). Remember to enclose these characters in quotes. Regular expressions are described in Chapter 22. Exit status is 0 if any lines match, 1 if none match, and 2 for errors.

See `grep` for the list of available options. Also see `fgrep`. `egrep` typically runs faster than those commands.

Examples

Search for occurrences of *Victor* or *Victoria* in *`file`*:

```
$ egrep 'Victor(ia)*' file
$ egrep '(Victor|Victoria)' file
```

Find and print strings such as *old.doc1* or *new.doc2* in *files*, and include their line numbers:

```
$ egrep -n '(old|new)\.doc?' files
```

enscript

enscript [*options*] [*files*]

Converts text files to PostScript for output to a printer or file. This conversion is necessary when printing text files from the command line to most laser printers, for example, because most laser printers are PostScript devices. enscript is a feature-rich application that allows you to modify the printed output in many ways. The following descriptions and examples cover enscript's basic operation; for a complete description, refer to enscript's manpage.

Used with no arguments, enscript receives text from standard input and sends it to the default printer. Otherwise, enscript converts the text files specified in *files*, and directs output to a named printer, file, or standard output as specified by *options* (or the default printer if no options are specified).

Options

-# *n*, -n *n*, --copies=*n*
: Print *n* copies of every page.

-a *pages*, --pages=*pages*
: Print selected *pages*, as specified in the following format:

  begin-end
  : Print from page number begin to page number end.

  -end
  : Print until page number end.

  begin-
  : Print from page number begin to the last page.

  page
  : Print only page number page.

  odd
  : Print only the odd numbered pages.

  even
  : Print only the even numbered pages.

-B, --no-header
: Don't print page headers.

-j, --no-job-header
: Don't print job header page.

--list-options
: List the current enscript option settings.

-r, --landscape
: Print the page in landscape mode, rotated 90 degrees.

-R, --portrait
: Print the page in portrait mode, the default.

-U *n*, --nup=*n*
: Print *n*-up; place *n* pages on each sheet of output.

--margins=*left:right:top:bottom*
: Print with margins of *left*, *right*, *top* and *bottom*, each specified in PostScript points. To use the default value for a margin, omit that argument.

Examples

Print pages 5 through 10, 2-up, of text document *notes.txt*:

```
$ enscript -a 5-10 -U 2 notes.txt
```

Print page 1 of text document *notes.txt*, setting a top margin of 50 points and a bottom margin of 25 points:

```
$ enscript -a 1 --margins=::50:25 notes.txt
```

---

env

```
env [options] [variable=value...] [command]
```

Displays the current environment or, if environment *variables* are specified, sets them to a new *value* and displays the modified environment. If *command* is specified, executes it under the modified environment.

Options

-, -i, --ignore-environment
: Ignore current environment entirely.

-u *name*, --unset *name*
: Unset the specified variable.

--help
: Print help message, and then exit.

--version
: Print version information, and then exit.

---

expand

```
expand [options] [files]
```

Expands tab characters into appropriate number of spaces. expand reads the named files or standard input if no files are provided. See also unexpand.

Options

-*tabs*, -t *tabs*, --tabs *tabs*
: *tabs* is a comma-separated list of integers that specify the placement of tab stops. If exactly one integer is provided, the tab stops are set to every *integer* spaces. By default, tab stops are eight spaces apart. With -t and --tabs, the list may be separated by whitespace instead of commas.

`-i, --initial`
: Convert tabs only at the beginning of lines.

`--help`
: Print help message and then exit.

`--version`
: Print version information and then exit.

Example

Cut columns 10 through 12 of the input data, even when tabs are used:

```
$ expand data | cut -c 10-12 > data.col2
```


expr

```
expr arg1 operator arg2 [operator arg3...]
```

Evaluates arguments as expressions and prints the result. Strings can be compared and searched. Arguments and operators must be separated by spaces. In most cases, an argument is an integer, typed literally or represented by a shell variable. There are three types of operators: arithmetic, relational, and logical. Exit status for `expr` is 0 (expression is nonzero and nonnull), 1 (expression is 0 or null), or 2 (expression is invalid).

`expr` is typically used in shell scripts to perform simple mathematics, such as addition or subtraction. It is made obsolete in the Korn shell by that program's built-in arithmetic capabilities.

Arithmetic Operators

Use the following operators to produce mathematical expressions whose results are printed:

`+`
: Add *arg2* to *arg1*.

`-`
: Subtract *arg2* from *arg1*.

`*`
: Multiply the arguments.

`/`
: Divide *arg1* by *arg2*.

`%`
: Take the remainder when *arg1* is divided by *arg2*.

Addition and subtraction are evaluated last, unless they are grouped inside parentheses. The symbols *, (, and) have meaning to the shell, so they must be escaped (preceded by a backslash or enclosed in single or double quotes).

Relational operators

Use relational operators to compare two arguments. Arguments can also be words, in which case comparisons assume `a < z` and `A < Z`. If the comparison statement is true, the result is 1; if false, the result is 0. Symbols < and > must be escaped.

= Are the arguments equal?

!= Are the arguments different?

> Is *arg1* greater than *arg2*?

>= Is *arg1* greater than or equal to *arg2*?

< Is *arg1* less than *arg2*?

<= Is *arg1* less than or equal to *arg2*?

Logical operators

Use logical operators to compare two arguments. Depending on the values, the result can be *arg1* (or some portion of it), *arg2*, or 0. Symbols | and & must be escaped.

| Logical OR; if *arg1* has a nonzero (and nonnull) value, the result is *arg1*; otherwise, the result is *arg2*.

& Logical AND; if both *arg1* and *arg2* have a nonzero (and nonnull) value, the result is *arg1*; otherwise, the result is 0.

: Similar to grep; *arg2* is a pattern to search for in *arg1*. *arg2* must be a regular expression in this case. If the *arg2* pattern is enclosed in \(\), the result is the portion of *arg1* that matches; otherwise, the result is simply the number of characters that match. By default, a pattern match always applies to the beginning of the first argument (the search string implicitly begins with a ^). To match other parts of the string, start the search string with .*.

Examples

Division happens first; result is 10:

```
$ expr 5 + 10 / 2
```

Addition happens first; result is 7 (truncated from 7.5):

```
$ expr \( 5 + 10 \) / 2
```

Add 1 to variable i; this is how variables are incremented in shell scripts:

```
$ i=`expr $i + 1`
```

Print 1 (true) if variable a is the string "hello":

```
$ expr $a = hello
```

Print 1 (true) if variable b plus 5 equals 10 or more:

```
$ expr $b + 5 \>= 10
```

In the following examples, variable p is the string "version.100". This command prints the number of characters in p:

```
$ expr $p : '.*'           Result is 11
```

Match all characters and print them:

```
$ expr $p : '\(.*\)'       Result is "version.100"
```

Print the number of lowercase letters at the beginning of p:

```
$ expr $p : '[a-z]*'        Result is 7
```

Match the lowercase letters at the beginning of p:

```
$ expr $p : '\([a-z]*\)'  Result is "version"
```

Truncate $x if it contains five or more characters; if not, just print $x. (Logical OR uses the second argument when the first one is 0 or null; i.e., when the match fails.) Double- quoting is a good idea, in case $x contains whitespace characters.

```
$ expr "$x" : '\(.....\)' \| "$x"
```

In a shell script, rename files to their first five letters:

```
$ mv "$x" `expr "$x" : '\(.....\)' \| "$x"`
```

(To avoid overwriting files with similar names, use `mv -i`.)

---

false

```
false
```

A null command that returns an unsuccessful (nonzero) exit status. Normally used in bash scripts. See also `true`.

---

fdisk

```
fdisk [device { -diskSize | -isDiskPartitioned | -installSize |
-sizeofExtended | -freeSpace | -freeWithoutUFS | -freeWithoutUFSorExt |
-isThereExtendedPartition | -isThereUFSPartition | -removePartitioning |
-bootPlusUFS | -dosPlusUFS integer | -setAvailableToUFS | -setExtendedToUFS |
-setExtAndAvailableToUFS | -setUFSActive | -script }] [-bootsectorOnly] [
-useAllSectors] [-useBoot0 [-boot0 filename]] [-heads integer] [-cylinders
integer] [-sectors integer]
```

Provides control over DOS partition maps on disk devices in Darwin x86 systems. Much of its functionality is devoted to managing an Apple UFS partition that Darwin uses as a boot volume. There can be only one Apple UFS partition on a disk.

When invoked without a device name argument, `fdisk` enters interactive mode, in which navigation is performed via a series of menus.

Options

`-boot0`
: Specify a nondefault file to use as the boot program for the `-useBoot0` flag.

`-bootPlusUFS`
: Repartition the disk to include an 8-MB booter partition (which is set active) and the remainder as an Apple UFS partition.

`-bootsectorOnly`
: Limit modification to include only the boot sector. Normally, the first sector of each new partition is erased, but this flag disables that behavior.

`-cylinders`
: Force an assumption of a disk geometry with the specified number of cylinders.

`-diskSize`
: Print the size of the specified device, in megabytes, to standard output.

`-dosPlusUFS`
: Repartition the disk to include a DOS partition of the specified size, in megabytes, and the remainder as an Apple UFS partition.

`-freeSpace`
: Print the size of the largest free area, in megabytes, to standard output.

`-freeWithoutUFS`
: Print the size of the largest free area, in megabytes, to standard output, as if there were no Apple UFS partition present.

`-freeWithoutUFSorExt`
: Print the size of the largest free area, in megabytes, to standard output, as if there were no Apple UFS or extended partitions present.

`-heads`
: Force an assumption of a disk geometry with the specified number of heads.

`-installSize`
: Print the size, in megabytes, of the area that would be taken by Darwin if it were to be installed. If the disk is partitioned, this is equal to the size of the Apple UFS partition; otherwise, it's equal to the size of the entire disk.

`-isDiskPartitioned`
: Print `Yes` to standard output if the disk has a DOS partition map on it, `No` if not.

`-isThereExtendedPartition`
: Print `Yes` to standard output if the disk has a DOS extended partition on it, `No` if not.

`-isThereUFSPartition`
: Print `Yes` to standard output if the disk has an Apple UFS partition on it, `No` if not.

`-removePartitioning`
: Erase the boot sector, which deletes the partition map and the boot program. After this, a Darwin installation will take the entire disk.

`-script`
: Read in a new set of partition entries from standard input.

`-sectors`
: Force an assumption of a disk geometry with the specified number of sectors per track.

`-setAvailableToUFS`
: After deleting any existing Apple UFS partition, create a new Apple UFS partition taking up the largest free area on the disk.

`-setExtAndAvailableToUFS`
: After deleting any existing Apple UFS and extended partitions, create a new Apple UFS partition taking up the largest free area on the disk.

`-setExtendedToUFS`
: Change an existing extended partition to Apple UFS.

`-setUFSActive`
: Make the Apple UFS partition the default boot partition on the disk.

`-sizeofExtended`
: Prints the size of the DOS extended partition, in megabytes, to standard output.

`-useAllSectors`
: Instruct `fdisk` to use all physical sectors on the disk, including those not seen by the BIOS.

`-useBoot0`
: Read in a new boot program from */usr/standalone/i386/boot0*.

`device`
: The disk device filename, e.g. */dev/disk0*.

---

fetchmail

`fetchmail [`*`options`*`] [`*`servers...`*`]`

Retrieves mail from mail servers and forwards it to the local mail delivery system. `fetchmail` retrieves mail from servers that support the common mail protocols POP2, POP3, IMAP2bis, and IMAP4. Messages are delivered via SMTP through port 25 on the local host and through your system's mail delivery agent (such as *sendmail*), where they can be read through the user's mail client. `fetchmail` settings are stored in the *~/.fetchmailrc* file. Parameters and servers can also be set on the command line, which will override settings in the *.fetchmailrc* file.

Options

`-a, --all`
: Retrieve all messages from server, even those that have already been seen but left on the server. The default is to only retrieve new messages.

`-A` *`type`*`, --auth` *`type`*
: Specify the type of authentication. *`type`* may be `password`, `kerberos_v5`, or `kerberos`. Authentication type is usually established by `fetchmail` by default, so this option isn't very useful.

`-B` *`n`*`, --fetchlimit` *`n`*
: Set the maximum number of messages (*n*) accepted from a server per query.

`-b` *`n`*`, --batchlimit` *`n`*
: Set the maximum number of messages sent to an SMTP listener per connection. When this limit is reached, the connection is broken and reestablished. The default of 0 means no limit.

-c, --check
: Check for mail on a single server without retrieving or deleting messages. Works with IMAP, but not well with other protocols, if at all.

-D *[domain]*, --smtpaddress *[domain]*
: Specify the *domain* name placed in RCPT TO lines sent to SMTP. The default is the local host.

-E *header*, --envelope *header*
: Change the header assumed to contain the mail's envelope address (usually "X-Envelope-to:") to *header*.

-e *n*, --expunge *n*
: Tell an IMAP server to EXPUNGE (i.e., purge messages marked for deletion) after *n* deletes. A setting of 0 indicates expunging only at the end of the session. Normally, an expunge occurs after each delete.

-F, --flush
: For POP3 and IMAP servers, remove previously retrieved messages from the server before retrieving new ones.

-f *file*, --fetchmailrc *file*
: Specify a nondefault name for the fetchmail configuration file.

-I *specification*, --interface *specification*
: Require that the mail server machine is up and running at a specified IP address (or range) before polling. The *specification* is given as *interface/ipaddress/mask*. The first part indicates the type of TCP connection expected (sl0, ppp0, etc.), the second is the IP address, and the third is the bit mask for the IP, assumed to be 255.255.255.255.

-K, --nokeep
: Delete all retrieved messages from the mail server.

-k, --keep
: Keep copies of all retrieved messages on the mail server.

-l *size*, --limit *size*
: Set the maximum message size that will be retrieved from a server. Messages larger than this size are left on the server and marked unread.

-M *interface*, --monitor *interface*
: In daemon mode, monitor the specified TCP/IP *interface* for any activity beside itself, and skip the poll if there is no other activity. Useful for PPP connections that automatically time out with no activity.

-m *command*, --mda *command*
: Pass mail directly to mail delivery agent, rather than send to port 25. The *command* is the path and options for the mailer, such as */usr/lib/sendmail -oem*. A %T in the command is replaced with the local delivery address, and an %F is replaced with the message's From address.

-n, --norewrite
: Don't expand local mail IDs to full addresses. This option disables expected addressing and should only be used to find problems.

-P *n*, --port *n*
: Specify a port to connect to on the mail server. The default port numbers for supported protocols are usually sufficient.

-p *proto*, --protocol *proto*
: Specify the protocol to use when polling a mail server. *proto* can be:

  POP2
  : Post Office Protocol 2.

  POP3
  : Post Office Protocol 3.

  APOP
  : POP3 with MD5 authentication.

  RPOP
  : POP3 with RPOP authentication.

  KPOP
  : POP3 with Kerberos v4 authentication on port 1109.

  IMAP
  : IMAP2bis, IMAP4, or IMAP4rev1. fetchmail autodetects their capabilities.

  IMAP-K4
  : IMAP4 or IMAP4rev1 with Kerberos v4 authentication.

  IMAP-GSS
  : IMAP4 or IMAP4rev1 with GSSAPI authentication.

  ETRN
  : ESMTP.

-Q *string*, --qvirtual *string*
: Remove the prefix *string*, which is the local user's hostid, from the address in the envelope header (such as "Delivered-To:").

-r *folder*, --folder *folder*
: Retrieve the specified mail *folder* from the mail server.

-s, --silent
: Suppress status messages during a fetch.

-t *seconds*, --timeout *seconds*
: Stop waiting for a connection after *seconds* seconds.

-U, --uidl
: For POP3, track the age of kept messages via unique ID listing.

-u *name*, --username *name*
: Specify the user *name* to use when logging into the mail server.

-V, --version
: Print the version information for fetchmail and display the options set for each mail server. Performs no fetch.

`-v, --verbose`
: Display all status messages during a `fetch`.

`-Z` *nnn*, `--antispam` *nnn*
: Specify the SMTP error *nnn* to signal a spam block from the client. If *nnn* is `-1`, this option is disabled.

fgrep

```
fgrep [options] pattern [files]
```

Search one or more *files* for lines that match a literal text string *pattern*. Exit status is 0 if any lines match, 1 if not, and 2 for errors.

See `grep` for the list of available options. Also see `egrep`.

Examples

Print lines in *file* that don't contain any spaces:

```
$ fgrep -v ' ' file
```

Print lines in *file* that contain the words in *spell_list*:

```
$ fgrep -f spell_list file
```

file

```
file [options] files
```

Classify the named *files* according to the type of data they contain. `file` checks the magic file (*/etc/magic*) to identify some file types.

Options

`-b` Brief mode: don't print filenames.

`-c` Check the format of the magic file (*files* argument is invalid with `-c`). Usually used with `-m`.

`-F` *separator*
: Print *separator* between file and type, instead of a colon.

`-f` *file*
: Read the names of files to be checked from *file*.

`-i` Print the MIME type of the file instead of a human-readable description.

`-k` Don't stop after the first match.

`-L` Follow symbolic links. By default, symbolic links are not followed.

`-m` *file*
: Search for file types in *file* instead of */etc/magic*.

`-N` Don't pad filenames for alignment.

-v Print the version.

-z Attempt checking of compressed files.

Many file types are understood. Output lists each filename, followed by a brief classification such as:

```
Apple QuickTime movie file (moov)
ASCII text
data
directory
gzip compressed data
empty
PDF document, version 1.4
Mach-O executable ppc
sticky symbolic link to private/tmp
```

Example

List all PDF Version 1.1 files:

```
$ file * | grep "PDF document, version 1.1"
```

find

find [*options*] [*pathnames*] [*conditions*]

An extremely useful command for finding particular groups of files (numerous examples follow this description). `find` descends the directory tree beginning at each *pathname* and locates files that meet the specified *conditions*. The default pathname is the current directory. The most useful conditions include `-print` (which is the default if no other expression is given), `-name` and `-type` (for general use), `-exec` and `-size` (for advanced users), and `-mtime` and `-user` (for administrators).

Conditions may be grouped by enclosing them in `\( \)` (escaped parentheses), negated with `!` (use `\!` in the C shell), given as alternatives by separating them with `-o`, or repeated (adding restrictions to the match; usually only for `-name`, `-type`, `-perm`). Modification refers to editing of a file's contents. Change refers to modification, permission or ownership changes, and so on; therefore, for example, `-ctime` is more inclusive than `-atime` or `-mtime`.

Options

-d Descend the directory tree, skipping directories and working on actual files first (and then the parent directories). Useful when files reside in unwritable directories (e.g., when using `find` with `cpio`).

-E When used with the `-regex` or `-iregex` conditions, interpret the regular expression as extended instead of basic. For more information on regular expressions, see Chapter 22.

-H If any of the pathnames given in the command line are symbolic links, consider the file information of the referenced files and not the links themselves. However, if the referenced file no longer exists, consider the link itself.

-L If any of the files encountered during the search are symbolic links, consider the file information of the referenced files and not the links themselves. However, if the referenced file no longer exists, consider the link itself.

-P If any of the files encountered during the search are symbolic links, consider the file information of the links themselves (the default behavior).

-s Move through directory contents in alphabetical order.

-x Don't scan filesystems (mounted volumes) other than the one that the command begins with.

-X When used with the -xargs action, identify and skip any files whose names contain characters used by -xargs as delimiters (', ", \, space, tab, and newline characters).

Conditions and actions

-amin *+n* | *-n* | *n*
: Find files last accessed more than *n* (*+n*), less than *n* (*-n*), or exactly *n* minutes ago. Note that find changes the access time of directories supplied as *pathnames*.

-anewer *file*
: Find files that were accessed after *file* was last modified.

-atime *+n* | *-n* | *n*
: Find files that were last accessed more than *n* (*+n*), less than *n* (*-n*), or exactly *n* days ago.

-cmin *+n* | *-n* | *n*
: Find files last changed more than *n* (*+n*), less than *n* (*-n*), or exactly *n* minutes ago. A change is anything that changes the directory entry for the file, such as a chmod.

-cnewer *file*
: Find files that were changed after they were last modified.

-ctime *+n* | *-n* | *n*
: Find files that were changed more than *n* (*+n*), less than *n* (*-n*), or exactly *n* days ago.

-delete *+n* | *-n* | *n*
: Delete found files and directories, operating as if the -d flag were being used as well (files first).

-empty
: Continue if file is empty. Applies to regular files and directories.

-exec *command* { } \;
: Run the Unix *command* from the starting directory on each file matched by find (provided command executes successfully on that file; i.e., returns a 0 exit status). When command runs, the argument { } substitutes the current file. Follow the entire sequence with an escaped semicolon (\;).

-execdir *command* { } \;
: Same as -exec, but run the Unix *command* from the directory holding the file matched by find.

-flags *[+ | -] flags, notflags*
: Find files by their file flag settings (see chflags). To specify flags that are set, list them in *flags*. To specify flags that are not set, list those flags (with their "no" prefixes) in *notflags*. To match files with at least all of the settings specified by both *flags* and *notflags*, use the - before *flags*. To match files with any of the flags specified in *flags* or *notflags*, use the + before *flags*. Without the - or the +, find finds only files with flag settings matching exactly with those in *flags* and *notflags*.

-fstype *fstype*
: Match files only on *type* filesystems. (Run sysctl vfs to view currently mounted filesystem types). You can also specify two pseudotypes, local and rdonly, which allows you to match files only on physically mounted volumes and read-only volumes, respectively.

-group *gname*
: Find files belonging to group *gname*. *gname* can be a group name or a GID number.

-iname *pattern*
: A case-insensitive version of -name.

-inum *n*
: Find files whose inode number is *n*.

-ipath *pattern*
: A case-insensitive version of -path.

-iregex *pattern*
: A case-insensitive version of -regex.

-links *n*
: Find files having *n* links.

-ls
: Write the list of found files to standard output as if provided by the ls -dgils command. Return true.

-maxdepth *num*
: Don't descend more than *num* levels of directories.

-mindepth *num*
: Begin applying tests and actions only at levels deeper than *num* levels.

-mmin *+n | -n | n*
: Find files last modified more than *n* (+*n*), less than *n* (-*n*), or exactly *n*.

-mtime *+n | -n | n*
: Find files that were last modified more than *n* (+*n*), less than *n* (-*n*), or exactly *n* days ago.

-name *pattern*
: Find files whose names match *pattern*. Filename metacharacters may be used but should be escaped or quoted.

-newer *file*
: Find files that have been modified more recently than *file*; similar to -mtime.

-nogroup
: The file's GID doesn't correspond to any group.

-nouser
: The file's UID doesn't correspond to any user.

-ok *command* { }\;
: Same as -exec, but prompt user to respond with y before *command* is executed.

-okdir *command* { } \;
: Same as -ok, but run the Unix *command*, from the directory holding the file matched by find.

-path *pattern*
: Find files whose names match *pattern*. Expect full pathnames relative to the starting pathname (i.e., don't treat / or . specially).

-perm *nnn*
: Find files whose permission flags (e.g., rwx) match octal number *nnn* exactly (e.g., 664 matches -rw-rw-r--). Use a minus sign before *nnn* to make a wildcard match of any unspecified octal digit (for example, -perm -600 matches -rw-******, where * can be any mode).

-print
: Print the matching files and directories, using their full pathnames. Return true.

-print0
: Print the matching files and directories, using their full pathnames and separating each with the ASCII NUL character. This allows find to properly work with the xargs utility and pathnames containing spaces, for example. Return true.

-prune
: Prevent find from descending into the directory found by the previous condition in the command line. Useful when used with an alternative condition (-o) that specifies which directories must be traversed. Return true.

-regex *pattern*
: Like -path but use grep-style regular expressions instead of the shell-like globbing used in -name and -path.

-size *n[c]*
: Find files containing *n* blocks, or if c is specified, *n* characters long.

-type *c*
: Find files whose type is *c*. *c* can be b (block special file), c (character special file), d (directory), p (FIFO or named pipe), l (symbolic link), s (socket), or f (plain file).

-user *user*
: Find files belonging to *user* (name or ID).

-xdev
: Search for files that reside only on the same filesystem as pathname.

Examples

List all files (and subdirectories) in your home directory:

```
$ find ~ -print
```

List all files named *chapter1* in the *~/Documents* directory:

```
$ find /Documents -name chapter1 -print
```

List all files beginning with *memo* owned by *ann*:

```
$ find /Documents -name 'memo*' -user ann -print
```

Search the filesystem (begin at root) for manpage directories:

```
$ find / -type d -name 'man*' -print
```

Search the current directory, look for filenames that don't begin with a capital letter, and send them to the printer:

```
$ find . \! -name '[A-Z]*' -exec lpr {}\;
```

Find and compress files whose names don't end with *.gz*:

```
$ gzip `find . \! -name '*.gz' -print`
```

Remove all empty files on the system (prompting first):

```
$ find / -size 0 -ok rm {} \;
```

Search the system for files that were modified within the last two days (good candidates for backing up):

```
$ find / -mtime -2 -print
```

Recursively grep for a pattern down a directory tree:

```
$ find ~/Documents -print0 | xargs -0 grep '[Nn]utshell'
```

Search the system excluding all but the system volume:

```
$ find / -path '/Volumes/*' -prune -o -name "*. doc" -print
```

fixmount

```
fixmount [-q] [-a | -d | -e] [-v [-h hostname_or_IP] | -r | -A] [-f]
nfs_server...
```

Communicates with the NFS mount daemon, mountd, to remove invalid records of client mounts from the NFS server. fixmount is run from the client, and when called without flags, prints the client's IP address to standard output if the server has a record of NFS mounts from the client.

`mountd` maintains records of which clients have mounted exports from the server, and writes the records to a file so that this information is retained through process or system restarts. (On most Unix platforms, this file is */etc/rmtab*; on Mac OS X, it's */var/db/mountdtab*.) Over time, this file accumulates a lot of outdated information, primarily due to clients rebooting or otherwise dropping their mounts without properly informing the server, or changing their hostnames.

The primary purpose of `fixmount` is to clear out the bogus entries from the file kept by `mountd`. On most Unix systems, it does this by comparing the current set of mounts on the client, as listed in */etc/mtab*, to the server's list of mounts from the client, and asking the server's `mountd` to remove any entries that don't match.

However, a Mac OS X system keeps a current list of mounts in the kernel, and doesn't use */etc/mtab*. Therefore, when `fixmount` checks this file and finds it empty (or nonexistent), it perceives all of the server's entries as bogus, even those that do match to current mounts on the client. This makes `fixmount`, at least as currently implemented, not very useful on Mac OS X.

Options

`-a`
: List mounts from the client in the form *`IP_addr:pathname`*. This is similar to `showmount -a`, but limited to information about the client on which `fixmount` is run.

`-A`
: Remove all of the entries for the client from the server's */var/db/mountdtab*.

`-d`
: List exports that are mounted on the client, instead of the client's IP address. This is similar to `showmount -d`, but limited to information about the client on which `fixmount` is run.

`-e`
: Print the server's list of NFS exports to standard output. This is the same as `showmount -e`.

`-f`
: Force all entries for the client to be interpreted as bogus. This makes `-f -r` equivalent to `-A`. On a Mac OS X client, it's as if this flag is always set.

`-h`
: Communicate with the server's `mountd` as if the client's hostname or IP address were that given by the argument to this option. This is useful when the client has changed its hostname or IP address, but the server retains invalid entries with the old information.

`-q`
: Minimize output from error messages.

`-r`
: Remove bogus entries for the client from the server's */var/db/mountdtab*.

`-v`
: Run the verification procedure to determine the list of bogus entries for the client (which is printed to standard output), but doesn't actually remove anything from the server's */var/db/mountdtab*.

fixPrecomps

```
fixPrecomps -help
fixPrecomps [-checkOnly] [-force] [-relroot directory] [-all | -precompsList
filename] [-precomps filename...] [-find_all_precomps] [-gcc2 | -gcc3all]
[-skipIfMissing] [-output directory] [-precompFlags flag...]
```

Compiles header files to improve performance for programs including them. When invoked without arguments, `fixPrecomps` reads any files in */System/Library/SystemResources/PrecompLists/* in alphanumeric order by filename. Normally this includes *phase1.precompList* and *phase2.precompList*. These files are expected to consist of lists of precompiled header filenames to generate. *fixPrecomps* then runs `cc -precomp` on the ordinary header files where the precompiled headers are either out of date (i.e., have modification times less recent than the ordinary headers) or nonexistent.

The headers listed in the *precompList* files have filename extensions of either *.p* or *.pp*. `fixPrecomps` finds ordinary headers with the same base filenames but extensions of *.h*. The *.p* headers are compiled with GCC Version 2 for use with C and Objective-C programs, while the *.pp* headers are compiled with GCC Version 2 for C++ and Objective-C++ programs. By default, `fixPrecomps` compiles headers with GCC version 3, in which case C/Objective-C precompiled header filenames end in *-gcc3.p*, and C++/Objective-C++ precompiled header filenames end in *-gcc3.pp*.

Options

`-all`
: Use all files contained in */System/Library/SystemResources/PrecompLists/*. This is the default.

`-checkOnly`
: For each header file listed in the *precompList* files, print a status message to standard output indicating whether the precompiled header exists and is up to date with the ordinary header.

`-find_all_precomps`
: Require specification of `-all`, `-precompList` or `-precomps`, but otherwise doesn't appear to do anything.

`-force`
: Produce precompiled headers even if they're up to date. Using this flag causes the `-checkOnly` flag to be ignored.

`-gcc2`
: Apply the command to GCC Version 2 C/Objective-C (*.p*) and C++/Objective-C++ (*.pp*) precompiled headers.

`-gcc3all`
: Apply the command to GCC Version 3 C++/Objective-C++ (*-gcc3.pp*) precompiled headers, as well as to those for C/Objective-C (*-gcc3.p*).

`-help`
: Print a usage statement to standard error.

`-output`
: Check for and create precompiled headers in locations relative to the specified directory. Intermediate directories must already exist, or compilation will fail.

`-precompFlags`
: Specify additional `cc` command-line flags to use when compiling headers.

`-precompList`
: Use only the *precompList* files specified.

`-precomps`
: Specify a list of precompiled headers to check or create.

`-relroot`
: Look for *System/Library/SystemResources/PrecompLists/* relative to the specified directory. The default is /.

`-skipIfMissing`
: Compile precompiled headers if they're out of date, but not if they don't exist. Using this flag causes the `-checkOnly` flag to be ignored.

FixupResourceForks

`FixupResourceForks [-nodelete] [-nosetinfo] [-q[uiet]]` *`pathname...`*

Recombines the resource fork and HFS metadata split out into a separate file (named *._filename*) with the file's data fork (in a file named *filename*), resulting in a single multiforked file (named *filename*) with HFS attributes. As such, this only works on HFS and HFS+ volumes. It reverses the effect of running `SplitForks`.

`FixupResourceForks` does a recursive descent into the directory specified by *pathname*, working on every file within it.

Options

`-nodelete`
: Prevent deletion of *._filename* after recombination with *filename*.

`-nosetinfo`
: Disable setting of HFS attributes on the recombined files.

`-quiet`
: Suppress printing the name of each recombined file to standard output.

fmt

`fmt [`*`goal`*` [`*`maximum`*`]] [`*`files`*`]`

Converts text to specified width by filling lines and removing newlines. Width is specified as being close to *`goal`* characters, but not over *`maximum`* characters wide (65 and 75 characters by default). Concatenate files on the command line, or read text from standard input if no file is specified. By default, preserve blank lines, spacing, and indentation. `fmt` attempts to break lines at the end of sentences and to avoid breaking lines after a sentence's first word or before its last.

fold

```
fold [option] [files]
```

Breaks the lines of the named *files* so they are no wider than the specified width (default is 80). `fold` breaks lines exactly at the specified width, even in the middle of a word. Reads from standard input when given - as a file.

Options

`-b` Count bytes, not columns (i.e., consider tabs, backspaces, and carriage returns to be one column).

`-s` Break at spaces only, if possible.

`-w` *width*
Set the maximum line width to *width*. Default is 80.

fs_usage

```
fs_usage [options] [processes]
```

Shows a continuous display of filesystem-related system calls and page faults. You must run `fs_usage` as root. By default, it ignores anything originating from `fs_usage`, `Terminal`, `telnetd`, `sshd`, `rlogind`, `tcsh`, `csh`, or `sh`, but shows all other system processes. To have `fs_usage` track only specific processes, specify those process names or IDs in *processes*.

Options

`-e` *[processes]*
Exclude from tracking those processes specified in *processes*. If no processes are given, exclude only the current `fs_usage` process.

`-f` *mode*
Filter output according to the *mode*, which must be either `network` or `filesys`.

`-w` Display in a more detailed, wider format. Lines longer than the window width will be wrapped.

fsck

```
fsck [-l num_procs] [-b block_num] [-m mode] [-c { 0 | 1 | 2 | 3 }] [-p | -n |
-y] device...
```

Performs consistency checks of UFS volumes, and attempts to fix any inconsistencies found.

Options

`-b` Specify an alternate super block for the filesystem.

`-c` Convert the filesystem to the specified version level. See the `fsck` manpage for details.

`-l` Limit the number of parallel `fsck` processes. Defaults to the number of disks.

-m Specify the permissions of the *lost+found* directory, where files that have become detached from their place in the directory hierarchy due to filesystem corruption can be located. The argument is an octal mode, as described in the chmod manpage. The default is 1777.

-n Automatically answer "no" whenever fsck asks to resolve an inconsistency.

-p Run in preening mode, in which only purely innocuous inconsistencies are resolved.

-y Automatically answer "yes" whenever fsck asks to resolve an inconsistency.

device
The volume's device filename, e.g., */dev/disk1s2*.

fsck_hfs

```
fsck_hfs -u
fsck_hfs [-d] [-f] [-r] { -q | -p | [-n | -y] } device...
```

Performs consistency checks of HFS and HFS+ volumes, and attempts to fix any inconsistencies found.

Options

-d Enable debugging output.

-f Force check even if the volume is marked as clean.

-n Automatically answer "no" whenever fsck_hfs asks to resolve an inconsistency.

-p Run in preening mode, in which only purely innocuous inconsistencies are resolved.

-q Check the filesystem but don't resolve any inconsistencies. Return filesystem status of clean, dirty, or failure to standard error.

-r Cause a rebuild of the volume's catalog btree to occur.

-u Print a usage statement to standard output.

-y Automatically answer "yes" whenever fsck_hfs asks to resolve an inconsistency.

device
The volume's device filename, e.g., */dev/disk1s2*.

fsck_msdos

```
fsck_msdos { -q | -p | [-n | -y] } device...
```

Performs consistency checks of FAT volumes and attempts to fix any inconsistencies found.

Options

-n Automatically answer "no" whenever `fsck_msdos` asks to resolve an inconsistency.

-p Run in preening mode, in which only purely innocuous inconsistencies are resolved.

-q Check the filesystem but don't resolve any inconsistencies. Print filesystem status to standard output.

-y Automatically answer "yes" whenever `fsck_msdos` asks to resolve an inconsistency.

device
: The volume's device filename, e.g., */dev/disk1s2*.

---

fstat

`fstat [options] [files]`

Displays a list of open files and their status. By default, `fstat` lists all open files on the system. If any pathnames are specified in *files*, however, only those files are listed.

Options

-f *[pathname]*
: List open files residing only on the same filesystem as *pathname*, or if *pathname* is not specified, the current working directory.

-M *pathname*
: Extract values for the name list from core file *pathname* instead of */dev/kmem*, the default.

-N *pathname*
: Extract the name list from kernel file *pathname* instead of */mach_kernel*, the default.

-n Display data numerically. For filesystems, show the device number instead of mount point. For special files, show the device number instead of its */dev* filename. For regular files, show permissions in octal instead of symbolic format.

-p *pid*
: List only those files opened by the process whose ID is specified in *pid*.

-u *username*
: List only those files opened by the user *username*.

-v Be verbose.

ftp

```
ftp [options] [hostname]
```

Transfers files to and from remote network site *hostname*. `ftp` prompts the user for a command. Type `help` to see a list of known commands, and use the `help` command to view help on a specific command.

The `ftp` client included with Mac OS X supports auto-fetch, which allows you to perform a download with a single command line. To auto-fetch a file, supply its location as an argument to `ftp` in one of several formats:

- `ftp` [*user@*]*host*:[*path*][/]
- `ftp` [`ftp://`[*user*[:*password*]@]host[:*port*]/*path*[/]]
- `ftp` [`http://`[*user*[:*password*]@]*host*[:*port*]/*path*]

Options

`-A` Force active mode for use with older servers.

`-a` Perform anonymous login automatically.

`-d` Enable debugging.

`-e` Disable command-line editing.

`-f` Perform a forced reload of the cache. Useful when transferring through proxies.

`-g` Disable filename globbing.

`-i` Turn off interactive prompting.

`-n` No autologin upon initial connection.

`-o` *pathname*
Save file as *pathname* when auto-fetching.

`-p` Enable passive mode (the default).

`-P` *port*
Specify alternate *port* number.

`-r` *wait*
Attempt to connect again after *wait* seconds if initial attempt fails.

`-R` When auto-fetching, resume incomplete transfers (if not transferring through a proxy).

`-t` Enable packet tracing.

`-T` *direction, maximum [,increment]*
Throttle transfer rates by specifying *direction* of transfer, *maximum* transfer speed in bytes/second, and an *increment* value that allows changing *maximum* on the fly. Direction can be `get` for incoming transfers, `put` for outgoing transfers, and `all` for both.

`-u` *url file [...]*
Upload *file* to *url* from the command line.

-v Verbose. Show all responses from remote server.

-V Disable verbose.

gcc_select

```
gcc_select [-v | --version] [-h | --help] [-l | --list]
gcc_select [-v | --version] [-n] [-force] [-root] [-dstroot pathname]
{ 2 | 3 | 3.x }
```

A shell script that sets the default version of GCC (either 2.95.2 (2), 3.1 (3), or some other version (specified as 3.*x*)) by creating various symlinks for compiler tools, libraries, and headers. With no arguments (or with just -v), the current default version is printed to standard output.

Options

-dstroot
: Specify the root-level directory in which changes are made. The default is */usr*.

-force
: Recreate symlinks for the specified version, even if it is already the current default version.

-h | --help
: Print a usage statement to standard output.

-l | --list
: List available GCC versions.

-n
: Print the list of commands that would be executed to standard output, but don't actually execute them.

-root
: Disable the initial check for *root* access before executing commands.

-v | --version
: Print the version of gcc_select to standard output.

GetFileInfo

```
GetFileInfo [options] pathname
```

Displays HFS+ file attributes (metadata) of file *pathname*. If you specify no options, GetFileInfo shows all the file's attributes. GetFileInfo is installed with the Developer Tools into */Developer/Tools*. Because this directory isn't in the shell's search path by default, you might to need to specify GetFileInfo's pathname to invoke it. See also SetFile.

Options

-a*[attribute]*
: Display the settings for those attributes that toggle on or off (sometimes called "Finder flags"). If *attribute* is empty, the settings of all attributes are displayed as a series of letters. If the letter is shown in uppercase, that

attribute is on (its bit is set). If the letter is shown in lowercase, that attribute is off. To view the setting for a single attribute (either 1 for on or 0 for off) specify that attribute by its letter in *attribute*. Refer to the following table for the specific attributes.

Attribute	Set | Unset	Meaning
Alias	A | a	File is/isn't an alias.
Bundle	B | b	File has/hasn't bundle resource.
Custom Icon	C | c	File has/hasn't a custom icon.
Desktop Item	D | d	File is/isn't on the desktop.
Extension	E | e	Filename extension is/isn't hidden.
Inited	I | i	File is/isn't inited.
Locked	L | l	File is/isn't locked.
Shared	M | m	Multiple users can/can't run a file at once (applies to application files).
INIT	N | n	File has/hasn't INIT resource.
System	S | s	File is/isn't a system file (locks name).
Stationary	T | t	File is/isn't a stationary file.
Invisible	V | v	File is/isn't invisible to Finder.

`-c` Display the file's four-character creator code.

`-d` Display the file's creation date.

`-m` Display the file's modification date.

`-t` Display the file's four-character type code.

Examples

Display all toggled attributes:

```
$ /Developer/Tools/GetFileInfo -a Takashi&Junichi.jpg
```

Display only the locked setting:

```
$ /Developer/Tools/GetFileInfo -aL Takashi&Junichi.jpg
```

gnutar

gnutar [*options*] [*tarfile*] [*other-files*]

Copies *files* to or restores *files* from an archive medium. An enhanced version of `tar`, `gnutar` is usually the preferred utility because `gnutar` can handle much longer pathnames than `tar`, and `gnutar`'s default omission of the leading slash in pathnames allows archives to be more easily opened on other systems. Note that until native drivers for tape drives exist for Mac OS X, `gnutar` can't write to tape. Note also that `gnutar` doesn't preserve resource forks or HFS metadata when copying files that contain them.

`gnutar` is installed on Mac OS X as part of Apple's Xcode Tools.

Function options

You must use exactly one of these, and it must come before any other options:

`-A, --catenate, --concatenate`
: Concatenate a second tar file on to the end of the first.

`-c, --create`
: Create a new archive.

`-d, --diff, --compare`
: Compare the files stored in *tarfile* with *other-files*. Report any differences, such as missing files, different sizes, different file attributes (such as permissions or modification time).

`--delete`
: Delete *other-files* from the archive.

`-r, --append`
: Append *other-files* to the end of an existing archive.

`-t, --list`
: Print the names of *other-files* if they are stored on the archive (if *other-files* aren't specified, print names of all files).

`-u, --update`
: Add files if not in the archive or if modified.

`-x, --extract, --get`
: Extract *other-files* from an archive (if *other-files* aren't specified, extract all files).

`--help`
: Display help information.

Options

`--atime-preserve`
: Preserve original access time on extracted files.

`-b, --block-size=n`
: Set block size to *n* 512 bytes.

`-B, --read-full-blocks`
: Form full blocks from short reads.

`--backup`
: If *tarfile* already exists, make a backup copy before overwriting.

`-C, --directory=directory`
: `cd` to *directory* before beginning `tar` operation.

`--checkpoint`
: List directory names encountered.

`--exclude=file`
: Remove *file* from any list of files.

`-f` *`arch`*, `--file=`*`filename`*
: Store files in or extract files from archive *`arch`*. Note that *`filename`* may take the form *`hostname`*`:`*`filename`*. Also, because Mac OS X has no native tape drive support, gnutar produces an error unless the `-f` option is used.

`-F` *`filename`*, `--info-script=`*`filename`*, `--new-volume- script=`*`filename`*
: Run the script found in *`filename`* when `tar` reaches the end of a volume. This can be used to automatically swap volumes with a media changer. This option implies `-M`.

`--force-local`
: Interpret filenames in the form *`hostname`*`:`*`filename`* as local files.

`-g`, `--listed-incremental`
: Create new-style incremental backup.

`-G`, `--incremental`
: Create old-style incremental backup.

`-h`, `--dereference`
: Dereference symbolic links.

`-i`, `--ignore-zeros`
: Ignore zero-sized blocks (i.e., EOFs).

`--ignore-failed-read`
: Ignore unreadable files to be archived. Default behavior is to exit when encountering these.

`-k`, `--keep-old-files`
: When extracting files, don't overwrite files with similar names. Instead, print an error message.

`-K`, `--starting-file=`*`file`*
: Start at *`file`* in the archive.

`-l`, `--one-file-system`
: Don't archive files from other filesystems.

`-L`, `--tape-length=`*`length`*
: Write a maximum of *`length`* 1024 bytes to each tape.

`-m`, `--modification-time`
: Don't restore file modification times; update them to the time of extraction.

`-M`, `--multivolume`
: Expect archive to multivolume. With `-c`, create such an archive.

`--mode=`*`filemode`*
: Set symbolic file mode (permissions) of added files to *`filemode`*.

`-N` *`date`*, `--newer=`*`date`*, `--after-date=`*`date`*
: Ignore files older than *`date`*.

`--newer-mtime=`*`date`*
: Ignore files whose modification times are older than *`date`*.

`--no-recursion`
: Don't descend into directories.

`--no-same-owner`
: Set the owner of the extracted files to be the current user, not the owner as defined in the archive.

`--no-same-permissions`
: Set the permissions of the extracted files to the default permissions for the current user, not as defined in the archive.

`--null`
: Allow filenames to be null-terminated with `-T`. Override `-C`.

`--numeric-owner`
: Use the ID numbers instead of names for file owners and groups.

`-o`, `--old`, *old-archive*, `--portability`
: Don't create archives with directory information that V7 `tar` can't decode.

`-O`, `--to-stdout`
: Print extracted files on standard out.

`--overwrite`
: Overwrite existing files when extracting.

`--overwrite-dir`
: Overwrite existing directory data when extracting.

`--owner=`*name*
: Set owner of added files to *name*.

`-p`, `--preserver-permissions`
: Keep ownership of extracted files same as that of original permissions.

`-P`, `--absolute-paths`
: Don't remove initial slashes (/) from input filenames.

`--preserve`
: Equivalent to invoking both the `-p` and `-s` options.

`--posix`
: Create archives that conform to POSIX standards. Such files aren't readable by older versions of `gnutar`.

`-R`, `--block-number`
: Display record number with each file in the archive.

`--record-size=`*size*
: Set size of records to *size* bytes, with *size* a multiple of 512.

`--recursive-unlink`
: Remove directories and files prior to extracting over them.

`--remove-files`
: Remove originals after inclusion in archive.

`--rsh-command=`*command*
: Don't connect to remote host with `rsh`; instead, use *command*.

`-s, --same-order, --preserve-order`
: When extracting, sort filenames to correspond to the order in the archive.

`-S, --sparse`
: Treat short files specially and more efficiently.

`--same-owner`
: Try to set ownership of extracted files as defined in the archive.

`--show-omitted-dirs`
: Show directories that were omitted during processing.

`--suffix=`*`c`*
: If *`tarfile`* already exists, make a backup copy before overwriting. Name the backup file by appending the character *`c`* to *`tarfile`* instead of the default "~".

`-T` *`filename`*, `--files-from` *`filename`*
: Consult *`filename`* for files to extract or create.

`--totals`
: Print byte totals.

`-U, --unlink-first`
: Remove files prior to extracting them.

`--recursive-unlink`
: Empty hierarchies before extracting directories.

`--use-compress-program=`*`program`*
: Compress archived files with *`program`* or uncompress extracted files with *`program`*.

`-v, --verbose`
: Verbose. Print filenames as they are added or extracted, or show permissions when files are listed.

`-V` *`name`*, `--label=`*`name`*
: Name this volume *`name`*.

`--version`
: Show version of `gnutar`.

`--volno-file=`*`n`*
: Force decimal number *`n`* to be used in `gnutar`'s prompt to change tapes.

`-w, --interactive, --confirmation`
: Wait for user confirmation (y) before taking any actions.

`-W, --verify`
: Check archive for corruption after creation.

`-z`
: Compress files with `gzip` before archiving them or uncompress them with `gunzip` before extracting them.

`-X` *`file`*, `--exclude-from` *`file`*
: Consult *`file`* for list of files to exclude.

--*[no-]*anchored
: Exclusion patterns match file name start (default: on).

--*[no-]*ignore-case
: Exclusion patterns ignore case (default: off, case-sensitive).

--*[no-]*wildcards
: Exclusion patterns use wildcards (default: on).

--*[no-]*wildcards-match-slash
: Exclusion pattern wildcards match "/" (default: on).

-z, --gzip, --ungzip
: Compress files with gzip before archiving them or uncompress them with gunzip before extracting them.

-Z, --compress, --uncompress
: Compress files with compress before archiving them or uncompress them with uncompress before extracting them.

[drive][density]
: Set drive (0-7) and storage density (l, m, or h, corresponding to low, medium, or high).

Examples

Create an archive of *~/Documents* and *~/Music* (c), show the command working (v), and write to an external volume, */Volumes/Backups/archive.tar*, saving the previous backup file as *archive.tar~ (--backup)*:

```
$ gnutar cvf /Volumes/Backups/archive.tar -backup ↵
~/Documents ~/Music
```

Extract only *~/Music* directory from *archive.tar* to the current directory:

```
$ gnutar xvf  ~/archive.tar Music
```

Compare extracted files with those in the archive (d):

```
$ gnutar dvf ~/archive.tar Music
```

---

grep

grep [*options*] *pattern* [*files*]

Searches one or more *files* for lines that match a regular expression *pattern*. Regular expressions are described in Chapter 20. Exit status is 0 if any lines match, 1 if none match, and 2 for errors. See also egrep and fgrep.

Options

-a, --text
: Don't suppress output lines with binary data; treat as text.

-A *num*, --after-context=*num*
: Print *num* lines of text that occur after the matching line.

-b, --byte-offset
: Print the byte offset within the input file before each line of output.

-B *num*, --before-context=*num*
: Print *num* lines of text that occur before the matching line.

--binary-files=*type*
: Treat binary files as specified. By default, grep treats binary files as such (*type* is binary). If a matching string is found within a binary file, grep reports only that the file matches; nothing is printed for nonmatching binary files. If *type* is without-match, grep assumes binary files don't match and skips them altogether. Same as -I. Using a *type* of text causes grep to treat binary files as text and print all matched lines. Same as -a.

-c, --count
: Print only a count of matched lines. With the -v or --invert-match option, count nonmatching lines.

-C*[num]*, --context=*[num]*, -*num*
: Print *num* lines of leading and trailing context. Default context is 2 lines.

-d *action*, --directories=*action*
: Define an *action* for processing directories. Possible actions are:

  read
  : Read directories like ordinary files (default).

  skip
  : Skip directories.

  recurse
  : Recursively read all files under each directory. Same as -r.

-e *pattern*, --regexp=*pattern*
: Search for *pattern*. Same as specifying a pattern as an argument, but useful in protecting patterns beginning with -.

-E, --extended-regexp
: Treat *pattern* as an extended regular expression. Same as using the egrep command.

-f *file*, --file=*file*
: Take a list of patterns from *file*, one per line.

-F *file*, --fixed-strings
: Treat *pattern* as a list of fixed strings. Same as using the egrep command.

-G *file*, --basic-regexp
: Treat *pattern* as a basic regular expression, the default behavior.

-h, --no-filename
: Print matched lines but not filenames (inverse of -l).

-H, --with-filename
: Print matched lines with filenames, the default behavior.

--help
: Display a help message.

-i, --ignore-case
: Ignore uppercase and lowercase distinctions.

-I Skip binary files. Same as --binary-files=without-match.

-l, --files-with-matches
: List the names of files with matches but not individual matched lines; scanning per file stops on the first match.

-L, --files-without-match
: List files that contain no matching lines.

--mmap
: For possibly better performance, read input using the mmap system call, instead of read, the default. Can cause unexpected system behavior.

-n, --line-number
: Print lines and their line numbers.

-q, --quiet, --silent
: Suppress normal output in favor of quiet mode; the scanning stops on the first match.

-r, --recursive
: Recursively read all files under each directory. Same as -d recurse.

-s, --no-messages
: Suppress error messages about nonexistent or unreadable files.

-v, --revert-match
: Print all lines that don't match pattern.

-V, --version
: Print the version number and then exit.

-w, --word-regexp
: Match on whole words only. Words are divided by characters that aren't letters, digits, or underscores.

-x, --line-regexp
: Print lines only if pattern matches the entire line.

-Z, --null
: Print the matching files using their full pathnames and separating each with the ASCII NULL character instead of the newline character. This allows grep to properly work with the xargs utility and pathnames that contain spaces, for example.

Examples

List the number of email messages from a specific domain:

```
$ grep -c '^From .*@mac\.com' mbox
```

List files that have at least one URL:

```
$ grep -Eil '*p:\/\/*' *
```

List files that don't contain *pattern*:

```
$ grep -c pattern files | grep :0
```

gunzip

```
gunzip [gzip options] [files]
```

Identical to gzip -d. Provided as a hard link to gzip. The -1 ... -9 and corresponding long-form options are not available with gunzip; all other gzip options are accepted. See gzip for more information.

gzcat

```
gzcat [gzip options] [files]
```

A link to gzip instead of using the name zcat, which preserves zcat's original link to compress. Its action is identical to gunzip -c. Also installed as zcat. See gzip for more information.

gzip

```
gzip [options] [files]
gunzip [options] [files]
zcat [options] [files]
```

Compresses specified files (or read from standard input) with Lempel-Ziv coding (LZ77). Rename compressed file to *filename.gz*; keep ownership modes and access/modification times. Ignore symbolic links. Uncompress with gunzip, which takes all of gzip's options, except those specified. zcat is identical to gunzip -c and takes the options -fhLV, described here. Files compressed with the compress command can be decompressed using these commands.

gzip doesn't preserve resource forks or HFS metadata when compressing files that contain them.

Options

-*n*, --fast, --best
: Regulate the speed of compression using the specified digit *n*, where -1 or --fast indicates the fastest compression method (less compression) and -9 or --best indicates the slowest compression method (most compression). The default compression level is -6.

-c, --stdout, --to-stdout
: Print output to standard output, and don't change input files.

-d, --decompress, --uncompress
: Same as gunzip.

-f, --force
: Force compression. gzip normally prompts for permission to continue when the file has multiple links, its *.gz* version already exists, or it is reading compressed data to or from a terminal.

`-h, --help`
: Display a help screen and then exit.

`-l, --list`
: Expects to be given compressed files as arguments. Files may be compressed by any of the following methods: `gzip`, `deflate`, `compress`, `lzh`, and `pack`. For each file, list uncompressed and compressed sizes (the latter being always `-1` for files compressed by programs other than `gzip`), compression ratio, and uncompressed name. With `-v`, also print compression method, the 32-bit CRC of the uncompressed data, and the timestamp. With `-N`, look inside the file for the uncompressed name and timestamp.

`-L, --license`
: Display the `gzip` license and quit.

`-n, --no-name`
: When compressing, don't save the original filename and timestamp by default. When decompressing, don't restore the original filename if present, and don't restore the original timestamp if present. This option is the default when decompressing.

`-N, --name`
: Default. Save original name and timestamp. When decompressing, restore original name and timestamp.

`-q, --quiet`
: Print no warnings.

`-r, --recursive`
: When given a directory as an argument, recursively compress or decompress files within it.

`-S` *`suffix`*, `--suffix` *`suffix`*
: Append .*suffix*. Default is `gz`. A null suffix while decompressing causes `gunzip` to attempt to decompress all specified files, regardless of suffix.

`-t, --test`
: Test compressed file integrity.

`-v, --verbose`
: Print name and percent size reduction for each file.

`-V, --version`
: Display the version number and compilation options.

---

halt

`halt [`*`options`*`]`

Prepares the system and then terminates all processes, usually ending with a hardware power-off. During preparation, all filesystem caches are flushed, and running processes are sent `SIGTERM` followed by `SIGTERM`.

Options

`-l` Don't log the halt via *syslog* (i.e., *mach_kernel: syncing disks*...).

`-n` Don't flush filesystem caches. Should not be used indiscriminately.

`-q` The filesystem caches are flushed, but the system is otherwise halted ungracefully. Should not be used indiscriminately.

---

hdid

```
hdid -help
hdid image_file [options]
```

Loads disk images, attaches them to device nodes (files in */dev*), and signals Disk Arbitration to mount them into the directory hierarchy.

`hdid` is a synonym for `hdiutil -attach` and takes the same set of options and arguments. See the `hdid` manpage for more details.

---

hdiutil

```
hdiutil command [cmd-specific_args_and_opts] [-quiet | -verbose | -debug]
[-plist]
```

Manages disk images, performing some of the same functions as the Disk Utility application. The Options section highlights some common uses, but the full set of commands (and associated arguments and options) is extensive and isn't detailed here. See the `hdiutil` manpage or run `hdiutil help` for more assistance.

Options

`attach`
: Attach a disk image to a device node and mount it. As arguments, it takes the filename of a disk image and a possible list of options, some of which are:

  `-autoopenrw`
  : Automatically open read/write volumes in the Finder after they're mounted.

  `-help`
  : Print a usage summary to standard output.

  `-mountpoint`
  : If there's only one volume in the disk image, mount it at mount point specified as an argument, instead of under */Volumes/*.

  `-mountroot`
  : Mount volumes under a directory specified as an argument instead of under */Volumes/*.

  `-noautoopenro`
  : Disable automatic opening of read-only volumes in the Finder after they're mounted.

`-nomount`
: Create device nodes in */dev* and attach the image or its partitions to them, but don't mount them.

`-noverify`
: Disable verification of disk images containing checksums.

`-readonly`
: Disable write access to the mounted image.

`-shadow`
: Pass modifications to the disk image through to a shadow image. Subsequent access to the modified data will be from the shadow, which allows effective read/write access to data on a disk image that shouldn't or can't be modified. This option takes the filename of a shadow disk image as an argument but defaults to the name of the attached image with a *.shadow* extension. The shadow image is created if it doesn't already exist.

`burn`
: Burns a disk image to an optical disk (a writable CD or DVD). As arguments, it takes the filename of a disk image and a possible list of options, some of which are:

`-erase`
: Erase an optical disk if the drive and media support erasure.

`-forceclose`
: Close the optical disk after burning the image, preventing any future burns to the disk.

`-fullerase`
: Perform a sector-by-sector erasure of an optical disk if the drive and media support it.

`-noeject`
: Disable ejection of the disk after burning.

`-optimizeimage`
: Optimize the size of the image for burning, reducing the size of HFS and HFS+ volumes to the size of the data on them.

`create`
: Create a blank disk image. It takes the filename for the disk image as an argument. One of these options is required to specify the size of the image:

`-megabytes`
: Specify the size of the image in megabytes. Takes an integer argument.

`-sectors`
: Specify the size of the image in 512-byte sectors. Takes an integer argument.

`-size`
: Specify the size of the image with a choice of unit. Takes an argument consisting of an integer concatenated with a letter, where the letter is `b`

(for bytes), k (for kilobytes), m (for megabytes), g (for gigabytes), t (for terabytes), p (for petabytes), or e (for exabytes).

`-srcfolder`
: Create an image large enough to hold the contents of a directory specified as an argument.

Finally, *create* can take a list of discretionary options, some of which are:

`-fs`
: Format the disk image with a filesystem, the format being given as an argument to this option. Possible formats are `HFS+`, `HFS`, `UFS`, and `MS-DOS`. After the image is created, it's attached, formatted, and detached.

`-stretch`
: If creating an HFS+ filesystem, initialize it so that it can later be stretched with `hdiutil resize`. Takes an argument with the same format as the `-size` option, which determines the maximum size to which the filesystem can be stretched.

`-volname`
: Specify the volume name for the image. Takes a string argument; the default volume name is `untitled`.

`detach`
: Unmount an image or its partitions and detach them from their device nodes. Takes a device name (e.g., `disk1`) as an argument.

`eject`
: Same as `detach`.

`header`
: Print the disk image header to standard output. Takes the filename of a disk image as an argument.

`help`
: Print an extensive usage summary to standard output.

`imageinfo`
: Print information about a disk image or device to standard output, including properties (such as whether the image is compressed, encrypted, or partitioned), format, size, and checksum. As arguments, it takes a device name (e.g., */dev/disk1*) or the filename of a disk image, and a possible list of options, some of which are:

`-checksum`
: Display only the checksum.

`-format`
: Display only the image format.

`info`
: Print the version of the DiskImages framework to standard output, as well as information about mounted images (such as image filename, format, associated device node, mount point, and mounting user's identity).

`internet-enable`
: After being applied to a disk image and when the image is mounted, its contents are automatically copied to the directory containing the image file, and then the image is unmounted and moved to the user's Trash. The effect is to replace the disk image by its contents, in place. It takes an argument of either `-yes`, `-no`, or `-query`, as well as a disk image filename.

`makehybrid`
: Create a hybrid HFS+/ISO-9660 disk image suitable for use on other operating systems. As an argument, it takes `-o` followed by an image source, which can be either another disk image or a directory. It also takes a list of discretionary options, some of which are:

  `-hfs`
  : Include HFS+ filesystem information in the image. This happens by default, unless the `-iso` or `-joliet` options are specified without `-hfs`.

  `-hfs-blessed-directory`
  : Specify the directory on an HFS+ volume containing a valid *BootX* file, which may created by the `bless` command.

  `-hfs-openfolder`
  : Specify the directory on an HFS+ volume that should be automatically opened in the Finder after mounting.

  `-iso`
  : Include ISO-9660 filesystem information in the image. This happens by default, unless the `-hfs` option is specified without `-iso`.

  `-joliet`
  : Include ISO-9660 filesystem information with Joliet extensions in the image. This happens by default, unless the `-hfs` or `-iso` options are specified without `-joliet`.

`mount`
: Same as `attach`.

`mountvol`
: Mount a device into the filesystem hierarchy using Disk Arbitration (similar to `diskutil mount`). Takes a device name (e.g., `disk1`) as an argument. This can be used to complete the process of mounting a disk image after using `hdiutil attach -nomount`.

`plugins`
: Print information about plug-ins for the DiskImages framework to standard output.

`pmap`
: Print the partition map of a disk image or device to standard output. As arguments, it takes a device name (e.g., */dev/disk1*) or the filename of a disk image, and a possible list of options.

`testfilter`
: Test whether a file is a valid disk image and return `YES` or `NO` to standard error.

`unmount`
: Unmount an image or its partitions without detaching them from their device nodes. Takes a device name (e.g., `disk1`) or a mount point as an argument.

`-debug`
: Enable debugging output to standard error.

`-plist`
: Display output in XML property list format, if the command can do it.

`-quiet`
: Minimize output.

`-verbose`
: Enable verbose output.

---

head

```
head [options] [files]
```

Prints the first few lines of one or more *`files`* (default is 10).

Options

`-n` Print the first *n* lines of the file.

`-n n`
: Print the first *n* lines of the file.

Example

Display the first 20 lines of `phone_list`:

```
$ head -20 phone_list
```

---

hfs.util

```
hfs.util { -m | -M } device mount_point { fixed | removable } { readonly |
writable } { suid | nosuid } { dev | nodev }
hfs.util -p device { fixed | removable } { readonly | writable }
hfs.util { -a | -k | -s | -u } device
hfs.util { -J | -U | -I } mount_point
```

Mounts HFS and HFS+ filesystems into the directory hierarchy.

Options

`-a` Enable (adopt) permissions on the volume, creating an entry for it in */var/db/volinfo.database* if one doesn't already exist. Unlike `disktool -A` or `vsdbutil -a`, this functions only on an unmounted volume.

`-I` Print information about the journal file to standard output.

`-J` Enable journaling on the volume.

`-k` Read the disk's UUID key and prints it to standard output. Only functions on an unmounted volume.

-m Mount the device.

-M Attempt to force the mount.

-p Probe the device and print the volume name to standard output.

-s Generate a new disk UUID key and set it on the volume. Only functions on an unmounted volume.

-u Unmount the device. This function doesn't appear to work.

-U Disable journaling on the volume.

device
  The disk device filename, e.g. *disk0s5*.

mount_point
  The directory on which the filesystem is mounted.

---

host

```
host [options] host [server]
host [options] domain [server]
```

Prints information about specified hosts or zones in DNS. Hosts may be IP addresses or hostnames; host converts IP addresses to hostnames by default and appends the local domain to hosts without a trailing dot. Default servers are determined in */etc/resolv.conf*. For more information about hosts and zones, refer to Chapters 1 and 2 of *DNS and BIND* (O'Reilly).

Options

-a All, same as -t ANY.

-c *class*
  Search for specified resource record class (in[ternet], cs[net], ch[aos], hs/hesiod, or any). Default is in. The chaos and csnet classes, although defined in RFC1035, are rejected as invalid classes by the host command.

-C Print the SOA (start of authority) records for the host.

-d Debugging mode. -dd is a more verbose version.

-l *domain*
  List all machines in *domain*.

-r No recursion. Don't ask contacted server to query other servers but require only the information that it has cached.

-s Chase signatures back to parent key (DNSSEC).

-t *type*
  Look for *type* entries in the resource record. Acceptable values for *type* are: a, ns, md, mf, cnames, soa, mb, mg, mr, null, wks, ptr, hinfo, minfo, mx, any, and * (careful, the shell loves those asterisks; be sure to escape them).

-v Verbose. Include all fields from the resource record, even time-to-live and class, as well as "additional information" and "authoritative nameservers" (provided by the remote nameserver).

-w Wait forever for a response from a queried server.

hostinfo

```
hostinfo
```

Prints basic information about the system to standard output, including Darwin version number, number and types of processors, amount of physical memory, current number of Mach tasks and threads running in the kernel, and CPU load.

Example

```
$ hostinfo
Mach kernel version:
         Darwin Kernel Version 7.0.0:
Wed Sep 17 20:12:58 PDT 2003; root:xnu/xnu-510.obj~1/RELEASE_PPC

Kernel configured for a single processor only.
1 processor is physically available.
Processor type: ppc750 (PowerPC 750)
Processor active: 0
Primary memory available: 320.00 megabytes.
Default processor set: 51 tasks, 114 threads, 1 processors
Load average: 0.18, Mach factor: 0.89
```

hostname

hostname [*option*] [*nameofhost*]

Sets or prints name of current host system. A privileged user can temporarily set the hostname with the nameofhost argument. Edit */etc/hostconfig* to make a permanent change.

Option

-s, --short
: Trim domain information from the printed name.

hwprefs

hwprefs [-h]
hwprefs [-v] *parameter*[=*value*] [*parameter*[=*value*]]...

Prints some information about the system to standard output. This is installed as part of the Computer Hardware Understanding Development (CHUD) set of developer tools.

Options

-h Print a usage statement to standard error.

`-v` Print information verbosely.

parameter
One of the following: `cpus` reports the number of CPUs (either `1` or `2`), `cpunap` reports whether the CPU may slow down to conserve energy (either `0` or `1`), `hwprefetch` reports the number of prefetch engines used by a G5 CPU (either `4` or `8`), and `ostype` reports the code name for the system's OS (either `Cheetah` (Mac OS X 10.0), `Puma` (10.1), `Jaguar` (10.2), `Smeagol` (10.2.7), or `Panther` (10.3)).

id

`id [options] [username]`

Displays information about yourself or another user: UID, GID, effective UID and GID if relevant, and additional GIDs.

Options

`-g` Print GID.

`-G` Print supplementary GIDs.

`-n` With `-u`, `-g`, or `-G`, print user or group name, not number.

`-p` Print the output in a more easily read format. Not used with other options.

`-r` With `-u`, `-g`, or `-G`, print real, not effective, UID or GID.

`-u` Print UID only.

ifconfig

`ifconfig [options] [interface address_family address parameters]`

Assigns an address to a network interface and/or configure network interface parameters. `ifconfig` is typically used at boot time to define the network address of each interface on a machine. It may be used at a later time to redefine an interface's address or other parameters. Without arguments, `ifconfig` displays the current configuration for a network interface. Used with a single *interface* argument, `ifconfig` displays that particular interface's current configuration.

Display Options

`-a` Display information about all configured interfaces. This is the default when no options and arguments are specified.

`-d` Display information about interfaces that are down.

`-L` Display address lifetime for IPv6 addresses.

`-l` Display all configured interfaces names only.

`-m` Display all supported media for specified interface.

`-u` Display information about interfaces that are up.

Arguments

interface
: String of the form *name unit*—for example, en0.

address
: Hostname or address in "dotted-octet" notation; for example, 172.24.30.12.

address_family
: Because an interface may receive transmissions in differing protocols, each of which may require separate naming schemes, you can specify the *address_family* to change the interpretation of the remaining parameters. You may specify inet (the default; for TCP/IP) or inet6.

dest_address
: Specify the address of the correspondent on the other end of a point-to-point link.

The following parameters may be set with ifconfig:

add/delete

[-]alias
: Create/delete an additional/existing network address for this interface.

anycast
: Specify address as an anycast address (inet6 only).

[-]arp
: Enable/disable use of the Address Resolution Protocol in mapping between network-level addresses and link-level addresses.

broadcast
: Specify address to use to represent broadcasts to the network (inet only). The default is the address with a host part of all 1s (i.e., x.y.z.255 for a class C network).

create/plumb *and* destroy/unplumb
: These commands perform operations related to interface cloning. However, Mac OS X itself doesn't support interface cloning. Therefore, the manpage descriptions of these parameters are of historical significance only.

[-]debug
: Enable/disable driver-dependent debugging code.

down
: Mark an interface "down" (unresponsive).

ether
: Same as lladdr.

[-]link[*0-2*]
: Enable/disable special link level processing modes. Refer to driver's manpage for more information.

lladdr *addr*
: Set the link-level *address* on an interface as a set of colon-separated hex digits; for example, 00:03:93:67:7a:4a.

`media` *type*
: Set the interface media type to *type*; for example, 10base5/ AUI.

`[-]mediaopt` *opts*
: Comma-separated list of media options for a supported media selection system.

`metric` *n*
: Set routing metric of the interface to *n*. Default is 0.

`mtu` *num*
: Set the interface's Maximum Transfer Unit (MTU) to *mtu*.

`netmask` *mask*
: Specify how much of the address to reserve for subdividing networks into subnetworks ((`inet` only). *mask* can be specified as a single hexadecimal number with a leading 0x, with a dot notation Internet address, or with a pseudonetwork name listed in the network table */etc/networks*.

`up` Mark an interface "up" (ready to send and receive).

---

info

`info [`*options*`] [`*topics*`]`

Info files are arranged in a hierarchy and can contain menus for subtopics. When entered without options, the command displays the top-level information file (usually */usr/local/info/dir*). When *topics* are specified, find a subtopic by choosing the first *topic* from the menu in the top-level information file, the next *topic* from the new menu specified by the first *topic*, and so on. The initial display can also be controlled by the `-f` and `-n` options.

Options

`--apropos` *string*
: Looks up *string* in all manual indices.

`-d` *directories*, `--directory` *directories*
: Search *directories*, a colon-separated list, for information files. If this option isn't specified, use the `INFOPATH` environment variable or the default directory (usually */usr/local/info*).

`--dribble` *file*
: Store each keystroke in *file*, which can be used in a future session with the `--restore` option to return to this place in `info`.

`-f` *file*, `--file` *file*
: Display specified info *file*.

`-h`, `--help`
: Display brief help.

`--index-search=`*string*
: Go to node pointed to by index entry *string*.

-n *node*, --node *node*
: Display specified *node* in the information file.

-O, --show-options, --usage
: Don't remove ANSI escapes from manpages.

-o *file*, --output *file*
: Copy output to *file* instead of displaying it at the screen.

-R, --raw-escapes
: Don't remove ANSI escapes from manpages.

--restore=*file*
: When starting, execute keystrokes in *file*.

--subnodes
: Display subtopics recursively.

--version
: Display version.

--vi-keys
: Use *vi*-like key bindings.

install

```
install [options] file1 file2
install [options] files directory
install -d [options] [file] directory
```

Used primarily in Makefiles to update files. install copies files into user-specified directories. Similar to cp, with additional functionality regarding inode-based information like UID, GID, mode, flags, etc.

Options

-b
: Create backup copies of existing target files by renaming existing *file* as *file.old*. See -B for specifying extension name (i.e., default is *.old*).

-B *suffix*
: Use *suffix* as a filename extension when -b is in effect.

-c
: Copy the specified file(s). This is the default behavior of the install command.

-C
: Copy the file. Don't change the modification timestamp if the target exists and is the same as the source.

-d
: Create any missing directories.

-f *flags*
: Set the file flags of the target file(s). Flags are a comma-separated list of keywords. See the chflags(1) manpage for further details.

-g *gid or groupname*
: Set GID of target file to *group* (privileged users only or user is member of specified group).

`-m` *mode*
: Set the mode of the target files to *mode*. The default is `0755`, or `rwxr-xr-x`.

`-M` Don't use `mmap(2)`.

`-o` *uid or username*
: Set ownership to *uid* or *username* or, if unspecified, to root (privileged users only).

`-p` Preserve modification times.

`-s` Strip binaries to enhance portability.

`-S` Safe copy. The source file is copied to temporary file and then renamed. The default behavior is to first unlink the existing target before the source is copied.

`-v` Verbose. `install` prints symbolic representations for each copy action.

---

installer

`installer` *options* `-pkg` *pkgpath* `-target` *volpath*

Installs standard Mac OS X package files from the command line. `install` is an alternative to the *Installer.app* GUI application.

Options

`-allow`
: Install over an existing version of the software, even when the version being installed is older. The package must have special support for this option.

`-config`
: Send the list of command-line arguments, formatted in *plist* XML, to standard output without performing the installation. If you direct the output to a file, you can use that file with the `-file` option to perform multiple identical installations.

`-dumplog`
: Log installer's messages to standard output.

`-file` *pathname*
: Read arguments from file *pathname*. The file needs to be a product of the `-config` option or a file of the same format.

`-help`
: Display a help screen, and then exit.

`-lang` *language*
: Identify *language* (specified in ISO format) as the default language of the target system. Used only with OS installations.

`-listiso`
: Display the languages `installer` recognizes, in ISO format.

-pkginfo
: List the packages to be installed without performing the installation. Metapackages contain multiple subpackages; this option lists those subpackages as well.

-plist
: When used with -pkginfo and -volinfo, format the output into *plist* XML.

-verbose
: Print more package and volume information. Used with -pkginfo and -volinfo.

-verboseR
: Print more package and volume information, formatted for parsing. Used with -pkginfo and -volinfo.

-vers
: Display the version of installer, and then exit.

-volinfo
: List the volumes mounted at the time the command is run without performing the installation.

Examples

List only available packages and target volumes:

```
$ installer -volinfo -pkginfo -pkg newpkg.pkg
```

Install newpkg.pkg on the current system volume:

```
$ installer -pkg newpkg.pkg -target /
```

Install newpkg.pkg, using arguments from installfile:

```
$ installer -pkg newpkg.pkg -file installfile
```

ipconfig

```
ipconfig getifaddr interface
ipconfig getoption { interface | "" } { option_name | option_code }
ipconfig getpacket interface
ipconfig ifcount
ipconfig set interface { BOOTP | DHCP }
ipconfig set interface { INFORM | MANUAL } IP_addr netmask
ipconfig waitall
```

Interacts with the IP Configuration Agent of configd to manage network configuration changes.

Options

getifaddr
: Print the specified network interface's IP address to standard output.

getoption
: Print the value of the specified DHCP option to standard output. If *interface* is specified, the option is interface-specific. If empty quotes are used instead,

the option is global. Option names and numeric codes are DHCP-standard (such as `host_name`, `domain_name`, `netinfo_server_address`, etc.).

`getpacket`
: Print DHCP transaction packets to standard output.

`ifcount`
: Print the number of network interfaces to standard output.

`set`
: Set the method by which the specified network interface is assigned an IP address. Using `BOOTP` or `DHCP` causes the system to attempt to contact a server of the appropriate type to obtain IP configuration information. Using `INFORM` sets the IP address locally, but initiates a DHCP request to obtain additional IP configuration information (DNS servers, default gateway, etc.). Using `MANUAL` indicates that all IP configuration information is set locally.

`waitall`
: Set the configurations of all network interfaces according to the specifications in */etc/iftab*.

join

```
join [options] file1 file2
```

Joins the common lines of sorted *file1* and sorted *file2*. Reads standard input if *file1* is `-`. The output contains the common field and the remainder of each line from *file1* and *file2*. In the following options, *n* can be 1 or 2, referring to *file1* or *file2*.

Options

`-a`*[n]*
: List unpairable lines in file *n* (or both if *n* is omitted).

`-e` *s*
: Replace any empty output field with the string *s*.

`-j`*n m*
: Join on the *m*th field of file *n* (or both files if *n* is omitted).

`-o` *n.m*
: Each output line contains fields specified by file number *n* and field number *m*. The common field is suppressed unless requested.

`-t`*c* Use character *c* as field separator for input and output.

`-v` *n*
: Print only the unpairable lines in file *n*. With both `-v 1` and `-v 2`, all unpairable lines are printed.

`-1` *m*
: Join on field *m* of *file1*. Fields start with 1.

`-2` *m*
: Join on field *m* of *file2*. Fields start with 1.

Examples

Assuming the following input files:

```
$ cat score
olga    81      91
rene    82      92
zack    83      93

$ cat grade
olga    B       A
rene    B       A
```

List scores followed by grades, including unmatched lines:

```
$ join -a1 score grade
olga 81 91 B A
rene 82 92 B A
zack 83 93
```

Pair each score with its grade:

```
$ join -o 1.1 1.2 2.2 1.3 2.3 score grade
olga 81 B 91 A
rene 82 B 92 A
```

---

jot

```
jot [option] [repetitions [begin [end [seed]]]]
```

Generates a list of random or sequential data *repetitions* lines long. Sequential lists start from the number given in the *begin* value and finish with the *end* value. Random data is generated using the seed value *seed*.

Options

`-b` *word*
: Print *word* only.

`-c`
: Print ASCII character equivalents instead of numbers.

`-n`
: Don't print a trailing newline character at the end of the list.

`-p` *precision*
: Print the data using the number of digits or characters specified by the number *precision*.

`-r`
: Generate random data. `jot` generates sequential data by default.

`-s` *string*
: Print the list separated by *string* instead of by newlines, the default.

`-w` *word*
: Print *word* along with the other generated data.

Examples

Return a list of sequentially numbered names:

```
$ jot -w box- 20 1 20
```

Return the ASCII values of numbers 43 to 52:

```
$ jot -c 10 43 52
```

kdump

```
kdump [option]
```

Decode and display a kernel trace file produced by `ktrace`. By default, `kdump` processes any `ktrace.out` file found in the current working directory.

Options

`-d` Show all numbers in decimal format.

`-f` *tracefile*
: Process the file *tracefile* instead of `ktrace.out`.

`-l` Continue to read and display the trace file as new trace data is added.

`-m` *maxdata*
: When decoding I/O data, show no more than *maxdata* bytes.

`-n` Don't decode completely; display some values, such as those from `ioctl` and `errno`, in their raw format.

`-R` With each entry, show time since previous entry (relative timestamp).

`-t` *tracepoints*
: Show only the traces specified in *tracepoints* (see `kdump`'s `-t` option).

`-T` With each entry, show seconds since the epoch (absolute timestamp).

kdumpd

```
kdumpd [-l] [-s directory [-u username] [-c | -C]] [-n] [directory]
```

Provides a service meant to accept transfers of kernel core dumps from remote Mac OS X clients. Based on `tftpd`, it offers a simplistic file drop service. Setting it up involves:

- Adding a `kdump` entry to */etc/services*, recommended on UDP port 1069.
- Creating a `kdump` service file in */etc/xinetd.d/*, modeled after that for `tftp`.
- Executing `sudo service kdump start`.

Once that's done, you can invoke `tftp` on a client system, enter `connect server_name 1069`, and then `put` *filename* to transfer a file. The file will be saved on the server in the directory specified in the arguments to *kdumpd*. There are restrictions: the filename can't include / or .., so the file is deposited into the target directory only; and the target file must not already exist.

This service is apparently not used by any current facility but may exist for future use by Apple.

Options

`-c` Same as `-C`. Using this option should reject the connection if the path including the client IP address doesn't exist, but a bug prevents it from doing so.

`-C` Add the client's IP address to the end of the *chroot* directory path. If this path doesn't already exist, it falls back to that specified for `-s`.

`-l` Enable logging via *syslog* using the `ftp` facility. However, logging is enabled by default, so this option doesn't actually do anything.

`-n` Suppress a negative acknowledgement if the client requests a relative pathname that doesn't exist.

`-s` Perform a *chroot* to the specified directory.

`-u` Change UID to the specified username. Defaults to `nobody`.

---

kill

`kill [`*`option`*`]` *`PID`*

This is the `/bin/kill` command; there is also a shell command of the same name that works similarly. Send a signal to terminate one or more process IDs (*`PID`*). You must own the process or be a privileged user. If no signal is specified, `TERM` is sent.

Options

`-l` List the signal names. (Used by itself.)

`-s` *`signal`*
: Send signal *`signal`* to the given process or process group. The signal number (from */usr/include/sys/signal.h*) or name (from `kill -l`). With a signal number of 9, the kill is absolute.

`-signal`
: Send signal *`signal`* to the given process or process group.

---

killall

`killall [`*`options`*`]` *`procname`*`...`

Kills processes specified by command or pattern match. The default signal sent by `killall` is `TERM` but may be specified on the command line. `killall` assembles and executes a set of kill commands to accomplish its task.

Options

`-c` *`procname`*
: Use with the `-t` or `-u` options to limit processes that sent a signal to those matching *`procname`*.

`-d` Print diagnostic information only about targeted processes; doesn't send signal.

-h, -help, -?
: Print usage and exit.

-l
: List known signal names.

-m
: Interpret the *procname* as a case-insensitive regular expression for selecting real process names to send a signal to.

-s
: Show the `kill` command lines that will send the signal but don't actually execute them.

-SIGNAL
: Send specified *signal* to process. *signal* may be a name (see `-l` option) or number.

-t *tty*
: Used to further select only those processes attached to the specified *tty* (procname tty), or to select all processes attached to the specified *tty* (i.e., no *procname* specified).

-u *user*
: Used to further select only those processes owned by the specified *user* (procname user), or to select all processes owned by the specified *user* (i.e., no *procname* specified).

-v
: Verbose output. Print the `kill` command lines that send the signal.

---

ktrace

`ktrace [`*options*`]` *command*

Trace kernel operations for process *command* and log data to file `ktrace.out` in the current working directory. The tracing continues until you either exit *command* or clear the trace points (with the `-c` or `-C` options). Use `kdump` to view the trace log.

Options

-a
: Append new data to the trace file instead of overwriting it.

-C
: Stop tracing all processes run by a user invoking `ktrace`. If this option is used with superuser privileges, the tracing of all processes is stopped.

-c
: Stop tracing process command.

-d
: Also trace any current child processes of the specified process.

-f *file*
: Log to *file* instead of *ktrace.out*, the default.

-g *pgid*
: Toggle tracing of all processes that are part of the process group *pgid*.

-i
: Also trace any future child processes of the specified process.

-p *pid*
: Toggle tracing of process *pid*.

`-t tracepoints`
: Trace only kernel operations specified in *tracepoints*. Use the appropriate letters from this list to indicate which type of operation(s) to trace:

`c` System calls

`i` I/O

`n` Name translations

`s` Signal processing

`u` Userland operations

`w` Context switches

Examples

Trace only system calls and I/O on process 489:

```
$ ktrace -t ci -p 489
```

Run the `atlookup` command and trace all of its kernel operations:

```
$ ktrace atlookup
```

Turn off tracing for all user processes:

```
$ ktrace -C
```

---

kuncd

```
kuncd [-d]
```

The Kernel-User Notification Center server, which handles communication to users from kernel processes. It's started as a bootstrap daemon, from */etc/mach_init.d/kuncd.plist* (processed by *register_mach_bootstrap_servers*). For more information, check out *http://developer.apple.com/documentation/DeviceDrivers/Conceptual/WritingDeviceDriver/KernelUserNotification/*.

Options/Usage

`-d` Enable debugging output.

---

languagesetup

```
languagesetup -h
languagesetup -langspec language
languagesetup [-English | -Localized]
```

Changes the default language used by the system. If invoked with no arguments, or with the `-English` or `-Localized` flags, it enters an interactive session in which the new language may be chosen from a menu.

Options

`-English`
: Present interactive prompts in English.

`-h` Print a usage statement to standard output.

-langspec
Specify the new system language on the command line, instead of interactively.

-Localized
Present interactive prompts in the system's default language.

last

last [*options*] [*users*]

Lists information about current and previous login sessions, including username and duration of each session. Sessions are listed one per line, newest first. To view only sessions from select users, specify those usernames in *users*.

Options

-f *file*
Read from log *file* instead of */var/log/wtemp*, the default.

-h *host*
Report only on those sessions initiated from machine *host*.

-*n* Display only the first *n* lines of output.

-t *tty*
Report only on those sessions initiated from device *tty*. To list Aqua logins, for example, specify console for *tty*.

leave

leave [[+]*time*]

Sets a time to be reminded that it's "time to leave." leave will remind you with a message at the command prompt five minutes, and then one minute, before the specified time. You'll be reminded again at the specified time and then every minute after until you either log out of that shell session or kill leave with kill -9 *pid*. Specify the time in the *hhmm* format. Use + before *time* to specify a relative time, hours, and minutes from the current time. Without any arguments, leave prompts you to enter a time in the same format.

less

less [*options*] [*filename*]

less is a program for paging through files or other output. It was written in reaction to the perceived primitiveness of more (hence its name). A number may precede some commands.

Options

-[z]*num*
Set number of lines to scroll to *num*. Default is one screenful. A negative *num* sets the number to *num* lines less than the current number.

`+[+]`*`command`*
: Run *`command`* on startup. If *`command`* is a number, jump to that line. The option `++` applies this command to each file in the command-line list.

`-?` Print help screen. Ignore all other options; don't page through file.

`-a, --skip-search-screen`
: When searching, begin after last line displayed. (Default is to search from second line displayed.)

`-b, --buffers=`*`n`*
: Use *`n`* buffers for each file (default is 10). Buffers are 1 KB in size.

`-B, --auto-buffers`
: Don't automatically allocate buffers for data read from a pipe. If `-b` specifies a number of buffers, allocate that many. If necessary, allow information from previous screens to be lost.

`-c, --clear-screen`
: Redraw screen from top, instead of scrolling from the bottom.

`-C, --CLEAR-SCREEN`
: Same as `-c`, but clear the screen before redrawing.

`-d, --dumb`
: Suppress dumb-terminal error messages.

`-e, --quit-at-eof`
: Automatically exit after reaching EOF twice.

`-E, --QUIT-AT-EOF`
: Automatically exit after reaching EOF once.

`-f, --force`
: Force opening of directories and devices; don't print warning when opening binaries.

`-F, --quit-if-one-screen`
: Automatically exit if the file fits on one screen.

`-g, --hilite-search`
: Highlight only string found by past search command, not all matching strings.

`-G, --HILITE-SEARCH`
: Never highlight matching search strings.

`-h, --max-back-scroll=`*`num`*
: Never scroll backward more than *`num`* lines at once.

`-i, --ignore-case`
: Make searches case-insensitive, unless the search string contains uppercase letters.

`-I, --IGNORE-CASE`
: Make searches case-insensitive, even when the search string contains uppercase letters.

-j, --jump-target=*num*
: Position target line on line *num* of screen. Target line can be the result of a search or a jump. Count lines beginning from 1 (top line). A negative *num* is counted back from bottom of screen.

-k, --lesskey-file=*file*
: Read *file* to define special key bindings.

-m, --long-prompt
: Display a more-like prompt, including percent of file read.

-M
: Prompt more verbosely than with -m, including percentage, line number, and total lines.

-n, --line-numbers
: Don't calculate line numbers. Affects -m and -M options and = and v commands (disables passing of line number to editor).

-N
: Print line number before each line.

-o, --log-file=*file*
: When input is from a pipe, copy output to *file* as well as to screen. (Prompt for overwrite authority if *file* exists.)

-O*file*
: Similar to -o, but don't prompt when overwriting file.

-p, --pattern=*pattern*
: At startup, search for first occurrence of *pattern*.

-P, --prompt=*prompt*
: Sets the three preset prompt styles:

  s
  : Set short, default prompt.

  m
  : Set medium prompt (specified by -m).

  M
  : Set long prompt (specified by -M).

  w
  : Set message printed while waiting for data.

  =
  : Set message printed by = command.

-q, --quiet, --silent
: Disable ringing of bell on attempts to scroll past EOF or before beginning of file. Attempt to use visual bell instead.

-Q
: Never ring terminal bell.

-r, --raw-control-chars
: Display "raw" control characters, instead of using ^x notation. Sometimes leads to display problems.

-s, --squeeze-long-lines
: Print successive blank lines as one line.

-S, --chop-long-lines
: Chop lines longer than the screen width, instead of wrapping.

`-t, --tag=`*`tag`*
: Edit file containing *tag*. Consult *./tags* (constructed by `ctags`).

`-T, --tags-file=`*`file`*
: With the `-t` option or `:t` command, read *`file`* instead of *./tags*.

`-u, --underline-special`
: Treat backspaces and carriage returns as printable input.

`-U, --UNDERLINE-SPECIAL`
: Treat backspaces and carriage returns as control characters.

`-V, --version`
: Display the lesser version number and a disclaimer.

`-w, --hilite-unread`
: Print lines after EOF as blanks instead of tildes (~).

`-x, --tabs=`*`n`*
: Set tab stops to every *n* characters. Default is 8.

`-X, --no-init`
: Don't send initialization and deinitialization strings from termcap to terminal.

`-y, --max-forw-scroll=`*`n`*
: Never scroll forward more than *n* lines at once.

Commands

Many commands can be preceded by a numeric argument, referred to as *`number`* in the command descriptions.

`SPACE, ^V, f, ^F`
: Scroll forward the default number of lines (usually one window).

`z`
: Similar to `SPACE`, but allows the number of lines to be specified, in which case it resets the default to that number.

`RETURN, ^N, e, ^E, j, ^J`
: Scroll forward. Default is one line. Display all lines, even if the default is more lines than the screen size.

`d, ^D`
: Scroll forward. Default is one-half the screen size. The number of lines may be specified, in which case the default is reset.

`b, ^B, ESC-v`
: Scroll backward. Default is one windowful.

`w`
: Like `b`, but allows the number of lines to be specified, in which case it resets the default to that number.

`y, ^Y, ^P, k, ^K`
: Scroll backward. Default is one line. Display all lines, even if the default is more lines than the screen size.

`u, ^U`
: Scroll backward. Default is one-half the screen size. The number of lines may be specified, in which case the default is reset.

`r, ^R, ^L`
: Redraw screen.

`R`
: Like `r`, but discard buffered input.

`F`
: Scroll forward. When an EOF is reached, continue trying to find more output, behaving similarly to `tail -f`.

`g, <, ESC-<`
: Skip to a line. Default is 1.

`G, >, ESC->`
: Skip to a line. Default is the last one.

`p, %`
: Skip to a *`position number`* percent of the way into the file.

`{`
: If the top line on the screen includes a {, find its matching }. If the top line contains multiple {'s, use *`number`* to determine which one to use to find a match.

`}`
: If the bottom line on the screen includes a }, find its matching {. If the bottom line contains multiple }'s, use *`number`* to determine which one to use to find a match.

`(`
: If the top line on the screen includes a (, find its matching). If the top line contains multiple ('s, use *`number`* to determine which one to use to find a match.

`)`
: If the bottom line on the screen includes a), find its matching (. If the bottom line contains multiple)'s, use *`number`* to determine which one to use to find a match.

`[`
: If the top line on the screen includes a [, find its matching]. If the top line contains multiple ['s, use *`number`* to determine which one to use to find a match.

`]`
: If the bottom line on the screen includes a], find its matching [. If the bottom line contains multiple]'s, use *`number`* to determine which one to use to find a match.

`ESC-^F`
: Behave like {, but prompt for two characters, which it substitutes for { and } in its search.

`ESC-^B`
: Behave like }, but prompt for two characters, which it substitutes for { and } in its search.

`m`
: Prompt for a lowercase letter and then use that letter to mark the current position.

' Prompt for a lowercase letter and then go to the position marked by that letter. There are some special characters:

' Return to position before last "large movement."

^ Beginning of file.

$ End of file.

^X^X
Same as '.

/pattern
Find next occurrence of *pattern*, starting at the second line displayed. Some special characters can be entered before *pattern*:

! Find lines that don't contain pattern.

* If current file doesn't contain *pattern*, continue through the rest of the files in the command-line list.

@ Search from the first line in the first file specified on the command line, no matter what the screen currently displays.

?pattern
Search backward, beginning at the line before the top line. Treats !, *, and @ as special characters when they begin *pattern*, as / does.

ESC-*/pattern*
Same as /*.

ESC-*?pattern*
Same as ?*.

n Repeat last pattern search.

N Repeat last pattern search, in the reverse direction.

ESC-n
Repeat previous search command but as though it were prefaced by *.

ESC-N
Repeat previous search command but as though it were prefaced by * and in the opposite direction.

ESC-u
Toggle search highlighting.

:e [filename]
Read in *filename* and insert it into the command-line list of filenames. Without *filename*, reread the current file. *filename* may contain special characters:

% Name of current file.

Name of previous file.

^X^V, E
Same as :e.

:n Read in next file in command-line list.

`:p` Read in previous file in command-line list.

`:x` Read in first file in command-line list.

`:d` Remove current from the list of files, effectively closing it.

`t` Go to the next tag. See the `-t` option for details about tags.

`T` Go to the previous tag.

`:f, =, ^G`
: Print filename, position in command-line list, line number on top of window, total lines, byte number, and total bytes.

`-` Expects to be followed by a command-line option letter. Toggles the value of that option or, if appropriate, prompts for its new value.

`-+` Expects to be followed by a command-line option letter. Resets that option to its default.

`--` Expects to be followed by a command-line option letter. Resets that option to the opposite of its default, where the opposite can be determined.

`_` Expects to be followed by a command-line option letter. Display that option's current setting.

`+`*`command`*
: Execute *`command`* each time a new file is read in.

`q, :q, :Q, ZZ`
: Exit.

`v` Not valid for all versions. Invoke editor specified by `$VISUAL` or `$EDITOR`, or `vi` if neither is set.

`!` *`[command]`*
: Not valid for all versions. Invoke `$SHELL` or `sh`. If *`command`* is given, run it and then exit. Special characters:

  `%` Name of current file.

  `#` Name of previous file.

  `!!` Last shell command.

`|` *`mark-letter command`*
: Not valid for all versions. Pipe fragment of file (from first line on screen to *`mark-letter`*) to *`command`*. *`mark-letter`* may also be:

  `^` Beginning of file.

  `$` End of file.

  `.`, *`newline`*
  : Current screen is piped.

Prompts

The prompt interprets certain sequences specially. Those beginning with `%` are always evaluated. Those beginning with `?` are evaluated if certain conditions are `true`. Some prompts determine the position of particular lines on the screen.

These sequences require that a method of determining that line be specified. See the -P option and the manpage for more information.

ln

```
ln [options] file1 file2
ln [options] files directory
```

Creates pseudonyms (links) for files, allowing them to be accessed by different names. In the Finder, links appear and work as aliases. In the first form, link *file1* to *file2*, where *file2* is usually a new filename. If *file2* is an existing file, it is removed first; if *file2* is an existing directory, a link named *file1* is created in that directory. In the second form, create links in *directory*, each link having the same name as the file specified.

Options

-f
: Force the link to occur (don't prompt for overwrite permission).

-n, -h
: Don't overwrite existing files.

-s
: Create a symbolic link. This lets you link across filesystems and also see the name of the link when you run `ls -l`. (Otherwise, you have to use `find -inum` to find any other names a file is linked to.)

locate

```
locate pattern
```

Searches a database of filenames and print matches. *, ?, [, and] are treated specially; / and . are not. Matches include all files that contain *pattern*, unless *pattern* includes metacharacters, in which case `locate` requires an exact match.

The locate database file is */var/db/locate.database*, which by default is updated as part of the weekly system maintenance cron job.

lock

```
lock [options]
```

Place a lock on the current shell session, preventing anyone from typing to the prompt without first entering a password or waiting until the end of the timeout period.

Options

-p
: Use the user's system password instead of prompting to create a new one-time password.

-t *timeout*
: Unlock the prompt in *timeout* minutes instead of the default 15 minutes.

lockfile

```
lockfile [options] filenames
```

Creates semaphore file(s), used to limit access to a file. When `lockfile` fails to create some of the specified files, it pauses for eight seconds and retries the last one on which it failed. The command processes flags as they are encountered (i.e., a flag that is specified after a file won't affect that file).

Options

`-sleeptime`
: Time `lockfile` waits before retrying after a failed creation attempt. Default is eight seconds.

`-!`
: Invert return value. Useful in shell scripts.

`-l` *`lockout_time`*
: Time (in seconds) after a lockfile was last modified at which it will be removed by force. See also `-s`.

`-ml`, `-mu`
: If the permissions on the system mail spool directory allow it or if `lockfile` is suitably setgid, it can lock and unlock your system mailbox with the options `-ml` and `-mu`, respectively.

`-r` *`retries`*
: Stop trying to create *`files`* after *`retries`* retries. The default is -1 (never stop trying). When giving up, remove all created files.

`-s` *`suspend_time`*
: After a lockfile has been removed by force (see `-l`), a suspension of 16 seconds takes place by default. (This is intended to prevent the inadvertent immediate removal of any lockfile newly created by another program.) Use `-s` to change the default 16 seconds.

logger

```
logger [options] [messages]
```

Logs messages to the system log (*/var/log/system.log*). Command-line messages are logged if provided. Otherwise, messages are read and logged, line-by-line, from the file provided via `-f`. If no such file is given, `logger` reads messages from standard input.

Options

`-f` *`file`*
: Read and log messages from *`file`*.

`-i`
: Log the PID of the `logger` process with each message.

`-p` *`priority`*
: Log each message with the given *`priority`*. Priorities have the form *`facility.level`*. The default is `user.notice`. See `syslog(3)` for more information.

-s Also log messages to standard error.

-t *tag*
: Add *tag* to each message line.

Example

Warn about upcoming trouble:

```
$ logger -p user.emerg 'Intruder Alert! Intruder Alert!'
```

---

look

```
look [options] string [file]
```

Looks through a sorted file and prints all lines that begin with *string*. Words may be up to 256 characters long. This program is potentially faster than `fgrep` because it relies on the *file* being already sorted, and can thus do a binary search through the file, instead of reading it sequentially from beginning to end.

With no *file*, `look` searches */usr/share/dict/words* (the spelling dictionary) with options `-df`.

Options

-d Use dictionary order. Only letters, digits, space, and tab are used in comparisons.

-f Fold case; ignore case distinctions in comparisons.

-t *char*
: Use *char* as the termination character, i.e., ignore all characters to the right of *char*.

---

lp

```
lp [options] [files]
```

Sends *files* to the printer. With no arguments, prints standard input. Part of the Common Unix Printing System (CUPS).

Options

-c Copy *files* to print spooler; if changes are made to *file* while it is still queued for printing, the printout is unaffected. This option has no effect when used with a CUPS server, which performs in a similar manner already.

-d *dest*
: Send output to destination printer named *dest*.

-E Force an encrypted connection if supported by the print server.

-h *host*
: Send print job to the print server *host*, `localhost` by default.

-H *action*
: Print according to the named *action*: hold (notify before printing), resume (resume a held request), immediate (print next; privileged users only).

-i *IDs*
: Override lp options used for request *IDs* currently in the queue; specify new lp options after -i. For example, change the number of copies sent.

-m
: Send mail after files are printed (not supported in CUPS as of Version 1.1.15).

-n *number*
: Specify the *number* of copies to print.

-o *options*
: Set one or more printer options. CUPS documentation describing these options is included with Mac OS X and viewable via a web browser using *http://127.0.0.1:631/sum. html#STANDARD_OPTIONS*.

-P *list*
: Print only the page numbers specified in *list*.

-q *n*
: Print request with priority level *n*, increasing from 1 to 100. The default is 50.

-s
: Suppress messages.

-t *title*
: Use *title* for the print job name.

-u *username*
: Cancel jobs belonging to *username*.

Example

Print five copies of a formatted manpage:

```
$ man -t niutil | lp -n 5
```

---

lpc

lpc [*command*]

Controls line printer; CUPS version. If executed without a command, lpc generates a prompt (lpc>) and accepts commands from standard input.

Commands

?, help *[commands]*
: Get a list of commands or help on specific commands.

exit, quit
: Exit lpc.

status *queue*
: Return the status of the specified print queue.

lpq

```
lpq [options]
```

Shows the printer queue. Part of the Common Unix Printing System (CUPS).

Options

+interval
: Repeat the lpq command every *interval* seconds until the queue is empty.

-a
: Show the jobs in the queues for all printers.

-E
: Force an encrypted connection if supported by the print server.

-l
: Be verbose.

-P *printer*
: Show queue for the specified *printer*.

lpr

```
lpr [options] files
```

Sends *files* to the printer spool queue. Part of the Common Unix Printing System (CUPS).

Options

-C, -J, -T *title*
: Use *title* for the print job name.

-E
: Force an encrypted connection if supported by the print server.

-l
: Assume print job is preformatted for printing and apply no further filtering. Same as -o raw.

-o *options*
: Set one or more printer options. CUPS documentation describing these options is included with Mac OS X and viewable via a web browser using *http://127.0.0.1:631/sum. html#STANDARD_OPTIONS*.

-p
: Print text files with pretty printing, adding a shaded header with date, time, job name, and page number. Same as -o prettyprint.

-P *printer*
: Output to *printer* instead of system default.

-r
: Remove the file upon completion of spooling.

-#*num*
: Print *num* copies of each listed file (100 maximum).

lprm

```
lprm [options] [jobnum]
```

Removes a print job from the print spool queue. You must specify a job number or numbers, which can be obtained from `lpq`. Used with no arguments, `lprm` removes the current job. Part of the Common Unix Printing System (CUPS).

Options

`-E` Force an encrypted connection if supported by the print server.

`-P` *printer*
: Specify printer name. Normally, the default printer or printer specified in the `PRINTER` environment variable is used.

`-` Remove all jobs in the spool.

lpstat

```
lpstat [options]
```

Prints the `lp` print queue status. With options that take a *list* argument, omitting the list produces all information for that option. *list* can be separated by commas or, if enclosed in double quotes, by spaces.

Options

`-a` *[list]*
: Show whether the *list* of printer or class names is accepting requests.

`-c` *[list]*
: Show information about printer classes named in *list*.

`-d` Show the default printer destination.

`-E` Force an encrypted connection if supported by the print server.

`-h` *host*
: Communicate with print server *host*, `localhost` by default.

`-l` Show a long listing of classes, jobs, or printers when used before `-c`, `-o`, or `-p`, respectively.

`-o` *[list]*
: Show job queues for printers in *list* or all printers if *list* isn't given.

`-p` *[list]*
: Show the status of printers named in *list* or all printers if *list* isn't given.

`-r` Show whether the print scheduler is on or off.

`-R` Show the job's position in the print queue when used before `-o`.

`-s` Summarize the print status (shows almost everything). Same as `-d -c -v`.

`-t` Show all status information (reports everything). Same as `-r -d -c -v -a -p`.

-u *user*
: Show request status for *user* or all users if user isn't given.

-v *[list]*
: Show device associated with each printer named in *list* or all printers if *list* isn't given.

-w *completed|not-completed*
: Only show completed or not completed print jobs, as appropriate. Option must appear before the -o option.

---

ls

```
ls [options] [names]
```

List contents of directories. If no *names* are given, list the files in the current directory. With one or more *names*, list files contained in a directory *name* or that match a file *name*. *names* can include filename metacharacters. The options let you display a variety of information in different formats. The most useful options include -F, -R, -l, and -s. Some options don't make sense together (e.g., -u and -c).

Options

-1 Print one entry per line of output.

-a List all files, including the normally hidden files whose names begin with a period.

-A List all files, including the normally hidden files whose names begin with a period. doesn't include the . and .. directories.

-b Print nonprintable characters with their C-style escape codes, such as \n for line feed and \t for tab. Characters without an escape code print with their octal values as, \xxx .

-B Print nonprintable characters with their octal codes as \xxx .

-c List files by status change time (not creation/modification time).

-C List files in columns (the default format).

-d Report only on the directory, not its contents.

-f Print directory contents in exactly the order in which they are stored, without attempting to sort them.

-F Flag filenames by appending / to directories, * to executable files, @ to symbolic links, | to FIFOs, = to sockets, and % to whiteouts.

-h List sizes from the -l option with units: bytes, kilobytes, etc.

-i List the inode for each file.

-k If file sizes are being listed, print them in kilobytes

-l Long format listing (includes permissions, owner, size, modification time, etc.).

-L Used with -l. List the file or directory referenced by a symbolic link rather than the link itself.

-n Used with -l. Displays GID and UID numbers instead of owner and group names.

-o Used with -l. Shows file flags (see chflags).

-p Mark directories by appending / to them.

-q Show nonprinting characters as ? (the default when printing to the terminal).

-r List files in reverse order (by name or by time).

-R Recursively list subdirectories as well as the specified (or current) directory.

-s Print size of the files in blocks.

-S Sort by file size, largest to smallest.

-t Sort files according to modification time (newest first).

-T Used with -l. Show complete time and date information.

-u Sort files according to the file access time.

-x List files in rows going across the screen.

-v Don't edit nonprinting characters for output (the default when not printing to the terminal).

-W Show whiteouts when listing directories on mounted filesystems.

Examples

List all files in the current directory and their sizes; use multiple columns and mark special files:

```
$ ls -asCF
```

List the status of directories */bin* and */etc*:

```
$ ls -ld /bin /etc
```

List C-source files in the current directory, the oldest first:

```
$ ls -rt *.c
```

Count the nonhidden files in the current directory:

```
$ ls | wc -l
```

---

lsbom

lsbom [*options*] *bomfile*

Prints the contents of a binary *BOM* ("bill of materials") file (*bomfile*) in human-readable format. By default, lsbom prints a line of information for each file listed in the *BOM*, as in this example:

```
./Documents/Install Log.txt 100664 0/80 1182 4086739704
```

This line shows, in order, the plain file's pathname, permissions (modes) in octal format, owner and GIDs, size, and checksum. When listing symbolic links, `lsbom` reports the size and checksum of the link itself, and also lists the pathname of the linked file. Device file listings include the device number but not the file size or checksum.

Options

`-b`
: List only block devices.

`-c`
: List only character devices.

`-d`
: List only directories.

`-f`
: List only files.

`-l`
: List only symbolic links.

`-m`
: When listing plain files, also display their modification dates.

`-s`
: Print only the file pathnames.

`-x`
: Don't show the permissions of directories and symbolic links.

`-arch` *`arch`*
: When listing fat binary files, show only the size and checksums of the code for chip type *`arch`*. Possible values for *`arch`* include `ppc`, `m68k`, `i386`, `hppa`, and `sparc`.

`-p` *`parameters`*
: Limit the content of each line as specified by *`parameters`*, which you can compose using any of the options in this list (but none more than once):

  `c` Show the checksum.

  `f` Show the filename.

  `F` Show the filename within quotes.

  `g` Show the GID.

  `G` Show the group name.

  `m` Show the octal file mode.

  `M` Show the symbolic file mode.

  `s` Show the file size.

  `S` Show the file size, formatted with commas.

  `t` Show the modification date in POSIX format (seconds since the epoch).

  `T` Show the modification date in human-readable format.

  `u` Show the UID.

  `U` Show the username.

  `/` Show the UID and GID, separated with a slash.

  `?` Show the username and group name, separated with a slash.

Examples

List the contents of *BOM* file *Installer.bom*:

```
$ lsbom Installer.bom
```

List only the paths of the directories in the *BOM file*:

```
$ lsbom -s -d Installer.bom
```

Format lines similar to those shown by the `ls -l` command:

```
$ lsbom -p MUGsTf Installer.bom
```


lsof

`lsof [options] [pathname]`

Lists open files, including regular files, directories, special files, libraries, network files, and others. The following descriptions and examples cover `lsof`'s basic operation; for a complete description, refer to `lsof`'s manpage.

Used without arguments, `lsof` lists all files opened by all active processes. Used with *pathname*, `lsof` lists the open files in the given filesystem mount point. If *pathname* is a file, `lsof` lists any processes having the given file open.

Selected Options

`-a` Recognize all list options as joined with "and" instead of the default "or."

`-b` Avoid `stat`, `lstat` and `readlink` functions, since they may block.

`-c` *chars*
: List files opened by processes whose command names begin with characters *chars*. *chars* can contain a regular expression if put between slashes (/). You can further define the expression by following the closing slash with `b`, to denote a basic expression, `i` to denote a case-insensitive expression, or `x` to denote an extended expression (the default).

`+c` *width*
: Print up to *width* characters of the command associated with a process. If *width* is 0, all characters are printed.

`+d` *pathname*
: List all open instances of the files and directories in *pathname*, including the directory *pathname* itself. This option doesn't search below the level of *pathname*, however.

`+D` *pathname*
: List all open instances of the files and directories in *pathname*, including directory *pathname* itself, searching recursively to the full depth of directory *pathname*.

`-i` *[address]*
: List all Internet files, or if specified, those with a Internet address matching *address*. Specify *address* as [*protocol*][@*host*][:*port*].

version

Specify IP version; 4 for IPv4, the default. IPv6 is not supported in this version of `lsof`.

protocol

Specify TCP or UDP.

host

Specify a host by name or numerically.

port

Specify a port number or service name.

`-l` Print UID numbers, instead of login names.

`-p` *[pid]*

List files opened by processes whose IDs are specified in the comma-separated list *pid*.

`+|-r` *[n]*

Operate in repeat mode. `lsof` lists open files as specified by the other options and then repeats the listing every 15 seconds (or *n* seconds, if specified). If `r` is prefixed with `+`, `lsof` repeats until the selection options produce no files to list. If `r` is prefixed with `-`, `lsof` repeats until the process is terminated with an interrupt or quit signal.

`-u` *[user]*

List files opened by users whose login names or UIDs are in the comma-separated list *user*. You can also specify a user whose files aren't to be listed by prefixing *user* with ^.

Examples

List processes that have your home directory opened:

```
$ lsof ~
```

List all open files in your home directory:

```
$ lsof +D
```

List the files opened by processes whose names begin with "i" and whose owner is "bob":

```
$ lsof -a -c i -u bob
```

List files using TCP port 80, repeating every two seconds until `lsof` is terminated:

```
$ lsof -i TCP:80 -r 2
```

---

machine

```
machine
```

Returns the system's processor type. A returned value of ppc750 indicates a PowerPC G3 chip, and ppc7400 indicates a PowerPC G4, for example.

mailq

```
mailq [option]
```

Lists all messages in the sendmail mail queue. Equivalent to sendmail -bp.

Option

-v Verbose mode.

mailstat

```
mailstats [options] [logfile]
```

Displays mail-arrival statistics. Parses a *procmail*-generated log file and displays a summary about the messages delivered to all folders (total size, average size, etc.). The log file is renamed as *logfile.old*, and a new *logfile* of size 0 is created.

Options

-k Keep log file intact.

-l Long display format.

-m Merge any errors into one line.

-o Use the old logfile.

-s Silent in case of no mail.

-t Terse display format.

makekey

```
makekey
```

Produces crypt password hashes. This can be used to automatically populate a password database from known passwords, or to make hashes of prospective passwords that can be subjected to cracking attempts before being put into use.

Options/Usage

makekey takes no command-line arguments. It accepts a character string on standard input, consisting of an eight-character password combined with a two-character *salt*, which is used to permute the DES password encryption algorithm. (Use man crypt for more information.) It prints a 13-character string to standard output, with the first two characters being the salt, and the other eleven characters being the password hash. The entire string is suitable for use as the password field in a standard Unix */etc/passwd*-format file or as the value of the passwd property in an Open Directory entry for a user employing Basic authentication.

Example

```
$ echo password12 | /usr/libexec/makekey
12CsGd8FRcMSM
```

man

```
man [options] [section] [title]
```

Displays information from the online reference manuals. `man` locates and prints the named *`title`* from the designated reference *`section`*.

Options

`-a` Show all pages matching title.

`-d` Display debugging information. Suppress actual printing of man pages.

`-f` Same as `whatis` command.

`-h` Print help and exit.

`-k` Same as `apropos` command.

`-m` *`systems`*
: Search *`systems`*' manpages. *`systems`* should be a comma-separated list.

`-M` *`path`*
: Search for manpages in *`path`*. Ignore `-m` option.

`-p` *`preprocessors`*
: Preprocess manpages with *`preprocessors`* before turning them over to `nroff`, `troff`, or `groff`. Always runs `soelim` first.

`-P` *`pager`*
: Select paging program *`pager`* to display the entry.

`-S` *`sections`*
: Define colon-separated list of *`sections`* to search.

`-t` Format the manpage with `troff`.

`-w` Print pathnames of entries on standard output.

Section names

Manpages are divided into sections, depending on their intended audience:

1 Executable programs or shell commands

2 System calls (functions provided by the kernel)

3 Library calls (functions within system libraries)

4 Special files (usually found in */dev*)

5 File formats and conventions

6 Games

7 Macro packages and conventions

8 System administration commands (usually only for a privileged user)

9 Kernel routines (nonstandard)

md5

```
md5 [options] [-s string] [files]
```

Calculates an md5 checksum value of the text provided in *string*, *files*, or from standard input. By default, when *string* or *files* is given, md5 prints those values first, followed by the checksum.

Options

-s *string*
: Calculate a checksum of the text in *string*.

-p
: Print the standard input followed by the checksum.

-q
: Operate in quiet mode. Print only the checksum.

-r
: Reverse the order of the output when string or files is given (checksum first).

-t
: Run the built-in speed test, which calculates a checksum from 100 MB of data.

-x
: Run the built-in test suite, which calculates checksums from seven short strings.

mDNS

```
mDNS [-E | -F | -A | -U | -N | -T | -M]
mDNS -B type domain
mDNS -L service_name _app_protocol._transport_protocol domain
mDNS -R service_name _app_protocol._transport_protocol domain port [string]...
```

A basic client for Rendezvous multicast DNS (mDNS), primarily used for testing local mDNS service. When invoked with no arguments, it prints a usage statement to standard error. In most instances, the command doesn't return on its own, so you'll need to use Ctrl-C to break out.

When registering or looking up a name like *website._http._tcp.local.*, *website* is the *service_name*, *http* is the *app_protocol*, *tcp* is the *transport_protocol*, and *local* is the *domain*. For example, to register such a service:

```
% mDNS -R website _http._tcp local 80 "my web site"
```

Options

-A
: Test mDNS by repeatedly adding, updating, and then deleting an HINFO resource record for *Test._testupdate._tcp.local.*.

-B
: Browse for services (although this doesn't seem to work).

-E
: Discover and list domains recommended for registration of services.

-F
: Discover and list domains recommended for browsing of services.

-L
: Look up a service, displaying its host address, port number, and TXT records if found.

-M Test mDNS by registering a service (*Test._testdualtxt._tcp.local.*) with multiple TXT resource records.

-N Test mDNS by registering a service (*Test._testupdate._tcp.local.*) with a large NULL resource record.

-R Register a service.

-T Test mDNS by registering a service (*Test._testlargetxt._tcp.local.*) with a large TXT resource record.

-U Test mDNS by repeatedly updating a TXT resource record for *Test._testupdate._tcp.local.*.

---

mDNSResponder

```
mDNSResponder [-d]
```

The server for Rendezvous multicast DNS (mDNS). It's started by the *mDNSResponder* startup item, creates a PID file in */var/run/*, and responds to TERM and INT signals by quitting cleanly.

Options

-d Run in debug mode, preventing daemonization, although it doesn't appear to be particularly useful in this state.

---

merge

merge [*options*] *file1 file2 file3*

Performs a three-way file merge. merge incorporates all changes that lead from *file2* to *file3* and puts the results into *file1*. merge is useful for combining separate changes to an original. Suppose *file2* is the original, and both *file1* and *file3* are modifications of *file2*. Then merge combines both changes. A conflict occurs if both *file1* and *file3* have changes in a common segment of lines. If a conflict is found, merge normally outputs a warning and puts brackets around the conflict, with lines preceded by <<<<<<< and >>>>>>>. A typical conflict looks like this:

```
<<<<<<< file1
relevant lines from file1
=======
relevant lines from file3
>>>>>>> file3
```

If there are conflicts, the user should edit the result and delete one of the alternatives.

Options

-A Output conflicts using the -A style of diff3. This merges all changes leading from *file2* to *file3* into *file1*, and generates the most verbose output.

-e Don't warn about conflicts.

-E Output conflict information in a less verbose style than -A; this is the default.

-L *label*
: Specify up to three labels to be used in place of the corresponding filenames in conflict reports. That is:

```
merge -L x -L y -L z file_a file_b file_c
```

generates output that looks as if it came from *x*, *y*, and *z* instead of from *file_a*, *file_b*, and *file_c*.

-p
: Send results to standard output instead of overwriting file1.

-q
: Quiet; don't warn about conflicts.

-V
: Print version number.

mkbom

```
mkbom [option] sourcedir bomfile
```

Creates a bill-of-materials, or *BOM* file. The new *BOM*, named in *bomfile*, lists the full contents of directory *sourcedir*. Included with each listing in the *BOM* is information about the listed file or directory, such as its permissions, size, and checksum. The Mac OS X Installer uses *BOMs* to determine what files to install, delete, or upgrade. See also `ditto` and `lsbom` for more information about working with *BOM* files.

Option

-s
: Create a simplified *BOM*, which includes only the pathnames of the listed files and directories.

mkdir

```
mkdir [options] directories
```

Creates one or more *directories*. You must have write permission in the parent directory in order to create a directory. See also `rmdir`. The default mode of the new directory is 0777, modified by the system or user's `umask`.

Options

-m
: Set the access *mode* for new directories. See `chmod` for an explanation of acceptable formats for *mode*.

-p
: Create intervening parent directories if they don't exist.

-v
: Verbose mode. Print directories as they're created.

Examples

Create a read-only directory named *personal*:

```
$ mkdir -m 444 personal
```

The following sequence:

```
$ mkdir work; cd work
$ mkdir junk; cd junk
$ mkdir questions; cd ../..
```

can be accomplished by typing this:

```
$ mkdir -p work/junk/questions
```

more

```
more [options] [files]
```

Displays the named *files* on a terminal, one screen at a time. See `less` for an alternative to `more`. Some commands can be preceded by a number.

Options

+num
: Begin displaying at line number *num*.

-num
: Set screen size to *num* lines.

+/pattern
: Begin displaying two lines before *pattern*.

`-c` Repaint screen from top instead of scrolling.

`-d` Display the prompt "Press space to continue, 'q' to quit" in response to illegal commands.

`-f` Count logical rather than screen lines. Useful when long lines wrap past the width of the screen.

`-l` Ignore form-feed (Ctrl-L) characters.

`-p` Page through the file by clearing each window instead of scrolling. This is sometimes faster.

`-r` Force display of control characters, in the form `^x`.

`-s` Squeeze; display multiple blank lines as one.

`-u` Suppress underline characters.

Commands

All commands in `more` are based on `vi` commands. An argument can precede many commands.

*num*SPACE
: Display next screen of text, or *num* more lines.

*num*z
: Display next lines of text, and redefine a screen to *num* lines. Default is one screen.

*num*RETURN
: Display *num* lines of text, and redefine a screen to *num* lines. Default is one line.

*num*d, ^D
: Scroll *num* lines of text, and redefine scroll size to *num* lines. Default scroll is 11 lines.

q, Q,
: Quit.

*num*s
: Skip forward *num* lines of text.

*num*f
: Skip forward *num* screens of text.

*num*b, ^B
: Skip backward *num* screens of text.

' Return to point where previous search began.

= Print number of current line.

/*pattern*
: Search for *pattern*, skipping to *num*th occurrence if an argument is specified.

n Repeat last search, skipping to *num*th occurrence if an argument is specified.

!*cmd*
: Invoke shell, and execute *cmd* in it.

v Invoke vi editor on the file, at the current line.

h Display the help information.

:n Skip to next file, skipping to *num*th file if an argument is specified.

:p Skip to previous file, skipping to *num*th file if an argument is specified.

:f Print current filename and line number.

. Re-execute previous command.

Examples

Page through *file* in "clear" mode and display prompts:

```
$ more -cd file
```

Format *doc* to the screen, removing underlines:

```
$ nroff doc | more -u
```

View the manpage for the grep command; begin near the word "BUGS" and compress extra whitespace:

```
$ man grep | more /BUGS -s
```

---

mount

```
mount [-t type]
mount [-d] [-f] [-r] [-u] [-v] [-w] { [-t types] -a | special | mount_point |
[-o mount_options] special mount_point]
```

Integrates volumes on local storage devices and network file servers into the system's directory hierarchy.

The first form of the command merely lists currently mounted volumes.

The second form of the command mounts volumes, with one of four possible sets of arguments. The -a flag causes all filesystems (possibly limited to those of a certain *type*) listed in */etc/fstab* or in the */mounts* directory of an Open Directory domain to be mounted, with the options given in the configuration. If only *special* or *mount_point* is provided, the associated fstab or Open Directory entry is used to determine what's mounted. The final alternative specifies both *special* and *mount_point*, and a possible list of options.

Options

-a
: Attempt to mount all filesystems listed in fstab or Open Directory, other than those marked with the noauto option.

-d
: Disable the actual mount, but do everything else. May be useful when used with the -v flag in a troubleshooting situation.

-f
: When using the -u flag and changing the status of a read-write filesystem to read-only, force the revocation of write access. Normally the change is denied if any files are open for writing at the time of the request.

-o
: Take a comma-separated list of options, which may include async, noauto, nodev, noexec, nosuid, union, and others. See the mount manpage for details.

-r
: Mount the filesystem for read-only access.

-t
: Restrict the use of the command to filesystems of the specified types presented in a comma-separated list, which may include hfs, ufs, afp, nfs, or others.

-u
: When used with -o, -r, or -w, change the status of a currently mounted filesystem to match the newly provided options.

-v
: Enable verbose output.

-w
: Mount the filesystem for read-write access.

special
: The form of this argument is particular to the type of filesystem being mounted, and could be a disk device name, a fixed string, or something involving a server name and directory. See the individual mount_type entries for details.

mount_point
: The directory on which the filesystem is mounted.

---

mount_afp

mount_afp [-i] [-o *mount_options*] afp:/[at]/[*username*[;AUTH=*auth_method*][:*password*]@]*afp_server*[:*port_or_zone*]/*share_name* *mount_point*

Mounts Apple Filing Protocol (AFP) shares as filesystem volumes. It takes an AFP URL and a mount point as arguments.

Options

-i Prompt for password if not specified in the AFP URL.

-o Takes -o options as listed in the mount manpage.

username
: The name to use for authentication to the AFP server. *username* may be null if the NO%20USER%20AUTHENT authentication method is used.

auth_method
: The name of the authentication method used. Examples include NO%20USER%20AUTHENT (no authentication required for guest-accessible shares), CLEARTXT%20PASSWRD (cleartext password), 2-WAY%20RANDNUM (two-way random number exchange), and CLIENT%20KRB%20V2 (Kerberos).

password
: The password to use for authentication. Note that specifying this on the command line exposes the password in a process listing.

afp_server
: The hostname or IP address of an AFP server.

port_or_zone
: A TCP port number if accessing the share over TCP/IP, or a zone name if accessing it over AppleTalk.

share_name
: The name of the AFP share you wish to access.

mount_point
: The directory on which the filesystem is mounted.

mount_cd9660

`mount_cd9660 [-e] [-g] [-j] [-r] [-s sector_num] device mount_point`

Mounts ISO-9660 CD-ROM filesystems into the directory hierarchy.

Options

-e Enable extended attributes.

-g Disable stripping version numbers from files, making all versions visible.

-j Disable Joliet extensions.

-r Disable Rockridge extensions.

-s Start the filesystem at the specified sector (given in 2048-byte blocks). Normally this is determined automatically.

device
: The CD device filename, e.g., */dev/disk1s2*.

mount_point
: The directory on which the filesystem is mounted.

mount_cddafs

```
mount_cddafs [-o mount_options] device mount_point
```

Mounts CDDAFS audio CD filesystems into the directory hierarchy.

Options

`-o` Take `-o` options as listed in the `mount` manpage.

device
: The CD device filename, e.g., */dev/disk1s2*.

mount_point
: The directory on which the filesystem is mounted.

mount_devfs

```
mount_devfs [-o mount_options] devfs mount_point
```

Mounts the *devfs* filesystem in */dev*, where block and character device special files exist.

Options

`-o` Take `-o` options as listed in the *mount* manpage. Not normally used for `mount_devfs`.

mount_point
: The directory on which the filesystem is mounted, normally */dev*.

mount_fdesc

```
mount_fdesc [-o mount_options] fdesc mount_point
```

Mounts the `fdesc` filesystem in */dev*. It contains the *fd* subdirectory, which contains one entry for each file descriptor held open by the process reading the contents of the directory. It also contains *stdin*, *stdout*, and *stderr*, which are symlinks to *fd/0*, *fd/1*, and *fd/2*, respectively; and *tty*, a reference to the controlling terminal for the process.

Options

`-o` Takes `-o` options as listed in the `mount` manpage. Normally includes the `union` option, which prevents mounting over and obscuring the *devfs* filesystem in */dev*.

mount_point
: The directory on which the filesystem is mounted, normally */dev*.

mount_ftp

```
mount_ftp [-o mount_options] [ftp://][username:password@]ftp_server:port_num
[/pathname] mount_point
```

Mounts FTP archives as filesystem volumes.

Options

`-o` Take `-o` options as listed in the `mount` manpage.

`username`
: The login name to use with an FTP server that requires authentication.

`password`
: The password to use with an FTP server that requires authentication. Note that specifying this on the command line exposes the password in a process listing.

`ftp_server`
: The hostname or IP address of an FTP server.

`port_num`
: The port number on which the server offers FTP service.

`pathname`
: The path to the directory you wish to access on the FTP server, relative to the site's default FTP root directory (e.g., */Library/FTPServer/FTPRoot* on Mac OS X Server). Defaults to */*.

`mount_point`
: The directory on which the filesystem is mounted. It must be an absolute pathname.

---

mount_hfs

```
mount_hfs [-w] [-o mount_options] device mount_point
mount_hfs [-e] [-x] [-u user_ID] [-g group_ID] [-m mode] [-o mount_options]
device mount_point
```

Mounts HFS and HFS+ filesystems into the directory hierarchy. The first form is applicable to HFS+ volumes, the second to HFS.

Options

`-e` Set the character set encoding. Defaults to `Roman`.

`-g` Set group ownership on files. Defaults to the mount point's group owner.

`-m` Set the maximum permissions for files. The argument is an octal mode, as described in the `chmod` manpage.

`-o` Take `-o` options as listed in the `mount` manpage.

`-u` Set ownership on files. Defaults to the mount point's owner.

`-w` Mount an HFS+ volume with its HFS wrapper, if one exists. An HFS wrapper is required for the volume to boot Mac OS 9.

`-x` Disable execute permissions.

`device`
: The disk device filename, e.g., */dev/disk0s5*.

`mount_point`
: The directory on which the filesystem is mounted.

mount_msdos

```
mount_msdos [-l | -s | -9] [-W filename] [-L locale] [-u user_ID] [-g group_ID]
[-m mode] [-o mount_options] device mount_point
```

Mounts DOS FAT filesystems into the directory hierarchy.

Options

`-9` Ignore files with Win95 long filenames and special attributes. This option may result in filesystem inconsistencies, so it's better to use `-s`.

`-g` Set group ownership on files in the volume. Defaults to the mount point's group owner.

`-l` List and generate long filenames and separate creation, modification, and access dates on files. This is the default if any long filenames exist in the volume's root directory, and neither `-s` nor `-9` have been specified.

`-L` Set the locale for character set conversions. Defaults to `ISO 8859-1`.

`-m` Set the maximum permissions for files in the volume. The argument is an octal mode, as described in the `chmod` manpage.

`-o` Take `-o` options as listed in the `mount` manpage.

`-s` Ignore and disable generation of long filenames and separate creation, modification, and access dates on files. This is the default if no long filenames exist in the volume's root directory, and `-l` has not been specified.

`-u` Set ownership on files in the volume. Defaults to the mount point's owner.

`-W` Specify a file containing character set conversion tables.

device
: The disk device filename, e.g., */dev/disk0s5*.

mount_point
: The directory on which the filesystem is mounted.

mount_nfs

```
mount_nfs [nfs_mount_options] [-o mount_options] nfs_server:pathname mount_point
```

Mounts Network File System (NFS) exports as filesystem volumes. `mount_nfs` can take a large number of options, most of which offer knobs to tune the performance of NFS mounts. Only a few are described in the "Options" section; see the manpage for full details.

Options

`-b` After an initial mount attempt fails, fork off a background process to continue trying the mount.

`-i` Make the mount interruptible, so that processes failing to access the mount can be terminated, instead of getting stuck in an uninterruptible state waiting on I/O.

-K Enable Kerberos authentication.

-m Specify a Kerberos realm to use with the -K option. Takes a realm name as an argument.

-o Takes -o options as listed in the mount manpage.

-s Make the mount soft, so that processes failing to access the mount eventually receive an error, instead of getting interminably stuck waiting on I/O.

-T Enable the use of TCP as the underlying network transport protocol, instead of the default UDP.

nfs_server
    The hostname or IP address of an NFS server.

pathname
    The pathname of the NFS export you wish to access.

mount_point
    The directory on which the filesystem is mounted.

---

mount_ntfs

```
mount_ntfs [-a] [-i] [-W filename] [-u user_ID] [-g group_ID] [-m mode]
[-o mount_options] device mount_point
```

Mounts NTFS filesystems into the directory hierarchy.

Options

-a Filenames are mapped to DOS 8.3 format.

-g Set group ownership on files in the volume. Defaults to the mount point's group owner.

-i Cause filename lookups to be case-insensitive.

-m Set the maximum permissions for files in the volume. The argument is an octal mode, as described in the chmod manpage.

-o Takes -o options as listed in the mount manpage.

-u Set ownership on files in the volume. Defaults to the mount point's owner.

-W Specify a file containing character set conversion tables.

device
    The disk device filename, e.g., */dev/disk0s5*.

mount_point
    The directory on which the filesystem is mounted.

mount_smbfs

```
mount_smbfs { -h | -v }
mount_smbfs [-u username_or_ID] [-g groupname_or_ID] [-f mode] [-d mode]
[-I hostname_or_IP] [-n long] [-N] [-U username] [-W workgroup_name]
[-O c_user[:c_group]/s_user[:s_group]] [-M c_mode[/s_mode]] [-R num_retries]
[-T timeout] [-o mount_options] [-x max_mounts] //
[workgroup;][username[:password]@]smb_server[/share_name] mount_point
```

Mounts Server Message Block (SMB) shares as filesystem volumes. It takes a share UNC and a mount point as arguments.

`mount_smbfs` can use the same configuration files used by *smbutil*: either *.nsmbrc* in the user's home directory or the global */usr/local/etc/nsmb.conf*, which overrides per-user files. The following example *.nsmbrc* demonstrates some of the available parameters:

```
[default]
username=leonvs
# NetBIOS name server
nbns=192.168.1.3

[VAMANA]
# server IP address
addr=192.168.1.6
workgroup=TEST

[VAMANA:LEONVS]
password= $$178465324253e0c07
```

The file consists of sections, each with a heading in brackets. Besides the `[default]` section, headings have a server name to which the parameters in the section apply, and can also include a username and a share name.

Sections of the configuration file may not be read properly unless the hostnames and usernames in the section headings are rendered in uppercase characters.

All sections and parameter definitions in *.nsmbrc* are optional; everything can be specified right on the `mount_smbfs` command line. It may come in handy for providing passwords for automated connections, when prompting for a password (which is the most secure method of providing it) is impractical. The value of the `password` parameter can be a cleartext password, but in this example is derived from the output of `smbutil crypt` *`password`*. While that's better than cleartext, don't trust the encryption too much, as it's fairly weak. Make sure you restrict permissions on *.nsmbrc* to prevent anyone reading your passwords.

Options

`-d`
: Specify directory permissions on the mounted volume, which default to the same as file permissions, plus an execute bit whenever a read bit is set. The argument is an octal mode, as described in the `chmod` manpage.

-f Specify file permissions on the mounted volume, which default to the same as those set on the mount point. The argument is an octal mode, as described in the chmod manpage.

-g Specify group ownership for files and directories on the mounted volume, which defaults to the same as that set on the mount point.

-h Print a brief usage statement to standard error.

-I Avoid NetBIOS name resolution, connecting directly to the hostname or IP address specified as an argument.

-M Assign access rights to the SMB connection.

-n With an argument of long, disable support for long filenames, restricting them to the "8.3" naming standard.

-N Suppress the prompt for a password. Unless a password is specified in a configuration file, authentication will fail for nonguest users.

-o Take -o options as listed in the mount manpage.

-O Assign owner attributes to the SMB connection.

-R Specify the number of times to retry a mount attempt. The default is 4.

-T Specify the connection request timeout (in seconds). The default is 15.

-u Specify ownership for files and directories on the mounted volume, which defaults to the same as that set on the mount point.

-U Specify a username for authentication. This may also be part of the UNC.

-v Print software version to standard error.

-W Specify an SMB workgroup or NT domain for authentication. This may also be part of the UNC.

-x Automatically mount all shares from the SMB server. The argument specifies a maximum number of shares that mount_smbfs is willing to mount from a server, to forestall resource starvation when the server has a very large number of shares. If the server has more shares than *max_mounts*, the mount attempt is cancelled.

workgroup
The name of the SMB workgroup or NT domain to use for authentication to the SMB server.

username
The name to use for authentication to the SMB server.

password
The password to use for authentication. Note that specifying this on the command line exposes the password in a process listing.

smb_server
The NetBIOS name of an SMB server.

share_name
The name of the SMB share you wish to access.

mount_point
The directory on which the filesystem is mounted.

mount_synthfs

```
mount_synthfs [-o mount_options] synthfs mount_point
```

Mounts a *synthfs* filesystem, which is a simple mapping of memory into the filesystem hierarchy (i.e., the contents of a *synthfs* filesystem are contained in memory). While creation of files in the filesystem is prevented (in fact, you may cause the system to hang after attempting to create files), directory hierarchies are allowed. This could be used to set up transient mount points for other volumes on, for example, read-only media with a shortage of spare directories to serve as mount points (like an installation CD).

Options

`-o` Take `-o` options as listed in the `mount` manpage.

mount_point
The directory on which the filesystem is mounted.

mount_udf

```
mount_udf [-e] [-o mount_options] device mount_point
```

Mounts Universal Disk Format (UDF) DVD-ROM filesystems into the directory hierarchy.

Options

`-e` Enable extended attributes.

`-o` Take `-o` options as listed in the `mount` manpage.

device
The DVD device filename, e.g., */dev/disk1*.

mount_point
The directory on which the filesystem is mounted.

mount_volfs

```
mount_volfs [-o mount_options] mount_point
```

Mounts the *volfs* filesystem in */.vol*. The *volfs* filesystem enables the Carbon File Manager API to map a file ID to a file, without knowing the BSD path to it. Thus, HFS aliases, which use file IDs, remain consistent, even if the targets of the aliases move around within the volume.

The */.vol* directory contains subdirectories named with numeric IDs, each associated with a volume on the system. While the directories appear empty if listed, with a file or directory ID, you can access any object on those volumes. A file ID is a unique number associated with each file on a volume (analogous to an inode number on a UFS-formatted filesystem) and can be viewed with the -i option of ls.

If you know a file's ID, you can access it as */.vol/vol_ID/file_ID*. If you know the ID of the directory the file is in, you can also access it as */.vol/vol_ID/dir_ID/filename*. The root directory of a volume always has a directory ID of 2, so you can map volume IDs to volumes with:

```
% cd /.vol/vol_ID/2; pwd
```


Options

-o
: Take -o options as listed in the mount manpage. Not normally used for mount_volfs.

mount_point
: The directory on which the filesystem is mounted, normally */.vol*.

mount_webdav

```
mount_webdav [-afile_descriptor] [-o mount_options] webdav_server[:port]
[/pathname] mount_point
```

Mounts directories from WebDAV-enabled servers as filesystem volumes.

Options

-a
: Specify a file descriptor associated with a file containing authentication information. See the mount_webdav manpage for details.

-o
: Take -o options as listed in the mount manpage.

webdav_server
: The hostname or IP address of a WebDAV server.

port
: The TCP port on which to access the server. Defaults to 80.

pathname
: The path to the directory you wish to access on the server, relative to the site's WebDAV root directory (e.g., */Library/WebServer/Documents* on Mac OS X Server). Defaults to /.

mount_point
: The directory on which the filesystem is mounted.

msdos.util

```
msdos.util -m device mount_point { fixed | removable } { readonly | writable }
{ suid | nosuid } { dev | nodev }
msdos.util -p device { fixed | removable } { readonly | writable }
msdos.util -u device
msdos.util -n device name
```

Mounts FAT (MS-DOS) filesystems into the directory hierarchy.

Options

-m Mount the device.

-n Reset the volume name of the device. This function doesn't appear to work.

-p Probe the device, and prints the volume name to standard output.

-u Unmount the device. This function doesn't appear to work.

device
: The disk device filename, e.g. *disk0s5*.

mount_point
: The directory on which the filesystem is mounted.

---

mv

`mv [option] sources target`

Moves or renames files and directories. In the following table, the source (first column) and target (second column) determine the result (third column):

Source	Target	Result
File	*name* (nonexistent)	Rename file to *name*.
File	Existing file	Overwrite existing file with source file.
Directory	*name* (nonexistent)	Rename directory to *name*.
Directory	Existing directory	Move directory to be a subdirectory of existing directory.
One or more files	Existing directory	Move files to directory.

`mv` doesn't preserve resource forks or HFS metadata when moving files that contain them. For such files, use `MvMac` instead.

Options

-f Force the move, even if target file exists; suppress messages about restricted access modes. Overrides previous -i and -n options.

-i Query user before removing files. Overrides previous -f and -n options.

-n Don't overwrite existing target files. Overrides previous -f and -i options.

-v Verbose; show files as they're being moved.

MvMac

`MvMac sources target`

Moves or renames files while preserving resource forks and HFS metadata. `MvMac` works like `mv`, but doesn't have any of `mv`'s options. `MvMac` is installed with the Xcode Tools into */Developer/Tools*. Since this directory isn't in the shell's search path by default, you might to need to specify `MvMac`'s pathname to invoke it.

netstat

```
netstat [options]
```

Shows network status. For all active sockets, prints the protocol, the number of bytes waiting to be received, the number of bytes to be sent, the port number, the remote address and port, and the state of the socket.

Options

`-A` Show the address of any protocol control blocks associated with sockets.

`-a` Show the state of all sockets, including server sockets (not displayed by default).

`-b` Modify the `-i` option display by providing bytes in and bytes out.

`-d` Modify the `-i` and `-w` options' display by providing dropped packets.

`-f` *`address_family`*
: Limit displayed information to the specified *`address_family`* where legitimate families are [`inet`, `inet6`, `unix`].

`-g` Display group address (multicast routing) information.

`-I` *`interface`*
: Display information for the specified *`interface`*.

`-i` Display state and packet transfer statistics for all auto-configured interfaces.

`-L` Display current listen queue sizes.

`-l` Modify display of `-r` option to include `mtu` information. As a standalone option, prints full IPv6 address.

`-M` *`core`*
: Extract information from specified *`core`* file instead of */dev/kmem*.

`-m` Display statistics related to network memory management routines

`-N` *`system`*
: Extract the name list from specified *`system`* instead of */kernel*.

`-n` Display network addresses using dotted octet notation (i.e., 172.24.30.1).

`-p` *`protocol`*
: Display statistics about *`protocol`* (see */etc/protocols* for names and aliases).

`-r` Display routing tables.

`-s`*`[s]`*
: Display per protocol statistics. Use of double `s` filters zero count statistics.

`-W` Don't truncate addresses.

`-w` *`wait`*
: Display network statistics every *`wait`* seconds.

nice

```
nice [option] [command [arguments]]
```

Executes a *command* (with its *arguments*) with lower priority (i.e., be "nice" to other users). With no arguments, nice prints the default scheduling priority (niceness). If nice is a child process, it prints the parent process's scheduling priority. Niceness has a range of -20 (highest priority) to 20 (lowest priority).

Option

-n *adjustment*, -adjustment, --adjustment=*adjustment*
: Run *command* with niceness incremented by *adjustment* (1 to 20); default is 10. A privileged user can raise priority by specifying a negative *adjustment* (e.g., –5).

nicl

```
nicl [options] datasource [command]
```

Modifies entries in the NetInfo database. You can manipulate directories and properties with nicl. The *datasource* may be the path to a NetInfo directory (such as /_) or the filesystem path of a NetInfo database (you must use the -raw option for this). Use -raw to work directly with the NetInfo database, such as */var/db/netinfo/local.nidb*. This is useful in cases when the NetInfo daemon is down (such as when you boot into single-user mode).

Options

-c
: Create a new data source.

-p
: Prompt for a password. You can use this instead of prefixing the command with sudo.

-P *password*
: Use the specified password.

-q
: Be quiet.

-raw
: Indicates that the *datasource* is a filesystem path to a NetInfo database.

-ro
: Open *datasource* as read-only.

-t
: Treat the domain as a tagged domain, which includes a machine name and a tagged NetInfo database.

-u *user*
: Use the specified user's identity when running the command. You'll be prompted for a password.

-v
: Be verbose.

-x500
: Use X.500 names (see the nicl manpage for more details).

Commands

`-append` *path key val ...*
: Append a value to an existing property. The property is created if it doesn't already exist.

`-copy` *path newparent*
: Copy the specified *path* to a new parent path.

`-create` *path [key [val ...]]*
: Create a NetInfo directory specified by *path*.

`-delete` *path [key [val ...]]*
: Destroy the specified path and all its contents. If you specify a key and/or value, only the specified key is deleted.

`-domainname`
: Print the NetInfo domain name of *datasource*.

`-flush`
: Flush the directory cache.

`-insert` *path key val index*
: Operate like `-append`, but instead of placing the value at the end, it inserts it at the specified index.

`-list` *path [key ...]*
: List all the NetInfo directories in the specified path. For example, to list all users, use `nicl / -list /users`.

`-merge` *path key val ...*
: Operate like `-append`, but if the value already exists, it is not duplicated.

`-move` *path newparent*
: Move the specified *path* to a new parent path.

`-read` *path [key ...]*
: Display all the properties of the specified path. For example, to see root's properties, use `nicl / -read /users/ root`.

`-search` *arguments*
: Perform a search within the NetInfo database. For complete details, see the `nicl` manpage.

`-rename` *path oldkey newkey*
: Rename a property.

`-resync`
: Resynchronize NetInfo.

`-rparent`
: Print the NetInfo parent of *datasource*.

`-statistics`
: Display NetInfo server statistics.

nidomain

`nidomain options`

Creates or destroys NetInfo databases. `nidomain` can also list which databases on a particular computer are serving which domains.

Options

`-l` *[host]*
: List which domains are served by machine *host*, or the local host if *host* is not specified.

`-m` *tag*
: Create a new local database to serve the NetInfo domain *tag*.

`-d` *tag*
: Destroy the local database serving domain *tag*.

`-c` *tag master/remotetag*
: Create the local database *tag*, cloned from the remote machine *master*'s database *remotetag*.

nidump

`nidump [-T timeout] (-r directory|format) [-t] domain`

Dumps NetInfo information in a flat-file format (such as the */etc/hosts* format) or in a raw format that uses a C-like syntax:

```
{
  "name" = ( "localhost" );
  "ip_address" = ( "127.0.0.1" );
  "serves" = ( "./local" );
}
```

Options

`-T` *timeout*
: Specify a timeout in seconds.

`-t`
: Treat the domain as a tagged domain, which includes a machine name and a tagged NetInfo database. For example, *abbot/local* refers to the local NetInfo domain of the machine named abbot.

`-r` *directory*
: Dump the directory in raw format. Directory should be a path to a NetInfo directory, such as */users/root* or */machines*.

format
: Specify a format corresponding to a Unix flat file of the same name. Can be: *aliases*, *bootptab*, *bootparams*, *ethers*, *exports*, *fstab*, *group*, *hosts*, *networks*, *passwd*, *printcap*, *protocols*, *resolv.conf*, *rpc*, *services*, or *mountmaps*.

domain
: Specify a NetInfo domain. For standalone machines, use a dot (.), which refers to the local domain.

---

nifind

```
nifind [options] nidir [domain]
```

Searches the root domain for the NetInfo directory *nidir* and returns the location and ID of the found directories. If *domain* is specified, searches the hierarchy only up to that domain.

Options

-a
: Search the entire NetInfo directory.

-n
: Don't search local directories.

-p
: Display the contents of the directories.

-T *n*
: Set the connection timeout to *n* seconds (default is 2).

-v
: Be verbose.

---

nigrep

```
nigrep regx [option]domain [nidir]
```

Searches the specified NetInfo domain using the regular expression *regx* and return the location and ID of the found directories. If *nidir* is specified, starts the search from that directory.

Option

-t
: Identify *domain* by a specified IP number or hostname and tag.

---

niload

```
niload  [-v] [-T timeout] [(-d|-m)] [(-p|-P password)]
[-u user] {-r directory|format} [-t] domain
```

Reads the Unix flat file format from standard input and loads it into the NetInfo database.

Options

-v
: Select verbose mode.

-T *timeout*
: Specify a timeout in seconds.

-d
: Specify that if a duplicate entry already exists, NetInfo deletes that entry before adding the new one. This can cause you to lose data if NetInfo is tracking information that isn't represented in the flat file. For example, if you dump the */users* directory to a flat passwd file format and load it back in with

niload -d, you will lose the picture, hint, and sharedDir properties for every user on your system because the passwd file doesn't have a field for those properties. Most of the time, the -m option is what you want.

-m
: Specify that if a duplicate entry already exists, niload will merge the changes. So, if you dump the */users* directory to a flat *passwd* file format, change a user's shell, and load that file back in with niload, NetInfo will keep the old shell. If you use the -m option, NetInfo will accept the new shell without the destructive side effects of the -d option.

-p
: Prompt for a password. You can use this instead of prefixing the command with sudo.

-P *password*
: Use the specified password.

If your shell history file is enabled, the -P option presents a security risk, since the password will be stored, along with the history of other shell commands. It is best to avoid using this option.

-u *user*
: Use the specified user's identity when running the command. You'll be prompted for a password.

-t
: Treat the domain as a tagged domain, which includes a machine name and a tagged NetInfo database.

domain
: Specify a NetInfo domain.

directory
: Denotes a path to a NetInfo directory.

format
: Specify a format corresponding to a Unix flat file of the same name. Can be: *aliases*, *bootptab*, *bootparams*, *exports*, *fstab*, *group*, *hosts*, *networks*, *passwd*, *printcap*, *protocols*, *rpc*, or *services*.

---

nireport

```
nireport [-T timeout] [-t] domain directory [property ...]
```

Lists all NetInfo groups.

Options

-T *timeout*
: Specify a timeout in seconds.

-t
: Treat the domain as a tagged domain, which includes a machine name and a tagged NetInfo database.

domain
: Specify a NetInfo domain.

directory
Denotes a path to a NetInfo directory.

property ...
Specify one or more NetInfo properties; e.g,, each user listed in the */users* directory has `name`, `passwd`, `uid`, and `gid` properties (as well as a few other properties). Every directory has a *name* property that corresponds to the directory name. For example, the */machines* directory's *name* property is `machines`.

You can use `nireport` to list any portion of the NetInfo directory. For example, to list the top-level directory, specify the local domain, the / directory, and the *name* property, as in `nireport . /` *name*.

niutil

`niutil` *command* `[-T` *timeout*`] [(-p|-P` *password*`)]`
`[-u` *user*`] [-R] [-t]` *arguments*

Uses `niutil` to modify entries in the NetInfo database. You can manipulate directories and properties with `niutil`.

Options

`-T` *timeout*
Specify a timeout in seconds.

`-p` Prompt for a password. You can use this instead of prefixing the command with `sudo`.

`-P` *password*
Use the specified password.

`-u` *user*
Use the specified user's identity when running the command. You'll be prompted for a password.

`-R` Retry the operation if the NetInfo server is busy.

`-t` Treat the domain as a tagged domain, which includes a machine name and a tagged NetInfo database.

Commands and arguments

`niutil -create` *options domain path*
Create a NetInfo directory specified by *path*. For example, the first step in creating a user is to create their directory with `niutil -create . /users/username`.

`niutil -destroy` *options domain path*
Destroy the specified path and all its contents.

`niutil -createprop` *options domain path propkey [val...]*
Create a property (specified by *propkey*) under the NetInfo directory specified by *path*. You can create a list by specifying multiple values.

`niutil -appendprop` *options domain path propkey val...*
Append a value to an existing property. The property is created if it doesn't already exist.

`niutil -mergeprop` *options domain path propkey val...*
This is like `-appendprop`, but if the value already exists, it is not added.

`niutil -insertval` *options domain path propkey val index*
This is like `-appendprop`, but instead of placing the value at the end, it inserts it at the specified index.

`niutil -destroyprop` *options domain path propkey...*
Delete the specified property. For an example, see the later section "Modifying a User."

`niutil -destroyval` *options domain path propkey val...*
Delete one or more values from a property.

`niutil -renameprop` *options domain path oldkey newkey*
Rename a property.

`niutil -read` *options domain path*
Display all the properties of the specified path. For example, to see root's properties, use `niutil -read . /users/ root`.

`niutil -list` *options domain path [propkey]*
List all the NetInfo directories in the specified path. For example, to list all users, use `niutil -list . /users`

`niutil -readprop` *options domain path propkey*
Display the values of the specified property.

`niutil -readval` *options domain path propkey index*
Display the value of the specified property at the given index. For example, to list the first member of the writers group, use `niutil -readval . /groups/ writers users 0`.

`niutil -rparent` *options domain*
Print the NetInfo parent of the specified domain.

`niutil -resync` *options domain*
Resynchronize NetInfo.

`niutil -statistics` *options domain*
Display NetInfo server statistics.

`niutil -domainname` *options domain*
Print the NetInfo domain name of the specified domain.

notifyd

`notifyd [-no_restart] [-no_startup] [-shm_pages` *integer*`]`

The notification server for the API described in the `notify(3)` manpage. (Use `man 3 notify` to display this page.) Using the API, processes may post notifications associated with arbitrary names, and other processes can register to be informed of such notification events. (A name should follow the convention used for Java classes: the reversed DNS domain name associated with the responsible organization, followed by one or more segments; e.g., `com.apple.system.timezone`.) `notifyd` sets up the shared memory used for the *notify_register_check* call, and directly answers *notify_check* requests for other notification methods (signal, Mach port, and file descriptor).

It also reads a configuration file, */etc/notify.conf*. Each line begins with one of two keywords: `reserve` or `monitor`. The `reserve` keyword lays out access restrictions for portions of the namespace. The arguments are a name, a user and a group that "owns" the name, and a set of read and write permissions for the user, the group, and others, similar to those applied to files. For example, the following line:

```
reserve com.apple.system. 0 0 rwr-r-
```

states that any names starting with *com.apple.system.* are owned by UID 0 (*root*) and GID 0 (*wheel*), and that anyone can receive notifications for these names, but only *root* (the owner) can post notifications.

The `monitor` keyword takes a name and a filename as arguments. When the specified file is changed, a notification is posted for the name. For example, the following line from the stock */etc/notify.conf* can be used by processes wishing to keep track of time zone changes:

```
monitor com.apple.system.timezone /etc/localtime
```

Another use would be to monitor changes to a daemon's configuration file. When the file is changed, the daemon or another process could receive notification and cause the daemon to automatically reread the configuration.

`notifyd` is started as a bootstrap daemon, from */etc/mach_init.d/notifyd.plist* (processed by *register_mach_bootstrap_servers*). It responds to HUP or TERM signals by restarting (unless the `-no_restart` flag was used), thus rereading */etc/notify.conf*. Before `notifyd` exits, it sends notifications for all registered names; after it restarts, processes registered for notifications must register again, as their tokens become invalid.

Options

`-no_restart`
: Disable automatic restart. Normally, if `notifyd` is killed, it's restarted within a few seconds.

`-no_startup`
: Apparently prevents `notifyd` from issuing notifications, while using all available CPU time. The purpose of this option is unknown.

`-shm_pages`
: Specify the number of pages (i.e., units of 4096 bytes) to reserve for shared memory (although it appears to use about twice that). Defaults to `1`.

nslookup

```
nslookup [-option...] [host_to_find | - [server ]]
```

Queries Internet domain name servers. `nslookup` has two modes: interactive and noninteractive. Interactive mode allows the user to query name servers for information about various hosts and domains or to print a list of hosts in a domain. Interactive mode is entered when either no arguments are provided (the default name server will be used), or the first argument is a hyphen and the second argument is the hostname or Internet address of a name server. Noninteractive mode is used to print just the name and requested information for a host or domain. It is used when the name of the host to be looked up is given as the first argument. Any of the *keyword=value* pairs listed under the interactive `set` command can be used as an option on the command line by prefacing the keyword with a –. The optional second argument specifies a name server.

Options

All options under the `set` interactive command can be entered on the command line, with the syntax - *keyword*[=*value*].

Interactive commands

`exit`
: Exit `nslookup`.

`finger` *[name] [>|>>filename]*
: Connect to finger server on current host, optionally creating or appending to *filename*.

`help, ?`
: Print a brief summary of commands.

`host` *[server]*
: Look up information for *host* using the current default server or using *server* if specified.

`ls -`*[*`adhs`*] -[*`t` *querytype] domain [>|>>filename]*
: List information available for *domain*, optionally creating or appending to *filename*. The `-a` option lists aliases of hosts in the domain. `-d` lists all contents of a zone transfer. `-h` lists CPU and operating system information for the domain. `-s` lists well-known services for the domain. `-t` lists all records of the specified type (see type table).

`lserver` *domain*
: Change the default server to *domain*. Use the initial server to look up information about *domain*.

`root`
: Change default server to the server for the root of the domain namespace.

`server` *domain*
: Change the default server to *domain*. Use the current default server to look up information about *domain*.

`set` *keyword[=value]*

Change state information affecting the lookups. Valid keywords are:

`all` Print the current values of the frequently used options to `set`.

`class=`*name(upper or lower class)*
: Set query class to `IN` (Internet; default), `CHAOS`, `HESIOD/HS`, or `ANY`.

`domain=`*name*
: Change default domain name to *name*.

`[no]debug`
: Turn debugging mode on or off.

`[no]d2`
: Turn exhaustive debugging mode on or off.

`[no]defname`
: Append default domain name to a single-component lookup name.

`[no]ignoretc`
: Ignore truncate error.

`[no]recurse`
: Tell name server to query or not query other servers if it doesn't have the information.

`[no]search`
: With `defname`, search for each name in parent domains of current domain.

`[no]vc`
: Always use a virtual circuit when sending requests to the server.

`port=`*port*
: Connect to name server using *port*.

`querytype=`*value*
: See `type=`*value*.

`retry=`*number*
: Set number of retries to *number*.

`root=`*host*
: Change name of root server to *host*.

`srchlist=`*domain-list*
: Where *domain-list* is a maximum of six slash (/) separated domain names.

`timeout=`*number*
: Change timeout interval for waiting for a reply to *number* seconds.

`type=`*value*
: Change type of information returned from a query to one of:

`A` Host's Internet address

`ANY` Any available information

Unix Command Reference

`CNAME`
: Canonical name for an alias

`HINFO`
: Host CPU and operating system type

`MD` Mail destination

`MG` Mail group member

`MINFO`
: Mailbox or mail list information

`MR` Mail rename domain name

`MX` Mail exchanger

`NS` Nameserver for the named zone

`PTR` Hostname or pointer to other information

`SOA` Domain start-of-authority

`TXT` Text information

`UINFO`
: User information

`WKS` Supported well-known services

`view` *`filename`*
: Sort and list output of previous `ls` command(s) with `more`. This appears to be nonfunctional in Mac OS X Version 10.2

ntfs.util

```
ntfs.util -m device mount_point { fixed | removable } { readonly | writable }
{ suid | nosuid } { dev | nodev }
ntfs.util -p device { fixed | removable } { readonly | writable }
ntfs.util -u device
ntfs.util -n device name
```

Mounts NTFS filesystems into the directory hierarchy.

Options

`-m` Mount the device.

`-n` Reset the volume name of the device.

`-p` Probe the device, and prints the volume name to standard output.

`-u` Unmount the device.

`device`
: The disk device filename, e.g., *disk0s5*.

`mount_point`
: The directory on which the filesystem is mounted.

ntp-wait

```
ntp-wait [-v] [-f] [-n num_tries] [-s time]
```

A Perl script that reports whether the local ntpd has synchronized yet. Returns 0 if synchronized, 1 if not.

Options

-f Cause ntp-wait to return 1 if an indeterminate result is received from ntpd; otherwise, ntp-wait returns 0.

-n Specify the number of times to try for a successful result before quitting. Defaults to 1000.

-s Specify the number of seconds between tries. Defaults to 6.

-v Enable verbose output to standard output.

ntptimeset

```
ntptimeset [-l] [-d]... [-v] [-s] [-c filename] [-u] [-S integer] [-V integer]
[-t timeout] [-H] [-a key_id] [-e delay]
```

Synchronizes the system clock in a manner similar to ntpdate, but in a way that attempts to compensate for current, possibly degraded, network conditions.

Options

-a Enable secure authentication with the key specified by the given identifier.

-c Specify the location of the configuration file. Defaults to */etc/ntp.conf*.

-d Enable debugging output.

-e Specify the delay, in seconds, caused by authentication. Normally this is negligible.

-H Simulate poor network conditions by dropping a proportion of network packets.

-l Enable logging to *syslog*.

-s Set the system clock. Otherwise, ntptimeset merely reports the clock's offset.

-S Specify a minimum number of servers that must respond. Defaults to 3.

-t Specify the time, in seconds, spent waiting for a server response. Defaults to 1.

-u Use an unprivileged client port.

-v Enable verbose output.

-V Specify a minimum number of servers that must respond with a valid time. Defaults to 1.

nvram

```
nvram [ -p] [-f filename] [name ] [= value ] ...
```

Modifies Open Firmware variables, which control the boot- time behavior of your Macintosh. To list all Open Firmware variables, use `nvram -p`. The Apple Open Firmware page is *http://bananajr6000.apple.com*.

To change a variable, you must run `nvram` as root or as the *super_user*. To set a variable, use *`variable=value`*. For example, to configure Mac OS X to boot verbosely, use `nvram boot-args=-v`. (Booting into Mac OS 9 or earlier resets this.) The table in this section lists Open Firmware variables. Some variables use the Open Firmware Device Tree notation (see the TechNotes available at the Apple Open Firmware page).

Be careful changing the `nvram` utility, since incorrect settings can turn a G4 iMac into a $2000 doorstop. If you render your computer unbootable, you can reset Open Firmware by zapping the PRAM. To zap the PRAM, hold down Option-⌘-P-R as you start the computer, and then release the keys when you hear a second startup chime.

Options

`-f` *`filename`*
: Read the variables to be set from *`filename`*, a text file of *`name=value`* statements.

`-p` Display all Open Firmware variables.

Variable	Description
auto-boot?	The automatic boot settings. If `true` (the default), Open Firmware automatically boots an operating system. If `false`, the process stops at the Open Firmware prompt. Be careful using this with Old World (unsupported) machines and third-party graphics adapters because the display and keyboard may not be initialized until the operating system starts (in which case you won't have access to Open Firmware).
boot-args	The arguments that are passed to the boot loader.
boot-command	The command that starts the boot process. The default is `mac-boot`, an Open Firmware command that examines the `boot- device` for a Mac OS startup.
boot-device	The device to boot from. The syntax is *`device`*`:`[*partition*],*path*:*`filename`*, and a common default is `hd:,\\:tbxi`. In the path, `\\` is an abbreviation for */System/Library/CoreServices*, and `tbxi` is the file type of the *BootX* boot loader. (Run */Developer/Tools/GetFileInfo* on *BootX* to see its type.)
boot-file	The name of the boot loader. (This is often blank because `boot-command` and `boot-device` are usually all that are needed.)
boot-screen	The image to display on the boot screen.
boot-script	A variable that can contain an Open Firmware boot script.
console-screen	A variable that specifies the console output device, using an Open Firmware Device Tree name.
default-client- ip	An IP address for diskless booting.
default-gateway- ip	A gateway address for diskless booting.

Variable	Description
default-mac- address?	Description not available at time of writing; see errata page at *http://www.oreilly.com/catalog/mosxian?*.
default-router- ip	A router address for diskless booting.
default-server- ip	An IP address for diskless booting.
default-subnet- mask	A default subnet mask for diskless booting.
diag-device	A private variable; not usable for security reasons.
diag-file	A private variable; not usable for security reasons.
diag-switch?	A private variable; not usable for security reasons.
fcode-debug?	A variable that determines whether the Open Firmware Forth interpreter displays extra debugging information.
input-device	The input device to use for the Open Firmware console.
input-device-1	A secondary input device (so you can have a screen and serial console at the same time). Use *scca* for the first serial port.
little-endian?	The CPU endian-ness. If `true`, initializes the PowerPC chip as little-endian. The default is `false`.
load-base	A private variable; not usable for security reasons.
mouse-device	The mouse device using an Open Firmware Device Tree name.
nvramrc	A sequence of commands to execute at boot time (if `use-nvramc?` is set to `true`).
oem-banner	A custom banner to display at boot time.
oem-banner?	The `oem` banner settings. Set to `true` to enable the `oem` banner. The default is `false`.
oem-logo	A 64-by-64 bit array containing a custom black-and-white logo to display at boot time. This should be specified in hex.
oem-logo?	The `oem` logo settings. Set to `true` to enable the `oem` logo. The default is `false`.
output-device	The device to use as the system console. The default is `screen`.
output-device-1	A secondary output device (so you can have everything go to both the screen and a serial console). Use *scca* for the first serial port.
pci-probe-mask	A private variable; not usable for security reasons.
ram-size	The amount of RAM currently installed. For example, 256 MB is shown as `0x10000000`.
real-base	The starting physical address that is available to Open Firmware.
real-mode?	The address translation settings. If `true`, Open Firmware will use real-mode address translation. Otherwise, it uses virtual-mode address translation.
real-size	The size of the physical address space available to Open Firmware.
screen-#columns	The number of columns for the system console.
screen-#rows	The number of rows for the system console.
scroll-lock	Set by page checking output words to prevent Open Firmware text from scrolling off the top of the screen.
selftest-#megs	The number of MB of RAM to test at boot time. The default is `0`.
use-generic?	The device node naming settings. Specify whether to use generic device node names such as "screen," as opposed to Apple hardware code names.
use-nvramrc?	The command settings. If this is `true`, Open Firmware uses the commands in *nvramrc* at boot time.
virt-base	The starting virtual address that is available to Open Firmware.
virt-size	The size of the virtual address space Open Firmware.

od

```
od [-c] [-a] [-b] [-B] [-o] [-O] [-d] [-D] [-i] [-I] [-l] [-L] [-f] [-e] [-
F] [-h] [-x] [-H] [-X] [-v] [filename]
```

Prints the contents of a file to standard output in a variety of formats. (If no filename is specified, it acts on the contents of standard input.) The name is an acronym for *octal dump*, from its default behavior of displaying files as series of octal numbers.

`od` has been deprecated in favor of `hexdump`; in fact, the two binaries are hard-linked to the same data. However, traditional `od` syntax applies when invoked by that name. See the `hexdump` manpage for more.

Options

`-a` Display content in 1-byte chunks of ASCII characters, hexadecimal numbers, and short strings representing control characters.

`-b` Display content in 1-byte chunks of octal numbers.

`-B` Display content in 2-byte chunks of octal numbers. This is the default.

`-c` Display content in 1-byte chunks of ASCII characters, octal numbers, and escape sequences representing control characters. This is probably the most commonly used option.

`-d` Display content in 2-byte chunks of unsigned decimal integers.

`-D` Display content in 4-byte chunks of unsigned decimal integers.

`-e` Display content in 8-byte chunks of decimal floating point numbers.

`-f` Display content in 4-byte chunks of decimal floating point numbers.

`-F` Same as `-e`.

`-h` Display content in 2-byte chunks of hexadecimal numbers.

`-H` Display content in 4-byte chunks of hexadecimal numbers.

`-i` Display content in 2-byte chunks of signed decimal integers.

`-I` Display content in 4-byte chunks of signed decimal integers.

`-l` Same as `-I`.

`-L` Same as `-I`.

`-o` Same as `-B`.

`-O` Display content in 4-byte chunks of octal numbers.

`-v` Disable the suppression of duplicate lines, which are normally represented by a single asterisk.

`-x` Same as `-h`.

`-X` Same as `-H`.

open

```
open file
open [-a application] file
open [-e] file
```

The open command can be used to open files and directories, and to launch applications from the Terminal application.

Options

-a *application*
: Use *application* to open the file.

-e *file*
: Force the use of Mac OS X's TextEdit application to open the specified *file*.

-f
: Read input from standard input and opens the text in TextEdit.

Examples

To open a directory in the Finder, use open, followed by the name of the directory. For example, to open the current directory, type:

```
$ open .
```

To open your Public folder in the Finder:

```
$ open ~/Public
```

To open the */Applications* folder in the Finder:

```
$ open /Applications
```

To open an application, you need only its name. For example, you can open Xcode (*/Developer/Applications*) with this command:

```
$ open -a Xcode
```

You aren't required to enter the path for the application—only its name—even if it is a Classic application. The only time you are required to enter the path is if you have two different versions of an application with similar names on your system.

You can also supply a filename argument with the -a option, which launches the application and open the specified file with that application. You can use this option to open a file with something other than the application with which it's associated. For example, to open an XML file in Xcode instead of the default text editor, TextEdit, you can use the following command:

```
$ open -a Xcode data.xml
```

To open multiple files, you can use wildcards:

```
$ open *.c
```

To force a file to be opened with TextEdit, use -e:

```
$ open -e *.c
```

The -e option opens only files in the TextEdit application; it can't open a file in another text editor, such as BBEdit. If you want to use TextEdit on a file that's owned by an administrator (or root), open -e won't work. You need to specify the full executable path, as in:

```
$ sudo /Applications/TextEdit.app/ ↵
Contents/MacOS/TextEdit filename
```

opendiff

`opendiff` *`file1 file2`* `[-ancestor` *`ancestor_file`*`] [-merge` *`merge_file`*`]`

Opens the two designated files in the FileMerge application.

Options

`-ancestor`
: Compare the two files against a common ancestor file.

`-merge`
: Merge the two files into a new file.

open-x11

`open-x11` *`app_name`*`...`

Starts specified X Window System applications using the X11 application.

Options

app_name
: The name of an executable X11 application. Those delivered with Mac OS X are in */usr/X11R6/bin/*. If located in a standard directory, the application pathname is not required.

osacompile

`osacompile [-l` *`language`*`] [-e` *`command`*`] [-o` *`name`*`] [-d] [-r` *`typeid`*`] [-t` *`type`*`]`
`[-c` *`creator`*`] [`*`file...`*`]`

Compiles into a new script file one or more text or compiled OSA script files or standard input.

Options

`-c` *`creator`*
: Assign the four-character file-creator code *creator* to the new script (the default is `osas`).

`-e` *`command`*
: Use *command* as a line of script to be compiled. You can use more than one -e option; each will specify a new line of script.

`-i` *`pathname`*
: Use the dictionary from the application *pathname* when compiling.

`-l OSAlang`
: Use OSA language *OSAlang* instead of the default AppleScript. Use the `osalang` command (described later in this chapter) to get information on all of the system's OSA languages.

`-o name`
: Use *name* as a filename for the new script instead of the default *a.scpt*.

`-r type:id`
: Place the resulting script in the resource fork of the output file, in the resource specified by *type:id*.

`-t type`
: Assign the four-character file-type code *type* to the new script (the default is `osas`).

`-x`
: Save file as execute only. This doesn't produce an applet, but a compiled script file that can't be viewed in Script Editor.

Examples

Use the filename *newscript* for a new script file, compiled from the source in *scripttext.txt*:

```
$ osacompile -o newscript scripttext.txt
```

Compile the file *scripttext.txt* into a compiled script called *newscript* (assuming that a JavaScript OSA scripting component exists on the system):

```
$ osacompile -l JavaScript rawscript.txt
```

---

osalang

`osalang [options]`

Lists the computer's installed OSA-compliant languages (i.e., languages that use Apple Events to communicate among applications). In the newness of Mac OS X, this command may only return "AppleScript" and "Generic Scripting System."

Options

`-d` Print only the default language.

`-l` List the name and description for each installed language.

`-L` List the name and a longer description for each installed language.

---

osascript

`osascript [options] [files]`

Executes an OSA script from *files*, or from standard input if *files* isn't specified.

Options

-e *command*
: Use *command* as a line of script to be compiled. You can use more than one -e option; each specifies a new line of script.

-l *OSAlang*
: Use OSA language *OSAlang* instead of the default AppleScript. Use the osalang command (described previously) to get information on all of the system's OSA languages.

-s *options*
: Provide output as specified in *options* with one or more of these flags:

  h Human readable (default)

  s Recompilable source

  e Send errors to standard error (default)

  o Send errors to standard output

Examples

To run a script that displays a dialog window from the Finder, first run osascript with no arguments, which allows you to enter the script into standard input:

```
$ osascript
tell app "Finder"
activate
display dialog "Mac OS X Rules!"
end tell
```

Press Ctrl-D to send an EOF, at which point osascript executes the script and prints the value returned:

```
button returned:OK
```

Run with the -s s option, the output is better formatted for subsequent parsing:

```
$ osascript -s s
tell app "Finder"
activate
display dialog "Mac OS X Rules!"
end tell
{button returned:"OK"} or argument/switch mismatch
```

---

passwd

passwd [-i *infosystem*] [-l *location*] [*username*]

Sets a user password in the designated directory service.

Options

-i Specify the directory service to use, which may be file, netinfo (the default), nis, or opendirectory.

-l Depending on the directory service being used, it's either a filename (defaults to */etc/master.passwd*), a NetInfo domain name or server/tag combo, a NIS domain name, or and Open Directory node name.

username
Designate whose password will be set. It defaults to that of the user running the command.

Unix Command Reference

paste

```
paste [options] files
```

Merges corresponding lines of one or more *files* into vertical columns, separated by a tab. See also `cut`, `join`, and `pr`.

Options

- Replace a filename with the standard input.

-d'*char*'
Separate columns with *char* instead of a tab. *char* can be any regular character or the following escape sequences:

You can separate columns with different characters by supplying more than one char:

\n Newline

\t Tab

\ Backslash

\0 Empty string

-s Merge subsequent lines from one file.

Examples

Create a three-column file from files *x*, *y*, and *z*:

```
$ paste x y z > file
```

List users in two columns:

```
$ who | paste - -
```

Merge each pair of lines into one line:

```
$ paste -s -d"\t\n" list
```

pax

```
pax [options] [patterns]
```

Portable Archive Exchange program. When members of the POSIX 1003.2 working group couldn't standardize on either `tar` or `cpio`, they invented this program. (See also `cpio` and `tar`.) Note that until native drivers for tape drives exist for Mac OS X, `pax` can't write to tape. Note also that `pax` doesn't preserve resource forks or HFS metadata when copying files that contain them.

pax operates in four modes, depending on the combinations of `-r` and `-w`:

List mode
: No `-r` and no `-w`. List the contents of a pax archive. Optionally, restrict the output to filenames and/or directories that match a given pattern.

Extract mode
: `-r` only. Extract files from a pax archive. Intermediate directories are created as needed.

Archive mode
: `-w` only. Archive files to a new or existing pax archive. The archive is written to standard output; it may be redirected to an appropriate tape device if needed for backups.

Pass-through mode
: `-r` and `-w`. Copy a directory tree from one location to another, analogous to `cpio -p`.

Options

Here are the options available in the four modes:

```
None:      c d f       n     s     v                   U G   T
-r:        c d f i k   n o p s   u v   D         Y Z E U G   T
-w:    a b   d f i       o   s t u v x   H L P X       U G B T
-rw:         d   i k l n   p s t u v   D H L P X Y Z   U G   T
```

`-a` Append files to the archive. This may not work on some tape devices.

`-b` *`size`*
: Use *`size`* as the blocksize, in bytes, of blocks to be written to the archive.

`-c` Complement. Match all file or archive members that don't match the patterns.

`-d` For files or archive members that are directories, extract or archive only the directory itself, not the tree it contains.

`-f` *`archive`*
: Use *`archive`* instead of standard input or standard output.

`-i` Interactively rename files. For each file, pax writes a prompt to */dev/tty* and reads a one-line response from */dev/tty*. The responses are as follows:

Return
: Skip the file.

A period
: Take the file as is.

new name
: Anything else is taken as the new name to use for the file.

EOF
: Exit immediately with a nonzero exit status.

`-k` Don't overwrite existing files.

-l Make hard links. When copying a directory tree (-rw), make hard links between the source and destination hierarchies wherever possible.

-n Choose the first archive member that matches each pattern. No more than one archive member will match for each pattern.

-o *options*
Reserved for format-specific options specified by the -x option.

-p *privs*
Specify one or more privileges for the extracted file. *privs* specify permissions or other characteristics to be preserved or ignored.

a Don't preserve file-access times.

e Retain the user and GIDs, permissions (mode), and access and modification time.

m Don't preserve the file modification time.

o Retain the user and group ID.

p Keep the permissions (mode).

-r Read an archive and extract files.

-s *replacement*
Use *replacement* to modify file or archive member names. This is a string of the form - s/*old*/*new*/[gp]. This is similar to the substitution commands in ed, ex, and sed. *old* is a regular expression, and *new* may contain & to mean the matched text and *n* for subpatterns. The trailing g indicates the substitution should be applied globally. A trailing p causes pax to print the resulting new filename. Multiple -s options may be supplied. The first one that works is applied. Any delimiter may be used, not just /, but in all cases, it is wise to quote the argument to prevent the shell from expanding wildcard characters.

-t Reset the access time of archived files to what they were before being archived by pax.

-u Ignore files older than preexisting files or archive members. The behavior varies based on the current mode:

Extract mode
Extract the archive file if it is newer than an existing file with the same name.

Archive mode
If an existing file with the same name as an archive member is newer than the archive member, supersede the archive member.

Pass-through mode
Replace the file in the destination hierarchy with the file in the source hierarchy (or a link to it) if the source hierarchy's file is newer.

-v In list mode, print a verbose table of contents. Otherwise, print archive member names on standard error.

-w Write files to standard output in the given archive format.

`-x` *`format`*
: Use the given format for the archive. The value of format is either `cpio` or `ustar`. The details of both formats are provided in the IEEE 1003.1 (1990) POSIX standard. The two formats are mutually incompatible; attempting to append using one format to an archive while using the other is an error.

`-B` Set the number of bytes that can be written to one archive volume. This option can only be used by a device that supports an end-of-file read condition such as a file or tape drive. This option shouldn't be used with a floppy or hard disk.

`-D` The file inode change time is checked to see if it is a newer version of the file.

`-E` *`limit,`*
: Set the number of read errors that can occur before `pax` will stop. *`limit`* can be from `0` to `none`. `0` causes `pax` to stop after the first read error; `none` keeps `pax` from stopping on any amount of errors. Caution should be used with `none` as it can put `pax` into an infinite loop if the archive is severely flawed

`-G` The group is used to select the file. To select by group number instead of group name, use a # in front of the number; to escape the #, use \.

`-H` If any of the pathnames given in the command line are symbolic links, follow only those links.

`-L` Follow all symbolic links.

`-P` Don't follow symbolic links. This is the default.

`-T` *`[from_date][,to_date][/[c][m]]`*
: Use either file modification date[*m*] or inode change time[*c*] to select files in a specified date range. The options c and `m` can be used together. The default option is `m`.

`-U` The user is used to select the file. To select by UID instead of username, use a # in front of the number; to escape the #, use \.

`-X` When traversing directory trees, don't cross into a directory on a different device (the `st_dev` field in the `stat` structure, see `stat`(2); similar to the `-mount` option of `find`).

`-Y` Similar to the `-D` option, with the exception that `pax` checks the inode change time after it has completed the filename modifications, and a pathname has been generated.

`-Z` Similar to the `-u` option, with the exception that `pax` checks the modification time after it has completed the filename modifications, and a pathname has been generated.

Example

Copy a home directory to a different directory (presumably on a bigger disk):

```
$ cd /Users
$ pax -r -w chuck/newhome
```

pbcopy

```
pbcopy [-help] [-pboard ( general | find | font | ruler )]
```

Copies standard input to the pasteboard buffer. The Clipboard is used to implement GUI copy, cut, and paste operations; drag-and-drop operations; and the Cocoa Services menu.

Options

`-help`
: Print a usage statement to standard output.

`-pboard`
: Specify the pasteboard to use: either the name used for general copying and pasting or a special-purpose pasteboard used for holding `find`, `font`, or `ruler` settings. Defaults to `general`.

pbpaste

```
pbpaste[-help] [-pboard ( general | find | font | ruler }] [-Prefer {
ascii | rtf | ps }]
```

Prints the contents of the Clipboard to standard output. The combination of `pbcopy` and `pbpaste` may be an interesting tool to use in scripting. However, the Clipboard can be modified by other processes at any time, which limits the tool's actual usefulness.

Options

`-help`
: Print a usage statement to standard output.

`-Prefer`
: Specify the output format to use if the desired format (ASCII, Rich Text Format, or PostScript) is available in the Clipboard.

`-pboard`
: Specify the pasteboard to use: either the name used for general copying and pasting or a special-purpose pasteboard used for holding `find`, `font`, or `ruler` settings. Defaults to `general`.

pdisk

```
pdisk
pdisk device { -diskSize | -isDiskPartitioned | -dump | -blockSize |
-initialize }
pdisk device { -partitionEntry | -partitionName | -partitionType |
-partitionBase | -partitionSize | -deletePartition } part_num
pdisk device { -setWritable | -setAutoMount } part_num { 0 | 1 }
pdisk device -makeBootable part_num boot_addr boot_bytes load_addr goto_addr
pdisk device -createPartition part_name part_type part_base part_size
pdisk device -splitPartition part_num part1_size part2_name part2_type
pdisk device -getPartitionOfType part_type instance_num
pdisk device -getPartitionWithName part_name instance_num
```

Provides control over Apple partition maps on disk devices in Macintosh systems.

Options

`-blockSize`
: Print the block size of the specified device, in bytes, to standard output.

`-createPartition`
: Add a partition to the partition map with the specified name, type (such as `Apple_HFS` or `Apple_UFS`), base (i.e., starting block number), and size (in blocks).

`-deletePartition`
: Delete the specified partition from the partition map.

`-diskSize`
: Print the size of the specified device, in megabytes, to standard output.

`-dump`
: Print the partition map on the specified device to standard output.

`-getPartitionOfType`
: Print the number of a partition with the specified type to standard output. An *`instance_num`* of `0` refers the lowest-numbered partition of the specified type, `1` refers to the second partition of that type, etc.

`-getPartitionWithName`
: Print the number of a partition with the specified name to standard output. An *`instance_num`* of `0` refers the lowest-numbered partition with the specified name, `1` refers to the second partition of that name, etc.

`-initialize`
: Create a partition map on the device.

`-isDiskPartitioned`
: Return `0` if the device has an Apple partition map on it, 1 if not.

`-makeBootable`
: Set the startup bit on a partition. This is unused by Mac OS X.

`-partitionBase`
: Print the starting block number of the specified partition to standard output.

`-partitionEntry`
: Print a line to standard output containing the name, type, base, and size of the specified partition.

`-partitionName`
: Print the name of the specified partition to standard output.

`-partitionSize`
: Print the size of the specified partition, in blocks, to standard output.

`-partitionType`
: Print the type of the specified partition to standard output.

-setAutoMount
: Set (1) or clears (0) the automount bit on a partition. This is unused by Mac OS X.

-setWritable
: Set (1) or clears (0) the writable bit on a partition.

-splitPartition
: Split an existing partition in two. The arguments include the size (in blocks) of the first partition formed from the split, and the name and type of the second partition.

device
: The disk device filename, e.g., */dev/disk0*.

Commands

pdisk enters interactive mode when invoked without arguments. Interactive commands that take arguments will prompt for any that are missing.

? Display a summary list of commands.

a Toggle the abbreviate flag. When in abbreviate mode, partition type names are shortened. For example, Apple_HFS is displayed as HFS.

d Toggle the debug flag. When in debug mode, some extra commands are enabled, including commands to display block contents and partition map data structures.

e *device*
: Edit the partition map on a device.

E *device*
: Should open a partition map for editing after prompting for a redefinition of the logical block size from the default 512 bytes, but this doesn't appear to work at present.

h Display a summary list of commands.

l *device*
: Display the partition map on a device.

L Display the partition maps on all devices.

p Toggle the physical flag. When in physical mode, block positions and sizes are reported according the physical limits of the partitions, which may not be the same as their logical limits.

q Quit interactive mode.

r Toggle the read-only flag. When in read-only mode, changes to the partition map are disallowed.

v Print the version number and release date of pdisk. (The output is currently far out of date, listing a release in 1997, when it was still used for MkLinux.)

`x` *device block_num*
: Display the contents of the block given by *block_num*. While it always appears to produce a bus error when called at this level, the same functionality is available from an expert level while editing a map, where it does work.

---

pdump

```
pdump [-v] [-s] [-h] [-p] [-d] [-d0] [-d1] [-d2] [-d3] [-d4] [-d5] [-d6]
[-st] [-i] [-e] [-x] [-if] [-t] [-o] [-k] [-m] [-class class] [-protocol
protocol] [-arch arch] [-f]
```

Prints information about precompiled header files to standard output. See the entry for `fixPrecomps` for more on precompiled headers.

Options

`-arch`
: Appears to do nothing.

`-class`
: List the method declarations for the specified class.

`-d` List all declarations.

`-d0` List type definition declarations.

`-d1` List class declarations.

`-d2` List category declarations.

`-d3` List protocol declarations.

`-d4` List enumerated constant declarations.

`-d5` List function declarations.

`-d6` List variable declarations.

`-e` List entry macros.

`-f` Appears to do nothing.

`-h` List included headers.

`-i` List all identifiers.

`-if` List conditional macros defined outside the precompiled header.

`-k` List "must keeps."

`-m` List method names and their classes.

`-o` List preprocessed tokens.

`-p` List paths to included headers.

`-protocol`
: List the method declarations for the specified protocol.

`-s` List bytes taken up by each of several kinds of elements in the precompiled header.

-st List all strings.

-t List all tags.

-v Enable verbose output.

-x List exit macros.

periodic

```
periodic name
```

Serves as a method of organizing recurring administrative tasks. periodic is used in conjunction with the cron facility, called by the following three entries from */etc/crontab*:

```
1   3   *   *   *   root    periodic daily
15  4   *   *   6   root    periodic weekly
30  5   1   *   *   root    periodic monthly
```

The facility is controlled by the */etc/defaults/periodic.conf* file, which specifies its default behavior. periodic runs all the scripts that it finds in the directory specified in *name*. If *name* is an absolute pathname, there is no doubt as to which directory is intended. If simply a name—such as daily—is given, the directory is assumed to be a subdirectory of */etc/periodic* or of one of the alternate directories specified in the configuration file's *local_periodic* entry.

periodic can also be executed from the command line to run the administrative scripts manually. For example, to run the daily script, run periodic as root using daily as its argument:

```
$ sudo periodic daily
```

The configuration file contains several entries for valid command arguments that control the location and content of the reports that periodic generates. Here are the entries related to daily:

```
# Daily options
...
daily_output="/var/log/daily.out"  Append report to a file
daily_show_success="YES"           Include success messages
daily_show_info="YES"              Include informational messages
daily_show_badconfig="NO"          Exclude configuration error
messages.
```

ping

```
ping [options] host
```

Confirms that a remote host is online and responding. ping is intended for use in network testing, measurement, and management. Because of the load it can impose on the network, it is unwise to use ping during normal operations or from automated scripts.

Options

`-c` *count*
: Stop after sending (and receiving) *count* `ECHO_RESPONSE` packets.

`-d` Set the `SO_DEBUG` option on the socket being used.

`-f` Flood `ping`-output packets as fast as they come back or 100 times per second, whichever is more. This can be very hard on a network and should be used with caution; only a privileged user may use this option.

`-i` *wait*
: Send a packet every *wait* seconds. Default is to wait 1 second between each packet. *wait* must be a positive integer value. This option is incompatible with the `-f` option.

`-l` *preload*
: Send *preload* number of packets as fast as possible before changing to default packet dispatch frequency. High packet losses are to be expected during preload delivery.

`-n` Numeric output only. No attempt is made to look up symbolic names for host addresses.

`-p` *digits*
: Specify up to 16-pad bytes to fill out packet sent. This is useful for diagnosing data-dependent problems in a network. The 32 most significant hexidecimal *digits* are used for the pattern. For example, `-p ff` causes the sent packet to be filled with all 1s, as does:

```
-p ffffffffffffffffffffffffffffffff0001
```

`-q` Quiet output; nothing is displayed except the summary lines at startup time and when finished.

`-r` Bypass the normal routing tables and send directly to a host on an attached network.

`-s` *packetsize*
: Specify number of data bytes to be sent. Default is 56, which translates into 64 ICMP data bytes when combined with the 8 bytes of ICMP header data. Maximum *packetsize* is 8192(2^13) - 8 = 8184.

`-v` Verbose; list ICMP packets received other than `ECHO_RESPONSE`.

`-R` Set the IP record route option, which stores the route of the packet inside the IP header. The contents of the record route will be printed if the `-v` option is given and will be set on return packets if the target host preserves the record route option across echoes or the `-l` option is given. Currently doesn't work in Mac OS X 10.2.1 (gets invalid argument error)

pl

```
pl [-input input_binary_file | -output output_binary_file]
```

Translates XML property list files into the more compact and readable key/value NeXT format. Also translates between this and a serialized binary format, in either direction. XML is read from standard input, NeXT-format data is read from standard input and written to standard output, and serialized binary data is read from and written to files specified with arguments.

Also see the manpage for `plutil`, which can check a file's property list syntax and translate directly between XML and binary (but not NeXT) formats.

Options

`-input`
: Specify a serialized binary file as input.

`-output`
: Specify a serialized binary file as output.

Examples

Translate XML property list to NeXT format:

```
$ cat foo.plist | pl
```

Translate XML property list to serialized binary format:

```
$ cat foo.plist | pl | pl -output foo.bin
```

Translate serialized binary file to NeXT format:

```
$ pl -input foo.bin
```

---

pmset

```
pmset [-a | -b | -c] action(s)
```

Modifies the system's power management settings. `pmset` is a command-line alternative to the Energy Saver System Preferences (Chapter 4). The settings apply system-wide and across reboots. Therefore, `pmset` requires root privileges to run.

Options

`-a` Use the settings that follow this flag when only the battery is in use and also when the power adapter is plugged in (the default).

`-b` Use the settings that follow this flag when only the battery is in use.

`-c` Use the settings that follow this flag only when the power adapter is plugged in.

Actions

`dim` *n*
: Dim the display after *n* minutes of idle time.

`sleep` *n*
: Put the computer to sleep after *n* minutes of idle time.

`slower 1 | 0`
: Set the processor performance setting to "reduced" (`1`) or "highest" (`0`).

`spindown` *n*
: Spin down the hard drive after *n* minutes of idle time.

`womp 1 | 0`
: Set the wake on magic packet ("wake for network administrator access") setting to on (`1`) or off (`0`).

Examples

Set the system to dim the display after 3 minutes and go to sleep after 10 minutes when using the battery:

```
$ pmset -b dim 3 sleep 10
```

Set both the battery-only and power adapter settings at once:

```
$ pmset -b dim 3 sleep 10 slower 1 -c dim 20 ↵
sleep 60 slower 0
```

---

postfix-watch

```
postfix-watch
```

Starts Postfix processes necessary to send email on demand. For a system that isn't providing mail service, Mac OS X runs those processes only when mail is queued for sending in */var/spool/postfix/maildrop*.

`postfix-watch` is started by the `Postfix` startup item.

---

pr

pr [*files*]

Converts a text file or files to a paginated, columned version, with headers. If – is provided as the filename, read from standard input.

Options

+*beg_pag*
: Begin printing on page *beg_pag*.

-*num_cols*
: Print in *num_cols* number of columns, balancing the number of lines in the columns on each page.

`-a` Print columns horizontally, not vertically.

`-d` Double space.

-e[*tab-char*[*width*]]
: Convert tabs (or *tab-chars*) to spaces. If *width* is specified, convert tabs to *width* characters (default is 8).

`-F` Separate pages with formfeeds, not newlines.

-h *header*
: Use *header* for the header instead of the filename.

-i*[out-tab-char[out-tab-width]]*
: Replace spaces with tabs on output. Can specify alternative tab character (default is tab) and width (default is 8).

-l *lines*
: Set page length to *lines* (default 66). If *lines* is less than 10, omit headers and footers.

-m
: Print all files, one file per column.

-n*[delimiter[digits]]*
: Number columns, or, with the -m option, number lines. Append *delimiter* to each number (default is a tab) and limit the size of numbers to *digits* (default is 5).

-o *width*
: Set left margin to *width*.

-r
: Continue silently when unable to open an input file.

-s*[delimiter]*
: Separate columns with *delimiter* (default is a tab) instead of spaces.

-t
: Suppress headers, footers, and fills at end of pages.

-v
: Convert unprintable characters to octal backslash format.

-w *page_width*
: Set the page width to *page_width* characters for multicolumn output. Default is 72.

---

printenv

printenv [*variables*]

Prints values of all environment variables or, optionally, only the specified *variables*.

---

ps

ps [*options*]

Reports on active processes. Note that you don't need to include a - before options. In options, *list* arguments should either be separated by commas or be put in double quotes.

Options

a
: List all processes.

c
: List the command name without the path.

e
: Include environment.

h
: Include a header with each page of information.

`j` List information for keywords: `user`, `pid`, `ppid`, `pgid`, `sess`, `jobc`, `state`, `tt`, `time`, and `command`.

`L` List all keywords.

`l` List information for keywords: `uid`, `pid`, `ppid`, `cpu`, `pri`, `nice`, `vsz`, `rss`, `wchan`, `state`, `tt`, `time`, and `command`.

`M` List each tasks threads.

`m` Sort by memory usage.

`O` Append the *`keywords`* that are in a list after the PID. The title of the *`keyword`* can be changed by using an = sign after the *`keyword`*. (*`keyword=newtitle`*)

`o` Same as `O` except it uses only the supplied keywords for the output of `ps`.

`p` List information for the supplied PID.

`r` List by CPU rather than by PID.

`S` Include child processes' CPU time and page faults.

`T` List information for standard input process.

`t`*`tty`*
: Display only processes running on *`tty`*.

`U` List processes belonging to username.

`u` List information for keywords: `user`, `pid`, `%cpu`, `%mem`, `vsz`, `rss`, `tt`, `state`, `start`, `time`, and `command`. The listing will be as if the `-r` option was supplied to `ps`.

`v` List information for keywords: `pid`, `state`, `time`, `sl`, `re`, `pagein`, `vsz`, `rss`, `lim`, `tsiz`, `%cpu`, `%mem`, and `command`. The listing will be as if the `-m` option was supplied to `ps`.

`w` Wide format. Don't truncate long lines.

`x` Include processes without an associated terminal.

Keywords

If there is an alias for the keyword, it's listed next to it.

Keyword	Description
`%cpu, pcpu`	Percentage of CPU used
`%mem, pmem`	Percentage of memory used
`acflag, acflg`	Accounting flag
`command`	Command and arguments
`cpu`	Short-term factor of CPU use
`flags, f`	Hexadecimal representation of process flags
`inblk, inblock`	Total amount of blocks read
`jobc T`	Count for job control
`ktrace`	Tracing flags
`ktracep`	Tracing vnode
`lim`	Limit of memory usage

Keyword	Description
`logname`	Username of user that started the command
`lstart`	Start time
`majflt, pagein`	Page fault totals
`minflt`	Page reclaim totals
`msgrcv`	Messages received total
`msgsnd`	Messages sent total
`nice, ni`	Value of nice
`nivcsw`	Involuntary context switches total
`nsigs, nsignals`	Signals taken total
`nswap`	Swap in/out totals
`nvcsw`	Voluntary context switch totals
`nwchan`	Wait channel
`oublk, oublock`	Blocks written total
`p_ru`	Amount of resources used out of resources used
`padd`	Address of swap
`pgid`	Group number for the process
`pid`	ID number of the process
`poip`	Progress of current pageouts
`ppid`	ID number of the parent process
`pri`	Scheduling priority
`re`	Core residency time
`rgid`	The real GID
`rlink`	Reverse link on run queue
`rss`	Resident set size
`rsz`	Resident set size + (text size/text use count) (alias `rssize`)
`rtprio`	Priority in real time
`ruid`	ID of the real user
`ruser`	Name of the user
`sess`	Pointer for the session
`sig, pending`	Signals that are pending
`sigcatch, caught`	Signals that have been caught
`sigignore, ignored`	Signals that have been ignored
`sigmask, blocked`	Signals that have been blocked
`sl`	Sleep time
`start`	Start time
`state, stat`	Sate of symbolic process
`svgid`	An executable setgid's saved GID
`svuid`	An executable setuid's saved UID
`tdev`	Device number of the control terminal
`time, cputime`	Total of user and system CPU time
`tpgid`	GID of the control terminal process
`tsess`	Pointer session of the control terminal

Keyword	Description
tsiz	Size of the text
tt	Name of control terminal
tty	The control terminals full name
uprocp	Pointer of the process
ucomm	Accounting name
uid	ID of the user
upr, usrpri	The scheduling priority after a system call as been made
user	Name of the user from UID
vsz, vsize	Listed in kilobytes the virtual size
wchan	Wait channel
xstat	Status of a zombie or stopped process; exit or stop

pwd

```
pwd [options]
```

Prints the full pathname of the current working directory.

Options

-L
Write the full pathname of the current working directory without resolving symbolic links.

-P
Write the full pathname of the current working directory with resolving symbolic links (-P is the default behavior).

rcp

```
rcp [options] file1 file2
rcp [options] file... directory
```

Copies files between two machines. Each *file* or *directory* is either a remote filename of the form *rname@rhost:path* or a local filename.

rcp doesn't preserve resource forks or metadata when copying files that contain them.

Options

-K
Suppress all Kerberos authentication.

-k
Attempt to get tickets for remote host; query krb_realmofhost to determine realm.

-p
Preserve modification times and modes of the source files.

-r
If any of the source files are directories, rcp copies each subtree rooted at that name. The destination must be a directory.

-x
Turn on DES encryption for all data passed by rcp.

reboot

```
reboot [options]
```

Prepares the system, terminates all processes, and then reboots the operating system. During preparation, all filesystem caches are flushed and running processes are sent a SIGTERM followed by SIGKILL.

Options

-l
: Don't log the halt via syslog (i.e., mach_kernel, syncing disks, etc.).

-n
: Don't flush filesystem caches. Should not be used indiscriminately.

-q
: The filesystem caches are flushed but the system is otherwise halted ungracefully. Should not be used indiscriminately.

register_mach_bootstrap_servers

```
register_mach_bootstrap_servers config_source
```

Registers a Mach port with the bootstrap task of mach_init on behalf of a specified daemon. (A Mach *task* is analogous to a process that runs within the kernel of Mac OS X; a *port* is used to communicate between tasks.) When another task sends a request to the bootstrap task for access to a port, mach_init starts up the associated daemon if necessary.

This serves as a replacement for certain startup items on Panther. Instead of launching services from */System/Library/StartupItems/* (processed by *SystemStarter*), files in */etc/mach_init.d/* are processed by *register_mach_bootstrap_servers*, which is called from */etc/rc*. (Per-user services are started by the login window application, which uses *register_mach_bootstrap_servers* to process */etc/mach_init_per_user.d/*.) One advantage of this over startup items is that a daemon can be run only when needed, if another process needs to communicate with it, thus reducing resource consumption.

Options

config_source
: Either an XML property list (*.plist*) file, or a directory containing such files. Each file is usually named after the associated daemon, and contains some of the following keys:

  command
  : The path to the server executable. This is a required key.

  isKUNCServer
  : Specify whether the daemon is *kuncd*, the Kernel-User Notification Center server, used by the kernel to communicate with users. Defaults to false.

  OnDemand
  : Specify whether the daemon should only be started when it first receives a request for its bootstrap port. If set to false, the daemon is started immediately. Defaults to true.

ServiceName

An identifier for the service. The name should follow the convention used for Java classes: the reversed DNS domain name associated with the responsible organization, followed by one or more segments specifically identifying the service (e.g., `com.apple.DirectoryService`). This is a required key.

username

The user under which the daemon is started.

renice

```
renice [priority] [options] [target]
```

Controls the scheduling priority of various processes as they run. May be applied to a process, process group, or user (*target*). A privileged user may alter the priority of other users' processes. *priority* must, for ordinary users, lie between 0 and the environment variable `PRIO_MAX` (normally 20), with a higher number indicating increased niceness. A privileged user may set a negative priority, as low as `PRIO_MIN`, to speed up processes.

Options

+num

Specify number by which to increase current priority of process, rather than an absolute priority number.

-num

Specify number by which to decrease current priority of process, rather than an absolute priority number.

`-g` Interpret *target* parameters as process GIDs.

`-p` Interpret *target* parameters as PIDs (default).

`-u` Interpret *target* parameters as usernames.

rev

```
rev [files]
```

Prints each line of each specified file. The order of the characters in each line is reversed. If no file is specified, `rev` reads from standard input.

rlogin

```
rlogin rhost [options]
```

Remote login. `rlogin` connects the terminal on the current local host system to the remote host system *rhost*. The remote terminal type is the same as your local terminal type. The terminal or window size is also copied to the remote system if the server supports it.

Options

-8 Allow an 8-bit input data path at all times.

-e*c* Specify escape character *c* (default is ~).

-d Debugging mode.

-k Attempt to get tickets from remote host, requesting them in the realm as determined by krb_realm-ofhost.

-l *username*
: Specify a different *username* for the remote login. Default is the same as your local username.

-x Turn on DES encryption for all data passed via the rlogin session.

-E Don't interpret any character as an escape character.

-K Suppress all Kerberos authentication.

-L Allow rlogin session to be run without any output postprocessing (i.e., run in litout mode).

---

rm

```
rm [options] files
```

Deletes one or more *files*. To remove a file, you must have write permission in the directory that contains the file, but you need not have permission on the file itself. If you don't have write permission on the file, you will be prompted (y or n) to override.

Options

-d Remove directories, even if they are not empty.

-f Remove write-protected files without prompting.

-i Prompt for y (remove the file) or n (don't remove the file).

-P Cause rm to overwrite files three different times before deleting them.

-r, -R
: If *file* is a directory, remove the entire directory and all its contents, including subdirectories. Be forewarned: use of this option can be dangerous.

-v Turn on verbose mode. (rm prints the name of each file before removing it.)

-W Undelete files on a union filesystem that whiteouts have been applied over.

---

rmdir

```
rmdir [options] directories
```

Deletes the named *directories* (not the contents). *directories* are deleted from the parent directory and must be empty (if not, rm -r can be used instead). See also mkdir.

Option

-p
: Remove *directories* and any intervening parent directories that become empty as a result; useful for removing subdirectory trees.

---

rsync

```
rsync [options] source destination
```

Transfers files from *source* to *destination*. rsync is a synchronization system that uses checksums to determine differences (instead of relying on modification dates) and does partial file transfers (transferring only the differences instead of the entire files).

rsync can use a remote shell (rsh by default) as a transport, in which case the remote host must have rsync installed as well. You can use a remote shell like ssh instead of the default by specifying that in *options*.

You can also use rsync without a remote shell, in which case rsync requires that the remote host run an rsync server daemon. For details on the advanced features of rsync, including running an rsync server, refer to rsync's manpage. The following descriptions and examples cover rsync's basic operation.

rsync doesn't preserve resource forks or HFS metadata when copying files that contain them.

The rsync *source* and *destination* arguments can be specified in several ways, as shown in the following table.

Source	Destination	Description
srcpath [...]	[user@]host:destpath	Transfer local directory *srcpath* to remote directory *destpath*.[a]
[user@]host: srcpath	destpath	Transfer remote directory *srcpath* to local directory *destpath*.[a]
[user@]host:srcpath		List contents of *srcpath* without transferring anything.[a]
srcpath [...]	[user@]host::destpath	Transfer local directory *srcpath* to remote directory *destpath*. [b]
[user@]host::srcpath	[destpath]	Transfer remote directory *srcpath* to local directory *destpath*, or list *srcpath* if *destpath* is not specified.[b]
rsync:// [user@]host[:port]:/ srcpath	[destpath]	Transfer remote directory *srcpath* to local directory *destpath*, or list *srcpath* if *destpath* is not specified.[b]
srcpath [...]	destpath	Transfer local directory *srcpath* to local directory *destpath*.

[a] Uses a remote shell as the transport and requires rsync on the remote host.

[b] Doesn't use a remote shell but requires an rsync server running on the remote host. Note the double colons (::), except for the URL format.

Selected options

`-a, --archive`
: Copy *source* recursively and save most file metadata in the copies, including owner, group, permissions, and modification times. Also copies symlinks (but not hard links). Equivalent to using `-rlptgoD`.

`-b, --backup`
: If a file in *source* already exists in *destination*, make a backup copy before overwriting. Name the backup file by appending ~ to the original filename.

`-D, --devices`
: Copy any character and block device files in *source* to *destination*.

`--delete`
: Delete any files in destination that aren't in source.

`-e` *command*, `--rsh=`*command*
: Use the remote shell *command* as the transport instead of the default `rsh`. The usual alternative is `ssh`.

`--existing`
: Don't add any new files to *destination*; update only what's there with any newer versions in *source*.

`--exclude=`*pattern*
: Exclude from transfer those files in *source* that match *pattern*. See `rsync`'s manpage for details on constructing exclude patterns.

`-g, --group`
: Preserve the groups of the source files in the copies.

`-I, --ignore-times`
: Transfer source files that have the same name, length, and date stamp as files in destination. The default behavior is to skip transfer of such files.

`-l, --links`
: Copy any symbolic links in source to destination.

`-o, --owner`
: Preserve the owners of the source files in the copies.

`-p, --perms`
: Preserve the permissions of the source files in the copies.

`--partial`
: Don't remove partially transferred files from *destination*. If a transfer is interrupted, this option allows a retried transfer to resume from where the failed attempt ended, instead of starting again from the beginning.

`-r, --recursive`
: Copy recursively. If any of the source files are directories, `rsync` copies each subtree rooted at that name.

`-t, --times`
: Preserve the modification times of the source files in the copies. Use this option whenever you want identical files excluded from subsequent transfers to the same directory.

`-u, --update`
: Don't transfer a file if it has a newer copy already existing in destination.

`-v, --verbose`
: Be verbose. Add vs for increased verbosity.

`-z, --compress`
: Compress data before transfer, which helps decrease transfer time over slower connections.

Examples

Transfer the entire local *~/Documents* directory into the folder named *Backups* on the machine at 192.168.2.56, using `rsh` as the transport:

```
$ rsync ~/Documents fred@192.168.2.56:Backups
```

Perform the same transfer using the archive and compress options as well as `ssh` as the transport:

```
$ rsync -aze ssh ~/Documents fred@192.168.2.56:Backups
```

A trailing slash on the source pathname causes `rsync` to transfer only the *contents* of that directory into the destination directory. This example transfers the contents of the remote */Backups/Documents* directory in the local *~/Temp* directory:

```
$ rsync -aze ssh fred@192.168.2.56:Backups/Documents/ ~/Temp
```

---

say

```
say [-v voice] [-o out.aiff] [-f file | string ...]
```

Uses Mac OS X's Speech Synthesis manager to speak the *file* or *string* using the default voice set in the Speech preference panel (System Preferences→Speech→Default Voice).

Options

string
: Text to be spoken using the default system voice; for example:

  ```
  $ say "I love Mac OS X"
  ```

  Notice how the system pronounces the "X" of "Mac OS X" as "ten."

`-f` *file*
: Specify a *file* to be read as input and spoken using the default system voice; for example

  ```
  $ say -f filename.txt
  ```

-v *voice*
: Use the specified voice instead of the default system voice; for example

```
$ say -v Fred "I love Mac OS X"
```

This uses the Fred *voice* to speak the *string*, "I love Mac OS X." The list of voices can be found in the Speech→Default Voices preference panel.

-o *out*.aiff
: Output the spoken text as an AIFF sound file; for example,

```
$ say -o ~/Desktop/iheartmosx.aiff -v Fred "I love Mac OS X"
```

This command uses the *voice* Fred to speak the *string* "I love Mac OS X," and save it as a sound file named *iheartmosx.aiff* on the Desktop. When outputting a sound file, the -o option *must* immediately follow the say command.

scp

scp [*options*] *file1 file2*
scp [*options*] *file... directory*

Securely copies files between two machines, using ssh as the transport. Each *file* or *directory* is either a remote filename of the form *rname@rhost:path* or a local filename.

scp doesn't preserve resource forks or metadata when copying files that contain them.

Options

-B
: Run in batch mode; don't prompt for passwords.

-c *cipher*
: Use the specified type of encryption, either blowfish, des, or 3des. (3des is the default.)

-C
: Turn on compression.

-F *filename*
: Use specified ssh configuration file.

-i *keyfile*
: Specify an identity file to use for authentication. The default is *$HOME/.ssh/identity*.

-o *keyword*
: Set configuration keyword.

-p
: Preserve modification times and modes of the source files.

-P *port*
: Select TCP port number.

-r
: If any of the source files are directories, scp copies each subtree rooted at that name. The destination must be a directory.

-S *pathname*
Use the local ssh executable located at *pathname*.

-q Run in quiet mode.

-v Be verbose.

-4 Use only IPv4 addresses.

-6 Use only IPv6 addresses.

---

screencapture

```
screencapture [-i [-s | -w | -W] | -m] [-x] { -c | pathname ...}
```

Saves the contents of the screen to a PDF file or to the Clipboard. Unless using the -i option to start an interactive screen capture, the contents of the entire display are captured.

Options

-c Save screenshot to the Clipboard for later pasting.

-i Initiate interactive screen capture. The mouse is used to select a region of the screen to capture. Pressing the spacebar toggles between this mouse selection mode and a window selection mode, in which clicking on a window captures the portion of the screen taken up by that window. Pressing the Control key saves the screenshot to the Clipboard. Pressing the Escape key cancels the interactive screen capture.

-m Capture only the main display, if multiple displays are in use.

-s Disable window selection mode in an interactive screen capture; only mouse selection is allowed.

-w Disable mouse selection mode in an interactive screen capture; only window selection is allowed.

-W Start an interactive screen capture in window selection mode instead of mouse selection mode.

-x Disable sound effects.

pathname
The name of a file in which to save the screenshot. You should terminate the filename with a *.pdf* extension.

---

script

```
script [option] [file]
```

Forks the current shell and makes a typescript of a terminal session. The typescript is written to *file*. If no *file* is given, the typescript is saved in the file *typescript*. The script ends when the forked shell exits, usually with Ctrl-D or exit.

Option

-a Append to file or typescript instead of overwriting the previous contents.

scselect

```
scselect [[-n] location]
```

Changes active network Location. With no arguments, a usage statement and a list of defined Locations (or "sets") is printed to standard output, along with an indication of which Location is currently active. Locations can be referred to by name or by integer ID.

Options

-n Change the active network Location, but doesn't apply the change.

scutil

```
scutil [-v] [-p]
scutil [-v] [-d] -r { hostname | IP_addr [IP_addr] }
scutil [-v] -w key [-t timeout]
scutil [-v] --get { ComputerName | LocalHostName }
scutil [-v] --set { ComputerName | LocalHostName } [hostname]
```

Provides control of the System Configuration framework's dynamic store. It's used to open an interactive session with `configd`, in which various commands are available to view and modify System Configuration keys.

As a quick example of interactive use, try this:

1. Invoke `scutil`. You will be placed at the `scutil` prompt.
2. Enter **`open`** to open the session with `configd`.
3. Enter **`list`**. You will see a set of keys, some of which are provided by the System Configuration framework (such as the keys in the `File:` domain), some of which are obtained from */Library/Preferences/SystemConfiguration/preferences.plist* (the `Setup:` keys), and some of which are published by the configuration agents (the `State:` keys).
4. Enter **`show State:/Network/Global/DNS`** to display the DNS dictionary. You should see a list of DNS servers and search domains configured on your system.
5. Enter **`close`**, then **`quit`**.

Options

-d Enable debugging output to standard error.

--get
  Print the system's computer name or Rendezvous hostname to standard output.

-p Enable a private API with additional commands, including `lock`, `unlock`, `touch`, `snapshot`, `n.file`, `n.signal`, `n.wait`, and `n.callback`.

`-r` Determine how the specified node (given as a hostname or an IP address) would be reached, printing the result to standard output. Possibilities include `Reachable`, `Directly Reachable Address` (the address is on the local network), and `Local Address` (the address resolves to the host on which the command is run). For systems with more than one network interface, two arguments may be given, where the first is the system's local address, and the second is the remote address. Note that this doesn't determine whether a machine at the specified address is currently active, only whether that address is reachable.

`--set`
: Set the system's computer name or Rendezvous hostname. If the new hostname isn't specified on the command line, it's taken from standard input.

`-t` Specify the timeout to wait for the presence of a data store key, in seconds. Defaults to `15`.

`-v` Enable verbose output to standard error.

`-w` Exit when the specified key exists in the data store or until the timeout has expired.

Commands

`scutil` enters interactive mode when invoked with no arguments.

`add` *`key`* [`temporary`]
: Add a key to the data store with the value of the current dictionary. The `temporary` keyword causes it to be flushed when the session to `configd` is closed.

`close`
: Close a session with `configd`.

`d.add` *`key`* [* | ? | #] *`value...`*
: Add an entry to the current dictionary. The optional type specifier can designate the values as arrays (*), booleans (?), or numbers (#).

`d.init`
: Create an empty dictionary.

`d.remove` *`key`*
: Remove the specified key from the current dictionary.

`d.show`
: Display the contents of the current dictionary.

`exit`
: Exit the `scutil` session.

`f.read` *`file`*
: Read prepared commands from a file.

`get` *`key`*
: Cause the value of the specified key to become the current dictionary.

`help`
: Print a list of available commands.

`list` *[regex]*
: List keys in the System Configuration data store. A regular expression may be specified to restrict which keys are listed.

`lock`
: Prevent changes to the data store by other processes.

`n.add` *key [pattern]*
: Request notification of changes to the specified key or to keys matching a regular expression (when the *pattern* argument is used).

`n.callback` *[verbose]*
: Send notifications via a callback function defined in the `scutil` code. This isn't particularly useful without modifying the source code.

`n.cancel`
: Cancel `n.watch` settings.

`n.changes`
: List changed keys that have been marked with notification requests and resets the state of notification.

`n.file` *[identifier]*
: Send notifications to a file descriptor. After issuing this command, the prompt returns only after a notification is received.

`n.list` *[pattern]*
: List keys upon which notification requests have been set. With the *pattern* argument, lists notification requests for keys matching regular expressions.

`n.remove` *key [pattern]*
: Remove notification requests for the specified key or regular expression (when the *pattern* argument is used).

`n.signal` *signal [process_ID]*
: Send notifications by signaling a process. If a PID isn't specified, the signal is sent to the `scutil` process. The signal is specified either as a name or a number (as described in the `kill` manpage).

`n.wait`
: Send notifications via Mach messaging.

`n.watch` *[verbose]*
: Cause changes to keys marked with notification requests to issue immediate notices, obviating the need to use `n.changes` to notice that the change has occurred.

`notify` *key*
: Send a notification for the specified key.

`open`
: Open a session with `configd`.

`q`
: Exit the `scutil` session.

`quit`
: Exit the `scutil` session.

`remove` *key*
: Remove the specified key from the data store.

`set` *key*
: Set the specified key to the value of the current dictionary.

`show` *key [pattern]*
: Same as `get key`, followed by *d.show*.

`snapshot`
: Save current store and session data to XML property lists in */var/tmp/*.

`touch` *key*
: "Touch" the specified key, spurring notifications as if it had changed, but leaving it unaltered.

`unlock`
: After issuing a `lock` command, allow other processes to make changes to the data store.

---

sdiff

```
sdiff [options] file1 file2
```

Compares two files to find differences and interactively merges them. Without the `-o` option, `sdiff` behaves like `diff-side-by-side`.

Options

`-a, --text`
: Treat all files as text files. Useful for checking to see if binary files are identical.

`-b, --ignore-space-change`
: Ignore repeating blanks and end-of-line blanks; treat successive blanks as one.

`-B, --ignore-blank-lines`
: Ignore blank lines in files.

`-d, --minimal`
: Ignore segments of numerous changes and output a smaller set of changes.

`-H`
: Speed output of large files by scanning for scattered small changes; long stretches with many changes may not show up.

`--help`
: Print brief usage message.

`-i, --ignore-case`
: Ignore case in text comparison. Upper- and lowercase are considered the same.

`-I` *regexp*, `--ignore-matching-lines=`*regexp*
: Ignore lines in files that match the regular expression *regexp*.

-l, --left-column
: For two-column output (-y), show only left column of common lines.

-s, --suppress-common-lines
: For two-column output (-y), don't show common lines.

-t, --expand-tabs
: Produce output with tabs expanded to spaces to line up tabs properly in output.

-v, --version
: Print version number of this version of sdiff.

-W, --ignore-all-space
: Ignore all whitespace in files for comparisons.

-w*n*, --width=*n*
: For two-column output (-y), produce columns with a maximum width of *n* characters. Default is 130.

-o *outfile*
: Send identical lines of *file1* and *file2* to *outfile*; print line differences and edit *outfile* by entering, when prompted, the following commands:

e
: Edit an empty file.

e b
: Edit both left and right columns.

e l
: Edit left column.

e r
: Edit right column.

l
: Append left column to *outfile*.

q
: Exit the editor.

r
: Append right column to *outfile*.

s
: Silent mode; don't print identical lines.

v
: Turn off "silent mode."

Example

Show differences using 80 columns and ignore identical lines:

```
$ sdiff -s -w80 list.1 list.2
```

SecurityServer

SecurityServer [-a *config_file*] [-d] [-E *entropy_file*] [-f] [-N *bootstrap_name*] [-t *max_threads*] [-T *thread_timeout*] [-X]

Provides services to the Security framework, including authorization and secure key management.

Options

-a Specify the configuration file for Authorization Services. Defaults to */etc/authorization*.

-d Run process in debug mode, and disables daemonization. Output is sent to standard error and to *syslog*.

-E Specify a file to use as a source of entropy for cryptographic operations. Defaults to */var/db/SystemEntropyCache*.

-f Force immediate initialization of the Common Security Services Manager (CSSM), the central access point for services provided by the Common Data Security Architecture (CDSA). Normally the CSSM is initialized when it is first needed.

-N Specify a service name used to register a Mach bootstrap port. Defaults to `SecurityServer`; any other setting prevents authorization from working.

-t Limit the number of Mach threads started by the `SecurityServer` process. Defaults to `100`.

-T Specify a timeout for Mach threads started by the `SecurityServer` process, in seconds. Defaults to `120`.

-X Direct `SecurityServer` to re-execute itself when in daemon mode, needed to work around Mach-related bugs in libraries.

---

sed

```
sed [options] [files]
```

Streams editor. Edits one or more *`files`* without user interaction. For more information on `sed`, see *sed and awk* (O'Reilly). The `-e` and `-f` options may be provided multiple times, and they may be used with each other.

Options

-a Treat all files as text and compare them.

-e *instruction*
: Apply the editing *`instruction`* to the files.

-f *script*
: Apply the set of instructions from the editing *`script`*.

-n Suppress default output.

---

service

```
service --list
service { --test-if-available | --test-if-configured-on } service
service service { start | stop }
```

A shell script used to list, start, and stop network services. Primarily this is an interface to services managed by `xinetd`, but it also includes support for Postfix (with a service name of `smtp`) and for receipt of faxes (`fax-receive`) on Panther.

Options

`--list`
: Print a list of services available for management to standard output.

`--test-if-available`
: Return `0` if the specified service is available on the system; `1` if not.

`--test-if-configured-on`
: Return `0` if the specified service is currently configured to run; `1` if not.

SetFile

`SetFile [`*`options`*`]` *`files`*

Sets the HFS+ file attributes (metadata) of *`files`*. `SetFile` is installed with the Xcode Tools (*/Developer/Tools*). Since this directory isn't in the shell's search path by default, you might to need to specify `SetFile`'s pathname to invoke it. See also `GetFileInfo`.

Options

`-a` *`attribute`*
: Set those file attributes that toggle on or off (sometimes called "Finder flags"). To set an attribute, provide that attribute's letter as uppercase in *`attribute`*. To unset an attribute, provide the letter in lowercase. You can specify multiple attributes at once; any not specified will retain their current setting in *`files`*. Refer to the following table for the specific attributes.

Attribute	Set | Unset	Meaning
Alias	A | a	File is/isn't an alias.
Bundle	B | b	File has/hasn't a bundle resource.
Custom Icon	C | c	File has/hasn't a custom icon.
Desktop Item	D | d	File is/isn't on the Desktop.
Extension	E | e	Filename extension is/isn't hidden.
Inited	I | i	File is/isn't init'ed.
Locked	L | l	File is/isn't locked.
Shared	M | m	Multiple users can/can't run file at once (applies to application files).
INIT	N | n	File has/hasn't INIT resource.
System	S | s	File is/isn't a system file (locks name).
Stationary	T | t	File is/isn't a stationary file.
Invisible	V | v	File is/isn't invisible to Finder.

`-c` *`creator`*
: Set the file's four-character creator code to *`creator`*.

`-d` *`date`*
: Set the file's creation date to date. Specify *`date`* in this format: `"mm/dd[yy]yy [hh:mm:[:ss] [AM | PM]]"`. Enclose *`date`* in quotes if it contains spaces.

-m *date*
: Set the file's modification date to *date*, specified as for -d.

-t *type*
: Set the file's four-character type code to *type*.

Example

Set the attributes of all files in the working directory whose names end with "jpg" to those of an unlocked GraphicConverter JPEG file, and give them all the same creation date:

```
$ /Developer/Tools/SetFile -a l -c GKON -t JPEG - d ↵
"07/01/03  00:00" *jpg
```

---

sftp

```
sftp [options] [hostname]
sftp [user@]hostname:[pathname]
```

Secure FTP. Transfers files to and from remote network site *hostname* using ssh as the transport. Once an sftp connection is made, sftp becomes interactive, prompting the user for a command. Type help to see a list of known commands.

If *pathname* is a directory, it becomes the initial remote working directory once the connection is made. If *pathname* is a file, sftp transfers that file into the local working directory, closes the connection, and exits without entering interactive mode.

Options

-b *filename*
: Run in batch mode, reading commands from *filename* instead of standard input.

-B *buffersize*
: Use a buffer size of *buffersize* bytes when transferring files instead of the default 32768 bytes.

-C
: Turn on compression.

-F *filename*
: Use specified ssh configuration file.

-o *keyword*
: Set configuration keyword.

-P *sftp-server_path*
: Connect to the local sftp-server program at *sftp-server_path*, instead of using ssh (for debugging purposes). The default location for the program on Mac OS X is */usr/libexec/sftp-server*.

-R *n*
: Allow up to *n* outstanding requests, instead of the default, 16.

-s *subsystem*
Invoke remote subsystem.

-S *pathname*
Use local ssh executable located at *pathname*.

-v Be verbose.

-1 Attempt a Version 1 connection.

showmount

```
showmount [-a | -d | -e] [-3] [nfs_server]
```

Queries the NFS mount daemon, mountd, to show which clients have mounted which directories from the NFS server. Called without flags, showmount prints a list of NFS client IP addresses to standard output; *nfs_server* defaults to localhost.

See the fixmount entry for more information.

Options

-3 Use NFS Version 3.

-a List clients with the exports they're mounting, in the form *IP_addr*:*pathname*.

-d List exports that are mounted on clients, instead of client IP addresses.

-e Print the server's list of NFS exports to standard output.

shutdown

```
shutdown [options] when [message]
```

Terminates all processing. *when* may be a specific time (in *hh*:*mm* format), a number of minutes to wait (in +*m* format), or now. A broadcast *message* notifies all users to log off the system. Processes are signaled with SIGTERM, to allow them to exit gracefully. Only privileged users can execute the shutdown command. Broadcast messages, default or defined, are displayed at regular intervals during the grace period; the closer the shutdown time, the more frequent the message.

Options

-c Cancel a shutdown in progress.

-f Reboot fast, by suppressing the normal call to fsck when rebooting.

-h Halt the system when shutdown is complete.

-k Print the warning message, but suppress actual shutdown.

-n Perform shutdown without a call to sync.

-r Reboot the system when shutdown is complete.

sips

```
sips [-h | --help | -H | --helpProperties]
sips [--debug] { -g | --getProperty } property image_or_profile_filename...
sips [--debug] { -x | --extractProfile } profile_filename image_filename...
sips [--debug] { -X | --extractTag } tag tag_filename profile_filename...
sips [--debug] { -v | --verify } profile_filename...
sips [--debug] { -s | --setProperty } property value [--out filename] image_or_
profile_filename...
sips [--debug] { -d | --deleteProperty } property [--out filename] image_or_
profile_filename...
sips [--debug] { -r | --rotate } degrees [--out filename] image_filename...
sips [--debug] { -f | --flip } { horizontal | vertical } [--out filename]
image_filename...
sips [--debug] { -c | --cropToHeightWidth | -p | --padToHeightWidth | -z |
resampleHeightWidth }height_pixels width_pixels[--outfilename] image_filename...
sips [--debug] { -Z | --resampleHeightWidthMax | --resampleHeight | --
resampleWidth } pixels [--out filename] image_filename...
sips [--debug] { -i | --addIcon } [--out filename] image_filename...
sips [--debug] { -e | --embedProfile | -E | --embedProfileIfNone | -m |
--matchTo } profile_filename [--out filename] image_filename...
sips [--debug] { -M | --matchToWithIntent } profile_filename { absolute |
relative | perceptual | satuation } [--out filename] image_filename...
sips [--debug] --deleteTag tag [--out filename] profile_filename...
sips [--debug] --copyTag src_tag dst_tag [--out filename] profile_filename...
sips [--debug] --loadTag tag tag_filename [--out filename] profile_filename...
sips [--debug] --repair [--out filename] profile_filename...
```

The Scriptable Image Processing System (SIPS) tool can manipulate images and ColorSync profiles from the command line.

ColorSync profiles are International Color Consortium (ICC) files that characterize the color properties of different devices, so that accurate color matching can be performed between them. There are ColorSync profiles located under */System/Library/ColorSync/Profiles/*, */Library/ColorSync/Profiles/*, */Library/Printers/*, and */Library/Image Capture/Devices/*, among other places. For more on ColorSync, see *http://www.apple.com/macosx/features/colorsync/*.

Options

`-c | --cropToHeightWidth`
: Crop an image to the specified size (in pixels). The image is cropped equally from both top and bottom, and from both sides.

`--copyTag`
: Copy the value of a tag in a ColorSync profile to another tag in the same profile.

`-d | --deleteProperty`
: Delete the specified property. A list of possible properties may be obtained with `sips -H`.

`--debug`
: Enable debugging output.

`--deleteTag`
: Delete the specified tag from a ColorSync profile.

`-e | --embedProfile`
: Embed the specified ColorSync profile into the image.

`-E | --embedProfileIfNone`
: Embed the specified ColorSync profile into the image only if another profile is not already embedded.

`-f | --flip`
: Flip an image in the specified direction.

`-g | --getProperty`
: Print the value of the specified property to standard output. A list of possible properties may be obtained with `sips -H`.

`-h | --help`
: Print a usage message to standard output.

`-H | --helpProperties`
: Print a list of image and profile properties to standard output.

`-i | --addIcon`
: Add an icon for an image file to its resource fork, which is used in Finder previews.

`--loadTag`
: Copy the value of a tag from a file to a ColorSync profile. (This is the opposite of `--extractTag`.)

`-m | --matchTo`
: Match an image to the specified ColorSync profile.

`-M | --matchToWithIntent`
: Match an image to the specified ColorSync profile with the given rendering intent. (Note the misspelled `satuation`; this is a typo in the `sips` code.)

`--out`
: Specify the filename of the modified image file. By default, `sips` modifies the file in place; this option lets you save the modified file under a different name, leaving the original unchanged.

`-p | --padToHeightWidth`
: Pad an image with blank space to the specified size (in pixels). The image is padded equally on both top and bottom, and on both sides.

`-r | --rotate`
: Rotate an image the specified number of degrees clockwise.

`--repair`
: Attempt to repair a malformed `desc` tag in a ColorSync profile. This is the same as the Repair operation under Profile First Aid in the ColorSync Utility application.

`--resampleHeight`
: Stretch or compress an image to the specified height (in pixels).

`--resampleWidth`
: Stretch or compress an image to the specified width (in pixels).

`-s | --setProperty`
: Set a property to the specified value. A list of possible properties may be obtained with `sips -H`.

`-v | --verify`
: Verify the syntax of a ColorSync profile. This is the same as the Verify operation under Profile First Aid in the ColorSync Utility application.

`-x | --extractProfile`
: Copy an embedded ColorSync profile from an image to a file with the specified name.

`-X | --extractTag`
: Copy the value of a tag (such as desc) from a ColorSync profile to a file with the specified name.

`-z | --resampleHeightWidth`
: Stretch or compress an image to the specified size (in pixels).

`-Z | --resampleHeightWidthMax`
: Stretch or compress an image while maintaining the aspect ratio. The largest dimension (height or width) is set to the specified size (in pixels).

Examples

Show the properties of a ColorSync profile (similar to what's displayed under the Profiles tab of the ColorSync Utility application):

```
$ sips -g all /Library/ColorSync/Profiles/WebSafeColors.icc
/Library/ColorSync/Profiles/WebSafeColors.icc
  size: 10644
  cmm: appl
  version: 2.2.0
  class: nmcl
  space: RGB
  pcs: Lab
  creation: 2003:07:01 00:00:00
  platform: APPL
  quality: normal
  deviceManufacturer: 0
  deviceModel: 0
  deviceAttributes0: 0
  deviceAttributes1: 0
  renderingIntent: perceptual
  creator: appl
  md5: 14487F1ED8F8947B15F6682BFCF21E00
  description: Web Safe Colors
  copyright: Copyright 2001 - 2003 Copyright Apple Computer Inc., all rights
reserved.
```

Convert a TIFF to a JPEG from the command line (also works for PNG, GIF, PICT, BMP, and other image formats):

```
$ sips -s format jpeg --out sample.jpeg sample.tiff
```


slogin

See ssh. (The slogin command file is a symbolic link to the ssh executable.)

slp_reg

```
slp_reg -l
slp_reg { -r | -d } URL [-a attribute_list]
```

Communicates with slpd to register services with the Service Location Protocol. Services are designated by SLP URLs.

Options

-a Specify an SLP attribute list.

-d Deregister the given service.

-l List registered services. This option is currently unimplemented.

-r Register the given service.

softwareupdate

```
softwareupdate [-h | --help | -l | --list]
softwareupdate { -i | --install | -d | --download } { -a | --all | -r |
--req | package? }
softwareupdate --ignored { none | add package ? | remove { -a | --all |
package ? } }
softwareupdate --schedule  { on | off }
```

A command-line version of the Software Update application, this checks for and installs Apple software updates. When invoked without arguments, it prints a usage statement to standard output.

Options

-d | --download
: Download the specified update packages to the directory specified in Internet Preferences (now part of Safari's General preferences), but don't install them. The arguments are the same as the -i or --install option. This is useful when downloading updates for clients of a Network Install server.

-h | --help
: Print a usage statement to standard output.

-i | --install
: Install the specified update packages: either an explicit list of packages (with names as given by the -l or --list flag), all uninstalled packages (-a or --all), or only those packages listed as required (-r or --req).

-l | --list
: Print a list of uninstalled updates to standard output, including package name, version number, size, and whether a reboot is required after the install.

--ignored
: Add or remove packages to or from the list of those ignored for the system.

--schedule
: Turn automatic checks for updates on or off.

---

sort

```
sort [options] [files]
```

Sorts the lines of the named *files*. Compare specified fields for each pair of lines, or, if no fields are specified, compare them by byte, in machine collating sequence. See also uniq, comm, and join.

Options

-b Ignore leading spaces and tabs.

-c Check whether *files* are already sorted, and if so, produce no output.

-d Sort in dictionary order.

-f Fold; ignore uppercase/lowercase differences.

-i Ignore nonprinting characters (those outside ASCII range 040-176).

-m Merge (i.e., sort as a group) input files.

-n Sort in arithmetic order.

-o*file*
: Put output in *file*.

-r Reverse the order of the sort.

-t*c* Separate fields with *c* (default is a tab).

-u Identical lines in input file appear only one (unique) time in output.

-zrecsz
: Provide recsz bytes for any one line in the file. This option prevents abnormal termination of sort in certain cases.

+*n* [-*m*]
: Skip *n* fields before sorting, and sort up to field position *m*. If *m* is missing, sort to end of line. Positions take the form *a.b*, which means character *b* of field *a*. If *.b* is missing, sort at the first character of the field.

-k *n[,m]*
: Similar to +. Skip *n*-1 fields and stop at *m*-1 fields (i.e., start sorting at the *n*th field, where the fields are numbered beginning with 1).

-M
: Attempt to treat the first three characters as a month designation (JAN, FEB, etc.). In comparisons, treat JAN < FEB and any valid month as less than an invalid name for a month.

-T *tempdir*
: Directory pathname to be used for temporary files.

Examples

List files by decreasing number of lines:

```
$ wc -l * | sort -r
```

Alphabetize a list of words, remove duplicates, and print the frequency of each word:

```
$ sort -fd wordlist | uniq -c
```

---

split

```
split [option] [infile] [outfile]
```

Splits *infile* into equal-sized segments. *infile* remains unchanged, and the results are written to *outfile*aa, *outfile*ab, and so on. (Default is xaa, xab, etc.). If *infile* is (or missing and default *outfile* is used), standard input is read.

Options

-*n*, -l *n*
: Split *infile* into *n*-line segments (default is 1000).

-b *n[km]*
: Split *infile* into *n*-byte segments. Alternate blocksizes may be specified:

k
: 1 kilobyte

m
: 1 megabyte

\-
: Take input from the standard input.

Examples

Break *bigfile* into 1000-line segments:

```
$ split bigfile
```

Join four files, then split them into 10-line files named *new.aa*, *new.ab*, and so on. Note that without the -, *new.* is as a nonexistent input file:

```
$ cat list[1-4] | split -10 - new.
```

SplitForks

```
SplitForks { -u | [-v] pathname }
```

Copies the resource fork and HFS attributes from a file named *filename* into a separate file named *._filename*, equivalent to an AppleDouble Header file. The original file retains the resource fork and HFS metadata as well.

If *pathname* refers to a file, that file's resource fork and metadata are split out. If *pathname* is a directory, `SplitForks` does a recursive descent into the directory, working on every file within it.

`FixupResourceForks` undoes the actions of `SplitForks`.

Options

`-u` Print a usage statement to standard output.

`-v` Enable verbose output.

spray

```
spray [options]
```

Similar to `ping`, `spray` sends RPC packets to a host and determines how many were received and their transit time. `spray` can cause a lot of network traffic, so use it cautiously.

Options

`-c` *count*
: Specify *count* packets to send.

`-d` *delay*
: Allow for *delay* microseconds between each packet.

`-l` *length*
: Set the RPC call message packet length to *length* bytes. Because all values are not possible, `spray` rounds to the nearest possible value.

srm

```
srm [option] file
```

Securely removes files or directories by overwriting, renaming, and truncating before unlinking. This prevents other users from undeleting or recovering any information about the file from the command line. `srm` is the brute force behind the Finder's Secure Empty Trash option.

`srm` can't remove write-protected files owned by another user, regardless of the permissions on the directory containing the file.

Options

-f, --force
: Ignore nonexistent files, and never prompt.

-i, --interactive
: Prompt before files are deleted.

-r, -R, --recursive
: Recursively remove the files of directories.

-s, --simple
: Delete the file, but only overwrite the file with a single pass.

-m, --medium
: Overwrite the file with seven U.S. Department of Defense-compliant passes (0xF6, 0x00, 0xFF, random, 0x00, 0xFF, random).

-z, --zero
: After overwriting, zero blocks used by file.

-n, --nounlink
: Overwrite the file, but don't rename or unlink it.

-v, --verbose
: Display what is being done.

--help
: Display help file information for the `srm` command.

--version
: Display the version information for `srm`.

---

ssh

```
ssh [-l user] host [commands]
ssh [options] [user@]host
```

The Secure Shell, `ssh` is a secure replacement for the `rsh`, `rlogin`, and `rcp` programs. `ssh` uses strong public-key encryption technologies to provide end-to-end encryption of data. There may be licensing/patent issues restricting the use of the software in some countries.

Options

-a
: Turn off authentication agent connection forwarding.

-A
: Turn on authentication agent connection forwarding.

-b *interface*
: Use the specified network interface (on a multiple interface machine).

-c *cipher*
: Use the specified type of encryption, either `blowfish`, `des` or `3des`. `3des` is the default.

-C
: Turn on compression.

-D
: Behave like a SOCKS4 server.

-e*c* Specify escape character *c*. Use the word "none" to disable any escape character.

-f Send ssh to the background.

-F *filename*
: Use specified configuration file.

-g Accept connections to local forward ports from remote hosts.

-i *keyfile*
: Specify an identity file to use for authentication. The default is *$HOME/.ssh/identity*.

-I *device*
: Used smartcard *device*.

-k Turn off Kerberos ticket forwarding.

-l *user*
: Log in as *user*.

-L *port1*:*host2*: *port2*
: Set up port forwarding from a local host to a remote host.

-m *algorithm*
: Use specified MAC algorithm(s).

-n Doesn't allow reading from STDIN.

-N Turn off remote command execution.

-o *keyword*
: Set configuration keyword.

-p *port*
: Select TCP port number.

-P Use a nonprivileged port is for outgoing connections.

-q Run in quiet mode.

-R *port1*:*host2*: *port2*
: Set up port forwarding from a remote host to a local host.

-s *subsystem*
: Invoke remote subsystem.

-t Turn on pseudo-*tty* distribution.

-T Turn off pseudo-*tty* distribution.

-v Be verbose.

-x Turn off X11 forwarding.

-X Turn on X11 forwarding.

-1 Attempt a Version 1 connection.

-2 Attempt a Version 2 connection.

-4 Use only IPv4 addresses.

-6 Use only IPv6 addresses.

strings

```
strings [options] files
```

Searches object or binary files for sequences of four or more printable characters that end with a newline or null.

Options

-a
: Search entire file, not just the initialized data portion of object files. Can also specify this option as –.

-o
: Display the string's offset position before the string.

-*num*
: Minimum string length is *num* (default is 4). Can also specify this option as -*n*.

stty

```
stty [options] [modes]
```

Sets terminal I/O options for the current device. Without options, stty reports the terminal settings, where a ^ indicates the Control key, and ^' indicates a null value. Most modes can be switched using an optional preceding dash (–, shown in brackets). The corresponding description is also shown in brackets. As a privileged user, you can set or read settings from another device using the syntax:

```
stty [options] [modes] < device
```

stty is one of the most complicated Unix commands. The complexity stems from the need to deal with a large range of conflicting, incompatible, and nonstandardized terminal devices—everything from printing teletypes to CRTs to pseudoterminals for windowing systems. Only a few of the options are really needed for day-to-day use. stty sane is a particularly valuable one to remember.

Options

-a
: Report all option settings.

-e
: Report current settings in BSD format.

-f *file*
: Use file instead of standard input.

-g
: Report current settings in stty format.

Control modes

0
: Hang up connection (set the baud rate to zero).

n
: Set terminal baud rate to *n* (e.g., 19200).

[-]clocal
: [Enable] disable modem control.

`[-]cread`
: [Disable] enable the receiver.

`[-]crtscts`
: [Disable] enable output hardware flow control using RTS/CTS.

`cs`*n*
: Select character size in bits (5 *n* 8).

`[-]cstopb`
: [One] two stop bits per character.

`[-]hup`
: [Don't] hang up connection on last close.

`[-]hupcl`
: Same as `[-]hup`.

`ispeed` *n*
: Set terminal input baud rate to *n*.

`[-]loblk`
: [Don't] block layer output. For use with `shl`; obsolete.

`ospeed` *n*
: Set terminal output baud rate to *n*.

`[-]parenb`
: [Disable] enable parity generation and detection.

`[-]parext`
: [Disable] enable extended parity generation and detection for mark and space parity.

`[-]parodd`
: Use [even] odd parity.

`speed` *num*
: Set *ispeed* and *opseed* to the same *num*.

Input modes

`[-]brkint`
: [Don't] signal INTR on break.

`[-]icrnl`
: [Don't] map carriage return (`^M`) to newline (`^J`) on input.

`[-]ignbrk`
: [Don't] ignore break on input.

`[-]igncr`
: [Don't] ignore carriage return on input.

`[-]ignpar`
: [Don't] ignore parity errors.

`[-]imaxbel`
: [Don't] echo BEL when input line is too long.

`[-]inlcr`
: [Don't] map newline to carriage return on input.

`[-]inpck`
: [Disable] enable input parity checking.

`[-]istrip`
: [Don't] strip input characters to seven bits.

`[-]iuclc`
: [Don't] map uppercase to lowercase on input.

`[-]ixany`
: Allow [only XON] any character to restart output.

`[-]ixoff`
: [Don't] send START/STOP characters when the queue is nearly empty/full.

`[-]ixon`
: [Disable] enable START/STOP output control.

`[-]parmrk`
: [Don't] mark parity errors.

Output modes

`[-]ocrnl`
: [Don't] map carriage return to newline on output.

`[-]olcuc`
: [Don't] map lowercase to uppercase on output.

`[-]onlcr`
: [Don't] map newline to carriage return-newline on output.

`[-]onlret`
: [Don't] perform carriage return after newline.

`[-]onocr`
: [Don't] output carriage returns at column zero.

`[-]opost`
: [Don't] postprocess output; ignore all other output modes.

`[-]oxtabs`
: [Don't] on output expand tabs to spaces.

Local modes

`[-]echo`
: [Don't] echo every character typed.

`[-]echoctl`
: [Don't] echo control characters as ^char, DEL as ^?.

`[-]echoe`
: [Don't] echo ERASE character as BS-space-BS string.

[-]echok
: [Don't] echo newline after KILL character.

[-]echoke
: [Don't] erase entire line on line kill.

[-]echonl
: [Don't] echo newline (^J).

[-]echoprt
: [Don't] echo erase character as *retcaeahc*/. Used for printing terminals.

[-]flusho
: Output is [not] being flushed.

[-]icanon
: [Disable] enable canonical input (ERASE and KILL processing).

[-]iexten
: [Disable] enable extended functions for input data.

[-]isig
: [Disable] enable checking of characters against INTR, QUIT, and SWITCH.

[-]lfkc
: Same as [-]echok. Obsolete.

[-]noflsh
: [Enable] disable flush after INTR, QUIT, or SWITCH.

[-]pendin
: [Don't] retype pending input at next read or input character.

[-]stappl
: [Line] application mode on a synchronous line.

[-]stflush
: [Disable] enable flush on synchronous line.

[-]stwrap
: [Enable] disable truncation on synchronous line.

[-]tostop
: [Don't] send SIGTTOU when background processes write to the terminal.

[-]altwerase
: [Don't] use a different erase algorithm when processing WERASE characters.

[-]mdmbuf
: Carrier Detect condition determines flow control output if on. If off, low Carrier Detect writes, return an error.

[-]xcase
: [Don't] change case on local output.

Control assignments

ctrl-char c
: Set control character to *c*. *ctrl-char* is one of the following: dsusp, eof, eol, eol2, erase, intr, kill, lnext, quit, reprint, start, status, stop, susp, switch, or werase.

min *n*
: With -icanon, *n* is the minimum number of characters that will satisfy the read system call until the timeout set with time expires.

time *n*
: With -icanon, *n* is the number of tenths of seconds to wait before a read system call times out. If the minimum number of characters set with min is read, the read can return before the timeout expires.

Combination modes

[-]evenp
: Same as [-]parenb and cs7[8].

ek
: Reset ERASE and KILL characters to # and @.

[-]nl
: [Un] set icrnl and onlcr. -nl also unsets inlcr, igncr, ocrnl, and onlret.

[-]oddp
: Same as [-]parenb, [-]parodd, and cs7[8].

[-]parity
: Same as [-]parenb and cs7[8].

[-]raw
: [Disable] enable raw input and output (no ERASE, KILL, INTR, QUIT, EOT, SWITCH, or output postprocessing).

sane
: Reset all modes to reasonable values.

tty
: Line discipline is set to TTYDISC.

[-]crt
: [Don't] set all CRT display modes.

[-]kerninfo
: [Don't] allow a STATUS character to display system information.

columns *num*, cols *num*
: Terminal size is set to *num* columns.

rows *num*
: Terminal size is set to *num* rows.

dec
: Digital Equipment Corporation mode set.

[-]extproc
: [Is not] Terminal hardware is doing some of the terminal processing.

size
: Terminal size is output as row number and column number.

su

`su [option] [user] [shell_args]`

Creates a shell with the effective user-ID *user*. If no *user* is specified, creates a shell for a privileged user (that is, becomes a superuser). Enter EOF to terminate. You can run the shell with particular options by passing them as *shell_ args* (e.g. , if the shell runs sh, you can specify -c *command* to execute *command* via sh or -r to create a restricted shell).

Options

-l
: Go through the entire login sequence (i.e., change to user's environment).

-c *command*
: Execute *command* in the new shell and then exit immediately. If *command* is more than one word, it should be enclosed in quotes—for example:

```
$ su -c 'find / -name \*.c -print' nobody
```

-f
: Start shell with -f option. In csh and tcsh, this suppresses the reading of the *.cshrc* file. In bash, this suppresses filename pattern expansion.

-m
: Don't reset environment variables.

sudo

`sudo [options] command`

Executes a command as the superuser or as another user on the system. Before sudo executes *command*, it prompts for the current account password (not root's).

sudo determines authorized users by consulting the file */etc/sudoers*. If the current user account is listed in */etc/sudoers* and is authorized there to run *command*, that user can then run subsequent sudo commands without being prompted for a password. However, if five minutes (the default value) passes between sudo commands, the user is prompted again for a password at the next sudo attempt and given another five minute window.

By default, Mac OS X includes the *admin* group in the *sudoers* file and gives that group authorization to run any command with sudo. Mac OS X accounts given administrator privileges become members of the *admin* group and thereby receive complete sudo privileges.

All attempts to use the sudo command are logged to the system log.

Options

-V
: Print the version number. When run by *root*, also list the options used at sudo's compilation.

-l
: List the commands that the current user is authorized to run with sudo.

-L
: List all option settings that can be used in the Defaults section of the *sudoers* file.

-h
: Print a usage statement.

-v
: Reset the timestamp, giving the user a new five-minute window to use sudo without being prompted for a password.

-k
: Kill the timestamp by setting it past the default timeout value. A password is not needed to use this option.

-K
: Kill the timestamp by removing it. A password doesn't need to be supplied.

-b
: Run *command* in the background, but don't allow use of shell job control to manipulate the process.

-p *prompt*
: Use *prompt* instead of the default password prompt. Within prompt, you can specify %u and %h to have them replaced by the current account name and local hostname, respectively

-u *user*
: Run the command as *user*, specified by either name or UID.

-s
: Begin a shell session as root or user, if -u is specified.

-H
: Set the HOME environment variable to the target user's home directory path. By default, sudo doesn't modify HOME.

-P
: Preserve the user's group vector instead of changing it to that of the target user.

-S
: Read password from standard input instead of prompting for it.

--
: Stop processing command-line arguments. This option makes the most sense when run with -s.

Examples

These examples assume that an appropriate *sudoers* file is in place. Refer to the sudoers manpage for more information on modifying the file.

List an otherwise protected directory:

```
$ sudo ls /Users/chuck
```

Edit the *hostconfig* file.:

```
$ sudo vi /etc/hostconfig
```

Edit a another user's *.login* file:

```
$ sudo -u max vi ~max/.login
```

sw_vers

```
sw_vers [option]
```

Displays the product name, version, and build version for the OS.

Options

`-productName`
: Display the name of the operating system, resulting in Mac OS X.

`-productVersion`
: Display the version number of the operating system.

`-buildVersion`
: Display the build number of the operating system.

Example

Display the version information for your system:

```
$ sw_vers
ProductName:    Mac OS X
ProductVersion: 10.3.2
BuildVersion:   7D24
```

systemkeychain

```
systemkeychain [-v] [-f] -C [password]
systemkeychain [-v] -t
systemkeychain [-v] [-c] [-k dest_keychain] -s keychain
```

Creates and manages the system keychain, */Library/Keychains/System.keychain*. (It also creates */var/db/SystemKey*, which presumably contains a randomly generated keychain password in encrypted form.) This keychain is used by system processes that run as *root*, such as daemons and boot processes, and is created automatically by the `SecurityServer` startup item.

Options

`-c` Create the destination keychain if it doesn't already exist.

`-C` Create a new system keychain, unless one already exists. The keychain password can be specified with an optional argument.

`-f` Force an overwrite of an existing system keychain when creating a new one.

`-k` Instead of adding a key to the system keychain, add it to the specified destination keychain.

`-s` Add a key to the system keychain that can be used to unlock the specified keychain.

`-t` Unlock the system keychain.

`-v` Enable verbose output.

system_profiler

```
system_profiler [-usage] | [-listDataTypes]
system_profiler [-xml] [dataType1 ... dataTypeN]
system_profiler [-xml] [-detailLevel -n]
```

Reports on the hardware and software of the system. Performs the same function as the System Profiler utility (*/Applications/Utilities*), except from the command line. This command replaces the *AppleSystemProfiler* command from Mac OS X 10.2 (Jaguar), located in */usr/sbin*.

Unix Command Reference

Options

The following options are available:

`-detailLevel -n`
: Specify the level of detail for the report with *n* being a number of:

  `-2` Brief overview data only

  `-1` Short data report

  `0` Standard data report

  `1` Extended data report

`-listDataTypes`
: List the available datatypes for the system.

`-usage`
: Display usage information and examples.

`-xml`
: Generate a report in XML format. The file will have a *.spx* file extension, which can be opened with the System Profiler.

Examples

Generate the standard System Profiler report and display it in the Terminal:

```
$ system_profiler
```

Show a listing of the available datatypes:

```
$ system_profiler -listDataTypes
```

Generate a report containing information about a specific datatype:

```
$ system_profiler dataTypeName
```

Generate an XML file containing a report that can be opened by the System Profiler utility and save it to the Desktop:

```
$ system_profiler -xml > ~/Desktop/SysReport.spx
```

SystemStarter

```
SystemStarter [options] [action [service]]
```

Utility to control the starting, stopping, and restarting of system services. The services that can be affected are described in the */Library/StartupItems* and */System/Library/StartupItems/* paths.

The action and service arguments are optional. If no service argument is specified, all startup items will be affected. When a specific startup item is given, that item and all the items that it depends upon, or that are dependent on it, will be affected.

Currently, `rc` calls `SystemStarter` at boot time. Because `SystemStarter` may eventually take over the role of `rc`, it's advisable to create custom startup items rather than continue to modify `rc`.

Options

`-g` Graphical startup

`-v` Verbose startup

`-x` Safe mode startup (a basic startup that only runs Apple items)

`-r` Keep running after last startup item completes (in graphical startup only)

`-d` Print debugging output

`-D` Print debugging output and shows dependencies

`-q` Quiet mode that silences debugging output

`-n` A pretend run mode that doesn't actually perform actions on any items

tail

```
tail [options] [file]
```

Prints the last 10 lines of the named file. Uses either `-f` or `-r`, but not both.

Options

`-f` Don't quit at the end of file; "follow" file as it grows. End with an INTR (usually `^C`).

`-F` Behaves the same as the `-f` option with the exception that it checks every five seconds to see if the filename has changed. If it has, it closes the file and opens the new file.

`-r` Copy lines in reverse order.

`-c` *num*
: Begin printing at *num*th byte from the end of file.

`-b` *num*
: Begin printing at *num*th block from the end of file.

-n *num*

Start at *num*th line from the end of file. -n is the default and doesn't need to be specified.

[+/-]

To start from the beginning of the file, use + before *num*. The default is to start from the end of the file; this can also be done by using a – before *num*.

Examples

Show the last 20 lines containing instances of .Ah:

```
$ grep '\.Ah' file | tail -20
```

Continually track the system log:

```
$ tail -f /var/log/system.log
```

Show the last 10 characters of variable name:

```
$ echo "$name" | tail -c -10
```

Reverse all lines in *list*:

```
$ tail -r list
```

---

talk

talk *user* [*@hostname*] [*tty*]

Exchanges typed communication with another *user* who is on the local machine or on the machine *hostname*. talk might be useful when you're logged in via modem and need something quickly, making it inconvenient to telephone or send email. talk splits your screen into two windows. When a connection is established, you type in the top half while *user*'s typing appears in the bottom half. Type ^L to redraw the screen and ^C (or interrupt) to exit. If *user* is logged in more than once, use *tty* to specify the terminal line. The *user* needs to have used mesg y.

Notes

Please note the following:

- There are different versions of talk that use different protocols; interoperability across different Unix systems is very limited.
- talk is also not very useful if the remote user you are "calling" is using a windowing environment because there is no way to know which *tty* to use to get their attention. The connection request can easily show up in an iconified window! Even if you know the remote *tty*, the called party must have done a mesg y to accept the request.

---

tar

tar [*options*] [*tarfile*] [*other_files*]

Copies *files* to or restores *files* from an archive medium. If any *files* are directories, tar acts on the entire subtree. Options need not be preceded by a dash (–, although they may be). Note that until native drivers for tape drives exist for Mac OS X, tar can't write to tape. Note also that tar doesn't preserve resource forks or metadata when copying files that contain them.

Function options

You must use exactly one of these, and it must come before any other options:

-c
: Create a new archive.

-r, u
: Append *other_files* to the end of an existing archive.

-t
: Print the names of *other_files* if they are stored on the archive (if *other_files* aren't specified, print names of all files).

x
: Extract *other_files* from an archive (if *other_files* aren't specified, extract all files).

Options

-b
: Set block size to 512 bytes.

-e
: If there is an error, stop.

-f *arch*
: Store files in or extract files from archive *arch*. The default is */dev/rst0*. Because Mac OS X has no native tape drive support, tar produces an error unless the -f option is used.

-h
: Dereference symbolic links.

-m
: Don't restore file modification times; update them to the time of extraction.

-O
: Create non-POSIX archives.

-o
: Don't create archives with directory information that v7 tar can't decode.

-p
: Keep ownership of extracted files the same as that of original permissions.

-s *regex*
: Using ed-style regular expressions, change filenames in the archive.

-v
: Verbose; print filenames as they are added or extracted.

-w
: Rename files with user interaction.

-z
: Compress files with gzip before archiving them, or uncompress them with gunzip before extracting them.

-C
: cd to *directory* before beginning tar operation.

-H
: If any of the pathnames given in the command line are symbolic links, follow only those links.

-L
: Follow all symbolic links.

-P
: Don't remove initial slashes (/) from input filenames.

-X Mount points will not be crossed.

-Z Compress files with compress before archiving them, or uncompress them with uncompress before extracting them.

Examples

Create an archive of */bin* and */usr/bin* (c), show the command working (v), and write to the file in your home directory, ~/archive.tar:

```
$ tar cvf ~/archive.tar /bin /usr/bin
```

List the file's contents in a format like ls -l:

```
$ tar tvf ~/archive.tar
```

Extract only the */bin* directory from *archive.tar* to the current directory:

```
$ tar xvf  ~/archive.tar bin
```

---

tee

tee [*options*] *files*

Accepts output from another command and sends it both to the standard output and to *files* (like a T or a fork in a road).

Options

-a Append to *files*; don't overwrite.

-i Ignore interrupt signals.

Example

View listing and save for later:

```
$ ls -l | tee savefile
```

---

telnet

telnet [*options*] [*host* [*port*]]

Accesses remote systems. telnet is the user interface that communicates with another host using the Telnet protocol. If telnet is invoked without *host*, it enters command mode, indicated by its prompt, telnet>, and accepts and executes the commands listed after the following options. If invoked with arguments, telnet performs an open command (shown in the following list) with those arguments. *host* indicates the host's official name. *port* indicates a port number (default is the Telnet port).

Options

-a Automatic login into the remote system.

-b *alias*
  Used to connect to an *alias* setup by ifconfig or another interface as the local address to bind to.

-c Tell `telnet` not to use a user's *.telnetrc* file.

-d Turn on socket-level debugging.

-e *[escape_char]*
: Set initial `telnet` escape character to *escape_char*. If *escape_ char* is omitted, there will be no predefined escape character.

-k Attempt to get tickets for remote host; query `krb_realmofhost` to determine realm.

-l *user*
: When connecting to remote system, and if remote system understands `ENVIRON`, send *user* to the remote system as the value for variable `USER`.

-n *tracefile*
: Open *tracefile* for recording the trace information.

-r Emulate `rlogin`. The default escape character is a tilde (~); an escape character followed by a dot causes `telnet` to disconnect from the remote host; a `^Z` instead of a dot suspends `telnet`; and a `]` (the default `telnet` escape character) generates a normal `telnet` prompt. These codes are accepted only at the beginning of a line.

-x Encryption is used if possible.

-8 Request 8-bit operation.

-E Disable the escape character functionality.

-F, -f
: Forward Kerberos authentication criteria if Kerberos is being used.

-K Disable automatic login to remote systems

-L Specify an 8-bit data path on output.

-S *tos*
: Set the IP type-of-service (TOS) option for the Telnet connection to the value *tos*.

-X *type*
: Turn off the *type* of authentication.

Commands

Control-Z
: Suspend `telnet`.

! *[command]*
: Execute a single command in a subshell on the local system. If *command* is omitted, an interactive subshell will be invoked.

? *[command]*
: Get help. With no arguments, print a help summary. If a *command* is specified, print the help information for just that command.

auth *argument ...*
: Control information sent through the `TELNET AUTHENTICATION` option.

`disable` *type*
: Authentication *type* is turned off.

`enable` *type*
: Authentication *type* is turned on.

`status`
: Status of authentication type is displayed.

`close`
: Close a Telnet session and return to command mode.

`display` *argument ...*
: Display all, or some, of the `set` and `toggle` values.

`encrypt` *arguments ...*
: Control information sent through the `TELNET ENCRYPT` option.

`disable` *type [input|output]*
: Encryption *type* is turned off.

`enable` *type [input|output]*
: Encryption *type* is turned on.

`start` *[input|output]*
: Encryption is turned on if it can be. If neither input or output is given, both will be started.

`status`
: Encryption status is displayed.

`stop` *[input|output]*
: Encryption is turned off. If neither input or output is given, both are stopped.

`type` *type*
: Encryption *type* is set.

`environ` *[arguments [...]]*
: Manipulate variables that may be sent through the `TELNET ENVIRON` option. Valid arguments for `environ` are:

`?`
: Get help for the `environ` command.

`define` *variable value*
: Define *variable* to have a value of *value*.

`undefine` *variable*
: Remove *variable* from the list of environment variables.

`export` *variable*
: Mark *variable* to have its value exported to the remote side.

`unexport` *variable*
: Mark *variable* to not be exported unless explicitly requested by the remote side.

`list`
: Display current variable values.

`logout`
: If the remote host supports the `logout` command, close the `telnet` session.

`mode` *[type]*
: Depending on state of Telnet session, *type* is one of several options:

  `?` Print out help information for the `mode` command.

  `character`
  : Disable `TELNET LINEMODE` option, or, if remote side doesn't understand the option, enter "character-at-a- time" mode.

  [-]`edit`
  : Attempt to [disable] enable the `EDIT` mode of the `TELNET LINEMODE` option.

  [-]`isig`
  : Attempt to [disable]enable the `TRAPSIG` mode of the `LINEMODE` option.

  `line`
  : Enable `LINEMODE` option, or, if remote side doesn't understand the option, attempt to enter "old line-by-line" mode.

  [-]`softtabs`
  : Attempt to [disable] enable the `SOFT_TAB` mode of the `LINEMODE` option.

  [-]`litecho`
  : [Disable] enable `LIT_ECHO` mode.

`open`*[-l user] host [port]*
: Open a connection to the named *host*. If no *port* number is specified, attempt to contact a Telnet server at the default port.

`quit`
: Close any open Telnet session and then exit `telnet`.

`status`
: Show current status of `telnet`. This includes the peer you are connected to, as well as the current mode.

`send` *arguments*
: Send one or more special character sequences to the remote host. Following are the arguments that may be specified:

  `?` Print out help information for `send` command.

  `abort`
  : Send Telnet `ABORT` sequence.

  `ao` Send Telnet AO sequence, which should cause the remote system to flush all output from the remote system to the user's terminal.

  `ayt` Send Telnet AYT (Are You There) sequence.

  `brk` Send Telnet BRK (Break) sequence.

`do` *cmd*
`dont` *cmd*
`will` *cmd*
`wont` *cmd*

Send Telnet DO *cmd* sequence, where *cmd* is a number between 0 and 255 or a symbolic name for a specific `telnet` command. If *cmd* is `?` or `help`, this command prints out help (including a list of symbolic names).

`ec` Send Telnet EC (Erase Character) sequence, which causes the remote system to erase the last character entered.

`el` Send Telnet EL (Erase Line) sequence, which causes the remote system to erase the last line entered.

`eof` Send Telnet EOF (End Of File) sequence.

`eor` Send Telnet EOR (End Of Record) sequence.

`escape`
Send current Telnet escape character (initially `^`).

`ga` Send Telnet GA (Go Ahead) sequence.

`getstatus`
If the remote side supports the Telnet `STATUS` command, `getstatus` sends the subnegotiation request that the server sends to its current option status.

`ip` Send Telnet IP (Interrupt process) sequence, which causes the remote system to abort the currently running process.

`nop` Send Telnet NOP (No operation) sequence.

`susp`
Send Telnet SUSP (Suspend process) sequence.

`synch`
Send Telnet SYNCH sequence, which causes the remote system to discard all previously typed (but not read) input.

`set` *`argument value`*
`unset` *`argument value`*

Set any one of a number of `telnet` variables to a specific value or to `True`. The special value `off` disables the function associated with the variable. `unset` disables any of the specified functions. The values of variables may be interrogated with the aid of the `display` command. The variables that may be specified are:

`?` Display legal `set` and `unset` commands.

`ayt` If `telnet` is in `LOCALCHARS` mode, this character is taken to be the alternate AYT character.

`echo`
This is the value (initially `^E`) that, when in "line-by-line" mode, toggles between doing local echoing of entered characters and suppressing echoing of entered characters.

eof If telnet is operating in LINEMODE or in the old "line-by-line" mode, entering this character as the first character on a line causes the character to be sent to the remote system.

erase
: If telnet is in LOCALCHARS mode or operating in the "character-at-a-time" mode, then when this character is entered, a Telnet EC sequence will be sent to the remote system.

escape
: This is the Telnet escape character (initially ^[), which causes entry into the Telnet command mode when connected to a remote system.

flushoutput
: If telnet is in LOCALCHARS mode, and the flushoutput character is entered, a Telnet AO sequence is sent to the remote host.

forw1
: If Telnet is in LOCALCHARS mode, this character is taken to be an alternate end-of- line character.

forw2
: If Telnet is in LOCALCHARS mode, this character is taken to be an alternate end-of- line character.

interrupt
: If Telnet AO is in LOCALCHARS mode, and the interrupt character is entered, a Telnet IP sequence is sent to the remote host.

kill
: If Telnet IP is in LOCALCHARS mode and operating in the "character-at-a-time" mode, then when this character is entered, a Telnet EL sequence is sent to the remote system.

lnext
: If Telnet EL is in LINEMODE or in the old "line-by-line" mode, then this character is taken to be the terminal's lnext character.

quit
: If Telnet EL is in LOCALCHARS mode, and the quit character is entered, a Telnet BRK sequence is sent to the remote host.

reprint
: If Telnet BRK is in LINEMODE or in the old "line-by- line" mode, this character is taken to be the terminal's reprint character.

rlogin
: Enable rlogin mode. Same as using -r command-line option.

start
: If the Telnet TOGGLE-FLOW-CONTROL option is enabled, this character is taken to be the terminal's start character.

stop
: If the Telnet TOGGLE-FLOW-CONTROL option is enabled, this character is taken to be the terminal's stop character.

`susp`
: If Telnet is in `LOCALCHARS` mode, or if the `LINEMODE` is enabled and the `suspend` character is entered, a Telnet SUSP sequence is sent to the remote host.

`tracefile`
: The file to which output generated by `netdata` is written.

`worderase`
: If Telnet BRK is in `LINEMODE` or in the old "line-by- line" mode, this character is taken to be the terminal's `worderase` character. Defaults for these are the terminal's defaults.

`slc` *[state]*
: Set the state of special characters when Telnet `LINEMODE` option has been enabled.

`?` List help on the `slc` command.

`check`
: Verify current settings for current special characters. If discrepancies are discovered, convert local settings to match remote ones.

`export`
: Switch to local defaults for the special characters.

`import`
: Switch to remote defaults for the special characters.

`toggle` *arguments [...]*
: Toggle various flags that control how Telnet responds to events. The flags may be set explicitly to `true` or `false` using the `set` and `unset` commands listed previously. The valid arguments are:

`?` Display legal `toggle` commands.

`autoflush`
: If `autoflush` and `LOCALCHARS` are both `true`, then when the `ao` or `quit` characters are recognized, Telnet refuses to display any data on the user's terminal until the remote system acknowledges that it has processed those Telnet sequences.

`autosynch`
: If `autosynch` and `LOCALCHARS` are both `true`, then when the `intr` or `quit` characters are entered, the resulting Telnet sequence sent is followed by the Telnet `SYNCH` sequence. The initial value for this `toggle` is `false`.

`binary`
: Enable or disable the Telnet `BINARY` option on both the input and the output.

`inbinary`
: Enable or disable the Telnet `BINARY` option on the input.

`outbinary`
: Enable or disable the Telnet `BINARY` option on the output.

`crlf`
: If this `toggle` value is `true`, carriage returns are sent as `CR-LF`. If it is `false`, carriage returns are sent as `CR- NUL`. The initial value is `false`.

`crmod`
: Toggle carriage return mode. The initial value is `false`.

`debug`
: Toggle socket level debugging mode. The initial value is `false`.

`localchars`
: If the value is `true`, then `flush`, `interrupt`, `quit`, `erase`, and `kill` characters are recognized locally, and then transformed into appropriate Telnet control sequences. Initial value is `true`.

`netdata`
: Toggle display of all network data. The initial value is `false`.

`options`
: Toggle display of some internal `telnet` protocol processing that pertains to Telnet options. The initial value is `false`.

`prettydump`
: When `netdata` is enabled, and if `prettydump` is enabled, the output from the `netdata` command is reorganized into a more user-friendly format, spaces are put between each character in the output, and an asterisk precedes any Telnet escape sequence.

`skiprc`
: Toggle whether to process *~/.telnetrc* file. The initial value is `false`, meaning the file is processed.

`termdata`
: Toggle printing of hexadecimal terminal data. Initial value is `false`.

`Verbose_enrypt`
: When encryption is turned on or off, Telnet displays a message.

`z`
: Suspend `telnet`; works only with `csh`.

---

test

`test` *`expression`* `[`*`expression`*`]`

Also exists as a built-in in most shells.

Evaluates an *`expression`* and, if its value is `true`, returns a zero exit status; otherwise, returns a nonzero exit status. In shell scripts, you can use the alternate form `[`*`expression`*`]`. This command is generally used with conditional constructs in shell programs.

File testers

The syntax for all of these options is `test` *`option file`*. If the specified file doesn't exist, the testers return `false`. Otherwise, they test the file as specified in the option description.

`-b` Is the file block special?

`-c` Is the file character special?

`-d` Is the file a directory?

`-e` Does the file exist?

`-f` Is the file a regular file?

`-g` Does the file have the `set-group-ID` bit set?

`-k` Does the file have the sticky bit set?

`-L`, `-h`
: Is the file a symbolic link?

`-p` Is the file a named pipe?

`-r` Is the file readable by the current user?

`-s` Is the file nonempty?

`-S` Is the file a socket?

`-t` *[file-descriptor]*
: Is the file associated with *`file-descriptor`* (or 1, which is standard output, by default) connected to a terminal?

`-u` Does the file have the `set-user-ID` bit set?

`-w` Is the file writable by the current user?

`-x` Is the file executable?

`-O` Is the file owned by the process's effective UID?

`-G` Is the file owned by the process's effective GID?

File comparisons

The syntax for file comparisons is `test` *`file1 option file2`*. A string by itself, without options, returns `true` if it's at least one character long.

`-nt` Is *`file1`* newer than *`file2`*? Check modification, not creation, date.

`-ot` Is *`file1`* older than *`file2`*? Check modification, not creation, date.

`-ef` Do the files have identical device and inode numbers?

String tests

The syntax for string tests is `test` *`option string`*.

`-z` Is the string 0 characters long?

`-n` Is the string at least 1 character long?

`=` *`string`*
: Are the two strings equal?

`!=` *`string`*
: Are the strings unequal?

< Does *string1* come before *string2*, based on their ASCII values?

> *Does string1* come after *string2*, based on their ASCII values?

Expression tests

Note that an expression can consist of any of the previous tests.

! *expression*
: Is the expression false?

expression -a *expression*
: Are the expressions both true?

expression -o *expression*
: Is either expression true?

Integer tests

The syntax for integer tests is `test` *integer1 option integer2*. You may substitute `-l` *string* for an integer; this evaluates to *string*'s length.

-eq Are the two integers equal?

-ne Are the two integers unequal?

-lt Is *integer1* less than *integer2*?

-le Is *integer1* less than or equal to integer2?

-gt Is *integer1* greater than *integer2*?

-ge Is *integer1* greater than or equal to *integer2*?

tftp

```
tftp [host [port]]
```

User interface to the TFTP (Trivial File Transfer Protocol), which allows users to transfer files to and from a remote machine. The remote *host* may be specified, in which case `tftp` uses *host* as the default host for future transfers.

Commands

Once `tftp` is running, it issues the prompt:

```
tftp>
```

and recognizes the following commands:

? *[command-name...]*
: Print help information.

ascii
: Shorthand for `mode ASCII`.

binary
: Shorthand for `mode binary`.

`connect` *`hostname [port]`*
: Set the *`hostname`*, and optionally the *`port`*, for transfers.

`get` *`filename`*
`get` *`remotename localname`*
`get` *`filename1 filename2 filename3...filenameN`*
: Get a file or set of files from the specified remote sources.

`mode` *`transfer-mode`*
: Set the mode for transfers. *`transfer-mode`* may be `ASCII` or `binary`. The default is `ASCII`.

`put` *`filename`*
`put` *`localfile remotefile`*
`put` *`filename1 filename2...filenameN remote- directory`*
: Transfer a file or set of files to the specified remote file or directory.

`quit`
: Exit `tftp`.

`rexmt` *`retransmission-timeout`*
: Set the per-packet retransmission timeout, in seconds.

`status`
: Print status information: whether `tftp` is connected to a remote host (i.e., whether a host has been specified for the next connection), the current mode, whether verbose and tracing modes are on, and the values for retransmission timeout and total transmission timeout.

`timeout` *`total-transmission-timeout`*
: Set the total transmission timeout, in seconds.

`trace`
: Toggle packet tracing.

`verbose`
: Toggle verbose mode.

tiff2icns

`tiff2icns [-noLarge]` *`input_filename`* `[`*`output_filename`*`]`

Converts TIFF image files to Apple icon (ICNS) files. If *`output_filename`* is not specified, the output file receives the same name as the input file, with the filename extension changed to *.icns*.

Option

`-noLarge`
: Prevent the creation of the highest resolution icons.

tiffutil

```
tiffutil { -dump | -info | -verboseinfo } input_file...
tiffutil { -extract  number | -jpeg [-fN] | -lzw | -none |
 -packbits } input_file [-out output_file]
tiffutil -cat input_file... [-out output_file]
```

Manipulates TIFF image files.

Options

`-cat`
: Concatenate multiple input files.

`-dump`
: Print a list of all tags in the input file to standard output.

`-extract`
: Extract an individual image from the input file, with `0` designating the first image in the file.

`-f`
: Specify the compression factor to use with JPEG compression. The value can range from `1` to `255`. The default is `10`.

`-info`
: Print information about images in the input file to standard output.

`-jpeg`
: Specify the use of JPEG compression when producing the output file.

`-lzw`
: Specify the use of Lempel-Ziv-Welch compression when producing the output file.

`-none`
: Specify the use of no compression when producing the output file.

`-out`
: Specify the name of the output file; defaults to *out.tiff*.

`-packbits`
: Specify the use of PackBits compression when producing the output file.

`-verboseinfo`
: Print lots of information about images in the input file to standard output.

time

```
time [option] command [arguments]
```

Executes a *command* with optional *arguments* and prints the total elapsed time, execution time, process execution time, and system time of the process (all in seconds). Times are printed on standard error.

Option

-p Print the real, user, and system times with a single space separating the title and the value, instead of a tab.

top

```
top [options] [number]
```

Full screen, dynamic display of global and per process resource usage by descending PID order.

Options

number
: top limits the total processes displayed to *number*.

-a Cumulative event counting mode. Counts are cumulative from top start time. -w and -k are superceded and ignored while - a is in effect

-d Delta event counting mode. Counts are deltas relative to a previous sample. -w and -k are superceded and ignored while -d is in effect.

-e Absolute event counting mode. Counts are absolute values from process start times. -w and -k are superceded and ignored while -e is in effect.

-k Report *kernal_task* memory map parameters: #MREGS, RPRVT, and RSHRD (and VPRVT with -w). Normally unreported and displayed as – .

-l *samples*
: Logging mode. Change display mode from periodic full screen updating to a sequential line mode output suitable for output redirection. The number of sequential snapshots is specified as *samples*.

-s *interval*
: Sampling interval. Default one second sample interval is replaced by *interval*.

-u Sort processes by decreasing CPU usage instead of by descending PID order.

-w Change the memory map and memory size parameters for all processes from counts to deltas, and adds a VPRVT column.

touch

```
touch [options] files
```

For one or more *files*, updates the access time and modification time (and dates) to the current time and date. touch is useful in forcing other commands to handle files a certain way; e.g., the operation of make, and sometimes find, relies on a file's access and modification time. If a file doesn't exist, touch creates it with a file size of 0.

Options

`-a` Update only the access time.

`-c` Don't create any file that doesn't already exist.

`-f` Try to update even if you don't have permissions.

`-h` The access or modification times of a symbolic link are changed. Access and modification time can be changed at the same time. The `-c` option is also applied.

`-m` Update only the modification time.

`-r` *`file`*
: Change times to be the same as those of the specified *`file`*, instead of the current time.

`-t` *`time`*
: Use the time specified in *`time`* instead of the current time. This argument must be of the format: *`[[cc]yy]mmddhhmm[.ss]`*, indicating optional century and year, month, date, hours, minutes, and optional seconds.

---

tr

```
tr [options] [string1 [string2]]
```

Translates characters; copies standard input to standard output, substituting characters from *`string1`* to *`string2`*, or deleting characters in *`string1`*.

Options

`-c` Complement characters in *`string1`* with respect to ASCII 001- 377.

`-d` Delete characters in *`string1`* from output.

`-s` Squeeze out repeated output characters in *`string2`*.

`-u` Guarantee that any output is unbuffered.

Special characters

Include brackets ([ ]) where shown.

`\a` ^G (bell)

`\b` ^H (backspace)

`\f` ^L (form feed)

`\n` ^J (newline)

`\r` ^M (carriage return)

`\t` ^I (tab)

`\v` ^K (vertical tab)

`\`*`nnn`*
: Character with octal value *nnn*.

\\ Literal backslash.

char1-char2
: All characters in the range *char1* through *char2*. If *char1* doesn't sort before *char2*, produce an error.

[*char1-char2*]
: Same as *char1-char2* if both strings use this.

[*char**]
: In *string2*, expand *char* to the length of *string1*.

[*char*number*]
: Expand *char* to number occurrences. [x*4] expands to xxxx, for instance.

[:*class*:]
: Expand to all characters in *class*, where *class* can be:

  alnum
  : Letters and digits

  alpha
  : Letters

  blank
  : Whitespace

  cntrl
  : Control characters

  digit
  : Digits

  graph
  : Printable characters except space

  lower
  : Lowercase letters

  print
  : Printable characters

  punct
  : Punctuation

  space
  : Whitespace (horizontal or vertical)

  upper
  : Uppercase letters

  xdigit
  : Hexadecimal digits

[=*char*=]
: The class of characters in which *char* belongs.

Examples

Change uppercase to lowercase in a file:

```
$ cat file | tr '[A-Z]' '[a-z]'
```

Turn spaces into newlines (ASCII code 012):

```
$ tr ' ' '\012' < file
```

Strip blank lines from *file* and save in *new.file* (or use 011 to change successive tabs into one tab):

```
$ cat file | tr -s "" "\012" > new.file
```

Delete colons from *file*; save result in *new.file*:

```
$ tr -d : < file > new.file
```

---

traceroute

```
traceroute [options] host [packetsize]
```

Traces the route taken by packets to reach network host. traceroute attempts tracing by launching UDP probe packets with a small TTL (time to live), then listening for an ICMP "time exceeded" reply from a gateway. *host* is the destination hostname or the IP number of host to reach. *packetsize* is the packet size in bytes of the probe datagram. Default is 38 bytes.

Options

-d
Turn on socket-level debugging.

-m *max_ttl*
Set maximum time-to-live used in outgoing probe packets to *max-ttl* hops. Default is 30 hops.

-n
Show numerical addresses; don't look up hostnames. (Useful if DNS is not functioning properly.)

-p *port*
Set base UDP port number used for probe packets to *port*. Default is (decimal) 33434.

-q *n*
Set number of probe packets for each time-to-live setting to the value *n*. Default is 3.

-r
Bypass normal routing tables and send directly to a host on an attached network.

-s *src_addr*
Use *src_addr* as the IP address that will serve as the source address in outgoing probe packets.

-t *tos*
Set the type-of-service in probe packets to *tos* (default 0). The value must be a decimal integer in the range 0 to 255.

-v Verbose; received ICMP packets (other than TIME_EXCEEDED and PORT_UNREACHABLE) will be listed.

-w *wait*
: Set time to wait for a response to an outgoing probe packet to *wait* seconds (default is three seconds).

true

```
true
```

A null command that returns a successful (0) exit status. See also false.

tset

```
tset [options] [type]
```

Sets terminal modes. Without arguments, the terminal is reinitialized according to the TERM environment variable. tset is used in startup scripts (*.profile* or *.login*). *type* is the terminal type; if preceded by a ?, tset prompts the user to enter a different type, if needed. Press the Return key to use the default value, *type*.

Options

-q, –
: Print terminal name on standard output; useful for passing this value to TERM.

-e*c* Set erase character to *c*; default is ^H (backspace).

-i*c* Set interrupt character to *c* (default is ^C).

-I Don't output terminal initialization setting.

-k*c* Set line-kill character to *c* (default is ^U).

-m*[port[baudrate]:type]*
: Declare terminal specifications. *port* is the port type (usually dialup or plugboard). *tty* is the terminal type; it can be preceded by ? as above. *baudrate* checks the port speed and can be preceded by any of these characters:

  > Port must be greater than *baudrate*.

  < Port must be less than *baudrate*.

  @ Port must transmit at *baudrate*.

  ! Negate a subsequent >, <, or @ character.

  ? Prompt for the terminal type. With no response, use the given type.

-Q Don't print "Erase set to" and "Kill set to" messages.

-r Report the terminal type.

-s Return the values of TERM assignments to the shell environment. This is commonly done via eval \'tset -s\' (in the C shell, surround this with the commands set noglob and unset noglob).

-V Print the version of ncurses being used.

Examples

Set TERM to wy50:

```
$ eval `tset -s wy50`
```

Prompt user for terminal type (default is vt100):

```
$ eval `tset -Qs -m '?vt100'`
```

Similar to above, but the *baudrate* must exceed 1200:

```
$ eval `tset -Qs -m '>1200:?xterm'`
```

Set terminal via modem. If not on a dial-in line, ?$TERM causes tset to prompt with the value of $TERM as the default terminal type:

```
$ eval `tset -s -m dialup:'?vt100' "?$TERM"`
```

---

tty

```
tty [option]
```

Prints the device name for your terminal. This is useful for shell scripts and commands that need device information. tty exits 0 if the standard input is a terminal, 1 if the standard input is not a terminal, and >1 if an error occurs.

Option

-s Suppress the terminal name.

---

udf.util

```
udf.util -m device mount_point
udf.util { -p | -u } device
```

Mounts UDF (DVD) filesystems into the directory hierarchy.

Options

-m Mount the *device*.

-p Probe the *device* and print the volume name to standard output.

-u Unmount the *device*.

device
  The DVD device filename, e.g., *disk1*.

mount_point
  The directory on which the DVD filesystem is mounted.

---

ufs.util

```
ufs.util { -k | -p | -s } device
ufs.util -n device name
```

Manipulates UFS filesystems.

Options

-k Read the disk's UUID key and print it to standard output.

-n Reset the volume name of the device. It takes effect after the next remount.

-p Probe the device and print the volume name to standard output.

-s Generate a new disk UUID key and set it on the volume.

device
: The disk device filename, e.g. *disk0s5*.

mount_point
: The directory on which the filesystem is mounted.

---

umount

```
umount [-f] [-v] [-t types] { -a | -A | -h hostname }
umount [-f] [-v] { special | mount_point }
```

Removes mounted volumes from the directory hierarchy.

Options

-a Unmount all filesystems listed in `fstab` or Open Directory.

-A Unmount all currently mounted filesystems, other than root's.

-f Attempt to force the unmount.

-h Unmount all filesystems currently mounted from the specified server.

-t Restrict the use of the command to filesystems of the specified types presented in a comma-separated list, which may include `hfs`, `ufs`, `afp`, `nfs`, or others.

-v Enable verbose output.

special
: The form of this argument is particular to the type of filesystem being mounted and can be a disk device name, a fixed string, or something involving a server name and directory. See the individual `mount_type` entries for details.

mount_point
: The directory on which the filesystem is mounted.

---

uname

```
uname [options]
```

Prints information about the machine and operating system. Without options, prints the name of the operating system.

Options

-a Combine all the system information from the other options.

-m Print the hardware the system is running on.

-n Print the machine's hostname.

-r Print the release number of the kernel.

-s Print the name of the operating system.

-p Print the type of processor.

-v Print build information about the kernel.

---

uncompress

```
uncompress [option] [files]
```

Restores the original file compressed by `compress`. The *.Z* extension is implied, so it can be omitted when specifying *`files`*.

The `-b`, `-c`, `-f`, and `-v` options from `compress` are also allowed. See `compress` for more information.

---

unexpand

```
unexpand [options] [files]
```

Converts strings of initial whitespace, consisting of at least two spaces and/or tabs to tabs. Reads from standard input if given no file or a given file named – .

Option

-a Convert all, not just initial, strings of spaces and tabs.

---

uniq

```
uniq [options] [file1 [file2]]
```

Removes duplicate adjacent lines from sorted *`file1`*, sending one copy of each line to *`file2`* (or to standard output). Often used as a filter. Specify only one of `-c`, `-d`, or `-u`. See also `comm` and `sort`.

Options

-c Print each line once, counting instances of each.

-d Print duplicate lines once, but no unique lines.

-f *n*
  Ignore the first *n* fields of a line. Fields are separated by spaces or by tabs.

-s *n*
  Ignore the first *n* characters of a field.

-u Print only unique lines (no copy of duplicate entries is kept).

-n Ignore the first *n* fields of a line. Fields are separated by spaces or by tabs.

+n Ignore the first *n* characters of a field. Both [-/+]*n* have been deprecated, but are still in this version.

Examples

Send one copy of each line from `list` to output file *list.new* (`list` must be sorted):

```
$ uniq list list.new
```

Show which names appear more than once:

```
$ sort names | uniq -d
```

Show which lines appear exactly three times:

```
$ sort names | uniq -c | awk '$1 == 3'
```

---

units

`units [options]`

Interactively supply a formula to convert a number from one unit to another. A complete list of the units can be found in */usr/share/misc/units.lib*.

Options

`-f filename`
: Use the units data in *filename*.

`-q` The prompts for "you have" and "you want" won't appear.

`-v` The version of `units` is listed.

[have-unit want-unit]
: A unit conversion can be entered from the command line instead of using the interactive interface.

---

unzip

```
unzip [-v]
unzip -Z [-v] [-M] [-s | -m | -l | -1] [-T] archive_filename [pathname...] [-x
pathname...]
unzip -Z [-v] [-M] [-2] [-h] [-t] [-z] archive_filename [pathname...] [-x
pathname...]
unzip [-q[q] | -v] [-M] [-l | -t | -z | -p | -c [-a[a]]] [-b] [-C] archive_
filename [pathname...] [-x pathname...]
unzip [-q[q] | -v] [-M] [-f | -u] [-a[a] | -b] [-C] [-L] [-j] [-V] [-X] [-n
| -o] [-d directory] archive_filename [pathname...] [-x pathname...]
```

Lists or extracts files from a ZIP archive (such as one created by the `zip` command). If the name of the archive file ends in *.zip*, that extension need not be specified in *archive_filename*. If *pathname* arguments are given, only archive items matching those arguments are processed; otherwise, `unzip` lists or extracts all items in the archive. When called with no arguments, it prints a usage statement to standard output.

Options

-a
: Convert text files in the archive to native format. For instance, it translates DOS linefeeds to Unix linefeeds on Mac OS X. When doubled (`-aa`), it attempts to convert all files, whether text or binary.

-b
: Treat all files as binary, so that no text conversions are attempted.

-c
: Extract file data to standard output.

-C
: Use case-insensitive matching of *pathname* arguments to archive items.

-d
: Extract files into the given directory. Otherwise, files are extracted into the current working directory.

-f
: Extract files only if they already exist, and if the modification timestamps in the archive are more recent than those on disk.

-j
: Discard the paths of archived files, so that all files are extracted into the same directory.

-l
: List archive contents, along with sizes, modification timestamps, and comments. More information is printed if `-v` is also used.

-L
: Convert filenames to lowercase if they were archived from a single-case filesystem (such as FAT). When doubled (`-LL`), all filenames are converted to lowercase.

-M
: Display output a page at a time.

-n
: Never overwrite existing files when extracting. By default, `unzip` prompts the user if an existing file would be overwritten.

-o
: Overwrite existing files when extracting, without prompting.

-p
: As `-c`, except that text conversions aren't allowed.

-q
: Minimize output. When doubled (`-qq`), produces even less output.

-t
: Perform a CRC check on archive items to determine if they have changed since being archived.

-u
: As `-f`, but also extract files that don't already exist on the disk.

-v
: Enable verbose output. If it's the only argument, print version information, compile settings, and environment variable settings to standard output.

-V
: For items archived on a VMS system, this retain file version numbers in filenames.

-x
: Exclude the files specified by the additional *pathname* arguments, which usually include wildcards to match filenames of a certain pattern.

-X
: Restore owner and group information for extracted files. Successful use of this flag will most likely require superuser privileges.

-z
: Print comments stored in the archive file to standard output.

-Z
: Provide more control over information displayed to standard output about archive contents. When invoked as the only argument, prints usage information for the following options to standard output:

-h Print archive name, size, and number of archived items.

-l As -s, but compressed size is also displayed.

-m As -s, but compression ratio is also displayed.

-M Display output a page at a time.

-s Print information about each item in the archive: permissions, version of zip used to create the archive, uncompressed size, file type, compression method, modification timestamp, and name. This is the default behavior if no other options are specified.

-t Print number of archived items, cumulative compressed and uncompressed sizes, and compression ratio.

-T Print timestamps in a sortable format, rather than the default human-readable format.

-v Enable verbose output.

-x Exclude the files specified by the additional *pathname* arguments, which usually include wildcards to match filenames of a certain pattern.

-z Print comments stored in the archive file.

-1 Print only filenames of archived items.

-2 As -1, but -h, -t, and -z flags may be used to print additional information.

Examples

List the contents of a ZIP archive:

```
$ unzip -lv whizprog.zip
```

Extract C source files in the main directory, but not in subdirectories:

```
$ unzip whizprog.zip '*.[ch]' -x '*/*'
```

uptime

```
uptime
```

Prints the current time, amount of time the system has been up, number of users logged in, and the system-load averages over the last one, five, and fifteen minutes. This output is also produced by the first line of the w command.

users

```
users [file]
```

Prints a space-separated list of each login session on the host. Note that this may include the same user multiple times. Consult *file* or, by default, */var/run/utmp*.

uudecode

```
uudecode [file]
```

Reads a uuencoded file and re-creates the original file with the permissions and name set in the file (see `uuencode`).

uuencode

```
uuencode[file] name
```

Encodes a binary *file*. The encoding uses only printable ASCII characters and includes the permissions and *name* of the file. When *file* is reconverted via `uudecode`, the output is saved as *name*. If the *file* argument is omitted, `uuencode` can take standard input, so a single argument is taken as the name to be given to the file when it is decoded.

`uuencode` doesn't preserve resource forks or metadata when copying files that contain them.

Examples

It's common to encode a file and save it with an identifying extension, such as *.uue*. This example encodes the binary file *flower12.jpg*, names it *rose.jpg*, and saves it to a *.uue* file:

```
$ uuencode flower12.jpg rose.jpg > rose.uue
```

Encode *flower12.jpg* and mail it:

```
$ uuencode flower12.jpg flower12.jpg | mail me@oreilly.com
```

uuidgen

```
uuidgen
```

Sends to standard output a generated Universally Unique Identifier (UUID). A UUID is a 128-bit value guaranteed to be unique. This is achieved by combining a value unique to the computer, such as the MAC Ethernet address, and a value representing the number of 100-nanosecond intervals since a specific time in the past.

vi

```
vi [options] [files]
```

A screen-oriented text editor based on ex. See Chapter 23 for more information on `vi` and ex. Options `-c`, `-C`, `-L`, `- r`, `-R`, and `-t` are the same as in ex.

Options

`-c` *command*
: Enter `vi` and execute the given `vi` *command*.

`-e`
: Edit in ex mode.

-F Don't make a temporary backup of the entire file.

-l Run in LISP mode for editing LISP programs.

-r *file*
Recover and edit *file* after an editor or system crash.

-R Read-only mode. Files can't be changed.

-S No other programs can be run, vi is put in secure edit mode.

-s This option works only when ex mode is being used. It enters into batch mode.

-t *tag*
Edit the file containing *tag* and position the editor at its definition.

-w*n* Set default window size to *n*; useful when editing via a slow dial-up line.

+ Start vi on last line of file.

+*n* Start vi on line *n* of file.

+/*pat*
Start vi on line containing pattern *pat*. This option fails if nowrapscan is set in your *.exrc* file.

---

view

view [*options*] [*files*]

Same as vi -R.

---

vm_stat

vm_stat [*interval*]

Displays Mach virtual memory statistics. The default view, without a specified interval, shows accumulated statistics. If interval is specified, vm_stat lists the changes in each statistic every interval seconds, showing the accumulated statistics for each item in the first line.

---

vmmap

vmmap *PID*

Displays the virtual memory regions associated with *PID*. vmmap displays the starting address, region size, read/write permissions for the page, sharing mode for the page, and the page purpose. This can be useful information for programmers especially, who often need to understand the memory allocation of a given process.

vndevice

```
vndevice { attach | shadow } device pathname
vndevice detach device
```

Attaches or detaches a virtual device node to or from a disk image file. (Note that the functionality of vndevice is incorporated within hdiutil.) Modifications to data on the attached disk image will instead be written to the virtual node, or *shadow image*, and subsequent access to that data will be from the shadow. This allows effective read/write access to data on a disk image which shouldn't or can't be modified.

Options

attach
: Attach a device node to a disk image designated by *pathname*.

detach
: Detach a device node from a disk image.

shadow
: Associate an attached device node to a shadow disk image designated by *pathname*.

device
: The device node filename, e.g., */dev/vn0*.

Examples

Create a disk image, attach a virtual device node to it, and mount it:

```
$ hdiutil create test.dmg -volname test -size 5m -fs HFS+ -layout NONE
$ sudo vndevice attach /dev/vn0 test.dmg
$ mkdir mount_point
$ sudo mount -t hfs /dev/vn0 mount_point
```

Wait a minute, and then:

```
$ touch mount_point/test_file
$ ls -l test.dmg
```

Note that the modification time on the disk image is current, reflecting the change you made by creating a test file.

Now set up shadowing. Unmount the volume first, then create the shadow disk image, attach the virtual node to it, and mount it again:

```
$ sudo umount /dev/vn0
$ hdiutil create shadow.dmg -volname shadow -size 5m -fs HFS+ -layout NONE
$ sudo vndevice shadow /dev/vn0 shadow.dmg
$ sudo mount -t hfs /dev/vn0 mount_point
```

Wait a minute, and then:

```
$ rm mount_point/test_file
$ ls -l test.dmg; ls -l shadow.dmg
```

The modification time on the test image wasn't updated, but the shadow image reflects the change you just made, indicating that writes are being passed through to the shadow.

Finish up by unmounting the volume and detaching the virtual node:

```
$ sudo umount /dev/vn0
$ sudo vndevice detach /dev/vn0
```


vsdbutil

```
vsdbutil { -a | -c | -d } pathname
vsdbutil -i
```

Enables or disables the use of permissions on a disk volume. This is equivalent to using the "Ignore Privileges" checkbox in the Finder's Info window for a mounted volume. The status of permissions usage on mounted volumes is stored in the permissions database, */var/db/volinfo.database*.

Options

`-a` Activate permissions on the volume designated by *pathname*.

`-c` Print the status of permissions usage on the volume designated by *pathname* to standard output.

`-d` Deactivate permissions on the volume designated by *pathname*.

`-i` Initialize the permissions database to include all mounted HFS and HFS+ volumes.

w

```
w [options] [user]
```

Prints summaries of system usage, currently logged-in users, and what they are doing. `w` is essentially a combination of `uptime`, `who`, and `ps -a`. Display output for one user by specifying *user*.

Options

`-h` Suppress headings and `uptime` information.

`-i` List by idle time.

`-M` *file*
: Use data from the supplied *file*.

`-N` *sysname*
: Use data from the supplied *sysname*.

`-n` List IP address as numbers.

wall

```
wall [file]
```

Writes to all users. `wall` reads a message from the standard input until an end-of-file. It then sends this message to all users currently logged in, preceded by "Broadcast Message from...". If *file* is specified, read input from that, rather than from standard input.

wc

```
wc [options] [files]
```

Prints byte, character, word, and line counts for each file. Prints a total line for multiple *files*. If no *files* are given, reads standard input. See other examples under `ls` and `sort`.

Options

`-c` Print byte count only.

`-l` Print line count only.

`-m` Print character count only.

`-w` Print word count only.

Examples

Count the number of users logged in:

```
$ who | wc -l
```

Count the words in three essay files:

```
$ wc -w essay.[123]
```

Count lines in the file named by variable `$file` (don't display the filename):

```
$ wc -l < $file
```

whatis

```
whatis keywords
```

Searches the short manpage descriptions in the `whatis` database for each *keyword* and prints a one-line description to standard output for each match. Like `apropos`, except that it searches only for complete words. Equivalent to `man -f`.

whereis

```
whereis files
```

Checks the standard binary directories for the specified programs, printing out the paths of any it finds.

Compatibility

The historic flags and arguments for the whereis utility are no longer available in this version.

which

```
which [commands]
```

Lists which files are executed if the named *commands* are run as a command. which reads the user's *.cshrc* file (using the source built-in command), checking aliases and searching the path variable. Users of the Bourne or Korn shells can use the built-in type command as an alternative.

Example

```
$ which file ls
/usr/bin/file
ls:      aliased to ls -sFC
```

who

```
who [options] [file]
```

Displays information about the current status of the system. With no options, lists the names of users currently logged in to the system. An optional system file (default is */var/run/utmp*) can be supplied to give additional information. who is usually invoked without options, but useful options include am i and -u. For more examples, see cut, line, paste, tee, and wc.

Options

-H
Print headings.

-m
Report only about the current terminal.

-T
Report whether terminals are writable (+), not writable (–), or unknown (?).

-u
Report terminal usage (idle time). A dot (.) means less than one minute idle; old means more than 24 hours idle.

am i
Print the username of the invoking user. (Similar to results from id.)

Example

This sample output was produced at 1:55 p.m. on January 15:

```
$ who -uH
USER     LINE     WHEN          IDLE     FROM
chuck    console  Jan 14 19:55 18:01
chuck    ttyp1    Jan 15 13:11    .
chuck    ttyp2    Jan 15 13:55    .
```

The output shows that the user chuck has been idle for 18 hours and 1 minute (18:01, under the IDLE column).

whoami

```
whoami
```

Prints current UID. Equivalent to `id -un`.

whois

`whois [option] name`

Queries the Network Information Center (NIC) database to display registration records matching *name*. Multiple *names* need to be separated by whitespace. The special *name* "help" will return more information on the command's use.

Option

`-h` Specify a different `whois` server to query. The default is *whois.internet.net*.

write

`write user [tty] message`

Initiates or responds to an interactive conversation with *user*. A `write` session is terminated with EOF. If the user is logged in to more than one terminal, specifies a *tty* number. See also `talk`; use `mesg` to keep other users from writing to your terminal.

xargs

`xargs [options] [command]`

Executes *command* (with any initial arguments) but reads remaining arguments from standard input instead of specifying them directly. `xargs` passes these arguments in several bundles to *command*, allowing *command* to process more arguments than it could normally handle at once. The arguments are typically a long list of filenames (generated by `ls` or `find`, for example) that get passed to `xargs` via a pipe.

Options

`-0` Expect filenames to be terminated by NULL instead of whitespace. Don't treat quotes or backslashes specially.

`-n` *args*
: Allow no more than *args* arguments on the command line. May be overridden by `-s`.

`-s` *max*
: Allow no more than *max* characters per command line.

`-t` Verbose mode. Print command line on standard error before executing.

`-x` If the maximum size (as specified by `-s`) is exceeded, exit.

Examples

Search for pattern in all files on the system, including those with spaces in their names:

```
$ find / -print0 | xargs -0 grep pattern > out &
```

Run `diff` on file pairs (e.g., *f1.a* and *f1.b*, *f2.a*, and *f2.b* ...):

```
$ echo $* | xargs -n2 diff
```

The previous line would be invoked as a shell script, specifying filenames as arguments. Display *file*, one word per line (same as `deroff -w`):

```
$ cat file | xargs -n1
```


yes

`yes [strings]`

Prints the command-line arguments, separated by spaces and followed by a newline, until killed. If no arguments are given, print `y` followed by a newline until killed. Useful in scripts and in the background; its output can be piped to a program that issues prompts.

zcat

`zcat [options] [files]`

Reads one or more *files* that have been compressed with `gzip` or `compress` and writes them to standard output. Reads standard input if no *files* are specified or if - is specified as one of the files; ends input with EOF. `zcat` is identical to `gunzip -c` and takes the options `-fhLV` described for `gzip`/`gunzip`.

zcmp

`zcmp [options] files`

Reads compressed files and passes them, uncompressed, to the `cmp` command, along with any command-line options. If a second file is not specified for comparison, looks for a file called *file.gz*.

zdiff

`zdiff [options] files`

Reads compressed files and passes them, uncompressed, to the `diff` command, along with any command-line options. If a second file is not specified for comparison, looks for a file called *file.gz*.

zgrep

```
zgrep [options] [files]
```

Uncompresses files and passes to grep, along with any command-line arguments. If no files are provided, reads from (and attempts to uncompress) standard input. May be invoked as zegrep or zfgrep; in those cases, invokes egrep or fgrep.

zip

```
zip [-h | -v]
zip [-q | -v] [-T] [-0 | -1 | -9] [-F[F]] [-o] [-f | -u] [-g] [-b directory]
[-J] archive_filename
zip [-q | -v] [-T] [-0 | -1 | -9] [-r [-D]] [-m] [-t MMDDYY] [-o] [-c] [-z]
[-X] [-j] [-k] [-l[l]] [-y] [-n suffix[:suffix]...] [ -f | -u] [-d] [-g]
[-b directory] [-A] archive_filename { pathname... | -@ } [{ -i | -x }
pathname...]
```

The files given by the *pathname* arguments are collected into a single archive file with some metadata (as with tar), where they are compressed using the PKZIP algorithm. The archive file is named with a *.zip* extension unless another extension is specified. If pathname is given as -, data to be archived and compressed is read from standard input; if *archive_filename* is -, the ZIP archive data is written to standard output instead of to a file. If *archive_filename* already exists, then the specified files are added to or updated in the existing archive. When called with no arguments, it prints a usage statement to standard output.

Unlike the creation of ZIP archives from the Finder, zip doesn't preserve resource or attribute forks.

Options

-A
: Adjust the file offsets stored in the ZIP archive to prepare it for use as a self-extracting executable archive.

-b
: When updating an existing archive, specify the directory in which the new archive is temporarily stored before being copied over the old. Normally the temporary file is created in the current directory.

-c
: Prompt for one-line comments associated with each file in the archive.

-d
: Remove files from an existing archive, instead of adding or updating them.

-D
: Disable the creation of directory entries in the archive.

-f
: Update files in an existing archive if the modification timestamps of the source files are more recent than those in the archive. Doesn't add new files to an existing archive.

-F
: Attempt to repair an archive file that has been corrupted or truncated. When doubled (-FF), it performs a more thorough analysis of the archive.

-g
: When updating an existing archive, attempt to append to the existing file, rather than creating a new file to replace the old.

-h
: Print a usage statement to standard output.

- `-i` Include only the files specified by the additional *pathname* arguments, which usually include wildcards to match filenames of a certain pattern.
- `-j` Discard the paths of archived files, retaining only the filenames.
- `-J` Strip data prepended to an archive, such as code to make the archive a self-extracting executable.
- `-k` Attempt to archive files using DOS-compatible names and attributes.
- `-l` Translate Unix-style newlines in files to DOS newlines. When doubled (`-ll`), convert DOS newlines to Unix newlines.
- `-m` Delete the source files after they've been archived.
- `-n` Disable compression for files with names ending in the specified strings.
- `-o` Set the modification timestamp of the ZIP archive to that of the most recently modified item in the archive.
- `-q` Minimize output.
- `-r` Perform a recursive traversal of directories specified in the *pathname* arguments, and archives their contents.
- `-t` Archive only files with modification timestamps more recent than the given date.
- `-T` Test the integrity of the ZIP archive created by the command. If the test fails, a preexisting archive file isn't overwritten, and source files aren't deleted (if using `-m`).
- `-u` Update files in an existing archive if the modification timestamps of the source files are more recent than those in the archive. Unlike `-f`, new files are also added.
- `-v` Enable verbose output. If it's the only argument, print version information, compile settings, and environment variable settings to standard output.
- `-x` Exclude the files specified by the additional *pathname* arguments, which usually include wildcards to match filenames of a certain pattern.
- `-X` Disable storage of file metadata in the archive, such as owner, group, and modification date.
- `-y` Archive symbolic links as symlinks, rather than archiving the targets of symlinks.
- `-z` Prompt for comments to be stored in the archive file.
- `-0` Disable compression.
- `-1` Compress more quickly, at the cost of space efficiency.
- `-9` Compress better, at the cost of time.
- `-@` Take the list of source files from standard input.

Examples

Archive the current directory into *source.zip*, including only C source files:

```
$ zip source -i '*.[ch]'
```

Archive the current directory into *source.zip*, excluding the object files:

```
$ zip source -x '*.o'
```

Archive files in the current directory into *source.zip* but don't compress *.tiff* and *.snd* files:

```
$ zip source -z '.tiff:.snd' *
```

Recursively archive the entire directory tree into one archive:

```
$ zip -r /tmp/dist.zip .
```

zprint

```
zprint [options] name
```

Displays information in columnar output about all memory zones. Using command-line switches, you can alter the formatting and amount of information displayed.

Options

`-w` Display the space allocated, but not in use, for each memory zone. The output for each zone is displayed in the right-most column.

`-s` Produce a sorted output of the memory zones in descending order beginning with the zone that wastes the most memory.

`-C` Override the default columnar format with a row-based display that also reduces the information fields shown.

`-H` Hide the default columnar headings. This may be useful when sorting output by column.

`name` is a substring of one or more memory zone names. Only memory zones matching this substring will be included in the output.

zmore

```
zmore [files]
```

Similar to `more`. Uncompresses files and prints them, one screen at a time. Works on files compressed with `compress`, `gzip`, or `pack`, and with uncompressed files.

Commands

Space
Print next screenful.

`i`*[number]*
Print next screenful, or *`number`* lines. Set *`i`* to *`number`* lines.

d, *Ctrl-D*
: Print next *i*, or 11 lines.

*i*z
: Print next *i* lines or a screenful.

*i*s
: Skip *i* lines. Print next screenful.

*i*f
: Skip *i* screens. Print next screenful.

q, Q, :q, :Q
: Go to next file, or, if current file is the last, exit zmore.

e, q
: Exit zmore when the prompt "--More--(Next file: file)" is displayed.

s
: Skip next file and continue.

=
: Print line number.

i/*expr*
: Search forward for *i*th occurrence (in all files) of *expr*, which should be a regular expression. Display occurrence, including the two previous lines of context.

*i*n
: Search forward for the *i*th occurrence of the last regular expression searched for.

!*command*
: Execute *command* in shell. If *command* isn't specified, execute last shell command. To invoke a shell without passing it a command, enter \!.

.
: Repeat the previous command.

---

znew

znew [*options*] [*files*]

Uncompresses *.Z* files and recompresses them in *.gz* format.

Options

-9
: Optimal (and slowest) compression method.

-f
: Recompress even if *filename.gz* already exists.

-t
: Test new *.gz* files before removing *.Z* files.

-v
: Verbose mode.

-K
: If the original *.Z* file is smaller than the *.gz* file, keep it.

-P
: Pipe data to conversion program. This saves disk space.

V
Appendixes

The final part of the book provides you with information on how to generate special characters from the keyboard without using the Character Palette, and wraps up with a list of Mac-related resources, such as books, magazines, web sites, and mailing lists.

The appendices in this part include:

- Appendix A, *Special Characters*
- Appendix B, *Resources*

Special Characters

Included with Mac OS X is the Keyboard Viewer application, which is a keyboard widget that allows you to see which character would be created by applying the Shift, Option, or Shift-Option keys to any key on the keyboard. To enable Keyboard Viewer, go to System Preferences→International→Input Menu and select the checkbox next to Keyboard Viewer. The Input menu will appear in the menu bar; to launch the Keyboard Viewer, simple select this item from the Input menu.

While this might seem useful, it can be a hassle to launch another application just to create one character, and copy and paste it into another program. Fortunately, one of the most little-known/-used features of the Mac OS is its ability to give you the same functionality within any application—making Keyboard Viewer unnecessary if you know what you're doing. Table A-1 lists these special characters. Keep in mind that this doesn't work for all font types, and some fonts—such as Symbol, Wingdings, and Zapf Dingbats—create an entirely different set of characters or symbols. For example, to create the symbol for the Command key (⌘), you would need to switch the font to Wingdings and type a lowercase *z*.

Table A-1. Special characters and their key mappings

Normal	Shift	Option	Shift-Option
1	!	¡	⁄
2	@	™	€
3	#	£	‹
4	$	¢	›
5	%	∞	ﬁ
6	^	§	ﬂ
7	&	¶	‡
8	*	•	°
9	(	ª	·

Table A-1. Special characters and their key mappings (continued)

Normal	Shift	Option	Shift-Option
0	)	º	‚
`	~	Grave (`)[a]	`
- (hyphen)	_ (underscore)	– (en-dash)	— (em-dash)
=	+	≠	±
[	{	“	”
]	}	‘	’
\	|	«	»
;	:	…	Ú
'	"	æ	Æ
,	<	≤	¯
.	>	≥	˘
/	?	÷	¿
a	A	å	Å
b	B	∫	ı
c	C	ç	Ç
d	D	∂	Î
e	E	Acute (´)[a]	´
f	F	ƒ	Ï
g	G	©	˝
h	H	˙	Ó
i	I	Circumflex (ˆ)[a]	ˆ
j	J	∆	Ô
k	K	˚	
l	L	¬	Ò
m	M	µ	Â
n	N	Tilde (˜)[a]	˜
o	O	ø	Ø
p	P	π	∏
q	Q	œ	Œ
r	R	®	‰
s	S	ß	Í
t	T	†	ˇ
u	U	Umlaut (¨)[a]	¨
v	V	√	◊
w	W	∑	„
x	X	≈	˛
y	Y	¥	Á
z	Z	Ω	¸

[a] To apply this accent, you must press another key after invoking the Option-*key* command. See Table A-2.

One thing you might have noticed in Table A-1 is that when the Option key is used with certain letters, it doesn't necessarily create a special character right away; you need to press another character key to apply the accent. Unlike the other Option-*key* commands, when used with the ` (backtick), E, I, N, and U characters, you can create accented characters as shown in Table A-2.

Table A-2. Option-key commands for creating accented characters

Key	Option-`	Option-E	Option-I	Option-N	Option-U
a	à	á	â	ã	ä
Shift-A	À	Á	Â	Ã	Ä
e	è	é	ê	˜e	ë
Shift-E	È	É	Ê	˜E	Ë
i	ì	í	î	˜i	ï
Shift-I	Ì	Í	Î	˜I	Ï
o	ò	ó	ô	õ	ö
Shift-O	Ò	Ó	Ô	Õ	Ö
u	ù	ú	û	˜u	ü
Shift-U	Ù	Ú	Û	˜U	Ü

For example, to create the acute-accented "e" in the word *résumé*, you type Option-E and then press the E key. If you want an uppercase acute-accented E (É), press Option-E and then Shift-E. Try this out with various characters in different fonts to see what sort of characters you can create.

B

Resources

The following is a list of resources for Mac OS X users, including books, magazines, mailing lists, and web sites.

Books

The following books are available for Mac users, administrators, and developers:

AppleScript: The Definitive Guide
By Matt Neuburg (O'Reilly)

AppleScript for Applications: Visual QuickStart Guide
By Ethan Wilde (Peachpit Press)

AppleWorks 6: The Missing Manual
By Jim Elferdink and David Reynolds (Pogue Press/O'Reilly)

Building Cocoa Applications: A Step-by-Step Guide
By Simson Garfinkel and Michael Mahoney (O'Reilly)

Carbon Programming
By K. J. Bricknell (Sams)

Cocoa Programming
By Scott Anguish, Erik Buck, and Donald Yacktman (Sams)

Cocoa Programming for Mac OS X
By Aaron Hillegass (Addison-Wesley)

Cocoa Recipes for Mac OS X: The Vermont Recipes
By Bill Cheeseman (Peachpit Press)

iMovie 3 & iDVD: The Missing Manual
By David Pogue (Pogue Press/O'Reilly)

iPhoto 2: The Missing Manual
By David Pogue, Joseph Schorr, and Derrick Story (Pogue Press/O'Reilly)

iPod & iTunes: The Missing Manual
By J.D. Biersdorfer (Pogue Press/O'Reilly)

Learning Carbon
By Apple Computer, Inc. (O'Reilly)

Learning Cocoa with Objective-C
By James Duncan Davidson and Apple Computer, Inc. (O'Reilly)

Learning the bash Shell
By Cameron Newham and Bill Rosenblatt (O'Reilly)

Learning Unix for Mac OS X Panther
By Dave Taylor and Brian Jepson (O'Reilly)

Mac 911
By Christopher Breen (Peachpit Press)

Mac OS 9: The Missing Manual
By David Pogue (Pogue Press/O'Reilly)

Mac OS X: The Missing Manual, Panther Edition
By David Pogue, (Pogue Press/O'Reilly)

Mac OS X Disaster Relief
By Ted Landau and Dan Frakes (Peachpit Press)

Mac OS X Java: Early Adopter
By Murray Todd Williams et al. (Wrox Press)

Mac OS X Panther Killer Tips
By Scott Kelby (New Riders Publishing)

Mac OS X Panther Pocket Guide
By Chuck Toporek (O'Reilly)

Mac OS X Panther for Unix Geeks
By Brian Jepson and Ernest E. Rothman (O'Reilly)

Mac OS X Panther Unleashed
By John Ray and William C. Ray (Sams)

Objective-C Pocket Reference
By Andrew M. Duncan (O'Reilly)

Office 2001 for Macintosh: The Missing Manual
By Nan Barber and David Reynolds (Pogue Press/O'Reilly)

Office X for Macintosh: The Missing Manual
By Nan Barber, David Reynolds, Tonya Engst (Pogue Press/O'Reilly)

Programming in Objective-C
By Stephen Kochen (New Riders)

REALbasic: The Definitive Guide
By Matt Neuburg (O'Reilly)

Secrets of the iPod
By Christopher Breen (Peachpit Press)

Switching to the Mac: The Missing Manual
By David Pogue (Pogue Press/O'Reilly)

Using csh & tcsh
By Paul DuBois (O'Reilly)

Magazines

The following print magazines are available for Mac users:

MacAddict
Published monthly, *MacAddict* is a magazine for users and power users. Each issue contains hardware and software reviews and is accompanied with a CD-ROM that contains free and shareware applications, as well as demo versions of games and the most popular graphics applications.

http://www.macaddict.com

Mac Design
Published monthly, *Mac Design* is a magazine for Mac-based graphic designers.

http://www.macdesignonline.com

macHOME
Published monthly, *macHOME* is a magazine for home-based Mac users. Each issue contains articles and tutorials on how to use your Mac.

http://www.machome.com

MacTech
Published monthly, *MacTech* is a magazine for Macintosh developers. Each issue contains articles and tutorials with code examples.

http://www.mactech.com

Macworld
Published monthly, each issue contains hardware and software reviews, as well as tutorials and how-to articles.

http://www.macworld.com

Mailing Lists

The mailing lists in this section can help you learn more about the Mac.

Apple-Run Mailing Lists

The following mailing lists are run by Apple:

applescript-studio
For scripters and developers who are using AppleScript Studio to build AppleScript-based applications for Mac OS X.

applescript-users
For scripters who are working with AppleScript.

carbon-development
: For Carbon developers.

cocoa-dev
: For Cocoa developers.

java-dev
: For Java developers.

mac-games-dev
: For Mac-based game developers.

mac-opengl
: For Mac-based OpenGL developers.

macos-x-server
: For network and system administrators who run the Mac OS X Server.

rendezvous
: Discussions on how to develop applications and devices that use Rendezvous.

scitech
: Discussions on Apple's support for science and technology markets.

studentdev
: For student developers.

weekly-kbase-changes
: Keep informed of weekly changes to Apple's Knowledge Base (KB).

For information on how to subscribe to these and other Apple-owned mailing lists, see *http://lists.apple.com*.

Apple also maintains a listing of miscellaneous Mac-related mailing lists at *http://lists.apple.com/cgi-bin/mwf/forum_show.pl*; click on the "Non-Apple Mailing Lists" link.

Omni Group's Mailing Lists

The following mailing lists are run by the Omni Group:

macosx-admin
: A technical list for Mac OS X system administrators.

macosx-dev
: A moderated list for Mac OS X application developers.

macosx-talk
: A list for general discussions about the Mac OS X operating system.

For more information on how to subscribe to these and other Omni lists, see *http://www.omnigroup.com/developer/ mailinglists*.

Resources

Web Sites

These are just a few of the many URLs every Mac user should have bookmarked.

Apple Sites

Apple's Mac OS X page
http://www.apple.com/macosx

Software Downloads page
http://www.apple.com/downloads/macosx

Apple's Support page
http://www.info.apple.com

Apple's Knowledge Base
http://kbase.info.apple.com

Apple Developer Connection (ADC)
http://developer.apple.com

Apple Store Locator
http://www.apple.com/retail

Bug Reporting
http://developer.apple.com/bugreporter

.Mac page
http://www.mac.com

Developers

Cocoa Dev Central
http://www.cocoadevcentral.com

Cocoa Dev Wiki
http://www.cocoadev.com

Mac DevCenter (by O'Reilly Network)
http://www.macdevcenter.com

Stepwise
http://www.stepwise.com

Discussions and News

Applelust
http://www.applelust.com

Apple Slashdot
http://apple.slashdot.org

MacCentral
http://www.maccentral.com

MacInTouch
http://www.macintouch.com

Mac Minute
http://www.macminute.com

Mac News Network
http://www.macnn.com

MacSlash
http://www.macslash.org

Rumor Sites

Apple Insider
http://www.appleinsider.com

MacRumors
http://www.macrumors.com

RumorTracker
http://www.rumortracker.com

SpyMac
http://www.spymac.com

Think Secret
http://www.thinksecret.com

Software

AquaFiles
http://www.aquafiles.com

Bare Bones Software
http://www.barebones.com

Fun with Fink
http://www.funwithfink.com

The Omni Group
http://www.omnigroup.com

Version Tracker
http://www.versiontracker.com/macosx

Tips, Tricks, Advice

Mac OS X FAQ
http://www.osxfaq.com

Mac OS X Hints
http://www.macosxhints.com

Index

Numbers

802.11b protocol and security, 286

Symbols

- & (ampersand)
  - ex, 647
- < > (angle brackets) ex, 646
- * (asterisk), 514
  - passwords set to, 363
    - quoting or escaping, 363
- @ (at)
  - ex, 647
  - tcsh, 585
- ' (backquote), 519
- ! (bang) ex, 646
- [ ] (brackets), 514
- : (colon)
  - ex editor, 613
  - :set command (ex), 647
  - tcsh null command, 586
- . (dot), 530
- .Mac (Apple's subscriber service)
  - accounts, 222
- .Mac (Internet panel), 157
- .Mac email, accessing from Safari, 223
- .Mac HomePage
  - creating Photo Album page, 224
  - publishing iMovie, 224
- .Mac member's HomePage, 223
- .Mac page, 976
- .Mac Slide Show, 223
- >> (double-arrow) icon (Finder toolbar), 53
- = (equals) ex, 646
- #! (hash bang), 530
  - tcsh shell, 586
- # (hash mark)
  - in shell scripts, 530
  - tcsh shell, 586
- : (null command), 530
- % (percent) bash job ID argument, 529
- | (pipe), 514
- ? (question mark), 514
- ~ (tilde)
  - bash, 514
  - ex, 647
  - tcsh, 581

A

- AB Action Plug-in for C (Xcode), 423
- AB Action Plug-in for Objective-C (Xcode), 423
- abbrev command (ex), 631
- About Application Name option (Application menu), 17
- About Finder option (Application menu), 68
- About QuickTime button (QuickTime Pro), 162
- About This Mac option (Apple menu), 10, 96
- ac command, 704
- accept command, 320

We'd like to hear your suggestions for improving our indexes. Send email to *index@oreilly.com*.

access mode, change, 733
accessibility, 201
system reading email message, 202
(see also speech recognition software; Universal Access)
accessing mounted volumes, 53
Accounts menu, 22
Accounts panel, 165
Accounts Preferences pane, 326–331
Limitation tab, 331
Login Options
Automatically log in as, 328
Display Login Window as, 327
Enable fast user switching, 328
Hide the Sleep, Restart, and Shut Down buttons, 328
Password Hint tab, 330
Password tab, 330
Picture tab, 330
Security tab, 330
Startup Items tab, 330
accounts, user (see user accounts)
Active Directory plug-in (Directory Access), 356
Active Network Ports option, 267
Activity Monitor, 187
add command (CVS), 474
Add to Favorites option (File menu), 69
add-on preferences, 118
Address Book, 183
address command (ex), 646
addsuffix variable (tcsh), 567
admin command (CVS), 445, 462–464
admin group, 332
Admin users (Mac OS X Panther), 166
administration
network, 334–337
system (see system administration)
administrative privileges, granting, 364
administrator
privileges, 203
finding out who has, 204
removing, 203
System Preferences and, 119
(see also root)
Advanced pane (Classic), 104
AFP (Apple Filing Protocol), 282, 378
access to shares, 713
URLs, 716
AFSUSER environment variable (tcsh), 572
afsuser variable (tcsh), 567
AirPort
adding menu extra for, 224
card, 206
configuration settings, 229
networks
enabling a computer to setup, 206
security, 347
switching from Ethernet, 206
security, 286
settings, 271–272
shared connections and, 230
sharing, 346
modem or Ethernet connection, 206
strength meter, 206
switching to from Ethernet, 230
wireless networking settings, 206
AirPort Admin Utility, 188
AirPort Base Station, 346
configuring, 206
AirPort option (Network pane), 271
AirPort options (Sharing panel), 346
Channel, 347
Enable encryption, 347
Network Name, 347
Password, 347
WEP key length, 347
AirPort Setup Assistant, 188
Aladdin Systems' Spring Cleaning, 192
alias command
bash, 531
tcsh, 586
aliases, 87
creating, 218
storing, 9
alloc command (tcsh), 587
Always open folders in a new window (Finder preference), 66
Always show file extensions (Finder preference), 67
ampersand (&) command (ex), 647
ampm variable (tcsh), 567
anacron, 350
analysis tool, 414
angle brackets (< >) command (ex), 646
annotate command (CVS), 474
anonymous FTP, 376
antialiasing
controlling, 119
fonts, 220

Apache
configuration, 375
modules, 376
Appearance Control Panel, 98
Personal preferences, 119
AppearanceSample example, 415
append command (ex), 631
Apple CD Audio Player, 100
Apple Developer Connection (ADC), 411, 976
Apple Events
overview, 399
remote, 371
Apple Filing Protocol (see AFP)
Apple Help Indexing Tool, 416
Apple Insider, 977
Apple menu, 9
changes in Mac OS X, 96
Option key and, 14
options
About This Mac, 10, 96
Dock, 12
Force Quit, 13
Get Mac OS X Software, 12
Location, 12
Log Out, 14
Recent Items, 12
Restart, 13
Shutdown, 13
Sleep, 13
System Preferences, 12
Recent Items submenu, 119
Restart option, 13
Shutdown option, 13
Apple Menu Options Control Panel, 98
Apple Open Firmware page, 870
Apple Remote Desktop, 163, 371
Apple Slashdot, 976
Apple Store Locator, 976
apple symbol (see Apple menu)
Apple System Profiler (see System Profiler)
Apple web sites, 976
Applelust, 976
@AppleNotOnBattery command, 350
appleping command, 704
Apple-run mailing lists, 974
Apple's
Knowledge Base, 976
Mac OS X page, 976
Mail application, 40
Services menu, 46
QuickTime web site, 162
Script Menu Extra, 397
subscriber service, 157
Support page, 976
AppleScript, 206, 397–410, 427
creating place for, 207
editor (see Script Editor)
extending, 403
flow control keywords, 402
folder, 183
folder actions, 406–408
identifying version, 206
programming, 398–409
quick-start guide, 399–403
resources, 410
scripts
creating, compiling, recording, and running, 404
saving, 405
source, 408
syntax, 401
testing scripts, 405
AppleScript Application (Xcode), 420
AppleScript Document-based Application (Xcode), 420
AppleScript Droplet (Xcode), 420
AppleScript script file inside a PDF Services folder, 303
AppleScript Studio, 408
Interface connections, 409
programming reference, 408
AppleScript Xcode Plugin (Xcode), 423
applescript-studio mailing list, 974
applescript-users mailing list, 974
AppleShare servers (AFP over IP or AppleTalk), 280
AppleSystemProfiler command, 236
Applet Launcher (Java), 189
AppleTalk, 356
as legacy communication protocol, 266
configuration, 270
Control Panel, 98
network interfaces, 705
printers, 711
configuration, 113
to be used with atprint, 710
viewing list of, 232
printing, 304
appletalk command, 336, 705
example, 706

AppleTalk Echo Protocol (AEP) request packets, 704
appletviewer command, 706
Application Environment, xv
Application menu, 17–18, 68
additional menus, 18
commands, 17
options
About Application Name, 17
About Finder, 68
Empty Trash, 68
Hide Application Name, 18
Hide Finder, 69
Hide Others, 18, 69
Preferences, 17, 68
Quit Application Name, 18
Secure Empty TrashNone, 68
Services, 17, 68
Show All, 18, 69
X11, 681
connecting to other X Windows Systems, 689
customizing, 687
Application (project type in Xcode), 420
Application Services layer, xiv
/Application Support folder (/Library folder), 252
Application Switcher, 23
applications, 82, 183–199
active versus inactive, 7
development, 413–415
force-quitting, 15
icons, 25
adding and removing, 26
installing, 191–199
linking to documents, 86
Mac OS 9, installing, 194
restricting user access, 203
standard menus, 18
uninstalling, 191
version information, 430
X11-based (see X11)
Applications folder
Preview, 186
Safari, 186
Sherlock, 186
Stickies, 187
TextEdit, 187
/Applications folder (/Developer folder), 412
Applications folders, 250
Applications (Mac OS 9) folder, 250
Applications option (Go menu), 71
application-to-document map in Mac OS X, 82
apply command, 706
examples, 707
apropos command, 707
apt-cache program (Fink), 700
apt-get command package (Fink), 700
Aqua, 3, 42
interactions with X11, 688
OSXvnc server, support by, 692
version of Qt for Mac OS X, 688
VNC client, 693
VNC viewers, 693
X11 full screen and rootless modes, 681
Aqua Human Interface Guidelines (see HIG)
AquaFiles, 977
archives in CVS, 444
args command (ex), 631
argv variable (tcsh), 567
Arrange option (View menu), 70
as Columns option (View menu), 70
as Icons option (View menu), 70
as List option (View menu), 70
Asia Text Extras, 188
asr command, 707–709
examples, 709
/Assistants folder (/Library folder), 253
asterisk (*), 514
at (@) command
ex, 647
tcsh, 585
at command, 709
examples, 710
at_cho_prn command, 710
atlookup command, 232, 710
examples, 711
atprint command, 232, 711
examples, 711
atq command, 712
atrm command, 712
atstatus command, 712
attribute forks, 247
/Audio folder (/Library folder), 253
Audio MIDI Setup, 188
authentication, 192, 387–392
BSD flat files, using, 356
relying solely upon, 358

Directory Access Authentication tab, 357
Linux-PAM, using, 354–355
NetInfo database and, 351
X11, configuring for, 687
AuthorizationTrampoline command, 712
autocorrect variable (tcsh), 567
autodiskmount command, 713
autoexpand variable (tcsh), 567
autolist variable (tcsh), 567
autologout variable (tcsh), 567
Automatically log in as option (Login Options), 168, 328
automount command, 713–717
automount daemon, 339
/automount directory, 261
autonomous system (AS), 335
AVI files, 186
awk command, 611

B

.backup files, 86
.bash_history file, 257
Back option (Go menu), 71
background images, 207
Background option (Icon View), 60
background processes, 504
viewing in Classic, 209
backslash_quote variable (tcsh), 567
backspace key, 515
Emacs, 652
backups of NetInfo database, 367
bang (!) (ex), 646
banner command, 717
Bare Bones Software, 977
basename command, 718
example, 718
bash shell, 508, 511–529
arithmetic expressions and operators, 525
built-in commands, 530–558
built-in shell variables, 523–525
command history, 526–529
command substitution, 527
fc command, 527
line-edit mode, 526
command-line editing, 515–518
Emacs mode, 515–516
vi mode, 517–518
commands, 246
case-sensitivity, 246
usage, 519
configuration files, 511
DISPLAY variable, enabling X11 forwarding, 689
features, 512
filename metacharacters, 514
invocation, options and arguments, 512
job control, 529
pattern matching, 514
prompt variables, 528
quoting, 518
redirection, usage, 520
special files, 514
syntax, 514–521
variables, 521–525
variable substitution, 522–523
vi mode editing, 515
batch command, 718
example, 718
battery power
Energy Saver panel, 139
low power warnings, 140
running on, 350
status in menu bar, 140
(see also Energy Saver panel)
battery status, 237
BBEdit, 46
bc command, 718–722
examples, 721
function keyword, 720
input/output keywords, 719
math library functions, 720
operators, 721
statement keywords, 719
bdelete command (ex), 632
beeps (system alert), for X11, 687
beginner's guide
to AppleScript, 399–403
to the Mac, 4
benchmark software, 414
bg command
bash, 531
tcsh, 585, 587
bg pid command, 504
biff command, 722
/bin directory, 260
bind command (bash built-in), 531
bindings (see keyboard shortcuts)

bindkey command (tcsh), 587
BinHex (.hqx) file compression, 197
bitmap fonts, 220
BlastApp example, 415
bless command, 722–725
  device options, 723
  examples, 724
  folder options, 722
  general options, 724
  info options, 724
Bluetooth
  adding menu extra for, 225
  menu extra, 22
  sending selected text to device, 47
Bluetooth File Exchange utility, 188
Bluetooth folder, 415
Bluetooth Monitor tool, 415
Bluetooth panel (System Preferences), 151
Bluetooth Serial Utility, 188
Bluetooth Setup Assistant, 188
Bombich Software, SMD application, 696
books (resources), 972–974
BootP, 270
bootstrap daemons, 380
Bourne shell, 511
brackets [ ], 514
branching (CVS), 446
break command
  bash built-in, 532
  tcsh, 588
breaksw command (tcsh), 588
Bresnik, Marcel, 338
BrickHouse, 342, 344
Bring All to Front option (Window menu), 71
broadcasting in
  Carbon applications, 399
  Cocoa applications, 399
browsers
  alternative, 285
  changing default, 287
browsing (web), 285–287
BSD Dynamic Library (Xcode), 422
BSD operating system
  flat files (see flat files)
  osx2x application, 690
BSD Static Library (Xcode), 423
buffer command (ex), 632
buffers, 652
buffers command (ex), 632
Bug Reporting, 976
build phases (Xcode), 425
Built Examples folder, 415
builtin command (bash), 532
built-ins command (tcsh), 588
Bundle (project type in Xcode), 421
bundles, 86, 421
Burn Disc option (File menu), 69
Burr, Steve, 700
bye command (tcsh), 588
ByHost folder, 679

C

C++ Tool (Xcode), 424
cache, identifying, 236
caching
  flushing cached credentials with sudo lookupd –flushcache, 364
  invalid credentials, caching by Directory Services, 358
cal command, 725
  examples, 725
Calculate all sizes option (List View), 63
calculator applications, 183
calendar command, 725
call waiting, disabling, 227
Camelbones project, 428
Camino browser, 287
cancel command, 320, 726
Carbon
  application development, 416
  broadcasting in, 399
Carbon Application (Xcode), 420
Carbon Bundle (Xcode), 422
Carbon Dynamic Library (Xcode), 422
Carbon Framework (Xcode), 422
Carbon Static Library (Xcode), 424
carbon-development mailing list, 975
case command
  bash, 532
  tcsh, 588
case-sensitivity, bash and zsh shell commands, 246
casual root abuse, 325
cat command, 726
  examples, 727
catalog variable (tcsh), 567

C/C++
C library, gethostent( ), 352
(see also Objective-C)
CCLEngine command, 727
cd command
bash built-in, 532
ex, 631
tcsh, 588
cd9660.util command, 729
cdpath variable (tcsh), 567
CD-RW discs, erasing, 213
CDs & DVDs panel (System Preferences), 132
cellular phones, communicating with, 151
center command (ex), 632
certtool command, 729
CFNotificationCenter class, 399
CFPlugIn Bundle (Xcode), 422
change command (ex), 632
Character Palette, 129
accessing from menu bar, 225
chdir command (tcsh), 589
checkgid command, 730
checkout command (CVS), 475
Chess, 183
chflags command, 731
examples, 731
chgrp command, 264, 732
Chicken of the VNC (Aqua VNC client), 693
Chinese Text Converter, 188
chkpasswd command, 732
chmod command, 217, 264, 733–734
examples, 734
Chooser, 100
configuring printers, 112
chown command, 264, 734
recursively setting home directory ownership, 364
chsh, chfn, and chpass commands, 364
CHUD Tools, 414
CIFS (Common Internet File System), 283
cksum command, 735
Class column (Property List Editor), 675
class paths, 441
Classic
Advanced pane, 104
application windows, 109
oddities, 110
applications, 27
force-quitting, 15, 110
managing, 106
memory and, 107
controls versus Aqua controls, 109
Dock and, 110
keyboard shortcut for starting and restarting, 209
launching from command line, 102
memory, 209
menu bar, 108
overview, 100
panel, 168
preferences panel, 101, 103
printing from, 112
restarting, 209
starting, 101–103
automatically, 209
when you log on, 102
tasks and settings, 208
viewing background processes, 209
Clean Up option (View menu), 70
cleaning up after installation, 199
clear command, 735
clock, removing from menu bar, 224
close command (ex), 632
Close option (File menu), 19
Close Window option (File menu), 69
CMM (Color Matching Module), 312
cmp command, 735
example, 736
Cocoa
application development, 416
broadcasting in, 399
Cocoa Application (Xcode), 420
Cocoa Bundle (Xcode), 422
Cocoa Dev Central, 976
Cocoa Dev Wiki, 976
Cocoa Document-based Application (Xcode), 420
Cocoa Dynamic Library (Xcode), 422
Cocoa Framework (Xcode), 422
Cocoa Static Library (Xcode), 424
cocoa-dev mailing list, 975
Cocoa-Java Application (Xcode), 420, 421
colcrt command, 736
colon (:)
ex editor, 613
:set command, 647
tcsh null command, 586

color
changing display to grayscale, 201
copying value from image into HTML document, 210
depth, 133
DigitalColor Meter, 189
hexadecimal value, 210
setting in Finder windows, 60
text highlighting, 119
X11 look and feel, customizing, 686
Color LabelNone option (File menu), 69
Color Matching Module (CMM), 312
color variable (tcsh), 567
colorcat variable (tcsh), 567
colored labels, 67
/ColorPickers folder (/Library folder), 253
ColorSync, 312–317
how it works, 312
profiles, 313
properties, 912
Quartz filters, 315–317
scripts, 317
using, 313
ColorSync Control Panel, 98
/ColorSync folder (/Library folder), 253
ColorSync Utility, 188, 313–315
Devices pane, 314
Filters Pane, 316
Color option, 316
Defaults option, 317
Domains option, 317
Images option, 317
PDF option, 317
Filters pane, 315, 316
Preferences pane, 314
Profile First Aid pane, 314
Profiles pane, 314
colrm command, 736
example, 736
column command, 737
Column View (Finder), 63
keyboard shortcuts, 64
options, 64
column widths, resizing, 65
COLUMNS environment variable (tcsh), 573
com.apple.PowerManagement.xml, 139
comm command, 737
example, 737
command command (bash), 533
command line
mode, accessing, 239
printing from, 231
command substitution
bash, 527
tcsh, 577, 578
command variable (tcsh), 567
command-line editing
bash, 515–518
tcsh, 581–584
Comments (Get Info window), 95
Comments option (List View), 63
commit command (CVS), 475
Common Internet File System (CIFS), 283
Common Unix Printing System (see CUPS)
communicating with wireless devices, 151
compgen command (bash), 533
complete command
bash, 533–535
tcsh, 589
complete=enhance variable (tcsh), 567
/Components folder (/Library folder), 253
compress command, 738
Computer option (Go menu), 71, 246
Concurrent Versions System (see CVS)
configd command, 738
configuration, AirPort, 229
configuration files
bash, 511
CVS client, 467
tcsh, 561
vi, 613, 647–650
configure script, 701
Connect to Server option (Go menu), 71, 281–284
Connection (QuickTime panel), 160
connections
dial-up configuration, 227
Ethernet configuration, 228
network speed, 229
VPN and, 228
Console utility, 188
contact information, searching Directory Services for, 358
content, finding files by, 78
Content index (Get Info window), 94

content-based searches, 234
ContentIndexing application, 79
contextual menus, 9
  Terminal versus xterm windows, 682
continue command
  bash, 535
  tcsh, 590
continue variable (tcsh), 568
continue_args variable (tcsh), 568
Control Panels, equivalents in Mac OS X, 98
Control Strip Control Panel, 98
Control-clicking in an xterm window, 682
converting files, text to PostScript, 769
Copies & Pages pane (Printer dialog), 297
copy command (ex), 633
copy keyword (AppleScript), 402
Copy option (Edit menu), 20, 70
copying and pasting
  files and folders, 88–92
  between X11 and Mac OS X applications, 688
    controlling with osx2x, 691
Core Services layer, xiv
CoreFoundation Tool (Xcode), 424
CoreServices Tool (Xcode), 424
correct variable (tcsh), 568
Cover Page option (Print dialog), 299
cp command, 739
  example, 739
cpio command, 739–741
  examples, 741
CpMac command, 741
CPU Monitor, 187
crash logs, 239
Create Archive of option (File menu), 69
create_nidb command, 741
Creator codes, 84–85
  common, 84
cron
  daily backups of NetInfo database, 367
  table, 349
  utilities, 349
crond, 349
crontab command, 742
C-s command (Emacs), 652
csh shell DISPLAY variable, enabling X11 forwarding, 689
Ctrl-key (Emacs)
  commands, 659–661
Ctrl-Z command
  bash, 529
  tcsh, 585
CUPS (Common Unix Printing System), 295
  access-control directives, 322
  configuring, 321
  system security, 322
cupsd.conf file, 321
curl command, 743
  examples, 744
cursor, changing style of, 238
custom icons, 218
Customize Toolbar option (View menu), 70
Customize Toolbar window, 52
cut command, 744
  examples, 744
Cut option (Edit menu), 20, 70
CVS (Concurrent Versions System), 444–489
  access methods, 465
  admin command, 445, 462–464
    security risks, 449
  administrator reference, 447–465
    CVSROOT environment variable, 448
  branching, 446
  checkoutlist file, 451
  client configuration files, 467
  client global options, 469
  commands
    for administrators, 462–465
    format of, 446
    for users, 473–489
  commitinfo file, 451
  common client options, 470–473
  config file, 452
  configuring, 466–468
  conflicts and merging, 445
  cvsignore file, 452
  CVSROOT directory, 449–458
    administrative file variables, 450
    files, 450
  cvswrappers file, 453
  environment variables, 466

CVS (*continued*)
global options, 447
global server option, 462
gotchas, 447
history file, 453
importing from RCS, 460
importing into CVS, 459, 460
code snapshots, 459
from PVCS, 461
from SCCS, 461
locking model, 445
loginfo file, 453
merging model, 445
modules file, 454
notify file, 456
passwd file, 456
password setup, 448
rcsinfo file, 457
readers file, 457
repositories, 444
creating, 448
making changes, 458
structure, 449
repository locators, 465
sandboxes, 444
creating, 468
CVS directory files, 469
.cvsignore files, 468
.cvswrappers files, 468
sharing, 461
structure, 468
security, 449
special files, 467
tagging, 445
taginfo file, 457
user reference, 465–489
users file, 457
verifymsg file, 458
writers file, 458
cwd variable (tcsh), 568
cycling through all of an application' s open windows, 43

D

.dfont extension, 220
.dmg files, 196
daemons, 339
bootstrap, 380
configuration file, monitoring, 865
managing, 380–384
StartupItems, 381–384
xinetd, 384
Darwin, xiv, 698
dynamic libraries versus ELF libraries, 429
files, 260
software installation strategies, 698
(see also Unix)
DarwinPorts web site, 685
Data Fork TrueType Font, 220
data forks, 246
data store for NetInfo and LDAP, 357
database-updating script, 80
Date & Time panel, 98, 169
date command, 745–747
examples, 746
Date Created option (List View), 62
Date (International preferences panel), 129
Date Modifier option (List View), 62
dates, 210
daily cron job, changing time for, 367
(see also Date & Time panel)
dc command, 747
examples, 747
dd command, 748–749
examples, 749
Debug mode (Xcode), 425
debugging tool, 414
declare command (bash), 535
default command (tcsh), 590
default shell, setting, 493
defaults command, 670, 750–752
commands, 750
complete reference for, 676–679
examples, 751
values, 751
warning, 751
defaults command-line program, 255
defaults database, 670–679
del key, 515
delete command (ex), 633
deleting files, 32, 393
(see also Trash)
Desktop
copying file to, 217
images, changing, 207
overview, 5

/Desktop directory (user directory), 251
desktop environments, 682, 685
 controlling all X11- and Mac OS X-based desktops, 690
 X11
 available from Fink, 685
 web sites for download and instructions, 685
Desktop panel, Personal preferences, 120
desktop printing, 308
dev files, 261
Developer Tools, 182
developer web sites, 976
development applications, 413–415
development tools (see Xcode Tools)
device drivers, 254
device profile registration (ColorSync), 313
dextract variable (tcsh), 568
df command, 752
DHCP (Dynamic Host Configuration Protocol), 270
 Internet Sharing and, 344
DialAssist Control Panel, 98
dialing automatically into the PPP server, 279
dialog boxes, 39
dial-up connections
 configuration, 227
 speed, 227
dialup networking, 275–279
dictionaries, nested, 672
dictionary attacks against password files, 352
diff command, 415, 752–756
 CVS, 476
diff3 command, 756
dig command, 336, 757
digital hub, 131
DigitalColor Meter, 189
Direct CG (AIPI), 681
directories
 permissions, 262
 user, 251
 (see also folders; bundles)
Directory Access application, 189, 351
 Authentication tab, 357
 caching of invalid credentials after changes to, 358
 Contact tab, 358
 directory service plug-ins, 355–357
Directory Services, 351–368
 configuring, 355–358
 Authentication tab, Directory Access, 358
 BSD flat files as sole authentication source, 358
 plug-ins supported by Directory Access, 356
 exporting directories with NFS, 365
 flat file counterparts, 366
 groups, managing, 360–362
 adding user to a group, 361
 creating groups with dscl, 361
 creating groups with niload, 361
 deleting groups, 362
 listing all GIDs, 360
 listing with nidump, 362
 hostnames and IP addresses, managing, 365
 NetInfo Manager, 358
 programming with, 352–355
 passwords, 352–355
 restoring the database, 367
 users and passwords, managing, 362–364
 adding users, 362
 creating user with dscl, 363
 creating user with niload, 363
 creating user's home directory, 363
 deleting user with dscl's delete command, 364
 granting administrative privileges, 364
 listing users with nidump, 364
 modifying user with dscl -create, 364
 utilities, 358
 list of, 359
DirectoryService command, 758
DirectoryService daemon, 352
dirname command, 759
dirs command
 bash, 536
 tcsh, 590
dirsfile variable (tcsh), 568
dirstack variable (tcsh), 568
disable command, 320

Discovery Services, 189
discussion web sites, 976
disk icons, 28
disk images, 196
  creating, 707
Disk Utility, 189
diskarbitrationd command, 759
disks
  erasing, 213
    CD-RW, 213
  images, creating, 212
  local, searches, 74
  mounting network, 280–285
  settings and tasks, 211
  unmounting, 33
disktool command, 759
diskutil command, 760–763
  options, 761–763
disown command (bash), 536
display
  changing from color to grayscale, 201
  settings, 213
    for persons with visual impairments, 201
  white on black, 202
DISPLAY environment variable (tcsh), 573
Display Login Window as option (Login Options), 167, 327
DISPLAY variable, enabling X11 forwarding in Terminal, 689
Displays panel (System Preferences), 133–138
ditto command, 763
  example, 764
  with --rsrc flag, 364
divider bar, Dock, 31
dmesg command, 764
DNS service discovery, 294
dnsquery command, 764
Dock, 24–31, 125
  appearance and behavior, 123
  application icons, 25, 26
  Classic and, 110
  context menu, 31
  divider bar, 31
  Finder, 31
  hacking the plist file, 125
  hiding, 125
  Home folder and, 29
  icons, 24
  interactive icons, 26
  keyboard shortcuts, 33
  launching applications from, 25
  menus, 27
    commands, 27
    iTunes, 28
  minimization of X11 windows to, 682
  relocating, 31
  resizing, 31
  using and configuring, 214
  X11, 681
Dock menu
  options
    Keep In Dock, 28
    Quit, 27
    Show In Finder, 28
Dock option (Apple menu), 12, 97
Dock panel (System Preferences), 123
document icons, 28
document windows, 36
documentation, 418
/Documentation folder
  (/Developer folder), 412
  (/Library folder), 254
document-based applications, 424
documents, 83
  linking to applications, 86
/Documents directory (user directory), 251
Documents folder, 250
documents, unsaved changes, 35
Domain Name Servers (Network pane), 269
domains, 248–250
dot (.), 530
dotfiles, 257
double-arrow (>>) icon (Finder toolbar), 53
dpkg command (Fink), 699
drawers, 40
Dreamweaver MX, 138
drives
  connecting to networked, 230
  erasing hard drives, 213
  formatted with HFS, 212
  partitioning hard drives, 213
  unmounting, 213

Drop Box directory, 251
Drop Box, file sharing and, 229
drutil command, 765–767
  options, 765–767
dscl utility
  adding users, 362
  adding users to group with merge command, 361
  delete command, 364
  deleting groups, 362
  groups, creating with, 361
  modifying user with -create command, 364
dselect command (Fink), 699
dspmbyte variable (tcsh), 568
DTEs (see desktop environments)
du command, 767
dual booting with Mac OS 9, 113
dual-fork file, 247
dual-processors, viewing load on, 239
dunique variable (tcsh), 568
Duplicate option (File menu), 69
DVD Player, 184
DVDs, 132
Dynamic Library (project type in Xcode), 422

E

.emacs file, 667
.exrc file, 650
eBay, 101
echo command, 768
  bash, 536
  example, 768
  tcsh, 590
echo variable (tcsh), 568
echo_style variable (tcsh), 568
echotc command (tcsh), 591
ed command, 611
ed, metacharacters, 608
edit command
  CVS, 476
  ex, 633
Edit menu, 19, 70
  options
    Copy, 20, 70
    Cut, 20, 70
    Find, Spelling, 20
    Paste, 20, 70
    Redo action, 20
    Select All, 20, 70
    Show Clipboard, 70
    Special CharactersNone, 70
    Undo, 70
    Undo action, 19
edit variable (tcsh), 568
EDITOR environment variable
  bash, 524, 526
  tcsh, 573
editors command (CVS), 476
egrep command, 768
  examples, 768
  patterns, 611
  searching with, 610
eject button for CD/DVD, 225
Eject option (File menu), 69
ELF libraries versus Darwin's dynamic libraries, 429
ellipsis, menu commands that end in, 8
ellipsis variable (tcsh), 568
else command (tcsh), 591
elvis text editor, 613
Emacs
  extending, 667
  running outside of Terminal, 669
Emacs editor, 651–666
  bindings, compared to vi bindings, 581
  buffers, 652
  command-line editing mode
    bash, 515–516
    tcsh, 582
  commands, 653–666
    buffer manipulation, 656
    capitalization, 656
    centering, 658
    Ctrl-key commands, 659–661
    cursor movement, 654
    deletion, 654
    essential commands, 653
    file handling, 653
    help, 652, 658
    indentation, 658
    macros, 658
    marking, 655
    Meta-key commands, 662
    paragraphs and regions, 655
    searching, 656
    special shell mode characters, 657
    stopping and undoing, 655

Emacs editor, commands (*continued*)
summary by name, 663–666
transposition, 655
windows, 657
word abbreviation, 656
common problems, 652
cutting and pasting in, 652
Del or Backspace, fixing in, 652
editing modes, 651
kill and yank, 652
point and mark, 652
windows, 652
email
client, 186
messages, 202
sending and receiving (see mail, services)
settings, 221
(see also mail)
Empty Project (project type in Xcode), 420
Empty Trash option (Application menu), 68
enable command, 320
bash, 537
Enable fast user switching option (Login Options), 168, 328
Enclosing Folder option (Go menu), 71
encrypted passwords, retrieving, 353
BSD flat files, using for authentication, 358
Panther and, 354
end command (tcsh), 591
(see also foreach command; while command)
endif command (tcsh), 591
endsw command (tcsh), 592
Energy Saver panel (System Preferences), 98, 138–142
enscript command, 232, 769
examples, 770
env command, 770
environment variables, 572
CVS, 466
tcsh, 572–574
equals (=) (ex), 646
erasing disks, 213
erasing files permanently, 33
Error Handling pane (Print dialog), 299
/etc directory, 260
BSD flat files, 356
/etc/crontab, 349
/etc/exports file, 365
/etc/group file
dumping /groups directory in file format, 361
enabling use of with Directory Services, 358
/groups directory versus, 360
/etc/hostconfig file, 383
/etc/hosts file, 365
/etc/master.passwd file, 362
/etc/pam.d directory, 355
/etc/passwd file, 362
enabling use of with Directory Services, 358
/etc/rc.init scripts, 382
/etc/sshd_config file, 689
eterm, replacement for xterm, 682
Ethernet
connection configuration, 228
MAC address for card, 228
switching to AirPort, 230
Ethernet option (Network pane), 272–274
eval command
bash, 537
tcsh, 592
Everywhere option, searches, 74
ex editor, 613, 618
command syntax, 629
command-line options, 618
commands
alphabetical summary, 631
vi, entering from, 629
:set command, 647
ex, metacharacters, 608
/Examples folder (/Developer folder), 412
exec command
bash, 538
tcsh, 592
execute bits, 264
execute permission, 261
exit command, 349
bash, 538
tcsh, 592
expand command, 770
example, 771
export command
bash, 538
CVS, 476

exporting
  directories with NFS, 365
  filesystems, 340
Exposé, 23–24
expr command, 771–773
  arithmetic operators, 771
  examples, 772
  logical operators, 772
  relational operators, 771
ext access method (CVS), 466
extensions, 84
  change program associated with, 217
  hiding/showing, 67
/Extensions folder (/Library folder), 254
Extensions Manager Control Panel, 99
/Extras folder (/Developer folder), 412
exusage command (ex), 633

F

false command, 773
FAQ (Mac OS X), 977
Fast User Switching, 22, 333–334
FAT (MS-DOS) filesystems, mounting, 855
FAT32 filesystem, 248
/Favorites folder (/Library folder), 254
Fax Alert script, 216
Fax button (Print dialog), 301
faxes, 307
  (see also Print & Fax preference pane)
faxing, 216
FBCIndex, 257
FBCLockFolder, 257
fc command (bash), 539
fcache file extension, 220
fdisk command, 773–775
Fetch (FTP application), 289
fetchmail command, 775–778
fg command
  bash, 539
  tcsh, 585, 592
fg pid command, 504
fgrep command, 778
  examples, 778
fignore variable (tcsh), 568
file command, 778
  ex, 633
  example, 779
File Exchange Control Panel, 99
File menu, 69
  commands, 19
  Open With, 69
  options
    Add to Favorites, 69
    Burn Disc, 69
    Close, 19
    Close Window, 69
    Color LabelNone, 69
    Create Archive of, 69
    Duplicate, 69
    Eject, 69
    Find, 69
    Get Info, 69
    Make Alias, 69
    Move to Trash, 69, 257
    New, 19
    New Finder Window, 69
    New Folder, 69
    Open, 19, 69
    Open Recent, 19
    Page Setup..., 19
    Print..., 19
    Save, 19
    Save As..., 19
    Show Original, 69
File Sharing Control Panel, 99
File Synchronization Control Panel, 99
FileMerge tool, 415
filenames
  illegal characters, 91
  rules, 91
  versus patterns, 607
files
  access mode, changing, 733
  archives, 929
    copying, 739
    copying or restoring files, 792
  comparing, 752, 756
  compression, 197
  deleting, 32
    (see also Trash)
  finding (see finding files)
  flags, change or view, 731
  forks, 246
  icons, 28
  manipulation, 216
  moving and copying, 88–92
  ownership
    changing, 732
    changing to newowner, 734

files (*continued*)
permissions, 261–264
viewing and modifying, 263
searches, keywords, 234
services, SLP and SMB protocols, 357
sharing, 370
Bluetooth File Exchange, 188
Drop Box, 251
sharing, Drop Box and, 229
sharing services, 378–380
transfer, 743, 896
secure, 908
types, 82–85
applications, 82
documents, 83
(see also documents)
filesystems
exporting, 340
HFS+, 245
journaled, fixing errors, 367
NFS (see NFS)
organization, 248–255
overview, 264
tables (see fstab file)
UFS, 245
(see also HFS+ filesystem; UFS)
filetest command (tcsh), 593
FileVault protection, 235, 392
find command, 81, 779–783
conditions and actions, 780–783
examples, 783
options, 779
Find option (File menu), 69
Find options (Finder), 75
Find, Spelling option (Edit menu), 20
Finder, 31
Advanced preferences pane, 67
Application menu (see Application menu)
bundles, 86
Column View, 63
keyboard shortcuts, 64
options, 64
Customize Toolbar window, 52
Edit menu (see Edit menu)
File menu (see File menu)
Find options, 75
folders, 85
force quitting, 16
Get Info window, 92–95
Go menu (see Go menu)
Help menu (see Help menu)
Icon View, 57
keyboard shortcuts, 57
options, 58–60
integration with X11, 681
keyboard shortcuts, 72
label preferences, 67
List View, 61, 61–63
arranging columns, 63
options, 62
sorting, 62
menus, 68–74
mounting through, 281
Move to Trash command, 257
overview, 49–52
preferences, 65–67, 219
Always open folders in a new window, 66
Always show file extensions, 67
changing through hidden files, 255
Languages for searching file contents, 67
New Finder Window shows, 65
Open new windows in Column View, 66
Show these items on the Desktop, 65
Show warning before emptying the Trash, 67
Spring-loaded folders and windows, 66
relaunching, 67
searches, 74
Everywhere option, 74
Home folder, 74
local disks, 74
results, 75
Selection option, 74
sections of, 49–51
settings, 219
Sidebar (see Sidebar)
toolbar
controls and icons, 51
customizing, 52
View menu (see View menu)
views, 56–67
Column, 63
Icon, 57
List, 61
Window menu (see Window menu)

Finder flags, 791
finding files, 74–81
  by content, 78
  search options, 76
  with grep, 81
  with the Terminal, 79–81
finger command, 336, 337
Fink, 699
  apt-cache program, 700
  apt-get command package, 700
  commands
    dpkg, 699
    dselect, 699
  downloading, 699
  Fun with Fink, documentation, 977
  Glade, 685
  glib, 685
fink command, 699
Fink Commander, 700
Fink package manager
  /sw directory, 686
  TightVNC, installing, 692
  VNC, installing on Mac OS X, 691
  web site, 685
  window managers and desktops for X11, 685
  X11-based applications and libraries, installing via, 688
Firefox, 287
Firewall (Sharing panel), 164, 344, 370
firewalls, 341–347
  enabling, 235
  rules, viewing, 342
  viewing ipfw's allow and deny rules, 343
fixmount command, 783
fixPrecomps command, 785
FixupResourceForks command, 786
flat files, 359, 366
  authentication, using for
    relying solely on, 358
    under Directory Access, 358
  Directory Services counterparts, 366
  in /etc, unification under Open Directory, 352
  group, /groups directory versus, 361
  and NIS, 356
flushing cached credentials, 364
fmt command, 786
fold command, 787
foldclose command (ex), 634
folders
  actions, 406–408
  Applications
    Preview, 186
    Safari, 186
    Sherlock, 186
    Stickies, 187
    TextEdit, 187
  double-clicking, 86
    with Command key, 86
  Finder and, 85
  Home, 4
    searches, 74
  icons, 28
  manipulating, 216
  moving and copying, 88–92
  special, 250
  Utilities
    Activity Monitor, 187
    AirPort Admin Utility, 188
    AirPort Setup Assistant, 188
    Asia Text Extras, 188
    Audio MIDI Setup, 188
    Bluetooth File Exchange, 188
    Bluetooth Serial Utility, 188
    Bluetooth Setup Assistant, 188
    ColorSync Utility, 188
    Console, 188
    DigitalColor Meter, 189
    Directory Access, 189
    Disk Utility, 189
    Grab, 189
    Installer, 189
    Java utilities, 189
    Keychain Access, 189
    NetInfo Manager, 189
    Network Utility, 190
    ODBC Administrator, 190
    Printer Setup Utility, 190
    StuffIt Expander, 190
    System Profiler, 190
    Terminal, 190
    X11, 190
foldopen command (ex), 634
Font Book, 184
Font Collections, 220
  creating, 220
  disabling, 221

fonts
duplicates, 221
management, 220
removing, 220
storing new, 220
/Fonts folder (/Library folder), 254
for command (bash), 539
Force Quit option (Apple menu), 13, 97
Force Quit window, 67
force-quitting applications, 15, 239
Classic, 15, 110
foreach command (tcsh), 593
fork access method (CVS), 466
Forward option (Go menu), 71
forwarding
X11, 689
Foundation Tool (Xcode), 424
Framework (project type in Xcode), 422
frameworks and libraries, 429
/Frameworks folder (/Library folder), 254
frozen system, 15, 239
fsck command, 787
fsck_hfs command, 788
fsck_msdos command, 788
fstab file, 340
fstat command, 789
fs_usage command, 787
FTP Access service, 163
ftp command, 790–791
FTP (File Transfer Protocol), 284, 288–290
access, 371
connecting to sites, 222
Fetch, 289
passive mode, 289
secure, 908
services, 376
full keyboard access, 201
full-screen and rootless modes, X11, 681, 682
toggling full-screen X11 and Aqua, 687
function command (bash), 540
function keys, 148

G

.gz files, 197, 198
gateways, 335
gcc_select command, 791
General Controls Control Panel, 99
General (Get Info window), 93
Generic Kernel Extension (Xcode), 423
Gestures, Inkwell, 155
Get Info option (File menu), 69
Get Info window (Finder), 92–95
Get Mac OS X Software option (Apple menu), 12, 97
GetFileInfo command, 791
examples, 792
gethostent( ), 352
getopts command (bash), 540
getpw* functions, passwords and, 352
gid property, 333
gid variable (tcsh), 568
GIF files, Preview, 186
GIMP (GNU Image Manipulation Program), 688
Gimp-print package, 323
Glade, on Fink web site, 685
glib, on Fink web site, 685
glob command (tcsh), 593
global command (ex), 634
GNOME desktop environment, 682
installing from Fink, 685
Mac OS X desktop displayed and controlled on Solaris machine, 695
menu bar, 5
Solaris machine connected to Mac OS X via VNC, 693
GNU
General Public License, 696
Image Manipulation Program (see GIMP)
project's calculator, 183
GNU Mac OS X Public Archive, 700
GNU-Darwin web site, 685
gnutar command, 792–797
examples, 797
function options, 793
options, 793–797
Go menu, 70
options
Applications, 71
Back, 71
Computer, 71, 246
Connect to Server, 71
Enclosing Folder, 71
Forward, 71
Go to Folder, 71, 246

Home, 71
iDisk, 71
Network, 71
Recent Folders, 71
Utilities option, 71
Go to Folder option (Go menu), 71, 246
Google, 702
goto command (tcsh), 594
Grab utility, 189
grabber, 65
graphical environments for Mac OS X, 680
graphical user interface (GUI) (see Aqua)
/Graphics Tools folder (/Developer/Applications folder), 413
Graphing Calculator, 183
grayscale, changing display to color, 201
grep command, 797–800
examples, 799
finding files with, 81
patterns, 611
searching with, 610
grid layout, 59
GROUP environment variable (tcsh), 572
group variable (tcsh), 568
groups, 221, 262, 360–362
adding, 204
adding user to admin group, 364
adding users to group with dscl merge command, 361
creating, 332
creating with dscl utility, 361
creating with niload, 361, 363
deleting with dscl's delete command, 362
listing all GIDs with nireport, 360
listing with nidump utility, 362
managing, 326
Groups & Files pane (Xcode), 417
Bookmarks, 418
Breakpoints, 418
Files and Classes, 418
Targets, 418
/groups directory, 360
gserver access method (CVS), 466
GTK+, on Fink web site, 685
GUI Emacs, 669
gunzip command, 800
gzcat command, 800
gzip command, 800
Gzip files, 197

H

.hqx files, 197
halt command, 801
handwriting recognition, 153
hard drives
erasing, 213
partitioning, 213
spindown time, 139
hardware
acceleration support, X11, 681
address (see MAC address)
identifying, 236
preferences panels, 131–156
Hardware preferences, 115
hash bang (#!), 530
tcsh shell, 586
hash command (bash), 540
hash mark (#)
in shell scripts, 530
tcsh shell, 586
hashstat command (tcsh), 594
hdid command, 802
hdiutil command, 802–806
options, 802–806
head command, 806
example, 806
header files, compiling, 785
/Headers folder (/Developer folder), 413
hearing impairments
alert cue for users with, 201
(see also accessibility)
Hearing pane (Universal Access panel), 173
help
Emacs, invoking in, 652, 658
help command
bash, 541
CVS, 477
ex, 634
Help menu, 20, 71
Mac Help option, 72
here document, using in group creation, 361
hexadecimal value for a color, 210

HFS filesystem, 248
identify whether a drive is formatted as, 212
HFS+ filesystem, 248
differences between UFS and, 245
hfs.util command, 806
hidden files, 255–261
changing Finder preferences, 255
Darwin, 260
dotfiles, 257
Mac OS 9, 258, 259
seeing, 255
Hide Application Name option (Application menu), 18
hide command (ex), 634
Hide Extension checkbox, 45
Hide Finder option (Application menu), 69
Hide Others option (Application menu), 18, 69
Hide the Sleep, Restart, and Shut Down buttons option (Login Options), 168, 328
Hide Toolbar option (View menu), 70
Hide/Show Status Bar option (View menu), 70
HIG (Aqua Human Interface Guidelines), 8
Hill, Brian, 342
hints, password, 204
histchars variable (tcsh), 568
histdup variable (tcsh), 568
histfile variable (tcsh), 568
histlit variable (tcsh), 568
history command
bash, 541
CVS, 477–479
tcsh, 594
history file for shell, 238
history variable (tcsh), 568
home directory, creating, 363
HOME environment variable (tcsh), 573
Home folder, 4, 29
searches, 74
Home (From pull-down menu), 44
Home option (Go menu), 71
home variable (tcsh), 568
host command, 807
HOST environment variable (tcsh), 573
hostconfig file, VNCSERVER variable, 697
hostinfo command, 808
hostname command, 808
hostnames, managing with Directory Services, 365
hosts, creating with niload, 365
hosts file, 365
HOSTTYPE environment variable (tcsh), 573
Hot Corners, 24
Howl, 294
HPATH environment variable (tcsh), 573
hup command (tcsh), 595
hwprefs command, 808

I

iApps, 182
iBook, Energy Saver panel, 139
IBPalette (Xcode), 423
iCab browser, 286
iCal, 182, 184
iChat, 184
adding menu extra for, 225
icns Browser (Aqua application), 415
Icon size option
(Icon View), 59
(List View), 62
Icon View (Finder), 57–58
keyboard shortcuts, 57
options, 58–60
IconComposer tool, 415
icons
adding and removing, 26
application, 25
bouncing at startup, 125
changing Preview, 94
custom, 218
disk, folder, and file, 28
Dock, bouncing at startup, 125
found (by default) along the bottom of the screen (see Dock)
hiding hard disk, 213
interactive Dock, 26
programs without, 26
proxy, 37
removing an icon that shows up in the side menu, 53
Trash, 32

id command, 809
iDisk
  available space, 222
  mounting, 223
  Public folder
    permissions, 158
    requiring passwords, 222
    viewing another's, 230
iDisk (From pull-down menu), 44
iDisk (Internet panel), 157
iDisk option (Go menu), 71
if command
  bash, 542
  tcsh, 595
if keyword (AppleScript), 402
ifconfig command, 265, 335, 336, 809–811
IFS filesystem, differences between HFS+ and, 245
ignoreeof variable (tcsh), 568
Image Capture, 184
ImageMagick, 688
images
  background, 207
  capturing (see Grab utility; screenshots)
  manipulating with GIMP (see GIMP)
IMAP services, 375
imapd daemon, 375
iMovie, 182, 185
  publishing on .Mac HomePage, 224
implicitcd variable (tcsh), 568
import command (CVS), 479
indexed hard drives, content-based searches and, 234
info command, 811
Info.plist file, 430
Infrared Control Panel, 99
infrared ports, adding menu extra for, 226
init command (CVS), 464
Ink, adding menu extra for, 226
Ink panel (System Preferences), 153–156
Inkwell application, 153–156
  Gestures, 155
  settings, 153
  Word List, 155
Input Menu (International preferences panel), 129
input (see I/O)
inputmode variable (tcsh), 568
insert command (ex), 635
install command, 812
Install Script Menu program, 397
Installed Updates (Software Update panel), 170
Installer, 189
installer command, 813
  examples, 814
installers, 191
Interface Builder, 182, 412, 428
Interface connections (AppleScript), 409
interface design Bible (see HIG)
interleaving windows, 42
International panel (System Preferences), 128
internationalization (see localization)
Internet & Network preferences, 115
Internet Connect application, 185, 279
Internet Control Panel, 99
Internet Explorer, 185, 286
Internet panel, 157
Internet panel (Sharing panel), 370
/Internet Plug-ins folder (/Library folder), 254
Internet radio station, 222
  (see also iTunes)
Internet settings, 221
Internet sharing, 344
  DHCP and, 344
Internet (Sharing panel), 164
I/O
  X11 interaction with input devices, 686
  X11 output, customizing, 686
IOKit Driver (Xcode), 423
IORegistryExplorer, 415
IP Address (Network pane), 269
IP addresses, 265, 335
  managing with Directory Services, 365
IP masquerading, 344
IP Printing, 305
IP sharing, 344
ipconfig command, 814
ipfirewall package, 342
ipfw command, 342
ipfw firewall package, 342
iPhoto, 182, 185
  creating Photo Album page, 224

IPv6 Address (Network pane), 269
ISO 9660 filesystem format, 248
ISP connection configuration, 227
iSync, 182, 185
iTunes, 100, 182, 186
iTunes (Dock menu), 28
iTunes Library, 251

J

Jar Bundler tool, 414
Java, 427
  applets, running, 706
  documentation browser (javadoc), 442
  javac compiler, 442
  options, 441
  programs
    class paths, 441
    running from command line, 440–442
  utilities
    Applet Launcher, 189
    Java Plugin Settings, 189
    JWS (Java Web Start), 189
Java AWT Applet (Xcode), 422
Java AWT Application (Xcode), 422
java command, 440
/Java folder (/Developer folder), 413
Java JNI Application (Xcode), 422
Java Plugin Settings, 189
Java (project type in Xcode), 422
Java Rendezvous, 294
Java Swing Applet (Xcode), 423
Java Swing Application (Xcode), 423
Java Tool (Xcode), 423
/Java Tools folder (/Developer/Applications folder), 414
JavaBrowser tool, 414
javac (Java compiler), 442
java-dev mailing list, 975
javadoc (Java documentation browser), 442
job control
  bash, 529
  tcsh, 584
jobs command, 504
  bash, 542
  tcsh, 595
jobs, viewing in the print queue, 231
join command, 815
  ex, 635
  examples, 816
jot command, 816
  examples, 816
journaled filesystem, fixing errors, 367
journaling, 247
JPEG files, Preview, 186
jumps command (ex), 635
JWS (Java Web Start), 189

K

k command (ex), 635
KDE desktop environment, 5, 682
  installing from Fink, 685
  Konqueror and Koffice on Mac OS X, 688
kdump command, 817
kdumpd command, 817
Keep arranged by option (Icon View), 60
Keep In Dock option (Dock menu), 28
Kerberos, 391
Kernel Environment layer, xiv
Kernel Extension (project templates in Xcode), 423
Kernel-User Notification Center server, 820
key bindings (see keyboard shortcuts)
key equivalents under X11, 686
key mappings of special characters, 969
keyboard
  access
    full, 201
    key combinations, 147
  language types, adding menu extra for, 224
  layout, selecting, 129
  layout (X11), customizing, 686
  navigation, 73
  option key special characters, 971
  Power-on button, 4
  startup, 4
Keyboard Control Panel, 99
Keyboard pane (Universal Access panel), 174
Keyboard panel (System Preferences), 142
keyboard shortcuts, 68–74
  Application menu, 68
  basic, 72

Classic, starting and restarting, 209
creating new sticky note, 47
Dock, 33
Edit menu, 70
Exposé, 24
File menu, 69
Finder
Column View, 64, 65
Icon View, 57
List View, 61
Finder Icon View, 58
for common commands, 8
Go menu, 70
Help menu, 71
log out, 4
menu commands, 8
overriding, 47
restarting, 4
sending text to Bluetooth device, 47
Show All Preferences, 117
shutdown, 4
startup, 4, 113
Universal Access, 201
View menu, 70
Window menu, 71
Zoom, 172
Keyboard Viewer application, 969–971
special characters option key, 971
/Keyboards folder (/Library folder), 254
Keychain Access, 99, 189, 225, 387–389
keychains, managing, 235
keynote presentation files, 86
keyword searches, 234
kill command, 506, 818
bash, 542
Emacs, 652
tcsh, 585, 596
kill –signal pid command, 504
killall command, 506, 818
killall –signal process-name command, 504
killdup variable (tcsh), 568
killring variable (tcsh), 568
Kind option (List View), 62
Konqueror (KDE web browser) ported to Mac OS X, 688
kserver access method (CVS), 466
kserver command (CVS), 465
ktrace command, 819
examples, 820
kuncd command, 820

L

.lproj folders, 130
Label position option (Icon View), 59
labels, colored, 67
LANG environment variable (tcsh), 573
Language (International preferences panel), 129
language preferences, 128
Languages for searching file contents (Finder preference), 67
Languages (Get Info window), 95
languages, programming, 425–428
languagesetup command, 820
last command, 821
Late Night Software Ltd's XML Tools.osax file, 403
Launcher Control Panel, 99
launching applications from the Dock, 25
layers of Mac OS X, xiv–xv
Layout pane (Printer dialog), 297
LC_CTYPE environment variable (tcsh), 573
LDAP, LDAPv3 plug-in, Directory Access, 356
leave command, 821
left command (ex), 635
less command, 821–828
commands, 824–828
options, 821–824
let command (bash), 543
libraries and frameworks, 429
/Library directory (user directory), 251
Library folders, 250, 252–255
/Application Support, 252
/Assistants, 253
/Audio, 253
/ColorPickers, 253
/ColorSync, 253
/Components, 253
/Documentation, 254
/Examples, 412
/Extensions, 254
/Favorites, 254
/Fonts, 254
/Frameworks, 254
/Internet Plug-ins, 254
/Keyboards, 254
/Preferences, 254
/Printers, 255

Library folders (*continued*)
/Scripting Additions, 255
/Scripts, 255
user specific, 252
/WebServer, 255
limit command (tcsh), 596
Limitations pane, 166
LINES environment variable (tcsh), 573
Linux default shell, 559
Linux-PAM, using to authenticate a user, 354–355
list command (ex), 635
List View (Finder), 61–63
arranging columns, 63
keyboard shortcuts, 61
options, 62
sorting, 62
listflags variable (tcsh), 568
listjobs variable (tcsh), 568
listlinks variable (tcsh), 569
listmax variable (tcsh), 569
listmaxrows variable (tcsh), 569
ln command, 828
local access method (CVS), 465
local command (bash), 543
local directory
browsing/modifying with NetInfo Manager, 358
Directory Services database, restoring, 367
displaying contents with nidump and nireport, 359
modifying with nicl utility, 360
local disks, Finder searches, 74
Local domain, 249
localization, 128
locate command, 79, 828
locating files (see finding files)
Location Manager Control Panel, 99
Location option (Apple menu), 12, 97
locations, network, 274
lock command, 828
locked items, empty trash, 218
Locked option (GetInfo), 93
lockfile command, 829
locking model (CVS), 445
log command
CVS, 480–482
tcsh, 597
log of software updates, 240
Log Out option (Apple menu), 14, 98
logger command, 829
example, 830
logging out, keyboard shortcuts, 4
login command
CVS, 482
tcsh, 597
Login Options pane, 167
login window, 327
logins
automatic
multiuser system, 204
turning off, 204
configuring, 203
from Windows system, 204
logging in, 3
logging out, 47
versus shutting down, 48
password, 203
changing, 203
remote, 290, 371
(see also passwords)
loginsh variable (tcsh), 569
LOGNAME environment variable (tcsh), 573
logout command
bash, 543
CVS, 482
tcsh, 598
logout variable (tcsh), 569
look command, 830
lookupd daemon, 352
–flushcache command, 358
lp command, 319, 830
example, 831
lpadmin command, 319
lpc command, 831
lpinfo command, 320
lpoptions command, 320
lpq command, 832
lpr command, 319, 832
LPR printer configuration, 113
lprm command, 320, 833
lpstat command, 320, 833
ls command, 255, 264, 834
examples, 835
ls -F command (tcsh), 598
lsbom command, 835–837
examples, 837

LS_COLORS environment variable (tcsh), 573
lsof command, 837
  examples, 838
lynx browser, 287
Lynx home page, 287

M

.Mac (Apple's subscriber service), 157
  accounts, 222
.Mac (Internet panel), 157
.Mac email, accessing from Safari, 223
.Mac HomePage
  creating Photo Album page, 224
  publishing iMovie, 224
.Mac member's HomePage, 223
.Mac page, 976
.Mac Slide Show, 223
MAC address, 206
  defined, 272
Mac DevCenter (by O'Reilly Network), 976
Mac Help option (Help menu), 72
MAC (media access control), 228
Mac Minute, 977
Mac News Network, 977
Mac OS 9
  applications, installing, 194
  Control Panels and their disposition in Mac OS X, 98
  dual-booting with, 113
  hidden files, 258, 259
  identifying version, 208
  obtaining, 101
  running applications on Mac OS X (see Classic)
  sheets and drawers, 110
  Special menu, changes in Mac OS X, 98
  /System Folder/Extensions folder, 254
Mac OS Extended Format, 245
Mac OS X
  Apple menu, 96
  application-to-document map, 82
  authentication lock, 193
  booting into when Mac OS 9 as default, 114
  built-in console login mode, 506
  changes since Mac OS 9, 96–100
  Desktop overview, 5
  development (see Xcode Tools)
  Directory Services architecture, 352
  emulation of right-mouse clicks, 682
  FAQ, 977
  firewalls, 341–347
  layers, xiv–xv
  menu bar (see menu bar)
  overview of Aqua, 4
  single-user mode, 347
  supported filesystem formats, 248
  version, identifying, 236
Mac OS X Hints, 977
Mac OS X Panther for Unix Geeks, 429
Mac OS X Panther, user account types, 166
MacCentral, 976
mac-games-dev mailing list, 975
mach file (Darwin), 260
machine command, 838
/machines file, 365
mach_kernel file (Darwin), 260
mach.sym file (Darwin), 260
MACHTYPE environment variable (tcsh), 573
MacInTouch, 976
mac-opengl mailing list, 975
macosx-admin mailing list, 975
macosx-dev mailing list, 975
macos-x-server mailing list, 975
macosx-talk mailing list, 975
MacPython-2.3 folder, 415
MacRumors, 977
MacScripter.net, 403
MacSlash, 977
magazines, 974
  Mac Design, 974
  MacAddict, 974
  macHOME, 974
  MacTech, 974
  Macworld, 974
mail, 186
  notification, 722
  retrieving from mail servers, 775
  services, 371
  (see also email)
Mail application (Apple), 40
  Services menu, 46
mail delivery agents (MDAs), 371, 374
MAIL environment variable (tcsh), 573

mail transport agents (MTAs), 371
  Postfix (see Postfix)
mail variable (tcsh), 569
mailing lists
  applescript-studio, 974
  applescript-users, 974
  carbon-development, 975
  cocoa-dev, 975
  java-dev, 975
  mac-games-dev, 975
  mac-opengl, 975
  macosx-admin, 975
  macosx-dev, 975
  macos-x-server, 975
  macosx-talk, 975
  Rendezvous, 975
  scitech, 975
  studentdev, 975
  weekly-kbase-changes, 975
mailq command, 839
mailstat command, 839
MainMenu.nib NIB file, 424
Make Alias option (File menu), 69
make clean command, 702
make install command, 702
make test, 702
/Makefiles folder (/Developer folder), 413
makekey command, 839
MallocDebug tool, 414
man command, 840
Managed users (Mac OS X Panther), 166
manpages
  flat file formats and, 366
  hosts and, 365
Manually option (Network pane), 269
Manually Using DHCP Router option (Network pane), 270
map command (ex), 636
mark command (ex), 636
marks command (ex), 636
marks (Emacs), 652
mask, network, 340
masquerading, 342
matchbeep variable (tcsh), 569
md5 command, 841
MDAs (mail delivery agents), 371, 374
mDNS command, 841
mDNSResponder command, 842
Media Keys (QuickTime panel), 162
memory
  identifying amount on system, 236
  in Classic, 209
  viewing status, 236
Memory Control Panel, 99
Memory section of Info window (Classic), 107
Memory/Versions (Classic Advanced control), 105
menu bar, 5
  adding items to, 224
  Classic, 108
  commands to be spoken and recognized, 202
  GNOME, 5
  KDE, 5
  key equivalents, X11, 686
  (see also Apple menu; Application menu; Dock menu; menus)
Menu Bar Clock (Date & Time panel), 169
menu extras, 21
  adding and controlling, 224–226
  AirPort, 224
  Bluetooth, 22, 225
  iChat, 225
  infrared ports, 226
  Ink, 226
  keyboard language types, 224
  moving, 22
  PCMCIA card status, 226
  PPPoE, 226
  removing, 22
  switching positions, 224
menulets (see menu extras)
menus
  commands, 8
    common, 19–20
    that end in ellipse, 8
  contextual menus, 9
  Dock, 27
  finder, 68–74
  keyboard shortcuts, 8
  overview, 7
  submenu headings, 8
  submenus, 9
  (see Application menu; menu bar)
merge command, 415, 842
merging model (CVS), 445

metacharacters
  listed by Unix program, 608
  replacement patterns, 610
  search patterns, 609
Meta-key (Emacs) commands, 662
Microsoft
  Remote Desktop Client (RDC), 697
  (see also Windows)
middle mouse button, simulation with Option-click, 682
Minimize Window option (Window menu), 20, 71
minimizing windows, 31
Mirror Displays checkbox, 134
mkbom command, 843
mkdir command, 218, 843
mkexrc command (ex), 636
modem configuration files, 227
Modem Control Panel, 99
Modem option (Network pane), 272
Modem pop-up menu, 272
modems
  automatically dialing into the PPP server, 279
  showing status in menu bar, 225
monitor
  displays, 133
  settings, 213
Monitors Control Panel, 99
more command, 844–845
  commands, 844
  options, 844
More Info (About This Mac), 12
Motif window manager (mwm), 688
mount command, 845
mount_afp command, 846
mount_cd9660 command, 847
mount_cddafs command, 848
mountd command and fixmount command, 783
mount_devfs command, 848
mount_fdesc command, 848
mount_ftp command, 848
mount_hfs command, 849
mounting disks
  diskarbitrationd command and, 759
  network disks, 280–285
  through Finder, 281
  through Terminal, 285
  unmounting an external drive or partition, 213
mount_msdos command, 850
mount_nfs command, 850
mount_ntfs command, 851
mount_smbfs command, 852–854
  options, 852
mount_synthfs command, 854
mount_udf command, 855
mount_volfs command, 854
mount_webdav command, 855
mouse, 226
  navigation without, 201
  trackpads, 144, 226
  using numeric keypad instead of, 202
mouse buttons
  emulation of three-button mouse in X11, 686
  xterm versus Terminal windows, 682
Mouse Control Panel, 99
Mouse Keys, 176
  numeric mouse controls, 176
Mouse pane (Universal Access panel), 175
Mouses panel (System Preferences), 143
move command (ex), 636
Move to Trash option (File menu), 69, 257
/Movies directory (user directory), 251
moving files and folders, 88–92
Mozilla browser, 286
MPEG files, 186
MS-DOS, 248
msdos.util command, 855
MTAs (mail transport agents), 371
multicast-DNS, 293
multihoming, 268
Multiple Users Control Panel, 99
multiuser systems, 251
/Music directory (user directory), 251
Music (QuickTime panel), 162
mv command, 217, 856
MvMac command, 856
mwm (Motif window manager), 688

N

.nib files, 428
Name & Extension (Get Info window), 94
name, changing computer, 237
naming (Rendezvous), 229

natd (Network Address Translation Daemon), 344
navigation without a mouse, 201
ncftp program, 289
nedit text editor, 688
NetInfo
  backing up database, 360
  browsing/modifying local directory, 358
  in Directory Services architecture, 351
  NFS and, 338
  plug-in supported by Directory Access, 357
  restoring/backing up database, 367
  utilities, 358
    list of, 359
NetInfo Manager, 189, 332, 351, 358
netstat command, 336, 857
network
  administration, 334–337
  disks
    mounting, 280–285
    security and, 286
  locations, 274
  mask, 340
  security
    AirPort, 347
    NFS, 341
  settings, fine-tuning, 265
  testing, 885
  (see also Airport)
Network Address Translation Daemon (natd), 344
network address translation (NAT), 342
network client connections to X11, 687
Network domain, 249
Network File System protocol (NFS), 284
network fileservers, browsing, 280
Network Information Service (NIS)
  flat files and, 356
Network option (Go menu), 71
Network panel, 159, 266–275
  system preferences, 274
Network Port Configurations table, 267
network printers, 296
network services
  running, 369–384
    through the Sharing pane, 369
Network utility, 190, 334
networked drive, connecting to, 230
networking, 265–294
  basics, 265–279
  dialup, 275–279
networks
  AirPort, switching to from Ethernet, 230
  connection speed, 229
  Ethernet, switching to from AirPort, 230
network-visible entities (NVEs), 710
new command (ex), 637
New Finder Window option (File menu), 69
New Finder Window shows (Finder preference), 65
New Folder option (File menu), 69
New option (File menu), 19
newgrp command (tcsh), 598
newowner, changing file ownership, 734
news web sites, 976
next command (ex), 637
NeXTSTEP programming language, 426
NFS (Network File System), 248, 284, 337–347
  access to shares, 713
  exporting directories with, 365
    options supported by Mac OS X, 365
  mounting, 338
    automount, 339
    static, 338
  network security and, 341
  server daemons, 339
nfsd daemons, 339
NFSManager, 338
nice command, 858
  tcsh, 598
nicl command, 360, 858–859
  commands, 859
  options, 858
  users, creating with, 363
nidomain command, 860
nidump command, 340, 359, 860
  dumping groups directory in /etc/group file format, 361
  groups, listing with, 362
  listing users with, 358, 364

nifind command, 861
nigrep command, 861
niload command, 359, 861
  adding users, 362
  creating a host, 365
  groups, creating with, 361
  users, creating with, 363
nireport command, 359, 362, 862
  listing all group IDs (GIDs), 360
  users, listing with, 362
NIS and flat files, 356
niutil command, 360, 863
No Limits button, 166
nobeep variable (tcsh), 569
noclobber variable (tcsh), 569
noding variable (tcsh), 569
noglob variable (tcsh), 569
nohlsearch command (ex), 637
nohup command (tcsh), 598
nohup vncserver command, 692
nokanji variable (tcsh), 569
non-human user accounts, 331
nonomatch variable (tcsh), 569
NOREBIND environment variable (tcsh), 574
nostat variable (tcsh), 569
Note Pad, 100
notify command (tcsh), 598
notify job control command (tcsh), 585
notify variable (tcsh), 569
notifyd command, 864
NSGlobalDomain, 672
nslookup command, 336, 866–868
  interactive commands, 866–868
  options, 866
ntfs.util command, 868
NTP (Network Time Protocol) server, 169
ntptimeset command, 869
ntp-wait command, 869
null command (:), 530
number command (ex), 637
number pad, using instead of mouse, 175
Numbers Control Panel, 99
Numbers (International preferences panel), 129
numeric keypad instead of the mouse, using, 202
nvi text editor, 613
nvram command, 870–871

O

ObjectAlloc tool, 414
Objective-C, 426
od command, 872
ODBC Administrator utility, 190
Omni Group, 977
  mailing lists, 975
  OmniWeb browser, 287
onintr command (tcsh), 599
open command, 873
  ex, 637
  examples, 873
Open Directory, 351
  (see also Directory Services)
open files, locating, 217
Open Firmware
  password, 389–391
  variables, modifying, 870
Open new windows in Column View (Finder preference), 66
Open option (File menu), 19, 69
Open Recent option (File menu), 19
open source Unix software, 701–702
Open with (Get Info window), 94
Open With option (File menu), 69
OpenGL, xv, 681
OpenGL Driver Monitor tool, 413
OpenGL Profiler tool, 413
OpenGL Shader Builder tool, 413
OpenLDAP web site, 356
OpenStep libraries, 426
OpenType fonts, 220
open-x11 command, 874
Opera browser, 287
Optimize Energy Settings (Energy Saver panel), 140
Option key
  holding down at startup, 114
  holding down while selecting Apple menu, 14
  special characters and, 971
Option-click, simulating middle-mouse button, 682
OroborOSX (web site), 685
OS X Package Manager, 192
OSA Extensions, 403
osacompile command, 874
osalang command, 875
osascript command, 875
  examples, 876

osaxen.com, 403
OSTYPE environment variable (tcsh), 574
osx2x application, 690
OSXGNU project, 192
OSXvnc application, 691
  launching with Share My Desktop (SMD), 696
  starting on Mac OS X machine with VNC server, 694
Output option (Print dialog), 298
output (see I/O; printing)
overhead projector display, 134
owd variable (tcsh), 569
owners, 262
Ownership & Permissions (Get Info window), 94

P

.prefPane files, 181
package managers, 698–701
PackageMaker tool, 415
PacketDecoder2 tool (BlueTooth), 415
Page Setup dialog, 309
  Format for menu, 310
  Orientation menu, 310
  Paper Size menu, 310
  Scale menu, 310
  Settings menu, 309
Page Setup... option (File menu), 19
/Palettes folder (/Developer folder), 413
Paper Feed option (Print dialog), 299
Paper Handling option (Print dialog), 298
partitioning a hard drive, 213
passive FTP mode, 289
passwd command, 876
Password panel (user account settings), 167
Password Security Control Panel, 99
passwords, 203, 352–355
  authenticating user with Linux-PAM, 354–355
  encrypted, Panther and, 354
  groups, setting for, 361
  hints, 204
  iDisk Public folder, 222
  Keychain Access, 189
  managing with Directory Services, 362–364
    setting password with passwd command, 363
    user created with dscl, 363
  Open Firmware, 389–391
  required, 204
  restricting, 203
  RSA SecurID, 292
paste command, 877
  examples, 877
Paste option (Edit menu), 20, 70
PATH environment variable (tcsh), 573
path separators, 246
path variable (tcsh), 569
paths, pop-up menu showing, 36
pattern matching
  examples of searching and replacing, 612
  filenames versus patterns, 607
  replacement patterns, 610
pax command, 877–880
  example, 880
  examples, 880
  options, 878–880
pbcopy command, 881
pbpaste command, 881
PCMCIA card status, adding menu extra for, 226
PDAs, communicating with, 151
PDF
  saving as, 300
PDF files
  converting full-color to grayscale, 210
  generating large numbers of, 303
  Preview, 186
  Quartz filters and, 316
PDF Services directory, 301–303
PDF Services folder
  aliases to folders inside, 302
  AppleScript script file inside, 303
  application files inside, 302
  folders inside, 302
  Unix tool file inside, 302
PDF workflow, 301–303
  adding Quartz filter, 303
pdisk command, 881–884
  commands, 883
  options, 882
pdump command, 884

PEF (Preferred Executable Format)
files, 416
PEFViewer tool, 416
percent (%), bash job ID argument, 529
/Performance Tools folder
(/Developer/Applications
folder), 414
periodic command, 885
Perl, 427
Camelbones project, 428
permissions, 261–264
changing, 217
iDisk Public folder, 158
viewing and modifying, 263
personal file sharing, 162, 370
Personal preferences, 115
Appearance panel, 119
Desktop panel, 120
Screen Saver panel, 120
Personal Web Sharing, 163, 251
persons with disabilities (see
accessibility)
PICT files, Preview, 186
Picture pane (user account
settings), 167
/Pictures directory (user directory), 251
pictures, setting in Finder windows, 60
ping command, 336, 885
pipe symbol (|)
using with Unix commands, 232
pipe symbol (|), 514
Pixie, 414
pkgInstall utility, 192
PKZip files, 197
pl command, 886
examples, 887
plist files, 670
structure of, 671
Plug-In (QuickTime panel), 160
plug-ins directory service, supported by
Directory Access, 355–357
Plug-ins (Get Info window), 95
pmset command, 887
examples, 888
point (Emacs), 652
POP services, 375
popd command
bash, 543
tcsh, 599
popd daemon, 375
pop-up menu showing an object's
path, 36
Port Scan tool, 337
port scanning, 337
portmap daemon, 339
portscan command, 336
POSIX, 608
character classes, 609
Postfix, 371–374
configuring local mailer, 372–374
configuring mail server, 374
good reference book on, 373
using, 372
postfix-watch command, 888
PostScript
converting text files to, 769
Level 1 fonts, 220
printers, printing to, 232
USB printer configuration, 113
PostScript converter, 318
PowerBook Energy Saver panel, 139
Power-on button, shutdown and, 13
PPP option (Network pane), 272
PPP (Point-to-Point protocol), 270
configuring, 275–279
connections, 727
server, automatically dialing
into, 279
PPPoE, adding menu extra for, 226
PPPoE option (Network pane), 272
pr command, 888
preference files, 671
(see also property lists)
preference panels, 115
PreferencePane (Xcode), 423
/Preferences folder (/Library
folder), 254
Preferences menu (X11), 686
Preferences option (Application
menu), 17, 68
preferences, system (see System
Preferences)
presentations using overhead
projector, 134
preserve command (ex), 637
Preview application, 186
Preview column (Finder Column
View), 63
Preview (Get Info window), 94
Preview icon, changing, 94
previous command (ex), 638

Print & Fax preference pane, 310–312
  Answer after rings, 311
  Default paper size in Page Setup, 311
  Email to (fax option), 312
  My Fax Number, 311
  Print on printer (fax option), 312
  Receive faxes on this computer, 311
  Save to (fax option), 312
  Selected printer in Print Dialog, 310
  Set Up Printers, 310
  Share my printers with other computers, 311
print administration
  command-line tools, 319
    accept command, 320
    cancel command, 320
    disable command, 320
    enable command, 320
    lpadmin command, 319
    lpinfo command, 320
    lp/lpr commands, 319
    lpoptions command, 320
    lprm command, 320
    lpstat command, 320
    reject command, 320
  web-based, 318
    Do Administration Tasks page, 319
    Download the Current CUPS Software page, 319
    Manage Jobs page, 319
    Manage Printer Classes page, 319
    Manage Printers page, 319
    On-Line Help page, 319
Print Center, 100
print command (ex), 638
Print dialog, 296–303
  application-specific options, 299
  ColorSync, 298
  Copies & Pages pane, 297
  Cover Page option, 299
  Error Handling pane, 299
  Fax button, 301
  Layout pane, 297
  Output option, 298
  Paper Feed option, 299
  Paper Handling option, 298
  Presets menu, 297
  Preview button, 300
  Printer Features option, 299
  Printer menu, 296
  Save to PDF button, 300, 301–303
  Scheduler option, 298
  simplified print sheet, 303
Print... option (File menu), 19
print queue, viewing jobs in, 231
printenv command, 889
  tcsh, 599
printer class, 307
printer pools, 307
Printer Setup Utility, 190, 303–308
  Add Printer, 304
  Create Desktop Printer, 308
  Fax List, 307
  Printer List window, 304–307
Printer Sharing service, 164
printers
  adding and deleting, 304
  AppleTalk, 711
    to be used with atprint, 710
  configuring, 231
    AppleTalk, 113
    LPR, 113
    PostScript USB printer, 113
    through Chooser, 112
    through Classic, 209
    USB (non-PostScript), 112
  discovering, 306
  drivers, 322
  interfaces, alternative, 318
  modifying list entry, 307
  network, 296
  PostScript, sending to, 232
  queues, 307
    Unix commands, 320
  setting pane, 297
  sharing, 371
    through cupsd.conf, 321
    through Sharing pane, 320
  SMB, 306
  USB, 296
/Printers folder (/Library folder), 255
printexitvalue variable (tcsh), 569
printf command (bash), 544
printing, 830
  AppleTalk, 304
  desktop, 308
  Directory Services pane, 306
  from Classic, 112
  options, application-specific, 300
  overview, 295
  Rendezvous, 306

saving settings, 299
SLP and SMB protocols, 357
Terminal command line, 231
to multiple printers, 307
USB sharing, 306
Windows Printing pane, 306
(see also CUPS)
/private
/etc directory, 260
/tmp directory, 260
/var directory, 260
/Private folder (/Developer folder), 413
process control commands, 504
process management, 504
backgrounded processes, 504
identifying which are running, 236
seeing processes, 504
Terminal, 502–506
Process Viewer, 26, 187
processes, seeing, 504–506
processor, identifying, 236
profiles, ColorSync, 188
programming AppleScript, 398–409
programming languages, 425–428
programs
identifying which are running, 236
running at scheduled times, 349
without icons, 26
Project Builder (see Xcode)
project building, 424
project templates in Xcode, 423
prompt variables (tcsh), 569
formatting substitutions, 570–572
promptchars variable (tcsh), 569
Property List column (Property List Editor), 675
Property List Editor, 416, 673, 750
using, 674–676
property lists, 670–673
com.apple
.dock, 125
.finder, 255
.finder, editing, 255
.LaunchServices, 82
.loginwindow, 327
naming conventions, 671
StartupParameters, 383
version, 430
viewing and editing, 673
(see also plist files)
proxies, 270
Proxies option (Network pane), 270
proxy icons, 37
ps command, 504, 889–892
keywords, 890
options, 889
with aux options, 505
x option, 505
pserver access method (CVS), 466
pserver command (CVS), 465
/Public directory (user directory), 251
Public folders
allow people to access, 235
Drop Box, 251
file sharing, 229
iDisk, viewing another, 230
sharing files and, 229
pushd command
bash, 544
tcsh, 600
pushdsilent variable (tcsh), 569
pushdtohome variable (tcsh), 569
Put Away command, 100
put command (ex), 638
pwd command, 892
bash, 544
PWD environment variable (tcsh), 574
Python, 428

Q

qall command (ex), 638
Qt libraries (X11-based), 688
Quartz Debug tool, 414
Quartz Extreme, xiv, 23
acceleration, 680
cube effect, 168
Quartz filters, 315–317
adding to PDF workflow, 303
PDF files and, 316
Quartz window manager, 680, 681, 683
question mark (?), 514
question mark icon in the Dock, 239
QuickDraw, xiv
QuickTime, xv
panel, 160
QuickTime (/Library folder), 255
QuickTime Player, 186
QuickTime Settings Control Panel, 99
Quit Application Name option (Application menu), 18
quit command (ex), 638
Quit option (Dock menu), 27

R

.rtfd files, 86
RAID (redundant array of independent disks), 213
RandR (Resize and Rotate) extension, 681
rannotate command (CVS), 474, 482
rcp command, 892
rdiff command (CVS), 482
read command
  bash, 545
  ex, 638
read permission, 261
readonly command (bash), 546
reboot command, 349, 368, 893
Rebuild Desktop (Classic Advanced control), 105
Recent Folders option (Go menu), 71
Recent Items option (Apple menu), 12, 97
recexact variable (tcsh), 569
recognize_only_executables variable (tcsh), 569
recover command (ex), 639
Redo action option (Edit menu), 20
redo command (ex), 639
refresh rates, 133
Registration button (QuickTime Pro), 162
rehash command (tcsh), 600
reject command, 320
release command (CVS), 483
Remote Access Control Panel, 99
remote Apple Events, 164, 371
remote copy, 892
Remote Desktop Client (RDC), Microsoft, 697
remote filesystems, mounting, 280
remote login services, 163, 290, 371, 377–378
remote shell (RSH), 378
REMOTEHOST environment variable (tcsh), 574
remove command (CVS), 484
removing an icon that shows up in the side menu, 53
renaming objects, 90
Rendezvous, 293, 306, 357
  mailing list, 975
Rendezvous, name change, 229
renice command, 894
Repeat After Me tool, 416
repeat command (tcsh), 600
Repeat with variable (AppleScript), 402
repositories (CVS), 444
  creating, 448
Resize and Rotate (RandR) extension, 681
resize command (ex), 639
resolution, 133
resource forks, 246
Resources folder, 130
Restart button, 328
Restart Classic (Classic Advanced control), 104
Restart option (Apple menu), 13, 98
Restart option, Apple menu, 13
restarting, 3
  keyboard shortcuts, 4
restricting applications, 203
results of searches, 75
return command (bash), 546
Return command (ex), 646
rev command, 894
revision control (see CVS)
rewind command (ex), 639
rich text documents, 86
right command (ex), 639
right-mouse clicks, 682
rlog command (CVS), 484
rlogin command, 894
rm command, 218, 895
rmdir command, 895
rmstar variable (tcsh), 569
root
  abuse, casual, 325
  acting as, 324
  directories, 250
  exploring, 257
  mounting filesystem as read/write, 367
  user account, 205, 326
rootless and full-screen modes, X11, 681
  toggling full-screen X11 and Aqua, 687
root-level commands, 325
route command, 265
Router (Network pane), 269

routing, 335
RPC calls, 339
rprompt variable (tcsh), 569
RSA SecurID password, 292
RSH (remote shell), 377, 378
rsync command, 896–898
  examples, 898
  options, 897
rtag command (CVS), 485
rumor web sites, 976
RumorTracker, 977
runaway process, 111
running older Mac applications on Mac OS X without booting into Mac OS 9 (see Classic)
rxvt, replacement for xterm, 682

S

.sit files, 197
.ssh directory, 257
Safari, 186
  accessing .Mac email from, 223
  context menus in, 9
  default home page, 222
  setting own stylesheet, 222
  specifying where files are downloaded, 221
  using with Rendezvous, 294
Sampler (Aqua application), 414
sandboxes (CVS), 444
Save As... option (File menu), 19, 45
Save option (File menu), 19
Save sheet, 45
savedirs variable (tcsh), 569
savehist variable (tcsh), 569
say command, 898
/sbin directory, 260
sbnext command (ex), 640
sbuffer command (ex), 639
scanning ports (see port scanning)
sched command (tcsh), 601
sched variable (tcsh), 569
scheduled times, running scripts and programs at, 349
Scheduler option (Print dialog), 298
scitech mailing list, 975
scp command, 899
Scrapbook, 100
Screen Saver panel (Personal preferences), 120
Screen Saver panel (System Preferences), 123
Screen Saver (Xcode), 423
screen savers, 123, 232
screencapture command, 900
screenshots, 233
  Grab utility, 189
script command, 900
  ex, 640
Script Editor, 403–406
  Apple Event-producing statements, 400
  creating, compiling, and running scripts, 404
  Formatting preferences, 404
  recording scripts, 404
  Save dialog
    Application Bundle option, 405
    Application option, 405
    Script Bundle option, 405
    Script option, 405
    Text option, 405
Script Menu
  adding to menu bar, 225
  enabling and removing, 206
  removing from menu bar, 225
Script Menu Extra, 397
Scriptable Image Processing System (SIPS) tool, 910
Scripting Additions, 207
/Scripting Additions folder (/Library folder), 255
scripts
  locating, 207
  running at scheduled times, 349
/Scripts folder (/Library folder), 255
scrollbar controls together, placing, 201
scselect command, 901
scutil command, 901–904
  commands, 902
  options, 901
sdiff command, 904
  example, 905
Search Domains (Network pane), 269
"Search for items whose", 75
  options, 76
"Search in" pop-up menu, 75
searches
  configuring for Directory Access Authentication tab, 358
  content-based, 234

searches (*continued*)
Finder, 74
Everywhere option, 74
Home folder, 74
local disks, 74
results, 75
Selection option, 74
keywords, 234
searching
and replacing examples, 612
for files (see finding files; pattern matching)
vi editor, in, 620
Secure Empty Trash, 33, 92
None option (Application menu), 68
secure FTP, 908
secure Internet protocols, 286
Secure Shell (see SSH)
security, 235, 385–394
authentication, 192, 387–392
AirPort networks, 347
AirPort-enabled Macs and, 286
CVS and, 449
default in Panther, 386
deleting files, 393
encrypted images, 392
filesystem, 392–394
Keychain Access, 387–389
network disks and, 286
physical, 394
screen savers, 233
Software Update, 386
Unix, 385
X11 features, configuring, 687
Security pane (user account settings), 167
security tips
AirPort networks, 286, 347
FTP, 289, 377
network disks, 286
NFS, 341
print servers, 321
Telnet, 290
SecurityServer command, 905
sed command, 611, 906
sed, metacharacters, 608
Seeing pane (Universal Access panel), 172
Select All option (Edit menu), 20, 70
select command (bash), 546
Selection option, searches, 74
server command (CVS), 465
Server Message Block (SMB), 283
service command, 906
Service Location Protocol (SLP), 357
Services menu, 46
Services option (Application menu), 17, 68
Services panel (Sharing panel), 370
Services (Sharing panel), 162
set command
bash, 547–549
ex, 640, 648–650
colon in (:set), 647
tcsh, 601
set keyword (AppleScript), 402
setenv command (tcsh), 601
SetFile command, 907
example, 908
settc command (tcsh), 602
settings and tasks, 200–241
Settings for (Energy Saver panel), 140
setty command (tcsh), 602
sftp command, 908
Share My Desktop (SMD), 696
/Shared directory (user directory), 251
shared folder, displaying contents, 212
sharing
connections, AirPort, 230
files, 370
Drop Box, 251
Drop Box and, 229
Public folder, 229
over AirPort, 346
printers, 371
Sharing panel, 162
AirPort options, 346
Channel, 347
Enable encryption, 347
Network Name, 347
Password, 347
WEP key length, 347
Apple Remote Desktop, 371
Firewall panel, 370
FTP Access, 371
Internet panel, 370
Personal File Sharing, 370
Personal Web Sharing, 371
Printer Sharing, 371
printers, 320
Remote Apple Events, 371
Remote Login, 371

running network services through, 369
Windows Sharing, 371
(see also Services panel)
sheets, 39
shell command (ex), 641
SHELL environment variable (tcsh), 574
shell scripts, comment character (#), 530
shell variables, tcsh shell, 567–570
shells
bash (see bash shell)
common features, 509
differing features, 510
history file, 238
overview, 507–510
setting default, 493
tcsh (see tcsh shell)
uses for, 508
Sherlock, 186
Sherlock Channel (Xcode), 423
shift command
bash, 549
tcsh, 602
SHLVL environment variable (tcsh), 573
shlvl variable (tcsh), 570
shopt command (bash), 549–551
Show All option (Application menu), 18, 69
Show All Preferences keyboard shortcut, 117
Show Clipboard option (Edit menu), 70
Show columns option (List View), 62
Show icon preview option (Icon View), 60
Show icons option (Column View), 64
Show In Finder option (Dock menu), 28
Show item info option (Icon View), 59
Show menu (Network pane), 267
Show Original option (File menu), 69
Show preview column option (Column View), 64
Show these items on the Desktop (Finder preference), 65
Show View Options option (View menu), 70
Show warning before emptying the Trash (Finder preference), 67
showmount command, 909
Shut Down button, 328
shutdown, 4
keyboard shortcuts, 4
shutdown command, 909
shutdown –h now command, 349
Shutdown option (Apple menu), 13, 98
shutting down, 47
versus logging out, 48
Sidebar (Finder), 53–56
dragging items, 55
icons, 53
preferences, 67
resizing, 55
Simple Finder button, 166
Simple Finder, restricting non-admin user, 206
SimpleSound, 100
SimpleText, 100
example, 415
Simplified users (Mac OS X Panther), 166
single-user mode, 347–349
booting in
to restore Directory Services database, 367
booting into, 348
exiting, 348
sips command, 910–913
examples, 912
options, 910–912
/Sites directory (user directory), 251
Size option (List View), 62
Sketch example, 415
Sleep option (Apple menu), 13, 98
Sleep timer (Classic Advanced control), 105
slide shows, 223
slogin command, 913
Slow Keys, 174
SLP (Service Location Protocol), 357
slp_reg command, 913
SMB (Server Message Block), 283, 357
printers, 306
share, 230
SMD (Share My Desktop), 696
Snap to grid option (Icon View), 59
snext command (ex), 640
Snort administrative tool, 337
SOAP web services, 412

Software Base Station (see AirPort Base Station)
Software Downloads page, 976
software installers, 191
Software Update, 386
  About This Mac, 12
  Control Panel, 99
Software Update panel, 170
Software Update preferences panel, 97
software updates
  installing, 170
  log, 240
software web sites, 977
softwareupdate command, 913
Some Limits button, 166
sort command, 914
  examples, 915
sound control, adding to menu bar, 225
Sound Control Panel, 99
sound effects for X11 system alert, 687
Sound panel (System Preferences), 150
source command
  bash, 551
  ex, 641
  tcsh, 603
speakable items, 181
special characters
  key mappings, 969
  option key, 971
Special CharactersNone option (Edit menu), 70
special files (CVS), 467
special folders in root directory, 250
Speech Control Panel, 99
Speech panel, 172
speech recognition software, 177–181
  settings, 201
Speech Synthesis manager, 898
Spin Control tool, 415
spindown time, hard drive, 139
split command, 915
  ex, 640
  examples, 915
SplitForks command, 916
spray command, 916
sprevious command (ex), 640
Spring Cleaning application, 192
Spring-loaded folders and windows (Finder preference), 66
SpyMac web site, 977
SRLanguageModeler tool, 416
srm command, 916
ssh command, 917–919
SSH (Secure Shell), 377, 917
  commercial version, using with X11 forwarding, 689
  using ssh with X11 forwarding, 689
  versus Telnet, 290
  VNC, using with, 692
    connections to Mac OS X Aqua desktops, 694–697
    TightVNC, 692
    tunneling VNC connection without TightVNC, 693
sshd_config file, enabling X11 forwarding, 689
Standard Apple Plug-ins (templates in Xcode), 423
Standard Tool (Xcode), 424
Standard users (Mac OS X Panther), 166
Start/Stop (Classic), 104
startup
  keyboard shortcuts, 4, 113
  Power-on button, 4
Startup Disk panel, 172
startup items, configuring, 380
Startup Items pane (user account settings), 167
Startup Manager, booting into specific drives, 114
Startup Options (Classic Advanced control), 104
StartupItems, 381–384
  manually running, 382
  StartupParameters.plist file, 383
  versus /etc/hostconfig file, 383
Static Library (templates in Xcode), 423
static mounting, 338
Stationary Pad option (GetInfo), 93
status command (CVS), 485
status variable (tcsh), 570
Stepwise, 976
Stickies, 35, 187
Sticky Keys, 174
sticky note shortcut, 47
stop command
  ex, 641
  tcsh, 585, 603
strings command, 919

stty command, 919–924
combination modes, 923
control assignments, 923
control modes, 919
input modes, 920
local modes, 921
options, 919
output modes, 921
studentdev mailing list, 975
StuffIt Expander, 190, 198
su command, 924
submenu headings, 8
submenus, 9
subnet, 340
Subnet Mask (Network pane), 269
subscriber service, Apple's, 157
substitute command (ex), 641
subwindows, 40
sudo command, 325, 924
example, 925
granting user privilege to use, 364
NetInfo utilities, using with, 360
sudo make install command, 702
Support page, Apple's, 976
suspend command
bash, 551
ex, 642
tcsh, 603
sview command (ex), 642
/sw directory, 686
switch command (tcsh), 603
switching to AirPort from Ethernet, 230
sw_vers command, 926
symlinks variable (tcsh), 570
system administration
acting as root, 324
overview, 324–350
system alert, configuring for X11, 687
system append-only (sappend) flag, 731
System domain, 249
System folder, 250
System Folder folder, 250
system immutable (schg) flag, 731
system information, 236
System panel (System Preferences), 115
System Preferences, 98, 115–181, 187
Accounts panel, 165
adding panes, 181
add-on preferences, 118
administrator and, 119
Bluetooth panel, 151
CDs & DVDs panel, 132
Classic panel, 168
Date & Time panel, 169
Displays panel, 133–138
Dock panel, 123
Energy Saver panel, 138–142
Hardware preferences, 115
Ink panel, 153–156
International panel, 128
Internet & Network preferences, 115
Internet panel, 157
Keyboard panel, 142
launching, 117
modifying user accounts, 364
Mouse panel, 143
Network panel, 159
Personal preferences, 115, 120
QuickTime panel, 160
Screen Effects panel, 123
Sharing panel, 162
Software Update panel, 170
Sound panel, 150
Speech panel, 172
Startup Disk panel, 172
System panel, 115
toolbars, 115, 116
hiding, 117
Universal Access panel, 172
System Preferences option (Apple menu), 12, 97
System Preferences panels, 118–176
System Profiler, 190
system status, 237
system updates, 237
systemkeychain command, 926
/System/Library/User Template directory, 363
system_profiler command, 927
SystemStarter command, 928
SystemStarter program, 384

T

t command (ex), 642
.tar files, 197, 198
tab window manager (twm), 685
VNC server and, 692
tag command
CVS, 485
ex, 642

Tagged Image File Format (TIFF), 85
tags command (ex), 642
tail command, 928
  examples, 929
talk command, 929
tar command, 929
  example, 931
targets (Xcode), 425
tasks and settings, 200–241
TCP/IP, 265
  commands, 334
  configuring, 269, 335
  overview, 334
  troubleshooting, 335
    tools, 336
TCP/IP Control Panel, 99
tcsh shell, 508, 559–606
  arithmetic operators, 575
  assignment operators, 574
  bitwise and logical operators, 575
  built-in commands, 585–606
  command completion, 581
  command history, 577–580
    command substitution, 577
    history modifiers, 579
    special aliases, 580
    word substitution, 578
  command structure, 563
  command-line editing, 581–584
    Emacs mode, 582
    vi mode, 583
  comparison operators, 575
  configuration files, 561
  DISPLAY variable, enabling X11 forwarding, 689
  environment variables, 572–574
  expressions, 574–577
    operator precedence, 574
    operators, 574–577
  file inquiry operators, 575–577
  formatting substitutions, prompt variable, 570–572
  invocation, options and arguments, 560
  job control commands, 584
  multiple redirection, 564
  quoting, 561
    characters, 562
  redirection, 563
  shell variables, 567–570
  special characters, 562
  special files, 561
  syntax, 561–564
  variables, 564–574
    modifiers, 565
    variable substitution, 564
tcsh variable (tcsh), 570
tee command, 931
  example, 931
telltc command (tcsh), 604
Telnet, 377
  versus SSH, 290
telnet command, 931–938
  commands, 932–938
  options, 931
templates in Xcode, 423
TERM environment variable (tcsh), 573
term variable (tcsh), 570
TERMCAP environment variable (tcsh), 574
Terminal, xv, 190
  browsing, 287
  commands, running as root, 325
  Connect to Server window, 500
  focus follows mouse, 502
  launching X11-based application from, 688
  mounting disks through, 285
  overview, 493
  preferences, 493–499
  printing, 231
  process control commands, 504
  process control keystrokes, 503
  process management, 502–506
    backgrounded processes, 504
    seeing processes, 504–506
  running Java programs, 440–442
  saving and loading terminal settings, 499–500
  scripting, 409
  Secure Keyboard Entry, 502
  setting a default shell, 493
  settings, 237
  split-view scrollback, 502
  window
    assign different title, 238
    changing background color and fonts, 238
    define number of lines, 238
  X11 forwarding enabled in, 689
  xterm windows versus Terminal windows, 682

Terminal Inspector window, 495–499
Buffer pane, 497
Color pane, 498
Emulation pane
Audible bell option, 497
Display pane, 497
Escape non-ASCII characters option, 496
Option click to position cursor option, 497
Paste newlines as carriage returns option, 497
Reverse linewrap option, 497
Strict VT-100 keypad behavior option, 497
Visual bell option, 497
Keyboard pane, 499
Delete key sends backspace option, 499
Key Mappings option, 499
Use option key as meta key option, 499
Processes pane, 496
Shell pane, 495
Use Settings as Defaults button, 499
Window pane, 498
terminating programs, 506
test command, 938–940
bash, 551–554
expression tests, 940
file comparisons, 939
file testers, 938
integer tests, 940
string tests, 939
test suite, 702
testing the network, 885
text
Asia Text Extras utility, 188
Chinese Text Converter, 188
IM Plugin Converter, 188
Text Control Panel, 99
text editors
dual mode versus modeless editing, 613
Emacs (see Emacs editor)
ex (see ex editor)
TextEdit, 187
vi (see vi editor)
text files, converting to PostScript, 769
Text size option
(Column View), 64
(Icon View), 59
(List View), 62
text smoothing (see antialiasing)
TextEdit, 187
text-processing utilities, 607
tftp command, 940
TFTP (Trivial File Transfer Protocol), 940
The Objective-C Programming Language Apple documentation, 426
Think Secret web site, 977
Thread Viewer tool, 415
TIFF files, Preview, 186
tiff2icns command, 941
tiffutil command, 942
TightVNC, 692
viewers for UNIX systems, 694
tilde (~)
bash, 514
ex command, 647
tcsh, 581
time, 210
(see also Date & Time panel)
time command, 942
tcsh, 604
Time (International preferences panel), 129
time variable (tcsh), 570
Time Zone (Date & Time panel), 169
times command (bash), 554
tips, tricks, advice web sites, 977
titlebar, 34
/tmp directory, 260
Tool (project templates in Xcode), 424
toolbars, 37
customizing, 37
hiding, 117
System Preferences
hiding, 117
window, 115
transparent button, 37
/Tools folder (/Developer folder), 413
tools (see Xcode Tools)
top command, 236, 943
touch command, 943
tperiod variable (tcsh), 570

tr command, 944–946
examples, 946
traceroute command, 229, 336, 946
TrackPad Control Panel, 99
trackpads, 144, 226
Transmit (FTP application), 289
Transport Setup button, 162
trap command (bash), 554
Trash
emptying locked items, 218
icon, 32
moving objects to, 92
new location, 25
turn off setting to confirm deletion, 218
/Trash directory, 257
Trolltech, Aqua version of Qt for Mac OS X, 688
troubleshooting
problems, 239
TCP/IP, 335
tools, 336
TruBlueEnvironment as a runaway process, 111
true command, 947
TrueType fonts, 220
try statements (AppleScript), 402
tset command, 947
examples, 948
tty command, 948
tty variable (tcsh), 570
twm (tab window manager), 685
VNC server and, 692
Type codes, 84–85
searching for files, 84
type command
bash, 555
typeset command (bash), 535

U

UDF filesystem format, 248
udf.util command, 948
UFS (Universal File System)
filesystem, 248
versus HFS+
path separators, 246
root, 246
ufs.util command, 948
uid variable (tcsh), 570
ulimit command (bash), 556
umask command
bash, 557
tcsh, 604
umount command, 949
unabbreviate command (ex), 642
unalias command
bash, 557
tcsh, 604
uname command, 949
uncomplete command (tcsh), 604
uncompress command, 950
undo command (ex), 643
Undo option (Edit menu), 19, 70
unedit command (CVS), 486
unexpand command, 950
unhash command (tcsh), 604
unhide command (ex), 643
Unicode, 130
uninstalling applications, 191
uniq command, 950
examples, 951
units command, 951
Universal Access
keyboard shortcuts, 201
panel, 172
Unix
directories
pipe symbol (|), use with Unix commands, 232
installing from source, 701–702
installing software, 698–702
metacharacters (see metacharacters)
networking, 334
open source software, 701–702
text-processing utilities, 607
VNC server, 691
(see also Darwin)
Unix command reference, 703–965
Unix file-transfer tools, 247
Unix tool file inside a PDF Services folder, 302
unlimit command (tcsh), 605
unmap command (ex), 643
unmounting disks, 33
external drives or partitions, 213
unsaved changes, 35
unset command
bash, 557
tcsh, 605
unsetenv command (tcsh), 605
until command (bash), 557

unzip command, 951–953
examples, 953
options, 952
update command
CVS, 486–488
Update (QuickTime panel), 162
Update Software (Software Update panel), 170
updating software, 170
uptime command, 953
USB Printer Sharing Control Panel, 99
USB printers, 296
USB printing, 306
non-PostScript printer configuration, 112
USB Prober tool, 416
Use preferences from home folder (Classic Advanced control), 105
Use relative dates option (List View), 63
user account
configuring, 330–331
user accounts
add button (+), 329
adding and removing, 202
administrator privileges, 203
finding out who has, 204
changing default shell, 494
configuring
Limitations option, 331
Password Hint option, 330
Password option, 330
Picture option, 330
Security option, 330
Startup Items option, 330
managing, 202–206, 326
minus button (–), 329
multiple, 22
non-human, 331
restricting to use Simple Finder, 206
root, 205
settings, 167
switching, 22
types for Mac OS X Panther, 166
user directories, 251
/Desktop, 251
/Documents, 251
/Library, 251, 252
/Movies, 251
/Music, 251
/Pictures, 251
/Public, 251
/Shared, 251
/Sites, 251
User domain, 249
USER environment variable (tcsh), 573
user specific Library folders, 252
user variable (tcsh), 570
users
home directory for, 363
managing with Directory Services, 362–364
adding users, 362
creating user with dscl, 363
creating user's home directory, 363
deleting user with dscl -delete, 364
granting administrative privileges, 364
listing all users with nireport, 362
listing users with nidump, 364
modifying user with dscl -create, 364
users command, 953
Users folders, 250, 251
Using BootP option (Network pane), 270
Using DHCP option (Network pane), 270
Using PPP option (Network pane), 270
utilities, 187–190
Utilities folder
Activity Monitor, 187
AirPort Admin Utility, 188
AirPort Setup Assistant, 188
Asia Text Extras, 188
Audio MIDI Setup, 188
Bluetooth File Exchange, 188
Bluetooth Serial Utility, 188
Bluetooth Setup Assistant, 188
ColorSync Utility, 188
Console, 188
DigitalColor Meter, 189
Directory Access, 189
Disk Utility, 189
Grab, 189
Installer, 189
Java utilities, 189
Keychain Access, 189

Utilities folder (*continued*)
NetInfo Manager, 189
Network Utility, 190
ODBC Administrator, 190
Printer Setup Utility, 190
StuffIt Expander, 190
System Profiler, 190
Terminal, 190
X11, 190
Utilities option (Go menu), 71
uudecode command, 954
uuencode command, 954
examples, 954
uuidgen command, 954

V

v command (ex), 643
Value column (Property List Editor), 676
/var directory, 260
/var/cron/tabs/, 349
/var/db/netinfo directory, 358
VENDOR environment variable (tcsh), 574
verbose variable (tcsh), 570
version
identifying, 236
information, 430
version command
CVS, 488
ex, 643
version control, 444
(see also CVS)
Version option (List View), 62
Version Tracker, 977
Mac OS X VNC viewers, 693
version variable (tcsh), 570
vi command, 954
ex, 643
vi editor, 613–650
address symbols, 630
bindings, compared to Emacs bindings, 581
command mode, 614
alphabetical key list, 627–629
command syntax, 615
command-line editing mode (bash), 515, 517–518
command-line options, 616–618
configuration, 647–650
~/.exrc file, 613, 647–650
edit commands, 622–624
changing text, 623
deleting text, 623
exiting, 624
multiple files, 625
saving, 624
text insertion, 622
editing operators, 615
enhanced versions, 613
ex (see ex editor)
files, opening, 616
insert mode, 614
line numbering, 621
macros, 626
marking position, 621
metacharacters, 608
miscellaneous commands, 627
movement commands, 619–622
character, 619
lines, 620
screens, 620
text, 619
operating modes, 613
searching, 620
:set command (ex), 647–650
shell, interacting with, 626
starting a session, 616
status-line commands, 615
tcsh command-line editing mode, 583
user-defined commands, characters for, 626
window commands, 625
view command, 955
view command (ex), 643
View menu
options
Arrange, 70
as Columns, 70
as List, 70
Clean Up, 70
Customize Toolbar, 70
Hide Toolbar, 70
Hide/Show Status Bar, 70
Show View Options, 70
viewers, VNC, 691
Mac OS X viewers, 693
vile text editor, 613
vim editor, 613
vipw utility, 358
Virtual Network Computer (see VNC)

virtual private network (VPN), 286
visiblebell variable (tcsh), 570
visual alert cue for a user with a hearing impairment, 201
visual command (ex), 644
VISUAL environment variable
  bash, 526
  tcsh, 574
visual impairments
  display settings for persons with, 201
  (see also accessibility)
viusage command (ex), 644
vmmap command, 955
vm_stat command, 955
VNC (Virtual Network Computer), 691–697
  components of, 691
  connecting to Mac OS X machine with VNC server, 693–697
  connections tunneled through SSH, 692
  installing on Mac OS X wtih Fink, 691
  launching, 692–694
  Macs connected to, controlling desktops, 690
  SSH, using with, 692
    TightVNC, 692
    tunneling connection over SSH without TightVNC, 693
  Windows machines, clients and servers for, 697
VNCDimension (Aqua VNC client), 693
vncserver command, 692, 693
VNCSERVER variable, 697
vndevice command, 956
voice settings, 201
volume control, showing in menu bar, 237
/Volumes directory, 261
VPN (Virtual Private Network), 286, 291–293
  connection configuration, 228
vsdbutil command, 957
vsplit command (ex), 644

W

w command, 957
wait command
  bash, 557
  tcsh, 605
waking a computer from sleep mode, 13
wall command, 958
  ex, 644
watch command
  CVS, 488
watch variable (tcsh), 570
watchers command (CVS), 489
watchlog command (tcsh), 605
wc command, 958
  examples, 958
web
  browsing, 285–287
  services, 375
  settings, 221
  sharing, 222
  sites, 976
web browsers, Safari, 186
Web Sharing Control Panel, 99
web sites
  setting shortcuts on Desktop, 222
Web-based Distributed Authoring and Versioning system (WebDAV), 284
web-based print administration, 318
/WebServer folder (/Library folder), 255
weekly-kbase-changes mailing list, 975
WEP encryption, 347
whatis command, 958
where command (tcsh), 605
whereis command, 958
which command, 959
  example, 959
  tcsh, 605
while command
  bash, 558
  tcsh, 606
who command, 959
  example, 959
who variable (tcsh), 570
whoami command, 960
whois command, 336, 960
Window Controller, 428

window managers
  Quartz, 681
  VNC, specifying for, 692
  X11, 683
    available from Fink, 685
Window menu, 20, 71
  options
    Bring All to Front, 71
    Minimize Window, 20, 71
Windows
  consulting Active Directory domain on server editions, 356
  VNC clients and servers for, 697
windows, 34–43
  controls, 34
  cycling through all of an application's open, 43
  document, 36
  drawers, 40
  interleaving, 42
  manipulating, 240
  minimizing, 31
  proxy icons, 37
  sheets, 39
  switching back and forth between, 20
  toolbars, 37
  types of, 39
Windows 2000 and AFP, 282
windows (Emacs), 652
Windows File Sharing service, 163
Windows NT and AFP, 282
windowshade feature, 35
WindowShade X application, 35
wireless devices, communicating with, 151
wireless network, AirPort configuration settings, 229
wnext command (ex), 644
Word List, Inkwell, 155
wordchars variable (tcsh), 570
working directories
  CVS, 444
WorldText example, 415
wq command (ex), 644
wqall command (ex), 644
write command, 960
  ex, 645
write permission, 261
www user account, 331

X

X command (ex), 645
X key, holding down at startup, 114
X Window System, 506
  Apple X11 distribution (see X11)
  connecting from Mac OS X to, 689
.xinitrc script, for X11 customization, 683
X11, 190, 680–697
  applications and libraries, installing via Fink, 688
  connecting to other X Window Systems, 689
    Applications menu, using, 689
    OSX2X, using, 690
  customizing, 683–688
    Applications menu, 687
    dot-files, desktops, and window managers, 683
    input devices, interaction with, 686
    output, 686
    security features, 687
  features of, 681
  forwarding, 689
  installing, 681
  interactions with Aqua, 688
  running, 681
    contextual menus in an xterm window, 682
    rootless and full-screen modes, 682
    xterm versus Terminal windows, 682
  VNC (Virtual Network Computer), 691–697
    connecting to Mac OS X VNC server, 693–697
    launching, 692–694
X11SDK, 681
xargs command, 960
  examples, 961
Xcode application, 412, 416–425, 426
  build phases, 425
  Debug mode, 425
  documentation, 418
  Groups & Files pane (see Groups & Files pane)
  new features, 417

project types, 420–424
targets, 425
window, 417
Xcode Tools, 85, 411–430
/Developer folder, 412–413
/Applications folder, 412
/Documentation folder, 412
/Examples folder, 412
/Extras folder, 412
/Headers folder, 413
/Java folder, 413
/Makefiles folder, 413
/Palettes folder, 413
/Private folder, 413
/Tools folder, 413
/Developer/Applications folder, 413–416
/Graphics Tools folder, 413
/Java Tools folder, 414
/Performance Tools folder, 414
/Utilities folder, 415
libraries and frameworks, 429
obtaining, 411
X11 SDK, 681
Xcode Tools CD-ROM, 411
Xfce desktop environment, 682
xfig/transfig drawing tool, 688
XFree86 Project, 680
xinetd, 384
xit command (ex), 645
XMethodsInspector application, 412
XML Tools.osax file, 403
XML-RPC
web services, 412
xmodmap utility, 682
xterm program, 506
customizing window in X11, 686
replacements for, 682

Y

yank command
Emacs, 652
ex, 645
yes command, 961

Z

z command (ex), 645
.zip files, 197
zcat command, 961
zcmp command, 961
zdiff command, 961
Zeroconf cross-platform technology, 294
zgrep command, 962
zip archives, 218
zip command, 962–964
examples, 964
options, 962
zmore command, 964
znew command, 965
Zoom keyboard shortcuts, 172
zprint command, 964
zsh shell command
case-sensitivity, 246

About the Authors

Chuck Toporek (*chuckdude@mac.com*) is a MacHead, through and through. He has used Macs since 1988, when he first cut his teeth on a Mac II system. Chuck is a senior editor for O'Reilly, mainly working on Macintosh-related books, and is also a member of the Program Committee for O'Reilly's Mac OS X Conference. He is a coauthor of *Hydrocephalus: A Guide for Patients, Families and Friends*, and author of two other Mac books from O'Reilly: the *Mac OS X Panther Pocket Guide* (now in its third edition) and *Inside .Mac*. In a former life, Chuck worked for print and online magazines, wrote articles and tutorials on Mac software and web design, and used Linux and Windows machines when a Mac wasn't around. When not crashing his mountain bike into the trees, he can be found reading, writing, or laying waste to aliens while playing *Halo*. Originally from a small town in Michigan, Chuck now lives in Portland, Oregon with his wife, Kellie Robinson (coauthor of the *Hydrocephalus* book), their cat Sophie, and far too many Pez dispensers.

Chris Stone (*cjstone@mac.com*) is a senior systems administrator (the Mac guy) at O'Reilly. He's written several Mac OS X-related articles for the O'Reilly MacDevCenter (*http://www.macdevcenter.com*) and contributed to *Mac OS X: The Missing Manual, Panther Edition,* published by Pogue Press/O'Reilly. Chris grew up on the San Francisco peninsula, went to Humboldt State University, and spent 10 years hidden away in the Japanese countryside before returning to California and settling in the North Bay area, where he now lives with his wife Miho and two sons Andrew and Jonathan.

Jason McIntosh (*jmac@jmac.org*) lives in Somerville, Massachusetts, and works as a senior web programmer with the Institute for Chemistry and Cellular Biology at Harvard Medical School in Boston. Previous technical publications include *Perl and XML* (coauthored with Erik T. Ray and published by O'Reilly), and an occasional series of columns and weblog entries on XML or Mac OS X for the O'Reilly Network, particularly *http://www.macdevcenter.com*. His primary hobby is playing and designing obscure board and card games. All these things, as well as other inventions and reflections, may be found at his online home at *http://www.jmac.org*. Jason has worked with Macintosh computers (selling them, administrating them, programming them, and writing about them) since 1991. He agrees that, yes, that is pretty funny about his name, now that you mention it.

Colophon

Our look is the result of reader comments, our own experimentation, and feedback from distribution channels. Distinctive covers complement our distinctive approach to technical topics, breathing personality and life into potentially dry subjects.

The animal on the cover of *Mac OS X Panther in a Nutshell* is a German shepherd. The model for this picture was Vinny, a search and rescue dog for the King County (Washington) sheriff's department. The German shepherd was hand-drawn from photographs of Vinny by his aunt, Lorrie LeJeune.

Search and rescue dogs are in quite a stressful field of work. In order for the dogs to be able to perform well, they must adapt to many different things—for example, diverse modes of travel, new people, all kinds of weather, and various types of terrain. Often, search and rescue dogs are medium to large in size. They are expected to be intelligent, strong, and generally even-tempered. The German shepherd is by no means the only breed of dog who takes on this line of work. Ultimately, search and rescue dogs must have a strong nose and be physically fit. It is a difficult job that requires the dedication and commitment of both the dog and its owner/partner.

Mary Anne Weeks Mayo was the copyeditor and production editor for *Mac OS X Panther in a Nutshell*. Colleen Gorman, Sarah Sherman, and Claire Cloutier provided quality control. Jamie Peppard and Mary Agner provided production assistance. Julie Hawks wrote (and did a mighty fine job on) the index.

Emma Colby designed the cover of this book, based on a series design by Edie Freedman. The cover image is an original illustration created by Lorrie LeJeune. Emma Colby produced the cover layout with QuarkXPress 4.1 using Adobe's ITC Garamond font.

Melanie Wang designed the interior layout, based on a series design by David Futato. Julie Hawks converted the Word files to FrameMaker 5.5.6 with a format conversion tool created by Erik Ray, Jason McIntosh, Neil Walls, and Mike Sierra that uses Perl and XML technologies. The text font is Linotype Birka; the heading font is Adobe Myriad Condensed; and the code font is LucasFont's TheSans Mono Condensed. The illustrations that appear in the book were produced by Robert Romano and Jessamyn Read using Macromedia FreeHand 9 and Adobe Photoshop 6. The tip and warning icons were drawn by Christopher Bing. This colophon was written by Mary Brady.

Related Titles Available from O'Reilly

Macintosh

AppleScript: The Definitive Guide
Appleworks 6: The Missing Manual
The Best of the Joy of Tech
iMovie 3 and iDVD: The Missing Manual
iPhoto2: The Missing Manual
iPod & iTunes: The Missing Manual, *2nd Edition*
Mac OS X Panther Pocket Guide
Mac OS X: The Missing Manual, *Panther Edition*
Mac OS X Unwired
Macintosh Troubleshooting Pocket Guide
Office X for the Macintosh: The Missing Manual
Running Mac OS X Panther

Mac Developers

Building Cocoa Applications: A Step-By-Step Guide
Cocoa in a Nutshell
Learning Carbon
Learning Cocoa with Objective-C, *2nd Edition*
Learning Unix for Mac OS X Panther
Mac OS X for Java Geeks
Mac OS X Hacks
Mac OS X Panther Hacks
Mac OS X Panther for Unix Geeks
Objective-C Pocket Reference
RealBasic: The Definitive Guide, *2nd Edition*

Keep in touch with O'Reilly

1. Download examples from our books

To find example files for a book, go to:

www.oreilly.com/catalog

select the book, and follow the "Examples" link.

2. Register your O'Reilly books

Register your book at *register.oreilly.com*

Why register your books? Once you've registered your O'Reilly books you can:

- Win O'Reilly books, T-shirts or discount coupons in our monthly drawing.
- Get special offers available only to registered O'Reilly customers.
- Get catalogs announcing new books (US and UK only).
- Get email notification of new editions of the O'Reilly books you own.

3. Join our email lists

Sign up to get topic-specific email announcements of new books and conferences, special offers, and O'Reilly Network technology newsletters at:

elists.oreilly.com

It's easy to customize your free elists subscription so you'll get exactly the O'Reilly news you want.

4. Get the latest news, tips, and tools

http://www.oreilly.com

- "Top 100 Sites on the Web"—PC Magazine
- CIO Magazine's Web Business 50 Awards

Our web site contains a library of comprehensive product information (including book excerpts and tables of contents), downloadable software, background articles, interviews with technology leaders, links to relevant sites, book cover art, and more.

5. Work for O'Reilly

Check out our web site for current employment opportunities:

jobs.oreilly.com

6. Contact us

O'Reilly & Associates
1005 Gravenstein Hwy North
Sebastopol, CA 95472 USA

TEL: 707-827-7000 or 800-998-9938
(6am to 5pm PST)

FAX: 707-829-0104

order@oreilly.com
For answers to problems regarding your order or our products.
To place a book order online, visit:

www.oreilly.com/order_new

catalog@oreilly.com
To request a copy of our latest catalog.

booktech@oreilly.com
For book content technical questions or corrections.

corporate@oreilly.com
For educational, library, government, and corporate sales.

proposals@oreilly.com
To submit new book proposals to our editors and product managers.

international@oreilly.com
For information about our international distributors or translation queries. For a list of our distributors outside of North America check out:

international.oreilly.com/distributors.html

adoption@oreilly.com
For information about academic use of O'Reilly books, visit:

academic.oreilly.com